What a resource! Whether you study the Bible, teach or preach it, or are planning to do a movie where you need to understand how people lived, the *Lexham Geographic Commentary on Acts through Revelation* is a treasure trove of information about first-century life. This is up to date and full of detail that not only will inform you but fascinate you as well. Just very well done.

—Darrell Bock, senior research professor of New Testament, Dallas Theological Seminary

Most New Testament professors are at best amateurs when it comes to geography and archaeology, and for many of us the geographical information is inaccessible, but the *Lexham Geographic Commentary on Acts through Revelation* brings it all together. Just what Bible readers, pastors, and professors need! An abundance of images, excellent scholarly descriptions and narratives, and first-rate scholarship all bundled into an accessible format. I will not study from Acts to Revelation without having this volume at my side.

—Rev. Canon Dr. Scot McKnight, professor of New Testament, Northern Seminary

The *Lexham Geographic Commentary on Acts through Revelation* is a worthy sequel to the award-winning *Lexham Geographic Commentary on the Gospels*. Over fifty entries by a range of scholars offer valuable insight into the geographical, social, and historical context of the book of Acts, the New Testament letters, and Revelation. An incredible amount of information that enables students better to understand the New Testament is available in this volume. Interspersed throughout are photographs, illustrations, and maps that enable the reader better to grasp the points being made in the text.

—Douglas J. Moo, Wessner Chair of Biblical Studies, Wheaton College

This volume fills a glaring lacuna in commentary literature by providing an in-depth and up-to-date discussion of the growth of the early Christian movement within its geographical contexts. Not only does it illuminate the reading of a vast number of biblical passages, it also bridges the gap between the subdisciplines of human and physical geography in presenting a strong case for the proper recognition of geography as a significant hermeneutical category. In so doing, it enriches our understanding of the nature of God's redemptive history that unfolds within a particular space and time. Biblical scholars and theologians alike have much to learn from this volume.

—David W. Pao, professor of New Testament and chair of the New Testament Department, Trinity Evangelical Divinity School

Geography and history are important! The *Lexham Geographic Commentary on Acts through Revelation* shows how they provide the framework for New Testament events and writings, and it gives discussions and insight that do not appear in most commentaries. The pictures of places and archaeologically significant data are very helpful, as are the bibliographical resources accompanying the articles. A quite helpful tool!

—Klyne R. Snodgrass, Professor Emeritus of New Testament, North Park Theological Seminary

Praise for the *Lexham Geographic Commentary on the Gospels*

A great number of the skills that contribute to solid biblical interpretation involve considering a text in one or another of its various contexts—linguistic, literary, historical, social, cultural, rhetorical, intertextual. But how often do we give adequate attention to the geographical and archaeological contexts of the events about which we read or the settings in which Jesus was raised, taught, acted, died, and rose again? This distinctive and clearly-focused commentary is replete with solid information about those geographical and archaeological contexts, and with connections to the Gospel texts (ranging from the secure to the suggestive, but always stimulating), that will admirably help us keep those physical contexts in view as we read, interpret, teach, and preach from the Gospels.

—David A. deSilva, Trustees' Distinguished Professor of New Testament and Greek, Ashland Theological Seminary

It is very rare for me to say in an endorsement that a work is "invaluable" and a "must purchase," but this is one of them. As one who has been writing commentaries for over thirty years, my only question is why someone didn't think of this a long time ago. My retirement project is doing a series of commentaries on the entire New Testament (nineteen volumes), and I just wish I had this five years ago when I started. Once I have this in hand, I will never write anything without consulting this "geographical commentary." I find it equally essential on general background issues as on geography itself. I am very impressed and cannot wait to start using it. Thank you, Barry, and thank you, Lexham Press! Now get me this material!

—Grant Osborne, professor emeritus, Trinity Evangelical Divinity School

This commentary focuses on the nexus of space, sociology, and theology as reflected in the Gospel text. Highlighting the socio-spatial background of each pericope enhances exegesis. This is especially true in the Gospels where the narrative shifts from place to place. The *Lexham Geographic Commentary on the Gospels* should be part of every Bible student's library.

—Philip Comfort, visiting professor of religion, Coastal Carolina University

LEXHAM GEOGRAPHIC COMMENTARY

on Acts through Revelation

LEXHAM GEOGRAPHIC COMMENTARY

on Acts through Revelation

Barry J. Beitzel, General Editor

Lexham Geographic Commentary on Acts through Revelation
Edited by Barry J. Beitzel

Lexham Press, 1313 Commercial St., Bellingham, WA 98225
LexhamPress.com

Print ISBN 9781683593423

Lexham Editorial: Douglas Mangum, James Spinti, and Erin Mangum
Cover Design: Bryan Hintz
Typesetting: ProjectLuz.com

25 26 27 28 29 30 31 / IN / 12 11 10 9 8 7 6 5 4 3

CONTENTS

ABBREVIATIONS

AB	Anchor Bible
ABD	*Anchor Bible Dictionary*. Edited by David Noel Freedman. 6 vols. New York: Doubleday, 1992
Ag. Ap.	Josephus' *Against Apion*
ANET	*Ancient Near Eastern Texts Relating to the Old Testament*. Edited by James B. Pritchard. 3rd ed. Princeton: Princeton University Press, 1969
ANF	*Ante-Nicene Fathers*. Edited by Alexander Roberts, James Donaldson, A. Cleveland Coxe, and Allan Menzies. 10 vols. American ed. New York: Christian Literature Publishing, 1885–1897
ANRW	*Aufstieg und Niedergang der römischen Welt: Geschichte und Kultur Roms im Spiegel der neueren Forschung. Part 2, Principat*. Edited by Hildegard Temporini and Wolfgang Haase. Berlin: de Gruyter, 1972–
Ant.	Josephus' *Jewish Antiquities*
b.	Babylonian Talmud
BA	*Biblical Archaeologist*
BAGRW	*Barrington Atlas of the Greek and Roman World*. Edited by Richard J. A. Talbert. Princeton, NJ: Princeton University Press, 2000
BAR	*Biblical Archaeology Review*
BASOR	*Bulletin of the American Schools of Oriental Research*
BBR	*Bulletin for Biblical Research*
BDAG	Bauer, W., F. W. Danker, W. F. Arndt, and F. W. Gingrich. *A Greek-English Lexicon of the New Testament and Other Early Christian Literature*. 3rd ed. Chicago: University of Chicago Press, 2000
BECNT	Baker Exegetical Commentary on the New Testament
BNP	*Brill's New Pauly: Encyclopaedia of the Ancient World*. Edited by H. Cancik, H. Schneider, and M. Landfester. 22 vols. Leiden: Brill, 2002–2012
BTB	*Biblical Theology Bulletin*
CIG	*Corpus Inscriptionum Graecarum*. Edited by August Boeckh. 4 vols. Berlin, 1828–1877
CIJ	*Corpus Inscriptionum Judaicarum*. Edited by Jean-Baptiste Frey. 2 vols. Rome: Pontifical Biblical Institute, 1936–1952
CurTM	*Currents in Theology and Mission*
DDD	*Dictionary of Deities and Demons in the Bible*. Edited by Karel van der Toorn, Bob Becking, and Pieter W. van der Horst. Leiden: Brill, 1995. 2nd rev. ed. Grand Rapids: Eerdmans, 1999

DJG	*Dictionary of Jesus and the Gospels*. Edited by Joel B. Green, Jeannine K. Brown, and Nicholas Perrin. 2nd ed. Downers Grove, IL: InterVarsity Press, 2013
DNTB	*Dictionary of New Testament Background*. Edited by Craig A. Evans and Stanley E. Porter. Downers Grove, IL: InterVarsity Press, 2000
EJ	*Encyclopaedia Judaica*. Edited by Fred Skolnik and Michael Berenbaum. 2nd ed. 22 vols. Detroit: Macmillan Reference USA, 2007
HA-ESI	*Ḥadashot Arkheologiyot–Excavations and Surveys in Israel (from 1999)*
ICC	International Critical Commentary
IEJ	*Israel Exploration Journal*
IG	*Inscriptiones Graecae*. Berlin: de Gruyter, 1924–
ISBE	*International Standard Bible Encyclopedia*. Edited by Geoffrey W. Bromiley. 4 vols. Grand Rapids: Eerdmans, 1979–1988
JAS	*Journal of Archaeological Science*
JBL	*Journal of Biblical Literature*
JETS	*Journal of the Evangelical Theological Society*
JSS	*Journal of Semitic Studies*
JTS	*Journal of Theological Studies*
LCL	Loeb Classical Library
Life	Josephus' *The Life*
LSJ	H. G. Liddell, R. Scott, and H. S. Jones. *A Greek-English Lexicon*. 9th ed. with rev. supp. Oxford: Clarendon, 1996
m.	Mishnah
MAB	*The New Moody Atlas of the Bible*. Edited by Barry J. Beitzel. Chicago: Moody Press, 2009
NEA	*Near Eastern Archaeology*
NEAEHL	*New Encyclopaedia of Archaeological Excavations in the Holy Land*. Edited by Ephraim Stern. 5 vols. Jerusalem: Israel Exploration Society, 1993, 2008
NICNT	New International Commentary on the New Testament
NIDB	*New Interpreter's Dictionary of the Bible*. Edited by Katharine Doob Sakenfeld. 5 vols. Nashville, TN: Abingdon, 2006–2009
NIGTC	New International Greek Testament Commentary
NovT	*Novum Testamentum*
NPNF[1]	*Nicene and Post-Nicene Fathers*, Series 1 (Vols. 1–8: Augustine; Vols. 9–14: Chrysostom). Edited by Philip Schaff. 14 vols. New York: The Christian Literature Company, 1886–1889
NPNF[2]	*Nicene and Post-Nicene Fathers*, Series 2. Edited by Philip Schaff and Henry Wace. 14 vols. New York: The Christian Literature Company, 1890–1900
NTApoc	*New Testament Apocrypha*. 2 vols. Revised ed. Edited by Wilhelm Schneemelcher. English trans. ed. Robert McL. Wilson. Louisville: Westminster John Knox, 2003
NTS	*New Testament Studies*
OGIS	*Orientis graeci inscriptiones selectae*. Edited by Wilhelm Dittenberger. 2 vols. Leipzig: Hirzel, 1903–1905
OTP	*The Old Testament Pseudepigrapha*. Edited by James H. Charlesworth. 2 vols. New York: Doubleday, 1983, 1985

PEQ	*Palestine Exploration Quarterly*
RPC	*Roman Provincial Coinage*. 10 vols. London: British Museum Press, 1992–
SBL	Society of Biblical Literature
SEG	*Supplementum epigraphicum graecum*. 8 vols. Amsterdam: J.C. Gieben, 1923–1971
SIG	*Sylloge Inscriptionum Graecarum*. Edited by Wilhelm Dittenberger. 4 vols. 3rd ed. Leipzig: Hirzel, 1915–1924
SHBC	Smyth & Helwys Bible Commentary
t.	Tosefta
TAM	*Tituli Asiae Minoris*. 7 vols. Vienna: Österreichische Akademie der Wissenschaften, 1901–2007
TDNT	*Theological Dictionary of the New Testament*. Edited by Gerhard Kittel and Gerhard Friedrich. Translated by Geoffrey W. Bromiley. 10 vols. Grand Rapids: Eerdmans, 1964–1976
Tg. Neof.	Targum Neofiti
TJ	*Trinity Journal*
TS	*Theological Studies*
TynBul	*Tyndale Bulletin*
UF	*Ugarit-Forschungen*
J.W.	Josephus' *Jewish War*
WBC	Word Biblical Commentary

SERIES PREFACE

To adapt a line from Ecclesiastes 12, "Of the writing of commentaries there is no end." Today's practitioners of biblical studies axiomatically regard the enterprise to be richly multi-faceted—even multidisciplinary. As a result of such breadth of inquiry, no one commentary series is capable of straddling the entire intellectual waterfront. When we see a "Layman's Commentary" series or a "Critical Commentary" series or an "Expositor's Commentary" series, we implicitly recognize and accept the fact that certain aspects of the biblical text will be emphasized while others may be treated more selectively or not at all. The same largely holds true for a "Theological Commentary" series, an "Exegetical Commentary" series, or a "Bible Backgrounds Commentary" series. Perhaps even more narrowly focused but still in this same tradition, one thinks of an "Arminian Commentary" series, a "Lutheran Commentary" series, and possibly even a "Woman's Commentary" series or a "South Asia Commentary" series. It has become understandably acceptable to us that no one commentary source can or should attempt to cover everything inherent in this widely diverse field. Accordingly, to refer to a "Geographic Commentary" series is merely to echo this same sentiment, while at the same time to attempt to delineate something of a distinctive approach and to define a particular focus of textual explication.

The conceptual premise of this commentary holds that geography is a legitimate, if commonly overlooked, hermeneutical category. Even cursory reflection leads one to the inescapable conclusion that words from God have been revealed in *real time* about *real people* in *real places*. And we think it *highly significant* that authors who spell out for us the biblical storyline in terms of "Who," "Why," "When," "How," "What," or "So What," frequently add the element of "Where," whether explicitly or implicitly. This fairly common tendency to weave the spatial dimension into the fabric of the Bible's narrative storyline actually sets the Scriptures apart from most other ancient holy writings. And it does this in quite striking and dramatic ways!

To be sure, sacred writings of each of the world's religions are designed to guide and nurture their devoted followers. But it must be stressed, other sacred writings do this in markedly different ways, insofar as geography is concerned. Let us take a glimpse at the sacred writings of the world's five largest religions. Thus, for example, the *Rigveda* (or *Rig-Veda*) of Hinduism is a complex of more than one thousand holy hymns, poetically expressing interest in establishing or maintaining cosmic/pantheistic order, which will bring to its faithful adherents a life of balance, bounty, and fertility on earth. The hymns reference a myriad of deities but few places. The *Rigveda* makes repeated mention of "seven rivers," but most are of uncertain or fluctuating identifications. It is noteworthy that the mention of these rivers relates thematically to the slaying of the god Vrdra, the dragon, thus releasing vast reservoirs of celestial water so that these seven rivers can be free to surge and to inundate the thirsty plains and deserts and to establish fertility across the land.

Likewise, in Buddhism's *Tripiṭaka* (or *Tipiṭaka*)—where concern focuses on Enlightenment and on its four noble truths designed to point out the way of morality, concentration, and knowledge—geography can be said to play a negligible, almost nonexistent role. The *Tripiṭaka* makes mention of fewer than three dozen place names, a great majority of which appear pragmatically in the text only to identify where Buddha stayed during the rainy season, where he gave a particular *sutta* (teaching), or where he spent a night during one of his itinerant journeys. Few places are found in these writings, and even these few seem to have neither narrative nor religious function of any sort.

Taoism's *Daodejing* (or *Dao De Jing*), from a quantitative perspective, is probably the least geographically-conscious ancient religious expression. The religion's essentially ascetic core priorities are focused elsewhere. I have found the Yangtze river identified twice in the text, in the context of ruling over kings, and the *Daodejing* may likewise make passing reference to an unnamed and unsituated river, stream, ravine, valley, or road. There is not much more.

Finally, Islam's *Qu'ran* (or *Koran*) bears the closest affinity to the Bible in terms of its spatial priorities. At the end of the day, however, the entire *Qu'ran* contains fewer geographical citations than can be found in Genesis 1–20 alone. Moreover, many of its locational referents appear ultimately to derive *from* the Bible: e.g., the Garden of Eden; Egypt; Mt. Sinai; Babylon; Media/Midian; and Gog and Magog. In fact, the *Qu'ran* tends to display a sharp antipathy towards towns and cities, where in its view sin abounds, people disobey God, and from where true believers have been evicted (doubtless reflecting Muhammad's own story in this regard). Islam's writings mention Mecca and Medina, as well as several people groups spread across the Arabian Peninsula (Russ; Yathrib; Tubba; Aad; Thamood), but not much more. Little wonder that an OCLC WorldCat bibliographic search for the entry "Atlas: Qur'an/Koran" yields but one entry.[1]

In vivid contradistinction to these other sacred writings, the Bible in all its canonical segments is replete with references to place names (by my rough count, nearly nine hundred distinct names, many attested multiple times), in addition to scores of names for mountains, bodies of water, deserts/wildernesses, regions, territories, provinces, and the like—including at times when geography is tellingly employed as a nexus of interpretation.

It is this distinctive and rather common *integration* of place names into the narrative by the biblical authors I wish to stress, not just the sheer quantity of references. Often an incident will be said to have occurred on a certain identified hill, in a particular designated valley, on a discrete named plain, or at a given denominated town. There are

1. Shawqī Abū Khalīl, *Atlas of the Qur'ân* (Riyadh and New York: Darussalam, 2003), appearing in four language editions. I am making a formal distinction here between an Atlas of the *Qur'an* and an Atlas of Islam. The latter bibliographical category, describing and portraying the growth of Islam throughout the Arabian Peninsula, across the Middle East and the Mediterranean world, and into Europe and to points beyond, is well represented in literature and is very useful.

times when the name of the place itself becomes an important part of the revelation, frequently including a wordplay or a pun on the name, so as to reinforce the event's explicit location in public consciousness and memory. Occasionally, an aspect of geography becomes a theological axis around which a major theme and/or a large portion of a book revolves such as fertility and the book of Deuteronomy, forestation and the book of Isaiah, hydrology and the book of Psalms, or agriculture and the book of Joel. Sometimes it is precisely a geographical reference or allusion that enables scholars to assign a book to a place of origin (e.g., Amos in Israel's northern kingdom; James in the eastern Mediterranean basin). Geography can be found as a significant component of biblical prophecy, whether a prophecy both given and realized in the Old Testament or fulfilled later in a New Testament narrative.

As I have argued elsewhere, many crucially important aspects of biblical history are said to have transpired *in very precise places* on earth—not just in empty space nor even in heaven.[2] In the Old Testament, covenantal faith is inextricably tied to place, and "land" becomes the prism of this faith. Land is the arena in which God acts mightily on behalf of his people. The ancestral narratives of the biblical patriarchs tell a story of place and offer spatial detail: early Israelite forebears lived in a named city within a given region (Ur of the Chaldeans), and they moved from there to take up residence at another place (Harran). While living at this latter location, the patriarch Abraham was singled out by God and commanded to move to yet another particular place (Canaan), where we are told he lived and worshiped in specified locations. And significantly, one must recall that many aspects of this primeval story are later rehearsed in the biblical text, often also precisely in the context of space.

Once in Canaan, Abraham and his descendants are promised definable land (הארץ, *hā'āreṣ*), further qualified with geographical boundaries. Many of the subsequent narratives are shaped in a certain trajectory because of this promise of land: the years in Egypt, the Exodus motif, the Sinai covenantal formulation, the conquest/settlement of the land, the Israelite kingdoms in the land, the captivity away from the land, the return to the land, and the New Israel in the land. It is not an overstatement to declare that during its later years of history, Israel's rootage in this covenantal "land" provides its faithful their foundational identity, security, and even prosperity.

When they were not in possession of their land, Israelites are often described by the biblical writers in terms that reflect the precarious connotations of landlessness, aimlessness, and estrangement. At such times they are called "sojourners," "wanderers," or "exiles." And whether removed to Egypt, Babylonia, or elsewhere, landlessness became tantamount to hopelessness. At the same time, it is a remarkable reality that biblical writers normally give us an indication of where Israel was, even when relocated outside their land: they were in Egypt, they were in Goshen, they journeyed to Sinai to receive the law, they lived for the better part of forty years at Kadesh-barnea,

2. Barry J. Beitzel, *The New Moody Atlas of the Bible* [*MAB*] (Chicago: Moody Press, 2009), 14–17; idem, *Biblica, the Bible Atlas: A Social and Historical Journey Through the Lands of the Bible* (London: Viking/Penguin, 2006), Foreword. Parts of this preface draw from sections of these works. Used with permission.

and so forth.[3] Later, when their kingdoms collapsed, they fled to Egypt or were taken captive to Transjordan, to Assyria, to Babylon, to Elam, or to Media.[4] While such information may seem extraneous to the modern reader, it is worth noting that this information is sometimes repeated in the text or is rehearsed in a later text. It is also from many of these same locations that Israel will come to settle in their land or later will be regathered to their land.

Israel's covenantal faith was very much based on and grounded in events that occurred *in certain places* in the world. There was an acute consciousness of a national home, a definable geographic domain in which even the soil was divinely consecrated, what one may call the "holy land" (Zech 2:12 [MT 2:16]—אדמת הקדש, *admath haqqodesh*; Ps 78:54—גבול קדשי, *gebul qodshi*; see also Dan 11:16, 41—ארץ הצבי, *erets-hatsevi*; compare Heb 11:9—εἰς γῆν τῆς ἐπαγγελίας, *eis gēn tēs epangelias*). It must be concluded that space/place plays an integral role in the whole of Old Testament history and theology.

Similarly, in the New Testament Gospels, one thinks of the location of Jesus' birth, his crucifixion, his resurrection, and his ascension. Also, much of the teaching of Jesus was clearly correlated to where he was situated at the time. He speaks of "living water" at Jacob's well (John 4:10), he calls himself the "bread of life" at Capernaum, where basaltic grain mills were manufactured (John 6:48); he declares Peter to be the "rock" against which not even the "gates of Hades" could prevail while at Caesarea Philippi, a site known for its associations with the underworld (Hades or hell) in ancient Near Eastern, Jewish, and Greek literature (Matt 16:18). In a same manner, while situated at certain locations, Jesus speaks of various kinds of soil, of thorns and thistles, of the strong east wind, of the flowers of the field, and of branches abiding in vines, and more.

Following the Gospels, one observes an unmistakable geographical correlation between the uniquely centrifugal form of the Great Commission (Acts 1:8: *from* Jerusalem, *then to* all of Judea and Samaria, and *finally to* the ends of the earth) and the way in which the early apostolic movement and the expansion of the early church are presented pervasively in both Acts and the Epistles. Once again geography is found to play a pivotal role in the biblical storyline.

So, is there a place for a "Geographic Commentary" in today's world? Consider this illustration. A patient begins to awaken from the anesthesia of an outpatient surgery. The attending physician soon happily discovers that the patient has become fully conscious and is quite aware of her circumstances: the patient can recall her name and address, if married the name of her spouse, if a parent the number and names of her children (and perhaps grandchildren), and, if quizzed, she can recite the password for her iPhone or the security code for her house. One might say this patient has regained full cognizance—except in one critical way. This patient has awakened in a new place, the unfamiliar location of a recovery room, and therefore she is unaware of her wider spatial surroundings. The patient cannot identify exactly where she is and, without

3. Refer to such texts as Gen 12:10; 13:1; 45:10; 46:34; 50:8; Exod 19; Num 10:11–12; 13:26; Deut 2:14. This segment of Israel's history is addressed in *MAB*, 106–14 (and maps 33–35).

4. Refer to such texts as 2 Kgs 15:29; 17:6; 18:11; 24:12–17; 25:6–12; 1 Chr 5:26; 8:6.; Ezra 2:59–63; Esth 2:6; Jer 52:28–30; Ezek 3:15; Dan 1:2–7. This segment of Israel's history is addressed in *MAB*, 194–95 (and map 81).

assistance, she would be unable immediately to locate the hospital's exit door or to find her car parked outside.

This patient, unmindful of her spatial surroundings, can be said to be suffering from a condition called "atopia." Atopia derives from a Greek word—actually the combination of a Greek negative particle prefixed to a noun referencing space or place (ἄ + τοπος = ἄτοπος, *atopos*)—and it means literally "no space/place" or "out of place."[5] Our patient lacks awareness of her spatial environs; she has atopia.

Behind this simple and inconsequential illustration lies a more profound reality. We can discover atopia at work in more than just recovery rooms. In America, what I will call "cultural atopia" can be observed across our educational systems, and, more generally, it has insinuated itself into our culture. Some twenty years ago, the widely-recognized educational authority, Alexander B. Murphy, asserted that from the 1960s through the 1980s, in the wake of the triumph of the social sciences and humanities, most academics in the United States considered the subject of geography to be a marginal discipline.[6] By the late 1980s, Murphy observed, Americans' general ignorance of geography, when compared to most other western countries, had become too widespread to ignore any longer. To the degree that Murphy's assessment is accurate, and there is an abundance of literature to support his claims, it seems we moderns, particularly in America, continue to some extent to live in a state of cultural atopia. Thus, for example, in a 1993 Gallup poll taken for the National Geographic Society, one in six Americans could not identify the continent of North America on an unmarked map of the world, and one in five could not identify on an unmarked map the particular state in which they resided. Feeling that somehow I must have misread or misunderstood these results in an article in the *Chicago Tribune*, I corresponded directly with George Gallup, who kindly confirmed in a personal letter that, in fact, these were the actual findings.

Nearer to our own time, Roper Public Affairs conducted a nationwide survey for the National Geographic Society, between the dates of December 17, 2005 and January 20, 2006. Among their findings were the following: After two Gulf wars, 63% of adult respondents could not identify Iraq on an unmarked map of the Middle East. Perhaps

---

5. For the etymology and meaning of "atopia" in several semantic fields, including medicine, see *The Oxford English Dictionary*, 2nd ed., suppl. vol. 1 (Oxford: Oxford University Press, 1993), 146c; *Webster's Third New International Dictionary, Unabridged* (Springfield, MA: Merriam-Webster, Inc.), 139b. Prefixing this privative to Greek lexemes can produce other words with a negative denotation, such as *a*gnostic, *a*theist, *a*millennial, or *a*symmetry. Adding other prefixes to this same Greek noun can produce words such as *u*topia (= "perfect space/place") or *dys*topia (= "bad/wicked space/place"). This Greek word occurs in the New Testament, either describing someone/something that is morally or behaviorally out of place (i.e. wrong, perverse, evil, degenerate; e.g. Luke 23:41; Acts 25:5; 2 Thess 3:2) or physically unusual, improper, unexpected, abnormal or out of place (e.g. Acts 28:6). The same word appears in very similar contexts in the works of Thucydides, Polybius, Philo, Dio Chrysostom, and Josephus, just as it appears in Ignatius' *Letter to the Magnesians*.

6. Alexander B. Murphy, "Rediscovering the Importance of Geography." *The Chronicle of Higher Education* 45.10 (October 30, 1998), A64–65. This situation has shown signs of some improvement over the past fifteen years; see "Geography's Place in Higher Education in the United States," *Journal of Geography in Higher Education* 31.1 (2007): 121–41, though atopia is still alive and well in today's culture.

more pertinent, with so many jobs leaving America for places like India, 47% of the respondents were unable to locate that country where their jobs may go. Still closer to home, 50% could not identify the State of New York (after the events of 9/11), and 34% could not identify Louisiana (after Hurricane Katrina). When told in the survey that escape from an approaching hurricane was possible only by evacuating to the northwest, 34% were unable to indicate correctly which way was northwest on a map. A wide array of other, more current, survey materials exist, and their findings generally follow this same cultural pattern.

I suppose results like these may evoke comments having to do with the need for a more robust understanding of world affairs or of what it means to be living in a global society with numerous globally-affected realities, but that is not where I wish to go. Rather, it seems to me that, as a consequence of this spatial malady or disquieting trend, if I may call it that, a rational argument can be adduced according to which this kind of spatial deficiency will inevitably carry over and bear tellingly upon *how we educate ourselves and others in biblical matters*: How we read and study our Bible, how we assess various elements found in a given biblical text, how we question and what sorts of questions we pose to the text, and the like. Those tutored in the American educational system are far more likely to follow their training and to ask questions of "Who," "Why," "How," "What," "When," but they are far less likely to ask questions of "Where." And, to the degree there is continuing validity to this line of reasoning, modernity and the modern church have now inherited what I shall call "biblical atopia," a lack of awareness of the spatial realia of the Bible, a malady in our contemporary world that may actually worsen as a result of certain tools of technology available in the computer age.

Biblical atopia, in my view, can manifest itself in different ways. It can appear, for example, as innocent exclusionism, simply failing to pose questions of "Where" and thereby failing to discern what must be seen as a conspicuous and deliberate geographical pattern found in the writings of the inspired biblical authors. It can also appear as ignorant romanticism. Some years ago I had a student in seminary who was joining the Trinity Middle Eastern Studies Program and was going to join us for a study tour of Israel and Sinai. She added that she could hardly wait to go home at Christmas and to share this good news with an elderly saint, a lady she much adored in her local church. When she returned after the holidays, she said to me, "I told my friend that I was going to be able to visit Mt. Sinai, Judea, Galilee, Jericho, Jerusalem, Bethlehem, Capernaum, and many other places associated with the lives of Abraham, Moses, David, Peter, and Jesus, thinking she would be delighted to hear such news." Instead, my student reported, the saintly woman had replied: "Well now, I know all those places are in the Bible, but I never thought of them as being on the earth."

Beyond innocent exclusionism or ignorant romanticism, biblical atopia can appear as idealized sentimentalism. Centuries of medieval art or poetry, or layers of preaching or meditation, can so idealize and sanctify the biblical storyline that one is led to imagine the land of promise as a veritable paradise, a glorious, magnificent, sacred, and utopian place of almost mythical proportions. This form of biblical atopia is likewise misguided and is out of step with the realistic presentation of biblical authors.

Finally, biblical atopia can appear today in the form of overt skepticism. Wanting perhaps quick and easy answers, some Bible readers may ask, "What difference does it *really* make where this or that biblical event took place? After all, it was very long ago and very far away."

As a response, I would strenuously argue that one must guard against *any* tendency to tacitly disregard what appears to be the priority of the inspired biblical writers, simply because of possible competing priorities in our modern world: Not only with names or discussions of places found in the biblical text, but also with names of persons, or identifiable conversations, or recorded dates, or narrative scenes and sequences, or even particular names for God, any of which may at times seem to us to be extraneous to a given plot and are therefore unworthy of our consideration in interpreting a text. Stated otherwise, in our search for answers to textual questions, or in our quest to discover meaning, relevance, and application in a biblical verse, paragraph, or chapter, we must be sure to exercise caution, lest we unwittingly create contemporary interpretative priorities that may, in fact, not align with those of the biblical authors, who, in the economy of biblical inspiration, can hardly be accused of including meaningless and trivial subject matter. We may not always be able to discern why a text reads as it does, but we *can* be certain that the text was not written to veil meaning or to add what the text's author regarded as extraneous and irrelevant details.

If the Christian gospel were simply a matter of otherworldliness, or if it were concerned only with applying spiritual or moral values, gaining an appreciation of the spatial dimension of the Bible would hardly matter, and seminal events in the Bible would hardly have been geographically encoded in the text by inspired biblical writers. But it is neither of these! Central to the *kerygma* of the New Testament is the foundational claim that God became Man at a definite moment in time and at a precise point in space. To be unaware of or to neglect the geographical DNA of the Bible or the biblical world will therefore often mean that one may run afoul of the biblical argument or that reality may dissolve into sentimentalism. The *Lexham Geographic Commentary* [LGC] seeks to address many "Where" questions.

Barry J. Beitzel
Bannockburn, Deerfield, IL
October 2018

VOLUME PREFACE

The second segment of the New Testament—from the book of Acts through the Revelation of John—is a compelling and courageous story of the outward thrust of the early apostolic movement and the subsequent growth of the early Christian church. Perhaps the basic outline of this story is most clearly reflected at the very beginning of the book of Acts, contained in Jesus' final earthly declaration: "But you [the apostles, who had accompanied Jesus to the summit of the Mount of Olives] will receive power when the Holy Spirit comes on you, and you will be my witnesses in Jerusalem, and in all Judea and Samaria, and to the ends of the earth" (Acts 1:8, NIV). Like concentric circles radiating from their epicenter, this grand story begins in Jerusalem and with Jewish people only (see Acts 1–7), it expands outwardly first to include the regions of Judea and Samaria (see Acts 8–12), and it comes finally to extend both to the ends of the earth and to include both Jew and gentile (see Acts 13–28). The Epistles that follow are but one of the profound consequences related to this outward radiating thrust of the early apostles.

At its quintessential core, this is very much a story of the proclamation of the gospel! But it is also a story that is couched contextually in a manner related to space, and actually in a magnificent way. For, by the time one nears the end of this initial chapter of the early Christian church—a period of some sixty fairly intense years—apostolic churches are known to have been established in Judea; in various cities throughout Phoenicia; across the vast Roman province of Syria; traversing the spacious expanse of Asia Minor, from the provinces of Cilicia and Cappadocia west to the Aegean Sea; on the Greek mainland, from the provinces of Macedonia and Achaia to the Peloponnesus, on several Mediterranean islands; and on the Italian peninsula. The story may begin in the Judean city of Jerusalem, but, in Acts, it ends in faraway Rome, and, in Revelation, it concludes on the remote Mediterranean island of Patmos. In between, these apostolic champions of the gospel are said to have presented their message in a wide array of Roman cities. They would then courageously travel across the miles—on physically challenging and largely unsafe international arteries, regional thoroughfares, or secondary pathways—so they could convey the good news to those who lived in the next municipal area.[1]

1. For the extensive travels of the apostle Paul, see *MAB*, 253. My own estimate of the mileage between cities known to have been visited by Paul on his various itineraries comes to a total of some 13,400 *air* miles. But when calculated according to the winding terrestrial roadways across the Roman Empire, the total distance would exceed that figure by a considerable margin. Additionally, one discovers what amounts to referenced but unchronicled Pauline itineraries: to Arabia (Gal 1:17), to Corinth (2 Cor 12:14; 13:1), and to Illyricum (Rom 15:19).

An international team of nineteen men and women have contributed to this volume and to our greater understanding of the spatial dimension of the early apostolic storyline. Professionally trained and with firsthand experience in various elements within the discipline, this stellar lineup includes some of the leading voices of apostolic geography known across the world, whether related to Canaan proper, or to the apostolic realms of Syria, Asia Minor, Greece, the Mediterranean islands, or Italy. Each contributor has published elsewhere on one or more aspects of biblical geography, and in some cases published prolifically, and I am exceedingly pleased to be able to present such an outstanding complement of fully-qualified scholars for this volume.

Moreover, the apostle also refers to shipwrecks of which we have no record (2 Cor 11:25), and then there is his expressed desire to visit Spain (Rom 15:24, 28; see also Rom 1:10-15). Looking beyond Paul, one must recognize the considerable distances involved relating to the writings of the apostle Peter. Assuming Petrine authorship, the epistle of 1 Peter was written from Rome, before AD 64–68, when Peter's life ended at the hands of the Emperor Nero. At the beginning of his epistle, Peter addresses "God's elect, exiles scattered throughout the provinces of Pontus, Galatia, Cappadocia, Asia, and Bithynia" (1 Pet 1:1, NIV). Perhaps in a manner similar to Revelation 1:4–4:22, where a courier apparently carried John's letter(s) to each of the seven churches, or similar to Colossians 4:15–17, where reference is made to Pauline writings that were to be read in several churches, the text of 1 Peter implies the activity of a courier conveying the apostle's writings from one Roman province to another and from one early church to another. Very rough mileage estimates entailed in this journey—crossing from Rome to the vicinity of modern Istanbul, then traversing the five contiguous Roman provinces, ending an Asia Minor circuit back near the coastline of the Aegean, assuming the courier looped through the heartland of the provinces and not the periphery, and assuming he did not return to Rome—represents a distance of some 1,800 miles, whether by land or sea. For the many difficulties and hazards of ancient travel, see Barry J. Beitzel, "Travel and Communication," *ABD* 6.644–48.

CHAPTER 1

TYPOLOGICAL GEOGRAPHY AND THE PROGRESS OF THE GOSPEL IN ACTS

Acts 1:8, 27:1–28:16; 28:30–31

Mark L. Strauss

KEY POINTS

- Geographical references in Luke-Acts function not only historically, but also theologically, typologically representing the progress of the gospel.
- In Luke's birth narrative (Luke 1–2), the good news begins in Jerusalem, symbolizing the roots of Christianity in the covenant promises of the Old Testament and Judaism.
- Jesus' Journey to Jerusalem, or Travel Narrative (Luke 9–19), is both a historical and theological journey; Jerusalem ambivalently represents both God's glorious salvation and Israel's stubborn resistance to the gospel.
- In Acts the progress of the gospel from Jerusalem, to Judea and Samaria, and to the ends of the earth (Acts 1:8) represents both the geographical and ethnic movements from Jerusalem to Rome and from Jews to gentiles.
- Paul's arrival in Rome, the center (not the "end") of the gentile world, confirms the continuing success of the gospel (Acts 28:30–31) and its unstoppable advance to all people everywhere (to the "ends of the earth"). The story is not yet over, though its conclusion has been written.

INTRODUCTION

The Book of Acts is without doubt the most geographically focused book in the New Testament. From beginning to end Acts is all about geography. It begins with an announcement that the gospel is to progress geographically from Jerusalem to the ends of the earth (1:8). It ends with a geographically rich sea voyage from Caesarea Maritima to Rome (27:1–28:16). In this latter trip alone, Luke refers to more than two dozen geographical locations.

This article, however, is not about the geography of Acts per se, which would be a massive study well beyond our scope.[1] Nor is it about the historical accuracy of Luke's geographical references, though that would also be a profitable study.[2] It is about Luke's geographical theology. For Luke, the journeys in Luke and Acts have not only historical significance, but also symbolic and theological significance. This article examines how Luke uses geography typologically to symbolize the paradox of the cross and ethnic progress of the gospel from Jews to all people everywhere.

ACTS 1:8 AND THE GEOGRAPHICAL AND THEOLOGICAL PLAN OF ACTS

Acts 1:8 has rightly been called the theme verse of the Book of Acts. According to Luke, following Jesus' resurrection and before ascending to heaven, he appeared to the disciples over a period of forty days, speaking about the central theme of his teaching in the gospel: *the kingdom of God*. Though Jesus had not established the kingdom in the political and nationalistic manner the disciples expected, they still wondered whether this was just a matter of timing. So they ask him, "Lord, are you restoring the kingdom to Israel at this time?" (Acts 1:6).[3] While Jesus does not explicitly reject the idea of a physical kingdom on earth, he responds that the "times or seasons" (χρόνους ἢ καιρούς, *chronous ē kairous*) of the kingdom are not to be their concern.[4] Instead, "you will receive power when the Holy Spirit comes on you; and you will be my witnesses in Jerusalem, and in all Judea and Samaria, and to the ends of the earth."

1. For detailed discussion of geographical locations in Acts, see the expanded edition of Eckhard J. Schnabel, *Acts*, (Grand Rapids: Zondervan, 2012). For Luke's conception of the world in his first century context, see J. M. Scott, "Luke's Geographical Horizon," in *The Book of Acts in Its Graeco-Roman Setting*, ed. D. W. J. Gill and C. Gempf, vol. 2 of *The Book of Acts in Its First Century Setting*, ed. Bruce W. Winter (Grand Rapids: Eerdmans, 1994), 484–583. For a specialized reading of Acts from the perspective of contemporary spatial theory of geography, see Matthew Sleeman, *Geography and the Ascension Narrative in Acts* (Cambridge: Cambridge University Press, 2009). Sleeman argues that spatial geography, particularly the relationship of heaven to earth following the ascension, is critically important in Luke-Acts, yet neglected by those who take a merely cartographical view of geography. For a summary and critique of Sleeman, see Douglas S. Huffman's review in *JETS* 54 (2011): 396–98.

2. For the accuracy of Luke's geographical references in Palestine, see Martin Hengel, "The Geography of Palestine in Acts," in *The Book of Acts in Its Palestinian Setting*, ed. Richard Bauckham, vol. 4 of *The Book of Acts in Its First Century Setting*, ed. Bruce W. Winter (Grand Rapids: Eerdmans, 1995), 27–78. For Luke's references throughout Acts see Colin J. Hemer, *The Book of Acts in the Setting of Hellenistic History*, ed. Conrad Gempf (Tübingen: Mohr Siebeck, 1989).

3. All translations are from the NIV unless otherwise stated.

4. For the presence of both present and future eschatology in Luke-Acts, see Darrell L. Bock, *A Theology of Luke and Acts* (Grand Rapids: Zondervan, 2012), ch. 20; Craig S. Keener, *Acts: An Exegetical Commentary* (Grand Rapids: Baker Academic, 2012), 1:682–88. As Keener points out, "Contrary to the later Gentile church's de-Judaized way of reading Scriptures, Jesus does not deny that Israel's restoration will come. Rather he merely warns the disciples it is not their place to know the *times* (1:7), the sort of detailed chronological map offered in some apocalyptic documents; instead, they must focus on their mission" (1:687; emphasis original).

Key themes of Acts emerge here: (1) the disciples as Jesus' representatives, fulfilling and completing his role in the world; (2) the eschatological Spirit of God as the guiding and empowering agent behind all they say and do; (3) the expansion of the gospel from its roots in Jerusalem to the ends of the earth.

AN OUTLINE OF ACTS?

Acts 1:8 is sometimes seen not only as a thematic introduction to Acts, but also the book's outline and structure:

1. The gospel to Jerusalem (chs. 1–7)
2. The gospel to Judea and Samaria (chs. 8–12)
3. The gospel to the ends of the earth (chs. 13–28)

This simple outline has a number of strengths: (1) All the events in chapters 1–7 occur in *Jerusalem*. (2) Acts 8:1, a key transitional statement following the martyrdom of Stephen, specifically refers to *Judea and Samaria* as the places to which the church was scattered. Most of the events in this middle section indeed take place in Judea or Samaria: Philip in Samaria (8:5–25); the Ethiopian eunuch—Judean road to Gaza (8:26–40); Peter's miracles at Lydda and Joppa (9:32–43); the conversion of Cornelius' family at Caesarea Maritima (10:1–11:18). (3) The missionary journeys of Paul that begin in chapter 13 climax with his arrival in Rome—the center of the gentile world and hence symbolic of the gospel's ultimate expansion to the *end of the earth*. In short, the ethnic movement of Acts—from Jews to Samaritans to gentiles—parallels the geographical movement, from Jerusalem/Judea, to Samaria, to the gentile world.

Yet there are also problems with this simple outline. The middle section does not quite work, since it includes not only the expansion of the gospel to Judea and Samaria, but also the establishment of the important church in Antioch, Syria (11:19–30), as well as Paul's conversion on the road to Damascus (9:1–19a), his time in Damascus (9:19b–25) and his return to Jerusalem (9:26–30). Luke's narrative in this middle section also returns to *Jerusalem* to recount the execution of James and Peter's miraculous release from jail (12:1–23). Finally, this simple geographical outline does not do justice to the length of the third section (chs. 13–28), which comprises more than half the book.

There are many other proposals concerning Luke's structure and design.[5] Many scholars note the summaries of the gospel's advance in 6:7; 9:31; 12:24; 16:5; 19:20; 28:31, which can yield the following outline: [6]

1. The church in Jerusalem (1:1–6:7)
2. The church in Judea and Samaria (6:8–9:31)
3. The gospel to the gentiles (ethnic, nongeographical) (9:32–12:24)
4. The gospel to Asia (12:25–16:5)
5. The gospel to Europe (but with a return to Ephesus) (16:6–19:20)
6. The gospel to Rome (19:21–28:31)

While this outline nicely combines geographical references and summary statements, it, too, has its problems and inconsistencies. First, there are a number of summary statements in Acts that it does not take into account (2:41, 47; 4:4; 5:14; 11:21; 13:48; 19:10). If Luke were structuring his volume around summaries, one would expect more consistency. Furthermore, there are some important sections in Acts that are not demarcated with summary statements. The Council of Jerusalem (15:1–35), for example, is often identified as both the structural and theological center point of Acts.[7] Yet here it is treated as a mere subsection of "the gospel to Asia." Similarly, it could be argued that Paul's break with Barnabas and the beginning of the second missionary journey (15:36–41) is a more important transition than the summary statement in 16:5. Furthermore, the designation "the gospel to Asia" used for 12:25–16:5 is much more apropos for Paul's ministry in Ephesus during his third missionary journey (19:1–41), rather than his outreach into Cyprus and Galatia on his first journey. During Paul's time in Ephesus, "all the Jews and Greeks who lived in the province of Asia heard the word of the Lord" (19:10).

In light of these difficulties, it is probably best not to expect from Luke the kind of precisely delineated outline sought by Western commentators. What is clear throughout Acts is that Luke is focused on *the unrelenting advance of the gospel*, and that this progress has critically important *ethnic* as well as *geographical* dimensions. In the discussion that follows we will trace the geographical and theological significance of the four place names mentioned in Acts 1:8—Jerusalem, Judea, Samaria, and the end of the earth.

THE GOSPEL TO JERUSALEM

The importance of Jerusalem and the temple in Luke-Acts is well document-

---

5. See Keener, *Acts*, 1:575–81, for various proposals.

6. Adapted from Ben Witherington III, *The Acts of the Apostles: A Socio-Rhetorical Commentary* (Grand Rapids, Eerdmans, 1998), 74.

7. I. H. Marshall, *Acts: An Introduction and Commentary* (Downers Grove, IL: InterVarsity Press, 1980), 256.

ed.[8] The Gospel contains thirty-one references to Jerusalem, compared to only thirteen in Matthew and eleven in Mark. The book of Acts has an additional sixty references. The Gospel begins and ends in the temple in Jerusalem. The opening scene has Zechariah offering incense in the temple, where he receives the angelic announcement of the birth of John the Baptist (1:5–25). The closing scene has the disciples returning to Jerusalem after the resurrection "with great joy" and staying "continually at the temple praising God" (24:53).

The Ambivalent Significance of Jerusalem in Luke-Acts

While clearly important for Luke's theology, Jerusalem plays an ambivalent role in Luke-Acts. On the one hand, Jerusalem is God's holy city, the place where his salvation will be achieved. The first announcement of salvation comes to Zechariah in the Jerusalem temple (1:11–17; compare Mal 4:5–6). His song of praise at John's birth celebrates that God is raising up "a horn of salvation for us in the house of his servant David ... salvation from our enemies" (1:69–71). This salvation is

8. J. K. Elliot, "Jerusalem in Acts and the Gospels," *NTS* 23 (1976–77), 462–69; M. Bachmann, *Jerusalem und der Tempel: Die geographisch-theologischen Elemente in der lukanischen Sicht des jüdischen Kultzentrums* (Stuttgart, Kohlhammer, 1980); J. Bradley Chance, *Jerusalem, the Temple, and New Age in Luke Acts* (Macon, GA: Mercer University Press, 1988); Ron C. Fay, "The Narrative Function of the Temple in Luke-Acts," *Trinity Journal* 27 (2006): 255–70; Mikeal C. Parsons, "The Place of Jerusalem on the Lukan Landscape: An Exercise in Symbolic Cartography," in *Literary Studies in Luke-Acts: Essays in Honor of Joseph B. Tyson*, ed. Richard P. Thompson and Thomas E. Phillips (Macon, GA: Mercer University Press, 1998), 155–71; Steve Walton, "A Tale of Two Perspectives? The Place of the Temple in Acts," in *Heaven on Earth: The Temple in Biblical Theology*, ed. T. Desmond Alexander and Simon Gathercole (Carlyle: Paternoster Press, 2004), 135– 49.

subsequently identified by the elderly Simeon, a righteous and devout man of Jerusalem, as the "consolation of Israel," the coming of the "Lord's anointed," and "your salvation ... a light for revelation to the Gentiles, and the glory of your people Israel" (2:25–32). The prophet Anna then identifies this same salvation as the "redemption of Jerusalem" (2:38). It is clear that, for Luke, Jerusalem is both the place where salvation will be achieved and the object and recipient of that salvation.

Yet beside this positive presentation lies a negative one. Jerusalem represents the rejection of God's messengers, the prophets, and the rejection of the gospel. In his prophetic role, Jesus must press on toward Jerusalem, "for surely no prophet can die outside Jerusalem!" (Luke 13:33). He then pronounces a judgment oracle against the city:

> "Jerusalem, Jerusalem, you who kill the prophets and stone those sent to you, how often I have longed to gather your children together, as a hen gathers her chicks under her wings, and you were not willing. Look, your house is left to you desolate. I tell you, you will not see me again until you say, 'Blessed is he who comes in the name of the Lord.'" (Luke 13:34–35)

Jerusalem's unwillingness to be "gathered" (ἐπισυνάγω, *episynagō*; 13:34) into the eschatological community of faith by answering Jesus' call will result in the city's desolation.

Similarly, as Jesus approaches Jerusalem for the last time he weeps over the city (Luke 19:41) and again predicts its destruction:

> "If you, even you, had only known on this day what would bring you peace—but now it is hidden from your eyes. The days will come upon you when your enemies will build an embankment against you and encircle you and hem you in on every side. They will dash you to the ground, you and the children within your walls. They will not leave one stone on another, because you did not recognize the time of God's coming to you." (Luke 19:42–44)

Jerusalem's destruction will result from the city's unwillingness to recognize God's "visitation" (ἐπισκοπή, *episkopē*; 19:44)[9] in the person of Jesus the Messiah.

These two passages, together with the parable of the tenant farmers (20:9–18), provide the backdrop for Jesus' discourse on the Mount of Olives. In response to the disciples' admiration of the beauty of the temple, Jesus predicts its destruction (21:5–6). Jerusalem will be besieged and destroyed (21:20–24) because of the city's rejection of God's visitation in the person of Jesus the Messiah (13:34; 19:44).

It is clear from these references that for Luke "Jerusalem" symbolically represents the obduracy of Israel's leaders, who are unfaithful guardians over the God's vineyard and who will reject and murder the owner of the vineyard's son (20:9–18). The result will be their destruction and the passing of the vineyard's guardianship to others (20:16).

9. This term is commonly used with reference to both judgment and redemption (Hebrew: פקד, *pqd*); judgment: Exod 20:5; 34:7; Num 14:18; Deut 5:9; Job 35:15; redemption/deliverance: Gen 50:24, 25; Exod 3:16; Ruth 1:6; 1 Sam 2:21; Ps 65:9.

Model of Herod's Temple

JERUSALEM AS DESTINATION IN THE GOSPEL: LUKE'S TRAVEL NARRATIVE

All three of the Synoptic Gospels have the same basic geographical outline. Jesus' public ministry begins in Galilee, with occasional forays into gentile territory. Jesus then heads to Jerusalem for Passover, where he challenges the religious leadership, is arrested, tried, and crucified, and then rises from the dead. In all three, the confession of Peter and Jesus' first passion prediction mark a key turning point, as Jesus begins to define his suffering role (Mark 8:27–33; Matt 16:13–23; Luke 9:18–22). In Mark's Gospel, the section that follows could be entitled "the revelation of the Messiah's suffering" (Mark 8:31–10:52) since Jesus three times predicts his death and then teaches his disciples about cross-bearing discipleship. Yet, surprisingly, the first mention of Jesus' Jerusalem destination does not come until Mark 10:32 ("They were on their way up to Jerusalem"), just before Jesus' third passion prediction. Jesus then arrives in Jerusalem a few paragraphs later (Mark 11:1–11). In other words, Jerusalem is not explicitly linked to Jesus' suffering fate until Mark 10:32. Matthew "corrects" this by mentioning Jesus' Jerusalem destination in Jesus' first passion prediction (Matt 16:21). Yet Jerusalem is not mentioned again in Matthew until the third passion prediction, where it appears in Mark (Matt 20:17).

Luke's Gospel stands in stark contrast to these other Synoptics, with a much greater emphasis on Jerusalem as Jesus' theological and geographical destination. At the transfiguration, Luke alone relates that the topic of conversation between Jesus, Moses, and Elijah was "his departure, which he was about to bring to fulfillment at Jerusalem" (9:31). Shortly after that, Luke notes the key turning point as Jesus sets out for Jerusalem: "As the time approached for him to be taken up to heaven, Jesus resolutely set out for Jerusalem" (9:51). This marks the beginning of Luke's so-called Travel Narrative or Journey to Jerusalem (9:51–19:27). Although Jesus does not head straight for Jerusalem, wandering from place to place, Luke repeatedly reminds us that he is traveling (9:57; 10:1, 38; 18:35; 19:1) and that his destination is Jerusalem (9:51–56; 13:22, 33; 17:11; 18:31; 19:11, 28, 41, 45). What in Mark takes a few paragraphs becomes in Luke an entire phase of Jesus' ministry (ten chapters!). Many of the stories and parables recounted during this journey concern God's love for the outsider: the poor, sinners, tax collectors, women, Samaritans, and gentiles.[10] Also prominent is the theme of reversal. The humble and contrite outsiders receive blessings, while the powerful and prideful insiders suffer loss.

For Luke, then, the journey to Jerusalem symbolically represents his messianic mission, a period of heightened resolve on Jesus' part to reach his Jerusalem goal and so fulfill the suffering role of the Messiah. Here again we see Luke's typological and theological geography in action. Jerusalem ambivalently represents both the place of Jesus' rejection and the place of God's glorious salvation.

FROM JERUSALEM OUTWARD

This strong emphasis on Jerusalem as the theological as well as geographical destination in the Gospel provides insight into Luke's presentation in Acts, where the gospel moves outward from Jerusalem to the ends of the earth. The whole of Luke-Acts can be viewed as a symbolic journey having Jerusalem as its center point. In the Gospel, Jesus journeys toward Jerusalem, which represents the promise of salvation found in the old covenant. At the climax and center point, salvation is achieved through Jesus' life, death, resurrection, and ascension. The message of salvation now goes forth from Jerusalem to the ends of the earth (24:47; Acts 1:8). Luke's Gospel represents *salvation achieved*; the book of Acts, *salvation announced*.

The idea of Jerusalem as the geographical and theological center of the earth has precedent in Judaism.[11] Philo says that Jerusalem is "situated in the center of the world."[12] The Book of Jubilees (second century BC), a retelling of the book of Genesis, similarly identifies Jerusalem as the "navel" of the world. In a passage on the table of nations from Genesis 10, the world is portrayed as circular and divided among the three sons of Noah, Shem, Ham, and Japheth, after the flood. The text says, "And he [Noah] knew that the garden of Eden was the holy of holies, and the dwelling of the LORD. And Mount Sinai (was) in the midst of the desert, and Mount Zion (was) in the midst of the navel of the earth. The three of these were created as holy places, one facing the other" (Jubilees 8:19).[13] This passage, which has

10. Well known parables include the good Samaritan (10:29–37), the rich fool (12:13–21), the great banquet (14:16–24), things lost (sheep, coin, and son; 15:1–32), the rich man and Lazarus (16:19–31), the persistent widow (18:1–8), and the Pharisee and the tax collector (18:9–14).

11. Philip S. Alexander, "Jerusalem as the Omphalos of the World: On the History of a Geographical Concept," *Judaism* 46 (1997): 147–58.

12. Philo, *Legatio ad Gaium* §294 (LCL). Cf. Josephus, *J.W.* 3.3.5 §§51–52, who identifies Jerusalem as the center of the country.

13. Translation from Orval S. Wintermute, "Jubilees," in *The Old Testament Pseudepigrapha*, ed. James H. Charlesworth (New Haven: Yale University Press, 2009), 2:73.

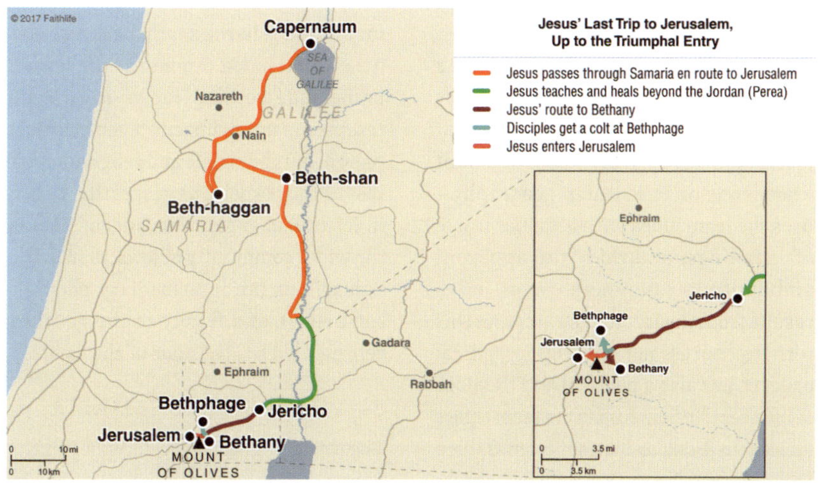

strong political implications, likely arose during the Hasmoneans period and was meant as polemic to defend Jewish territorial claims.[14]

Luke, too, presents Jerusalem as the center of the world and the focal point of God's redemptive activity, but for a different reason. The salvation promised and achieved in Judaism (symbolized by Jerusalem) was all along intended for the whole world. Luke's geographical typology therefore presents the gospel moving outward from its center both geographically and ethnically.

THE GOSPEL TO JUDEA

The second geographical reference in Acts 1:8 is Judea. Luke refers to Judea eleven times in his Gospel and twelve times in Acts, together more than half the references in the New Testament (forty-five times). Curiously, Luke uses the term in two different ways. Sometimes he uses it of Judea proper, the southern district of Palestine distinct from Galilee and Samaria. For example, Luke carefully differentiates Pilate's governorship over Judea from Herod Antipas' reign in Galilee (Luke 3:1). Similarly Joseph heads south "from the town of Nazareth in Galilee to Judea, to Bethlehem the town of David" (Luke 2:4). Other times Judea for Luke apparently encompasses all of Palestine. After describing Jesus' ministry in Nazareth and Capernaum, Luke says that, "he kept on preaching in the synagogues of Judea" (4:44). At his trial, Jesus' accusers claim that, "He stirs up the people all over Judea by his teaching, starting in Galilee and all the way here." (23:5). The same thing happens in Acts. Luke clearly distinguishes Judea from Galilee and Samaria in Acts 9:31, but then treats Judea as encompassing Galilee in 10:37, where John preaches "throughout Judea ... beginning in Galilee."

Some commentators attribute this to Luke's inadequate knowledge of

14. Alexander, "Jerusalem as the Omphalos of the World," 151.

Palestinian geography. This, however, would be surprising in light of Luke's historical and geographical accuracy elsewhere. Dean P. Béchard notes that Josephus—who hardly has a deficient knowledge of Palestinian geography—uses the term Judea with a similar range of meanings, and that "the apparent ambiguity in Josephus's use of Judea results from the fact that he employs this term to express not only topographical concept but also a political and theological concept." [15] Sometimes the term refers strictly to Judea as distinct from Galilee, Samaria, and Perea. Other times it refers to the shifting jurisdictions over which the Romans placed their vassals or governors. For example, Pilate can be called governor of Judea, even though he rules both Judea and Samaria (but not Galilee, the jurisdiction of Herod Antipas). Still other times Josephus uses Judea in a theological sense for what he elsewhere calls "the land of the Jews." In these contexts, "Judaea often signifies what Josephus and his fellow Jews believe to be the homeland God has apportioned to his chosen people as a lasting inheritance."[16] Significantly, when Josephus uses the term in this latter sense of the Jewish homeland, he includes Judea, Galilee, and Perea, but not Samaria.[17]

Josephus' use of the term provides insight into Luke's, and more specifically the outline set forth in Acts 1:8. While Luke is well aware of the distinct province of Judea in the south, he is also cognizant that Judea can mean "the Jewish homeland," so that "Judea" in Acts 1:8 represents not primarily a geo-political region, but the ethnic and religious progress of the gospel. The gospel that began in Jerusalem expands to "Judea," that is, the wider community of Jews, then to the Samaritans (an intermediary people—see below), and finally to the gentiles, represented by "the ends of the earth."

THE GOSPEL TO SAMARIA

The third geographical reference in 1:8 is Samaria. The term can refer to the city that was the capital of the northern kingdom of Israel during the monarchy (ninth and tenth centuries BC) but here no doubt refers to the geographical and political region between Judea and Galilee, west of the Jordan River.

BACKGROUND OF THE SAMARITANS

The origin of the Samaritans is controversial.[18] The Samaritans viewed themselves as pure Israelites, the authentic heirs of the religion of Abraham and the patriarchs. Despite conquest and upheaval, they had maintained their ancestral connection to the land. First-century Jews, by contrast, considered the Samaritans to be a half-breed race, descendants of foreign colonists who had intermarried with the Israelites of the northern kingdom after the Assyrian conquest. They considered Samaritan religion to be a syncretism

---

15. Dean Philip Béchard, "The Theological Significance of Judaea in Luke-Acts," in *The Unity of Luke-Acts*, ed. Joseph Verheyden (Leuven: Leuven University Press, 1999) 675–91, esp. 677–79.

16. Béchard, "Theological Significance," 679–80.

17. Béchard, "Theological Significance," 680–81.

18. See Alan D. Crown, ed., *The Samaritans* (Tübingen: Mohr Siebeck, 1989); H. G. M. Williamson and M. Kartveit, "Samaritans," *DJG* 832–36.

0 15 30 Miles
0 15 30 Kilometers
N
MEDITERRANEAN SEA
Sidon
ITUREA
Damascus
SYRIA
PHOENICIA
Litani River
Pharpar River
Tyre
Panias (Caesarea Philippi)
TRACHONITIS
Kedesh
GAULANITIS
Lake Huleh
Hazor
Acco
Chorazin
Bethsaida
BATANEA
Raphana
Capernaum
Arbela
GALILEE
Sepphoris
Tiberias
Hippos
Yarmuk River
Ashtaroth
Canatha (Kenath)
Sea of Galilee
AURANITIS
Geba
Nazareth
Gadara
Abila
Dor
Edrei
Scythopolis (Beth-shan)
DECAPOLIS
Caesarea Maritima (Strato's Tower)
Pella
Dion
Sebaste (Samaria)
Gerasa (Jerash)
W. Faria River
Jordan River
Amathus
SAMARIA
Antipatris (Aphek)
Shechem
Jabbok River
Yarkon River
Alexandrium
Joppa
Phasaelis
PEREA
Gophna
Tyrus
Philadelphia (Amman)
Jamnia
Emmaus (Nicopolis)
Jericho
Azotus (Ashdod)
Cypros
Livias
Esbus (Heshbon)
Jerusalem
Ascalon (Ashkelon)
Betogabris (Beth-guvrin)
Bethlehem
Hyrcania
Medeba
Herodium
Eastern Desert
JUDEA
Callirrhoe
Gaza
Marisa (Mareshah)
Hebron
Machaerus
Adora
Dibon
DEAD SEA
Arnon River
IDUMEA
Masada
Beersheba
Besor Brook
Malatha
Mampsis
Zered River
NABATEA
KINGDOM OF HEROD THE GREAT
City
Site of Herodian fortress
Decapolis city
Cities Herod gave to his sister Salome
Boundary of Herod the Great's Kingdom
Boundary of domain given to Archelaus, son of Herod, by Augustus Caesar in (4 BC), when Herod died
Boundary of domain given to Herod Antipas, son of Herod, by Augustus Caesar in (4 BC), when Herod died
Boundary of domain given to Herod Philip, son of Herod, by Augustus Caesar in (4 BC), when Herod died
Semi-independent municipality
Syrian Province
Copyright 2016 Faithlife / Logos Bible Software

of Israelite worship and pagan idolatry (see 2 Kings 17:24–41).[19] According to the biblical record, the enmity between Jews and Samaritans began following the Babylonian exile, when the Jews rebuffed the Samaritans' efforts to join in the rebuilding of the temple (Ezra 4). As a result, the Samaritans built their own temple on Mount Gerizim (John 4:20). Hatred between Jews and Samaritans reached a high point during the Hasmonean period, when John Hyrcanus conquered Samaria and destroyed the temple on Mount Gerizim.[20] This animosity provides the background for Gospel texts about the Samaritans.

LUKE AND THE SAMARITANS

Luke's special interest in the Samaritans is well known.[21] Mark doesn't mention the Samaritans at all, and Matthew mentions them only once, in Jesus' instructions to the Twelve *not* to "enter any town of the Samaritans" (Matt 10:5). By contrast, Luke has three episodes in his Gospel that concern Samaritans (Luke 9:51–55; 10:25–37; 17:16–18), all of which have some positive component. In addition, he reports the evangelization of the Samaritans by Philip in Acts 8.

The first episode in the Gospel occurs in the introduction to the Travel Narrative (Luke 9:51–55). Jesus clearly welcomes contact with the Samaritans since he has sent messengers ahead to a Samaritan village to prepare for his visit (9:52). Hearing of his Jerusalem goal, however, the Samaritans refuse hospitality. In an honor and shame culture, this affront demands a response, and James and John audaciously offer to call down fire from heaven against the Samaritan village. Jesus responds by rebuking them. Such violent retribution is not the way of the servant Messiah, who calls for love even for enemies (Luke 6:27, 35). The implication is that Samaria remains the object of God's grace rather than his judgment.

The second episode is the parable of the good Samaritan (Luke 10:25–37), which Jesus tells in response to the scribal question, "and who is my neighbor?" Here a despised Samaritan is shockingly depicted as one who shows self-sacrificial love even for his enemy. The third episode is Jesus' healing of ten men with leprosy (Luke 17:16–18). On the surface the pericope teaches the importance of gratitude, as only one of those healed returns to thank Jesus. Yet the narrator concludes, "and he was a Samaritan" (17:18). It is the outsider who is most grateful for the salvation that Jesus provides. This picks up the major theme of reversal that runs throughout Luke-Acts. While the poor, the sick, the sinners, the tax collectors, and other outsiders joyfully repent and receive the forgiveness of sins, the rich and powerful, the religious elite, and other insiders, reject Jesus' kingdom announcement and so will suffer loss.

These episodes prepare for the evangelization of Samaria by Philip in Acts 8, after the dispersion of Hellenistic Jewish Christians following the stoning of Stephen. But how does Luke view

19. Theologically, the Samaritans treated only the Torah as fully authoritative and had their own version—the Samaritan Pentateuch. They had no expectations for a Davidic messiah, but instead were expecting a Moses-like deliverer known as the Taheb.

20. Josephus, *Ant.* 13.9.1 §§254–56.

21. Morton S. Enslin, "Luke and the Samaritans," *Harvard Theological Review* 36 (1943), 277–97.

Mount Gerizim

the Samaritans? Are they (1) essentially Jewish; (2) halfway between Jews and gentiles; (3) or fully gentile. Against the first option is Luke 17:18, where Jesus refers to the Samaritan who returns to thank Jesus as "this foreigner" (ὁ ἀλλογενὴς οὗτος, *ho allogenēs houtos*). If Samaritans are foreigners, they are not Jewish. Are they then to be considered gentiles? As Darrell Bock points out, Luke's narrative suggests otherwise: "Though boundaries are certainly being pushed in Acts 8–9, these expansions do not seem to have the same epochal character as Peter's encounter with Cornelius in Acts 10."[22] Luke clearly views Acts 10 as *the key turning point* initiating the gentile mission. First, Peter's vision of unclean animals (symbolizing gentiles) has no parallel in the conversion of the Samaritans, who are not treated as unclean in the same way as gentiles. Furthermore, Peter and John head to Samaria to affirm the Samaritan's reception of the gospel without opposition from the Jerusalem church.[23] By contrast, in the Cornelius episode, Peter is severely criticized for entering the home of a gentile (11:2). Acts 10–11 is clearly a significant advance over anything that has come before—including the conversion of Samaria. Third, Luke delays recounting the conversion of gentiles in Antioch until after the Cornelius episode, even though chronologically it likely began earlier, shortly after Stephen's stoning (11:19–24). His purpose is to highlight that it was Peter, the revered apostle, rather than Hellenistic-Jewish Christians,

22. Darrell L. Bock, *Acts* (Grand Rapids: Baker Academic, 2007), 324–25.

23. Luke likely sees the delay in the coming of the Spirit upon the Samaritans as God's way of ensuring the unity of the Jewish and Samaritan Christians—an important step in light of the hatred between Jews and Samaritans. The delay of the Spirit confirms for the Samaritans

who initiated the gentile mission (an important part of Luke's apologetic for the gentile mission). That no such reordering is necessary with the Samaritans in chapter 8 would suggest that they are not viewed as gentiles.

It would seem, then, that Luke views the Samaritans as an intermediary people between Jews and gentiles. They have much in common with Judaism, worshiping the same God and reading (some of) the same Scriptures. They are not pagans. But they *are* outsiders to the people of God and so surprising recipients of God's grace. Joel Green comes to a similar conclusion: "Luke's narrative presupposes an awareness of the Samaritans' status as foreigners (from a perspective within Judaism) who are not as peripheral to conventional understandings of God's purpose as Gentiles would be, but who are nonetheless not expected to exemplify the graciousness of God."[24] This point further confirms the assertion that Acts 1:8 represents not just a geographical, but a theological and ethnic expansion of the gospel.

THE GOSPEL TO THE ENDS OF THE EARTH

Of the four geographical references in Acts 1:8, this one is the most debated. "To the end of the earth" (ἕως ἐσχάτου τῆς γῆς, *heōs eschatou tēs gēs*) is almost certainly an allusion to Isaiah 49:6.[25] But to what does it refer? Is it primarily a geographical reference or an ethnic one? Scholars have proposed various referents, including (1) Rome; (2) Spain; (3) Ethiopia; (4) the gentiles; (5) diaspora Jews; or (6) a general reference to the farthest reaches of the inhabited world.[26]

Ethiopia or Spain have been suggested since similar phrases are used in Greco-Roman literature of the farthest reaches of the known world. These edges would be Spain in the west, Ethiopia in the south, India or possibly China in the east, and perhaps the Scythians (or the arctic) in the north (see Col 3:11). E. Earle Ellis argues for Spain, and particularly the city of Gades, which Strabo describes as a city "at the end of the earth."[27] This is supported by the fact that in Romans 15:24, 28, Paul is making plans to go to Spain. Clement of Rome, writing shortly after the time of Paul, claims that the apostle reached "the limits of the west" (τὸ τέρμα τῆς δύσεως, *to terma tēs dyseōs*; 1 Clement 5:6–7), a probable reference to Spain. Yet it seems unlikely that the phrase would be so specific and limited to one place and direction. This is especially so since Spain is never mentioned and plays no role in Acts, either as a destination or a goal.

---

their dependence on the Jerusalem church and confirms for the Jerusalem church that Samaritans can indeed be saved.

24. Joel B. Green, *The Gospel of Luke* (Grand Rapids: Eerdmans, 1997), 405.

25. The phrase also occurs in other LXX texts, Isa 45:22; 48:20; 62:10–11; Jer 16:19; 38:8 [31:8], although Isa 49:6 is the most likely background, especially in light of the allusions to it in Luke 2:32 and Acts 13:47.

26. See T. S. Moore, "To the End of the Earth: The Geographical and Ethnic Universalism of Acts 1:8 in Light of Isaianic Influence on Luke," *JETS* 40 (1997): 389–99.

27. Strabo, *Geography* 1.1.6; 1.2.31; 2.3.5; 2.4.2. E. Earle Ellis, "'The End of the Earth' (Acts 1:8)," *BBR* 1 (1991): 123–31; James S. Romm, *The Edges of the Earth in Ancient Thought: Geography, Exploration, and Fiction* (Princeton: Princeton University Press, 1992).

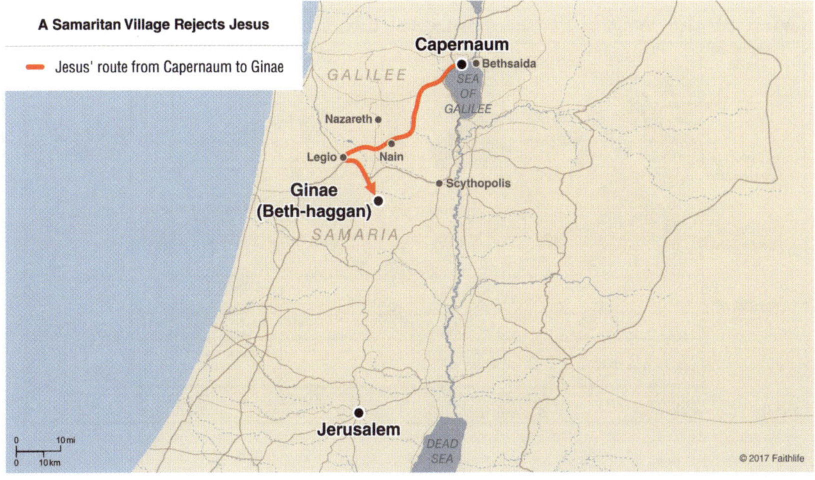

Rome makes good sense in the narrative progression of Acts, since the book begins in Jerusalem and ends in Rome.[28] Rome may also be supported by Psalms of Solomon 8:15, where the conqueror who came from the "end of the earth" likely refers to the Roman general Pompey coming to overrun Jerusalem in 63 BC. As Ellis points out, however, this does not point unambiguously to Rome, since Pompey came to the east after a command in Spain in 77–71 BC.[29] A greater problem with Rome is that it is hardly at the ends of the earth. Indeed, it is the very center of the Roman world. As Schnabel points out, "Rome is not portrayed as a goal or fulfillment of the early Christian mission, but as a new starting point from which the gospel was proclaimed 'with all boldness and without hindrance' (28:31)."[30]

A reference to gentiles makes good sense from the context of Isaiah 49:6, where the nations/gentiles are specifically mentioned: "I will also make you a light for the gentiles [גּוֹיִם, *goyim*; ἔθνη, *ethnē*] that my salvation may reach to the ends of the earth."[31] Other allusions to Isaiah 49:6 in the Lukan corpus also point to the gentiles. This is true of Simeon's prophecy in Luke 2:32, where the messiah will be "a light for revelation to the gentiles, and the glory of your people

28. This view is taken by many commentators, including Hans Conzelmann, *A Commentary on the Acts of the Apostles* (Philadelphia: Fortress Press, 1987), 7, and Joseph A. Fitzmyer, *The Acts of the Apostles: A New Translation with Introduction and Commentary* (New Haven: Yale University Press, 2010), 206–7.

29. Ellis, "End of the Earth," 125.

30. Schnabel, *Acts*, 79. See also Schnabel's essay in the present volume: "Jesus' Missionary Commission and the Ends of the Earth."

31. Bock, *Acts*, 65; David W. Pao, *Acts and the Isaianic New Exodus* (Grand Rapids: Baker Academic, 2002), 84–86, 92–95.

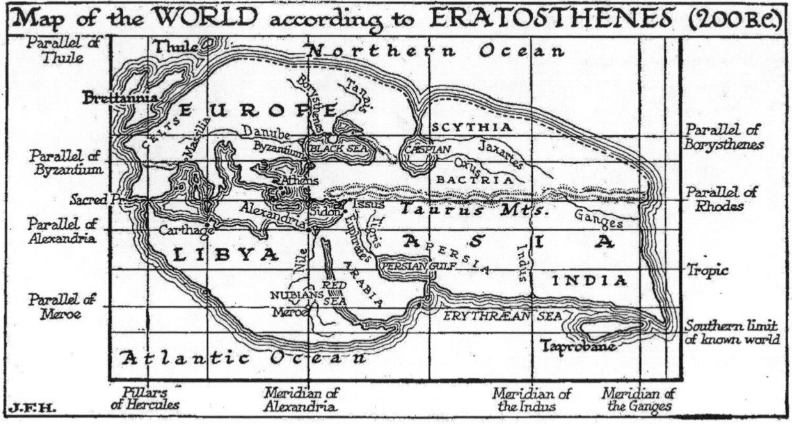

Reconstructed Map of Eratosthenes Depicting the Ancient World (ca. 2nd century BC)

Israel." It is also true in Acts 13:47, where Isaiah 49:6 is cited by Paul to justify his turning to the gentiles following rejection by many Jews in Antioch-Pisidia.

It should be noted, however, that when Paul reaches Rome at the end of Acts, the mission to the Jews does not end. Indeed, the Christians who greet Paul as he approaches Rome (Acts 28:14–15) disappear from the narrative in the next passage and he preaches to the Jewish leaders in Rome (28:17–28). Luke's intention seems to be to end the book with the same pattern that has occurred throughout Acts: (1) some Jews respond positively (v. 24a); (2) the majority reject the message (vv. 24b–28); (3) Paul turns to the gentiles (v. 28); (4) the gospel advances "unhindered" (vv. 30–31). You can chain the gospel messenger, but you can't chain the gospel message.

CONCLUSION

It would seem best to treat the phrase "to the end of the earth" (1:8) as geographical, ethnic, and (especially) *theological*. It refers to *the fulfillment of Scripture through the continuing advance of the gospel to every people, tribe, and nation in the farthest corners of the inhabited world*. Does this include the Jews? Of course. But from Luke's perspective, that is a given. The promise of salvation came through Israel and was for "the glory of your people Israel" (Luke 2:32), and so Paul will continue to go to the Jews first (cf. Rom 1:16). But what is remarkable and earthshaking is that this gospel that began in Jerusalem is moving unceasingly outward from its Jewish foundation to the whole world. In Luke's story, the reality that the gospel—despite every obstacle thrown in its path—has reached Rome, the heart of the gentile world, confirms that it will continue on its unstoppable journey to the farthest corners of the earth. The story that began in Jerusalem is not yet over. In some ways it is just beginning. Yet its ending is assured because it has already been written—both in the prophets (Isa 49:6, etc.) and in Jesus' pronouncement: "You will be my witnesses in Jerusalem ... and to the ends of the earth" (1:8).

BIBLIOGRAPHY

Alexander, Philip S. "Jerusalem as the Omphalos of the World: On the History of a Geographical Concept." *Judaism* 46 (1997): 147–58.

Bachmann, M. *Jerusalem und der Tempel: Die geographisch-theologischen Elemente in der lukanischen Sicht des jüdischen Kultzentrums*. Stuttgart, Kohlhammer, 1980.

Béchard, Dean Philip. "The Theological Significance of Judaea in Luke-Acts." Pages 675–91 in *The Unity of Luke-Acts*. Edited by Joseph Verheyden. Leuven: Leuven University Press, 1999.

Bock, Darrell L. *A Theology of Luke and Acts*. Grand Rapids: Zondervan, 2012.

———. *Acts*. Grand Rapids: Baker Academic, 2007.

Chance, J. Bradley. *Jerusalem, the Temple, and New Age in Luke-Acts*. Macon, GA: Mercer University Press, 1988.

Charlesworth, James H., ed. *The Old Testament Pseudepigrapha*. 2 vols. New Haven: Yale University Press, 2009.

Conzelmann, Hans. *A Commentary on the Acts of the Apostles*. Philadelphia: Fortress, 1987.

Crown, Alan D., ed. *The Samaritans*. Tübingen: Mohr Siebeck, 1989.

Elliot, J. K. "Jerusalem in Acts and the Gospels." *NTS* 23 (1976–1977): 462–69.

Ellis, E. Earle. "'The End of the Earth' (Acts 1:8)." *BBR* 1 (1991): 123–31.

Enslin, Morton S. "Luke and the Samaritans." *Harvard Theological Review* 36 (1943): 277–97.

Fay, Ron C. "The Narrative Function of the Temple in Luke-Acts." *Trinity Journal* 27 (2006): 255–70.

Fitzmyer, Joseph A. *The Acts of the Apostles: A New Translation with Introduction and Commentary*. New Haven: Yale University Press, 2010.

Green, Joel B. *The Gospel of Luke*. Grand Rapids: Eerdmans, 1997.

Hemer, Colin J. *The Book of Acts in the Setting of Hellenistic History*. Edited by Conrad Gempf. Tübingen: Mohr Siebeck, 1989.

Hengel, Martin. "The Geography of Palestine in Acts." Pages 27–78 in *The Book of Acts in Its Palestinian Setting*. Edited by Richard Bauckham. Volume 4 of *The Book of Acts in Its First Century Setting*. Edited by Bruce W. Winter. Grand Rapids: Eerdmans, 1995.

Huffman, Douglas S. Review of *Geography and the Ascension Narrative in Acts*, by Matthew Sleeman. *JETS* 54 (2011): 396–98.

Keener, Craig S. *Acts: An Exegetical Commentary*. 4 vols. Grand Rapids: Baker Academic, 2012–2015.

Marshall, I. H. *Acts: An Introduction and Commentary*. Downers Grove, IL: InterVarsity Press, 1980.

Moore, T. S. "To the End of the Earth: The Geographical and Ethnic Universalism of Acts 1:8 in Light of Isaianic Influence on Luke." *JETS* 40 (1997): 389–99.

Pao, David W. *Acts and the Isaianic New Exodus*. Grand Rapids: Baker Academic, 2002.

Parsons, Mikeal C. "The Place of Jerusalem on the Lukan Landscape: An Exercise in Symbolic Cartography." Pages 155–71 in *Literary Studies in Luke-Acts: Essays in Honor of Joseph B. Tyson*. Edited by Richard P. Thompson and Thomas E. Phillips. Macon, GA: Mercer University Press, 1998.

Romm, James S. *The Edges of the Earth in Ancient Thought: Geography,*

Exploration, and Fiction. Princeton: Princeton University Press, 1992.

Schnabel, Eckhard J. *Acts*. Grand Rapids: Zondervan, 2012.

Scott, J. M. "Luke's Geographical Horizon." Pages 484–583 in *The Book of Acts in Its Graeco-Roman Setting*. Edited by D. W. J. Gill and C. Gempf. Volume 2 of *The Book of Acts in Its First Century Setting*. Edited by Bruce W. Winter. Grand Rapids: Eerdmans, 1994.

Sleeman, Matthew. *Geography and the Ascension Narrative in Acts*. Cambridge: Cambridge University Press, 2009.

Walton, Steve. "A Tale of Two Perspectives? The Place of the Temple in Acts." Pages 135–49 in *Heaven on Earth: The Temple in Biblical Theology*. Ed. T. Desmond Alexander and Simon Gathercole. Carlyle: Paternoster, 2004.

Williamson, H. G. M. and M. Kartveit, "Samaritans." *DJG* 832–36.

Wintermute, Orval S. "Jubilees." Pages 35–142 in vol. 1 of *The Old Testament Pseudepigrapha*. Edited by James H. Charlesworth. 2 vols. New Haven: Yale University Press, 2009.

Witherington, Ben, III. *The Acts of the Apostles: A Socio-Rhetorical Commentary*. Grand Rapids, Eerdmans, 1998.

CHAPTER 2

THE TOPOGRAPHY OF JERUSALEM IN THE BOOK OF ACTS

Acts 1:6–13; 2:1–12, 38–46; 3:11; 4:3–22; 5:12–18, 21–41; 6:9–7:60; 9:1–12; 12:1–11; 21:26–37; 22:24–23:31

Eckhard J. Schnabel

KEY POINTS

- For the earliest followers of Jesus, Jerusalem was the first center of their life and mission.
- The life of the Jerusalem church was not focused on the temple: the believers met on the Temple Mount, but they also met in private homes.
- The early church did not seem to have regarded Jerusalem with its topography and its institutions as a holy city, as God's presence in the temple had been replaced in significance with God's presence in the crucified and risen Jesus Messiah.

INTRODUCTION

The book of Acts refers to sixteen locations in Jerusalem, some of which can be identified in the topography of the city. The locations in Jerusalem are connected with the community of Jesus' followers, with the apostles' evangelistic work, and with the Jewish leaders who tried to curb the church's activities.

JERUSALEM AND JESUS' ASCENSION ON THE MOUNT OF OLIVES (ACTS 1:6–12)

The last encounter between the risen Jesus and the eleven disciples took place on the Mount of Olives on the ridge overlooking Bethany to the east and, across the Hinnom Valley, Jerusalem to the west (Luke 24:50; Acts 1:12). The ridge of the

Mount of Olives is 200 to 260 feet (60 to 80 m) above Jerusalem. Josephus says that the Mount of Olives is five stadia (0.6 miles or 925 m) from Jerusalem.[1] Jesus and the disciples had a clear view of Jerusalem and the Temple Mount. Jesus' answer to the disciples' question whether the restoration of the kingdom to Israel is imminent (Acts 1:6), stating, "you will receive power when the Holy Spirit comes on you; and you will be my witnesses in Jerusalem, and in all Judea and Samaria, and to the ends of the earth" (Acts 1:8), expands the focus of the Jewish people on the holy city of Jerusalem and the traditional Jewish territories of Judea and Samaria to all regions of the world in which the population was predominantly polytheistic (gentile), with no region excepted, not even the peoples who live at the ends of the earth.[2] If Jesus had raised his arms in the direction of the geographical terms in his final commission, he would have pointed first straight ahead to Jerusalem directly in front of the disciples, then to Judea (same direction), to Samaria to the right (north); then, if he continued in a circle, beyond the Dead Sea and Arabia toward Babylonia and India (east); to the southern end of the Dead Sea toward Africa and Ethiopia (south); beyond Jerusalem to the Mediterranean Sea and toward Macedonia, Achaia, Rome, and Spain (west); beyond Samaria to Asia Minor and Scythia (north). While Jerusalem was the center of the apostles' mission for the next twelve years, the focus of their life and work was the communities of followers of Jesus that they would establish around the Mediterranean and beyond.

After Jesus had left them, the disciples descended the western slopes of the Mount of Olives, passing south of Gethsemane across the Kidron Valley, entering the city through the gate in the northwestern section of the City of David (about 656 feet [200 m] north of the Pool of Siloam),[3] or further south through the gate at the foot of Mount Zion near the entrance to the Tyropoeon Valley,[4] or further west, in the Valley of Hinnom, through the gate and tower complex that gave access to a road that ran between the upper city and the lower city, often identified as the Gate of the Essenes.[5]

THE UPPER ROOM (ACTS 1:13; 2:1)

The "upper room" (τὸ ὑπερῷον, *to hyperōon*) in Acts 1:13 is identified by some scholars with the room where Jesus celebrated his last meal with the disciples (Mark 14:15; Luke 22:12: ἀνάγαιον, *anagaion*, also means "room upstairs"), and with an upstairs room in the house of Mary, the mother of John Mark in which followers of Jesus assembled (Acts 12:12). Luke's readers would probably assume that the "one

---

1. Josephus, *Ant.* 20.169; in *J.W.* 5.70, he uses the figure of six stadia (0.7 miles or 1.1 km).

2. See chapter 4,"Jesus' Missionary Commission and 'the Ends of the Earth.'"

3. See H. Geva, "Jerusalem: The Second Temple Period," *NEAEHL* 2:722, 728, for the gates in the southern wall.

4. This may have been the Dung Gate referred to in Neh 3:14; some scholars identify this gate as the Gate of the Essenes.

5. Josephus, *J.W.* 5.145; see also 11QTemple (11Q19) XL, 14. See also Bargil Pixner, Doron Chen, and Shlomo Margalit, "Mount Zion: The 'Gate of the Essenes' Reexcavated," *Zeitschrift des Deutschen Palästina-Vereins* 105 (1989): 85–95; Rainer Riesner, "Josephus' 'Gate of the Essenes' in Modern Discussion," *Zeitschrift des Deutschen Palästina-Vereins* 105 (1989): 105–9.

Valleys of Hinnom (Left), Tyropoeon (Center), and Kidron (Right) in Jerusalem

place" where the disciples had gathered on Pentecost (Acts 2:1) is the "room upstairs" of Acts 1:13. The identification of the two sites is both possible and plausible,[6] but cannot be demonstrated.[7] The identification of the site of Jesus' last supper and the site of the upper room in which Jesus' disciples met is the reason why Jerome translates the two different expressions of Mark 14:15/Luke 22:12 and Acts 1:13 with the same Latin term, *cenaculum*.[8]

Luke does not specify the location of the two-story house in view here. A localization depends on early church tradition. Cyril of Jerusalem provides the earliest explicit localization of the house with the upper room in which Jesus celebrated the last supper as being on Sion, the southwestern hill of the upper city; he states in a catechetical lecture of AD 348, standing at the site of Golgotha in the Church of the Holy Sepulcher, that the Holy Spirit descended at Pentecost "upon the Apostles in the form of fiery tongues here in Jerusalem, in the Upper Church of the Apostles."[9] This is the first reference to a church on Sion, a hill that is higher than the site of the Church of the Holy Sepulcher (thus "Upper Church"). Hesychius of Jerusalem (ca. AD 440) also

6. See Theodor Zahn, *Die Apostelgeschichte des Lucas*, 2 vols. (Leipzig: Deichert, 1921–1922), 1:43–45.

7. For the following discussion see also Eckhard J. Schnabel, *Jesus in Jerusalem: April 2–10, A.D. 30* (Grand Rapids: Eerdmans, 2018), chapter 2.8.

8. Hence the term Cenacle that is commonly used for the upper room.

9. Cyril of Jerusalem, *Catecheses* 16.4: ἡ ἀνωτέρα τῶν ἀποστόλων Ἐκκλησία (*hē anōtera tōn apostolōn Ekklēsia*); see Leo P. McCauley and Anthony A. Stephenson, *St. Cyril of Jerusalem: Works*, 2 vols. (Washington, DC: Catholic University of America Press, 1969–1970), 78. See also Rainer Riesner, *Essener und Urgemeinde in Jerusalem: Neue Funde und Quellen*, 2nd ed. (Giessen: Brunnen, 1998), 78–83.

locates the Last Supper on Sion.[10] Eusebius states that the Christians who had left Jerusalem at the outbreak of the Jewish revolt in AD 66 returned in AD 73/74 under the leadership of Simon son of Kleopha, forming "a very large church of Jews in Jerusalem" who rebuilt their center as a synagogue.[11] Second century sources mention an ancient synagogue used by Jewish Christians.[12] Some suggest that this synagogue and the later church were built at the site of the house with the upper room in which the apostles met in the early days of the church in Jerusalem.[13] This is the smaller of the two churches in Jerusalem shown on the Madaba Map (sixth century)—the Hagia Sion Basilica built by the bishop of Jerusalem, John II, in AD 386–394. An inscription in the Basilica of St. Martin in Tours (France), dated to AD 470–474, originally connected with a mural depiction of the Hagia Sion Basilica in Jerusalem, calls this church (for the first time) "Mother of All Churches" (*mater ecclesiarum*), and asserts that the "throne," that is, the *cathedra*, the chair or seat of the apostle James, can be seen in the church.[14] The Hagia Sion Basilica was restored by Modestus before AD 630 and rebuilt and expanded by the Crusaders around AD 1140 as the church of Sancta Maria in Monte Sion.[15] Muslim troops destroyed the basilica in 1219. The Cenacle that tourists are shown today in the Benedictine abbey Dormitio Mariae (since 1998 Hagia Maria Sion) was built AD 1229–1244.

THE PLAZA AT THE HULDA GATES (ACTS 2:5–12, 41)

The Upper Room would not have been able to accommodate the hundreds, indeed thousands of residents of Jerusalem and festival pilgrims who heard the disciples speak in unlearned languages (Acts 2:5–13) and listened to Peter's explanation (Acts 2:14–40). It is plausible to assume a change of location between Acts 2:4 and Acts 2:5 from the upper room in a private home to a public venue.[16] The public venue might have been the plaza in front of the Hulda Gates at the southern entrance to the Temple Mount. The plaza had roughly

---

10. Hesychius, *Quaestiones*; see Donatus Baldi, *Enchiridion Locorum Sanctorum: Documenta S. Evangelii loca respicientia*, 2nd ed. (Jerusalem: Franciscan Printing Press, 1982), 479–81.

11. Eusebius, *Historia ecclesiastica* 3.11; *Demonstratio evangelica* 3.5.

12. Epiphanius, *De mensuribus et ponderibus* 14. See also Baldi, *Enchiridion*, 477–78.

13. Bargil Pixner, "Mount Zion, Jesus, and Archaeology," in *Jesus and Archaeology*, ed. James H. Charlesworth (Grand Rapids: Eerdmans, 2006), 309–22; see also Jerome Murphy-O'Connor, "The Cenacle—Topographical Setting for Acts 2:44–45," in *The Book of Acts in Its Palestinian Setting*, ed. Richard Bauckham, vol. 4 of *The Book of Acts in Its First-Century Setting*, ed. Bruce W. Winter (Grand Rapids: Eerdmans, 1995), 303–21.

14. Baldi, *Enchiridion*, 483 n. 1; Calvin B. Kendall, *The Allegory of the Church: Romanesque Portals and their Verse Inscriptions* (Toronto: University of Toronto Press, 1998), 37.

15. Jack Finegan, *The Archeology of the New Testament: The Life of Jesus and the Beginning of the Early Church*, rev. ed. (Princeton: Princeton University Press, 1992), 232–38 (nos. 205, 209); Bargil Pixner, *Paths of the Messiah and Sites of the Early Church from Galilee to Jerusalem: Jesus and Jewish Christianity in Light of Archaeological Discoveries*, ed. Rainer Riesner (San Francisco: Ignatius Press, 2010), 319–59; David C. Clausen, *The Upper Room and Tomb of David: The History, Art and Archaeology of the Cenacle on Mount Zion* (Jefferson, NC: McFarland, 2016).

16. Craig S. Keener, *Acts: An Exegetical Commentary*, 4 vols. (Grand Rapids: Baker, 2012–15), 1:796–97.

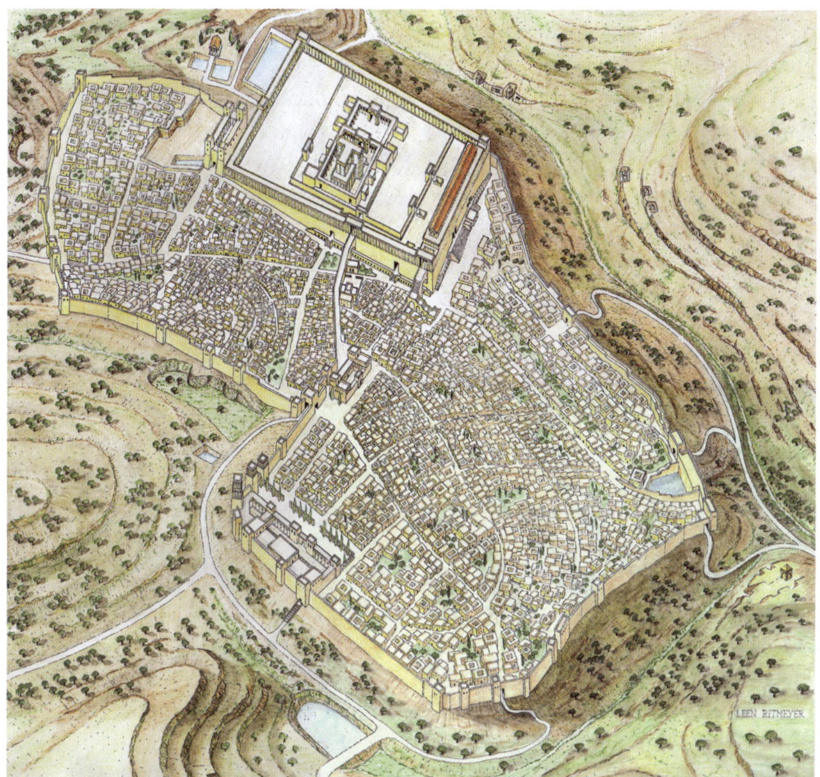

Jerusalem in the First Century

the same footprint as the Royal Portico, 787 feet long by 108 feet wide (240 x 33 m). Assuming three people per square meter, the plaza could easily hold twenty-four thousand persons.[17] Another possibility is the outer court of the temple (see nos. 5, 16).[18]

IMMERSION POOLS IN JERUSALEM (ACTS 2:38, 41; 21:26)

Luke reports that Peter called on the residents of Jerusalem and pilgrims who listened to, understood, and accepted his proclamation of Jesus' death and resurrection and of the significance of the outpouring of the Holy Spirit to immerse themselves in water as a sign of repentance and purification, which "about three thousand" did (Acts 2:38, 41). Paul, in the context of his desire to demonstrate that he does not teach the annulment of the Mosaic Law, "purified himself" (Acts 21:26), that is, he immersed himself in one of the immersion pools.

17. For crowd sizes, see G. Keith Still, "Crowd Safety and Risk Analysis," http://www.gkstill.com/Support/crowd-density/CrowdDensity-1.html.

18. Martin Hengel, "The Geography of Palestine in Acts," in Bauckham, *The Book of Acts in Its Palestinian Setting*, 4:27–78, 37; Keener, *Acts*, 1:797.

The Greek term *baptizō* (βαπτίζω) used in Acts 2:38, 41 refers to immersion in water for the purpose of purification.[19] Archaeological excavations have discovered 164 immersion pools (מקואות, *miqva'ot*) in Jerusalem dating to the late Second Temple period.[20] Clusters of *miqva'ot* existed around the Temple Mount. Two large pools built to accommodate the ritual purification needs of large numbers of people were the Pool of Siloam (130–200 x 230 feet [40–60 x 70 m], with steps on at least three of the four sides) in the Tyropoeon Valley near the southern city gate and the Pool of Bethesda (the southern basin, which has an impressive flight of steps along the western side, measures 154 x 170 feet [47 x 52 m]) at the northeast corner of the Temple Mount.[21]

The immersion of three thousand Jews who confessed their faith in the crucified and risen Jesus Messiah in the large public immersion pools of Jerusalem was not only physically possible but not even unique: the thousands of festival pilgrims that were in the city for Pentecost would all have immersed themselves in one of the *miqva'ot* before ascending to the Temple Mount.

SOLOMON'S COLONNADE ON THE TEMPLE MOUNT (ACTS 3:11; 5:12)

According to Acts 3:11; 5:12, the Jerusalem church met in Solomon's Colonnade (στοὰ Σολομῶντος, *stoa Solomōntos*; NRSV: "Solomon's Portico"). A stoa or portico (Lat. *porticus*) was an open colonnade with a roof over the hall to a rear wall. Some stoas, like Solomon's Portico, had an additional interior row of columns that supported the ridge of the roof. A stoa provided shade from the sun and

Southern Wall of the Temple Mount

19. Eckhard J. Schnabel, "The Meaning of βαπτίζειν in Greek, Jewish, and Patristric Literature," *Filologia Neotestamentaria* 24 (2011): 3–40.

20. Jodi Magness, *Stone and Dung, Oil and Spit: Jewish Daily Life in the Time of Jesus* (Grand Rapids: Eerdmans, 2011), 17 n. 6; see also Yonatan Adler, "The Ritual Baths Near the Temple Mount and Extra-Purification Before Entering the Temple Courts: A Reply to Eyal Regev," *IEJ* 56 (2006): 209–15.

21. Ronny Reich and Eli Shukron, "The Siloam Pool in the Wake of Recent Discoveries," in *New Studies on Jerusalem, Vol. 10*, ed. Eyal Baruch and Avi Faust (Ramat-Gan: Bar-Ilan University, 2004), 137–40; Shimon Gibson, "The Pool of Bethesda in Jerusalem and Jewish Purification Practices of the Second Temple Period," *Proche-Orient chrétien* 55 (2005): 270–93; Urban C. von Wahlde, "Archaeology and John's Gospel," in Charlesworth, *Jesus and Archaeology* (Grand Rapids: Eerdmans, 2006), 523–86, 560–66; Shimon Gibson, *The Final Days of Jesus: The Archaeological Evidence* (New York: HarperOne, 2009), 59–80. See also Gordon Franz, "Jesus at the Pool of Bethesda," in *Lexham Geographic Commentary on the Gospels*, ed. Barry J. Beitzel (Bellingham, WA: Lexham Press, 2017), 125–33; Elaine A. Phillips, "Healing by Living Waters at the Pool of Siloam," in *Lexham Geographic Commentary on the Gospels*, ed. Barry J. Beitzel (Bellingham, WA: Lexham Press, 2017), 365–73.

Southern Wall of the Temple Mount (Model)

shelter from the rain; it served as a social meeting point and was used for political, religious, and commercial activities. The outer court (later dubbed "Court of the Gentiles") was surrounded by four stoas. The stoa on the east was called Solomon's Colonnade. As the stoas on the northern and western side, it measured (1433 x 49 feet (437 x 15 m), with a height of 41 feet (12.5 m).[22] Josephus describes these three stoas as follows:

> The porticoes, all in double rows, were supported by columns five and twenty cubits high—each a single block of the purest white marble—and ceiled with panels of cedar. The natural magnificence of these columns, their excellent polish and fine adjustment presented a striking spectacle, without any adventitious embellishment of painting or sculpture. (*J.W.* 5.190–192 [LCL])

The "all" in Acts 5:12 ("Many signs and wonders among the people happened at the hands of the apostles. They were all meeting with one mind in Solomon's Portico;" [author's translation]) is related by some commentators to the apostles mentioned in the first part of the statement.[23] In view of Acts 2:44–46; 5:11, a reference to all believers is more plausible.[24] Since the apostles taught believers both on the Temple Mount and "from house to house" (Acts 5:42), it is possible that

22. The eastern side of the outer court was 1541 feet (470 m), and the width of the Royal Stoa was 108 feet (33 m), which leaves 1437 feet (437 m) for Solomon's Colonnade. See Ehud Netzer, *The Architecture of Herod, the Great Builder* (Grand Rapids: Baker Academic, 2008), 160, 164–65.

23. Joseph A. Fitzmyer, *The Acts of the Apostles: A New Translation with Introduction and Commentary* (New York: Doubleday, 1998), 328.

24. Thus NIV: "And all the believers used to meet together in Solomon's Colonnade;" see also I. Howard Marshall, *The Acts of the Apostles: An Introduction and Commentary* (Leicester: Inter-Varsity Press, 1980), 115; Jacob Jervell, *Die Apostelgeschichte* (Göttingen: Vandenhoeck & Ruprecht, 1998), 200–201.

Pool of Siloam (Lower Basin)

the assemblies of the Jerusalem believers mentioned in 4:23, 31, 32–37; 5:2, 21, 42; 11:1–18, 22; 15:4–29; 21:17–25 took place in Solomon's Colonnade.

HOUSES IN JERUSALEM (ACTS 2:46; 5:42)

According to Acts 5:42, the Jerusalem believers met on the Temple Mount "and from house to house" (*κατ' οἶκον, kat' oikon*). One of the houses in which followers of Jesus met was the two-story house with the upper room in which the twelve apostles met (Acts 1:13; see above, "The Upper Room"). Another house mentioned by Luke is "the house of Mary the mother of John, also called Mark, where many people had gathered and were praying" (Acts 12:12). Mary[25] was evidently a wealthy woman: she owned a substantial house with a courtyard and an outer gate (12:13).[26]

The so-called Western House, excavated in the Herodian Quarter, is an example of the large residence of a wealthy family, located in the northern

25. The New Testament mentions six women with the name of Mary: 1. Mary, the mother of Jesus; 2. Mary Magdalene, a disciple of Jesus; 3. Mary of Bethany, the sister of Martha, a disciple of Jesus; 4. Mary, the mother of James and Joseph, a disciple of Jesus who was at the tomb on Easter morning; 5. Mary, the wife of Clopas, a disciple of Jesus who witnessed Jesus' crucifixion; 6. Mary, the mother of John Mark. The Jewish name was also used later by Christians; *Lexicon of Greek Personal Names* (http://www.lgpn.ox.ac.uk/) lists fifty-five persons with the name.

26. C. K. Barrett, *The Acts of the Apostles*, 2 vols. (Edinburgh: T & T Clark, 1994–1998), 1:584 ("a large house with a large gateway in which was set a wicket-door that would be used for ordinary purposes"); see also Eckhard J. Schnabel, *Acts* (Grand Rapids: Zondervan, 2012), 539; Keener, *Acts*, 2:1903.

Temple Mount from Southwest

part of the upper city between Herod's Palace and the Temple Mount.[27] The house covered an area of sixty-five by fifty-two feet (21 x 17 m). The basement contained water installations, including a bathroom, two large and two small *miqva'ot*, three cisterns, and a deep pool, as well as service (store) rooms. The bathroom, including the bathtub, was paved with mosaics. No remains of the living quarters of the first floor have survived.

SANHEDRIN BUILDING (ACTS 4:3-22; 5:21-41; 6:12-7:56; 22:30-23:10, 14)

Peter and John (Acts 4:3–22), the twelve (Acts 5:21–41), Stephen (6:12–7:56), and Paul (22:30–23:10, 14) were forcibly taken to the Sanhedrin (συνέδριον, *synedrion*; Hebraized as סַנְהֶדְרִין, *sanhedrin*), the high court of Jerusalem, where they were interrogated, threatened, and in the case of Stephen, sentenced to death. It was in the Sanhedrin that Jesus had been sentenced to death. Four locations have been suggested for the meeting of Jerusalem's judicial court.[28]

(1) According to the Mishnah, the Sanhedrin met in the Chamber of Hewn Stone (לִשְׁכַּת הַגָּזִית, *lishkat haggazit*), located in the southeast corner of the inner enclosure that gave access both to the Court of the Priests and the Court of Israel. This chamber (thirty-nine by thirty-six feet [12 x 11 m]) was evidently large enough for the assembly of the members of the Sanhedrin, whose number cannot be ascertained for the AD 30s.

27. The following description is taken from Nahman Avigad, *The Herodian Quarter in Jerusalem: Wohl Archaeological Museum* (Jerusalem: Keter, 1991), 23–29.

28. See m. Sanhedrin 11:2; m. Middot 5:4. The later text b. Yoma 25a states that this structure was "like a great basilica" (כמין בסלקי גדולה, *kmyn bslqy gdwlh*). See also Netzer, *Architecture of Herod*, 156. The following discussion is adapted from Schnabel, *Jesus in Jerusalem*, ch. 2.11.

(2) Another rabbinic tradition relates that forty years before the destruction of the city, in other words, around AD 30, the Sanhedrin moved from its previous location in the Chamber of Hewn Stone to the Hanut (חָנוּת, *chanut*),[29] perhaps a reference to the Royal Stoa at the southern side of the outer court of the temple complex. Some have suggested that the Sanhedrin met in an apsis at the east end of the Royal Stoa.[30] This suggestion is rendered implausible if E. Netzer is correct in his assertion that the entrances to the Royal Stoa on the short sides included "a courtyard flanked by a few side rooms that were needed for the stationing of the king's guard, as dressing rooms, and for the storage of ceremonial utensils."[31]

(3) Some scholars assume that there was both a "city council" (βουλή, *boulē*) and the Sanhedrin (the "supreme court"), the former located in the area of the Huldah Gates south of the Temple Mount.[32] Remains of two structures have been discovered between the staircases leading to the Double and Triple Gates on the south side of the Temple Mount. The building on the east is identified as a public building, which may have been one of the council houses.[33] It is not inconceivable that the apostles were taken, at least on some occasions, to this civic body.

(4) Many scholars think that the Sanhedrin was located immediately west of the Temple Mount. The term translated as "hewn stone" (גָּזִית, *gazit*) is translated in the LXX as *xystos* (ξυστός; 1 Chron 22:2; Amos 5:11), a term that describes a walking place in the grounds of a gymnasium or a covered colonnade;[34] this means that the Hebrew expression which localizes the meeting place of the Sanhedrin could be understood as "the Hall beside the Xystos." According to Josephus, the council building was located in the upper city between the Temple Mount and the Xystos, standing near the Xystos.[35] The Xystos was the covered colonnade of the gymnasium (a place of study, philosophical discussion, and athletic activities) built during the Maccabean period (1 Macc 1:14-15; 2 Macc 4:11–15), which was now used as a public plaza. The Xystos was connected with the Temple Mount at the Kipunus Gate (Wilson's Arch) by a bridge. Remains of a magnificent hall dating to the Second Temple period have been discovered immediately south of

29. Or חֲנוּיּוֹת (*chanuyyot*), "shops;" b. Shabbat 15a; b. Sanhedrin 41a.

30. Kathleen Ritmeyer and Leen Ritmeyer, "Reconstructing Herod's Temple Mount," in *Where Christianity Was Born*, ed. H. Shanks (Washington, DC: Biblical Archaeological Society, 2006), 80–101, 90.

31. Netzer, *Architecture of Herod*, 170.

32. See t. Hagigah. 2:9; t. Sanhedrin 7:1.

33. Ritmeyer and Ritmeyer, "Reconstructing Herod's Temple", 95; Leen Ritmeyer, *The Quest: Revealing the Temple Mount in Jerusalem* (Jerusalem: Carta, 2006), 76.

34. See LSJ, s.v. "ξυστός."

35. Josephus, *J.W.* 5.144: "Beginning in the north at the tower called Hippicus, it [i.e., the first wall] extended to the Xystus, and then joining the council-chamber (*tē boulē*) terminated at the western portico of the temple" (LCL); 6:354: "But on the next [day], they [i.e., Titus' troops] set fire to the Archives, the Acra, the council-chamber, and the region called Ophlas" (LCL). For the information that the Xystos was connected with the Temple Mount by a bridge see *J.W.* 2.344. See also Emil Schürer, *The History of the Jewish People in the Age of Christ (175 B.C.–A.D. 135)*, revised by G. Vermes et al. (Edinburgh: T&T Clark, 1973–1987), 2:223–24.

The Sanhedrin

The Jewish high court of justice consisted of 71 men and was led by the high priest. The council could decide almost any fate of its people—except the death penalty, which was decided by the Romans. The court was located within the Chamber of Hewn Stone inside Herod's Temple.

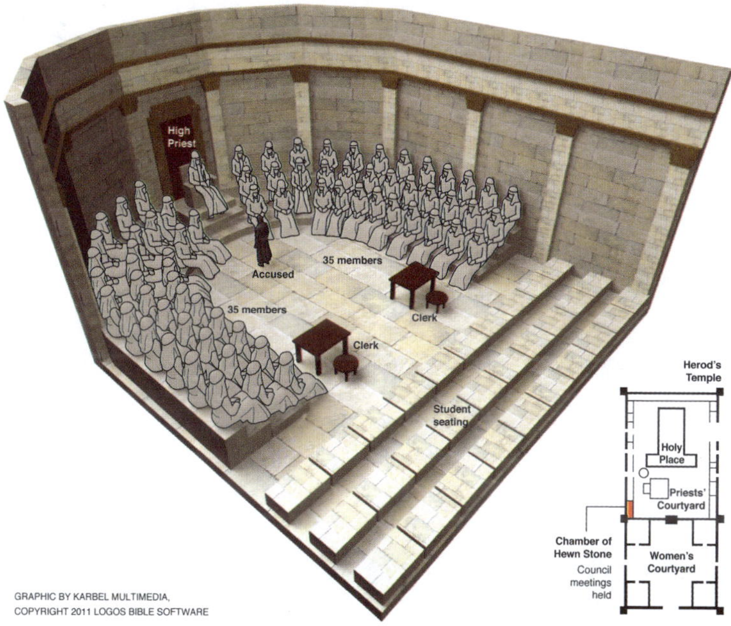

the bridge (Wilson's Arch), north of the monumental stairway (Robinson's Arch).[36] When the hall was discovered it was called Masonic Hall; later it was referred to, incorrectly, as Hasmonean Hall; a more appropriate term is Herodian Hall. The hall measured 46 by 84 feet (14 x 25.5 m), with a height of 19.6 feet (6 m); it had a monumental double doorway set in the eastern side. The vaulted ceilings of the hall and the column that one can see today date to a later period. This hall is described by Hillel Geva as follows:

> The walls are built of ashlars. Pilasters at the corners and along the walls originally bore Corinthian capitals, one of which is preserved in the northeastern corner. In the eastern wall was a double door with a lintel. Today the hall has a vaulted ceiling, of later construction, supported

36. Dan Bahat, "The Western Wall Tunnels," in *Ancient Jerusalem Revealed: Excavations 1993–1999*, repr. and exp. ed., ed. Hillel Geva (Jerusalem: Israel Exploration Society, 2000), 178–79; Bahat, *The Jerusalem Western Wall Tunnel* (Jerusalem: Israel Exploration Society, 2013), 113–28; Bahat asserts that the proposed identification of the hall with Josephus' Xystus cannot be verified (*Jerusalem Western Wall*, 135 n. 35).

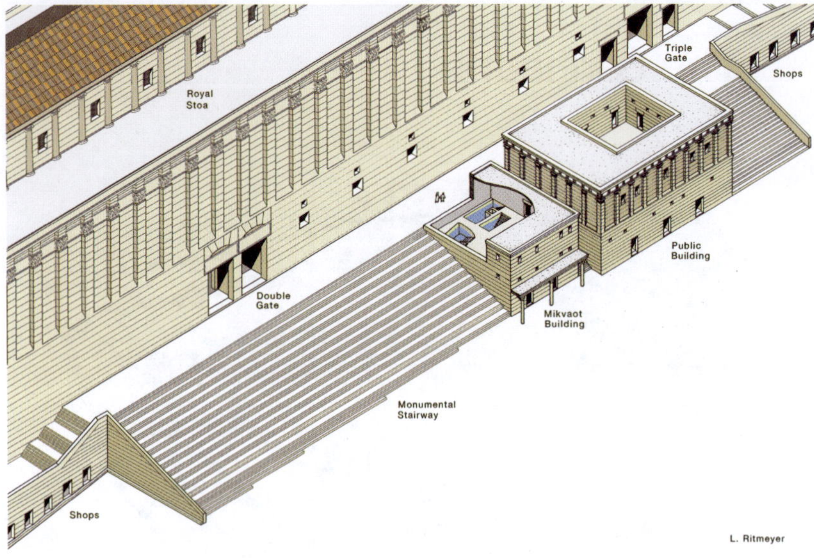

Double and Triple Gates Buildings

on a central pillar. The original hall was presumably part of a large Herodian public building that some scholars have identified with the Chamber of Hewn Stones (the Xystos) or with the Council Building, both referred to by Josephus as being in this area.[37]

The Herodian Hall is the most likely site of the Sanhedrin building at the time of the apostles.

THE STREETS OF JERUSALEM (ACTS 5:15; 23:21)

Luke reports that people brought their sick relatives out of their homes "into the streets" and laid them on beds and mats so that Peter's shadow might fall on some of them and heal them (Acts 5:15). According to Acts 23:21, over forty enemies of Paul wait in ambush to kill him when, as they hope, the Roman commander brings Paul from the Antonia Fortress to the Sanhedrin building. In the Herodian Quarter a narrow alley only six feet (1.9 m) wide was excavated.[38] This was probably typical for the streets in the residential areas of Jerusalem.

Perhaps the largest street of Jerusalem ran from the south gate through the Tyropoeon Valley and along the west side of the Temple Mount. The street was forty-one feet (12.5 m) wide and was paved with impressive stones, some five feet (1.5 m) wide and eight inches (20 cm) thick; the upper side of the paving stones had

37. Geva, "Jerusalem," 742; with reference to Josephus, *J.W.* 5.144. See also Meir Ben-Dov, *In the Shadow of the Temple: The Discovery of Ancient Jerusalem* (New York: Harper & Row, 1985), 178–80; Klaus Bieberstein, *A Brief History of Jerusalem: From the Earliest Settlements to the Destruction of the City in AD 70* (Wiesbaden: Harrassowitz, 2017), 125.

38. Avigad, *Herodian Quarter*, 39.

Herodian Hall from Model of Jerusalem

marginal dressing "but a rough surface to prevent slippage."[39] It is possible that this is where people took their sick relatives, hoping to "catch Peter" when he walked to Solomon's Colonnade on the Temple Mount; and the Roman commander would have used this street to take Paul from the Antonia Fortress on the northwest corner of the Temple Mount to the Sanhedrin building.

SYNAGOGUES IN JERUSALEM (ACTS 6:9)

Stephen, one of the seven (Acts 6:5–6), was active as a witness for the crucified and risen Jesus Messiah in the synagogues of Jerusalem (Acts 6:9). The syntax of the Greek sentence does not allow a determination regarding the number of synagogues mentioned by Luke. He could refer to one "Synagogue of Freedmen" which was attended by diaspora Jews from different regions of the Mediterranean world, including Jews from Cyrene and Alexandria and from cities in the provinces of Cilicia and Asia; thus NIV: "Opposition arose, however, from members of the Synagogue of the Freedmen (as it was called)—Jews of Cyrene and Alexandria as well as the provinces of Cilicia and Asia—who began to argue with Stephen."[40] However, in Acts 24:12 Paul mentions "synagogues" (plural) in Jerusalem. Also, it would be strange if diaspora Jews from Africa, Egypt, and Asia Minor would all be "freedmen" (*libertinoi*), former slaves who had been manumitted. The term *libertinoi*, a Greek transliteration of Lat. *libertini*, is most likely a reference to Jews

39. Bahat, "Western Wall Tunnels," 188.
40. Barrett, *Acts*, 1:323; Fitzmyer, *Acts*, 358.

from Rome who had been taken there as slaves (perhaps in connection with Pompey's conquest of Jerusalem in 63 BC) and who were manumitted by their Roman masters, or to descendants of emancipated Jewish slaves from Rome. If the freedmen, the Cyrenian Jews, and the Alexandrian Jews attend different synagogues, while the Jews from Cilicia and Asia gather in one synagogue, we have four synagogues. If each group met in a different synagogue, we have a total of five synagogues; thus Schnabel: "Then some members of the synagogue of freedmen, as it was called, of the Cyrenians, and of the Alexandrians, and of those from Cilicia and Asia, came forward to debate with Stephen."[41]

The existence of a synagogue in Jerusalem has been confirmed by the discovery of the Theodotos inscription (see page 157) which honors a certain

> Theodotos son of Vettenos, priest and archisynagogos, son of an archisynagogos, grandson of an archisynagogos ... [who] built the synagogue for the reading of the Law and teaching the commandments, and the guest-house and the (other) rooms and water installations (?) for the lodging of those who are in need of it from abroad, which (= the synagogue?) his forefathers the elders and Simonides founded.[42]

The Greek lettering allows specialists to date the inscription and thus the building to the late first century BC or the early first century AD. Since Vettenos is a Latin name, this family seems to have returned from Rome to live in Jerusalem. It is thus possible, but not certain, that Theodotos was the president of the "synagogue of the freedmen" mentioned by Luke.

PRISONS IN JERUSALEM (ACTS 4:3; 5:18, 21–22; 12:1–11; 21:34, 37)

There were several prisons in Jerusalem: Josephus uses the plural term *desmōtēria* (δεσμωτήρια), which is not surprising given the large numbers of prisoners that he mentions.[43] Luke mentions (and implies) several prisons in Jerusalem.

(1) *Prison in the Sanhedrin building*. The priests, the captain of the temple guard, and some Sadducees arrested Peter and John who are teaching in Solomon's Colonnade on the Temple Mount, put them into prison (τήρησις, *tērēsis*) for the night (Acts 4:3) and took them to a meeting of the Sanhedrin the next day (Acts 4:5). This prison was presumably located in the Sanhedrin building south of the bridge from the Kipunus Gate (Wilson's Arch) to the upper city (see above, "Sanhedrin Building"). Stephen was probably taken to the Sanhedrin prison as well (between the statement that Stephen's opponents "seized" him and the statement that they "brought him before the Sanhedrin;" Acts 6:12).

41. Schnabel, *Acts*, 344; see also Schürer, *History of the Jewish People*, 2:428; Lee I. Levine, *The Ancient Synagogue: The First Thousand Years*, 2nd ed. (New Haven: Yale University Press, 2005), 56.

42. J. J. Price, in Hannah M. Cotton, et al., *Corpus Inscriptionum Iudaeae / Palaestinae I: Jerusalem. Part 1: 1–704* (Berlin: de Gruyter, 2010), 53–56 (no. 9), translation page 54.

43. Josephus, *J.W.* 4.353, 385; 5.526. See also Brian M. Rapske, *The Book of Acts and Paul in Roman Custody*, vol. 3 of *The Book of Acts in Its First-Century Setting*, ed. Bruce W. Winter (Grand Rapids: Eerdmans, 1994), 137.

Herodian Street in Front of Western Wall of Temple Mount

(2) *The public jail.* The high priest and fellow Sadducees arrested the twelve, presumably as they were teaching in Solomon's Colonnade (Acts 5:21) and put them "in the public jail" (ἐν τηρήσει δημοσίᾳ, *en tērēsei dēmosia*; Acts 5:18; in 5:19 the term *phylakē* (φυλακή) is used, in 5:21, 23 the term *desmōtērion* (δεσμωτήριον). This prison had doors or a gate (Acts 5:19). This may have been the same jail in which Peter and John had been detained earlier; this is particularly true if the suggestion is correct that *dēmosia* is an adverb referring to the fact that they were jailed "publicly."[44] If *dēmosia* is taken as an adjective characterizing the prison in terms of its use as "public jail/prison" (NASB, NIV, NRSV), it may refer to a different prison. If the latter is correct, one can assume that the "public prison" was close to the Temple Mount in the upper city where other official buildings were located.

(3) *The prison in Herod's palace (praetorium).* The prison of Herod was probably located in his palace on the west side of the city, which the Roman prefect used as his Praetorium. This is where Jesus was kept during the Roman trial.[45] Since King Herod Agrippa I (AD 41–44) replaced the Roman prefect as the governing authority in Judea for several years, Peter's incarceration in Acts 12:3–5, which dates to this period, could be located in Herod's prison; if so, James, who was executed by Agrippa (Acts 12:2), would have been in this prison as well.

(4) *The prison in the Antonia Fortress.* After Paul was rescued by the Roman tribune from being lynched in the outer court of the temple by Jewish antagonists, he was taken into custody in the "barracks" (παρεμβολή, *parembolē*) of the Antonia Fortress (21:34, 37)[46] on the northwest corner of the Temple Mount (see below). Once Paul was inside the for-

44. Barrett, *Acts*, 1:283.

45. Mark 15:1, 7, 17; Luke 23:1, 13–25; John 18:28–29, 33.

46. Acts 22:24; 23:10, 16, 32.

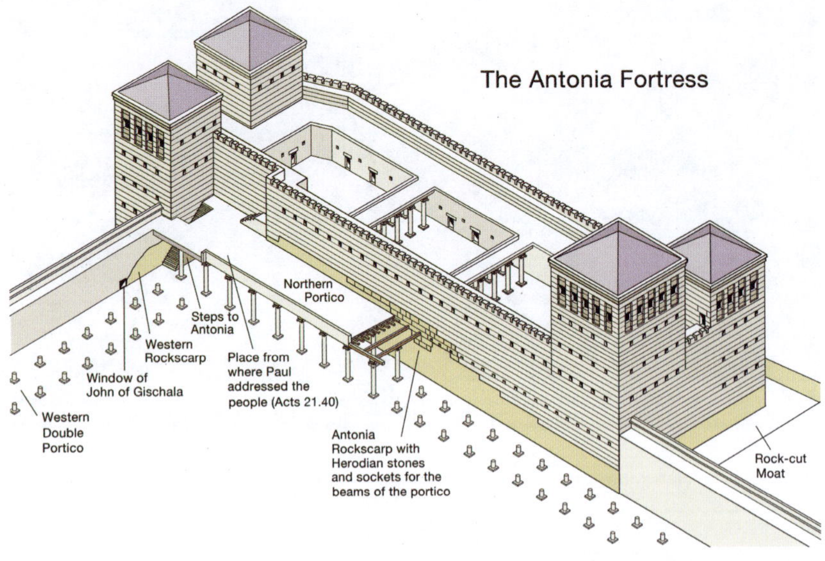

tress, probably in the courtyard of the barracks, the tribune orders that he be interrogated under torture—"with the whip," leather thongs, often with pieces of metal or bone that tore into the flesh, attached to a wooden handle—for which the soldiers stretched him out, spreading him in a forward position thus creating a tense posture of his upper body so that the blows would inflict maximum damage on the naked skin. Paul is spared this harsh interrogation only when he points out that he is a Roman citizen. Fearful of the consequences of his actions, the tribune seemed to have removed the chains from Paul (Acts 22:22); he kept him in custody in the Antonia overnight, and on the next day, before taking him to the Sanhedrin building, he "released" him, further slackening the custodial arrangements, perhaps removing all bonds before taking him to the Sanhedrin.[47] Since Agrippa I had full control of Jerusalem in AD 41–44, James and Peter, if they were not incarcerated in Herod's palace, could have been imprisoned in the Antonia as well (Acts 12:2, 3–5).

PLACE OF EXECUTION (ACTS 7:57–60)

After his interrogation in the Sanhedrin, which apparently ended in a death sentence (implied in Acts 7:57: the Jewish leaders covered their ears to prevent hearing further blasphemies), Stephen was dragged "outside of the city" where he was stoned (Acts 7:58). In territories controlled by Roman governors, only the proconsul or prefect had the right to impose capital sentences. Stephen's killing by Jews, who stone him outside the city according to Jewish law,[48] is best understood as "an act of establishment violence" which was a "legally legitimate killing of an irregular nature by those

47. Schnabel, *Acts*, 925; Rapske, *Paul in Roman Custody*, 146.

48. Lev 24:14; Num 15:35; see also m. Sanhedrin 6:1.

present."[49] Stephen was taken, perhaps, from the Sanhedrin building adjacent to the western wall of the Temple Mount across the upper city past Herod's palace (*praetorium*) through a gate in the western city wall to the site where executions took place, perhaps to Golgotha, a former quarry where executions were carried out;[50] alternately, Stephen might have been taken from the Sanhedrin building south along the main street in the Tyropoeon Valley past the Pool of Siloam to the gate in the southern wall of the city to the Hinnom or Kidron Valley.

RESIDENCE OF THE HIGH PRIEST (ACTS 9:1–2)

According to Acts 9:1–2, Saul went to the high priest, that is, to Caiaphas (AD 18–36/37), asking for letters to the synagogues in Damascus requesting cooperation in the efforts to locate and arrest followers of Jesus. Presumably Saul contacted Caiaphas in the high priest's residence, which may have been the villa excavated in the Herodian Quarter excavations by N. Avigad.[51]

RESIDENCE OF KING HEROD AGRIPPA I (ACTS 12:1–4)

The trial of James, one of the twelve, who was found guilty and subsequently executed (Acts 12:1–2), and the planned trial of Peter (Acts 12:4), presumably took place at the palace of King Herod I, Agrippa I's grandfather, which was used by the Roman prefects as *praetorium* and vacated when Agrippa I became king in AD 41 (until AD 44).[52]

More specifically, the site of the trial was the judge's bench (βῆμα, *bēma*) that stood "at a place called The Stone Pavement, or in Hebrew Gabbatha" (John 19:13). The Greek term *lithostrōtos* (λιθόστρωτος) means "paved with stones" or "mosaic or tessellated pavement."[53] The Hebrew (or Aramaic) term "Gabbatha" (Γαββαθα, *Gabbatha*) is not a translation of *lithostrōtos* but the Hebrew name for this location.[54] The excavations of Magen Broshi along the western Old City wall in the 1970s uncovered a gateway complex midway along the western Old City wall south of the citadel. Shimon Gibson suggests that the Lithostrotos was located at this monumental gateway adjacent to Herod's palace; the gateway had a large courtyard (ninety-eight by thirty-six feet [30 x 11 m]) situated between two fortification walls and two large towers.[55] Josephus reports that Florus, the Roman prefect, placed the *bēma* in front of the palace in which he resided (*J.W.* 2.301), which seems to confirm Gibson's sugges-

---

49. Torrey Seland, *Establishment Violence in Philo and Luke: A Study of Non-Conformity to the Torah and Jewish Vigilante Reactions* (Leiden: Brill, 1995), 241, 242; see also Schnabel, *Acts*, 391.

50. Matt 27:33; Mark 15:22; Luke 23:33; John 19:17. See also Benjamin A. Foreman, "Locating Jesus' Crucifixion and Burial," in *Lexham Geographic Commentary on the Gospels*, ed. Barry J. Beitzel (Bellingham, WA: Lexham Press, 2017), 504–17.

51. Schnabel, *Jesus in Jerusalem*, ch. 2.9, 2.10. See also Benjamin A. Foreman, "From the Upper Room to the Judgment Seat," in *Lexham Geographic Commentary on the Gospels*, ed. Barry J. Beitzel (Bellingham, WA: Lexham Press, 2017), 483–503.

52. See Foreman, "From the Upper Room to the Judgment Seat."

53. LSJ, s.v. "λιθόστρωτος"; see also BDAG, s.v. "λιθόστρωτος."

54. For the following comments see Schnabel, *Jesus in Jerusalem*, ch. 2.13.

55. Magen Broshi and Shimon Gibson, "Excavations along the Western and Southern Walls of the Old City of Jerusalem," in Geva, *Ancient Jerusalem Revealed*, 153; Shimon Gibson, "The

Herod's Palace from Model of Jerusalem

tion. The gateway, which seems to have been built at the time of King Herod, evidently led directly into the compound of Herod's Palace. If half of the courtyard of the gateway complex could be used by audiences watching trials, a densely packed crowd would have numbered around eight hundred people.[56] Places of execution in the Hinnom Valley or at the site of Golgotha could easily be reached through this gate.

OFFICES IN THE INNER ENCLOSURE OF THE TEMPLE (ACTS 21:26)

After Paul agreed to demonstrate to the Jewish Christians of Jerusalem that he does not teach the abandonment of the Mosaic Law, "he went to the temple to give notice of the date when the days of purification would end and the offering would be made" for the four believers who had made a vow (Acts 21:26). Paul seemed to have entered[57] the inner court, going to the Place of the Hearth located in the northwest corner of the inner enclosure, which "served as a sort of supervision center for all activities carried out in the Temple, both in the daytime (concerning the incoming sacrifices) and at night (when the guard shifts were dispatched;" it was used by the priests and Levites who were on duty, and "by Jewish males bringing sacrifices, who

Trial of Jesus at the Jerusalem Praetorium: New Archaeological Evidence," in *The World of Jesus and the Early Church: Identity and Interpretation in Early Communities of Faith*, ed. Craig A. Evans (Peabody, MA: Hendrickson, 2011), 112–18.

56. Assuming five persons per square yard (m²), the upper limit for standing or viewing spaces, above which the risk of trips or falls increases significantly; see Still, "Crowd Safety," http://www.gkstill.com/Support/crowd-density/CrowdDensity-1.html.

57. The imperfect *eisēei* (εἰσῄει) could indicate that Paul entered the inner courts several times, perhaps due to the fact that the four men were purified on different days.

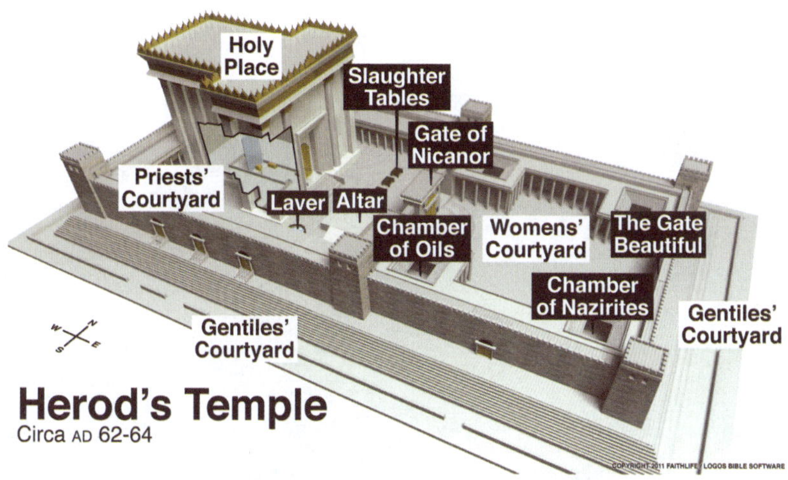

were allowed to enter its northern half in order to obtain the token needed for bringing sacrifices."[58] Nazirites boiled their offerings in the Chamber of the Nazirites, one of the four segregated areas in the Court of Women, each measuring sixty-five by sixty-five feet (20 x 20 m), located in the southeast corner of the court (m. Middot 2:5).

INNER COURTS, GATES, AND THE OUTER COURT OF THE TEMPLE (ACTS 21:27–30, 32–33)

When Paul was seized in the inner court of the temple (Acts 21:27–29) by Jews who thought that he had profaned the temple, they dragged him out of the court whereupon "the gates were shut" (Acts 21:30). If Paul was seized in the Place of the Hearth (see above), he would have been dragged through the gate of this structure in the northwest corner of the inner enclosure, across the elevated walkway and down twelve (or fourteen) steps, through a door in the balustrade with the warning inscriptions, into the northern section of the outer court (Court of the Gentiles). The gates that were shut would have been the gate of the Place of the Hearth and the gate in the balustrade opposite the Place of the Hearth. If he was seized in the Court of the Israelites, he would probably have been dragged through the Nicanor Gate into the Court of Women and through the Beautiful Gate into the eastern section of the outer court. In this case, the gates that were shut would have been the Nicanor Gate and the Beautiful Gate.

The attempted lynching of Paul (Acts 21:31) and his rescue by the Roman commander and his soldiers (Acts 21:32–33) took place in the outer court, either north of the temple between the inner enclosure and Solomon's Stoa (if he was seized in the Place of the Hearth), or east of the temple between the Court of Women and the Royal Stoa (if he was seized in the Court of the Israelites).

---

58. Netzer, *Architecture of Herod*, 158; on the Place of the Hearth, see Netzer, *Architecture of Herod*, 155–56. See m. Middot 1:6–9; m. Middot 1:1; for the rooms of the Place (Chamber) of the Hearth and their functions.

Antonia Fortress from Model of Jerusalem

THE ANTONIA FORTRESS (ACTS 21:31–32; 22:24–29; 23:10–11, 16–31)

Paul, after his arrest in the outer court of the temple, was taken to "the barracks" (*parembolē*), that is, to the Antonia Fortress at the northwestern end of the Temple Mount where Roman auxiliary forces were stationed (Acts 21:31–32, 22:24–29).[59] He stayed there as a prisoner until his transfer to Caesarea (23:10–11, 16–31).[60]

BIBLIOGRAPHY

Adler, Yonatan. "The Ritual Baths Near the Temple Mount and Extra-Purification Before Entering the Temple Courts: A Reply to Eyal Regev." *IEJ* 56 (2006): 209–15.

Avigad, Nahman. *The Herodian Quarter in Jerusalem: Wohl Archaeological Museum*. Jerusalem: Keter, 1991.

Bahat, Dan. *The Jerusalem Western Wall Tunnel*. Jerusalem: Israel Exploration Society, 2013.

———. "The Western Wall Tunnels." Pages 177–90 in *Ancient Jerusalem Revealed: Excavations 1993–1999*. Reprinted and exp. ed. Edited by Hillel Geva. Jerusalem: Israel Exploration Society, 2000.

Baldi, Donatus. *Enchiridion Locorum Sanctorum: Documenta S. Evangelii loca respicientia*. 2nd ed. Jerusalem: Franciscan Printing Press, 1982.

Barrett, C. K. *The Acts of the Apostles*. 2 vols. Edinburgh: T&T Clark, 1994–1998.

59. See Josephus, *J.W.* 5.238–247. See also Netzer, *Architecture of Herod*, 120–26; Ritmeyer, *Temple Mount*, 123–31.

60. For details on the Antonia Fortress see Eckhard Schnabel, "Paul as a Prisoner in Judea and Rome," chapter 32 in this volume, page 398.

Ben-Dov, Meir. *In the Shadow of the Temple: The Discovery of Ancient Jerusalem*. New York: Harper & Row, 1985.

Bieberstein, Klaus. *A Brief History of Jerusalem: From the Earliest Settlements to the Destruction of the City in AD 70*. Wiesbaden: Harrassowitz, 2017.

Broshi, Magen, and Shimon Gibson. "Excavations along the Western and Southern Walls of the Old City of Jerusalem." Pages 147–55 in *Ancient Jerusalem Revealed: Excavations 1993–1999*. Reprinted and exp. ed. Edited by Hillel Geva. Jerusalem: Israel Exploration Society, 2000.

Clausen, David C. *The Upper Room and Tomb of David: The History, Art, and Archaeology of the Cenacle on Mount Zion*. Jefferson, NC: McFarland, 2016.

Cotton, Hannah M., Leah Di Segni, Werner Eck, Benjamin Isaac, Alla Kushnir-Stein, Haggai Misgav, Jonathan Price, Israel Roll, and Ada Yardeni, eds. *Corpus Inscriptionum Iudaeae / Palaestinae I: Jerusalem. Part 1: 1–704*. Berlin: de Gruyter, 2010.

Finegan, Jack. *The Archeology of the New Testament: The Life of Jesus and the Beginning of the Early Church*. Revised ed. Princeton: Princeton University Press, 1992.

Fitzmyer, Joseph A. *The Acts of the Apostles: A New Translation with Introduction and Commentary*. New York: Doubleday, 1998.

Foreman, Benjamin A. "From the Upper Room to the Judgment Seat." Pages 483–503 in *Lexham Geographic Commentary on the Gospels*. Edited by Barry J. Beitzel. Bellingham, WA: Lexham Press, 2017.

———. "Locating Jesus' Crucifixion and Burial." Pages 504–17 in *Lexham Geographic Commentary on the Gospels*. Edited by Barry J. Beitzel. Bellingham, WA: Lexham Press, 2017.

Franz, Gordon. "Jesus at the Pool of Bethesda." Pages 125–33 in *Lexham Geographic Commentary on the Gospels*. Edited by Barry J. Beitzel. Bellingham, WA: Lexham Press, 2017.

Geva, Hillel. "Jerusalem: The Second Temple Period." *NEAEHL* 2:717–52.

Gibson, Shimon. *The Final Days of Jesus: The Archaeological Evidence*. New York: HarperOne, 2009.

———. "The Pool of Bethesda in Jerusalem and Jewish Purification Practices of the Second Temple Period." *Proche-Orient chrétien* 55 (2005): 270–93.

———. "The Trial of Jesus at the Jerusalem Praetorium: New Archaeological Evidence." Pages 97–118 in *The World of Jesus and the Early Church: Identity and Interpretation in Early Communities of Faith*. Edited by Craig A. Evans. Peabody, MA: Hendrickson, 2011.

Hengel, Martin. "The Geography of Palestine in Acts." Pages 27–78 in *The Book of Acts in Its Palestinian Setting*. Edited by Richard Bauckham. Volume 4 of *The Book of Acts in Its First-Century Setting*. Edited by Bruce W. Winter. Grand Rapids: Eerdmans, 1995.

Jervell, Jacob. *Die Apostelgeschichte*. Göttingen: Vandenhoeck & Ruprecht, 1998.

Keener, Craig S. *Acts: An Exegetical Commentary*. 4 vols. Grand Rapids: Baker Academic, 2012–2015.

Kendall, Calvin B. *The Allegory of the Church: Romanesque Portals and their Verse Inscriptions*. Toronto: University of Toronto Press, 1998.

Levine, Lee I. *The Ancient Synagogue: The First Thousand Years*. 2nd ed. New Haven: Yale University Press, 2005.

Magness, Jodi. *Stone and Dung, Oil and Spit: Jewish Daily Life in the Time of Jesus*. Grand Rapids: Eerdmans, 2011.

Marshall, I. Howard. *The Acts of the Apostles. An Introduction and Commentary*. Leicester: Inter-Varsity Press, 1980.

McCauley, Leo P., and Anthony A. Stephenson. *St. Cyril of Jerusalem: Works*. 2 vols. Washington, DC: Catholic University of America Press, 1969–1970.

Murphy-O'Connor, Jerome. "The Cenacle—Topographical Setting for Acts 2:44–45." Pages 303–21 in *The Book of Acts in Its Palestinian Setting*. Edited by Richard Bauckham. Volume 4 of *The Book of Acts in Its First-Century Setting*. Edited by Bruce W. Winter Grand Rapids: Eerdmans, 1995.

Netzer, Ehud. *The Architecture of Herod, the Great Builder*. Grand Rapids: Baker Academic, 2008.

Phillips, Elaine A. "Healing by Living Waters at the Pool of Siloam." Pages 365–73 in *Lexham Geographic Commentary on the Gospels*. Edited by Barry J. Beitzel. Bellingham, WA: Lexham Press, 2017.

Pixner, Bargil. "Mount Zion, Jesus, and Archaeology." Pages 309–22 in *Jesus and Archaeology*. Edited by James H. Charlesworth. Grand Rapids: Eerdmans, 2006.

———. *Paths of the Messiah and Sites of the Early Church from Galilee to Jerusalem: Jesus and Jewish Christianity in Light of Archaeological Discoveries*. Edited by Rainer Riesner. San Francisco: Ignatius Press, 2010.

Pixner, Bargil, Doron Chen, and Shlomo Margalit. "Mount Zion: The 'Gate of the Essenes' Reexcavated." *Zeitschrift des Deutschen Palästina-Vereins* 105 (1989): 85–95.

Rapske, Brian M. *The Book of Acts and Paul in Roman Custody*. Volume 3 of *The Book of Acts in Its First-Century Setting*. Edited by Bruce W. Winter. Grand Rapids: Eerdmans, 1994.

Reich, Ronny, and Eli Shukron. "The Siloam Pool in the Wake of Recent Discoveries." Pages 137–40 in *New Studies on Jerusalem, Vol. 10*. Edited by Eyal Baruch and Avi Faust. Ramat-Gan: Bar-Ilan University, 2004.

Riesner, Rainer. *Essener und Urgemeinde in Jerusalem: Neue Funde und Quellen*. 2nd ed. Giessen: Brunnen, 1998.

———. "Josephus' 'Gate of the Essenes' in Modern Discussion." *Zeitschrift des Deutschen Palästina-Vereins* 105 (1989): 105–9.

Ritmeyer, Kathleen, and Leen Ritmeyer. "Reconstructing Herod's Temple Mount." Pages 80–101 in *Where Christianity Was Born*. Edited by H. Shanks. Washington, DC: Biblical Archaeological Society, 2006.

Ritmeyer, Leen. *The Quest: Revealing the Temple Mount in Jerusalem*. Jerusalem: Carta, 2006.

Schnabel, Eckhard J. *Acts*. Grand Rapids: Zondervan, 2012.

———. *Jesus in Jerusalem: April 2–10, A.D. 30*. Grand Rapids: Eerdmans, 2018.

———. "The Meaning of βαπτίζειν in Greek, Jewish, and Patristic Literature." *Filologia Neotestamentaria* 24 (2011): 3–40.

Schürer, Emil. *The History of the Jewish People in the Age of Christ (175 B.C.–A.D. 135)*. Revised by Geza Vermes, Fergus Millar, Matthew Black, and Martin

Goodman. Edinburgh: T&T Clark, 1973–1987.

Seland, Torrey. *Establishment Violence in Philo and Luke: A Study of Non-Conformity to the Torah and Jewish Vigilante Reactions*. Leiden: Brill, 1995.

Still, G. Keith. "Crowd Safety and Risk Analysis." http://www.gkstill.com/Support/crowd-density/CrowdDensity-1.html.

Wahlde, Urban C. von. "Archaeology and John's Gospel." Pages 523–86 in *Jesus and Archaeology*. Edited by James H. Charlesworth. Grand Rapids: Eerdmans, 2006.

Zahn, Theodor. *Die Apostelgeschichte des Lucas*. 2 vols. Leipzig: Deichert, 1921–1922.

CHAPTER 3

THE THREEFOLD EXPANSION OF THE EARLY CHURCH: JERUSALEM, JUDEA, AND SAMARIA

Acts 1:6–8

Cyndi Parker

KEY POINTS

- The Gospel of Luke contains a journey narrative from Galilee to Jerusalem, and the book of Acts provides the companion narrative from Jerusalem to the "ends of the earth."
- Instructions for the expansion of the early church from Jerusalem to Judea, Samaria, and the ends of the earth provides the organizing structure for the book of Acts.
- The list of place names in Acts 1:8 is more than a geographical designation. Each place is a cultural product derived from a combination of memory, religion, sociology, and politics.
- The expansion of the early church demonstrates there are no boundaries limiting the restoration offered by God's kingdom as long as the story of restoration is fully embedded in the events in Jerusalem.

INTRODUCTION

The Book of Acts opens with a brief conversation in which Jesus assures the disciples that they "will receive power when the Holy Spirit comes on you; and you will be my witnesses in Jerusalem, and in all Judea and Samaria, and to the ends of the earth" (Acts 1:8, NIV).[1] The instruction to take the gospel message out of Jerusalem is often explained as a geographical ref-

1. Unless otherwise stated, all quotes are from the NASB.

erence moving in concentric circles from the smallest location to the next larger location. While this explanation is true, the instruction has a more complex and nuanced meaning beyond geography. Given that Jesus is talking to his Galilean disciples, one would expect a purely geographical list to include Jerusalem, Judea, Samaria, and *Galilee*—especially since Jesus spent most of his public ministry in Galilee.[2] But Galilee is omitted in favor of "the ends of the earth." A preferable explanation to the place names acknowledges that the places mentioned in Acts 1:8 are a cultural product derived from a combination of memory, religion, sociological, and political associations. Their nuanced meaning deserves careful attention.

CONNECTIONS BETWEEN LUKE AND ACTS

The book of Acts is recognized as the second volume of the work started in the Gospel of Luke in which the author recorded "all that Jesus began to do and to teach" (Acts 1:1, compare Luke 1:3). The book of Acts continues the narrative from Luke but shifts the focus to the Holy Spirit and the witness of the disciples. Further continuity is preserved between these two books with the themes of "journey" and "restoration."

Luke's Gospel contains a journey narrative in chapters 9–19 (see map on page 9). The Galilean disciples follow Jesus to Jerusalem where they witness his death and resurrected presence. The book of Acts continues the journey theme but reverses the travel direction from Jerusalem outward, and from the suffering of Jesus to the restoration of his kingdom.[3] The disciples who traveled with Jesus to Jerusalem received the "spatial manifesto" (to be a witness in Jerusalem, Judea, Samaria, and ends of the earth)[4] that pushes them in an outward trajectory but only with the empowerment of the Holy Spirit.[5] The spread of the gospel is a major theme for Acts—in fact, the "spatial manifesto" provides the organizing structure for the book that focuses on the witnesses who are empowered by the Holy Spirit and sent out from Jerusalem.[6]

In addition to the journey theme, Acts continues the Gospel's idea of kingdom restoration. In response to the disciples' question, "Lord, are you at this time going to restore the kingdom to Israel?" (1:6), Jesus replies but does not directly answer the question. The disciples' hope for the restoration of the kingdom portrays a persistent confusion about the kingdom of God, restoration of Israel, and the (presumed) national independence (see

---

2. Ben Witherington III suggests that the omission is due to the author of Acts not knowing details about the evangelization of Galilee even if he is familiar with the fact the first disciples were Galilean (Ben Witherington III, *The Acts of the Apostles: A Socio-Rhetorical Commentary* [Grand Rapids: Eerdmans, 1998], 11).

3. John B. Polhill, *Acts* (Nashville: Broadman & Holman, 1992), 86; Matthew Sleeman, *Geography and the Ascension Narrative in Acts* (Cambridge: Cambridge University Press, 2009), 64.

4. Sleeman, *Geography and the Ascension Narrative*, 67, 69.

5. Notice how the disciples are told not to leave Jerusalem until the Holy Spirit comes upon them (Acts 1:4, 8), which happens in Acts 2.

6. Acts records the good news spreading from Jerusalem (chs. 1–7) to Judea and Samaria (chs. 8–12), and to the ends of the earth (chs. 13–28), see F. F. Bruce, *The Book of the Acts*, revised ed. (Grand Rapids: Eerdmans, 1988), 36; Polhill, *Acts*, 86.

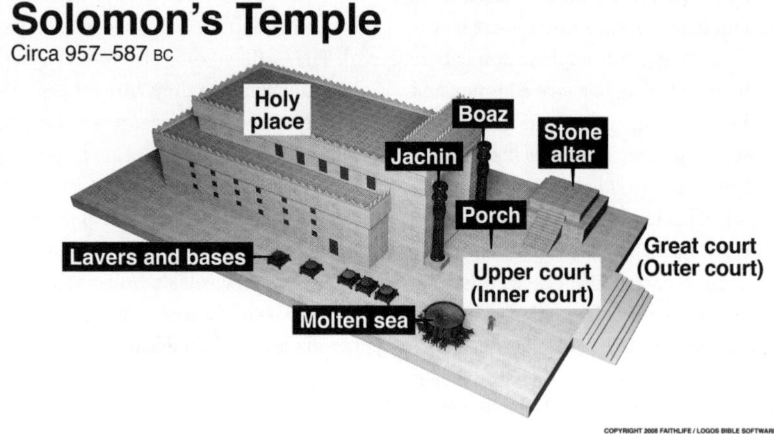

Luke 22:24–27). Jesus' response is not a simple yes or no answer.[7] Jesus says the date and time are not to be known, but there is a vision for the ongoing work. "You will receive power when the Holy Spirit comes on you" (Acts 1:8a). These words connect back to the ministry of John the Baptist who predicted the type of baptism Jesus would require (Acts 1:5; see also Luke 3:16; Matt 3:11). Jesus was baptized, the Holy Spirit descended upon him, and Jesus began his public ministry. Likewise, the disciples are to wait for the Holy Spirit to arrive, and in the Spirit's power be released into a new ministry. The author of Acts purposefully connects the disciples to a line of Holy Spirit enabled work, from John the Baptist to Jesus and now to them.[8]

Jesus' instructions in Acts 1:8 explain the disciples' continuing mission. Repentance for the forgiveness of sins will be preached to all nations starting in Jerusalem. The "spatial manifesto" dismantles the Jewish expectation of deliverance from Rome and a return of self-rule to Israel even while maintaining Israel at the heart of the change.[9]

Jerusalem, Judea, Samaria, and the ends of the earth are not neutral geographical markers; they present a cultural way of seeing the world. Places and memory are interlinked, so that every memory recalls a place, and every place preserves an associated memory. For the Jews, memory of their Israelite history was embedded into the rocks and dirt around them making place both a teaching tool and a memory trigger. Jesus effectively used his physical locations to communicate with his audience.[10] For the disciples who followed Jesus, the geography not only held the ancient memory embedded in the land but also the recent

7. Bruce, *Book of Acts*, 35.

8. Bruce, *Book of Acts*, 36.

9. Sleeman, *Geography and the Ascension Narrative*, 70.

10. See *Lexham Geographic Commentary on the Gospels*, ed. Barry J. Beitzel (Bellingham, WA: Lexham, 2016) for detailed examples.

lived-memory of their time with Jesus. Recounting all the biblical events and religious and cultural developments in each region named in Acts 1:8 is unrealistic in this article, but these brief overviews encourage readers to recall the depth of memory held by each place.[11]

JERUSALEM

Jerusalem was the destination for the exilic Jews choosing to return to their historic place of residence and to the city that held the memory of God's presence among his people. The city was the political and religious capital for a united kingdom under David and the subsequent southern kingdom of Judah. The religious reforms of Hezekiah and Josiah centralized even more authority in Jerusalem. The final destruction of the city in 586 BC completed the exile of the Israelites, and the city became the subject of songs and wistful memories. Understandably, Jerusalem was the focal point for Jews in the Second Temple period because it held the memory of the time long past when they were an independent kingdom with a king "after God's own heart" (1 Samuel 13:14, see also Acts 13:22).

The significance of the city was encapsulated not only in the memory of the past but also in the presence of the temple, a significant fact when considering the connection between Luke and Acts. The temple is a central theme in Luke's Gospel, which begins and ends in the temple (1:8–10 and 24:53).[12] Luke's Gospel also portrays the life and ministry of Jesus at the temple, from his infant dedication and the blessing of Simeon (2:21–39), to Jesus' astute interactions with the teachers in the temple courts (2:41–50), to the final week Jesus spent in Jerusalem teaching in the temple (19:45–48). Even after the death and resurrection of Jesus, the Gospel of Luke ends with Jesus ascending to heaven and the disciples returning to the temple (24:53). The book of Acts takes up the temple theme and begins with a focus on the initial events in or around the temple in Jerusalem.

The combination of the historical and religious significance of Jerusalem and the temple creates the anchor point of the gospel message as well as the key starting point for the spread of the good news. When the Holy Spirit empowers those waiting in the upper room, crowds of people gather to investigate the unusual event. According to Acts 2:9–11, people in the crowd came from the eastern frontier of the Roman Empire to the western edge of the empire, including Egypt and northern Africa (see map on page 95). If they all took Peter's message back home with them, then theoretically, one could argue that with one sermon Peter reaches the "ends of the earth." However, all the people in the crowd, both Jews and converts to Judaism (2:11a), were ideologically focused on the Jerusalem temple. When Peter addressed the crowd, he used insider language. His sermon was predicated on knowledge of Joel and Psalms 16 and 110, so the message only reached those familiar with Israelite history and writings. Following Peter's sermon, Acts records Peter and John healing a man in the temple in chapters 3 and 4 and then describes the early community of believers in chapters 4 and 5. So through

11. For a discussion of some of the relevant events and cultural background, see Mark L. Strauss, "Typological Geography and the Progress of the Gospel in Acts," chapter 1 in this volume.

12. Polhill, *Acts*, 86.

Judean Hill Country

the early chapters of Acts, the focus of the narrative remains on the temple, and as long as the message stayed in Jerusalem, it inhabited a Jewish, temple-centric story.

JUDEA

Although greatly influenced by Greco-Roman thought, the Judean hill country fostered a consistently conservative Jewish mindset. The diverse landscape of Judea held many of the memories of Old Testament stories, from the earliest beginnings of Israelite society to the home territory of King David and to the heartland of the southern kingdom of Judah. This was the land to which the exiled Jews returned when Persia granted them religious freedom and financial support to rebuild Jerusalem and the temple.

Although the gospels record Jesus' interactions with people in Judea, most of those activities were in or around Jerusalem.[13] The gospels record a resistance from the Jews in Judea to Jesus. The problem may be due in part to the mountainous terrain. The tight horizon lines and the difficult ascents through the hills presented geographical obstacles that obstructed interactions with outsiders. People living in the core of Judea did not have their conservative views challenged because outsiders had to exert considerable effort to reach those communities. A group of traders or bands of Roman soldiers did not haphazardly wander through towns nestled in the bends and folds of the Judean hills. The conservative worldview of Judeans along with the "ivory tower" reputation of the scholars at the Jerusalem temple may have led to the resistance Jesus faced when in Judea.[14]

The conservative nature of Judea is also noticeable in early Roman politics.

13. For a detailed discussion of Jesus' interactions in Judea, see Chris McKinny, "The Words and Teachings of Jesus in the Context of Judea," in Beitzel, *Lexham Geographic Commentary on the Gospels*, 338–55.

14. The point is obscured in English translations, because the Greek word *Ioudaios* (Ἰουδαιος) can be translated as a geographical reference (Judean) or as the name of a group of people (Jew). As an example, the regional variety in how people responded to Jesus is evident in John 7:1 where it is recorded that Jesus left Judea to go to Galilee for "the Jews

Herod the Great, while establishing his authority and legitimacy to rule, built several palaces in the hill country, including his palace in Jerusalem. When Herod died, the control of Judea and Samaria passed first to his son Archelaus and then to Roman governors who quickly moved the primary place of governance out of the temple-centric Judean hills to the Rome-centric coastal city of Caesarea Maritima.[15]

As Acts tells the story of the gospel leaving Jerusalem, the message reached the Jews first and with astonishing success. Acts 5 says the people from surrounding towns in Judea went to Jerusalem to see what was happening. News of the events in Jerusalem was spreading, and the communities that had previously resisted Jesus now sought explanations for what they heard.

Up to this point, the narrative in Acts is not wholly unexpected. Jerusalem and Judea were anticipated places of restoration. Those regions preserve memories of the old Davidic kingdom, and they were expected locations for a newly established kingdom of God. But core Jewish ideas of restoration would be stretched with the next move to Samaria.

SAMARIA

The geographical regions of Judea and Samaria were considered one political unit by Rome but not by the people who lived there (see map on page 11). Their territories held memories of the past that reinforced the separation between populations.

Samaria preserved memories of the Israelite past in its soil, rocks, and hills just as the hills to the south did. Several patriarchal stories are connected with the city of Shechem, which was also the chosen burial place of Joseph (Josh 24:32). The two hills surrounding Shechem, Mount Ebal and Mount Gerizim, sat as constant reminders of the renewed covenant between God and his people (Deut 11:29–32; Josh 8:30–35).[16] Shechem was chosen as the first capital of the Northern Kingdom of Israel (1 Kings 12:25), but the politically savvy King Omri moved the capital to Samaria (1 Kings 16:24)—the city that ultimately gave its name to the surrounding region. The fall of the Northern Kingdom to Assyria is marked by the destruction of the city of Samaria in 722 BC.

The history of the people living in the Samarian hill country after the Assyrian conquest is complicated due to a limited number of extrabiblical documents. The Bible records how Assyria replaced the Israelite population in the Northern Kingdom with other peoples (2 Kgs 17:24). The newcomers embraced a version of Yahwistic theology, although they practiced according to their earlier customs (2 Kgs 17:25–41). Not all of the northern Israelites were exiled because several from the northern tribes responded to the religious reforms made by Hezekiah and Josiah and even contributed to the

---

were seeking to kill him." However, "the Jews" were the primary population in both Judea and Galilee. Jesus would not leave the Jewish Judea to go to the Jewish Galilee to escape the Jews! More likely, Jesus left Judea for Galilee because the *Judeans* were trying to kill him.

15. See Paul Wright, "The Geography of Caesarea Maritima," chapter 16 in this volume.

16. A detailed analysis of the connection between memory and place—especially Mount Ebal and Mount Gerizim—is available in Cynthia Parker, "Deuteronomy's Place: An Analysis of the Placial Structure of Deuteronomy" (PhD diss., University of Gloucestershire, 2015).

Mount Ebal (Right) and Mount Gerizim (Left)

refurbishing of the temple (2 Chron 30:3–11, 18; 34:9). People from this core Samarian hill country became the Samaritan people, but the exact history of who they are and how their variation on Yahwistic beliefs developed is unclear.

Generations later conflicts sprung up between the Jews who returned to Judea from exile and the already well-established Samaritan community to the north (Neh 4 and 6). These initial conflicts developed into deep hostility between the Jews and Samaritans.[17]

Despite the historic animosity between the Jews and Samaritans, Luke records how Jesus purposefully interacted with Samaritans (Luke 9:52–54; 10:33–37; 17:11–19). Through his own life and teachings Jesus demonstrated how the gospel message included the Samaritans along with the Jews. The book of Acts continues this message and records how the great persecution that hit the young Christian community in Jerusalem forced people to flee to the surrounding areas of Judea and Samaria, having a great impact on several Samaritan villages (Acts 8:1, 4–25).

ENDS OF THE EARTH

The final portion of the "spatial manifesto" moves the horizon from "Israel" to the ends of the earth (see Isa 49:6)—a concept addressed in great detail elsewhere in this commentary.[18] Significant to notice here, however, is that the geographical markers dismantle the restrictions on restored space. God's kingdom is not just for Israel even if Jerusalem is at

17. For a detailed account of the complex history between the people in Samaria and Judea, see Gary Knoppers, *Jews and Samaritans: The Origins and History of Their Early Relations* (Oxford: Oxford University Press, 2013).

18. See, especially, Eckhard J. Schnabel, "Jesus' Missionary Commission and the Ends of the Earth," chapter 4 in this volume.

the head.[19] The "witnessing space is projected as breaching the ethnic divides that define Israel-space."[20] The "ends of the earth" requires reaching beyond specific places with Israelite and Jewish memory and beyond the experienced spaces the disciples shared with Jesus.

While the book of Acts follows the expansion theme, there remains a consistent return to that which anchors the gospel message. The good news flowed out to other places but connected those audiences back to the core of Jerusalem and the events there—the life, death, and resurrection of Jesus. Gentiles living throughout the Roman Empire did not have the same narrative, history, or memory preserved in their surrounding landscapes, but they were invited to acknowledge all that was preserved in the Jewish story. The Holy Spirit empowered the disciples to move outward and to ultimately include the gentiles, for no boundary limited the restoration offered by God's kingdom as long as the story of restoration was fully embedded in the events in Jerusalem.

BIBLIOGRAPHY

Beitzel, Barry J., ed. *Lexham Geographic Commentary on the Gospels*. Bellingham, WA: Lexham Press, 2016.

Bruce, F. F. *The Book of the Acts*. Revised ed. Grand Rapids: Eerdmans, 1988.

McKinny, Chris. "The Words and Teachings of Jesus in the Context of Judea." Pages 338–55 in *Lexham Geographic Commentary on the Gospels*. Edited by Barry J. Beitzel. Bellingham, WA: Lexham Press, 2016.

Parker, Cynthia. "Deuteronomy's Place: An Analysis of the Placial Structure

19. Sleeman, *Geography and the Ascension Narrative*, 70.

20. Sleeman, *Geography and the Ascension Narrative*, 71.

of Deuteronomy." PhD diss., University of Gloucestershire, 2015.

Knopper, Gary. *Jews and Samaritans: The Origins and History of Their Early Relations*. Oxford: Oxford University Press, 2013.

Polhill, John B. *Acts*. Nashville: Broadman & Holman, 1992.

Sleeman, Matthew. *Geography and the Ascension Narrative in* Acts. Cambridge: Cambridge University Press, 2009.

Witherington, Ben, III. *The Acts of the Apostles: A Socio-Rhetorical Commentary*. Grand Rapids: Eerdmans, 1998.

CHAPTER 4

JESUS' MISSIONARY COMMISSION AND THE ENDS OF THE EARTH

Acts 1:8

Eckhard J. Schnabel

> KEY POINTS
>
> - Jesus sends the Twelve to "the end of the earth" (Acts 1:8).
> - The phrase "end(s) of the earth" is used by ancient geographers to refer to specific regions.
> - The "ends of the earth" are Spain (west), Scythia (north), Ethiopia/Nubia (south), and India (east).
> - The evidence in the New Testament and in early Christian texts suggests that the apostles understood the phrase "ends of the earth" in a geographical sense, and planned their missionary work accordingly.

THE ENDS OF THE EARTH

Jesus' missionary commission in Matthew 28:19 focuses on the ethnic dimension of the scope of the work of the Twelve: they are called to make disciples of "all nations" (πάντα τὰ ἔθνη, *panta ta ethnē*). The term ἔθνη (*ethnē*) refers to peoples "united by kinship, culture, and common traditions."[1] In Acts 1:8, Jesus' commission is formulated in geographical terms: "you will receive power when the Holy Spirit comes on you; and you will be my witnesses in Jerusalem, and in all Judea and Samaria, and to the ends of the earth" (ἕως ἐσχάτου τῆς γῆς, *heōs eschatou tēs gēs*). The phrase "ends of the earth" (ἔσχατον τῆς γῆς, *eschaton tēs gēs*, lit. "end of the earth") is interpreted in the following ways.

1. METAPHORICAL INTERPRETATION

Some interpret the phrase "the end(s) of the earth" in a general, metaphorical

1. BDAG, s.v. "ἔθνος." Biblical citations are taken from the NIV, unless otherwise indicated.

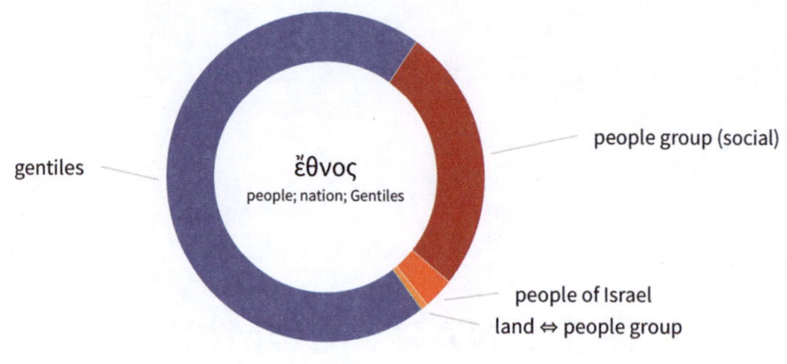

sense: the phrase "alludes to a worldwide mission, and probably also to a mission to both Jews and Gentile in the Diaspora."[2] This interpretation can be linked with the possibility that Luke alludes to Isaiah 49:6, where Yahweh says of his servant: "I will also make you a light for the Gentiles, that my salvation may reach to the ends of the earth" (*heōs eschatou tēs gēs*). Since Jesus' commission refers to three specific geographical terms—Jerusalem, Judea, Samaria—it is preferable to interpret the phrase "the end(s) of the earth" as a geographical term as well.

2. Rome

In Psalms of Solomon 8:15 ("He brought someone from the end of the earth, one who attacks in strength; he declared war against Jerusalem, and her land"),[3] the phrase ἀπ' ἐσχάτου τῆς γῆς (*ap' eschatou tēs gēs*) very probably refers to Rome, the foreign power that God had used to punish Israel for its sins, presumably a reference to the conquest of Jerusalem by the Roman general Pompey (Gnaeus Pompeius Magnus) in 63 BC. This reference, which dates to a Jewish text written in the middle of the first century BC, has been linked with the fact that the book of Acts ends in Rome: Acts 1:8 is a programmatic statement of the geographical expansion of the Christian movement from Jerusalem to Rome.[4] It should be noted, however, that while Pompey was indeed a Roman general,

2. Ben Witherington, *The Acts of the Apostles: A Socio-Rhetorical Commentary* (Grand Rapids: Eerdmans, 1998), 111, who approvingly quotes Rudolf Pesch, *Die Apostelgeschichte* (Neukirchen-Vluyn: Neukirchener Verlag, 1986), 1:70, who argues that Acts 1:8 should be read in the light of Luke 24:47: "the gospel must go to all people." Compare Richard I. Pervo, *Acts* (Philadelphia: Fortress, 2008), 44, who interprets the phrase as "a symbol of universality." A general reference to the gentiles is assumed by Willem C. van Unnik, "Der Ausdruck ΕΩΣ ΕΣΧΑΤΟΥ ΤΗΣ ΓΗΣ (Apostelgeschichte 1.8) und sein alttestamentlicher Hintergrund [1966]," in *Sparsa Collecta* (Leiden: Brill, 1973), 386–401; compare also David W. Pao, *Acts and the Isaianic New Exodus* (Tübingen: Mohr Siebeck, 2000), 93–94. Jacob Jervell, *Die Apostelgeschichte* (Göttingen: Vandenhoeck & Ruprecht, 1998), 116, interprets in terms of the Jewish diaspora.

3. *OTP* 2:659.

4. See Hans Conzelmann, *Acts of the Apostles* (Philadelphia: Fortress, 1987), 7; Joseph A. Fitzmyer, *The Acts of the Apostles* (New York: Doubleday, 1998), 206–7; compare F. F. Bruce, *The Acts of the Apostles: The Greek Text with Introduction and Commentary* (Grand Rapids: Eerdmans,

he came to the east in 67 BC after having commanded troops between 77–71 BC in Spain, which means the phrase "end of the earth" could refer here to Spain. More importantly, one should note that Luke knows and uses the Septuagint, in which the phrase "from/to end(s) of the earth" (ἀπό/ἕως ἐσχάτου τῆς γῆς, *apo/heōs eschatou tēs gēs*) is used in Deuteronomy 28:49 for any foreign enemy of Israel that comes from far away; in Isaiah 8:9; Jeremiah 10:13; 51:16 for distant lands; in Isaiah 45:22; 48:20; 49:6; 62:11; and Jeremiah 16:19 for all distant peoples; and in Jeremiah 6:22; 50:41 for the Babylonians.[5] In light of these references, there is no a priori reason why Acts 1:8 would have been intended, or understood, to refer specifically to the city of Rome. The phrase "end(s) of the earth" most often referred to the far reaches of the inhabited world, a meaning that was never applied to the city of Rome, which was located in the center of the Mediterranean. Rome was the capital of the Roman Empire—it would have been absurd to describe the power center of the Roman Empire with the label "end of the earth." Finally, Luke does not portray Rome in Acts 27–28 as the goal or end point of the mission of the earliest missionaries: he does not relate who established the church in the capital of the empire.

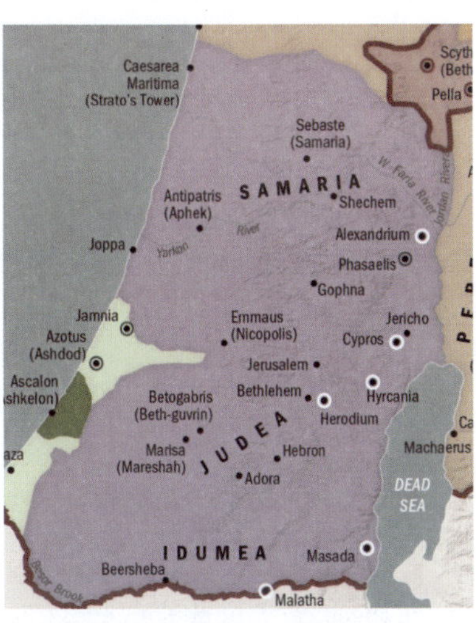

Location of Jerusalem, Judea, and Samaria

3. Ethiopia or Spain

Since Acts 8:27 mentions an Ethiopian eunuch who is eventually converted to faith in Jesus, and since Ethiopia is described by Greek geographers as a land at the end of the earth, some have assumed that the fourth geographical term in Acts 1:8 refers to Ethiopia.[6] Others have suggested that Luke has Spain in mind, the goal of Paul's missionary work in the west (Rom 15:24, 28), also a land described by contemporary geographers as being at the "end of the earth."[7] Both of these proposals are too restrictive. The formulation in the singular ("the end") does not require an interpretation in terms of a single region:

1990), 103; also C. K. Barrett, *The Acts of the Apostles* (Edinburgh: T & T Clark, 1994–98), 1:80, who interprets the phrase in terms of Rome as representative of the entire world.

5. The phrase "the farthest point (or end) of the earth" (ἀπ' ἄκρου/ἄκρων τῆς γῆς, *ap' akrou/akrōn tēs gēs*) is used for Assyria (Isa 5:26) and Babylonia (Isa 43:6).

6. See Timothy C. G. Thornton, "To the End of the Earth: Acts 1.8," *Expository Times* 89 (1977–78): 374–75.

7. See Earle E. Ellis, "'The End of the Earth' (Acts 1:8)," *BBR* 1 (1991): 123–32. For critical interaction, see Eckhard J. Schnabel, *Early Christian Mission* (Downers Grove: InterVarsity Press, 2004), 374–75.

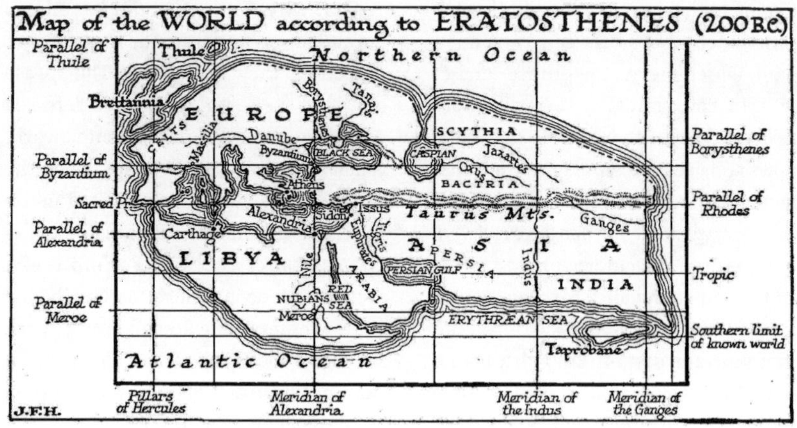

Reconstructed Map of Eratosthenes Depicting the Ancient World (ca. 2nd century BC)

the wording corresponds to Isaiah 49:6, where a worldwide mission that reaches the gentiles is in view. This passage and other Old Testament references suggest a global interpretation, which can be specific in geographical terms in the context of references in Greco-Roman texts that use the term "end(s) of the earth."[8] As regards Spain, it should be noted that the commission of Acts 1:8 was given to the eleven disciples, not to Paul.

4. SPAIN, SCYTHIA, ETHIOPIA/NUBIA, INDIA

Ancient authors repeatedly use the phrase "ends (τὰ ἔσχατα, *ta eschata*) of the earth" to designate regions in the west, north, south, and east.[9] It is thus plausible to interpret the phrase "end of the earth" in Acts 1:8 in geographical terms, referring to specific regions at the farthest reaches of the earth.

(1) The Western End of the Earth: Spain, Specifically the Region of Gades

While Gaul, Germania, and Britannia constituted the western border regions of the Roman Empire—Britannia was annexed in AD 43—and while the Arctic was known to ancient geographers, it was Spain, specifically the city of Gades (see below), that was described by Strabo and others as located "at the end of the earth."[10] The region of Gades with the "promon-

8. See James S. Romm, *The Edges of the Earth in Ancient Thought: Geography, Exploration, and Fiction* (Princeton: Princeton University Press, 1992); Schnabel, *Early Christian Mission*, 372–76; idem, *Acts* (Grand Rapids: Zondervan, 2012), 79–80.

9. Compare Strabo, *Geographica* 1.1.6; 1.2.31; 2.3.5; 2.4.2; Philostratus, *Vita Apollonii* 6.1.1; Philo, *Cherubim* 99; *Dreams* 1.134; *Migration* 181.

10. Strabo, *Geographica* 3.1.8; compare 1.2.31; 2.5.14; 3.1.4; see Lucan, *Pharsalia* 3.454; Juvenal, *Satirae* 10.1–2; Silius, *Punica* 17.637. Note that Strabo also knows the Canary Islands, as lying "to the westward of the most western Maurusia [i.e., Morocco]" (*Geographica* 1.1.5). See Andrew

tory of Iberia which they call the Sacred Cape is the most westerly point of the inhabited world."[11] Diodorus Siculus also located Gades "at the end of the inhabited world."[12] Spain (Greek Ἰβηρία, *Ibēria*, Latin *Hispānia*), described in extensive detail by Strabo in Book 3 of his *Geography*, was considered a *provincia pacata* from around 19 BC, after Octavian (Augustus) had completed the subjugation of the Iberian, Celtiberian, and Cantabrian populations (Romans had entered Spain in 218 BC).[13] In the first century AD, Spain was divided into three provinces: Hispania Tarraconensis on the east coast, with Tarraco (modern Tarragona) as the capital; Hispania Lusitania on the west coast, with Augusta Emerita (modern Mérida) as the capital; and Hispania Baetica on the south coast, with Corduba (modern Córdoba) as the capital, one of the most Romanized provinces of the Roman Empire.[14] Gades (modern Cádiz), located on three islands off the southern, Atlantic coast, west of Gibraltar, was a large city owing its wealth to shipping, the fishing industry, and the fertility of the region.[15] A main attraction of Gades was the temple of Hercules (Hercules Gaditanus), established by the Phoenicians as a temple of Melqart, modeled on the god's temple of Tyre.[16] The two pillars which stood in front of the temple were referred to as the "pillars of Hercules" and were said to have been set up "as boundary markers for the world."[17] The temple seems to have

Fear, "Journey to the End of the World," in *Pilgrimage in Graeco-Roman and Early Christian Antiquity: Seeing the Gods*, ed. J. Elsner and I. Rutherford (Oxford: Oxford University Press, 2005), 319–31.

11. Strabo, *Geographica* 2.5.14.

12. Diodorus Siculus 25.10.1: τὰ ἔσχατα τῆς οἰκουμένης (*ta eschata tēs oikoumenēs*).

13. P. Barceló, "Hispania, Iberia I.D," *BNP* 6:388. See Simon J. Keay, *Roman Spain* (Berkeley: University of California Press, 1988); Geza Alföldy, "Spain," in *The Augustan Empire, 43* B.C.–A.D. *69*, volume 10 of *Cambridge Ancient History*, ed. A. K. Bowman, E. Champlin, and A. Lintott (Cambridge: Cambridge University Press, 1996), 449–63; John S. Richardson, *The Romans in Spain* (Oxford: Blackwell, 1996); Andrew T. Fear, *Rome and Baetica: Urbanization in Southern Spain c. 50 BC–AD 150* (Oxford: Clarendon, 1996); Leonard A. Curchin, *Roman Spain: Conquest and Assimilation* (New York: Routledge, 1991; repr. 2014).

14. Strabo, *Geographica* 3.2.15: "The Turdetanians, however, and particularly those that live about the Baetis, have completely changed over to the Roman mode of life, not even remembering their own language any more. And most of them have become Latins, and they have received Romans as colonists, so that they are not far from being all Romans." See also P. Barceló, "Hispania, Iberia I.F," *BNP* 6:388.

15. Strabo, *Geographica* 3.5.3, claiming that as regards the size of Gades' population, it was ranked second only to Rome. See also Pliny, *Naturalis historia* 3.1.8; P. Barceló and H. G. Niemeyer, "Gades," *BNP* 5:635–637; *BAGRW*, Map 26, D5.

16. See Andrew Fear, "Journey," 319–27; F. Graf, "Hispania, Iberia IV," *BNP* 6:397: the Melqart/Heracles temple was "one of the central sanctuaries of the western Mediterranean."

17. Philostratus, *Vita Apollonii* 5.1: ὅρια τῆς γῆς (*horia tēs gēs*). The identification of the "Pillars of Heracles" with the rocky headlands of Gabal Musa and Gabal at-Tariq (Gibraltar), which line the straits of Gibraltar, is wrong; Barceló and Niemeyer, "Gades," *BNP* 5:636. See Pliny, *Naturalis historia* 2:67, on the circumnavigation of the western, northern, eastern, and southern oceans "which flow completely around the globe," making it (allegedly) possible to sail from Spain to Ethiopia and from India to Germania!

Roman Theater at Gades

had an oracle who interpreted dreams. Gades' remote location at the western limit of the known world as well as its religious appeal appear to have prompted Apollonius of Tyana (c. AD 15–100) to visit Gades after he visited India.[18] Pliny provides the distances of land travel from the Ganges in India to Gades in Spain—a total of 8,945 miles (14,396 km).[19] The voyage from Gades to Rome took about six days of sailing;[20] the outward journey would have taken longer due to the currents in the straits of Gibraltar, prompting some travelers to put in at Malaca (modern Málaga) and make the last leg of the journey on foot.[21]

(2) The Northern End of the Earth: Scythia

While ancient geographers knew about the Arctic as the northernmost region, the Roman poet Propertius (c. 50–5 BC) describes the Scythians as the people who lived "at the end of the earth." This description is part of his comment on the city of Borysthenes, founded by colonists on the northwestern coast of the Black Sea.[22] For Greek and Roman authors, "Scythia" described the regions to the north and the east of their sphere of control: the region from the river Danube to the river Don, as far as the Caucasus Mountains to the Volga River, north of the

18. Philostratus, *The Life of Apollonius of Tyana*, ed. and trans. Christopher P. Jones, Loeb Classical Library 16–17 (Cambridge: Harvard University Press, 2005), 15–16; Andrew Fear, "Journey," 328–29.

19. Pliny, *Naturalis historia* 2.112.

20. Pliny, *Naturalis historia* 19.1; compare Plutarch, *Galba* 7.

21. Andrew Fear, "Journey," 330.

22. Propertius, *Elegiae* 2.7.18: *gloria ad hibernos lata Borysthenidas*.

Black Sea.[23] In the popular imagination, Scythia was a desolate steppe inhabited by nomadic cattle breeders and archers, uncivilized people who blinded, scalped, and flayed their enemies and who drank wine unmixed with water. After the political unification of the tribal confederations who lived in this vast region (the Sacae, Callipidae, Alazonae, Aroteres) in the sixth century BC, they formed a kingdom in the fourth century. Ionian cities such as Naxos, Miletus, and Samos and Doric cities such as Corinth, Megara, and Sparta had established colonies on the coast of the Black Sea in the seventh and sixth centuries; on the northwestern coast, these included Tomis, Histria, Tyras, Nikonion, and Olbia.[24] The Greeks brought grain, wool, staple fiber plants, dried fish, precious metals, and slaves.[25] Since the second century BC, the capital of Scythia was located in Neapolis (modern Simferopol) in the Crimea (Ukraine).[26] In the first century BC, the southern region of the Crimea was subjugated by the Bosporan Kingdom (based on the Kerch peninsula on the Cimmerian Bosporus).[27] In the middle of the first century AD, the Scythians were able to free themselves from Bosporan rule, but military conflicts continued. In AD 61, on the orders of Emperor Nero, Roman

23. See *BAGRW*, Maps 23, 84. On Scythia, see Iris von Bredow, "Scythae," *BNP* 13:149–160; Ellis Hovell Minns, *Scythians and Greeks: A Survey of Ancient History and Archaeology on the North Coast of the Euxine from the Danube to the Caucasus* (1913; repr. Cambridge: Cambridge University Press, 2013); Michael Rostovtzeff, *Skythien und der Bosporus* (Berlin: Schoetz, 1931; repr., Stuttgart: Steiner, 1993); Tamara Talbot Rice, "The Scytho-Sarmatian Tribes of South-Eastern Europe," in Fergus Miller, *The Roman Empire and its Neighbours*, reprint, 2nd ed. (London: Duckworth, 1981; repr., 1996), 281–93; Renate Rolle, *The World of the Scythians* (Berkeley: University of California Press, 1989); Askold Ivantchik, "The Scythian 'Rule Over Asia': The Classical Tradition and the Historical Reality," in *Ancient Greeks West and East*, ed. Gocha R. Tsetskhladze (Leiden: Brill, 1999), 497–520; Christopher J. Tuplin, ed., *Pontus and the Outside World: Studies in Black Sea History, Historiography, and Archaeology* (Leiden: Brill, 2004).

24. *BAGRW*, Map 23, B4, D2, E2, G4, I4; Map 84, B3, E1, C4. See also Gocha R. Tsetskhladze, ed., *Greek and Roman Settlements on the Black Sea Coast* (Bradford: Loid, 1994); Gocha R. Tsetskhladze, ed., *The Greek Colonisation of the Black Sea Area: Historical Interpretation of Archaeology* (Stuttgart: Steiner, 1998); Demetrios V. Grammenos and Elias K. Petropoulos, eds., *Ancient Greek Colonies in the Black Sea*, 22 vols. (Oxford: Archaeopress, 2007). The colonies of Chersonesos, Theodosia, Pantikapaion, Phanagoreia, Tanais, and Gorgippia eventually belonged to the Bosporan Kingdom; archaeological evidence indicates that there was a Jewish presence in the Bosporan Kingdom (see Irina A. Levinskaya, *The Book of Acts in Its Diaspora Setting*, Vol. 5 in *The Book of Acts in Its First-Century Setting* [Grand Rapids: Eerdmans, 1996], 105–16; Lee I. Levine, "The Hellenistic-Roman Diaspora CE 70–CE 235: The Archaeology Evidence," in *The Cambridge History of Judaism Volume III: The Early Roman Period*, ed. W. Horbury, W. D. Davies, and J. Sturdy [Cambridge: Cambridge University Press, 1999], 991–1024, 1010–14).

25. Bredow, "Scythae," *BNP* 13:159, who points to the Scythian "police" force at Athens, mentioned by Aristophanes, *Equites* 665; *Lysistrata* 433–75.

26. *BAGRW*, Map 23, H4.

27. See *BAGRW*, Map 87, Insert. On the Bosporan Kingdom, see Iris von Bredow, "Regnum Bosporanum," *BNP* 12:443–450.

Mosaic Floor Visible in the Ruins of the Archaeological Site at Chersonesos

troops were stationed in Chersonesos, which also served as a naval base.[28] In the (former) Greek colonies, Greek was spoken. The presence of Jews is attested for Olbia,[29] although it is not known when Jews settled there.

(3) The Southern End of the Earth—Ethiopia (Nubia)

Homer described the Ethiopians as "the farthermost of men," a phrase that Strabo understands as a reference to "the ends of the earth, on the banks of Oceanus."[30] Herodotus mentions an army that marched to Ethiopia "to the ends of the earth."[31] The Greeks used the term Αἰθίοψ (*Aithiops*) for the people living south of Egypt—the people of the ancient cultures of Nubia (Kush, modern southern Sudan), south of the first cataract of the Nile River (at Syene/Elephantine, modern Aswan), especially the region between the third and sixth cataract. Greek explorers visited "Ethiopia" since the sixth century BC. In 330 BC the capital was moved from Napata to Meroë.[32]

28. See Josephus, *J.W.* 2.367; Iris von Bredow and S. R. Tokhtas'ev, "Chersonesus [3].A" *BNP* 3: 214.

29. Levinskaya, *Diaspora*, 219–22; David Noy, Alexander Panayotov, and Hanswulf Bloedhorn, *Inscriptiones Judaicae Orientis. Vol. I: Eastern Europe* (Tübingen: Mohr Siebeck, 2004), 254–61.

30. Strabo, *Geographica* 1.1.6: "Homer assuredly makes it plain that the Ethiopians live at the ends of the earth (ἔσχατοι, *eschatoi*), on the banks of the Oceanus: that they live at the end of the earth, when he speaks of 'the Ethiopians that are sundered in twain, the farthermost of men' (ἔσχατοι ἀνδρῶν, *eschatoi andrōn*)"; see Homer, *Odyssey* 1.23.

31. Herodotus, *Historiae* 3.25: τὰ ἔσχατα γῆς (*ta eschata gēs*).

32. See *BAGRW*, Map 82 B3, D5. For Nubia, see S. Seidlmayer, "Nubia," *BNP* 9:867–70; Laszlo Török, *Der meroitische Staat. Untersuchungen und Urkunden zur Geschichte des Sudan im Altertum* (Berlin: Akademie-Verlag, 1986); David N. Edwards, *Upper Nubia in the 1st millennium* A.D. (Oxford: BAR International, 1989); Peter L. Shinnie, *Ancient Nubia* (New York: Kegan

The *Barrington Atlas* indicates the following settlements between Napata and Meroë: Marru, Alana, Sakole (?), Scammos, Gora, Abale, Darou, Galim, Seserem, Mallo, Sakolche, and Tadu. Archaeological investigations have established that Meroë was a royal city with a palace complex, numerous temples, including the temple of the sun, and iron works.[33] In Musawwarat, south of Meroë, three major temples were discovered.[34] There were regular contacts between Rome and the Ethiopians. During the first century AD, Nero sent an expedition with the task of exploring Nubia; the expedition established that the length of Nubia measured 975 (Roman) miles (1,433 km, or 890 miles),[35] which corresponds rather exactly to the distance from Aswan (first cataract) to Meroë.

Nubian Pyramids at Meroë

Temple Ruins at Musawwarat

(4) The Eastern End of the Earth: India

Procopius, writing in the sixth century AD, refers to Roman soldiers posted on the eastern border of Persia and India as living "at the ends of the inhabited world."[36] Mesopotamian ships sailed to India as early as 2800 BC; Herodotus describes India in an excursus on ethnographical matters.[37] The Greek translation of the book of Esther mentions India as the eastern border of the empire of King Ahasuerus (Esth 1:1; 8:9). The later Additions to Esther mention India in a description of the geography of the Persian Empire (13:1; 16:1).

Knowledge of India in the West increased dramatically with Alexander's military campaign in the eastern Persian regions of Sogdiana and Bactria.[38]

Paul, 1996), 95–118; Derek A. Welsby, *The Kingdom of Kush: The Napatan and Meroitic Empires* (Princeton: Wiener, 1998); Edwin M. Yamauchi, *Africa and the Bible* (Grand Rapids: Baker Academic, 2004), 149–82; Schnabel, *Early Christian Mission*, 682–83.

33. See Peter L. Shinnie and Rebecca J. Bradley, *The Capital of Kush 1: Meroe Excavations 1965–1972* (Berlin: Akademie Verlag, 1980); Peter L. Shinnie and Julie R. Anderson, *The Capital of Kush 2: Meroe Excavations 1973–1984* (Wiesbaden: Harrassowitz, 2004).

34. See Fritz Hintze, *Musawwarat es Sufra. Band I.1, 2. Der Löwentempel* (Berlin: Akademie-Verlag, 1971/1993).

35. Pliny, *Naturalis historia* 6.35.184.

36. Procopius, *De bellis* 2.3.52; compare 6.30.9.

37. Herodotus, *Historiae* 3.98–106.

38. See *BAGRW*, Map 6, B2. See also H. J. Nissen, "Sogdiana," *BNP* 13:605–606; H. Treidler and B. Brentjes, "Bactria," *BNP* 2:455–57; K. Karttunen, "India," *BNP* 6:769–73; H. J. Drexhage, "India, trade with," *BNP* 6:773–77; Jakob Seibert, *Die Eroberung des Perserreiches*

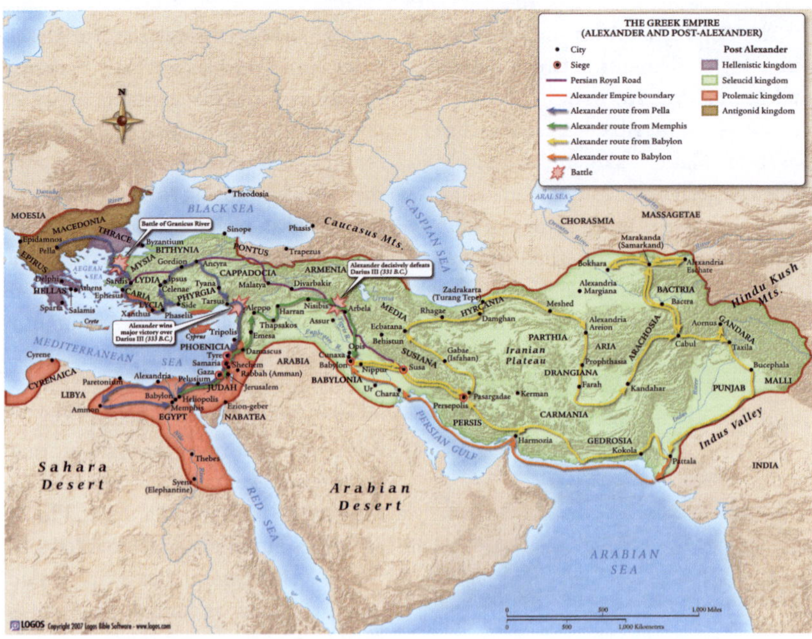

Sogdiana was the region between the rivers Iaxartes and Oxus, with the capital of Marakanda (modern Samarkand, Uzbekistan). The capital of Bactria, on both sides of the river Oxus, corresponding approximately to modern Afghanistan, was Zariaspa (modern Balkh). Alexander conquered the Indus Valley from Bactria in the north all the way to the Indian Ocean, establishing several Hellenistic settlements—e.g., Alexandria Oxiana (perhaps modern Termez), Alexandria in Paropamisos (perhaps modern Begram), and others. An important urban center was Taxila (35 km, or 22 miles, northwest of Rawalpindi, Pakistan), very probably the capital of King Gondophares (AD 20–46), who controlled the region of Kabul, Arachosia, and Gandhara.[39]

durch Alexander d. Gr. auf kartographischer Grundlage (Wiesbaden: Reichert, 1985); Rosa Maria Cimino, ed., *Ancient Rome and India: Commercial and Cultural Contacts Between the Roman World and India* (New Delhi: Munshiram Manoharlal Publishers, 1994); Klaus Karttunen, "Graeco-Indica (2)," in *Athens, Aden, Arikamedu: Essays on the Interrelations Between India, Arabia and the Eastern Mediterranean*, ed. M.-F. Boussac and J.-F. Salles (New Delhi: Centre de Sciences Humaines, 1995), 11–20; Klaus Karttunen, *India and the Hellenistic World* (Helsinki: Finnish Oriental Society, 1997); Schnabel, *Early Christian Mission*, 479–95; Grant Parker, *The Making of Roman India* (Cambridge: Cambridge University Press, 2008); Getzel M. Cohen, *The Hellenistic Settlements in the East from Armenia and Mesopotamia to Bactria and India* (Berkeley: University of California Press, 2013), 225–333; K. S. Mathew, ed., *Imperial Rome, Indian Ocean Regions and Muziris: New Perspectives on Maritime Trade* (New York: Routledge, 2017).

39. See *BAGRW*, Map 6, C3. See also Saifur Rahman Dar, "Gondophares and Taxila," in *St. Thomas and Taxila: A Symposium on Saint Thomas*, ed. J. Rooney (Rawalpindi: Christian

Dharmarajika Stupa (Buddhist Monument) at Taxila

There were two main routes to India: the overland caravan route via Damascus, Palmyra, Seleucia, Babylon, Vologesias, and Spasinu Charax (Maysan, Jebel Khayabi) near the head of the Persian Gulf,[40] and the route via the Nile River and the Red Sea, the main route in the Augustan period.

Trade with India was mostly controlled by merchants from Alexandria in Egypt who owned fleets of ships transporting goods destined for India on the Nile River as far as Coptos (modern Qift), a journey of twelve days if the Etesian winds were blowing.[41] At Coptos, camel caravans transported the goods across the desert—the shortest route from the Nile to the Red Sea, about 175 km (110 miles)—to Myos Hormos (modern Quseir el-Qadim), and from there by ship through the Red Sea via the (modern) Straits of Hormuz across the Indian Ocean, utilizing the monsoon winds blowing west to east in June/July; the return journey in December/January followed the same route. According to Strabo, 120 ships sailed every year from Myos Hormos to India.[42] Pliny reports that every year 100 million sesterces were spent on goods from India, China, and Arabia.[43]

Important towns on India's west coast that were involved in the trade

Study Centre, 1988), 16–30; R. Morton Smith, *Kings and Coins in India: Greek and Śaka Self-Advertisement* (New Delhi: Harman, 1997), 109–18, who dates his reign to AD 19–48; Ahmad Hasan Dani, *The Historic City of Taxila* (Tokyo: Centre for East Asian Cultural Studies, 1986); Dilip K. Chakrabarti, *The Archaeology of Ancient Indian Cities* (Delhi: Oxford University Press, 1995; repr., 1998), 174–81.

40. See *BAGRW*, Map 3, C3, E3.

41. Pliny, *Naturalis historia* 6.102.

42. Strabo, *Geographica* 2.5.12; compare 17.1.13; 17.1.45; Pliny, *Naturalis historia* 6.100–104.

43. Pliny, *Naturalis historia* 12.84; compare 6.101; 21.11.

between India and the Roman Empire were Barbarikon, Barygaza, Muziris, and Nelkynda;[44] on the east coast, Chaberis Emporion, Podouke (Arikamedu), and Dandagoula (Paloura).[45]

(5) *Jewish Geography*

Educated Jews knew the regions which Greek and Roman geographers located at the "ends of the earth." Josephus mentions the Scythians, Gades, Ethiopia, and India.[46] He believed that the Indians were descendants of Shem.[47]

5. RELEVANT NEW TESTAMENT EVIDENCE

Luke does not signal how the Twelve understood the phrase "the ends of the earth" in Jesus' commission in Acts 1:8. As stated earlier, the fact that the commission mentions three geographical terms—Jerusalem, Judea, Samaria—strongly suggests that "end of the earth" should be understood in a geographical sense. Luke mentions one of the regions that Greek and Roman geographers located at the "ends of the earth." In Acts 8:27, Luke describes the man whom Philip meets on the road to Gaza as "an Ethiopian eunuch, an important official in charge of all the treasury of the Kandake (which means 'queen of the Ethiopians')." The reference indicates that Luke has some information about the "Ethiopians" and their political system—the queens of Nubia had the title "Kandake"[48]—and about the court official from this region whose conversion to faith in Jesus as Messiah he relates in Acts 8:26–39. Irenaeus (c. AD 130–202) and Eusebius (AD 260–340) state that the converted Ethiopian was the first missionary to Ethiopia.[49]

The apostle Paul plans a mission to Spain (Rom 15:24, 28), and he mentions Scythians (Col 3:11)—referring to two regions that geographers described as regions at the ends of the earth. Several early Christian writers say that Paul did in fact reach Spain, implying that he was released from the imprisonment in Rome

44. See *BAGRW*, Map 5, B1, C2, D4, D5.

45. See *BAGRW*, Map 5, D4, E3.

46. For Scythians, see Josephus, *J.W.* 7.90, 244; *Ant.* 1.124; for Gades, *J.W.* 2.363, for Ethiopia, *J.W.* 2.382; *Ant.* 1.131; *Ag. Ap.* 1.169; for India, *J.W.* 2.385; *Ant.* 1.38; *Ag. Ap.* 1.144.

47. Josephus, *Ant.* 1.147.

48. See Strabo, *Geographica* 17.1.54; Pliny, *Naturalis historia* 6.11.29.

49. Irenaeus, *Against Heresies* 4.23.2: "Immediately when [Philip] had baptized him, he departed from him. For nothing else [but baptism] was wanting to him who had been already instructed by the prophets: he was not ignorant of God the Father, nor of the rules as to the [proper] manner of life, but was merely ignorant of the advent of the Son of God, which, when he had become acquainted with, in a short space of time, he went on his way rejoicing, to be the herald in Ethiopia of Christ's advent [*praeco futurus in Aethiopia Christi adventus*]." Eusebius, *Historia ecclesiastica* 2.1.13: "But as the preaching of the Savior's Gospel was daily advancing, a certain providence led from the land of the Ethiopians an officer of the queen of that country, for Ethiopia even to the present day is ruled, according to ancestral custom, by a woman. He, first among the Gentiles, received of the mysteries of the divine word from Philip in consequence of a revelation, and having become the first-fruits of believers throughout the world, he is said to have been the first on returning to his country to proclaim the knowledge of the God of the universe and the life-giving sojourn of our Savior among men; so that through him in truth the prophecy obtained its fulfillment, which declares that 'Ethiopia stretches out her hand unto God' [Ps 68:31; 67:32 LXX]."

reported by Luke (Acts 28). Clement of Rome says that Paul "came to the limits of the West" (1 Clement 5.7; the term δύσις (*dysis*), "west," is often used for Spain). The author of the Muratorian Canon says that Paul proceeded from the city of Rome to Spain (line 39). According to the apocryphal Acts of Peter (AD 180–190), Paul left Rome and went to Spain (Acts of Peter 1). Many scholars accept this tradition.[50]

The reference to "Scythians" in Colossians 3:11 possibly implies the presence of a Scythian slave in the church of Colossae.[51] It is not impossible that the reference implies that Paul, who wrote to the Christians in Colossae (probably in AD 61 from Rome),[52] knew of a successful mission in Scythia. When the apostles left Jerusalem in AD 41/42 as a result of the persecution of the church by King Herod Agrippa I (AD 41–44), during which James was executed (Acts 12:1–2; Peter's execution was scheduled for the time after Passover, Acts 12:3–4),[53] one of them might well have traveled to Scythia. Origen (c. AD 200–240) claims to know that the apostle Andrew preached the gospel in Scythia.[54] This agrees with the apocryphal Acts of Andrew and Matthias (c. AD 350), a text that has Matthias and Andrew preach the gospel among people who eat human flesh (Acts of Andrew and Matthias 1); the Greeks described the people living on the northern coast of the Black Sea as cannibals (Herodotus, *Historiae* 4.106).[55]

Coin Depicting Gondophares, the Indo-Parthian King, at Taxila

Early Christian traditions assert that the apostle Thomas went to India—the "end of the earth" in the East. The Acts of Thomas, written c. AD 200–240 in Edessa, speaks of contacts between Thomas and Gondophernes (Gondophares), the Indo-Parthian ruler in Taxila between AD 20–46 (Acts of Thomas 17–29). Both the king and his brother, along with many Indians, came to faith in Jesus (30–61); later, Thomas traveled to the

50. See Schnabel, *Early Christian Mission*, 1274–75.

51. See Johann Albert Bengel, *Gnomon Novi Testamenti*, Editio octava (1742; repr., Stuttgart: Steinkopf, 1887), 806; O. Michel, "Σκύθης," *TDNT* 7:449–50; Douglas A. Campbell, "Unravelling Colossians 3.11b," *NTS* 42 (1996): 120–32.

52. See D. A. Carson and Douglas J. Moo, *An Introduction to the New Testament*, 2nd ed. (Grand Rapids: Zondervan, 2005), 521–22.

53. Note that in Acts 11:30; 21:18 "elders" are mentioned as the group leading the church in Jerusalem, replacing the "apostles" who are mentioned in the earlier chapters of Acts. Note the texts that state that the apostles left Jerusalem twelve years after Jesus' death and resurrection: Acts of Peter 5; Apollonios (in Eusebius, *Historia ecclesiastica* 5.18.14); Acts of Thomas 1:1; Origen (in Eusebius, *Historia ecclesiastica* 3.1.1).

54. Origen, according to Eusebius, *Historia ecclesiastica* 3.1.1.

55. Note that the apocryphal text Acts of Andrew does not mention a mission of Andrew to Scythia; the author relates Andrew's ministry in Pontus, Thrace, Macedonia, and Achaia. On an apostolic mission to Scythia, see Schnabel, *Early Christian Mission*, 906.

land of Mizdaios where members of the royal family and other Indians were converted (62–568, 82–158, 170). The available evidence indicates that this tradition is historically possible.[56] While it has not been possible to identify the land of Mizdaios, the story of Thomas' departure from Taxila to another region in India may have a historical background: after Gondophernes' death, the Kushan tribes from central Asia under the leadership of Kujala Kadphises put pressure on the Punjab for several years and eventually conquered Taxila in AD 59. If Thomas left Taxila traveling south on the Indus River, he would have reached Barbarikon, the main port city on the Indian Ocean, from where he could have travelled south to Muziris (modern Cranganore) and Nelkynda (modern Nirkunnam), two important trading posts on the coast in Malabar, and from there to Podouke (Arikamedu; modern Virampatnam near Pondicherry) on the east coast. Muziris was located in the kingdom of the Chera, Nelkynda in the kingdom of the Panya (Pandya), and Podouke in the kingdom of the Chola. This scenario agrees with the tradition of the church of South India (in Kerala, on the southwest coast) that the apostle Thomas engaged in missionary work in all three kingdoms of southern India and established churches.[57]

The evidence outlined above suggests that it is possible, even likely, that the apostles understood the reference to the "ends of the earth" in Jesus' commission (Acts 1:8) literally in a geographical sense and that they were concerned to make sure that Spain, Scythia, Ethiopia, and India were reached with the good news of Jesus, Israel's Messiah and Savior of the world.

BIBLIOGRAPHY

Alföldy, Geza. "Spain." Pages 449–63 in *The Augustan Empire, 43 B.C.–A.D. 69*. Volume 10 in *Cambridge Ancient History*. Edited by A. K. Bowman, E. Champlin, and A. Lintott. Cambridge: Cambridge University Press, 1996.

Barrett, C. K. *The Acts of the Apostles*. 2 vols. International Critical Commentary. Edinburgh: T & T Clark, 1994–1998.

Bengel, Johann Albert. *Gnomon Novi Testamenti*. Editio octava. 1742. Repr., Stuttgart: Steinkopf, 1887.

Bruce, F. F. *The Acts of the Apostles: The Greek Text with Introduction and Commentary*. 3rd revised and enlarged edition. Grand Rapids: Eerdmans, 1990.

Campbell, Douglas A. "Unravelling Colossians 3.11b." *NTS* 42 (1996): 120–32.

Carson, D. A., and Douglas J. Moo. *An Introduction to the New Testament*. 2nd edition. Grand Rapids: Zondervan, 2005.

Chakrabarti, Dilip K. *The Archaeology of Ancient Indian Cities*. Delhi: Oxford University Press, 1995.

Cimino, Rosa Maria, ed. *Ancient Rome and India: Commercial and Cultural Contacts Between the Roman World and India*. New Delhi: Munshiram Manoharlal Publishers, 1994.

Cohen, Getzel M. *The Hellenistic Settlements in the East from Armenia and Mesopotamia to Bactria and India.*

56. See the discussion in Schnabel, *Early Christian Mission*, 880–95.

57. For the history of the so-called "Thomas Christians," see Benedict Vadakkekara, *Origin of India's St Thomas Christians: A Historiographical Critique* (Delhi: Media House, 1995).

Berkeley: University of California Press, 2013.

Conzelmann, Hans. *Acts of the Apostles*. Translated by J. Limburg, A. T. Kraabel, and D. H. Juel. Hermeneia. Philadelphia: Fortress, 1987.

Curchin, Leonard A. *Roman Spain: Conquest and Assimilation*. New York: Routledge, 1991. Repr., 2014.

Dani, Ahmad Hasan. *The Historic City of Taxila*. Tokyo: Centre for East Asian Cultural Studies, 1986.

Dar, Saifur Rahman. "Gondophares and Taxila." Pages 16–30 in *St. Thomas and Taxila: A Symposium on Saint Thomas*. Edited by J. Rooney. Rawalpindi: Christian Study Centre, 1988.

Edwards, David N. *Upper Nubia in the 1st Millennium* A.D. Oxford: BAR International, 1989.

Ellis, Earle E. "'The End of the Earth' (Acts 1:8)." *BBR* 1 (1991): 123–32.

Fear, Andrew T. *Rome and Baetica: Urbanization in Southern Spain c. 50 BC–AD 150*. Oxford: Clarendon, 1996.

Fear, Andrew. "Journey to the End of the World." Pages 319–31 in *Pilgrimage in Graeco-Roman and Early Christian Antiquity: Seeing the Gods*. Edited by J. Elsner and I. Rutherford. Oxford: Oxford University Press, 2005.

Fitzmyer, Joseph A. *The Acts of the Apostles*. Anchor Bible 31. New York: Doubleday, 1998.

Grammenos, Demetrios V., and Elias K. Petropoulos, eds. *Ancient Greek Colonies in the Black Sea 2*. 2 vols. Oxford: Archaeopress, 2007.

Hintze, Fritz. *Musawwarat es Sufra. Band I.1, 2. Der Löwentempel*. Berlin: Akademie-Verlag, 1971/1993.

Ivantchik, Askold. "The Scythian 'Rule Over Asia': The Classical Tradition and the Historical Reality." Pages 497–520 in *Ancient Greeks West and East*. Edited by Gocha R. Tsetskhladze. Leiden: Brill, 1999.

Jervell, Jacob. *Die Apostelgeschichte*. Göttingen: Vandenhoeck & Ruprecht, 1998.

Karttunen, Klaus. "Graeco-Indica (2)." Pages 11–20 in *Athens, Aden, Arikamedu: Essays on the Interrelations Between India, Arabia and the Eastern Mediterranean*. Edited by M.-F. Boussac and J.-F. Salles. New Delhi: Centre de Sciences Humaines, 1995.

———. *India and the Hellenistic World*. Helsinki: Finnish Oriental Society, 1997.

Keay, Simon J. *Roman Spain*. Berkeley: University of California Press, 1988.

Levine, Lee I. "The Hellenistic-Roman Diaspora CE 70–CE 235: The Archaeology Evidence." Pages 991–1024 in *The Cambridge History of Judaism Volume III: The Early Roman Period*. Edited by W. Horbury, W. D. Davies, and J. Sturdy. Cambridge: Cambridge University Press, 1999.

Levinskaya, Irina A. *The Book of Acts in Its Diaspora Setting*. Grand Rapids: Eerdmans, 1996.

Mathew, K. S., ed. *Imperial Rome, Indian Ocean Regions and Muziris: New Perspectives on Maritime Trade*. New York: Routledge, 2017.

Minns, Ellis Hovell. *Scythians and Greeks: A Survey of Ancient History and Archaeology on the North Coast of the Euxine from the Danube to the Caucasus*. 1913. Repr., Cambridge: Cambridge University Press, 2013.

Noy, David, Alexander Panayotov, and Hanswulf Bloedhorn. *Inscriptiones*

Judaicae Orientis. Vol. I: Eastern Europe. Tübingen: Mohr Siebeck, 2004.

Pao, David W. *Acts and the Isaianic New Exodus*. Tübingen: Mohr Siebeck, 2000.

Parker, Grant. *The Making of Roman India*. Cambridge: Cambridge University Press, 2008.

Pervo, Richard I. *Acts*. Hermeneia. Philadelphia: Fortress, 2008.

Pesch, Rudolf. *Die Apostelgeschichte*. 2 vols. Neukirchen-Vluyn: Neukirchener Verlag, 1986.

Philostratus. *The Life of Apollonius of Tyana*. Edited and translated by Christopher P. Jones. Loeb Classical Library 16–17. Cambridge, MA: Harvard University Press, 2005.

Richardson, John S. *The Romans in Spain*. Oxford: Blackwell, 1996.

Rolle, Renate. *The World of the Scythians*. Berkeley: University of California Press, 1989.

Romm, James S. *The Edges of the Earth in Ancient Thought: Geography, Exploration, and Fiction*. Princeton: Princeton University Press, 1992.

Rostovtzeff, Michael. *Skythien und der Bosporus*. Berlin: Schoetz, 1931. Repr., Stuttgart: Steiner, 1993.

Schnabel, Eckhard J. *Acts*. Zondervan Exegetical Commentary on the New Testament 5. Grand Rapids: Zondervan, 2012.

———. *Early Christian Mission*. 2 vols. Downers Grove: InterVarsity Press, 2004.

Seibert, Jakob. *Die Eroberung des Perserreiches durch Alexander d. Gr. auf kartographischer Grundlage*. Wiesbaden: Reichert, 1985.

Shinnie, Peter L. *Ancient Nubia*. New York: Kegan Paul, 1996.

Shinnie, Peter L., and Julie R. Anderson. *The Capital of Kush 2: Meroe Excavations 1973–1984*. Wiesbaden: Harrassowitz, 2004.

Shinnie, Peter L., and Rebecca J. Bradley. *The Capital of Kush 1: Meroe Excavations 1965–1972*. Berlin: Akademie Verlag, 1980.

Smith, R. Morton. *Kings and Coins in India: Greek and Śaka Self-Advertisement*. New Delhi: Harman, 1997.

Talbert, Richard J. A., ed. *Barrington Atlas of the Greek and Roman World*. Princeton: Princeton University Press, 2000.

Talbot Rice, Tamara. "The Scytho-Sarmatian Tribes of South-Eastern Europe." Pages 281–93 in *The Roman Empire and its Neighbours*. Edited by Fergus Millar. 2nd edition. London: Duckworth, 1981. Repr., 1996.

Thornton, Timothy C. G. "To the End of the Earth: Acts 1.8." *Expository Times* 89 (1977–78): 374–75.

Török, Laszlo. *Der meroitische Staat. Untersuchungen und Urkunden zur Geschichte des Sudan im Altertum*. Berlin: Akademie-Verlag, 1986.

Tsetskhladze, Gocha R., ed. *Greek and Roman Settlements on the Black Sea Coast*. Bradford: Loid, 1994.

———, ed. *The Greek Colonisation of the Black Sea Area: Historical Interpretation of Archaeology*. Stuttgart: Steiner, 1998.

Tuplin, Christopher J., ed. *Pontus and the Outside World: Studies in Black Sea History, Historiography, and Archaeology*. Leiden: Brill, 2004.

Unnik, Willem C. van. "Der Ausdruck ΕΩΣ ΕΣΧΑΤΟΥ ΤΗΣ ΓΗΣ (Apostelgeschichte 1.8) und sein alttestamentlicher Hintergrund

[1966]." Pages 386–401 in *Sparsa Collecta*. Leiden: Brill, 1973.

Vadakkekara, Benedict. *Origin of India's St Thomas Christians: A Historiographical Critique*. Delhi: Media House, 1995.

Welsby, Derek A. *The Kingdom of Kush: The Napatan and Meroitic Empires*. Princeton: Wiener, 1998.

Witherington, Ben. *The Acts of the Apostles: A Socio-Rhetorical Commentary*. Grand Rapids: Eerdmans, 1998.

Yamauchi, Edwin M. *Africa and the Bible*. Grand Rapids: Baker Academic, 2004.

CHAPTER 5

A SABBATH-DAY'S JOURNEY FROM THE MOUNT OF OLIVES

Acts 1:12

Perry G. Phillips

KEY POINTS

- Luke states Jerusalem was "a Sabbath day's journey" from the Mount of Olives.
- The rabbis determined the distance of a Sabbath day's journey was two thousand cubits.
- The narrative in Acts reveals the disciples walked a greater distance than two thousand cubits, complicating our understanding of Luke's use of the term.
- Six suggestions are advanced to explain Luke's use of "a Sabbath day's journey."
- Jesus' ascension on the Mount of Olives relates to the prophecy of Zechariah 14:4 and Jesus' statements about his return in his Olivet discourse.

THE CONTEXT OF THE ASCENSION

Forty days have passed since Jesus' resurrection. The time has come for him to ascend to the Father. In companionship with his disciples, he ascended the Mount of Olives to the vicinity of Bethany[1] and bid his disciples to remain in Jerusalem until the coming of the Holy Spirit (Acts 1:4). He ascended into heaven and disappeared in the clouds. Mesmerized by the event, the disciples continued staring at the sky until shaken into present reality (no doubt) by two angels who

1. Bethany appears many times in connection with Jesus (for example, Mark 11:11, 12), which is not surprising. When visiting Jerusalem, Galileans stayed on the east slopes of the Mount of Olives at Bethany and Bethphage. See Joachim Jeremias, *Jerusalem in the Time of Jesus: An Investigation into Economic and Social Conditions during the New Testament Period* (Philadelphia: Fortress, 1969), 62.

told them Jesus would return the same way they saw him go up into heaven. The disciples returned to Jerusalem from the Mount of Olives, a distance of "a Sabbath day's journey" (σαββάτου ἔχον ὁδόν, *sabbatou echon hodon* [Acts 1:12]).[2]

"A SABBATH DAY'S JOURNEY"

The Sabbath was not only meant for rest, it was also the sign of the covenant at Sinai (Exod 31:13, 16). As such, the rabbis fastidiously kept the Sabbath in painstaking detail, including determining how far one could walk on that holy day.

According to the rabbis, the distance one could travel on the Sabbath—a Sabbath day's journey—was rooted in Exodus 16:29: "Remain each of you in his place; let no one go out of his place on the seventh day" (ESV). The rabbis differentiated between "in his place" and "out of his place." Specifically, the Mekilta of Rabbi Ishmael, a rabbinic midrash on the book of Exodus, states the following:

> *Abide Ye Every Man in His Place.* That is, within four cubits.
>
> *Let No Man Go Out of His Place.* That is, beyond two thousand cubits.[3] And as soon as they heard this, they accepted it and observed the Sabbath, as it is said: "So the people rested on the seventh day."[4]

---

2. Literally, "having a journey of a Sabbath." See the note in LEB.

3. The rabbis based this distance on the admonition to remain two thousand cubits from the ark (Josh 3:4) and upon the two-thousand-cubit distance of Levitical pasturelands from city walls (Num 35:5). See Adam L. Porter, "Sabbath Day's Journey," *NIDB* 5:10–11.

4. Jacob Z. Lauterbach, *Mekilta de-Rabbi Ishmael: A Critical Edition on the Basis of the Manuscripts and Early Editions with an English Translation, Introduction, and Notes* (Philadelphia: Jewish Publications Society of America, 1933), 2:122.

Rabbi Akiva and Rabbi Eliezer also discuss the topic in the Mishnah:

> On that day, Rabbi Akiva expounded [the verse], (Numbers 35:5) "You shall measure outside the city on the eastern outskirts, two thousand cubits..." (Numbers 35:5), and another verse says (Numbers 35:4) "... from the wall of the city and outward, one thousand cubits around." It is impossible to say one thousand cubits, for it already said two thousand cubits, and it is impossible to say two thousand cubits, for it already said one thousand cubits. How does it work? One-thousand cubits is for the open land, and two thousand cubits is the Sabbath border [the distance one can travel from the city on Sabbath]." Rabbi Eliezer, son of Rabbi Yosi the Galilian [*sic*] says, one thousand cubits is for the open land, and two thousand cubits is for fields and orchards.[5]

Further information is provided in the Babylonian Talmud, where the topic is discussed at length in Tractate Eruvin.[6] Louis Jacobs summarizes the rabbinic regulations as follows:

> The rabbis placed no restrictions on freedom of movement within one's town, but they prohibited any walking outside the town beyond a distance of 2,000 cubits (a little more than half a mile [805 m]). This boundary is known as the *teḥum shabbat* (Sabbath limit). It is, however, permitted to place, before the Sabbath, sufficient food for two meals at the limits of the 2,000 cubits; then, by a legal fiction known as *eruv*, this place becomes one's "abode" for the duration of the Sabbath, so that the 2,000 cubits may then be walked from there.[7]

The Targum of Ruth 1:16 also indicates familiarity with the two-thousand-cubit rule for the allowable limit of travel on the Sabbath:

> Ruth said, "Do not urge me to leave you, to back from after you *for I desire to be a proselyte." Naomi said, "We are commanded to keep*

5. Mishnah Sotah 5:3, translation from Sefaria.org (https://www.sefaria.org/Mishnah_Sotah.5.3?lang=en&with=all&lang2=en).

6. See, especially, b. Eruvin 41b–61b. The Sabbath limit is also discussed in b. Eruvin 21a, 72b–73a, and 82a–b.

7. Louis Jacobs, "Sabbath: The Laws and Customs of the Sabbath," *EJ* 17:619; see also Zvi Kaplan, "Eruv," *EJ* 6:484–85; Yitzhak Dov Gilat, "Eruvin," *EJ* 6:485–86.

5 stades

≈ 900 meters

≈ 0.6 miles / 984.3 yards / 2,952.8 feet / 35,433.1 inches

≈ 0.6 Roman miles / 1 Sabbath day's journey / 4.5 furrow lengths / 327.3 reeds / 492.1 fathoms ...

A little more than 3 Tower Bridges

> *Sabbaths and holy days so as not to walk beyond two thousand cubits."* (emphasis original)[8]

How are the rabbinic teachings relevant to Luke's statement about distance? Specifically, two thousand cubits equal five *stadia*. Luke tells us that the ascension took place "as far as Bethany"[9] (Luke 24:50: ἕως πρὸς Βηθανίαν, *heōs pros Bēthanian*). John 11:18 indicates that Bethany lay about fifteen *stadia* from Jerusalem, which is on the *eastern* side of the Mount of Olives, which is beyond the summit, the traditional location for the ascension.[10] But a Sabbath day's journey of five *stadia* from Jerusalem puts one on the *western* side of the mount, about one-third the distance to Bethany.[11] Superficially, this looks like a problem with Luke's geography.

SUGGESTED RESOLUTIONS TO THE "PROBLEM"

SUGGESTION 1

Luke is referring merely to the distance one traverses crossing the Kidron Valley from Jerusalem, thereby conforming to the distance as recorded by Josephus.[12] The disciples, however, were near Bethany, so Josephus' distances fall short as well. But the main difficulty is that this suggestion detaches Luke's statement from its context. Luke has made it clear that the ascension occurred at Bethany, so the most reasonable interpretation is that he is referring to the disciples' trek

8. G. R. B. Beattie, *The Targum of Ruth: Translated with Introduction, Apparatus, and Notes* (Collegeville, MN: Liturgical Press, 1994), 20. The Targums are Aramaic interpretive translations of the books of the Hebrew canon.

9. So the ESV, NASB, LEB, RSV, and HCSB. The NIV has "in the vicinity of Bethany." But the preposition *pros* implies "up to" (Bo Reicke, "πρὸς," *TDNT* 6:721.)

10. A point emphasized by Edward Robinson on his visit to Jerusalem. E. Robinson, *Biblical Researches in Palestine, and in the Adjacent Regions: Journal of Travels in the Year 1838*, 3 vols., 11th ed. (Boston: Crocker and Brewster, 1874), 254, n.1; 415–16.

11. Here's the math: If one takes a regular cubit as 18 inches = 1.5 feet, then 2000 cubits is 3000 feet. One *stadium* is about 607 feet; hence, 15 *stadia* = 9105 feet, about three times the allowed rabbinic distance. Cubit lengths varied somewhat, but the same argument obtains.

12. Josephus gives two distances from Jerusalem to the Mount of Olives. First, he mentions that Vespasian set up a camp on the Mount of Olives six stadia from Jerusalem (*J.W.* 5:67–70). When discussing the false prophet from Egypt (who claimed he could destroy Jerusalem), Josephus tells us the prophet and his followers went up the Mount of Olives a distance of five stadia from Jerusalem (*Ant.* 20:167–72). Josephus, however, is relating the distance from Jerusalem to *the locations of two events* that occurred on the Mount of Olives. He is not setting a distance to the mountain per se.

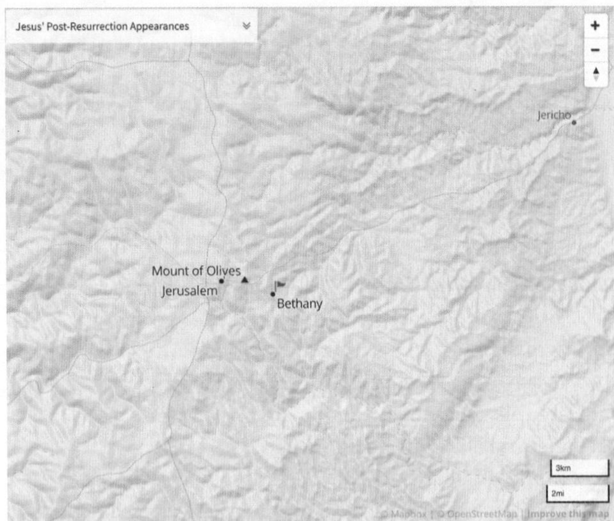

Locations of Bethany and Jerusalem

from Bethany to Jerusalem—a total distance greater than a Sabbath day's journey. That is, Luke is focusing on the disciples, not on the geography. As such, this suggestion fails to be persuasive.

SUGGESTION 2

The church father John Chrysostom (fourth century) suggested that the ascension took place on a Sabbath and that Luke used the expression so as not to give offense to the Jews.[13] To him, the mention of forty days is approximate, being more of a theological time period than an actual period. But his thesis lacks evidence, for from early times the ascension has been commemorated on a Thursday, unless, of course, Chrysostom had a general Sabbath in mind as, for example, the first and last days of the Feast of Tabernacles also called "Sabbaths" (Heb: שַׁבָּתוֹן, *shabbaton*; Lev 23:39). But even then, there is no evidence that the ascension took place on any known Sabbath.

SUGGESTION 3

Four centuries ago John Lightfoot (1602–1675) suggested that "Bethany" was not only the name of the town of Bethany, but also the name of the environs of the town, and that its environs extended to Bethphage, which was a Sabbath day's journey from Jerusalem. As such, the ascension did not take place at the town

13. Chrysostom states, "'Then returned they unto Jerusalem from the mount called Olivet, which is from Jerusalem a Sabbath day's journey.' 'Then returned they,' it is said: namely, when they had heard. For they could not have borne it, if the angel had not (ὑπερέθετο) [*hyperetheto*] referred them to another Coming. It seems to me, that it was also on a Sabbath-day that these things took place; for he would not thus have specified the distance, saying, 'from the mount called Olivet, which is from Jerusalem a Sabbath day's journey,' unless they were then going on the Sabbath-day a certain definite distance ("Homilies on the Acts of the Apostles," Homily 3 [*NPNF*[1] 11:17]).

of Bethany, well beyond a Sabbath day's distance from Jerusalem, but rather took place on the *border* of the *environs* of Bethany, near Bethphage, thereby restricting the distance from Jerusalem to a Sabbath day's journey.[14] Interestingly, in his commentary on Acts, Lightfoot appears to reject his own proposal that "Bethany" referred to the environs of the town rather than to the town itself.[15] This writer finds Lightfoot's arguments in his Acts commentary more persuasive. Luke has the town, not its environs in mind.

SUGGESTION 4

Luke mentions that the disciples worshiped Jesus with great joy before returning to Jerusalem (Luke 24:52). Did the worship occur at the location of the ascension? Maybe the disciples gathered at that place where Jesus often met with them (John 18:2), which does not appear to have been far from Jerusalem given that Jesus and the disciples walked thither after the Lord's Supper. Luke's use of "Sabbath day's journey," therefore, recapitulates numerous occasions when the disciples walked back and forth to Jerusalem on their excursions with Jesus from the place where they often met.[16]

SUGGESTION 5

Although we do not know the exact location of Bethphage,[17] we do know that the rabbis considered Bethphage as part of Jerusalem.[18] Moreover, a walk from Jerusalem to Bethphage fell within

---

14. John Lightfoot, *Hebrew and Talmudical Exercitations* in *The Whole Works of Rev. John Lightfoot, D.D.*, ed. Rev. John Rogers Pitman, 13 vols. (London: J. F. Dove, 1823–25), 12:219. In Lightfoot's words, "Our Saviour led out his disciples, when he was about to ascend, to the very first brink of that region or tract of mount Olivet which was called 'Bethany,' and was distant from the city [of Jerusalem] a sabbath day's journey. And so far [i.e., "And as far as," meaning a Sabbath day's journey] from the city itself [again, Jerusalem] did that tract extend which was called 'Bethphage:' and when he was come to that place where the bounds of Bethphage and Bethany met and touched one another, he there ascended." He also promoted the boundary thesis in *The Chorographic Works* (in *Whole Works*, 10:78–79). Lightfoot's works are available online at https://biblicalstudies.org.uk/book_lightfoot_works.html.

15. Lightfoot, *A Commentary on the Acts of the Apostles*, in *Whole Works*, 8:30. He opposed the "boundary" proposal here for three reasons: (1) "It is rare in Scripture to find open fields, called by the name of a town, when there is no expression that the fields are meant" (page 30). (2) When the prefix "Beth-" appears with other named locations, it refers to a city or to a town, not to a region. (3) All other mentions of "Bethany" in Luke refer to the town, not to the region. Why switch meaning here?

16. Lightfoot suggested the following: "And so may we conceived it [i.e., where Jesus often met with his disciples] was the common haunt of others of the city, upon such times, and such occasions of prayer and meditation, to resort thither, for the delightsomeness of the place, and the helpfulness of it, by the delight and solitariness, to contemplation. And, therefore, the evangelist may be conceived to use this expression for the measure betwixt it and the city, 'a sabbath-day's journey,' because it was most remarkably so; not only upon obligation, but for delight, and the people's common sabbath-day's walk" (Lightfoot, *Whole Works*, 8:31–32).

17. A.D. Riddle, "The Passover Pilgrimage from Jericho to Jerusalem." *Lexham Geographic Commentary of the Gospels*, ed. Barry J. Beitzel (Bellingham, WA: Lexham Press, 2017), 402, 403.

18. Riddle, "Passover Pilgrimage," 404. Riddle points to m. Menahot 11:2 and to b. Pesahim 63b. To these references one can add b. Menahot 78b; Pesahim 91a, 95b; Sanhedrin 14a. Particularly relevant is the comment by Rashi in the last reference: "Bethphage—a place

Mount of Olives

the confines of a Sabbath day's journey since the rabbis did not restrict the distance one could walk within the confines of one's own town.[19] As such, after witnessing the ascension at Bethany, the disciples' walk back to Bethphage—considered part of Jerusalem—comports with a Sabbath day's journey regardless of their starting point within the walls of Jerusalem proper.[20] More generally, the extended boundary of Jerusalem was a nice accommodation to the Jewish community on the east side of the mount who wished to participate in Sabbath temple activities without contravening the Sabbath distance regulation.

SUGGESTION 6

Luke freely acknowledges his use of historical documents and of personal interviews upon which he based his writings (Luke 1:3). Perhaps he found this expression in his materials, and although a strange expression to him personally, he felt it served his readers to use "a sacred measure for a sacred story."[21]

In short, many suggestions attempt to explain Luke's use of "a Sabbath day's journey." And although we do not know fully Luke's purpose, one can, however, legitimately doubt that he intended to give simply the geographical distance between Jerusalem and the Mount of

located from the wall of the city [Jerusalem] and/but judged as Jerusalem in all matters" (author's translation.) In short, Jerusalem's environs included Bethphage.

19. b. Eruvin 51a.

20. Both Mark 11:1 and in Luke 19:29 mention Bethany and Bethphage together and expressly state that both are on the Mount of Olives.

21. Proposed by Wilhelm Michaelis ("ὁδός," *TDNT* 5:69 n. 90). Also, as Craig Keener points out, "Luke mentions the Sabbath day's journey to show their proximity to the holy city (fulfilling Luke 24:49) but also to indicate they continued to observe the law (cf. early chapters of Acts)," *Acts: An Exegetical Commentary* (Grand Rapids: Baker Academic, 2012), 1:735.

Olives or to tally the walking distance of the disciples on the day of the ascension.[22]

WHY THE MOUNT OF OLIVES?

Why did the ascension occur on the Mount of Olives? Since Jesus will return "the same way he went up," we find a tight correlation between Jesus' ascension and his second coming when "on that day his feet will stand on the Mount of Olives, east of Jerusalem" (Zech 14:4).

Further, it was on the Mount of Olives, in the course of his Olivet discourse, that he spoke of his coming "in the clouds with great power and glory" (Mark 13:26; compare Matt 24:30; Luke 21:27). Geographically and theologically, the Mount of Olives makes an obvious connection between the ascension and the second coming.[23]

CONCLUSION

Luke states that the distance between Jerusalem and the Mount of Olives is a Sabbath day's journey. But to where on the Mount of Olives? The ascension was near Bethany, about fifteen stadia from Jerusalem, whereas rabbinic evidence points to a Sabbath day's journey's being two thousand cubits, or about five stadia. We do not know why Luke chose to mention the Jerusalem/Mount of Olives distance in terms of a Sabbath day's journey, but it is clear that Luke's use of the expression does not span the total distance traversed by the disciples. As for the Mount of Olives, it is the logical location for the ascension, for it geographically connects Jesus' ascension and his prophesied return forecast in his Olivet discourse and prophesied by Zechariah.

BIBLIOGRAPHY

Beattie, G. R. B. *The Targum of Ruth: Translated with Introduction, Apparatus, and Notes*. The Aramaic Bible 19. Collegeville, MN: Liturgical Press, 1994.

Chrysostom, John. "Homilies on the Acts of the Apostles and the Epistle to the Romans." *NPNF*[1] Vol. 11.

Gilat, Yitzhak Dov. "Eruvin." *EJ* 6:485–86.

Jacobs, Louis. "Sabbath: The Laws and Customs of the Sabbath." *EJ* 17:619–20.

Jeremias, Joachim. *Jerusalem in the Time of Jesus: An Investigation into Economic and Social Conditions during the New Testament Period*. Philadelphia: Fortress, 1969.

Josephus. *The Works of Josephus*. Translated by H. St. J. Thackeray et al. 10 vols. LCL. Cambridge: Harvard University Press, 1926–1965.

Kaplan, Zvi. "Eruv." *EJ* 6:484–85.

Keener, Craig S. *Acts: An Exegetical Commentary*. 4 vols. Grand Rapids: Baker Academic, 2012–2015.

22. I disagree with Richard Longenecker that "We may therefore estimate that their journey from the place of the ascension back to Jerusalem was a bit over a kilometer, or about 3/4 mile." Richard N. Longenecker, "Acts," in *Luke through Acts*, in *The Expositors Bible Commentary*, ed. Tremper Longman III and David E. Garland, rev. ed. (Grand Rapids: Zondervan, 2007), 10:723.

23. Although the ascension occurred near Bethany, today's commemorative locations are at one of the summits of the Mount of Olives. See Stephen Langfur, "The Mount of Olives." (http://www.netours.com/content/view/162/47/). The prominent bell tower of the Russian Ascension Convent marks another commemorative location (https://biblewalks.com/sites/RussianAscensionChurch.html).

Langfur, Stephen. "The Mount of Olives." http://www.netours.com/content/view/162/47/.

Lauterbach, Jacob Z. *Mekilta de-Rabbi Ishmael: A Critical Edition on the Basis of the Manuscripts and Early Editions with an English Translation, Introduction, and Notes*. 2 vols. Philadelphia: Jewish Publications Society of America, 1933.

Lightfoot, John. *The Whole Works of the Rev. John Lightfoot, D.D.* Edited by Rev. John Rogers Pitman. 13 vols. London: J. F. Dove, 1823–1825.

Longenecker, Richard N. "Acts." Pages 663–1102 in *Luke through Acts*. Vol. 10 of *The Expositors Bible Commentary*. Edited by Tremper Longman III and David E. Garland. 12 vols. Revised ed. Grand Rapids: Zondervan, 2007.

Michaelis, Wilhelm. "ὁδός." *TDNT* 5:42–114.

Porter, Adam L. "Sabbath Day's Journey." *NIDB* 5:10–11.

Reicke, Bo. "πρὸς." *TDNT* 6:721.

Riddle, A.D. "The Passover Pilgrimage from Jericho to Jerusalem." Pages 395–407 in *Lexham Geographic Commentary of the Gospels*. Edited by Barry J. Beitzel. Bellingham, WA: Lexham Press, 2017.

Robinson, Edward G. *Biblical Researches in Palestine, and in the Adjacent Regions: Journal of Travels in the Year 1838*. 3 vols. 11th ed. Boston: Crocker and Brewster, 1874.

"Russian Ascension Convent." https://biblewalks.com/sites/RussianAscensionChurch.html.

CHAPTER 6

THE LOCATION OF PENTECOST AND GEOGRAPHICAL IMPLICATIONS IN ACTS 2

Acts 2:1-41

Chris McKinny

KEY POINTS

- The events of Pentecost most likely took place on the Temple Mount, and not in the Cenacle.
- The traditional evidence identifying the Cenacle with an early Christian community and Jerusalem's first church is compelling, if not yet proven archaeologically.
- The appearance of the Holy Spirit at Pentecost in the Jerusalem temple complex should be understood against the historical, theological, and geographical backdrop of the Old Testament.

INTRODUCTION

This essay will discuss the geographical location of Pentecost (Acts 2) and investigate several possible intertextual links between the location of Pentecost and past events at the temple. Peter's Pentecost sermon in Acts 2 explicitly references Joel 2:28–32; Psalm 16:8–11; and Psalm 110:1. These explicit references will be briefly discussed, but the primary purpose of this essay is to suggest and examine the implicit presence of other Old Testament texts related to the geographical movements of the Holy Spirit in Peter's sermon.

Before we begin the task of locating the events of Pentecost and examining its intertextuality, it is important to briefly recount the events of Pentecost. Acts 2 records the outpouring of the Holy Spirit upon the "believers" (see Acts 1:15) who were gathered together "in one place" on the day of Pentecost (2:1).[1] The coming of the Spirit is described both audibly as "a mighty rushing wind," which filled "the entire house where they were sitting," and visually "as divided tongues of fire," which "rested on each one of them" (2:2–3). As a result of this "filling" of the Spirit, those gathered there spoke in other tongues (2:4), which quickly bewildered many pious Jews who inexplicably recognized their own language being spoken by Galilean Jews (2:5–13). In response to this, Peter delivered a sermon to those present that explained the significance of the coming of the Spirit (2:14–41). Specifically, Peter would argue that the outpouring of the Holy Spirit was a sign that the "last days" had arrived (quoting Joel 2:28–32), and that the impetus for these developments was the resurrection of Jesus the Messiah whom they had crucified (quoting Ps 16:8–11) and was currently exalted at the right hand of God (quoting Ps 110:1). Finally, Peter concluded his sermon by calling on his hearers to repent and be baptized (Acts 2:36–41).

As noted above, Peter's sermon is based on the exposition (or Jewish "midrashic exegesis")[2] of three Old Testament passages (Joel 2:28–32; Ps 16:8–11; 110:1), which he interprets as being fulfilled in the person and work of Jesus. This sermon and these passages are of obvious importance for understanding the role of the Holy Spirit in the book of Acts, and subsequently to the lives of believers in the church. They also present significant christological interpretations and arguments associated with Jesus' redemptive work and status as the invested Messiah and Son of God. In Peter's sermon, these passages serve as the Old Testament, big picture evidences for why the local and diasporic Jews gathered at the temple for the festival of Pentecost should believe that "this" Jesus, whom they had crucified, was made "both Lord and Messiah" by God (Acts 2:36). Given the literal holy ground that Peter was speaking on, there are a wealth of implied intertextual connections linking the appearance of God's Spirit on the temple that would have presumably been apparent to the Jews present at Pentecost and the readers of Luke's account. Stated another way, Peter's main point can be understood by interpreting his arguments from the Scriptures that he explicitly cites. However, the implied biblical data that are not referenced add further weight and significance to Peter's claims of Christ's status as deity and death-defier. In light of this premise, we will attempt to demonstrate some of the geographically related intertextual links between the Old Testament and Pentecost. But first, let us examine the setting and possible locations for the events of Pentecost.

THE TIMING OF PASSOVER, CHRIST'S ASCENSION, AND PENTECOST

Passover is part of the seven-day long Feast of Unleavened Bread beginning on the fifteenth day of Nisan/first month (that is, during March and/or April). Jesus was crucified on either the day of

1. Unless otherwise indicated, Scripture quotations are from the English Standard Version (ESV).

2. I. Howard Marshall, "Acts," in *Commentary on the New Testament Use of the Old Testament*, ed. G. K. Beale and D. A. Carson (Grand Rapids: Baker Academic, 2007), 532.

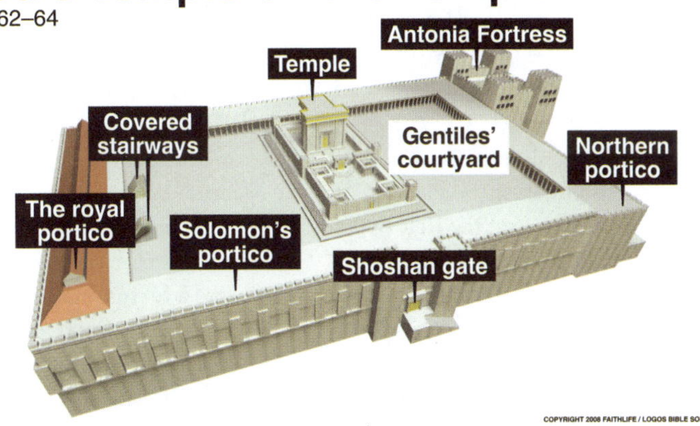

Passover or the day after (either the fifteenth or sixteenth of Nisan).[3] According to Acts 1:3, Jesus "appeared to them during forty days" and specifically commanded them to not leave Jerusalem as they were to wait for the baptism of the Holy Spirit, which he promised would occur "not many days from now" (Acts 1:4–5). Since Pentecost/the Feast of Weeks occurred seven weeks following Passover (Lev 23:15–16; Deut 16:9), then it seems obvious that Luke was indicating Jesus' ascension (Acts 1:9–11) occurred a few days or so before Pentecost.[4]

Awaiting the coming of the Spirit, the disciples along with the "women, Mary the mother of Jesus, and his brothers" stayed in an "upper room" (τὸ ὑπερῷον ἀνέβησαν, *to hyperōon anebēsan*) (Acts 1:14). With regard to this building, traditionally the "upper room" of Acts 1:13 has been associated with the same structure (τὸ κατάλυμα/ἀνάγαιον μέγα, *to katalyma/anagaion mega*) that is mentioned in accounts of the Last Supper (see Mark 14:14–15; Luke 22:11–12), as well as the place where the disciples were staying following Christ's crucifixion (Luke 24:33; John 20:19–29), and Pentecost (Acts 2:1–4). Others identify this same building with the home of Mary and John Mark (her son), due to the fact that Peter came to Mary's house following his imprisonment and miraculous release from Herod Agrippa I (Acts 12:12; compare Mark 14:51–52).[5] We will now survey the available evidence and suggest the location for the events of Pentecost.

---

3. See discussion in Harold W. Hoehner, *Chronological Aspects of the Life of Christ* (Grand Rapids: Zondervan, 1978), 68–83.

4. Craig S. Keener, *Acts: An Exegetical Commentary* (Grand Rapids: Baker Academic, 2012), 1:797–98. On the Israelite calendar of feasts, see chart on page 697.

5. For example, Bargil Pixner, *Paths of the Messiah and Sites of the Early Church from Galilee to Jerusalem: Jesus and Jewish Christianity in Light of Archaeological Discoveries* (San Francisco: Ignatius Press, 2010), 319–59.

THE SETTING OF THE APOSTLES' RECEIVING THE HOLY SPIRIT: THE UPPER ROOM OR THE TEMPLE MOUNT?

TEXTUAL EVIDENCE

It should be noted that we are only attempting to pinpoint the location of the apostles' reception of the Holy Spirit (Acts 2:1–4). Thus, we are not questioning the location of the reaction of the multiethnic multitude (Acts 2:5–13) or of Peter's sermon (Acts 2:14–40). It would seem obvious that these events clearly took place on the Temple Mount. This is made clear by the reference to many Jewish worshipers hearing their own native tongues on the lips of the Aramaic-speaking disciples (Acts 2:6–12). In addition, Acts 2:41 indicates that those "who received his [Peter's] word were baptized, and there were added that day about three thousand souls." This number should be compared to the "120" in Acts 1:15, who were present at the selection of Matthias as the replacement for Judas (Acts 1:15–26). The setting of this earlier event is clearly the upper room (Acts 1:13). However, there seems to be a time gap between Acts 1:26 and 2:1, as noted by the reference to "when the day of Pentecost arrived." Thus, the events of Acts 1:15–26 (the selection of Mattathias) and Acts 2:1–4 (the outpouring of the Spirit upon the disciples) are separate events, even if the setting of the latter has not been certainly determined. In any event, the baptism of three thousand people is clearly a mass religious event that would have required a large facility with available ritual baths.[6] Excavations around (various) and beneath the Temple Mount (by Charles Warren in the 1860s) revealed numerous ritual baths and cisterns that would have been available to Second Temple Jewish worshipers.[7] Therefore, we can conclude that the majority of Acts 2 occurred on the Temple Mount and its environs, but the location of the event in Acts 2:1–4 remains debated.

From a textual standpoint, the location of Pentecost may possibly be connected to the upper room of Acts 1:14 by the reference in Acts 2:1–2. The latter indicates that the outpouring of the Spirit occurred where they were "all together in one place" and describes the Spirit's rushing wind noise that "filled the entire house." However, a literary

Mikveh near Southern Steps of Temple Mount

6. See Craig S. Keener, *The IVP Bible Background Commentary: New Testament*, 2nd ed. (Downers Grove, IL: InterVarsity Press, 2014), 322.

7. See discussion in Leen Ritmeyer, *The Quest: Revealing the Temple Mount in Jerusalem* (Jerusalem: Carta, 2006), 221–33.

connection between these two passages is not definitive, as no transition from the presumed upper room location to the Temple Mount is included in Acts 2:4–5. Moreover, Acts 2:6 indicates that the multitude heard "this sound" (that is, the rushing wind of Acts 2:2), so in order to hold to the traditional view (see below) that Pentecost occurred in the upper room (that is, on the western hill) then one must assume that the apostles moved from there to the Temple Mount after receiving the Holy Spirit.

TRADITIONAL EVIDENCE

While the evidence for locating the outpouring of the Spirit in Acts 2:1–4 from the book of Acts is relatively inconclusive, Byzantine tradition clearly favored a connection between the upper room of the Last Supper and the location of Pentecost connecting both events with the Cenacle/Tomb of David on Mt. Zion.[8] The two earliest traditions come from Cyril of Jerusalem (approximately AD 315–373)[9] and Epiphanius of Constantia/Salamis (approximately AD 315–403),[10] who connected the Upper Church of the Apostles or the Church of God with the events of Pentecost. Notably, Epiphanius' referred to the Church of God beside the "seven synagogues which alone remained standing in Zion." While not mentioning the church directly, the anonymous Pilgrim of Bordeaux (writing in approximately AD 333) provides even earlier testimony corroborating Epiphanius' statement about seven synagogues on Mount Zion

---

8. Also known as the Mother of All Churches, the Church of the Apostles, the Church of God, the Coenaculum, the Church of the Upper Room, and so on. See discussion in Clemens Kopp, *The Holy Places of the Gospels* (New York: Herder, 1963); Anson F. Rainey and R. Steven Notley, *The Sacred Bridge: Carta's Atlas of the Biblical World* (Jerusalem: Carta, 2006), 370; see also the discussion in Jerome Murphy-O'Connor, *The Holy Land: An Oxford Archaeological Guide from Earliest Times to 1700*, 5th ed. (Oxford: Oxford University Press, 2008), 115–18; see especially David Christian Clausen, *The Upper Room and Tomb of David: The History, Art and Archaeology of the Cenacle on Mount Zion* (Jefferson, NC: McFarland, 2016).

9. "We know the Holy Ghost, who spake in the Prophets, and who on the day of Pentecost descended on the Apostles in the form of fiery tongues, here, in Jerusalem, in the *Upper Church of the Apostles*; for in all things the choicest privileges are with us. Here Christ came down from heaven; here the Holy Ghost came down from heaven. And in truth it were most fitting, that as we discourse concerning Christ and Golgotha here in Golgotha, so also we should speak concerning the Holy Ghost in the *Upper Church*" (*Catechetical Lectures*, Lecture XVI.4; emphasis added). See translation in Cyril of Jerusalem, *St. Cyril of Jerusalem's Lectures on the Christian Sacraments: The Procatechesis and the Five Mystagogical Catecheses*, trans. Frank L. Cross (Crestwood, NY: St. Vladimir's Seminary Press, 1951). Apparently, Cyril of Jerusalem also mentioned that the supposed bones of James (the brother of Jesus) were temporarily interned near the church, see Clausen, *Upper Room and Tomb of David*, ch. 3.

10. "And he [Hadrian] found the temple of God trodden down and the whole city devastated save for a few houses and *the church of God*, which was small, where the disciples, when they had returned after the Savior had ascended from the Mount of Olives, went to the upper room. For there it had been built, that is, in that portion of Zion which escaped destruction, together with blocks of houses in the neighborhood of Zion and the seven synagogues which alone remained standing in Zion, like solitary huts, one of which remained until the time of Maximona the bishop and Constantine the king, 'like a booth in a vineyard,' as it is written" (quoting Isa 1:8; Epiphanius, *Weights* 54c; emphasis added). Epiphanius of Salamis, *Epiphanius' Treatise on Weights and Measures: The Syriac Version*, trans. James E. Dean, (Chicago: University of Chicago Press, 1935), 30.

Cenacle, Traditional Site of the Last Supper

(that is, the western hill).[11] After visiting the pool of Siloam and the Gihon Spring the Pilgrim writes,

> On this side one goes up Sion, and sees where the house of Caiaphas the priest was, and there still stands a column against which Christ was beaten with rods. Within, however, inside the wall of Sion, is seen the place where was David's palace.[12] *Of seven synagogues which once were there, one alone remains*; the rest are ploughed over and sown upon, as said Isaiah the prophet.[13]

These traditions indicate that the western hill of Jerusalem was still in ruins during the fourth century AD. Within these ruins, only one of the seven synagogues remained with the rest presumably destroyed in either the AD 70 destruction by Titus or following the Bar Kokhba Revolt in AD 132–135. Notably, this lone remaining synagogue (see Epiphanius and the Pilgrim) is distinct from the "the church of God"

11. According to Murphy-O'Connor, the Byzantine tradition relating the western hill of Jerusalem to Zion is rooted in a misunderstanding of Micah 3:12, which employs synonymous parallelism instead of referring to two (or three) different hills in Jerusalem, see Murphy-O'Connor, *Holy Land*, 115.

12. These traditions connecting Zion and the palace of David (see 2 Sam 5:11–12) with the western hill of Jerusalem are indicative of Byzantine confusion regarding the location of the original settlement of Jerusalem.

13. Actually Mic 3:12; compare Isa 1:8; Pilgrim of Bordeaux, *Itinerary from Bordeaux to Jerusalem*, trans. Aubrey Stewart (London: Palestine Pilgrim's Text Society, 1887), 23 (emphasis added).

(Epiphanius), which was built in the small area of the western hill that "escaped destruction." Eusebius (*Ecclesiastical History* 3.5.3) and Epiphanius (*Weights* 54a) relay that the Jewish-Christian community of Jerusalem, which had fled to Pella during the Jewish Revolt, returned to Jerusalem following the AD 70 destruction. Subsequently, they apparently resided in the city until the arrival of Hadrian (see Eusebius, *Proof of the Gospel* 3.5.124d). Later Byzantine tradition held that it was this community that built the church on Mount Zion connected with the Last Supper and Pentecost.[14] In the late fourth century AD, the large Hagia Sion church[15] was built on the western hill in near proximity to the preexisting Upper Church of the Apostles. Christian pilgrim accounts, iconographic,[16] and archaeological evidences (see below), indicate that these two buildings were separate, but nearby structures are as late as the seventh century.

To this point, we can conclude the following. First, Byzantine tradition connecting the Upper Church of the Apostles with the upper room of the Last Supper and Pentecost is well attested by the earliest Christian sources. Second, to my knowledge there does not appear to be a rival Byzantine tradition connecting Pentecost (whether the entire event or only the witness of the multitude and Peter's sermon) with the Temple Mount. Third, it seems abundantly clear that there was an early Jewish-Christian community on the western hill, who built a church there at least sometime before Cyril of Jerusalem (approximately AD 350). While it is possible that this church has not been located, it seems probable that the building known today as the Church of the Upper Room and the Tomb of David is in fact the original church built at some point before the mid-fourth century AD.[17]

ARCHAEOLOGICAL EVIDENCE

Possible archaeological support tying Pentecost to the Cenacle comes from the suggestions of Bargil Pixner. Pixner developed a complex theory that incorporated the biblical text, the above referenced traditions, and J. Pinkerfield's unpublished excavations of the floor of the "Tomb of David" in 1949.[18] Pinkerfield claimed that the building was origi-

14. See sources in David Christian Clausen, "Can the Cenacle on Mount Zion Really Be the 'Upper Room' of Jesus's Last Supper?" *The Bible and Interpretation* May (2016), http://www.bibleinterp.com/articles/2016/05/cla408003.shtml; Clausen, *Upper Room and Tomb of David.*

15. The ruins of Hagia Sion are located beneath Dormition Abbey, which was constructed in the early twentieth century.

16. These include two sixth century AD depictions of the Hagia Sion church with a small church (presumably the Cenacle) in immediate proximity: the Medeba Map's depiction of Jerusalem and a similarly dated mosiac from the Church of Santa Maria Maggiore in Rome. Clausen, "Can the Cenacle on Mount Zion," 10–11; Clausen, *Upper Room and Tomb of David*, ch. 3.

17. See Clausen, *Upper Room and Tomb of David*, chs. 12–14 who persuasively argues for this view against the suggestions of an original Jewish synagogue or a pagan Mithraeum.

18. Before he could finish his report, Pinkerfield was murdered (along with three others) by Jordanian soldiers during an archaeological tour of Ramat Raḥel in 1956.

Courtyard in Front of the Cenacle with Dormition Abbey on Mt. Zion

nally a synagogue constructed in the Late Roman period.[19] In response to this, Pixner agreed that it was a synagogue, but suggested that it should be dated to the first century AD since it was built using Herodian-style masonry. He further hypothesized that this synagogue was none other than the room of the Last Supper (as well as the home of John Mark), the location of Pentecost, and the church/synagogue that is referenced by Cyril of Jerusalem, Epiphanius, and the Pilgrim of Bordeaux.[20] While future excavations in the Cenacle might indicate the viability of Pixner's theory, several scholars point out that there is very little archaeological evidence in support of Pinkerfield or Pixner's conclusions suggesting that the original structure was a synagogue.[21] A recent, limited excavation inside of the Cenacle and in the adjacent courtyard by Amit Reem seemed to indicate that the building was constructed in the fourth century AD.[22]

19. J. Pinkerfield, "'David's Tomb': Notes on the History of the Building: Preliminary Report," *Bulletin of the Louis Rabinowitz Fund for the Exploration of Ancient Synagogues*, 3 (1960): 41–43; Clausen, "Can the Cenacle on Mount Zion," 3.

20. See discussion in Pixner, *Paths of the Messiah*, 319–59.

21. For example, Murphy-O'Connor, *Holy Land*, 155–58; Clausen, *Upper Room and Tomb of David*, ch. 12.

22. Amit Reem, "The Tomb of David on Mount Zion: Theories versus Archaeological Reality," *Hidushim Ba'archiologiyah Shel Yerushalayim Usvivoteha* 7 (2013): 185–86 [in Hebrew]; see also Reem and Ilya Berkovich, "New Discoveries in the Cenacle: Reassessing the Art,

CONCLUSION

The Church of the Upper Room has early Christian tradition connecting it with both the location of the Last Supper and Pentecost. This tradition is probably based on a supposed textual connection between Acts 1:13 and 2:1–4. But as we have seen, Acts 2:1–4 does not necessarily have to be connected with the upper room. Therefore, I would conclude that this early Christian tradition connecting Pentecost with the upper room probably originated from a misreading of Acts 1–2 and not an independent Pentecost tradition. Nevertheless, this negative conclusion concerning the location of Pentecost does not mean that one should determine that the Cenacle was not the location of the Last Supper (as well as other possible connections, see above). Regarding the archaeology, we must remain cautious, but it appears that the Cenacle was either constructed or underwent significant building activity in the fourth century AD. This evidence matches the contemporary references to the Upper Church of the Apostles, if not their attestations to earlier building activity and occupation by Jewish-Christians during the Early and Late Roman periods.[23]

Therefore, if the Church of the Upper Room should not be connected with Pentecost, then it seems highly probable that the entirety of the Pentecost event (including Acts 2:1–4) took place in the temple precinct. From a historical and archaeological perspective, this conclusion clearly matches the purposes of the Herodian Temple Mount as a place for mass religious gatherings. In addition, it is worth mentioning that religious Jews were supposed to be worshiping in the temple during the festival of Pentecost (Acts 20:6; 1 Cor 16:8), as well as during Passover (for example, John 11:55) and Tabernacles (for example, John 7:2). So, by referencing Pentecost (Acts 2:1), Luke is allowing for the inference that the disciples were in the temple because that would be the obvious location for celebrating the feast. In addition, locating Pentecost entirely on the Temple Mount implies intertextual geographical parallels between the descent of the Holy Spirit on believers and the activities of Yahweh's Spirit (in various forms) in the Old Testament.

GEOGRAPHICALLY RELATED INTERTEXTUAL IMPLICATIONS OF PENTECOST

In light of the conclusion above, we will now turn our attention to the numerous intertextual allusions between the Old Testament (and the Gospel of Luke) and Acts 2.[24] We will organize these pos-

Architecture and Chronology of the Crusader Basilica on Mount Sion," *New Studies in the Archaeology of Jerusalem and Its Region* 10 (2016): 56*–92* for an interesting new analysis of the Crusader chapel.

23. In light of these references, it seems likely that a post-AD 70 church (or a Jewish-Christian religious structure, as it unclear if the term "church" would have been used for such a structure during this period) was constructed on the western hill, which is either represented by the Cenacle or in its immediate proximity.

24. There are certainly more than I discuss below, as my focus is primarily on the geographical implications associated with the intertextual allusions. For example, the reference to drunk priests and prophets in Isa 28:1–15 may be linked with Peter's initial statement "these people are not drunk, as you suppose, since it is only the third hour of the day" (Marshall, "Acts," 531).

sible allusions chronologically, but our intention is to show both the chronological and geographical development of the relationship between the Holy Spirit and God's people with specific emphasis to the Temple Mount.[25]

THE REVERSAL OF BABEL: GENESIS 11:1–9; ACTS 2:5–13

The first allusion to an Old Testament passage is rather obvious—the reversal of the confusion of languages at the tower of Babel (Gen 11:1–9) with the supernatural ability to understand foreign speech in their original language at Pentecost (Acts 2:5–13).[26]

- Compare the "whole world … moved eastward to the plain of Shinar and settled there" (Gen 11:1) to the gathering together of Jews from "every nation under heaven" (Acts 2:5).
- Compare the "whole earth had one language and the same words" (Gen 11:1) to "each one was hearing them [the disciples] speak in their own language" (Acts 2:6).
- Compare the confusion after the change of languages (Gen 11:7–9) to the "bewilderment" of understanding those hearing their own language come out of a Galilean mouth (Acts 2:6, 12).
- Compare the "plain of Shinar" and "Babel" (Gen 11:1, 9) to the first Jews mentioned in "Parthians, Medes, Elamites, and residents of Mesopotamia" (Acts 2:9) who are clearly identified with Jews of the Babylonian diaspora.
- Compare the preceding table of nations in Genesis 10 (who are the subject of Gen 11:1–9) to the list of Jews from all over the known world in Acts 2:8–11.
- Compare the source of the language confusion in Genesis 11:5–8 (Yahweh)[27] to the source of the language understanding in Acts 2:11 (that is, God, see also Acts 1:8)

Finally, the intertextual link between Babel and Pentecost points to the conclusion that the coming of the Holy Spirit would undo the division of peoples and their "scattering over all the earth" (Gen 11:8) by inaugurating a new era of "understanding" between the nations, even those who are "far off" (Acts 2:39; see also Acts 10:44–48). Moreover, it also implies that God was opening a new way to heaven for at least three thousand (Acts 2:41) of the "devout men from every nation under heaven" (Acts 2:5), after the failed attempt at Babel to reach heaven by means of "brick, stone, and mortar" (Gen 11:4). With regard to the three-fold geographical

25. When it comes to determining the viability of intertextual allusions or echoes, as a general guiding principle we should pay close attention to Paul's instruction to the Corinthians (compare especially his association of Christ with "the spiritual Rock that followed them" 1 Cor 10:4). See the discussion of method in Abner Chou, *The Hermeneutics of the Biblical Writers: Learning to Interpret Scripture from the Prophets and Apostles* (Grand Rapids: Kregel, 2018). With specific reference to Luke's use of the Old Testament, see Ben Witherington III, *The Acts of the Apostles: A Socio-Rhetorical Commentary* (Grand Rapids: Eerdmans, 1998), 123–27.

26. Contra Marshall, who does not see any "concrete evidence" for this connection ("Acts," 532).

27. With the plural "us" in Gen 11:7.

Pieter Bruegel the Elder's "Construction of the Tower of Babel"

outline of the events of the Book of Acts (Acts 1:7: Jerusalem/Judea, Samaria, and the end of the earth), the reversal of Babel at Pentecost is the first step in the process that will culminate in the apostle's bringing the gospel "to the ends of the earth."

THE GIVING OF THE LAW: EXODUS 24:12–18; ACTS 2:1–13

There are no explicit textual allusions between Pentecost (Acts 2) and the giving of the Law (Exod 24:12–18).[28] However, Second Temple Jewish literature plainly points to the fact that contemporary Jews believed that Pentecost was the day when the law was given at Sinai.[29] Specifically, it was understood that Moses was given a covenant that had already been given to Noah ("on heavenly tablets"), which had been lost until Sinai (Jubilees 6:15–23). Against this contemporary backdrop, parallels between the two events are relatively straightforward.

- Both events contain fiery theophanies (Exod 24:16–17; Acts 2:3–4; compare also Christ's "cloud" in Acts 1:9). Both events are connected with a new covenant (Luke 22:20; Jer 31:31).
- Both events use a prophetic messenger to explain the significance of what God has done (Moses, Exod 25:1–2; Peter, Acts 2:14). Regarding this, James VanderKam points to the possible echo of a rabbinic

28. James C. VanderKam, "Weeks, Feast of," *ABD* 6:897.

29. Marshall, "Acts," 531.

Summit of Mount Sinai

tradition in which all the foreign speakers heard the giving of the Law from Sinai in their seventy languages (b. Shabbat 88b).[30]

- Finally, one can also point to the subsequent spiritual anointing of the seventy elders at the tent of meeting in Numbers 11:25.[31] This event directly links the transfer of Yahweh's Spirit from Moses to the elders at his place of residence (that is, the tent of meeting). Moses' following statement to Joshua in Numbers 11:29 indicates the hope that one day "all Yahweh's people were prophets, that Yahweh would put his Spirit on them!" This text likely lies behind Joel 2:29,[32] and is therefore particularly relevant to the outpouring of the Spirit at Pentecost.

THE "CLOUD" OF YAHWEH IN THE SOLOMONIC TEMPLE

The next allusion is connected to an intertextual chain that can be traced back to

30. See discussion in VanderKam, "Weeks, Feast of," 6:897. B. Shabbat 88b reads as follows, "with regard to the revelation at Sinai, Rabbi Yoḥanan said: What is the meaning of that which is written: "The Lord gives the word; the women that proclaim the tidings are a great host" (Ps 68:12)? It means that each and every utterance that emerged from the mouth of the Almighty divided into seventy languages, a great host," Adin Even-Israel Steinsaltz, "Shabbat 88b," in *William Davidson Talmud*, Sefaria (Jerusalem: Koren, 2017), https://www.sefaria.org/Shabbat.88b.3?lang=bi&with=all&lang2=en.

31. "Yahweh came down in the cloud spoke to him [Moses], and took some of the Spirit that was on him and put it on the seventy elders" (Num 11:25).

32. Marshall, "Acts," 531.

the theophanies associated with Yahweh's cloud seen at the giving of the law (Exod 24:15–18), throughout the wilderness wanderings (for example, Exod 13:21–22; Num 14:14), and his residence in the tent of meeting after its construction (Exod 33:9; Num 12:5; Deut 31:15). Significantly, the rest of my suggested allusions are geographically localized to the temple precinct as a result of Solomon building "the house of Yahweh" (1 Kgs 6) and, subsequently, Yahweh's physical indwelling of his house (1 Kgs 8:10–13).

On this occasion (which is probably a parallel to the Feast of Tabernacles, compare 1 Kgs 8:2), Solomon assembled all of the leaders of Israel and had the priests bring up the "ark of Yahweh, the tent of meeting, and all the of the holy vessels that were in the tent ... to its place in the inner sanctuary of the house, in the Most Holy Place [that is, the holy of holies], beneath the wings of the cherubim" (1 Kgs 8:4–6).[33] With his physical mobile throne and his treasures secured in his new residence, Yahweh appeared once more in his theophanic cloud that "filled the house of Yahweh, so that the priests could not stand to minister because of the cloud, for the glory of Yahweh filled the house of Yahweh" (1 Kgs 8:10–11). In my opinion, Solomon's inauguration of Yahweh's temple is clearly parallel to the events of Pentecost. Consider the following parallels:

- Both events feature the gathering of Israelites/Jews from everywhere (the kingdom/diaspora) to the temple in Jerusalem (1 Kgs 8:1; Acts 2:5).
- Both groups witnessed the astonishing, supernatural physical manifestation of God's Spirit in the form of cloud (1 Kgs 8:10–13) and tongues of fire (Acts 2:1–5).
- Both events specifically reference the "house" being filled by Yahweh's Spirit (1 Kgs 8:10; Acts 2:2). From my perspective, this intertextual link is one of the main reasons why the events of Pentecost should be located on the Temple Mount.[34]
- Both events were followed by the main leader (Solomon/Peter) delivering a long oration directed at explaining the significance of what the crowd had just seen (1 Kgs 8:12–61; Acts 2:14–40).

This last parallel requires some unpacking. For Solomon (1 Kgs 8:12–61), Yahweh's presence in this new house meant the fulfillment of Solomon's end of the Davidic covenant (2 Sam 7; compare 8:12–26) and the perpetuation of the Mosaic covenant with its blessings and cursing (for example, Deut 32–33, compare 1 Kgs 8:31–61). Significantly, Solomon also expressed his humility and incredulity that the uncontainable Yahweh would graciously choose to reside in a permanent structure from which he would hear the "pleas of your servant [Solomon and Davidic kings] and of your people" (1 Kgs 8:27–30).

Likewise, Peter employed Joel 2:28–32 to explain the supernatural phenomenon that they had just observed—namely the outpouring of Yahweh's Spirit (Joel 2:29) upon them. In its contemporary First

33. For the location of the holy of holies currently beneath the Dome of the Rock, see discussion in Ritmeyer, *Quest*, 312–17.

34. See discussion in Keener, *Acts*, 1:796–97.

Temple setting (as well as Peter's day), the prophecy of Joel is based on the basic understanding that Yahweh's Spirit was not at that time upon individual people (except for unusual circumstances, for example, Elisha in 2 Kgs 2), but resided in the inner sanctuary of the temple. Therefore, it stands to reason that Joel 2:28–32 is textually linked to 1 Kings 8 (as well as 2 Chron 5–6). Accordingly, the prophecy of Joel concerns a future event that will shift the localization of Yahweh's Spirit from a physical structure to a spiritual people (see also Jer 3:15–18; Zech 12:10). Therefore, Peter was claiming that the prophecy of Joel was currently being fulfilled before their very eyes. In light of the connections that we have outlined above, Peter was also implicitly referencing the earlier indwelling of the Solomonic temple on which Joel's prophecy is based. Peter, like Solomon, then explained that this amazing change had occurred on account of the life, death, and resurrection of Jesus, the son of David (Acts 2:32–41; compare Solomon's use of the Davidic covenant above). But he also makes the bombastic claim that Jesus received the "promise of the Holy Spirit" from the Father and was the one "who poured out this that you yourselves are seeing and hearing" (Acts 2:33). In this regard, Peter proclaimed that Jesus was responsible for the filling of Yahweh's new temples (that is, the disciples) with his Spirit, in the same way that Yahweh was responsible for filling his physical temple in the days of Solomon. To underscore this intertextual link, compare Jesus' "cloud" that the disciples saw at his ascension a few days before the events of Pentecost (Acts 1:9).

THE DEPARTURE OF YAHWEH'S SPIRIT FROM THE SOLOMONIC TEMPLE: EZEKIEL 8–11

In relation to what we have discussed above, it is worth mentioning that according to the prophetic visions of Ezekiel, Yahweh's Spirit departed from the Solomonic temple in the years before its destruction (Ezek 8–11).[35] In this vision, the Spirit is personified as a mobile throne with "whirling wheels" (for details see Ezek 10:2, 9–17; compare 1:5–21) and also as a "cloud with brightness around it and fire flashing forth continually" (Ezek 10:3; compare 1:4). With regard to the latter description, the cloud is obviously linked with 1 Kings 8:10–13, and it seems probable that the fire (πυρός, *pyros*, in the LXX) of Ezekiel 1:4 and 10:6 can be connected to the "tongues of fire [*pyros*]" of Acts 2:3.[36]

Besides similar imagery between the depictions of Yahweh's Spirit, Ezekiel's multistep departure of Yahweh's glory/Spirit from the Solomonic temple in Ezekiel 10–11 can be linked to the outpouring of the Holy Spirit at Pentecost. First, before the departure of the Spirit, Ezekiel 11:19–20 indicates that a "new spirit" would be placed within the returning Israelites. This is a clear con-

35. The return of Yahweh's Spirit to the temple (from the Mount of Olives—"coming from the east") is also predicted in Ezek 43:1–9, which is the reverse vision of Ezek 8–11 (compare 43:3). Whether or not this was fulfilled or partially fulfilled at Pentecost is a matter of theological debate that goes beyond the scope of our discussion.

36. Marshall, "Acts," 531–32; see also Darrell L. Bock, *Acts*, 2 vols. (Grand Rapids: Baker Academic, 2007) who in his discussion on Acts 2:2–3 connects Philo's discussion of "fire" in *Decalogue* 11.46 and several Old Testament passages.

nection to Christ's outpouring of the Holy Spirit on Pentecost (Acts 2:33). Second, Ezekiel's address was to those who were "far off among the nations ... those scattered among the nations" (Ezek 11:16), which mirrors the addressees of Peter's sermon in Acts 2:39 (compare Joel 2:32). Third, Jesus ascended from the same location that the Spirit had departed to—the Mount of Olives (Acts 1:12; Ezek 11:22; see also Zech 14:4). Therefore, Jesus' outpouring of the Spirit at Pentecost is a geographical reversal of the Spirit's departure in Ezekiel 8–11. This geographical reversal is all the more intriguing when one considers that after mirroring the path of the Spirit from the Mount of Olives (Jesus, Acts 1:7–11) to the temple courts (Acts 2:1–5), the Spirit entered the disciples instead of reentering through the torn curtain of the holy of holies (Luke 23:45; Matt 27:51; Mark 15:38; compare Heb 10:20), and thereby fulfilled the prediction of the prophets (for example, Ezek 11:19–20).[37]

THE RETURN OF YAHWEH'S SPIRIT IN AND FROM HIS SON: LUKE 3:16; ACTS 2:33

On a related point, there does not appear to be a clear reference to the return of Yahweh's Spirit to Zerubbabel's temple. In my view, there are a number of textual parallels between Ezra 3 and 1 Kings 6–8 and the parallel passage of 2 Chronicles 2–6 (for example, celebration of the Feast of Tabernacles: 1 Kgs 8:2; Ezra 3:4; receiving cedars from Tyre and Sidon via Joppa: 2 Chr 2:16; Ezra 3:7). These parallels likely indicate that Ezra's presentation of the return to and rebuilding of the temple is attempting to follow in the steps of its glorious predecessor. However, these similarities stop abruptly with a huge difference at their conclusion. As we have seen, when Solomon inaugurated the temple (1 Kgs 8:1–12), Yahweh's Spirit filled it and the people rejoiced. However, when the exiles finished inaugurating the temple—just at the point where one would expect to see the theophanic cloud return—nothing supernatural happened. In fact, Ezra 3:12–13 indicates that the "old men" who had seen Solomon's temple wept over the sight of the new one. While it is obviously incorrect to state that Yahweh's Spirit was not active during the Second Temple period, it seems significant that (to my knowledge) no reference is made to the return of Yahweh's Spirit to its former home on Zion.

Against this backdrop, one should pay close attention to the Gospel predictions and depictions of Christ's role in returning the Spirit both to its rightful home (that is, the temple) and its new home (that is, the hearts of his disciples). John the Baptist's announcement of the Messiah who "will baptize you with Holy Spirit and fire" (Luke 3:16; compare John 1:26) is a prediction that was fulfilled in Jesus' outpouring of the Holy Spirit on Pentecost. Luke makes this clear within Peter's appeal at the end of the sermon (Acts 2:38–40), which employs very similar language to Luke 3:16, 21–22. Therefore, in its main context within Luke-Acts, Pentecost serves as the fulfillment of Christ's ultimate destiny that was promised by his forerunner. Still, one must also be attuned to the fact that the Gospel writers depicted Christ's life and minis-

37. A similar geographical connection can be seen in the use of spirit/river imagery flowing from the temple in Joel 3:18; Ezek 47:1–12; Zech 13:1; 14:8 which appear to be some of "the Scriptures" that Jesus was referring to in John 7:37–39.

try as being "filled with the Spirit" following his baptism by John (for example, Matt 4:1; Luke 4:1). As a logical inference, and even though this is never explicitly highlighted in the Gospels, one should not miss that Christ's actions in the temple (for example, Luke 4:9; compare Luke 9:31) represented an actual physical return of God's Spirit to his former residence. Nevertheless, Peter grounds his culminating argument in two great truths that are explicitly tied to location (or geography). First, the risen Jesus was currently seated at the right hand of the throne of God. Second, this Jesus had poured out the Holy Spirit in their midst (Acts 2:32–36).

CONCLUSION

In conclusion, and despite early Christian tradition to the contrary, the events of Pentecost should be entirely localized to the Temple Mount. This localization underscores numerous implied intertextual parallels between the appearances and activities of Yahweh's Spirit from his residences (that is, Sinai, tabernacle, and Jerusalem temple) and the outpouring of Yahweh/Jesus' Spirit upon the disciples in Acts 2. The absence of the Holy Spirit from the temple following its departure (Ezek 11) and the prediction of Christ's "baptism with the Holy Spirit and fire" (Luke 3:16) represent the major turning point in this geographical change from physical to spiritual. Notably, the anointing of the Holy Spirit upon the hearts of the followers of Jesus from Pentecost onward is one of the major pieces of Christ's culminating redemptive work that supersedes the need for a physical, atoning temple with its various cultic protections and rituals (priests, curtains of separation, and the rest) The transformation of the abode of the Spirit from a physical mountain, tent, or building, to a spiritual, sacerdotal people has massive implications for believers. This point is made clear by the temple imagery of Peter (1 Pet 2:9), John (Rev 1:6; 5:10; compare "kingdom of priests" Exod 19:5–6), Paul (1 Cor 6:19), and the writer of Hebrews (especially Heb 9:6–22). Therefore, one can take immense joy when observing the geographical movements of the Holy Spirit that Peter (as recorded by Luke) described and implied during his Acts 2 sermon. In response, we might also, like Solomon did when witnessing Yahweh's cloud filling "the whole house" (1 Kgs 8:27; Acts 2:2), marvel that our uncontainable God through the manifestation of his Spirit would choose to reside in his redeemed people, and thereby make them living, breathing temples of God (see 1 Pet 2:4–5).

BIBLIOGRAPHY

Bock, Darrell L. *Acts*. 2 vols. Grand Rapids: Baker Academic, 2007.

Chou, Abner. *The Hermeneutics of the Biblical Writers: Learning to Interpret Scripture from the Prophets and Apostles*. Grand Rapids: Kregel, 2018.

Clausen, David Christian. "Can the Cenacle on Mount Zion Really Be the 'Upper Room' of Jesus's Last Supper?" *The Bible and Interpretation*, May 2016. http://www.bibleinterp.com/articles/2016/05/cla408003.shtml.

———. *The Upper Room and Tomb of David: The History, Art and Archaeology of the Cenacle on Mount Zion*. Jefferson, NC: McFarland, 2016.

Cyril of Jerusalem. *St. Cyril of Jerusalem's Lectures on the Christian Sacraments: The Procatechesis and the Five Mystagogical Catecheses*. Translated by Frank L. Cross. Crestwood, NY: St. Vladimir's Seminary Press, 1951.

Epiphanius of Salamis. *Epiphanius' Treatise on Weights and Measures: The Syriac Version*. Translated by James E. Dean. Chicago: University of Chicago Press, 1935.

Hoehner, Harold W. *Chronological Aspects of the Life of Christ*. Grand Rapids: Zondervan, 1978.

Keener, Craig S. *Acts: An Exegetical Commentary*. 4 vols. Grand Rapids: Baker Academic, 2012–2015.

———. *The IVP Bible Background Commentary: New Testament*. 2nd ed. Downers Grove, IL: InterVarsity Press, 2014.

Kopp, Clemens. *The Holy Places of the Gospels*. New York: Herder, 1963.

Marshall, I. Howard. "Acts." Pages 513–605 in *Commentary on the New Testament Use of the Old Testament*. Edited by G. K. Beale and D. A. Carson. Grand Rapids: Baker Academic, 2007.

Murphy-O'Connor, Jerome. *The Holy Land: An Oxford Archaeological Guide from Earliest Times to 1700*. 5th ed. Oxford: Oxford University Press, 2008.

Pilgrim of Bordeaux. *Itinerary from Bordeaux to Jerusalem*. Translated by Aubrey Stewart. London: Palestine Pilgrim's Text Society, 1887.

Pinkerfield, J. "'David's Tomb': Notes on the History of the Building: Preliminary Report." *Bulletin of the Louis Rabinowitz Fund for the Exploration of Ancient Synagogues* 3 (1960): 41–43.

Pixner, Bargil. *Paths of the Messiah and Sites of the Early Church from Galilee to Jerusalem: Jesus and Jewish Christianity in Light of Archaeological Discoveries*. San Francisco: Ignatius Press, 2010.

Rainey, Anson F., and R. Steven Notley. *The Sacred Bridge: Carta's Atlas of the Biblical World*. Jerusalem: Carta, 2006.

Reem, Amit. "The Tomb of David on Mount Zion: Theories versus Archaeological Reality." *Hidushim Ba'archiologiyah shel Yerushalayim Usvivoteha* 7 (2013): 175–96 [in Hebrew].

Reem, Amit, and Ilya Berkovich. "New Discoveries in the Cenacle: Reassessing the Art, Architecture and Chronology of the Crusader Basilica on Mount Sion." *New Studies in the Archaeology of Jerusalem and Its Region* 10 (2016): 56*–92*.

Ritmeyer, Leen. *The Quest: Revealing the Temple Mount in Jerusalem*. Jerusalem: Carta, 2006.

Steinsaltz, Adin Even-Israel. "Shabbat 88b." In *William Davidson Talmud*. Jerusalem: Koren, 2017. https://www.sefaria.org/Shabbat.88b.3?lang=bi&with=all&lang2=en.

VanderKam, James C. "Weeks, Feast of." *ABD* 6:895–97.

Witherington, Ben, III. *The Acts of the Apostles: A Socio-Rhetorical Commentary*. Grand Rapids: Eerdmans, 1998.

CHAPTER 7

EARLY CHURCH DEMOGRAPHICS

Acts 2:5–11; 6:1–10; 10:1–45; 19:23–41

Elaine A. Phillips

KEY POINTS

- There was a seamless connection between the array of early Jewish communities inside and outside Jerusalem and the earliest believers in the resurrected Jesus.
- The diversity within the Jewish communities from which the congregations of believers arose reflected geopolitical, sociological, and worldview distinctions.
- Among the new assemblies of believers, there were those of the circumcision party, God-fearing gentiles, and full-fledged proselytes.

INTRODUCTION

From the outset, the early groups of believers in Jerusalem were "untidily diverse."[1] This is not a surprise; Zion was the spiritual home and pilgrimage destination for Jews and admirers of Judaism from all points of the known world. Luke depicts both the worlds from which the Jewish faithful came as well as their allegiances in Jerusalem. These serve as backdrops for the emergence of the communities of those whose lives were transformed by the risen Christ and who would be "witnesses ... even to the ends of the earth" (Acts 1:8).[2] These earliest Christian communities did not perceive a boundary line between themselves and their fellow Jews.[3] Instead, ethnicities and social placement were more visible.

1. Craig C. Hill, *Hellenists and Hebrews: Reappraising Division within the Earliest Church* (Minneapolis: Fortress, 1992), 4.

2. Unless otherwise noted, all Scripture translations are from the NRSV.

3. James D. G. Dunn, *Unity and Diversity in the New Testament: An Inquiry into the Character of Earliest Christianity*, 2nd ed. (London: SCM, 1990), 239. As two representative samples

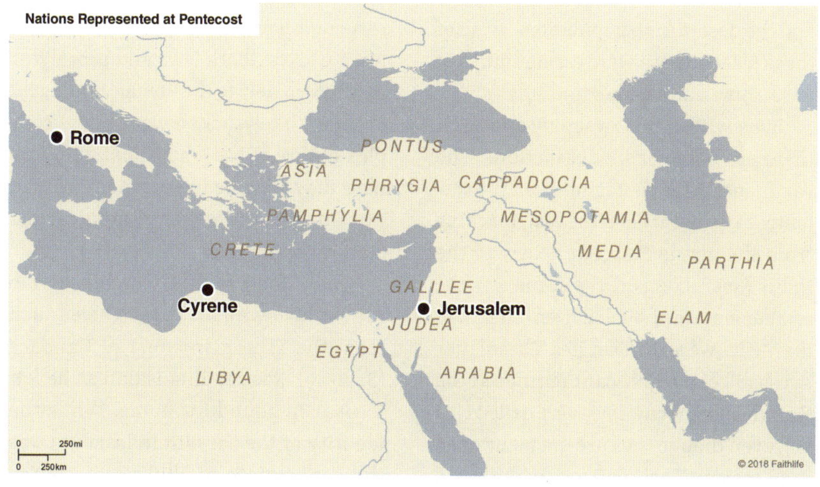

JEWS "FROM EVERY NATION UNDER HEAVEN" (ACTS 2:5–11; 8:26–39)

The Feast of Weeks (Pentecost) was one of the three pilgrim festivals during which God's faithful people were to appear before the Lord (Deut 16:9–12). That may partially explain the cosmopolitan nature of those who were present in Jerusalem (2:5–11),[4] unaware that they were on the cusp of an entirely transformative event. The "attendance list" is multifaceted and selective. In broad strokes, Luke subtly crosses the divide between eastern regions characteristically at enmity with the Roman Empire, and western provinces under Rome's sway. He places Judea, geopolitically vulnerable on the eastern fringes of the Roman Empire, in between these two groups. Further, he singles out the city of Rome as it represented in the minds of his audience "the ends of the earth" (1:8). As a geographical postscript, he adds Crete as a significant island entity

of the complex issues involved, see Joel Marcus, "Jewish Christianity," and Margaret M. Mitchell, "Gentile Christianity," in *The Cambridge History of Christianity: Origins to Constantine*, edited by Margaret M. Mitchell and Frances M. Young (Cambridge: Cambridge University Press, 2006), 87–102, 103–24.

4. There are those who think that these were primarily not pilgrims but diaspora Jews who had returned to live in Jerusalem. See Ben Witherington III, *The Acts of the Apostles: A Socio-Rhetorical Commentary* (Grand Rapids: Eerdmans, 1998), 135–36; and Richard N. Longenecker, "Acts," in *Expositor's Bible Commentary*, ed. Tremper Longman III and David E. Garland, rev. ed. (Grand Rapids: Zondervan, 2007), 736–37. In response, however, the same descriptive participle (κατοικοῦντες, *katoikountes*, "inhabiting, living in, staying") appears in both verses 5 and 9. Verse 9 references "those living in Mesopotamia, Judea, and Cappadocia" who were among the throngs in Jerusalem. Further, the *katoikountes* of verse 5 also included "visitors from Rome" (2:10).

and the desert Arab populations. In all of these places, there were communities of Jews, some quite long-standing.[5]

Even within this sweeping approach, there are noteworthy distinctions. The Parthians, listed first, embodied the contemporary threat from the east, reaching from the fertile crescent nearly to the Indus River. Long off the scene was the smaller empire of Media. Even older than the Medes were the Elamites. These latter two had been significant entities at the time the northern tribes were exiled (722 BC), even though they are not mentioned in 2 Kings 17.[6] Their memory in the broad geographical context of "Mesopotamia" no doubt persisted. While some skepticism has been expressed regarding the surprise of the Judeans in this Jewish context, the point is that the speakers were Galileans, a distinction observed by Judeans, perhaps with some regional conceit.[7]

Turning to the west, the Roman provinces listed start with Cappadocia in the east, move north to Pontus, west to Asia, and south to Pamphylia. Phrygia was an ancient ethnicity crossing several first century provincial boundaries. North Africa (Egypt and Cyrene) completed the picture of the Mediterranean as a "Roman lake," closed by "visitors from Rome" itself. Because they are specifically noted as "visitors," it is likely that they returned home bearing witness to the risen Christ. "Both Jews and proselytes" may refer solely to the Roman contingent or, more likely, acknowledges the complex nature of the whole audience. And here they all were in Jerusalem. We can just imagine the welter of political and cultural exchanges!

One of these faithful worshipers warranted his own narrative. The eunuch from the Ethiopian court of Candace (8:26–39) was reading Isaiah as he left Jerusalem bound for home. While the identity of the Servant in Isaiah 53 was the centerpiece of Philip's discourse, the wider Isaianic context is striking. Eunuchs and foreigners who joined themselves to the Lord would be given an everlasting name (Isa 56:1–8), a heartening promise against the backdrop of his marginalized status (Deut 23:1).[8]

Additional named representatives of Judaism's diaspora included Barnabas, a Levite (4:36), and Mnason, both from Cyprus (21:16).

AN EARLY CONFRONTATION IN JERUSALEM: HELLENISTS VS. HEBRAISTS (ACTS 6:1–10; 9:29; 11:20[9])

On what basis were these two groups divided to the point of requiring intervention from the leadership of all the disciples

5. M. Stern, "The Jewish Diaspora," in *The Jewish People in the First Century: Historical Geography, Political History, Social, Cultural and Religious Life and Institutions*, ed. S. Safrai and M. Stern (Assen: Van Gorcum, 1974), 117–83.

6. They were among Jeremiah's list of those to whom the cup of God's wrath would be given (Jer 25:25).

7. John 7:52 records a similar disdain for Galilee on the part of residents of Jerusalem.

8. Whether "eunuch" in this context simply meant "court official" or implied his physical condition, the label undoubtedly carried a stigma.

9. There are textual variants in regard to Acts 11:20; some of the earliest and best manuscripts read *Hellēnas* (Ἕλληνας) in place of *Hellēnistas* (Ἑλληνιστάς). This may be because the context clearly indicates these were non-Jews.

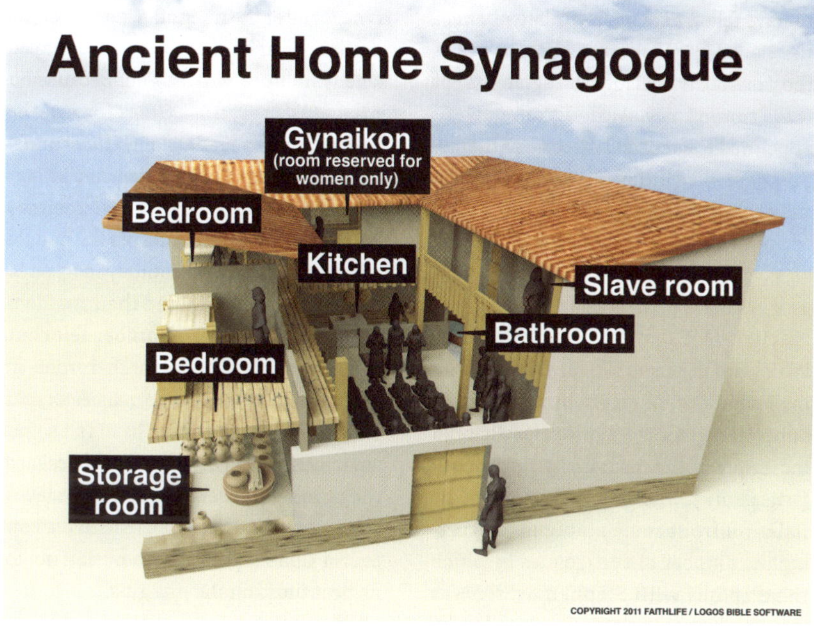

in Jerusalem (6:1)? A common interpretation, going back to John Chrysostom, has focused on language. Diaspora Jews living in Jerusalem worshiped in a Greek-language environment, while those native to Jerusalem spoke Hebrew (or Aramaic).[10] Embedded, however, in these language environments were also worldviews, some shaped by the philosophy, literature, and language of the Greco-Roman world,[11] and the others by deep allegiance to torah and all that involved. In the worshiping assemblies, some traditional and some less so, the dialogue would have been ongoing and vibrant. The complexity of the situation is demonstrated by Paul himself, a native of Cilicia who spoke Greek, and yet referred to himself as a Hebrew of the Hebrews, a Pharisee in terms of interpretation of the law, and zealous for the covenant (Phil 3:4–7; see also 2 Cor 11:22). Early on, he argued with Hellenists in Jerusalem (9:29) who seemed to be contending for a more traditional interpretation of their Judaism.

In the context of Acts 6, the point is that the Hellenists had separate synagogues because worship was in Greek. This isolation meant that structures intended to assist vulnerable members of all the Jewish communities had broken down; in particular, care of widows was neglected. If the names of the seven subsequently chosen for ministry (6:5) reflect their cultural background, the task seems

10. Witherington, *Acts of the Apostles*, 242. The term, Hellenists, does not appear in other contemporary literature. See Longenecker, "Acts," 802–5, for the range of suggested interpretations.

11. It reflected their "intellectual orientation" (Longenecker, "Acts," 804). See also Dunn, *Unity and Diversity*, 268–70.

to have fallen exclusively to members of the Hellenist group, those best aware of the previously overlooked segment(s) of their community. Although they were appointed to serve, at least two of them—Stephen and Philip—also spoke powerfully as witnesses for Jesus.[12]

WHO ATTENDED WHICH SYNAGOGUES? (ACTS 6:9; 13:42–52; 17:4,12)

Who were the members of these gatherings where Stephen encountered such opposition? As we explore additional indicators of the cosmopolitan nature of Jerusalem's Jewish communities, we initially confront some ambiguity regarding the number of synagogues in which the disputes with Stephen arose. Was there only one, primarily attended by freedmen from a range of Roman provinces? Or does the verse imply two synagogues, one of freedmen from Cyrene and Alexandria, and a second of those from Cilicia and Asia? Some even contend that there were five separate synagogues.[13] In any case, Stephen met vigorous opposition coming from traditional Hellenists.

SOCIAL STRATIFICATIONS[14]

In this vibrant context, Luke chose to highlight Stephen's confrontation in the synagogue of the freedmen, possibly hinting at a social boundary that also shaped who worshiped with whom. Because *libertinos* (Λιβερτῖνος) is a Greek form of the Latin word for freed slaves (*lībertīnus*), and because it is here connected to specific place names, this synagogue may have included descendants of people taken into slavery by Pompey in 63 BC to Rome.[15] Once they gained their freedom, perhaps a significant number felt compelled to relocate and plant their roots in Zion, the homeland of their ancestors. At the same time, they may have felt somewhat marginalized. We cannot disregard the parallel between these freed slaves and Israel's own heritage, read in the context of God's repeated admonition not to neglect those on the margins.

Moving outside Jerusalem and into the first missionary enterprise, Luke notes that Jews in Pisidian Antioch incited prominent women and men of the city against Paul (13:50), suggesting that segments of the Jewish population were influential in civil affairs. On a positive note, Jewish synagogues in Thessalonica and Berea also included prominent women and men (17:4,12), many of whom believed the words of Paul and Silas.

---

12. This possibly points to an additional separation between the two groups. If the core leaders remained devoted to teaching the Hebrew-speaking gatherings, then it was necessary for Stephen—and later Philip—to teach *their* people (Longenecker, "Acts," 812).

13. Two seems the best interpretation, based on the use of *tōn* (τῶν) introducing each group (H. Strathmann, "Λιβερτῖνοι," *TDNT* 4:265–66).

14. See Witherington, *Acts of the Apostles*, 210–13, who suggests that Luke is more mindful of social status in the early church, perhaps because he was writing to Theophilus, a person of presumably higher social standing.

15. Strathmann, "Λιβερτῖνοι," 265. Regarding Caesar Augustus, Philo noted, "He was aware that the great section of Rome on the other side of the Tiber is occupied and inhabited by Jews, most of whom were Roman citizens emancipated. For having been brought as captives to Italy they were liberated by their owners" (*On the Embassy to Gaius*, 155). According to Suetonius, for a period of time *libertini* referred not to individuals who themselves were set free, but to their sons (*Claudius*, 5.24).

"Jews and God-fearers" Inscription on a Theater Seat at Miletus

LOCATIONS OF ORIGIN

Coming from the coast of northern Africa, Cyrenians and Alexandrians may have shared sufficient cultural characteristics to worship together.[16] The same might have been true of Cilicia and Asia. Whatever specific contexts they represented, they were united in their opposition to Stephen, being thoroughly persuaded of their received Jewish heritage and ruffled by Stephen's teaching.

LEVELS OF ALLEGIANCE TO THE GOD OF ISRAEL: THE DEVOUT, THE GOD-FEARERS, AND THE CONVERTS (10:1–45; 13:16, 26; 16:11–15; 17:17; 18:7)

There is an enormous amount of literature devoted to these related groups. The issues are complex, particularly as there were inevitably multiple levels of attraction to and participation in Judaism. Those who were "devout" were also those who had a healthy fear of God. Just what was involved in the further commitment of conversion seems to have differed depending on location in space and time. Nevertheless, one feature seems relatively stable; even though (male) converts underwent circumcision, adopted practices of the Torah, and eschewed idolatry, they were still generally called proselytes and viewed as separate from Jews by those who were Jews.[17] Some of these individuals, though not all, would come to belief in the risen Lord as Paul and his companions preached in the synagogues strategically located throughout the Roman provinces in Asia Minor and Greece.

---

16. Josephus (referencing Strabo) indicated the close relationship of organized Jewish groups in Egypt and Cyrene. In Alexandria, a great part of the city was given over to the Jewish community (*Ant.*, 14:110–118). The particular importance of Cyrene might also be suggested by the mention of Niger, a friend of Herod from Cyrene (13:1).

17. See Shaye J. D. Cohen, "Crossing the Boundary and Becoming a Jew," *Harvard Theological Review* 82 (1989):13–33; and Scot McKnight, "Proselytism and Godfearers," in *Dictionary of New Testament Backgrounds*, ed. Craig A. Evans and Stanley E. Porter (Downers Grover, IL: InterVarsity Press, 2000), 835–47.

Pool on the Gangites River, Possible Location of Lydia's Baptism

THE DEVOUT AND THE GOD-FEARERS[18]

The adjective *eusebēs* (εὐσεβής, "devout") describes those individuals who were attracted to Judaism. Among them was Cornelius, a Roman centurion who gave to the poor, prayed, and whose household joined him in his devotion to God (10:2). Cornelius also feared (φοβέω, *phobeō*) God (10:22); friends and relatives close to him respected him sufficiently to gather when he summoned them to hear Peter (10:24). Peter's address would have brought great encouragement, affirming that God-fearers found favor with God (10:35).

God-fearers in the synagogues throughout the Mediterranean world provided the ready audience for Paul in his missionary journeys. Speaking in the synagogue in Antioch in Pisidia, he acknowledged the presence of men of Israel—also calling them sons of Abraham—and "you who fear God" (13:16, 26).

Lydia, *sebomenē ton theon* (σεβομένη τὸν θεόν, "devoted to God") and a wealthy merchant, was attending a riverside prayer service in Philippi, heard Paul speak and was baptized (16:14). When Paul and Silas moved along to Thessalonica, they encountered prominent individuals, some of whom were also among the devout (σεβομένων, *sebomenōn*) Greeks (17:4). Upon his arrival in Athens, Paul reasoned in the synagogue with the Jews and with the devout persons (σεβομένοις, *sebomenois*) who were also there (17:17). His reception in the Jewish community of Corinth was significantly less friendly, so he went to the house of Titius Justus, a person who worshiped (σεβομένου, *sebomenou*) God (18:7). It just so happened that his house was next-door to the synagogue.

There continued to be some naysayers. The aforementioned women of high-standing in Pisidian Antioch were

18. With specific reference to Antioch, Josephus noted that the Jews were "constantly attracting to their religious ceremonies multitudes of Greeks, and these they had in some measure incorporated with themselves" (*J.W.* 7.45).

also devout, but were caught up in the efforts to run Paul and Barnabas out of town (13:50).

PROSELYTES[19]

Proselytes (προσήλυτος, *prosēlytos*) were generally viewed as full-fledged converts to Judaism, accepting the yoke of the Torah, most notably circumcision for men. Nevertheless, the three narratives in Acts that specify proselytes characteristically distinguish them from Jews, perhaps a subtle but persistent status indicator. They were present at Pentecost (2:11). One of the Hellenists chosen to serve at table was Nicolaus, a proselyte from Antioch, last in the list (6:5). "Jews and devout proselytes" to Judaism heard Paul and Barnabas with enthusiasm (13:43), even though the following Sabbath the tide of Jewish opinion turned against them (13:45).

DISTINCTIONS AND SELF-DESIGNATIONS IN THE EMERGING CHURCH (19:23–41; 22:3–5; 24:4–27)

DISCIPLES

While the term "disciples" (μαθητής, *mathētēs*) appears frequently in the Gospels and Acts, it is absent from the rest of the New Testament. The Greek term was widely used as early as the sixth century BC, referring to one who learned by following a way of life set forth by the master. Although an equivalent word in Hebrew does not surface frequently, the concept was common in Jewish sources.[20]

Luke likely employed "disciples" to indicate continuity from the Gospel narratives—"disciples of Jesus"—to the geographical spread of the early Christian movement through the Roman world.[21] Christians did not refer to themselves this way; they tended to use "brothers" (ἀδελφοί, *adelphoi*). Perhaps Paul did not use "disciples" because it did not say *enough* in terms of the radical transformation resulting from belief in the risen Savior and participation in the Body of Christ. The "disciples of the Teacher," as portrayed in the Gospels, now served and witnessed to their risen Lord.[22]

BELIEVERS AMONG TRADITIONAL JEWS

In two instances, this group is simply designated "believers among the circumcised" (10:45) or "those of the circumcision" (11:2) who were critical of Peter. It is instructive to return briefly to the response to Peter's sermon at Pentecost. Three thou-

---

19. Jewish communities reflected in later rabbinic literature recognized those who were attracted to the God of Israel. While the majority of rabbinic texts view proselytes with favor, there were those who disdained these converts (McKnight, "Proselytism and Godfearers," 840–42). In an extensive discourse on Exod 22:20 ("you shall not afflict or oppress the stranger"), the rabbis read *gerim* (גרים, "strangers") as proselytes, beloved in every respect as the Israelites were. This specific meaning—converts—developed after the close of the biblical period. At the end of the pericope, *yr 'y hshmym* (יראי השמים, "those who fear heaven") are distinguished from the categories of "beloved strangers" (*Mekilta de-Rabbi Ishmael* Nezikin 18).

20. Paul Trebilco, *Self-designations and Group Identity in the New Testament* (Cambridge: Cambridge University Press, 2012), 208–13.

21. Jerusalem (6:1–7; 9:1, 26; 15:10); Damascus (9:10, 19, 25—here "Paul's disciples"); Joppa (9:38); Antioch on the Orontes (11:26, 29; 14:28); Antioch in Pisidia (13:52); Lystra and Derbe (14:20–22; 16:1); Galatia and Phrygia (18:23); Achaia (18:27); Ephesus (19:1, 9, 30; 20:1, 30); Tyre (21:4); Caesarea (21:16).

22. Trebilco, *Self-designations and Group Identity*, 225–32.

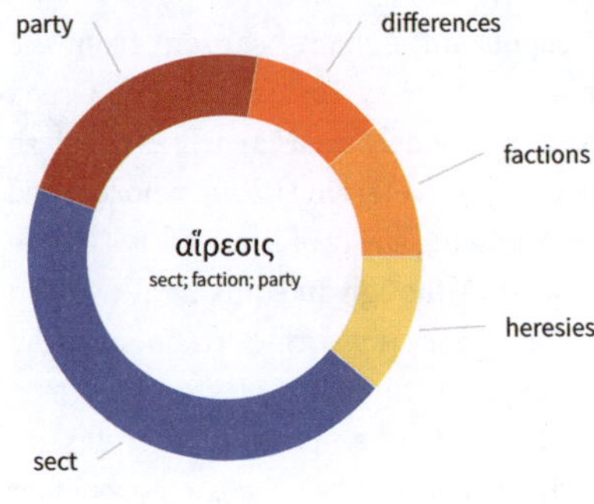

sand of the "house of Israel" were baptized, devoted themselves to study and fellowship, attended the temple, and were steadily joined by additional believers (2:36–47). These would constitute the backbone of the Jerusalem group, whether Hellenists or Hebraists. No wonder they had a high profile in the context of the outpouring of the Spirit on the gentiles and in the aftermath of that event, the critical discussion in Jerusalem about the status of these gentiles (Acts 15). The group coalesced at this point; Luke called them "certain ones from the party [αἱρέσεως, *haireseōs*] of the Pharisees" (15:5). *Hairesis* (αἵρεσις) occasionally carried a negative connotation, implying "sect" or "heresy"; Paul was accused of being a figurehead for the "sect" of the Nazareans (24:5). At the same time, against the wider Jewish Hellenistic backdrop, the word simply meant "school"[23] and signified social identity around meaningful teaching.

THE WAY

As the Church moved forward, a new descriptive label appears to have become well-known in short order. Saul, an outsider when we first encounter him, was pursuing men and women still affiliated with the synagogue who belonged to "the way" (9:1–2). He persecuted those faithful to "this way" to death (22:4). His own later declaration of commitment reveals the substance of their belief—he worshiped "the God of our fathers, believing everything laid down by the Law and written in the Prophets, having a hope in God … that there will be a resurrection of both the just and the unjust" (24:14–15). Their affirmations were not aberrant, even though outsiders called them a "sect" (verse 14).[24] Felix, in whose presence Paul made this statement, also knew the group as "the way" (24:22).

Luke's narrative of the events in Ephesus provides further indication that believers were increasingly known as "the way." After Paul taught in the synagogue for three months, they were the target of hostile opposition. Paul moved to the hall of Tyrannus, a public forum for teaching the word of the Lord (19:8–10). During those two years, his public rout of the magic industry and condemnation of idolatry prompted a major disturbance against "the way" (19:23–41).[25]

Because "way" is laced throughout the Old Testament and was common in daily first-century usage, it was a perfect identifier for the growing church. In the Old Testament, God's people were repeatedly admonished to choose the "way of righteousness," and walk in the "way of Torah." The signature passage, both for the Qumran community and for the

23. Heinrich Schlier, "Αἵρεσις," *TDNT* 1:180–184.

24. This framed the matter in "us" versus "them" terms (Trebilco, *Self-designations and Group Identity*, 248).

25. The prior arrival of Apollos—rhetorically polished, knowing "the way of the Lord," but needing further instruction in "the way of God"—may also be part of the back story (18:25–26).

Gospel narratives, was Isa 40:3–5. For the former, their study and practice of torah would prepare the way of the Lord; for the latter, the preparation was John the Baptist's declaration that Jesus was the Way in whom the glory of the Lord would be revealed.[26] There were further implications; followers of Jesus were to take the way Jesus walked. Thus, "way" became "theological shorthand, expressing their conviction about who Jesus was—the Way, the Truth, and the Life—and the significance of following him."[27]

ALREADY A "GLOBAL" CHURCH

We perhaps tend to think of our own generation's church as global in ways that it has never been in prior centuries. Nevertheless, this brief survey of the remarkably diverse backgrounds, beliefs, and affirmations of the church depicted in Acts may disabuse us of that notion. We are also reminded that differences led to fractiousness then just as they do now. Despite varying party allegiances, however, the terms that consistently recur are "brothers" (that is, family members), "believers" in the transforming power of the resurrected Christ and His Holy Spirit, and followers of "the way." Both insiders and outsiders recognized these extraordinary assemblies were radically different as they journeyed on the path set before them, led by Jesus—the Way to the Father, the embodiment of Truth, and the Source of Life everlasting.

BIBLIOGRAPHY

Cohen, Shaye J. D. "Crossing the Boundary and Becoming a Jew." *Harvard Theological Review* 82 (1989): 13–33.

Dunn, James G. D. *Unity and Diversity in the New Testament: An Inquiry into the Character of Earliest Christianity*. 2nd edition. London: SCM, 1990.

Hill, Craig C. *Hellenists and Hebrews: Reappraising Division within the Earliest Church*. Minneapolis: Fortress, 1992.

Josephus. *The Jewish War; Jewish Antiquities*. Translated by H. St. J. Thackeray et al. 9 vols. LCL. Cambridge: Harvard University Press, 1926–1965.

Lauterbach, Jacob Z., ed. *Mekilta de-Rabbi Ishmael*. 3 vols. Philadelphia: Jewish Publication Society, 1976.

Longenecker, Richard N. "Acts." In *Expositor's Bible Commentary*. Edited by Tremper Longman III and David E. Garland. Revised ed. Grand Rapids: Zondervan, 2007.

Marcus, Joel. "Jewish Christianity." Pages 87–102 in *The Cambridge History of Christianity: Volume 1 Origins to Constantine*. Edited by Margaret M. Mitchell and Frances M. Young. Cambridge: Cambridge University Press, 2006.

McKnight, Scot. "Proselytism and Godfearers." Pages 835–47 in *Dictionary of New Testament Backgrounds*. Edited by Craig A. Evans and Stanley E. Porter. Downers Grover, IL: InterVarsity Press, 2000.

Mitchell, Margaret M. "Gentile Christianity." Pages 103–24 in *The Cambridge History of Christianity: Origins to Constantine*. Edited by Margaret M. Mitchell and Frances M. Young. Cambridge: Cambridge University Press, 2006.

26. Trebilco, *Self-designations and Group Identity*, 249–55.

27. Trebilco, *Self-designations and Group Identity*, 266.

Philo. *On the Embassy to Gaius*. Translated by F. H. Colson. LCL 379. Cambridge: Harvard University Press, 1962.

Schlier, Heinrich. "Αἵρεσις." *TDNT* 1:180–84.

Strathmann, H. "Λιβερτῖνοι." *TDNT* 4:265–66.

Stern, M. "The Jewish Diaspora." Pages 117–83 in *The Jewish People in the First Century: Historical Geography, Political History, Social, Cultural and Religious Life and Institutions*. Edited by S. Safrai and M. Stern. Assen: Van Gorcum, 1974.

Suetonius. *The Lives of the Caesars*. Translated by J. C. Rolfe. 2 vols. LCL. Cambridge: Harvard University Press, 1914.

Trebilco, Paul. *Self-designations and Group Identity in the New Testament*. Cambridge: Cambridge University Press, 2012.

Witherington, Ben, III. *The Acts of the Apostles: A Socio-Rhetorical Commentary*. Grand Rapids: Eerdmans, 1998.

CHAPTER 8

GEOGRAPHY OF THE NATIONS IN JERUSALEM FOR PENTECOST

Acts 2:7–11

Paul H. Wright

KEY POINTS

- Acts 2:9–10 provides a representative list of diaspora Jewish communities.
- Jews of the diaspora never lost their tie to the land of Israel where their ancestors had first encountered God.
- The act of pilgrimage for festivals like Pentecost kept the diaspora Jews connected to the land of Israel.
- Only about 1 percent of diaspora Jews traveled to Jerusalem for one of the pilgrimage festivals each time one was celebrated.

PENTECOST AND PILGRIMAGE FESTIVALS

Pentecost (Greek πεντηκοστή, *pentēkostē*, "fiftieth," or Hebrew שָׁבֻעוֹת, *Shavuot*, "weeks"), is the second of the great pilgrimage festivals in the annual calendar of ancient Israel. Originally, *Shavuot* celebrated the end of the wheat harvest fifty days (seven weeks plus one day) after Passover (Lev 23:15–21). By the time of the New Testament, Pentecost had also come to mark the covenant that God made with Israel through Moses on Mount Sinai (Jubilees 6:17–19).[1] The calendar sequence and the grand narrative of Israel's founding national epic both frame Pentecost by two other pilgrimage festivals. These are Passover (Hebrew פֶּסַח, *Pesach*) at the beginning of the barley harvest in early spring marking Israel's exodus from Egypt, and Tabernacles or Booths (Hebrew סֻכּוֹת, *Sukkoth*) at the time when the summer fruit is gathered after a rainless summer, recalling God's provision of Israel during

1. M. D. Herr, "The Calendar," in *The Jewish People in the First Century*, ed. Shmuel Safrai and Menahem Stern (Assen: Van Gorcum, 1974), 2:858–60.

their forty years of wilderness wandering (see the chart of the Israelite festival calendar on page 697).

The celebration of these festivals in the diaspora corresponded to the agricultural cycle in the land of Israel, even if that cycle was out of sync with the growing seasons in other parts of the Jewish world. Although Jews living in the diaspora, outside of the historic borders of the land of Israel, tended to assimilate to the larger languages and cultures of the peoples among whom they lived, most, at their core, continued to consider themselves as "Hebrews living abroad."[2] The differences between Judaism in Judea and diaspora Judaism were matters of degree, not of kind. The Jews of the diaspora were unique among peoples of the ancient world in that, in spite of centuries of physical absence from their homeland, they never lost their tie to the places where their ancestors had first encountered God.[3] The Jews' sacred scriptures, the Hebrew Bible, were fully integrated with their forefathers' experiences in the land of Israel. The Holy City of Jerusalem was their compass, their blueprint, the tangible map by which a Jew knew how to be a Jew wherever he or she lived, a place of roots that would not die. Even though Philo and the earliest writers of the Sibylline Oracles were natives of Alexandria, their writings focused on Jerusalem and the temple rather than edifices on their own Egyptian soil. In describing the extent of the diaspora, for instance, Philo states:

> As for the holy city, I must say what befits me to say. While she [Jerusalem], as I have said, is my native city she is also the mother city not of one country, Judea, but of most of the others in virtue of the colonies sent out at diverse times to the neighboring lands.[4]

The growth of the local synagogue in the diaspora communities kept the Jewish identity alive by focusing its liturgical and educational role, which was centered on the holidays, on Jerusalem. Because the Sanhedrin functioned as the high court for Jewish life even in the diaspora, it was Jerusalem that determined the first day of each new year, thereby fixing the days when all Jews would together celebrate the three pilgrimage festivals, regardless of their place of residence.[5] Indeed, the act of pilgrimage welded the diaspora Jews to

---

2. Here the literature, both primary and secondary, is vast. See, for instance, Menahem Stern, "The Jewish Diaspora," in Safrai, *The Jewish People in the First Century*, 1:117–83; Shmuel Safrai, "Relations between the Diaspora and the Land of Israel," in Safrai, *The Jewish People in the First Century*, 1:184–215; Emil Schürer, *The History of the Jewish People in the Age of Jesus Christ*, rev. Géza Vermès, Fergus Millar, and Martin Goodman (Edinburgh: T&T Clark, 1986), 3.1:1–176; Victor Tcherikover, *Hellenistic Civilization and the Jews*, trans. S. Applebaum (New York: Atheneum, 1979), 269–377; Rachel Hachlili, *Ancient Jewish Art and Archaeology in the Diaspora* (Leiden: Brill, 1998), 11–12; Oskar Skarsaune, *In the Shadow of the Temple: Jewish Influences on Early Christianity* (Downers Grove, IL: InterVarsity Press, 2002), 23–102; and Leonard V. Rutgers, *The Jews in Late Ancient Rome: Evidence of Cultural Interaction in the Roman Diaspora* (Leiden: Brill, 1995).

3. Robert L. Wilken, *The Land Called Holy: Palestine in Christian History and Thought* (New Haven, CT: Yale University Press, 1992), 21.

4. Philo, *Embassy to Gaius* 281 (LCL).

5. S. Safrai, "Relations between the Diaspora," 204–7.

the land of Israel—and, because it was an experience shared across the diaspora, it bound Jewish communities in the diaspora to each other as well.[6]

While there is no evidence that the three great pilgrimage festivals were celebrated on a regular basis during the time of the Old Testament—in fact, the writer of Chronicles admits that Passover in Jerusalem was celebrated rather infrequently (2 Chron 30:1–3, 26; 35:18)—by the first century AD they had become major events in Jerusalem. In the process, that city, a place otherwise tucked into the dry hills of Rome's southeastern frontier, grew to become a bustling, cosmopolitan center where a jumble of languages from across the known world could be heard. (The same holds true today.) Michael Avi-Yonah estimates that the diaspora numbered five million persons in the first century, one-fifth of whom lived in Egypt.[7] The population of Judea (including Samaria and Galilee) was about half that of the diaspora, with approximately fifty thousand to one hundred thousand people calling Jerusalem home. Scholars generally estimate that Jerusalem's population doubled during the pilgrimage festivals, in effect bringing about 1 percent of diaspora Jewry to the city each time they were celebrated.[8] From the point of view of the residents of Jerusalem, this was a lot of people; if we would ask anyone among the 99 percent who stayed home, likely they would say that hardly anyone made the trip, but held in especially high regard those who did.

Remains of Synagogue at Dura-Europos

THE GEOGRAPHICAL LIST OF ACTS 2:9–10

It is with this context that the crowds celebrating the Pentecost that followed the Passover punctuated by the first Easter filled Jerusalem with a babel of languages from across the diaspora (see map on page 95). Acts 2:9–10 gives a list of peoples and places present that day: "Parthians, Medes and Elamites, and residents of Mesopotamia, Judea and Cappadocia, Pontus and Asia, Phrygia and Pamphylia, Egypt and the parts of Libya near Cyrene, visitors from Rome (both Jews and converts to Judaism), Cretans and Arabs."[9]

Textual and archaeological sources reveal that all of these regions had Jewish communities at the time of the New Testament. The data are plentiful; a brief survey of even a selection of data related to the peoples and places mentioned in Acts 2 gives us a map and an approximate timeline of the spread of the diaspora by the time of the New Testament.

---

6. S. Safrai, "Relations between the Diaspora," 203.

7. Michael Avi-Yonah, "Historical Geography of Palestine," in Safrai, *The Jewish People in the First Century*, 1:108–9.

8. Skarsaune, *In the Shadow of the Temple*, 91.

9. Unless otherwise noted, Scripture quotations are from the New International Version (NIV).

PARTHIANS

The Parthian Empire encompassed lands of the ancient Near East that lay east of Roman control, including the Persian plateau and Mesopotamia. Most of the Jews under Parthian control lived in Babylon (southern Mesopotamia) and the plain of Elam to the east, where the Jewish community dated back to the exile in the early sixth century BC (2 Kgs 25:11; 2 Chron 36:20; Jer 52:15, 25–26; Ezek 1:1–3).[10] Others lived among the Medes north and east of Babylon, likely remnants of the dispersion of the northern kingdom of Israel (2 Kgs 17:6; 18:11), and the exile of Nebuchadnezzar (Jer 25:25; Esth 1:19; Tob 3:7). Josephus mentioned Jewish communities in Nisibis and Nearda/Nehardea on the Euphrates (*Ant.* 18.312, 379), Charax Spasinu near the Persian Gulf (*Ant.* 20.43) and Seleucia and Ctesiphon on the Tigris (*Ant.* 18.374, 377), noting that in Babylon there were "countless myriads [of Jews] whose number cannot be ascertained" (*Ant.* 11.133; 15.39). Cuneiform sources also attest to a Jewish presence in various Babylonian cities as early as the sixth century BC.[11] Among these are texts that record the agribusiness activities of four generations of the Jewish Murashu family in the fifth and sixth centuries BC. Perhaps the most complete archaeological finds for the diaspora anywhere are the remains of the buildings and syna-

10. Schürer, *History of the Jewish People,* 3.1:5–10; Stern, "Jewish Diaspora," 170–79.

11. Ran Zadok, *The Jews in Babylonia during the Chaldean and Achaemenian Periods according to the Babylonian Sources* (Haifa: University of Haifa, 1979).

gogue at Dura-Europos.[12] Situated at a busy crossroads on the mid-Euphrates, this city alone could have counted for many of the languages of Pentecost, as inscriptional evidence attests to Greek, Latin, Aramaic, Hebrew, Syriac, Middle Persian, Palmyrene, and Safaitic spoken by residents of the city.

ANATOLIA (ASIA MINOR)

Sources also attest to a Jewish presence in many of the regions of Anatolia.[13] Most frequently mentioned are various cities in the western province of Asia Minor proper, including Ephesus, Miletus, Pergamum, Thyatira, and Smyrna. Josephus spoke of Jews living in Sardis as early as the fourth century BC (*Ag. Ap.* 1.179; 2.39); the impressive archaeological remains of a synagogue there postdate the time of the New Testament. Josephus also mentioned that Antiochus III (early second century BC) moved two thousand Jewish families from Babylon to Phrygia, a district straddling Asia Minor and Galatia (*Ant.* 12.148–149). Attested diaspora communities in Phrygia include Laodicea, Hierapolis, and Apamea. Philo referred to Jews dwelling in Pamphylia, a province on the southern Anatolian coast, and in remote places such as Pontus on the coast of the Black Sea (*Embassy to Gaius* 281). Inscriptional evidence supports Philo's claims. That Jews lived in Cappadocia, in central and eastern Anatolia, is confirmed by various passages in the Mishnah and Talmud (m. Ketuboth 13:11; y. Yebamoth 16.4; y. Shebiith 9.5; y. Pe'ah 1.4; y. Kilaim 8.1; y. Shabbath 2.2), and from Josephus' account that Alexander, son of Herod the Great, married a Cappadocian princess (*Ant.* 16.11).

Outer Courtyard of Synagogue at Sardis

EGYPT

The diaspora presence was strongest in Egypt,[14] with Jews forming the majority population in two of Alexandria's five districts by the first century AD (Philo, *Flaccus* 55). Judeans had originally fled to Egypt to avoid exile to Babylon (Jer 43:5–44:30), although there is some evidence to posit a Judean military colony there a century earlier. The Elephantine papyri, dating from the sixth to the early fourth centuries BC, include letters and legal texts sent between Jerusalem and the Jewish community in Elephantine, a Nile island in Upper Egypt at modern Aswan. These letters mention a Jewish

12. Fergus Millar, *The Roman Near East, 31 BC–AD 337* (Cambridge: Harvard University Press, 1993), 445–52; Hachlili, *Ancient Art and Archaeology*, 39–45, and passim.

13. Schürer, *History of the Jewish People*, 3.1:17–38; Tcherikover, *Hellenistic Civilization and the Jews*, 287–89; Stern, "Jewish Diaspora," 143–57.

14. Schürer, *History of the Jewish People*, 3.1:38–60; Tcherikover, *Hellenistic Civilization and the Jews*, 269–87; Stern, "Jewish Diaspora," 122–33.

temple in Elephantine, destroyed in the late fifth century BC but then rebuilt.[15] A second Jewish temple, built by the Jerusalem high priest Onias III in the second century BC, stood at Leontopolis (Tell el-Yehudiah) in the province of Heliopolis, in the southeastern Nile delta (*J.W.* 1.33; 7.423). Both were places of sacrifice, yet their presence seems not to have minimized the role of Jerusalem for the Egyptian diaspora. The Hebrew Bible was translated into Greek (the Septuagint) in Alexandria in the mid-third century BC, an indication of the desire of its diaspora population to solidify its Jewishness in the Hellenistic world.

Elephantine Island

CYRENE

The parts of Libya near Cyrene filled the bend of the North African coast west of Alexandria, directly south of Greece. Jews arrived in Cyrenaean Libya as early as the late fourth century BC, sent there by Ptolemy I Soter (*Ag. Ap.* 2.44). While the large Jewish presence in Cyrene enjoyed legal protection, the local inhabitants did not always treat it well (*Ant.* 14.115; 16.160).[16]

ROME

We can assume a Jewish presence in Rome prior to the second century BC as well, not on specific textual evidence but by implication due to the spread of the diaspora through the eastern and central Mediterranean by that time.[17] Pompey bolstered the Jewish population in Rome when he brought Jewish captives there following his conquest of Judea in 63 BC (Philo, *Embassy to Gaius* 155). Certainly many other Jews were attracted to the possibilities of living in the capital of the Roman Empire, and thrived under the favorable conditions established there by Julius Caesar as well. By the first century AD, Rome boasted at least eleven synagogues, concentrated on the right bank of the Tiber River (Trastevere). Jews also lived in Italian cities southward as far as Pompei.[18] In full view of the emperor, their fortunes rose and fell with the changing attitudes and priorities of the reigning Caesar.

CRETANS

Jews are known to have lived among the Cretans (Philo, *Embassy to Gaius* 282), as well as on other Greek islands. The Jewish population of Crete was large enough to prompt Tacitus (*Histories* 5,2) to record

15. Bezalel Porten, "Aramaic Letters: The Jedaniah Archive from Elephantine," in *The Context of Scripture: Archival Documents from the Biblical World*, ed. William W. Hallo and K. Lawson Younger, Jr. (Leiden: Brill, 2002), 3:116–132; and Porten, "Elephantine Papyri," *ABD* 2:449.

16. Schürer, *History of the Jewish*, 3.1:60–62; Tcherikover, *Hellenistic Civilization and the Jews*, 290–91; Stern, "Jewish Diaspora," 133–37.

17. Schürer, *History of the Jewish People*, 3.1:73–86; Stern, "Jewish Diaspora," 160–70.

18. Stern, "Jewish Diaspora," 167–68.

Island of Crete

the rumor that the Jewish people had originated there.

ARABS

By "Arabs," the writer of Acts certainly means the Nabateans, a people who, according to Josephus, controlled the "the whole country extending from the Euphrates to the Red Sea" in the first century AD (*Ant.* 1.220–221). This was the traditional territory of the Arabs who had descended from Ishmael (Diodorus 2,48.1; Gen 25:12–18). Documentary evidence for Jews in Arabia prior to the Byzantine Period is sparse, though we can posit it based on the strength of the diaspora in surrounding lands (Babylon, Syria, Judea and Egypt).[19] Some Jews must have fled into Arabia to escape Rome's heavy hand after the destruction of Jerusalem in AD 70; the Mishnah (Shabbat 6:6) assumes a Jewish presence there.

THE MEANING OF THE GEOGRAPHICAL LIST

Taken together, this and other data suggest that the diaspora was born of many factors over hundreds of years between the end of the period of the Old Testament and the beginning of the time of the New. Some left Israel by force: the historic sources mention exile, expulsion, capture in war, and forced migration. But many other Jews left—or, once forced out of their homelands, decided to stay where they were—because living conditions in other parts of the world were better than those they had left behind. Life in Babylon and Egypt, or the Aegean or Rome could be quite pleasant for a foreigner, with social and economic opportunities characteristic of an empire's heartland not found on the frontier. And the dry, rocky land of Judea was everyone's frontier, although one that was necessary to control and cross. As such, the land bridge of the southern Levant was a natural springboard for the movement of populations to other parts of the known world.

The list of peoples in Jerusalem for Pentecost recorded in Acts 2 gives the geographical name for diaspora communities that lay within the borders of the Roman Empire, but the gentilic for those lying outside of Rome's control. The list covers the longitudinal dimension of the world of the Bible, linking the ancient Near East with the Mediterranean basin. The order of the peoples and lands mentioned proceeds generally east to west, following a northern line into Europe and then a southern line across North Africa before swinging back to the eastern desert. By doing so, it starts and ends with lands that lay outside of Rome's political control. This overall move from east to west might be expected, given the ancient Semites' practice of orienting themselves to the east, but is also consistent with the overall movement of God's people from east to west in the

19. Schürer, *History of the Jewish People*, 3.1:15–17.

biblical narrative (for example, the westward travels of Abraham, Ezra, and Paul).

Perhaps the key issue geographically is what is *not* included in the list. Josephus, quoting Strabo, states that "this people [the Jews] has already made its way into every city, and it is not easy to find any place in the habitable world which has not received this nation and in which it has not made its power felt" (*Ant.* 16.115 [LCL]).

Josephus made similar claims as casual references in his writings elsewhere (*Ag. Ap.* 2.282; *J.W.* 2.398–399), as did the Alexandrian Philo, who twice listed specific countries where there was a Jewish presence in the first century AD (*Flaccus* 45–46; *Embassy to Gaius* 281–282). Philo's lists include Egypt, Phoenicia, Syria, Pamphylia, Cilicia, Asia as far as Bithynia and Pontus, Thessaly, Boeotia, Macedonia, Aetolia, Attica, Argos, Corinth, the Peloponnese, Euboea, Cyprus, Crete, and regions beyond the Euphrates. We should note that in spite of these claims that the Jews filled the known world, a careful reading of the literary evidence, coupled with the results of archaeology, shows that the diaspora communities were not spread throughout the entire Roman world but rather clustered around certain areas of the empire, primarily in the eastern, Greek-speaking coastal regions. Scholars generally regard the list in Acts 2 to be reliable in that it is comparable to the lists of Philo, though we are not sure if Luke's derives from a source other than an eyewitness of the Pentecost event.

In any case, the list of Acts 2 certainly does not provide an exhaustive register of the diaspora in the first century. Except for Crete, Acts 2 does not mention Jewish communities in Greece or Macedonia at all. This is unexpected given Philo's emphasis of these two regions in his listing of places that had Jewish communities. Galatia and Cilicia are also absent, even though literary and archaeological sources attest to a Jewish presence in central and southeastern Anatolia as well.[20] The same holds true for Cyprus, also not mentioned by Luke. All of these were places frequented in the itineraries of the Apostle Paul, which only heightens their absence in the Acts 2 list.

Jews from Syria are also not included. All three of the districts of the Roman province of Syria—the Phoenician coast, the northern tier from Seleucia and Antioch through Palmyra (Tamor) to the Euphrates, and the city of Damascus—are attested in the sources as having Jewish communities in the first century AD.[21] Indeed, Josephus noted that Jews were "particularly numerous in Syria," especially in Antioch, "where intermingling is due to the proximity of the two countries" (*J.W.* 7.43). Phoenicia reached as far south as Dora (Dor) on the Mediterranean coast just above Caesarea, and over to Cadasa (Kadesh) on the eastern slope of the Upper Galilean hills; both were places within easy pilgrimage distance to Jerusalem, as was Damascus. Moreover, the coin that the Jerusalem authorities accepted for the temple tax was the Tyrian shekel, an indication not only of what made for good coinage but of an intertwined economy as well. For all of this, Luke does not record that

20. Schürer, *History of the Jewish People*, 3.1:28–36; Tcherikover, *Hellenistic Civilization and the Jews*, 291; Stern, "Jewish Diaspora," 147–49, 154–55.

21. Schürer, *History of the Jewish People*, 3.1:13–15; Tcherikover, *Hellenistic Civilization and the Jews*, 289–90; Stern, "Jewish Diaspora," 137–42.

Jewish voices from Syria were heard in Jerusalem at Pentecost. His list might simply be representative, as, apparently, were the lists of Philo. Or, because Luke's omission of significant Jewish diaspora communities cannot readily be explained on normal demographic grounds, it may just reflect an actual situation on the ground: the eyewitnesses of the Pentecost event actually heard, or remembered to have heard, only *some* of the languages present. If so, the list's incompleteness may be the best witness of its authenticity.

Most surprising, however, is not that the list omits Syria but that it includes Judea. Certainly most of the people who attended the Pentecost festivities in Jerusalem any given year were Judeans and not part of the diaspora at all. Yet the Judean voice was specifically mentioned along with the rest. The issue of hearing strange Judean tongues in Jerusalem makes sense only if they had an accent that was sufficiently distinct from the Galilean Jewish accent of Jesus' disciples to warrant notice (compare Matt 26:73):

> Utterly amazed, they [the mix of Jews present] asked: "Are not all these men who are speaking Galileans? Then how is it that each of us hears them in his own native language? ... We hear them declaring the wonders of God in their own tongues!" (Acts 2:7–8, 11)

If nothing else, the inclusion of Judea in the list of Acts 2, nestled nicely with a representative list of the diaspora communities, serves to tie the Jewish homeland to its frontier, uniting the Jewish communities worldwide to each other and Jerusalem in the process.

BIBLIOGRAPHY

Avi-Yonah, Michael. "Historical Geography of Palestine." Pages 78–116 in vol. 1 of *The Jewish People in the First Century: Historical Geography, Political History, Social, Cultural and Religious Life and Institutions*. Edited by Shmuel Safrai and Menahem Stern. Assen: Van Gorcum, 1974–1976.

Diodorus. *Diodorus of Sicily*. Translated by C. H. Oldfather, Charles L. Sherman, C. Bradford Welles, Russel M. Geer, and Francis R. Walton. LCL. Cambridge: Harvard University Press, 1935–1967.

Hachlili, Rachel. *Ancient Jewish Art and Archaeology in the Diaspora*. Leiden: Brill, 1998.

Herr, M. D. "The Calendar." Pages 834–64 in vol. 2 of *The Jewish People in the First Century: Historical Geography, Political History, Social, Cultural and Religious Life and Institutions*. Edited by Shmuel Safrai and Menahem Stern. Assen: Van Gorcum, 1974–1976.

Josephus. *Against Apion*. Translated by H. St. J. Thackeray. LCL. Cambridge: Harvard University Press, 1926.

———. *Jewish Antiquities*. Translated by H. St. J. Thackeray. 9 vols. LCL. Cambridge: Harvard University Press, 1930–1965.

———. *The Jewish War*. Translated by H. St. J. Thackeray. 3 vols. LCL. Cambridge: Harvard University Press, 1927–1930.

Millar, Fergus. *The Roman Near East, 31 BC–AD 337*. Cambridge: Harvard University Press, 1993.

Philo. *Flaccus*. Translated by F. H. Colson. LCL. Cambridge: Harvard University Pess, 1941.

———. *The Embassy to Gaius*. Translated by F. H. Colson. LCL. Cambridge: Harvard University Press, 1962.

Porten, Bezalel. "Aramaic Letters: The Jedaniah Archive from Elephantine." Pages 116–32 in vol. 3 of *The Context of Scripture: Archival Documents from the Biblical World*. Edited by William W. Hallo and K. Lawson Younger. Leiden: Brill, 2002.

———. "Elephantine Papyri." *ABD* 2:445–55.

Rutgers, Leonard V. *The Jews in Late Ancient Rome: Evidence of Cultural Interaction in the Roman Diaspora*. Leiden: Brill, 1995.

Safrai, Shmuel. "Relations between the Diaspora and the Land of Israel." Pages 184–215 in vol. 1 of *The Jewish People in the First Century: Historical Geography, Political History, Social, Cultural and Religious Life and Institutions*. Edited by Shmuel Safrai and Menahem Stern. Assen: Van Gorcum, 1974–1976.

Schürer, Emil. *The History of the Jewish People in the Age of Jesus Christ*. Revised by Géza Vermès, Fergus Millar, and Martin Goodman. 3 vols. Edinburgh: T&T Clark, 1986.

Skarsaune, Oskar. *In the Shadow of the Temple: Jewish Influences on Early Christianity*. Downers Grove, IL.: InterVarsity Press, 2002.

Stern, Menahem. "The Jewish Diaspora." Pages 117–83 in vol. 1 of *The Jewish People in the First Century: Historical Geography, Political History, Social, Cultural and Religious Life and Institutions*. Edited by Shmuel Safrai and Menahem Stern. Assen: Van Gorcum, 1974–1976.

Tacitus. *Histories*. Translated by Clifford H. Moore. LCL. 2 vols. Cambridge: Harvard University Press, 1925–1931.

Tcherikover, Victor. *Hellenistic Civilization and the Jews*. Translated by S. Applebaum. New York: Atheneum, 1979.

Wilkin, Robert L. *The Land Called Holy: Palestine in Christian History and Thought*. New Haven, CT: Yale University Press, 1992.

Zadok, Ran. *The Jews in Babylonia during the Chaldean and Achaemenian Periods according to the Babylonian Sources*. Haifa: University of Haifa, 1979.

CHAPTER 9

THE JERUSALEM TEMPLE IN THE BOOK OF ACTS

Acts 2:46–3:10; 5:20–42; 21:26–30

Todd Bolen

KEY POINTS

- The early church participated in fellowship, teaching, and evangelism in the temple courts, especially Solomon's Colonnade.
- The Beautiful Gate cannot be identified with certainty, but it was heavily trafficked, provided access to the temple courts, and was located near Solomon's Colonnade.
- Paul was attacked in the temple courts because of the accusation that he brought a gentile beyond the barrier wall that excluded gentiles from the Court of the Women.

INTRODUCTION

The role of the Jerusalem temple in the early church is easy to overlook given the transformational realities brought about through the death and resurrection of Jesus. But one need not claim that Christians were participating in the full range of sacrifices to recognize how central the temple was for the first believers who were living in Jerusalem. For Jews who had grown up visiting the temple, and for disciples of Jesus who learned from their Lord there, it is not surprising that much of the practice of the first Christians occurred in the temple courts. This essay provides cultural detail gleaned from archaeology and ancient sources to describe important features of the temple complex that are mentioned in the book of Acts, including the Beautiful Gate, Solomon's Colonnade, and the partition wall.

BELIEVERS IN THE TEMPLE COURTS

Following the birth of the church on Pentecost, Jerusalem became the central place for the gathering of believers. Some

Herod's Temple on the Temple Mount

Size comparison

time later, persecution would disperse all but the apostles throughout Judea and Samaria (Acts 8:1), but until then the hub of activity was in the Holy City. It is not surprising that Acts indicates that believers met regularly in the temple area, for this was not only the place of worship, but its enormous precincts facilitated the gathering of the increasingly large crowds.

The word used by Luke for "temple" throughout the book of Acts is the word *hieron* (ἱερόν). This word is often translated into English as simply "temple" (e.g., ESV, NASB), but it indisputably signifies not the temple building proper, but the larger temple complex that included the plazas, colonnades, and outer buildings.[1] What did the early Christians do when they came to the temple compound? Acts 2:46 says that they met together in the temple courts every day. The sentence structure in the Greek suggests that they also ate together here.[2] The notice that Peter and John were ascending to the temple at the hour of prayer indicates that believers prayed here as well (3:1). Their healing of a lame man at the entrance suggests that other healings and miracles took place here on other occasions (3:2–10; see also 5:12). When an astonished crowd gathered around the apostles, Peter preached to them with the result that many believed and were added to the church (3:11–4:4). After the apostles were arrested and imprisoned, an angel of the Lord released them and sent them back to the temple courts to continue preaching and teaching (5:18–26). This they continued to do, despite opposition, day after day, both in the temple area and in the houses of Jerusalem (5:42).

Following his conversion on the road to Damascus, Paul visited Jerusalem where he came up to the temple to pray (22:17). Here the Lord appeared to him in a vision (22:18). After more than a decade of missionary work among the gentiles, Paul returned to Jerusalem. The apostle immersed himself in a ritual bath (מִקְוֶה, *mikveh*) and then went up to the temple to give notice for a forthcoming offering (21:23–26). In sum, these reports in the

1. Only priests were allowed inside the temple building at certain times to carry out various rituals; see Luke 1:9.

2. Eckhard J. Schnabel, *Acts*, exp. digital ed. (Grand Rapids: Zondervan, 2012), Acts 2:46–47b.

book of Acts demonstrate that the early church in Jerusalem made the temple courts a regular place for fellowship, discipleship, and evangelism. This is not surprising given the central role of the temple during the ministry of the Lord (Matt 26:55; John 2:14–21; 5:14; 7:14; 8:2; 10:23; 18:20).

Western Wall

What do we know today about the temple complex where the believers spent so much time? Though the Romans destroyed the city of Jerusalem and much of the Temple Mount in AD 70, archaeological investigation and ancient texts reveal much. To begin with, the walls of the Temple Mount are still standing, though not to their original height. From this we know exactly how large the area was. The rectangular compound had a length of 1,574 feet (492 m) on its western wall and a length of 902 feet (282 m) on its southern. Altogether, the Temple Mount measured 172,000 square feet (144,000 m²), the equivalent of twenty-seven American football fields. Visitors to the Temple Mount today often are surprised by just how spacious the area is. In recent years, the complex has held three hundred thousand Muslims gathered here for prayer in the month of Ramadan.[3] The apostles took advantage of this vast space to preach to large crowds, and as the church grew in numbers, there was plenty of room to accommodate the new believers.

The early Christians entered the temple area through one of at least eight gates. The most popular gates for access were those coming up from the historic center of Jerusalem to the south. Crowds could easily stream through the monumental Double and Triple Gates, remains of which stand today. Four gates accessed the Temple Mount on the west, including one now known as Warren's Gate, one over Wilson's Arch, a third known as Barclay's Gate, and a fourth over Robinson's Arch. These provided direct access from the heart of the city in the first century. The single gates on the north (Tadi Gate) and on the east (Susa Gate) are less known, and they seem to have had limited or restricted use (m. Middot 1.3).

The first believers were surrounded by extraordinary beauty and monumental architecture. Later rabbis, who were no admirers of King Herod, declared that "he who has not seen the Temple of Herod has never seen a beautiful building" (b. Baba Batra 4a). According to Josephus, the temple was built of gleaming white limestone overlaid with gold (*J.W.* 5.222). So bright was its appearance when the sun rose, Josephus wrote, that

3. Daniel K. Eisenbud, "Over 300,000 Muslims Attend Ramadan Overnight Prayers at Al-Aksa Mosque," *Jerusalem Post*, June 22, 2017, http://www.jpost.com/Israel-News/Over-300000-Muslims-attend-Ramadan-overnight-prayers-at-Al-Aksa-Mosque-497661.

onlookers had to avert their gaze to avoid being blinded (*J.W.* 5.222).[4]

The temple building was surrounded by courts and colonnades. Immediately in front of the temple, the Court of the Israelites was restricted to Jewish men who brought their sacrifices to the priests serving at the altar. Before that, the Court of the Women was open to all Jewish men, women, and children who had been purified. There is no indication in the temple texts in Acts that the early church gathered in these smaller courtyards. Instead, the believers assembled in the much larger Court of the Gentiles, which was open to all. This court encompassed the other courts on all four sides and was itself enclosed by covered colonnades along the walls of the Temple Mount.

Jesus and Disciples in Solomon's Colonnade by James Tissot (c. 1886)

The colonnades around the temple complex provided shelter from the sun, wind, and rain. The early church regularly met in Solomon's Colonnade, quite possibly continuing the practice from the days of Jesus' ministry (John 10:23; Acts 3:11; 5:12). While nothing remains of the superstructure of Solomon's Colonnade,[5] Josephus describes the colonnades as having a single nave measuring 48 feet (15 m) across with a row of columns on each side that were 40 feet (12.5 m) high (*J.W.* 5.190).[6] Solomon's Colonnade ran along the eastern side of the Temple Mount, and it may have been named after Solomon because the eastern wall of the Temple Mount was the oldest of them all.[7] To the south, the believers would have seen the inspiring Royal Stoa, which was 914 feet (278 m) long, 124 feet (38 m) wide, and 95–105 feet (30–33 m) tall.[8] Compared to other buildings, Josephus wrote that "this cloister deserves to be mentioned better than any other under the sun" (*Ant.* 15.412). Whether the early Christians would have participated in any of its economic or judicial activities is not

4. For more about the grandeur and enormity of the Temple Mount, see Todd Bolen, "Magnificent Stones and Wonderful Buildings of the Temple Complex," in *Lexham Geographic Commentary on the Gospels*, ed. Barry J. Beitzel (Bellingham, WA: Lexham, 2017), 462–75.

5. A capital believed to be from Solomon's Colonnade was recently discovered in the Temple Mount Sifting Project; see Yori Yalon, "Section of 2nd Temple-era Column Found at Temple Mount Dig," *Israel Hayom*, April 4, 2017, http://www.israelhayom.com/2017/04/04/section-of-2nd-temple-era-column-found-at-temple-mount-dig/.

6. Josephus' claim that the stones were thirty-two feet (10 m) long and ten feet (3 m) high seems hyperbolic given what has been discovered in the archaeological remains.

7. King Herod expanded the Temple Mount on the northern, western, and southern sides. Thus the eastern wall was the only pre-Herodian construction, but scholars today do not agree how much earlier it is. It is possible that it was built before the exile and thus during the time when Solomon's temple was still standing. Hillel Geva, "Jerusalem: The Second Temple Period," *NEAEHL* 2:743. See also, Josephus, *J.W.* 5.185.

8. Leen Ritmeyer, *The Quest: Revealing the Temple Mount in Jerusalem* (Jerusalem: Carta, 2006), 91–94.

Model of Herod's Temple

known.[9] What is abundantly clear is that despite the hostility of the temple leadership, the first Christians gathered daily in the temple courts to teach and proclaim the good news of the Messiah (Acts 5:42).

THE LAME MAN AT THE BEAUTIFUL GATE

While many miracles were apparently performed on the Temple Mount (Acts 5:12), the only one recorded in the book of Acts is the healing of a crippled man. This man, lame from birth, sat begging daily at the "temple gate called Beautiful" (3:2–6). Unfortunately, the absence of this name in other ancient sources has led to much speculation regarding its location. The text provides three indicators of where we should look: (1) the Beautiful Gate was used by the apostles when going up to the temple area (3:1–2); (2) the Beautiful Gate provided access to the temple area (3:8); and (3) the Beautiful Gate may have been near Solomon's Colonnade (3:11). Five gates have been proposed and may be considered briefly.[10]

1. The Corinthian Gate is a prime candidate, for Josephus describes how beautiful this gate was (*J.W.* 5.201).[11] But its location close to the temple proper between the Court of the

9. If the Sanhedrin met in the Royal Stoa at this time, the apostles may have been on trial here (Acts 4:5–21; 5:27–41; 22:30–23:10).

10. The most significant discussions of this issue are to be found in Kirsopp Lake, "Localities in and near Jerusalem Mentioned in Acts," in *The Acts of the Apostles*, ed. F. J. Foakes Jackson and Kirsopp Lake (London: Macmillan, 1933; repr., Grand Rapids: Baker, 1979), 5:479–86; Justin Taylor, "The Gate of the Temple Called 'The Beautiful' (Acts 3:2,10)," *Revue Biblique* 106 (1999): 549–62; Craig S. Keener, *Acts: An Exegetical Commentary* (Grand Rapids: Baker Academic, 2012–2015), 2:1047–50.

11. Josephus describes the gate closest to the temple as being the one gate not covered in gold (see *J.W.* 2.411; 6.293). The Mishnah records that the one nongold gate was Nicanor's Gate (m. Middot 2.3). But since much literature in recent years identifies Nicanor's Gate as the one providing access to the Court of the Women (our Eastern Gate below), we have chosen to not use this term here to avoid that point of confusion.

Israelites and the Court of the Women makes this an improbable choice, for it is unlikely that a man with such a serious infirmity would have been permitted access this deep into the worship area. Furthermore, because only men were allowed to pass through this gate into the Court of the Israelites, the beggar would have had fewer opportunities for contributions.

2. The Eastern Gate provided access to the Court of the Women from the Court of the Gentiles.[12] This proposal has several advantages, including the gate's proximity to Solomon's Colonnade and the high traffic that would have passed this way. It is reasonable to assume that the lame man would have been permitted to sit outside the Court of the Women and within the area open to the gentiles.

3. There is yet a third gate approaching from the east. The Shushan (Susa) Gate led from outside the city walls directly into the temple complex. As with the previous two gates, no trace of this structure has been found to date, but it is presumed that this gate gave immediate access to Solomon's Colonnade. Its depiction of Shushan's palace would have made it look beautiful (m. Middot 1.3). The weakness of this view is that fewer visitors would have entered the temple courts from outside the city, thus making this a less attractive place to beg.

4. A fourth option is the gate above Robinson's Arch on the southern end of the western wall. Atop a monumental staircase arising from the Tyropoeon Valley, this gate must have served many visitors, providing access to the Royal Stoa and the Court of the Gentiles.[13] One problem with identifying this as the Beautiful Gate is that it is located on the opposite side of the Temple Mount from Solomon's Colonnade, about 960 feet (300 m) away.

5. The Double Gate on the southern wall is a fifth possibility.[14] This mon-

Remains of Robinson's Arch

12. The Western Text of 3:11 supports the idea that this was an interior gate of the temple courts, thus aligning with either the first or second view given here.

13. Schnabel, *Acts*, Acts 3:2.

14. This view is advanced by Temple Mount expert Leen Ritmeyer, "The Beautiful Gate of the Temple in Jerusalem," Ritmeyer Archaeological Design, December 14, 2010, http://

> umental structure has the chief advantage of being the most popular gate for accessing the temple courts. It would not be surprising, then, if this was the gate regularly used by the apostles and deemed to be ideal by a man begging for his living. Portions of the interior of this gate are preserved today and are noteworthy for their exquisite beauty.[15] If this was the Beautiful Gate, the lame man would have walked and leapt through the still-existing subterranean passageway up to the temple courts in front of the Royal Stoa.

In our assessment, a decision is difficult between views 2 and 5. Both could fit well the text of Acts 3, and without further description of this gate or its location, we cannot be certain. In any case, the spectacle of the formerly lame beggar jumping and praising the Lord was a powerful testimony to those present at the temple that day, such that Peter had the opportunity to speak to the crowd before the temple guard arrived and arrested him.

PAUL AND THE DIVIDING WALL OF PARTITION

The temple continued to be a place of Christian presence in the decades before the Romans destroyed it in AD 70. Though it is not mentioned in connection with the Jerusalem Council or Paul's second missionary journey, its significance is seen in a request given to Paul following his third missionary journey. In order to quiet talk that Paul was teaching against Jewish customs, Paul was advised to pay the expenses of four men who had taken a vow. Paul purified himself and went to the temple (Acts 21:20–26). When the seven days of purification were nearly over, Paul was seized in the temple courts by Jews from the diaspora who accused him of bringing gentiles into the temple area. Paul's opponents were beating him severely when the Romans intervened and arrested him. Paul was permitted to speak to the crowd before he was confined in the Roman barracks (Acts 21:27–22:24).

This episode is clarified by knowledge of a couple points of geography. The first concerns the presence of a 4.5-foot (1.4-m) high wall that separated the Court of the Gentiles from the Court of the Women. Josephus records that along this wall inscriptions in Greek and Latin warned gentiles from trespassing into the sacred area (*J.W.* 5.193–94; 6.125; *Ant.* 15.417). In 1871 an intact Greek copy was discovered about 160 feet (50 m) from the Temple Mount, and in 1935 a fragmentary copy of another Greek inscription was found in a tomb near St. Stephen's Gate.[16] These inscriptions confirm Josephus' record, stating that "No foreigner may enter within the railing and enclosure that surround the Temple. Anyone apprehended shall have himself to blame for his consequent death!"[17] The false charge

www.ritmeyer.com/2010/12/14/the-beautiful-gate-of-the-temple/. For more details on the Double Gate, see Ritmeyer, *Quest*, 67–74.

15. Hershel Shanks, *Jerusalem's Temple Mount: From Solomon to the Golden Dome* (New York: Continuum, 2007), 82.

16. P. Kyle McCarter, Jr., *Ancient Inscriptions: Voices from the Biblical World* (Washington, DC: Biblical Archaeology Society, 1996), 129–30.

17. McCarter, *Ancient Inscriptions*, 130.

Temple Balustrade Inscription

against Paul was that he had brought a gentile beyond this wall. Paul would later observe that unlike the temple, the church had no such division between Jew and gentile, for Christ "has destroyed the barrier, the dividing wall of hostility" (Eph 2:14 NIV).

The second point is that King Herod had constructed a large fortress on the northern end of the Temple Mount that he named after his one-time friend Mark Antony (Josephus, *Ant.* 18.92; *J.W.* 5.238–47). This imposing structure overlooked the temple grounds, providing the Roman soldiers with a view of the riot that broke out on Paul's account. When the soldiers arrested Paul, they led him up a staircase from the temple grounds to the Antonia Fortress, probably located in the northwest corner behind the present-day Ghawanima minaret.[18] It was from these steps that Paul addressed the Jews in Jerusalem for the last time (Acts 21:40).

CONCLUSION

That the temple was central in the life of the early Christians is not surprising given the sanctuary's prominence in Jerusalem. While there is no clear indication that the church ever participated in sacrifice after Jesus' death,[19] the believers enjoyed fellowship, teaching, and evangelism in the temple courts and particularly in Solomon's Colonnade. Of the many apostolic miracles in the temple area, Luke records only the one of the lame man at the Beautiful Gate. Paul's presence here some decades later provoked a riot that could have caused his death but ultimately brought about his imprisonment and journey to Rome. Our knowledge of ancient sources along with discoveries

18. Ritmeyer, *Quest*, 127.

19. Schnabel, *Acts*, Acts 3:1.

Fragment of Temple Warning Inscription

from artifacts and archaeological investigation provides clarity to some, but not all, of the historical and geographic questions provoked by Luke's accounts of these events in the temple courts.

BIBLIOGRAPHY

Bolen, Todd. "Magnificent Stones and Wonderful Buildings of the Temple Complex." Pages 462–75 in *Lexham Geographic Commentary on the Gospels*. Edited by Barry J. Beitzel. Bellingham, WA: Lexham, 2017.

Eisenbud, Daniel K. "Over 300,000 Muslims Attend Ramadan Overnight Prayers at Al-Aksa Mosque." *Jerusalem Post*, June 22, 2017. http://www.jpost.com/Israel-News/Over-300000-Muslims-attend-Ramadan-overnight-prayers-at-Al-Aksa-Mosque-497661.

Geva, Hillel. "Jerusalem: The Second Temple Period." *NEAEHL* 2:717–57.

Keener, Craig S. *Acts: An Exegetical Commentary*. 4 vols. Grand Rapids: Baker Academic, 2012–2015.

Lake, Kirsopp. "Localities in and near Jerusalem Mentioned in Acts." Pages 474–86 in vol. 5 of *The Acts of the Apostles*. Edited by F. J. Foakes Jackson and Kirsopp Lake. London: Macmillan, 1933. Repr., Grand Rapids: Baker, 1979.

McCarter, P. Kyle, Jr. *Ancient Inscriptions: Voices from the Biblical World*. Washington, DC: Biblical Archaeology Society, 1996.

Ritmeyer, Leen. "The Beautiful Gate of the Temple in Jerusalem." Ritmeyer Archaeological Design, December 14, 2010. http://www.ritmeyer.com/2010/12/14/the-beautiful-gate-of-the-temple/.

———. *The Quest: Revealing the Temple Mount in Jerusalem*. Jerusalem: Carta, 2006.

Schnabel, Eckhard J. *Acts*. Expanded digital edition. Grand Rapids: Zondervan, 2012.

Shanks, Hershel. *Jerusalem's Temple Mount: From Solomon to the Golden Dome*. New York: Continuum, 2007.

Taylor, Justin. "The Gate of the Temple Called 'The Beautiful' (Acts 3:2,10)." *Revue Biblique* 106 (1999): 549–62.

Yalon, Yori. "Section of 2nd Temple-era Column Found at Temple Mount Dig." *Israel Hayom*, April 4, 2017. http://www.israelhayom.com/2017/04/04/section-of-2nd-temple-era-column-found-at-temple-mount-dig/.

CHAPTER 10

THE GEOGRAPHY OF WORSHIP: FROM TEMPLE TO SYNAGOGUE TO CHURCH

Acts 2:46; 6:9; 11:22, 26; 13:14–15; 14:1; 18:4; 19:8

Benjamin A. Foreman

KEY POINTS

- Worship at the end of the First Temple period was fully centralized in the temple.
- Local congregations of worship probably formed sometime in the exile after Jerusalem was destroyed, and eventually developed into what we now call "synagogues."
- The synagogue did not replace the temple; the two existed alongside each other for several hundred years.
- The concept of the local church grew out of the synagogue. Christians completely separated from the synagogue sometime after the destruction of the Second Temple.

INTRODUCTION

Most western Christians today probably give little thought to the role of geography in worship. They may select a church based on its proximity to their house, the style of music, theology, or any number of reasons, but what they may not realize is that the concept of a local gathering in a building near their home is totally foreign to the Old Testament. Formal worship for the people of Israel was not a weekly local meeting, but a national, triannual jamboree at one central location (Deut 16:16). The shift from one central place of worship to many local assemblies occurred very late in Israel's history. This essay will trace this geographical movement in order to shed some light on where the concept of the local church originated.

WORSHIP AT THE END OF THE FIRST TEMPLE PERIOD

The nature and practice of Israel's worship in the Old Testament is highly disputed.

Because our topic here is the geography of New Testament worship, we will sidestep the debate and focus rather on some of the regulations for worship outlined in Deuteronomy. Since most scholars agree the book was the "law of the land" from at least the seventh century BC onward, the book is a convenient place to look for insight into how the Israelites were meant to worship Yahweh at the end of the First Temple period.

One of the key themes trumpeted in the book of Deuteronomy is the centralization of Israel's worship. This is stated most clearly in 12:5–6:

> "But you shall seek the place that the Lord your God will choose out of all your tribes to put his name and make his habitation there. There you shall go, and there you shall bring your burnt offerings and your sacrifices, your tithes and the contribution that you present, your vow offerings, your freewill offerings, and the firstborn of your herd and of your flock."[20]

Although the high places are not mentioned in this passage (or at all in Deuteronomy), these verses clearly oppose them. Deuteronomy outlaws all local, ritual sacrifice.[21]

In addition to limiting ritual sacrifice to the chosen place, the book also requires the men of Israel to celebrate the national festivals there (see the chart of Israelite festivals on page 697):

> "Three times a year all your males shall appear before the Lord your God at the place that he will choose: at the Feast of Unleavened Bread, at the Feast of Weeks, and at the Feast of Booths. They shall not appear before the Lord empty-handed." (Deut 16:16)

How the men were to celebrate the Passover is a relevant issue for our discussion. According to Leviticus 23:7–8, the Israelites were to hold a "sacred assembly" (מִקְרָא־קֹדֶשׁ, *miqra qodesh*) on both the first and seventh day of the feast. The Hebrew for "sacred assembly" is literally "a holy summons" or "a holy reading," and thus seems to designate a national gathering for worship, perhaps including the reading and teaching of Scripture.[22] In Deuteronomy 16:6, the Israelites are instructed to eat the Passover sacrifice at the central sanctuary on the evening of the fourteenth of Abib (= Nisan), and then on the following morning, they are to "return to their tents." The meaning of this phrase is important because if the intent was for the Israelites to return home, the second "sacred assembly" would be celebrated in the local villages throughout

---

20. All biblical quotations are from the ESV unless otherwise noted. Although some have tried to argue Deut 12:5 speaks of regional sanctuaries (and not one sole sanctuary), Wenham has shown this interpretation is unsustainable (Gordon J. Wenham, "Deuteronomy and the Central Sanctuary," *TynBul* 22 [1971]: 110–11).

21. A distinction should be made between ritual sacrifice and special instances of sacrifice. Special occasions of local sacrifice are not forbidden in Deuteronomy. See Jeffrey Niehaus, "The Central Sanctuary: Where and When?," *TynBul* 43 (1992): 3–30.

22. Gordon J. Wenham, *The Book of Leviticus* (Grand Rapids: Eerdmans, 1979), 301.

the country.[23] This, then, might be taken as an early precursor to local worship in the villages, similar to what would later become a synagogue. In the end, however, this seems unlikely since there is no indication in the text that the first "sacred assembly" was to be celebrated any differently from the second. The "tents" mentioned in Deuteronomy 16:7 most likely were temporary shelters set up to house visitors for the holidays.[24]

Deuteronomy also commands the priests to read the law at the central place of worship every seven years at the Feast of Booths (Deut 31:9–11). The priests—who served in the sanctuary—were charged with teaching the law (Lev 10:11; Deut 31:9; Jer 18:18), and therefore the law, it seems, was primarily studied in the temple.[25] Although there were exceptions to this (for example, 2 Chr 17:7–9), there is little evidence the Israelites regularly met together outside of the temple to study the law.[26]

Interestingly, Deuteronomy gives us very little information about prayer at the central sanctuary. It does record a response the Israelites were supposed to voice when giving the firstfruits offering (Deut 26:5–10), or when paying the tithe of produce (Deut 26:13–15), but no comprehensive instructions are given regarding what should be prayed when the worshipers present their offerings and sacrifices. Several psalms refer to sacrifice (for example, Ps 20:3; 26:6; 107:22) and may have accompanied their sacrifices, but this is unclear. Although people may have offered individual, spontaneous prayers from their homes and facing the temple (see Pss 5:8; 28:2; 138:2; 1 Kgs 8:44, 48; Dan 6:1), "Liturgical prayer was not an institution independent of other cultic acts, as it has come to be in synagogue services."[27]

The distinction between singing and prayer is not always clear since songs of worship often *are* prayers. Singing, however, was part of ancient Israelite worship.[28] In 1 Chronicles 25, David appointed twenty-four classes of singers from three main families (Asaph, Jeduthun, and Heman). The Old Testament gives us very little indication of what these singers sang, but it is likely that at least some of their songs are preserved in the book of Psalms (Israel's "hymnbook"). Deuteronomy, however, does not elaborate on this.

From this brief overview, it is clear that formal worship was meant to be a

23. See, for example, Peter T. Vogt, "Centralization and Decentralization in Deuteronomy," in *Interpreting Deuteronomy: Issues and Approaches*, ed. David G. Firth and Philip Johnston (Downers Grove, IL: InterVarsity Press, 2012), 136.

24. P. C. Craigie, *The Book of Deuteronomy* (Grand Rapids: Eerdmans, 1976), 244.

25. Isaiah 2:3 (= Micah 4:2) may also imply that the law was primarily studied in the temple. See Roland de Vaux, *Ancient Israel: Vol. 2 Religious Institutions* (New York: McGraw-Hill, 1965), 353–55.

26. Although parents were required to teach the law to their children (Deut 6:7), they clearly did not have personal scrolls in their houses. The command, therefore, is for the fathers to teach their families what they have learned at the central place of worship. For an excellent treatment of the communal and individual aspect of Israel's commitment to the covenant, see Christopher J. H. Wright, *Old Testament Ethics for the People of God* (Leicester: Inter-Varsity Press, 2004), esp. 363–83.

27. De Vaux, *Ancient Israel: Religious Institutions*, 2:457.

28. See De Vaux, *Ancient Israel: Religious Institutions*, 2:382.

Solomon's Temple

corporate, centralized affair at the end of the First Temple period. The temple was the focal point for sacrifice, celebration of festivals, study of the Scriptures, and prayer/singing. By New Testament times, however, the Jews were worshiping in local synagogues throughout the country. When did this geographical shift in worship occur?

HISTORY OF THE SYNAGOGUE

Josephus implies the concept of the synagogue goes back to Moses:

> "He [Moses] appointed the Law to be the most excellent and necessary form of instruction, ordaining, not that it should be heard once for all or twice or on several occasions, but that every week men should desert their other occupations and assemble to listen to the Law and to obtain a thorough and accurate knowledge of it, a practice which all other legislators seem to have neglected" (*Ag. Ap.* 2.175 [LCL]).[29]

Clear evidence for this in the Old Testament, however, is entirely lacking. Solid attestation to synagogues comes only several centuries after the destruction of the First Temple, much later than we would expect. But before looking at this evidence, a brief note about the word "synagogue" is in order.

TERMINOLOGY

The English word "synagogue" derives from a transliteration of the Greek *synāgogē* (συναγωγή) and has the general meaning "collecting" or "bringing

29. For further examples of the antiquity of the synagogue in Jewish tradition see H. H. Rowley, *Worship in Ancient Israel: Its Forms and Meaning* (Philadelphia: Fortress, 1967), 213–14.

together, assembling."[30] The term occurs over two hundred times in the Septuagint for the gathering of waters (Gen 1:9), harvest (Exod 34:22), or other things. In the Septuagint, it most frequently translates the Hebrew word *edah* (עֵדָה)—referring to the gathered community of Israel.[31]

Sometime toward the end of the Second Temple period the term took on a more specialized sense and was used either for the congregation assembled for worship or for the building in which they gathered. In the New Testament, the term is used in both ways, sometimes even within the same chapter (for example, Acts 13:14 [building], 13:43 [assembly]).[32] When studying the development of the synagogue, therefore, it is important to determine whether the people or the building is intended.

Another common word for synagogues is *proseuchē* (προσευχή, meaning "prayer"). This term almost exclusively designates synagogues of the diaspora. Some scholars see a clear difference between the way the two terms are used, but this is hard to prove.[33] The two words were apparently synonymous.

HISTORY

The origin and early development of the synagogue is about as elusive as the location of the *Flor de la Mar's* treasure. The earliest literary references come from Hellenistic Egypt. For example, a stele dating to the reign of Ptolemy III Euergetes (246–221 BC) records the dedication of a synagogue in Arsinoe-Crocodilopolis (sixty-two miles [100 km] southwest of Cairo): "On behalf of king Ptolemy, son of Ptolemy, and queen Berenice his wife and sister and their children, the Jews in Crocodilopolis (dedicated) the *proseuchē*."[34] Approximately

30. BDAG, 963.

31. See L. Coenen, "Church, Synagogue," *The New International Dictionary of New Testament Theology*, ed. Colin Brown (Grand Rapids: Zondervan, 1986), 292–95.

32. This example is from Lee I. Levine, *The Ancient Synagogue: The First Thousand Years* (New Haven: Yale University Press, 2000), 1.

33. For example, some argue *proseuchē* is only used for diaspora synagogues since this would be inappropriate for synagogues in Israel which are closer to the temple—the ultimate "house of prayer" (for example, Isa 56:7). Exceptions to the rule, however, make the theory less convincing; see Stephen K. Catto, *Reconstructing the First-Century Synagogue: A Critical Analysis of Current Research* (New York: T&T Clark, 2007), 15–16.

34. William Horbury and David Noy, *Jewish Inscriptions of Graeco-Roman Egypt* (Cambridge: Cambridge University Press, 1992), no. 117.

Delos Synagogue

twenty other references to synagogues have been recovered in Egyptian inscriptions dating from the mid-third century BC through the Roman period. These inscriptions are significant since they are "considerably earlier than any other Diaspora evidence known to date."[35] Most of the other literary references to synagogues date to the first century BC and later (Philo, Josephus, NT, etc.).[36]

Although the oldest references to synagogues come from Egypt, no ancient synagogue has yet been found there. The oldest known synagogue is probably the one excavated on the Greek island of Delos in the Aegean Sea. It has been dated to the mid-second century BC, and if this is correct, it predates all others found to date by nearly a century.[37]

Within the land of Israel, the literature implies there were synagogues all throughout the country in the first century AD (the literary evidence prior to this is questionable). The Talmud, for example, claims there were 480 synagogues in Jerusalem (for example, y. Megilla 3.1). This number is obviously inflated, but Acts 6:9 implies there were at least 5 in

35. Levine, *Ancient Synagogue*, 75.

36. For a nice overview of the literary evidence from the first century see Catto, *First-Century Synagogue*, 14–48.

37. André Plassart, "La Synagogue Juive de Délos," *Revue Biblique* 11 (1914): 522–34. More recently see L. M. White, "The Delos Synagogue Revisited: Recent Fieldwork in the Graeco-Roman Diaspora," *Harvard Theological Review* 80 (1987): 133–60.

Jerusalem.[38] Matthew writes that Jesus went "throughout all Galilee, teaching in their synagogues" (Matt 4:23), and extrabiblical writers (for example, Philo and Josephus) also indicate synagogues were widespread in the first century.[39]

In the land of Israel, however, the archaeological attestation to first century BC/AD synagogues is not very impressive. Approximately nine have been found in total (at Gamla, Jericho, Masada, Kh. Cana, Jerusalem [inscription only], Herodion, Kiryat Sefer, Capernaum, Magdala).[40] Although these meager numbers may be surprising, it is important to remember that in some villages the community of worshipers may have gathered in domestic or public buildings, and thus the buildings themselves may not always be clearly identifiable in the archaeological record.[41]

One particularly important find is the Theodotus inscription, discovered in 1913.[42] Originally part of a synagogue in the City of David, the engraving notes the synagogue ruler (Gk. *Theodotos*, θεόδοτος) constructed the building for the

38. For example, David A. Fiensy, "The Composition of the Jerusalem Church," in *The Book of Acts in Its Palestinian Setting*, ed. Richard Bauckham, vol. 4 of *The Book of Acts in Its Palestinian Setting*, ed. Bruce W. Winter (Grand Rapids: Eerdmans, 1995), 233–34.

39. See Catto, *First-Century Synagogue*, 23–48.

40. See pages 698–99 for images of the archaeological sites of the synagogues at Gamla, Masada, Herodion, and Magdala. Scholars sometimes quibble over the dates and thus the number of first-century synagogues may vary a bit depending on one's opinion. For an overview with bibliography, see Catto, *First-Century Synagogue*, 82–105. For a preliminary discussion of the synagogue at Magdala see: M. Zapata-Meza and R. Sanz-Rincón, "Excavating Mary Magdalene's Hometown," *BAR* 43.3 (2017): 37–42.

41. Catto, *First-Century Synagogue*, 105.

42. Gerald M. Fitzgerald, "Notes on Recent Discoveries" *Palestine Exploration Fund Quarterly Statement* 53 (1921): 175–86. See page 157 for an image of the inscription.

reading of the law, the study of the commandments, ritual bathing, and hosting guests from out of town. Most scholars agree the inscription dates to sometime before the destruction of the temple, and some even speculate this is the synagogue of the freedmen in Acts 6:9.[43] Part of the significance of the inscription is that it sheds unambiguous insight into the function of synagogues in the first century AD.

In spite of the gaping holes in the early literary and archaeological evidence, scholars have not shied away from filling in the gaps.[44] Some believe the idea of the synagogue goes all the way back to the First Temple period.[45] Support for this is usually found in passages like Psalm 74:8, which mentions the "meeting places" of God (מוֹעֲדֵי־אֵל, *mo'adei el*) scattered throughout the land, or Jeremiah 39:8, which states the Babylonians destroyed the "house of the people" (בֵּית הָעָם, *beit ha'am*)—-a popular name in later Judaism for synagogues.[46] Scholars who believe they reach back to First Temple times also speculate Josiah's reforms (2 Kgs 23) would have inspired local, non-sacrificial acts of worship to arise.[47]

The most popular view traces the origin of the synagogue to Babylon during the exilic period.[48] According to this theory, the destruction of the temple forced the Jews to create an alternative form of worship. The evidence for this is also thin, but a few scattered references to the elders gathering around Ezekiel to hear the word of the Lord (Ezek 8:1; 14:1), or the mention of *miqdash me'at* (מִקְדָּשׁ מְעַט) in Ezek 11:16 are garnered in support.[49]

Jewish tradition (for example, y. Megilla 4.1) has typically seen Ezra's reading of the law as the inspiration for the synagogue since the reading of the Torah is one of the main activities associated with it. This argument is weak, though, since the law was read at the temple as well (Deut 31:9–11).

Still others believe the synagogue originated in Egypt in the Hellenistic period. The starting point for this view is usually the recognition that the earliest references to synagogues come from the third century in Egypt, and other parallels between the activities in the synagogue and those of Hellenistic Egypt are also highlighted.[50] Another theory looks

---

43. L. H. Vincent, "Découverte de La Synagogue Des Affranchis à Jérusalem," *Revue Biblique* 30 (1921): 247–77.

44. The next few paragraphs draw heavily from Levine, *Ancient Synagogue*, 22–26.

45. For example, Louis Finkelstein, "The Origin of the Synagogue," in *The Synagogue: Studies in Origins, Archaeology and Architecture*, ed. Joseph Gutman (New York: Ktav, 1975), 3–13.

46. This view goes at least as far back as Rashi (see his commentary on Jer 39:8).

47. See Lee I. Levine, "The Second Temple Synagogue: The Formative Years," in *The Synagogue in Late Antiquity*, ed. Lee I. Levine (Philadelphia: American Schools of Oriental Research, 1987), 9.

48. For example, Rowley, *Worship in Ancient Israel*, 224–27.

49. The phrase can be translated "small sanctuary" and Targum Jonathan even renders "synagogue" (*betei kenishta*, בָּתֵּי כְנִישְׁתָא) in Ezek 11:16.

50. See J. Gwyn Griffiths, "The Legacy of Egypt in Judaism," in *The Early Roman Period*, vol. 3 of *The Cambridge History of Judaism*, ed. William Horbury, W. D. Davies, and John Sturdy (Cambridge: Cambridge University Press, 1999), 1028–36.

to the Hasmonean period and credits the Pharisees of Judea as the innovators.[51]

More recently, Levine has proposed that the synagogue arose because of a shift in urban planning. According to him, the Israelites would gather at the city gates for social and religious purposes in the Old Testament period, but when city gates were no longer built with open squares or adjacent rooms in the Hellenistic period, the Jews constructed public buildings to satisfy the need. These buildings eventually came to be known as "synagogues."[52]

Detailed interaction with all these views is obviously not possible here. While the precise origin of the synagogue is far from certain, perhaps even "unknowable,"[53] the destruction of the focal point of ancient Israel's worship (the First Temple) almost certainly would have generated the need to create an alternative. Exactly what other factors contributed to the development of the synagogue is uncertain. What is clear, however, is that Jewish worship underwent a radical geographical transformation several hundred years (at the very least) before Jesus. By New Testament times, worship in the synagogues was in full swing throughout the Jewish world. What did they do in these meetings?

ACTIVITIES

In New Testament times, synagogues were used for a variety of activities, one of which was education. The Talmudic reference mentioning the 480 synagogues in Jerusalem also states that each had one school for the study of the Talmud and another for the study of the Mishnah (y. Megilla 3.1). Although the number is dubious, the passage likely reflects the historical reality that they were also used as schools. A synagogue is most likely where Paul was educated at the feet of Gamaliel (Acts 22:3). The Theodotus inscription makes it clear they also were sometimes used for hosting travelers, and some even had special rooms to help facilitate this. As public buildings, they were also the natural venue for communal meals, making decisions on public matters, and sometimes even administering justice (see Acts 22:19).

By far the most important activity of the synagogue was the study of the law.[54] This is the first point mentioned in the Theodotus inscription, and this is clear from many other texts. Philo, for example, writes:

> "For that day [i.e., Sabbath] has been set apart to be kept holy and on it they abstain from all other work and proceed to sacred spots which they call synagogues.... Then one takes the books and reads aloud and another of especial proficiency comes forward and expounds what is not under-

51. E. Rivkin, "Ben Sira and the Non-Existence of the Synagogue," in *In the Time of Harvest: Essays in Honor of Abba Hillel Silver*, ed. Daniel J. Silver (New York: Macmillan, 1963), 320–54.

52. See the full argument in Levine, *Ancient Synagogue*, 26–41.

53. Shaye J. D. Cohen, "The Temple and the Synagogue," in Horbury, *Early Roman Period*, 298.

54. As Catto notes, "Within virtually any 'synagogue' gathering on a Sabbath, in any geographical location, this could have been a common element [in the first century]" (*First-Century Synagogue*, 150).

stood." (Philo, *Quod omnis probus liber sit*, 81–82 [LCL])

The importance of studying the law is clear from James' statement in Acts 15:21 as well: "For from ancient generations Moses has had in every city those who proclaim him, for he is read every Sabbath in the synagogues." Like many other things, the first-century Torah reading cycle is debated, but many scholars believe that in Israel, the entire Torah was read on the sabbath in the synagogue over a three-year or three-and-a-half-year period.[55] As is clear from Philo's statement (and the New Testament), once the Torah was read it was then expounded.

In addition to reading and studying the Torah, the Jews also read from the Prophets (the *haftarah*) on the Sabbath. This is clear from Luke 4:16–30 where Jesus enters a synagogue in Nazareth, reads from Isaiah 61:1–2, and announces the passage has been fulfilled in him. In Acts 13:15 Luke tells us Paul read from the Law *and* the Prophets in the synagogue of Antioch in Pisidia. In New Testament times, it seems, the lectionary for the Prophets was not yet fixed and apparently the speaker had the freedom to choose which passage to read.[56]

Interestingly, although *proseuchē* ("prayer") was the most popular word for synagogues outside of Israel, we do not have widespread evidence of liturgical prayer in these assemblies prior to the destruction of the temple. In the New Testament, the only mention of prayer in connection to a synagogue is in Matthew 6:5–6. This has led some scholars to conclude communal prayer was not known prior to the destruction of the temple. Catto, however, has garnered some evidence of this in synagogues, and thus, although liturgical prayer clearly played a more dominant role after the destruction of the temple, it apparently also had a place in pre-70 synagogues.[57]

In summary, synagogues were the locus for both secular and religious activities. Except for sacrifice, all the elements of worship were decentralized and transferred to these local assemblies. It is important to note, however, that synagogues never replaced the temple. Since sacrifice could take place only in the temple, the two institutions existed side by side for several hundred years. The Christian community, however, did not share this view.

THE RISE OF THE CHURCH

BEFORE THE ASCENSION

Throughout his ministry, Jesus routinely went to the synagogue on the Sabbath (Luke 4:16; "as was his custom") and traveled to the temple to celebrate the festivals and teach (John 2:13; 5:1; 7:14). The New Testament depicts a close tie between Jesus and the Jewish institutions of his day, and although he certainly faced opposition, the Gospels give no clear indication of his intention to break away from the synagogue or temple. Even after the ascension, the apostles initially continued to pray and teach in the temple (Acts 3:1).

Given the continuity between Jesus and first-century Judaism, it is surpris-

55. Levine, *Ancient Synagogue*, 140.

56. Note Luke 4:17 says Jesus "found" the passage he wanted to read.

57. See Catto, *First-Century Synagogue*, 142.

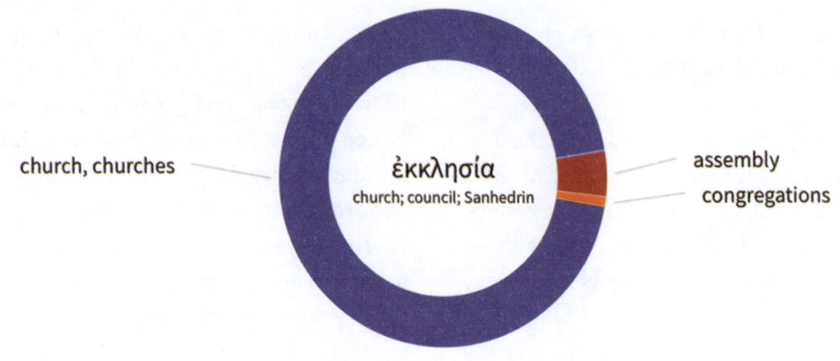

ing Jesus' followers never referred to their assemblies as "synagogues" (James 2:2 is the only exception).[58] On the other hand, prior to the ascension they apparently did not identify themselves as the "church" (ἐκκλησία, *ekklēsia*) either. The term *ekklēsia* ("church") occurs only three times in the Gospels—-Matt 16:18 and 18:17 (twice). Only after the resurrection did the believers begin using the word *ekklēsia* for their community.[59] What led the followers of Jesus to separate from the synagogue?

THE PARTING OF WAYS

The New Testament makes it clear churches were founded very early. For example, Luke records there were churches in Jerusalem (Acts 11:22) and Antioch (11:26) already several years prior to the Jerusalem Council in AD 48/49 (Acts 15).[60] At this point, however, there still was not a total separation between Christians and the synagogue/temple. Paul continued to teach in the synagogues (Acts 13:15; 14:1; 18:4; 19:8) and wished to celebrate Pentecost at the temple (Acts 20:16).[61] The final breakaway from Judaism seems to have coincided with the destruction of the Second Temple, or perhaps even later.[62] But rather than attempt to pinpoint when the parting of ways occurred, we will briefly examine some factors that led to this separation.

The early Christian message can be summed up in one word: Jesus. Nearly everything the early Christians claimed about him was rejected by the Jewish establishment. For example, their claim that he is the messiah who has been

58. Coenen, "Church, Synagogue," 296.

59. The word "church" is derived from the Greek verb "to call." Thus, the community of believers are those who have been "called" (or "elected") to follow Jesus. Unlike modern usage, Paul always employs the word to refer to the people (not the building). Although smaller communities are called "churches" (for example, 1 Cor 16:19; Rom 16:5), they are all part of one universal church. See Coenen, "Church, Synagogue," 296–305.

60. References to "the church" in Acts 5:11; 8:1, 3; 9:31 might simply refer to the followers of Jesus, not the assembly of believers on Sundays.

61. For a discussion of Paul's continued relationship with Judaism, see Reidar Hvalvik, "Paul as a Jewish Believer—According to the Book of Acts," in *Jewish Believers in Jesus*, ed. Oskar Skarsaune and Reidar Hvalvik (Peabody, MA: Hendrickson, 2007), 121–53.

62. See James D. G. Dunn, *The Parting of the Ways: Between Christianity and Judaism and Their Significance for the Character of Christianity* (London: SCM, 1991), 238–43.

resurrected from the dead (Acts 2:31; 3:26; 4:2; 17:3; etc.) was too much for the Sadducees who did not believe in the resurrection (Acts 22:8). But their faith in Jesus was even more radical than this. As N. T. Wright eloquently notes, "The early Christians spoke of Jesus as the one who had embodied the living presence of the creator god, and of his own spirit as the one who continued to make that god present in the lives and assemblies of the early church."[63] Put more softly, the early Christians believed Jesus was to be identified in some way with the God of Israel. Most scholars recognize this high Christology is evident in at least several early texts (for example, 1 Cor 8:6; Phil 2:6–11; Col 1:15–20), all agree it is full-blown in the Gospel of John.[64] For many first-century Jews, this was more than they could swallow (see "Excursus: Belief in Jesus as God" below).[65]

Since the early Christians believed Jesus was the lamb of God, the final sacrifice, they naturally concluded sacrifices are no longer necessary. This was an important (and visible) difference in their temple-worship practice. Sacrifice was the central activity of the temple, yet the early Christians "treated the temple as if it were the supreme synagogue."[66] They taught and prayed there, but never sacrificed.[67] Pulling various strands of evidence together, Skarsaune concludes, "the faction led by James—presumably the whole Aramaic-speaking community—seems to have completely ignored the sacrificial cult of the temple. This created tension between them and the Sadducees, and later with the Diaspora Jews who were zealous for the temple."[68]

The person of Jesus also replaced the centrality of the Torah. Jesus claimed to have fulfilled the law (Matt 5:17–18), and Paul preached Christ is the end of the law (Rom 10:4). As Coenen notes, "Once the Law of Moses had effectively taken central place in its [the synagogue] life, liturgy, and institution ... the idea of the synagogue must have seemed so rigid to

63. N. T. Wright, *The New Testament and the People of God* (Minneapolis: Fortress, 1992), 368.

64. For a solid defense of early high Christology, see Larry W. Hurtado, *Lord Jesus Christ: Devotion to Jesus in Earliest Christianity* (Grand Rapids: Eerdmans, 2003); Hurtado, *How on Earth Did Jesus Become a God? Historical Questions about Earliest Devotion to Jesus* (Grand Rapids: Eerdmans, 2005); Richard Bauckham, *Jesus and the God of Israel: God Crucified and Other Studies on the New Testament's Christology of Divine Identity* (Grand Rapids: Eerdmans, 2008); Simon Gathercole, *The Pre-Existent Son: Recovering the Christologies of Matthew, Mark, and Luke* (Grand Rapids: Eerdmans, 2006). For a concise introduction to early Christology, see Hurtado, *Honoring the Son: Jesus in Earliest Christian Devotional Practice* (Bellingham, WA: Lexham Press, 2018).

65. Belief in a divine plurality, however, is not totally foreign to first-century Judaism. For an accessible treatment of two Jewish texts that move in that direction, see Daniel Boyarin, *The Jewish Gospels: The Story of the Jewish Christ* (New York: New Press, 2012), 71–101.

66. Oskar Skarsaune, *In the Shadow of the Temple: Jewish Influences on Early Christianity* (Downers Grove, IL: InterVarsity Press, 2002), 157.

67. The only exception is Acts 21:23–26, but this seems to have been a concession. As Skarsaune notes, "Romans 3:25 shows that Paul could have attached no atoning quality to these sacrifices, which in any case were probably not conceived of as having such a quality." (Skarsaune, *In the Shadow of the Temple*, 157).

68. Skarsaune, *In the Shadow of the Temple*, 160.

the Christian that he separated from it in favor of a reformed Christian assembly."[69]

Finally, the resurrection of Jesus on Sunday led to the choice of this day as the new day for worship (Acts 20:7; 1 Cor 16:2; Rev 1:10). Exactly how the transition from the Sabbath to Sunday took place is unclear, but as Wilson notes, one motive for this was "the purely pragmatic need for regular, separate gatherings to cater to distinctive Christian needs."[70] Effectively, this change in the day of worship led to a total break from the synagogue. Christian worship in the temple was no longer necessary, and in the synagogue no longer feasible.

CONCLUSION

Although the geographical shift in worship from temple to synagogue to church has a long and complicated history, the general outline is clear. At the end of the First Temple period, worship was fully centralized: sacrifice, the study of Scripture, and all other liturgical activities belonged exclusively to the domain of the temple. A creative alternative to worship apparently formed in the wake of the catastrophe of 587/586 BC. Instead of burying their worship with the rubble of the temple, the Jews began to gather weekly in local venues and transferred all non-sacrificial elements of worship to these provincial assemblies. Interestingly, once the pipedream of rebuilding the temple became a reality, the temple never regained its status as the sole sanctuary for worship. Temple and synagogue supplemented each other for several hundred years, and Jews unanimously recognized the necessity of both.

In Jesus a new theology was born. Since Christ's death rendered sacrifices unnecessary, Christians completely abandoned the temple, and in time irreconcilable differences in theology led to a total break with the synagogue as well. A new day of worship (Sunday) was selected to commemorate the resurrection of Jesus, and local churches became the new place for Christian worship—a practice that has continued for two thousand years.

I would like to close with a few reflective comments on how geography may affect Christian worship. In my opinion, the decentralization of the church has both advantages and disadvantages. On the positive side, local assemblies provide more convenient access to worship and thus help facilitate greater participation (in theory at least). Additionally, smaller regional churches are more conducive to ministry: people's needs are better identified and cared for at the local level than at the national level. In a similar vein, local assemblies provide a broader selection for Christians to choose from. People naturally have different style preferences, and local assemblies help to accommodate these variegated penchants. Negatively, local worship tends to promote a sense of individualism. Geography divides, and Christians who gather for worship only in their neighborhood congregation risk losing sight of the full mosaic. The church is not just a regional flock, but a web of believers spread across the globe. Also, the decentralization of the church inevitably eases the incursion of unorthodoxy. Removing the central governing body and throwing

---

69. Coenen, "Church, Synagogue," 297.

70. Stephen Wilson, *Related Strangers: Jews and Christians 70–170 C.E.* (Minneapolis: Fortress, 1995), 233.

the responsibility of oversight into the lap of individual churches can be dangerous. Orthodoxy is more easily preserved in a centralized system of worship. In the end, perhaps the church would be better served if local congregations were to occasionally assemble for worship with other flocks of Christians. Periodic semi-centralized worship services might help mitigate some of the risks just mentioned and would be a visual reminder that the local congregation is only one piece of the beautiful puzzle called "the church."

EXCURSUS: BELIEF IN JESUS AS GOD—TWO EARLY EXAMPLES

It is sometimes claimed in popular works and some pseudo-scholarship that Christians prior to the Council of Nicea (AD 325) did not believe Jesus was God. Dan Brown, for example, recently advanced this idea in his popular book *The Da Vinci Code*. Jesus' divinity, according to Brown, was the result of a "relatively close vote" at the Council of Nicea.[71]

While such an assertion might be raw material for entertaining fiction, it has no basis in historical reality. Not only was the "vote" not "relatively close" by any standard,[72] it is clear from a sea of Christian texts that the early Christians worshiped Jesus as God from New Testament times onward.[73] This can be seen in some of the early Christian material culture as well. Two examples will be discussed here.

1. THE MEGIDDO MOSAIC[74]

In 2005 archaeologists uncovered the foundations of a large Christian prayer hall under a prison compound near Megiddo. Preserved in the floor of the prayer hall is a beautiful mosaic picturing two fish, various geometric designs, and three Greek inscriptions. One of these inscriptions mentions a woman named Akeptous who donated a communion table to the prayer hall. Significantly, Jesus is expressly called God in the inscription: "The God-loving Akeptous has offered the table to God Jesus as a memorial."

Based on the style of letters and the language used in the mosaic, the excavators date the construction of the building to around AD 230, and believe it was abandoned in the late third century AD when the Sixth Roman Legion relocated to the area. If this dating is correct, the Megiddo prayer hall is the oldest Christian building in Israel, perhaps even anywhere, and contains one of the oldest Christian inscriptions found to date.[75] The significance of this discovery, therefore, can

71. Dan Brown, *The Da Vinci Code* (New York: Anchor Books, 2003), 306.

72. The historical sources disagree on the exact number in attendance (they range from 250 to over 300). In any event, five, perhaps only two, of the several hundred attendees sided with Arius who argued against the deity of Christ (Socrates Scholasticus, *Ecclesiastical History*, II.8; see also II.9 where only Theonas and Secundus are mentioned).

73. See especially Bauckham, *Jesus and the God of Israel*, 127–51.

74. This section is based on the helpful summary in Edward Adams, "The Ancient Church at Megiddo: The Discovery and an Assessment of Its Significance," *Expository Times* 120.2 (2008): 62–69. For the more complete preliminary report, see Yotam Tepper and Leah Di Segni, *A Christian Prayer Hall of the Third Century CE at Kefar 'Othnay (Legio): Excavations at the Megiddo Prison 2005* (Jerusalem: Israel Antiquities Authority, 2006).

75. The Dura-Europos house church (in modern Syria) is generally held to be the oldest known Christian place of worship. The house was built in AD 231 and converted into a church

Megiddo Mosaic

hardly be overemphasized: one of the earliest Christian inscriptions, found in the earliest Christian church, identifies Jesus as God.

2. *NOMINA SACRA*[76]

Another example that illuminates the early Christian belief about Jesus is a scribal phenomenon known as the *nomina sacra*. This Latin term (meaning "sacred names") refers to the early Christian practice of writing certain words in an abbreviated form "to indicate their sacred character."[77] Rather than spell out these words completely, scribes usually wrote just the first and last letter of the word (sometimes also a middle letter was included) and drew a horizontal line above the letters to distinguish them from the rest of the text. In the earliest Christian manuscripts (middle- to late-second century AD) four words were consistently written as *nomina sacra*: Jesus, Christ, Lord, and God.[78] This is significant since the key words for Jesus and God were given equal scribal veneration.

The *nomina sacra* are apparently a Christian adaptation of a Jewish prac-

in AD 240/241. The Megiddo Christian prayer hall, therefore, is ten years older (if the archaeologist's dating is correct).

76. The information for this section is from Larry W. Hurtado, "The Origin of the *Nomina Sacra*: A Proposal," *JBL* 117 (1998): 655–73; Hurtado, *Lord Jesus Christ*, 625–27.

77. Hurtado, "Origin of the *Nomina Sacra*," 655.

78. Hurtado argues that the *nomina sacra* practice probably goes back to the first century. Over the next two centuries the custom was altered somewhat. By the Byzantine period fifteen words were written as *nomina sacra*, most of which included one or two medial letters.

The earliest papyrus of Jude (P72), ca. AD 175. Instances of *nomina sacra* are circled.

tice. In the Second Temple period, Jewish scribes began expressing their reverence for *YHWH* (God's personal name) by writing his name in a special way. The Dead Sea Scrolls copyists, for example, typically replaced the tetragrammaton (*YHWH*) with four or five dots or transcribed it with Paleo-Hebrew letters. In Greek scrolls, scribes frequently wrote the divine name with Hebrew or Paleo-Hebrew letters, or in abbreviated form with Hebrew letters.

These two factors combined—(1) the equal treatment of Jesus' name and God's, and (2) that the practice has its antecedent in the Jewish tradition of abbreviating God's personal name—strongly suggest that the earliest *nomina sacra* reflect the belief in the divinity of Jesus. Some scholars, therefore, rightly propose these four early *nomina sacra* should more properly be termed *nomina divina* ("divine names").

BIBLIOGRAPHY

Adams, Edward. "The Ancient Church at Megiddo: The Discovery and an Assessment of Its Significance." *Expository Times* 120.2 (2008): 62–69.

Bauckham, Richard. *Jesus and the God of Israel: God Crucified and Other Studies on the New Testament's Christology of Divine Identity*. Grand Rapids: Eerdmans, 2008.

Boyarin, Daniel. *The Jewish Gospels: The Story of the Jewish Christ*. New York: New Press, 2012.

Brown, Dan. *The Da Vinci Code*. New York: Anchor Books, 2003.

Catto, Stephen K. *Reconstructing the First-Century Synagogue: A Critical Analysis of Current Research*. New York: T&T Clark, 2007.

Coenen, L. "Church, Synagogue." Pages 291–307 in *The New International Dictionary of New Testament Theology*. Edited by Colin Brown. Grand Rapids: Zondervan, 1986.

Cohen, Shaye J. D. "The Temple and the Synagogue." Pages 298–325 in *The Early Roman Period*. Volume 3 of *The Cambridge History of Judaism*. Edited by William Horbury, W. D. Davies, and John Sturdy. Cambridge: Cambridge University Press, 1999.

Craigie, P. C. *The Book of Deuteronomy*. Grand Rapids: Eerdmans, 1976.

Dunn, James D. G. *The Parting of the Ways: Between Christianity and Judaism and Their Significance for the Character of Christianity*. London: SCM, 1991.

Fiensy, David A. "The Composition of the Jerusalem Church." Pages 213–36 in *The Book of Acts in Its Palestinian Setting*. Edited by Richard Bauckham. Volume 4 of *The Book of Acts in Its Palestinian Setting*. Edited by Bruce W. Winter. Grand Rapids: Eerdmans, 1995.

Finkelstein, Louis. "The Origin of the Synagogue." Pages 3–13 in *The Synagogue: Studies in Origins, Archaeology and Architecture*. Edited by Joseph Gutman. New York: Ktav, 1975.

Fitzgerald, Gerald M. "Notes on Recent Discoveries." *Palestine Exploration Fund Quarterly Statement* 53 (1921): 175–86.

Gathercole, Simon. *The Pre-Existent Son: Recovering the Christologies of Matthew, Mark, and Luke*. Grand Rapids: Eerdmans, 2006.

Griffiths, J. Gwyn. "The Legacy of Egypt in Judaism." Pages 1025–51 in *The Early Roman Period*. Volume 3 of *The Cambridge History of Judaism*. Edited by William Horbury, W. D. Davies, and John Sturdy. Cambridge: Cambridge University Press, 1999.

Horbury, William, and David Noy. *Jewish Inscriptions of Graeco-Roman Egypt*. Cambridge: Cambridge University Press, 1992.

Hurtado, Larry W. *Honoring the Son: Jesus in Earliest Christian Devotional Practice*. Bellingham, WA: Lexham Press, 2018.

———. *How on Earth Did Jesus Become a God? Historical Questions about Earliest Devotion to Jesus*. Grand Rapids: Eerdmans, 2005.

———. *Lord Jesus Christ: Devotion to Jesus in Earliest Christianity*. Grand Rapids: Eerdmans, 2003.

———. "The Origin of the *Nomina Sacra*: A Proposal." *JBL* 117 (1998): 655–73.

Hvalvik, Reidar. "Paul as a Jewish Believer—According to the Book of Acts." Pages 121–53 in *Jewish Believers in Jesus*. Edited by Oskar Skarsaune and Reidar Hvalvik. Peabody, MA: Hendrickson, 2007.

Levine, Lee I. *The Ancient Synagogue: The First Thousand Years*. New Haven: Yale University Press, 2000.

———. "The Second Temple Synagogue: The Formative Years." Pages 7–31 in *The Synagogue in Late Antiquity*. Edited by Lee I. Levine. Philadelphia: American Schools of Oriental Research, 1987.

Niehaus, Jeffrey. "The Central Sanctuary: Where and When?" *TynBul* 43 (1992): 3–30.

Plassart, André. "La Synagogue Juive de Délos." *Revue Biblique* 11 (1914): 523–34.

Rivkin, E. "Ben Sira and the Non-Existence of the Synagogue." Pages 320–54 in *In the Time of Harvest: Essays in Honor of Abba Hillel Silver*. Edited by Daniel J. Silver. New York: Macmillan, 1963.

Rowley, H. H. *Worship in Ancient Israel: Its Forms and Meaning*. Philadelphia: Fortress, 1967.

Skarsaune, Oskar. *In the Shadow of the Temple: Jewish Influences on Early Christianity*. Downers Grove, IL: InterVarsity Press, 2002.

Tepper, Yotam, and Leah Di Segni. *A Christian Prayer Hall of the Third*

Century CE at Kefar 'Othnay (Legio): Excavations at the Megiddo Prison 2005. Jerusalem: Israel Antiquities Authority, 2006.

Vaux, Roland de. *Ancient Israel: Volume 2 Religious Institutions*. New York: McGraw-Hill, 1965.

Vincent, L. H. "Découverte de La Synagogue Des Affranchis à Jérusalem." *Revue Biblique* 30 (1921): 247–77.

Vogt, Peter T. "Centralization and Decentralization in Deuteronomy." Pages 118–38 in *Interpreting Deuteronomy: Issues and Approaches*. Edited by David G. Firth and Philip Johnston. Downers Grove, IL: InterVarsity Press, 2012.

Wenham, Gordon J. *The Book of Leviticus*. Grand Rapids: Eerdmans, 1979.

———. "Deuteronomy and the Central Sanctuary." *TynBul* 22 (1971): 103–18.

White, L. M. "The Delos Synagogue Revisited: Recent Fieldwork in the Graeco-Roman Diaspora." *Harvard Theological Review* 80 (1987): 133–60.

Wilson, Stephen. *Related Strangers: Jews and Christians 70–170 C.E.* Minneapolis: Fortress, 1995.

Wright, Christopher J. H. *Old Testament Ethics for the People of God*. Leicester: Inter-Varsity Press, 2004.

Wright, N. T. *The New Testament and the People of God*. Minneapolis: Fortress, 1992.

Zapata-Meza, M., and R. Sanz-Rincón. "Excavating Mary Magdalene's Hometown." *BAR* 43.3 (2017): 37–42.

CHAPTER 11

THE PERSECUTION OF THE EARLIEST CHRISTIANS IN GEOGRAPHICAL PERSPECTIVE

Acts 5:17–41; 7:52–8:3; 9:1–2; 12:1–11; 13:44–14:7; 16:16–24; 19:23–41; 21:27–25:12; 2 Cor 11:23–27; Heb 10:32–34; 1 Pet 3:13–17; 4:12–19; Rev 2:9–10

Eckhard J. Schnabel

KEY POINTS

- Followers of Jesus were persecuted in the first century in all Roman provinces except Cyprus, Cilicia, and Pamphylia.
- Cities in which the early Christians were persecuted include Jerusalem and Caesarea in Roman Judea, in Damascus and Antioch in the province of Syria; Pisidian Antioch, Iconium, and Lystra in the province of Galatia; Philippi, Thessalonica, and Berea in the province of Macedonia; Corinth in the province of Achaia; Ephesus and Pergamum in the province of Asia; and in the city of Rome.
- Persecution ranges from harassment, verbal abuse, denunciation before local courts, and judicial proceedings to beatings, exile, and execution.

INTRODUCTION

This essay surveys the extent of the persecution of Christians in the first century AD by listing twenty-seven different persecution events mentioned or alluded to by the New Testament writers or known from other early Christian writings. The term "persecution" is used here to describe the aggressive harassment and deliberate ill-treatment of the followers of Jesus, ranging from verbal abuse, denunciation before local magistrates, and initiating court proceedings to beatings, floggings, banishment from a city, exile, execution, and lynch killings. The Greek term *diōgmos* (διωγμός), usually translated as "persecution," is defined as "a program or process designed to harass and oppress someone."[1]

PERSECUTION IN JERUSALEM, JUDEA (1)

Peter and John who speak to a crowd of people in Solomon's Portico are taken into custody and taken to the Sanhedrin, Israel's highest court, whose members undertake a legal investigation into their activities (Acts 4:1–22). They order the apostles to stop proclaiming Jesus, and they threaten further action if they disobey. These events probably happened in AD 30, perhaps in mid-April, given that Jesus had been executed by crucifixion on April 8 (Nisan 14; see page 697 for a chart of the Israelite calendar).

PERSECUTION IN JERUSALEM, JUDEA (2)

Caiaphas, the high priest, and the Sadducees arrest the twelve apostles who preach in Solomon's Portico in the temple (Acts 5:17–41). The apostles spend a night in prison. The next morning they are taken to the Sanhedrin to be tried in the highest court of the land; some seek their execution. After the intervention of Gamaliel, the Sanhedrin decides to punish the apostles by flogging, and they are ordered to refrain from teaching about Jesus. These events presumably also happened in the spring of AD 30.

PERSECUTION IN JERUSALEM, JUDEA (3)

Greek-speaking Jews who belonged to the local synagogues of Jerusalem accuse Stephen of speaking against the temple and the law (Acts 6:9–12). They arrest Stephen, incite the people of Jerusalem, and initiate legal proceedings (Acts 6:12–15). Caiaphas presided over the trial that resulted in Stephen's execution (Acts 7:1, 54, 57–60). This third persecution event in Jerusalem probably dates to AD 31–32.

PERSECUTION IN JERUSALEM, JUDEA (4)

Following Stephen's execution, Caiaphas and the Sanhedrin (Acts 7:1, 54–60) took active measures against the church in Jerusalem. Saul (Paul) was actively involved in this persecution, which targeted individual Christians' families: he went from house to house, dragging off both men and women and putting them into prison (Acts 8:3). Many of the believers were forced to leave the city, fleeing to towns in Judea and Samaria (Acts 8:1, 4–5) where they were presumably taken in by relatives and friends, or by other followers of Jesus. Some of these Jewish Christian refugees traveled to the Mediterranean coast and headed in a northerly direction, reaching Phoenicia, a region that belonged to the province of Syria, and eventually Antioch, the capital of the province (Acts 11:19–20). These events happened sometime in AD 31–32.

PERSECUTION IN DAMASCUS, SYRIA (1)

Saul expanded the persecution of believers beyond Jerusalem, obtaining letters

---

1. BDAG, s.v. διωγμός. James A. Kelhoffer, *Persecution, Persuasion and Power: Readiness to Withstand Hardship as a Corroboration of Legitimacy in the New Testament* (Tübingen: Mohr Siebeck, 2010), 8, defines "persecution" and "unjust suffering" interchangeably to designate "any undeserved penalty or punishment—whether real, imagined, anticipated, or exaggerated." Some of the material in this essay is adapted from Eckhard J. Schnabel, "Persecution in the Early Christian Mission according to the Book of Acts," in *Rejection: God's Refugees in Biblical and Contemporary Perspective*, ed. Stanley E. Porter (Eugene, OR: Pickwick, 2015), 141–80; an extended version of this essay is published in *JETS*.

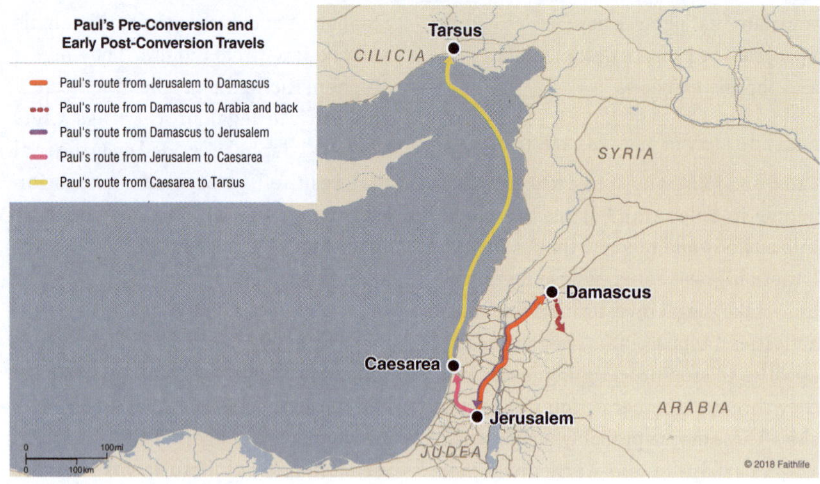

from the high priest requesting the authority to arrest local followers of Jesus and take them to Jerusalem for trial and punishment (Acts 9:1–2; 22:5). These events also date to the years AD 31–32.

PERSECUTION IN ARABIA/NABATEA

The representative of the Nabatean king Aretas attempted to arrest Saul (2 Cor 11:32–33) where he had been preaching the gospel (see Gal 1:17 in the context of Gal 1:23). He had ordered his men to guard the gates of Damascus so that Saul could be seized when he left the city. The Nabatean persecution of Saul may be dated to AD 32/33.

PERSECUTION IN DAMASCUS, SYRIA (2)

Jews of Damascus conspired to kill Saul, closely watching the city gates "day and night" to catch Saul (Acts 9:23–24). The arrest would either result in a lynch killing, in a trial in Damascus before the local magistrates, or in Saul's transfer to Petra, the capital of the Nabatean kingdom, to be tried and convicted there. The plot of the Jews of Damascus dates to AD 33/34.

PERSECUTION IN JERUSALEM, JUDEA (5)

The Greek-speaking Jews of Jerusalem plan to kill Saul when he visits Jerusalem for the first time after his conversion, forcing Paul to leave the city and go to Cilicia (Acts 9:28–30). This event must have happened around AD 33/34.

PERSECUTION IN ANTIOCH, PROVINCE OF SYRIA

The information given by Luke that "the disciples were called Christians first at Antioch" (Acts 11:26) probably implies denunciations against Jesus' followers in the capital of the province of Syria before the local courts or before the proconsul. The linguistic form of the term "Christians" (Χριστιανοί, *Christianoi*) indicates that it was coined by Latin speakers, which suggests that the followers of Jesus had come to the attention of city magistrates. Perhaps Jewish citizens brought

Bust of Claudius

legal charges before the magistrates of the city (as happened in Thessalonica; see Acts 17:5–9) or before the Roman proconsul of the province (as happened in Corinth; see Acts 18:12–14). Or Syrian citizens brought legal charges before the magistrates of the city (as happened in Philippi; see Acts 16:19–39) or the proconsul. These events could have taken place in AD 37/38 or, if Paul was active in Antioch at the time, in AD 39/40.

PERSECUTION IN ROME (1)

Claudius issued an edict in AD 41 commanding the Jews living in Rome to adhere to their ancestral way of life and to refrain from holding assemblies.[2] This edict should be understood in the context of unrest in the Jewish community in Rome, which is most plausibly related to the missionary activity of Jewish Christians in the capital of the empire that caused quarrels in the local synagogues.[3] The measure would have impacted not only the synagogues but the Christians as well.

PERSECUTION IN JERUSALEM, JUDEA (6)

Herod Agrippa I, whom the emperor had put in charge over Judea and Samaria in AD 41, initiated court proceedings against the apostles on death penalty charges (Acts 12:1). He executed James with the sword, and he arrested Peter, whom he evidently had convicted on a death penalty charge, setting a date for his execution after the Passover (Acts 12:2–4). It is only by a miracle that Peter escaped from prison (Acts 12:6–11). The date of these events is linked in Acts 11:4 with the Passover festival, which in AD 41 fell on April 5.[4]

Coin Depicting Herod Agrippa I

2. Cassius Dio, *Roman History* 60.6.6; see also Louis H. Feldman and Reinhold Meyer, *Jewish Life and Thought Among Greeks and Romans: Primary Readings* (Minneapolis: Fortress, 1996), 332 (nos. 10, 32).

3. See Rainer Riesner, *Paul's Early Period: Chronology, Mission Strategy, Theology* (Grand Rapids: Eerdmans, 1998), 167–79; Helga Botermann, *Das Judenedikt des Kaisers Claudius: Römischer Staat und Christiani im 1. Jahrhundert* (Stuttgart: Steiner, 1996), 103–40.

4. Cf. Riesner, *Paul's Early Period*, 118–22, for arguments that this persecution began in AD 41, at the latest in AD 42.

PERSECUTION IN PISIDIAN ANTIOCH IN PHRYGIA, PROVINCE OF GALATIA

In Pisidian Antioch, Jews contradict Paul's preaching "and heaped abuse on him" (Acts 13:45); the term βλασφημέω (*blasphēmeō*) means here "slander, revile, defame." When the church grew and when the gospel was preached throughout the entire region, the Jewish leaders "incited" (παροτρύνω, *parotrynō*) prominent women who had been attending the synagogue as well as the city magistrates, hoping to provoke a strong emotional reaction against the two missionaries. They "stirred up persecution" (ἐπήγειραν διωγμόν, *epēgeiran diōgmon*) and eventually "expelled" (ἐξέβαλον, *exebalon*) them from the region (Acts 13:50). These events took place in AD 46.

PERSECUTION IN ICONIUM IN LYCAONIA, PROVINCE OF GALATIA

In Iconium, Jewish and gentile residents, including the local magistrates (ἄρχοντες, *archontes*), conspire to "mistreat" (ὑβρίζω, *hybrizō*) the missionaries and "stone" (λιθοβολέω, *lithoboleō*) Paul and Barnabas, forcing them to leave the city (Acts 14:5–6). These events took place in AD 46.

PERSECUTION IN LYSTRA IN LYCAONIA, PROVINCE OF GALATIA

In Lystra, the residents are "convinced" (πείθω, *peithō*) by Jews from Pisidian Antioch and Iconium to take action against Paul and Barnabas (Acts 14:19). They "stoned" (λιθάζω, *lithazō*) Paul, an incident that Paul refers to in 2 Cor 11:25. Then they drag Paul's body through the streets and through one of the gates to a place outside the city, thinking that he is dead (Acts 14:19). These events also date to AD 46.

PERSECUTION IN ROME (2)

In AD 49 the emperor Claudius issued a second edict against the Jews of Rome, ordering them to leave the city of Rome (see Persecution in Antioch, Province of Syria). Suetonius reports Claudius' measures against "men of foreign birth" (*peregrinae condicionis homines*) and specifies that "since the Jews constantly made disturbances at the instigation of Chrestus, he expelled them from Rome" (*Judaeos impulsore Chresto assidue tumultuantes Roma expulit* [Suetonius, *Divus Claudius* 25.3–4]). The edict was a reaction to severe disturbances that prompted Claudius to order the expulsion of the Jews from the city of Rome. The most plausible interpretation of Suetonius' statement understands the *Chrestus* who is named as the instigator of the disturbances as a reference to Jesus Christ.[5] The edict intended to address disturbances provoked by the missionary outreach of Jewish followers of Jesus who preached that Jesus was the Messiah (Greek Χριστός, *Christos*). The edict of expulsion was directed at all the Jews living in Rome, not only the Christians.

The letter to the Hebrews, probably written for a Jewish Christian group in the city of Rome, reflects the reality of past, present, and imminent persecu-

5. See E. Mary Smallwood, *The Jews under Roman Rule: From Pompey to Diocletian; A Study in Political Relations* (Leiden: Brill, 1976), 210–16; Botermann, *Judenedikt*, 50–136; recently Silvia Cappelletti, *The Jewish Community of Rome from the Second Century B.C. to the Third Century C.E.* (Leiden: Brill, 2006), 77–78.

Possible Site of the Philippian Jail Where Paul and Silas Were Imprisoned

tion.[6] It cannot be determined when the letter was written, but a date before the Neronian persecution of Christians (see Persecution in Rome [3]) is plausible: it seems that none of the members of the church had suffered martyrdom (Heb 12:4). It is possible that the persecution mentioned in the letter took place in connection with Claudius' edict of AD 49.[7] The author reminds the believers that they had "endured in a great conflict full of suffering" (Heb 10:32), which is specified in the next sentences: some of them had been "made a public spectacle through denunciations and afflictions," some had been prisoners, and some had suffered the "seizure" of their possessions (Heb 10:33–34; cf. 13:3).[8] The denunciations (ὀνειδισμοί, *oneidismoi*) prompted four types of punishments, presumably after court cases in which Christians were found guilty.[9] First, they were made a public spectacle in the theater (θεατρίζω, *theatrizō*) where a hostile crowd hurled insults at them. Second, they suffered physical punishments (θλίψεις, *thlipseis*), such as public floggings and beatings. Third, they were incarcerated (δεσμίοι,

6. See Hans-Friedrich Weiss, *Der Brief an die Hebräer* (Göttingen: Vandenhoeck & Ruprecht, 1991), 76; Paul Ellingworth, *The Epistle to the Hebrews: A Commentary on the Greek Text* (Grand Rapids: Eerdmans, 1993), 28–29; Peter Lampe, *From Paul to Valentinus: Christians at Rome in the First Two Centuries* (Minneapolis: Fortress, 2003), 76–77.

7. See Craig R. Koester, *The Epistle to the Hebrews: A New Translation with Introduction and Commentary* (New York: Doubleday, 2001), 52.

8. Translation from Koester, *Hebrews*, 458. Bruce W. Winter, *Divine Honours for the Caesars: The First Christians' Responses* (Grand Rapids: Eerdmans, 2015), 270, interprets *oneidismoi* in terms of "verbal abuses;" thus most English translations.

9. For the following see Winter, *Divine Honours*, 268–72.

desmioi), awaiting trial and sentencing. Fourth, they suffered the confiscation of their possessions (ἁρπαγῇ τῶν ὑπαρχόντων, *harpagē tōn hyparchontōn*). The most plausible charge on which the Christians were convicted was the charge of *mājestās* ("treason") on account of their weekly meetings, violating Augustus' legislation on associations (from which Jews were explicitly exempt).[10] A fifth punishment may be hinted at in Heb 13:12–14 where the believers are admonished to accept suffering "outside the city gate ... outside the camp," expressions interpreted by Bruce Winter as referring to exile, a punishment that involved the loss of citizenship and all property.[11] Court cases in which Christians of Rome were sentenced to "exile" (*exilium*) could well have taken place in connection with Claudius' expulsion of the Jews from Rome in AD 49.

PERSECUTION IN PHILIPPI, PROVINCE OF MACEDONIA

In Philippi, the owners of the fortune-telling slave girl who was liberated from the spirit that had been speaking through her seized Paul and Silas and accused them before the magistrates of causing a disturbance in the city and of introducing new and unlawful customs (Acts 16:18–21). The punishment for these charges could range, depending on the specific charges, from eviction, loss of citizenship, forfeiture of private assets, and even to the death penalty. The citizens supported the accusations of the slave girl's owners. The magistrates ordered the lictors (bailiffs) to strip Paul and Silas and beat them with rods, a punishment that usually accompanied other penalties (Acts 16:22–24). These events date to August/October AD 49.

PERSECUTION IN THESSALONICA, PROVINCE OF MACEDONIA

Jews in Thessalonica who opposed Paul recruited "bad characters" (NIV), organized a crowd who started a riot, and looked for Paul and Silas with the intention to drag them before the assembly of the city, evidently hoping that the citizens would indict and sanction the visiting teachers (Acts 17:5). After they failed to locate Paul and Silas, they took Jason, presumably Paul's host, before the politarchs (πολιτάρχης), the senior magistrates of the city. Paul and Silas are accused of two offenses: they upset the stability in other regions of the empire and they have now come to Thessalonica where they are also upsetting the stability of peace and order; and they violate the decrees of the emperor by advocating loyalty to a certain Jesus rather than to the emperor in Rome (Acts 17:6–7). Since the magistrates could not interrogate the visiting teachers, they took bail from Jason and other believers, whom they evidently forced to vouch for the good behavior of Paul and Silas or for their departure from the city (Acts 17:9). The situation was dangerous: the Thessalonian immediately took Paul and Silas to Berea (Acts 17:10). These events date to October or November AD 49.

PERSECUTION IN BEREA, PROVINCE OF MACEDONIA

In Berea, the local citizens are incited by Jews from Thessalonica, with the result that Paul had to leave the city while Silas

10. See Olivia F. Robinson, *The Criminal Law of Ancient Rome* (London: Duckworth; Baltimore: Johns Hopkins University Press, 1995), 80.

11. Winter, *Divine Honours*, 278–85.

Bema at Corinth

and Timothy were able to stay (Acts 17:11–15). These events probably date to December AD 50.

PERSECUTION IN CORINTH, PROVINCE OF ACHAIA (1)

In Corinth, Jews who opposed Paul slandered him, perhaps asserting that he blasphemes God since he teaches that the crucified Jesus is God's Messiah rather than a man cursed by God (see Deut 21:22–23). As a result of the opposition, Paul abandoned his teaching in the synagogue (Acts 18:6–7). The opposition continued—Paul evidently considered leaving the city, a plan that is abandoned only after God assured Paul in a vision that he will not be harmed (Acts 18:9–10). The opposition reached a climax when some Jews "made a united attack" by seizing Paul and taking him to the judicial bench (βῆμα, *bēma*), a platform in the forum of the city (Acts 18:12).[12] The Jewish leaders initiated trial proceedings by forcing Paul to appear before Gallio, the governor of the province of Achaia, hoping that he would agree to judicial proceedings. Paul is accused of "persuading the people to worship God in ways contrary to the law" (Acts 18:13). The specific charges may have resembled those advanced by the Jews in Thessalonica, who had accused Paul of proclaiming Jesus as king, implying that Paul wanted to instigate a rebellion against the emperor and against Roman rule in the provinces. Or, the Corinthian Jews appealed to Claudius' edict that had decreed that the Jews should be allowed to practice their customs without interference, arguing that Paul disturbed law and order with his new religious teach-

12. See Mary E. H. Walbank, "The Foundation and Planning of Early Roman Corinth," *Journal of Roman Archaeology* 10 (1997): 121–22.

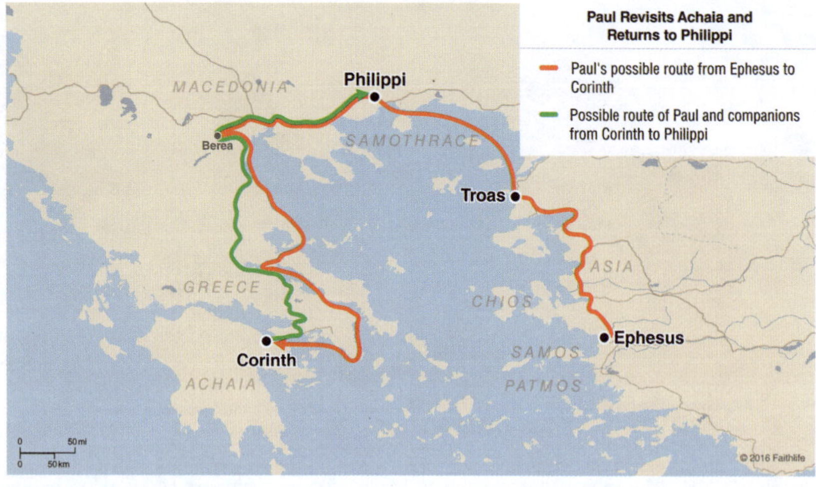

ing.[13] Or, they accused Paul of introducing a new religious cult whose weekly meetings were not exempt from the imperial ban on weekly meetings of associations and clubs.[14] Gallio dismissed the case against Paul, rejecting the legal merits of the charges: the accusations are neither a matter of "criminal behavior" nor a serious case of "deception."[15] These events took place in AD 50–51, the Gallio incident probably in July/August AD 51.

PERSECUTION IN EPHESUS, PROVINCE OF ASIA

In Ephesus, Demetrius, the leader of the guild of the silversmiths, incited the citizens to defend the preeminence of the goddess Artemis Ephesia against the growing Christian movement (Acts 19:23–28). Rather than taking legal action, Demetrius galvanized the population: people rushed into the theater for an impromptu popular assembly, dragging along Gaius and Aristarchus, Paul's travel companions, who were evidently denounced before the crowd, the public shame (and possible physical harm) was intended to suppress the influence of the new group of the followers of Jesus. The situation was so dangerous that the believers and local officials prevented Paul from going into the theater (Acts

13. See Adrian Nicolas Sherwin-White, *Roman Society and Roman Law in the New Testament* (Oxford: Clarendon,. 1963; repr., Grand Rapids: Baker, 1992), 99–107.

14. See Wendy Cotter, "The Collegia and Roman Law: State Restrictions on Voluntary Associations, 64 BCE–200 CE," in *Voluntary Associations in the Graeco-Roman World*, ed. John S. Kloppenborg and S. G. Wilson (London: Routledge, 1996), 74–89; Bruce W. Winter, "Gallio's Ruling on the Legal Status of Early Christianity (Acts 18:14–15)," *TynBul* 50 (1999): 217–18.

15. NIV translates in Acts 18:14 "some misdemeanor or serious crime," which misses the meaning of the Greek terms ἀδίκημα (*adikēma*) and ῥᾳδιούργημα (*rhadiourgēma*).

19:29–34). Gaius and Aristarchus seem to have been set free after the γραμματεύς (*grammateus*, city clerk) managed to quiet the crowd, warning of the detrimental consequences of mob violence, suggesting that they can file legal charges against Paul and his associates (Acts 19:35–41). Paul's departure from Ephesus (Acts 20:1) suggests that he decided to leave promptly in order to preempt a legal case before the local courts or the proconsul. These events probably date to June/July AD 55.

Persecution in Corinth, Province of Achaia (2)

Jews in Corinth planned to harm Paul during the sea voyage from Corinth to Syria and Jerusalem for the Passover Festival (Acts 20:3). The discovery of the plot prompted Paul to take the land route to Macedonia, embarking in Assos (Acts 20:14). These events date to April AD 57.

Persecution in Jerusalem, Judea (7)

Back in Jerusalem, when Paul visited the temple to demonstrate that he does not teach Jewish believers to neglect the Mosaic law, Jews from the province of Asia saw him in one of the inner courts of the temple; they stirred up the crowds of Jewish pilgrims and seized Paul, thinking that he had profaned the temple by bringing Trophimus, a gentile Christian from Ephesus, into the inner court (Acts 21:27–29). Paul is dragged from one of the inner courts into the outer court; a lynch killing was averted only when the commander of the Roman cohort stationed in the Antonia fortress intervened (Acts 21:30–33; see image on page 38). The commander then sought to extract a confession from Paul by torture, which is prevented only when Paul mentioned that he was a Roman citizen (Acts 22:24–29). After a hearing in the Sanhedrin that was inconclusive (Acts 22:30–23:10), and after a plot of Jerusalem Jews to kill Paul was uncovered (Acts 23:12–22), Paul is transferred as a prisoner to Caesarea. These events took place in May AD 57.

Persecution in Caesarea, Judea

The high priest Ananias and other Jewish leaders initiated legal proceedings against Paul in Caesarea before Felix, the Roman prefect of Judea, evidently with the goal of obtaining a death sentence (Acts 24:1–9). Despite the fact that Paul's guilt cannot be proven, Felix refused to release him: Paul remained in custody, awaiting the resolution of his case. Two years later, when Porcius Festus arrived in the province as the new prefect, Paul's opponents plan to ambush and kill Paul during a requested transfer of the case to Jerusalem (Acts 25:2–3). Since Paul feared that he would not get a fair hearing, he appealed to be tried by the emperor, a right that he had as a Roman citizen (Acts 25:1–12). Paul is transferred from Caesarea to Rome as a prisoner in AD 59/60, two years after his arrest in Jerusalem.

Persecution in Rome (3)

Paul is a prisoner in Rome at least for the two years from AD 60–62. If the Jewish leaders who had initiated legal proceedings against Paul in Judea did not show up in Rome, together with the requisite witnesses who could prove the charges against Paul, the case against Paul might have been dismissed—or not, if Nero, who was emperor since AD 54, regarded Paul as a threat.

If the letter to the Hebrews is connected with the city of Rome (see "Persecution in Rome [2]" on page 146), the threat of a new, possibly more severe persecution could imply imminent events not long before AD 64 when, after the fire that raged in Rome from 19–28 July, Nero persecuted and killed Christians (Tacitus, *Annales* 15.44).

PERSECUTION IN THE PROVINCES OF PONTUS-BITHYNIA, GALATIA, CAPPADOCIA, ASIA

The believers in "Pontus, Galatia, Cappadocia, Asia, and Bithynia" (1 Pet 1:1) face trials (1 Pet 1:5–6) and unjust suffering (1 Pet 3:9, 14)—mostly verbal abuse, as is indicated by the terms "slander" (καταλαλέω, *katalaleō*; 1 Pet 2:12; 3:16), "disparage" (ἐπηρεάζω, *epēreazō*; 1 Pet 3:16), "malign" (βλασφημέω, *blasphēmeō*; 1 Pet 4:4), and "reproach" (ὀνειδίζω, *oneidizō*; 1 Pet 4:14).[16] The fact that the believers have reason to be afraid (1 Pet 3:6) suggests that the verbal abuse at least implied more intimidating measures against the believers, if it did not indeed go hand in hand with denunciations before local magistrates. Given the experiences of Paul in Asia Minor, it would be surprising if the believers in the northern provinces would never have been denounced to the local authorities, who would force them to give a "defense" (ἀπολογία, *apologia*) of their faith (1 Pet 3:15). The statement in 1 Pet 4:16 ("if you suffer as a Christian") supports this interpretation: the term Χριστιανός (*christianos*) implies contacts between the followers of Jesus and Latin speakers that used this term to ridicule the believers in Jesus Messiah and that would consist of the local elites in these provinces (see "Persecution in Jerusalem, Judea [6]" on page 145).

Bust of Nero

PERSECUTION IN ROME (4)

The apostles Paul and Peter were martyred in the Neronian persecution.[17] Eusebius, who dates the death of Paul and Peter to Nero's thirteenth year (13 October AD 66–12 October AD 67), writes: "It is recorded that in Nero's reign Paul was beheaded in Rome itself, and that Peter likewise was crucified and the record is confirmed by the fact that the cemeteries there are still called by the names of Peter

16. See John H. Elliott, *1 Peter: A New Translation with Introduction and Commentary* (New York: Doubleday, 2000), 100.

17. The earliest reference is 1 Clement 5, which mentions neither the circumstances nor the date of their death.

and Paul" (*Ecclesiastical History* 2.25; trans. Williamson).[18]

PERSECUTION IN THE CHURCHES OF THE PROVINCE OF ASIA

Believers in the church in Philadelphia were pressured by local Jews to deny the name of Jesus (Rev 3:8–9). In Smyrna, members of the synagogue denounced followers of Jesus to the local authorities, perhaps alleging that their professed loyalty to Jesus implied disloyalty to the emperor.[19] Such denunciations had resulted in, or might soon lead to, the imprisonment of believers (Rev 2:9–10). At Pergamum, the believer Antipas had been put to death (Rev 2:13).

Further passages in Revelation also provide evidence for persecution. John, the author, had evidently been denounced to the authorities, tried in a local court and sentenced to "relegation to an island" (*relegatio ad insulam*), which did not normally involve loss of Roman citizenship or property, or perhaps to "deportation to an island" (*deportatio ad insulam*), which was permanent and involved loss of all rights and property—specifically to the island of Patmos (Rev 1:9). Unlike Antipas, John was not executed, perhaps because he belonged to a higher social class, or because his prophecies were regarded not as treason but as pernicious superstition, which was punished with a more lenient sentence.[20] John's readers know believers "who had been slain because of the word of God and the testimony they had maintained" (Rev 6:9); who were beheaded (Rev 20:4); who had died as martyrs as a result of their testimony (Rev 12:11; see also 11:7–8; 14:13; 16:6; 17:6; 18:24) and who thus "came out of the great tribulation" (Rev 7:14). The situation that John's prophecy implies can be dated from the early 70s to the late 90s AD, while an earlier date during the reign of Nero (AD 54–68) or shortly thereafter continues to be advocated.[21]

CONCLUSION

Seven instances of persecution are related for Jerusalem in Roman Judea, four for the city of Rome, three for the province of Syria (Damascus [2x] and Antioch), three for the province of Galatia (Pisidian Antioch, Iconium, and Lystra), three for the province of Macedonia (Philippi, Thessalonica, and Berea), two

---

18. Alfred Schöne, *Eusebi Chronicorum: Armeniam versionem latine factam ad libros manuscriptos recensuit H. Peterman* (Berlin: Weidmann, 1975–1876), 2:156–157 (Armenian version); Jerome's Latin translation dates their death to Nero's fourteenth year, i.e., AD 67/68. See also Acts of Paul 11; Acts of Peter 30–41; Ascension of Isaiah 4.2–3; Epiphanius, *Panarion* 27.6.6. As regards Nero's personal involvement, one needs to keep in mind that Nero was in Greece from autumn AD 66 to the end of AD 67 or the beginning of 68; Jerome Murphy-O'Connor, *Paul: A Critical Life* (Oxford: Oxford University Press, 1996), 371, with reference to Ceslas Spicq, *Les Épîtres pastorales*, 4th ed. (Paris: Gabalda, 1969), 146.

19. See Craig R. Koester, *Revelation: A New Translation with Introduction and Commentary* (New Haven: Yale University Press, 2014), 97, 280.

20. For the view that John was of a higher social class, see David E. Aune, *Revelation*, 3 vols. (Dallas: Word, 1997–98), 1:79–80. For the view that they were not treason, see Koester, *Revelation*, 243, with reference to Adela Yarbro Collins, *Crisis and Catharsis: The Power of the Apocalypse* (Philadelphia: Westminster, 1984), 102.

21. See Aune, *Revelation*, 1:lxv, lxx for the later dates. See Thomas B. Slater, "Dating the Apocalypse to John," *Biblica* 84 (2003): 252–58 for the reign of Nero.

for the province of Achaia (Corinth), one for Caesarea in Roman Judea, one for Arabia, an undetermined number for the province of Asia (Ephesus and Asia), and an undetermined number for the provinces of Pontus-Bithynia, Galatia, and Cappadocia. The only provinces of the Roman Empire for which no persecution is reported are Cyprus, Cilicia, and Pamphylia (and Spain and Egypt, provinces for which we have no explicit record of missionary activity in the first century).

BIBLIOGRAPHY

Aune, David E. *Revelation*. 3 vols. Dallas: Word, 1997–1998.

Botermann, Helga. *Das Judenedikt des Kaisers Claudius: Römischer Staat und Christiani im 1. Jahrhundert*. Stuttgart: Steiner, 1996.

Cappelletti, Silvia. *The Jewish Community of Rome from the Second Century B.C. to the Third Century C.E.* Leiden: Brill, 2006.

Collins, Adela Yarbro. *Crisis and Catharsis: The Power of the Apocalypse*. Philadelphia: Westminster, 1984.

Cotter, Wendy. "The Collegia and Roman Law: State Restrictions on Voluntary Associations, 64 BCE–200 CE." Pages 74–89 in *Voluntary Associations in the Graeco-Roman World*. Edited by John S. Kloppenborg and S. G. Wilson. London: Routledge, 1996.

Ellingworth, Paul. *The Epistle to the Hebrews: A Commentary on the Greek Text*. Grand Rapids: Eerdmans, 1993.

Elliott, John H. *1 Peter: A New Translation with Introduction and Commentary*. New York: Doubleday, 2000.

Feldman, Louis H., and Reinhold Meyer. *Jewish Life and Thought Among Greeks and Romans: Primary Readings*. Minneapolis: Fortress, 1996.

Kelhoffer, James A. *Persecution, Persuasion and Power: Readiness to Withstand Hardship as a Corroboration of Legitimacy in the New Testament*. Tübingen: Mohr Siebeck, 2010.

Koester, Craig R. *The Epistle to the Hebrews: A New Translation with Introduction and Commentary*. New York: Doubleday, 2001.

———. *Revelation: A New Translation with Introduction and Commentary*.

New Haven: Yale University Press, 2014.

Lampe, Peter. *From Paul to Valentinus: Christians at Rome in the First Two Centuries*. Minneapolis: Fortress, 2003.

Murphy-O'Connor, Jerome. *Paul: A Critical Life*. Oxford: Oxford University Press, 1996.

Riesner, Rainer. *Paul's Early Period: Chronology, Mission Strategy, Theology*. Grand Rapids: Eerdmans, 1998.

Robinson, Olivia F. *The Criminal Law of Ancient Rome*. London: Duckworth; Baltimore: Johns Hopkins University Press, 1995.

Schnabel, Eckhard J. "Persecution in the Early Christian Mission according to the Book of Acts." Pages 141–80 in *Rejection: God's Refugees in Biblical and Contemporary Perspective*. Edited by Stanley E. Porter. Eugene, OR: Pickwick, 2015.

Schöne, Alfred. *Eusebi Chronicorum: Armeniam versionem latine factam ad libros manuscriptos recensuit H. Peterman*. Berlin: Weidmann, 1875–1876.

Sherwin-White, Adrian Nicolas. *Roman Society and Roman Law in the New Testament*. Oxford: Clarendon, 1963. Repr. Grand Rapids: Baker, 1992.

Slater, Thomas B. "Dating the Apocalypse to John." *Biblica* 84 (2003): 252–58.

Smallwood, E. Mary. *The Jews under Roman Rule: From Pompey to Diocletian; A Study in Political Relations*. Leiden: Brill, 1976.

Spicq, Ceslas. *Les Épîtres pastorales*. 4th ed. Paris: Gabalda, 1969.

Walbank, Mary E. H. "The Foundation and Planning of Early Roman Corinth." *Journal of Roman Archaeology* 10 (1997): 95–130.

Weiss, Hans-Friedrich. *Der Brief an die Hebräer*. Göttingen: Vandenhoeck & Ruprecht, 1991.

Winter, Bruce W. *Divine Honours for the Caesars: The First Christians' Responses*. Grand Rapids: Eerdmans, 2015.

———. "Gallio's Ruling on the Legal Status of Early Christianity (Acts 18:14–15)." *TynBul* 50 (1999): 213–24.

CHAPTER 12

THE THEODOTUS SYNAGOGUE INSCRIPTION AND ITS RELATIONSHIP TO THE BOOK OF ACTS

Acts 6:9

Chris McKinny

KEY POINTS

- The Theodotus Synagogue Inscription was found beside the remains of a first century BC/AD synagogue on the southeastern side of the City of David (not in the area of the Ophel, near the Temple Mount, as is commonly thought).
- The synagogue and its inscription has been identified with the "Synagogue of the Freedman" in Acts 6:9, which might also indicate that the synagogue was the home synagogue of Stephen, Simon of Cyrene, and the apostle Paul.
- Recent excavations in the City of David, particularly those in connection with the Herodian Stepped Street, when taken together with unique material from Luke in the Gospel of Luke and Acts demonstrate that Luke was very familiar with the Lower City of Jerusalem.

INTRODUCTION

Between 1913–1914 and again in 1923–1924, Raymond Weill carried out the first above-ground, large-scale excavations in the City of David.[1] Weill's excavations primarily took place along the southeastern

1. The first excavations in Jerusalem were the tunneling activities of Charles Warren in the 1860s, Bliss and Dickie in the 1890s, and Montague Parker in 1909–1911. Weill was also the first Jewish archaeologist to excavate in Jerusalem, see Ronny Reich, "Weill, Raymond," in *The Oxford Encyclopedia of Archaeology in the Near East*, ed. Eric Meyers (Oxford: Oxford University

Theodotus Synagogue Inscription

slopes of the City of David.[2] The rudimentary techniques of Weill's excavation, which corresponded to contemporary scholars of his day, makes reassessment of his work difficult. In broad terms, Weill exposed a large Herodian quarry with two large "tombs" that he identified with the "tomb of David" and the Davidic dynasty (see 1 Kgs 2:10). Presently, most scholars understand that these "tombs" are in fact underground (barrel-shaped) cellars of late Second Temple period Jewish homes in the Lower City of Jerusalem.[3] Significantly, just to the south of these cellars Weill found several water installations including a stepped *mikveh* (Jewish ritual bath) and an adjoining cistern.[4] Within the cistern, Weill found several architectural pieces including an Ionic capital, dressed masonry fragments, and a large Greek dedicatory inscription mentioning a synagogue and accompanying lodging and water facilities.

Unquestionably, the inscription—known as the Theodotus Synagogue Inscription—was the most important find of Weill's excavation. Weill and later scholars (for example, Ronny Reich) connected the water cistern and *mikveh* with the "water installations" mentioned in the inscription.[5] Thus, it seems probable that a first century AD synagogue existed

Press, 1997), 5:343–44; see also Raymond Weill, *La Cité de David, I–II: Compte rendu des fouilles exécutées à Jérusalem, sur les site de la ville primitiv; 2, Texte* (Paris: Geuthner, 1947); Weill and Louis-Hugues Vincent, *The City of David: Revisiting Early Excavations; English Translations of Reports by Raymond Weill and L. H. Vincent*, ed. Hershel Shanks and Ronny Reich (Washington, DC: Biblical Archaeology Society, 2004).

2. Further excavations also were undertaken further to the north in "Channel II" (also known as the Canaanite or Siloam tunnel) (Ronny Reich, *Excavating the City of David: Where Jerusalem's History Began* [Jerusalem: Israel Exploration Society, 2011], 85–86).

3. For example, Reich, *Excavating the City of David*, 73–74.

4. Reich, *Excavating the City of David*, 75–76.

5. Reich, *Excavating the City of David*, 73–74.

in the southeastern part of the Lower City of Jerusalem while the Herodian temple was still standing.[6] Subsequently, many scholars have suggested a connection between the inscription and the "Synagogue of the Freedmen" that is mentioned in Acts 6:9.[7] The basis for this identification is the language of the inscription (Greek), the Latin/Roman name of the father (Vettenos) of the founder (Theodotus), and the mention of accommodations for needy travelers of the Jewish diaspora. While I accept the probability (if not the certainty) of this proposal, recent excavations in the City of David give further information concerning the geographical and archaeological context of the synagogue during the first century AD.

THE THEODOTUS SYNAGOGUE INSCRIPTION AND THE SYNAGOGUE OF THE FREEDMEN (ACTS 6:9)

Below, I have reproduced the translation of the Theodotus Synagogue Inscription from the original publication after English translation from French.

> Theodotus, son of Vettenos, priest and chief of the synagogue, son of a synagogue head, grandson of a synagogue head, built this the synagogue for the reading of Torah and the teaching of the instruction in the commandments, and the guest house with its rooms and water installations as lodging for needy [pilgrims] from the Diaspora. The foundations[8] were laid by his ancestors, the elders and Simonides.[9]

While Theodotus ("God gave" in Greek) is listed as the builder of the synagogue, the inscription later states that "the foundations were laid by his ancestors" which might indicate that Theodotus renovated the synagogue or perhaps rebuilt it after it was damaged. It is also possible that Theodotus built the synagogue in its entirety in its present location (Weill's excavation). According to this hypothetical reconstruction, Theodotus would have built a new structure after moving to that location from somewhere else in the city. We will discuss the archaeological context below, but there is universal agreement that the synagogue was destroyed in AD 70 and was therefore built sometime before this massive destruction.[10] Accordingly, and assum-

6. John S. Kloppenborg, "The Theodotus Synagogue Inscription and the Problem of First-Century Synagogue Buildings," in *Jesus and Archaeology*, ed. James H. Charlesworth (Grand Rapids: Eerdmans, 2006), 236–82.

7. For example, see C. K. Barrett, *The Acts of the Apostles: Vol. 1; Preliminary Introduction and Commentary on Acts 1–14* (Edinburgh: T&T Clark, 2004) with bibliography.

8. Translated as "foundation stone" in K. C. Hanson and D. E. Oakman, *Palestine in the Time of Jesus: Social Structures and Social Conflicts* (Minneapolis: Fortress, 1998), 73–74.

9. Interestingly, the inscription, although found in 1913, was not publicly known until 1921 as a result of World War I (in which Weill served on the French side), Raymond Weill and Théodore Reinach, "L'Inscription de Théodotos," *Revue Des Études Juives* 71 (1921): 30–31; Weill and Vincent, *City of David*, 86–90; Reich, *Excavating the City of David*, 74–75.

10. For example, Reich, *Excavating the City of David*, 72; Eric M. Meyers and Mark A. Chancey, *Alexander to Constantine: Archaeology of the Land of the Bible* (New Haven, CT: Yale University Press, 2012), 209.

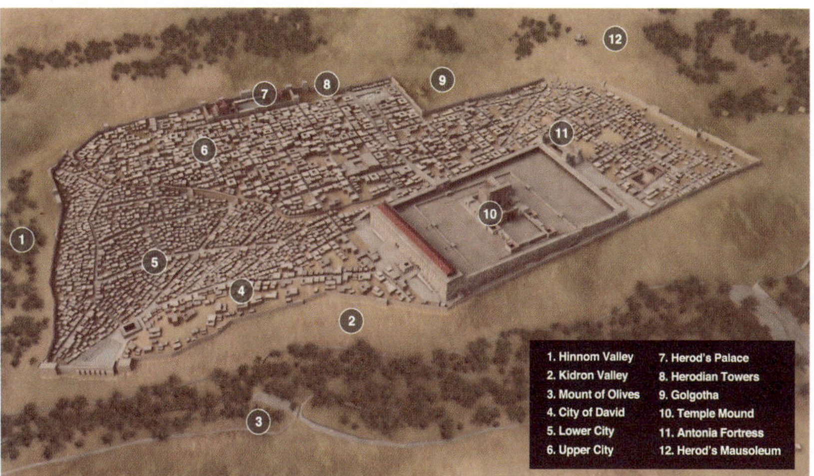

The Upper City (#1), Lower City (#2), and City of David (#3) of 1st Century Jerusalem

ing some type of renovation to an existing structure by Theodotus perhaps this renovation could be related to the major 31 BC (or spring 30 BC) earthquake mentioned by Josephus (*J.W.* 1.370; *Ant.* 15.211). In any case, the mention of three generations who functioned as the "chief of the synagogue" as well as the reference to the building or rebuilding of the synagogue and its adjoining compartments would seem to indicate that the congregation was active for at least most of the first century AD and perhaps even earlier in the first century BC.

While the exact dating and history of Theodotus' synagogue will likely remain unknown, the mention of the title "chief of synagogue" (ἀρχισυνάγωγος, *archisynagōgos*) can be further clarified by several other New Testament occurrences of this title (compare Jairus of Capernaum, Mark 5:22, 35–38; Luke 8:41, 49; unnamed ruler of Galilean synagogue, Luke 13:14; multiple rulers of synagogue in Antioch in Pisidia, Acts 13:15; Crispus and Sosthenes rulers of the Corinthian synagogue, 18:8, 17). The position of chief or ruler of the synagogue was clearly accompanied by wealth and prestige as noted by Theodotus' identification as priest and synagogue head, as well as the material wealth required to build or rebuild the synagogue. This reality is further evidence against the premise that the Lower City of Jerusalem (that is, the eastern hill/City of David) was the poorer neighborhood of Jerusalem in comparison to the Upper City (that is, the western hill).[11]

Regarding Simonides, it is unclear if this figure is the same as the grandfather of Theodotus, who also served as a chief of synagogue. Vettenos, the father of Theodotus, is the most important name in the inscription. Vettenos is likely related to the Roman *gens Vettena*, and there is

11. See, for example, Doron Ben-Ami and Yana Tchekhanovets, "The Lower City of Jerusalem on the Eve of Its Destruction, 70 C.E.: A View From Hanyon Givati," *BASOR* 364 (November 2011): 61–85.

a widespread opinion that he received this name due to a relationship between himself and the Vetteni or Vettienei families of Rome.[12] Scholars have further suggested that either Vettenos or perhaps Theodotus were the freedman (that is, a freed Roman slave) of the "Synagogue of the Freedmen" that is mentioned in Acts 6:9.[13] Additional evidence comes from later rabbinic references to a Jerusalem synagogue used by Alexandrians and Tarsians (that is, from Tarsus the capital of Cilicia).[14] Given that Acts 6:9 indicates that Hellenistic Jews from Cyrene, Alexandria, Cilicia, and Asia were part of the Synagogue of the Freedmen, it is therefore possible to link Simon of Cyrene (Matt 27:32; Mark 15:21; Luke 23:26), Saul/Paul of Tarsus (for example, Acts 9:11, 30; 11:25), and Stephen (most likely a Hellenist Jew; Acts 6:5) with this synagogue. Craig Keener suggests that Saul/Paul and Stephen "grew up" in this synagogue.[15] This is supported by the reference to Cilicia (Paul's home country)[16] in connection with the synagogue (Acts 6:9) and Saul's introduction in the book of Acts at the end of the stoning of Stephen (Acts 7:58). While we must remain cautious, this proposal seems compelling even if it is based on several pieces of fragmentary evidence. Assuming the basic viability of this suggestion, let us examine recent archaeological work in the City of David that helps contextualize Theodotus' diasporic/Hellenistic synagogue in the Lower City of first century AD Jerusalem.

ARCHAEOLOGICAL AND GEOGRAPHICAL CONTEXT

As we have demonstrated, the Theodotus Synagogue Inscription has immense historical value irrespective of its archaeological context as it is a direct witness to first century BC–AD synagogues, the Jewish diaspora, and religious practices in Jerusalem before the AD 70 destruction of Jerusalem. Moreover, as we have argued, its identification with the "Synagogue of the Freedmen" is a definite possibility, even if it cannot be determined with certainty. On the other hand, because Weill's excavations are not widely known, very few scholars have dealt with the archaeological stratigraphic significance of where this synagogue was located in relationship to the newly uncovered Herodian street that transects the Lower City/City of David north-south from the Temple Mount to the Siloam Pool. Despite numerous sec-

12. Anders Runesson, Donald D. Binder, and Birger Olsson, *The Ancient Synagogue from Its Origins to 200 C.E.: A Source Book* (Leiden: Brill, 2008), 54.

13. For example, Ben Witherington III, *The Acts of the Apostles: A Socio-Rhetorical Commentary* (Grand Rapids: Eerdmans, 1998), 256; Darrell L. Bock, *Acts*, 2 vols. (Grand Rapids: Baker Academic, 2007), 270; Craig S. Keener, *Acts: An Exegetical Commentary: Volume 2; 3:1–14:28* (Grand Rapids: Baker Academic, 2014), 394–97.

14. See t. Megillah 3:6 (224); y. Megillah 3:1, 73d.35 (Jerusalem synagogue of the Alexandrians); b. Megillah 26a (Jerusalem synagogue of the Tarsians or coppersmiths). See discussion in Joachim Jeremias, *Jerusalem in the Time of Jesus* (London: SCM, 1969), 65–66; Barrett, *Acts*, 324; Craig S. Keener, *The IVP Bible Background Commentary: New Testament*, 2nd ed. (Downers Grove, IL: InterVarsity Press, 2014), 335; Keener, *Acts*, 2:393–94.

15. Keener, *Acts*, 2:395–96.

16. "I [Paul] am a Jew, born in Tarsus in Cilicia, but brought up in this city [Jerusalem], educated at the feet of Gamaliel" (Acts 22:3 ESV).

Location of Theodotus Inscription

ondary sources listing the discovery of the Theodotus inscription being located either immediately south of the Temple Mount or in the Temple Mount excavations,[17] it is clear that Weill found the Theodotus inscription on the southeastern slopes of the City of David. This location is less than 110 yards (100 m) north of the pool of Siloam.[18] While the inscription is in secondary use, it seems clear that it originated from a nearby building that was either destroyed by quarrying activities or, more likely, was located to the west beneath the old street that was not excavated by Weill. This street remains one of the main north-south streets in the City of David until today.

Recent excavations have added substantial archaeological data for understanding Jerusalem in the first century AD.[19] Beginning in the Ophel (that is, just south of the Temple Mount), Eilat Mazar's renewed excavations have shown a wide range of late Second Temple period activ-

17. For example, Steven Fine, "Synagogue Inscriptions," in Meyers, *Oxford Encyclopedia of Archaeology*, 5:114; Philip A. Harland, *Travel and Religion in Antiquity* (Waterloo, ON: Wilfrid Laurier University Press, 2011), 57; Jodi Magness, *The Archaeology of the Holy Land: From the Destruction of Solomon's Temple to the Muslim Conquest* (Cambridge: Cambridge University Press, 2012), 288.

18. Reich, *Excavating the City of David*.

19. For context, see that all of these excavations have occurred after the conclusion of Reich's summary treatment of Jerusalem's archaeology (Reich, *Excavating the City of David*, 270–72).

Aerial of Southern End of the City of David

ities including (announced in 2018) the discovery of a massive cave located just to the southwest of the staircase of the Huldah Gates.[20] While it was just exposed and further analyses might change her conclusions, this cave was apparently used throughout the late Second Temple period, and by the Jewish rebels during the siege of Jerusalem between AD 67–70.[21]

Further to the south, Yuval Gadot's excavation revealed that the western slope of the Kidron Valley was used as an enormous garbage depositing zone that was utilized by the entire city during the first century AD.[22] On the east side of the eastern hill/City of David, excavations headed by Doron Ben Ami have revealed a large palatial structure that he has con-

20. Eilat Mazar, ed., *The Ophel Excavations to the South of the Temple Mount: Final Reports Volume 1* (Jerusalem: Shoham, 2015); for past excavations in the Ophel, see summary in Mazar, *The Complete Guide to the Temple Mount Excavations* (Jerusalem: Shoham, 2002).

21. Brent Nagtegaal, "Dozens of Coins From Final Year of Jewish Revolt Discovered in Jerusalem Cave," *The Trumpet*, March 26, 2018, https://www.thetrumpet.com/17069-rare-jewish-revolt-coins-discovered-in-jerusalem-cave; https://www.youtube.com/watch?v=Cz4hgd2XdtI.

22. For example, Yuval Gadot and Yonatan Adler, "A Quantitative Analysis of Jewish Chalk Vessel Frequencies in Early Roman Jerusalem: A View from the City's Garbage Dump," *IEJ* 66 (2016): 202–19. This excavation continues the earlier work of Reich related to the Early Roman city dump of Jerusalem; see Guy Bar-Oz et al., "'Holy Garbage': A Quantitative Study of the City-Dump of Early Roman Jerusalem," *Levant* 39 (2007): 1–12, https://doi.org/10.1179/lev.2007.39.1.1.

nected with the "palace of Queen Helena of Adiabene" (Josephus, *Ant.* 20.17–95; *J.W.* 2.530; 4.567; 5.147) along with many other earlier remains.[23] On the west side of these excavations and running the entire length of the central or Tyropean Valley, Reich and Eli Shukron excavated a drainage tunnel of an Early Roman street[24] and now the street itself is being excavated by Nahshon Szanton, Joe Uziel, and Moran Hagbi.[25] This Herodian street ran from the Antonia Fortress (northwest corner of the Temple Mount) to the Siloam Pool.[26]

In recent years, excavations to the northwest of the partially exposed Siloam Pool (previously by Reich and Shukron) show that the pool was accessed by a stepped street. This street transects the entire City of David. Significantly, it seems that the Herodian stepped street passed near ("a few dozen meters") the Theodotus Synagogue.[27] In addition, a segment of another Herodian street (or perhaps the same street, see above) connected to the northwestern corner of the pool of Siloam was also excavated by Reich and Shukron.[28] The extent of this street as well as the main central/Tyropean Valley branch have yet to be determined as excavations are ongoing.[29] However, a comparison of the coordinates between the likely location of the Theodotus Synagogue (that is, beneath the unexcavated street, see fig. 1 on page 701) and the street running northwest from the pool of Siloam indicates that these two locations are possibly only separated by around 80–120 feet (25–40 m) from one another. Regarding the date of these streets, it is now appar-

23. See especially Ben-Ami and Tchekhanovets, "Lower City of Jerusalem"; Ben-Ami and Tchekhanovets, "A Roman Mansion Found in the City of David," *IEJ* 63 (2013): 164–73; see remains that may possibly be connected with the Seleucid Akra, Ben-Ami and Tchekhanovets, "'Then They Built up the City of David with a High, Strong Wall and Strong Towers, and It Became Their Citadel' (I Maccabees 1:33)," *City of David Studies of Ancient Jerusalem* 11 (2016): 19*–29*; see also Doron Ben-Ami, "Notes on the Iron IIA Settlement in Jerusalem in Light of Excavations in the Northwest of the City of David," *Tel Aviv* 41 (2014): 3–19, https://doi.org/10.1179/0334435514Z.00000000030.

24. Reich, *Excavating the City of David*, 244–48.

25. Nahshon Szanton and Joe Uziel, "On the Question of the Stepped Stone Monument from the Second Temple Period in the City of David," *City of David Studies of Ancient Jerusalem* 10 (2015): 19–40; Uziel, Szanton, and Moran Hagbi, "Monumental Building Projects in Jerusalem in the Days of Pontius Pilate: A Numismatic View from the Stepped Street in the Tyropoeon Valley," *New Studies in the Archaeology of Jerusalem and its Region* 10 (2016): 99–114 [in Hebrew]; Szanton and Ayala Zilberstein, "'The Second Hill, Which Bore the Name of Acra, and Supported the Lower City…' A New Look at the Lower City of Jerusalem in the End of the Second Temple Period," *New Studies in the Archaeology of Jerusalem and Its Region* 10 (2016): 30–47.

26. Reich, *Excavating the City of David*, 225–43.

27. Nir Hasson, quoting Yuval Baruch, "Ancient Jerusalem Road Hints at Possible Reason for Jewish Revolt Against Rome," *Haaretz*, January 2, 2017, https://www.haaretz.com/archaeology/.premium-ancient-jerusalem-road-hints-at-possible-reason-for-jewish-revolt-against-rome-1.5480317.

28. Reich, *Excavating the City of David*, 232–44, see especially fig. 162.

29. I would like to express my gratitude to Joe Uziel and Nahshon Szanton for sharing with me the preliminary results of their excavation of the stepped street.

ent that these Herodian streets[30] were actually built during the governance of Pontius Pilate (AD 26–36) as made evident by coins bearing his insignia found beneath the paving stones. These streets came to an exceptionally violent end in AD 70 with the Roman sack of Jerusalem. Thus, we have a very tight chronological window (between AD 26–36)[31] to connect Pontius Pilate's building activities in this zone of Jerusalem to events mentioned in the Gospels (for example, John 9 and Luke 13:4)[32] and the book of Acts (Acts 6:9).[33]

---

30. It is possible that it is only a single very, wide street (Joe Uziel personal communication).

31. The excavators note evidence of an earlier street dating to either the Hasmonean or Herodian period. This earlier street seems to have been destroyed by the stepped street (Szanton and Zilberstein, "'Second Hill," 34 n. 8).

32. Chris McKinny, "Southern Temple Mount Excavations," in *Lexham Geographic Commentary on the Gospels*, ed. Barry J. Beitzel (Bellingham, WA: Lexham, 2018), 453–54.

33. As an aside to these important chronological, geographical, and archaeological details, given the location of the current excavation (that is, along the southwestern slopes of the City of David) it seems possible that Uziel, Szanton, and Hagbi may be on the verge of an even more significant discovery—the tomb of David. In the Old Testament, the tomb(s) of David (and subsequently the tombs of his descendants) were clearly localized in the City of David (see 1 Kgs 2:10; 2 Kgs 9:28; 2 Chr 32:33). The most important reference related to the location of David's tomb is Neh 3:16, which indicates that the building of the wall of Jerusalem (the context seems to be referring to the eastern wall of the city along the Central Valley) was "repaired to a point opposite the tombs of David, as far as the artificial pool, and as far as the house of the mighty men" [compare the location of Bathsheba/Uriah's house to David's in 2 Sam 11:2–13]. In the preceding verse, the reference to the "Pool of Shelah of the king's garden" should most likely be connected with the pool of Siloam (for example, John 9:7, 11; Josephus, *J.W.* 5.145; m. Sukkah 4:9) and the king's garden mentioned in connection with the burials of Manasseh and Amon (2 Kgs 21:18, 26 [that is, the garden of Uzza]; see also 2 Kgs 25:4). Taken together, these references would seem to indicate that the tomb of David (and perhaps also his palace, G. Barkay personal communication) were located near the pool of Siloam. Accordingly, and assuming the reconstruction outlined above, the tomb should be located north of the pool of Siloam as the south (Hinnom Valley), east (Kidron Valley), and west (rise of Western Hill) can be excluded for topographic reasons. The current excavators have revealed a "stepped podium" along the eastern side of the street and described the street as passing near a monumental structure, which is located to the north of the pool of Siloam on the eastern side of the street; see Szanton and Uziel, "On the Question of the Stepped Stone Monument"; Uziel, Szanton, and Hagbi, "Monumental Building Projects"; Szanton and Zilberstein, "'Second Hill," 32–33*, Fig. 1 n. 6. The tomb of David is mentioned several times in the Early Roman period, these include Peter's famous reference in Acts 2:29 and Josephus' (via Nicolaus of Damascus) recounting of John Hyrcanus and Herod the Great's (attempted) plundering of the tomb (*Ant.* 16.179–184; t. Baba Batra 1:11; see also Cassius Dio 69.14 who mentions the destruction of the tomb of Solomon following the Bar Kokhba Revolt). With regard to Herod the Great, Josephus relayed that Herod "built a propitiatory monument of that fright he had been in; and this of white stone, at the mouth of the sepulcher, and that at a great expense also. And even Nicolaus his historiographer makes mention of this monument built by Herod, though he does not mention his going down into the sepulcher" (*Ant.* 16.182–183 [Whiston]). In my opinion it seems possible that the above mentioned monumental building on the eastern side of the stepped street could be the Herodian Second Temple period monument/complex over the presumable location of the tomb of David. Finally, it should be noted that the traditional location for the tomb of David beneath the Cenacle is incorrect, as it is based on the faulty Byzantine assumption that Mount Zion was located on the Western Hill of Jerusalem—contra the notes

Corner Steps of Pool of Siloam

CONCLUSION: THE INSCRIPTION IN ITS LUKAN CONTEXT

In light of the recent archaeological excavations in the southern part of the Lower City, it is now possible to examine Luke's references to this region of Jerusalem against its archaeological and geographical context. Two references to this region occur only in Lukan material—the Synagogue of the Freedman (Acts 6:9) and the disaster of the collapse of the Siloam tower (Luke 13:4). As we have demonstrated, the proposal to connect the Synagogue of the Freedmen with the Theodotus Synagogue Inscription and its accompanying architectural features remains a viable historical reconstruction. Moreover, it is particularly intriguing to consider that this structure was the "home synagogue" of Saul/Paul and Stephen (Acts 6:9; 7:58). If this proposal is correct, then it seems likely that Luke was informed about this synagogue by Paul (compare Col 4:14; 2 Tim 4:11; Phlm 24), and that Luke himself would have visited this area of the city during his research for his books (that is, Luke-Acts). While the identity of the enigmatic Siloam tower (Luke 13:4) remains elusive,[34] the timing of its construction during the reign of Pontius Pilate closely matches the excavation data connecting Pilate to the stepped street. The collapse of the Siloam tower would have taken place in approximately AD 30–33 (depending on one's view of the date of the crucifixion) and Stephen's stoning would have occurred a short time later. Thus, the archaeological evidence related to Pontius Pilate demonstrates Luke's accuracy regarding the dating of the Siloam tower. These details would seem to make clear that Luke was very familiar with the locations that he describes. One can imagine Luke visiting the Lower City of Jerusalem seeing the Siloam Pool with its accompanying fortifications (Luke 13:4), passing near Theodotus' Synagogue by walking on the stepped street (Acts 6:9)—perhaps even passing the tomb of David (Acts 2:29, see note above) before eventually making his way to the Temple Mount (Luke 2:21–38, 41–51). In each instance, he would use these settings as the backdrop of his unique material in his Gospel and the book of Acts.

BIBLIOGRAPHY

Bar-Oz, Guy, Ram Bouchnik, Ehud Weiss, Lior Weissbrod, Daniella E. Bar-Yosef Mayer, and Ronny Reich. "'Holy Garbage': A Quantitative Study

in John D. Currid and David W. Chapman, eds., *ESV Archaeology Study Bible* (Wheaton, IL: Crossway, 2018), 1600.

34. It is possible that this tower was related to the fortification of the city built around the pool of Siloam, see, for example, Keener, *IVP Bible Background Commentary*, 215.

of the City-Dump of Early Roman Jerusalem." *Levant* 39 (2007): 1–12. https://doi.org/10.1179/lev.2007.39.1.1.

Barrett, C. K. *The Acts of the Apostles, Vol. 1: Preliminary Introduction and Commentary on Acts 1–14*. Edinburgh: T&T Clark, 2004.

Ben-Ami, Doron. "Notes on the Iron IIA Settlement in Jerusalem in Light of Excavations in the Northwest of the City of David." *Tel Aviv* 41 (2014): 3–19. https://doi.org/10.1179/0334435514Z.00000000030.

Ben-Ami, Doron, and Yana Tchekhanovets. "The Lower City of Jerusalem on the Eve of Its Destruction, 70 C.E.: A View From Hanyon Givati." *BASOR* 364 (November 2011): 61–85.

———. "A Roman Mansion Found in the City of David." *IEJ* 63 (2013): 164–73.

———. "'Then They Built up the City of David with a High, Strong Wall and Strong Towers, and It Became Their Citadel' (I Maccabees 1:33)." *City of David Studies of Ancient Jerusalem* 11 (2016): 19*–29*.

Bock, Darrell L. *Acts*. 2 vols. Grand Rapids: Baker Academic, 2007.

Currid, John D., and David W. Chapman, eds. *ESV Archaeology Study Bible*. Wheaton, IL: Crossway, 2018.

Fine, Steven. "Synagogue Inscriptions." Pages 114–18 in volume 5 of *The Oxford Encyclopedia of Archaeology in the Near East*. Edited by Eric Meyers. Oxford: Oxford University Press, 1997.

Gadot, Yuval, and Yonatan Adler. "A Quantitative Analysis of Jewish Chalk Vessel Frequencies in Early Roman Jerusalem: A View from the City's Garbage Dump." *IEJ* 66 (2016): 202–19.

Hanson, K. C., and Douglas E. Oakman. *Palestine in the Time of Jesus: Social Structures and Social Conflicts*. Minneapolis: Fortress, 1998.

Harland, Philip A. *Travel and Religion in Antiquity*. Waterloo, ON: Wilfrid Laurier University Press, 2011.

Hasson, Nir. "Ancient Jerusalem Road Hints at Possible Reason for Jewish Revolt Against Rome." *Haaretz*, January 2, 2017. https://www.haaretz.com/archaeology/.premium-ancient-jerusalem-road-hints-at-possible-reason-for-jewish-revolt-against-rome-1.5480317.

Jeremias, Joachim. *Jerusalem in the Time of Jesus*. London: SCM, 1969.

Josephus, Flavius. *The Works of Josephus: Complete and Unabridged.* Translated by William Whiston. Peabody: Hendrickson, 1987.

Keener, Craig S. *Acts: An Exegetical Commentary*. 4 vols. Grand Rapids: Baker Academic, 2012–2015.

———. *The IVP Bible Background Commentary: New Testament*. 2nd ed. Downers Grove, IL: InterVarsity Press, 2014.

Kloppenborg, John S. "The Theodotus Synagogue Inscription and the Problem of First-Century Synagogue Buildings." Pages 236–82 in *Jesus and Archaeology*. Edited by James H. Charlesworth. Grand Rapids: Eerdmans, 2006.

Magness, Jodi. *The Archaeology of the Holy Land: From the Destruction of Solomon's Temple to the Muslim Conquest*. Cambridge: Cambridge University Press, 2012.

Mazar, Eilat. *The Complete Guide to the Temple Mount Excavations*. Jerusalem: Shoham, 2002.

———, ed. *The Ophel Excavations to the South of the Temple Mount: Final Reports Volume 1*. Jerusalem: Shoham, 2015.

McKinny, Chris. "Southern Temple Mount Excavations." Pages 442–61 in *Lexham Geographic Commentary on the Gospels*. Edited by Barry J. Beitzel. Bellingham, WA: Lexham, 2018.

Meyers, Eric M., and Mark A. Chancey. *Alexander to Constantine: Archaeology of the Land of the Bible*. New Haven, CT: Yale University Press, 2012.

Nagtegaal, Brent. "Dozens of Coins From Final Year of Jewish Revolt Discovered in Jerusalem Cave." *The Trumpet*, March 26, 2018. https://www.thetrumpet.com/17069-rare-jewish-revolt-coins-discovered-in-jerusalem-cave. https://www.youtube.com/watch?v=Cz4hgd2XdtI.

Reich, Ronny. *Excavating the City of David: Where Jerusalem's History Began*. Jerusalem: Israel Exploration Society, 2011.

———. "Weill, Raymond." Pages 343–44 in volume 5 of *The Oxford Encyclopedia of Archaeology in the Near East*. Edited by Eric Meyers. Oxford: Oxford University Press, 1997.

Runesson, Anders, Donald D. Binder, and Birger Olsson. *The Ancient Synagogue from Its Origins to 200 C.E.: A Source Book*. Leiden: Brill, 2008.

Szanton, Nahshon, and Joe Uziel. "On the Question of the Stepped Stone Monument from the Second Temple Period in the City of David." *City of David Studies of Ancient Jerusalem* 10 (2015): 19–40.

Szanton, Nahshon, and Ayala Zilberstein. "'The Second Hill, Which Bore the Name of Acra, and Supported the Lower City…' A New Look at the Lower City of Jerusalem in the End of the Second Temple Period." *New Studies in the Archaeology of Jerusalem and Its Region* 10 (2016): 30*–47*.

Uziel, Joe, Nahshon Szanton, and Moran Hagbi. "Monumental Building Projects in Jerusalem in the Days of Pontius Pilate: A Numismatic View from the Stepped Street in the Tyropoeon Valley." *New Studies in the Archaeology of Jerusalem and its Region* 10 (2016): 99–114. [In Hebrew]

Weill, Raymond. *La Cité de David, I–II: Compte rendu des fouilles exécutées à Jérusalem, sur les site de la ville primitiv; 2, Texte*. Paris: Geuthner, 1947.

Weill, Raymond, and Théodore Reinach. "L'Inscription de Théodotos." *Revue Des Études Juives* 71 (1920): 30–56.

Weill, Raymond, and Louis-Hugues Vincent. *The City of David: Revisiting Early Excavations; English Translations of Reports by Raymond Weill and L. H. Vincent*. Edited by Hershel Shanks and Ronny Reich. Washington, DC: Biblical Archaeology Society, 2004.

Witherington, Ben, III. *The Acts of the Apostles: A Socio-Rhetorical Commentary*. Grand Rapids: Eerdmans, 1998.

CHAPTER 13

SAMARIA: TOO WICKED TO REDEEM?

Acts 8:4–25

John A. Beck

> KEY POINTS
>
> - Samaria (also known as Sebaste) was among the most heinous, contemptible, and depraved cities in the promised land.
> - When Philip shared the good news about Jesus there, the Holy Spirit led many to saving faith, including a well-known practitioner of sorcery.
> - If Samaria can be saved, then no place is too wicked to be redeemed.

INTRODUCTION

We expect the good news about the risen Christ to spread throughout the world (Matt 28:19), something Luke affirms by organizing the contents of Acts geographically. He traces the gospel's movements from Jerusalem into all Judea and Samaria and on to the ends of the earth (Acts 1:8). But this language leaves us unprepared for the powerful story that unfolds in Acts 8. Philip took the good news about Jesus to one of the most heinous, contemptible, and depraved cities in the promised land, Samaria (renamed Sebaste by Herod the Great). His bold move became a test case for the power of the gospel, a case that convincingly answered this question. Can a place as wicked as Samaria/Sebaste repent and find redemption from sin?

STORY SUMMARY

Our story begins in Jerusalem as a great persecution broke out against the church. Philip fled north. As he traveled, he spoke to those he met along the way about Jesus. His gospel teaching was confirmed by miracles. Shrieking spirits abandoned their hosts and disabled people were healed. Even a well-known practitioner of sorcery, Simon Magus, joined those who believed and were baptized by Philip. He had amazed others with his power and now Simon was amazed at what was hap-

pening in his city. Forgiven and freed, the very character of the city changed. Luke says it this way: "So there was great joy in that city" (Acts 8:8).[1]

News like this gets around. When it arrived in Jerusalem, the Jewish believers in Jesus dispatched Peter and John on behalf of the church in Jerusalem to get firsthand information on all that was happening. When they arrived, they prayed for the new believers. When they laid hands on them, the citizens of this perverse place "received the Holy Spirit" (8:17). When Simon saw this, he could not resist his old urges. He asked Peter and John if he could purchase the secret to this amazing miracle. Peter replied with a sharply worded rebuke intended to call Simon to repent. Then Peter and John returned to Jerusalem, preaching the good news in many Samaritan villages along the way.

CITY IDENTIFICATION

This is a compelling story and one that would have power in any location. But when we add the geographical setting to this storyline, the narrative becomes even more potent. To get the setting right will require us to consider several strands of evidence.

On three different occasions (8:5, 8, 9), Luke calls the place a *polis* (πόλις). In his Gospel, Luke uses this Greek word somewhat loosely. It can refer to communities that are very different in size—a village like Nazareth (Luke 1:26), a town like Capernaum (Luke 4:31), or a city like Jerusalem (Luke 19:41). However in Acts, Luke's habit is to use the term for larger urban centers like Jerusalem (Acts 7:58), Caesarea Philippi (25:23), Pisidian Antioch (13:44), and Philippi (16:12). What is more, Luke uses a second term in this story, *kōmē* (κώμη). This term is used for

1. Unless otherwise specified all translations are from the New International Version (NIV).

a community that is much smaller than a *polis*, something akin to the smaller towns of the Roman district of Samaria where the majority of people lived (8:25). All of this suggests that Luke is using *polis* here in a more specialized sense. In contrast to *kōmē*, the setting of this story is a large city.

But is it just any city or is Luke directing our attention to a specific city? In 8:5, the NIV has "Philip went down to a city in Samaria." The ESV has "Philip went down to the city of Samaria." These two translations reflect a difference in the Greek manuscripts of Acts. When the evidence is weighed, those that include the definite article are more likely reflecting Luke's intentions.[2] "The city" is the better translation choice.

That brings us to the word Samaria. This proper noun can refer either to a Roman district north of Judea, known as Samaria, or to an Old Testament city called Samaria, known as Sebaste in the New Testament era. The word, Samaria, appears eleven times in the New Testament. Most of those references are to the district (Luke 17:11; John 4:4, 5; Acts 1:8; 8:25; 9:31; 15:3). This includes the final mention of Samaria in our story where the context calls for us to understand it in that way. But the first four times the word Samaria is used in our story, it is referring to the city of Samaria/Sebaste, starting in Acts 8:5. Here the Greek grammar allows for two possible translations. It could be "the city (of the district) of Samaria"[3] or "the city of Samaria."[4] In the first instance, the reference would be to the major *polis* in the district, of which there is only one, Samaria/Sebaste.[5] In the second, the author is referencing the same city directly by using its Old Testament name.

The internal evidence also provides support for this city identification, because it is just where we would expect to find someone like Simon Magus. Prior to Philip's arrival, he is the one who received all the attention in this story. So who was he and where would we expect to find a man like him? Let's start with who he was *not*. The early church fathers identified him as the father of Gnosticism.[6] But there is nothing in Luke's description of this man that would support that.[7] Rather Luke describes him as a well-known practitioner of sorcery (8:9–10). People presumed that he had the ability to manipulate fate

2. Bruce M. Metzger, *A Textual Commentary on the Greek New Testament*, rev. ed. (New York: United Bible Society, 1994), 311. Even those who chose to translate without the article, due to apparent conflicts they find within the story when identifying the setting with Sebaste, affirm that the manuscripts with the definite article preserve the more likely reading. See Ben Witherington III, *The Acts of the Apostles: A Socio-Rhetorical Commentary* (Grand Rapids: Eerdmans, 1998), 282; and Craig S. Keener, *Acts: An Exegetical Commentary* (Grand Rapids: Baker Academic, 2013), 2:1494.

3. This treats the genitive in 8:5 as a partitive genitive.

4. This treats the genitive in 8:5 as an appositional genitive. This option is favored by Moisés Silva, ed., *New International Dictionary of New Testament Theology and Exegesis*, 2nd ed. (Grand Rapids: Zondervan, 2014), 4:243.

5. Keener, *Acts*, 2:1494 and David G. Peterson, *The Acts of the Apostles* (Grand Rapids: Eerdmans, 2009), 280.

6. For an overview see, Keener, *Acts*, 2:1509–1510.

7. C. K. Barrett, *The Acts of the Apostles* (Edinburgh: T&T Clark,1994), 1:397.

and unseen forces that could be used to help or harm others.[8] Through his magic arts he beguiled people into thinking he was more than he was. Luke tells us that people called him, "the Great Power of God" (8:10). This title sets him apart from the ordinary citizen of the city, perhaps even suggesting that he was divine.[9]

So where would we expect to meet a man like this in the Roman district of Samaria? This district was the home of the Samaritans who practiced a religion that was similar to, but not identical to Judaism of the first century. To this day, they affirm their belief in one God (the Lord), one prophet (Moses), one holy book (Torah), and one holy mountain (Mount Gerizim). Their theology had many points of similarity with the Jewish faith because they drew their teachings from the Torah, the first five books of the Old Testament. This included Deuteronomy 18:9–13 that expressly forbids associating oneself with any form of magic or sorcery. It is hard to imagine that Simon would have found a welcoming audience among these Samaritans. But the city of Samaria/Sebaste was an island of Greco-Roman paganism within the district of Samaria. It is exactly in such a hellenized city that someone like Simon would find the acclaim and the interested following that Simon has in our story.[10]

When all this evidence is weighed, the city that is the setting for Philip's teaching, healing, and powerful response is not so ambiguous after all. We join Barry Beitzel in his assumption that this city was "almost certainly Sebaste."[11]

HOW DID PEOPLE THINK ABOUT SAMARIA?

We need to consider how the early church in Jerusalem would have thought about the district of Samaria and then how they would have thought about the city of Samaria/Sebaste. In the Gospels, we have three winsome stories about Samaritans: the parable of the good Samaritan (Luke 10:25–37), the story of a grateful Samaritan healed of leprosy (Luke 17:11–17), and the story of a Samaritan woman from Sychar (John 4:1–26). The power of all these stories resides in depicting an *exceptional* Samaritan rather than the *expected* Samaritan. The baseline is built on the Assyrian deportation/importation strategy apparent in 2 Kings 17:24–41. When the Assyrians exiled members of the northern kingdom, they imported non-Israelites into this part of the promised land. Eventually these newcomers intermarried with descendants of Abraham and adopted some of their religious beliefs. Their descendants were neither fully Jewish ethnically nor fully orthodox in their Judaism.

> [They] persisted in their former practices. Even while these people were worshiping the Lord, they were serving their idols. To this day their children and grandchildren continue to do as their ancestors did. (2 Kgs 17:40b–41)

8. Barrett, *Acts of the Apostles*, 1:397 and Keener, *Acts*, 2:1503–1505.

9. Darrell L. Bock, *Acts* (Grand Rapids: Baker Academic, 2007), 327.

10. Ironically, some commentators see this as the very reason to reject Sebaste as the setting for the story. While acknowledging someone like Simon fits in the milieu of Sebaste, they see his adherents as religious Samaritans who do not. See Keener, *Acts*, 2:1489; Bock, *Acts*, 325.

11. Barry J. Beitzel, *The New Moody Atlas of the Bible* (Chicago: Moody, 2009), 251.

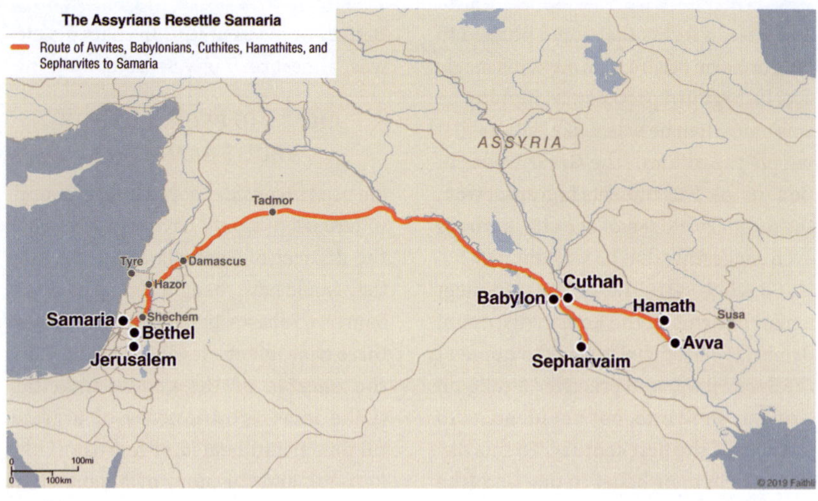

Apart from the exceptions noted in the stories above, the Gospels do little to change this perception. When Jesus sent out the twelve to announce that the kingdom of heaven had arrived, he told them to avoid gentiles and all towns of the Samaritans (Matt 10:5). When Jesus was on his way to Jerusalem for the last time, a Samaritan village snubbed him (Luke 9:51–55). And John explains the terse and unwelcoming words of the woman at the well by offering this parenthetical observation: "For Jews do not associate with Samaritans" (4:9b). Most Jewish-Christian believers would have viewed Samaritans with a general distrust if not disdain.

Samaria/Sebaste's reputation was even worse. It was home to some of the most disreputable people in the Old Testament. King Omri was among the worst of the kings who ruled Israel. He purchased a hill from a man named Shemer and founded a new capital for the northern kingdom on that hill, calling it Samaria (1 Kgs 16:23–24). His son, Ahab, ruled from that city along with Jezebel, a Phoenician princess who brought her infamous passion for Baal into the promised land. This couple added to their ignominy by building a temple for Baal in their capital city (2 Kgs 16:30–32). The negative perception of Samaria was cemented into place by this unholy trinity—Ahab, Jezebel, and Baal. When the Assyrians invaded, they targeted and destroyed this capital of Israel. In a subsequent era, Herod the Great reestablished it (27 BC), naming it Sebaste.[12] But the name change did nothing to improve our perception of the place. Herod built a massive temple, 115 feet by 79 feet (35 x 24 m), with a 90-foot-wide (27.5 m) staircase at the highpoint of the city (likely on the same spot that Ahab and Jezebel built the earlier temple to Baal). This temple was meant to honor his patron Caesar Augustus, a nod to the growing pagan tradition of emperor

12. The name change was in honor of Caesar Augustus. Sebaste (σεβαστή, *sebastē*) was the Greek equivalent of the Latin "Augustus."

worship.[13] So whether we are looking far back into the Old Testament or examining the evidence from the time of Herod, Samaria/Sebaste was a thoroughly pagan city. Ahab and Jezebel, Herod, and Simon the sorcerer secure our impressions that Samaria/Sebaste is a reprehensible, pagan place that lived outside the realm of hope or rehabilitation.

THE RHETORICAL ROLE OF SAMARIA/SEBASTE IN THE STORY

That is why the story of Samaria/Sebaste has such rhetorical power. Luke left many stories from the time of Peter and John's return to Jerusalem untold, village stories in which Samaritans certainly came to know Jesus as the savior. But he could not help but tell this Samaria/Sebaste story because the city itself plays a key role in delivering the lesson to be learned.[14]

First of all, note that in telling the story Luke persistently reminds us of where we are. The term for city, *polis*, is used three times (8:4, 8, 9). The word, Samaria, is used five times in this story (of eleven times in the New Testament). Four of those times, it refers to the city of Samaria/Sebaste (8:4, 9, 14).

Our expectations for the place run low and they diminish even farther when we see who is spearheading the mission effort. Philip is not the apostle Philip, but an assistant to the apostles in Jerusalem. He along with seven others were appointed to look after practical tasks like the distribution of food among the widows of the church in Jerusalem so that the apostles could give their time to prayer and ministry of the word (Acts 6:1–6). There is no doubt that our Philip was a good and faithful man. But he was not an apostle. And if there were ever a time for an apostle, Samaria/Sebaste was it. The Lord had used Elijah and Elisha to address the apostasy of Samaria in the Old Testament. Nothing less appeared to be necessary to address the pagan world of Sebaste in the New Testament.

But when Philip brought the gospel things changed here. Evil spirits flee their hosts. Diseases leave the bodies of the afflicted. Joy fills the place as the good news of Jesus death and resurrection bring assurance of forgiveness. In fact, even Simon the sorcerer believed and was baptized. All of this is occurring in a place that gave us Ahab and Jezebel and a temple to the emperor of Rome. I appreciate the shock that must have seized the church in Jerusalem. They quickly dispatched the two whom we might have picked to evangelize Sebaste, Peter and John. But please note. They did not come to fix things. They did not reevangelize or rebaptize. They came to see for themselves if such a powerful change could occur in such an impious place. It had. And when they laid their hands on their new brothers and sisters, the Holy Spirit came upon them just as he

13. John McRay, *Archaeology and the New Testament* (Grand Rapids: Baker, 1991), 145–48.

14. I take this position in contrast to the view that the setting has little to contribute to the telling of the story. For example, Marshall observes, "Whatever be the identification (of the city), it has no significance for the story as such." I. Howard Marshall, *The Book of Acts: An Introduction and Commentary* (Downers Grove, IL: InterVarsity Press, 2007), 154 n. 1.

had in Jerusalem on Pentecost.[15] Samaria/Sebaste had been redeemed!

APPLICATION

Could this still happen today? That is the question I have as I leave this story. Can a place or a person with such a horrible reputation like Samaria/Sebaste come to know the Lord? Whom do we write off as irredeemable? What places do we walk by, certain that they are beyond help and beyond hope? What person do we discount because of their past? Samaria/Sebaste is the test case meant to change our perspective. If a place as bad as that can be redeemed, there is no place and no person I should write off.

That includes me. Because when sin gets its hold on us and guilt builds within, we too can feel irredeemable. That in spite of passages that totally refute the notion. "The blood of Jesus, his Son, purifies us from all sin" (1 John 1:7). When those misgivings arise, it marks the time to reread the story of Samaria/Sebaste. No one has a worse history than that place. If it can be redeemed, so can I.

BIBLIOGRAPHY

Barrett, C. K. *The Acts of the Apostles*. 2 vols. Edinburgh: T&T Clark, 1994.

Beitzel, Barry J. *The New Moody Atlas of the Bible*. Chicago: Moody, 2009.

Bock, Darrell L. *Acts*. Grand Rapids: Baker Academic, 2007.

Bruce, F. F. *The Book of Acts*. Revised ed. Grand Rapids: Eerdmans, 1988.

Keener, Craig S. *Acts: An Exegetical Commentary*. 4 vols. Grand Rapids: Baker Academic, 2012–2015.

Marshall, I. Howard. *The Book of Acts: An Introduction and Commentary*. Downers Grove, IL: InterVarsity Press, 2007.

McRay, John. *Archaeology and the New Testament*. Grand Rapids: Baker, 1991.

Metzger, Bruce M. *A Textual Commentary on the Greek New Testament*. Revised ed. New York: United Bible Society, 1994.

Peterson, David G. *The Acts of the Apostles*. Grand Rapids: Eerdmans, 2009.

Silva, Moisés, ed. *New International Dictionary of New Testament Theology and Exegesis*. 2nd ed. 5 vols. Grand Rapids: Zondervan, 2014.

Witherington, Ben, III. *The Acts of the Apostles: A Socio-Rhetorical Commentary*. Grand Rapids: Eerdmans, 1998.

15. Apparently there was a delay in the giving of this gift so that it could be witnessed by Peter and John and then relayed to confirm the story that was circulating in Jerusalem (Bruce, *Book of Acts*, 170; Witherington, *Acts of the Apostles*, 289).

CHAPTER 14

THE ROMAN ROAD SYSTEM AROUND THE MEDITERRANEAN

Acts 8:26; 20:1–3; 23:23–33; 28:13–16; Romans 15:19

Mark Wilson

KEY POINTS

- Roads were built initially to transport Roman legions to areas of conflict.
- The empire's expansion required governors to build roads for the provincial infrastructure.
- Milestones not only informed travelers but also served as imperial propaganda markers.
- Evangelistic activities from Jerusalem to Rome were facilitated along existing road networks.
- Apostolic journeys can be localized on major roads such as the *Via Appia* and the *Via Sebaste*.

CONSTRUCTION OF ROADS

The adage, "All roads lead to Rome," is reversed in this discussion. The construction of roads leading from Rome toward the eastern Mediterranean began in the third century BC. Around 20 BC Augustus placed a Golden Milestone (*Milliarium Aureum*) in the Forum to acknowledge that Rome was the hub of the empire's road system (Cassius Dio 54.8.4). However, the early church developed in the opposite direction—from Jerusalem to Rome—as seen in the book of Acts (1:8; 28:16). The established Roman road system will be connected to the spread of the gospel seen in the later New Testament.

Local roads were built initially to connect Rome with its surrounding cities.[1]

1. The following general information on roads is drawn, passim, from Romolo Augusto Staccioli, *The Roads of the Romans* (Los Angeles: Getty, 2003).

Golden Milestone (*Milliarium Aureum*)

The building of consular roads brought an expansion of the road system throughout the Italian peninsula. The principal arterial roads followed the natural communication routes that had existed throughout history. The road system eventually extended throughout the provinces as the empire expanded. These roads developed for several reasons. They facilitated the movement of legions to established military bases along the empire's borders, especially during threats from enemies like the Parthians. Peripheral roads linked the military outposts on the outer boundary (*limes*) of provinces. Such roads were built by legionary troops and later maintained by local authorities through whose territory the road passed. They also allowed intercity and interprovincial communication and commerce. These roads likewise carried pilgrims to temples like Artemis' in Ephesus (Acts 19:24–26), to oracles like Apollo's in Claros and Didyma (Philostratus, *Life of Apollonius* 4.1), to healing centers like Asclepius' in Pergamum (Aelius Aristides, *Orations* 53.1–5), and to Jewish sacred feasts in Jerusalem like Pentecost (Acts 2:5–11).[2]

The construction of roads was celebrated by ancient authors. Plutarch observed that they were made in a straight line partly of quarried stone and partly with tightly rammed masses of earth (*Life of Caius Gracchus* 7.1–2). Bridges were built to cross depressions and riverbeds, thus allowing passage all year and providing raised roadbeds with a uniform height and an agreeable appearance. Roads were measured by Roman miles, and fixed stones were used to mark the distances. Strabo observed that, while the Greeks gave little attention to infrastructure, the Romans invested themselves in projects like paving roads and constructing aqueducts (*Geography* 5.3.8; 4.6.6). They paved roads, cut hills, and filled valleys, so that merchandise could be conveyed by carriage from the ports. Augustus was particularly concerned with building as many roads as he possibly could. Tacitus noted that an important reason for constructing solid roads and bridges over marshy areas was to convey heavy troops (*Annales* 4.73). Josephus confirms this aspect: behind the advance military guard came the road-makers who straightened out bends and leveled rough places so Vespasian's army would not experience exhaustion during difficult marches (*J.W.* 3.118).[3] Trajan's Column in Rome depicts several scenes (nos. 19, 23, 41, 56) showing the Roman military constructing roads and bridges during deployment.[4]

2. For more on pilgrimage travel in antiquity, see Robert L. Cioffi, "Travel in the Ancient World," Oxford Handbooks Online (2016), 16–19; https://dx.doi.org/10.1093/oxfordhb/9780199935390.013.110.

3. For other comments by ancient authors, see Cornelius van Tilburg, *Traffic and Congestion in the Roman Empire* (London: Routledge, 2007), 11–15.

4. See page 700 for images of the Cichorius plates for two more of these scenes.

Trajan's Column (Cichorius Plate) Scene 19 (Center): Building a Bridge

FEATURES OF ROMAN ROADS

The *cursus publicus* (postal service), inaugurated in the Republican era but reorganized by Augustus, employed young men to carry messages to and from the provinces. Later regular couriers on horseback (*tabellarii*), sometimes with fast carts, carried imperial communications (Suetonius, *Life of Augustus* 49.3). Every seven to ten miles (11–16 km) *mutationes* (horse-changing stations) were established. Riders could cover approximately fifty miles (80 km) a day. Regular travelers stopped at *mansiones*, usually located one day's journey apart. These provided all types of services and provisions for travelers including inns, restaurants, carpenters, blacksmiths, and veterinarians. A relief, now in Rome's Museum of National Civilizations, shows an innkeeper leaning out the window of his *mansio* and watching the arrival of two guests in a carriage.[5] The standard width of paved roads was fourteen Roman feet (13.5 ft; 4.1 m), but this could narrow to three and six-tenths feet (1.1 m) or expand to twenty-three feet (7 m) depending on terrain and location. Usually roads were curbed, then ridged to facilitate the runoff of water. Bridges and viaducts carried travelers across the many rivers and ravines that coursed through the mountains and countryside.[6] Some roads even featured sidewalks to allow pedestrian traffic.

Milestones called *milliaria* began to appear in the Republican period. The oldest known milestone was placed at Mile 53 of the *Via Appia* sometime between 255–253 BC. Caius Gracchus passed the *lex viaria* ("road law") in 123 BC and "measured off every road by miles ... and planted stone pillars in the ground to mark the distances" (Plutarch, *Life of Caius Gracchus* 7.2). The Roman mile (RM) consisted of 1,000 paces (*millia passum*)

5. https://www.agefotostock.com/age/en/Stock-Images/Rights-Managed/DAE-10327264.

6. For the documentation and discussion of over five hundred bridges, see Colin O'Connor, *Roman Bridges* (Cambridge: Cambridge University Press, 1993). For pictures of and information on these bridges, see https://en.wikipedia.org/wiki/List_of_Roman_bridges.

Ancient Roman Bridge in Aleppo, Syria

5 feet each equaling 5000 Roman feet. This was standardized by Agrippa in 29 BC with an approximate equivalent of 4,860 English feet (0.92 mi [1482 m]). The milestones identified the road builder or repairer, usually an emperor or governor, and indicated the direction and distance traveled or yet to be traveled, usually from its roadhead (*caput viae*). Outside of Italy these milestones assumed an additional function: "as an assertion—symbolized by the very massiveness of the road-markers—of Roman territorial possession in Asia Minor."[7] While French's comment may be limited to Asia Minor, his observation rings true empire-wide, for Roll asserts similarly about milestones in Judea that "their primary role was to propagandize the idea of Rome and its Empire."[8]

An extra-urban feature that developed outside Rome in the third century BC was the appearance of tombs outside the city gate. The names of local elites were announced on these sepulchral monuments. Exedrae and benches were provided for travelers, and sepulchral inscriptions appealed to them: "Hey, traveler, come here and rest a moment." This necropolis pattern was replicated in cities throughout the empire with a noteworthy example being Asian Hierapolis with over two thousand tombs and sarcophagi outside its city gates leading to Philadelphia and Laodicea.[9] Travelers also erected votive altars to enlist divine assistance for their journeys. One such altar is inscribed with *salvos ire*, wishing a safe outbound journey, and *salvos venire*, wishing a safe return. Another votive

7. David H. French, *Milestones: Republican*, fascicle 3.1 of *Roads and Milestones of Asia Minor* (Ankara: British Institute of Archaeology at Ankara, 2012), 8.

8. Israel Roll, "The Roman Road System in Judaea," *Jerusalem Cathedra* 3 (1983): 153.

9. Francesco D'Andria, *Hierapolis of Phrygia (Pamukkale): An Archaeological Guide* (Istanbul: Ege Yayınları, 2003), 48–62, 205–9.

relief expresses similar wishes for a safe journey and shows two sets of feet, the ones on the right outbound and those on the left inbound.[10]

ROMAN ROADS AROUND THE MEDITERRANEAN

ROADS IN ITALY

As the city of Rome expanded its territory southward into the Italian peninsula, one of the first roads to be built was the *Via Appia*. Named after its builder, the Roman censor Appius Claudius Caecus, the first section was constructed as a military road in 312 BC during the Second and Third Samnite Wars. Its initial phase covered 132 RM (122 mi. [196 km]) to Capua.[11] Throughout the next century the road was extended in stages until it reached Brundisium (modern Brindisi) in 191 BC, a distance of 365 RM (336 mi. [541 km]).[12] Ovid made this journey from Rome in ten days, averaging 36 RM a day (*Pontus* 4.5.8). Brundisium became "a strategic crossing point into Greece and a bridgehead for the conquest of the east."[13] Statius called the *Via Appia: Appia longarum ... regina viarum* ("queen of long roads"; *Silvae* 2.2). Its construction and related infrastructure served as a model for subsequent road construction throughout the empire.

On his captivity journey, Paul landed at Rome's port of Puteoli where he spent seven days. From Puteoli the *Via Campania* first passed through the rock-cut pass with stone walls revetted in a building technique called *opus reticulatum*. This *Montagna Spaccata* ("Broken Mountain") is still used for traffic today. At Capua the *Via Campania* connected with the *Via Appia*. Outside Tarracina (modern Terracina) a canal paralleled the road through the Pontine marshes, a nineteen-mile (30.6 km) section called the *Decennovium*. Travelers could take a "red-eye" through the night in a barge pulled by mules along its banks. Horace tells humorously that the arrangement did not always work out (*Satires* 1.5.9–23). Perhaps the centurion Julius was able to requisition a barge for official use to transport Paul along the *Decennovium* (Acts 27:1). Nevertheless, a messenger must have been

Votive Altar with Inscription *salvos ire*

10. Daniela Velestino, *La Galleria Lapidaria dei Musei Capitolini* (Rome: De Luca, 2015), 70–71.

11. See the section on the *Via Appia* in Ray Laurence, *The Roads of Roman Italy: Mobility and Cultural Change* (London: Routledge, 1999), 13–21.

12. For details related to mileage along the *Via Appia*, see http://www.straderomane.it/en/strade/r0001/r0001_en.htm.

13. Giuseppina Pisani Sartorio, "Origins and Historic Events," in *The Appian Way: From Its Foundation to the Middle Ages*, ed. Ivana Della Portella (Los Angeles: Getty, 2004), 20.

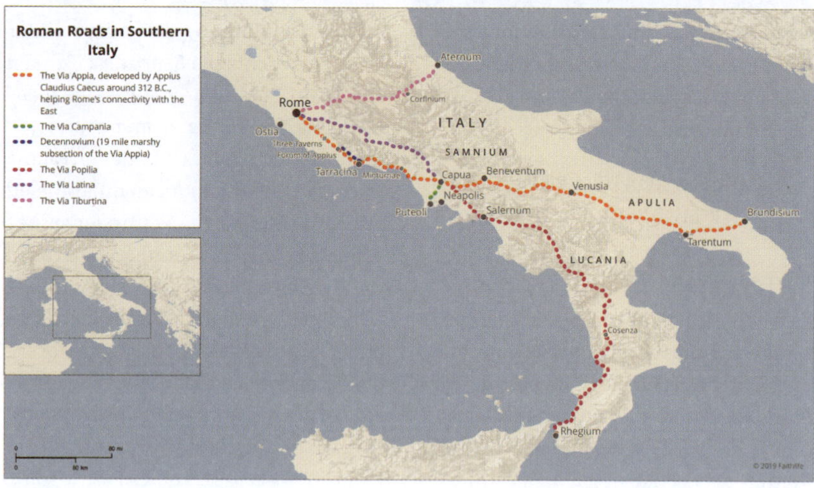

sent from Puteoli to Rome because Roman believers met Paul first at the Forum of Appius (modern Borgo Faiti). This *mansio* at RM 43 was named after the censor who founded the road.[14] Horace also stopped at the Forum of Appius, observing it was "full of boatmen and crooked innkeepers" (*Satires* 1.5.3–4).[15] Other believers met Paul at RM 35 at Three Taverns (*Tres Tabernae*), another way station that provided food and refreshment. Both groups accompanied Paul on the *Via Appia* for the remainder of his journey into Rome (Acts 28:13–16).

ROADS IN THE BALKANS

Around 146 BC the governor Gnaeus Egnatius began a road project across the Balkan Peninsula to link the Adriatic to his province of Macedonia on the Aegean Sea.[16] Before 56 BC the road had been extended through Thrace to Byzantium (Cicero, *On the Consular Provinces* 2.4).[17] Its length was 746 RM (696 mi. [1,120 km]). Travelers wishing to continue east from the port of Brundisium ferried across the Adriaticum (modern Adriatic) either to Dyrrachium or Apollonia (Strabo, *Geography* 7.7.4,8; he calls the former city by its Greek name Epidamnus). Branches of the *Via Egnatia* terminated at these Adriatic ports in the province of Illyricum. The remains of a *mutatio* are found at Ad Quintum (modern Bradashesh). Lychnidos (modern Ohrid) was the last major city in eastern

14. Gijs Tol et al., "Minor Centres in the Pontine Plain: The Cases of Forum Appii and Ad Medias," *Papers of the British School at Rome* 82 (2014): 116–18.

15. *Horace's Satires and Epistles*, trans. Jacob Fuchs (New York: Norton, 1977).

16. For a beautifully illustrated volume on the *Via Egnatia* with excellent maps (albeit in Greek), see Giannes Lolos, *Εγνατία Ὁδός* (Athens: Olkos, 2009); for a practical guide for visiting the route today and its related archaeological sites, see Marietta van Attekum and Holger de Bruin, *Via Egnatia on Foot: A Journey into History* (Driebergen: Via Egnatia Foundation, 2014).

17. Constantine around AD 337 constructed the Milion in Constantinople to mark the eastern starting point of the *Via Egnatia*. The monument was modeled after Augustus' Golden Milestone in Rome.

Illyricum. Heraclea Lyncestis (modern Bitola) was the first major Macedonian city, then Edessa where a branch ran south to Berea. After Pella came the provincial capital Thessalonica on the Aegean coast. Eastward the road ran through Apollonia, Amphipolis, Philippi, and back to the coast at Neapolis.

On his second and third journeys Paul transshipped through Neapolis where he connected with the *Via Egnatia* (Acts 16:11; 20:1–3; 1 Cor 16:5; 2 Cor 1:16; 2:13; 7:5; Phil 4:15; 1 Tim 1:3). On the second journey Paul was forced to flee from Thessalonica down the coastal road that turned inland to Berea (Acts 17:10). From Berea some fellow believers took him back to the coast where he embarked either by ship perhaps from Pydna to Piraeus, the port of Athens, or he traveled overland through the rugged mountains of northern Achaia (Acts 17:14–15). When Paul preached in Illyricum, probably during the third journey, the *Via Egnatia* carried him westward to Dyrrachium (Rom 15:19). Silas, the messenger for 1 Peter, traveled the *Via Appia* to Brundisium. He then ferried to Dyrrachium and traversed the *Via Egnatia* through Thrace to Byzantium. There he boarded a boat to Pontus, landing probably in Amisus, to begin his ambulatory visitation of churches in the provinces listed in 1 Peter 1:1.

ROADS IN GREECE

Corinth, rebuilt by Julius Caesar in 46 BC, became the capital of the newly formed province of Achaia in 27 BC. There was little imperial interest in building or repairing roads here until the reign of Trajan, who installed the first milestones. Susan Alcock explains, "In part, this must be explained by the province's broken and dissected topography (encouraging marine transport), in part to its military unimportance."[18] For this reason Paul's arrival in Achaia from coastal Macedonia was probably through Piraeus, the port of Athens (Acts 17:14–15). Paul's journey to Corinth (Acts 18:1) fol-

18. Susan E. Alcock, *Graecia Capta: The Landscapes of Roman Greece* (Cambridge: Cambridge University Press, 1993), 121.

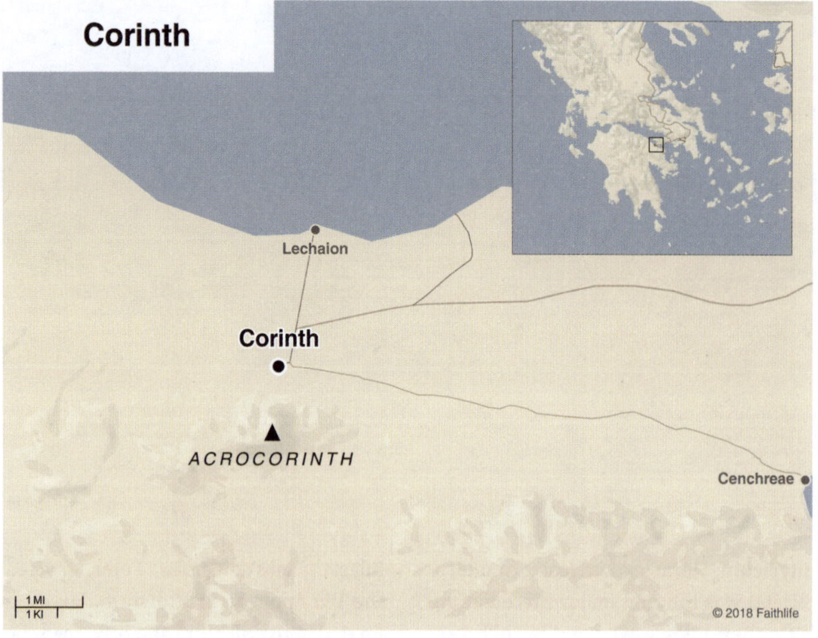

lowed the Scironian road via Megara that entered the Peloponnese after crossing the Isthmus of Corinth. Hadrian later widened the road to two lanes so chariots could pass (Pausanias 1.44.6). Corinth was a major transportation hub for the province. Roads led to its northern port of Lechaion on the Gulf of Corinth and its eastern port on the Saronic Gulf—Cenchrae, a sailing point for Paul and home of Phoebe (Acts 18:18; Rom 16:1). A road network to the northwest connected it with the imperial colonies of Patrai and Nicopolis, where Paul later spent a winter (Titus 3:12). Paul's plan to pass through Achaia on his third journey (Acts 19:21; compare 20:1) suggests that he might have taken the overland route south from Berea via Larissa to Athens and Corinth.[19] An edict dating from Claudius regulated the demands of the *cursus publicus* around Tegea in the central Peloponnese (*ILS* 214). Paul's letters suggest multiple churches in Achaia,[20] so these would have developed along such established roads (1 Thess 1:7; 2 Cor 1:1; 11:10).

19. *BAGRW*, maps 55, 58, 59 show few roads in Achaia. For maps of the first-century AD road network in Achaia see Alcock, *Graecia Capta*, 123; and Athanasios D. Rizakis, "Town and Country in Early Imperial Greece," *Pharos: Journal of the Netherlands Institute at Athens* 20 (2014): 242.

20. Jerry A. Pattengale, "Achaia," *ABD* 1:53 claims at least twenty churches by the start of Nero's reign in AD 54; however, the source of that number is unstated.

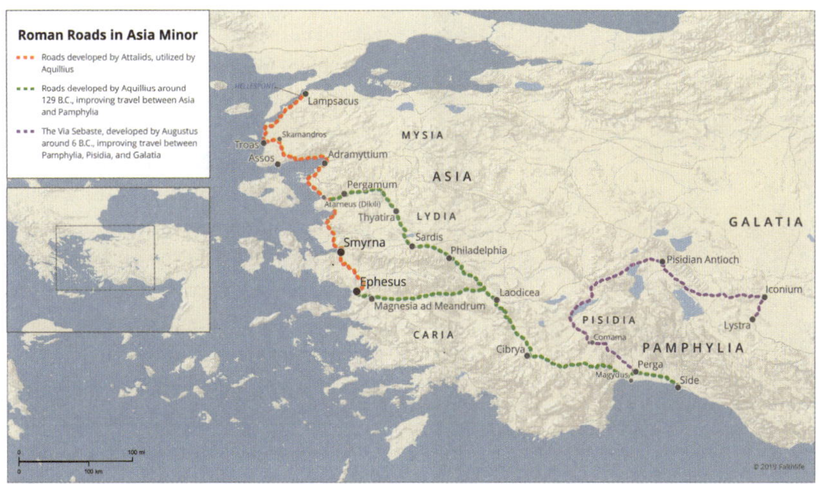

ROADS IN ASIA MINOR[21]

When Attalus III bequeathed his kingdom to the Romans in 133 BC and after the rebellion of Aristonicus was squelched four years later, the Roman Senate voted to receive Asia into the Roman Empire in 129 BC. The governor Manius Aquillius immediately began to expand the road system in the province. He utilized existing roads developed by the Attalids for military and commercial purposes. One road ran north from Ephesus through Smyrna and past Pergamum to Lampsacus on the Hellespont (Dardanelles; modern Çanakkale Boğazı). The measurement on a milestone found near Dikili indicates Ephesus as the *caput viae*. Paul connected with this road at Adramyttium on his second journey coming from Mysia. A spur near Skamandros took him west to the coastal port of Troas (Acts 16:8). Here Paul transshipped to the Macedonian port of Neapolis (Acts 16:11). Paul probably took this road when he left Ephesus after the riot, traveling again to Troas (Acts 20:1; 2 Cor 2:12). The messenger delivering Revelation to the seven churches traversed this road to visit Ephesus, Smyrna, and Pergamum (Rev 1:11).

Manius Aquillius developed another road to link the Aegean and Mediterranean Seas. Branches began at Pergamum and Ephesus and merged at Laodicea before crossing the Taurus Mountains to pass through Perga before it terminated at Side.[22] The messenger delivering Revelation to the seven churches used the branch from Pergamum to visit Thyatira, Sardis, Philadelphia, and Laodicea (Rev 1:11). In 6 BC Augustus improved the road segment from Perga to Lake Ascania for a section of his new *Via Sebaste* that then

21. Monographs covering all Roman roads in Asia Minor—the lifetime work of David French—are available for free download at: https://biaa.ac.uk/publications/item/name/electronic-monographs.

22. For the discussion of Republican roads in Asia Minor, see French, *Milestones: Republican*, 9–12.

Republican Milestone from Side Erected by Governor Manius Aquillius

branched to the north and east through Pisidian Antioch and terminated at Lystra. An Augustan milestone, still standing in situ in the pass at Döşeme, numbers 139 RM to Pisidian Antioch, the road's *caput viae*.[23] Paul's landfall on the first journey, probably at Magydus the seaport of Perga, brought him inland through a rock-cut pass with sidewalks, still in existence, to the connection with the *Via Sebaste*.[24]

On his third journey Paul walked along a sacred way that ran southward from Troas. A nine-arched bridge, still preserved, carried him across the Satnioeis River. From the Apollo temple at the Smintheum Paul continued to the port of Assos where he boarded a ship carrying his companions (Acts 20:13–14).[25]

Later in that journey Paul landed at Miletus and sent a messenger, probably Trophimus, to Ephesus to gather the church's elders. They exited through Ephesus' eastern Magnesian Gate and first traveled to its sister city, Magnesia ad Meandrum. From there a road situated between Mount Mycale and the Gulf of Latmus continued southwest past Priene. To cross the gulf near the mouth of the Meander River, a ferry was required to reach Miletus, where Paul addressed the elders (Acts 20:17–38).[26]

Peter's first letter was delivered by a messenger, probably Silas (Silvanus), to churches in the provinces of Pontus, Galatia, Cappadocia, Asia, and Bithynia (1 Pet 1:1; 5:12). A comprehensive road system connected the capitals and other major cities in these provinces. A knowledge of this road network has allowed the

23. G. H. R. Horsley and S. Mitchell, *The Inscriptions of Central Pisidia: Including Texts from Kremna, Ariassos, Keraia, Hyia, Panemoteichos, the Sanctuary of Apollo of the Perminoundeis, Sia, Kocaaliler, and the Dǫ̈seme Bǒgazi* (Bonn: Habelt, 2000), 168–69.

24. Mark Wilson, "Saint Paul in Pamphylia: Intention, Arrival, Departure," *Adalya* 19 (2016): 236–38.

25. Glen L. Thompson and Mark Wilson, "Paul's Walk to Assos: A Hodological Inquiry into Its Geography, Archaeology, and Purpose," in *Stones, Bones and the Sacred: Essays on Material Culture and Ancient Religion in Honor of Dennis E. Smith*, ed. Alan Cadwallader (Atlanta: SBL Press, 2016), 278–83.

26. Mark Wilson, "The Ephesian Elders Come to Miletus: An Annaliste Reading of Acts 20:15–18a," *Verbum et Ecclesia* 34 (2013): 3–6.

reconstruction of a viable itinerary for Silas, with accompanying insights into the demographics of these early Petrine churches.[27]

ROADS IN CYPRUS

After the Ptolemies moved the capital to Paphos from Salamis in the late fourth century BC, a road system developed to link the ends of the island. It passed along the southern coast below the Troodos Mountains.[28] In 58 BC Cyprus was annexed to Rome but did not become its own province until 22 BC. Paphos continued as the Roman provincial capital, although Salamis served as one of the four district centers. After Paul and Barnabas preached in the synagogues in Salamis, the latter's hometown (Acts 13:5), they along with John Mark traveled southwest through the cities of Kition, Amathus, and Kourion. They undoubtedly spoke in any synagogues existing in these cities. They then passed through Palai Paphos, home of the famous temple of Aphrodite. In Paphos they met the provincial governor Sergius Paulus whose *patria* (family) was from Pisidian Antioch (Acts 13:7–12). The governor apparently offered an introduction to the leaders of the Roman colony there. This suggested to Paul that their evangelistic efforts should turn northward to Pamphylia and Galatia.[29] Presumably Barnabas and John Mark followed a similar itinerary across Cyprus when they

27. See Mark Wilson, "Peter's Christian Communities in Asia Minor," chapter 46 in this volume for a detailed discussion.

28. For maps of Cyprus's road system during the Hellenistic and Roman Imperial periods, see Tønnes Bekker-Nielsen, *The Roads of Ancient Cyprus* (Copenhagen: Museum Tusculanum, 2004), 102 fig. 12, 14 fig. 13, and 110 fig. 14.

29. Stephen Mitchell, "Population and Land in Roman Galatia," *ANRW* 7.2:1073–74.

returned to the island on their second journey (Acts 15:39).[30]

ROADS IN SYRIA

Antioch on the Orontes served as the capital of the Seleucid Empire (281 BC), then Pompey made it the capital of the new Roman province of Syria in 64 BC. The city sat at the apex of an important road system in the northeastern corner of the Mediterranean Sea. In the first century AD the Euphrates River (modern Fırat) was the eastern boundary of the Roman Empire, and ongoing problems with the Parthians required the Romans to base at least two legions in Antioch to secure that border.[31] A road led approximately 125 miles (201 km) northeast to the major ford at Zeugma/Apamea. Another road ran south connecting Antioch with the major coastal cities of Roman Syria: Laodicea ad Mare (modern Latakia), Tripolis (modern Tripoli), Berytus (modern Beirut), Sidon (modern Saida), and Tyre (modern Sour). The road then entered Judea passing through Ptolemais (modern Acre) to Caesarea Maritima.[32] The road led inland from the coast through Antipatris and Lydda before ascending to Jerusalem. Cities along this route were conveniently located a day's journey apart, thus providing

30. For the hypothesis that Alexandria was the original destination of the first journey, see Thomas W. Davis and Mark Wilson, "The Destination of Paul's First Journey: Asia Minor or North Africa?" *Pharos Journal of Theology* 97 (2016): 1–14.

31. During Trajan's reign that increased to four legions and an equal number of auxiliary troops totaling around forty thousand; see Michael Maas, "People and Identity in Roman Antioch," in *Antioch The Lost Ancient City*, ed. Christine Kondoleon (Princeton: Princeton University Press, 2000), 15.

32. A section of this road, 164 feet long (50 m), was found north of Acco near Shave Ziyyon; see http://www.hadashot-esi.org.il/report_detail_eng.aspx?id=22789&mag_id=122.

travelers convenient facilities for room and board. [33] Journeys between Antioch and Jerusalem are mentioned numerous times: by Agabus and his fellow prophets (Acts 11:27–28); by Paul and Barnabas for famine relief (Acts 11:29–30; Gal 2:2), by Paul and Barnabas for the apostolic council (Acts 15:3–4, 30),[34] by Paul for the second journey return (Acts 18:22); by the so-called Judaizers (Acts 15:1; Gal 2:12); and by Peter (Gal 2:11).[35]

Northwest of Antioch a road led through the Syrian Gates (modern Belen Geçidi) to descend to the Mediterranean coast, then north through Alexandria ad Issum before passing the Syrian/Cilician Gates into Cilicia. Cilicia's three main cities were Mopsuestia (modern Misis), Adana, and Tarsus. All were situated on major rivers: respectively the Pyramus (modern Ceyhan), Sarus (modern Seyhan), and Cydnus (modern Berdan). Roman bridges spanning the rivers still remain in these Cilician cities.[36] When Barnabas traveled to Tarsus to bring Paul back to Antioch, this was the route that he used (Acts 11:25–26). The letter drafted by the Jerusalem council presumes this itinerary:

33. Kevin Butcher, *Roman Syria and the Near East* (Los Angeles: Getty, 2003), 128–29. Butcher provides a map of a similar journey made by Theophanes and his retinue around AD 317–323 that took eighteen days from Antioch to Raphia, south of Gaza (p. 132 fig. 43).

34. A diversion from Ptolemais through Samaria is mentioned here, probably to connect with Samaritan believers in Sebaste and Shechem (Acts 8:5, 14; 9:31).

35. An alternate inland route via Damascus was also possible; see Barry Beitzel, *The New Moody Atlas of the Bible* (Chicago: Moody, 2009), 254, 255 map 108.

36. O'Connor, *Roman Bridges*, 127.

Antioch, Syria, Cilicia (Acts 15:23). On his second and third journeys Paul traveled this route before traversing the Cilician Gates north of Tarsus into the heartland of Asia Minor (Acts 15:41–16:1; 18:23).

Roads in Arabia

After Paul's conversion on the road outside of Damascus (Acts 9:3–8), he traveled to Arabia (Gal 1:17). In the first century AD Arabia was the land of the Nabateans, the descendants of Ishmael, and of the Idumeans who had converted to Judaism under John Hyrcanus I in the late second century BC.[37] The road from Damascus led southeast through Soada (modern As Suwayda) and Bostra (modern Busra). There the road turned southwest to Philadelphia (modern Amman). It then turned south to run east of the Dead Sea all the way to Petra, the capital of the kingdom. Much of this route was later incorporated into the *Via Nova Traiana* built from AD 111–114 between Bostra and the Red Sea port Aela (modern Elath/Aqaba). The reference to Sinai in Arabia (Gal 4:25) has suggested to Martin Hengel and Anna Maria Schwemer that Paul might have extended his journey southeast into the northern Hejaz to Hegra/Hagra (modern Mada'in Saleh). A Jewish community lived in Hegra in the first century AD,[38] and a Jewish tradition localized the holy mountain Sinai nearby.[39] Caravans plied these trade routes carrying frankincense and other precious spices from southern Arabia to Rome (Pliny, *Natural History* 12.32.63–65).

Roads in Judea

During the Hellenistic period a group of Greek cities were built in the Galilee region, later known as the Decapolis (Mark 5:20; 7:31). A series of roads were constructed to connect these cities and their adjoining regions. However, any specifics about their nature or alignment are unknown. Many of the earlier roads, according to Roll, "were gradually converted by the Romans into built and engineered imperial highways."[40] These roads facilitated intra- and interregional commerce and communication in Judea. However, the earliest documented roads come from the time of the Jewish revolt in AD 66. The first Roman milestone dates to AD 69 when Traianus, the father of the emperor Trajan, was commander and overseer of road construction from Caesarea to Scythopolis.[41]

---

37. For a discussion of these sites in modern Syria and Jordan, see Eckhard Schnabel, *Early Christian Mission* (Downers Grove, IL: InterVarsity Press, 2004), 2:1033–45.

38. Jane Taylor, *Petra and the Lost kingdom of the Nabateans* (London: Tauris, 2001), 163.

39. Martin Hengel and Anna Maria Schwemer, *Paul Between Damascus and Antioch: The Unknown Years* (Louisville, KY: Westminster John Knox, 1997), 113–16.

40. Israel Roll, "Between Damascus and Megiddo and Megiddo: Roads and Transportation in Antiquity across the Northeastern Approaches to the Holy Land," in *Man near a Roman Arch: Studies Presented to Prof. Yoram Tsafrir*, ed. Leah Di Segni et al. (Jerusalem: Israel Exploration Society, 2009), 11.

41. Benjamin Isaac observes that when Judea was a subunit of Syria administered by equestrian officials the roads were not marked by milestones. He continues, "This process was initiated only when senatorial commanders were in charge of Judaea as a separate province. It may be noted that these Flavian milestone-inscriptions are the only ones that mention the names of military commanders or governors in Judaea" ("Roman Roads, Physical Remains, Organization and Development," *Scripta Classica Israelica* 34 [2015]: 41)

From the Hasmonean period two routes ran westward from Jerusalem toward the coast and merged at Lydda before continuing to Joppa. The northern route ran through Lower Beit Horon and Modiʿin while the southern route passed Emmaus (Luke 24:13). After Pompey conquered Palestine in 63 BC, his representative Gabinius reorganized the political structure by dividing it into five administrative districts. Jerusalem was one of the district centers along with Gadara, Amathus, Jericho, and Sepphoris (Josephus, *J.W.* 1.170). The Lower Beit Horon-Modiʿin route became more settled and thus began to carry increased traffic.[42] Peter probably traveled on the northern route to Lydda and Joppa (Acts 9:32–38). Later he took the coastal road to Caesarea when Cornelius' messengers came to Joppa to fetch him (Acts 10:5–9, 22–24). Philip as well as Peter and John traveled north on the central ridge road to Samaria (Acts 8:5, 14). Philip later took the road through the hill country past Beth Guvrin[43] to meet the Ethiopian eunuch who was traveling along the desert road near Gaza (Acts 8:26).[44]

Saul, later Paul, traveled from Jerusalem to Damascus to persecute the disciples there (Acts 9:1–3). There were several ways he could reach Scythopolis, a transportation node in the southern Galilee. He could travel northward through Samaria.[45] Or he could descend along the Wadi Qilt (Heb. *Nahal Prat*) to

42. Andrea M. Berlin, "Jewish Life before the Revolt: The Archaeological Evidence," *Journal for the Study of Judaism* 36 (2005): 422–23.

43. Seventeen milestones dating to the late Roman period have been discovered along this route. Five are now displayed at the KKL-JNF Archaeological Garden: http://www.kkl-jnf.org/about-kkl-jnf/green-israel-news/december-2016/roman-milestones-givat-yeshayahu/.

44. The eunuch's mode of transport is usually translated "chariot" (ἅρμα, *harma*), but this is unlikely. It was more probably a richly ornamented single-axle carriage called a *carpentum* used by officials and the elite.

45. Beitzel, *New Moody Atlas of the Bible*, 255 map 108; compare 249 map 105.

Jericho (compare Luke 10:33), then proceed either through the Transjordanian highlands[46] or follow the west bank of the Jordan River.[47] From Scythopolis the road ran north to the Sea of Galilee where it forked. The road on the lake's eastern side steered northeastward from above Hippus through Gaulanitis toward Damascus (Rainey-Notley). The road on the lake's western side passed through Tiberius and Capernaum, then continued northward into the Jordan River valley. A fork at Hazor turned northeastward again through Gaulanitis to Damascus (Beitzel).[48] A third possible route continued northward along the Jordan to connect with the Herodian road mentioned by Josephus (*J.W.* 3.10.7). This route ran eastward from Tyre past Caesarea Philippi through Trachonitis to Damascus (*BAGRW*). Archaeological realia from these routes include numerous late Roman milestones found near Scythopolis and a well-preserved Roman bridge at Caesarea Philippi.[49]

After being taken into custody in Jerusalem at the end of his third journey, Paul was secretly taken to Caesarea (sixty-eight miles [109 km]) under the protective command of two centurions commanding two hundred soldiers, seventy cavalrymen, and two hundred spearmen. Paul was provided a horse to ride (Acts 23:23–24). At Antipatris the foot soldiers were allowed to return to Jerusalem, while the cavalry escorted Paul the remainder of the trip (twenty-six miles [42 km]; Acts 23:31–33). That such an auxiliary cohort could travel at night suggests that they were marching on a built and engineered road between Jerusalem and Caesarea, the provincial capital and residence of the governor Felix. Acts thus provides important textual evidence for an imperial road in Judea before the Jewish revolt.[50]

ROADS AND TRAVEL

Travel by sea was the preferred option because of speed, ease, and cost. However, the Mediterranean was closed during the winter and unpredictable in the late fall and early spring. Travel at this time was dangerous, as Paul well knew (2 Cor 11:25; see also Acts 27:9–12). Even when sea-lanes were open, winds could be fickle, and travelers were subject to the availability of a ship sailing in the right

46. Anson F. Rainey and R. Steven Notley, *Carta's New Century Handbook and Atlas of the Bible* (Jerusalem: Carta, 2007), 241 with map.

47. See *BAGRW*, map 69.

48. Israel Roll, "Between Damascus and Megiddo," 10 map 4 does not show this as an option in the Roman period.

49. For a list of these milestones see http://milestones.kinneret.ac.il/en/info-about-milestones/inscriptions-on-milestones/; for the bridge see John Francis Wilson, *Caesarea Philippi: Banias the Lost City of Pan* (London: Tauris, 2004), 52, also illustration 45.

50. Under Elagablus (AD 219/220) the Romans did major construction work on the northern route from Jerusalem to Antipatris through Gopha. However, the road south from Antipatris to Lydda/Diospolis continued to be maintained as well; see Israel Roll, "Roman Milestones in the Vicinity of Aphek-Antipatris,"in *Aphek-Antipatris I: Excavation of Areas A and B, the 1972 to 1976 Seasons*, ed. Moshe Kochavi, Pirhiyah Beck, and Esther Yadin (Tel Aviv: Emery and Claire Yass Publications in Archaeology, 2000), 41–44, 40 fig. 4.1 for a map.

direction.[51] The book of Acts and the New Testament letters depict a combination of land and sea travel for the journeys of Paul and for Silas' delivery of Peter's first letter. Even Revelation was carried from the island of Patmos before delivery could begin from Ephesus to the other seven churches.

For his land journeys Paul primarily walked (for example, πεζεύω, *pezeuō*; Acts 20:13). Perhaps pack animals were used occasionally. However, fodder and water would be a constant need, and predators like lions were an ever-present danger in the mountains. Personal necessities such as food, clothing, and water would be carried in something resembling a modern backpack. A goat-hair sheet could also provide basic shelter from inclement weather when a *mansio* or synagogue hostel was not available.[52] Paul eloquently described the challenges of travel:

> I have been constantly on the move. I have been in danger from rivers, in danger from bandits ... in danger in the city, in danger in the country, in danger at sea.... I have often gone without sleep; I have known hunger and thirst and have often gone without food; I have been cold and naked. (2 Cor. 11:26–27 NIV)

Regarding bandits, Paul traveled on the desolate borders of Bithynia and Mysia during his second journey (Acts 16:7–8). A bandit-overlord named Cleon preyed here in the late first century BC (Strabo, *Geography* 12.8.8–9). In this same region Paul likely encountered some of Cleon's successors.

CONCLUSION

Travel was ubiquitous in the Roman Empire. The itinerary of Herod the Great in 14 BC demonstrates this: from Caesarea he sailed to Rhodes, Cos, Chios, Lesbos, Byzantium, landing at Sinope. From Pontus he traveled overland through Paphlagonia, Cappadocia, and Phrygia arriving in Ephesus and then sailing back to Samos (Josephus, *Ant.* 16.17–23). The epitaph of Flavius Zeuxis, a merchant from Hierapolis, declares that on seventy-two occasions he made the dangerous passage around Cape Malea at the tip of the Peloponnesus below Corinth.[53] Zeuxis thus made thirty-six roundtrips to Rome during his lifetime from the Lycus valley, a distance by land and sea of 2310 miles (3718 km).[54] Eckhard Schnabel estimates that Paul traveled approximately 15,000 miles (25,000 km) during his journeys, of which about 8700 miles (14,000 km) were by land.[55] While this figure may appear large to modern travelers, it is

51. William M. Ramsay, "Roads and Travel (in NT)," in *A Dictionary of the Bible*, ed. James Hastings (Edinburgh: T&T Clark, 1898), 5:376–83. Cicero (*Atticus* 5.8.1) was delayed for twelve days in Brundisium waiting for passage on a ship.

52. For these and other factors related to ancient travel, see Mark Wilson, "Paul's Journeys in 3D: The Apostle as Ideal Ancient Traveller," *Journal of Early Christian History* 8 (2018): 13–17.

53. Tullia Ritti, *An Epigraphic Guide to Hierapolis (Pamukkale)* (Istanbul: Ege Yayınları, 2006), 67–70.

54. This figure was calculated on Orbis from nearby Laodicea ad Lycum: http://orbis.stanford.edu/.

55. Eckhard Schnabel, *Paul the Missionary: Realities, Strategies and Methods* (Downers Grove, IL: InterVarsity Press, 2008), 122.

significantly less than the sum of Zeuxis' travels: 83,160 miles (133,848 km). As Laurence observes,

> The need to travel would seem to be part of the experience of the Roman Empire.... There is evidence in some form for travel or the need to undertake journeys on the part of individuals from all parts of the empire.[56]

Thus the apostles traveling along Roman roads to preach the gospel would be viewed as part of a larger empire-wide movement.

BIBLIOGRAPHY

Alcock, Susan E. *Graecia Capta: The Landscapes of Roman Greece*. Cambridge: Cambridge University Press, 1993.

Attekum, Marietta van, and Holger de Bruin. *Via Egnatia on Foot: A Journey into History*. Driebergen: Via Egnatia Foundation, 2014.

Beitzel, Barry. *The New Moody Atlas of the Bible*. Chicago: Moody, 2009.

Bekker-Nielsen, Tønnes. *The Roads of Ancient Cyprus*. Copenhagen: Museum Tusculanum, 2004.

Berlin, Andrea M. "Jewish Life before the Revolt: The Archaeological Evidence." *Journal for the Study of Judaism* 36 (2005): 417–70.

Butcher, Kevin. *Roman Syria and the Near East*. Los Angeles: Getty, 2003.

Cioffi, Robert L. "Travel in the Ancient World." Oxford Handbooks Online, 2016. https://dx.doi.org/10.1093/oxfordhb/9780199935390.013.110.

Davis, Thomas W., and Mark Wilson. "The Destination of Paul's First Journey: Asia Minor or North Africa?" *Pharos Journal of Theology* 97 (2016): 1–14.

D'Andria, Franceso. *Hierapolis of Phrygia (Pamukkale): An Archaeological Guide*. Istanbul: Ege Yayınları, 2003.

French, David H. *Milestones: Republican*. Fascicle 3.1 of *Roads and Milestones of Asia Minor*. Ankara: British Institute of Archaeology at Ankara, 2012.

Hengel, Martin, and Anna Maria Schwemer. *Paul between Damascus and Antioch: The Unknown Years*. Louisville, KY: Westminster John Knox, 1997.

Horace. *Horace's Satires and Epistles*. Translated by Jacob Fuchs. New York: Norton, 1977.

Horsley, G. H. R., and S. Mitchell. *The Inscriptions of Central Pisidia: Including Texts from Kremna, Ariassos, Keraia, Hyia, Panemoteichos, the Sanctuary of Apollo of the Perminoundeis, Sia, Kocaaliler, and the Dǫseme Bŏgazi*. Bonn: Habelt, 2000.

Isaac, Benjamin. "Roman Roads, Physical Remains, Organization and Development." *Scripta Classica Israelica* 34 (2015): 41–48.

Laurence, Ray. "Afterword: Travel and Empire." Pages 167–76 in *Travel and Geography in the Roman Empire*. Edited by Colin Adams and Ray Laurence. London: Routledge, 2001.

———. *The Roads of Roman Italy: Mobility and Cultural Change*. London: Routledge, 1999.

Lolos, Giannes. *Εγνατία Ὀδός*. Athens: Olkos, 2009.

Maas, Michael. "People and Identity in Roman Antioch." Pages 13–21 in *Antioch The Lost Ancient City*. Edited

56. Ray Laurence, "Afterword: Travel and Empire," in *Travel and Geography in the Roman Empire*, ed. Colin Adams and Ray Laurence (London: Routledge, 2001), 169.

by Christine Kondoleon. Princeton: Princeton University Press, 2000.

Mitchell, Stephen. "Population and Land in Roman Galatia." *ANRW* 7.2:1053–81.

O'Connor, Colin. *Roman Bridges*. Cambridge: Cambridge University Press, 1993.

Pattengale, Jerry A. "Achaia." *ABD* 1:53.

Rainey, Anson F., and R. Steven Notley. *Carta's New Century Handbook and Atlas of the Bible*. Carta: Jerusalem, 2007.

Ramsay, William M. "Roads and Travel (in NT)." Pages 375–402 in vol. 5 of *A Dictionary of the Bible*. Edited by James Hastings. 5 vols. Edinburgh: T&T Clark, 1898–1923.

Ritti, Tullia. *An Epigraphic Guide to Hierapolis (Pamukkale)*. Istanbul: Ege Yayınları, 2006.

Rizakis, Athanasios D. "Town and Country in Early Imperial Greece." *Pharos: Journal of the Netherlands Institute at Athens* 20 (2014): 239–65.

Roll, Israel. "Between Damascus and Megiddo: Roads and Transportation in Antiquity across the Northeastern Approaches to the Holy Land." Pages 1–20 in *Man near a Roman Arch: Studies Presented to Prof. Yoram Tsafrir*. Edited by Leah Di Segni, Yizhar Hirshfeld, Joseph Patrich, and Rina Talgam. Jerusalem: Israel Exploration Society, 2009.

———. "Roman Milestones in the Vicinity of Aphek-Antipatris." Pages 39–46 in *Aphek-Antipatris I: Excavation of Areas A and B, the 1972 to 1976 Seasons*. Edited by Moshe Kochavi, Pirhiyah Beck, and Esther Yadin. Tel Aviv: Emery and Claire Yass Publications in Archaeology, 2000.

———. "The Roman Road System in Judaea." *Jerusalem Cathedra* 3 (1983): 136–61.

Sartorio, Giuseppina Pisani. "Origins and Historic Events." Pages 14–39 in *The Appian Way: From Its Foundation to the Middle Ages*. Edited by Ivana Della Portella. Los Angeles: Getty, 2004.

Schnabel, Eckhard. *Early Christian Mission*. 2 vols. Downers Grove, IL: InterVarsity Press, 2004.

———. *Paul the Missionary: Realities, Strategies and Methods*. Downers Grove, IL: InterVarsity Press, 2008.

Staccioli, Romolo Augusto. *The Roads of the Romans*. Los Angeles: Getty, 2003.

Taylor, Jane. *Petra and the Lost Kingdom of the Nabateans*. London: Tauris, 2001.

Thompson, Glen L., and Mark Wilson. "Paul's Walk to Assos: A Hodological Inquiry into Its Geography, Archaeology, and Purpose." Pages 269–313 in *Stones, Bones and the Sacred: Essays on Material Culture and Ancient Religion in Honor of Dennis E. Smith*. Edited by Alan Cadwallader. Atlanta: SBL Press, 2016.

———. "The Route of Paul's Second Journey in Asia Minor: In the Steps of Robert Jewett and Beyond." *TynBul* 67 (2016): 217–46.

Tilburg, Cornelius van. *Traffic and Congestion in the Roman Empire*. London: Routledge, 2007.

Tol, Gils, Tymon de Haas, Kayt Armstrong, and Peter Attema. "Minor Centres in the Pontine Plain: The Cases of Forum Appii and Ad Medias." *Papers of the British School at Rome* 82 (2014): 109–34.

Velestino, Daniela. *La Galleria Lapidaria dei Musei Capitolini*. Rome: De Luca, 2015.

Wilson, John Francis. *Caesarea Philippi: Banias the Lost City of Pan*. London: Tauris, 2004.

Wilson, Mark. "The Ephesian Elders Come to Miletus: An Annaliste Reading of Acts 20:15–18a." *Verbum et Ecclesia* 34 (2013): 1–9.

———. "Paul's Journeys in 3D: The Apostle as Ideal Ancient Traveller." *Journal of Early Christian History* 8 (2018): 1–19.

———. "The Route of Paul's First Journey to Pisidian Antioch." *NTS* 55 (2009): 471–83.

———. "Saint Paul in Pamphylia: Intention, Arrival, Departure." *Adalya* 19 (2016): 229–50.

———. "The 'Upper Regions' and the Route of Paul's Third Journey from Apamea to Ephesus." *Scriptura* 117 (2018): 1–21.

CHAPTER 15

THE DESERT ROAD BETWEEN JERUSALEM AND GAZA

Acts 8:26–40

Paul H. Wright

KEY POINTS

- Philip's encounter with the Ethiopian eunuch in Acts 8 marks the moment the gospel begins to move from "Samaria, and to the ends of the earth" (Acts 1:8).
- The passage contains a number of clues to the encounter's geographical context.
- Considerations of topography make the natural route from Jerusalem to Gaza fairly easy to determine.

GEOGRAPHICAL CLUES IN ACTS 8:26–40

Philip's encounter with the Ethiopian eunuch occurs at a critical juncture in the narrative flow of the book of Acts, marking the moment when the gospel message first moved from "Samaria, and to the ends of the earth" (Acts 1:8).[1] The introductory verse, Acts 8:26, provides a number of geographical clues that allow careful readers to place Philip's encounter within a likely geographical context: "Now an angel of the Lord said to Philip, saying, 'Go south to the road—the desert road—that goes down from Jerusalem to Gaza.'" The text adds that the eunuch was riding in a chariot (Acts 8:28) and that he found water sufficient to be baptized along the way (Acts 8:36). In terms of method, our search should take into account the following geographical clues:

1. Unless otherwise noted, Scripture quotations come from the New International Version (NIV).

"SOUTH"

The phrase *kata mesēmbrian* (κατὰ μεσημβρίαν) means "about noon" (see Zeph 2:4, LXX), although here it is usually taken idiomatically as the directional "toward the south," that is, toward the position where the sun appears in the sky about noon. Within this context, *kata mesēmbrian* does not modify the relative position of Gaza to Jerusalem, a direction that, by compass, is west-southwest, but rather the relationship of Philip to the road that connects the two cities. Incidentally, because Gaza functioned as the historic gateway for persons in Judea traveling to Egypt and points in the inhabited south beyond, "south" is also the functional directional for Gaza even though its compass direction from Jerusalem is west-southwest.

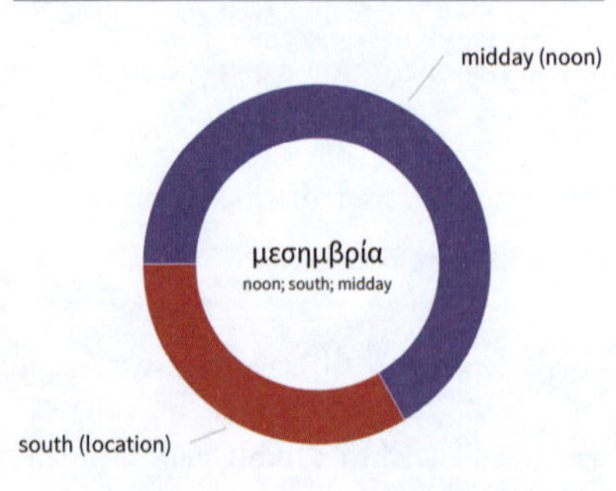

"DESERT"

The Greek term *erēmos* (ἔρημος, "desert, wilderness") references places that are generally deserted, uncultivated, and empty of a permanent human presence. While deserts or areas termed "wilderness" in the New Testament certainly qualify as *erēmos* (1 Macc 5:24; Matt 3:1), so do open stretches of steppe land or grassland. There were, for instance, plenty of *erēmos* places around the busy Sea of Galilee. These include areas outside of the cities where Jesus would slip away to be alone (Luke 5:16), places beyond the fields where the Gergasene demoniac would wander (Luke 8:29), and the site of the feeding of the five thousand, with towns close enough to buy bread (Luke 9:12). The object modified by *erēmos* in Acts 8:26 is not stated, though most readers assume that it refers to the portion of the road between Jerusalem and Gaza where Philip was to go, rather than to the city of Gaza itself. Gaza had been razed by Alexander Jannaeus in 96 BC, then rebuilt, according to Josephus, by the Syrian procurator Gabinius in 57 BC (*Ant.* 13.358–364; 14.88). Strabo (*Geography* 16.2.30), on the other hand, mentioned that Gaza remained uninhabited (μένουσα ἔρημος, *menousa erēmos*) in his day (the early first century AD).

"ROAD … GOES DOWN … JERUSALEM TO GAZA"

"Goes down" is the expected verb given the reality that travelers normally ascend on their journey to Jerusalem (for example, Ps 122:3–4; Jer 31:6; Acts 15:2; 21:15; 25:9). Jerusalem lies between 2400 and 2500 feet (730–760 m) in elevation while the tel of ancient Gaza (Tell Ḥarube/Tell ʿAzza) sits on a small rise about 160 feet (50 m) above sea level three miles (5 km) inland. The phrase about the road "from Jerusalem to Gaza" suggests the most direct, or the most natural, route between the two cities.

"CHARIOT" AND "WATER"

That the eunuch was riding in a chariot (Acts 8:28) indicates a route suitable for chariot travel, even in the hill country of Judea. There was also "some water" along the road in sufficient quantity for the eunuch and Philip to go "down into the water" for baptism (8:36–39). Water

Sea of Galilee and Surrounding Terrain

sufficient for baptism indicates an available supply of "living," or running, water near the route.

ROMAN ROADS

Our tendency is to look first for textual and archaeological evidence of a Roman road between Jerusalem and Gaza. Roman roads were massive engineering achievements, leaving behind trails of stone that attest to the absolute competence of Rome's skills in empire building. Eventually, approximately one thousand miles of paved Roman roads were constructed in the province of Syria-Palestine, though only bits and pieces of their roadbeds, paving, curbing, milestones, and ancillary structures such as bridges and water reservoirs can be seen today.[2]

Because Roman roads were used primarily for imperial purposes (military and administrative activities), their network expanded as Rome solidified its frontier. Although Josephus spoke of the Romans building roads as part of their efforts to move troops more efficiently during the Great Revolt (for example, *J.W.* 3.118, 141), their biggest prompt to fully meld Judea into the empire came with the annexation of the Nabatean realm in AD 106. The earliest known milestone in the province of Judea, which dates to AD 56, belongs to the coastal road connecting Antioch with Ptolemais.[3] This is a likely location because the natural port at Ptolemais (Acco) was the easiest landing point for the deep-water ships used by Rome. The earliest milestone in the hill country of Judea dates to AD 120, well after the destruction of the Jerusalem temple and not long before the emperor

2. Israel Roll, "The Roman Road System in Judea," in *The Jerusalem Cathedra*, ed. Lee I. Levine (Jerusalem: Yad Ben-Zvi, 1983), 3:136.

3. David F. Graf, Benjamin Isaac, and Israel Roll, "Roads and Highways: Roman Roads," *ABD* 5:785.

Roman Road from Jerusalem to Beth-guvrin

Hadrian founded the city as a polis, Aelia Capitolina, in AD 135.[4]

By the end of the second century AD both Aelia Capitolina and Betogabris (Beth-guvrin) had become hubs of the Roman road network. Betogabris was renamed Eleutheropolis by the emperor Septimius Severus in AD 200. A road angling from Aelia Capitolina (Jerusalem) to the coast via Betogabris appears on the thirteenth century *Tabula Peutingeriana*,[5] which dates the data shown on at least this part of the map to the mid-second century AD. Eusebius (*Onomasticon* 48:18; 168:22) speaks of towns along the Roman road on the descent from Eleutheropolis to Gaza. Gaza itself does not seem to have been an important hub for Rome other than in the city's traditional role as a gateway to Egypt. Its ancient port was likely not as suitable for larger, open sea vessels as were the ports at Ptolemais and Caesarea further up the coast.

Consistent with these texts, archaeologists have uncovered remains of a Roman road connecting Jerusalem with Betogabris/Eleutheropolis.[6] These include a section of bedrock-cut steps forming a portion of the roadbed in the lower part of the Judean hills descending into the Elah Valley, a portion of the road just south of the Elah Valley adjacent to the moshav Giv'at Yishayahu (currently covered by the pavement of modern

4. Roll, "The Roman Road System in Judea," 142; Graf, Isaac and Roll, "Roads and Highways," 786.

5. Israel Finkelstein, "The Holy Land in the Tabula Peutingeriana: A Historical-Geographical Approach." *PEQ* 111 (1979): 27–34; Ekkehard Weber, "The Tabula Peutingeriana and the Madaba Map," in *The Madaba Map Centenary, 1897–1997*, ed. Michele Piccirillo and Eugenio Alliata (Jerusalem: Studium Biblicum Franciscanum, 1998), 41–46.

6. Zecharia Kallai, "Remains of the Roman Road Along the Mevo-Beitar Highway" *IEJ* 15 (1965): 195–203; Yohanan Landau, "Milestones near Giv'at Yishayahu" *Bulletin of the Jewish Palestine Exploration Society* 28 (1964): 232–35.

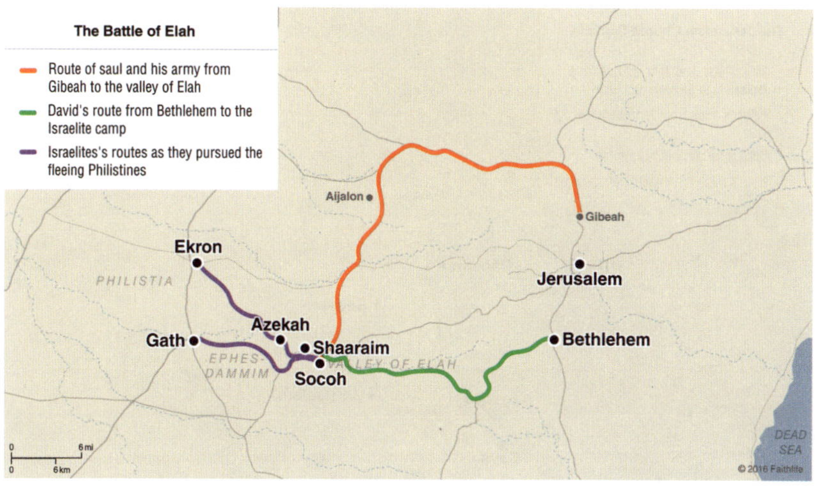

Highway 38), and a number of milestones from the second century AD marking the mileage to and from Eleutheropolis.

There is no evidence that this Roman road network was operative, as such, in the early AD 30s when Philip met the Ethiopian eunuch. The question, rather, becomes what might the relationship between the Roman road network and the natural routes known from earlier periods be, including the road from the time of the Herodian dynasty? In this case, geographical logic alone would indicate that the Roman road between Jerusalem and Gaza followed the earlier natural route, at least in its main line. The principle, simple in conception and logical as to facts on the ground, is that main routes (such as this one) connected main cities, in this case Jerusalem to Hellenistic Marisa (near Betogabris) and then Gaza.

THE NATURAL ROUTE FROM JERUSALEM TO GAZA

Based on considerations of topography, the location of main cities and water resources, the natural route from Jerusalem to Gaza is fairly easy to determine. From Jerusalem travel normally would proceed southward along the watershed ridge to a point just west of Bethlehem, then follow the top of a continuous ridge separating the Sorek from the Elah wadi systems to the point where the hill country drops into the Judean Shephelah (foothills) at the beginning of the broad Elah Valley (modern Highway 375). The bedrock-cut roadbed steps mentioned above are visible just east of this point. It is likely that we can see a young David tracking the same ridge as he takes supplies to his brothers in Saul's army facing the Philistine forces of Goliath (1 Sam 17:17–20). A shortcut between Jerusalem and the top of this ridge tracks southwestward out of Jerusalem along what is today Jerusalem's ʿAza (Gaza) Road, then into the southern, Rephaim branch of the Sorek wadi before climbing the ridge west of the site of Battir, the last stand of the Bar-Kokhba revolt (AD 135). From the entrance to the Shephelah the

natural routes tracks westward along the edge of the Elah Valley to a point just south of the ancient site of Azekah (which was uninhabited in the first century AD), then angles south-southwestward via a narrow side valley to Marisa/Betogabris/Eleutheropolis (the line of modern Highway 38) and then to the vicinity of ancient Lachish (also not inhabited in the first century). From there the route would have followed the flow of the Nahal Shiqma (Wadi el-Ḥesi) westward to a point on the coast just north of Gaza. The entire route, including its hilly, upper stretch via Bethlehem, avoided terrain that would preclude chariot travel.

Although we do not know where Philip was when he received the angelic call, this route does seem to be the best fit of the biblical data. The episode opens with Philip somewhere in Samaria, working his way back toward Jerusalem (Acts 8:25). Philip could have headed directly west from southern Samaria toward the coast and then due south to Gaza, following the route well-trodden from earliest antiquity by conquerors and caravaneers making their way longitudinally along the coastal plain. But his call either took him back to Jerusalem first, or had him work his way southward from Samaria so as to intercept the Jerusalem–Gaza road somewhere along its upper length. It was on the westward run out of Marisa where Philip most likely met the Ethiopian eunuch.[7] The level portion of the coastal plain that lies a bit further north, forming a triangle between Joppa, Gezer, and Yavneh (Jamnia), is well-watered, covered with rich alluvial soil and, historically, home to a relatively dense population. The area of the plain on the run between Marisa and Gaza, by contrast, is a rolling, drier steppe land with wide, open empty spaces between its towns. This is a good fit for the descriptor *erēmos*. Yet there was also run-

7. This proposed itinerary is, of course, tentative, but does account well for the available textual and geographical data.

ning water in the vicinity. Several springs can be found along the valley formed by the Nahal Shiqma in the eastern part of the coastal plain, where the natural water runoff from the highest part of the Judean hills around Hebron, directly east, would have created stretches of flowing, "living" water. Immediately afterward, we find Philip in Azotus (Ashdod), a thriving city three miles (4.8 km) off the coast but due north of and perhaps half-a-day's walk from this *erēmos* place. The narrative fails to provide any information about how much time took place between Philip's call and his arrival in Azotus, but the entire trip normally would have taken perhaps three days.

Why might it be important that Philip was called to travel toward Gaza in the first place? Historically, Gaza was the location of Egypt's persistent penetration into Canaan. Yet for all of Egypt's imperial presence in the homeland of ancient Israel, it was to Egypt that Israel and then the Jews repeatedly traveled, sometimes to stay. The litany of instances is long. Among them we find Joseph and his extended family (Gen 46:1–34), Jeroboam (1 Kgs 12:1–2), Jeremiah (Jer 43:1–13), the infant Jesus (Matt 2:13–14), disciples of John the Baptist (Acts 18:24–25), Philo and a thriving Jewish diaspora in Elephantine and Alexandria in the first century AD. Many Jews were very much at home in Egypt during this time, and so it was the direction of Gaza, "the outpost of Africa, the door of Asia" (in the words of George Adam Smith)[8] that was a natural first outlet for the gospel's penetration to "the ends of the earth" (Acts 1:8).

BIBLIOGRAPHY

Finkelstein, Israel. "The Holy Land in the Tabula Peutingeriana: A Historical-Geographical Approach." *PEQ* 111 (1979): 27–34.

Graf, David F., Benjamin Isaac, and Israel Roll. "Roads and Highways: Roman Roads." *ABD* 5:782–87.

Josephus. *Jewish Antiquities*. Translated by H. St. J. Thackeray. 9 vols. LCL. Cambridge: Harvard University Press, 1930–1965.

———. *The Jewish War*. Translated by H. St. J. Thackeray. 3 vols. LCL. Cambridge: Harvard University Press, 1927–1930.

Kallai, Zecharia. "Remains of the Roman Road along the Mevo-Beitar Highway." *IEJ* 15 (1965): 195–203.

Landau, Yohanan. "Milestones near Giv'at Yishayhu." *Bulletin of the Jewish Palestine Exploration Society* 28 (1964): 232–35 (in Hebrew).

Roll, Israel. "The Roman Road System in Judea." Pages 136–61 in vol. 3 of *The Jerusalem Cathedra*. Edited by Lee I. Levine. Jerusalem: Yad Ben-Zvi, 1983.

Smith, George Adam. *The Historical Geography of the Holy Land*. London: Hodder and Stoughton, 1894.

Strabo. *The Geography of Strabo*. Translated by Horace Leonard Jones. 8 vols. LCL. Cambridge: Harvard University Press, 1917–1932.

Weber, Ekkehard. "The Tabula Peutingeriana and the Madaba Map." Pages 41–46 in *The Madaba Map Centenary, 1897–1997*. Edited by Michele Piccirillo and Eugenio Alliata. Jerusalem: Studium Biblicum Franciscanum, 1998.

8. George Adam Smith, *The Historical Geography of the Holy Land* (London: Hodder and Stoughton, 1894), 135.

CHAPTER 16

THE GEOGRAPHY OF CAESAREA MARITIMA

Acts 8:40; 9:30; 10:1–48; 12:19; 18:22; 21:7–16; 23:23–35; 25:1–27:3

Paul H. Wright

KEY POINTS

- The location of Caesarea Maritima was ill-suited for a commercial center, but the site became the largest and most influential port in the eastern Mediterranean.
- The architecture of the port of Caesarea reflects the grandeur of its founder, Herod the Great.
- Caesarea represents both the intrusive reality of Roman power in Judea and unlimited opportunities to launch the gospel to the ends of the earth.

INTRODUCTION

The geographical situation of Caesarea Maritima is a bit of a paradox. Caesarea is stunning, perfectly situated to serve Herod's grand purpose of linking Judea with Rome and fashioned with a level of technological skill that surpassed what was being built elsewhere in the empire. Yet, Herod chose to build Caesarea on a plot of ground that was particularly ill-suited for constructing the infrastructure necessary for such a worthy port, a place that was advantageous on neither its seaward nor landward side. The incongruity is striking, but so is the genius behind the site. These become apparent when we view the geography of Caesarea through three lenses: the location of the city, the architecture of the city, and the image of the city.

LOCATION

Caesarea is located on the northwestern corner of the Sharon Plain, twenty-three miles (37 km) south of the promontory of Mount Carmel and thirty-three miles (53 km) north of Joppa. Structurally, the Sharon Plain is composed of three lon-

gitudinal zones.[1] The westernmost is defined by three parallel ridges of *kurkar*, a limey, rough, tan sandstone formed from calcified dunes. Of these ridges, one forms the sporadic cliff line along the shore, while a second, which is lower, runs more continuously one-half mile (0.8 km) inland. The sands covering the shore have washed in from the Sahara and Sinai coasts by the counterclockwise movement of the Mediterranean's currents. A break in the westernmost *kurkar* ridge south of Caesarea allows these sands to penetrate inland, over time forming sizeable dunes and completely covering the second ridge. The third *kurkar* ridge, the so-called red ridge because it is covered with red sands, lies another two miles (3 km) further east. These three *kurkar* ridges run concurrent with the coast, defining its straight-line shape. This geographical reality may lie behind the name Sharon, if it derives from the Hebrew root *yashar* (ישר), "straight" or "smooth."[2] The Sharon's second zone, lying east of the red ridge, is comprised of a band of low, jumbled hills of brown-red *ḥamra* sands. East of that, the third zone, a shallow trough of alluvial soil, rises to the foothills of Samaria (the tribal regions of Ephraim and Manasseh).

Historically, runoff from the Samaria hills onto the Sharon Plain has tended to back up among these *kurkar* ridges and

1. Yehuda Karmon, *Israel: A Regional Geography* (London: Wiley-Interscience, 1971), 14–20.

2. The same Hebrew root may describe the generally smooth or flat topography of the plain; see J. Simons, *The Geographical and Topographical Texts of the Old Testament: A Concise Commentary in 32 Chapters* (Leiden: Brill 1959), 83. This follows the pattern of natural regions being designated by terms that describe a geographical phenomenon characteristic of the region; for example, *Shephelah* = "lowland," *Negev* = "dry land," *Mishor* = "tableland," *Bashan* = "flat land," and *Edom* = "red (land)."

ḥamra hills, creating large expanses of overgrown, seasonal swampland that resisted easy cultivation, impeded travel, and promoted water-borne disease. This has been especially prominent in the central Sharon Plain but less so in the north, where overall elevations are a bit higher. The prophet Isaiah called this exuberance of nature "the splendor of Sharon" (Isa 25:2), relating its natural bounty to the messianic age.[3] But for practical purposes, the entire Sharon, save for the alluvial trough lining its eastern end, did not attract much permanent settlement in ancient times. Until, that is, Herod got ahold of the place. The soils of the Sharon are fertile if the water flow can be controlled by human intervention, and this process seems to have begun only with the founding of Caesarea. Herod didn't live long enough to see all of his intentions realized, but he did set the stage to transform the Sharon Plain into a valuable economic zone. Caesarea ended up possessing the largest usable territory of any Greco-Roman city (*polis*) in the province of Judea, stretching an estimated twenty-one miles (35 km) north to south and eastward in places as far as seventeen miles (27 km) from the coast, an area that covered nearly three hundred fifty square miles (906.5 km^2).[4] How much of this territory was already converted to arable farmland that could support the economy of Caesarea in the first century AD is unknown, but it likely was very little.

Easier to estimate are the lines of the highways that connected Caesarea with points inland in the time of the New Testament.[5] The historic route, which was tracked by traders and empires for millennia, ran along the seam between the Sharon Plain and the rise of the Samaria hills, from Antipatris (Acts 23:31) to the Megiddo pass. It continued on to points in the Great Plain (that is, the Jezreel Valley; Jdt 1:8; Josephus, *Life* 115; *J.W.* 2.188, etc.), and its connections beyond.[6] But there seems also to have been a north-south passage along the coast, tracking the moist sand at the seashore and/or pushing through the brush-covered dunes just east of the first *kurkar* ridge. Though carrying mainly local traffic prior to the Hellenistic period, this route gained importance with the establishment of Greek and Roman control of the coastal plain and their subsequent penetration into the hills of Judea and Samaria. There are no natural east-west routes through the Sharon Plain; historically this has tended to isolate the coastline from the main longitudinal route running at the edge of the Samaria foothills. But with the establishment of the port of Caesarea, east-west corridors must have developed. Their exact routes in the time of the New Testament can be conjectured based on local topography and the principle that main routes connected main cities, linking smaller cities and villages in the process. We should

3. Unless otherwise indicated, Scripture quotations are from the New International Version (NIV).

4. Kenneth G. Holum et al., *King Herod's Dream: Caesarea on the Sea* (New York: Norton, 1988), 75.

5. Yehuda Karmon, "Geographical Influences on the Historical Routes in the Sharon Plain," *PEQ* 93 (1961): 43–60; David Dorsey, *The Roads and Highways of Ancient Israel* (Baltimore: Johns Hopkins University Press, 1991), 72–74.

6. Dorsey, *Roads and Highways*, 70–72.

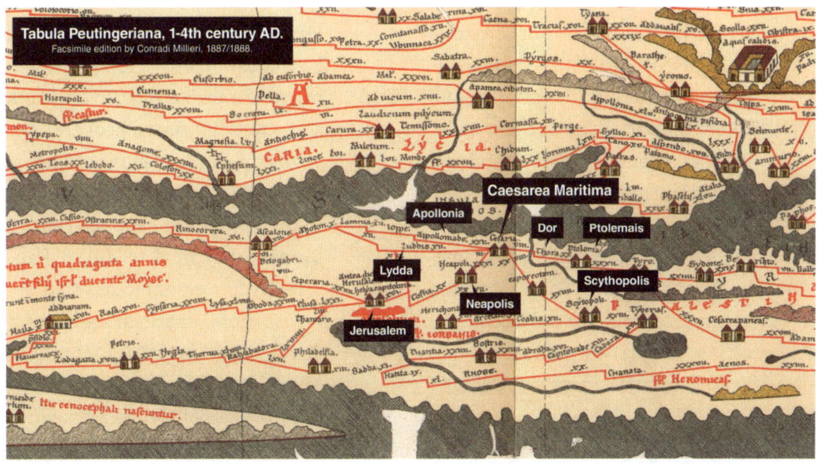

Peutinger Map: Five Routes Leading to Caesarea

note that the primary initiative for establishing Roman roads in Judea should be attributed to the emperor Hadrian who, following the Bar Kokhba revolt of AD 132–135, turned Jerusalem into the *polis* Aelia Capitolina, renamed the province of Judea "Syria-Palaestina," and bolstered the number of imperial troops stationed there. Yet we might reasonably assume that the routes linking inland Judea and Samaria with Caesarea were already being established in Herod's day. While sufficient archaeological remains in the Sharon Plain that would verify the line of these routes during the Second Temple period are lacking, enough archaeological data-points from the Late Roman and Byzantine periods (bridges, paving stones, and village remains) do exist to confirm the suggestion.

All of this is consistent with the *Tabula Peutingeriana* (Peutinger Map), a document preserving data from as early as the second century AD that depicts five routes converging on Caesarea.[7] The five are:

1. A road running north along the coast from Caesarea to Dora (Dor), Ptolemais, and the Phoenician ports beyond. This road functioned in tandem with parallel sea traffic that plied the same ports. Several milestones dating to AD 56 mark the line of this route between Ptolemais and Antioch.[8]

7. Karmon, "Geographical Influences," 53–57; Israel Roll, "The Roman Road System in Judea," in *The Jerusalem Cathedra*, ed. Lee I. Levine (Jerusalem: Yad Ben-Zvi, 1983), 3:136–61; David F. Graf, Benjamin Isaac, and Israel Roll, "Roads and Highways: Roman Roads," *ABD* 5:782–87; Ekkehard Weber, "The Tabula Peutingeriana and the Madaba Map," in *The Madaba Map Centenary, 1897–1997*, ed. Michele Piccirillo and Eugenio Alliata (Jerusalem: Studium Biblicum Franciscanum, 1998), 44.

8. Graf, Isaac, and Roll, "Roads and Highways," 785.

2. A road heading east from Caesarea to Kapor'otnai (Kefar Otni) near the tel of Megiddo, and then on to Scythopolis. The earliest milestone of a Roman road in the inland portion of the province of Judea was found along this route near modern Afula, erected in the name of Vespasian in AD 69.[9] This route connected Rome to the Decapolis cities on the empire's eastern, Transjordanian frontier.

3. A road heading east-southeast from Caesarea to Neapolis (Shechem) in the Samaria hills. This route, which connected two of Herod's Augusteum temples, linked Rome to an area of the hill country that was more culturally open to Hellenism than were the hills around Jerusalem.

4. A road heading south-southeast from Caesarea to the inland coastal cities of Antipatris (Aphek), Lydda (Lod), and Yavneh, with a branch to Jerusalem that followed the "public road leading up to Bethhoron" (Josephus, *J.W.* 2.228).[10] This ancient natural route was certainly paved by Hadrian if not already improved by Titus for his conquest of Jerusalem in AD 70.[11] It was along this route that we can posit Peter's flight from Jerusalem down to Caesarea to escape a death sentence handed out by Herod Agrippa I in approximately AD 43 (Acts 12:19). The Apostle Paul also most likely took this route as he hurried up to Jerusalem from Caesarea for the Pentecost of AD 57, following his third missionary journey (Acts 20:15–16). The journey covered sixty-four miles (103 km), a distance that would be hard to do quickly in the late spring heat and coastal humidity typical to Judea. Paul found it convenient to stay the first night out of Caesarea at the home of one Mnason of Cyprus (Acts 20:16). Mnason's village is unnamed, but that he was "of Cyprus" provides evidence that the roads crossing the Sharon were becoming settled with interests that faced west. A few days later Paul reversed the trip in all due haste after being arrested in Jerusalem; he was escorted to Antipatris by a quick night trip under horse and spear guard, then sent on to a two-year long rendezvous with the Roman governor Felix at Caesarea (Acts 23:23–35).

5. A road heading south along the coast from Caesarea to Apollonia, Joppa, and eventually Egypt. There is no substantive archaeological evidence for this being a formal Roman road prior to the *Tabula Peutingeriana*, even though Titus' march from Alexandria to Caesarea in early AD 70 to finish off the Jewish revolt (*J.W.* 4.656–663) necessitated a path suitable for moving his legionary troops. It is on this route that we can track Philip as he worked his way along

---

9. Roll, "Roman Road System," 140; Graf, Isaac, and Roll, "Roads and Highways," 785.

10. All quotations from the works of Josephus derive from the Loeb Classical Library translations (LCL).

11. Israel Roll, "Roman Roads in Western Samaria," *PEQ* 118 (1986): 122–25, 127–29.

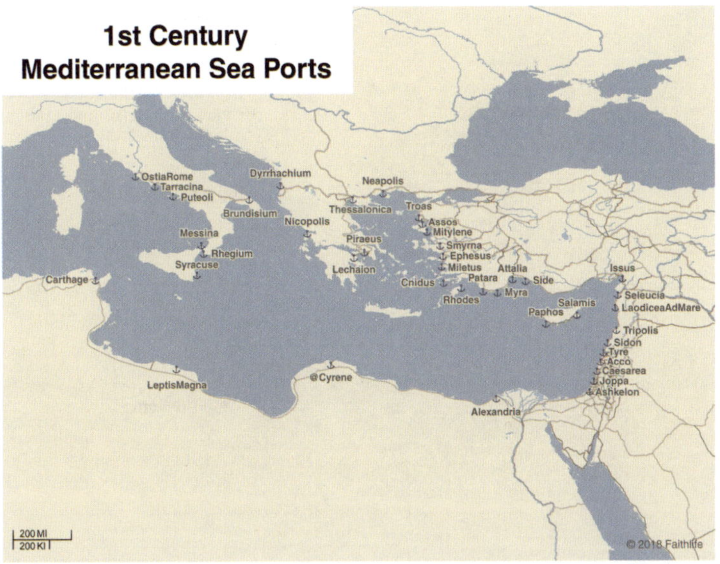

the coast from Azotus (Ashdod) to Caesarea following his encounter with the Ethiopian eunuch (Acts 8:40). Somewhat later, Peter made the walk from Joppa to Caesarea in two days (Acts 10:23–24), having been summoned by both Cornelius, a centurion "in what was known as the Italian Regiment" (Acts 10:1) and the Spirit of God (Acts 10:17–22).

To the west, of course, Caesarea opened up to the sea-lanes of the Mediterranean. Long-distance shipping lanes between Caesarea and the north African coast likely carried Jewish pilgrims to the crowded Pentecost festival of Acts 2:5–11.

The busiest sea-lane was the shipping lane up and down the Levantine coast, frequented by small vessels that plied their wares from port to port. Saul of Tarsus sailed back home from Caesarea this way, after meeting Jesus on the road to Damascus (Acts 9:30). His approach to Judea at the conclusion of his third missionary journey took him down the coast from Tyre to Ptolemais and then Caesarea, each an easy day's journey apart (Acts 21:7–16). Paul sailed back up the coast on his subsequent journey to Rome on an Adramyttian ship, so named because it was working its way back to its home port, Adramyttium on the Aegean coast of Asia Minor (Acts 27:1–2). His journey from Caesarea to Sidon took just one day (Acts 27:3), helped, no doubt, by the current.[12]

Caesarea was also port of call for the north Mediterranean shipping lanes from Rome via Greece, the Aegean, and Cyprus. Heading home at the end of his second and third missionary journeys, Paul's ships put sail to wind to skirt

12. For a common-sense understanding of the speed of Paul's travels by sea, see William M. Ramsay, *St. Paul: The Traveler and Roman Citizen*, updated and rev. ed., ed. Mark Wilson (Grand Rapids: Kregel, 2001), 222–28.

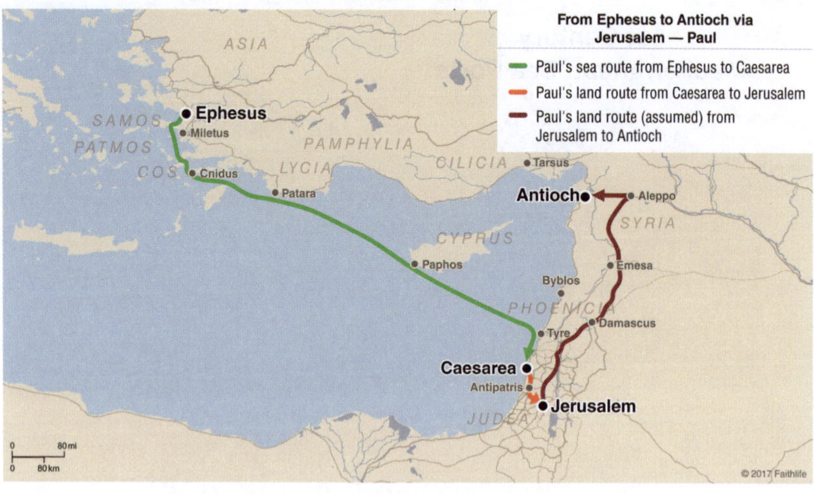

Cyprus along its southern, open-sea flank, landing eventually at Caesarea (Acts 18:22; 21:1–3). Indeed, whenever Paul returned to Judea by sea, he seems to have landed at the Caesarea harbor.

We must keep in mind that the port of Caesarea served not only peoples of the Mediterranean, but also those who brought goods from the east, including points in Arabia and via the Red Sea. Caesarea was Herod's port to the west, but land routes linked it to equally viable and lucrative markets facing east. Herod the Great reaped the economic benefits of controlling a true land between.[13]

All of this speaks to the bigger picture. But why did Herod choose this *specific* spot to construct his gateway to Rome when there already were well-established ports in the area? By far the most likely candidate might have been Ptolemais, the southernmost of the line of Phoenician ports hugging the rugged coastline north of Mount Carmel. Ptolemais was blessed with every natural geographical advantage, having a hooked seacoast for a harbor and a wide, level inland connection to the Great Plain and Transjordan behind. Fifteen miles (24 km) south of the Carmel promontory was Dora (Dor), proven to be an effective port in the Persian and Hellenistic periods. On a gentle bend in the coastline another forty miles (64 km) south lay Joppa, not as protected as Ptolemais but sufficient to serve local shipping needs. These were Herod's obvious options. Between Dora and Joppa, the coastline afforded no natural anchorages save for breaks in the *kurkar* ridge where ships could dock in calm seas. And even these spots were not conducive to shipping over the long term, for along the entire length the surf pounds the shoreline, eating away its edge and causing the *kurkar* ridge to crumble onto the beach, leaving shelves of sharp rock just below

13. For the phrase "land between" and its characterization of Judea, see James M. Monson, *Regions on the Run: Introductory Map Studies in the Land of the Bible* (Rockford, IL: Biblical Backgrounds, 1998).

View from the Ruins of Herod's Palace Looking Toward the Harbor at Caesarea Maritima

the waterline to wreck ships buffeted by the winds. Josephus described the situation this way:

> For the whole sea-board from Dora to Joppa, midway between which the city [of Caesarea] lies, was without a harbor, so that vessels bound for Egypt along the coast of Phoenicia had to ride at anchor in the open when menaced by the southwest wind; for even a moderate breeze from this quarter dashes the waves to such a height against the cliffs, that their reflux spreads a wild commotion far out to sea (*J.W.* 1.409)

The erudite historical geographer George Adam Smith took a longer view, one that speaks of persistent human frustration in trying to tame the Sharon seacoast: "While the cruelty of many another wild coast is known by the wrecks of ships, the Syrian shore south of Carmel is strewn with the fiercer wreckage of harbours."[14]

Eight miles (13 km) south of Dora was Strato's Tower, a small port that by the late first century BC had fallen on hard times (Josephus said it was "dilapidated;" *J.W.* 1.408). The name Strato is the Greek form of *'Abd-ashtart*, who were two Sidonian kings from the fourth century BC. The site probably was first settled by one of them; the earliest pottery dates to that time. Strato's Tower is first mentioned in historical sources in the Zenon Papyri.[15] These texts record the visit of one Zenon, chief administrator to the finance minister of Ptolemy II Philadelphus, to Judea, Syria, and Phoenicia in 259 BC. Zenon, we read, landed at Strato's Tower, then made his way inland back down to Judea. His

14. George Adam Smith, *The Historical Geography of the Holy Land* (London: Hodder and Stoughton, 1894), 131.

15. Michael Avi-Yonah, *The Holy Land: A Historical Geography from the Persian to the Arab Conquest (536 BC–AD 640)* (Jerusalem: Carta, 2002), 39.

itinerary suggests that Strato's Tower was already the southernmost Phoenician port that had viable inland connections to Judea. The city was conquered and fortified by a local petty Hellenistic ruler named Zoilus in the late second century BC (Josephus, *Ant.* 13.324), then incorporated into the Hasmonean kingdom in approximately 103 BC by Alexander Jannaeus (Josephus, *Ant.* 13.334–337). We likely can date the earliest Jewish presence in Caesarea from that time. With the arrival of Roman control in the Levant half a century later, Mark Antony returned control of the Judean and Phoenician coasts, except Tyre and Sidon, to Egypt (specifically to Cleopatra VII). His grant shut Herod off from the sea (Josephus, *Ant.* 15.95; *J.W.* 1.361–362). But after the battle of Actium and following Antony and Cleopatra's suicide in 30 BC, Octavian (soon to be Caesar Augustus) gave the coastal areas south of Mount Carmel to Herod in order to secure a loyal Roman coast along the southern Levant (Josephus, *Ant.* 15.217; *J.W.* 1.396). This finally allowed Herod access to the sea, and with it came his best chance to earn the reputation "the Great" (see a map of Herod's kingdom on page 11).

What practical advantage did Strato's Tower, by now a dilapidated town on a contrary coastline, give Herod over the other ports on the coast? The most obvious is that while Ptolemais was the doorway of Galilee and Joppa and had a natural connection to Jerusalem, Strato's Tower, rebuilt as Caesarea, commanded a midpoint that gave Herod equal access to, and hence control of, both. It also provided immediate access to Sebaste, the rebuilt (and renamed) historic capital of Samaria (Josephus, *Ant.* 15.296; *J.W.* 1.403). Caesarea and Sebaste were the most important of the *polei* founded by Herod the Great and should be seen as twin anchors for Rome's control of the province of Judea. Herod named both after the emperor (*Sebaste* is the Greek form of the Latin *Augustus*, "venerable"). We might add that with the establishment of Caesarea and Sebaste as *polei*, together with the Decapolis city of Scythopolis already in place further east, Herod created a demographic line that strategically separated the Jews of Judea from the Jews of Galilee. Because the two largest centers of Jewish population under Herod's control were not, as a result, contiguous territories, the political influence of the Jews in their ancestral homeland was weakened to Herod's benefit. A further geographical advantage of Caesarea is that the city was able to develop the largest arable inland territory of all of the coastal towns lying between Mount Carmel and Joppa due to its location at the northern—and hence slightly higher and less swampy—end of the Sharon Plain. But perhaps most importantly, Herod founded Caesarea in a place where he was not beholden to the established economic, social, and political interests of others. The residents of Joppa had never gotten over his conquest of their city in 38 BC (Josephus, *Ant.* 14.396; *J.W.* 1.292) and Ptolemais was under the political control of Phoenicia, a province where Herod held no responsibility or rights.[16] The area of Strato's Tower, on the other hand, was essentially virgin territory on which Herod erected the gateway for

16. Avi-Yonah, *Holy Land*, 39.

a new political reality in the southern Levant.[17]

ARCHITECTURE

A second lens through which to view the geography of Caesarea is its architecture. Josephus described Herod's building activities in Caesarea at great length (*J.W.* 1.408–415; *Ant.* 15.331–341), portraying it as an archetypal Mediterranean Greek city (*polis*). By and large, the excavated remains of Caesarea corroborate Josephus' description, with some important exceptions. They also show a careful connection with the site's geography, that is, in the choice of building materials, the location and orientation of its major structures, and in methods of engineering and construction.

Josephus stated that Herod built Caesarea in just twelve years (*Ant.* 15.341). This is a fantastically short period of time if we consider the immense technological challenges involved and that the Jerusalem temple complex alone was forty-six years in the making (John 2:20). It is likely that Herod was able to start construction at Caesarea only after he had subdued his kingdom, and the economy of Judea had gained enough momentum to fund his massive building projects. This suggests a date in the late 20s BC. Josephus assigned the ceremony that celebrated Caesarea's founding to the twenty-eighth year of his reign (counting from 37 BC, the year Herod conquered Jerusalem), noting that it coincided with the 192nd Olympiad that, according to Western dating, was celebrated from 13 to 9 BC (*Ant.* 16.136). This places the initial phase of the city's construction in the twelve years from approximately 22 to 10 BC. Like all thriving cities, Caesarea was never "finished."

The relevant question is, how much of Caesarea was already in place by the time of the events described in the book of Acts? Josephus mentioned several structures that he attributed to Herod: the harbor, a grid street pattern with underground sewers, houses, palaces, the Augusteum temple, an amphitheater, a theater, civic halls and public places (*J.W.* 1.408–415; *Ant.* 15.331–341). It seems from archaeology that at least some of these structures (the theater, Augusteum, amphitheater, and artificial harbor) were the first ever buildings of these types constructed in the region. On the other hand, Caesarea is not mentioned in Strabo's *Geography* while other places on the Levantine coast are (*Geography* 2.5.39; 16.2.25). This suggests that Strabo, a contemporary of Herod, either did not know Caesarea, was not sufficiently impressed to include the city in his geographical itinerary, or the place wasn't yet quite as grand as Josephus, writing some seven decades later, made it out to be. Modern visitors to the site should beware: most of the currently excavated remains date later than the first century AD. These include structures from the Late Roman through Byzantine periods (warehouses, baths, columned streets, the Mithraeum, public latrines, houses, the synagogue, and an octagonal church) and from the time of the Crusades (the sloped wall,

17. We might note that for his part, Josephus also seems to have held a special affinity for Herod's Caesarea and the city's role as the seat of Roman government in Judea in the first century AD. It may be personal: after Josephus had surrendered his person to the Romans following the Jewish defeat at Jotapata in the Galilee (AD 67), he married a lady from Caesarea (*Life* 414–415).

Aerial View of the Ruins of Caesarea Maritima

moat, citadel, gate, and cathedral), as well as the mosque and houses constructed by Bosnian Muslim immigrants in the late nineteenth century.

One of Josephus' more obvious exaggerations is his assertion that Herod built Caesarea "entirely ... with white stone" (*J.W.* 1.408) and "got no material suitable for so great a work from the place itself but completed it with materials brought from outside at great expense" (*Ant.* 15.332). While later builders at Caesarea imported both marble and granite, Herod himself used locally quarried *kurkar*, sometimes (as in the case of the Augusteum) plastering it with thick, white stucco to appear as stone of better quality. Though of *kurkar*, the buildings and structures themselves were constructed "in a style worthy of the name which the city bore" (*J.W.* 1.415). Archaeological remains show that some were erected in the Corinthian order.[18] Other than the building stone itself, everything about the architecture and civic layout of Herod's Caesarea shouts "West!"

The harbor at Caesarea, which Herod named Sebastos, must have been the most impressive structure on site, given Josephus' attention to the details of its construction (*J.W.* 1.411–414; *Ant.* 15.333–339). It was also the main reason for the existence of the city in the first place and, given the constantly moving water and shifting sands along the coast, likely the most challenging project that Herod built anywhere. The Roman architect Vitruvius, another contemporary of Herod, provided detailed engineering instructions as to how to build an artificial harbor "if we have no natural harbor suitable for protecting ships from a stormy sea" (*On Architecture* 5.12.2 [LCL]). His recommended blueprint matches, in all essential details, the

18. On the Corinthian order, see Vitruvius, *On Architecture*, 4.1.1–12.

Aerial View of Caesarea Harbor

archaeological remains of the Caesarea harbor. The harbor was built just south of an area of broken *kurkar* that apparently served as a quay for Strato's Tower in the Hellenistic period.[19] The anchorage consisted of three basins enclosing a total area of fifty acres (20 hectares), together forming a harbor that was, according to Josephus, larger than Piraeus, the port of Athens (*J.W.* 1.410).

Workmen dug the inner anchorage into the shoreline at a place where there likely was already a second Hellenistic harbor; today it is completely silted up and covered by an expansive grassy lawn. Stratification of the soil suggests that already in the first century AD this inner anchorage needed constant dredging to keep it from being silted in due to the action of the currents and waves. The middle anchorage was a natural bay, equivalent to the harbor enclosed by the modern breakwater, built with piers of ashlar *kurkar* facing into the harbor. The outer anchorage, the largest of the three, was constructed in the open water by means of a huge mole, or breakwater, circling offshore from southeast to northwest for a third of a mile (500 m). Another mole ran straight back to shore, with a gap between the two through which ships entered the harbor from the northwest. These breakwaters were up to two hundred feet (60 m) wide at their underwater base, with an above-water surface wide enough, according to Josephus, for a broad promenade lined with towers and warehouses, numerous quays facing inward, and immense statues at the harbor entrance. The breakwaters were constructed by the use of huge wooden frames filled with rubble that was cemented together by concrete made with lime and *pozzolana*, a brown

19. For archaeology of the harbor see Avner Raban, "Maritime Caesarea," *NEAEHL* 1:286–90; and Yosef Porath et al., "Caesarea," *NEAEHL* 5:1680–83.

volcanic ash from central Italy that hardened when it came in contact with water. When finished, they mediated the competitive action of the currents that pushed along the coast from the south, and the wind-driven waves crashing ashore from the west-northwest. Herod constructed a second breakwater a bit outside of the harbor moles that further served to deflect the force of the waves even though it did not rise above the waterline. Unfortunately, natural forces of destruction started to tear away at the harbor as soon as it had been built. By the mid-second century AD, the surface of the harbor had dropped below the waterline, making the approach to Caesarea dangerous for ships. The cause may have been the action of the shifting sand and waves, or the earthquake of AD 130;[20] two geological fault-lines run on a north-south line directly underneath Herod's outer anchorage. Lying in silent witness is the wreckage of seventeen ships from Roman times that ran into the submerged breakwater. The shoreline south of the ruined port served as a makeshift harbor until the moles were restored to use in the early sixth century AD.

Herod built an Augusteum, a temple to the self-declared divine Caesar, on a platform rising above the eastern line of the inner anchorage. In it, he placed a huge statue of the emperor (Josephus, *J.W.* 1.414). The facade of the Augusteum faced the harbor though the building itself was set at a 30-degree angle off the city's grid street pattern. This way it dominated the view from both directions. Enough architectural pieces have been found to posit a building in the Corinthian order soaring to a height of seventy-two feet (22 m) above the top of the platform on which it stood.[21] Mariners could easily have seen the gleaming white Augusteum from some distance out to sea; the building would help guide them into the safety of the harbor. Grateful for a safe journey, they would ascend to the Augusteum from the innermost quay by means of a grand staircase sixty-six feet (20 m) wide. Herod built a second Augusteum, larger in size, at Sebaste. On a clear day its long white limestone wall was also likely visible dead ahead to sharp-eyed sea captains heading into the Caesarea port. Together, these Augusteums marked Rome's gigantic stride up into the now-Hellenized heartland of Samaria.

The city itself was basically semicircular, a shape that Vitruvius (*On Architecture* 1.5.2) recommended was proper for defense. The line of Caesarea's city wall, scribing an arch over a mile (2 km) long, is visible in aerial photos (see aerial view on page 239). A portion of the Herodian city wall and a round tower have been found south of the theater, and a gate flanked by two round towers along the northern line of the city.[22] Josephus did not mention a city wall at Caesarea but he did state that Herod "built a fortress for the entire nation in the place formerly called Straton's [*sic*] tower" (*Ant.* 15.293).

Nothing of the streets from Herod's Caesarea have been found, but enough of the grid plan from the Late Roman and Byzantine periods have been uncovered,

---

20. D. H. Kallner-Amiran, "A Revised Earthquake-Catalogue of Palestine," *IEJ* 1 (1950–1951): 225.

21. Porath, "Caesarea," 1666, 1670; Ehud Netzer, *The Architecture of Herod, the Great Builder* (Grand Rapids: Baker Academic, 2006): 103–6.

22. Netzer, *Herod, the Great Builder*, 99.

Barrel-Vaulted Warehouse

with vaulted sewers beneath, to posit that Herod's streets and sewer system followed the same plan.[23] Archaeologists have uncovered four north-south streets running parallel to the shore and probably twelve running east-west at right angles, together defining housing blocks (*insulae*) 260 feet (80 m) wide. After AD 6, when Caesarea became the Roman capital of Judea, the area southeast of the Augusteum grew to be an area of wealthy houses, replete with frescoed walls and mosaic floors.[24]

Remains of barrel-vaulted warehouses in the area between the southern Crusader wall and the theater contained many shards of amphora (pottery vessels for maritime shipping) from North Africa, Italy, Spain, and the Aegean dating to the first century AD. These attest to a brisk trade in commodities such as wine, oil, and *garum* (fermented fish guts soaked in salt—a costly delicacy).[25] Herod's warehouses were likely in the same location.[26]

Herod built a "very costly" palace at Caesarea in a setting that was strikingly different than his palace fortresses in the Judean desert (Josephus, *Ant.* 15.331). Those were islands of comfort amidst rolling waves of barren hills; this prom-

23. Josephus, *J.W.* 1.413; *Ant.* 15.340; Porath, "Caesarea," 1674–76; Netzer, *Herod, the Great Builder*, 96.

24. Porath, "Caesarea," 1658.

25. Inscribed amphorae mentioning *garum* have been found at both Masada and Herodium. According to data provided by the Roman historian Pliny, one amphora of *garum* in the first century could cost the equivalent of three times the average annual salary of a Roman legionnaire. See Barry J. Beitzel, "Herod the Great: Another Snapshot of His Treachery?" *JETS* 57 (2014): 312–13; Roi Porat, Rachel Chachy and Yakov Kalman, *Herodium: Final Reports of the 1972–2010 Excavations Directed by Ehud Netzer, Vol. 1: Herod's Tomb Precinct* (Jerusalem: Israel Exploration Society, 2015), 370.

26. Netzer, *Herod, the Great Builder*, 100–101.

ontory palace was set as the bow of a ship heading into the sea. The palace was built on a jut of wave-pounded *kurkar* extending 330 feet (100 m) offshore. It comprised a two-story rectangle of frescoed rooms enclosing a rock-cut, colonnaded pool coated with hydraulic plaster, adorned with a statue in the middle (the base of the statue remains).[27] The pool seems to have been filled with fresh water, providing a safe, private place for swimming and bathing. An upper part of the palace, connected by stairs off the northeastern corner of the promontory, is usually identified as the Praetorium. This was the administrative wing of the palace and likely included quarters for the Praetorian Guard as well as holding cells for prisoners. The archaeological evidence suggests that this wing was erected by the earliest Roman governors rather than by Herod, although Acts 23:25 attributes the place to him. Overlying Byzantine remains preserve its character today. The compound likely served as the living headquarters of the Roman governors during the time of the New Testament. It can also reasonably be seen as the location of the trials of Paul before Festus and Agrippa II (Acts 25:1–26:32). From the Praetorium, Paul would have had constant view of the comings and goings of the harbor, with a persistent tug on his heart to travel to Rome.

Pillars from the Upper Level of Praetorium

Josephus spoke of a building "on the south side of the harbor, farther back, an amphitheater large enough to hold a great crowd of people, and conveniently situated for a view of the sea" (*Ant.* 15.341). Most scholars assume that this was the city's hippodrome (*circus*), the magnificent remains of which fill the space between the harbor and the promontory palace.[28] Because its stalls and starting gates date to the time of Herod, the hippodrome is the best candidate for the site of the games that Herod celebrated in honor of the inauguration of the city (Josephus, *J.W.* 1.415; *Ant.* 16.136–139). The structure was built according to the city's grid plan, aligned with the city streets and seashore.[29] A large portion was actually erected on artificial fill. Prior to the construction of the hippodrome, the shoreline lay somewhat to the east.

27. Netzer, *Herod, the Great Builder*, 106–12.

28. It is a problem of matching terms (theater, amphitheater, stadium, hippodrome) with archaeological remains, several combinations of which fit the data at Caesarea. Archaeologists have found two theater-type structures, two amphitheater-type structures and two hippodrome-type structures at Caesarea, some of which were constructed after the first century AD. Unfortunately, one term that Josephus didn't use was "hippodrome." See Yosef Porath, *Caesarea Maritima, Vol. 1, Herod's Circus and Related Buildings, Part 1: Architecture and Stratigraphy* (Jerusalem: Israel Antiquities Authority, 2013), 21–29.

29. Porath, "Caesarea," 1675; Netzer, *Herod, the Great Builder*, 116–18.

The newly completed harbor breakwater trapped sand to its south and over the course of three to five years (based on modern parallels) filled in the shoreline sufficiently so that the hippodrome could be built.[30]

Restored Theater at Caesarea

Caesarea's theater, originally built by Herod, is the earliest in Judea yet excavated.[31] Atypically it faces west, so that the late afternoon sun would shine in the faces of the audience rather than light up the performers. In *Antiquities of the Jews*, Josephus mentioned the theater just before noting that the amphitheater was "conveniently situated for a view of the sea" (*Ant.* 15.341). He may have gotten his referents mixed up: a west-facing theater would have warranted explanation, whereas half of the spectators in the hippodrome sat with their backs to the sea anyway. The theater had seating for four thousand people. Like the walls and columns of the Augusteum, its *kurkar* orchestra wall was plastered and painted to imitate marble. It was in this locus of all-things-Roman that Herod Agrippa I presented himself as a god, then was "eaten by worms and died" (Acts 12:20–23; compare Josephus, *Ant.* 19.343–350). The theater was modified repeatedly over the next four centuries, with as many as fourteen renovations attested archaeologically. One modification reused a stone bearing a partially broken inscription mentioning Pontius Pilate, confirming his title as *praefectus* (a Roman governor of equestrian rank).[32] This inscription also mentions that Pilate built a Tiberium, which would ordinarily be understood as a temple dedicated to Tiberius (AD 14–37). However, because Tiberius refused deification, this Tiberium may have been some other structure. In any case, archaeologists have not yet unearthed a temple to Tiberius in Caesarea.

The water table at Caesarea is quite high, lying in some places a scant three feet (1 m) below the surface of the ground. As a result, the city was supplied by several nearby springs; the main one, ʿAin el-Balad, "village spring," is close to the remains of the synagogue. These must have been inadequate for the growing needs of the ancient city, however, so Herod brought in additional water from springs on the southern slope of Mount Carmel four miles (7 km) to the northeast of the city. To do so, he constructed an aqueduct, a structure that Josephus failed to mention. Herod's workmen dug a portion of the northern length of the aqueduct as a tunnel running along the

30. Porath, *Caesarea Maritima*, 68, 199. See page 702 for an image of a hippodrome at Caesarea.

31. Netzer, *Herod, the Great Builder*, 112–15.

32. Lee I. Levine, *Roman Caesarea: An Archaeological-Topographical Study* (Jerusalem: Hebrew University Institute of Archaeology, 1975), 19–21.

first *kurkar* ridge. The southern portion is raised on arches in places where the ridge had broken away; this is the eastern half of the so-called high-level aqueduct.[33] The emperor Hadrian doubled the flow to approximately 800,000 gallons (3000 cubic meters) per hour[34] by adding the western half of the aqueduct in AD 130. The date of a low-level aqueduct nearby, which seems to have brought water for irrigation, is unknown. A sophisticated set of waterworks, including pools, channels, and dams, was developed in the northern Sharon Plain over the next few centuries, with roads and bridges intertwined. With it, the entire region became a textbook example of the capacity of human intervention to shape nature for the common good, irrespective of the potential and priorities of Rome.

Aqueduct Along the Beach at Caesarea

IMAGE

Geography is concerned not only with material matters such as landforms and location, or the impact of resources and terrain on architecture and city planning, but with worldview. *Place* evokes emotions of belonging, carrying images of order and security for those who call it home.[35] The very existence of the ancient farmers and shepherds who lived in the desert-facing, high hill country of Judea was rooted on dry land ecosystems. For them, the sea was something "other," something unknown, something uncontrollable, and something not useful for life (Isa 57:19–21).[36] Unlike the Phoenicians, Greeks, and Romans who had learned to embrace the sea (compare Ps 107:23–30; Ezek 27:1–36), the sea was the unapproached *border* of Israel (Josh 15:12; 16:3; 17:9; 19:29), something that in their cosmology was pushed back so that people could live (Gen 1:9–10; 7:1–9:17; Exod 14:21–30; Rev 21:1).

When Herod built Caesarea-on-Sea (Josephus, *J.W.* 2.266–267; 7.20) as a fully functioning Greek city from the sandy ground up, he intended its buildings and institutions to establish a new reality in Judea. The impression of Caesarea on first-time Jewish visitors was likely similar to that which the Apostle Paul felt when he first visited Athens (Acts 17:16). Away out on the wave-battered frontier of the province of Judea, Caesarea exuded the stigma of an intrusive civi-

33. Netzer, *Herod, the Great Builder*, 101–3; Levine, *Roman Caesarea*, 30–36; Avraham Negev, "The High Level Aqueduct at Caesarea," *IEJ* 14 (1964): 237–49.

34. Levine, *Roman Caesarea*, 30; Daniel Sperber, *The City in Roman Palestine* (New York: Oxford University Press, 1998), 132–33.

35. Jeff Malpas, *Place and Experience: A Philosophical Topography* (Cambridge: Cambridge University Press, 1999), 15–16.

36. Yamm, the deified sea, was the Canaanite god of chaos and cosmic disorder. See Fritz Stolz, "Sea," *DDD* 1390–1402.

lization. The theater, built as the repository of performances where people (to borrow a phrase) "spent their time doing nothing but talking about and listening to the latest ideas" (Acts 17:21), was especially troubling to the Jewish soul. And its physical orientation seems to be meaningful: the audience sat with their backs to Jerusalem, their eyes seaward to the glories of Rome. When Peter fell into a trance on the coastal rooftop down shore in Joppa he saw "something like a large sheet being let down to earth by its four corners" (Acts 10:11), full of squirming things he knew to be both unclean and inappropriate for his *kosher* Jewish convictions. The word for sheet, *othonē* (ὀθόνη), is the Greek word for the sail of a square-rigged Mediterranean ship, and it was at Caesarea three anxious days later that Peter, face to face, encountered—then accepted—the fact that the gospel was even meant for the world that was crashing his shore.

Why did Herod build here? Partly just to show that he could. And what better place to do so than this *kurkar*-ridden coast? Here Herod "triumphed over nature ... notwithstanding the totally recalcitrant nature of the site" (Josephus, *J.W.* 1.410–411). At the same time, Josephus noted that Caesarea was, "from its advantageous situation, suited for the exercise of [Herod's] liberality" (*J.W.* 1.408). Given its recalcitrant nature, perhaps for Herod the place was most advantageous *precisely because* it provided a site suitable for his megalomania. But Herod also built Caesarea where he did for practical reasons, fronting what was expedient for his own magnanimity to meet Rome's need for control. A necessary corollary was Herod's propensity to bend the Judean soul toward Rome in the process.

Pontius Pilate Inscripton

The mixed demographics of first century AD Caesarea ensured that Jewish-gentile tensions always lay close to the surface, with the Jews (a minority population in the city) no doubt enjoying the personal opportunities a city as cosmopolitan as this offered, while at the same time pushing back the more troubling of its hellenizing tendencies. But the governing seat of a foreign occupying power seems always to be a place where tensions between locals and interlopers are on parade (for example, Josephus, *J.W.* 2.266–70; 284–292; 7.361–363). It all finally erupted in the Great Revolt, which began in AD 66 here in Caesarea, ostensibly sparked by pagan cultic practices in close proximity to the synagogue (*J.W.* 2.296). Rome responded by using Herod's port to tighten the screws: the general Vespasian established his headquarters in Caesarea, from which he and his legions quickly subdued the coast and Galilee and from which his son, Titus, marched to subdue

Jerusalem four years later (*J.W.* 3.409–413; 4.88; 5.41–42; 7.20; Tacitus, *Histories* 5.1).

In AD 69 Vespasian was first hailed as emperor by his troops in Caesarea (Tacitus, *Histories* 2.78–80); Josephus added that this happened "on Jewish soil" (*J.W.* 6.312–313). The collocation is apt, for it marked the reality that the ancient Near East and the Mediterranean basin were now firmly bound together at exactly their natural seam. For it is on the coastal plain of Judea and Samaria that "the ends of the earth" (Acts 1:8) begins, with Caesarea pulling Jews both willing and recalcitrant out to sea. Caesarea first shows up in the book of Acts at just the right time, following Phillip's encounters in Samaria and with the Ethiopian eunuch, and just after the call of Saul of Tarsus (Acts 8:4–10:1). For all of its Romeward intentionality, Caesarea was the launchpad for the inexorable spread of the gospel through the message and ministry of the Apostle Paul.

POSTSCRIPT

The Christian community at Caesarea played a significant role in the development of the historical geography of the Bible. The brilliant scholar Origen lived in Caesarea from AD 231 to 250, where he founded an influential school of Christian life and thought. His magisterial collection of manuscripts, many of which he wrote himself, was enlarged by Pamphilus (died AD 309), who established a library that ended up being second in size only to that of Alexandria. Pamphilus' student Eusebius (c. AD 260–340), the prolific bishop of Caesarea, produced not only the first comprehensive written history of the church but also a geographical catalog called the *Onomasticon*.[37] In it, Eusebius attempted to identify biblical sites based on data available to him in the fourth century AD. The *Onomasticon* remains an invaluable primary source for biblical geographers and offers a wonderful window into the sacred geography of the early church.

BIBLIOGRAPHY

Avi-Yonah, Michael. *The Holy Land: A Historical Geography from the Persian to the Arab Conquest (586 BC–AD 640)* Jerusalem: Carta, 2002.

Beitzel, Barry J. "Herod the Great: Another Snapshot of His Treachery?" *JETS* 57 (2014): 309–22.

Dorsey, David. *The Roads and Highways of Ancient Israel*. Baltimore: Johns Hopkins University Press, 1991.

Freeman-Grenville, G. S. P., Rupert L. Chapman III, and Joan E. Taylor. *The Onomasticon by Eusebius of Caesarea: Palestine in the Fourth Century A.D.* Jerusalem: Carta, 2003.

Graf, David F., Benjamin Isaac, and Israel Roll. "Roads and Highways: Roman Roads." *ABD* 5:782–87.

Holum, Kenneth G., Robert L. Hohlfelder, Robert J. Bull, and Avner Raban. *King Herod's Dream: Caesarea on the Sea*. New York: Norton, 1988.

Josephus. *Jewish Antiquities*. Translated by H. St. J. Thackeray, Ralph Marcus, Allen Wikgren, and Louis H. Feldman. 6 vols. LCL. Cambridge: Harvard University, 1930–1965.

---

37. R. Steven Notley and Ze'ev Safrai, *Eusebius, Onomasticon: The Place Names of Divine Scripture* (Leiden: Brill, 2005); and G. S. P. Freeman-Grenville, Rupert L. Chapman III, and Joan E. Taylor, *The Onomasticon by Eusebius of Caesarea: Palestine in the Fourth Century A.D.* (Jerusalem: Carta, 2003).

———. *The Jewish War*. Translated by H. St. J. Thackeray. 2 vols. LCL. Cambridge: Harvard University, 1927–1930.

———. *The Life and Against Apion*. Translated by H. St. J. Thackeray. LCL. Cambridge: Harvard University, 1926.

Kallner-Amiran, D. H. "A Revised Earthquake-Catalogue of Palestine." *IEJ* 1 (1950–1951): 223–46.

Karmon, Yehuda. "Geographical Influences on the Historical Routes in the Sharon Plain." *PEQ* 93 (1961): 43–60.

———. *Israel: A Regional Geography*. London: Wiley-Interscience, 1971.

Levine, Lee I. *Roman Caesarea: An Archaeological-Topographical Study*. Jerusalem: Hebrew University Institute of Archaeology, 1975.

Malpas, Jeff. *Place and Experience: A Philosophical Topography*. Cambridge: Cambridge University Press, 1999.

Monson, James M. *Regions on the Run: Introductory Map Studies in the Land of the Bible*. Rockford, IL: Biblical Backgrounds, 1998.

Netzer, Ehud. *The Architecture of Herod, the Great Builder*. Grand Rapids: Baker Academic, 2006.

Negev, Avraham. "The High Level Aqueduct at Caesarea." *IEJ* 14 (1964): 237–49.

Notley, R. Steven, and Ze'ev Safrai. *Eusebius, Onomasticon: The Place Names of Divine Scripture*. Leiden: Brill, 2005.

Porat, Roi, Rachel Chachy, and Yakov Kalman. *Herodium: Final Reports of the 1972–2010 Excavations Directed by Ehud Netzer, Vol. 1: Herod's Tomb Precinct*. Jerusalem: Israel Exploration Society, 2015.

Porath, Yosef. *Caesarea Maritima, Vol. 1: Herod's Circus and Related Buildings, Part 1: Architecture and Stratigraphy*. Jerusalem: Israel Antiquities Authority, 2013.

Porath, Yosef, Kenneth Holum, Avner Raban and Joseph Patrich. "Caesarea." *NEAEHL* 5:1656–1684.

Raban, Avner. "Maritime Caesarea." *NEAEHL* 1:286–91.

Ramsay, William M. *St. Paul: The Traveler and Roman Citizen*. Updated and revised edition. Edited by Mark Wilson. Grand Rapids: Kregel, 2001.

Roll, Israel. "Roman Roads in Western Samaria." *PEQ* 118 (1986): 113–34.

———. "The Roman Road System in Judea." Pages 136–61 in vol. 3 of *The Jerusalem Cathedra*. Edited by Lee I. Levine. Jerusalem: Yad Ben-Zvi, 1983.

Simons, J. *The Geographical and Topographical Texts of the Old Testament: A Concise Commentary in 32 Chapters*. Leiden: Brill, 1959.

Smith, George Adam. *The Historical Geography of the Holy Land*. London: Hodder and Stoughton, 1894.

Sperber, Daniel. *The City in Roman Palestine*. New York: Oxford, 1998.

Stolz, Fritz. "Sea." *DDD* 1390–1402.

Strabo. *The Geography of Strabo*. Translated by Horace Leonard Jones. 8 vols. LCL. Cambridge: Harvard University, 1917–1932.

Tacitus. *Histories*. Translated by Clifford H. Moore. LCL. Cambridge: Harvard University, 1925.

Vitruvius, *On Architecture*. Translated by F. Granger. LCL. Cambridge: Harvard University, 1962.

Weber, Ekkehard. "The Tabula Peutingeriana and the Madaba Map." Pages 41–46 in *The Madaba Map Centenary, 1897–1997*. Edited by Michele Piccirillo and Eugenio Alliata. Jerusalem: Studium Biblicum Franciscanum, 1998.

CHAPTER 17

THE ROAD FROM JERUSALEM TO DAMASCUS

Acts 9:1–19; 22:3–16; 26:12–18

Paul H. Wright

> KEY POINTS
>
> - Paul likely traveled between Jerusalem and Damascus using an established route.
> - The natural topography of the region suggests four possible routes.
> - A route through the Jordan Valley makes sense for Jewish travelers starting in Jerusalem.

LOCATING THE ROAD PAUL TOOK TO DAMASCUS

The book of Acts relates the story of the conversion of Saul of Tarsus on the road to Damascus three times. The first instance describes the event in real time (Acts 9:1–19). The second and third are Paul's own retelling of his conversion experience, first as part of his oral defense before the Jewish authorities in Jerusalem after he was arrested for allegedly bringing Greeks into restricted areas of the temple compound (Acts 22:3–16) and again as he restated his defense before King Agrippa II in Caesarea two years later (Acts 26:12–18). The only significant geographical referent in these narratives is that Paul encountered Jesus as he "neared" or "came near" to Damascus (Acts 9:3; 22:6 NIV; using the verb ἐγγίζω, *engizō*). Details as to which road he might have taken from Jerusalem are wholly lacking in the text, but there are several possibilities.

ROMAN ROADS

Logic might suggest that our search begin with the network of imperial roads that Rome built across their empire to link its provinces and major cities with each other, but especially to Rome itself. These roads were constructed to speed the movement of legionary troops and others traveling on imperial business,

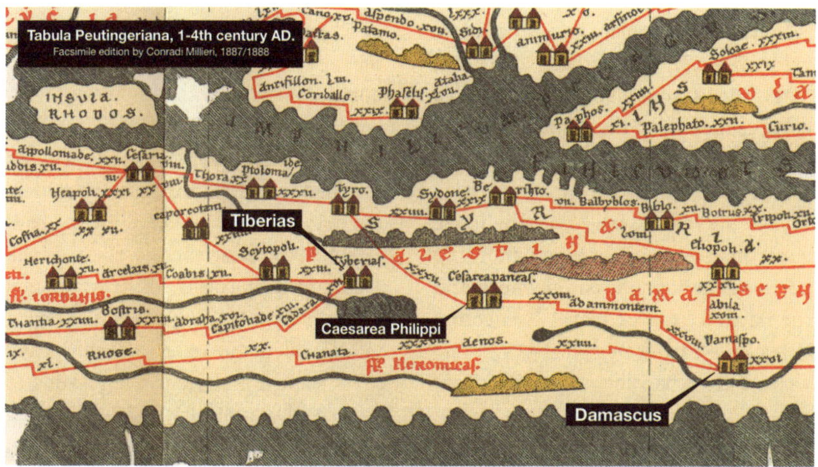

Peutinger Map: Damascus to Tiberias

and to create a web of economic arteries that would link the disparate parts of the empire into a mutually dependent whole. As the empire grew, so did its network of roads, reaching the province of Judea as early as the mid-first century AD.[1] The earliest known milestone in Judea, dating to AD 56, two decades after Paul's journey to Damascus, belonged to the coastal road connecting Antioch with Ptolemais. A milestone dating to AD 69 mentions the road connecting Legio (near the ruins of Megiddo) with Scythopolis (ancient Beth-shean), erected by the Tenth Roman Legion (*Fretensis*). This is the earliest evidence of a Roman road penetrating the province of Judea (later Syria-Palaestina) inland, in this case through the Jezreel Valley (the "Great Plain"; *J.W.* 2.188, and so on). This was the easiest line of travel between the coast and Transjordan. The earliest milestone from the hill country of Judea dates to AD 120, well after the destruction of the Jerusalem temple and not long before the Emperor Hadrian founded Jerusalem as a polis, a Greco-Roman style city-state, called Aelia Capitolina in AD 135. We might justifiably suppose that Damascus was linked to the empire by a Roman road in the first century AD as well, since during the reign of Tiberius (AD 14–37) Rome housed four of its twenty-five legions there (Tacitus, *Annales* 4.5). It certainly was by the early second century AD as Rome solidified its hold in Transjordan during the reigns of Trajan (AD 98–117) and Hadrian (AD 117–138) following their takeover of the Nabatean realm in AD 106.

The *Tabula Peutingeriana* shows a trunk road running from Tiberias to Damascus via Caesarea Philippi, circling the southern end of Mount Hermon. This map of the Roman Empire was drawn on parchment in the thirteenth century AD but is likely based on a map from the

1. Israel Roll, "The Roman Road System in Judea," in *The Jerusalem Cathedra*, ed. Lee I. Levine (Jerusalem: Yad Ben-Zvi, 1983), 3:138–44; David F. Graf, Benjamin Isaac, and Israel Roll, "Roads and Highways: Roman Roads," *ABD* 5:785–86.

fourth or fifth centuries AD and certainly preserves even earlier data.[2] The route that it shows from Tiberias to Damascus must be the line of the Roman road that was in use at least as early as the second century AD. Does it likely preserve Paul's line of travel as well? The operative question is, what might the relationship between the Roman road network and the natural lines of travel connecting cities from earlier periods be? With no written or archaeological evidence that a route from Jerusalem to Damascus had already been formally incorporated into the Roman road network, let alone paved, in the AD 30s, what evidence might there be for proposing the location of a route or routes between the two cities?

POSSIBLE ROUTES

We must consider two primary criteria. The first is the principle that main routes connected main cities; the second is that routes tended to follow the shortest paths of least resistance between points. Because the location of main cities in the southern Levant changed over time, so did main lines of travel within and between its regions. The natural geographical features, on the other hand, such as topography, terrain, and available water sources, have remained largely stable over time, and this has tended to keep the number of options that the main routes might have traversed to a minimum. Once the key cities are known for any given period, the most likely line of travel between them can be reasonably surmised, even absent specific archaeological or textual information.

The natural lines of topography in the province of Judea run generally north-south, and the main routes—both those incorporated into the Roman road network and the natural routes that had traversed the land for millennia prior—followed these lines. From west to east, these corridors are: (1) the Mediterranean coast; (2) the watershed of the Judean highlands and the broad inland valleys of Samaria; (3) the Jordan River valley; and (4) the highlands of Transjordan east of its great dividing gorges (the Yarmuk, Jabbok, Arnon, and Zered canyons). Damascus, lying along the eastern front of the Mount Hermon range, was the primary northern terminus point for all four, although much of the coastal traffic also carried on straight north to Phoenicia.

As a result, there are several "Damascus roads," depending on one's point of departure. For Paul's journey, logic would eliminate the first and fourth lines of route as viable candidates since they would have been too circuitous for his journey. The second is possible. This route follows the watershed northward out of Jerusalem, then drops into a series of intermountain valleys in Samaria to Neapolis and Sychar (both adjacent to ancient Shechem) before continuing through a narrow trough north-northeastward to the Decapolis city Scythopolis (ancient Beth-shean) where it enters the Jordan Valley. From there this central route joins the Jordan Valley route and tracks northward to the Sea of Galilee and beyond. Its main advantage is that it is the shortest of the four; the draw-

2. Israel Finkelstein, "The Holy Land in the Tabula Peutingeriana: A Historical-Geographical Approach," *PEQ* 111 (1979): 27–34; Ekkehard Weber, "The Tabula Peutingeriana and the Madaba Map," in *The Madaba Map Centenary, 1897–1997*, ed. Michele Piccirillo and Eugenio Alliata (Jerusalem: Studium Biblicum Franciscanum, 1998), 41–46.

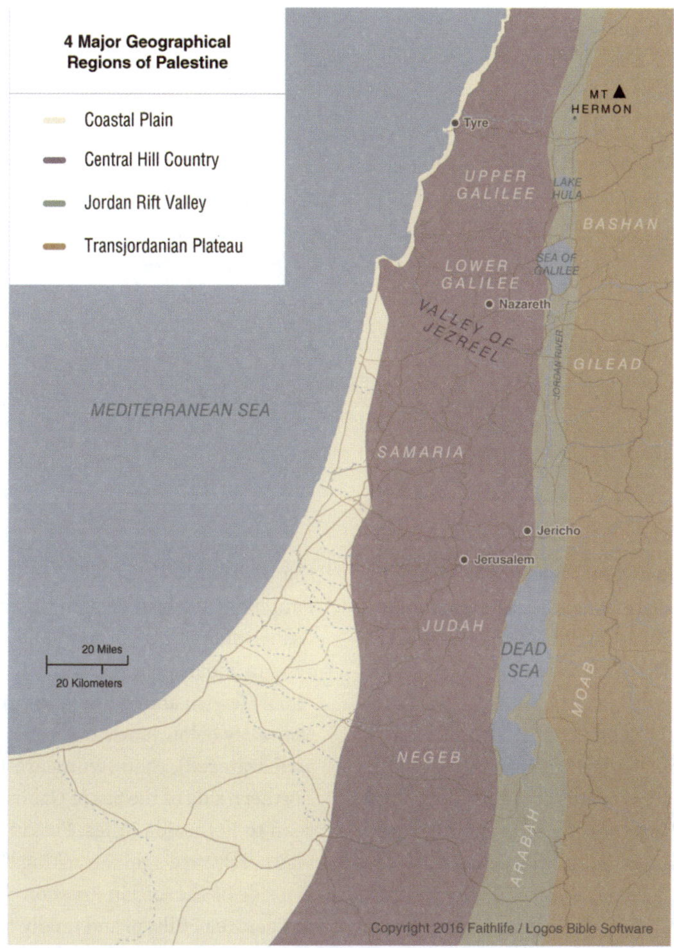

back, at least as customarily understood, is that in the time of the New Testament it traversed the length of Samaria, a place through which Jews of the first century were, by and large, reticent to travel.[3]

The third of our options, the longitudinal route through the Jordan Valley, is the most likely. Historically, the eastern side of the Jordan Valley has always been more heavily populated, and hence more heavily traveled, than its western side. This is primarily due to geographical factors. The westward-facing Gilead hills, which rise steeply out of the Jordan Valley toward the east, receive heavy amounts of rainfall during the rainy season. Most

3. A number of primary sources challenge the commonly held idea that Jews avoided travel through Samaria. These texts indicate that Jews owned lands, agricultural fields, and homes with miqva'ot in Samaria, could eat food prepared by Samaritans, and travel on paths in Samaria declared by the rabbis to be ritually clean (m. Orlah 3:7; t. Avodah Zarah 3:1; m. Arakhin 3:2; m. Kelim 17:5; y. Avodah Zarah 5:4; t. Mikvaot 6:1; and y. Avodah Zerah 5:4).

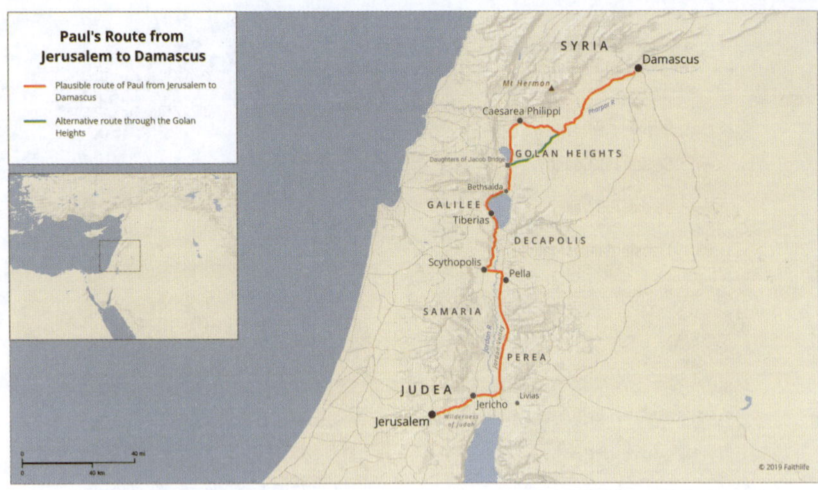

of its runoff flows through the dramatic Jabbok River (Wadi Zerqa) gorge into the Jordan Valley, carrying fertile alluvial soil with it. The result is a large tract of arable land extending outward from the point where the Jabbok River connects with the Jordan Valley. Smaller tracts line the valley at the mouths of the smaller Gilead wadis. Together, these tracts support a much larger population than does the western Jordan Valley, which, by contrast, is a semi-arid desert ecosystem in the rain shadow of the Judean and Samaria hills. That the Jordan Valley is also relatively flat, unlike the hilly route through Samaria, adds to the ease of travel there.

PAUL'S LIKELY ROUTE TO DAMASCUS

The practice in the biblical world was to name routes after the main destination point of the traveler. For this reason, we can see Paul leaving Jerusalem and descending through the wilderness of Judea on the road to Jericho, crossing the southern end of the Jordan Valley (its widest point) on the road to Livias, then turning northward on the road to the Decapolis city of Pella. From there, Paul likely crossed back to the western, Galilee side of the Jordan Valley on the road to Tiberias (a region that was primarily Jewish and, unlike the portion of the valley below Judea and Samaria, also well-watered), then swung around the northern side of the Sea of Galilee on the road to Bethsaida Julias. From there, it was northward again, tracking the eastern side of the Jordan River on the road to Caesarea Philippi and finally running east and north around the broad sweep of the Mount Hermon range on the road to Damascus. Paul may have taken a shortcut, off the line of what was to become the main Roman road, angling instead northeastward across the Golan Heights from the so-called bridge of Jacob's Daughters. The name "bridge of Jacob's Daughters" dates only to Crusader times, but it marks an ancient passage over the Jordan River about eight miles (13 km) north of the Sea of Galilee. A slight rise just north of the Pharpar River (see 2 Kgs 5:12) some twelve miles (19.3 km) south of Damascus affords the first view of the city, which dominates the broad, well-watered plain extending eastward from Mount Hermon. It is perhaps here that Paul first saw the light.[4]

Due to inherent difficulties of travel, this trip, about 130 miles (210 km) long, likely would have taken several days or up to a week unless Paul were in a real hurry. He most likely would have overnighted in cities or large villages along the way rather than be exposed to the open elements (although he had plenty of that on his later journeys; see 2 Cor 11:25–27), if possible, in places where a rabbi could keep the scruples of his convictions. This also favors a journey on the eastern side of the Jordan Valley, which in part tracked through the region of Perea, an area with a viable Jewish population. Paul would have had to cross a 20-mile (32 k) stretch under the control of the Decapolis cities (Pliny, *Natural History* 5.16, 74) south and east of the Sea of Galilee, with a sizeable gentile population. This would not have posed any particular threat however, since we can assume that from his earliest years Paul was fluent in the language and culture of the Greeks and certainly had become resourceful enough to know how to keep kosher in their regions if he wanted to.

Straight Street in Damascus

Paul ended his journey blinded, being led by hand into the walled city of Damascus to a house on the street called Straight (Acts 9:8–11). Scholars have generally identified this street with the city's *Cardo Maximus* (or, *Decumanus Maximus* since it runs east-west), a fifty-foot (15 m) wide, columned, straight (though slightly bent) thoroughfare along which archaeologists have found remains of a theater and a palace. This was, perhaps, the longest and most prominent street in Roman Damascus.

CONCLUSION

It was only at the very end of his journey from Jerusalem, in a place lying beyond the northern border of the land of ancient Israel, that Paul met the risen Jesus. But why when he "neared Damascus" (Acts 9:3 NIV)? Surely there were other places where he also suspected that there might be believers in Jesus. The conversion of Saul of Tarsus is a tipping point in the narrative flow of the book of Acts, with the action shifting in the next episodes out to Joppa and Caesarea on the coast, and then into the wide world of the Mediterranean (Acts 9:32–10:48). For ancient Israel, Damascus was the gateway from which the longest list of frightful conquerors had entered their land—the Arameans in the days of Ahab, then the Assyrians, the Babylonians, the Persians, the Seleucids, and finally Rome itself by

4. William M. Ramsay, *St. Paul: The Traveler and Roman Citizen*, rev. and updated by Mark Wilson (Grand Rapids: Kregel, 2001), 44.

the hands of Pompey. This northeastern gateway represented the most ominous throughway for Israel, an open sieve with a litany of threats flowing through, compromising their very existence. Because Rome stationed legionary troops in Damascus in the first century AD, the city perhaps most represented "Rome away from home" for the Jews of Judea. As such, Damascus seems a most appropriate location for the conversion of Saul, a Jewish rabbi who would follow Jesus' command to carry the gospel message out of Jerusalem and to a waiting Roman world.

BIBLIOGRAPHY

Finkelstein, Israel. "The Holy Land in the Tabula Peutingeriana: A Historical-Geographical Approach." *PEQ* 111 (1979): 27–34.

Graf, David F., Benjamin Isaac, and Israel Roll. "Roads and Highways: Roman Roads." *ABD* 5:782–87.

Josephus. *The Jewish War*. Translated by H. St. J. Thackeray. 3 vols. LCL. Cambridge: Harvard University Press, 1927.

Pliny. *Natural History*. Translated by H. Rackham. 10 vols. LCL. Cambridge: Harvard University Press, 1942–1962.

Ramsey, William M. *St. Paul: The Traveler and Roman Citizen*. Revised and updated by Mark Wilson. Grand Rapids: Kregel, 2001.

Roll, Israel. "The Roman Road System in Judea." Pages 136–61 in vol. 3 of *The Jerusalem Cathedra*. Edited by Lee I. Levine. Jerusalem: Yad Ben-Zvi, 1983.

Tacitus. *Annals*. Translated by John Jackson. 3 vols. LCL. Cambridge: Harvard University Press, 1931–1937.

Weber, Ekkehard. "The Tabula Peutingeriana and the Madaba Map." Pages 41–46 in *The Madaba Map Centenary, 1897–1997*. Edited by Michele Piccirillo and Eugenio Alliata. Jerusalem: Studium Biblicum Franciscanum, 1998.

CHAPTER 18

PAUL'S MISSIONARY WORK IN SYRIA, NABATEA, JUDEA, AND CILICIA

Acts 9:19–30; 11:25–30

Eckhard J. Schnabel

KEY POINTS

- Paul began to carry out the missionary commission given to him by the risen Jesus immediately after his conversion in Damascus.
- The first two phases of Paul's missionary work are located in Damascus (province of Syria) and in Nabatea/Arabia (probably Petra).
- The third and fourth phases of Paul's missionary work are located in Jerusalem (Roman Judea) and in Cilicia (probably Tarsus).
- The fifth phase of Paul's mission took place in Syria, in particular in Antioch, the capital of the province where Roman authorities called Jesus' followers "Christians."
- The selection of areas of missionary work depended on proximity, existing contacts, persecution, and, in the case of Arabia, perhaps on historical considerations.

INTRODUCTION

In my view, the traditional division of Paul's missionary work into three "journeys," first devised by J.A. Bengel in his preface to the Book of Acts in his *Gnomon Novi Testamenti* and promoted in the headings of Bible translations, Bible atlases, biblical maps, and commentaries, does not reflect the reality of Paul's missionary work.[1] This approach

1. Johann Albrecht Bengel, *Gnomon Novi Testamenti*, 8th ed. (Stuttgart: Steinkopf, 1887), 410–11.

Roman Triumphal Arch on "Straight Street"

Temple of Zeus in Damascus

ignores the first ten years of Paul's missionary work in Syria, Nabatea, Judea, and Cilicia, and it overemphasizes Paul's repeated visits to Jerusalem and Syrian Antioch as regards their significance of Paul's mission. It is preferable to analyze Paul's mission in terms of territories and Roman provinces. I have organized Paul's missionary work in terms of sixteen periods or phases. This chapter covers the first five of these phases (see the chart on page 702 for all sixteen periods).

MISSIONARY WORK IN DAMASCUS, SYRIA

Paul's mission in Damascus (Acts 9:19–22) is the first phase of his missionary work.[2] Immediately after his conversion in Damascus (Acts 9:1–19), Paul preached the gospel of Jesus, the crucified and risen Messiah, in the local synagogues (Acts 9:20, 22; 26:20). Jesus had commissioned Paul to be his envoy (Acts 9:15; 22:15; 26:16–18; see also Rom 1:1) in Damascus—and this is the city in which Paul began to proclaim the gospel whose content he knew full well from his previous encounters with Jesus' followers whom had persecuted. The fact that Jews of Damascus later collaborated with the local representative of the Nabatean king Aretas IV in the effort to have Paul arrested and put on trial (2 Cor 11:32) suggests that Paul's evangelism in Damascus had considerable success.

Damascus was an old trading town situated in an oasis at the western edge of the Arabian Desert, about 170 miles (270 km) north of Jerusalem. Damascus belonged to the Nabatean kingdom of Aretas III from 85–72 BC, to the Armenian kingdom of Tigranes from 72–69 BC, and to the Roman province of Syria after 64 BC. The takeover by the Romans led to major building activities in Damascus; the connection between the eastern and the western parts of the

2. See Eckhard J. Schnabel, *Early Christian Mission*, 2 vols. (Downers Grove, IL: InterVarsity Press, 2004), 2:1031–32; Schnabel, *Paul the Missionary: Realities, Strategies, and Methods* (Downers Grove, IL: InterVarsity Press, 2008), 59–60.

city was expanded as the main east-west thoroughfare (Lat. *decumanus maximus*, according to Acts 9:11 called "Straight Street"). The renovated temple dedicated to Zeus/Jupiter was the largest temple complex in Syria in the Roman period. Herod I built a theater and a gymnasium in the city (Josephus, *J.W.* 1.422).

MISSIONARY WORK IN ARABIA/NABATEA

Paul's mission in Arabia is the second phase of his missionary work.[3] Paul asserts in Gal 1:17 that when God called him to preach the gospel among the gentiles, he immediately obeyed and went into Arabia, returning to Damascus later. In 2 Cor 11:32–33 Paul reports that the ethnarch of King Aretas wanted to arrest him in Damascus (see also Acts 9:23–25). Paul's stay in Arabia (Nabatea), the region south of Syria that included Moab and Edom and extended south to the Gulf of Aqaba, must have provoked unrest that King Aretas IV (9 BC–AD 40) wanted to put down by arresting Paul. A very plausible reason for unrest provoked by Paul's presence in Arabia is missionary work among both the Jewish communities and the local population in the cities of Arabia. The reason for proclaiming the gospel in Arabia might be connected with the fact that the Jews regarded the Arabs as descendants of Ishmael, the son of Abraham. Since the forced conversion of the Idumeans, the descendants of Esau,

3. For Paul's mission in Arabia, see Jerome Murphy-O'Connor, *Paul: A Critical Life* (Oxford: Oxford University Press, 1996), 81–85; Martin Hengel and Anna Maria Schwemer, *Paul Between Damascus and Antioch: The Unknown Years* (Louisville: Westminster John Knox, 1997), 106–26; Schnabel, *Early Christian Mission*, 2:1032–45; Schnabel, *Paul*, 60–65.

by John Hyrcanus (135–104 BC), the Arab Nabateans were the closest relatives of the Jews who were gentiles. Herod Antipas, the tetrarch of Galilee, had married the daughter of King Aretas IV in AD 23. If Paul was converted in AD 31/32, he spent AD 32/33 in Arabia. Aretas' capital was at Petra in central Arabia; towns between Petra and Damascus in which Paul might have preached the gospel are (from north to south) Sakkaia, Shahba, Kanatha, Suweida, Bostra, Gerasa, Philadelphia, Heshbon, Medaba, Dibon, Rabbatmoaba, Charakmoaba.

MISSIONARY WORK IN JERUSALEM (JUDEA)

Paul's mission in Jerusalem is the third phase of his missionary work.[4] When it became impossible to continue the mission in Arabia and in Damascus, Paul returned to Jerusalem and preached the gospel in the local synagogues in which Greek-speaking Jews met (Acts 9:26–29; 22:17; 26:20; Gal 1:18–19).[5] Paul wanted to stay despite a plot to kill him, but the risen Jesus told Paul to leave the city and go to the gentiles (Acts 22:18–21). In Rom 15:19, a statement in which Paul describes the scope of his entire missionary work, he states that he preached the gospel in Jerusalem.

MISSIONARY WORK IN CILICIA

Paul's mission in Cilicia is the fourth phase of his missionary work.[6] Jerusalem believers took Paul to Caesarea sending him to Tarsus in Cilicia (Acts 9:30). Paul

4. See Schnabel, *Early Christian Mission*, 2:1045–46; Schnabel, *Paul*, 65–66.

5. See Schnabel, "The Persecution of the Earliest Christians in Geographical Perspective," chapter 11 in this volume.

6. See Schnabel, *Early Christian Mission*, 2:1046–48, 1054–69; Schnabel, *Paul*, 69–71.

writes later that when he was in Syria and Cilicia, the churches in Judea had not met him after his conversion, but they heard that he was proclaiming the faith that he had tried to destroy (Gal 1:21–24). Tarsus was a logical choice for continued missionary work: Paul grew up in Tarsus (Acts 9:11; 21:39; 22:3), and there was evidently nobody else proclaiming the gospel in Cilicia. It seems that Paul was active not only in Tarsus, the capital of the province, but in other towns—in Hierapolis (Kastabala), Anazarbos, Epiphaneia, Aigaiai, Mallos, Mopsuestia, and Adana in eastern Cilicia; Zephyrion, Soloi, Kalanthia, Sebaste, Olba, and Korykos in central Cilicia. When Barnabas wanted to recruit Paul for ministry in Antioch, the capital of Syria, he went to Tarsus to look for Paul; it evidently took some time to find him (Acts 11:25–26). Since Paul's family had both Tarsian and Roman citizenship and thus was one of the most prominent Jewish families in Tarsus, the verbs "look for" and "find" suggests that Paul was active in other Cilician towns besides Tarsus. Paul engaged in missionary work in Cilicia (and Syria) for eight or nine years (AD 34–42). Luke's report about the Apostles' Council confirms that there were churches in Cilicia (Acts 15:23, 41).

Basalt Street in Tarsus

When the Roman general and senator Pompey reorganized the east in 68 BC, Cilicia was united with Lycia, Pamphylia, and Pisidia and organized as the province of Cilicia, with the city of Tarsus as the capital. When Cappadocia became an imperial province under Tiberius in AD 17, the province of Cilicia was divided between Galatia and Syria. Strabo describes in detail the flourishing literary and philosophical life in Tarsus, praising the scholars from Tarsus, many of whom were active in Rome:

> The people at Tarsus have devoted themselves so eagerly, not only to philosophy, but also the whole round of education in general, that they have surpassed Athens, Alexandria, or any other place that can be named where there have been schools and lectures of philosophers. (Strabo, *Geography* 14.5.13 [LCL])

Dio Chrysostom describes Tarsus, together with Ephesus and Smyrna, around AD 100 as one of the three greatest cities in Asia Minor (Dio Chrysostom, *First and Second Tarsic Discourses*).

MISSIONARY WORK IN SYRIA

Paul's mission in Syria, with a focus on Antioch, is the fifth phase of his missionary work.[7] Paul reports in Gal 1:21 that after his conversion, and before his first visit to Jerusalem as a follower of Jesus, he preached the gospel in "the regions of Syria and Cilicia." The fact that the Jerusalem believers took Paul to Caesarea probably suggests that he embarked on

7. See Schnabel, *Early Christian Mission*, 2:1069–72; Schnabel, *Paul*, 71–74.

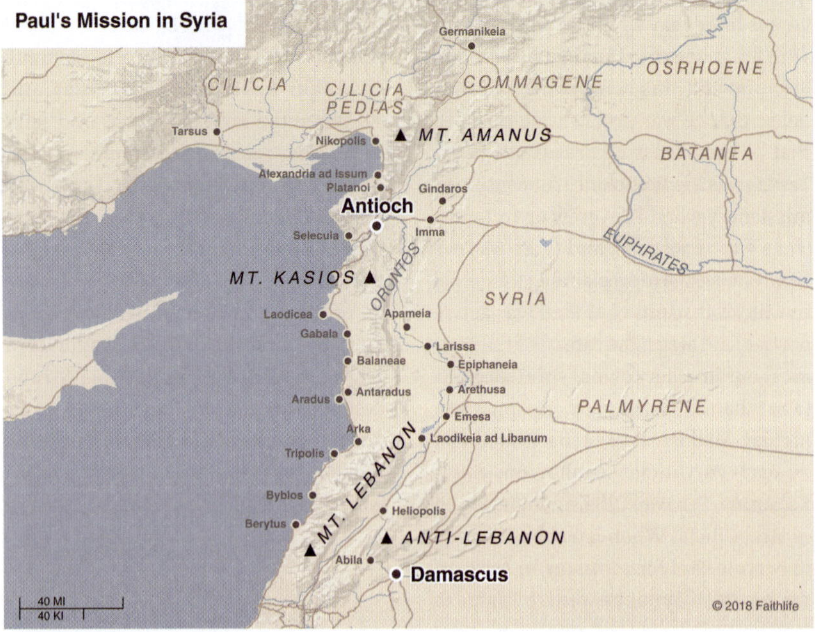

a ship headed toward Tarsus in Cilicia. It is not impossible, however, to assume that Paul took the land route along the Mediterranean coast, which would have allowed him to preach the gospel in cities in which Greek-speaking Jerusalem believers had already preached (Acts 8:4; 11:19) located in western Syria: Berytus, Aphaka, Byblos, Tripolis, Arka (Caesarea ad Libanum), Aradus, Antaradus, Balaneae, Paltus, Gabala, Laodicea, and Seleucia on the Orontes. If Paul took the sea route to Cilicia and proclaimed the gospel in Syria during AD 34–42, he could have preached in towns in northwest Syria, adjacent to Cilicia: in Germaniceia, Nicopolis, Gindaros, Imma, Platanoi, Alexandria ad Issum (from north to south). Also, Paul could have returned to Damascus during these nine years, using the Christian community in Damascus as base of operations and preaching the gospel in southern central Syria: in Abila, Heliopolis, Laodicea ad Libanum, Emesa, Arethusa, Epiphaneia, Larissa, and Apameia. Luke's report about the Apostles' Council confirms that there were churches in Syria besides the church in Antioch (Acts 15:23, 41).[8]

As a result of Barnabas' request, Paul left Cilicia and moved to Antioch on the Orontes, the capital of the province of Syria, where he was active from around AD 42–44, teaching "great numbers of people" (Acts 11:25–26). Luke reports that "the disciples were called Christians first at Antioch" (Acts 11:26). The term "Christians" (Χριστιανοί, *Christianoi*, "Messiah people") occurs in the New Testament only here, in Acts 26:28 (on the

8. For Paul's mission in Syria, see Schnabel, *Early Christian Mission*, 2:1048–54; Schnabel, *Paul*, 66–67.

lips of Herod Agrippa II), and in 1 Pet 4:16 (in the context of legal prosecution). The term was not a self-designation of the followers of Jesus who called themselves "the brothers (and sisters)" (οἱ ἀδελφοί, *hoi adelphoi*) "the believers" (οἱ πιστεύοντες, *hoi pisteuontes*), "the holy ones" (οἱ ἅγιοι, *hoi hagioi*), "the assembly" (ἐκκλησία, *ekklēsia*, "church"), "the disciples" (οἱ μαθηταί, *hoi mathētai*), "the way" (ἡ ὁδός, *hē hodos*). The term *Christianoi* was a name given by outsiders to those who believed that Jesus was the Messiah (Greek Χριστός, *Christos*, for Hebrew הַמָּשִׁיחַ, *ha-mashiakh*, Aramaic מְשִׁיחָא, *meshikha*, "the Anointed One"), the awaited royal Savior.[9] Jews called the followers of Jesus *Natsrayya* or *Notsrim* ("Nazarenes"). Greeks would have used formulations such as *Christeioi* or *Christikoi* if they had wanted to coin a term designating people whose identity is focused on their faith in Jesus as the *Christos*, the Messiah.[10] The suggestion that the term was coined by Latin speakers is plausible, more specifically the suggestion that members of the Roman provincial administration coined the term *Christiani*, Grecized as *Christianoi*, as a result of an encounter with followers of Jesus.[11] Martin Hengel suggests that, "perhaps the new church had to register in the provincial capital with the magistrates of the city or of the province of Syria as a Jewish 'special synagogue' or 'religious association,' i.e., as *collegium*, συναγωγή or ἔρανος."[12] Since followers of Jesus came to the attention of city magistrates in various cities as troublemakers, accused as such by either Jewish or non-Jewish residents (Acts 16:19–39; 17:5–9; 18:12–14; 19:23–40), it is very likely that this had happened in Antioch as well and that the Roman magistrates coined the term *Christiani* as a designation for

---

9. The term *Christianoi* (Lat. *Christiani*) is used by Roman authors (Tacitus, *Annales* 15.44; Suetonius, *Nero* 16.2; Pliny, *Epistles* 10.96; 10.97) and by Josephus (*A.J.* 18.64). It is only in the second century that Christian writers use the term; cf. Ignatius of Antioch, *To the Romans* 3:2; *To the Ephesians* 11:2; *To the Magnesians* 4:1; *To Polycarp* 7:3; *To the Trallians* 6:1; Didache 12:4.

10. Hengel and Schwemer, *Paul*, 453 n. 1171. See also Edwin A. Judge, "Judaism and the Rise of Christianity: A Roman Perspective," in *The First Christians in the Roman World: Augustan and New Testament Essays*, ed. James R. Harrison (Tübingen: Mohr Siebeck, 2008), 431–44, 363, who points to the Greek-speaking synagogues in Rome who used the Greek suffix *-esioi* in their names.

11. For the term as coined by Latin speakers, see Erik Peterson, "Christianus," in *Frühkirche, Judentum und Gnosis: Studien und Untersuchungen* (Rome: Herder, 1959), 64–87. Note the terms *Caesariani*, *Pompeiani*, *Augustiani* as political "party" labels in Rome. See also Marta Sordi, *The Christians and the Roman Empire* (Norman: University of Oklahoma Press, 1986), 15; Hengel and Schwemer, *Paul*, 225–30; David Horrell, "The Label Χριστιανός: 1 Peter 4:16 and the Formation of Christian Identity," *JBL* 126 (2007): 362; Paul Trebilco, *Self-Designations and Group Identity in the New Testament* (Cambridge: Cambridge University Press, 2012), 277. As coined as a result of encounters with provincial administration, see Peterson, "Christianus"; Justin Taylor, "Why were the Disciples First Called 'Christians' at Antioch? (Acts 11,26)," *Revue Biblique* 101 (1994): 75–94; Schnabel, *Early Christian Mission*, 1:792–96; Horrell, "Label", 363–64; Trebilco, *Self-Designations*, 278.

12. Martin Hengel and Anna Maria Schwemer, *Paulus zwischen Damaskus und Antiochien: Die unbekannten Jahre des Apostels* (Tübingen: Mohr Siebeck, 1998), 342, my translation (expansion of Hengel and Schwemer, *Paul*, 226).

the followers of Jesus.[13] The new appellation *Christiani/Christianoi* suggests that the missionary work of the church of Antioch was effective and expanding and thus came to the attention of the Roman authorities.

BIBLIOGRAPHY

Bengel, Johann Albrecht. *Gnomon Novi Testamenti*. 8th ed. Stuttgart: Steinkopf, 1887.

Hengel, Martin, and Anna Maria Schwemer. *Paul Between Damascus and Antioch: The Unknown Years*. Louisville: Westminster John Knox, 1997.

———. *Paulus zwischen Damaskus und Antiochien: Die unbekannten Jahre des Apostels*. Tübingen: Mohr Siebeck, 1998.

Horrell, David. "The Label Χριστιανός: 1 Peter 4:16 and the Formation of Christian Identity." *JBL* 126 (2007): 361–81.

Judge, Edwin A. "Judaism and the Rise of Christianity: A Roman Perspective." Pages 431–41 in *The First Christians in the Roman World: Augustan and New Testament Essays*. Edited by James R. Harrison. Tübingen: Mohr Siebeck, 2008.

Murphy-O'Connor, Jerome. *Paul: A Critical Life*. Oxford: Clarendon, 1996.

Peterson, Erik. "Christianus." Pages 64–87 in *Frühkirche, Judentum und Gnosis: Studien und Untersuchungen*. Rome: Herder, 1959.

Riesner, Rainer. *Paul's Early Period: Chronology, Mission Strategy, Theology*. Grand Rapids: Eerdmans, 1998.

Schnabel, Eckhard J. *Early Christian Mission*. 2 vols. Downers Grove, IL: InterVarsity Press, 2004.

———. *Paul the Missionary: Realities, Strategies, and Methods*. Downers Grove, IL: InterVarsity Press, 2008.

Sordi, Marta. *The Christians and the Roman Empire*. Norman: University of Oklahoma Press, 1986.

Taylor, Justin. "Why were the Disciples First Called 'Christians' at Antioch? (Acts 11,26)." *Revue Biblique* 101 (1994): 75–94.

Trebilco, Paul. *Self-Designations and Group Identity in the New Testament*. Cambridge: Cambridge University Press, 2012.

13. See Horrell, "Label", 367. Rainer Riesner, *Paul's Early Period: Chronology, Mission Strategy, Theology* (Grand Rapids: Eerdmans, 1998), 114, suggests that the term was coined in connection with the anti-Jewish unrest triggered in AD 39/40 by Caligula's directive that his statue be erected in the temple of Jerusalem. See also Judge, "Judaism," 363: the term arose "from the questions posed for Romans over the political loyalty of the followers of Christ."

CHAPTER 19

PETER'S MINISTRY IN CAESAREA MARITIMA

Acts 10:1–11:18

John A. Beck

KEY POINTS

- The early Jewish-Christian church in Jerusalem was uncertain about how to include gentiles into their growing movement and so isolated themselves from gentiles.
- Peter's ministry in Caesarea Maritima helped him see that the gospel should be taken to the gentiles.
- The Holy Spirit changed the perspective and practices of the Jerusalem church by replicating the Jerusalem Pentecost story in Caesarea Maritima.

INTRODUCTION

It is only natural that we know and love some Bible places more than others because some locations have hosted stories that are particularly warm and uplifting. For example, Bethlehem holds a special place in our hearts because it hosted the birth of Jesus. Likewise, we know and love Jerusalem because it fills us with hope and peace since it is the location where Jesus died and rose from death to redeem us. We cherish these stories and these places.

Caesarea on the sea (or Caesarea Maritima) is not that kind of place. But it should be, particularly for those of us who do not count Abraham as our biological father. The story of Caesarea is a story that changed the church. It is our "Pentecost" story. Here the Holy Spirit replicated the Jerusalem Pentecost miracle to show that we and those like us belong in the church just as much as our Jewish brothers and sisters. As such, it is one of the most important stories in the book of Acts.[1]

1. Darrell L. Bock, *Acts* (Grand Rapids: Baker Academic, 2007), 380.

Aerial View of Joppa

LOCATIONS

The larger story is one that flows between three locations: Jerusalem, Joppa, and Caesarea Maritima. Let's start by getting to know each of them so we can appreciate their roles in this narrative.

Jerusalem needs little introduction. Nestled into the northern reaches of the Judean hill country, the holy city of Jerusalem is arguably the most important city in the plan of salvation. David conquered this city and made it the capital of his kingdom. Solomon built the Lord's temple here. Further, Jerusalem claims top billing among all Bible places because it witnessed the culminating moments of the redemption story. This is where God made peace with us at the cross and empty tomb. After the resurrection, Jerusalem remained the primary geographic focus for the first seven chapters of Acts, playing host to the ascension of Jesus, Pentecost, and many other stories that transition us from the time of Jesus to the time of his church on earth. In our narrative, it is mentioned only twice (10:39; 11:2). But its importance in the story is undeniable because it provides the setting for the culminating scene (11:1–18). The story that began in Joppa and moved to Caesarea is incomplete until it comes to Jerusalem.

Joppa is the Old Testament port of Jerusalem, residing on the Mediterranean Sea about thirty-four miles (54.7 km) northwest of Jerusalem. The biblical authors mention it as the seaport through which cedar logs passed on their way from the sea to Jerusalem so that they could be used in the building and subsequent rebuilding of the temple (2 Chr 2:16; Ezra 3:7). But its most well-known story involves a prophet named Jonah. The Lord had sent this reluctant missionary to Assyria. But Jonah tried to evade the assignment by getting on a ship that would take him to the other side of the world. Joppa was the seaport from which he sailed (Jonah 1:1–3). Peter ends up here because of an urgent invitation delivered

Aerial View of Caesarea Maritima

by the friends of Dorcas, a most charitable lady who had died. Peter went to Joppa and called her back to life (Acts 9:36–42). Afterward, Peter remained in Joppa and that is where we find him at the start of our story. At six occurrences (10:5, 8, 23, 32; 11:5, 13), Joppa is the most frequently mentioned of the three locations, providing the setting for fourteen and a half verses (10:9–23a). Like Jerusalem, it is primarily Jewish in orientation in this era.[2]

That brings us to the geographical focal point of our story, Caesarea Maritima, another seaport located thirty-two miles (55 km) north of Joppa. (Note this is not Caesarea Philippi, a city located at the southern base of Mount Hermon). It is mentioned three times (10:1, 24; 11:11) but provides the setting for the bulk of the story, thirty-three and a half verses (10:1–8, 23b–48). What happens here gets most of our attention and hosts the dramatic events that change the church. Herod the Great built this amazing seaport to connect him to the culture and commodities of the European world that he so deeply loved.[3] He named the city in honor of his Roman patron, Caesar Augustus. After Herod's death, it became the seat of the Roman prefects and was dominated by gentiles and their pagan culture.[4] For those who felt at home in Europe, this was the most Roman experience the Middle East offered.[5] But for many observant Jews, it was cultural pollution of the highest order that turned the promised land into something other than the Lord intended it to be. While the

2. Craig S. Keener, *Acts: An Exegetical Commentary* (Grand Rapids: Baker Academic, 2013), 2:1758.

3. For an in-depth look at the archaeology that reflects this Roman heritage, see Ehud Netzer, *The Architecture of Herod, the Great Builder* (Grand Rapids: Baker Academic, 2006), 94–118.

4. C. K. Barrett, *The Acts of the Apostles* (Edinburgh, T&T Clark, 1994), 1:436.

5. John A. Beck, *Discovery House Bible Atlas* (Grand Rapids: Discovery House, 2015), 293.

city did have a Jewish presence, it was the quintessential Roman city of the province of Judea.

This is what makes Caesarea stand apart from Jerusalem and Joppa. Jerusalem has had a longstanding role to play in the plan of salvation. It championed the worship of one deity in one temple. Of course, Caesarea saw things very differently. Here we find multiple temples dedicated to multiple deities, including a temple built at the highest point of the city in honor of the Roman emperor. Monotheism was a foreign notion. The residents of this city were far from the kingdom of God not only in their religious views but also with respect to their theological vocabulary. In the pagan world of Caesarea, there was no need for terms like repentance, forgiveness, conversion, and faith. In short, the worlds of Jerusalem/Joppa and Caesarea were separated by a great cultural and linguistic gulf; one that is filled by our story. As we expect, Jerusalem/Joppa had something to teach Caesarea. But ironically it is Caesarea that also has something to teach Jerusalem.

PLACES AND PEOPLE

With that introduction to the places, let's see how they shape the people and story that evolves between them, starting with Peter in Joppa. We know a great deal about Peter from the Gospels and from the early chapters in Acts. He was the leader of the Jewish-Christian church in Jerusalem and served as its primary spokesperson.[6] But as our story begins, Peter was not in Jerusalem but rather in the Jewish seaport of Joppa, geographically closer to where gentiles lived but somewhat uncertain as to what to do with them.

This tension existed, in part, due to the dietary laws of Leviticus 11 that played a role in keeping God's chosen people separated from gentiles (Dan 1:8–16). Old Testament law not only defined which animals could be eaten and which must be avoided but also how animals that could be eaten were slaughtered and prepared for a meal. Given the complexity, the observant Jew who wanted to honor the kosher food restrictions would be very concerned about having their diet compromised in a gentile's home, where non-kosher food or kosher food improperly prepared could mingle with food that could be eaten. Consequently, it became the norm to avoid dining with gentiles (Jub 22:16; 3 Macc 3:4). These dietary practices put an obstacle in the path of the Jewish believers in Jesus who were to extend the kingdom of God into the lives of gentiles. Peter himself had spoken of this expansion (Acts 2:39; 3:25). He had heard Jesus declare all food clean (Mark 7:19). But like most in the Jewish-Christian orbit, Peter had not figured out how to make peace between the need to evangelize gentiles and the felt need to avoid eating a meal with them.

We meet Peter about noon when hunger was stirring inside him. As Peter was praying on the rooftop looking out over the Mediterranean Sea, he saw a sheet, or better a sail, let down from heaven by its four corners with lunch aboard. In it, Peter saw animals of all kinds both kosher and not. "Get up, Peter. Kill and eat." (Acts 10:13).[7] Could this voice

6. Keener, *Acts*, 2:1728.

7. All translations are the author's unless otherwise noted.

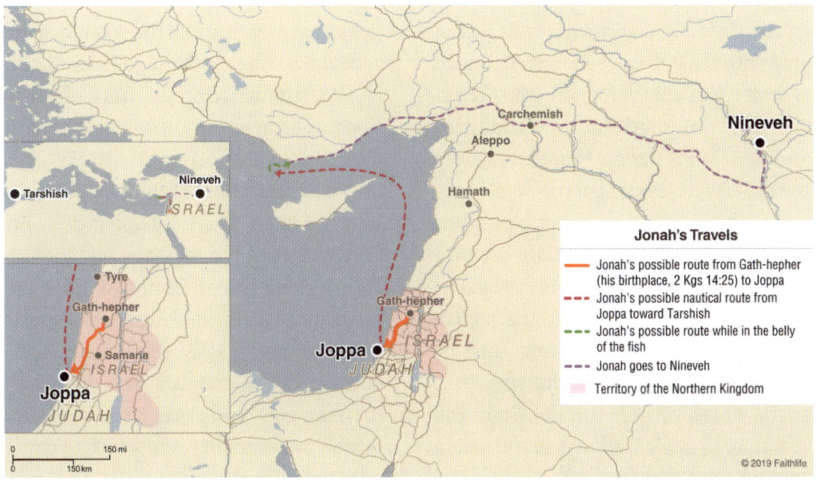

from heaven be trusted? Was this a test? Peter pushed back with strong language insisting that he had never eaten anything "impure or unclean" (10:14). Then the voice boomed a second time. "Do not call anything impure that God has made clean." (10:15) This happened three times, enough to confirm that an important point was being made. But what was it? Just then a shout rang through the compound. "Is Peter there?" It came from a small group of gentiles who had come to Joppa from Caesarea with an invitation to travel with them back to their port city.

This is the moment we feel a bit of geographic déjà vu, connecting us to another Joppa story that has the same ring to it. In this story, the Lord had told Jonah to leave the promised land and travel to the Assyrian city of Nineveh. From Jonah's point of view, this was a horrible idea and he did everything he could to avoid the invitation to speak to gentiles. He went to Joppa where he boarded a ship that would take him as far away from his assignment as he could possibly get. But the Lord's call to visit the gentile world was not so easily avoided. Jonah was thrown from the ship into the water and then spent three days within a large fish. The experience changed his mind and off Jonah went to do what the Lord had asked of him. Peter was on the same waterfront Jonah visited, faced by a similar call to visit gentiles. Both seemed to be using Joppa as a means of isolating themselves from gentiles. Perhaps it was the memory of a reluctant Jonah, in part, that moved Peter to follow a different course of action than Jonah took. Peter did not fully understand what the Lord wanted, but off he went to the place he would rather avoid, Caesarea Maritima.

The invitation to which Peter responded came from Cornelius. The first things we learn about him are worrisome (10:1). His name indicates he was of European heritage, a gentile from pagan Caesarea. That is enough to raise our suspicions about him. But it gets worse. He is a Roman army officer associated with the Italian Regiment. This man of status was a leader among the occupiers of the promised land who had taxed and oppressed people like Peter. From the observant Jewish perspective, there was nothing appealing about him. Then comes the surprising twist. He is a God-fearer. Although he was not prepared to become a full convert to the Jewish faith (which included circumcision), he was drawn to the monotheism, synagogue worship, and ethics of God's Old Testament people.[8] What is more, he is a man who put that faith into practice. He and his household prayed regularly and gave generously to those in need (10:2). Like Peter, Cornelius also had a vision that directed him to send envoys south to Joppa. Here the geography is important. Note that Cornelius was not directed to go to Joppa but to bring Peter to Caesarea.

The Caesarea story that follows is told in great detail (10:23b–48). When Peter arrived, upward of fifty highly motivated people were waiting for him.[9] Peter immediately gave voice to the reservations that lingered. "You are well aware that it is against our law for a Jew to associate with or visit a gentile. But God has shown me that I should not call anyone impure or unclean." (10:28) He sounds less than convinced. But he is beginning to connect the vision in Joppa to the experience he is having in Caesarea. The words "impure and unclean" are the same words Peter had used earlier in Joppa to describe the contents of the linen sail (10:14), words that the voice from heaven corrected. When Cornelius summarized his vision, Peter took one more step. The Pentecost preacher told these gentiles the "good news of peace through Jesus Christ" (10:36), summarizing the story of salvation just as he had in Jerusalem (compare Acts 2:14–40 and 10:37–43).

Then something absolutely astounding happened. The Holy Spirit came on all who heard the message just like he had in Jerusalem on Pentecost. Here the geography is critical. Gentiles *in Caesarea* were having exactly the same experience as Jews *in Jerusalem*. The symmetry between event and place "astonished" the Jewish believers in Jesus who had come with Peter from Joppa (10:45). There was only one thing to do. Peter took the lead. "Surely no one can stand in the way of their being baptized with water" (10:47). That is what they had done in Jerusalem on Pentecost. That is what they would do here in Caesarea. And now we see the whole point of Peter's vision, the invitation, and the fact that this was a Caesarea story rather than one that took place in either Joppa or Jerusalem. Peter's vision in Joppa made it clear that the food laws were no longer an obstacle. Gentiles did not have to become Jewish to join the ranks of the church. And kosher food laws were no longer an obstacle to table fellowship. Peter got it and acted on the new information. He remained with these gentiles in Caesarea for a few days (10:48). It is not stated directly but we can discern implicitly that this involved having meals with gentiles.

We expect this stunning news about Caesarea to make its way back to the holy city. But how will the Jewish-Christian believers react to it? Joppa had Peter. Caesarea had Cornelius. But Jerusalem

8. F. F. Bruce, *The Book of Acts*, rev. ed. (Grand Rapids: Eerdmans, 1988), 203.

9. Keener, *Acts*, 2:1786.

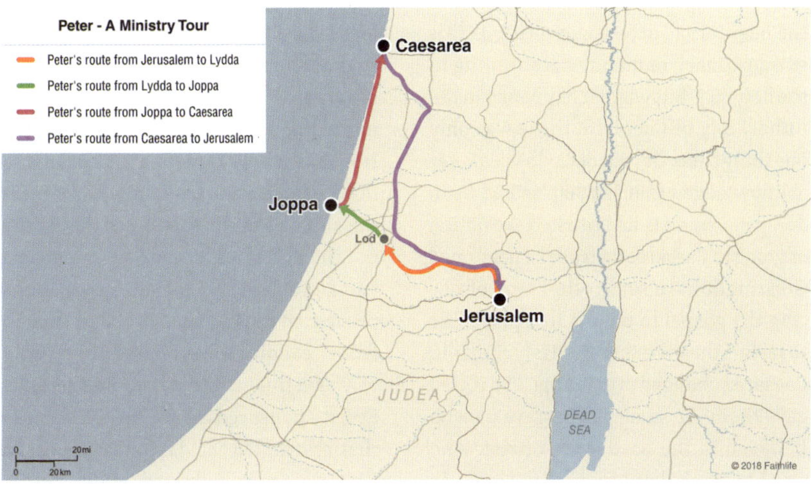

does not have a single figure by which we measure the reaction. Instead there is a group within the Jerusalem church that is the focus of the dissent. When Peter returned to Jerusalem, "the circumcised believers criticized him and said, 'You went into the house of uncircumcised men and ate with them'" (11:2–3). The picture in their minds is both geographical and unattractive. They imagine Peter going into the gentile, pagan world of Caesarea. They see the lavish palace, the theater, the horseracing stadium, the temple to Augustus, the loose morals, and the non-kosher food that filled the place. What was Peter thinking! No godly person enters a den of iniquity like this. And what did he do when he arrived? Unlike Jonah who preached a fire-and-brimstone sermon about Nineveh's impending destruction, Peter went into a gentile, centurion's home and spoke about Jesus and forgiveness. He baptized them. And then to top it off, he ate with them, practicing table fellowship that violated all the best practices of the Jerusalem church. It is this eating that was the sticking point and stood for the rest (11:3) "Shame on you Peter, shame on you!"

Peter took a breath and then the fiery apostle calmly told them the story. He was content to stay in Joppa, eating only kosher food with other Jewish believers. But then the vision came. In relating its contents, he emphasized the words "impure and unclean" (11:8) that the voice from heaven corrected. "Do not call anything impure that God has made clean." (11:9b) Right on the heels of the vision, people who fit that category of "impure and unclean" were at his door with an invitation. "The Spirit told me to have no hesitation about going with them." (11:12) Peter went to Caesarea along with six others from Joppa who became witnesses of all that followed. And wow was there something to see. Peter's sermon was followed by a special giving of the Holy Spirit "as he had come upon us at the beginning" in Jerusalem (11:15). This extraordinary moment was stunning in the holy city. But when it happened in the unholy city of Caesarea, there was only one thing to do. Get out of God's way. Peter acknowledged that is what he had been doing in Joppa. He had resisted the notion of going to Caesarea because *he* presumed God might have some other way of getting the gospel to people in a place like that. But the giving of the Holy Spirit in Caesarea changed everything. "So if God gave them the same gift he gave us who believed in the Lord Jesus Christ, who was I to think that I could stand in God's way?" (11:17) That is when the lightning bolt struck in Jerusalem. This Caesarea story that had changed Peter's perspective now changed Jerusalem. "When they heard this, they had no further objections and praised God saying, 'So then, even to gentiles God has granted repentance that leads to life.'" (11:18)

Gentiles did not have to become Jews and Jews did not have to become gentiles.[10] In order to receive forgiveness and become full members of the church, gentiles did not have to yield to the full array of Old Testament laws including circumcision. This is not the last time this issue rises in the early church. We see the Jerusalem church having a heated discussion about it in Acts 15. But the Lord had spoken in irreversible fashion, anchoring the view in the geography. Joppa had a problem as evidenced by Peter. The Jewish-Christian church was reluctant to engage socially with gentiles. And that worked against the full realization of the Great Commission. Caesarea helped Joppa solve that problem. But Caesarea also had a problem that could be solved by Joppa. God fearing, gentile families like that of Cornelius needed a fuller revelation of the plan of salvation that did not reside anywhere in that city. So the Holy Spirit brought Joppa to Caesarea so that Cornelius and his family could meet the story of forgiveness. But that is the not the end of the story. Jerusalem also had a problem. Old social constructions prevented the Jewish-Christian church from reaching people like the family of Cornelius in Caesarea. So the Holy Spirit sponsored an event in Caesarea that resembled the day of Pentecost in Jerusalem to help the Jerusalem church see that it had brothers and sisters in Caesarea. From beginning to end, this is a place-based story. Each place has a role to play and no place can be removed from the story without doing harm to the integrity of the lesson.

APPLICATION

This Caesarea story is a story that still speaks to us today. In particular, it addresses the malady of our own minimalism. When we keep the church small and like us, it is a more comfortable church. We avoid navigating the complexity of different language groups and different social customs that make church harder than we think it should be. While we consciously will say that the church we want is an international church, we need to inspect our own set of "food laws." These assumptions and personal preferences can unconsciously inform our policies and practices. And we can begin to send people quiet but clear messages that our church is a place where a certain kind of people belong and where others don't.

10. Bock, *Acts*, 410.

A trip to Caesarea Maritima can change that. Here is a place that seems unlikely to produce results. Just look at the place! Everyone there appeared to bask in a pagan mindset. They even lacked the basic vocabulary for a conversation about salvation through Jesus. We know places like that. And this is where Peter's Joppa vision still speaks to us. What "impure and unclean" categories have I established that the Lord wants removed? When we see what the Holy Spirit can do in a place like Caesarea, we join Peter in asking the astonished question. "Who was I to think that I could stand in God's way?" People of all places, cultural groups, languages, and even disreputable places are waiting to hear that Jesus has taken away their sin. This Caesarea story is meant to change the church, our church ... and us.

BIBLIOGRAPHY

Barrett, C. K. *The Acts of the Apostles*. 2 vols. Edinburgh: T&T Clark, 1994.

Beck, John A. *Discovery House Bible Atlas*. Grand Rapids: Discovery House, 2015.

Bock, Darrell L. *Acts*. Grand Rapids: Baker Academic, 2007.

Bruce, F. F. *The Book of Acts*. Revised ed. Grand Rapids: Eerdmans, 1988.

Keener, Craig S. *Acts: An Exegetical Commentary*. 4 vols. Grand Rapids: Baker Academic, 2012–2015.

Netzer, Ehud, *The Architecture of Herod, the Great Builder*. Grand Rapids: Baker Academic, 2006.

CHAPTER 20

PETER AND THE CENTURION CORNELIUS:

ROMAN SOLDIERS IN THE NEW TESTAMENT

Acts 10:1–11:18; 13:6–12; Eph 6:10–17

J. Carl Laney

KEY POINTS

- The Roman army was a well-organized fighting unit with specialized jobs, training, and military equipment.
- Roman soldiers mentioned in the New Testament are generally presented in a positive light, many showing serious interest in spiritual matters.
- The apostle Paul had contact with Roman soldiers, and his writings reflect his knowledge of their military training and equipment.
- Archaeological discoveries and inscriptions reflect active participation by Roman soldiers in early Christianity.

INTRODUCTION

Josephus, the Jewish historian, informs readers that the vast empire of Rome did not come about as a "gift of fortune" but as the "prize of valor."[1] He attributes the greatness of the Roman empire to its well-trained, disciplined, and efficient army. Having described their unified movements, quick response to commands, and ability to overcome obstacles, Josephus comments:

> No wonder that the Empire has extended its boundaries on the east to the Euphrates, on the west to the ocean, on the south to the most fertile traces of Libya, on the north to the Ister and the Rhine.

1. Josephus, *J.W.* 3.71. Translations from Josephus' works are from the Loeb Classical Library edition.

> One might say without exaggeration that, great as are their possessions, the people that won them are greater still.[2]

Why should Christians be knowledgeable about the Roman army? First, there are numerous references in the New Testament to the Roman army. Second, members of the Roman army had a prominent place in the lives of Jesus and the apostle Paul. Third, imagery from the equipment of the Roman army is used to describe Christian service and spiritual warfare.

Praetorian Guard

ORGANIZATION OF THE ROMAN ARMY

A key factor in the success of the Roman army was its military organization. As the U.S. president is the "commander-in-chief" of the military, so the Roman army was under the supreme authority of the emperor (*imperātor*).

The Praetorian Guard. To protect the emperor, his family, and the city of Rome, Emperor Augustus (27 BC–AD 14) created an elite body of troops known as the Praetorian Guard. Bedoyere points out that the term "Praetorian Guard" is relatively modern. The Romans knew the imperial bodyguard as the *cohortes praetoriae* ("the praetorian cohorts").[3] The Praetorian Guard numbered around ten thousand soldiers who were recruited from the city of Rome and Italy. They regarded themselves as a cut above the rest of Rome's military: they had higher pay, higher status, better conditions, and a shorter period of service than ordinary soldiers.[4] In addition to protecting the emperor, the Praetorian Guard enforced laws, maintained public order, and accompanied the emperor should he decide to lead the army into battle. The Praetorian Guard became a powerful political force in Rome. In AD 42 soldiers of the Praetorian Guard led the assassination of Caligula (AD 37–41) and then installed Claudius (AD 41–54) on the throne. The Praetorian Guard was disbanded in the fourth century by Constantine (AD 274–337).[5] Paul was in custody of the Praetorian Guard during his first Roman imprisonment (Phil 1:13), which provided an opportunity for him to witness to this elite group of Roman soldiers.

The Legionaries. There were two kinds of Roman soldiers—the legionaries and the auxiliaries. Roman legionaries were

2. Josephus, *J.W.* 3.107–8.

3. Guy De La Bedoyere, *Praetorian: The Rise and Fall of Rome's Imperial Bodyguard* (New Haven: Yale University Press, 2017), 5.

4. John Wilkes, *The Roman Army* (Cambridge: Cambridge University Press, 1972), 26.

5. Lesley Adkins and Roy Adkins, *Introduction to the Romans* (Secaucus, New Jersey: Chartwell Books, 1991), 35.

Roman Soldiers

Roman citizens and were recruited from established Roman provinces. The Latin name for a Roman legionary was *miles gregarius*, meaning "common soldier."[6] They served for about twenty-five years with far better pay and conditions than those of auxiliaries. The legionaries were totally devoted to serving Rome and were not to marry during their years of service, although this was relaxed at the end of the second century.[7] Each legion was commanded by a Roman nobleman, called a legate (*lēgātus*), who was chosen by the emperor himself. The legate was assisted by six military tribunes, who were professional soldiers proficient in the art of war and military leadership. The Roman legion, consisting of about 5,300 soldiers, was divided into ten cohorts of 480 men, each of which was divided into six centuries. Originally a century had one hundred men, as the name implies. Although it was eventually reduced to eighty men, the name "century" was retained. A century was divided into ten parties of ten men each who shared a tent, a cook kettle, and other equipment. The emperor Trajan's (AD 98–117) army had thirty legions, but the number varied depending on the needs of the time. Josephus records that the Roman legions played an important part in the Jewish War.[8] General Titus, who later succeeded his father Vespasian and ruled as emperor (AD 79–81), assembled two legions (Legion XII and Legion XV) at Caesarea and approached Jerusalem from the north. He was joined by Legion X, which had wintered at Jericho, and by Legion V, which had wintered at Emmaus. The Jewish rebels were no match for a Roman army of about eighty thousand soldiers, and the city was captured and burned and the walls destroyed by the end of September, AD 70.[9]

The Auxiliaries. The word "auxiliary" comes from the Latin word for "help." The auxiliary soldiers "helped" the Roman army of legionaries. They were recruited from the border provinces and were not usually Roman citizens, although they received Roman citizenship at the end of their term of service.[10] In the time of Emperor Trajan (AD 98–117), there were about 220,000 auxiliary soldiers, as compared with 159,000 legionaries.[11] The auxiliaries were recruited for special jobs

6. Wilkes, *Roman Army*, 31.

7. Wilkes, *Roman Army*, 31.

8. Josephus, *J.W.*, 6.67–70.

9. Josephus, *J.W.*, 6.434–35.

10. A. C. Bouquet, *Everyday Life in New Testament Times* (New York: Charles Scribner's Sons, 1953), 21.

11. Wilkes, *Roman Army*, 5.

that the legionaries were not trained to do. The Romans preferred hand-to-hand combat, so they recruited soldiers from the provinces who were skilled at archery and could fight on horseback. Roman legions would have included small cavalry units, but most of the Roman cavalry were auxiliaries.

The Cohorts. The cohort was a unit of soldiers within a legion. While there were ten cohorts in a Roman legion, not all cohorts were the same. The First Cohort was the senior cohort, and it differed from the other nine in two ways: First, it had only five centuries, but six centurions. The sixth centurion was the "chief centurion" of the legion. His rank was *primus pilus*, "number one javelin." Second, the first cohort had 600 extra men who supported the troops as clerks and craftsmen rather than fighting in battles.[12] Some cohorts bore names that honored figures in Roman history, as in the case of the cohort of the centurion Julius, which was named in honor of Emperor Augustus (Acts 27:1). Cornelius served in the Italian cohort, named for its place of origin (Acts 10:1). There were two cohorts of auxiliary troops stationed in Jerusalem at the Antonia Fortress in the early first century AD. A third cohort guarded the provincial capital Caesarea. Two additional cohorts, including one of cavalry, served the province of Judea.[13]

"The Centurion" by James Tissot (c. 1886)

SPECIAL JOBS IN THE ROMAN ARMY

In every century, soldiers were assigned to special jobs: craftsmen who could repair armor, clerks who kept records of equipment and pay, engineers responsible for the design of roads and bridges, soldiers who could build and maintain siege weapons, blacksmiths who could make weapons, cartwrights who could build wagons and repair broken wheels, and baggage-masters to make sure that equipment was properly packed and transported to the next camp.[14] When Augustus learned that more soldiers died of wounds than were killed in battle, he introduced the medical corps to perform surgeries and attend the wounded.[15]

In addition, the *signifer* carried the Roman *sīgnum*, or standard. The chief standard bearer, the *aquilifer*, carried the standard with a gold or silver eagle (*aquila*) on top. This symbol of Rome was so prized that it was a terrible dis-

12. Wilkes, *Roman Army*, 33.

13. Jona Lendering, "Judea," in www.livias.org/articles/place/Judaea (published 1997; last modified June 5, 2017).

14. Wilkes, *Roman Army*, 21

15. Bouquet, *Everyday Life in New Testament Times*, 21.

Roman Standard Bearer

grace to lose it. Legionaries would defend the *aquila* with their lives and fight for years to retrieve it if it was captured by the enemy. The *cornicen* served as the trumpeter for the legion and used his *cornū*, or horn, to signal the troops. The *optiō* (from Latin *optō*, "to choose") was an executive officer who was selected to be the next in line to become a centurion when one was killed or retired. The *tesserarius* was a junior officer in the legion who was responsible to get the password from the commander. The password was written on a block of wood called a *tessera*. The *imaginifer* carried a bronze image (*imāgō*) of the emperor to remind the soldiers whom they served and to help them focus their loyalty on him in the heat of battle.

TRAINING AND EQUIPMENT IN THE ROMAN ARMY

Roman soldiers won so many battles because they were well trained and highly disciplined. They were first and foremost fighting men, and physical fitness was essential. New recruits were drilled in the rigors of running, jumping, climbing over obstacles, and marching. Paul recognized the hard training of Roman soldiers when he wrote to Timothy, "Suffer hardship with me, as a good soldier of Christ Jesus" (2 Tim 2:3).[16]

Roman soldiers practiced the actual movements they would use in battle. They learned how to march in straight lines, turn from a column to a battle line, open and close ranks, form a wedge to break through enemy lines, and form a circle or "orb" (*orbis*) with their shields if surrounded by the enemy. One of the most famous of the Roman soldiers' formations was the *testudo*, which enabled them to advance slowly with protecting shields on all sides and over their heads. Soldiers practiced hand-to-hand combat with wicker shields and wooden swords to avoid injury. Their constant drill with swords, shields, and spears made the Roman soldiers experts in the art of warfare.

The Jewish historian Josephus lauds the peacetime training for Roman soldiers. He writes:

> For their nation does not wait for the outbreak of war to give men their first lesson in arms; they do not sit with folded hands in peace time only to put them in motion in the hour of need. On the contrary, as though they had been born with weapons in hand, they never have a truce from training, never wait for emergencies to arise. Moreover, their peace maneuvers are no less strenuous than veritable warfare;

16. Unless otherwise noted, Scripture quotations are from the New American Standard Bible (NASB).

Roman *Testudo* (Tortoise) Formation

> each soldier daily throws all his energy into his drill, as though he were in action. Hence that perfect ease with which they sustain the shock of battle; no confusion breaks their customary formations, no panic paralyses, no fatigue exhausts them; and as their opponents cannot match these qualities, victory is the invariable and certain consequence. Indeed, it would not be wrong to describe their maneuvers as bloodless combats and their combats as sanguinary maneuvers.[17]

A few paragraphs later, Josephus adds:

> This perfect discipline makes the army an ornament of peace-time and in war welds the whole into a single body; so compact are their ranks, so alert their movements in wheeling to right or left, so quick their ears for orders, their eyes for signals, their hands to act upon them ... no wonder that the empire has extended its boundaries on the east to the Euphrates, on the west to the ocean, on the south to the most fertile tracts of Libya, on the north to the Ister and the Rhine. One might say without exaggeration that, great as are their possessions, the people that won them are greater still.[18]

In addition to his weapons and shield, a fully equipped Roman soldier carried about ninety pounds of tools and military gear. Most important was the sol-

17. Josephus, *J.W.* 3.72–75.

18. Josephus, *J.W.* 3.105–7.

Much of what we know about the Roman military armor and equipment comes from the images on Trajan's Column which celebrates Rome's triumphs (AD 113)

dier's helmet, which was made of bronze over a leather skullcap. The helmet had hinged cheek pieces and a curved extension that provided protection for the soldier's neck. Wearing a helmet was a distinct advantage, since their enemies had no such protection. Body armor protected the upper part of the soldier's body, front and back. Strips of metal were secured with leather cords to create something like a vest—with the front and back buckled together, allowing the soldier's arms to move freely. Around his waist, the soldier wore a wide belt with thick leather strips hanging down in front. The belt protected the soldier's groin and thighs while allowing for freedom of movement. Sturdy sandals were especially important for soldiers, who traveled on foot. A legionary wore sandals with thick leather soles and hobnails to help avoid slipping in a muddy and bloody battlefield. Strips were worn inside the sandals during wintry conditions. For protection, Roman soldiers had shields, which consisted of laminated wood covered with tough leather and trimmed around the edges with iron or bronze. Shields were curved, offering protection not only in front but on the sides of the soldier.[19] The apostle Paul uses the familiar images of the Roman military equipment to teach the Ephesians lessons of spiritual warfare (Eph 6:10–17).

Two offensive weapons were used to attack the enemies of Rome. Each soldier had two throwing spears made with sharp points which would bend after penetrating an enemy's shield. Since the enemy couldn't dislodge the spear, it could not be thrown back. After throwing their spears, the legionaries would charge the enemy to engage them with hand-to-hand combat. Each soldier carried a sword on his left side and a nine-inch dagger on his right. The double-edged sword was the soldier's most important weapon. Although the sword was sharp on both sides, Roman soldiers were taught to thrust and stab rather than slash at the enemy.[20]

In addition to a soldier's personal equipment, the Roman army used deadly artillery pieces. The *onager* (Latin for

19. Further details on the legionary equipment can be found in Wilkes, *Roman Army*, 12–13.
20. Wilkes, *Roman Army*, 12–13.

Catapult

Ballista

"wild ass") was a catapult which could hurl fifty-pound stones up to four hundred yards (365 meters) against enemy cities and forts. Each legion had about ten of these powerful military machines. The *ballista*, mounted on mule drawn carts, was a weapon capable of firing arrows and other projectiles. The arrows were sometimes smeared with burning pitch and set enemy defenses on fire. There were about fifty to sixty *ballistae* assigned to each legion. To assault city walls, the Romans used a siege tower, which provided protection for the advancing army. Once the tower reached the wall of the city, a heavy ram, swinging back and forth, would be used to break through the wall or gate as archers shot arrows into the city from the top of the tower. Josephus records how Vespasian constructed three fifty-foot siege towers for his attack on Jotopata.[21] He reports how a ninety-foot siege tower with a great battering ram was rolled up a ramp against the walls of the fortress Masada shortly before Masada was captured.[22]

John the Baptist and the Soldiers (Luke 3:14)

Luke records that John the Baptist was preaching a message of repentance in the district around the Jordan River when the crowds were questioning him asking, "Then what shall we do?" (Luke 3:10). John answers simply by saying that they should carry out God's command to show true, neighborly love (compare Lev 19:18). Some tax collectors wanted to know what specific application this had for them. Jesus replied, "Collect no more than what you have been ordered to" (Luke 3:12). Some soldiers approached John with a similar question, "And what about us, what shall we do?" (Luke 3:14). Luke does not say whether they were Jewish or Roman soldiers, but the latter is more likely since they may have been enforcing the collection of taxes.[23] In the Roman empire, power was obtained and protected by soldiers and money, "and the two were closely connected" since the military payroll was often obtained by force of arms.[24] Subjects in Roman provinces had little redress when Roman

21. Josephus, *J.W.* 3.283–85.

22. Josephus, *J.W.* 7.305–10.

23. Norval Geldenhuys, *Commentary on the Gospel of Luke* (Grand Rapids: Eerdmans, 1951), 139.

24. J. B. Campbell, *The Emperor and the Roman Army, 31 BC–AD 235* (Oxford: Clarendon Press, 1984), 181.

troops used force or false charges to supplement their income.[25] Emperors sometimes made large payments to the Roman troops as a bribe to secure their loyalty. Distribution of money to the Praetorian Guard and other troops "became a regular feature of imperial accessions, designed to bind the army to the emperor in goodwill and mutual benefit."[26] It is in light of this background that John the Baptist provided the soldiers with a three-fold application of his message, "Do not take money from anyone by force, or accuse anyone falsely, and be content with your wages" (Luke 3:14). What is particularly significant about this account is that John does not ask these soldiers to abandon their military careers, as if to imply that military service was inappropriate for Christians.[27] He simply asks them as soldiers not to abuse their power.

THE CENTURION AT CAPERNAUM (MATTHEW 8:5–13; LUKE 7:1–10)

Matthew and Luke record an encounter Jesus had with at centurion which sheds light on the authority of an officer in the Roman army had over his men. The incident took place at Capernaum after Jesus had preached his Sermon on the Mount (Matt 5–7; Luke 6:17–49). Capernaum, located on the northwest shore of the Sea of Galilee is one of the cities most frequently mentioned in the Gospels. Situated on the main road linking Damascus with the Mediterranean coast, Capernaum was strategically located for travel, trade, and the collection of taxes and tariffs on the caravans traveling this international coastal highway. Matthew Levi collected taxes for the Roman government at Capernaum before being called by Jesus (Matt 9:9). Jesus relocated to Capernaum after being rejected in his own hometown of Nazareth (Matt 4:13), taught in the synagogue (John 6:24–59), and lodged there in Peter's house (Mark 1:29–35). Josephus describes Capernaum and the surrounding region as being fertile and well watered.[28] The site has been excavated and preserves a limestone synagogue dated to the end of the second century or beginning of the third century AD[29] and an octagonal Byzantine structure built around what is believed to have been Peter's house.

What would a Roman centurion be doing in Capernaum? It is possible that the centurion had come from a legion stationed in the Roman province of Syria where three legions of auxiliaries were stationed.[30] But since he was highly regarded by the people of Capernaum and had built their synagogue (Luke 7:2–5), it is more likely that he was stationed in Capernaum both for reasons of security and to enforce the collection of customs and taxes. Gundry suggests the possibility that the term "centurion" is being used loosely for a military offi-

25. Leon Morris, *Luke: An Introduction and Commentary*, TNTC (Downers Grove, IL: InterVarsity Press, 1988),114.

26. Campbell, *The Emperor and the Roman Army*, 187.

27. John F. Shean, *Soldiering for God: Christianity and the Roman Army* (Leiden: Brill, 2010), 145.

28. Josephus, *J.W.* 3.516–21.

29. Abraham Negev, ed., *Archaeological Encyclopedia of the Holy Land* (Jerusalem: Weidenfeld & Nicolson, 1972), 73.

30. Bouquet, *Everyday Life in New Testament Times*, 21.

Front Interior of Synagogue at Capernaum

cial in the service of Herod Antipas, the tetrarch of the region.[31]

What is clear about this centurion is that he understands the military concept of "chain of command." When Jesus entered Capernaum, the centurion approached Jesus, entreating him to come and heal his paralyzed servant. When Jesus agreed to do what the centurion asked (Matt 8:7), the centurion said that he felt unworthy for Jesus to enter his home. The centurion didn't want for Jesus to be ceremonially defiled by entering the house of a gentile.[32] Instead, if Jesus would "just say the word" (Matt 8:8), his servant would be healed. Verse 9 reveals that the military experience of the centurion served as the basis for such confidence. The centurion was a soldier who knew the importance of obeying authority. He obeyed those in authority over him and expected the soldiers under him to do the same. Robertson observes, "As a military man he had learned obedience to his superiors and so expected obedience to his commands, instant obedience."[33] The significance of the military in this account is noted by Shean who comments, "This is probably one of the earliest instances in Christian

31. Robert Gundry, *Matthew: A Commentary on His Literary and Theological Art* (Grand Rapids: Eerdmans, 1982), 141.

32. It is helpful to note that in rabbinic literature, the house of a gentile was considered ritually unclean (m. Oholoth 18.7).

33. A. T. Robertson, *Word Pictures in the New Testament* (Nashville: Broadman Press, 1930), 1:65.

Hasmonean Palace, Model of Jerusalem

literature where a military analogy is used to describe ... the obedience of the congregation to that of a faithful body of soldiers."[34]

After hearing the words of the centurion, Jesus marveled and said that this gentile soldier had exhibited greater faith than anyone in Israel (Matt 8:10)! He adds that believing gentiles coming from lands outside of Israel ("from east and west") like the Roman centurion would enjoy a place of honor in his kingdom while unbelieving Jews would be excluded (Matt 8:11–12). The severity of the judgment on those excluded (v. 12) is said to have "no equal in rabbinic and apocalyptic literature."[35] In this narrative, the centurion "serves as a precursor to the reception of the gospel by the Gentiles."[36] Others would follow in his footsteps, affirming their faith in Jesus.

SOLDIERS AT THE CROSS (MATT 27:27–54; MARK 15:16–39; LUKE 23:26–47; JOHN 19:17–37)

Roman soldiers played an active part in the crucifixion of Jesus Christ. The Gospels record that the trial of Jesus ended with Pilate delivering up Jesus "to be crucified" (Matt 27:26, Mark 15:15, John 19:16). Then the Roman soldiers took Jesus into the praetorium where the cohort gathered to mock and abuse him (Matt 27:27; Mark 15:16; John 18:28). The *praetōrium* is a Latin term which originally denoted the residence of the commanding officer or general in a Roman fort or camp. The name is derived from the Latin *praetor* ("leader") which designated the highest ranking officer in the camp or fort. *Praetorium* could be literally translated, "the place of the man who goes before others."[37] The praeto-

34. John F. Shean, *Soldiering for God*, 144.

35. Gundry, *Matthew*, 146.

36. William A. Simmons, *Peoples of the New Testament World* (Peabody, MA: Hendrickson, 2008), 269.

37. Bedoyere, *Praetorian*, 7.

rium could be a tent or a building in a more permanent or established fort. In the Gospels, the word is used to refer to the headquarters of the Roman prefect or governor in Jerusalem. Since Caesarea was the official center for Roman rule in Judea, Pilate would have resided at the praetorium when his duties required him to visit Jerusalem.

A major question for students of the New Testament is whether the references to the praetorium in the Gospels (Matt 27:27; Mark 15:16; John 18:28,33; 19:19) refer to the old Hasmonean palace, Herod's palace (made available to the prefect for Jerusalem visits), or the Antonia Fortress which was located just north of the Herodian temple platform.

Although no traces of the building have been discovered, Josephus indicates that the Hasmonean palace was located on the western side of the upper city of Jerusalem (a little north of the modern Jewish Quarter).[38] King Agrippa (AD 37–44) built a large apartment in the palace from which he enjoyed gazing into the temple courts while eating his meals.[39] The earliest Christian tradition identifies the Hasmonean palace with the praetorium.[40]

Another possible location for the praetorium is Herod's Palace located at the highest point of the Western Hill just south of Jerusalem's Jaffa Gate. The palace banqueting halls, bedrooms, garden walks and magnificent towers are described in detail by Josephus.[41] Although Christian tradition has identified the praetorium with the Antonia Fortress which was located on an outcrop of limestone at the northwest corner of the temple platform, excavations of the nearby pavement, the *Lithostrotos* (λιθόστρωτος), are dated to the days of Hadrian (AD 117–138) rather than Pilate (AD 26–36).[42] Since Mark identifies "the palace" (*tes aules*) as "the Praetorium" (πραιτώριον, *praitorion*) in Mark 15:16, and the same term is used to describe Herod's seaside palace in Caesarea (Acts 23:35), Rainey and Notley conclude that the praetorium should be identified with Herod's palace rather than the Antonia Fortress.[43]

While the traditional view identifying the praetorium with the Antonia Fortress no longer enjoys favor, it is still worthy of consideration. This fortress was built over an earlier Hasmonean fortress (the Baris) by King Herod and named for his friend Mark Anthony. Josephus reports that a Roman cohort was permanently quartered in the Antonia Fortress so they could repress any insurrection which might take place during the Jewish religious festivals as they apparently did on at least one occasion (Luke 13:1).[44] While some might object that a fortress was not

38. Josephus, *J.W.* 2.344.

39. Josephus, *Ant.* 20.189–91.

40. Emil G. Kraeling, *Rand McNally Bible Atlas* (New York: Rand McNally, 1966), 405.

41. Josephus, *J.W.* 5.176–81.

42. P. Benoit, "The Archaeological Reconstruction of the Antonia Fortress" in *Jerusalem Revealed: Archaeology of the Holy City 1968–1974* (New Haven and London: Yale University Press, 1976), 87–88.

43. Anson F. Rainey and R. Steven Notley, *The Sacred Bridge* (Jerusalem: Carta, 2006), 365–66.

44. Josephus, *J.W.* 5.244.

Model of Jerusalem from the time of Jesus with Herod's Palace in the foreground and the towers of Antonia Fortress in the background.

a suitable place for a Roman prefect to reside while visiting Jerusalem, Josephus reports that "The interior resembled a palace (*basileion*) in its spaciousness and appointments, being divided into apartments of every description and for every purpose, including cloisters, baths and broad courtyards for the accommodation of troops; so that its possession of all conveniences it seems a town, from its magnificence a palace (*basileion*)."[45] Josephus uses the Greek word βασίλειον (*basileion*, "kingly dwelling" or "palace") twice in describing the Antonia Fortress. Since the purpose of Pilate's coming to Jerusalem during Passover was to command Roman soldiers in dealing with potential trouble in the Jewish temple (compare Acts 21:27–31),[46] the Antonia Fortress may have served as the residence of Pilate during the trial of Jesus.[47] According to Benoit, the pavement with the Convent of the Sisters of Zion which has been identified as "the pavement" (*lithostroton*) mentioned in John 19:13 dates from the time of Hadrian, but "the fortress of Antonia stood on the mass of rock where the Omariyya school stands today."[48] Since no excavation has taken place on this site, it cannot be definitively

45. Josephus, *J.W.* 5.240–41.

46. As in the case of the outrage that followed Pilate's placing in Jerusalem military standards featuring the emblem of the emperor reported by Josephus, *Ant.* 18.55–59.

47. Jack Finegan, *The Archaeology of the New Testament* (Princeton: Princeton University Press,1969), 158.

48. Benoit, "The Archaeological Reconstruction of the Antonia Fortress," 89.

dated. Further research is necessary to arrive with any degree of certainty over the location of Pilate's praetorium.[49]

After he was condemned to be crucified, the Roman soldiers led Jesus from the pavement where he was tried into the praetorium where he was stripped, mocked, and beaten (Matt 27:28–31). Once a defendant was found guilty and condemned to be executed, the crucifixion would be carried out by an official known as the *carnifix serarum*, the "flesh nailer." A soldier at the head of the procession carried the *titulus*, an inscription written on wood, which stated the defendant's name and the crime for which he had been condemned. Later the *titulus* was attached to the victim's cross for passersby to see the charges against the victim. Somewhere along the route to Golgotha stood Simon, who was from the province of Cyrenaica in northern Africa. Possibly he was visiting Jerusalem to participate in the feast of Passover when he was compelled by the Roman soldiers to help Jesus carry his cross. Roman soldiers had the authority to command such services of residents in the provinces where Rome ruled. While Christian art traditionally depicts Jesus carrying the upright beam as well as the cross piece, a condemned prisoner would only carry the *patibulum* or cross-piece.

None of the gospel writers provides details of the procedures used in crucifixion. They simply record that "they crucified him" (Matt 27:35; Mark 15:24; Luke 23:33; John 19:18). The readers of the Gospels were all too aware of this form of execution and the excruciating suffering the victims experienced.

Immediately after the death of Jesus a centurion who had been charged with "keeping guard over Jesus" (Matt 27:54) made an astonishing confession. When he saw "the way that he [Jesus] breathed his last," the soldier declared, "Truly, this man was the Son of God" (Matt 27:54; Mark 15:39). Luke's account records that the centurion "began praising God, saying, "Certainly this man was innocent [or righteous]" (Luke 23:47). There is great debate over whether the centurion was thinking of Jesus a member of the Roman pantheon or acknowledging him as deity in the Christian sense. Simmons argues that instead of affirming Jesus' deity, the soldier was merely acknowledging that Jesus had simply "fulfilled his divine commission."[50] On the other hand, it would seem rather anticlimactic for the writers of the Synoptic Gospels to end their account of Jesus' death on such a trivial note. It appears that the execution of Jesus caused the centurion to "revise his opinion of the executed revolutionary."[51] The placement of the centurion's words in the narrative along with the theological understanding of the term "Son of God" suggests that the soldier was so powerfully impressed with the events of the day and Jesus' words on the cross that "he saw the hand of the living God, and acknowledge that the claims of Christ had after all been genuine."[52]

49. For further study see Bedoyere, *Praetorian.*

50. Simmons, *Peoples of the New Testament World*, 270.

51. John Pobee, "The Cry of the Centurion—A Cry of Defeat" in *The Trial of Jesus*, ed. Ernst Bammel (Naperville, IL: Alec R. Allenson Inc., 1970), 101.

52. Geldenhuys, *The Gospel of Luke*, 612.

Caesarea Maritima, where the centurion Cornelius came to faith through Peter's witness.

CORNELIUS AND HIS HOUSEHOLD (ACTS 10:1–48; 11:1–18)

The book of Acts tells the story of the advance of God's kingdom from Jerusalem, to Judea and Samaria, and to the remotest part of the Roman world (Acts 1:8). Luke's account of the conversion of Cornelius, a *gentile* centurion, is a significant milestone in the progression of this story. The fact that this story is told twice—first in Acts 10 and then repeated in Acts 11—points to the importance of this account in Luke's narrative. The gospel had advanced from Jerusalem, to Judea and Samaria, and was now going to transform the life of a gentile soldier in a very gentile city.[53]

Cornelius was a centurion in the Roman army, but was probably not Roman by birth. Since no Roman legionaries were stationed in Judea at this time in the first century AD, he was most likely a member of the auxiliary troops recruited from the provinces.[54] He was a member of the "Italian cohort" which, although originally established in Italy, had been moved to Syria.[55] Since Caesarea was the center for the Roman administration of Judea, Cornelius was stationed there as part of the security forces to protect Roman interests and keep the peace. The name "Cornelius" may have been taken from the Roman general P. Cornelius Sulla who is remembered for having freed ten thousand slaves in 82 BC.[56]

53. Josephus notes that "Caesarea was one of the largest cities of Judea with a population consisting chiefly of Greeks"—i.e., gentiles (*J.W.* 3.409).

54. Simmons, *Peoples of the New Testament World*, 270.

55. I. Howard Marshall, *The Acts of the Apostles: An Introduction and Commentary*, TNTC (Grand Rapids: Eerdmans Publishing 1980), 183.

56. F. F. Bruce, *The Book of Acts* (Grand Rapids: Eerdmans, 1954), 214.

Although Cornelius was not a follower of Jesus, Luke reports that he was "a devout man and one who feared God with all his household, and gave many alms to the Jewish people and prayed to God continually" (Acts 10:2). The prayers and generosity of Cornelius are also mentioned by the angelic messenger (Acts 10:4). It is clear that Cornelius believed in the God of the Jews and was committed to honoring him from a sincere and submissive heart. However, Cornelius still needed to "be saved" through the cleansing blood of the Savior Jesus (Acts 11:14).

As God prepared the heart of Cornelius to respond to the gospel, so God prepared the heart of Peter to present the gospel to a *gentile*! Luke records the details of Peter's extraordinary vision on a housetop in Joppa in which he is presented with a sheet full of food regarded by the Jews as levitically unclean (Lev 11:1–23). Peter is instructed by a heavenly voice, "Get up, Peter, kill and eat!" (Acts 10:13). Peter protests that he has always observed the Jewish food laws and has never partaken of unclean foods. But the voice responded, "What God has cleansed, no longer consider unholy" (Acts 10:15). Peter was still puzzling over the meaning of the vision when he heard a knock on the door by messengers from Cornelius who informed Peter that a God-fearing centurion was was waiting in Caesarea to "hear a message from you" (Acts 10:22).

When Peter entered Caesarea two days later (Acts 10:23–24), he was met by Cornelius along with his relatives and close friends (Acts 10:24). Peter, it seems, had begun to understand the meaning of his vision and announced that while it was not considered lawful for Jews to have social contact with unbelieving gentiles, God had shown him that he should not regard any person as "unholy or unclean" (Acts 10:28). He further acknowledges that "God is not one to show partiality, but in every nation the person who fears Him and does what is right is welcome to Him" (10:34–35). In response to Peter's preaching of the gospel (10:38–43), Cornelius and his family embraced Jesus by faith, received the Holy Spirit and were identified as followers of Jesus through the ritual of water baptism (10:44–48).

The conversion of Cornelius, a *gentile* soldier was a significant milestone in the growth of God's kingdom in the first century. Up until this time, the gospel had gone from the Jews, to the Samaritans (half-Jews), but now with Cornelius the gospel had reached those completely outside the community of those who embraced the Mosaic law and traditions. When the church leaders in Jerusalem received Peter's report they announced, "Well now, God has granted to the Gentiles also the repentance that leads to life" (Acts 11:18). Who would have imagined that a Roman soldier stationed in occupied Judea would lead the way for gentile inclusion in the church of Jesus Christ. Simmons comments, "This long, detailed account in Acts 10 and 11 demonstrates that the gospel is not just for Jews, but for Gentiles as well."[57]

SERGIUS PAULUS, COMMANDER AT CYPRUS (ACTS 13:6–12)

On their first missionary journey, Paul and Barnabas, accompanied by John Mark, preached first in the synagogues of the port and commercial center

57. Simmons, *Peoples of the New Testament World*, 271.

Archaeological Remains at Paphos

of Salamis, and then traveled west to the capital at Paphos. There Paul and Barnabas were invited into the court of the Roman governor or *prōcōnsul*, Sergius Paulus, to inform him of the message they were preaching (Acts 13:7). Bruce identifies him with Lucius Sergius Paullus who was one of the curators of the Tiber in the reign of Claudius,[58] although Marshall follows van Elderen who argues that the proconsul mentioned in this text is more likely Quintus Sergius Paullus mentioned in an inscription discovered on Cyprus.[59] As proconsul in the province of Cyprus, Sergius Paulus was appointed by the senate to serve as Rome's representative, ruler and commander of the Roman soldiers stationed there. His belief in the message of the gospel no doubt smoothed the way for the missionary work on Cyprus (Acts 13:12).

SOLDIERS AND THE APOSTLE PAUL

The apostle Paul had several contacts with Roman soldiers resulting from the riot which took place in the Jerusalem temple (Acts 21:27–30). Seeing Paul in the temple courts, he was accused by the Jews of preaching against their people and their law, and defiling the holy temple! Viewing the ensuing riot from their nearby garrison, the Antonia Fortress, located at the northwest corner of the temple area, "the commander of the cohort" along with some "soldiers and centurions" ran to Paul's rescue before he would be beaten to death (Acts 21:31–32).

58. Bruce, *Acts*, 264.

59. Marshall, *Acts: An Introduction and Commentary*, 233; B. van Elderen, "Some Archaeological Observations on Paul's First Missionary Journey," *Apostolic History and the Gospel*, ed. W. Ward Gasque and Ralph P. Martin (Exeter: Paternoster Press, 1970), 150–61.

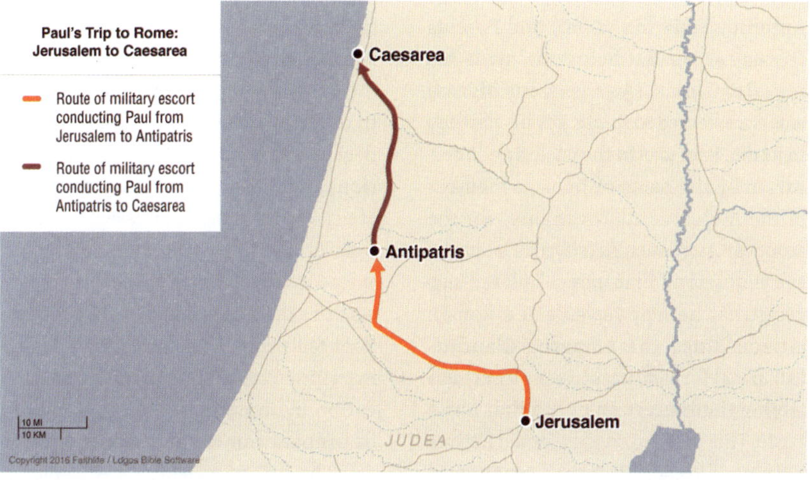

The commander of the cohort is identified by name as Claudius Lysias in the letter he sent to the Roman governor or procurator, Antonius Felix (AD 52–60), regarding the case. The designation used to describe the commander (Acts 21:31) is *chiliarchos* (χιλίαρχος), literally "ruler of a thousand." While a cohort was normally 480 legionaries, the soldiers stationed in Jerusalem were auxiliary troops which were divided into units of five hundred and one thousand men.[60] For this reason the commander, whose rank is denoted in Latin by *tribunus militum*, is designated in Acts as *chiliarchos*, "commander of a thousand."[61] The commander immediately took charge of the situation, ordering Paul to be put in chains, while he inquired as to the cause of the commotion. When he learned that Paul was not a rebel, but a Jewish citizen of Tarsus, he granted permission for Paul to speak in his own defense to the gathered crowd (Acts 22:40–23:21). When Paul's account of his Damascus road experience and commission to preach to the gentiles only intensified the riot, the commander sent Paul to the barracks of the Antonia Fortress to be interrogated by scourging (Acts 22:24). But Paul's appeal to his Roman citizenship was respected by the commander and the apostle was spared from the cruel *flagrum* or scourge. Rumors of a plot to assassinate Paul led to his being transferred to Caesarea to await further legal action under the custody of the procurator Felix (Acts 23:23–35). To ensure his safety, Paul was accompanied by a small army, including two centurions, two hundred soldiers, seventy horsemen, and two hundred spearmen!

Paul remained in Caesarea for two years under the custody of procurators

60. Wilkes, *Roman Army*, 29.

61. Bruce, *Book of Acts*, 458n32.

Antonius Felix (AD 52–60) and Porcius Festus (AD 60–62) before he made his "appeal to Caesar" (Acts 25:11) and his case was transferred to Rome. For his journey to Rome, Paul was in the custody of a centurion by the name of Julius, a member of the Augustan cohort (named for the emperor Augustus; Acts 27:1). The use of the centurion's first name, "Julius," suggests that he may have been a Roman citizen since the emperor Claudius (AD 41–54) forbade noncitizens from identifying themselves on only a first name basis. This privilege was reserved for free citizens of Rome.[62] From the beginning to the end of Paul's journey to Rome, Julius treated Paul with consideration and respect, allowing him to go ashore and visit friends at Sidon (Acts 27:3), intervening to protect Paul's life during the shipwreck (Acts 27:42–43), and allowing Paul to stay with friends for a week in Puteoli before continuing the journey north by foot (Acts 28:14). There is no indication that Julius became a believer as a result of his time with Paul, but we can be assured that the apostle would not have missed the opportunity to share his faith.

SOLDIERS IN EARLY CHRISTIANITY

What becomes clear as we have considered the depictions of Roman soldiers in the record of the New Testament is "their persistently positive character despite the unsavory reputation soldiers enjoyed in other genres of ancient literature."[63] Besides the biblical references to centurions and the Roman military, a number of references in mosaic inscriptions shed light on the faith of Roman soldiers in early Christianity. One of the most recent was the discovery in 2005 of a mosaic floor featuring three inscriptions.[64] The inscriptions were found during an excavation by inmates of an Israeli prison in preparation for an expansion project. The prison was built near ancient Megiddo on a site where soldiers of the Sixth Roman Legion made camp in the time of the emperor Hadrian (AD 76–138) and remained there throughout most of the third century AD.[65] The site, which became known as Legio, was strategically located to control travel along a branch of the international coastal leading to Galilee and Damascus. According to Yotam Tepper, the Israeli archaeologist in charge of the excavation, the mosaic floor was part of a building which appears to have been a place for Christian worship. Since the building does not follow the traditional basilica plan of early churches, Tepper doesn't call it a church. He writes, "The Legio Christian hall of worship is certainly not a church in the architectural sense of the term."[66] But the

62. Simmons, *Peoples of the New Testament World*, 273n38, citing Suetonius, *The Twelve Caesars* 5.25.3.

63. Shean, *Soldiering for God*, 145.

64. Scott Wilson, "Site May Be 3rd Century Place of Christian Worship," *Washington Post Foreign Service* (November 7, 2005). See page 138 for an image of the Megiddo Prison Mosaic.

65. Matthew J. Adams, Jonathan David, and Yotam Tepper, "Legio: Excavations at the Camp of the Roman Sixth Ferrata Legion in Israel," *Biblical History Daily* (May 1, 2014), https://www.biblicalarchaeology.org/daily/biblical-sites-places/biblical-archaeology-sites/legio/.

66. Yotam Tepper and Leah Di Segni, *A Christian Prayer Hall of the Third Century CE at Kefar 'Othnay (Legio)*, (Jerusalem: Israel Antiquities Authority, 2006), 46.

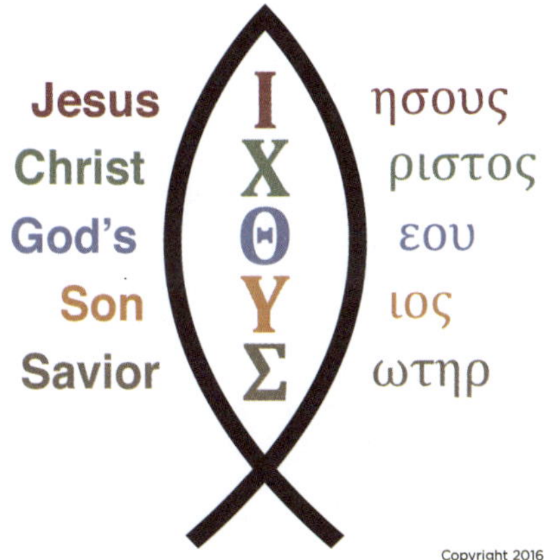

The ichthus (fish) was an early Christian symbol.

three inscriptions reveal a clear link with Christian worship during a time before Constantine legalized Christianity for the Roman empire.

The largest of the mosaics, featuring the early Christian symbol of two fish, includes an inscription in ancient Greek which reads, "Gaianos, also called Porphyrio, centurion, our brother, having sought honor with his own money, has made this mosaic. Brouti has carried out the work."[67] Other than the Bible, this is the earliest mention of a Roman army officer who appears to have been a follower of Jesus. Like the centurion at Capernaum who financed the building of the community synagogue (Luke 7:5), so this soldier had financed the creation of this mosaic. The inscription documents the faith of a Roman military officer before Christianity was recognized as an official religion. The second inscription mentions four women of the community. The third inscription is considered the most significant archaeologically. It reads, "The God-loving Aketous has offered this table to the God Jesus Christ, as a memorial."[68] The "table" may refer to an altar or, recalling the Last Supper, a place where Christians gathered to remember Jesus and celebrate the eucharist. The latter is suggested by the phrase, "as a memorial" (1 Cor. 11:24–25). In a press briefing, Tepper reported that the inscriptions "contribute to the study of the Roman army in the Eastern Roman Empire, Christian theology, the status of Christianity prior to the Byzantine period, and the cultural relations with the ancient Jewish settlement nearby."[69]

Excavations at the site of Dura-Europos, a fortress city located in modern Syria on the banks of the Euphrates River, provides evidence of the close association of the Roman military with early Christianity. The emperor Trajan occu-

67. Adams, David, and Tepper, "Legio."

68. Adams, David, and Tepper, "Legio."

69. "The Israel Antiquities Authority recommends the prison to be transferred to a new location," press release, 2006.

pied the city in AD 114, and it was later expanded and fortified by the Romans. Discoveries at the site include a Roman camp, a palace for the Roman commander, temples dedicated to various Greek and Roman gods, a Jewish synagogue and a house dedicated to Christian worship.[70] It is well known that the earliest Christian meeting places were private homes which were adapted and expanded to accommodate a gathering of believers.[71] Archaeologists at Dura-Europos uncovered a private residence joined to a "hall-like room" which apparently functioned as a meeting room. Graffiti on the walls leave no doubt that this was a meeting place for Christians. The graffiti read, "One God in heaven," "Remind Christ of Proclus among yourselves," and "Remind Christ of the humble Siseos."[72] Frescos on the walls of the baptistry room, featuring the Good Shepherd, the healing of the paralytic, and Jesus and Peter walking on the water, are believed to be some of the earliest depictions of the ministry of Jesus.[73] What is especially significant about this discovery is the fact that it was located in such close proximity to the Roman garrison. The fact that Roman soldiers tolerated the presence of a church in a major Roman garrison town "reveals that the history of the early Church was not simply a story of pagan persecution."[74]

One of the best known Roman soldiers who became an early follower of Jesus was Saint Sebastian, believed to have been martyred around AD 288 during emperor Diocletian's (AD 244–312) persecution of Christians. The accounts of Sebastian are blended with legend, but it is believed that he was born in Gaul, went to Rome, and joined the army during the reign of Marcus Aurelius Carinus (AD 283–285) who reigned in the western empire. Sebastian distinguished himself in his service to the emperor and was promoted to serve in the Praetorian Guard, the elite military group responsible for protecting the emperor. Sebastian became a follower of Jesus during a time when Christianity was not an authorized religion and converts were likely to be persecuted. His refusal to swear allegiance to the emperor led to the sentence of death by a firing squad of archers. According to legend, Sebastian was tied to a tree or a post and shot with arrows. He was left for dead, but he was rescued by a widow who nursed him back to health. Later he presented himself to Diocletian (AD 284–305) and rebuked him for persecuting Christians. Sebastian was then beaten to death with a club. His body was tossed in a sewer, but it was retrieved and buried near Rome's catacombs. The seventeenth century basilica of Saint Sebastian remembers the life of a Roman soldier who was a fervent and faithful follower of Jesus.[75]

---

70. Negev, *Archaeological Encyclopedia of the Holy Land*, 93.

71. Everett Ferguson, *Backgrounds of Early Christianity* (Grand Rapids: Eerdmans, 1987), 104.

72. Jack Finegan, *Light from the Ancient Past: The Archaeological Background of the Hebrew Christian Religion*, Vol. 2 (London: Oxford University Press, 1969), 449.

73. John McKay and Bennett Hill, *A History of World Societies* (New York: MacMillan, 2011), 166.

74. Simon James, "Dura-Europos: Pompeii of the Syrian Desert" (Simon James's Homepage, updated June 19, 2003), https://www.le.ac.uk/ar/stj/dura/index.htm.

75. Shean, *Soldiering for God*, 214–15.

While Saint Sebastian is probably one of the best known Roman soldiers who became a follower of Jesus, funerary epitaphs[76] identifying persons of faith in the Roman military indicate that there were others. Shean comments, "Surviving inscriptions represent the most tangible and unequivocal form of evidence we have for the presence of Christians in the Roman army."[77] Roman soldiers in the New Testament are an example of Gentile openness to the truth of the gospel. Cornelius and others in Rome's military led the way for Jew-gentile diversity in the body of Christ, the church.

BIBLIOGRAPHY

Adams, Matthew J., Jonathan David, and Yotam Tepper. "Legio: Excavations at the camp of the Roman Sixth Ferrata Legion in Israel." *Biblical History Daily* (May 1, 2014). https://www.biblicalarchaeology.org/daily/biblical-sites-places/biblical-archaeology-sites/legio/

Adkins, Lesley, and Roy Adkins. *Introduction to the Romans*. Secaucus, NJ: Chartwell Books, 1991.

Bedoyere, Guy de la. *Praetorian: The Rise and Fall of Rome's Imperial Bodyguard*. New Haven: Yale University Press, 2017.

Benoit, P. "The Archaeological Reconstruction of the Antonia Fortress." In *Jerusalem Revealed: Archaeology of the Holy City, 1968–1974*. Edited by Yigael Yadin. New Haven: Yale University Press, 1976.

Bouquet, A. C. *Everyday Life in New Testament Times*. New York: Charles Scribner's Sons, 1953.

Bruce, F. F. *The Book of Acts*. NICNT. Grand Rapids: Eerdmans, 1954.

Campbell, J. B. *The Emperor and the Roman Army*. Oxford: Clarendon Press, 1984.

Ferguson, Everett. *Backgrounds of Early Christianity*. Grand Rapids: Eerdmans, 1987.

Finegan, Jack. *The Archaeology of the New Testament*. Princeton: Princeton University Press, 1969.

———. *Light from the Ancient Past: The Archaeological Background of the Hebrew Christian Religion*. Vol. 2. London: Oxford University Press, 1969.

Geldenhuys, Norval. *Commentary on the Gospel of Luke*. NICNT. Grand Rapids: Eerdmans, 1951.

Gundry, Robert. *Matthew: A Commentary on His Literary and Theological Art*. Grand Rapids: Eerdmans, 1982.

James, Simon. "Dura-Europos: Pompeii of the Syrian Desert." Simon James's Homepage. Updated June 19, 2003. https://www.le.ac.uk/ar/stj/dura/index.htm.

Kraeling, Emil G. *Rand McNally Bible Atlas*. New York: Rand McNally, 1966.

Lendering, Jona "Judea," in www.livias.org/articles/place/Judaea Published 1997; last modified June 5, 2017.

Marshall, I. Howard *The Acts of the Apostles: An Introduction and Commentary*. TNTC. Grand Rapids: Eerdmans, 1980.

McKay, John, and Bennett Hill. *A History of World Societies*. New York: MacMillan, 2011.

76. An epitaph, from the Greek *epi* (upon) and *taphos* (tomb) is an inscription on a tombstone which is written in memory of the deceased.

77. Shean, *Soldiering for God*, 185.

Morris, Leon. *Luke: An Introduction and Commentary*. TNTC. Downers Grove, IL: InterVarsity Press, 1988.

Negev, Abraham, ed. *Archaeological Encyclopedia of the Holy Land*. Jerusalem: Weidenfeld & Nicolson, 1972.

Pobee, John. "The Cry of the Centurion—A Cry of Defeat." Pages 91–102 in *The Trial of Jesus*. Edited by Ernst Bammel. Naperville, IL: Alec R. Allenson Inc, 1970.

Rainey, Anson, and R. Steven Notley. *The Sacred Bridge*. Jerusalem: Carta, 2006.

Robertson, A. T. *Word Pictures in the New Testament*. 6 vols. Nashville: Broadman Press, 1930–1933.

Shean, John F. *Soldiering for God: Christianity and the Roman Army*. Leiden: Brill, 2010.

Simmons, William A. *Peoples of the New Testament World*. Peabody, MA: Hendrickson, 2008.

Tepper, Yotam, and Leah Di Segni. *A Christian Prayer Hall of the Third Century CE at Kefar 'Othnay (Legio)*. Jerusalem: Israel Antiquities Authority, 2006.

Van Elderen, B. "Some Archaeological Observations on Paul's First Missionary Journey." Pages 150–61 in *Apostolic History and the Gospel*. Edited by W. Ward Gasque and Ralph P. Martin. Exeter: Paternoster Press, 1970.

Wilkes, John. *The Roman Army*. Cambridge: Cambridge University Press, 1972.

Wilson, Scott. "Site May Be 3rd Century Place of Christian Worship." *Washington Post Foreign Service* (November 7, 2005).

CHAPTER 21

THE GEOGRAPHIC IMPORTANCE OF ANTIOCH ON THE ORONTES

Acts 6:5; 11:19–30; 13:1–3; 14:26–28; 15:1–3,22–35; 18:22–23

Elaine A. Phillips

KEY POINTS

- Third largest city of the Roman Empire in the first centuries BC and AD
- Strategic location between western and eastern geo-political entities
- Greco-Roman ideals and worldview deeply embedded in cultural fabric
- Early Christian community in Antioch was at the forefront of the move to include gentiles

GEOGRAPHICAL CONTEXT AND STRATEGIC LOCATION

The phrase, "on the Orontes," distinguishes this Antioch from five additional cities in Syria alone that bore the same name.[1] The headwaters of the Orontes River are in Lebanon's Beqaʿ Valley between the Lebanon and Anti-Lebanon mountain ranges. The river winds north for approximately two hundred miles (320 km) into Syria before swinging west, breaking through the Lebanon and Taurus ranges, and flowing southwest to the Mediterranean Sea. Antioch was founded approximately twenty miles (32 km) inland from what would become Seleucia Pieria, one of the best harbors on the eastern Mediterranean. In antiquity, the Orontes was navigable between Antioch and the sea.

1. Seleucus named ten more cities outside Syria Antioch in honor of his father; in remembrance of his mother, he named five cities Laodicea; his Persian wife, Apamea, garnered four named cities; and he named nine cities after himself (Fatih Cimok, *Antioch on the Orontes*, 2nd ed. [Istanbul: A Turizm Yayınları, 1994], 11–12).

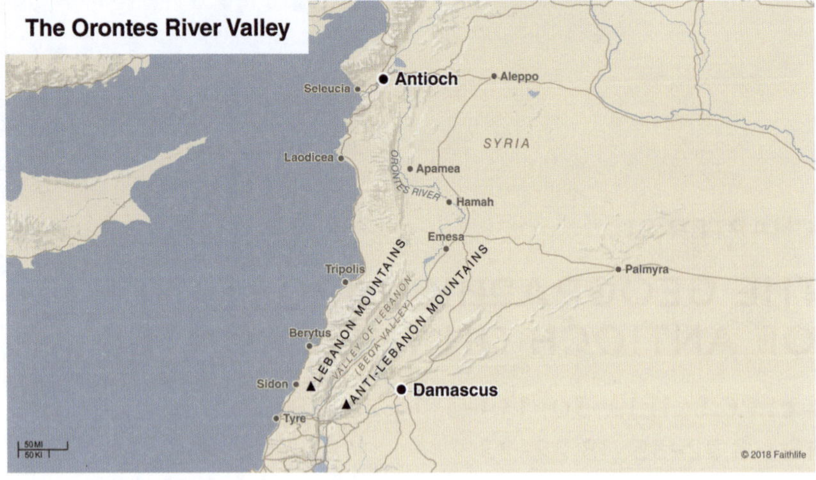

The ancient city was on the east side of the river at the edge of the Amuk plain.[2] Mount Silpius rose behind Antioch to the east. The Beilan pass provided access through the mountains to the north and west to the region of Cilicia. Antioch had control of the network of land connections between Anatolia, the upper Euphrates region, and points south. Seleucia and Antioch were at a key eastern Mediterranean terminus of the major Eurasian transport route, popularly called the "Silk Road."[3] Although only tracks across immense expanses of desert and mountains, this "modest non-road became one of the most transformative super highways in human history—one that transmitted ideas, technologies, and artistic motifs, not simply trade goods."[4]

The geological composition of the region is limestone. Much of the average rainfall (45 in. [114 cm] per year) percolates into natural underground cavities and fissures and issues forth in springs. Approximately five miles (8 km) to the south of Antioch lay the ancient city of Daphne, known for its abundant water supply. On the plateau around Daphne as well as the plain of Antioch, the staple crops of wheat, olive oil, and grapes, along with a variety of vegetable produce, made this an agriculturally desirable area. It was a beautiful location and

2. The following geographical summary is distilled from Glanville Downey, *A History of Antioch in Syria: From Seleucus to the Arab Conquest* (Princeton: Princeton University Press, 1961), 46–63. Strabo, *Geography* 16.2.4–8, describes the region and its primary cities.

3. Valerie Hansen, *The Silk Road: A New History* (Oxford: Oxford University Press, 2012), 6–8. The label was proposed in 1877 by a German geographer working in China.

4. Hansen, *Silk Road*, 5. The goods in transit were paper, spices, metals, saddles, glass, chemicals, in addition to silk—a relatively minor commodity. Chinese documents elucidate primarily the rich connections within China and indicate little direct connection with the Roman Empire. Nevertheless, as early as the fifth century BC, Herodotus (*Histories* 5.52–53) provided the continuity between Europe, Asia, and western China as he detailed the major thoroughfare across the whole of the Anatolian plateau as far as Susa.

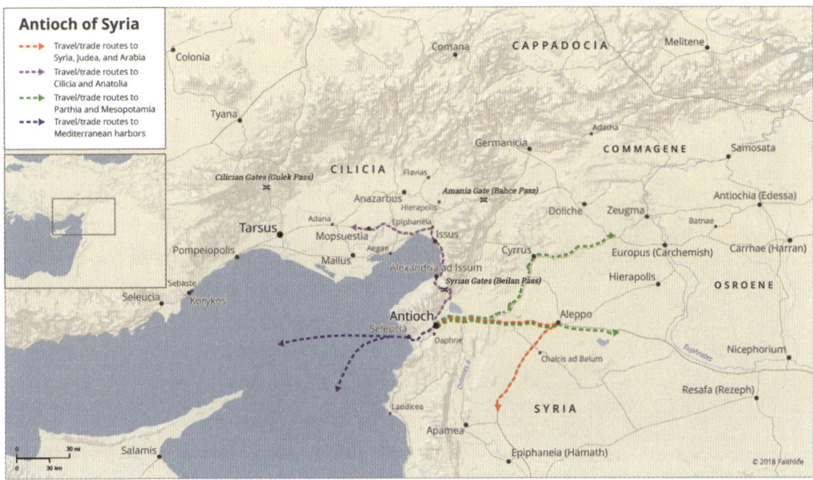

its distance from the coast enhanced the security factor; it took a day for hostile forces to arrive from the sea.

In antiquity, sources indicate that part of the expanded city lay on an island. This is a seismically active region and historical sources record a number of severe earthquakes. Some of them, along with river silting, have likely contributed to the disappearance of the separate island.

CULTURAL HISTORY

Although ancient legends about the origin of Antioch suggest that there may have been a settlement prior to the third century BC, the city was founded and named in 300 BC by Seleucus I Nicator.[5] In the aftermath of Alexander the Great's sweep across the eastern Mediterranean and his sudden death, the four top contenders to be his successor squabbled over the fracturing empire.[6] When Seleucus defeated Antigonus in 301 at Ipsus, he not only solidified his control over Syria and upper Mesopotamia; he also expanded his political control west to the Aegean Sea. Establishing his capi-

5. Cimok, *Antioch on the Orontes*, 9–10. Later rabbinic tradition claims that Nebuchadnezzer met with the Great Sanhedrin at Daphne, the southern suburb of Antioch (y. Sheqalim 6.2). For rabbinic Judaism, Antioch was an even more significant city than Alexandria. See Carl H. Kraeling, "The Jewish Community at Antioch," *JBL* 51 (1932): 132–33. For the founding by Seleucus I Nicator, see Strabo, *Geography* 16.2.4. See also Josephus, *Ant.* 12.119.

6. Downey's presentation of the history of the city is dependent on the work of John Malalas, a sixth century writer who lived in Antioch until the Persian conquest of the city in AD 540 when it seems he departed for Constantinople. His sweeping presentation of history starts with Adam, interfacing Old Testament narratives, Greek mythology, New Testament vignettes, and works of Apocrypha, often fancifully embellishing them (*The Chronicle of John Malalas*, translated by Elizabeth Jeffreys, Michael Jeffreys, Roger Scott et al. [Melbourne: Australian Association for Byzantine Studies, 1986]). In addition, the writings of Libanius, a fourth century philosopher native to Antioch, reflect the intellectual climate of the city. For an assessment of these sources, see Downey, *History of Antioch*, 38–42.

tal at this intersection between east and west was a bid for allegiance from both.[7]

Tetradrachm Bearing Image of Antiochus I Soter

One of the nine cities Seleucus named after himself was Seleucus Pieria, downriver from Antioch on the Mediterranean coast. It appears Seleucus originally intended that location as his capital, but his son, Antiochus I Soter, moved the capital upriver to Antioch. From the start, the population of Antioch was diverse, including Athenians, Macedonians, Cretans, and Cypriots, along with slaves and retired soldiers. At some point, Jews became a significant part of the community. Josephus claimed that the Jews in Antioch were accorded the same rights as Greek citizens by the successors to Antiochus Epiphanes.[8] They would have been surrounded by worshipers of Athena, Zeus, and Apollo (thought to be founders and protectors of the Seleucid dynasty), and an array of additional major and minor deities.[9]

Growing friction between the Seleucids and Rome during the reign of Antiochus III (223–187 BC) eventually led to his defeat at Magnesia (190 BC) and the treaty of Apamea (188 BC). His successor, Antiochus IV Epiphanes (175–163 BC), a former hostage in Rome and resident of Athens, had absorbed Greco-Roman culture and intended to upgrade Antioch accordingly. He added a temple for Jupiter Capitolinus, a new *agora* (ἀγορά), a *bouleutērion* (βουλευτήριον) where the council of elders met, and a new quarter of the city, called Epiphania. He celebrated extravagant games and associated himself with Zeus—thus the moniker *epiphanēs* (ἐπιφανής, "god manifest"). When Antiochus Epiphanes plundered the Jerusalem temple and took sacred vessels to Antioch, some Jews were taken captive as well.[10]

7. Downey, *History of Antioch*, 61.

8. *J.W.* 7.44. There is some discussion as to the implications of this statement. In *Ant.* 12.119, Josephus indicates that the Jews of Antioch had privileges immediately upon the founding of the capital because they served in the military for the Seleucid kings. See Appendix C in vol. 7 of *Antiquities* (LCL, trans. Ralph Marcus [Cambridge: Harvard University Press], 737–42) for consideration of these conflicting claims. Whenever those rights were granted, it is likely that since the time of the Seleucids, Jews generally had the right to follow their own laws and thus preserve their religious identity (Kraeling, "Jewish Community," 138–39). That would exempt them from participation in the civic polytheistic rituals.

9. Downey, *History of Antioch*, 75–76.

10. Details distilled from Downey, *History of Antioch*, 95–109. See also 1 Macc 1:23–24, 32, and Josephus, *Ant.* 12.251. Both Jewish and Christian sources refer to these captives as the "third exile" (y. Sanhhedrin 10.6; Wayne A. Meeks and Robert L. Wilkens, *Jews and Christians*

Bust of Antiochus III

Political developments in the second and first centuries BC were complicated by the threat of Parthians beyond the eastern frontier and interference from Egypt. Following the two-decade-long rule of Tigranes of Armenia, who had taken the city in 83 BC, Pompey annexed Syria to the Roman Empire in 64 BC and established Antioch as the capital of Syria, giving the region greater stability in the face of the uneasy Parthian frontier.[11]

When Julius Caesar arrived in Antioch in 47 BC, he gave the city freedom, anticipating their continued support in his civil war against the Senate. The benefits for Antioch included a new theater, an amphitheater, an aqueduct, and a basilica, named the Caesareum after himself.[12] After Caesar's assassination, Herod the Great marched to Antioch to help Mark Antony repulse the Parthian invasion of 40 BC. When Octavian (Augustus) defeated Antony at Actium in 31 BC, Herod succeeded in ingratiating himself with Augustus; Herod continued to visit and invest heavily in the city.[13] For his part, Augustus declared Syria an imperial province, and the legate of Syria was headquartered at Antioch along with anywhere between two and four legions.[14]

Bust of Caesar Augustus (Octavian)

Augustus visited Antioch twice (31–30 and 20 BC) and both visits spurred on extensive building activity, undertaken by Herod and others.[15] Antioch boasted

in Antioch in the First Four Centuries of the Common Era [Missoula, MT: Scholars Press, 1978], 3; Kraeling, "Jewish Community," 134).

11. Downey, *History of Antioch*, 143. The ongoing tensions on Rome's eastern frontier were interwoven with the geography of the region from Antioch to Damascus. See Fergus Millar, *The Roman Near East: 31 BC–AD 337* (Cambridge: Harvard University Press, 1993), 33–43.

12. Richard N. Longenecker, "Antioch of Syria," in *Major Cities of the Biblical World*, ed. R. K. Harrison (Nashville: Nelson, 1985), 12–13.

13. Kraeling, "Jewish Community," 133, 147.

14. Downey, *History of Antioch*, 151–64. See also Millar, *Roman Near East*, 31–33.

15. Downey, *History of Antioch*, 169.

the earliest monumental colonnaded thoroughfare—two Roman miles long (1.8 miles; 3 km) with 3200 columns—entertainment complexes, and temples to Jupiter Capitolinus, Dionysius, and Pan.[16] Cicero described Antioch, the third largest city in the empire, as "a renowned and populous city, the seat of brilliant scholarship and artistic refinement." (*Pro Archia* 4).

Bust of Gaius Caligula

In the third year of Gaius Caligula's reign (AD 40), however, several events, described by Malalas, rocked Antioch. One was a severe earthquake (AD 37); a second was the burning of synagogues in AD 40. While the details of the unrest that led to the synagogue attacks are obscure, there may have been a connection with the imprudent decision of Caligula to have a statue of himself placed in the Jerusalem temple. The protests against this desecration would have commenced with the Jewish leadership in Antioch as they appealed to the governor, Petronius. Anti-Jewish sentiment may have followed.[17] This reconstruction of events suggests a significant and visible Jewish population, conservatively estimated at about forty-five thousand in the time of Augustus and ranging upwards to sixty-five thousand in the following century.[18]

The reign of Claudius (AD 41–54) was marked by several years of famine in succession (AD 45–47) in Syria, Palestine, and Egypt (Acts 11:27–30) and another severe earthquake.[19] In AD 66, Vespasian's forces assembled at Antioch in order to deal with the unrest in Caesarea and Jerusalem that led to the first Jewish revolt and the destruction of the Second Temple in AD 70.[20] All of this was the backdrop for the early decades of the burgeoning church.

"FIRST CALLED 'CHRISTIANS' IN ANTIOCH"

Antioch's position between east and west, the heavy military presence, the deeply ingrained Hellenistic worldviews, and the long-standing Jewish community all contributed to the rich and complicated fabric of the city in the first century AD. The initial notice of Antioch in the New

16. Cimok, *Antioch on the Orontes*, 17.

17. Kraeling, "Jewish Community," 148–50. See also Meeks and Wilkins, *Jews and Christians*, 4, and Josephus' account (*Ant.* 18.261–72). The description of Malalas is quite different. He intimated that two factions that sound suspiciously like competing political parties began the devastating riot in the theater (*Chronicle* 10:20).

18. Kraeling, "Jewish Community," 136.

19. Longenecker, "Antioch of Syria," 17. See also Josephus, *Ant.* 20.51–53.

20. Downey, *History of Antioch*, 199, 201, 275–76. See further Meeks and Wilkins, *Jews and Christians*, 15–16.

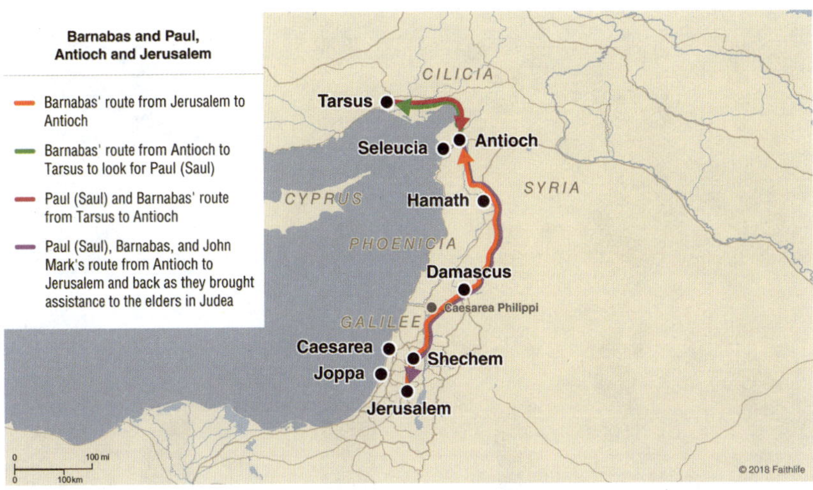

Testament concerns Nicolas, a convert to Judaism, who was chosen to serve the Jerusalem church (Acts 6:5). Perhaps he was among those pilgrims who responded to the message at Pentecost (Acts 2) and remained in Jerusalem rather than returning home. When refugees from persecution in Jerusalem fled following the martyrdom of Stephen, some of them came to Antioch and an intercultural ministry began as disciples from Cyprus and Cyrene preached not only to Hellenized Jews but also to Greeks (Acts 11:19–21).

As the believers were flourishing in this vibrant cultural environment, Barnabas was sent from the apostolic authorities in Jerusalem to monitor the community (Acts 11:22). Shortly thereafter, he brought Saul from Tarsus and they spent a year with the Antioch congregation (Acts 11:25–26). The designation "Christians" marked the movement at that point, although it is unclear why the label was originally given. Possibly it was originally intended by outsiders as a derogatory name, or perhaps Roman authorities used it to distinguish the new "sect."[21] The label did not seem to catch on until the end of the first century when Ignatius, third bishop of Antioch in the latter decades of the first century, warned against being called "Christians" but not living in a manner befitting of the name.[22] In the interval, Luke and Paul characteristically called believers in Jesus "the Way" as their recognition spread from Damascus (Acts 9:2) to Ephesus

21. Paul Trebilco, *Self-designations and Group Identity in the New Testament* (Cambridge: Cambridge University Press, 2012), 276–82; Downey, *History of Antioch*, 198, 275–76.

22. *Epistle to the Magnesians* 4. He also admonished his readers to live according to the principles of "Christianity" (*Magnesians* 10). In the longer recension of *Magnesians* 10, he made a point of saying that Isaiah's prophecy, "the people shall be called by a new name ... and shall be a holy people" (Isa 62:2, 12) was first fulfilled in Syria (i.e., Antioch), quoting Acts 11:26.

The cave church of St. Peter on Mount Silpius. According to tradition, it is here that Peter first preached in Antioch. The facade of the church was built during the Crusades.

(Acts 19:9, 23) and circled back around to Paul's witness in Jerusalem (Acts 22:4) and Caesarea (Acts 24:14, 22).

There was regular traffic between the Jerusalem church and Antioch. Prophets came from Jerusalem; Agabus predicted the famine that occurred during the reign of Claudius and accordingly the church in Antioch took up a collection for Jerusalem (Acts 11:27–30). Antioch was the scene of early Judaizing efforts (Acts 15:1–3; see also Gal 2:11–12), no doubt because it was perceived by all parties as wielding substantial influence. Following the decision of the council in Jerusalem, Paul and Barnabas, along with Judas and Silas, returned first to Antioch to deliver the letter from the council. Paul and Barnabas stayed for some additional time (Acts 15:22–35). At the crossroads for military and commercial traffic and the locus of east/west cultural exchange, Antioch was the perfect gateway to gentile ministry and served as the headquarters for Paul's missionary travels (Acts 13:1–3; 14:26–28; 18:22–23).

ANTIOCH AS A CENTER IN EARLY CHRISTIANITY

Antioch was a prominent center for the preservation and transmission of the biblical text in the tumultuous second and third centuries AD. In contrast to third-century Alexandria, where scribes were influenced by centuries of careful textual criticism, the focus in Antioch was a readable edition; at the end of the third century AD, Lucian of Antioch produced a recension of the Septuagint that smoothed out difficult readings.[23]

23. Kurt Aland and Barbara Aland, *The Text of the New Testament: An Introduction to the Critical Editions and to the Theory and Practice of Modern Textual Criticism*, trans. Erroll

The exegetical school in Antioch also reacted against the allegorical method that had dominated Alexandrian interpretation of Scripture since Philo's influential interpretive work for the Hellenistic Jewish community in the first century AD. The focus in Antioch was on the historical context and clear meaning of the text, perhaps influenced by the connections between Jews and Christians in the city.[24] Finally, interwoven with these textual and hermeneutical developments were complex ongoing challenges to orthodoxy, particularly as the Arian controversy swept through the church.[25]

BIBLIOGRAPHY

Aland, Kurt, and Barbara Aland. *The Text of the New Testament: An Introduction to the Critical Editions and to the Theory and Practice of Modern Textual Criticism*. Translated by Erroll F. Rhodes. Grand Rapids: Eerdmans, 1987.

Cicero. *Pro Archia*. Translated by N. H. Watts. LCL. Cambridge: Harvard University Press, 1923.

Cimok, Fatih. *Antioch on the Orontes*. 2nd ed. Istanbul: A Turizm Yayınları, 1994.

Comfort, Philip. *Encountering the Manuscripts: An Introduction to New Testament Paleography and Textual Criticism*. Nashville: Broadman & Holman, 2005.

Downey, Glanville. *A History of Antioch in Syria: From Seleucus to the Arab Conquest*. Princeton: Princeton University Press, 1966.

Eusebius. *The Church History*. NPNF2.1.

Hansen, Valerie. *The Silk Road: A New History*. Oxford: Oxford University Press, 2012.

Herodotus. *Histories*. Translated by A. D. Godley. 4 vols. LCL. Cambridge: Harvard University Press, 1922.

Ignatius. *Letter to the Magnesians*. *ANF* 1.

Josephus. *The Jewish War; Jewish Antiquities*. Translated by H. St. J. Thackeray et al. 9 vols. LCL. Cambridge: Harvard University Press, 1926–1965.

Kraeling, Carl H. "The Jewish Community at Antioch." *JBL* 51 (1932): 130–60.

Longenecker, Richard N. "Antioch of Syria." Pages 8–21 in *Major Cities of the Biblical World*. Edited by R. K. Harrison. Nashville: Nelson, 1985.

Malalas, John. *The Chronicle of John Malalas*. Translated by Elizabeth Jeffreys, Michael Jeffreys, Roger Scott et al. Melbourne: Australian Association for Byzantine Studies, 1986.

Meeks, Wayne A., and Robert L. Wilkens. *Jews and Christians in Antioch in the First Four Centuries of the Common Era*. Missoula, MT: Scholars Press, 1978.

Millar, Fergus. *The Roman Near East: 31 BC—AD 337*. Cambridge: Harvard University Press, 1993.

Strabo. *Geography*. Translated by Horace Leonard Jones. 8 vols. LCL.

F. Rhodes (Grand Rapids: Eerdmans, 1987), 64–65; Philip Comfort, *Encountering the Manuscripts: An Introduction to New Testament Paleography and Textual Criticism* (Nashville: Broadman & Holman, 2005), 262–79.

24. Meeks and Wilkins, *Jews and Christians*, 21–34; Kraeling, "Jewish Community," 155. We know there was significant contact as John Chrysostom warned his parishioners of the seductive attraction of the synagogue.

25. Downey, *History of Antioch*, 327–53.

Cambridge: Harvard University Press, 1917–1932.

Trebilco, Paul. *Self-designations and Group Identity in the New Testament*. Cambridge: Cambridge University Press, 2012.

CHAPTER 22

FAMINES IN THE LAND

Acts 11:27–30

Paul H. Wright

KEY POINTS

- Famine was an ever-present potential danger in ancient Israel and the Levant.
- Ancient Israel required at least twelve inches of rainfall annually to avoid drought and famine.
- The famine mentioned in Acts 11 caused severe grain shortages in Rome itself.

INTRODUCTION

The Hebrew word *ra'av* (רָעָב) and the Greek word *limos* (λιμός) both mean "hunger," but they can also refer to the most severe form of hunger—"famine." Famines, or the threat of famine, are mentioned frequently enough in the Bible for us to assume that the slow grip of starvation lurked ever at the door of ancient Israel, its reality sufficiently severe so as to be imbedded in the consciousness of everyone trying to wrest a living from Judea's stony heartland hills. The culminating testimony in Psalm 136, that great hymn of thanksgiving expressing the Lord's everlasting lovingkindness, (כִּי לְעוֹלָם חַסְדּוֹ, *ki le'olam hasdo*), is that he "gives food to every creature" (Ps 136:25).[1] This is indication enough that daily sustenance was never taken for granted in the ancient world, and that life was full enough if the hunger pains were gone. The ponderous language in the Bible, especially the Old Testament, about famine can be explained partly because the land of ancient Israel was so prone to them, and partly because the Bible's overall prophetic tenor prompted its authors to use the reality of famines as images of even larger realities, namely divine judgment and separation from God.

1. Unless otherwise indicated, Scripture quotations are from the New International Version (NIV).

Wheat Field in Upper Galilee

CAUSES AND CONDITIONS OF FAMINE

DROUGHT

Famine could strike the land of ancient Israel for any number of reasons. The most frequent, certainly, were climate related. Israel's homeland is a narrow band of territory, only partly arable, squeezed between the Mediterranean Sea and the north Arabian and Sinai deserts (see map on page 225). The severe drop of the Rift Valley cleaves this already thin band in two, drawing the arid landscape of the Sinai up into its heartland. Rainfall amounts average between twenty and forty inches (500–1000 mm) per year in the western, northern, and higher sections of the land, but a scant two to eight inches (50–200 mm) annually south, east, and in the lower parts of the Rift. The key factor is that the distance between the wet and the arid sections of the land is, in most places, only a few dozen miles (35–50 km). Rainfall, moreover, is seasonal, falling during the five to six months between the autumn (early) rains and the spring (latter) rains (Deut 11:14). The result is that in any given year, even the slightest shift in international weather patterns can tip the balance from being wet enough for bumper crops over to famine. The regions closest to, or facing, the slopes dropping out of the Judean hills toward the south and east, such as the Judean wilderness or sections of the Negev, are most vulnerable to crop failure due to a lack of adequate rainfall, though no region is exempt. Even Galilee, the most agriculturally productive region in the southern Levant, was subject to famine due to significant variations in climate.[2]

Year by year, the surest indicator of famine in ancient Israel was if rainfall amounts did not exceed twelve inches (300 mm) annually, the amount necessary for the staple of life, wheat, to mature. Grain crops (wheat and barley) are the most vulnerable since they are sown annually and have shallow root systems. Orchard crops (for example, olives, figs, pomegranates, and grapes), which are more typically found in the higher, wetter elevations, have deep roots and can withstand longer periods of drought.

There is no cause given in the book of Ruth for the famine that hit Bethlehem in the days of the judges (Ruth 1:1); we can explain it by lack of rainfall, but Bethlehem was never a town of abounding resources that could temper the effects of a bleak year when the harvest was poor.

The template examples of famine in the Bible are in the patriarchal narratives. As soon as Abram arrived in the marginal zone that was the Negev, the area that was to become his home, he faced a famine, (of course!), and so chose to move on to the storehouses of Egypt (Gen 12:9–10). A milder famine chased his son Isaac from Beer-sheva to Gerar, a Canaanite city state only ten miles (16 km) to the west; that is, Isaac moved from a portion of the Negev that receives six inches (150 mm) of rain annually to one that is blessed with more than twelve (300 mm) and hence is less susceptible to the ravages of famine (Gen 26:1). A generation later it was back to Egypt when a more severe famine again struck the land (Gen 41:56–42:5).

Because of the perennial (though fluctuating) flow of the Nile, the Tigris, and the Euphrates rivers, coupled with the possibility of irrigation, the Egyptian and Mesopotamian river civilizations were largely able to mitigate against famine in the ancient world. As a result, they tended to be places to which peoples from marginal lands such as Canaan would migrate for food. Still, a number of texts indicate that there were plenty of years in which the Nile flood was low and Egypt, too, was not able to feed its own population. These include the seven lean years (the years of gaunt cattle)[3] during the time of Joseph (Gen 41:1–55) as well as the century of Egypt's First Intermediate Period (Dynasties 7–10; approximately 2160–2055 BC). This latter period was a time of general disorder and economic decline across Egypt, where "the whole country [became] like locusts going upstream and downstream (in search of food)."[4]

2. Morten H. Jensen, "Climate, Droughts, Wars, and Famines in Galilee as a Background for Understanding the Historical Jesus," *JBL* 131 (2012): 315. See page 697 for a chart of the agricultural calendar of the Levant.

3. Illustrative reliefs of the effects of famine on people and cattle in Egypt can be seen in James B. Pritchard, *The Ancient Near East in Pictures Relating to the Old Testament* (Princeton: Princeton University Press, 1954), 101–2.

4. Ian Shaw, *The Oxford History of Ancient Egypt* (Oxford: Oxford University Press, 2000), 128–29. Note as well John A. Wilson, "The Admonitions of Ipu-Wer," in *Ancient Near Eastern Texts Relating to the Old Testament*, ed. James B. Pritchard (Princeton: Princeton University Press, 1955), 441–44; and Nili Shupak, "The Admonitions of an Egyptian Sage: The Admonitions of Ipuwer," in *Canonical Compositions from the Biblical World*, vol. 1 of *The Context of Scripture*, ed. William W. Hallo and K. Lawson Younger (Leiden: Brill, 1997), 93–98.

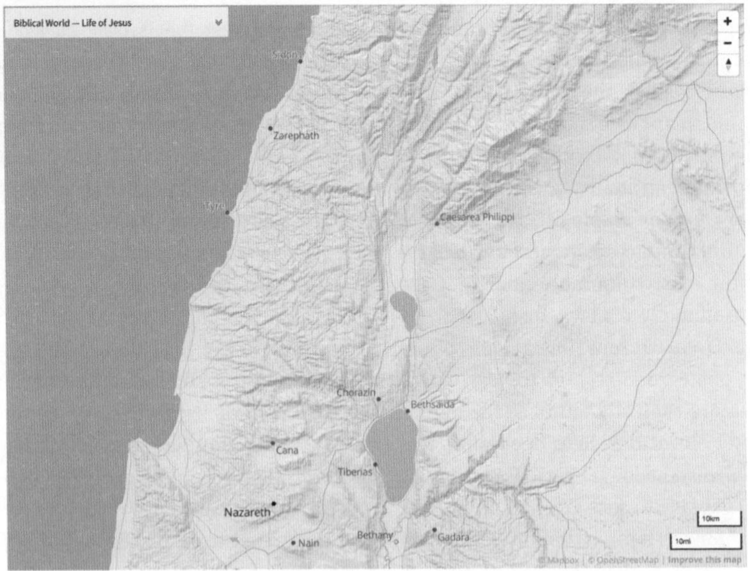

This reality of periodic famine in Egypt and the Levant persisted into the time of the New Testament. The Roman world was especially dependent on the grain harvests from the Nile Delta and northern Transjordan (the Bashan), and shortages there had an immediate impact on food supplies back in Rome.[5]

The port cities of Tyre and Sidon generally relied on foodstuffs from Israel to feed the workers who maintained the wealthy Phoenician trade network (Ezek 27:17; Acts 12:20). The downside was that in years of famine, the people of ancient Israel lacked the resource base from which to secure food for themselves. And it was their capital city, Jerusalem, that seems to have been especially prone to famine. There are perhaps two geographical reasons for this. One, of all of the cities on the watershed, it is toward Jerusalem that the eastern wilderness encroaches the closest. Second, Jerusalem lacks a sufficient number of easily arable fields in its immediate vicinity that could sustain its own growing population, especially in years of insufficient rainfall.

PESTILENCE OR PLAGUE

A second cause of famine in the ancient world was pestilence or plague, commonly understood to be swarms of locusts. Joel 1:4 mentions four kinds of locust (gnawing, swarming, creeping, then stripping) in a sequence of utter destruction:

> What the gnawing locust has left,
> the swarming locust has eaten;
> And what the swarming locust has left, the creeping locust has eaten;
> And what the creeping locust has

5. Bruce W. Winter, "Acts and Food Shortages," in *The Book of Acts in Its Graeco-Roman Setting*, ed. David W. J. Gill and Conrad Gempf, vol. 2 of *The Book of Acts in Its First Century Setting*, ed. Bruce W. Winter (Grand Rapids: Eerdmans, 1994), 61–69.

> left, the stripping locust has eaten.
> (Joel 1:4 NASB)

Unlike conditions of inadequate rainfall that developed slowly over the course of a year, swarms of locust could appear off the open desert suddenly, with no human recourse, and could devour a field of green wheat or barley in a few short hours. The threat of locust was eradicated from the Middle East only in the middle of the twentieth century AD, with the introduction of airplane-sprayed pesticides.

Locust

WAR

Famines were also caused by warfare, and here the consequences were devastating. The best-case scenario for the victim was when an enemy simply invaded his or her land, capturing and seizing the crops in the process. In the days of Gideon, bands of Midianites, Amalekites, and "other eastern peoples," all desert dwellers, pushed into the arable land of Israel. They were probably driven by hunger in the lands from which they came, and by devouring the fields of Israel "like swarms of locusts" (Judg 6:3, 5) created hunger in their wake. At least the people subdued could flee and try to find new fields to plant. Much more severe was the result of famine caused by siege. Here the goal was to cut off the food supply of a people huddled behind the walls of their city in order to force surrender. The walled cities in ancient Judah were places of political, military, or economic control, and so the object of particularly brutal attack during an invasion. Architectural evidence of storehouses and elaborate water systems in cities such as Megiddo, Hazor, Gezer, Beer-sheva, and Jerusalem attest to the measures taken to withstand prolonged siege. The biblical authors spared no detail in describing the effects of famine due to siege. The siege of Samaria by the Aramean king Ben-hadad in the days of Elisha the prophet was horrendous (2 Kgs 6:24–31), with the defenders of the city resorting to cannibalism. Nebuchadnezzar was able to break through the walls of Jerusalem only after a siege of eighteen months when the city's residents were weakened for lack of food (2 Kgs 25:3; Jer 52:6). Jerusalem faced severe famine again during the siege of Titus in AD 70; Josephus went to great length to describe the horrors its residents faced in the unfortunate choice of a quick death by the sword or a slow death by starvation (*J.W.* 6.193–213).

AN ACT OF GOD

A final cause of famine in the biblical world—and this is the one most often mentioned by the biblical writers—is that of a specific act of God. Sometimes famines were unexplained other than being due to the will of God (2 Kgs 8:1), a kind of fatalism that was common across the ancient world and remains so in much of the modern one. But more often the prophets used the threat of famine as a wake-up call to stir their stubborn and recalcitrant people to righteous living on the principle that pain is God's "megaphone to arouse a deaf world"[6] (for example, Deut 28:23–24; 1 Kgs 17:1). Frequently it is part of the triumvirate of judgment: "sword, famine, and plague" (2 Chron 20:9; Jer 14:12; 21:7; 24:10; Ezek 6:11–12). Having numbered Israel, David's God-imposed choice of retribution was seven years of famine, three months of the sword, or three days plague (2 Sam 24:13); in reality, famine was the normal end result of the other two. Ezekiel spoke of God's four severe judgments on Jerusalem: the sword, famine, wild beasts, and plague (Ezek 14:21); John's vision included the four horses of the apocalypse: conquest, war, famine, and death (Rev 6:1–6). In each instance, a progression can be seen: war leads to famine, which leads to desperate beasts, which leads to death.

CONDITIONS OF POVERTY

Each of these causes of famine was aggravated by general conditions of poverty that seemed to blanket most of the ancient world, most of the time. Herodotus (*Histories* 7.102.1) noted that "poverty is always the foster-sister of Greece," a fifth-century BC version of what is more familiar to us in Dicken's London: "This boy is Ignorance. This girl is Want."[7] Jesus was nothing but realistic when he said, "For you will always have the poor among you" (John 12:8), acknowledging a mass of people trapped in subsistence living, barely eking out an existence, living on the edge of hunger and want, consumed by the daunting task of sheer physical survival. At least the masses living in the countryside could forage for wild vines and grubs (2 Kgs 4:39). Every year held the potential of two hungry gaps, one just before the spring harvest and another before the summer fruit ripened, when the stores ran low and what was left to eat was likely spoiled, rancid or moldy. "'What makes bitter things sweet?' asked Alcuin, the Yorkshire schoolmaster who went to reform Frankish education for the emperor Charlemagne in the eighth century. 'Hunger.'"[8]

FAMINES IN SECOND TEMPLE LITERATURE

Our sources from the Second Temple period mention several instances of food shortages or famine in Judea, some caused by siege, others by natural disaster, and most, perhaps not coincidentally, coinciding with a political disaster that tightened the screws of foreign control over the Jewish homeland.[9] During the Maccabean struggle for independence, the city of Beth-zur north of Hebron surrendered to the Seleucid king Antiochus V Eupator after running out of food (1 Macc 6:48–54; Josephus, *Ant.* 12.378). The sources note that the food supply throughout the land was low due to the Sabbatical year, during which fields lay fallow (see Exod 23:10–11; Lev 25:1–7). In 63 BC, the year that Pompey brought Judea under Roman political control, a strong wind devastated the crops of the

---

6. C. S. Lewis, *The Problem of Pain* (New York: Macmillan, 1973), 81.

7. Charles Dickens, *A Christmas Carol*, stave 3. (London: Chapman & Hall, 1843), 118.

8. Robert Lacey and Danny Danziger, *The Year 1000: What Life was Like at the Turn of the First Millennium* (London: Little, Brown, 1999), 57.

9. A listing and discussion is provided by Joachim Jeremias, *Jerusalem in the Time of Jesus: An Investigation into Economic and Social Conditions during the New Testament* (London: SCM, 1969), 140–144 and Jensen, "Climate, Droughts, Wars, and Famines in Galilee," 319–22.

Terrain near the Dead Sea

whole country, resulting in hunger and severe inflation (Josephus, *Ant.* 14.28).

Famine gripped Jerusalem in 37 BC as Herod the Great laid siege to the city, his culminating conquest of the province of Judea (Josephus, *Ant.* 14.471; *J.W.* 1.347). Again, Josephus noted that the famine was aggravated because it was the Sabbatical year. In Herod the Great's thirteenth year, 25–24 BC, a prolonged drought caused famine, sickness, and plague throughout Judea. People resorted to butchering their flocks for something to eat, which resulted in a shortage of wool for clothing (*Ant.* 15.299–316). Josephus added that Herod himself suffered for want of tax revenue as a result. But perhaps the most gruesome famine in the Second Temple Period was that which was caused by Titus' siege of Jerusalem in AD 70 (*J.W.* 6.193–213).

FAMINE DURING THE REIGN OF CLAUDIUS

The famine most noted in the New Testament is the one that struck the Roman world during the reign of Claudius, mentioned in Acts 11:27–28:

> During this time some prophets came down from Jerusalem to Antioch. One of them, named Agabus, stood up and through the Spirit predicted that a severe famine would spread over the entire Roman world. (This happened during the reign of Claudius).

Several contemporary sources also mention this famine.[10] The Roman senator and historian Tacitus records that Rome suffered a shortage of grain during the reign of Claudius (AD 41–54); at one point there was enough food in the city to last

10. See Peter Garnsey, *Famine and Food Supply in the Graeco-Roman World: Responses to Risk and Crisis* (Cambridge: Cambridge University Press, 1988); Winter, "Acts and Food Shortages," 63–65.

no more than fifteen days. The crowds turned against the emperor and mobbed him in the Forum; he escaped only by the intervention of troops. Much of Rome's grain supply came from Egypt; Tacitus bemoaned the fact that "the life of the Roman nation has been staked upon cargo-boats and accidents" (*Annales* 13.43). Writing a century and a half after the event, Dio Cassius mentioned that Claudius, prompted by a famine caused by shortages in Rome's import of grain, made improvements in the harbor of Rome (*Roman History* 60.11). Josephus added that the famine occurred in Tiberius Alexander's term as procurator of Judea (AD 46–48), and that it was severe enough to cause hyperinflation (*Ant.* 3.320–21; 20.101).

Joachim Jeremias notes that the year 47–48 was a Sabbatical year, so that if the harvest had failed the year prior, the effects of the famine would have been multiplied.[11] This suggestion rests on two premises, both doubtful. The first is that enough people kept the Sabbatical year so as to make a significant difference in the total amount of crops harvested; the second is that, facing the very real consequences of famine that included starvation, sickness, and even death, the religious scruples of the populace would override their pangs for survival.

EFFECTS OF FAMINE

The Bible and contemporary sources provide enough descriptions of famine for us to weave together a patterned sequence of its effects, from anxiety to hunger to desperate acts of survival and then death. The timeframe could unfold over years (Gen 45:6–7; 2 Kgs 8:1), with innumerable moments to consider one's fate or devise urgent means of survival. The first anxious moments, which happen nearly every autumn, accompany the changing weather patterns when wind-driven clouds blow in from the west but carry no rain (Prov 25:14). The ground cracks; the cisterns run dry; the wild donkeys stand on bare heights to sniff the air for moisture (Jer 14:3–6). The weather is capricious—one city has rain; its neighbor doesn't (Amos 4:7–8). Slowly but surely the grass withers everywhere and springs dry to a trickle (1 Kgs 18:5). The livestock also suffers, and farmers everywhere have to decide whether or not to slaughter their animals so they themselves can eat (1 Kgs 17:7; 18:5). Wild animals are also affected, and so climb up into to the settled areas to rip and tear into whatever livestock they can still find (Ezek 5:17). In a normal year, the dry roots of desert plants revive with the scent of water (Job 14:7–9); in years of famine, the roots themselves are killed (Isa 14:30). Farmers may sow much but harvest little; their families eat, but never enough to be satisfied; sheep produce wool, but their coats are not sufficient to weave warm clothing (Hag 1:6). Eventually the people are weakened for lack of nutrition, especially the young who, lacking body mass, faint in the streets (Lam 2:11–12). The body no longer contains enough moisture to sweat, with the skin becoming hot as an oven (Lam 5:10); Josephus adds that "famine courses through [the victim's] intestines and marrow" (*J.W.* 6.204), driving people to acts of desperation. It would have been better, the writer of Lamentations notes, to have been killed suddenly by the sword than to waste away in the agony of hunger (Lam 4:9–10).

11. Jeremias, *Jerusalem in the Time of Jesus*, 143.

The Negev

At this point, our sources pull no punches in describing the desperate means to which hunger-stricken people will go to live, "snatching from each other the pitiful supports of life" (Josephus, *J.W.* 6.194). These are, perhaps, the most extreme indicator of the human drive to survive. Inflation runs wild, with people paying exorbitant prices to eat things not fit or proper for human consumption. Bits of salt plants and deserts shrubs (Job 30:4), tufts of withered grass (Josephus, *J.W.* 6.198) and pig food (Luke 15:14–16) end up on the menu, with doves' dung (Heb. חֲרֵי־יוֹנִים , *hare yonim*, a hapax legomenon; 2 Kgs 6:25) and even human excrement (2 Kgs 18:27) fair game. Josephus spoke of people trapped in Jerusalem during the siege of Titus who gnawed at "objects which even the filthiest of brute beasts would reject" such as shoe and belt leather (*J.W.* 6.197). A comparative instance is reported by Bar Hebraeus, who wrote of people forced to "pick the grains of barley from the dung of horses and donkeys and eat them"[12] during a severe famine that struck the Middle East in the tenth century AD. Worst of all was cannibalism, which the biblical writers and Josephus recount with horror (2 Kgs 6:28–29; Lam 4:10; *J.W* 6.201–13). Disease runs rampant (Jer 14:18); families are destroyed with no one left to mourn or bury the dead (Jer 14:16; 16:4). The ramifications for social and political instability are enormous, with classical sources speaking of riots and civil unrest in times of severe grain shortage.[13] Seneca summed up the situation curtly: "Hungry people do not listen to reason" (*On the Shortness of Life* 18.5).

RESPONSES TO FAMINE

Faced with these prospects, what recourse did people have? One was to turn to the local fertility gods and god-

12. Bar Hebraeus, *Ktābā d-maktbānūt zabnē*, E. A. Wallis Budge, ed. and trans., *The Chronography of Gregory Abu Faraj* (Oxford: Oxford University Press, 1932), 1:164.

13. Winter, "Acts and Food Shortages," 69–71; Jensen, "Climate, Droughts, Wars, and Famines in Galilee," 322–24.

desses; the need to overcome capricious weather patterns was likely the reason that there were so many of them in the first place! Sometimes, we read in the sources, governments or wealthy benefactors got involved.[14] Josephus noted that during the prolonged drought of 25–24 BC, Herod the Great was not able to by grain from his near neighbors since they, too, were affected by the conditions, and he lacked the available cash reserves to purchase grain anyway. To compensate, Herod cut up the gold and silver decorations of his palace to buy grain from Egypt, ever the ancient world's granary, and rationed it as food and seed to his own people as well as to the neighboring provinces (*Ant.* 15.306–9). Josephus added that Herod's motives were utilitarian: to gain political favor among the people.

Josephus also recorded the story that during the reign of Claudius, Queen Helena of Adiabene visited Jerusalem and found the city "hard pressed by famine, and many were perishing from want of money to purchase what they needed" (*Ant.* 20.51–53). Ever the ready benefactor, the queen purchased grain and dried figs from Egypt to relieve the hungry people of Judea. Her favor is recorded as being genuine.

But since the generosity of benefactors or government programs aimed at mitigating the ravages of famine were liable to be infrequent, unreliable, and of mixed motives, the masses typically must have fallen back to whatever devices they could muster, seizing or relying on whatever human or natural resources lay at hand. Elimelech and Naomi, for instance, chose to leave their Bethlehem home for the higher, wetter tableland of Moab off to the east (Ruth 1:1); at least that region was home to distant kinfolk, the tribe of Reuben (Num 32:1–5).

For their part, the earliest Christians gained the reputation of helping each other, whatever the need (Acts 2:44–47; 5:1–2). The Apostle Paul reported that churches in Macedonia and Achaia, which were certainly more prosperous than their Judean counterparts, collected offerings "for the poor among the saints in Jerusalem" (Rom 15:26). And so it is fitting that the writer of the book of Acts uses the famine that hit Jerusalem during the reign of Claudius to point out the generosity of the church in Antioch, a prosperous city on the main trade route connecting the Mediterranean Sea with the Upper Euphrates: "The disciples, each according to his ability, decided to provide help for the brothers living in Judea. This they did, sending their gift to the elders by Barnabas and Saul" (Acts 11:29–30; see also Gal 2:10). The helpful camaraderie of the early church gained renown. Through it, the consequences of a famine "of hearing the words of the LORD" (Amos 8:11) were also alleviated.

BIBLIOGRAPHY

Budge, E. A. Wallis, ed. and trans. *The Chronography of Gregory Abu Faraj*. 2 vols. Oxford: Oxford University Press, 1932.

Dickens, Charles. *A Christmas Carol*. London: Chapman & Hall, 1843.

Dio Cassius. *Roman History*. Translated by Earnest Cary. 9 vols. LCL. Cambridge: Harvard University Press, 1914–1927.

Garnsey, Peter. *Famine and Food Supply in the Graeco-Roman World: Responses*

14. Winter, "Acts and Food Shortages," 72–75.

to Risk and Crisis. Cambridge: Cambridge University Press, 1988.

Herodotus. *Histories*. Translated by A. D. Godley. Revised edition. 4 vols. LCL. Cambridge: Harvard University Press, 1938–1946.

Jensen, Morten H. "Climate, Droughts, Wars, and Famines in Galilee as a Background for Understanding the Historical Jesus." *JBL* 131 (2012): 307–24.

Jeremias, Joachim. *Jerusalem in the Time of Jesus: An Investigation into Economic and Social Conditions during the New Testament*. London: SCM, 1969.

Josephus. *Jewish Antiquities*. Translated by H. St. J. Thackeray. 9 vols. LCL. Cambridge: Harvard University Press, 1930–1965.

———. *The Jewish War*. Translated by H. St. J. Thackeray. 3 vols. LCL. Cambridge: Harvard University Press, 1927–1930.

Lacey, Robert, and Danziger, Danny. *The Year 1000: What Life Was Like at the Turn of the First Millennium*. London: Little, Brown, 1999.

Lewis, C. S. *The Problem of Pain*. New York: Macmillan, 1973.

Pritchard, James B. *The Ancient Near East in Pictures Relating to the Old Testament*. Princeton: Princeton University Press, 1954.

Seneca. *On the Shortness of Life*. Translated by John W. Basore. LCL. Cambridge: Harvard University Press, 1932.

Shaw, Ian. *The Oxford History of Ancient Egypt*. Oxford: Oxford University Press, 2000.

Shupak, Nili. "The Admonitions of an Egyptian Sage: The Admonitions of Ipuwer." Pages 93–98 in *Canonical Compositions from the Biblical World*. Volume 1 of *The Context of Scripture*. Edited by William W. Hallo and K. Lawson Younger. Leiden: Brill, 1997.

Tacitus. *Annals*. Translated by John Jackson. 3 vols. LCL. Cambridge: Harvard University Press, 1931–1937.

Wilson, John A. "The Admonitions of Ipu-Wer." Pages 441–444 in *Ancient Near Eastern Texts Relating to the Old Testament*. Edited by James B. Pritchard. Princeton: Princeton University Press, 1955.

Winter, Bruce W. "Acts and Food Shortages." Pages 59–78 in *The Book of Acts in Its Graeco-Roman Setting*. Edited by David W. J. Gill and Conrad Gempf. Volume 2 of *The Book of Acts in Its First Century Setting*, Edited by Bruce W. Winter. Grand Rapids: Eerdmans, 1994.

CHAPTER 23

THE DEATH OF HEROD AGRIPPA I IN CAESAREA MARITIMA

Acts 12:5–23

Todd Bolen

KEY POINTS

- Agrippa I's rule over Galilee, Samaria, Perea, and Judea constituted a return to the glory days of King Herod.
- The accounts of Josephus and the book of Acts are complementary and provide a fuller report of the events surrounding the death of Agrippa.
- An analysis of Josephus' account reveals that Herod Agrippa I died in the hippodrome, not the theater.
- The Jewish king Agrippa was struck down for accepting praise as a god not far from the temple where the Roman emperor was worshiped as a god.

INTRODUCTION

The reign of Herod Agrippa I marked an astonishing return to power for the waning Herodian dynasty.[1] When King Herod died in 4 BC, his kingdom was divided among three of his sons. Within a decade, his son Archelaus was deposed and his territory in Judea turned over to a Roman prefect. The other two sons, Antipas and Philip, continued to rule over other regions, but more than three decades passed before Herod's grandson, Agrippa I, was able to regain control over the full extent of Herod's former domain (see page 705 for a chart of the Herodian dynasty). This restoration came about through Agrippa's savvy political skills and the relationships he developed with the imperial family in the years he lived in Rome.

The focus of this essay is on Herod Agrippa's gruesome death in Caesarea,

1. This essay incorporates material previously posted at *The Bible and Interpretation*, http://www.bibleinterp.com/opeds/agrippa357926.shtml. Used by permission.

reported both in the book of Acts and in Josephus' *Antiquities*. But the story is more impressive when one is aware of Agrippa's meteoric rise to power. Within the span of one year, from AD 36 to 37, Agrippa went from a Roman prison cell to ruler over the northern territories of Philip and Lysanias in Gaulanitis, Trachonitis, Batanea, and Abilene (see map on page 11). Agrippa's imprisonment was the result of an impertinent remark suggesting his preference for Caligula over Tiberius, but when the former became emperor, Agrippa was rewarded for his loyalty. Within two years, Agrippa was given the title of king and granted the territories of Galilee and Perea in place of his deposed uncle, Herod Antipas. Two years later, in AD 41, Caligula was dead and Agrippa's presence in Rome facilitated the installment of Claudius as the next emperor. Again Agrippa was rewarded, this time with consular rank and the addition of Judea, Samaria, and Idumea to his kingdom. For the first time in thirty-five years, Jerusalem was ruled by a Jew, and Agrippa was on the verge of surpassing his grandfather's power and prestige.[2]

With the tremendous support of Rome in place, Agrippa also sought to ingratiate himself with the Jewish people. He reduced taxes, began construction on Jerusalem's "Third Wall," and honored the Jewish laws (Josephus, *Ant.* 19.293, 299, 326).[3] When Caligula attempted to install a statue of himself in the Jerusalem temple, Agrippa intervened so that the edict was canceled (Josephus, *Ant.* 18.289–304). In several regional disputes, Agrippa acted on behalf of the Jews (Josephus, *Ant.* 19.300–311). His efforts succeeded admirably, for later Jewish writings speak highly of this king (m. Bikkurim 3:4; m. Sotah 7:8). This is the backdrop for Agrippa's persecution of the early church.

Head of Agrippa Based on Depiction from Coin

Agrippa's execution of the apostle James and his imprisonment of the apostle Peter certainly encouraged the Jewish leaders who were strongly opposed to the budding Christian movement (Acts 12:1–4). It must have seemed that his power was absolute and his popularity ever-increasing. Only a few years into his reign, Agrippa seemed unstoppable, and the church must have felt quite vulnerable. But the Lord was at work, and in response to the prayers of the believers, Peter was set free and Agrippa was struck down (Acts 12:5–23). The circumstances of the king's death are intriguing, and this essay will look at the details of that event, with a particular focus on its location as reported by Josephus.

2. Though King Herod is popularly known as "Herod the Great," this title was never used for him in his lifetime. By contrast, Agrippa used the title for himself (Peter Richardson, *Herod: King of the Jews and Friend of the Romans* [Minneapolis: Fortress, 1999], 12, 211, 313).

3. All translations of Josephus are from Whiston.

THE ACCOUNTS OF ACTS AND JOSEPHUS

The death of Herod Agrippa I is one of the few events that is reported by both the book of Acts and Josephus (Acts 12:19-23; *Ant.* 19.343-50). Most scholars believe that the two reports had independent sources, and though they agree in several respects, Josephus' longer account contains more details, including the incident's occasion, location, and aftermath.[4] Acts records that Herod gave the address in Caesarea, and Josephus places it in the theater of Caesarea. Acts does not say anything about the time of day, but Josephus writes that it occurred early in the morning.

Acts connects the episode with the resolution of a quarrel with the people of Tyre and Sidon but says of the public address itself only that it occurred "on the appointed day." Josephus relates that Agrippa appeared to the crowd on the second day of a festival intended to honor Caesar. Both sources speak of Herod's clothing, but whereas Acts says simply that he was "wearing his royal robes," Josephus describes the garments as made "wholly of silver" and when "illuminated by the fresh reflection of the sun's rays ... was so resplendent as to spread a horror over those that looked intently upon him" (*Ant.* 19.344). Josephus indicates that the crowd hailed Agrippa as a god because of his radiant clothing, but Luke's brief account may imply that they did so in response to the sound of Agrippa's voice. Both agree that Agrippa accepted the crowd's enthusiastic praise and died shortly thereafter.

HEROD AGRIPPA'S RESIDENCE IN CAESAREA

Excavations at Caesarea are helpful in reconstructing this event.[5] The city had been founded by King Herod in 22 BC as a port city to connect the land of Israel to the West. Agrippa had surely sailed in and out of the city's harbor on his many journeys to Rome. Overlooking the harbor, a temple dedicated to the emperor and the goddess Roma appealed to the city's gentile residents.

Unlike the Roman prefects who preceded him, Agrippa chose not to live in Caesarea. Instead he opted to dwell in Jerusalem, residing in his grandfather's palace on the city's Western Hill. Sometime after the Passover in which he had planned to bring Peter to trial, Agrippa traveled down to Caesarea to stay for a time. Here he undoubtedly took up residence in Herod's promontory palace, for we know that both his predecessor Marullus and his successor Felix lived here (Acts 23:35).[6] This palace was situated in close proximity to the city's theater and hippodrome, and its western wing was surrounded on three

---

4. One who argues that Acts is dependent upon Josephus is Richard I. Pervo, *Acts: A Commentary* (Minneapolis: Fortress, 2009), 301, 312–13. Among those who see the accounts as independent is Colin J. Hemer, *The Book of Acts in the Setting of Hellenistic History*, ed. Conrad H. Gempf (Tübingen: Mohr Siebeck, 1989), 166.

5. For more extended discussions of the city, see the essays by Paul H. Wright, "Geography of Caesarea Maritima"; and John A. Beck, "Peter's Ministry in Caesarea Maritima," chapter 19 in this volume.

6. Eckhard J. Schnabel, *Acts*, expanded digital ed. (Grand Rapids: Zondervan, 2012), Acts 12:18–19.

Promontory Palace of King Herod

sides by the Mediterranean Sea.[7] The upper palace included an audience hall, a complex of rooms, and a large peristyle courtyard. On the morning in which he was struck down, Agrippa left this palace and proceeded to his appointed place to address the crowd.

THE OCCASION AND LOCATION OF HEROD AGRIPPA'S DEATH

According to Josephus, Agrippa's speech and subsequent demise occurred in the theater (θέατρον, *theatron*). On this basis, tourists today visit the Herodian theater and envision the event occurring in this semi-circular entertainment venue. A closer analysis of Josephus' account, however, indicates that the hippodrome, rather than the theater, was the setting for Herod's public address.[8]

The first clue in Josephus that suggests this location is the speech's timing at "the beginning of the day" (ἀρχομένης ἡμέρας, *archomenēs hēmeras*). Dressed in a

7. Netzer, Burrell, and Gleason identified this as a palace built by King Herod (Ehud Netzer, *The Architecture of Herod, the Great Builder* [Tübingen: Mohr Siebeck, 2006], 106–12), but excavations by the Israel Antiquities Authority date its construction to the early Roman governors (Yosef Porath, "Caesarea: The Israel Antiquities Authority Excavations," *NEAEHL* 5:1658). Josephus states that Herod adorned the city with a "very costly palace" (*Ant.* 15.331). Richardson observes the architectural similarities between this palace and those attributed to Herod at Jericho, Masada, and Herodium (Richardson, *Herod*, 181). Whether built during Herod's rule or after, the palace would have properly belonged to Agrippa when he was king.

8. It should be noted that what Josephus called an "amphitheater" is considered by scholars today to be a circus/hippodrome or a hippo-stadium on the basis of clear evidence of horse-racing activity (Porath, "Caesarea," 1658; Joseph Patrich, "Caesarea: The Combined Caesarea Expeditions Excavations; Areas CC, KK, and NN," *NEAEHL* 5:1675; Netzer, *Architecture*

Aerial View of the Ruins of Caesarea Maritima

garment made "wholly of silver," Agrippa dazzled the crowd when his robes were "illuminated by the fresh reflection of the sun's rays upon it." The theater, however, faces west. If the king was positioned on the stage, the sun would not have reached over the multistoried seating area before midmorning. And if he was speaking from a throne in the seating area, the sun would not have reflected off his clothes until even later. The hippodrome, by contrast, has only twelve rows of seating, and the sun would have quickly risen over them. Agrippa may well have been addressing the crowd from the western side of the hippodrome where the sun reflected off his clothes early in the morning.

The second indication that Agrippa was struck down in the hippodrome is the occasion of his death. Acts says only that it transpired "on the appointed day" (τακτῇ δὲ ἡμέρᾳ, *taktē de hēmera*), but Josephus describes the event occurring on the second day of a festival in honor of Caesar in which a great multitude was assembled. Scholars identify this festival with either the quinquennial celebration of the city's founding, on March 5, AD 44, or a celebration of Emperor Claudius' birthday on August 1 of that same year. The former was originally organized by King Herod in 12 BC.[9] It was styled after the Olympic Games, but called "Caesar's Games" (Josephus, *J.W.* 1.415). These games included combats and horse races (Josephus, *Ant.* 16.136–41), and were conducted in the hippodrome, not in the theater, as the latter was designed for dramatic performances. The emperor's birthday was also celebrated with sporting events, and so this occasion also best suits a setting in the hippodrome.

A third piece of supporting evidence can be adduced from Josephus' report of

of Herod, 118). As will be shown below, Josephus' imprecise terminology here supports the conclusion of this study.

9. Richardson, *Herod*, 282 n. 85.

Hippodrome of Caesarea

an encounter between Pilate and a large crowd about a decade earlier (*J.W.* 2.172). When the Roman governor sent standards with Caesar's image into Jerusalem, a large delegation traveled to Caesarea to entreat Pilate to remove these offensive placards. Josephus writes that "on the next day Pilate sat upon his *bēma* [βῆμα] in the great stadium [μεγάλῳ σταδίῳ, *megalō stadiō*]."[10] The word for stadium more naturally refers to the hippodrome, particularly with the modifier "great."[11] Luke's reference to the *bēma* as the location for Agrippa's speech likely refers to this same *bēma*.[12]

Finally, it should be noted that Josephus' use of terms designating buildings of entertainment is known to be imprecise. Regarding Jerusalem he states at one point that Herod built a theater and an amphitheater (*Ant.* 15.268), and elsewhere he mentions a hippodrome (*J.W.* 2.44; *Ant.* 17.255). None of these buildings have been discovered in Jerusalem today, and most scholars conclude that only one of them, or at most two, existed, and that Josephus referred to a single building by multiple terms. The Jerusalem model at the Israel Museum, for instance, reconstructs only a theater.[13] In other words, if Josephus could refer to an amphitheater as a hippodrome in Jerusalem, he certainly could have identified a hippodrome as a theater in Caesarea. He appears to have made precisely this mistake in describing sporting events and horse races as occurring in the theater of Jerusalem (*Ant.* 15.269–85).[14]

The lines of evidence thus converge to locate the hippodrome of Caesarea as the place where the Roman governor's *bēma* was located, and it was here where the crowds gathered to hear Agrippa's address in advance of the day's games.

10. Whiston incorrectly translates *megalō stadiō* as "open market place."

11. Henry George Lidell, Robert Scott, and Henry Stuart Jones, "στάδιον," *A Greek-English Lexicon.* 9th ed. with revised supplement (New York: Oxford University Press, 1996), 1631. The theater seated 4,000–5,000 spectators while the hippodrome in Herod's day held 7,500. See Netzer, *Architecture of Herod*, 113–15 and Porath, "Caesarea," 1659.

12. English translations variously render *bēma* as throne, rostrum, or platform.

13. In the past, a hippodrome was located southwest of the Temple Mount, but it has since been removed (David Amit, *Model of Jerusalem in the Second Temple Period* [Jerusalem: Israel Museum, 2009], 64).

14. This observation was made by Richardson, who notes that the building where the trophies were hung was for animal contests, yet Josephus calls it a theater (*Herod*, 187 n. 42).

Location of the Temple of Roma

Unlike the theater, the design of the hippodrome best suits illumination of Agrippa's garments by the rays of the early morning sun.

One other aspect is elucidated by an understanding of the event's location. Immediately adjacent to the northern end of the hippodrome was the imperial temple, the center of worship of the emperor and the goddess Roma.[15] The crowds that hailed Agrippa that day were very familiar with the practice of honoring the emperor as a god. Only a few years earlier, Agrippa's close friend, Emperor Caligula, demanded that he be revered as a god. One way that Caligula signaled his desire for worship was by the clothing he wore, oftentimes dressing himself in the attire of one of the deities.[16] Whether Agrippa intended by his dress to provoke a similar reaction or not, his failure to resist such acclaim brought divine judgment. As Josephus tells it, the king recognized that his punishment was just—the intense pain apparently brought moral clarity—for he declared with irony that "I, who was called immortal by you, am now under sentence of death" (*Ant.* 19.347).

Luke's brief account could suggest that Agrippa died immediately. Josephus' longer report describes an immediate collapse, followed by five agonizing days in the palace before the king expired. Luke writes that Agrippa was eaten by worms, and Josephus records that he died from excruciating pain in his belly. The paral-

15. This temple was apparently depicted on Agrippa's coins in the last year of his rule (Duane W. Roller, *The Building Program of Herod the Great* [Berkeley: University of California Press, 1998], 139). More details about the archaeological results of the excavation of the temple can be found in Netzer, *Architecture of Herod*, 103–6 and Lisa C. Kahn, "King Herod's Temple of Roma and Augustus at Caesarea Maritima," in *Caesarea Maritima: A Retrospective after Two Millenia*, ed. Avner Raban and Kenneth G. Holum (Leiden: Brill, 1996), 130–45.

16. Caligula's custom of dressing himself as a living deity has led some to believe that Agrippa was intending to provoke the crowd's acclamations by virtue of his ostentatious costume. In the temple that Caligula built for himself in Rome, he erected a golden statue, and each day its clothes were changed to match the ones the emperor was wearing (Suetonius, *Gaius Caligula* 22.2). At various times, he would act or dress as if he were Jupiter, Neptune, Apollo, or another of the gods or goddesses. See Werner Eck, "Caligula," *BNP* 2:956.

lel should not be missed: just as Agrippa resembled King Herod in his expansive rule, so he resembled him in his gruesome death (*Ant.* 19.169–73).[17]

CONCLUSION

In some ways, the record of Agrippa's death seems out of place in Acts. After all, the episode does not include the apostles, the church, or the spread of the gospel. Yet Luke saw fit to include this event in his account of the church's beginning. He did so to affirm God's power over those who would attack the apostles and destroy the church. If Herod Agrippa can be struck down in a moment, surely no earthly power can stop the spread of the gospel to the ends of the earth. As the book of Acts continues, it will be at this very city of Caesarea where the apostle Paul will testify of the Lord Jesus to Agrippa's son, and from here he will set sail to preach the good news in the emperor's court.

BIBLIOGRAPHY

Amit, David. *Model of Jerusalem in the Second Temple Period.* Jerusalem: Israel Museum, 2009.

Eck, Werner. "Caligula." *BNP* 2:955–57.

Hemer, Colin J. *The Book of Acts in the Setting of Hellenistic History*. Edited by Conrad H. Gempf. Tübingen: Mohr Siebeck, 1989.

Kahn, Lisa C. "King Herod's Temple of Roma and Augustus at Caesarea Maritima." Pages 130–45 in *Caesarea Maritima: A Retrospective after Two Millenia*. Edited by Avner Raban and Kenneth G. Holum. Leiden: Brill, 1996.

Liddell, Henry George, Robert Scott, and Henry Stuart Jones. *A Greek-English Lexicon.* 9th ed. with revised supplement. New York: Oxford University Press, 1996.

Netzer, Ehud. *The Architecture of Herod, the Great Builder*. Tübingen: Mohr Siebeck, 2006.

Patrich, Joseph. "Caesarea: The Combined Caesarea Expeditions Excavations; Areas CC, KK, and NN." *NEAEHL* 5:1668–80.

Pervo, Richard I. *Acts: A Commentary*. Minneapolis: Fortress, 2009.

Porath, Yosef. "Caesarea: The Israel Antiquities Authority Excavations." *NEAEHL* 5:1656–65.

Richardson, Peter. *Herod: King of the Jews and Friend of the Romans*. Minneapolis: Fortress, 1999.

Roller, Duane W. *The Building Program of Herod the Great*. Berkeley: University of California Press, 1998.

Schnabel, Eckhard J. *Acts*. Expanded digital edition. Grand Rapids: Zondervan, 2012.

17. Perhaps even Luke's use of the name "Herod" in this pericope, instead of Agrippa, was intended to evoke the comparison for readers familiar with the history.

CHAPTER 24

PAUL'S MISSIONARY WORK IN CYPRUS, GALATIA, AND PAMPHYLIA

Acts 13:1–14:28

Eckhard J. Schnabel

KEY POINTS

- The sixth phase of Paul's mission was his work in Paphos and Salamis on Cyprus, the seventh phase in Pisidian Antioch, Iconium, Lystra, and Derbe in the province of Galatia, and the eighth phase in Perga in the province of Pamphylia.
- The selection of areas of missionary work depended on existing and new contacts, persecution, and proximity.

MISSIONARY WORK IN SALAMIS AND PAPHOS ON THE ISLAND OF CYPRUS

Paul's mission in Cyprus (Acts 13:4–12) is the sixth phase of his missionary work.[1] The reason Barnabas and Paul go to Cyprus is surely the fact that Barnabas was originally from Cyprus (Acts 4:36) and that Jerusalem believers who had to flee included families who were originally from Cyprus and who proclaimed the gospel in Antioch on the Orontes and also in cities in Cyprus (Acts 11:19–20).

Since Barnabas had been sent by the apostles in Jerusalem to consolidate the emerging church in Antioch, it was a logical step for Barnabas to decide to do the same on Cyprus. Barnabas and Paul,

1. See page 702 for a table of the phases of Paul's missionary work. For Paul's mission on Cyprus, see Eckhard J. Schnabel, *Early Christian Mission*, 2 vols. (Downers Grove, IL: InterVarsity Press, 2004), 1077–89; Schnabel, *Paul the Missionary: Realities, Strategies, and Methods* (Downers Grove, IL: InterVarsity Press, 2008), 75–77. See also Schnabel, "Paul's Missionary Work in Syria, Nabatea, Judea, and Cilicia," chapter 18 in this volume.

together with John Mark, traveled from Antioch to Seleucia (sixteen miles [25 km]) where they embarked on a ship bound for Cyprus, a distance of about sixty-two miles (100 km). Seleucia was an important port city on the Syrian coast, with an artificial inner harbor and an outer harbor that served as a base for the imperial fleet.[2]

The first station of the missionary team was Salamis where Paul preached in synagogues (Acts 13:5; note the plural συναγωγαῖ, *synagōgai*). Salamis had been the most important city of Cyprus in the fifth and fourth centuries BC, as indicated by monumental royal tombs. The statement that "they traveled through the whole island until they came to Paphos" suggests missionary work in the towns located on the road between Salamis in the east and Paphos in the west of the island, a distance of 112 miles (180 km): Thremitos, Kition, Amathus, and Kourion.[3] Paphos was the seat of the Roman governor; the city had a gymnasium, theater, and amphitheater; the temple of Aphrodite was the most famous sanctuary in antiquity devoted to the worship of the goddess. The reference to Salamis and Paphos suggests that there were churches at least in these two cities. In Paphos, the governor Sergius Paulus was converted. The proconsul of Cyprus at the time of Paul's visit is most likely identical with Lucius Sergius Paulus who is mentioned in an inscription from the city of Rome that lists him as one of five curators of the Tiber River during the principate of Claudius.[4]

2. Nigel Pollard, *Soldiers, Cities and Civilians in Roman Syria* (Ann Arbor: University of Michigan Press, 2000), 56–60, 279–83.

3. Unless otherwise indicated, Scripture quotations are from the New International Version (NIV).

4. *Corpus Inscriptionum Latinarum* VI 31545 = *Inscriptiones Latinae Selectae* II 5926; see Schnabel, *Early Christian Mission*, 1085. For this identification see: Stephen Mitchell, *Anatolia: Land, Men, and Gods in Asia Minor*, 2 vols. (Oxford: Oxford University Press, 1995), 2:6–7; Cilliers

Salamis on the Island of Cyprus

Jewish communities are attested for Cyprus in the second century BC (1 Macc 15:23). Philo describes Cyprus as "full of Jewish colonies" (*On the Embassy to Gaius* 282). According to a rabbinic text, the Jews of Cyprus regularly donated wine for the temple in Jerusalem that was used for the incense offering on the Day of Atonement (y. Yoma 4.5 [41d]).

Cyprus was annexed by the Romans in 58 BC. In 30 BC the island became a Roman province; in the same year Augustus granted half of the income from the local copper mines to Herod I and left the other half for Herod to administer.[5] Cyprus was divided into the four districts of Paphos, Salamis, Amathus, and Lapethos (the latter on the north coast). The governor Sergius Paulus (Acts 13:7) is one of two governors documented for the principate of Claudius (AD 41–54); T. Cominius Proculus (AD 43/44) would have been his successor.

DISTANCES TRAVELED IN THE SIXTH PHASE

Distance Traveled by Ship:

- from Antioch (Syria) to Salamis: 220 km (137 miles)
- from Paphos (Cyprus) to Perga (Pamphylia): 300 km (186 miles)
- **Total: 520 km (323 miles)—between 4–10 days**

Breytenbach, *Paulus und Barnabas in der Provinz Galatien: Studien zu Apostelgeschichte 13f.; 16,6; 18,23 und den Adressaten des Galaterbriefes* (Leiden: Brill, 1996), 39.

5. Josephus, *J.W.* 16.127–129. See also Hans Hauben, "Herod the Great and the Copper Mines of Cyprus," *Ancient Society* 35 (2006): 175–95.

Distances Traveled on Foot:

- Salamis to Paphos: 180 km (112 miles)—7 days[6]

MISSIONARY WORK IN PISIDIAN ANTIOCH, ICONIUM, LYSTRA, AND DERBE IN THE PROVINCE OF GALATIA

Paul's mission in Antioch, Iconium, Lystra, and Derbe in southern Galatia (Acts 13:13–14:23) is the seventh phase of his missionary work.[7] The conversion of Sergius Paulus (Acts 13:12) seemed to have played a significant role in Paul's travel plans. If Paul had planned on missionary work in large cities, he would have stayed in Perga (Acts 13:13) after reaching the mainland of Asia Minor (on Perga see below). The fact that John Mark left Paul and Barnabas after reaching Perga, returning to Jerusalem (Acts 13:13), suggests that the next phase of Paul's missionary work had not been planned but was triggered by new factors. Some have suggested that it was a severe case of malarial fever that prompted Paul to travel north into the Taurus Mountains, seeking relief in the higher elevations of the Anatolian Plateau.[8] This proposal does not explain why Paul and Barnabas headed straight for Pisidian Antioch: towns closer to the coast but already in higher elevations, and larger than Pisidian Antioch, included Olbasa, Comama, Cremna, Sagalassus. A more plausible suggestion for Paul's travel route is the fact that Sergius Paulus, the governor of Cyprus, had connections with Pisidian Antioch: inscriptions found in the area indicate that the family of the Sergii Pauli owned estates in southern Galatia.[9] The visit to Pisidian Antioch may have been suggested by Sergius Paulus, "no doubt providing [Paul] with letters of introduction to aid his passage and his stay."[10] The mission to Antioch led to the mission in Iconium, Lystra, and Derbe.

FROM PERGA TO PISIDIAN ANTIOCH

Paul and Barnabas disembarked either at Attaleia or at Magydus. The river port

6. Assuming fifteen miles (25 km) per day; see Rainer Riesner, *Paul's Early Period: Chronology, Mission Strategy, Theology* (Grand Rapids: Eerdmans, 1998), 311, who assumes an average of fifteen to twenty miles (20–30 km) per day of walking by foot. Justinian, *Digest* 2.11.1, quoting Gaius, assumes that the time allocated for a party to appear in court is based on a travel day of 20,000 paces, or 20 Roman miles (which equals 18.3 miles [29.6 km]). See also Mark Wilson, "Paul's Journeys in 3D: The Apostle as Ideal Ancient Traveller," *Journal of Early Christian History* 8 (2018): 1–19, who suggests that when we factor in the ascent of the Via Sebaste, 1.42 days should be added, that is, a median walking pace would result in 35 days of walking by foot.

7. Schnabel, *Early Christian Mission*, 1089–1122; Schnabel, *Paul the Missionary*, 77–88. See also Schnabel, "Paul's Missionary Work in Syria, Nabatea, Judea, and Cilicia," chapter 18 in this volume.

8. See Gal 4:13, where Paul asserts that he came to Galatia and preached the gospel there "because of an illness." See also William M. Ramsay, *St. Paul the Traveller and the Roman Citizen*, updated and rev. ed., ed. M. Wilson (Grand Rapids: Kregel, 2001), 90–92; F. F. Bruce, *Commentary on Galatians* (Grand Rapids: Eerdmans, 1982), 208–9.

9. See page 317 for an image of one of the inscriptions. The latest discussion of the Sergii Pauli and their relationship to Pisidian Antioch is Michel Christol and Thomas Drew-Bear, "Les Sergii Paulli et Antioche," in *Actes du Ier congres international sur Antioche de Pisidie*, ed. T. Drew-Bear, M. Tashalan, and C. J. Thomas, (Paris: Boccard, 2002), 177–91.

10. Mitchell, *Anatolia*, 2:7.

at Perga, which was navigable in the first century via the Kestros (modern Aksu) River,[11] seems to have been used as a canal rather than for oceangoing ships.[12] They had three options for their journey from Perga to Pisidian Antioch.[13]

Option One: The Eastern Route

The eastern route began at Perga, traversed the plain of Pamphylia crossing the Kestros River and the Eurymedon (Köprücay) River, traveling via Aspendos and Side to Etenna, crossing the Taurus Mountains at the Kesik Beli pass before reaching Mistea (Claudiocaesarea) at Lake Karalis, turning northwest toward Neopolis and Pisidian Antioch. This route is 149 miles (240 km) long.[14] This option is the least plausible: the natural terminus for this route was Iconium, not Pisidian Antioch.[15]

Option Two: The Central Route

The central route followed the Kestros River before it climbed the deep, rocky valleys of the Taurus Mountains[16] to Adada; from there the main route continued northeast to Timbriada and through the hills above Lake Limnae (modern Egirdir Gölü) to Malos, Dabenae, and

11. Douglas A. Campbell, "Paul in Pamphylia (Acts 13.13–14a; 14.24b-26): A Critical Note," *NTS* 46 (2000): 597–98.

12. Mark Wilson, "Saint Paul in Pamphylia: Intention, Arrival, Departure," *Adalya* 19 (2016): 236–38.

13. The following options are taken from Mark Wilson, "The Route of Paul's First Journey to Pisidian Antioch," *NTS* 55 (2009): 471–83.

14. See *BAGRW*, map 65, E4/F4/F3/G2/F1. This option is preferred by John McRay, *Paul: His Life and Teaching* (Grand Rapids: Baker Academic, 2003), 120–21; and Jack Finegan, *The Archaeology of the New Testament: The Mediterranean World of the Early Christian Apostles* (Boulder, CO: Westview, 1981), 90.

15. Mitchell, *Anatolia*, 1:70.

16. Sections of the Roman road can still be seen in the village Sütcüler.

Pisidian Antioch.[17] This route is 114 miles (183 km) long, the shortest of the three options, which is the reason why the central route is marked as the route that Paul traveled in most Bible atlases.[18]

Option Three: The Western Route

The western route followed the paved Roman road built by the legate Cornutus Arruntius Aquila, built around 6 BC under the direction of Augustus (Greek Σεβαστός, *Sebastos*), linking the Roman colonies of Comama, Cremna, Parlais, Antioch, Iconium, and Lystra established by Augustus.[19] The Augustan milestones along this route are orientated toward Pisidian Antioch as the *caput viae*, the "head" of the road. From Perga the road traversed the flat region of western Pamphylia, climbing into the Taurus Mountains through the Klimax Pass (modern Doseme Bogazi), passing through Comama (*Colonia Iulia Augusta Prima Fida Comama*), Lysinoe (Lysinia) on the western shore of Lake Askania, and Apollonia (Soziopolis) before reaching Antioch. This route is 140 miles (225 km) long.[20]

Most likely Paul and Barnabas took this western route, traveling from Perga to Pisidian Antioch on the *Via Sebaste*: the western route was the easiest route into the Anatolian highlands, and Sergius Paulus would surely have suggested this route.[21]

PISIDIAN ANTIOCH

Pisidian Antioch was founded by Seleukos I Nicator (348–281 BC) or Antiochos II (261–246 BC) to safeguard Seleucid interests. The city belonged to the region of Phrygia; since it was located near the border to Pisidia, it was called "Pisidian Antioch" to distinguish it from other cities with the name Antioch.[22] Antioch was refounded by Augustus as a Roman

---

17. *BAGRW*, Map 65, E4/E3/F2/F1. See also Frederic W. Farrar, *The Life and Work of St. Paul* (New York: Dutton, 1896), 204; Étienne de Mesmay, *Sur les routes de l'apôtre Paul en Turquie* (Paris: Parole et Silence, 2005), 38–42.

18. For a survey of the route marked in Bible atlases, see Wilson, "Paul's First Journey", 480–81.

19. David H. French, "The Roman Road-System of Asia Minor," *ANRW* 7:707–9.

20. *BAGRW*, maps 65 (Lycia-Pisidia), E3/D3/D2/D1, and 62 (Phrygia), E1/F1. Adapted and modified from Schnabel, *Early Christian Mission*, 1074, where a visit to Ariassos was assumed, prompting the figure of 174 miles (280 km) for the western route from Perga to Antioch (which was also assumed for the return journey). For the towns mentioned in this paragraph, see Schnabel, *Early Christian Mission*, 1091–92 (Attaleia), 1096–97 (Komama), 1097 (Lysinoe/Lysinia), 1098 (Apollonia, Soziopolis), 1098–1103 (Antioch), with historical and archaeological information.

21. David H. French, "Acts and the Roman Roads of Asia Minor," in *The Book of Acts in Its Graeco-Roman Setting*, ed. D. W. J. Gill and C. Gempf, vol. 2 of *The Book of Acts in Its First Century Setting*, ed. Bruce W. Winter (Grand Rapids: Eerdmans, 1994), 49–68, 52; and Stephen Mitchell and Marc Waelkens, *Pisidian Antioch: The Site and its Monuments* (London: Duckworth, 1998), 12; also Wilson, "Paul's First Journey", 482.

22. The Gazetteer in *BAGRW* lists eighteen towns with the name Antioch, spelled either Antiocheia or Antiochia (listed from west to east): Antiocheia ad Chrysaoron (Alabanda) in the province of Asia (map 61, F2), Antiochia ad Maeandrum in the province of Asia (map 65, A2); Antiochia (Pisidian Antioch) in Phrygia in the province of Galatia (map 62, F5); Antiochia Castellum in Isauria in the province of Galatia (map 66, B3); Antiochia ad Cragum

colony with the official name *Colonia Caesarea Antiocheia*, the most important of his new colonies in south Galatia and an important center of the imperial cult in the region, even though it occupied, in terms of urban infrastructure, the fourth place in Pisidia after Selge, Termessos, and Sagalassus. It is estimated that Antioch had about ten thousand inhabitants, including about three thousand veterans of Augustus' army.[23]

Paul's preaching in the synagogue of Antioch (Acts 13:14–45) and among the non-Jewish population (Acts 13:46–48), both in the city and in the surrounding region (Acts 13:49)—over fifty villages are attested for the territory that Antioch controlled—was successful, so much so that the Jewish leaders contacted wives of the local aristocracy who managed to get the leading men of the city (the *duoviri*) to expel the missionaries (Acts 13:50).[24] Paul and Barnabas then traveled east on the *Via Sebaste*, passing through Neapolis and Pappa (Tiberiopolis) before reaching Iconium.

ICONIUM, LYSTRA, AND DERBE

Iconium was an old Phrygian city that Augustus refounded as the *Colonia Iulia Augusta Iconium*. The theater of the city was financed with imperial and private funds. Paul and Barnabas spent considerable time in Iconium (Acts 14:3). They were forced to leave on account of a plot by Jewish and gentile citizens to stone them. From Iconium the missionaries traveled on the road leading south—probably still the *Via Sebaste*[25]—to Lystra, where Augustus had established the military colony of *Colonia Iulia Felix Gemina Lystra*. The epithet "*gemina*" suggests that veterans of two Roman legions were stationed in the colony.[26] Luke reports the healing of a lame man in Lystra, the attempt of the local Lycaonian speaking population to honor Barnabas and Paul as manifestations of Zeus and Hermes, and the instigation of the local citizens by Jews from Antioch and Iconium that led to Paul being stoned (Acts 14:6–20). From Lystra, the missionaries traveled south, passing through Belören (name of ancient town unknown), then east, passing through Kodylessos, Posala, Pyrgoi,

in the province of Lycia/Pamphylia (map 66, A4); Antiochia ad Cydnum (Tarsus) in the province of Cilicia (map 66, F3); Antiochia ad Sarum (Adana) in the province of Cilicia (map 66, G3); Antiochia ad Pyramum (Mallos) in the province of Cilicia (map 66, G3); Antiochia (on the Orontes River) in the province of Syria (map 67, C4); Antiochia ad Euphratem in the region of Osrhoene/Parthia (map 67, F2); Antiochia ad Callirhoem (Edessa) in the region of Osrhoene/Parthia (map 67, H2); Antiochia ad Chrysorhoam (Gerasa) in the Decapolis/ Nabatea (map 69, C5); Antiochia Arabis (Antoninopolis) in Armenia (map 89, B3); Antiochia (Nisibis) in Armenia (map 89, D3); Antiochia (or Alexandria, Spasinou Charax) in Mesene/ Babylonia (map 93, D3); Antiocheia Persidos in Persia (map 94, A5); Antiochia (Alexandria, Merv) in Bactria (map 98, C1).

23. Barbara Levick, *Roman Colonies in Southern Asia Minor* (Oxford: Clarendon, 1967), 93–94.

24. See Schnabel, "The Persecution of the Earliest Christians in Geographical Perspective," chapter 11 in this volume.

25. French, "Acts and the Roman Roads," 53.

26. Gertrud Laminger-Pascher suggests the *Legio VII* and the *Legio IV Macedonica* (Gertrud Laminger-Pascher, *Die kaiserzeitlichen Inschriften Lykaoniens. Faszikel I: Der Süden*, [Wien: Österreichische Akademie der Wissenschaften, 1992]), 118.

Stadium at Perga

Ilistra and Laranda before reaching Derbe (Claudioderbe). Luke reports that the proclamation of the gospel in Derbe resulted in "a large number of disciples" (Acts 14:21).

THE RETURN TRIP

It is possible that after their stay in Derbe, Paul and Barnabas considered the possibility of returning to Antioch via Tarsus, traveling from Derbe first in a northeasterly direction passing through Sidamaria, Cybistra, and Tynna (Dana), then turning south passing through Podandos and the Cilician Gates to Tarsus, a distance of 130 miles (210 km).[27] Instead, they returned to Lystra, Iconium, and Antioch—a distance of 205 miles (330 km)—strengthening the new believers and appointing elders (Acts 14:21–23). It is quite possible that they used the short central route (option two noted above) for the journey from Pisidian Antioch to Perga: the text states that Paul and Barnabas traveled "through Pisidia."[28]

DISTANCES TRAVELED IN THE SEVENTH PHASE

The distances that Paul traveled in the course of his missionary work in southern Galatia—a total of 687 miles (1105 km)—are as follows:

- Perga to Pisidian Antioch via the western route: 157 miles (253 km):
- Perga to Comama: 42 miles (68 km)
- Comama to Apollonia: 71 miles (115 km)

27. On the roads north of the Cilician Gates, see Jacopo Turchetto, "Beyond the Myth of the Cilician Gates: The Ancient Road Network of Central and Southern Cappadocia," in *La Cappadoce Méridionale: de la préhistoire à la période byzantine*, ed. D. Beyer, O. Henry, and A. Tibet (Istanbul: Institut Français d'Études Anatoliennes Georges Dumézi, 2015), 179–200.

28. Wilson, "Paul's First Journey", 482–83.

Galaticae et Pamphyliae Inscription from Perga

- Apollonia to Antioch: 43 miles (70 km)
- Pisidian Antioch to Iconium, Lystra, Derbe: 156 miles (251 km):
- Antioch to Iconium: 48 miles (78 km)
- Iconium to Lystra: 21 miles (34 km)
- Lystra to Derbe: 86 miles (139 km)
- Derbe to Pisidian Antioch, via Lystra and Iconium: 156 miles (251 km)
- Pisidian Antioch to Perga via the central route: 114 miles (183 km):
- Antioch to Malos: 34 miles (55 km)
- Malos to Adada: 30 miles (48 km)
- Adada to Perga: 50 miles (80 km)
- **Total: 583 miles (938 km)—thirty-eight days (six weeks, assuming Paul rested one day a week)**

MISSIONARY WORK IN PERGA IN THE PROVINCE OF PAMPHYLIA

Paul's mission in Perga (or Perge following the Greek Πέργη, *Pergē*[29]) in Pamphylia (Acts 14:24–25) is the eighth phase of his missionary work.[30] Luke's report of Paul's proclamation of the gospel in Perga, the capital of the province of Pamphylia, is related in six words of Greek text, reduced to the basic process of missionary work: *kai lalēsantes en Pergē ton logon* (καὶ λαλήσαντες ἐν Πέργῃ τὸν λόγον, "and they preached the word in Perga"; Acts 14:25). Luke does not provide any details for Paul's mission in Perga: he evidently reckons that his readers would

29. It is necessary to note that many English translations (e.g., ESV, KJV, NASB, NIV, NKJV, NLT, NRSV), and even BDAG, s.v. Πέργη, render the name Πέργη in English as "Perga" (thus also William M. Ramsay, *The Historical Geography of Asia Minor* [London: Murray, 1890], 393–94, 415) even though the proper transliteration of the Greek name of the city is *Pergē*. This spelling persists in biblical studies despite the fact that classical historians uniformly use the spelling "Perge" (e.g., LSJ, s.v. βωμίς 2; ἐγχωνεύω; ἐπίστασις VI; etc; *BAGRW*, map 65, E4; W. Martini, "Perge," *BNP* 10:773–775; G. E. Bean and S. Mitchell, "Perge," in *The Oxford Classical Dictionary*, ed. Simon Hornblower and Anthony Spawforth, 4th ed. [Oxford: Oxford University Press, 2012], 1106–7; David Magie, *Roman Rule in Asia Minor to the End of the Third Century after Christ* (Princeton: Princeton University Press, 1975], passim). Nevertheless, in conformity with the vast preponderance of biblical literature, we shall employ the spelling "Perga" throughout the present volume.

30. See Schnabel, *Early Christian Mission*, 1122–24; Schnabel, *Paul the Missionary*, 88–89. See also Schnabel, "Paul's Missionary Work in Syria, Nabatea, Judea, and Cilicia," chapter 18 in this volume.

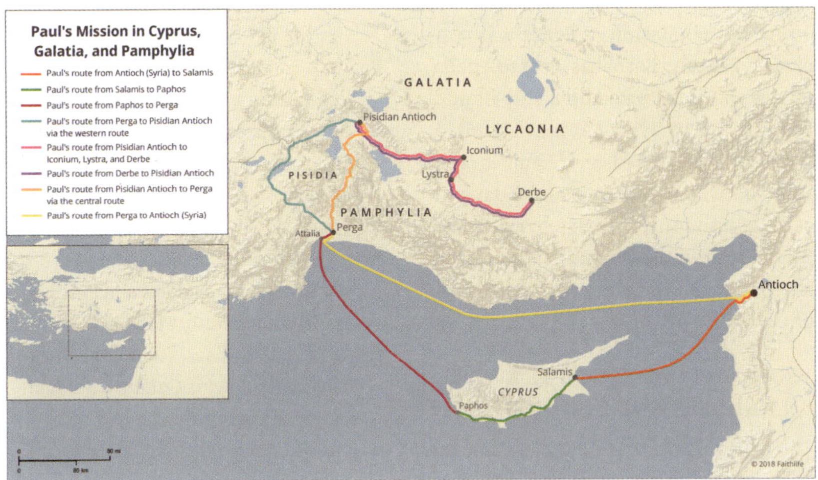

fill in the details of the Pamphylian mission from the events of Paul's mission in Antioch, Iconium, Lystra, and Derbe. The apocryphal *Acts of Paul* mention Christians in Pisidia and Pamphylia, specifically in Perga.[31]

Perga was an ancient city, mentioned in Hittite documents, allegedly settled by Greeks after the Trojan War, later controlled by the Seleucid kings, the kings of Pergamum, and eventually by the Romans. Perga competed with Side for the rank of the first city in Pamphylia. The theater of Perga could hold fourteen thousand spectators. The life and culture of the city is reflected in inscriptions that document the presence of physicians, philosophers, philologists, athletes, actors, poets, singers, mimes, musicians, and dancers, some of whom were active in other regions, for example, in Ephesus, Pergamum, Tlos, Thyatira, Sparta and Rome.[32]

It has been assumed that Pamphylia—a part of the new Roman province of Cilicia after 55 BC, of the province of Asia after 49 BC, of the province of Galatia after 25 BC—became province Pamphylia-Lycia in AD 43, that is, two years before Paul arrived in the region in AD 45/46.[33] More recently it has been argued, on the basis of two inscriptions from Perga, that Pamphylia was part of the *provincia Galaticae et Pamphyliae*, detached and joined with Lycia only at the time of Vespasian (AD 69–79).[34]

31. *Acts of Paul* 5; the text mentions Thrasymachus and Cleon with their wives Aline and Chrysa as believers from Perga.

32. Hartwin Brandt, *Gesellschaft und Wirtschaft Pamphyliens und Pisidiens im Altertum* (Bonn: Habelt, 1992), 145; Schnabel, *Early Christian Mission*, 1122–24.

33. Stephen Mitchell, "Pamphylia," in *Oxford Classical Dictionary*, 1071–72.

34. First asserted by Brandt, *Gesellschaft und Wirtschaft*, 98; see also Sencer Şahin, "Ein Vorbericht über den Stadiasmus Provinciae Lyciae in Patara," *Lykia* 1 (1994): 130–37; Şahin, *Die Inschriften von Perge*, 2 vols. (Bonn: Habelt, 1999-2004), 1:31 n. 49; 2:138–39 n. 46.6; Fatih Onur, "Two Procuratorian Inscriptions from Perge," *Gephyra* 5 (2008): 65.

After the mission in Perga was concluded, Paul and Barnabas went to Attalia where they embarked on a ship bound for Antioch in Syria (Acts 14:25–26), a sea journey of three hundred miles (480 km), between four and eight days of sailing, assuming a direct journey to the Syrian coast without stops in ports on the south coast of Cilicia or on the south coast of Cyprus.

SUMMARY OF PAUL'S TRAVELS IN GALATIA AND IN PAMPHYLIA

- By ship: Antioch (Syria) to Salamis (Cyprus): 137 miles (220 km)
- Cyprus: Salamis to Paphos: 112 miles (180 km)—seven days
- By ship: Paphos (Cyprus) to Perga (Pamphylia): 186 miles (300 km)
- Galatia: Perga to Pisidian Antioch via the western route: 157 miles (253 km)—ten days
- Pisidian Antioch to Iconium, Lystra, Derbe: 156 miles (251 km)—ten days
- Derbe to Pisidian Antioch, via Lystra and Iconium: 156 miles (251 km)—ten days
- Pisidian Antioch to Perga via the central route: 114 miles (183 km)—seven days
- By ship: Perga to Antioch: 330 miles (530 km)
- **Total by foot: 695 miles (1118 km)—forty-five days**
- **Total by ship: 652 miles (1050 km)—between eight to nineteen days**

BIBLIOGRAPHY

Bean, G. E., and S. Mitchell. "Perge." Pages 1106–7 in *The Oxford Classical Dictionary*, ed. Simon Hornblower and Anthony Spawforth. 4th ed. Oxford: Oxford University Press, 2012.

Brandt, Hartwin. *Gesellschaft und Wirtschaft Pamphyliens und Pisidiens im Altertum*. Bonn: Habelt, 1992.

Breytenbach, Cilliers. *Paulus und Barnabas in der Provinz Galatien: Studien zu Apostelgeschichte 13f.; 16,6; 18,23 und den Adressaten des Galaterbriefes*. Leiden: Brill, 1996.

Bruce, F. F. *Commentary on Galatians*. Grand Rapids: Eerdmans, 1982.

Campbell, Douglas A. "Paul in Pamphylia (Acts 13.13–14a; 14.24b-26): A Critical Note." *NTS* 46 (2000): 595–602.

Christol, Michel, and Thomas Drew-Bear. "Les Sergii Paulli et Antioche." Pages 177–91 in *Actes du Ier congres international sur Antioche de Pisidie*. Edited by T. Drew-Bear, M. Tashalan, and C. J. Thomas. Paris: Boccard, 2002.

Farrar, Frederic W. *The Life and Work of St. Paul*. New York: Dutton, 1896.

Finegan, Jack. *The Archaeology of the New Testament: The Mediterranean World of the Early Christian Apostles*. Boulder, CO: Westview, 1981.

French, David H. "Acts and the Roman Roads of Asia Minor." Pages 49–58 in *The Book of Acts in Its Graeco-Roman Setting*. Edited by D. W. J. Gill and C. Gempf. Volume 2 of *The Book of Acts in Its First Century Setting*. Edited by Bruce W. Winter. Grand Rapids: Eerdmans, 1994.

———. "The Roman Road-System of Asia Minor." *ANRW* 7:698–729.

Hauben, Hans. "Herod the Great and the Copper Mines of Cyprus." *Ancient Society* 35 (2006): 175–95.

Laminger-Pascher, Gertrud. *Die kaiserzeitlichen Inschriften Lykaoniens: Faszikel I; Der Süden*. Wien: Österreichische Akademie der Wissenschaften, 1992.

Levick, Barbara. *Roman Colonies in Southern Asia Minor*. Oxford: Clarendon, 1967.

Magie, David. *Roman Rule in Asia Minor to the End of the Third Century after Christ*. Princeton: Princeton University Press, 1950.

Martini, W. "Perge," *BNP* 10:773–775.

McRay, John. *Paul: His Life and Teaching*. Grand Rapids: Baker Academic, 2003.

Mesmay, Étienne de. *Sur les routes de l'apôtre Paul en Turquie*. Paris: Parole et Silence, 2005.

Mitchell, Stephen. *Anatolia: Land, Men, and Gods in Asia Minor*. 2 vols. Oxford: Oxford University Press, 1995.

———. "Pamphylia." Pages 1071–72 in *The Oxford Classical Dictionary*. Edited by Simon Hornblower and Anthony Spawforth. 4th ed. Oxford: Oxford University Press, 2012.

Mitchell, Stephen, and Marc Waelkens. *Pisidian Antioch: The Site and its Monuments*. London: Duckworth, 1998.

Onur, Fatih. "Two Procuratorian Inscriptions from Perge." *Gephyra* 5 (2008): 53–66.

Pollard, Nigel. *Soldiers, Cities and Civilians in Roman Syria*. Ann Arbor: University of Michigan Press, 2000.

Ramsay, William M. *The Historical Geography of Asia Minor*. London: Murray, 1890.

———. *St. Paul the Traveller and the Roman Citizen*. Updated and rev. ed. Edited by M. Wilson. Grand Rapids: Kregel, 2001.

Riesner, Rainer. *Paul's Early Period: Chronology, Mission Strategy, Theology*. Grand Rapids: Eerdmans, 1998.

Şahin, Sencer. *Die Inschriften von Perge*. 2 vols. Bonn: Habelt, 1999–2004.

———. "Ein Vorbericht über den Stadiasmus Provinciae Lyciae in Patara." *Lykia* 1 (1994): 130–37.

Schnabel, Eckhard J. *Early Christian Mission*. 2 vols. Downers Grove. IL: InterVarsity Press, 2004.

———. *Paul the Missionary: Realities, Strategies, and Methods*. Downers Grove, IL: InterVarsity Press, 2008.

Turchetto, Jacopo. "Beyond the Myth of the Cilician Gates: The Ancient Road Network of Central and Southern Cappadocia." Pages 179–200 in *La Cappadoce Méridionale: de la préhistoire à la période byzantine*. Edited by D. Beyer, O. Henry, and A. Tibet. Istanbul: Institut Français d'Études Anatoliennes Georges Dumézi, 2015.

Wilson, Mark. "Paul's Journeys in 3D: The Apostle as Ideal Ancient Traveller." *Journal of Early Christian History* 8 (2018): 1–19. DOI: 10.1080/2222582X.2017.1411204

———. "The Route of Paul's First Journey to Pisidian Antioch." *NTS* 55 (2009): 471–83.

———. "Saint Paul in Pamphylia: Intention, Arrival, Departure." *Adalya* 19 (2016): 229–50.

CHAPTER 25

BARNABAS, JOHN MARK, AND THEIR MINISTRY ON CYPRUS

Acts 13:4–13; 15:36–39

Mark Fairchild

KEY POINTS

- The beginnings and the growth of the church in Cyprus are not well known.
- A large Jewish presence on Cyprus during the first century AD is evident from ancient sources.
- Sergius Paulus, the proconsul of Cyprus, converted to Christianity in spite of opposition from a Jewish magician, Elymas (Bar-Jesus).
- Barnabas, a native Cypriot, and his cousin John Mark accompanied Paul on an early mission to Cyprus, but only Barnabas and John Mark returned for a second mission.
- The apocryphal Acts of Barnabas provides us with an account of Barnabas and Mark's second mission to Cyprus, but the document is late and historically suspect.

INTRODUCTION

Christianity spread to Cyprus, the easternmost island in the Mediterranean Sea, early in the first century. This was due in large part to the efforts of Barnabas and John Mark. The details of their ministry on the island are largely lost and the brief descriptions in Acts provide us with a mere glimpse of those early years. Several late traditions purport to fill in the historical gaps, but their credibility is questionable. This essay attempts to assess these traditions and to survey the history, culture, and geography of the island to see if we might find clues that will augment our understanding of Christianity on Cyprus.

Acts introduced Barnabas as a diaspora Jew from Cyprus who was a Levite. His name was Joseph, but the apostles

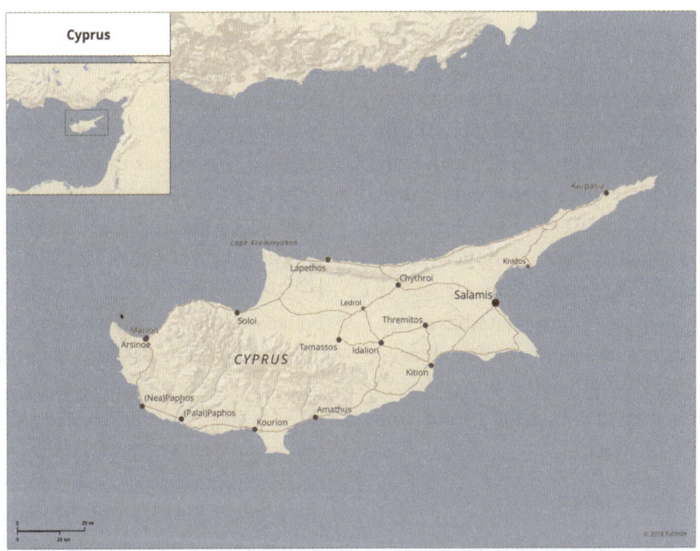

gave him the name Barnabas—son of encouragement (Acts 4:36). Clement of Alexandria and Eusebius assert that Barnabas was one of the seventy disciples sent out by Jesus to proclaim the coming kingdom.[1] He was in Jerusalem shortly after the outpouring of the Holy Spirit on Pentecost and sold a piece of land, contributing the proceeds of the sale for the needs of the early Jerusalem Christian community. Following Paul's conversion when nobody trusted the sincerity of his new faith, Barnabas befriended Paul and introduced him to the Jerusalem church (9:27).

John Mark is mentioned only in Acts, where he is described as having a Jewish name (John) and a Roman name (Mark). However, this John Mark is probably the same as the Mark mentioned in Paul's letters (Col 4:10, Phlm 24) and 1 Peter 5:13. The early church traditions support this identification. Early church traditions also claim that later in life Mark followed Peter to Rome and wrote the second Gospel from what he remembered of Peter's preaching. Originally, Mark lived in Jerusalem (Acts 12:12; 13:13) and in his letter to the Colossians Paul alluded to Mark as Barnabas' cousin (Col 4:10). Since Barnabas was a native Cypriot and he sold what land he owned in Jerusalem (Acts 4:37), it is likely he lived with Mark while he was in Jerusalem.[2]

Following the dispersion of Christians from Jerusalem and Judea after the death of Stephen, many Jewish Christians came to Phoenicia, Cyprus, and Antioch (Acts 11:19) sharing the gospel with fellow Jews in those areas. It is possible that Barnabas made his way to Cyprus at this time in order to share the gospel with family and friends on the island. Located only about sixty miles (96.5 km) off the Syrian coast, Cyprus had a large Jewish population.

1. Clement of Alexandria, *Stromata* 2:20; Eusebius *Ecclesiastical History* 1.12.
2. It was common for extended family members to reside in the homes of relatives.

Turning his attention more specifically to Antioch, Luke noted that some men from Cyprus and Cyrene came to Antioch and began ministering to the Greeks as well as the Jews (11:20). Even though Cypriots are mentioned in this verse, it is not likely that Barnabas was among this first group that came to Antioch. Later when the Jerusalem church heard of the large number of converts in Antioch, they sent Barnabas to Antioch to strengthen the church (11:22). Barnabas may have been redirected from Cyprus to Antioch.

THE EARLY MISSION TO CYPRUS

In time, both Paul and John Mark joined Barnabas in Antioch. The three of them departed for Cyprus with Barnabas as the leader of the mission (Acts 13:3–5). Luke's narrative is clear that the Holy Spirit sent the group on the mission, but it is probable that the choice of the mission's itinerary was Barnabas' decision. Barnabas was familiar with the land, the roads, and the people. As a native Cypriot, he also had relatives on the island that needed to hear the gospel. Additionally, if he was involved in ministry in Cyprus prior to being called to Antioch, Barnabas wanted to continue his earlier work in Cyprus.

Throughout this mission, including the journey into Galatia, Barnabas and Paul prioritized ministry to the Jews. In city after city, the apostles first proclaimed the gospel in the synagogues. This was the routine at Salamis (13:5), Pisidian Antioch (13:14, 44), Iconium (14:1), probably Lystra (14:19) and at the other locations as well. This followed Paul's belief that God's message first and foremost had to be proclaimed to the Jewish people: "I am not ashamed of the gospel, for it is the power of God for salvation to everyone who believes, to the Jew first and also to the Greek" (Rom 1:16, ESV).

Cyprus was close to Palestine and it should not be surprising to find that Jews settled on the island early.[3] Funerary inscriptions indicate that a Jewish settlement existed on Cyprus as early as the Achaemenid period in the fourth century BC.[4] By the first century AD literary sources indicate that Cyprus had a large Jewish population. Philo, around AD 40, made note of Jewish colonies on Cyprus (Philo, *Legatio ad Gaium* 282). Dio Cassius described a large Jewish uprising on Cyprus at the time of Trajan.[5] In his discussion of magic, Pliny the Elder recounted a large sect of Jewish magicians on Cyprus.[6] The apostles met one

---

3. According to Zdzislaw J. Kapera, "We can suppose that practically in each of the eighteen known cities there were some Jewish colonies and synagogues" (Kapera, "The Jewish Presence in Cyprus before AD 70," *Scripta Judaica Cracoviensia* 7 [2009]: 37).

4. Michael Heltzer, "Epigraphic Evidence Concerning a Jewish Settlement in Kition (Larnaca, Cyprus) in the Achaemenid Period (IV cent. B.C.E.)," *Aula Orientalis* 7 (1989): 189–206.

5. If Dio Cassius' figures are anything close to accurate, the Jewish population on Cyprus must have been very large. Dio Cassius wrote that the Jews of Cyprus led by Artemion rose up against the Romans during Trajan's reign around AD 117 and slaughtered two hundred forty thousand Greeks and Romans. After Martius Turbo put down the rebellion, a decree was issued banning all Jews from the island (Dio Cassius, *History* 68.322). Dio's figures have been called into question, but nonetheless Dio's account reflects a huge Jewish population in the first century.

6. "There is another sect adept in the magic arts who come from Moses, Jannes, and Lotapea, and the Jews, thousands of years after Zoroaster, but more recent is their branch

Salamis Gymnasium

of those, Bar-Jesus (Elymas), at Paphos (Acts 13:6–12) and the Roman procurator of Judea, Felix, utilized a Cypriot magician named Atomus a few years later (Josephus, *Ant.* 20.142–144).[7] Additionally, several inscriptions found at Cyprus are evidence of a significant Jewish presence on the island.[8]

SALAMIS

Barnabas, Paul, and John Mark departed from Seleucia Pieria, the Mediterranean port of Antioch and sailed to the eastern port of Cyprus, Salamis. There, they began ministry in the synagogues of the city (Acts 13:5). Salamis was a large city and was the capital of the island before being supplanted by Paphos in the second century BC. The plural "synagogues" suggests that a number of Jews lived in the city. The fact that Salamis was crushed during the Jewish revolt during Trajan's reign is evidence that Salamis was largely Jewish. The patron deity of Salamis was Zeus Olympios and a large temple of his was located on the periphery of the city's large agora. The temple was originally built during the late Hellenistic period and was reconstructed during the Roman Imperial period.

From Salamis the apostles traveled west to Paphos. The western interior of Cyprus contains the island's highest mountain range, the Trogodos range. The mountains compel most travelers from the east to take the southern coastal road

of magic practiced in Cyprus" (Pliny the Elder, *Natural History* 30.2). Mitford believes the collection of curse tablets from Cyprus (#127–142) "were doubtless drafted by a Jewish sorcerer" (T. B. Mitford, *The Inscriptions of Kourion* [Philadelphia: American Philosophical Society, 1971], 134, 246–83).

7. Elsewhere Josephus mentioned the prosperous Jewish communities in Egypt and Cyprus during the Hellenistic period (*Ant.* 13.284).

8. T. B. Mitford, "New Inscriptions from Early Christian Cyprus," *Byzantion* 20 (1950): 110–16.

to the capital. A milestone dating to the time of Augustus informs us that this route was refurbished prior to the time of the apostle's journey.[9] The route would have taken the group from Salamis to Tremithous, Kition, Amathous, Kourion, Palaipaphos, and Paphos and would have involved a total of 110 miles (177 km).

TREMITHOUS

Tremithous was located about twenty-one miles (34 km) southwest and inland from Salamis via a Roman road. A horoscope inscription found at the site shows that Jews in the community utilized a Jewish calendar.[10] Takashi Fujii's examination of inscriptions on Cyprus shows that four calendars were used throughout the first two centuries and that the various communities adapted their calendars according to their own customs while also superficially acknowledging the imperial calendar.[11]

KITION

From Tremithous the apostles would have traveled around thirteen miles (21 km) south to Kition on the coast.[12] The remaining journey to Paphos would have followed the coastal road for the distance. We have already mentioned the Jewish funerary inscriptions at Kition that establish a Jewish presence at the site in the fourth century BC. Josephus explained that the word "Kittim" referred to the islands and maritime countries. But, more specifically, Josephus identified Cyprus as Kittim and asserted that the word came from Chethimos, grandson of Japheth, the founder of the city Kition. Those origins are doubtful, but Kition was a port city with a Jewish population during the first century that maintained contact with the Jewish mainland. Kition was the birthplace of Zeno (334–262 BC) the father of Stoic philosophy. Later, on Paul's journey to Athens, Paul had an opportunity to debate with the Stoic philosophers (Acts 17:18).

AMATHOUS

Thirty-four miles (54.7 km) further west along the coast Barnabas, Paul, and John Mark would have arrived at Amathous. Over two hundred curse tablets have been found at Amathous, which leads scholars to believe that the city was a center for magic.[13] These date to the late second to the early third century AD and may be connected with Jewish magic.[14] Legend has it that Aphrodite was born on the island and numerous cults to Aphrodite are found in Cyprus. Aphrodite was worshiped as the primary deity in Amathous,

9. David W. J. Gill, "Paul's Travels through Cyprus (Acts 13:4–12)," *TynBul* 46 (1995): 221–23.

10. Sacha Stern, "A 'Jewish' Birth Record, *Sambat-*, and the Calendar of Salamis," *Zeitschrift für Papyrologie und Epigraphik* 172 (2010): 105–14.

11. Takashi Fujii, *Imperial Cult and Imperial Representation in Roman Cyprus* (Stuttgart: Steiner, 2013), 152–56.

12. The Acts of Barnabas, 17, claims that Barnabas and Paul converted and baptized a man named Heraclius at Kition.

13. Andrew Wilburn, *Materia Magica: The Archaeology of Magic in Roman Egypt, Cyprus, and Spain* (Ann Arbor: University of Michigan Press, 2012), 169–218.

14. So Mitford, *Inscriptions of Kourion*, 134. The curse tablets cited by Mitford are now believed to have come from Amathous. A Jewish association with these curse tablets is also supported by Pieter Willem van der Horst, "The Jews of Ancient Cyprus," *Zutot: Perspectives on Jewish Culture* 3 (2003): 118–19.

and the cult at Amathous was one of the earliest. Aphrodite Amathusia, the local expression of Aphrodite, was famous throughout the Hellenistic and Roman periods. A first century BC temple to her has been excavated on the acropolis flanked by two massive six-foot (1.8 m) water vases.

Fifth Century Statue of Aphrodite from Cyprus

KOURION

Moving on from Amathous, the apostles traveled further west along the coast to Kourion, about fifteen miles (24 km) distant. The city was built on a cliff overlooking the sea, over three hundred feet (91.5 m) above the water. An earlier settlement was located further inland, but sometime during the fifth or fourth century BC, the city relocated to its current site. The chief deity at Kourion was Apollo Hylates and his sanctuary was located a mile (1.6 km) west of the city where worship was conducted as early as the eighth century BC. Excavations at the site indicate that the city flourished during the Hellenistic and Roman periods and a great deal of construction took place during that time. The city was devastated by earthquakes in AD 332 and 342, but recovered in the early Byzantine period.

One home, the House of Eustolios, was destroyed in those earthquakes but was rebuilt by the wealthy Eustolios. Several mosaic inscriptions remain in the house. One of them extolled the civic benefactions of Eustolios after the earthquakes, claiming that he took care of Kourion as Phoebus Apollo once did. Another mosaic inscription in the same house asserted that the house was strengthened not by stones and iron, but rather by the venerated signs of Christ. The two mosaics illustrate the transition from paganism to Christianity (see page 706 for images of these mosaics).

Kourion

PALAIPAPHOS

Around 312 BC Nikokles, king of the Paphian kingdom, established a new capital city, Nea Paphos (New Paphos), about ten miles (16 km) west of the older Palaipaphos (Old Paphos). The new site had a natural port and was more strate-

Sanctuary of Aphrodite

gically positioned. Nea Paphos was probably populated in part with displaced residents of Marion, a city to the north that was destroyed by Ptolemy Soter in 312 BC. Palaipaphos continued to exist and flourished up through the Hellenistic and Roman periods.

Barnabas, Paul, and John Mark would have arrived at Palaipaphos first, twenty miles (32 km) to the west of Kourion. The origins of Old Paphos are not clear. Legends go back to Kinyras, who was mentioned in the Iliad. Kinyras allegedly established a sanctuary for Aphrodite, who was born in the sea and came ashore at Paphos. Homer mentioned the sacred site at Paphos and the temple constructed there was the most famous temple of Aphrodite in the Mediterranean world as well as the most sacred site on the island of Cyprus. The temple has been excavated, but little has survived.

PAPHOS

Passing on from Palaipaphos, the apostles would have arrived at Nea Paphos, ten miles (16 km) further down the road. Here, according to the biblical text (Acts 13:6–12), they met Sergius Paulus and Elymas (Bar-Jesus). The capital of Cyprus was transferred from Salamis to Nea Paphos sometime during the second century BC and at that time the city came to be known simply as Paphos. Sergius Paulus was appointed proconsul of the island by the Romans. Such appointments were usually for one year. Four inscriptions have been suggested as references to Sergius Paulus, but none of these are entirely conclusive.[15] Nevertheless,

15. A first century boundary stone from Rome probably from the time of Claudius (*GIL* 6.31545) referred to L[ucius] Sergius Paulus as a curator of the Tiber. Some scholars have suggested that this Sergius Paulus went to Cyprus shortly after his curatorship. Another first century inscription from Soloi in Cyprus (*Inscriptiones Graecae ad res Romanas pertinentes* III.930) mentioned the proconsul Sergius, but it is not clear that this is the same

L. Sergius Paulus Inscription from Pisidian Antioch

these several inscriptions have led many scholars to conclude that one or more of these inscriptions refer to the proconsul Sergius Paulus mentioned in Acts 13. The L. Sergius Paulus inscription found at Pisidian Antioch is particularly interesting and has led some scholars to suggest that the proconsul had family in Pisidian Antioch and requested Paul, Barnabas and John Mark to travel there to share the gospel with the proconsul's relatives.

The encounter with Bar-Jesus (Elymas) at Paphos is not entirely surprising, given Pliny's comments and the well-known presence of Jewish magicians on the island. The magician's association with Sergius Paulus suggests that he was functioning as an advisor to the governor. Magicians were frequently employed by political leaders as astrologers and necromancers who were skilled at issuing curses against opponents. However, the impotent power of Elymas' magic was no match for the force of the Almighty and Elymas walked away blind. Sergius Paulus walked away with a new faith.

Sergius Paulus who was proconsul during Paul's visit. A third inscription was found at Kytharia, Cyprus and contained the name Quintus Sergius [Paulus]. The name Paulus is conjecture and epigraphists have debated whether this inscription dates to the time of Caligula (which would be too early) or Claudius. The fourth inscription (*Inscriptiones Graecae ad res Romanas pertinentes* III.935) was found at Pisidian Antioch and alluded to L[ucius] Sergius Paulus, son of L[ucius] Sergius Paulus. Various arguments have been proffered to connect these inscriptions to Acts 13, but none of them are compelling. See Bastian Van Elderen. "Some Archaeological Observations on Paul's First Missionary Journey," in *Apostolic History and the Gospel: Biblical and Historical Essays Presented to F. F. Bruce on His 60th Birthday*, ed. W. Ward Gasque and Ralph P. Martin. (Exeter: Paternoster, 1970), 152–57; Douglas A. Campbell, "Possible Inscriptional Attestation to Sergius Paul[l]us (Acts 13:6–12), and the Implications for Pauline Chronology," *Journal of Theological Studies* 56 (2005): 1–29.

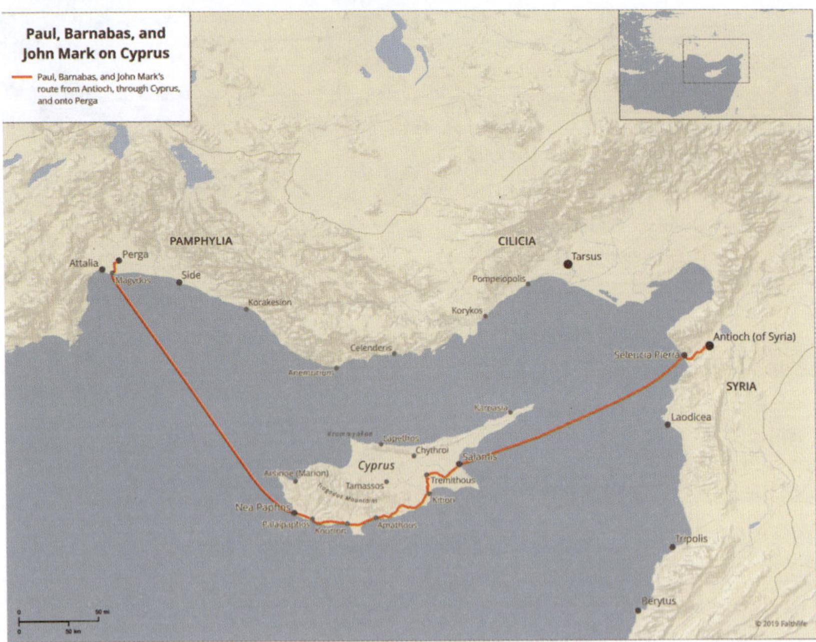

END OF THE EARLY MISSION

The mission continued as the apostles sailed from Paphos to the Anatolian mainland, probably putting into port at Magydos and traveling another seven miles (11.25 km) north to Perga. At this point John Mark departed from the mission and returned to Jerusalem, leaving Barnabas and Paul to continue on their own to Pisidian Antioch and Lycaonia. The reasons for Mark's departure are not clear, but the incident disturbed Paul to such a degree that he refused to let Mark join them on another mission. Barnabas was equally insistent that Mark should accompany the apostles and the disagreement between Barnabas and Paul resulted in a split. Paul took Silas and departed for Syria and Cilicia, while Barnabas and John Mark returned to Cyprus.

BARNABAS AND JOHN MARK'S RETURN MISSION ON CYPRUS

The New Testament mentioned nothing more about the exploits of Barnabas and John Mark on Cyprus. However, later traditions passed on folklore and traditions of questionable value. The Acts of Barnabas, supposedly written by John Mark, described a journey by Barnabas and Mark departing from Laodicea in Syria and arriving at a number of sites in Rough Cilicia.[16] From there they sailed south to Cyprus and landed at Krommyakon. Their journey continued east to the northern coastal town of Lapethos and then moved inland to

16. The ship was blown off course and landed at Korasion, Pityoussa, Akonesiai, and Anemurium (Acts of Barnabas 11–13). The ports were sequentially located along the Cilician coast from east to west.

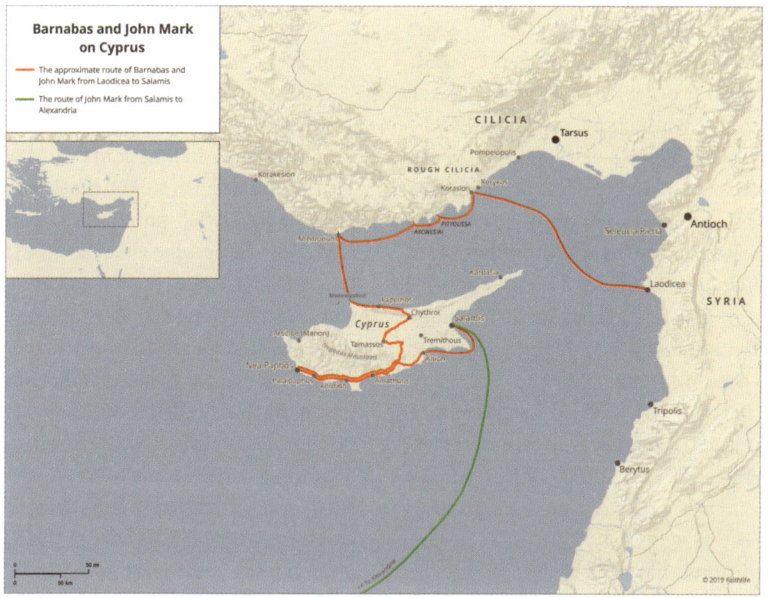

Lampadistos[17] and Tamassos. Barnabas and Mark crossed the Trogodos Mountains and arrived at Palaipaphos and Paphos. There they met Bar-Jesus, the magician that they met on the first journey to the island. Bar-Jesus opposed Barnabas and Mark and stirred up the Jewish communities along the southern coast. He pursued Barnabas and Mark as they continued to move to the east. They traveled to Kourion, Amathous, and Kition. In each location, Barnabas and Mark were harassed by the residents as Bar-Jesus continued to stir up trouble. Taking a ship from Kition, they finally arrived at Salamis. There, at the instigation of Bar-Jesus, Barnabas was seized and burned to death (Acts of Barnabas 23).[18] Mark escaped and fled to Alexandria, Egypt where he engaged in a ministry to the Egyptians for several years.

As with many of the apocryphal gospels and acts, there is a mixture of truth and legend. Many of the early traditions were forgotten over the centuries and the traditions that persisted slowly changed. However, it would be a mistake to dismiss the early church traditions entirely. Most scholars date the Acts of Barnabas in the fifth century, but certain details stand out. The geography of the document is accurate and the itinerary is plausible.[19]

17. Lampadistos is the only city or town on the itinerary that is unknown.

18. The traditional tomb of Barnabas lies underground at the monastery of St. Barnabas outside the city walls of Salamis.

19. Philip H. Young, "The Cypriot Aphrodite Cult: Paphos, Rantidi and Saint Barnabas," *Journal of Near Eastern Studies* 64 (2005): 37: "the geographical and cultural details of the account in the Acts of Barnabas are so specific and different from the story told in Acts that they demonstrate that the writer had a firsthand knowledge of Cyprus and was, most likely, a native of the island himself."

The journey along the southern coast from Paphos to Salamis corresponds (in reverse order) with our conjectured journey from Acts 13. Additionally, the legendary aspects of the narrative are modest compared to other postapostolic Acts. Eusebius (*Ecclesiastical History* 2.16) repeated an earlier tradition that Mark ministered in Alexandria and several other patristic authors made the same claim, although they do not agree with the time of his arrival.

Perhaps the Acts of Barnabas preserves nothing more than an early travel narrative of Barnabas' and John Mark's second mission to the Cyprus. This travel narrative was fleshed out with weaker traditions that still circulated on the island in the fifth century. For those who are more skeptical of the traditions, even this may be going too far. For some the Acts of Barnabas was written too late to be of any value historically.

CONCLUSION

The earliest Christian ministry on the island of Cyprus is sketchy. Acts 11:19 reports that Christians fleeing from the persecution associated with the lynching of Stephen came to Cyprus and preached the Christian faith to Jews on the island. Neither the names of the evangelists nor the details of this ministry were given in this singular verse. Later, Barnabas, Paul, and John Mark sailed to Cyprus and began a ministry on the island (Acts 13:2–13). But even this brief account offers us few details of the journey. After Paul and Barnabas split up, Barnabas took John Mark and returned to Cyprus (Acts 15:39). Thereafter, they completely disappear from the biblical narratives. More information about this second mission appears in a document written about four hundred years later, the Acts of Barnabas, but the historical value of this book is suspect.

The early Christian evangelists began their work sharing the gospel in Jewish communities. Ancient sources, as well as inscriptions, indicate that Cyprus had a large Jewish population, so it is reasonable to assume that the missions focused upon cities, towns, and villages with a Jewish presence. The topography of the land, coupled with the presence of known Roman roads, suggest that ministry on the first (and perhaps the second) mission was conducted in the cities of Salamis, Kition, Amathous, Kourion, Palaipaphos, and Nea Paphos along with smaller communities along the way. Several traditions report Barnabas' martyrdom at Salamis where today a tomb is reportedly the place where his remains were buried.

BIBLIOGRAPHY

Bekker-Nielsen, Tonnes. *The Roads of Ancient Cyprus*. Copenhagen: Museum Tusculanum, 2004.

Burkiewicz, Lukasz. "The Beginnings of Christianity in Cyprus: Religious and Cultural Aspects." *Folia Historica Cracoviensia* 23 (2017): 13–36.

Cagnat, René, Jules Toutain, Georges Lafaye, and Victor Henry. *Inscriptiones Graecae Ad Res Romanas Pertinentes/Auctoritate et Impensis Academiae Inscriptionum et Litterarum Humaniorum Collectae et Editae*. Paris: Leroux, 1901–1927.

Campbell, Douglas A. "Possible Inscriptional Attestation to Sergius Paul[l]us (Acts 13:6–12), and the Implications for Pauline Chronology." *Journal of Theological Studies* 56 (2005): 1–29.

Christou, Demos. *Paphos Archaeological Guide and Historical Review*. Nicosia: Kailas, 2008.

Clement of Alexandria, *Stromateis: Books 1–3*. Translated by John Ferguson. Washington, DC: Catholic University of America Press, 1991.

Davis, Thomas W. "The Jewish Diaspora in Ptolemaic and Roman Cyprus: Some Speculations." *Journal of Ancient Egyptian Interconnections* 10 (2016): 39–44.

———. "Saint Paul on Cyprus." Pages 405–23 in *Do Historical Matters Matter to Faith? A Critical Appraisal of Modern and Postmodern Approaches to Scripture*. Edited by James K. Hoffmeier and Dennis R. Magary. Wheaton, IL: Crossway, 2012.

Dio Cassius. *Roman History: Books 61–70*. Translated by Earnest Cary. LCL 176. Cambridge: Harvard University Press, 1925.

Eusebius. *Ecclesiastical History*. Translated by Kirsopp Lake. LCL 153. Cambridge: Harvard University Press, 1926.

Fujii, Takashi. *Imperial Cult and Imperial Representation in Roman Cyprus*. Stuttgart: Steiner, 2013.

Gill, David W.J. "Paul's Travels through Cyprus (Acts 13:4–12)." *TynBul* 46 (1995): 219–28.

Heltzer, Michael. "Epigraphic Evidence Concerning a Jewish Settlement in Kition (Larnaca, Cyprus) in the Achaemenid Period (IV cent. B.C.E.)." *Aula Orientalis* 7 (1989): 189–206.

Horst, Pieter Willem van der. *Jews and Christians in Their Graeco-Roman Context: Selected Essays on Early Judaism, Samaritanism, Hellenism, and Christianity*. Tübingen: Mohr Siebeck, 2006.

———. "The Jews of Ancient Cyprus." *Zutot: Perspectives on Jewish Culture* 3 (2003): 110–20.

Jones, Alan H. M. *The Cities of the Eastern Roman Provinces*. 2nd ed. Oxford: Clarendon, 1971.

Josephus. *Jewish Antiquities: Book 20*. Translated by Louis H. Feldman. LCL 456. Cambridge: Harvard University Press, 1965.

Kapera, Zdzislaw J. "The Jewish Presence in Cyprus before AD 70." *Scripta Judaica Cracoviensia* 7 (2009): 33–44.

Kollmann, Bernd. *Joseph Barnabas: His Life and Legacy*. Collegeville, MN: Liturgical Press, 2004.

Mitford, T. B. "The Cults of Roman Cyprus." *ANRW* 18.3:2176–2211.

———. *The Inscriptions of Kourion*. Philadelphia: American Philosophical Society, 1971.

———. "Some New Inscriptions from Early Christian Cyprus." *Byzantion* 20 (1950): 105–75.

Panteli, Stavros. *Place of Refuge: A History of the Jews in Cyprus*. London: Elliot & Thompson, 2003.

Parker, Pierson. "John and John Mark." *JBL* 79 (1960): 97–110.

Philo. *On the Embassy to Gaius*. Translated by F. H. Colson. LCL 379. Cambridge: Harvard University Press, 1962.

Pliny. *Natural History: Books 28–32*. Translated by William H. S. Jones. LCL 418. Cambridge: Harvard University Press, 1963.

Reilly, Wendell Stephen. "Saint Mark the Disciple of Saint Peter and Saint Paul." *Catholic Biblical Quarterly* 1 (1939): 223–31.

Snyder, Glenn E. "The Acts of Barnabas: A New Translation and Introduction." Pages 317–36 in volume 1 of *New Testament Apocrypha: More*

Noncanonical Scriptures. Edited by Tony Burke and Brent Landau. Grand Rapids: Eerdmans, 2016.

Stern, Sacha. "A 'Jewish' Birth Record, *Sambat*-, and the Calendar of Salamis." *Zeitschrift für Papyrologie und Epigraphik* 172 (2010): 105–14.

Stewart, Charles Anthony. "The First Vaulted Churches in Cyprus." *Journal of the Society of Architectural Historians* 69 (2010): 162–89.

Trebilco, Paul R. *Jewish Communities in Asia Minor*. Cambridge: Cambridge University Press, 1991.

Van Elderen, Bastian. "Some Archaeological Observations on Paul's First Missionary Journey." Pages 150–161 in *Apostolic History and the Gospel: Biblical and Historical Essays Presented to F. F. Bruce on His 60th Birthday*. Edited by W. Ward Gasque and Ralph P. Martin. Exeter: Paternoster, 1970.

Wilburn, Andrew. *Materia Magica: The Archaeology of Magic in Roman Egypt, Cyprus, and Spain*. Ann Arbor: University Michigan Press, 2012.

Young, Philip H. "The Cypriot Aphrodite Cult: Paphos, Rantidi and Saint Barnabas." *Journal of Near Eastern Studies* 64 (2005): 23–44.

CHAPTER 26

THE SOCIAL AND GEOGRAPHICAL WORLD OF PISIDIAN ANTIOCH

Acts 13:13–52; 14:24–28; 16:6; 18:23

David A. deSilva

KEY POINTS

- Pisidian Antioch was a major hub of the Pauline mission, especially if Galatians addresses churches in South Galatia.
- Pisidian Antioch, founded by Antiochus I, was refounded by Augustus as a Roman colony and populated with thousands of his veterans and their families.
- The archaeological site of Pisidian Antioch is dominated by the sprawling complex of the Augusteum (a temple to the divine Augustus).
- Paul's proclamation of the gospel in Antioch would have been heard as a challenge to the dominant story of deliverance through a divine agent celebrated in and around the Augusteum.

PISIDIAN ANTIOCH IN THE BIBLICAL STORY

According to Acts 13, Paul and Barnabas were commissioned by the church in Syrian Antioch to go out as missionaries. They first preached the gospel throughout the island of Cyprus and then sailed to the mainland, landing at Perga in the region of Pamphylia. They journeyed along the *Via Sebaste*, or "Augustan Road," north into the region of Pisidia, to another Antioch, a city that would become an important landmark on the map of Paul's missionary work. Despite immediate hostility from members among the Jewish community, Paul and Barnabas appear to have planted the seeds of a congregation there before they were driven out of the city by the Jewish community's leaders in concert with the governing authorities.

From Pisidian Antioch they journeyed east along the *Via Sebaste* to Iconium and Lystra, making a short detour to

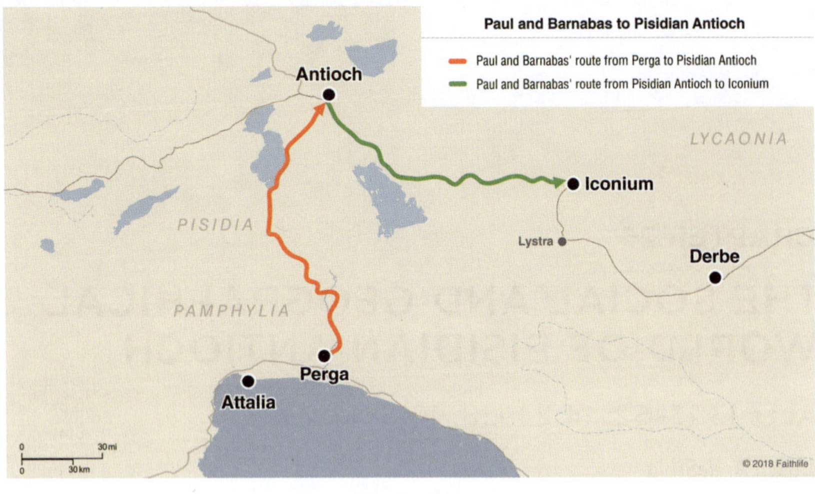

Derbe as well. Paul and Barnabas visit Antioch again on their way back from Derbe to Perga, "strengthening the disciples' souls, encouraging them to persevere in the faith, ... appointing elders for them in every congregation" (Acts 14:21–23). It seems probable that the author of Acts imagines Paul visiting Pisidian Antioch yet again when he speaks of Paul, Timothy, and Silas traveling through Phrygia and Galatia in Acts 16:6, in the early phases on Paul's second missionary journey. Paul would visit the congregation here a fourth time, then, at the outset of his third missionary journey to Ephesus as he passes again through Phrygia and Galatia, "strengthening all the disciples" (Acts 18:23; compare the same language in 14:22).

Although a matter of longstanding debate, many scholars believe that Paul's Letter to the Galatians was addressed to the congregation in Pisidian Antioch and its sister churches in Lystra and Iconium, all of which fall within the Roman province of Galatia during the time of Paul's active ministry.[1] If this accounting is correct, it would make Pisidian Antioch as important a hub for the Pauline mission as it was for the imperial highway system and imperial cult that put the city squarely on the Roman map.

THE POLITICS OF PISIDIAN ANTIOCH IN TIME AND SPACE

Antioch was founded by Antiochus I in the early third century BC, one of many cities that would be named "Antioch" or "Seleucia" in honor of the rulers of the Seleucid Empire. Though technically within the region of Phrygia, the city sat close to the Pisidian border and came to be called "Pisidian" Antioch to distinguish it from the many other Antiochs in Asia Minor and Syria (including Syrian Antioch, the city from which Paul and

1. See the discussion in David deSilva, *The Letter to the Galatians* (Grand Rapids: Eerdmans, 2018), 28–48.

Anatolian Moon God, Men

Barnabas set out on their first missionary journey). Very little remains today of the Hellenistic-period city. The ruins of a temple dedicated to the Anatolian moon god "Men," standing just a few miles outside the city, date back to the second century BC. The worship of Men is thought to have been imported by the city's first settlers, many of whom came from the westernmost part of Turkey where Men was a prominent deity. The theater in the heart of the city also dates back originally to the Hellenistic period, though it was remodeled and expanded significantly during the late Roman period. At its grandest, it extended over the road that ran alongside the original, smaller theater. Pedestrian and wheeled traffic continued to pass through a tunnel that had been provided under the top tier of seats.

Although Paul is remembered to have preached his first two sermons in Antioch in a Jewish synagogue, there is no direct archaeological evidence of a Jewish presence in the city, despite the overzealous claims of archaeologists to have found such evidence below the fourth century Christian basilica or the fourth century "Church of St. Paul." The literary evidence, however, is strong. Josephus records that, when the region of Phrygia was becoming unruly under Antiochus III, the king resettled two thousand Jewish families

Apse of Fourth Century Church of St. Paul

Part of the aqueduct bringing water into Antioch. The shifting terrain has buried almost all trace of the lower course of arches.

from Babylonia to the "most important places" within the regions of Phrygia and Lydia to stabilize the situation (*Ant.* 12.146–153 [LCL]). These settlers were granted land for houses and crops, distributions of food until their crops became productive, and exemption from taxes for ten years, ensuring their goodwill toward the crown. Antioch would surely have been one of these "important places."

Phrygia and Galatia came under direct Roman rule in 25 BC, united in the new Roman province of Galatia. Antioch was at first a terminus of, and later a major junction of, the *Via Sebaste* or "Augustan Road," built by Augustus in 6 BC to facilitate troop movement to the eastern frontier. Augustus himself elevated the city's status to that of a Roman colony—the *Colonia Caesarea Antiochia*—and injected new life into the city by settling upward of three thousand veterans and their families there. These families would have felt a strong bond of personal loyalty to the *Pater Patriae* (the "father of the fatherland," a title given to Augustus and his successors) as their own families' patron. The city's water supply was dramatically increased to accommodate the growing population. A new aqueduct, a two-story arched structure, was constructed to bring in water from the hills north of the city. The aqueduct brought water to the *castellum aquae*, the principal reservoir, and a *nymphaeum*, an ornate pool from which residents could draw water, both on the north side of the city. This *nymphaeum* was provided with a large paved courtyard. A modest but adequate bath complex was added west of the *nymphaeum* later in the first century AD.

Prominent among the ruins of the city are many pieces of the original water

Shops or Offices on the *Decumanus Maximus*

pipes that carried water throughout the city, both from the aqueduct and from the older springs that had supplied the city prior to its refounding as a Roman colony. Remains of this water system are also evident in the great open square in the heart of the city, perhaps originally supplying another public fountain. Running water was also supplied to public latrines, both flushing the waste and providing water for personal hygiene. One of the easily overlooked achievements of the Roman Empire was its emphasis on supplying running water throughout its cities. After the Byzantine period, people would not again enjoy this level of sanitation, personal hygiene, and ready availability of clean water until after the Renaissance.

The city's internal roads were also improved. In the typical Roman fashion, there was a major north-south road called the *Cardo Maximus* and a major east-west road called the *Decumanus Maximus*. The *Cardo* began at the *nymphaeum* and continued south past shops and major public buildings till it intersected with the *Decumanus*. The full extent of the *Cardo* south of the *Decumanus* awaits further excavation. The *Decumanus* ran west from the *Cardo* past the theater, latrine, and another host of shops. Its eastern wing also awaits further excavation. A stretch of three or four shops or offices along the *Decumanus* are particularly well preserved, probably because they were once covered by the renovated and extended theater.

Very few public buildings survive or have been uncovered on the site. The city no doubt had an assortment of temples. An inscription bears a dedication to "Jupiter, Best and Greatest" and a cult statue of the same has been discovered on site, suggesting the presence of

The foundations of the Augusteum in the midst of a sprawling courtyard and remains of the semicircular portico.

a temple to the chief of the Greek and Roman pantheon (see page 706 for an image of the inscription). By far the most impressive structure on the site today, as no doubt in Paul's lifetime as well, is the Augusteum, a monumental temple built to honor Augustus as a god, likely completed by the turn of the era. The temple had a footprint of about 85 (26 m) by 50 feet (15.25 m), with an estimated original height of between 45 (13.75 m) and 55 feet (16.75 m). A colossal cult image of Augustus would have sat within the temple, visible through a pair of large doors in the front (see image on page 703). The sacred space was rendered far more impressive by the construction of a two-story semicircular portico behind the temple. Straight porticoes extended from the tips of the semicircle past the temple, creating an open courtyard—the sacred precinct of the temple—of about 300 square feet (27.8 sq. m). Remnants of the ornate carvings that once adorned the architraves of temple and porticoes alike, featuring the common sacrificial motif of garlands and the heads of bulls, litter the surrounding area. These decorations are reminiscent of the sacrifices that would have been performed here to honor Augustus on the twenty-third of every month, in celebration of his birthday on September 23, expressing loyalty and gratitude to the emperor for his divine gifts and as particular benefactor of this colony, as well as to petition the other gods, like Jupiter Best and Greatest, for the emperor's continued well-being during his lifetime. The worship of Augustus continued long after his death and his official recognition by the Senate as a god, after which it was customary to refer to him as "the Divine Augustus" in all public inscriptions.

The city fathers and rich donors further aggrandized this monument by constructing a massive gateway, called a propylaeum, to the sacred area. Although almost nothing remains of this building today except for its footprint, this was originally a tall structure decorated with statues of members of the imperial family. One of these showed a male figure, perhaps Augustus himself, with a barbarian kneeling before him as a captive. Such art communicated a clear message to the indigenous inhabitants around Antioch: one way or another, they would submit to Roman rule.

During the reign of Tiberius, a rich citizen named Titus Baebius Asiaticus paved a large open area in front of the propylaeum, naming it "Tiberius Square" in honor of Augustus's successor. Surrounded by shops, bars, and restaurants, this area functioned as a place for recreation and commerce. Some of the few remaining paving stones still bear the markings of the game boards that had been scratched into them in antiquity. Citizens gathered to enjoy some of the benefits of the imperial peace here in the shadow of the great Augusteum complex.

One of the most important inscriptions from the Augustan period is the *Res Gestae Divi Augusti*, "the things accomplished by the divine Augustus."[2] The emperor composed this text himself in the months prior to his death, intending it to be the epitaph on his life's achievement. The inscription speaks of his deliverance of the Roman world from civil war (i.e., the war he himself waged against Marc Antony and Cleopatra VII, effectively brought to an end with Octavian's victory in the naval battle at Actium in 31 BC), his successful neutralizing of threats to the borders, his lavish benefactions upon the Roman people, the staggering number of public buildings erected at his expense (that is, from his share in the spoils of war), his diligence in rewarding veterans, and the many public honors awarded to him on account of his virtue. Augustus ordered that this lengthy document be engraved on bronze plates and placed in front of his mausoleum in Rome. A copy in both Latin and Greek was found inscribed in the ancient temple of Rome and Augustus in Ancyra (modern Ankara), in Apollonia in Pisidia, and here in Pisidian Antioch on the propylaeum in front of the Augusteum. About a hundred pieces of this inscription, which appears to have been intentionally demolished at some point in antiquity, were found in the area of Tiberius Square. Many of these pieces are now assembled, like a jigsaw puzzle missing many of its pieces, in the museum in the modern town of Yalvaç that adjoins the archaeological site.

Res Gestae Divi Augusti Inscription

2. See page 707 for an image of a replica of the inscription. The full text in English can be found in Alison E. Cooley, *Res Gestae Divi Augusti: Text, Translation, and Commentary* (Cambridge: Cambridge University Press, 2009); and in Frederick W. Danker, *Benefactor: An Epigraphic Study of a Graeco-Roman and New Testament Semantic Field* (St. Louis: Clayton, 1982), 256–80. The Latin text and an older translation can also be found in F. W. Shipley, trans., *Velleius Paterculus; Res Gestae Divi Augusti*, LCL 152 (Cambridge: Harvard University Press, 1924).

Fragments of an inscription ascribing divine honors to the emperor.

Two sentences from the *Res Gestae* are particularly appropriate as we consider Antioch. Augustus recalls how "citizens everywhere, privately as individuals and collectively as municipalities, sacrificed unremittingly at all the shrines on behalf of my health." The Augusteum in Pisidian Antioch was one such temple where such sacrifices were offered. In another place, Augustus recalls how "In Africa, Sicily, Macedonia, the two Spanish provinces, Achaia, Asia, Syria, Narbonian Gaul, and Pisidia, I settled colonies of soldiers." Pisidian Antioch was one of these colonies.

THE CHALLENGE OF PAUL'S GOSPEL IN PISIDIAN ANTIOCH

The sociospatial world of Pisidian Antioch, being prominently centered around the expansive cult site of the Augusteum, suggests that Paul's audience—both his converts *and* their unsupportive neighbors—would have heard significantly political overtones in his proclamation of a "son of a god" (see, e.g., Acts 13:33) who came as a "savior" (Acts 13:23; cf. 13:26) to bring deliverance to the whole world, whose coming was "good news" ("gospel") for all people.

The term "gospel" (εὐαγγέλιον, *euangelion*), no doubt as common in Paul's preaching (see the use of the verb form in Acts 13:32; 14:7; and the noun form in Acts 20:24) as it was in his letters (Gal 1:6, 7, 11; 2:2, 5, 7, 14, just to browse a letter quite likely sent to the Christians in Antioch), appears in imperial as well as Christian contexts, though in plural forms rather than the singular typical in Christian discourse. An inscription from Priene in the province of Asia, dated to about 9 BC, looks back to Augustus' birth as "the beginning of good news (*euangeliōn*)" for the whole world.[3] Josephus applies the term to Vespasian's accession to imperial powers at the end of the civil wars of AD 68–69 (*J.W.* 4.656). A gymnasiarch

3. For the full text, translation, and discussion, see Danker, *Benefactor*, 215–18.

in Pergamum also uses the term when honoring Augustus.[4]

Augustus was lauded as "son of the deified [Julius]" (*divi filius*) on the legends of coins and in public inscriptions, as were his own successors in relationship to him ("son of the deified Augustus," *divi Augusti filius*) after his death and formal divinization by the Senate. While Latin distinguishes between a "god" (*deus*) and a "deified being" (*divus*), Greek does not. Augustus and many of his successors were called "son of God" (υἱὸς θεοῦ, *huios theou*), using the phrase that would also be applied verbatim to Jesus in the New Testament and, no doubt, in the early preaching of Christian missionaries.

Augustus was also hailed as "savior" (σωτήρ, *sōtēr*), another common way to speak of Jesus in early Christian discourse. What Paul calls "this present evil age" (Gal 1:4), from which deliverance is desperately needed, the majority in Pisidian Antioch would have celebrated, along with other pro-Roman elements throughout the Mediterranean, as the Golden Age of the Augustan Peace. When Paul identifies that "Savior" (Acts 13:23; Eph 5:23; Phil 3:20; 2 Tim 1:10), that agent of deliverance, as Jesus, "the Son of God" (Rom 1:4; 2 Cor 1:19; Gal 2:20; Eph 4:13), he applies titles commonly ascribed to the emperor in Rome to an executed Judean. His message would have been heard in Antioch as a challenge to imperial ideology on all fronts, as would the witness of Christians increasingly during the first three centuries of the church throughout the empire.

BIBLIOGRAPHY

Cooley, Alison E. *Res Gestae Divi Augusti: Text, Translation, and Commentary*. Cambridge: Cambridge University Press, 2009.

Danker, Frederick W. *Benefactor: An Epigraphic Study of a Graeco-Roman and New Testament Semantic Field*. St. Louis: Clayton, 1982.

Demirer, Ünal. *Pisidian Antioch: St. Paul, Sanctuary of Men, Yalvaç Museum*. Ankara: Dönmez Offset, 2002.

deSilva, David. *The Letter to the Galatians*. Grand Rapids: Eerdmans, 2018.

Gazda, Elaine, and Diana Ng, eds. *Building a New Rome: The Imperial Colony of Pisidian Antioch (25 BC–AD 700)*. Ann Arbor: Kelsey Museum of Archaeology, 2011.

Mitchell, Stephen, and Marc Waelkens. *Pisidian Antioch: The Site and Its Monuments*. London: Duckworth with the Classical Press of Wales, 1998.

Shipley, F. W., trans. *Velleius Paterculus; Res Gestae Divi Augusti*. LCL 152. Cambridge: Harvard University Press, 1924.

Taylor, Lily Ross. *The Divinity of the Roman Emperor*. Middleton, CT: American Philological Association, 1931.

---

4. *Inscriptiones Graecae ad res Romanas pertinentes* 4.317; see Lily Ross Taylor, *The Divinity of the Roman Emperor* (Middleton, CT: American Philological Association, 1931), 275.

CHAPTER 27

PAUL'S MISSIONARY WORK IN MACEDONIA AND ACHAIA

Acts 16:6–18:28

Eckhard J. Schnabel

KEY POINTS

- The ninth phase of Paul's missionary work took place in Philippi, Thessalonica, and Berea in the province of Macedonia.
- The tenth phase of Paul's mission focused on Athens and Corinth in the province of Achaia.
- The selection of areas of missionary work aimed at proclaiming the gospel in areas west of previous areas of missionary work.
- After unsuccessful attempts to work in cities in Asia Minor, Paul moved to Europe and preached the gospel in Macedonia, then Achaia.
- The areas for missionary work were selected through planning supported by divine guidance, persecution, and geographical proximity.

PAUL'S VISIT TO THE CHURCHES IN SYRIA, CILICIA, AND SOUTHERN GALATIA

Paul's plan to start missionary work in the province of Asia (see below) included a visit to the churches that he had established during the fourth, fifth, and seventh phases of his mission: the churches in Syria, in Cilicia, and in southern Galatia (see page 702 for a chart of the phases of Paul's missionary work). A main reason for taking the land route to the province of Asia was the fact that the letter that informed the churches about the decision of the Apostles' Council that had taken place in Jerusalem was addressed to the gentile believers not only in Antioch but also in other towns of Syria and Cilicia (Acts 15:23), as well as the desire of Paul to visit the churches in southern Galatia—in Pisidian Antioch,

Iconium, Lystra, Derbe—to see "how they are doing" (Acts 15:36).

Paul traveled from Jerusalem, where the Apostles' Council had taken place, to Antioch in Syria (Antioch on the Orontes) and from there to cities in northern Syria, Cilicia, and southern Galatia (Acts 15:41–16:5).

Distance traveled by foot:

- Jerusalem (Judea) to Antioch (Syria): 391 miles (630 km)—twenty-five days
- Antioch (Syria) via Planatoi and Alexandria (Syria) to Epiphaneia, Anazarbos, Adana, to Tarsus (Cilicia): 152 miles (244 km)—eight days
- Tarsus (Cilicia) to Derbe (Galatia): 130 miles (210 km)—five days
- Derbe to Pisidian Antioch, via Lystra and Iconium: 156 miles (251 km)—ten days

PAUL'S PLANS OF MISSIONARY WORK IN THE PROVINCE OF ASIA

After having proclaimed the gospel in Damascus, Arabia, Cilicia, Syria (especially Antioch), Cyprus, and southern Galatia, Paul planned the next phase of his missionary work to take place in the province of Asia (Acts 16:6).

It should not be assumed too quickly that Paul planned to go to Ephesus.[5] From Pisidian Antioch, Paul could have traveled on the *Via Sebaste* west-southwest to Apollonia (Mordiaion) and from there to Apameia (Apameia Cibotos, also Celaenae, modern Dinar) which had a large Jewish community.[6] From there, Paul had two main options.

5. *Pace* Eckhard J. Schnabel, *Early Christian Mission*, 2 vols. (Downers Grove, IL: InterVarsity Press, 2004), 2:1131; Craig S. Keener, *Acts: An Exegetical Commentary*, 4 vols. (Grand Rapids: Baker, 2012–15), 3:2328; for the following see the modified argument in Eckhard J. Schnabel, *Paul the Missionary: Realities, Strategies, and Methods* (Downers Grove, IL: InterVarsity Press, 2008), 89, 268–69.

6. *BAGRW*, Map 62, F5/E5, Map 65, E1/D1.

Option one: Paul could have traveled southwest and then west to the Lycus Valley in the region of the upper Meander River, going to Colossae, Laodicea (an important assize center), to Hierapolis and Tripolis, to Antioch ad Maeandrum, Tralles, and Magnesia, and from there via Maiandros and Priene to Miletus (with a significant Jewish community) to the south—or to Ephesus to the northwest.

Option two: Paul could have traveled from Apamea, following a route through the central region of the province, to Eumeneia, Sebaste, Akmonia, Temenouthyrai, and Blaundos, and from there to the valley of the Hermus River to Philadelphia and Sardis (an old royal city, with a significant Jewish population); from Sardis, Paul could have reached Smyrna to the west or, via Maiboza, Thyatira and Pergamum to the northwest.

Luke notes that Paul abandoned his plans to do missionary work in the province of Asia because the Holy Spirit "prevented" him, perhaps through a dream, a vision, or a prophetic message (Acts 16:6). According to Acts 15:32, Silas, one of his travel companions, was a prophet. The intervention of the Spirit might have been connected with the missionary work that other Christians had started in cities in southern and central Asia, or with future hostility of citizens or officials in some of these cities—the kind of hostility leading to eviction in Pisidian Antioch, Iconium, and Lystra, causing major difficulties for his missionary work.[7]

PAUL'S PLANS OF MISSIONARY WORK IN THE PROVINCE OF PONTUS-BITHYNIA

When Paul's plan to preach the gospel in the province of Asia had to be abandoned, he and his coworkers "attempted to go to Bithynia" (Acts 16:7), evidently with the goal of starting missionary work in the cities of Nicea, Nicomedia, and Chalcedon.[8] Bithynia became a Roman province in 74 BC when the king Nikomedes IV bequeathed his kingdom to the Romans. Pompey organized the province *Pontus et Bithynia* by integrating Pontic regions into the new province.

It seems that Paul and his team had left Pisidian Antioch and crossed into the province of Asia, presumably taking the route from Apollonia (Galatia) to Apamea (Asia)—traveling "through the region of Phrygia and Galatia" (Acts 16:6), most likely a reference to the region of Phrygia Paroreius, occupying the territory either side of Sultan Da, ethnically Phrygian and politically part of the province of Galatia in the east and part of the province of Asia in the west.[9] It should be noted that Paul had not been prohibited by the Spirit to *travel* in the province of Asia. As Paul aimed at Bithynia, he would have turned north at Apameia, aiming to

7. The latter suggestion has been made by David H. French, "Acts and the Roman Roads of Asia Minor," in *The Book of Acts in its Graeco-Roman Setting*, ed. D. W. J. Gill and C. Gempf, vol. 2 of *The Book of Acts in Its First Century Setting*, ed. Bruce W. Winter (Grand Rapids: Eerdmans, 1994), 57–58.

8. See Schnabel, *Early Christian Mission*, 1:842–48, for details on these cities in Bithynia.

9. Stephen Mitchell, *Anatolia: Land, Men, and Gods in Asia Minor*, 2 vols. (Oxford: Oxford University Press, 1995), 2:3; see also Glen L. Thompson and Mark Wilson, "The Route of Paul's Second Journey in Asia Minor: In the Steps of Robert Jewett and Beyond," *TynBul* 67 (2016): 223–24.

travel north via Synnada, Prymnessus, and Kotiaeum to Dorylaion, located in the northeast region of the province of Asia on the border with Bithynia.[10] It was probably at Dorylaion that the Holy Spirit prevented Paul and his team from entering Bithynia (Acts 16:7).

Having been prevented to preach the gospel in the province of Asia (west of Galatia) as well as in the province of Bithynia-Pontus (north and northwest of Galatia), and not wanting to return to Antioch without opening up new areas of missionary work, Paul evidently decided that God wanted him to preach the gospel in Europe and headed toward Troas.[11] If correct, the dream vision in Troas (Acts 16:9–10), the port of embarkation for ships bound for Macedonia, would have confirmed Paul's third plan of missionary work, rather than suggest a new course of action.

PAUL'S TRAVEL THROUGH MYSIA TO TROAS

The journey from the northern region of the province of Asia bordering on Bithynia to Troas, located on the northern part of the east coast, is described by Luke with the phrase "passing by Mysia" (Acts 16:8). Strabo found it difficult to describe the borders of the region of Mysia (*Geography* 12.4.4).[12] The northern part of Mysia was called Mysia Abrettene, the southern part Mysia Abbaeitis. Paul presumably turned south at Dorylaion,

10. For the travel route, see Schnabel, *Early Christian Mission*, 2:1139–47; Thompson and Wilson, "Paul's Second Journey," 228–32. It is thus much less plausible to assume that Paul traveled from Apamea in a southwesterly direction to the valley of the Lycus River, traveling via Laodicea, Hierapolis, Tripolis, Philadelphia, and Sardis to Troas, as suggested by Giovanni Uggeri, "Sulle strade di San Paolo in Anatolia: Il secondo e il terzo viaggio," in *Seminario di studi Paolo di Tarso: Il messaggio, l'immagine, i viaggi; Studi in memoria di Luigi Padovese*, ed. S. Uggeri Patitucci and L. Padovese (Palermo: Officina di studi medievali, 2011), 134.

11. See W. Paul Bowers, "Paul's Route Through Mysia: A Note on Acts XVI.8," *Journal of Theological Studies* 30 (1979): 507–11.

12. See Schnabel, *Early Christian Mission*, 2:1144–45, for details.

returning to Kotiaeum; since he aimed to reach Troas, he must have traveled to Hadrianuthera (modern Balıkesir), located in northern Mysia in the plain of Apias on the Macestus River. Two routes have been suggested for the journey from Kotiaeum (modern Kütahya) to Hadrianuthera. A northern route ran due west from Kotiaeum, across the hills to the valley of the Rhyndakos River to Hadrianeia and from there to Hadrianuthera.[13] While there is a modern road (D230) connecting Hadrianeia and Hadrianuthera, there is no evidence for a route in this area in antiquity. A southern route ran from Kotiaeum southwest to Aizanoi (in the Ryndakos Valley) and Kadoi (in the upper reaches of the Hermus River), then west to Synaos, Ankyra Sidera (in the Macestus Valley) and to Hadrianuthera.[14] There is no evidence for an ancient route between Ankyra Sidera and Hadrianuthera, but it is plausible to assume that the track of the modern highway (D240) through the Macestus Valley was the route of a connection between the cities in antiquity.

From Hadrianuthera, Paul traveled west via Pionia (in the valley of the Enbeilos River) to Adramyttium, from there along the Mediterranean coast to Antandros and Gargara, then turning north, across the western ridge of Mount Ida to Skamandros and then west to Troas.[15]

The route from Pisidian Antioch to Dorylaion and, via Hadrianuthera, to Troas, was 590 miles (950 km), which required thirty-eight days of walking (six weeks, assuming Paul rested one day a week).

PAUL'S MISSIONARY WORK IN PHILIPPI, THESSALONICA, AND BEREA IN THE PROVINCE OF MACEDONIA

Paul's missionary work in Philippi, Thessalonica, and Berea in the province of Macedonia was the ninth period of his missionary work.[16]

---

13. *BAGRW*, Map 62, C3/B2/A2 (from Kotiaeum to Hadrianeia; Hadrianuthera is on Map 56, F2). Mary T. Boatwright, *Hadrian and the Cities of the Roman Empire* (Princeton: Princeton University Press, 2000), 189, mentions a road connection Hadrianeia and Hadrianuthera but provides no evidence. Thompson and Wilson, "Paul's Second Journey," 234, note that the Optimal Path Analysis run from Kütahya to Balikesir in two route planning programs prefer the northern route (noting concerns). Some have assumed an even more northerly route: via the Rhyndakos Valley to the area around Cyzicus and then along the south shores of the Sea of Marmara and the Hellespont to Troas; see William M. Ramsay, *St. Paul the Traveller and the Roman Citizen*, updated and rev. ed., ed. M. Wilson (Grand Rapids: Kregel, 2001), 158; Jean Bérard, "Recherches sur les itinéraires du saint Paul en Asie Mineure," *Revue Archéologique* 6 (1935): 69, 81.

14. *BAGRW*, Map 62, C3/B3/B4/A3 (from Kotiaeum to Ankyra Sidera). See also French, "Acts and the Roman Roads," 54; Thompson and Wilson, "Paul's Second Journey," 234–37.

15. See Thompson and Wilson, "Paul's Second Journey," 237–43, with a discussion of Robert Jewett, "Mapping the Route of Paul's 'Second Missionary Journey' from Dorylaeum to Troas," *TynBul* 48 (1997): 10–16, who suggests a route from Hadrianuthera to Troas that ran north of the Ida Mountains; Thompson and Wilson, "Paul's Second Journey," 238, point out that there are no modern roads running east to west north of Mount Ida, and neither French nor *BAGRW* depict such an east-west route in antiquity.

16. See "Paul's Missionary Work in Syria, Nabatea, Judea, and Cilicia," chapter 18 in this volume. See also Schnabel, *Early Christian Mission*, 2:1125–1169; Schnabel, *Paul*, 92–98. For

Agora at Philippi

Paul embarked in Troas and sailed via Samothrace to Neapolis, the port city of Philippi in the province of Macedonia (Acts 16:11). The sea journey from Troas to Neapolis is 137 miles (220 km); the island of Samothrace (and the city with the same name) lies halfway between Troas and Neapolis.

Macedonia, the northern region of what we call Greece, became the leading power of the Greek-speaking world at the time of the kings Philip II (382–336 BC) and his son Alexander III the Great (356–323 BC) who exported Greek culture to the eastern Mediterranean regions. Macedonia became a Roman province in 148 BC. Colonies of veterans of the Roman army were established in Dyrrhachium, Dion, Pella, Philippi, Cassandreia, and Stobi. Combined into a single province with Achaia in AD 15, the emperor Claudius organized Macedonia again as a separate province in AD 44, five years before Paul's arrival. The capital of the province was Thessalonica.[17]

From Neapolis, Paul and his companions traveled to Philippi, only ten miles (16 km) to the northwest (Acts 16:12), on the *Via Egnatia*. Construction of this east-west route across Macedonia

Berea, Thessalonica, and Berea, see *BAGRW*, Map 51, C3, Map 50, C3/B3.

17. For details, see Schnabel, *Early Christian Mission*, 2:1150–51; on the cities of Neapolis, Philippi, Thessalonica, and Berea—and the cities Paul passed through during his travels in Macedonia—see Schnabel, *Early Christian Mission*, 2:1149–69. For Macedonia. see Nicholas G. L. Hammond and Frank W. Walbank, *A History of Macedonia*, 3 vols. (Oxford: Clarendon, 1972–1988); David W. J. Gill, "Macedonia," in *The Book of Acts in Its Graeco-Roman Setting*, ed. D. W. J. Gill and C. Gempf, vol. 2 of *The Book of Acts in Its First Century Setting*, ed. Bruce W. Winter (Grand Rapids: Eerdmans, 1994), 397–417.

Shop Ruins at the Thessalonica Agora

from Dyrrhachium and Apollonia on the Adriatic to Neapolis on the Aegean coast and to Byzantium (Constantinople) was begun in 145 BC and finished around 130BC; it was the quickest route from the city of Rome to the East.[18]

Philippi is mentioned in ancient sources on account of the battle in 42 BC in which Mark Antony and Octavian (Augustus) defeated Brutus and Cassius, the murderers of Julius Caesar, which took place in the vicinity, and the naval battle of Actium in 31 BC in which Augustus won a decisive victory over Mark Antony. Augustus refounded Philippi in 27 BC as a new Roman colony with the name *Colonia Iulia Augusta Philippensis*, which was granted the *ius Italicum*, resulting in tax exemption of the land that the citizens owned. Two temples located in the forum were dedicated to the worship of the emperor. In the first century, Philippi had between five thousand and ten thousand inhabitants.

Luke reports the conversion of Lydia, a dealer in purple cloth from Thyatira (Acts 16:13–15), the exorcism involving a slave girl (Acts 16:16–18), the confrontation with the owners of the slave girl that led to accusations before the local authorities who beat Paul and Silas and threw them into prison (Acts 16:16–24), the conversion of the jailer (Acts 16:25–34), and the public rehabilitation of the missionaries and departure of Paul and his team (Acts 16:35–40).

After Philippi, Paul traveled west on the *Via Egnatia*, across the Plain of Daton north of Mount Pangaion, Lake Prasias to the west, reaching Amphipolis, a coastal town, then across the valley of Lake Bolbe

18. For the *Via Egnatia*, see Gill, "Macedonia," 409–10.

via Bormiskos, Arethusa, and Apollonia before reaching Thessalonica, located at the northeastern end of the Thermaic Gulf at the foot of Mount Kissos. Luke mentions Amphipolis and Apollonia in his travel report (Acts 17:1). Luke reports Paul's preaching the gospel in the synagogue, the conversion of some Jews and a large number of God-fearers—gentiles attending synagogue activities—and prominent women, a commotion in the city caused by Jewish opponents of Paul, the initiation of court proceedings against the missionaries, the demand that Jason, one of the new believers, post bail, and Paul's hurried departure (Acts 17:1–10).

Thessalonica, which had been founded by the Macedonian king Cassander in 315 BC, soon eclipsed the old Macedonian capital Pella, a two-day journey to the northwest. When Macedonia was established as a senatorial province in 148 BC, Thessalonica was granted autonomous self-rule and became the provincial capital. When Claudius reorganized Macedonia in AD 44, the city remained the capital of the province. The city had between twenty thousand and forty thousand inhabitants.[19]

The next stop was Berea, over a day's journey (21 miles [34 km]) south of the *Via Egnatia*, located on a terrace above the Haliacmon River at the southernmost of the three passes across the Bermion Mountains. The city seems to have been the seat of the provincial assembly (κοινόν, *koinon*) since Augustus. The decision to begin missionary work in Berea was probably due to the fact that the Jewish believers in Thessalonica who took Paul to Berea thought that he would be safe there. Luke reports great interest in the gospel among the Jewish population and many conversions, both of Jews, prominent Greek women, and many gentiles (Acts 17:10–12).

Distance traveled:

- Neapolis to Philippi: 10 miles (16 km)—0.6 days
- Philippi to Thessalonica: 100 miles (160 km)—6.4 days
- Thessalonica to Berea: 46 miles (75 km)—3 days
- **Total:** 156 miles (251 km)—10 days

PAUL'S MISSIONARY WORK IN ATHENS AND CORINTH IN THE PROVINCE OF ACHAIA

Paul's missionary work in Athens and Corinth in the province of Achaia was the tenth period of his missionary work.[20]

The province of Achaia was organized as a senatorial province in 27 BC, comprising central Greece (Attica, Boeotia), the Peloponnese, Epirus, Aetolia, Thessaly, and the Ionian islands. Combined in AD 15 with Macedonia and organized as an imperial province, it was again admin-

19. Christoph vom Brocke, *Thessaloniki: Stadt der Kassander und Gemeinde des Paulus; eine frühe christliche Gemeinde in ihrer heidnischen Umwelt*, (Tübingen: Mohr-Siebeck, 2001), 71–72. Rainer Riesner, *Paul's Early Period: Chronology, Mission Strategy, Theology* (Grand Rapids: Eerdmans, 1998), 341, thinks that if one includes the people living in the villages controlled by Thessalonica, the total population could have reached between sixty-five thousand and one hundred thousand people.

20. See Schnabel, "Paul's Missionary Work in Syria, Nabatea, Judea, and Cilicia," chapter 18 in this volume. See also Schnabel, *Early Christian Mission*, 2:1169–1197; Schnabel, *Paul*, 98–107.

istered as a separate senatorial province in AD 44, six years before Paul's arrival. The seat of the provincial government was Corinth.

Paul was taken by believers from Berea to the coast (Acts 17:14), while Silas and Timothy stayed in the city. The believers who escorted Paul took him all the way to Athens (Acts 17:15). The reference to the "sea" in Acts 17:14 may suggest to Luke's readers that Paul and the Berean believers sailed to Athens, embarking at Pydna—a journey of about 285 miles (460 km). Since this would have required fares for each person, it is possible that the phrase "those who escorted Paul" in Acts 17:15 suggests travel by land.[21] Since Paul's life had been in danger in all three Macedonian cities in which he had preached the gospel, it might have seemed advisable not to take a ship to Athens, which involved the possibility of encountering enemies from Philippi or Thessalonica, but to travel by land.

Little is known about the roads in Achaia during the first century: "In Achaia proper, no real imperial interest in road building or repairs seems to be indicated until the time of Trajan."[22] If Paul and the Berean believers traveled to Athens by foot, they would have traveled, after reaching Pydna on the coast, south on the coastal road, through Dion and Heracleion with Mount Olympus towering above the narrow coastal plain. They turned west at Homolion, passing through Gonnoi, turning south passing through Larissa, Pherai, Pyrassos on the Gulf of Pagasaeus, Halos, Pteleon, and Antrones. Turning west along the Gulf of

21. A sea journey is assumed by David W.J. Gill, "Achaia," in *The Book of Acts in Its Graeco-Roman Setting*, ed. D. W. J. Gill and C. Gempf, vol. 2 of *The Book of Acts in Its First Century Setting*, ed. Bruce W. Winter (Grand Rapids: Eerdmans, 1994), 433–53, 441; Keener, *Acts*, 3:2564.

22. Susan E. Alcock, *Graecia Capta: The Landscapes of Roman Greece* (Cambridge: Cambridge University Press, 1993), 121; see also Gill, "Achaia," 439. For the route from Berea to Athens described in this paragraph, see *BAGRW*, Map 50, B3/C4, Map 55, D1/D2/D3/D4; Map 58, E1/F1/F2.

Maliacus, they passed through Echinus and Lamia. They turned south, crossing from Macedonia into Achaia, walking through the Thermopylae and reaching Alpenos, Nikaia, and Thronion. Crossing Mount Cnemis they came to Elateia, Parapotamioi, Panopeos, and Chaeroneia on the west side of Lake Copais. Traveling along the south shore of the lake, they passed through Lebadeia, Coronea, Haliartos, eventually reaching Thebes. Crossing the eastern ridges of Mount Helicon at Potniai or Skolos, they reached Tanagra in the valley of the Asopus River. Travelling southeast, they crossed the northeastern ridges Mount Parnassus passing through Aphidna. They crossed Mount Pentelicus at Oeum Deceleicum and, passing through the plain of the Cephissus River, they reached Athens. This route from Berea to Athens is 320 miles (515 km), a distance that required twenty-one days (nearly four weeks) of travel.

Luke reports Paul's missionary work in the local synagogues before Jewish audiences and in the agora, the center of Athens, before gentiles audiences (Acts 17:17), and then focuses on Paul's argument before the Areopagus Court that he does not introduce new deities to the city that would require action by the court and the people's assembly (Acts 17:18–33). Several Athenians became believers (Acts 17:34).

The golden age of Athens, the so-called Pentecontaetia, the Great Fifty Years from the end of the campaign of Xerxes (479 BC) who burned the Acropolis to the beginning of the Pelopponesian War (431 BC), was long past when Paul arrived in AD 50. Athens came under Roman control in 86 BC. Augustus repeatedly visited Athens and helped finance the rebuilding of temples and civic buildings, which motivated the Jewish king Herod I to make donations to Athens as well. The population of Athens in the first century is estimated at thirty thousand people.

From Athens, Paul traveled along the Saronic Gulf via Eleusis, Megara, and Isthmia to Corinth, a distance of fifty-three miles (86 km). For Paul's missionary work in Corinth, Luke reports the eviction from the synagogue, conversion of many Jews and gentiles, divine encouragement to stay in the city despite the opposition, and the unsuccessful attempt of Corinthian Jews to initiate legal proceedings against Paul before Gallio, the governor of the province of Achaia (Acts 18:1–18).

Corinth was strategically located at the southwest end of the isthmus separating the Peloponnese and Attica. The city was known for its pottery industry (Corinthian vases), metal manufacture (an alloy known as Corinthian bronze), and carpet weaving. Because Corinth led the resistance of the Greek cities against Rome, the Roman Senate decreed that the city must be destroyed, a decision that was carried out in 146 BC by the general Lucius Mummius. In 44 BC Julius Caesar refounded the city as a Roman colony (*Colonia Laus Iulia Corinthus*) and settled three thousand freed slaves and veterans in the city. The new colony was intended to safeguard the Roman control of the trade with the eastern Mediterranean. Roman Corinth flourished quickly. The Panhellenic games in nearby Isthmia returned to the control of Corinth around AD 50, the year of Paul's arrival in the city. Roman Corinth had about eighty thousand inhabitants; if we include the towns and villages that Corinth controlled, another twenty thousand people might be added.

Ruins of Corinth

When his missionary work in Corinth was complete, Paul decided to return to Jerusalem and Antioch (Acts 18:18, 22–23). He accompanied Aquila and Priscilla who went from Corinth to Ephesus, and sailed from there to Caesarea (Acts 18:19–22).

SUMMARY OF PAUL'S TRAVELS IN JUDEA, SYRIA, AND CILICIA, AND DURING HIS MISSION IN MACEDONIA AND ACHAIA

- Jerusalem (Judea) to Antioch (Syria): 391 miles (630 km)—twenty-five days
- Antioch (Syria) to Tarsus (Cilicia), via Anazarbos: 152 miles (244 km)—eight days
- Tarsus (Cilicia) to Antioch (Galatia), via Derbe, Lystra, Iconium: 286 miles (461 km)—fifteen days
- Antioch to Troas, via Apamea, Dorylaion, Hadrianuthera: 590 miles (950 km)—thirty-eight days
- *Travel by ship*: Troas (Asia) to Neapolis (Macedonia): 137 miles (220 km)
- Neapolis (Macedonia) to Berea, via Philippi, Thessalonica: 156 miles (251 km)—ten days
- Berea to Athens (Achaia): 320 miles (515 km)—twenty-one days
- Athens to Corinth (Achaia): 53 miles (86 km)—three days
- *Travel by ship*: Corinth (Achaia) to Caesarea (Judea), via Ephesus: 870 miles (1400 km)[23]
- Caesarea to Jerusalem (Judea), via Joppe: 75 miles (120 km)—five days
- Jerusalem to Antioch (Syria): 391 miles (630 km)—twenty-five days
- **Total by foot:** 2415 miles (3887 km)—155 days (twenty-six weeks)
- **Total by ship:** 1006 miles (1620 km): between 12–30 days (two-five weeks)

23. Assuming no stops, which in reality would have been unrealistic.

BIBLIOGRAPHY

Alcock, Susan E. *Graecia Capta: The Landscapes of Roman Greece*. Cambridge: Cambridge University Press, 1993.

Bérard, Jean. "Recherches sur les itinéraires du saint Paul en Asie Mineure." *Revue Archéologique* 6 (1935): 57–90.

Boatwright, Mary T. *Hadrian and the Cities of the Roman Empire*. Princeton: Princeton University Press, 2000.

Bowers, W. Paul. "Paul's Route Through Mysia: A Note on Acts XVI.8." *Journal of Theological Studies* 30 (1979): 507–11.

Brocke, Christoph vom. *Thessaloniki: Stadt der Kassander und Gemeinde des Paulus; eine frühe christliche Gemeinde in ihrer heidnischen Umwelt*. Tübingen: Mohr-Siebeck, 2001.

French, David H. "Acts and the Roman Roads of Asia Minor." Pages 49–58 in *The Book of Acts in its Graeco-Roman Setting*. Edited by D. W. J. Gill and C. Gempf. Volume 2 of *The Book of Acts in Its First Century Setting*. Edited by Bruce W. Winter. Grand Rapids: Eerdmans, 1994.

Gill, David W. J. "Achaia." Pages 433–53 in *The Book of Acts in Its Graeco-Roman Setting*. Edited by D. W. J. Gill and C. Gempf. Volume 2 of *The Book of Acts in Its First Century Setting*. Edited by Bruce W. Winter. Grand Rapids: Eerdmans, 1994.

———. "Macedonia." Pages 397–417 in *The Book of Acts in Its Graeco-Roman Setting*. Edited by D. W. J. Gill and C. Gempf. Volume 2 of *The Book of Acts in Its First Century Setting*. Edited by Bruce W. Winter. Grand Rapids: Eerdmans, 1994.

Hammond, Nicholas G. L., and Frank W. Walbank. *A History of Macedonia*. 3 vols. Oxford: Clarendon, 1972–1988.

Jewett, Robert. "Mapping the Route of Paul's 'Second Missionary Journey' from Dorylaeum to Troas." *TynBul* 48 (1997): 1–22.

Keener, Craig S. *Acts: An Exegetical Commentary*. 4 vols. Grand Rapids: Baker Academic, 2012–2015.

Mitchell, Stephen. *Anatolia: Land, Men, and Gods in Asia Minor*. 2 vols. Oxford: Oxford University Press, 1995.

Ramsay, William M. *St. Paul the Traveller and the Roman Citizen*. Updated and rev. ed. Edited by M. Wilson. Grand Rapids: Kregel, 2001.

Riesner, Rainer. *Paul's Early Period: Chronology, Mission Strategy, Theology*. Grand Rapids: Eerdmans, 1998.

Schnabel, Eckhard J. *Early Christian Mission*. 2 vols. Downers Grove, IL: InterVarsity Press, 2004.

———. *Paul the Missionary: Realities, Strategies, and Methods*. Downers Grove, IL: InterVarsity Press, 2008.

Thompson, Glen L., and Mark Wilson. "The Route of Paul's Second Journey in Asia Minor: In the Steps of Robert Jewett and Beyond." *TynBul* 67 (2016): 217–46.

Uggeri, Giovanni. "Sulle strade di San Paolo in Anatolia: Il secondo e il terzo viaggio." Pages 125–73 in *Seminario di studi Paolo di Tarso: Il messaggio, l'immagine, i viaggi; Studi in memoria di Luigi Padovese*. Edited by S. Uggeri Patitucci and L. Padovese. Palermo: Officina di studi medievali, 2011.

CHAPTER 28

PAUL AT THE AREOPAGUS IN ATHENS

Acts 17:15–34

Joshua W. Jipp

KEY POINTS

- The Areopagus was an Athenian institution devoted to matters of justice, law, and governance.
- The Areopagus was remembered for playing a leading role in the death of Socrates who was charged with introducing foreign deities into Athens.
- Paul's speech in Acts 17:22–31 presumes some basic knowledge of the institution of the Areopagus, Stoic and Epicurean philosophy, and the trial of Socrates.

INTRODUCTION

For most readers of the Acts of the Apostles, Paul's speech to the Stoic and Epicurean philosophers at the Areopagus is one of the literary high points of Acts. A. D. Nock famously referred to Luke's literarily "brilliant picture" of Paul in Athens.[1] Paul's speech draws upon popular philosophical language and argumentation to set forth the identity of God as the creator of the universe who has revealed himself in Jesus Christ. While Paul is waiting for Silas and Timothy (Acts 17:15), he takes a tour of Athens and observes the remarkable number of idols and images in the city (17:16). While preaching in the synagogue and the marketplace every day, he is accosted by some Athenians and taken to the Areopagus where they demand the right to hear more about Paul's strange preaching (17:19–20). A robust interpretation of the speech requires some understanding of the geography of Athens,

1. A. D. Nock, "The Book of Acts: Review of Dibelius, *Aufsätze zur Apostelgeschichte*," *Gnomon* 25 (1953): 506.

Mars Hill in Athens

especially some awareness of the history, prestige, and function of the Areopagus.

THE HISTORY, FUNCTION, AND PRESTIGE OF THE ATHENIAN AREOPAGUS

The Areopagus (the "hill of Ares," Ἄρειον πάγον, *Areion pagon*) refers, depending upon the context and the time period of the source, to either the location on the hill and/or an Athenian assembly that engaged in governmental or judicial tasks.[2] The Areopagus was located on a hill northwest of the Acropolis and south of the Agora (Herodotus, *Histories* 8.52); this may have been the same location where Paul preached his message every day (Acts 17:17). Thus, references to the "Areopagus" may refer to either the hill, the council, or both.[3] By the time of Luke's writing of Acts, many scholars suppose that the Areopagus no longer met on the hill but rather met more frequently in the *Stoa Basileios* near the Agora (Demosthenes, *Against Aristogeiton 1* 22–23).[4] Yet there are good reasons for supposing that the Areopagus council continued to meet on the hill.[5]

The predemocratic origins of the Areopagus are shrouded in mystery, and it may be that the council existed to provide wisdom and guidance to the Athenian rulers. It seems that with the rise of Athenian democracy, the primary task of the Areopagus was to carry out judicial verdicts, especially in homicide cases (Lycurgus, *Against Leocrates* 61–64; Lysis 6.14; 10.11). Plutarch notes that many suppose that Solon was the creator of the Areopagus, but he argues strongly

2. See further Peter J. Rhodes, "Areopagus," *BNP* 1:1046–48.

3. See here C. J. Hemer, "Paul at Athens: A Topographical Note," *NTS* 20 (1974): 342.

4. Craig Keener, *Acts: An Exegetical Commentary* (Grand Rapids: Baker Academic, 2014), 3:2600; see, however, T. D. Barnes, "An Apostle on Trial," *JTS* 22 (1969): 408.

5. See further Barnes, "An Apostle on Trial," 409.

that the institution actually predates Solon and his reforms (Plutarch, *Solon* 19). During the time of Solon, all ex-archons became members of the council.[6] Aristotle also says that during the time of Solon the Areopagus was entrusted with guarding the laws and dispensing penalties against those who disturbed the public order (Aristotle, *Constitution of Athens* 3.3.6). Aristotle further notes that the members of the council of the Areopagus were appointed by wealthy, noble-born archons. The wealth and status of the members further enhanced the prestige of the institution.

Numerous texts celebrate the Areopagus as a bastion of justice and fairness. Pausanius passes on the legend that the Athenians named the Areopagus as such because the god Ares was the first to be tried there (Pausanius, *Descriptions of Greece* 38.5). The actual hill appears, therefore, to have carried significant symbolic resonances. Aeschylus's *Eumenides* (the final tragedy in his *Oresteia*) concludes with Athena's establishment of the council of the Areopagus who adjudicate a proper trial for the defendant, Orestes (Aeschylus, *Eumenides* 470–489, 680–684). Demosthenes praises the Areopagus as one of Athens' premier institutions:

> There are many institutions of ours the like of which are not to be found anywhere, but among them one especially peculiar to ourselves and venerable,—I mean the court of the Areopagus (*Against Aristocrates* 65 [LCL]).

Demosthenes passes on the myth from Aeschylus' *Eumenides* concerning the council's founding by the gods to mediate justice in cases of homicide (*Against Aristocrates* 66). It is the only tribunal, further, that no tyrant, oligarchy, or democracy has deprived of its jurisdiction in mediating Athenian justice. Isocrates' *Areopagiticus* presents an oration praising the virtues of the Areopagus and arguing for an even further increase in its powers. Hubert Martin states the prestige and honor of the Areopagus well:

> The council of the Areopagus was a body hallowed by its unique origins, and as such it exercised certain functions deeply rooted in religious tradition as to be virtually sacrosanct.[7]

The Areopagus also played a deciding role in the death or martyrdom of Socrates. In fact, a number of scholars have suggested that Luke depicts Paul as a new Socrates or a Socrates-like figure in Acts 17.[8] Socrates was, of course, that pesky philosopher who never left Athens and spent all of his time in Athens in the agora conversing with whoever happened to be present.[9] As Socrates was charged with introducing foreign deities to Athens (Plato, *Euthyphro* 1C; 2B; *Apology* 24B; Xenophon, *Memorabilia* 1.1.1) so is

---

6. Theodore John Cadoux and P. J. Rhodes, "Areopagus," in *Oxford Classical Dictionary*, ed. Simon Hornblower and Antony Spawforth, 3rd ed. (Oxford: Oxford University Press, 1996), 151.

7. Hubert H. Martin, Jr., "Areopagus," *ABD* 1:371.

8. I have argued this as well and draw here from my article "Paul's Areopagus Speech of Acts 17:16–34 as *Both* Critique *and* Propaganda," *JBL* 131 (2012): 567–88.

9. Plato, *Apology* 1.17C; 17.30B; Xenophon, *Memorabilia* 1.1.10; Diogenes Laertius, *Lives* 2.21; Dio Chrysostom, *Oration* 54.3.

Bust of Socrates

Paul charged with the same infraction (Acts 17:18b–20).

The popular resonances of the Areopagus as the Athenian judicial council continued into the time of the Roman Cicero who stated that "if someone says that the Republic of Athens is governed by the Council, we must understand him to mean, by the Council of the Areopagus" (*On the Nature of the Gods*, 2.74 [LCL]; see also *Letter to Atticus* 1.5; 5.6). Cicero also provides evidence that some Romans citizens joined the Areopagus council (Cicero, *Balbus* 12.30).[10] It is clear that even with the rise of Roman imperial rule the Areopagus continued to wield its authority and judicial functions well into the period of the late Roman empire.[11]

The primary classical sources present a multifaceted picture of a significant cultural, Athenian institution devoted to laws, verdicts, and governance—even if the exact role of the council shifted at times depending upon the larger political climate.[12] Presumably Luke's audience is intended to grasp the popular resonances of the Areopagus as the primary governing council over Athens, a council invested with the role of being the caretaker of legislative, judicial, religious, cultural, and political matters.[13]

PAUL BEFORE THE AREOPAGUS IN ACTS 17

How does our understanding of the ancient and venerable institution of the Athenian Areopagus influence our interpretation of Acts 17:16–34?[14]

First, Luke presents Paul and his gospel as confronting the elite religious, cultural, and legal institutions of Athens. Within this text, Luke refers to the Athenian agora (Acts 17:17), the Stoic and Epicurean philosophers (17:18), Athenian interest in the divine (17:21–22), an altar

10. Craig Keener, *Acts*, 3:2601.

11. David W. J. Gill, "Achaia," in *The Book of Acts in Its Graeco-Roman Setting*, ed. David W. J. Gill and Conrad Gempf, vol. 2 of *The Book of Acts in its First Century Setting*, ed. Bruce W. Winter (Grand Rapids: Eerdmans, 1994), 447; Barnes, "An Apostle on Trial," 411–14.

12. For a helpful study devoted to the history and changes of the Areopagus, see Christopher W. Blackwell, "The Council of the Areopagus," in *Dēmos: Classical Athenian Democracy*, ed. C. W. Blackwell (The Stoa: A Consortium for Electronic Publication in the Humanities [www.stoa.org], 2003), http://www.stoa.org/projects/demos/areopagus.pdf.

13. See Gill, "Achaia," 447–48; Martin, "Areopagus," 1:370–72.

14. What follows represents a summarized and greatly revised version of my more detailed argument in "Paul's Areopagus Speech of Acts 17:16–34," 575–87.

to an unknown god (17:23), and lines from the Stoic Cleanthes and Aratus (17:28). The institution of the Areopagus as the setting for Paul's speech (17:19), then, contributes to Luke's depiction of Paul as engaging and confronting the religious, philosophical, and culturally elite Athenians. On the one hand, Luke's depiction of Paul at the Areopagus indicates that his gospel message is no sectarian, backwoods superstition but a message worthy to receive attention from society's most prestigious and elite institutions. On the other hand, at a number of points, Luke emphasizes that Paul's engagement of the Athenians is one of conflict.[15] For example, in Paul's initial tour of Athens, Luke notes that Paul's spirit is provoked due to the fact that "he was seeing the city was full of idols" (θεωροῦντος κατείδωλον οὖσαν τὴν πόλιν, *theōrountos kateidōlon ousan tēn polin*; 17:16).[16] Whereas the Roman elite Cicero sees the Romans as the cultural heirs of the venerable traditions of ancient Athens "from which education, science, belief in the gods, agriculture, justice, and law derives" (*Pro Flacco* 62), the Lukan attribute of Athens is that it is "a luxuriant forest of idols."

Second, as noted briefly above, the parallels between Luke's characterization of Paul and the trial and death of Socrates provides the opportunity for Paul to give a defense speech before the tribunal of the Areopagus where he "proclaims the good news of Jesus and the resurrection (ὅτι τὸν Ἰησοῦν καὶ τὴν ἀνάστασιν εὐηγγελίζετο, *hoti ton Iēsoun kai tēn anastasin euēngelizeto*, 17:18b).[17] In other words, there are a variety of clues that suggest Luke has constructed Paul's time in Athens as a trial scene. Luke speaks of the Athenians as accusing Paul of "introducing" (εἰσφέρεις, *eisphereis*, 17:20) foreign deities, and this resonates with memories of Socrates, as this verb was used to depict the charge against Socrates (Xenophon, *Apology* 10–11; Justin, *First Apology* 5.4, *Second Apology* 10.5).[18] Luke portrays Paul as a Socrates-like figure in order to depict the event as a kind of mock trial between early Christianity and Athens as the epicenter of pagan philosophy and culture. According to Xenophon, the charge brought against

15. This stands against a vast number of interpreters who read the speech as placid philosophical discourse over shared religious conceptions of God, humanity, and creation. See, for example, Martin Dibelius, who, by starting with the speech proper, underestimates the importance of the speech's introduction and thereby concludes that the author's tone is one of enlightening his audience (Dibelius, "Paul on the Areopagus," in *Studies in the Acts of the Apostles*, ed. Heinrich Greeven, trans. Mary Ling [London: SCM Press, 1956], 53–56).

16. On the adjective *kateidōlos* (κατείδωλος), see R. E. Wycherley, "St. Paul at Athens," *JTS* (1968): 619–21, who argues that the prefix means something to the effect of "luxuriant with."

17. On the parallels between Paul and Socrates, see Karl Olav Sandnes, "Paul and Socrates: The Aim of Paul's Areopagus Speech," *Journal for the Study of the New Testament* 50 (1993): 13–26; Eckhard Plümacher, *Lukas als hellenistischer Schriftsteller: Studien zur Apostelgeschichte* (Göttingen: Vandenhoeck & Ruprecht, 1972), 97–99; Loveday C. A. Alexander, "Acts and Intellectual Biography," in *Acts in its Ancient Literary Context: A Classicist Looks at the Acts of the Apostles* (London: T&T Clark, 2005), 61–68; C. Kavin Rowe, *World Upside Down: Reading Acts in the Graeco-Roman Age* (Oxford: Oxford University Press, 2009), 31–33.

18. See here the clear discussion by Bertil Gärtner, *The Areopagus Speech and Natural Revelation*, trans. Carolyn Hannay King, (Uppsala: Lund, 1955), 54–55; Also, see Sandnes, "Paul and Socrates," 21–22.

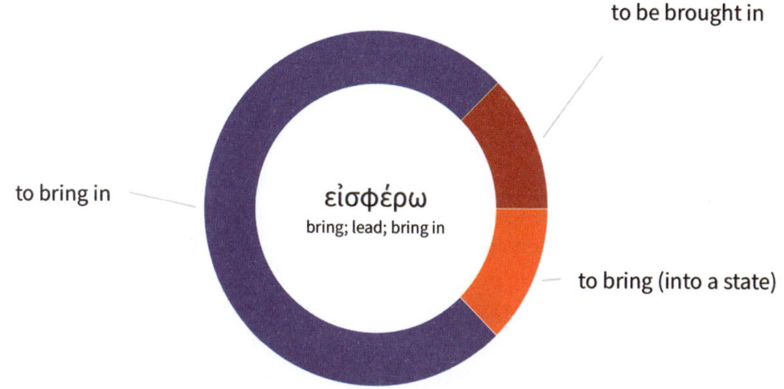

Socrates is that he "does evil, for he does not acknowledge the gods whom the state acknowledges, while introducing other, novel divine beings" (*Memorabilia* 1.1.1).[19] Likewise, of Paul, the philosophers claim that he "seems to be a herald of foreign deities" (ξένων δαιμονίων δοκεῖ καταγγελεύς εἶναι, *xenōn daimoniōn dokei katangeleus einai*; 17:18b) and that he is bringing forth "some strange/foreign things into our ears" (ξενίζοντα ... τινα ... εἰς τὰς ἀκοὰς ἡμῶν, *xenizonta ... tina ... eis tas akoas hēmōn*; 17:20a). One should not underestimate the extent to which ancient pagan cities could be hostile and suspicious of introducing foreign deities into the life of the city (for example, Josephus, *Ag. Ap.* 2.262, 265).[20] Thus, the language of Acts 17:19 might be better translated as "they grasped him (ἐπιλαβόμενοί τε αὐτοῦ, *epilabomenoi te autou*) and led him to the Areopagus, saying: 'We have the right to know what this teaching is which you are speaking of.'"[21] Luke's use of the verb *epilambanomai* (ἐπιλαμβάνομαι) often has the connotations of forceful seizure of those proclaiming the gospel, and that fits Luke's context well here (for example, Acts 16:19; 18:17; 21:30, 33; see also Luke 23:26).[22]

Third, the setting of Paul's speech as the Areopagus, the Athenian tribunal, further confirms this episode as something of a trial scene. While there is some ambiguity as to whether Luke understands the "Areopagus" to be the actual hill of Ares or the Athenian council (or both!), a few factors within Acts lead me to concur with Timothy D. Barnes that Luke refers to "the effective government of Roman Athens and its chief court."[23] For example, and first, the extensive

19. English translation of Xenophon follows Hans-Josef Klauck, *Magic and Paganism in Early Christianity: The World of the Acts of the Apostles* (Edinburgh: T&T Clark, 2000), 76.

20. See Richard I. Pervo, *Acts: A Commentary* (Minneapolis: Fortress, 2009), 427; also see Robert Garland, *Introducing New Gods: The Politics of Athenian Religion* (London: Duckworth, 1992), 10.

21. Further support for this translation is provided by Bruce W. Winter, "On Introducing Gods to Athens: An Alternative Reading of Acts 17:18–20," *TynBul* 47 (1996): 81–83.

22. So Rowe, *World Upside Down*, 29.

23. Barnes, "An Apostle on Trial," 413; also, Pervo, *Acts*, 428.

echoes between Paul and Socrates highlight the judicial function of the court. Second, the epithet used to describe "Dionysius the Areopagite" may suggest that he is a member of the Athenian council (17:34). Third, it makes more sense to imagine Paul speaking "in the midst of an assembly," not on the middle of a hill, based on 17:22a where Paul is "standing in the midst of the Areopagus" (ἐν μέσῳ τοῦ Ἀρείου πάγου, *en mesō tou Areiou pagou*) and in 17:33 where, again, Paul is spoken of as leaving "from their midst" (ἐκ μέσου αὐτῶν, *ek mesou autōn*). The language suggests that Paul is "in the midst" of some of the members of the Areopagus council, not that he is "in the middle of the hill."[24] Most important, however, is the simple fact that the Areopagus, as we have seen extensively, was entrusted with the city's care in judicial and political matters. Paul is granted the opportunity to proclaim Jesus and his resurrection from the dead among one of the most revered councils of the ancient world, and yet its association with mediating Athenian justice—not least against Socrates' supposed religious innovations—strikes a strong note of conflict between Paul and his audience. The Athenians declare that they have the "right" or "authority" to hear about Paul's so-called foreign gods (17:19b) and will form a decision regarding the "strong doctrines" Paul is proclaiming (17:20). It may be that the Areopagus here is tasked with an educational responsibility and present an informal inquiry to Paul to give an explanation for his strange teachings.[25]

PAUL'S SPEECH IN ACTS 17:22–31

Paul's speech draws upon features of Hellenistic philosophy, especially Stoic traditions, to present the Christian movement as a legitimate and superior philosophy.[26] The primary topics of the speech, namely, monotheism, the critique of temples and sacrifices, the deity's providential arrangement of the seasons, and the unity of humanity, resonate quite clearly with Stoic philosophy. These similarities function to call the Athenians to turn from their ignorant worship of the deity by showing them that the Christian movement is the fulfillment of the best aspects of their history and traditions.[27] Like the Stoics, Paul too proclaims that the singular God: (1) is the creator of all things and, therefore, does not dwell in human-made temples (οὐκ ἐν χειροποιήτοις ναοῖς κατοικεῖ, *ouk en cheiropoiētois naois kataoikei*; Acts 17:24); (2) is not rightly worshiped through human priestly sacrifices since he is the creator of everything (17:25); (3) has implanted internally within humans a desire to seek him (17:27); and (4) cannot be imaged through idols or created material since humanity alone is the offspring and likeness of God (17:28–29). Not only the topics themselves but the similarity of their internal logic and reasoning demonstrate close similarities to Stoic thinking. And again, the fact that the Stoic philosophers make up the dramatic audience of the sermon (17:18), along with Paul's

24. Gärtner, *The Areopagus Speech and Natural Revelation*, 55–56.

25. Gärtner, *The Areopagus Speech and Natural Revelation*, 59.

26. For further discussion on the topic of this section, see my article "Does Paul Translate the Gospel in Acts 17:22–31," *Perspectives in Religious Studies* 45.4 (2018): 361–76.

27. My argument throughout this section has been articulated in more detail throughout Jipp, "Paul's Areopagus Speech of Acts 17:16–34."

Athenian Acropolis and Its Many Temples

explicit quotation from the well-known Stoic Aratus (17:28b) and the general reference to the Athenian poets (17:28a) suggests that Luke has crafted the sermon in such a way as to invite both the dramatic audience of the Athenians and readers of Acts to engage in comparison between Hellenistic philosophy and Paul's proclamation of the gospel.

If Paul is to be understood as chastising his audience for being "excessively superstitious" (17:22b), which makes good sense in light of his reference to having encountered an altar to "an unknown god" (17:23), then Paul is charging his audience of engaging in irrational worship. The motivation for establishing altars to unknown gods stems from anxiety that one has not placated every god possible.[28] Thus, when Paul declares that he will now proclaim to them the one "whom they have worshiped in ignorance" (17:23b), he turns the table on the Athenians by declaring that they are the superstitious ones who worship in ignorance.[29] Paul's invocation of the Stoic poets and Aratus functions to make the point that the singular human Jesus of Nazareth, the one who died and has been raised from the dead, is God's appointed judge of the world (17:31)—a point that most of the audience finds absurd (17:32).

Paul has articulated and defended his proclamation of the gospel, centered upon Jesus and his resurrection from the dead, before the historic, venerable council of the Athenian Areopagus. And while many of them mock and some delay their consideration of the matter (17:32a), some of the men believed and joined Paul (17:32b). Even one of the Areopagites, Dionysius, along with his wife Damaris were persuaded by Paul's message (17:34), thereby further legitimating Luke's portrait of the gospel as no crude superstition and deserving of careful consideration.

28. See Klauck, *Magic and Paganism in Early Christianity*, 82–83.

29. Paul refers to their worship as "ignorant" or "without knowledge" three times in his speech (17:23 twice; 17:30).

BIBLIOGRAPHY

Alexander, Loveday C. A. "Acts and Intellectual Biography." Pages 43–68 in *Acts in Its Ancient Literary Context: A Classicist Looks at the Acts of the Apostles*. London: T&T Clark, 2005.

Barnes, T. D. "An Apostle on Trial." *Journal of Theological Studies* 20 (1969): 407–19.

Blackwell, Christopher W. "The Council of the Areopagus." In *Dēmos: Classical Athenian Democracy*. Edited by C. W. Blackwell. The Stoa: A Consortium for Electronic Publication in the Humanities (www.stoa.org), 2003. http://www.stoa.org/projects/demos/areopagus.pdf

Cadoux, Theodore John, and P. J. Rhodes. "Areopagus." Page 151 in *Oxford Classical Dictionary*. Edited by Simon Hornblower and Antony Spawforth. 3rd ed. Oxford: Oxford University Press, 1996.

Dibelius, Martin. "Paul on the Areopagus." Pages 26–77 in *Studies in the Acts of the Apostles*. Edited by Heinrich Greeven. Translated by Mary Ling. London: SCM Press, 1956.

Garland, Robert. *Introducing New Gods: The Politics of Athenian Religion*. London: Duckworth, 1992.

Gärtner, Bertil. *The Areopagus Speech and Natural Revelation*. Translated by Carolyn Hannay King. Uppsala: Lund, 1955.

Gill, David W. J. "Achaia." Pages 433–53 in *The Book of Acts in Its Graeco-Roman Setting*. Edited by David W. J. Gill and Conrad Gempf. Volume 2 of *The Book of Acts in Its First Century Setting*. Edited by Bruce W. Winter. Grand Rapids: Eerdmans, 1994.

Hemer, C. J. "Paul at Athens: A Topographical Note." *NTS* 20 (1974): 341–50.

Jipp, Joshua W. "Does Paul Translate the Gospel in Acts 17:22-31." *Perspectives in Religious Studies* 45.4 (2018): 361–76.

———. "Paul's Areopagus Speech of Acts 17:16–34 as *Both* Critique *and* Propaganda." *JBL* 131 (2012): 567–88.

Keener, Craig. *Acts: An Exegetical Commentary*. 4 vols. Grand Rapids: Baker Academic, 2012–2015.

Klauck, Hans-Josef. *Magic and Paganism in Early Christianity: The World of the Acts of the Apostles*. Edinburgh: T&T Clark, 2000.

Martin, Hubert H., Jr. "Areopagus." *ABD* 1:370–72.

Nock, A. D. "The Book of Acts: Review of Dibelius, *Aufsätze zur Apostelgeschichte*." *Gnomon* 25 (1953): 497–506.

Pervo, Richard I. *Acts: A Commentary*. Minneapolis: Fortress, 2009.

Plümacher, Eckhard. *Lukas als hellenistischer Schriftsteller: Studien zur Apostelgeschichte*. Göttingen: Vandenhoeck & Ruprecht, 1972.

Rhodes, Peter J. "Areopagus." *BNP* 1:1046–48.

Rowe, C. Kavin. *World Upside Down: Reading Acts in the Graeco-Roman Age*. Oxford: Oxford University Press, 2009.

Sandnes, Karl Olav. "Paul and Socrates: The Aim of Paul's Areopagus Speech." *Journal for the Study of the New Testament* 50 (1993): 13–26.

Winter, Bruce W. "On Introducing Gods to Athens: An Alternative Reading of Acts 17:18–20." *TynBul* 47 (1996): 71–90.

Wycherley, R. E. "St. Paul at Athens." *Journal of Theological Studies* (1968): 619–21.

CHAPTER 29

WHAT HAS ATHENS TO DO WITH JERUSALEM?

Paul's Areopagus Speech in Context

Acts 17:16–34

Benjamin A. Foreman

KEY POINTS

- Athens was neither a large, nor politically important, city in the first century AD.
- Although Athens was a thoroughly polytheistic city, new gods could not be introduced into the pantheon without the express permission of the Areopagus council. Paul, therefore, was brought before the council to see if he was propagating the worship of unsanctioned gods.
- While Paul's speech has points of contact with Hellenistic thinking, it is a thoroughly Christian message.

INTRODUCTION

In a scathing treatise against Christian heresies, the Carthaginian lawyer and church father Tertullian (approximately AD 160–220) famously asks, "What indeed has Athens to do with Jerusalem?" (*De praescriptione haereticorum* 7). Although Tertullian polemically poses this rhetorical question to show the futility of philosophy, it encapsulates quite nicely the topic of this essay.

According to the narrative in Acts, Paul traveled to Athens on his second missionary journey, sometime in AD 50 or 51. As is the case wherever Jesus is preached, the response to his message there was mixed. Some Athenians responded positively (Luke explicitly names two of them), but others mocked him (Acts 17:32–34). No other passage in Acts, however, has produced such a massive volume of secondary literature.[1] Scholars have raised questions

1. Note Bruce's comment: "Probably no ten verses in Acts have formed the text for such

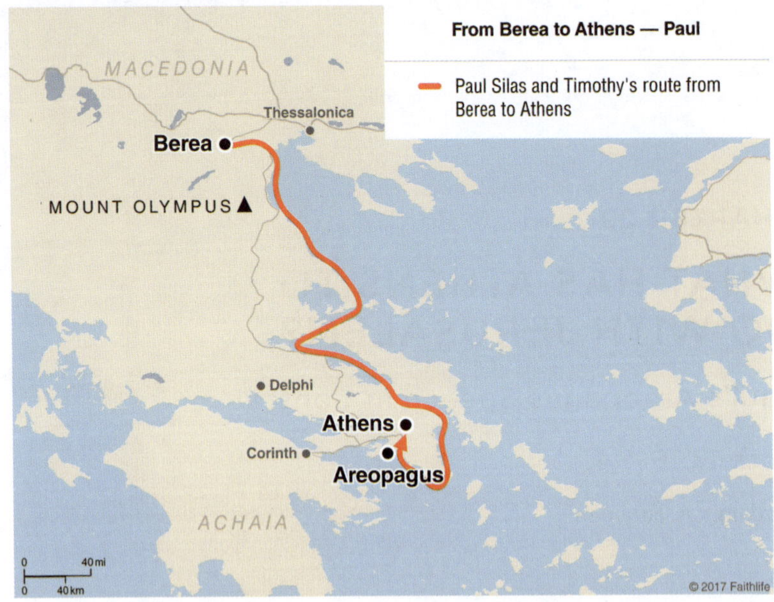

about the authenticity of Paul's speech, its content, context, and whether it is even a Christian message. Since the focus of this commentary is on matters related to the spatial setting of the New Testament, this essay will focus on the cultural milieu of Athens and consider the extent to which Paul conformed the content of his message to his audience (and by extension, his location).

To provide some cultural context on the city of Athens, it is helpful first to briefly compare the city with Jerusalem. Contrary to popular belief, the answer to Tertullian's question is, "Really quite a lot." The contextual worlds of Athens and Jerusalem were not as distant from each other as many assume—both were thoroughly Hellenistic cities. Nevertheless, one key feature clearly distinguished Athens from Jerusalem, and this, we will see, is what Paul picks up on in his Areopagus speech.

THE HELLENIZATION OF JERUSALEM

The city of Jerusalem underwent massive changes in the first century AD. Prior to Agrippa I's construction of the third wall in AD 41–44, Jerusalem fanned out over an area of approximately 230 acres (93 ha).[2] Numerous impressive buildings peppered the city's landscape, but all were dwarfed by the city's chef-d'oeuvre: the temple. What made the temple so significant was not just the building itself, but the entire Temple Mount complex. In Herod's day, the Temple Mount occupied about one sixth of the city's total area (thirty-six acres [14.5 ha]) and was

an abundance of commentary as has gathered around Paul's Areopagus speech." (F. F. Bruce, *Commentary on the Book of Acts*, rev. ed. [Grand Rapids: Eerdmans, 1988], 333).

2. This figure includes the area enclosed by the first and second wall. For a description of the three walls surrounding Jerusalem see Josephus, *J.W.* 5.142–155.

"the largest single temple complex in the ancient world."[3]

Although Jerusalem of the first century AD retained an undoubtedly Jewish character, the threads of Hellenism were thoroughly woven into the fabric of society. Herod built the first theater of the country in Jerusalem, and "all around the theater were inscriptions concerning Caesar and trophies of the nations which he had won in war" (Josephus, *Ant.* 15.272 [LCL]).[4] He also built an amphitheater "in the plain" (Josephus, *Ant.* 15.268; the location is also uncertain), which may have served as the hippodrome Josephus also mentions (*Ant.* 17.255; *J.W.* 2.44).

Jerusalem's domestic architecture also bore the marks of Greek/Roman influence. One poignant example comes from a massive house (called the Palatial Mansion) uncovered in the priestly quarter on Jerusalem's Western Hill. The 6500 square foot (604 m²) residence, which belonged to a priestly family, was beautified on the inside with painted frescoes that "clearly resemble the wall paintings at Pompeii."[5] Imitation ashlar masonry—a construction style originating in Greece—ornamented the mansion's large reception hall, and a Doric frieze adorned the wall of an adjacent room. In the surrounding area Corinthian and Ionic capitals were also found.[6] Greek influence extended also to their burial practices. The Tomb of Absalom in the Kidron Valley, for example, is "a fusion of Ionic, Doric, Egyptian, and Hellenistic-Roman styles,"[7] and even private burials were influenced by Greco-Roman practice.[8]

Hellenism penetrated more than just Jerusalem's architecture. Based on the number of Greek inscriptions found on ossuaries in Jerusalem, Martin Hengel estimates that about 10–20 percent of the Jewish population spoke Greek as their mother tongue. Some synagogue services were even conducted in Greek (e.g., Acts 6:9)—as the Greek Theodotus

3. Magen Broshi, "The Archaeology of Palestine 63 BCE–CE 70," in *The Early Roman Period*, vol. 3 of *The Cambridge History of Judaism*, ed. William Horbury, W. D. Davies, and John Sturdy (Cambridge: Cambridge University Press, 2008), 3. For the Temple Mount's fascinating history, see Leen Ritmeyer, *The Quest: Revealing the Temple Mount in Jerusalem* (Jerusalem: Carta, 2006).

4. Herod's theater has yet to be found. The Israeli Antiquities Authority recently uncovered a later "theater" (perhaps an odeon [used for musical productions] or *bouleutērion* [for assemblies relating to public affairs]) under Wilson's Arch near the Western Wall. The archaeologists, however, have dated it to sometime after AD 70, suggesting it may have still been under construction during the Bar Kokhba revolt (AD 132–135). See the preliminary press release: https://www.timesofisrael.com/massive-section-of-western-wall-and-roman-theater-uncovered-after-1700-years/.

5. Nahman Avigad, *Discovering Jerusalem* (Nashville: Nelson, 1980), 99.

6. See Avigad, *Discovering Jerusalem*, 81–203, for further examples.

7. Broshi, "Archaeology of Palestine," 36–37.

8. Bond notes that some Jewish tombs were found with coins in them. According to her, this reflects the pagan practice of placing coins in the eyes or mouth of the deceased. She also argues the very use of stone ossuaries ("bone boxes") for secondary burial is a development of Roman practice (Helen K. Bond, *Caiaphas: Friend of Rome and Judge of Jesus?* [Louisville: Westminster John Knox, 2004], 2–3).

Tomb of Absalom, Kidron Valley

inscription implies.[9] According to Hengel, "The most important center of Greek language in Jewish Palestine was the capital, Jerusalem."[10]

In short, "Herod's Jerusalem was a Hellenistic city through and through, which had been decked in splendor as a result of the king's ambition."[11] But despite Hellenism's widespread influence on Jerusalem, there still was one area in which the city remained untouched: Jerusalem was a one-temple city tolerating no cultic images. The inhabitants of Jerusalem were so devoted to the first and second commandments, that when Pilate, for example, attempted to parade the bust of the emperor through Jerusalem, the city nearly erupted into riots.[12] In that sense, Jerusalem was not Athens.

9. For further information, see B. Foreman, "The Geography of Worship: From Temple to Synagogue to Church," chapter 10 in this volume, and C. McKinny, "The Theodotus Synagogue Inscription and Its Relationship to the Book of Acts," chapter 12 in this volume.

10. Martin Hengel, *The "Hellenization" of Judaea in the First Century after Christ* (Eugene, OR: Wipf and Stock, 2003), 9.

11. Hengel, *Hellenization of Judaea*, 33.

12. Josephus, *Ant.* 18.55–59. Gaius Caligula also attempted to erect a statue of himself in the temple of Jerusalem. But given the Jews' threat to revolt if he carried through with the plan, Agrippa eventually convinced him not to bring the statue to Jerusalem (cf. Philo, *Legatio ad Gaium* 30.207; 43.346; Tacitus, *Annales* 12.54; Josephus, *Ant.* 18.289–301).

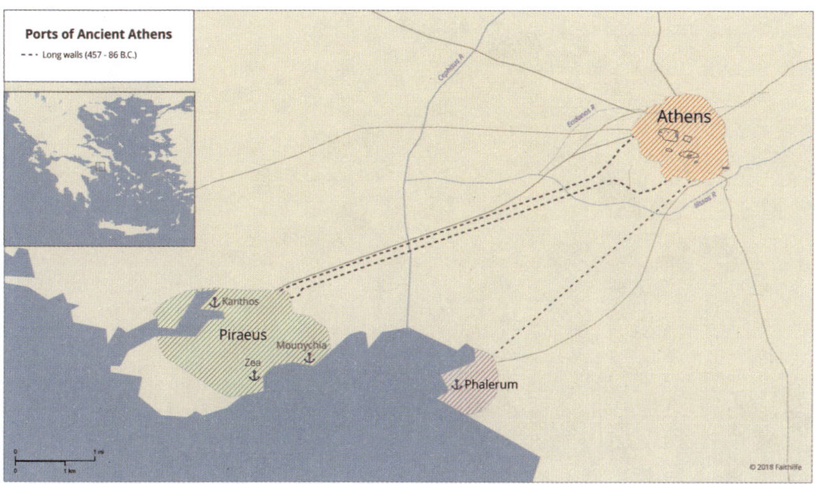

THE CITY OF ATHENS

THE PORTS

The city of Athens sits on a plain in a large triangular peninsula known in antiquity as Attica. Athens was the region's most important city—the peninsula was divided into 139 districts and were all governed from there. Although the city's original harbor was at Phalerum (four miles [6.4 km] to the southeast), in the fifth century BC the prominent politician Themistocles incorporated Piraeus (five miles [8 km] to the southwest) into the city as well (Pausanias, *Graeciae descriptio* 1.1.2). With three large deep-water harbors, it became Athens's primary port. Kanthos was the largest wharf and served as the principal commercial harbor. Zea was the main war harbor, and while Mounychia was the smallest harbor, it still contained some eighty-two ship sheds.[13]

Luke tells us Paul traveled from Berea to Athens by sea (Acts 17:14). Since Piraeus was the chief cosmopolitan port, he probably would have sailed into this marina, perhaps docking at Kanthos, the main commercial harbor. According to Pausanias, "The most noteworthy sight in the Peiraeus [Piraeus] is a precinct of Athena and Zeus" (*Graeciae descriptio* 1.1.3 [LCL]). Paul's first sight, therefore, would have been the Athenian idols. From there it was a five mile (8 km) walk to the heart of the city.

THE BUILDINGS

Settlement in Athens reaches all the way back to the late Neolithic period (ca. 4000 BC), though little is known about the city until the Bronze Age. After passing though several centuries of darkness, the city finally reached its zenith in the fifth century BC (known as the Classical period). Its rise began with the famous battle of Marathon in 490 BC, which resulted in the Athenians' successful expulsion of the Persians from Attica. A decade later, however, the Persian king Xerxes (mentioned in Esther) returned

13. This paragraph is a summary of John M. Camp, *The Archaeology of Athens* (New Haven: Yale University Press, 2001), 294–97.

Parthenon

with a larger force and ran the Athenians out of their city. Although the Persians burned and destroyed most of the city, the sweetness of their victory was short-lived. The Athenians soon scored a major naval victory at the port of Salamis, and the following year the Persians suffered a humiliating defeat at Plataea (479 BC). These key battles shifted the tide of war in favor of Athens, and the Persians soon hobbled home licking their wounds. To keep the Persians at bay, the Greek city-states formed a confederacy, and in due course the Athenians found themselves at the head of this coalition (called the Delian League). With money now flowing into the Athenian coffers, the citizens set about rebuilding their city. Over the next thirty years (ca. 460–429 BC), "Athens was adorned with some of the greatest works ever known—paid for by the tribute from its empire."[14]

The flowering city also became an intellectual powerhouse. As Connolly and Dodge note, a person wandering the streets of Athens at that time might have bumped into the sculptor Phidias, the dramatists Sophocles and Euripides, the comedy writer Aristophanes, the historian Thucydides, or the philosopher Socrates—who was teaching pupils such as Plato and Xenophon. Such a volume of erudite prowess is unmatched in any other period: "Never in history have so

14. William R. Biers, *The Archaeology of Greece: An Introduction*, rev. ed. (Ithaca: Cornell University Press, 1987), 188. According to Biers, one-sixth of the empire's tribute went to the city of Athens.

many great people been alive at the same time, let alone living in the same town."[15]

Many of the major historical monuments seen by Paul were built by the fifth-century citizenry. Like the Temple Mount in Jerusalem, Athens's most famous monument (the Parthenon) was built on the highest part of the city—the acropolis. Although smaller than the Temple Mount, the Athenian acropolis is visually impressive.[16] Standing on the southern side of the acropolis, the Parthenon (built from 447–438 BC) contained six large porticoes, and was designed to house the large, forty-foot tall (12 m), statue of Athena Parthenos.[17] Just in front of the building was the altar of Athena. Lining the acropolis were other sanctuaries and temples such as the Erechtheion, and temples to Nike, Pandion, Zeus, Roma and Augustus, and others. Leading up to the acropolis was an impressive monumental staircase (called the Propylaia), built entirely out of marble.[18]

Just to the west was the Areopagus ("Mars Hill"), the hill where the city's council met to discuss matters pertaining to the city (see the discussion below).[19] Apparently, the council met in the open air, since according to Camp, "The rock top has some quarried and worn surfaces, but there is little to indicate the presence of a council chamber or the nature of any other possible facilities."[20] Just below the Areopagus was the Greek agora—the historic marketplace of the city. The large temple of Hephaestus, the Hephaisteion, sat in this area as well, as did the temple of Ares, the Royal Stoa, the Stoa of Attalos, and a number of other covered walkways used for discussions and other religious purposes.

Approximately seven hundred feet (213.3 m) to the east of the Greek agora lay the Roman forum. Initiated by Julius Caesar, it was completed by Caesar Augustus sometime in the final decade of the first century BC. By Paul's day it had overtaken the Greek agora as the main market of the city.[21] In addition to serving as a commercial center, it was also a place for religious activity since the temple of Ares, an altar for Zeus, a stoa of Zeus, and a podium temple to the Eleusinian divinities, were all located there.[22] To the

15. Peter Connolly and Hazel Dodge, *The Ancient City: Life in Classical Athens and Rome* (Oxford: Oxford University Press, 1998), 9.

16. The oval acropolis is approximately 450 feet long (north/south) by 1000 feet wide (east/west) (137 x 305 m). The Temple Mount is about 1500 feet long (north/south) by 950 feet wide (east/west) (457 x 289.5 m). See chart on page 708.

17. See the description in Pausanias, *Graeciae descriptio* 1.24.

18. For a helpful, accessible discussion of these monuments, see Konstantinos Tsakos, *The Acropolis: The Monuments and the Museum; A Guide to the History and Archaeology* (Athens: Hesperos, 2000).

19. This is well argued in Timothy D. Barnes, "An Apostle on Trial," *Journal of Theological Studies* 20 (1969): 408–10.

20. Camp, *Archaeology of Athens*, 265. *Pace* McRay who says it was "undoubtedly covered in marble in Paul's day." (John R. McRay, "Athens," *Dictionary of New Testament Background*, ed. Craig A. Evans and Stanley E. Porter [Downers Grove, IL: InterVarsity Press, 2000], 140).

21. Camp, *Archaeology of Athens*, 193.

22. Daniel J. Geagan, "Roman Athens, Some Aspects of Life and Culture, I: 86 B.C.–A.D. 267," *ANRW* 7.1:380–81.

The Areopagus (Mars Hill)

southeast of the acropolis stood a large temple for the Olympian Zeus. In Paul's day it was still under construction, for although the Athenians began to build the temple in the fifth century BC, it was not completed until the time of Hadrian (2nd century AD).

In short, a large assortment of religious buildings and monuments peppered the streets and hills of Athens. The contrast between the sole sanctuary in Jerusalem and the almost innumerable temples and idols in Athens could hardly have been greater.

PAUL IN ATHENS

Although Athens may still have been an iconic city in the minds of many in the first century AD, it by no means was a major political player in the Roman world. Its peak in the fifth century was followed by a five-hundred-year downward trajectory. The city saw a brief resurgence in the first century BC when Augustus renovated many of its historic monuments (and even added many new ones), but Roman interest in Athens receded after his death. Over the next century, the only other Roman emperor to visit the city was Trajan (approximately AD 98–117).[23] When Paul came to the city in approximately AD 50 it had a population of only around 30,000 (see table below for comparison).[24]

Luke does not say if Paul visited the acropolis or other public monuments. As was his custom in other cities (Acts 13:5, 14; 14:1; 17:1, 10; 18:4, 19; 19:8), he made his way to the synagogue to preach the message of Jesus to the city's Jewish residents (Acts 17:17). In 1977 archaeologists recovered a small marble fragment from

23. Geagan, "Roman Athens," 383.

24. Eckhard J. Schnabel, *Acts* (Grand Rapids: Zondervan, 2012), 722. McRay ("Athens," 139) lowers the number to 25,000.

Roman Forum

a pottery assemblage originally excavated in the Greek agora in 1933. The stone is etched with a menorah and a lulav (a palm branch used in the festival of tabernacles) and therefore the excavator believes it was originally part of the marble facade of a synagogue. Fascinating as this suggestion may be, the building is dated to sometime between AD 267–396 and therefore cannot be the synagogue from Paul's day.[25] So far, no synagogue from the first century has been found in Athens, but since many Jewish synagogues convened in private residences, Paul may simply have "reasoned" (v. 17) with the Jews in a local home.[26]

City	Estimated Population in the First Century[27]
Rome	1.2 million
Alexandria	500,000–600,000
Antioch	200,000–600,000
Ephesus	200,000–250,000
Corinth	150,000–300,000
Jerusalem	80,000
Athens	30,000

25. See discussion in A. T. Kraabel, "The Diaspora Synagogue: Archaeological and Epigraphic Evidence since Sukenik," in *Ancient Synagogues: Historical Analysis and Archaeological Discovery*, ed. Dan Urman and Paul V. M. Flesher (Leiden: Brill, 1995), 125–26.

26. See B. Foreman, "The Geography of Worship: From Temple to Synagogue to Church," chapter 10 in this volume.

27. Population estimates vary considerably among scholars. The numbers in the table are taken from the following sources: Rome—Connolly and Dodge, *Ancient City*, 127; Alexandria—Dorothy I. Sly, *Philo's Alexandria* (London: Routledge, 1996), 44–51; Antioch—Frederick W. Norris, "Antioch of Syria," *ABD* 1:265 (number does not include slaves or

Paul also conversed with the Athenians in the agora (marketplace) (v. 17). This is probably a reference to the Roman forum, the main marketplace in Paul's day. Interestingly, the crowd understood Paul to be a "preacher of foreign divinities (pl.)" (v. 18). Paul, of course, was not advocating multiple gods, but to polytheistic ears, "Jesus" (m.) and "*anastasis*" (ἀνάστασις, f.), the Greek word for "resurrection," sounded like a reference to two deities.[28]

Preaching two divinities to a city swimming in a sea of gods is not what concerned the Athenians. What troubled them was his (supposed) propagation of *foreign* deities. Strange as it may seem, the introduction of new gods into the city for worship had to be officially sanctioned by the Areopagus council (the governing body of Athens).[29] Four and a half centuries earlier (399 BC) Socrates was brought before the five-hundred-member council in Athens and accused of rejecting the gods of the city and *teaching new deities* (Plato, *Apology*, 24B, 26C; Xenophon, *Memorabilia*, 1.1.1, 3).[30] Although many of the council members initially sided with Socrates, they eventually turned on him, and Socrates was sentenced to death by poisoning (the famous hemlock). Even Josephus knew the introduction of new deities was under the jurisdiction of the council. He writes about an Athenian

population of surrounding region); Ephesus—Harold Hoehner, *Ephesians: An Exegetical Commentary* (Grand Rapids: Baker Academic, 2002), 88, cf. n. 6; Corinth—John R. McRay, "Corinth," in Evans, *Dictionary of New Testament Background*, 228 (number does not include slaves); Jerusalem—Broshi, "Estimating the Population of Ancient Jerusalem," *BAR* 4.2 (1978): 13–14.

28. "Jesus" may have been interpreted as a divinized power of healing or restoration (Bruce, *Acts*, 331), and "*Anastasis*" may have been understood as a personification of the afterlife (Schnabel, *Acts*, 726).

29. Barnes, "An Apostle on Trial," 411–14.

30. The sources also say he was accused of leading the children astray.

priestess who was put to death because, "someone accused her of initiating people into the mysteries of foreign gods; this was forbidden by their law, and the penalty decreed for any who introduced a foreign god was death" (*Ag. Ap.* 2.268 [LCL]).[31] Concerned, therefore, that Paul may be proposing the worship of new deities without the express permission of the council, the people brought Paul to the Areopagus for further examination.[32]

The word Areopagus literally means "the hill of Ares." In Greek mythology, Ares was the god of war and was known as Mars to the Romans—hence the Latin name "Mars Hill." There is some debate about whether Paul was brought to the top of the traditional hill or somewhere else. Since "Areopagus" (Greek: Ἄρειος πάγος, *Areios pagos*) can refer specifically to the council or the hill, some believe the location of Paul's speech cannot be pinpointed since (in their view) the council met in various locations throughout the city.[33] As Barnes has shown, however, the traditional explanation is still the best: Paul was led up the hill to meet with the council.[34]

PAUL'S SPEECH IN CONTEXT

Standing atop the open-air rock outcropping of the Areopagus and facing north, Paul had a clear view of the acropolis (500 feet [152.5 m] to his right), the Greek agora (550 feet [167.6 m] below him), the Roman Forum (700 feet [213.3 m] to the right of the Greek agora), the temple of Hephaestus (350 feet [106.7 m] to left of the Greek agora), and numerous other public monuments. From the vista spread before him, one thing could not be missed: the Athenians were passionately devoted to their gods.

Capitalizing on the city's religiosity, Paul begins his speech with a personal observation: "I found also an altar with this inscription, 'To the unknown god'" (v. 23). As scholars note, several ancient sources refer to Athenian altars dedicated to unknown gods. For example, Pausanias, who visited Athens sometime around AD 150 writes that at the harbor of Phalerum (as at Piraeus) there stood temples for Athena and Zeus (among others), and "altars of the gods named Unknown" (Pausanias, *Graeciae descriptio* 1.1.4 [LCL]).[35] Paul's reference to the unknown god of Athens, however, was not just a good introduction to his speech. Paul was not a fan of hemlock; this was part of his defense: "What therefore you worship as unknown, this I proclaim to you" (v. 23). Although somewhat crafty, his argument was simply that in preaching Christ and the resurrection, he was not introducing new gods to the city.

---

31. For more references see C. Kavin Rowe, *World Upside Down: Reading Acts in the Graeco-Roman Age* (Oxford: Oxford University Press, 2010), 194 n. 117.

32. Bock, objects to the interpretation that Paul was put on trial at the Areopagus since "no description in the outcome of the scene really points to that kind of an event [i.e., an arrest and trial]" (Darrell L. Bock, *Acts* [Grand Rapids: Baker Academic, 2007], 562). As Barnes notes, however, "The almost uniform practice of the Roman world was an informal process, with hardly any rules to circumscribe either procedure of penalties or the nature of the charge" (Barnes, "An Apostle on Trial," 413–14).

33. E.g., Camp, *The Archaeology of Athens*, 195.

34. See Barnes, "An Apostle on Trial."

35. See McRay, "Athens," 140, for more references.

Since he merely was giving a name to an unknown god they already worshiped, the council had no basis for indictment.[36]

After briefly laying out his defense, Paul quickly moves on to describe who this "unknown" God is: he is both creator and Lord of all (vv. 24).[37] This would have been foreign to Athenian ears, for the belief in one God as sole creator and sole ruler of all things is, according to Bauckham, "what distinguished [Israel's] God as unique from all other reality, including beings worshipped as gods by Gentiles."[38] Athenians most definitely did not believe in one creator God who is Lord of all, and standing before the Areopagus, Paul makes the following four subsidiary points about this one God:

1. The God who created all things does not dwell in human temples, nor does he need anything from humans (vv. 24–25).
2. This one God who created everything is knowable and near (26–28a). Some commentators believe Paul quotes (v. 28a) from the sixth-century BC Greek philosopher Epimenides, but this is uncertain.[39] A more important point to notice is Paul connects the nearness of God to the Old Testament creation story: "From one man he made every nation of the human race ... so that they would search for God and perhaps grope around for him and find him, though he is not far from each one of us" (vv. 26–27 NET).
3. The one creator God cannot be imaged (vv. 28b–29). Paul's argument here is quite subtle and works at two levels. First, he quotes from a Greek poem called *Phaenomena* (written in 301 BC), and states that if we are god's offspring (as the poem asserts), then it is foolish to make images of him, since "we ought not to think that the divine being is like gold or silver or stone, an image formed by the art and imagination of man" (v. 29). In the poem Paul refers to, however, the Stoic author Aratus claims we are the offspring of *Zeus* (compare v. 28). But clearly Paul is not equating Yahweh with Zeus.[40] He quotes from Aratus, rather, to show the Athenians that even within their

36. I say his argument was "crafty" because at a deeper level Paul was arguing against himself. If the true god is unknown to them, then by definition Paul is introducing to them a new god—new to them at least.

37. Rowe powerfully argues that when Peter's assertion that *Jesus* is Lord of all (10:36) is read against Paul's statement here that *God* is Lord of all (17:24), "Peter's speech makes a bold Christological claim.... God's universal Lordship is expressed in the Lordship of Jesus Christ." See the full argument in Rowe, *World Upside Down*, 103–16, 140–156 [105, 112].

38. Richard Bauckham, *Jesus and the God of Israel: God Crucified and Other Studies on the New Testament's Christology of Divine Identity* (Grand Rapids: Eerdmans, 2008), 9.

39. E.g., Bruce, *Acts*, 338–39. C. K. Barrett, *A Critical and Exegetical Commentary on the Acts of the Apostles, Volume 2: Introduction and Commentary on Acts XV–XXVIII* (Edinburgh: T&T Clark, 1998), 846–47, believes it goes back to Paul or Luke.

40. Rowe notes the Jewish philosopher Aristobulus (second century BC) quotes from the same poem and does precisely this—he posits "an ultimate metaphysical identity between the high god of the pagans (Zeus) and the high god of the Jews (God of Israel)" (Rowe, *World Upside Down*, 38).

Propylaia Leading to Acropolis

own religious system, the Athenian idolatry is silly since these images are nothing more than "the art and imagination of man" (v. 29). In other words, Paul lifts a line from Aratus simply to show that if we have been brought forth from god (as they believe), then it is foolish to think we can bring gods—through idols—into existence.[41] His main critique, therefore, is of the Athenian idolatry, yet he does so from within their own system of thinking.

On the other hand, his words cannot be divorced from what he stated earlier about the one Creator who brought forth the entire human race from one man (v. 26). When verse 29 is heard within the wider context of Paul's speech, it is clear the "divine being" of whom we are his offspring (v. 29), is, in Paul's mind, Yahweh of Genesis 1. Thus, his critique of the Athenian idolatry from within their own system is not made at the expense of equating Yahweh with Zeus. In *neither* system of belief does it make sense to make an image of God. His argument, therefore, is just as compelling when heard with Hellenistic or with Hebraic ears.

4. This God who created all things is also a judge who demands repentance (vv. 30–32). God's judgment, according to Paul, will be carried out by "a man" whom he has appointed and raised from the dead (v. 31). Although Jesus is not named, he is clearly implied.

41. As Rowe rightly remarks, although some of the philosophers may have broadly agreed with Paul's skepticism of the idol rituals, "many—probably most—ancients took their images rather more sincerely" (Rowe, *World Upside Down*, 35).

Temple of Hephaestus

Luke notes Paul's listeners included Epicurean, Stoic, and "other" (οἱ δέ, *hoi de*) philosophers (v. 18).[42] Several of Paul's statements in his speech would have resonated with his Greek listeners. For example, several philosophical schools in Athens would have agreed with Paul (#1) that God cannot be contained in a temple, nor is he in need of anything—Socrates, Seneca, and Lucian, all recognized the foolishness of "serving" the gods.[43] Epicurean philosophers would have agreed with Paul (#2) that God is knowable,[44] and Stoics would have nodded approvingly of his statement (#2) that God is near.[45] Additionally, the Stoics (obviously) would have concurred (#3) that humans are the offspring of "god." Because of these and other points of correspondence with Greek philosophy, some believe Paul in his Areopagus speech establishes common ground with his listeners and builds on this to point them to Christ.[46] Or put in more theological terms, Paul moves from natural or general revelation to special revelation.[47] Others argue Paul's discourse is not an evangelistic message, but strictly

42. Although space does not permit us to interact here with these two schools of philosophy, a helpful overview for the non-specialist can be found in Everett Ferguson, *Backgrounds of Early Christianity*, 3rd ed. (Grand Rapids: Eerdmans, 2003), 354–78.

43. See. n. 39 above.

44. Epicureans, however, argued God is known through reason (rather than revelation). As Epicurus writes, "[Knowledge of God] is according to the notion of God indicated by the common sense of mankind ... for there are gods, and the knowledge of them is manifest" (quoted in Schnabel, *Acts*, 730).

45. For examples, see Rowe, *World Upside Down*, 37.

46. E.g., Dean E. Flemming, *Contextualization in the New Testament: Patterns for Theology and Mission* (Downers Grove, IL: InterVarsity Press, 2005), 75–79.

47. E.g., John R. W. Stott, *The Message of Acts: The Spirit, the Church, and the World* (Leicester: Inter-Varsity Press, 1990), 286: "[Paul's speech] indicates that glimmerings of truth, insight

(and only) a defense against the charge of introducing foreign deities.[48]

Neither of these views, in my opinion, accurately represents what Paul is doing in Act 17:22–31. As we have seen, the points of correspondence with Hellenistic thinking serve different functions. Paul refers to the Athenian worship of the unknown god not to show them Yahweh through their own religion, but to defend himself against the charge of introducing new deities into the city. At the same time, he uses this as a springboard to explain who this one true God is: He is both Creator and Lord of all. The rest of his speech is tied directly to this central thrust. Although certain statements may have resonated with his Greek audience, Paul uses these phrases to reformulate their thinking. Thus, while he occasionally uses the cast of Hellenistic thinking, he fills it with a Christian core. The basis of Paul's message is not natural revelation but special revelation. As Rowe rightly notes, "The line from Aratus's *Phaenomena* and other allusions are removed from their original interpretive frameworks and embedded within a different framework, one that stretches from Gen 1 through the resurrection of Jesus to the last day."[49]

In conclusion, Paul's Areopagus speech was a Christian message through and through. His message is not a Hellenistic presentation of the gospel, nor is it in any real sense a dialogue with Greek philosophy. His contacts with Greek philosophy are merely entry points into the ears of his audience. The core of Paul's teaching did not change depending on his location. Commentators who note Paul did not mention the cross, should also remember the entire speech takes just over one and a half minutes to read out loud. Paul almost certainly said more than just what Luke wrote.[50]

So, what has Athens to do with Jerusalem? Tertullian answered his own question as follows:

> Away with all attempts to produce a mottled Christianity of Stoic, Platonic, and dialectic composition! We want no curious disputation after possessing Christ Jesus, no inquisition after enjoying the gospel! With our faith, we desire no further belief. For this is our palmary [praiseworthy] faith, that there is nothing which we ought to believe besides. (*De praescriptione haereticorum* 7 [*ANF* 3:246])

If the interpretation given above is correct, Paul very likely would have agreed.

BIBLIOGRAPHY

Avigad, Nahman. *Discovering Jerusalem*. Nashville: Nelson, 1980.

Barnes, Timothy D. "An Apostle on Trial." *Journal of Theological Studies* 20 (1969): 407–19.

Barrett, C. K. *A Critical and Exegetical Commentary on the Acts of the Apostles, Volume 2 : Introduction and Commentary on Acts XV–XXVIII*. Edinburgh: T&T Clark, 1998.

Bauckham, Richard. *Jesus and the God of Israel: God Crucified and Other Studies*

from general revelation may be found in non-Christian authors."

48. Schnabel, *Acts*, 745.

49. Rowe, *World Upside Down*, 40.

50. As Stott rightly points out, "How could he proclaim the resurrection without first mentioning the death which preceded it?" (Stott, *Acts*, 289).

on the New Testament's Christology of Divine Identity. Grand Rapids: Eerdmans, 2008.

Biers, William R. *The Archaeology of Greece: An Introduction*. Revised ed. Ithaca: Cornell University Press, 1987.

Bock, Darrell L. *Acts*. Grand Rapids: Baker Academic, 2007.

Bond, Helen K. *Caiaphas: Friend of Rome and Judge of Jesus?* Louisville: Westminster John Knox, 2004.

Broshi, Magen. "The Archaeology of Palestine 63 BCE–CE 70." Pages 1–37 in *The Early Roman Period*. Volume 3 of *The Cambridge History of Judaism*. Edited by William Horbury, W. D. Davies, and John Sturdy. Cambridge: Cambridge University Press, 2008.

———. "Estimating the Population of Ancient Jerusalem." *BAR* 4.2 (1978): 10–15.

Bruce, F. F. *Commentary on the Book of Acts*. Revised ed. Grand Rapids: Eerdmans, 1988.

Camp, John M. *The Archaeology of Athens*. New Haven: Yale University Press, 2001.

Connolly, Peter, and Hazel Dodge. *The Ancient City: Life in Classical Athens and Rome*. Oxford: Oxford University Press, 1998.

Ferguson, Everett. *Backgrounds of Early Christianity*. 3rd ed. Grand Rapids: Eerdmans, 2003.

Flemming, Dean E. *Contextualization in the New Testament: Patterns for Theology and Mission*. Downers Grove, IL: InterVarsity Press, 2005.

Geagan, Daniel J. "Roman Athens, Some Aspects of Life and Culture, I: 86 B.C.–A.D. 267." *ANRW* 7.1:371–437.

Hengel, Martin. *The "Hellenization" of Judaea in the First Century after Christ*. Eugene, OR: Wipf & Stock, 2003.

Hoehner, Harold. *Ephesians: An Exegetical Commentary*. Grand Rapids: Baker Academic, 2002.

Kraabel, A. T. "The Diaspora Synagogue: Archaeological and Epigraphic Evidence since Sukenik." Pages 95–126 in *Ancient Synagogues: Historical Analysis and Archaeological Discovery*. Edited by Dan Urman and Paul V. M. Flesher. 2 vols. Leiden: Brill, 1995.

McRay, John R. "Athens." Pages 139–40 in *Dictionary of New Testament Background*. Edited by Craig A. Evans and Stanley E. Porter. Downers Grove, IL: InterVarsity Press, 2000.

———. "Corinth." Pages 227–31 in *Dictionary of New Testament Background*. Edited by Craig A. Evans and Stanley E. Porter. Downers Grove, IL: InterVarsity Press, 2000.

Norris, Frederick W. "Antioch of Syria." *ABD* 1:265–69.

Ritmeyer, Leen. *The Quest: Revealing the Temple Mount in Jerusalem*. Jerusalem: Carta, 2006.

Rowe, C. Kavin. *World Upside Down: Reading Acts in the Graeco-Roman Age*. Oxford: Oxford University Press, 2010.

Schnabel, Eckhard J. *Acts*. Grand Rapids: Zondervan, 2012.

Sly, Dorothy I. *Philo's Alexandria*. London: Routledge, 1996.

Stott, John R. W. *The Message of Acts: The Spirit, the Church, and the World*. Leicester: Inter-Varsity Press, 1990.

Tsakos, Konstantinos. *The Acropolis: The Monuments and the Museum; A Guide to the History and Archaeology*. Athens: Hesperos, 2000.

CHAPTER 30

THE SOCIAL AND GEOGRAPHICAL SIGNIFICANCE OF ALEXANDRIA

Acts 18:24–28

Benjamin A. Foreman

KEY POINTS

- Apollos of Alexandria was part of the largest community of Jews living outside of the land of Israel in the first century.
- Famous for its public monuments, scholasticism, and grain export, the city of Alexandria was the second most important city in the Roman Empire, second only to Rome.
- The gospel message arrived in Alexandria very early, perhaps within ten years of Jesus' ascension.
- Apollos, an eloquent and learned man, probably came to faith in his hometown, and may have received some of his training in an erudite school in Alexandria.

INTRODUCTION

Alexandria is the only Egyptian city mentioned in the New Testament. Considering Egypt was home to the largest Jewish community outside of the land of Israel in the first century AD, this is somewhat surprising.[1] A steady stream of foot traffic flowed between Jerusalem and Alexandria in Jesus' day (they are separated by about 335 miles [536 km]), yet the city is mentioned only four times in the New Testament—and not in connection to any specific event. The New Testament authors focus primarily on Paul's missionary activity, and since he planted his gospel seeds mainly in Asia

1. All dates are AD unless otherwise noted.

Minor and Europe, the New Testament is totally silent about how and when the Christian message journeyed into Egypt.

The gospel, however, seems to have reached Egypt very soon after Jesus' ascension. Acts 18:24–28 records that a fiery Alexandrian Jew named Apollos embraced Jesus as Messiah sometime before the early 50s and became a formidable mouthpiece for the faith in Ephesus and Corinth. In New Testament times, Apollos' native Alexandria was one of the most important cities in the Roman Empire, and this essay will highlight the sociospatial significance of this vibrant metropolis. But before looking at Alexandria in some detail, a word on Israel's contact with Egypt in general is necessary.

ISRAEL'S NEXUS WITH EGYPT

Israel's flirtation with Egypt reaches all the way back to the seeds of Israel's own history.[2] Already in the days of the patriarchs, drought in Canaan drove Abraham down to Egypt in search of greener pastures (Gen 12:10). Although his stay was short-lived, Jacob's descent to the rich, Nile-watered soils of Egypt, planted the nation into the "breadbasket of the world" for several hundred years (Gen 15:13; Exod 12:40).

Israel's exodus from Egypt by no means eliminated all contact between the two nations. When threatened by Solomon, the fledgling Jeroboam fled to the land of the pharaohs and found an ally in Shishak (1 Kgs 11:40). In the mid-seventh century BC (during Manasseh's

2. The words "Egypt" or "Egyptians" occur just over 750 times in the Old and New Testaments. This is quite high compared to the number of times other nations are mentioned, and is an indication of the importance of Egypt to Israel's history. See page 709 for a chart of nations mentioned in the Bible.

Largely brick remains of a Roman town inhabited in the sixth century BC, including the remains of a Jewish temple.

reign) an Israelite kernel began to form on Elephantine Island near Aswan. The burgeoning community eventually built a temple there (sometime in the mid-sixth century BC), and the sanctuary serviced the Jews of south Egypt for about 150 years.[3] On the eve of Jerusalem's destruction, Jeremiah states there were numerous nuclei of Jewish communities throughout Egypt (Jer 24:8), some even down as far as the "land of Pathros" (Jer 44:1)—a regional term for Upper Egypt south of Thebes. Many of these Jews probably settled the area sometime during the tempestuous last days of the kingdom of Judah. In the exilic period, a large portion of those left in the wake of the Babylonian conquest fled to the eastern delta of Lower Egypt and established a community at Tahpanhes (= Tell Defneh; see Jer 42–43).[4]

Throughout the Second Temple period pockets of Jewish communities continued to form and grow throughout Egypt. The son of the ousted high priest Onias III made his way to the Nile delta around 170 BC and built another Jewish temple at Leontopolis (Tell el-Yehudiyyeh) in

3. This temple was destroyed in an anti-Jewish riot in 410 BC, rebuilt, then went out of use again shortly thereafter. See James C. VanderKam, *An Introduction to Early Judaism* (Grand Rapids: Eerdmans, 2001), 147–50.

4. Although some Israelites stayed behind (how many is debated), the language of Jer 42:1 ("all the people from the least to the greatest") and 43:5–6 ("all the remnant ... men, women, children, princesses, and every person") implies a large portion of the remaining Israelites fled to Egypt.

Lower Egypt.[5] Although there is some dispute about the date, this temple seems to have operated for nearly two and a half centuries.[6] By the first century there were, according to Philo, over one million Jews within Egypt's borders (*In Flaccum* 43). The largest, richest, and most erudite city in this flourishing country was Alexandria.

GEOGRAPHY OF ALEXANDRIA

Founded by Alexander the Great in 331 BC, Alexandria quickly became a multicultural metropolis whose success was unrivaled by any other city in the Mediterranean world. As Mondésert notes, "[Alexandria was] the most brilliant city in the Empire on account of its commercial activity and it maritime importance, its ethnic and religious cosmopolitanism, its library and its schools, its scientific and artistic resources and its fashionable life."[7]

The city owed its success mainly to its location. It not only opened its front door to the Mediterranean Sea, it was also shielded by a large island about one mile (1.6 km) off shore. This natural breakwater, called Pharos, created optimal conditions for a harbor. Additionally, the city had the advantage of being bordered by a large lake to the south, called Mareotis.

---

5. Josephus contradicts himself when describing this temple's construction. In *J.W.* 7.420–432 he claims Onias III built it, but credits Onias IV with its construction in *Ant.* 12.387–388 and 13.62–73. The account in *Jewish Antiquities* is probably correct since 2 Macc 4:33–34 says Onias III was killed at Daphne near Antioch.

6. Josephus (*J.W.* 7.436) claims it stood for 343 years, but this does not work chronologically. The figure should probably be reduced by 100 years.

7. Claude Mondésert, "Philo of Alexandria," in *The Cambridge History of Judaism, Vol. III: The Early Roman Period*, ed. William Horbury, W. D. Davies, and John Sturdy (Cambridge: Cambridge University Press, 2008), 878–79.

Since a web of canals connected Mareotis to the harbor and the Nile River, the lake effectively became a parking garage for merchant ships sailing in and out of Egypt. According to Strabo, who lived in Alexandria for over five years, more goods were exchanged between vessels on the lake than in the harbor.[8] In addition to this, the sea and the lake also created a pleasant climate unlike anywhere else in Egypt (*Geographica* 17.1.7). In short, Alexandria was an international hub whose residents could enjoyably feast on Mediterranean fancies with one hand and African delicacies with the other.

Climate and exotic imports aside, Alexandria was important to Rome because it sat at the head of one of the largest grain-producing countries in the Roman Empire. According to Erdkamp, "Grain was the most important item of food in antiquity ... [and] is more central to our understanding of the Roman economy and society than, for instance, olive oil or wine."[9] Although estimates vary, some believe Rome required approximately 150,000–200,000 tons (136,000–181,500 metric tons) of grain every year to feed its population.[10] Egypt's role in supplying Roman grain has been variously interpreted, but Erdkamp convincingly argues "Egypt provided the largest part of the corn consumed by Rome."[11] Since all of Egypt's shipments funneled through Alexandria, the city was essentially the grain capital of the Roman Empire.

Bust of Alexander the Great

The vessels delivering the grain to the "Eternal City" varied in size. The largest ships could carry a load of up to 1100 US tons (1,000 metric tons), but ships with a maximum payload of 385 US tons (350 metric tons) were more common. Given the huge demand, Rome offered its citizens various incentives to use their ships for transporting grain, and therefore smaller craft also played a significant role in meeting Rome's colossal quota.[12]

Paul journeyed to Rome aboard two Alexandrian ships (Acts 27:6; 28:11). The

8. Horace Leonard Jones, *The Geography of Strabo*, LCL (London: Heinemann, 1917), xx–xxi.

9. Paul Erdkamp, *The Grain Market in the Roman Empire: A Social, Political, and Economic Study* (Cambridge: Cambridge University Press, 2005), 317.

10. Peter Garnsey, "Grain for Rome," in *Trade in the Ancient Economy*, ed. Peter Garnsey, Keith Hopkins, and C. R. Whittaker (Berkeley: University of California Press, 1983), 118–119; quoted in Barry J. Beitzel, *The New Moody Atlas of the Bible* (Chicago: Moody, 2009), n. 601.

11. See Erdkamp, *Grain Market*, 226–30.

12. For more details see Erdkamp, *Grain Market*, 178.

Pharos of Alexandria

first, which wrecked off the coast of Malta, is explicitly called a grain vessel (27:38) and seems to have been a very large craft since it carried 276 people in addition to its cargo (v. 37). The size of the second ship is unclear.

The streets of Alexandria were lined with many impressive monuments. Most famous was the lighthouse—called Pharos, after the island. Jutting out of the eastern-most part of the island, the lighthouse extended several hundred feet into the Alexandrian sky and projected a light some one hundred miles (160 km) into the Mediterranean. The structure, which was built in the early Hellenistic period and stood for some 1500 years, was so impressive it earned itself a spot on the list of the seven ancient wonders of the world.[13]

Stretching down from the harbor into the center of the city was a public sector called Bruchium, which Strabo estimates constituted about "one-fourth or even one-third" of the city (*Geographica* 17.1.8 [LCL]). One of the most imposing structures in this precinct was a temple called Caesareum. It commemorated Augustus Caesar's takeover of the city in 30 BC, and in 22 BC he transported two ancient obelisks (dating back to the reign of Thutmose III, ca. 1479–1425 BC) from Heliopolis and displayed them at the entrance to the temple. One of the obelisks was thrown down by an earthquake in the thirteenth century, but the other stood for nearly nineteen centuries right where the Roman engineers placed it. In 1881 the standing obelisk was removed by the Americans, shipped to New York, and placed in Central Park, where it can still be seen today.[14]

South of Caesareum stood the royal mausoleum (the "Soma"), which housed Alexander the Great's body.[15] The famous library of Alexandria was also in this area, probably in the building Strabo refers to

13. For a more complete description, see Dorothy I. Sly, *Philo's Alexandria* (London: Routledge, 1996), 22–24.

14. The fallen obelisk was taken to London in the 1830s and exhibited along the Thames. The fascinating story of these obelisks (popularly referred to as "Cleopatra's Needles") is recounted (with beautiful pictures) in Henry H. Gorringe, *Egyptian Obelisks* (London: Nimmo, 1885), 1–76, 96–109.

15. After Alexander's body was embalmed in Babylon, the intention was for it to be buried in the northern Seleucid kingdom. His funerary procession, however, was attacked and his body was taken to Alexandria; B. W. R. Pearson, "Alexander the Great," *Dictionary of New Testament Background*, ed. Craig A. Evans and Stanley E. Porter (Downers Grove, IL: InterVarsity Press, 2000), 22.

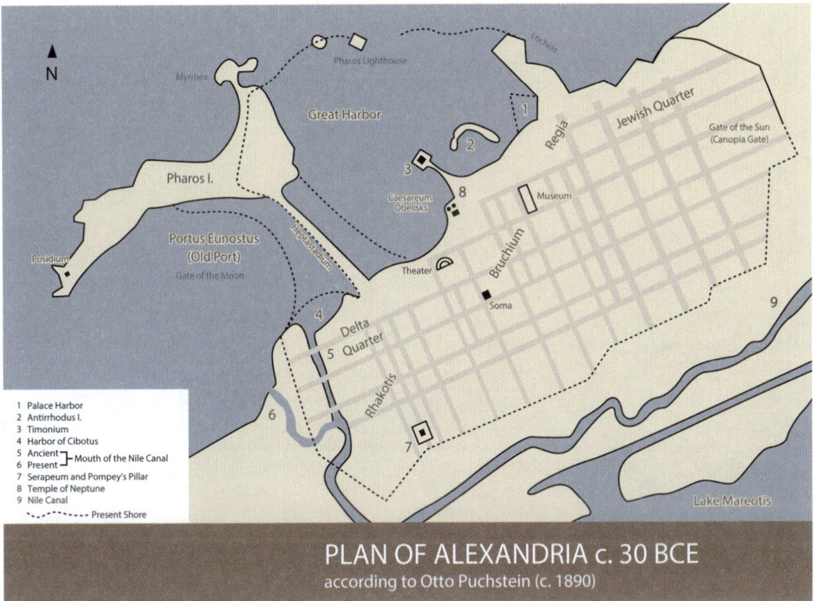

PLAN OF ALEXANDRIA c. 30 BCE
according to Otto Puchstein (c. 1890)

as the "Museum."[16] Unparalleled in its extent, it was constructed with the ambitious goal of collecting "all the books in the world" (Letter of Aristeas 9), the Old Testament being translated into Greek (the Septuagint) for this purpose (more on the Septuagint below). Scholars estimate the library's stockpile was somewhere between four hundred thousand to seven hundred thousand scrolls. In the southwestern part of the city was a temple devoted to Alexandria's protector god Serapis (called "Serapeum"), and a hippodrome, theater, gymnasium, and other civic buildings were also scattered throughout the city. Unfortunately, very little of the ancient city has survived until today. In 297 the emperor Diocletian erected a massive column atop the ruins of the Serapeum to commemorate his victory over an uprising in the city. This column, mistakenly referred to as "Pompey's Pillar," and a Roman theatre from the second century, are the only major ancient monuments visible in the city today.[17]

This cosmopolitan metropolis was home to one of the "largest and most important [Jewish communities] of the

16. There is some debate on where the library was. For an in-depth discussion see Hélène Fragaki, "La Bibliothèque d'Alexandrie: Questions de Topographie et d'Architecture," in *The Library of Alexandria: A Cultural Crossroads of the Ancient World*, ed. Christophe Rico and Anca Dan (Jerusalem: Polis Institute Press, 2017), 3–42.

17. The above map of Alexandria is based on: William Shepherd, *Historical Atlas* (New York: Holt, 1911), 34–35. Courtesy of the University of Texas Libraries, The University of Texas at Austin. Perry-Castañeda Library Map Collection.

Roman Triumphal Column "Pompey's Pillar"

Greek-speaking Diaspora."[18] One of the loudest Jewish voices of the first century was a resident of Alexandria and a contemporary of Apollos—Philo.

THE JEWS OF ALEXANDRIA

According to the historical sources (*Ant.* 12.7; Letter of Aristeas 13), the first Jews to arrive in Alexandria were forcibly settled there by Ptolemy I Soter (reigned 323–283 BC). Once in the city, however, they were given "equal civic rights with the Macedonians," and their favorable treatment inspired many more Jews to stream to the city "of their own accord" to search for better fortunes (*Ant.* 12.8–9). By the first century, the city had been partitioned into five districts, each named after the first five letters of the Greek alphabet. Two of these were settled principally by Jews, and the other quarters had a sprinkling of Jews as well (Philo, *In Flaccum* 55). In Josephus' view, their concentration into two districts permitted them to "be free to observe their rules more strictly" (*J.W.* 2.488). Although religion may have been a factor, Philo writes there were synagogues "in every district of the city" (*Legatio ad Gaium* 132 [LCL]), and since "those who belonged to the artisan class tended to cluster with other persons who shared their trade," the real reason for the distillation of the Jews into two primary areas may have been more pragmatic than religious.[19]

Josephus figures Egypt, excluding Alexandria, had a total population of 7.5 million in his day (*J.W.* 2.385). Because

18. Birger A. Pearson, "Earliest Christianity in Egypt: Some Observations," in *The Roots of Egyptian Christianity*, ed. Birger A. Pearson and James E. Goehring (Philadelphia: Fortress, 1986), 145.

19. Sly, *Philo's Alexandria*, 43.

Diodorus (*Bibliotheca Historica* 52.6) claims there were 300,000 freedmen in the city (ca. 60 BC), and considering population density statistics, Sly estimates there were between 500,000–600,000 residents in first-century Alexandria. Since Jews occupied two of the city's five quarters (and were in other districts as well), there may have been around 180,000 Jews living in the city in Apollos' day.[20]

According to Josephus, the Jews "settled by the sea without a harbour, close beside the spot where the waves break on the beach" (*Ag. Ap.* 2.33 [LCL]). Since most of the city was sheltered by the island of Pharos, this is clearly an allusion to the northeast, the region beyond the Lochias promontory (see map). Elsewhere, Josephus informs us that one of the Jewish quarters was the delta district (*J.W.* 2.495). Many scholars simply combine both of those references and assume the delta district was in the northeast. As Pearson points out, however, a papyrus document from 13 BC unmistakably situates the delta quarter in the *northwestern* part of the city.[21] Josephus' references to the Jewish districts in *Against Apion* and *Jewish War*, therefore, apparently refer to separate quarters on opposite sides of the city—one in the northwest, one in the northeast. As we will see, this precision is important since it will help us to assess the historical value of the traditions concerning the arrival of the gospel in Alexandria.

By far the most prominent Jew residing in Alexandria in those days was Caius Julius Philo. Born into a rich Jewish Alexandrian family in ca. 20 BC, Philo received a Greek and Jewish education (*De Congressu Eruditionis Gratia* 74–76; *De Specialibus Legibus* 2.229–230), and spent much of his life writing works that integrated both systems of belief. As one scholar notes, "No other author in antiquity has attempted with so much boldness the confrontation and symbiosis of Judaism with another philosophy and another culture."[22] The voluminous treatises he left behind (about two thousand pages) have earned him a reputation as one of the most important figures in first-century Judaism.

Scholars typically cluster his writings into several categories: historical works, expositions of the law, allegorical commentaries, and philosophical treatises.[23] His texts are a treasure trove for scholars interested in studying streams of Jewish thinking in the first century.[24]

Alexandrian Jews enjoyed the freedom to live and worship as they pleased for several hundred years, but blissful life did not last forever.[25] Although Jews were

20. See Sly, *Philo's Alexandria*, 44–51.

21. The document states the Kibotos harbor, which according to Strabo (*Geography* 17.1.10) was an artificial harbor within the harbor of Eunostos, was "in delta." See Pearson, "Earliest Christianity," 146–47.

22. Mondésert, "Philo of Alexandria," 877.

23. Mondésert, "Philo of Alexandria," 879.

24. Interestingly, his thinking made only a small ripple in the Jewish world. His works were preserved exclusively by Christian scholars, and according to Mondésert, "In general Judaism knew absolutely nothing about him for fifteen hundred years, until in the sixteenth century Azariah ben Moses dei Rossi ... revived his name and his writings"; Mondésert, "Philo of Alexandria," 877.

25. This paragraph is a summary of Sly, *Philo's Alexandria*, 167–80.

the largest minority community of the city, most of the residents were Greek or Macedonian, and relations between the two groups took a turn for the worse in the mid-30s. The Greek community was unhappy with the preferential treatment the Romans were giving to the Jews of Alexandria, and the sentiment of the city's Greek community reached a boiling point in 38. Beginning with civil disorder, Greek acrimony quickly snowballed into a full-fledged pogrom against the Jews. Synagogues were desecrated or demolished, Jews were forced to eat pork or tortured, others were scourged (some to death), and some even crucified. By the time the dust settled, the Jews had been hounded out of "every quarter of the city" and corralled "into a very narrow space as if into a pen" (Philo, *In Flaccum* 124).

The Jews responded by sending a delegation to Rome in 39/40 to protest their persecution. Philo was chosen to head up the commission, and in Rome he attempted to convince the Emperor Gaius Caligula that the Jews were good citizens and should be given the same rights as Greek citizens.[26] Although he ultimately failed, that he was chosen to head up the delegation shows he was apparently the most influential and highly regarded Jew in Alexandria.

Little else is known about Philo's personal life. He probably died around 50 since he writes he was "an old man" when he was sent to Rome in 39/40. Although he is not mentioned in the New Testament, his nephew Marcus Julius Alexander married Agrippa II's sister Bernice (*Ant.* 19.276), before whom Paul gave his testimony in Caesarea (Acts 25:13, 23).[27] Another nephew of his, Tiberius Julius Alexander, seems to have abandoned his Jewish faith, since Josephus writes he "did not stand by the practices of his people" (*Ant.* 20.101). This nephew was appointed procurator of Judea from 46–48, prefect of Egypt in 66, and counselor to Titus in the war against the Jews in 69–70 (*J.W.* 5.46).

THE ARRIVAL OF CHRISTIANITY IN EGYPT

Although "the Alexandrian Jewish community of that time [first century A.D.] is probably the most well documented of the entire Jewish Diaspora," our knowledge of when and how the gospel first reached Egypt is very limited.[28] Since the New Testament focuses on the progression of the Christian message through Asia Minor and Europe, we are dependent almost entirely on early tradition to reconstruct the history of early Egyptian

26. Greek citizens were given an exemption from poll tax (or given a lower rate), whereas the native Egyptian population had to pay the tax in full. The Greeks wanted the Romans to grant the Jews the same status as the Egyptian population. See Peter Borgen, "Philo of Alexandria," *ABD* 5:336.

27. Bernice's private life was at best questionable, scandalous at worse. Her marriage to Philo's nephew lasted about a year, ending with his death in 44. Soon after his death she married her uncle Herod Chalcis and bore him two sons. When he died in 48 she lived "a long time" as a widow (*Ant.* 20.145), and was still unmarried when Paul met her in Caesarea in 60. Rumors of an incestuous affair with her brother Agrippa II, however, prompted her to marry Polemo king of Cilicia, hoping this would dispel the gossip. This marriage was short-lived as well, however, and ended with her desertion of Polemo (*Ant.* 20.145–146).

28. Birger A. Pearson, *Gnosticism and Christianity in Roman and Coptic Egypt* (London: T&T Clark, 2004), 82.

Roman Odeion at Alexandria

Christianity. Recent study, however, has helped to shed some light.[29]

The earliest extant tradition on the descent of Christianity to Egypt comes from Eusebius (approximately 260–340), who writes:

> They say that this Mark [the gospel writer] was the first to be sent to preach in Egypt the Gospel which he also put into writing, and was the first to establish churches in Alexandria itself. The number of men and women who were there converted at the first attempt was so great, and their asceticism was so extraordinarily philosophic, that Philo thought it right to describe their conduct and assemblies and meals and all the rest of their manner of life. (*Historica Ecclesiastica* 2.16 [LCL])

Eusebius states elsewhere that Mark arrived in Alexandria in the third year of Claudius' rule (i.e., 43; *Chronicle*) and left the city to meet Peter in Rome in the eighth year of Nero's rule (i.e., 62; *Historica Ecclesiastica* 2.24). He apparently had no information on how or when Mark died since he does not elaborate on this.[30]

Eusebius's testimony might be viewed with suspicion since he also claims Philo met Peter in Rome, and "welcomed, reverenced, and recognized the divine mission of the apostolic men of his day" (2.17.2).[31] It is clear from Philo's own writings, however, that he never converted to

29. Much of this section relies on Pearson's work in: "Earliest Christianity," 132–60; *Gnosticism and Christianity*, 100–113.

30. See Pearson, "Earliest Christianity," 139 n. 30.

31. Although Runia rightly notes Eusebius does not explicitly say Philo was a Christian, Eusebius comes very close to doing so. Later Byzantine commentators refer to him as Philo the bishop. See David T. Runia, *Philo in Early Christian Literature: A Survey* (Minneapolis: Fortress, 1993), 3–7.

Christianity.[32] Nevertheless, Eusebius's account agrees with early Egyptian tradition and should not be rejected so quickly.

According to the Copts, Mark first came to the city in 48, 55, 68, or 61 (the sources do not agree), and became the first of what is now an unbroken succession of over 115 patriarchs.[33] His first convert in the city was a cobbler he miraculously healed. Coming to faith, the man was baptized, and many others also believed and were baptized. Public sentiment eventually turned on Mark, however, and after appointing a successor to the patriarchy, he sailed to Rome where he met Peter and Paul. Several years later he returned to Alexandria, and on Easter of 68 he was killed by a violent mob under the pretense he was trying to overthrow the city's idols.[34]

One of the main sources for this tradition is a fourth century work called the Martyrium Marci. Although some of the material in this piece is probably legendary, Pearson has shown it reflects the topography of the city in the first century.[35] In Martyrium Marci Mark is active in the northwestern and northeastern areas of Alexandria (the two Jewish districts), whereas the heart of Christian activity in the fourth century was in Bruchium, the center of the city. Additionally, some

32. For an in-depth treatment of Philo's view of the messiah, see Richard D. Hecht, "Philo and Messiah," in *Judaisms and Their Messiahs at the Turn of the Christian Era*, ed. Jacob Neusner, William Scott Green, and Ernest S. Frerichs (Cambridge: Cambridge University Press, 1987), 139–68.

33. Coptic tradition relies heavily on a tenth century work called *The History of the Patriarchs of the Coptic Church of Alexandria*, compiled chiefly by Sawirus ibn al-Muqaffa. For more on this work, see Thomas C. Oden, *The African Memory of Mark* (Downers Grove, IL: InterVarsity Press, 2011), 64–76.

34. Aziz S. Atiya, *A History of Eastern Christianity* (London: Mehuen, 1968), 25–28.

35. See the full argument in Pearson, *Gnosticism and Christianity*, 100–113.

of the sites within the city in the narrative were outside of the city in the fourth century when Martyrium Marci was written. These geographical details are important because if the piece was entirely composed in the fourth century, it would have reflected the layout of the city in that time. This suggests Martyrium Marci preserves "a continuity of tradition between the first century and the fourth century."[36] Since this matches Eusebius's claim that Mark was the first to bring the gospel to Alexandria in the first half of the first century AD, the tradition appears to be authentic.

Some manuscripts of Acts 18:25 specifies Apollos "had been instructed *in his homeland* in the word of the Lord." Although it is unclear whether this tradition is reliable, it is certainly possible, perhaps even probable. According to the chronology of Acts, Apollos came to Ephesus sometime before Paul's third missionary journey (approximately 52–55). The gospel almost certainly reached Alexandria before that. Those in Jerusalem for Pentecost in Acts 2 included Jews from Egypt and Libya (2:10), and some of the three thousand converts (Acts 2:41) may have included Alexandrians (or other north Africans who would have traveled through Alexandria on their way home). Acts 6:8 specifically mentions Alexandrian Jews in the debate with Stephen, and considering also the international character of the city, Jews would have caught wind early on of the budding Christian community in Judea. Apollos could have heard the gospel from any of these sources, or even from Mark himself. Mark may have made several visits to Alexandria, the first perhaps even as early as 43, as Eusebius claims.[37] In short, the gospel almost certainly spread to Alexandria years before 52, and since the New Testament gives no indication otherwise, there is no reason to believe Apollos did not come to faith in his homeland.

APOLLOS IN CONTEXT

As the tentacles of the gospel extended throughout the Mediterranean world, various heretical teachings began to sprout up among the field of believers. One heresy that took deep root in the nascent Alexandrian church was Gnosticism.[38] This teaching appeared very early, and some even believe Apollos was caught up in this web of unorthodoxy. The argument runs as follows: (1) Apollos was an influential teacher in the young Corinthian church (Acts 19:1; 1 Cor 1:12; 3:5; 4:6); (2) Gnosticism had a powerful influence on both the Jewish (e.g., Philo) and Christian (e.g., Teachings of Silvanus [2nd century]) population of Alexandria; (3) Paul is arguing against Gnosticism in 1 Cor 1–4; (4) Apollos must therefore have picked up this teaching in Alexandria—perhaps from Philo himself—and passed it on to the new believers in Corinth.[39]

---

36. Pearson, *Gnosticism and Christianity*, 109–10.

37. Pearson remarks Martyrium Marci may hint that Mark made multiple trips to Alexandria. See Pearson, "Earliest Christianity," 139 n. 34.

38. It is difficult to define Gnosticism since the term is used broadly. In general, the belief system stresses the importance of knowledge (*gnōsis*) for salvation and drives a sharp wedge between the physical and transcendent realms. For a concise summary see Everett Ferguson, *Backgrounds of Early Christianity* (Grand Rapids: Eerdmans, 2003), 301–13.

39. See Pearson, *Gnosticism and Christianity*, 95–99.

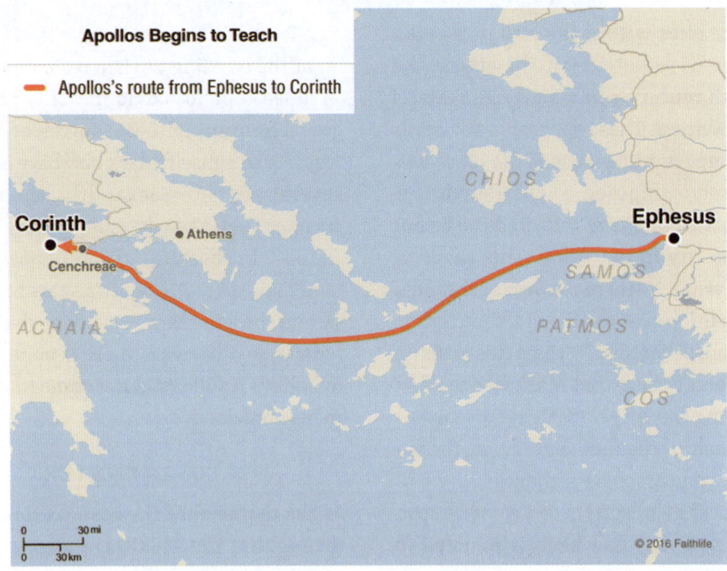

This conclusion is not supported by the New Testament. Although Apollos had a deficient understanding of the gospel ("he knew only the baptism of John"; Acts 18:25), Luke also writes Apollos "*taught accurately* the things concerning Jesus" (18:25). Moreover, Paul does not view Apollos as a threat but as a colleague in 1 Corinthians, which is why Paul "strongly urged him to visit" the Corinthians (1 Cor 16:12).[40] Although Apollos' Alexandria was heavily influenced by gnostic philosophy, there is little evidence he himself fell prey to this false teaching.

As an Alexandrian Jew, Apollos would have bargained for fish, written poetry, and dreamed, in Greek. Although Luke states he was a "learned" or "eloquent" (*logios*) man (Acts 18:24), Hebrew would have been for him, as for most Alexandrians, the language of distant ancestors. Even Philo knew little or no Hebrew and quoted freely from the Septuagint.[41] But far from viewing it as an inferior translation, Jewish Alexandrians highly acclaimed it. It was in their city, on the Island of Pharos (Philo, *De Vita Mosis* 2.35–36), that the translators, working "under prophetic inspiration" (*De Vita Mosis* 2.37), produced this "accurate" translation "requiring no revision" (Letter of Aristeas 301, 310–311). Alexandrians (many non-Jews included) celebrated this literary masterpiece by gathering on Pharos every year to "reverence the place in which the first light of interpretation shone forth" (*De Vita Mosis* 2.41). The Septuagint was the Bible of Apollos, Philo, and most first-century

40. Schnabel suggests Apollos "may have baptized people with an emphasis on repentance and forgiveness of sins, without explaining the association of immersion in water with the life, death, and resurrection of Jesus." Eckhard J. Schnabel, *Acts*, (Grand Rapids: Zondervan, 2012), 785.

41. Mondésert, "Philo of Alexandria," 894.

Jews in general. When Apollos "powerfully refuted the Jews in public, showing by the Scriptures that the Christ was Jesus" (Acts 18:28), he almost certainly did this in Greek and from the Septuagint—whether in Alexandria, Ephesus, or Corinth.[42]

Apollos was a compelling apologist. Luke describes him as a "learned [or "eloquent"] man" (Acts 18:24) who "spoke boldly in the synagogues" (18:26), and "powerfully refuted Jews in public" (18:28). Although we can only speculate where he acquired these rhetorical skills, it is not too far-fetched to assume he received some of his training in an erudite school in Alexandria, perhaps even from Philo himself.[43]

The New Testament, of course, does not tell us when or why Apollos left Alexandria, though public opinion toward believing Jews would certainly not have encouraged him to stay. As a Jew he would have experienced opposition from the Greek residents, as a Christian he would have encountered resistance from the Jewish community. We will never know whether Apollos left his native city because of political unrest or for other reasons. But whatever his motivation, the fiery African preacher became a powerful tool for the gospel in Asia Minor and Europe.

BIBLIOGRAPHY

Atiya, Aziz S. *A History of Eastern Christianity*. London: Mehuen, 1968.

Beitzel, Barry J. *The New Moody Atlas of the Bible*. Chicago: Moody, 2009.

Borgen, Peder. "Philo of Alexandria." *ABD* 5:333–42.

Erdkamp, Paul. *The Grain Market in the Roman Empire: A Social, Political, and Economic Study*. Cambridge: Cambridge University Press, 2005.

Ferguson, Everett. *Backgrounds of Early Christianity*. Grand Rapids: Eerdmans, 2003.

Fragaki, Hélène. "La Bibliothèque d'Alexandrie: Questions de Topographie et d'Architecture." Pages 3–42 in *The Library of Alexandria: A Cultural Crossroads of the Ancient World*. Edited by Christophe Rico and Anca Dan. Jerusalem: Polis Institute Press, 2017.

Garnsey, Peter. "Grain for Rome." Pages 118–30 in *Trade in the Ancient Economy*. Edited by Peter Garnsey, Keith Hopkins, and C. R. Whittaker. Berkeley: University of California Press, 1983.

Gorringe, Henry H. *Egyptian Obelisks*. London: Nimmo, 1885.

Hecht, Richard D. "Philo and Messiah." Pages 139–68 in *Judaisms and Their Messiahs at the Turn of the Christian Era*. Edited by Jacob Neusner, William Scott Green, and Ernest S. Frerichs. Cambridge: Cambridge University Press, 1987.

Jones, Horace Leonard. *The Geography of Strabo*. 8 vols. LCL. London: Heinemann, 1917.

Mondésert, Claude. "Philo of Alexandria." Pages 877–900 in *The Cambridge History of Judaism, III: The Early Roman Period*. Edited by

42. Had Apollos confronted Philo, or any other Jew with the Christian message, the debate would not have been over the legitimacy of the Greek translation, but over the interpretation of the Greek Scriptures.

43. See Bruce W. Winter, *Philo and Paul Among the Sophists* (Cambridge: Cambridge University Press, 1997).

William Horbury, W. D. Davies, and John Sturdy. Cambridge: Cambridge University Press, 1999.

Oden, Thomas C. *The African Memory of Mark*. Downers Grove, IL: InterVarsity Press, 2011.

Pearson, B. W. R. "Alexander the Great." Pages 20–23 in *Dictionary of New Testament Background*. Edited by Craig A. Evans and Stanley E. Porter. Downers Grove, IL: InterVarsity Press, 2000.

Pearson, Birger A. "Earliest Christianity in Egypt: Some Observations." Pages 132–60 in *The Roots of Egyptian Christianity*. Edited by Birger A. Pearson and James E. Goehring. Philadelphia: Fortress, 1986.

———. *Gnosticism and Christianity in Roman and Coptic Egypt*. London: T&T Clark, 2004.

Runia, David T. *Philo in Early Christian Literature: A Survey*. Minneapolis: Fortress, 1993.

Schnabel, Eckhard J. *Acts*. Grand Rapids: Zondervan, 2012.

Sly, Dorothy I. *Philo's Alexandria*. London: Routledge, 1996.

VanderKam, James C. *An Introduction to Early Judaism*. Grand Rapids: Eerdmans, 2001.

Winter, Bruce W. *Philo and Paul Among the Sophists*. Cambridge: Cambridge University Press, 1997.

CHAPTER 31

PAUL'S MISSIONARY WORK IN THE PROVINCES OF ASIA AND ILLYRICUM

Acts 19:1–41; 20:1–38; 21:1–16

Eckhard J. Schnabel

KEY POINTS

- The eleventh phase of Paul's missionary work took place in the province of Asia, focused on Ephesus.
- The mission in Asia allowed Paul to implement his plans to preach the gospel in western Asia Minor.
- The twelfth phase of Paul's mission was a brief spell in the province of Illyria.
- The mission in Latin-speaking Illyricum provided a new church-planting opportunity.

PAUL'S VISIT TO THE CHURCHES IN JUDEA, SYRIA, CILICIA, AND SOUTHERN GALATIA

After his mission in Macedonia and Achaia, Paul had accompanied Aquila and Priscilla to Ephesus on the way to Jerusalem (Acts 18:18–19). When Ephesian Jews invited him to spend time in the city (Acts 18:20–21), Paul continued his journey to Syria: he traveled to Caesarea and Jerusalem in Roman Judea (Acts 18:22) and then continued to Antioch in Syria (Acts 18:22) where he spent "some time" (Acts 18:23). Luke does not tell us the purpose of Paul's visit in Caesarea, Jerusalem, and Antioch in AD 51/52; it is plausible to assume that he gave a report of his church visits in Syria, Cilicia, and Galatia communicating the decisions of the Apostles' Council (AD 48/49), and of his missionary work in Macedonia and Achaia (AD 49–51).

Paul set out from Antioch (Syria), presumably in the spring of AD 52, "and traveled from place to place throughout the region of Galatia and Phrygia, strengthening all the disciples" (Acts 18:23).

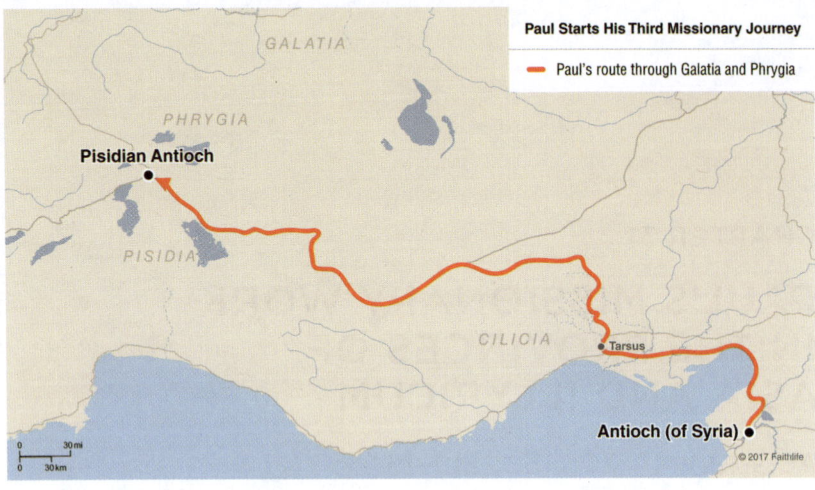

Luke's travel notice is extremely compressed. Since Paul aimed for Ephesus, the notice implies that Paul took the land route: as at the beginning of the ninth phase of his missionary work,[1] Paul traveled through northern Syria (via Planatoi, Alexandria) and eastern Cilicia (Epiphaneia, Anazarbos, Adana, Tarsus), visiting the churches he had established during the fourth and fifth phase of his missionary work, as well as southern Galatia visiting the churches in Derbe, Lystra, Iconium, and Antioch. The land route from Antioch in Syria to Antioch in Galatia amounted to a distance of 438 miles (705 km), which required twenty-eight days or five weeks of travel.

PAUL'S TRAVEL FROM PISIDIAN ANTIOCH TO EPHESUS (ASIA)

The phrase "the region [χώρα, *chōra*] of Galatia and Phrygia" in the travel notice of Acts 18:23 is most plausibly understood as (1) a reference to Lycaonian and Phrygian regions that had been incorporated in the Roman province of Galatia—Derbe, Lystra, and Iconium in Lycaonian Galatia, and Antioch in Phrygian Galatia (Pisidian Antioch), and (2) as well as a reference to Asian Phrygia, that is, those regions of Phrygia that had become part of the province of Asia and through which Paul traveled after his visit to the churches in Derbe, Lystra, Iconium, and Antioch.[2] Luke takes up Paul's travel to Ephesus in Acts 19:1: "Paul took the road through the interior and arrived at Ephesus" (NIV). Which route did Paul take from Pisidian Antioch (in southern Galatia) to Ephesus (Asia)? The Greek phrase *ta anōterika merē* (τὰ ἀνωτερικὰ μέρη) and thus Paul's route from Pisidian

1. See Schnabel, "Paul's Missionary Work in Macedonia and Achaia," chapter 27 in this volume.

2. Colin J. Hemer, *The Book of Acts in the Setting of Hellenistic History*, ed. C.H. Gempf (Tübingen: Mohr Siebeck, 1989), 120, 205; Eckhard J. Schnabel, *Early Christian Mission*, 2 vols. (Downers Grove, IL: InterVarsity Press, 2004), 2:1199.

Antioch via Apamea (modern Dinar) to Ephesus has been variously interpreted.[3]

POSSIBLE ROUTES

Option 1. An inner route through Lydia: the expression in Acts 19:1 refers to the mountains of Asia and Phrygia with the headwaters of the Meander and Hermus Rivers, suggesting a route via Tavium in the eastern region of northern Galatia, Thyatira, and Sardis.[4]

Option 2. An upper route through the northern regions of coastal Bithynia and the Mysian shore of the Propontis and the Aegean Sea, suggesting a route north to the Sea of Marmara.[5]

Option 3. An upper route through the valleys of the Cayster and Hermus Rivers via Smyrna, with the suggestion that Paul might have wanted to visit the important cities of Philadelphia, Sardis, and Smyrna.[6]

Option 4. An upper route toward the valleys of the Lycus and Meander Rivers, suggesting a route from Apamea to Laodicea, turning north toward Hierapolis, and Tripolis, then across the mountains into the Kogamus River Valley west to Philadelphia and Sardis, then south across the Tmolus Mountains into the valley of the Cayster River to Ephesus.[7]

Option 5. An upper route through the Cayster Valley: Luke's "higher districts" refer to the region of the upper Meander and upper Cayster valleys,[8] specifically to the "the traverse of the hill-road" that ran from Apamea to the Cayster Valley north of the Messogis Mountains.[9] I have reconstructed this route as follows.[10] Paul traveled from Pisidian Antioch west-southwest on the *Via Sebaste* to Apollonia (Mordiaion), west across the mountains and along the northern shore of Lake Aulutrene to Apameia; from there

3. The following survey relies on Mark Wilson, "The 'Upper Regions' and the Route of Paul's Third Journey from Apamea to Ephesus," *Scriptura* 117 (2018):1–21; see there for relevant critiques of these proposals.

4. William J. Conybeare and John S. Howson, *The Life and Epistles of St. Paul*, 2 vols. 2nd ed. (London: Longmans & Roberts, 1856), 2:5–6.

5. David H. French, "Acts and the Roman Roads of Asia Minor," in *The Book of Acts in Its Graeco-Roman Setting*, ed. D. W. J. Gill and C. Gempf, vol. 2 of *The Book of Acts in Its First Century Setting*, ed. Bruce W. Winter (Grand Rapids: Eerdmans, 1994), 55.

6. Mauricio S. Monroy, *The Church of Smyrna: History and Theology of a Primitive Christian Community* (Frankfurt: Lang, 2015), 162.

7. Giovanni Uggeri, "Sulle strade di San Paolo in Anatolia: Il secondo e il terzo viaggio," in *Seminario di studi Paolo di Tarso: il messaggio, l'immagine, i viaggi; Studi in memoria di Luigi Padovese*, ed. Stella Uggeri Patitucci and Luigi Padovese (Palermo: Officina di studi medievali, 2011), 134, 137.

8. William M. Ramsay, *The Church in the Roman Empire Before A.D. 170* (London: Hodder & Stoughton 1893; repr., Boston: Adamant, 2004), 94; Ramsay, *St. Paul the Traveller and the Roman Citizen* (London: Hodder & Stoughton, 1896), 265; followed by F. F. Bruce, *The Acts of the Apostles: The Greek Text with Introduction and Commentary*, 3rd revised and enlarged ed. (Grand Rapids: Eerdmans, 1990), 405.

9. Hemer, *Book of Acts*, 120, 187; Rainer Riesner, *Paul's Early Period: Chronology, Mission Strategy, Theology* (Grand Rapids: Eerdmans, 1998), 286; as possibility in Craig S. Keener, *Acts: An Exegetical Commentary*, 4 vols. (Grand Rapids: Baker Academic, 2012–2015), 3:2815.

10. Schnabel, *Early Christian Mission*, 2:1200.

he traveled in the upper Meander Valley northwest to Homodena, Eumeneia (Fulvia), Sebaste,[11] then south to Blaundos and into the valley of the Kogamos River; traveling west, Paul would have reached Philadelphia (modern Alaşehir) and Sardis (modern Sart); from Sardis, Paul would have turned south, crossing the Tmolus Mountains into the Cayster Valley, traveling via Hypaipa, Larisa[12] and Thyaira to Ephesus.[13] This route is two hundred miles (322 km) long.

Option 6. A southern route from Apamea via Laodicea to the valley of the Meander River,[14] suggesting a route from Apamea southwest via Anaua (Sanaos) north of Lake Sanaos, then west to Colossae and Laodicea ad Lycum

11. A direct route from Sebaste to Blaundos is suggested in *BAGRW*, map 62, B5/C5 (indicated by arrows at Blaundos and Sebaste; the route would have run north of the Sindros River). It was not necessary to travel via Temenouthyrai (nor via Akmonia, a considerable detour, which might only have been motivated by the desire to visit the Jewish community there).

12. There is a route from Larisa south via Tyrrha (Thyaira) to Ephesus, which is more plausible than the route via Metropolis suggested in Schnabel, *Early Christian Mission*, 2:1198, 1203; see Wilson, "Paul's Third Journey."

13. *BAGRW*, map 62, F5/E4/D5/C5/B4/B5/A5; map 56, H5/G5/F5; map 61, F1/E1/F2. I suggested that Paul might have crossed the Tmolus Mountains before reaching Philadelphia via a possible road connecting the Kogamos Valley with Tarigya, Diginda, Daredda, Koloe, and Nikaia and the Cayster Valley (Schnabel, *Early Christian Mission*, 2:1200); while I continue to think that this might have been possible, I no longer regard it as likely: the route across the Tmolus range from Sardis south to Hypaipa seems to have been more prominent.

14. Wilson, "Paul's Third Journey".

in the valley of the Lycus River, a side-arm of the upper Meander River; from Laodicea Paul would have continued west, passing through Karoura, Antioch on the Meander, Tralles, and Magnesia before reaching Ephesus.[15] This route is 173 miles (279 km) long.

ANALYSIS

Option 6 is the shorter and much more convenient route. This route requires that the phrase *ta anōterika merē* (τὰ ἀνωτερικὰ μέρη) is interpreted in terms of "interior regions" (ESV, NIV, NRSV), and the verb *katerchomai* (κατέρχομαι, "come down") in Acts 19:1[16] is either connected with Pisidian Antioch and Apamea, which are at higher altitudes, or taken in a more general sense.[17] If Paul wanted to get from Pisidian Antioch to Ephesus as quickly as possible, this would have been the logical route to take.

Option 5 interprets both terms more consistently as indicating regions of higher altitude (RSV: "upper country").[18] The argument that has sometimes been advanced that Paul traveled through the highlands in order to avoid the scorching heat of the region around Ephesus is hardly plausible: Paul wanted to proclaim the gospel in Ephesus, which would not have made it possible to escape the heat of the Mediterranean coast. A more plausible reason for the longer route via the Cayster Valley might have been a recurrence of malaria that Paul had suffered from earlier and which would have thought to be ameliorated in higher altitudes.[19]

PAUL'S MISSIONARY WORK IN EPHESUS AND IN THE PROVINCE OF ASIA

Paul most probably arrived in Ephesus in the late summer of AD 52. Luke reports for Paul's mission in Ephesus nine incidents: (1) Paul arrives in Ephesus and encounters followers of John the Baptist (Acts 19:1–7). (2) Paul proclaims the gospel in the synagogue (Acts 19:8–9). (3) He relocates his preaching and teaching activity from the synagogue to the lecture hall of Tyrannus where Paul was active for two years, a base of operation from which he reached the entire province of Asia (Acts 19:9–10). (4) Miracles that happened in Paul's ministry (Acts 19:11–12). (5) The fiasco involving Jewish exorcists who are beaten up by the evil spirits they attempted to drive out has an enormous impact on the population (Acts 19:13–16). (6) More Jews and Greeks are converted, and the church grows as they confess their sins and burn magic texts (Acts 19:17–20). (7) Paul decides to visit Macedonia, Achaia, Jerusalem, and Rome (Acts 19:21–22). (8) A riot instigated

---

15. *BAGRW*, map 65, D1/C2/B2/A2, map 61, H2/G2/F2/E2.

16. This is the preferred reading in Nestle-Aland, 26th edition, attested in P74vid, ℵ , A, E, and other manuscripts.

17. *Katerchomai* is defined in BDAG as "to move in a direction considered the opposite of up but not necessarily with suggestion of a gradient," with the suggested gloss "come down" (BDAG, s.v. "κατέρχομαι 1"). See also Wilson, "Paul's Third Journey": "whichever route Paul used, he descended in elevation toward the coast."

18. The verb *katerchomai* in nine of fifteen uses in Luke-Acts describes geographical movement from higher to lower altitudes: Luke 4:31; 9:37; Acts 8:5; 9:32; 11:27; 12:19; 15:1, 30; 21:10, in Acts the "going down" from Jerusalem to other regions and cities.

19. See Schnabel, "Paul's Missionary Work in Cyprus, Galatia, and Pamphylia," chapter 24 in this volume.

Theater at Ephesus

by the silversmiths grips the citizens who assemble in the theater, a dangerous situation that the city clerk is able to defuse (Acts 19:23–41). (9) Paul departs from Ephesus and travels to Macedonia (20:1).

As Acts 19:10 and passages in Paul's letters to the Corinthian Christians indicate, further events took place during Paul's mission in Ephesus: Mission to other cities in the province of Asia—Acts 19:10; Epaphras establishes churches in Colossae, Hierapolis, Laodicea—Col 1:7; 4:12; Apollos arrives from Corinth and Paul writes a letter to Corinth—1 Cor 16:12; 5:9; Chloe's people arrive from Corinth and Paul sends Timothy to Corinth—1 Cor 1:11; 4:17; Paul sends 1 Corinthians to Corinth—1 Cor 16:8; Paul plans to travel to Jerusalem via Macedonia and Corinth—1 Cor 16:3–6; Acts 19:21; Paul organizes a collection for the poor believers in Jerusalem—1 Cor 16:1; Rom 15:26–27; Timothy returns from Corinth, then is sent to Macedonia—Acts 19:22; Paul visits Corinth to address problems in the church 2 Cor 13:2; Paul sends Titus to Corinth with "severe letter"—2 Cor 2:4, 13; Riot in Ephesus—Acts 19:23–41; Paul suffers serious affliction in the province of Asia—2 Cor 1:8.

The city of Ephesus (near modern Selçuk) was one of the most important cities of the ancient world, with a population of probably two hundred thousand. When the province of Asia was established as the first Roman province in Asia Minor in 133 BC, Ephesus was granted the status of a free city (*civitas libera atque foederata*).[20] Julius Caesar, who visited Ephesus in 48 BC, was honored with a monument whose inscription acclaims him as "the god descending from Ares

20. Stephen Mitchell, "The Administration of Roman Asia from 133 BC to AD 250," in *Lokale Autonomie und römische Ordnungsmacht in den kaiserzeitlichen Provinzen vom 1. bis 3. Jahrhundert*,

and Aphrodite and the savior of human life." In 30–29 BC Augustus made Ephesus the seat of the provincial governor. The political status of the city and its harbor, the largest in Asia Minor, contributed to the economic growth of Ephesus. The theater seated twenty-four thousand spectators. The worship of Artemis Ephesia was the dominant cult of the city. Jews are attested in Ephesus since the Seleucid period; some received citizenship rights from king Antiochus III (261–246 BC). Josephus quotes an edict of the Roman consul Lucius Lentulus, issued in 49 BC, that granted the Jews of Ephesus exemption from military service.[21]

The fact that Paul stayed in Ephesus for over two years—from late summer AD 52 to the spring of AD 55—and that the entire province of Asia "heard the word of the Lord" while Paul was based in Ephesus suggests that Paul traveled to other cities preaching and establishing churches, as he had done during his previous missionary work. It appears that during Paul's mission in Ephesus, Epaphras established the churches in Colossae, Laodicea, and Hierapolis. We know from Rev 1:11; 2:1–3:22, that churches existed, besides Ephesus and Laodicea, in Smyrna, Pergamum, Thyatira, Sardis, and Philadelphia. The report in Acts 20:15, 17–38 suggests that a church existed in Miletus. A church in Troas is attested in Acts 20:6–12; 2 Cor 2:12–13; 2 Tim 4:13. Since Luke does not indicate whether Paul traveled to other cities in the province of Asia, and since Paul does not provide such details either, it is impossible to specify travel routes for Paul's wider ministry in the province.

PAUL'S MISSION IN THE PROVINCE OF ILLYRICUM

Paul left Ephesus in the spring of AD 55 and traveled through Macedonia, encouraging the believers (Acts 20:1–2), presumably in the churches he had established in Philippi, Thessalonica, and Berea, before he arrived "in Greece" where he stayed for three months (Acts 20:2–3), most plausibly a very compacted reference to the fact that Paul stayed in Corinth over the winter of AD 55/56—writing his letter to the believers in the city of Rome during this period—traveling to Jerusalem in the early spring of AD 56.

Luke provides no details concerning Paul's travel route. Paul may have left Ephesus by ship, heading straight for the Macedonian port of Neapolis (283 miles [455 km]) or he may have taken the coastal road, visiting churches north of Ephesus, for example, Smyrna, Pergamum, Adramyttium, and Troas, a journey of 193 miles (310 km), before crossing the Aegean Sea to Neapolis (137 miles [220 km]). The latter is more likely, given the statement in 2 Cor 2:12 (written not long after Paul left Ephesus) that Paul preached the gospel in Troas. After arriving in Neapolis (Macedonia), he would have traveled to Philippi, Thessalonica, and Berea (156 miles [251 km]).

Paul states in Rom 15:19 that he preached the gospel "from Jerusalem all

---

ed. W. Eck and E. Müller-Luckner (Munich: Oldenbourg, 1999), 17–46.

21. Josephus, *J.W.* 14.228; the Jews of Ephesus are often mentioned by Josephus: *Ant.* 12.125–126; 14.223–227, 228–229, 230, 234, 237–240, 262–264; 16.27–28, 167–168, 172–173. See also Jerome Murphy-O'Connor, *St. Paul's Ephesus: Texts and Archaeology* (Collegeville, MN: Liturgical Press, 2008), 78–85; Paul R. Trebilco, *The Early Christians in Ephesus from Paul to Ignatius* (Grand Rapids: Eerdmans, 2007), 37–51.

the way around to Illyricum." Since Paul did in fact preach the gospel in Jerusalem (the third phase of his mission),[22] the two geographical terms in the statement should be interpreted inclusively, which means that Paul proclaimed the gospel in Illyricum. The mission to Illyricum can be interpolated in Luke's statement in Acts 19:21 that Paul wanted to travel through Macedonia and Achaia before returning to Jerusalem and then traveling via Rome to Spain (Rom 15:23–29). The reason for traveling to Illyricum might have been connected with the fact that Illyricum was Latin-speaking as was Spain, the next major goal of Paul's mission.[23] A further reason might be connected with the fact that the difficulties in the church in Corinth he had to deal with during his time in Ephesus had been addressed, at least temporarily, and that Paul was eager to engage in pioneer missionary work again.[24]

Illyricum was the first Roman province on the eastern Adriatic coast, organized in 167 BC as a Roman territory that was part of the Illyrian kingdom, "the Illyrian territory of the Parthini and Atintani south of Lissus in the hinterland of Dyrrhachium. ... This protectorate was probably the source of the Roman idea of I[llyricum]."[25] The province of Illyria, established perhaps by Sulla, included large parts of Dalmatia and Pannonia that later became independent provinces.

On leaving Berea (Macedonia), Paul would have traveled north along the foot of Mount Bora (Bermion), passing near Edessa, to reach the *Via Egnatia*, which he would have followed east, passing

22. See Schnabel, "Paul's Missionary Work in Syria, Nabatea, Judea, and Cilicia," chapter 18 in this volume.

23. F. F. Bruce, *Paul: Apostle of the Free Spirit* (Exeter: Paternoster, 1977), 317.

24. Jerome Murphy-O'Connor, *Paul: A Critical Life* (Oxford: Oxford University Press, 1996), 316; I do not agree with the view that Paul had not been involved in missionary work for a few years while coworkers such as Epaphras had established new churches.

25. M. Šašel Kos, "Illyricum," *BNP* 6: 733; the following point, page 734.

through Edessa and Arnisa, the last city in the Lynkos region before crossing over the Kirli Derven Pass into Illyricum; the next cities were Heracleia in the Erigon valley and Lychnidos on a lake with the same name; crossing the Candaviae Mountains, Paul arrived in the Gernusus Valley, which opened into the coastal plain with the port cities of Dyrrhachium and Apollonia further south.[26] The chronology of Paul's mission allows only the summer of AD 56 for a mission to Illyricum. If Paul preached the gospel in the traditional Illyrian territory, he would have been in Dyrrhachium and Apollonia.[27] If he aimed at the province of Illyricum, he would have traveled north from Dyrrhachium, reaching Scodra, Risinium (Rhizon), or Epidaurum.[28]

The journey from Berea to Dyrrhachium was around 205 miles (330 km); Apollonia was 22 miles (36 km) south of Dyrrhachium. North of Dyrrhachium, on the land route, were Scodra (32 miles [52 km]), Risinium (68 miles [110 km]), and Epidaurum (99 miles [160 km]).

The journey to Corinth could most easily have been accomplished by ship, from any of these port cities, a distance of 364 miles (585 km) from Dyrrhachium, 475 miles (765 km) from Epidaurum. Paul may have passed through Nicopolis in southern Epirus (Macedonia), where he decided at a later time to spend the winter (Tit 3:12), when the ship that took him to Corinth made a stop there. Or, Paul took the land route from Illyricum to Corinth (around 300 miles [485 km]), passing on the inland route[29] through Byllis, Hekatompedon, Antigoneia, Hadrianopolis, Phanota, Photike, Ephyra (Kichyros), Nicopolis, Stratos, Pleuron, Calydon, across the sea to Patrai, then to Aigion, Aigai, and Sicyon before reaching Corinth.[30]

Remains of Roman Harbor at Troas

PAUL'S RETURN TO JERUSALEM

Paul wanted to sail to Syria to reach Jerusalem, a plan that was thwarted due to the discovery of a plot of Corinthian

26. *BAGRW*, map 49, E3/D3/D2/C2/B2/B3. For details see Schnabel, *Early Christian Mission*, 2:1250–57; Schnabel, *Paul the Missionary: Realities, Strategies, and Methods* (Downers Grove, IL: InterVarsity Press, 2008), 112–13. David W. J. Gill assumes that the term Illyria in Rom 15:19 refers to the region of Dalmatia: Paul sailed from Dyrrhachium or Apollonia northward along the Adriatic coast (David W. J. Gill, "Macedonia," in *The Book of Acts in Its Graeco-Roman Setting*, ed. D. W. J. Gill and C. Gempf, vol. 2 of *The Book of Acts in Its First-Century Setting*, ed. Bruce W. Winter [Grand Rapids: Eerdmans, 1994], 399, 410).

27. *BAGRW*, map 49, B2/B3.

28. *BAGRW*, map 49, B1; map 20, G7; see also 7; Schnabel, *Paul the Missionary*, 113.

29. The coastal route from Dyrrhachium and Apollonia to Nicopolis would have taken Paul through Aulon, Chimaira, Phoinike, past Bouthroton and Gitana through Phaskomelia, past Elaias Limen to Nicopolis. See *BAGRW*, map 49, B3, map 54, B2/B3.

30. Schnabel, *Early Christian Mission*, 2:1256. See also *BAGRW*, map 49, B3, map 54, B2/B3/C3/D4, map 55, A4/B4/C4, map 58, B1/C1/C2.

Jews (Acts 20:3). Paul decided to travel north to Macedonia—either by sea or by land, the latter less likely considering Paul's desire to be in Jerusalem by Pentecost[31]—crossing from Europe to Asia Minor at Neapolis, sailing to Troas (Acts 20:6–7).

From Troas, Paul traveled by foot to Assos (Acts 20:13)—on the coastal road on the Sacred Way to the temple dedicated to Apollo Smintheum, via Kolonai and Larisa through the Halesian Plain, and from there in the valley of the Satnioeis River to Assos.[32] The reasons for Paul taking the land route, in contrast to his companions who sailed, are unclear. Suggestions from ministry concerns in Troas which delayed Paul's departure, a tactical maneuver in the context of dangers from Jewish opponents, the dangers of the circumnavigation of Cape Lectum, the desire to avoid sea sickness, training of church leaders from Troas, the desire to save money, the desire to demonstrate his physical robustness to his younger coworkers, the desire to have time for solitude.[33] The best suggestions refer either to the warnings of the Spirit that Paul faces prison and hardship in Jerusalem (Acts 20:22–23), Paul gaining time to reflect on the Spirit's warnings and providing him with the opportu-

31. The journey by foot from Corinth to Neapolis via Berea, Thessalonica, Berea would be 528.4 miles [852 km], lasting thirty-four days or six weeks.

32. For detailed description see Glen L. Thompson and Mark Wilson, "Paul's Walk to Assos: A Hodological Inquiry into Its Geography, Archaeology, and Purpose," in *Stones, Bones, and the Sacred: Essays on Material Culture and Ancient Religion in Honor of Dennis E. Smith*, ed. A. H. Cadwallader (Atlanta: SBL Press, 2016), 278–90.

33. See Thompson and Wilson, "Paul's Walk", 294–305, for a critique.

nity to demonstrate with his walk on the Sacred Way that he is not afraid,[34] or to the possibility that Paul might have been visiting believers in the area.[35]

Assos

From Assos, Paul sailed via Mytilene, Chios, and Samos to Miletus (Acts 20:14–15), where he met with the elders of the church in Ephesus (Acts 20:17–38). From Miletus Paul and his companions sailed via Kos, Rhodes, Patara, Cyprus, to Tyre (Acts 21:1–5). After meeting with the believers, they sailed to Ptolemais (Acts 21:7), then to Caesarea (Acts 21:8–14) and Jerusalem to the house of a Cypriote believer with the name Mnason (Acts 21:15–16).

SUMMARY OF PAUL'S TRAVELS DURING HIS MISSION IN THE PROVINCES OF ASIA AND ILLYRICUM

- Antioch (Syria) to Antioch (Galatia), via Tarsus: 438 miles (705 km)—twenty-eight days (five weeks)
- Pisidian Antioch to Ephesus (Asia), via the Cayster Valley: 200 miles (322 km)—thirteen days
- Ephesus to Troas, via the coastal road: 193 miles (310 km)—twelve days
- *By ship*: Troas (Asia) to Neapolis (Macedonia): 137 miles (220 km)
- Neapolis to Berea, via Philippi, Thessalonica: 156 miles (251 km)—ten days
- Berea to Dyrrhachium (Illyricum): 205 miles (330 km)—thirteen days
- *By ship*: Dyrrhachium to Corinth: 364 miles (585 km)
- *By ship*: Corinth to Neapolis (Macedonia): 285 miles (460 km)—between four and nine days
- *By ship*: Neapolis to Troas (Asia): 137 miles (220 km)

---

34. Thompson and Wilson, "Paul's Walk", 302–5. However, it should be noted that Paul could have reflected on the Spirit's warning during the two to three week journey by ship from Assos to Caesarea, and there is reason why Paul needed to demonstrate his courage to his coworkers by walking on the Sacred Way: traveling to Jerusalem despite repeated warnings by Christian prophets was "demonstration" enough that Paul was not afraid.

35. Eckhard J. Schnabel, *Acts* (Grand Rapids: Zondervan, 2012), 837 n. 24. This possibility is too readily dismissed by Thompson and Wilson, "Paul's Walk", 301, with reference to C. K. Barrett, *The Acts of the Apostles*, 2 vols. (Edinburgh: T&T Clark, 1994–1998), 2:957, who asserts that there is "nothing to suggest that he made an evangelistic tour through the district"—the suggestion of Thompson and Wilson is no less speculative than the assumed possibility that there were believers in the area. The existence of Christians in villages has been undervalued; see Thomas A. Robinson, *Who Were the First Christians? Dismantling the Urban Thesis* (Oxford: Oxford University Press, 2017).

- Troas to Assos: 31 miles (50 km)—two days
- *By ship*: Assos to Miletus: 199 miles (320 km)
- *By ship*: Miletus (Asia) to Tyre (Syria): 211 miles (940 km)
- *By ship*: Tyre to Caesarea, via Ptolemais: 56 miles (90 km)[36]
- Caesarea to Jerusalem (Judea), via Joppe: 75 miles (120 km)—five days
- **Total by foot:** 1297 miles (2088 km)—eighty-four days (fourteen weeks)
- **Total by ship:** 1762 miles (2835 km)—twenty to fifty-two days (between three to seven weeks)

BIBLIOGRAPHY

Barrett, C. K. *The Acts of the Apostles*. 2 vols. Edinburgh: T&T Clark, 1994–1998.

Bruce, F. F. *The Acts of the Apostles: The Greek Text with Introduction and Commentary*. 3rd revised and enlarged ed. Grand Rapids: Eerdmans, 1990.

———. *Paul: Apostle of the Free Spirit*. Exeter: Paternoster, 1977.

Conybeare, William J., and John S. Howson. *The Life and Epistles of St. Paul*. 2 vols. 2nd ed. London: Longmans & Roberts, 1856.

French, David H. "Acts and the Roman Roads of Asia Minor." Pages 49–58 in *The Book of Acts in Its Graeco-Roman Setting*. Edited by D. W. J. Gill and C. Gempf. Volume 2 of *The Book of Acts in Its First Century Setting*. Edited by Bruce W. Winter. Grand Rapids: Eerdmans, 1994.

Gill, David W. J. "Macedonia." Pages 397–417 in *The Book of Acts in Its Graeco-Roman Setting*. Edited by D. W. J. Gill and C. Gempf. Volume 2 of *The Book of Acts in Its First Century Setting*. Edited by Bruce W. Winter. Grand Rapids: Eerdmans, 1994.

Hemer, Colin J. *The Book of Acts in the Setting of Hellenistic History*. Edited by C. H. Gempf. Tübingen: Mohr Siebeck, 1989.

Keener, Craig S. *Acts: An Exegetical Commentary*. 4 vols. Grand Rapids: Baker Academic, 2012–2015.

Kos, M. Šašel. "Illyricum." *BNP* 6:732–735.

Mitchell, Stephen. "The Administration of Roman Asia from 133 BC to AD 250." Pages 17–46 in *Lokale Autonomie und römische Ordnungsmacht in den kaiserzeitlichen Provinzen vom 1. bis 3. Jahrhundert*. Edited by Werner Eck and Elisabeth Müller-Luckner. Munich: Oldenbourg, 1999.

Monroy, Mauricio S. *The Church of Smyrna: History and Theology of a Primitive Christian Community*. Frankfurt: Lang, 2015.

Murphy-O'Connor, Jerome. *Paul: A Critical Life*. Oxford: Oxford University Press, 1996.

———. *St. Paul's Ephesus: Texts and Archaeology*. Collegeville, MN: Liturgical Press, 2008.

Ramsay, William M. *The Church in the Roman Empire Before A.D. 170*. London: Hodder & Stoughton, 1893. Repr. Boston: Adamant, 2004.

36. The journey by ship from Assos to Caesarea was 839 miles (1350 km), taking between ten and twenty-five days (1.4 to 3.6 weeks).

———. *St. Paul the Traveller and the Roman Citizen*. London: Hodder & Stoughton, 1896.

Riesner, Rainer. *Paul's Early Period: Chronology, Mission Strategy, Theology*. Grand Rapids: Eerdmans, 1998.

Robinson, Thomas A. *Who Were the First Christians? Dismantling the Urban Thesis*. Oxford: Oxford University Press, 2017.

Schnabel, Eckhard J. *Acts*. Grand Rapids: Zondervan, 2012.

———. *Early Christian Mission*. 2 vols. Downers Grove, IL: InterVarsity Press, 2004.

———. *Paul the Missionary: Realities, Strategies, and Methods*. Downers Grove, IL: InterVarsity Press, 2008.

Thompson, Glen L., and Mark Wilson. "Paul's Walk to Assos: A Hodological Inquiry into Its Geography, Archaeology, and Purpose." Pages 269–313 in *Stones, Bones, and the Sacred: Essays on Material Culture and Ancient Religion in Honor of Dennis E. Smith*. Edited by A. H. Cadwallader. Atlanta: SBL Press, 2016.

Trebilco, Paul R. *The Early Christians in Ephesus from Paul to Ignatius*. Grand Rapids: Eerdmans, 2007.

Uggeri, Giovanni. "Sulle strade di San Paolo in Anatolia: Il secondo e il terzo viaggio." Pages 125–73 in *Seminario di studi Paolo di Tarso: il messaggio, l'immagine, i viaggi; Studi in memoria di Luigi Padovese*. Edited by Stella Uggeri Patitucci and Luigi Padovese. Palermo: Officina di studi medievali, 2011.

Wilson, Mark. "The 'Upper Regions' and the Route of Paul's Third Journey From Apamea to Ephesus." *Scriptura* 117 (2018): 1–21.

CHAPTER 32

PAUL AS A PRISONER IN JUDEA AND ROME

Acts 21:1–28:28

Eckhard J. Schnabel

KEY POINTS

- After Paul's arrest in the outer court of the temple in Jerusalem, he spent time in the Antonia Fortress and in the building of the Sanhedrin.
- After his transfer to Caesarea Maritima, Paul was in prison in the *praetorium* of the prefect of the Roman province of Judea.
- Luke relates with some geographical detail, in precise nautical terms, Paul's transfer from Caesarea to the city of Rome.
- The fourteenth phase of Paul's missionary work lasted for at least two years when he was a prisoner in Rome waiting for his Jewish opponents to arrive from Judea.

INTRODUCTION

When Paul returned to Jerusalem after his missionary work in Ephesus and in Illyricum, he was nearly killed in the outer court of the temple when Jewish pilgrims from the province of Asia recognized him and thought that he had profaned the temple by taking one of his gentile companions into the inner courts (Acts 21:27–31). This took place shortly after Pentecost (Acts 20:16), which was on May 29 in the year AD 57. Paul planned to travel to Rome, probably in early summer of the same year, before traveling to Spain, either in the fall of AD 57 or in the spring of AD 58. Instead, he spent two years as a prisoner in Caesarea (AD 57–59; Acts 24:27), and, after his transfer to the city of Rome, at least two years as a prisoner in the capital of the empire (AD 60–62; Acts 28:30). Paul was imprisoned in three geographical locations.

PAUL IN THE ANTONIA FORTRESS IN JERUSALEM

After the Roman commander of the auxil-

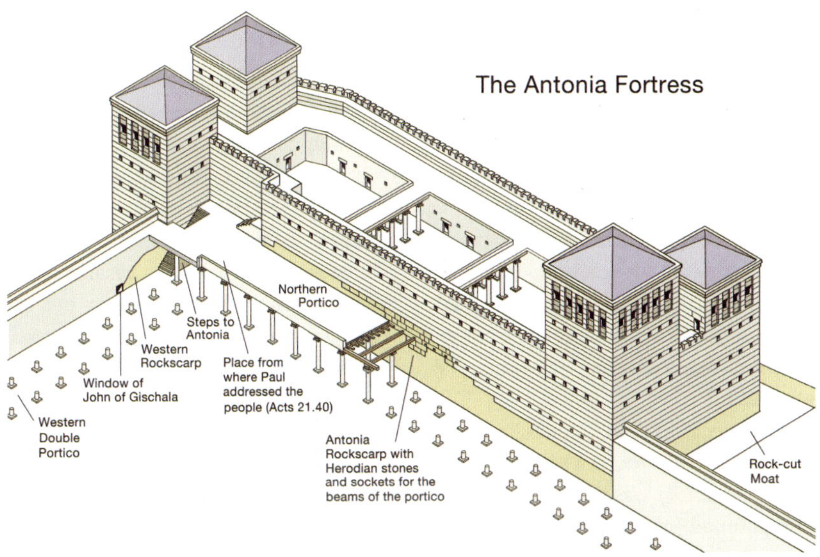

iary troops rescued Paul from being killed in the outer court of the temple (Acts 21:31–35), allowing Paul to address the crowds and defend himself (Acts 22:1–21), he took Paul to "the barracks" (παρεμβολή, *parembolē*) of the Antonia Fortress (see page 79 for an illustration of the Temple Mount).

When Herod the Great built the enormous plaza of the Temple Mount, he removed large parts of the rocky hill on the northwest section, leaving vertical rock scarps almost thirty feet (9 m) high in some places, forming an ideal foundation for the new fortress built by Herod replacing the Baris.[1] Josephus provides a detailed description of the Antonia in *J.W.* 5.238–46.[2] The Antonia was built as a *tetrapyrgion*, a central structure with towers at each of the four corners; three towers were about 82 feet (25 m) high, the fourth tower at the southeast corner was 115 feet (35 m) high, soaring an astonishing 164 feet (50 m) above the outer court of the temple.[3] The four towers were connected by walls, and the entire structure—perhaps 394 feet from east to west and 148 feet wide (120 x 45 m)—seems to have been surrounded by a wall, with a space of 6 to 10 feet (2–3 m) allowing

1. While some scholars locate Herod's Antonia at the site of the Hasmonean Baris (on the basis of Josephus, *Ant.* 15.403), Bahat cites archaeological evidence for the suggestion that the Baris was south of the Antonia; Ritmeyer thinks that the Baris was located at the northwest corner of the square Temple Mount, while the Antonia was at the northwest corner of Herod's extension of the Temple Mount to the north.

2. Shorter comments are found in Josephus, *J.W.* 1.401; *Ant.* 15.292, 403–9, 424; 18.91–92.

3. See Netzer, *Architecture of Herod*, 125. Ritmeyer, *Temple Mount*, 130, reckons Josephus' 50 cubits to be 86 ft (26.25 m).

the movement of guards and defenders.[4] The upper structure, which was 66 feet (20 m) high, might have had four stories. The interior of the Antonia "resembled a palace in its spaciousness and appointments, being divided into apartments of every description and for every purpose, including cloisters, baths and broad courtyards for the accommodation of troops; so that from its possession of all conveniences it seemed a town, from its magnificence a palace." (Josephus, *J.W.* 5.241 [LCL])

The barracks of the Antonia evidently included a prison to which Paul, in chains (Acts 21:33; 22:29), was taken (Acts 22:24).[5] The planned interrogation by torture (Acts 22:25) would probably have taken place in one of the courtyards. Learning that Paul was a Roman citizen, the Roman commander evidently removed the chains (Acts 22:29), although he kept Paul in custody in the Antonia—perhaps in a room in the barracks, outside of the prison cells—because the charges against Paul had not been clarified. The Antonia was only one-third of a mile (500 m), as the crow flies, from Golgotha, the site of Jesus' crucifixion. The next day the commander took Paul to the Sanhedrin building for a meeting with the Jewish authorities; after the meeting erupted in a shouting match, he took Paul back into the barracks of the Antonia (Acts 23:10).[6]

PAUL IN THE PRAETORIUM IN CAESAREA

When a plot of Jerusalem Jews who plan to kill Paul is discovered, the Roman commander transfers Paul from the Antonia Fortress to the praetorium of the Roman prefect of Judea in Caesarea (Acts 23:12–35; see map on page 414). During the transfer via Antipatris to Caesarea (Acts 23:31–32), Paul was under heavy protective guard, accompanied by two hundred soldiers, seventy cavalrymen, and two hundred bowmen who are commanded by two centurions (Acts 23:23). While the size of this force seems excessive to some, it can be defended on account of two factors: the situation in Judea, particularly in the open countryside, was unstable when Felix was prefect, with the activities of Jewish insurgents increasing; it was conventional military strategy to factor in the size of one's own and of the enemy's troops, which in this case was ten to one (note the more than forty conspirators, Acts 23:13).[7]

Antipatris (Aphek in the Old Testament) was located in the coastal plain, about thirty-seven miles (60 km) northwest of Jerusalem, reached either on a southerly route via Moza (Ammaous), Aialon, Emmaus (Nicopolis), and Lydda (thirty-five miles [56 km]); a central route via Bethoron, Caphar Ruta, Modiin, Hadid (Adida), and Lydda (thir-

---

4. For the dimensions of the wall, see Pierre Benoit, "L'Antonia d'Hérode le Grand et le forum oriental d'Aelia Capitolina," in *Exégèse et Théologie IV* (Paris: Cerf, 1982), 311–46. Remains of the rockscarp suggest that the moat might have been 160 feet (48 m) wide; see Ritmeyer, *Temple Mount*, 130. For the space for movement of guards, see Netzer, *Architecture of Herod*, 125.

5. See the section on the prison in the Antonia in chapter 2 (pages 33–34).

6. See the discussion of the Sanhedrin building in chapter 2 (pages 27–30).

7. For the instability of the countryside, see Josephus, *Ant.* 20.161–72; *J.W.* 2.264–65, 271. A few years later, in October AD 66, an entire Roman army was defeated (*J.W.* 2.540–55). For the military strategy, see Xenophon, *Cyropaedia* 1.4.18–19; Diodorus Siculus 13.111.1; Plutarch, *Themistocles* 9.4; Diogenes Laertius 1.83. For a comprehensive discussion, see Craig S. Keener, *Acts: An Exegetical Commentary*, 4 vols. (Grand Rapids: Baker Academic, 2012–2015), 3:3319–26.

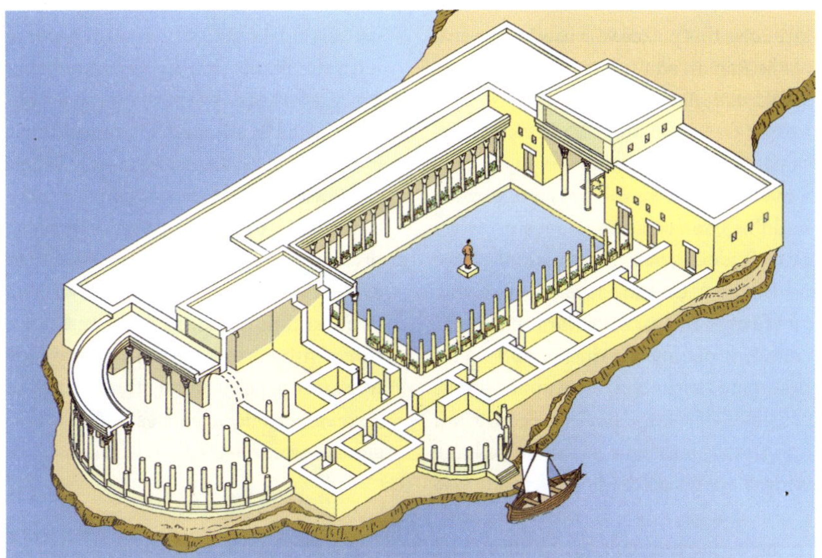

Illustration of Herod's Palace at Caesarea

ty-six miles [58 km]); or a northerly route via Gophna, Thamna, and Ramathaim/Arimathaia (thirty-three miles [53 km]). The city had been reestablished by the Roman general Pompey under the name Arethusa, and refounded by Herod the Great in 9 BC as Antipatris in honor of his father Antipater (Josephus, *Ant.* 14.75; 16.142–43; *J.W.* 1.417). When the evangelist Philip visited "every city" between Azotos and Caesarea during his missionary travels (Acts 8:39–40), he presumably preached in Antipatris as well. The infantry would not have been able to reach Antipatris in one day. They either accompanied the cavalry escort during the night hours, or there was a full day of marching between the night during which they left Jerusalem and their arrival in Antipatris. The reference "the next day" in Acts 23:32 refers either to the departure of the infantry escort before the centurions and Paul reached Antipatris, or to the morning after their arrival in Antipatris on the second day of travel.[8] In Antipatris, the troops and their prisoner would have stayed in the fortress that Herod the Great had built on the acropolis.[9] Since the region between Antipatris and Caesarea (about thirty-one miles [50 km]) was largely gentile, the regular soldiers could return to Jerusalem while Paul was taken with the lighter cavalry escort to the provincial capital.

Caesarea Maritima was built by Herod the Great between 22–10 BC, including a palace on the small peninsula south of the harbor (called "Promontory Palace"). After AD 6, when Judea became a Roman

8. Brian M. Rapske, "Acts, Travel, and Shipwreck," in *The Book of Acts in its Graeco-Roman Setting*, ed. D. W. J. Gill and C. Gempf (Grand Rapids: Eerdmans, 1994), 1–47, 11–14.

9. P. Beck and M. Kochavi, "Aphek (in Sharon): The Roman Period," *NEAEHL* 1:70.

territory, this palace was used as the seat of the Roman administration, that is, as *praetorium* (Acts 23:35).[10] The palace/praetorium was a two-story building consisting of two wings. The lower palace (264 x 216 feet [80 x 66 m]) was a luxurious building constructed around a peristyle court surrounded by columns and a large central pool. On the east side was a cluster of larger rooms, with a large hall in the center, probably the dining and reception room (*triclinium*). The upper palace consisted of a large peristyle courtyard (210 x 137.75 feet [64 x 42 m]) and a large wing of rooms on the northern side (210 x 78.75 feet [64 x 24 m]), with a large hall in the western part of the building that may have served as an audience hall. A room near the entrance to the upper palace was a room with a mosaic whose Latin text suggests that it belonged to the prison wing of the praetorium; the Latin text reads: *Spes bona / adiutorib(us) / offici / custodiar(um)* ("A happy future for the assistants in the office of the prison administration").[11]

Paul spent two years in Caesarea since Felix, the Roman prefect, did not decide the case: he frequently conversed with Paul, who explained the gospel to him, but he also wanted to grant a favor to the Jews (Acts 24:1–27). When the new prefect, Festus, wanted to do the Jews a favor when they asked that Paul be transferred from Caesarea to Jerusalem (Acts 25:9), Paul seemed to realize that matters might take a turn for the worse, with the result that he requested that his case be heard by the emperor, a right that he had as a Roman citizen and that Festus granted (Acts 25:10–12). When the Jewish king Herod Agrippa II came to Caesarea to pay his respects to the new prefect, Paul has another opportunity to explain the gospel (Acts 25:1–26:32). The two years in Caesarea constituted the thirteenth period of Paul's missionary work (see page 702 for a table listing the sixteen periods or phases of Paul's missionary work).

PAUL'S TRANSFER FROM CAESAREA TO THE CITY OF ROME

Paul was taken as prisoner from Caesarea in Judea to the city of Rome. Julius, a centurion, took Paul and other prisoners on board a ship from Adramyttium, a port city in the west coast of the province of Asia, located between Pergamum and Troas opposite the island of Lesbos. The ship plied "ports along the coast of the province of Asia" (Acts 27:2), traveling perhaps as far as Alexandria in Egypt, now being on the journey back to its home port. Luke describes the route of the ship with impressive nautical detail (Acts 27:3–8).

They sailed from Caesarea north to Sidon on the Syrian coast; then they sailed "under the lee" (ὑπεπλεύσαμεν, *hypepleusamen*), that is, on the side of Cyprus that protected the ship from

---

10. Netzer, *Architecture of Herod*, 106–12; see also Barbara Burrell, "Palace to Praetorium: The Romanization of Caesarea," in *Caesarea Maritima: A Retrospective after Two Millenia*, ed. Avner Raban and Kenneth G. Holum (Leiden: Brill, 1996), 228–47.

11. Hannah M. Cotton and Werner Eck, "Governors and Their Personnel on Latin Inscriptions from Caesarea Maritima," *The Israel Academy of Sciences and Humanities Proceedings* 7:7 (2001): 230–32. Since the mosaic was laid later than the mid-first century AD, and since this section of the praetorium might have been added as late as the second century, it is impossible to be certain about the prison in which Paul was kept; see Werner Eck, *Rom und Judaea* (Tübingen: Mohr Siebeck, 2007), 88.

Downward view at Myra from in front of the granary across the marshlands where vestiges of the ancient Roman harbor remain.

the wind: the prevailing autumnal west winds forced the ship to pass Cyprus on the eastern and northern side of the island; the original course apparently would have taken the ship to Paphos on the south coast of Cyprus, but that proved impossible. As they sailed between northern Cyprus and the southern coast of Asia Minor, the progress of the ship against the autumn winds "was assisted by local on-shore and off-shore breezes, and by the westerly trend of the currents along the south Anatolian coasts."[12]

They landed at Myra in Lycia (Acts 27:5). The Western text includes the information that the voyage from Sidon to Myra took fifteen days.[13] The addition is hardly original, but it gives a plausible time for the journey in adverse conditions. As the Adramyttium ship continued along the coast of Asia Minor, Julius transferred the prisoners to a ship sailing for Italy. Myra was, together with Patara (cf. Acts 21:1), the principal port for the Alexandrian grain ships who took on board provisions after having crossed the Mediterranean. Egypt provided a third of the grain that the city of Rome needed annually.[14] The journey from Rome to Egypt took at least a month or two, if one left at the earliest possible date in the month of April, sailing against the prevailing northwesterly winds; the return journey "downhill" could take as

12. Colin J. Hemer, *The Book of Acts in the Setting of Hellenistic History* (Tübingen: Mohr Siebeck, 1989), 133.

13. Manuscripts 614. 1127. 1292. 1611. 1890. 2138. 2147. 2412. 2652, and Latin and Syriac manuscripts; see Holger Strutwolf, et al., *Die Apostelgeschichte*, 4 vols. (Stuttgart: Deutsche Bibelgesellschaft, 2017), 1.2:1011.

14. See Greg H. R. Horsley and Stephen R. Llewelyn, eds., *New Documents Illustrating Early Christianity* (North Ryde: Macquarie University; Grand Rapids: Eerdmans, 1981–2012), 7:112–29; Robert Sallares, "Grain Trade, Grain Import," *BNP* 5:976–981.

Kaloi Limenes

little as two or three weeks. Provided a quick turn-around in Rome and fast reloading in Alexandria, ships could squeeze in a second crossing before the season closed. The ship that Julius and his party of prisoners boarded was most likely a grain ship on its second crossing of the year, trying to reach Rome just before the onset of the winter season.

The journey from Myra to Rome is reported in great detail by Luke due to the storm resulting in being shipwrecked on the island of Malta (Acts 27:6–28:14). Luke describes eleven stages of the journey.[15]

STAGE 1

From Myra (Lycia), the ship sailed west, reaching the area south of Cnidus, a city on the western tip of the peninsula in southwestern Caria (Acts 27:7). Cnidus remained a free city even within the Roman province of Asia.[16] They did not anchor in the port of Cnidus.

STAGE 2

From off Cnidus the ship sailed southwest toward Crete, sailing around the cape at the northeastern tip of the island Crete called Samonion Promontory (Salmone), then along the southern coast of the island (Acts 27:7–8).

STAGE 3

The ship reached Kaloi Limenes ("Fair Havens;" Acts 27:8), about 1.2 miles (2 km) west of Lasea (Lasaia). The bay offered good anchorage, except from the southeast winds in the winter months, although offshore islands provided some protection from the southwest. This set-

15. Acts 27:5, 7, 8, 16, 17, 27; 28:1, 12, 13, 14. See *BAGRW*, map 65, C5; map 61, E4; map 60, F2/C3/B3; map 37, C1–E1; map 38, B1 (Berenice); map 35, G2 (Lepcis Magna); map 1, F3 / map 47 (Malta insert); map 47, G4/H1; map 44, F4/D3/C2; map 43, E4/D3/C2–B2.

16. Hans Kaletsch, "Cnidus," *BNP* 3:489–90.

tlement of Kaloi Limenes, which Luke calls "a place" (τόπος, *topos*) was not large, nor was the town of Lasea to whose territory the bay belonged (see page 417 for a map of Paul's journey from Caesarea to Fair Havens).

Stage 4

Despite the warning of Paul, who was an experienced traveler, the centurion opted to stay on the ship, whose owner and pilot decided to set sail, hoping to winter in Phoenix, a port with better facilities further west. It seems that just after the ship had rounded Cape Matala, it was caught by "a wind of hurricane force, called the Northeaster" (εὐρακύλων, *eurakylōn*) that swept down from the mountains of Crete, across the open plain of Mesara.[17] The crew was unable to head into the wind—they were forced to surrender the ship to the wind (Acts 27:13–15).

Stage 5

The only geographical marker mentioned by Luke between Crete and the shipwreck on Malta is the island of Cauda, which they passed to the west (Acts 27:16), thirty nautical miles (55 km) west-southwest of Cape Matala (Crete).

Stage 6

Unable to establish the course of the ship since navigation was impossible due to the cloud cover (Acts 27:20), the ship was driven southwest for fourteen days (Acts 27:27). The crew feared that the ship would be driven into the Syrtis and run aground on sandbars (Acts 27:17). The term "Syrtis" refers to the Greater Syrtis or *Syrtis Maior* (modern Gulf of Sidera), which is the eastern part of the coastal waters west of Cyrenaica between Berenice and Lepcis Magna in northern Africa, a notorious navigational hazard repeatedly mentioned with fear in contemporary literature.[18] It has been estimated that with a drift of 36.5 nautical miles (67.6 km) in twenty-four hours, the ship would have drifted from Cauda to Malta—a distance of 476 nautical miles (882 km)—in slightly over thirteen days (see page 420 for a map of journey from Fair Havens to Malta).[19] Luke calls the body of water between Crete and the Syrtis "the Adriatic Sea" (Acts 27:27), a term that refers here to the sea between Crete and Sicily.[20]

Stage 7

The ship approached land on the fourteenth night of the storm and ran aground on a sandbar in the early day-

---

17. Hemer, *Book of Acts*, 141; see also Colin J. Hemer, "Euraquilo and Melita," *Journal of Theological Studies* 26 (1975): 100–111. The term *eurakylōn* is a hybrid term from the Greek *euros* (Εὖρος, "east") and Latin *aquilo* ("north").

18. According to Strabo, *Geography* 17.3.20, the difficulty with the Syrtis is that its deep waters "contain shallows, and the result is, at the ebb and the flow of the tides, that sailors sometimes fall into the shallows and stick there, and that the safe escape of a boat is rare. On this account sailors keep at a distance when voyaging along the coast, taking precautions not to be caught off their guard and driven by winds into these gulfs" (LCL).

19. Hemer, *Book of Acts*, 145.

20. According to Ptolemy, *Geography* 3.15.1, Crete is bordered on the west by the Adriatic Sea. The Adriatic Sea should be distinguished from the "Adriatic Gulf" located between Italy and Dalmatia (modern Yugoslavia), which is the modern referent of the term "Adria" (see Hemer, *Book of Acts*, 146 n. 129). Heinz Warnecke, *Die tatsächliche Romfahrt des Apostels Paulus* (Stuttgart: Katholisches Bibelwerk, 1987), argues that the ship was driven toward the Adriatic (Gulf) and

light hours; once they were on land they discovered that they had landed on the island of Malta (Acts 27:27–28, 39–41; 28:1). The most likely sites of the shipwreck are (1) the bay north of the channel between the mainland and St. Paul's Islands (Salmonetta Island); (2) Mistra Bay, south of Selmun Bay on the west side of St. Paul Bay; (3) the small bay south of Qawra Point, on the eastern side of the peninsula that separates St. Paul's Bay from Salina Bay to the west.[21]

The island of Malta is located at the narrowest point of the Mediterranean, between Sicily and Tunisia; it measures eighteen miles (29 km) by eight miles (13 km). The neighboring island of Gaulos to the northwest belongs to Malta. The northeast coast has two major sandy bays, Mellieha Bay in the west, and St. Paul's Bay. The two natural harbors are located at the east end of the island. Malta belonged since 218 BC to the province of Sicilia (Sicily).

St. Paul's Island

There are three possibilities for the estate of Publius, the chief official of the Roman administration on the island, based on archaeological explorations that have unearthed the remains of Roman villas (marked on the map as E1–3): (1) San Pawl Milqi, at the southern end of Salina Bay; (2) Xemxija, west of St. Paul's Bay; (3) Wardija (Taʿl-Ghazzelin), situated on the rocky shore on the southeast side of St. Paul's Bay, where a Roman bath complex has been discovered.[22]

STAGE 8

After three months, the centurion was able to book passage on an Alexandrian ship that had spent the winter in Malta (Acts 28:11). It was probably late January or early February when they were able to sail to Syracuse (Acts 28:12), a city on the east coast of Sicily, founded by the Corinthians in 733 BC, under Roman control since 211 BC, the seat of the provincial government. Syracuse had one of the largest natural harbors in the

that the shipwreck took place not at Malta but at Cephallania, the largest of the Ionian islands west of Greece (*BAGRW*, map 1, H3; map 54, D5), but his argument is partly based on his (mis) understanding of *eurakylōn* as "a dynamic wind shifting from northeast to east." For a critique of Warnecke, see Jürgen Wehnert, "Gestrandet. Zu einer neuen These über den Schiffbruch des Apostels," *Zeitschrift für Theologie und Kirche* 87 (1990): 67–99.

21. Richard J. Bauckham, "The Estate of Publius on Malta (Acts 28:7)," in *The Christian World Around the New Testament* (Grand Rapids: Baker Academic, 2017), 340–44; see also Eckhard J. Schnabel, *Acts: Expanded Digital Edition* (Grand Rapids: Zondervan, 2012), at Acts 27:41. The bay north of the channel between the mainland and St. Paul's Islands is the suggestion of Bauckham ("Estate of Publius," 343). For the area from Salina Bay to the west, see Eugene P. Teuma, *San Pawl Il-Bahar: A Guide* (Hal-Qormi: Dormax, 2003), who notes the presence of lead anchor stocks found near Qawra Point, "the largest ever recovered from any Roman Period wreck site."

22. Bauckham, "Estate of Publius," 346–50.

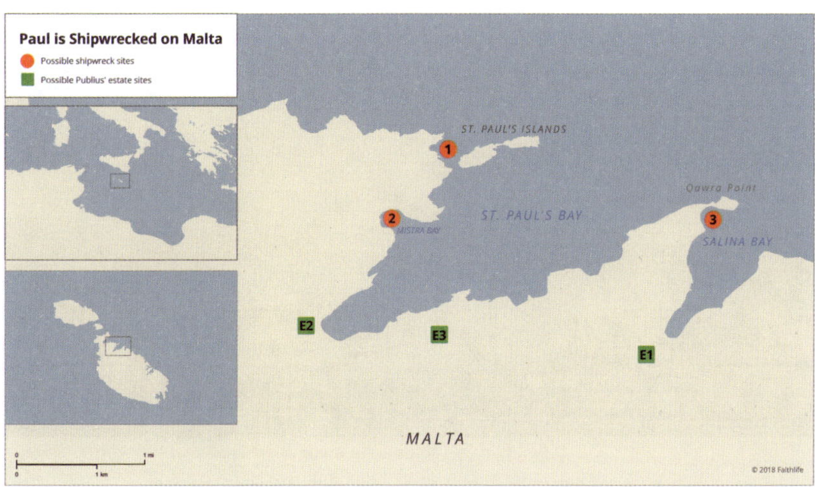

Mediterranean. The voyage from Malta to Syracuse was about eighty nautical miles (150 km), which could be completed in a good day of sailing.

STAGE 9

After three days they sailed from Syracuse to Rhegium (Regium Iulium) (Acts 28:13), at the southern entrance of the Straits of Messina, which were only seven miles (11 km) wide near Rhegium, a voyage of sixty-five nautical miles (120 km). Rhegium, situated on the tip of the Italian peninsula in Calabria, opposite the Sicilian city of Messina, prospered after the earthquake of 19 BC when Augustus settled veterans of his army in the city.

STAGE 10

They sailed from Rhegium (Regium Iulium) along the west coast of southern Italy to Puteoli on the north shore of the Bay of Naples, about twenty-five miles (40 km) west of Pompeii at the foot of Mt. Vesuvius, a voyage of about 175 nautical miles (325 km), completed in two days (Acts 28:13). Puteoli was the major port of the city of Rome due to its natural harbor, which was protected by a breakwater, with fifteen enormous piers.[23] The emporium stretched for one and a one-quarter miles (2 km) along the shore west of the mole. Passengers disembarked at Puteoli and traveled overland to Rome, while the cargo of grain was taken to Portus, the new harbor at Ostia built by Claudius at the mouth of the Tiber river. The city handled most of the trade with the eastern provinces of the empire, as well as the grain imports from Egypt. Many of Rome's elites owned villas in Puteoli, which was connected with the city of Rome by the *Via Appia*, a coastal route conceived by Appius Claudius Caecus, consul in 307 BC. The road, paved in black basalt, and flanked by level pedestrian footpaths and by tombs, villas, and

23. Strabo notes, "By mixing the sand-ash (i.e., *pozzuolana* or tuff) with the lime, they can run jetties out into the sea and thus make the wide-open shores curve into the form of bays, so that the greatest merchant-ships can moor therein with safety" (*Geography* 5.4.6 [LCL]).

Bay of Naples with Mount Vesuvius in the Background

pleasant rest and refreshment facilities, ran from Porta Capena in Rome to Brundisium in Calabria on the Adriatic (365 miles [587 km]).

STAGE 11

In Puteoli, Paul and his companions were greeted by Christian believers with whom they were able to stay for a week (Acts 28:14). Roman Christians who had been informed of Paul's imminent arrival in the city traveled south, some as far as Forum Appii, a market town on the *Via Appia* about thirty-eight miles (62 km) southeast of Rome, others as far as a place called "Three Taverns" (Latin *Tres Tabernae*), about thirty miles (48 km) from Rome, located at the crossing of the road from Norba in the Lepinus Hills to Antium on the coast.[24]

PAUL IN ROME

Paul, traveling on the *Via Appia* among the prisoners under the command of the centurion Julius, accompanied by believers from the capital, entered the city of Rome at the *Porta Capena* in the valley between the southwestern slopes of Caelian Hill and Aventinus Minor (see page 426 for a map of Paul's journey from Malta to Rome).[25]

The passive formulation "Paul was allowed to live by himself" (Acts 28:16) points to a Roman official who took

24. It took Horace two days to get from Rome to the Forum of Appius. Very ambitious travelers could reach the Forum of Appius from Rome in one day. Horace says that the Forum of Appius was "crammed with boatmen and stingy tavern-keepers;" he complains about the poor drinking water of the town, which made him ill (Horace, *Satires* 1.5.1–6 [LCL]). Cicero mentions Three Taverns several times in his letters (*Epistulae ad Atticum* 1.13.1; 2.10; 2.12.2; 2.13.1), one of which was written from the Forum of Appius (2:10). See Hemer, *Book of Acts*, 156 n. 157.

25. Andrea Carandini, ed., *The Atlas of Ancient Rome: Biography and Portraits of the City* (Princeton: Princeton University Press, 2017), I, 359 (S. Gozzini); for the *Via Appia* and the *Porta Capena*, see Carandini, *Atlas of Ancient Rome*, II, tables Ib (H), 145, 148, and additional tables 26, 31, 35, 36.

responsibility once the centurion Julius presented Paul as a prisoner. The reading of the Western and Byzantine text is either an inference on the basis of assumptions about Roman administration or it preserves reliable information.[26] The *stratopedarchēs* was probably a subordinate of the *praefectus praetorii*, an officer who probably served as the "head administrator of the *officium* of the Praetorian Guard."[27] The Praetorian Prefect at the time was Sextus Afranius Burrus, who held the post from AD 51–62; during the transfer of rule to Nero in AD 54, he guaranteed the loyalty of the Praetorian Guard, and, together with Seneca, guided Nero's politics in the early years; he died in AD 62, supposedly poisoned by Nero.[28] Assuming that Paul was taken to the Praetorian Prefect, Paul would have been taken through the center of the city from the *Porta Capena* to the so-called *Porta Clausa* and to the barracks of the Praetorian Guard (*Castra Praetoria*) located just outside the city walls on the northeast side of the city—past the east side of the Circus Maximus, Nero's Colossus on the east side of the Temple of Rome and Venus, and via the *Vicus Sandalarius* and the *Vicus Collis Viminalis*.[29] It is plausible to assume that the lodgings in which Paul was allowed to live by himself were near the barracks of the Praetorian Guard.

Paul was in Rome as a prisoner at least for two years, during which he was able to explain the gospel to the Jews of Rome (Acts 28:23–24), proclaiming the kingdom of God and teaching about the Lord Jesus Christ "with all boldness and without hindrance" (Acts 28:31). This was the fourteenth phase of Paul's missionary work.

BIBLIOGRAPHY

Bahat, Dan. *The Jerusalem Western Wall Tunnel*. Jerusalem: Israel Exploration Society, 2013.

Bauckham, Richard J. "The Estate of Publius on Malta (Acts 28:7)." Pages 337–51 in *The Christian World Around the New Testament*. Grand Rapids: Baker Academic, 2017.

Beck, P., and M. Kochavi. "Aphek (in Sharon): The Roman Period." *NEAEHL* 1:64–72.

Benoit, Pierre. "L'Antonia d'Hérode le Grand et le forum oriental d'Aelia Capitolina." Pages 311–46 in *Exégèse et Théologie IV*. Paris: Cerf, 1982.

Burrell, Barbara. "Palace to Praetorium: The Romanization of Caesarea."

26. Manuscripts of the Western and Byzantine text tradition read: "the centurion delivered the prisoners to the *stratopedarchēs*; but Paul was allowed …" For full evidence, see Strutwolf, *Apostelgeschichte*, 1.2:1068.

27. Adrian Nicolas Sherwin-White, *Roman Society and Roman Law in the New Testament* (Oxford: Clarendon, 1963; repr., Eugene, OR: Wipf & Stock, 2004); Harry W. Tajra, *The Trial of St. Paul: A Juridical Exegesis of the Second Half of the Acts of the Apostles* (Tübingen: Mohr Siebeck, 1989), 177–79.

28. W. Eck, "Afranius [3]," *BNP* 1:289–90.

29. For the *Castra Praetoria*, see Carandini, *Atlas of Ancient Rome*, I, 460–61 (M. C. Capanna); II, table 184, 190, and also additional tables 6, 11 (with the so-called *Porta Clausa* on the south side); for the *Porta Viminalis*, see Carandini, *Atlas of Ancient Rome*, II, tables Ib (D), 123 and additional tables 6, 11; for the *Vicus Sandalarius*, see Carandini, *Atlas of Ancient Rome*, II, 104, additional tables 20; for the *Vicus collis Viminalis*, see II, table 180, and additional tables 10 (unmarked a.t. 15, 11); see also I, 323–41 (F. Fraioli).

Pages 228–47 in *Caesarea Maritima: A Retrospective after Two Millenia*. Edited by Avner Raban and Kenneth G. Holum. Leiden: Brill, 1996.

Carandini, Andrea, ed. *The Atlas of Ancient Rome: Biography and Portraits of the City*. Princeton: Princeton University Press, 2017.

Cotton, Hannah M., and Werner Eck. "Governors and Their Personnel on Latin Inscriptions from Caesarea Maritima." *Israel Academy of Sciences and Humanities Proceedings* 7.7 (2001): 215–40.

Eck, Werner. "Afranius [3]." *BNP* 1:289–90.

———. *Rom und Judaea*. Tübingen: Mohr Siebeck, 2007.

Hemer, Colin J. *The Book of Acts in the Setting of Hellenistic History*. Tübingen: Mohr Siebeck, 1989.

———. "Euraquilo and Melita." *Journal of Theological Studies* 26 (1975): 100–111.

Horsley, Greg H. R., and Stephen R. Llewelyn, eds. *New Documents Illustrating Early Christianity*. North Ryde: Macquarie University; Grand Rapids: Eerdmans, 1981–2012.

Kaletsch, Hans. "Cnidus." *BNP* 3:489–490.

Keener, Craig S. *Acts: An Exegetical Commentary*. 4 vols. Grand Rapids: Baker Academic, 2012–2015.

Lichtenberger, Achim. *Die Baupolitik Herodes des Großen*. Wiesbaden: Harrassowitz, 1999.

Netzer, Ehud. *The Architecture of Herod, the Great Builder*. Tübingen: Mohr Siebeck, 2006. Repr.. Grand Rapids: Baker Academic, 2008.

Rapske, Brian M. "Acts, Travel, and Shipwreck." Pages 1–47 in *The Book of Acts in its Graeco-Roman Setting*. Edited by D. W. J. Gill and C. Gempf. Volume 2 of *The Book of Acts in Its First Century Setting*. Edited by Bruce W. Winter. Grand Rapids: Eerdmans, 1994.

Ritmeyer, Leen. *The Quest: Revealing the Temple Mount in Jerusalem*. Jerusalem: Carta, 2006.

Sallares, Robert. "Grain Trade, Grain Import." *BNP* 5:976–981.

Schnabel, Eckhard J. *Acts: Expanded Digital Edition*. Grand Rapids: Zondervan, 2012.

Schwartz, Daniel R. "'Stone House,' *Birah*, and Antonia during the Time of Jesus." Pages 341–48 in *Jesus and Archaeology*. Edited by James H. Charlesworth. Grand Rapids: Eerdmans, 2006.

Sherwin-White, Adrian Nicolas. *Roman Society and Roman Law in the New Testament*. Oxford: Clarendon,. 1963. Repr.. Eugene, OR: Wipf & Stock, 2004.

Strutwolf, Holger, Georg Gäbel, Annette Hüffmeier, Gerd Mink, and Klaus Wachtel, eds. *Die Apostelgeschichte*. 4 vols. Stuttgart: Deutsche Bibelgesellschaft, 2017.

Tajra, Harry W. *The Trial of St. Paul: A Juridical Exegesis of the Second Half of the Acts of the Apostles*. Tübingen: Mohr Siebeck, 1989.

Teuma, Eugene P. *San Pawl Il-Bahar: A Guide*. Hal-Qormi: Dormax, 2003.

Warnecke, Heinz. *Die tatsächliche Romfahrt des Apostels Paulus*. Stuttgart: Katholisches Bibelwerk, 1987.

Wehnert, Jürgen. "Gestrandet. Zu einer neuen These über den Schiffbruch des Apostels." *Zeitschrift für Theologie und Kirche* 87 (1990): 67–99.

CHAPTER 33

PAUL'S JOURNEY TO ROME

Acts 27:1–28:15

J. Carl Laney

KEY POINTS

- Travel and shipping was done year-round in the Mediterranean Sea, but stormy weather increased the danger from late fall to early spring.
- Among the many Mediterranean Sea ports, Alexandria, Myra, and Puteoli were among the most important for shipping wheat from the Egyptian delta to Rome.
- Luke records Paul's exciting and danger-filled travel itinerary from Caesarea to Rome (Acts 27:1–28:15).
- Paul's first imprisonment or "house arrest" after arriving in Rome provided considerable freedom for witness and writing letters to churches (Ephesians, Philippians, and Colossians).

KEY QUESTIONS

The Book of Acts records that after being detained for two years in Caesarea under the custody of Roman authorities (Acts 23:31–26:32), Paul journeyed by sea to Rome, having appealed for his case to be heard by Caesar (Acts 25:11). In classic epic style, Luke recounts the voyage, shipwreck, and final land segment of Paul's journey to Rome (Acts 27:1–28:16). But readers of the New Testament are left with lots of questions. What was it like to travel by ship on the Mediterranean Sea during the Greco-Roman period? Was it relatively safe to travel by ship? Was there a known and regular schedule for Mediterranean shipping and travel? What kinds of cargo did the ships carry? What background for Paul's journey to Rome would be helpful for readers of the New Testament? Answers to these questions will enable us better understand Paul's life, travels, and ministry.

MEDITERRANEAN SEA TRAVEL

While a network of paved Roman roads provided for relatively safe travel in the first century, sea travel was faster, but

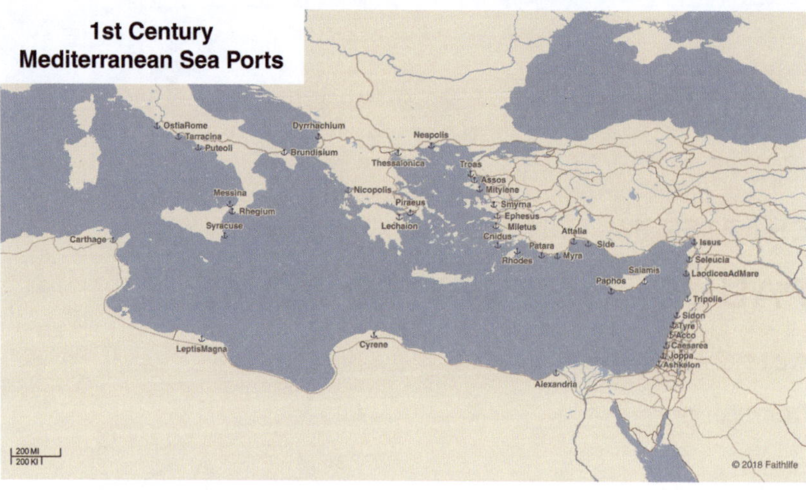

more hazardous. According to Jerome Murphy-O'Connor, regular storms "effectively closed" the Mediterranean Sea for travel during winter.[1] This opinion is supported by Pliny the Elder, who reports that "Spring opens the sea to voyagers." (*Natural History* 2:47 [LCL]). However, in the same paragraph, Pliny provides additional information indicating that merchant ships sailed during the winter. He continues, "Yet the severity of the storms does not entirely close up the sea. In former times, pirates were compelled, by the fear of death, to rush into death, and to brave the winter ocean; now we are driven to it by avarice." Apparently military vessels also sailed during the stormy winter months. Josephus writes of a ship sent on a military mission that encountered three continuous months of severe stormy weather (*J.W.*, 2:200–203 [LCL]). The difficulty of navigating through winter fog and heavy cloud cover (obscuring the sun, stars, and other navigational landmarks) was another reason the Mediterranean Sea was usually closed for ship travel during the winter months, but there were exceptions to this general pattern.[2]

It is also important to understand that weather on the Mediterranean Sea differs from one quadrant to another. Barry Beitzel points out that the northwestern quadrant remains quite stormy, even during the summer, while the southeastern quadrant is rarely stormy, even in winter.[3] Ancient shipping manifests indicate that in the southeastern region of the Mediterranean Sea there was year-round open sea trade and travel. Generally speaking, we can conclude that some parts of the Mediterranean Sea were open for travel year-round, whereas some parts were dangerous for travel in the fall (September and October) and spring (between March and May), while the larger part of the

1. Jerome Murphy-O'Connor, "On the Road and on the Sea with St. Paul," *Bible Review* 1 (Summer 1985): 38.

2. Murphy-O'Connor, "On the Road and on the Sea," 45.

3. Barry J. Beitzel, *The New Moody Atlas of the Bible* (Chicago: Moody, 2009), 264.

Mediterranean was extremely dangerous between November and February. This background helps explains why Paul recommended staying at Fair Havens rather than sailing on (Acts 27:9–10) and why after the shipwreck, the sailors wintered on Malta before continuing their journey (Acts 28:11).

13th Century Mosaic Depicting the Pharos Lighthouse of Alexandria

Sea travel in the ancient world was radically different than a modern Mediterranean cruise. Ships plying the Mediterranean waters were intended for cargo. Passengers were "nothing more than an incidental benefit to the owner."[4] Since there was no cabin, passengers lived on the deck of the ship, the only shade being provided by the mainsail. Drinking water was generally provided; there was no food service. Passengers carried their own provisions for their journey. There were no set schedule or published fares. A traveler would simply go to the harbor, find a ship being loaded, inquire about the destination, haggle about the fare, come aboard, and then pray for a safe voyage. In a satirical poem, the Greek poet Horace suggests that "the ship was first conceived by a sadistic degenerate whose mission was to destroy humanity."[5] Paul's experience at sea may well support this assessment (2 Cor 11:25; Acts 27:39–44).

MEDITERRANEAN SHIPPING AND PORTS

A vast network of Roman roads provided for efficient travel during the Roman period by donkey or on foot. But travel by ship was faster, even though more hazardous. Shipping on the Mediterranean was primarily for the purpose of transporting goods or troops, not passengers. The shipping lanes were determined by the direction of the wind, which varied depending on the season. The prevailing wind during the summer was most consistently from the northwest.[6] Consequently, a journey by sea from Puteoli, in the Bay of Naples, to Alexandria was an easy, ten to twenty-day trip. But going in the opposite direction was quite a different matter. Ships carrying wheat from Alexandria customarily went north to the port of Myra, where the centurion Julius found a ship for Paul and the other prisoners (Acts 27:5–6). Ships then worked their way west against the prevailing winds to reach the boot of Italy where they turned north to Puteoli.

Shipping in the first century AD was enhanced by more than twenty well-established seaports. The most noteworthy

4. Murphy-O'Connor, "On the Road and on the Sea," 46.
5. Cited in Murphy-O'Connor, "On the Road and on the Sea," 47.
6. Murphy-O'Connor, "On the Road and on the Sea," 45.

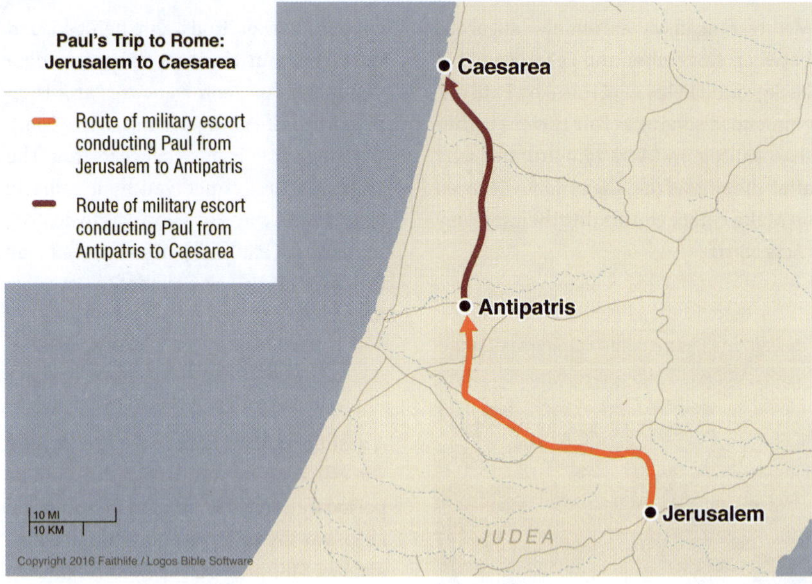

on the eastern Mediterranean coast was Caesarea Maritima, a port built by King Herod in honor of his patron, the emperor Augustus. On the north coast of Africa was Alexandria, founded by Alexander the Great in 331 BC and noted for its famous lighthouse, the Pharos of Alexandria. Directly north of Alexandria and across the Mediterranean Sea was Myra where granaries were built by the emperor Hadrian to serve the Roman army. A similar granary was built at Patara, a port west of Myra. Ancient Corinth had harbors on both sides of the slender isthmus where it was situated, giving access to both the Aegean and the Adriatic Seas. Leptis Magna, on the north coast of Africa just south of Sicily, was famous for the vast quantities of olive oil that were shipped from its port to Rome. Puteoli, situated in the Bay of Naples, was the main port of entry for passengers and cargo going to Rome before Claudius (10 BC–AD 54) began building the port of Ostia at the mouth of the Tiber River, a project that was completed by Nero in AD 62.

ALEXANDRIA'S WHEAT FLEET

The delta of Egypt was the breadbasket for the Roman Empire, and the people of Rome depended heavily on grain imported from Egypt to meet their needs. Consequently, there was a well-established shipping industry in the Mediterranean Sea. The biggest and best ships sailing the Mediterranean Sea in the first century were vessels that brought Egyptian grain to Rome.[7] These ships were about 180 feet (55 m) in length, 50 feet (15 m) in width, and about 44 feet (13.5 m) from the deck to the bottom of the hold.[8] Such a ship could carry enough

7. Murphy-O'Connor, "On the Road and on the Sea," 46.

8. Lucian, *Navigium*, 5 (trans. H. W. Fowler and F G. Fowler, *The Works of Lucian of Samosota* [Oxford: Clarendon Press, 1905]).

grain to feed every person in Attica for a year.[9] It is estimated that the city of Rome needed to import 150,000 to 200,000 tons (136,000 to 180,000 metric tons) of grain annually to meet this need.[10] With the aid of southeasterly winds, a grain ship sailing from Rome to Alexandria to pick up another load could make the 1200 mile trip in ten to twenty days. The return trip with a load of grain could take much longer, as illustrated by Paul's experience (Acts 27–28).

PAUL'S TRAVEL ITINERARY

BACKGROUND FOR THE JOURNEY

Paul had been imprisoned in Caesarea since his arrest in Jerusalem as a result of a riot that took place in the temple area (Acts 21:27–32). A threat against his life led to Paul being transferred to Caesarea, Rome's administrative center for Judea in the first century.

Paul defended himself against the accusations of his Jewish countrymen before the Roman prefects Felix and Festus, but they had not granted his release. After a long period of delay, Paul exerted his right as a Roman citizen and appealed to Caesar (Acts 24:11). The appeal required that Paul's case be transferred to Rome. Paul began his journey to Rome late in the fall of AD 59, after two years of imprisonment in Caesarea. Carl Rasmussen suggests that it was late fall by the time he reached Crete since "the fast" (Day of Atonement) had already past (Acts 27:9).[11] Paul and some other prisoners were escorted to Rome by a Roman soldier named Julius who served as "a centurion of the Augustan cohort" (Acts 27:1). The account in Acts was written by Luke, who accompanied Paul on this journey (Acts 27:1, 28:16) and was a participant in the events recorded.

Centurions (*centuriō* in Latin) were the professional soldiers in the Roman army.[12] Each centurion commanded one hundred legionaries. Although the number was reduced to eighty by the time of the emperor Trajan (AD 98–117), the original name was retained.[13] Centurions were responsible for training men in their own centuries and leading them into battle. In addition to assigning daily duties, posting guards, and carrying out inspections, centurions had to account for all the military equipment that was assigned to the century.

What kind of men were chosen as centurions? Polybius, the Greek historian (200–118 BC) writes that the Romans "wish the centurions not so much to be venturesome and daredevil as to be natural leaders, of steady and sedate spirit. They do not desire them so much to be men who will initiate attacks and open the battle, but men who will hold their ground when worsted and hard-pressed and be ready to die at their posts." (*Histories* 6.24.8–9 [LCL]). Julius must have been such a man as this. He

9. Lucian, *Navigium*, 6 (Fowler).

10. Peter Garnsey, "Grain for Rome," in *Trade in the Ancient Economy*, ed. Peter Garnsey, Keith Hopkins, and Charles R. Whittaker (Berkeley: University of California Press, 1983), 118–19.

11. Carl G. Rasmussen, *Zondervan NIV Atlas of the Bible* (Grand Rapids: Zondervan, 1989), 186–87.

12. For more information on the Roman army, see Laney, "Peter and the Centurion Cornelius: Roman Soldiers in the New Testament," chapter 20 in this volume.

13. John Wilkes, *The Roman Army* (Cambridge: Cambridge University Press 1972), 33.

The ancient harbor at Caesarea Maritima from which Paul sailed for Rome.

was a centurion who had been assigned to a cohort (five hundred soldiers) named in honor of the emperor Augustus (31 BC–AD 14). As a trusted Roman army officer, Julius appears to have been given the special assignment of escorting prisoners to Rome.

FROM CAESAREA TO SIDON (ACTS 27:1–3)

Caesarea rose to its greatness during the rule of King Herod. When Caesar Augustus confirmed him as king of Judea, Herod showed his gratitude by building a great city on the site of a small Phoenician anchorage, "Straton's Tower." Herod's engineers built a massive harbor, theater, amphitheater, palace, and a temple dedicated to the deified emperor Augustus (Josephus, *J.W.* 1.408–414). A decade after Herod's death (4 BC), Caesarea became the seat of the Roman prefects (governors) of Judea and one of the leading maritime cities of the eastern Mediterranean.[14]

Luke records that Paul sailed from Caesarea on an "Adramyttian ship which was about to sail to the regions along the coast of Asia" (Acts 27:2). Adramyttium is a port city located on the coast of Asia (modern Turkey) at the head of a gulf facing the large island of Lesbos. The port city is southeast of Troas from which Paul sailed to Neapolis on his second journey (Acts 16:11). Adramyttium was apparently the home port for the ship and Julius, Paul's escort, knew that the vessel would be stopping at various ports on its journey home. He knew that at one of these ports he would be able to find a ship going to Rome. Although the port exists no longer, the ancient city is remembered today in the name of the small, nearby village, Edremid (or Adramiti).

The Adramyttian ship was a coasting vessel that would have stopped to overnight at various ports on its return to

14. Robert J. Bull, "Caesarea Maritima: The Search for Herod's City," *BAR* 8.3 (May/June 1982), 24–40; Robert L. Hohlfelder, "Caesarea beneath the Sea," *BAR* 8.3 (May/June 1982): 42–47; Yosef Porath, "Vegas on the Med: A Tour of Caesarea's Entertainment District," *BAR* 30.5 (Sept/Oct 2004): 24–35.

Adramyttium. Luke records that the ship stopped at Sidon where Julius "treated Paul with consideration" (Acts 27:3), allowing him to go ashore to receive hospitality and care from his friends. Sidon, a principal port of ancient Phoenicia, is located about seventy miles (112 km) north of Caesarea and about thirty miles (48 km) north of Tyre. The importance of the city in the biblical record is reflected by the fact that it is mentioned thirty-four times in Scripture. Sidon and Tyre are often linked together in the New Testament. Jesus said that the people of these cities would have repented after witnessing his miracles in contrast with those of Chorazin and Bethsaida (Matt 11:21–22; Luke 10:13–14). The modern Lebanese city of Sidon (Sayda) is built over the ancient ruins, making archaeological excavation nearly impossible.

FROM SIDON TO MYRA (ACTS 27:4–5)

The next section of Paul's sea voyage took him along the Mediterranean seacoast from Sidon to Myra. Luke records that the ship "sailed under the shelter of Cyprus" (Acts 27:4) because of contrary winds. Since the prevailing winds on the eastern Mediterranean coast during the summer months come from the west, Paul's ship sailed east and north of Cyprus to reach Myra.[15] On an earlier voyage during a different season of the year, Paul sailed from Patara (west of Myra) to Phoenicia more directly, passing Cyprus on the left (Acts 21:1–3). After sailing for a time protected by Cyprus from the prevailing westerly winds, Paul's ship crossed the open sea to reach the south coast of the Roman provinces of Cilicia and Pamphylia (Asia Minor) to reach Myra.

15. James Smith, *The Voyage and Shipwreck of St. Paul* (Grand Rapids: Baker, 1978), 68.

Granary at Myra

Myra was one of the most important cities of the Roman province of Lycia. Strabo notes that the city itself lay two miles inland from the harbor (*Geography* 14.3.7). The importance of Myra was due to its location directly north of Alexandria, making it one of the chief ports for the wheat fleet that carried grain from the fertile delta of Egypt to feed the masses of people in Rome. The delta region of Egypt was the "chief granary of Rome, and the corn trade between Alexandria and Rome was of the highest importance."[16] In view of its strategic location for shipping, the Romans constructed there a large imperial granary that existed in the time of Paul and was later enlarged by Hadrian (AD 117–138) and is still largely intact at classical Myra.[17] According to Beitzel's personal observations and measurements, the granary had eight parallel storage magazines, each measuring about 120 feet (36.5 m) in depth, 25 inches (63.5 cm) width, and appear to have stood 25–30 feet (7.5–9 m) high. The interior walls are cyclopean in construction, with an arched stone ceiling, whereas the outer wall contains ten courses of finished masonry, finished with a molded cornice and a facade front with featuring ornamentation and an inscription. Beitzel comments, "The Myra wheat granary manifests a refinement and quality of architectural craftsmanship and the sheer size of storage capacity that speak eloquently of the critical importance early Rome placed on the safe transfer to its dietary lifeblood from Egypt."[18]

Although once a flourishing city, as evidenced by its magnificent theater and rock-cut tombs, Myra has become a ruin remembered primarily because of a saint named Nicholas who became the bishop of the church of Myra (AD 300–350). Nicholas had a reputation for generosity and is said to have provided three daughters of a poor man with dowry so that they could enter an honorable marriage.[19] This story provides the background for the custom of giving gifts in celebration of the saint's day (December 6th).

16. F. F. Bruce, *Commentary on the Book of Acts* (Grand Rapids: Eerdmans, 1954), 502.

17. Pers. comm., Barry J. Beitzel (October 31, 2017).

18. Pers. comm., Barry J. Beitzel (October 31, 2017).

19. Serif Yenen, *Turkish Odyssey: A Traveler's Guide to Turkey and Turkish Culture* (Istanbul: Yenen, 1997), 439.

Nicholas is remembered today during the Christmas season as Santa Claus in the US, Father Christmas in England, and Père Noël in France.

FROM MYRA TO FAIR HAVENS (ACTS 27:6–12)

At Myra, Julius secured passage for Paul and the other prisoners on an Alexandrian grain ship headed for Rome (Acts 27:6). This was a large ship, loaded with a cargo of grain along with 276 passengers. There is a question about the original reading of this text.[20] The fourth-century Greek text Vaticanus reads "about seventy-six." While the number 276 seems large, it would have included the sailors, soldiers, and passengers. Josephus reports that there were 600 travelers on the ship that took him to Italy (*Life*, 3.15).

Paul's journey to Rome progressed slowly after leaving Myra because the wind was contrary, pushing them away from their destination (Acts 27:7). Sailing against wind coming from the northwest was possible by taking advantage of the better-protected coastline and the ship was able to make it as far as Cnidus, a small island off the western end of a peninsula extending from the southwest coast of Asia.The island is now called Cape Krio and is connected to the mainland by a sandy isthmus.

Since the winds coming from the northwest did not permit further westerly progress, the ship sailed south "under the shelter of Crete" (Acts 27:7). The sheltered side of Crete would be along the south coast of the island. To reach the southern coast of Crete, Paul's ship rounded Cape Salmone, which extends like an elephant's upraised trunk from the west coast of the island.

Sailing was still difficult along the south coast of Crete, but the ship was able to reach Fair Havens near the city of Lasea, identified with the ruins lying to the east of the small bay.[21] Fair Havens has been identified with the harbor that retains the ancient name (*Kaloi Limenes*) and is located two miles east of Cape Matala. The harbor would provide temporary shelter from the westerly winds but was not suitable as a winter shelter.[22]

Luke records that Paul's journey was delayed considerably as the captain waited for improved sailing conditions. But the Day of Atonement ("the fast"), occurring in September or October, was already past. Sailing during the winter season was hazardous, and Luke notes that it had already become so. The Day of Atonement fell on October 5 in AD 59, and this accords well with Luke's description of the situation.[23] Although Paul had little say in the matter, he had already survived three shipwrecks (Acts 11:25) and didn't want to repeat the experience! So Paul began to admonish (and "kept at it," as indicated by the imperfect tense of the Greek verb) the ship's captain of the dangers of sailing on. Wintering at Fair Havens would preserve not only the ship and its cargo, but also the lives of the passengers.

---

20. Bruce M. Metzger, *A Textual Commentary on the Greek New Testament* (London: United Bible Societies, 1971), 499–500.

21. Bruce, *Book of Acts*, 504. Lasea is mentioned by Pliny the Elder, *Natural History*, 4.59.

22. A. T. Robertson, *Word Pictures in the New Testament: Vol. 3, The Acts of the Apostles* (Nashville: Broadman,1930), 459.

23. Bruce, *Book of Acts*, 506.

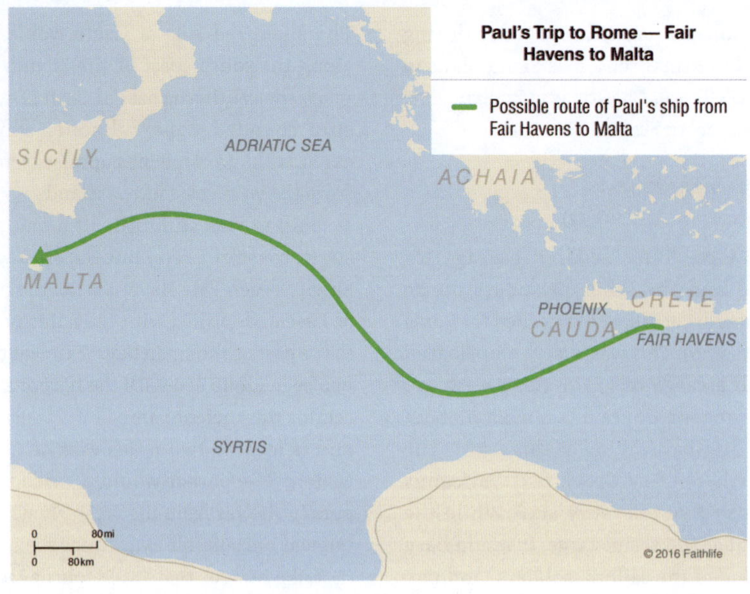

Concluding that Fair Havens was not a suitable harbor for wintering, the decision was made to depart for the harbor at Phoenix, which would provide greater protection for the ship against the winter storms. The harbor of Phoenix has been identified with Lutro, a port thirty-four miles (54.4 km) east of Cape Matala. Smith quotes a modern sea captain as saying that this harbor "is the only bay where a vessel could be quite secure in winter."[24] But Luke's description of the harbor as "facing southwest and northwest" doesn't seem to match this situation. A better choice is Phineka, which appears to preserve the ancient name Phoenix and fits Luke's description better. Although Smith favors Lutro as Luke's Phoenix, F. F. Bruce concludes that Luke's description of Phoenix fits "less well" with Lutro than Phineka.[25]

The Storm at Sea (Acts 27:13–26)

The decision to travel on appears to have been confirmed by a gently blowing south wind that enabled the ship to sail west close to the south shore of Crete (Acts 27:13). Luke describes the vessel as "coasting along Crete." Suddenly, everything changed as a violent, northwest wind rushed down from the seven thousand foot (2100 m) mountains of central Crete. Luke describes this wind as "Euraquilo," a hybrid word combining the Greek *euros* (Εὖρος, "east wind") with the Latin *aquilo* ("northeast"), indicating that the wind came from an east, northeast direction.[26] Caught in the grip of this fierce wind, the ship was unable to reach Phoenix and was driven from the protective coastlands of Crete out into the stormy Mediterranean Sea.

Luke records that the ship found

24. Smith, *Voyage and Shipwreck of St. Paul*, 91 n. 1.
25. Bruce, *Book of Acts*, 508 n. 32.
26. Robertson, *Acts of the Apostles*, 464.

Harbor at Cauda

some shelter from the small island of Cauda, identified today with Gavdos, located about twenty-five miles (40 km) from the south coast of Crete (Acts 27:16).[27] The island offered some protection for the ship against the northeasterly wind and it was there on calmer seas that the sailors took several steps to improve their situation. First, the sailors took steps "to secure the boat." The word "boat" (σκάφη, *skaphē*) refers not to Paul's ship, but rather to a light boat or skiff that would be towed behind the ship in good weather, but hauled aboard and lashed down to avoid being lost in a storm. This small boat would be used for transportation when the ship was anchored offshore. Second, the sailors used cables or ropes to undergird the ship to protect the wooden hull from the pounding of the waves and shifting of the cargo as the vessel rode out the storm. Pliny the Elder explains that one of the chief dangers faced by Mediterranean sailors was "not only breaking up the spars but the hull itself." (*Natural History* 2.132). The third step taken by the sailors was to "lower the gear." The word translated "gear" (σκεῦος, *skeuos*) may refer to the ship's sail, tackle, or rigging, or sea anchor that would slow the speed of the wind blown ship. All three of these possibilities would be helpful in riding out a bad storm on the open sea.

The actions taken by the sailors to secure the ship were taken for fear that they might "run aground on the shallows of Syrtis" (Acts 27:17). If the ship was blown far enough south by the northeast wind, it would reach "Syrtis," the dangerous sandbanks (possibly "quicksands") off the coast of North Africa. Strabo describes this region as containing shallows along with deep waters where ships can run aground, and escape is rare (*Geography* 17.3.20). Dio Chrysostom (AD 40–120) explains:

> But those who have once sailed into it find egress impossible; for shoals, cross-currents, and long sandbars extending a great distance out make the sea utterly impassable or troublesome. For

27. Cauda is preferred over the textual variant, "Clauda." See Metzger, *Textual Commentary*, 498.

> the bed of the sea in these parts is not clean, but as the bottom is porous and sandy it lets the sea seep in, there being no solidity to it. (*Discourse* 5:8–10 [LCL]).

Little wonder that the sailors on Paul's ship were fearful of drifting into this region.

The following day further action was taken for the safety of the passengers and crew. In order to lighten the load so that the ship would ride higher on the waves, the sailors began to jettison the cargo. Similar action was taken by the sailors of Jonah's ship in the face of a fierce storm (Jonah 1:5). On the third day of the storm an even more drastic action was taken. Ancient Mediterranean sailing ships would customarily carry spare tackle in case of damage or breakage. Smith suggests that Luke's word *σκευή* (*skeue*) refers to the main spar pole that supported the sail.[28] Luke, who watched this unfolding drama, adds that the sailors (perhaps with passengers assisting) cast the spare tackle overboard "with their own hands" (Acts 27:19).

The storm continued raging, darkening the sky and blotting out the sun and stars for "many days" (Acts 27:20). Seasickness along with weakness from lack of food and feelings of despair diminished all hope of survival. At this point godly Paul could not resist saying, "Men, you ought to have followed my advice and not set sail from Crete" (Acts 27:21). But Paul went on to assure his fellow travelers that while the ship would be lost, their lives would be saved (Acts 27:22). His encouragement was not merely the result of wishful thinking. Previously Paul had warned that the loss of life was likely if they left Fair Havens (Acts 27:10), but now he explains that his view had changed. Paul had received a message from God, delivered by his angel, that he would "stand before Caesar" and that the lives of those sailing with him would be spared (Acts 27:24). Paul told his fellow travelers, "keep up your courage" (Acts 27:25) and expect to run aground (literally "fall out") on an island (Acts 27:26).

The Preparations for Landing (Acts 27:27–38)

Fourteen long nights after leaving Fair Havens and being caught in the storm found Paul's ship being "driven through" (διαφέρω, *diapherō*) the sea of *Adrias* (Ἀδρίας). In antiquity this term referred not only to the gulf located between the boot of Italy and Greece, but the central part of the Mediterranean Sea between Sicily and Achaia.[29] According to Smith, this is where one would expect to find a ship driven by the wind from Crete. Smith interviewed several experienced sea captains about the rate of drift by a ship being driving along on the Mediterranean by a winter storm. He learned that under such conditions as described by Luke, a ship like Paul's would drift about thirty-six and a half miles (58.4 km) in twenty-four hours.[30] This would put the ship in close proximity to the Island of Malta and the traditional location of Paul's fourth shipwreck, known today as St. Paul's Bay.

---

28. Smith, *Voyage and Shipwreck of St. Paul*, 116.
29. Bruce, *Book of Acts*, 515.
30. Smith, *Voyage and Shipwreck of St. Paul*, 126.

St. Paul's Island and Bay

The sound of breakers crashing on the shore may have alerted the sailors that their vessel was approaching land (Acts 27:27). Luke records that the sailors used their nautical skills to measure the depth of the water and discovered that the water was becoming more shallow. The word "fathom" (ὀργυιά, *orguia*) refers to the distance between two outstretched hands, approximately six feet (1.8 m), and is used chiefly to measure the depth of water. Since it was dark and and the sailors feared that the ship would be dashed on the rocky shoreline, they set out anchors (ἄγκυρα, *ankyra*, is used also in Heb 6:19) to secure the ship. Casting out four anchors seems to have been a precaution against the possibility of a rope breaking or a single anchor failing to hold.

Luke records that the sailors, fearing for their lives, attempted to escape from the doomed ship by pretending to set out anchors from the bow of the ship (Acts 27:30). Paul realized their real intentions and warned Julius and the soldiers that without the sailor's help in beaching the ship, their own lives would be in jeopardy (Acts 27:31). The assurance of survival (Acts 27:24) depended in part on the responsible actions of the ship's crew. Immediate action was taken by the soldiers, who cut the ropes attached to the dinghy, letting it fall into the sea (Acts 27:32).

Since it had been fourteen days since Paul's ship had been caught in the storm and the passengers were weak from hunger, Paul urged them to eat some food to gain strength for what lay ahead (Acts 27:34). The apostle set an example for all believers when he led in a prayer of thanksgiving. The words "gave thanks" translate the Greek word *eucharisteō* (εὐχαριστέω) from which the term Eucharist is derived. A. T. Robertson suggests that this may recall the Lord's Supper (Acts 2:42), but for the passengers and crew, this was an ordinary meal.[31]

Encouraged by Paul's reassurance (Acts 27:34) and strengthened by food (Acts 27:36), the weary travelers began to lighten the ship by casting its cargo of wheat into the sea (Acts 27:38). The purpose of this drastic measure was to enable the ship to ride higher in the water, enabling it to get closer to the shore before running aground on the beach. The voyage would be a total loss for the owner of the vessel, but perhaps the captain retained hopes of saving the ship.

The Shipwreck on Malta (Acts 27:39–44)

Beck observes that Acts 27 records the most detailed report of a shipwreck from the records of the ancient world.[32] After a long and wakeful night, dawn broke, but the sailors could not recognize the land to which the storm and wind had driven them. However, they could see a bay with a sandy beach and resolved to sail the ship onto what appeared to be a safe place to land the vessel (27:39). The sailors worked together to accomplish several simultaneous actions (27:40). First, having no further use of the anchors, they released the ropes, leaving the stone anchors in the sea. Second, they loosened the ropes that had secured the rudders during the storm. Ancient ships had a pair of paddle-like rudders that were tied down when a ship was anchored. Third, they raised the mainsail and headed for the beach.

The forward motion of the vessel was suddenly halted when it struck a reef "where the two seas met" (Acts 27:41), referring to the zone between the sea and the bay. Crossing the bar from open sea to a harbor is often quite treacherous. In modern times sea pilots with specialized training and experience are often hired for this purpose. The ship was solidly grounded and it wasn't long before the powerful force of the waves began shattering the planks in the stern.[33] Not wishing for their prisoners to escape, the soldiers planned to kill their prisoners (Acts 27:42), but Julius was determined to fulfill his duty by bringing Paul safely to Rome and intervened. Taking charge of the situation, he ordered those who could swim to jump overboard and the rest to use pieces of timber or other items from the ship to get to shore. Luke concludes his account of the shipwreck assuring his readers that "all were brought safely to land" (Acts 27:44).

Luke continues his narrative in the next chapter of Acts, reporting that Paul and his fellow travelers had arrived on the island of Malta (Acts 28:1). The traditional location of the shipwreck is known as "St. Paul's Bay," which is also the name of the nearby town. The bay associated with Paul's shipwreck is actually on an island separated from the mainland of Malta by a narrow channel that has been identified by Smith as the place "where the two seas met."[34] Smith goes on to explain how this reference, along with

---

31. Robertson, *Acts of the Apostles*, 472.

32. John A. Beck, *The Baker Illustrated Guide to Everyday Life in Bible Times* (Grand Rapids: Baker, 2013), 239.

33. I observed this very thing taking place when a rented sailboat came too close to the shore and was grounded on sand in Monterey Bay. By the next morning the stern had been broken open by the waves and seawater and sand had filled the boat.

34. Smith, *Voyage and Shipwreck of St. Paul*, 142.

Statue of St. Paul on St. Paul's Island

Luke's mention of the "rocks" (Acts 27:29) and the sandy "beach" (Acts 27:39), agree completely with the situation one finds at the traditional site. Ramsay agrees with his assessment.[35] A great deal can change along a coastline in two thousand years and readers should be careful about identifying the actual location of Paul's shipwreck on Malta.

PAUL'S MINISTRY ON MALTA (ACTS 28:1–10)

When the sailors, soldiers, passengers, and prisoners had made it safely to shore, it was discovered the island they had landed on was Melita, known today as Malta (Acts 28:1). Bruce suggests that because the name *Melita* is a Canaanite word for "refuge"; Paul would have recognized the significance of the island as a place of "refuge" for the passengers and crew.[36] The non-Greek-speaking natives or "barbarians" (οἱ βάρβαροι, *hoi barbaroi*) demonstrated their kindness and hospitality by starting a fire on the beach to warm the wet and weary travelers (Acts 28:2). While picking up wood to add to the fire, Paul encountered a viper (likely poisonous) that latched onto his hand (Acts 28:3). This led the Maltese people to conclude that Paul must have been a murderer—worthy of death—but divine justice (δίκη, *dikē*) was not going to let him escape. When Paul shook the snake from his hand and suffered no harm from the incident (28:5), the people concluded that he was a god (28:6)! This was similar to what happened in Lystra where Paul and Barnabas were mistakenly identified with the Greek gods Hermes and Zeus (Acts 14:12).

35. William Michael Ramsay, *St. Paul the Traveller and Roman Citizen*, (New York: Putnam's Sons, 1898), 341.

36. Bruce, *Acts of the Apostles*, 521.

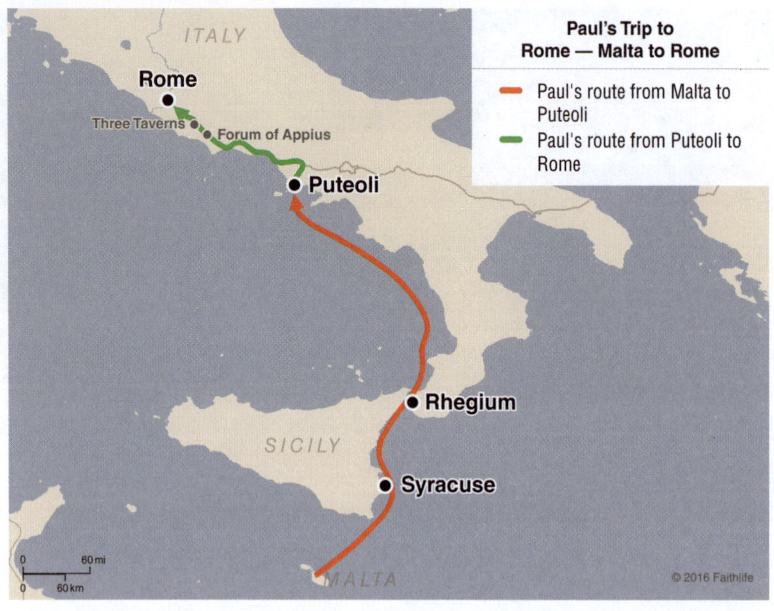

Not only was Paul spared the effects of a deadly snakebite, he went on to engage in a ministry of miracles, healing the father of Publius, a leading public figure on the Island (28:8). Paul continued with this ministry of healing, providing miraculous cures for people with a variety of illnesses. The miracles were not an end in themselves but reflect the New Testament pattern of presenting signs to verify and confirm the truth of the gospel message (Matt 4:23; John 20:30–31).

FROM MALTA TO PUTEOLI (ACTS 28:11–13)

Paul and his fellow passengers and prisoners spent the winter on the Island of Malta. It was not until early spring that the Mediterranean would be regarded as somewhat safe for sea travel. The delay of "three months" would have them departing Malta sometime around early February. Luke records that Paul left Malta on another "Alexandrian ship" that was carrying wheat to Rome (Acts 28:11). He comments that this particular ship featured on its bow the "Twin Brothers," Pollux and Castor. These twin gods were sons of Zeus, and were regarded as the patrons of sailors. Viewing their stars in the Gemini constellation during a dark night at sea was believed to bring sailors good fortune. The poet Horace (65–68 BC) honors them in his *Odes* when he writes, "To the greedy sea and the light breezes, Pollux and his brother Castor carry me safely through the stormy Aegean, all with the aid of my double-oared skiff." (*Odes* 30.62–64 [LCL]). The images of Pollux and Castor may have been carved and secured to the ship or simply painted on the bow.

Leaving Malta, the ship sailed north to Syracuse, an important port on the southeast coast of Sicily and the capital of the Roman government of Sicily (Acts 28:12). After three days, perhaps engaged with trade, Paul's journey continued across the narrow, two-mile (3.2 km) wide Strait of Messina to Rhegium

(Acts 28:13) located on the tip of the boot of Italy. Known as Reggio today, Rhegium was a busy port having been destroyed by an earthquake in 91 BC and rebuilt by the emperor Augustus. A day after Paul's arrival at Rhegium, a wind arose from the south enabling the ship to reach Puteoli the following day (Acts 28:13). Puteoli was the principal port of southern Italy and the great emporium of the Alexandrian wheat fleet. Known as Pozzuoli today, this final port of Paul's journey by ship was located on the north side and most sheltered part of the Bay of Naples, about five miles (88 km) west of Naples. Since Rome lacked a harbor of its own, Puteoli was the main port for Rome even though the city was about 170 miles (272 km) away. The completion of a harbor at Ostia, just nineteen miles (30.5 km) from Rome in the time of the emperor Hadrian (AD 98–117) diminished the commercial importance of Puteoli.[37] It took three ships for Paul to reach Puteoli from Caesarea. The rest of his journey would be by foot along the famous Appian Way.

FROM PUTEOLI TO ROME (ACTS 28:14–15)

Hearing of Paul's arrival, some brothers in the faith invited Paul to stay with them for a time. Julius, perhaps needing to care for some official business, must have agreed to this arrangement and Paul stayed at Puteoli for seven days before continuing his journey (Acts 28:14). Luke records that some Christians in Rome who had heard of Paul's arrival, came south along the Appian Way to meet him and accompany the apostle to his destination (Acts 28:15). The Appian Way was one of the most important and strategic roads in Italy, stretching from Rome to Brundisium in southeast Italy. The road is named for Appius Claudius Caecus (340–273 BC) a wealthy Roman official who completed the first section of the road in 312 BC. Like other Roman roads, the primary purpose was for the movement of military troops and supplies. But travelers going to and from Rome benefited from these well-built, paved roads.

Some of the Christians coming to meet Paul joined him at the town of Appii Forum, a market town forty-three miles (69 km) south of Rome. The word *forum* is the Roman equivalent to the Greek *agora* (ἀγορά) and refers to the town center, which featured the market and public buildings. Others who came out to welcome Paul met him at the Three Taverns, thirty-three miles (53 km) south of the city. The English word "taverns" (Latin *taberna*) has connotations today that are not implied by the original text. It simply refers to a place providing hospitality where travelers can obtain food and lodging. Forbes suggests that the word "taverns" may simply refer to "buildings."[38] Three Taverns was an important stopover on the Appian Way where three roads joined the major route leading to Rome.

At last Paul reached Rome, the "eternal city" on the Tiber River (28:14). When Paul entered Rome through Porta Appia (the gate known today as Porta San Sebastiano), he had reached the very heart of the ancient world. As a missionary strategist, Paul had longed to minister here at the hub and focal point of the Roman Empire (Rom 15:23). Although he was a prisoner, Paul now had an opportu-

37. Todd Bolen, "Puteoli," http://www.BiblePlaces.com/puteoli.

38. S. Russell Forbes, *The Footsteps of St. Paul in Rome: An Historical Memoir from the Apostle's Landing at Puteoli to His Death, A.D. 62–64* (New York: Nelson, 1887), 20.

Appian Way

nity for witness and ministry that would radiate to all parts of the Roman world.

Paul's Situation in Rome (Acts 28:16–31)

As Luke brings his account of Paul's journey to a conclusion, he provides some important information about the apostle's situation in Rome. Although a prisoner of Rome, he had a good deal of freedom. This is quite different from the situation Paul describes in 2 Tim 4:6–18 during what appears to be his second Roman imprisonment. Luke reports that Paul was allowed to "stay by himself with the soldier who was guarding him" (Acts 28:16). The soldier would have been a member of an elite military unit, the Praetorian Guard (Phil 1:13). They were a powerful group of soldiers whose primary function was to guard the emperor and the imperial palace in Rome. They were a pampered unit that received far more pay than the ordinary legionary pay and could retire after sixteen years of service.[39] Paul's words to the Philippians indicate that the members of the Praetorian Guard took turns guarding him, providing Paul with the opportunity to testify to each of these elite soldiers (Phil 1:13).

Luke also explains that Paul was able to stay "in his own rented quarters" (Acts 28:30). It seems that Paul was under detention or house arrest rather than being incarcerated in a regular prison, although he does mention "wearing this chain" in Acts 28:20. Luke describes his lodging as being of sufficient size to accommodate large numbers of visitors (Acts 28:23). Luke makes it clear that these accommodations were rented at Paul's own expense, rather than that of the Roman government (Acts 28:30). During the two years of waiting for his hearing before the emperor Nero (AD 37–68), Paul had the freedom to welcome guests, preach the kingdom of God, and carry on correspondence (Acts 28:31). It is believed that Paul wrote his letters

39. Lesley Adkins and Roy Adkins, *Introduction to the Romans* (Secaucus, NJ: Chartwell,1991), 35.

to the Ephesians, Philippians, Colossians, and Philemon during this time in Rome.[40]

BIBLIOGRAPHY

Adkins, Lesley, and Roy Adkins. *Introduction to the Romans*. Secaucus, NJ: Chartwell, 1991.

Beck, John A. *The Baker Illustrated Guide to Everyday Life in Bible Times*. Grand Rapids: Baker, 2013.

Beitzel, J. Barry. *The New Moody Atlas of the Bible*. Chicago: Moody, 2009.

Bolen, Todd. "Puteoli." http://www.BiblePlaces.com/puteoli.

Bruce, F. F. *The Book of Acts*. Grand Rapids: Eerdmans, 1954.

Bull, Robert J. "Caesarea Maritima: The Search for Herod's City." *BAR* 8.3 (May/June 1982): 24–40.

Forbes, S. Russell. *The Footsteps of St. Paul in Rome: An Historical Memoir from the Apostle's Landing at Puteoli to His Death, A.D. 62–64*. New York: Nelson, 1887.

Fowler, H. W., and F. G. Fowler. *The Works of Lucian of Samosota*. Oxford: Clarendon, 1905.

Garnsey, Peter. "Grain for Rome." Pages 118–30 in *Trade in the Ancient Economy*. Edited by Peter Garnsey, Keith Hopkins, and Charles R. Whittaker. Berkeley: University of California Press, 1983.

Hohlfelder, Robert L. "Caesarea beneath the Sea." *BAR* 8.3 (May/June 1982): 42–47.

Metzger, Bruce M. *A Textual Commentary on the Greek New Testament*. London: United Bible Societies, 1971.

Murphy-O'Connor, Jerome. "On the Road and on the Sea with St. Paul." *Bible Review* 1 (Summer 1985): 38–47.

Porath, Yosef. "Vegas on the Med: A Tour of Caesarea's Entertainment District." *BAR* 30.5 (Sept/Oct 2004): 24–35.

Ramsay, William Michael, *St. Paul the Traveller and Roman Citizen*. New York: Putnam's Sons, 1898.

Rapske, B. M. "Acts, Travel and Shipwreck." Pages 29-36 in *The Book of Acts in Its Graeco-Roman Setting*. Edited by D. W. J. Gill and C. Gempf. Volume 2 of *The Book of Acts in Its First Century Setting*. Edited by Bruce W. Winter. Grand Rapids: Eerdmans, 1994.

Rasmussen, Carl G. *Zondervan NIV Atlas of the Bible*. Grand Rapids: Zondervan, 1989.

Robertson, A. T. *Word Pictures in the New Testament: Vol. 3, The Acts of the Apostles*. Nashville: Broadman, 1930.

Smith, James. *The Voyage and Shipwreck of St. Paul*. Grand Rapids: Baker, 1978.

Wilkes, John. *The Roman Army*. Cambridge: Cambridge University Press, 1972.

Yenen, Serif. *Turkish Odyssey: A Traveler's Guide to Turkey and Turkish Culture*. Istanbul: Yenen, 1997.

40. For a consideration of what happened after the two years of Paul's house arrest, see Laney, "Paul's Travels After Acts," chapter 36 of this volume.

CHAPTER 34

THE SOCIAL AND GEOGRAPHICAL WORLD OF ROME

Acts 18:2; 19:21; 23:11; 28:14, 16; Rom 1:7, 15; 2 Tim 1:17

David A. deSilva

KEY POINTS

- Though Rome appears rarely in the biblical narrative as a setting for events, it looms large throughout the New Testament as the political and conceptual center of the empire within which Jesus and the movement born in his name were embedded.
- The public spaces of Rome told a story of a city that rose to world domination under the watchful care of the gods; many of its spaces told the story of the godlike achievements of Julius Caesar and his adopted son Octavian, celebrated as "son of a god" and bringer of peace and order.
- From the opulence of Roman building programs to the provision of free grain for Rome's two hundred thousand families, the city well-merited the critique of provincials like John the Seer, whose Revelation critiques Roman policy and practice throughout.
- The story of the Jewish War (from a Roman point of view, the pacification of the uprising in Judea) was told in the architecture of the Flavian period, from the Temple of Peace built by Vespasian to display the artifacts from the temple, to the Arch of Titus, to the Colosseum built with the spoils of the Jewish War.
- An important innovation in Jewish practice was imposed by Vespasian as a form of war reparations: The tax once collected for the temple of Yahweh was now expanded and used for the temple of Jupiter on the Capitoline Hill.
- The archaeology of the housing and support structures for the "Roman in the street" provides important windows into the likeliest settings for the typical house church in the city of Rome, though the possibility exists that a *few* well-to-do Romans converted and would host gatherings of the assembly.

ROME IN THE BIBLICAL STORY

For all its importance as the center of empire throughout the New Testament period, the physical spaces of Rome intersect disproportionately rarely with the biblical story. It emerges as Paul's destiny late in Acts as a result of his appealing his case to be heard in the highest courts of the empire (Acts 25:11–12), which seems to be the manner in which a word from the Lord to Paul finds fulfillment (19:21; 23:11), but upon Paul's arrival at last in the capital city we see him only in his own rented dwelling meeting with local leaders of the Jewish community, all the while with his Roman guard on duty (28:16–31). Paul wrote what is arguably his most substantial letter to the Christians in Rome, but we learn surprisingly little about their own conditions there from Paul's letter—no doubt because he himself had not yet been to the city itself nor interacted with more than a few dozen Christians who find themselves in Rome at the time of his writing (Rom 16:3–16). In 2 Timothy, we find notice that one Onesiphorus had successfully navigated the urban jungle of Rome to bring relief and support to Paul during one of his imprisonments there (1:16–18).

Rome was perhaps the most permanent home for Aquila (originally a native of Pontus in northern Turkey) and Priscilla, who lived there for an undisclosed period prior to the Emperor Claudius' expulsion of Jews from Rome because of some disturbances caused by one "Chrestus" (Suetonius, *Claudius* 25.4; Acts 18:2). While this is an attested slave name in the period, it is tempting to believe that Suetonius misunderstood the cause of these disturbances, which were really the result of inner-Jewish conflict over claims concerning "Christus."[1] It was this expulsion, dated to AD 49, that brought Priscilla and Aquila to Corinth and, thus, into Paul's orbit (see map on page 465). This important couple found their way back to Rome prior to Paul's writing of his letter, in which he sends fond greetings to his erstwhile partners in mission (Rom 16:3–4).

The origins of the Christian communities in Rome are shrouded in mystery. According to Luke, Jewish and gentile Godfearing pilgrims from Rome were present at Pentecost to hear Peter's inspired proclamation of the good news (Acts 2:10–11).[2] Some of these may have been won to the new movement and eventually taken its confession and way of life back to Rome with them. The list of greetings that Paul sends along with his letter, on the other hand, is also a list of associates and relatives of Paul who may themselves have been instrumental in building up the Christian community there, if not planting some sizable portion of it themselves (Rom 16:3–16).[3] The movement grew sufficiently large to be noticed by Nero and his informants and selected for scapegoating; its mem-

1. E. Mary Smallwood, *The Jews Under Roman Rule: From Pompey to Diocletian*, 2nd ed. (Leiden: Brill, 1981), 210–11.

2. On the origins and history of the Jewish community in Rome, see Smallwood, *Jews Under Roman Rule*, 128–43, 201–19; Harry J. Leon, *Jews of Ancient Rome*, rev. ed. (Peabody, MA: Hendrickson, 1995).

3. The notices of the "hard work" of many of these sisters and brothers may refer to their church-planting and nurturing activity in Rome, as is at the very least the case for the Mary of Rom 16:6.

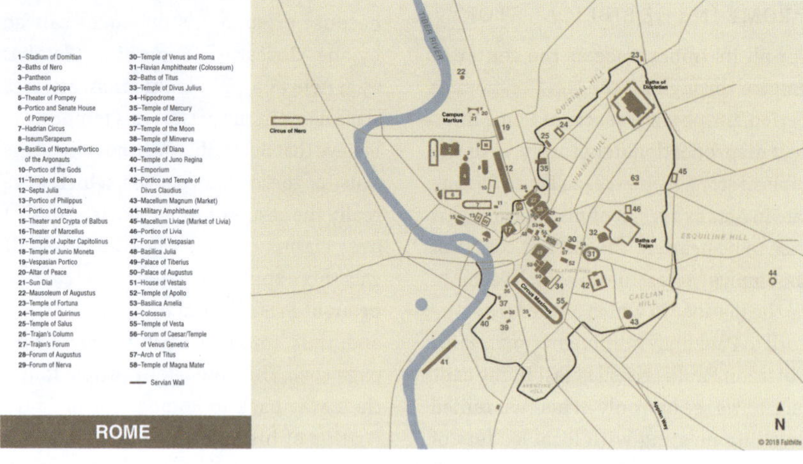

ROME

bers apparently also lived in sufficiently high tension with their neighbors for this scapegoating to be greeted without resistance—and perhaps even with pleasure—by the general population of the city (Tacitus, *Annales* 15.44).

The reader of the New Testament is nevertheless aware of Rome and its impact upon the Mediterranean at every turn. The life of Jesus and the written corpus of the New Testament all take shape within the frame of Roman imperialism, as, for example, the presence of the imperial machinery of prefects, tribunes, centurions, and soldiers in Judea bear repeated witness (Matt 8:5–13; 27:1–2, 11–54, 62–66; Acts 10:1–2, 17–46; 21:30–39; 22:22–29; 23:10; 23:16–26:32). Rome is the ideological center of the world into which the church was born—a center *against* which many of the early church's leaders defined the ideology of the new movement. In some instances, this opposition remains somewhat subtle, as in Luke's depiction of "good news" that means "peace" for the world coming by means of the birth of a "savior" who is *not* Augustus (Luke 2:1–20), or in Luke's reassertion of a geography that places Jerusalem at the center of the world and Rome at "the ends of the earth" (1:8) by virtue of being the location at which the story of the gospel's progress ends. In other instances, this opposition is overt and unsparing, as in John's caustic portrayal of Roman imperialism, its mechanisms, its effects, and its destiny in a *just* universe (Rev 17:1–19:10).

THE CITY OF ROME

The geographic location of Rome is well suited to a city that would grow in importance over the centuries since its first settlement. Located primarily on the eastern shore of the river Tiber in a great bend of the river as well as at a juncture where several established ancient land routes crossed the river at a low point, it was well-placed for trade by land and water, and later for the coordination of communications and movements throughout a larger empire. The Tiber River emptied into the Mediterranean about twenty miles (32 km) downriver from Rome at the port of Ostia, giving the city fairly ready access to sea trade.

The seven hills across which the city eventually spread—the Palatine,

Capitoline, Quirinal, Viminal, Esquiline, Caelian, and Aventine—provided a defensible position for a growing settlement and, later, city. Speaking of the city as *urbs septicollis* (a seven-hilled city) was a common poetic way of referring to Rome (Virgil, *Georgics* 2.535; *Aeneid* 6.784; Ovid, *Tristia* 1.4.69; Martial, *Epigrams* 4.64.11). Plutarch and Varro both refer to an obscure festival called *Septimontium*, which may be connected with the growth of the city to encompass these seven hills (Plutarch, *Quaestiones romanae et graecae.* 69; Varro, *De lingua Latina* 6.24). All but the Caelian were enclosed within the city's walls in the Republican period (already by the fourth century BC wall associated with Servius Tullius, one of Rome's kings).[4] By the time of Augustus, the city had outgrown its walls (most of which had either fallen into disrepair or been hidden as the city literally grew up around and against them on both sides). Rome's transition from a walled city to an open city with no need of defensive fortifications was a result of Augustus' establishment of the Roman peace—which meant both bringing an end to the civil wars and pushing back the frontiers of potentially hostile forces so far from the city of Rome as to render walls superfluous. The legions on the frontiers, as it were, became the city's walls.

The city of Rome was the beating heart of the empire that encompassed the lands around the entire Mediterranean. The symbol of the eagle standing in victory and domination over the globe was an apt depiction of the power and influence of the city's power brokers. This city was indeed "the great city that rules over the kings of the earth" (Rev 17:18). It was also the parasitic and insatiable consumer of the world's goods, for which John would sharply criticize it (Rev 18:1–24). The grandeur of Rome came from its siphoning off the resources and wealth of its conquered territories and vassal states around the Mediterranean. While Rome only had emperors beginning in the late first century BC, it had an empire from the early years of the second century BC as it began to take over the lands of Greece and North Africa. The public architecture of the city was designed above all to impress, to create a visual image that matched its leaders' propaganda about its greatness, its eternity, and its achievement. Brick and marble everywhere gave eloquent testimony to Rome's grandeur, power, and wealth.

Depiction of Roman Eagle on Globe in Area of the Temple of Apollo and Portico of Octavia

THE ROMAN FORUM

If Rome was the heart of the empire, the Roman Forum was the heart of Rome (see map on page 710). Here the politics and piety of the city blended together to pro-

4. Peter Connolly and Hazel Dodge, *Ancient City: Life in Classical Athens and Rome* (Oxford: Oxford University Press, 1998), 108.

Basilica Julia

claim that Rome's power was the result of the gods' purposes and beneficence. Official public orations and addresses were made from a rostrum in the center west of the Forum.[5] Legal proceedings, both civil and criminal, were heard in the basilicas—expansive, columned, covered buildings like the Basilica Aemilia and the even grander Basilica Julia, which also provided offices for several governmental functionaries. Julius Caesar had undertaken the construction of the latter basilica, funding the operation with spoils from the conquest of Gaul (including the proceeds from the sale of tens of thousands of prisoners of war into slavery). Across the forum, the Senate—composed essentially of Rome's male millionaires from its most distinguished families—met in the Curia Julia to decide Roman policy to the extent that Julius' successors, the emperors, would allow them. Julius had prepared for the renovation of this structure, though his assassination in 44 BC left it to his successor, Octavian, to execute.[6] Julius also began the first major expansion of the Republican Forum, building the Forum of Caesar north and northwest of the Curia Julia. This created additional public spaces for offices, meetings, and the conducting of the business of empire,

5. Paoli Guidobaldi, *The Roman Forum* (Milan: Electa, 1997), 24, 26.

6. Guidobaldi, *Roman Forum*, 15; Amanda Claridge, *Rome: An Oxford Archaeological Guide*, 2nd ed. (Oxford: Oxford University Press, 2010), 71.

Curia of Julius Caesar

all under the watchful shadow of a new temple to *Venus Genetrix*.[7] The epithet of the goddess refers to the myth of Venus' having given birth to Anchises, father of the Trojan Aeneas, the mythical hero of the Roman people whose story is told in Virgil's *Aeneid*. Julius also traced the mythical ancestry of the Julii family line back through this line to the goddess, making his new forum a blatant witness to his own propaganda.

THE TEMPLES

The business of the Roman Forum took place under the watchful eye of the gods. A temple toward the east end of the forum was dedicated to Vesta, the goddess of the hearth. Six virgin priestesses tended the sacred fire that represented the hearth not just of a single family, but of the entire Roman people—the larger family of which the emperor himself was the head (as *Pater Patriae*). These Vestal Virgins lived in a villa adjacent to the temple. Their celibacy during their thirty-year term as priestesses bought them freedom from being under a man's authority and often gave them significant influence with the emperors and their court.[8] A temple to Castor and Pollux stood between the temple of Vesta and the Basilica Julia to the west. Castor and Pollux were twins and half-brothers at the same time: both were born of Leda, but Pollux had been sired by Zeus disguised as a swan while Castor was the son of Leda's mortal husband. They were famous for their brotherly affection, typified in Pollux's gift of half of his immortality to Castor so that they could share six months in Olympus at the price of sharing six months in Hades. They are seen in the constellation Gemini and were the patron gods of sailors and cavalry.[9] Indeed, the twin brothers watched over the path of the Alexandrian grain ship that took Paul from Malta to Puteoli as

Temple of Castor and Pollux

7. Claridge, *Rome*, 163–68.

8. Guidobaldi, *Roman Forum*, 55–57; Claridge, *Rome*, 105–8.

9. See Strabo, *Geography* 1.3.2: "the Dioscuri were called 'guardians of the sea' and 'saviors of sailors'" (LCL).

the ship's figurehead (Acts 28:11). Castor was also an important precedent for a mortal becoming divine, and no doubt eased developments for the emperors and their worship in Rome after their deaths.

The iconic temple of Saturn, the mythic father of Jupiter, Neptune, and Hades, stood near the west end of the Forum at a slight elevation (that is, on the beginning rise of the Capitoline Hill). It had originally been erected before the period of the Republic.[10] Today the front six Ionic columns still stand, along with their architrave and a small portion of the pediment. This temple served also as the treasury of Rome, guarded by the ancient god. A legend written upon the architrave commemorates the rebuilding of the temple after a disastrous fire. The first line of this inscription—*Senatus populusque Romanus*, "The Roman Senate and People"—is incidentally the source of the famous acronym *SPQR* seen everywhere in Rome and on things Roman. A temple to Concordia, reaching back to the early Republic but rebuilt in AD 10 after a fire, stood to the north of the temple of Saturn, and a portico to the "Counseling Gods"—all twelve Olympians—was added to the west.[11]

Overshadowing the whole atop the Capitoline Hill to the west of the Forum stood the temple of Jupiter, Juno, and Minerva, the foundations of which are still visible, enclosed within the Capitoline Museum. Representations on a number of coins and carved reliefs suggest that the temple had four columns at its front during the late Republic and early Imperial period, but was rebuilt more grandly under Vespasian, spreading to a size that required the support of six columns.[12] Atop a second plateau of the same hill sat the temple of *Juno Moneta*, which was also close by the State Mint (hence the eventual association of Juno's epithet *Moneta*, "she who warns," with the word for money).[13] The central archives (the *tabularium*) was also built into the Capitoline Hill, overlooking the Roman Forum.

Coin Depicting Temple of Jupiter Capitolinus

IMPERIAL PALACES

If the business of the Forum happened under the watchful eye of the gods, it happened also under the watchful eyes of the living emperors and their families,

10. Guidobaldi, *Roman Forum*, 30; Claridge, *Rome*, 83–84.

11. Claridge, *Rome*, 80, 83; Guidobaldi, *Roman Forum*, 29.

12. Coins from the Republican period minted under M. Volteius show the facade of the temple with four columns and three pairs of bronze doors opening to each of the three sacred areas (*cellae*) of the divine trio. Sesterces minted under Vespasian show the restored temple with six columns, this time also showing the doors open to reveal the three cult images within.

13. S. Pescarin, *Rome: A Guide to the Eternal City* (New York: Barnes and Noble, 2000), 24.

whose palaces spread across the sides and top of the Palatine Hill to the south of the Forum. On the western Palatine sat the house of Augustus and Livia along with an older temple to *Magna Mater* (the great mother goddess) and a new temple to Apollo, built by Augustus.[14] Tiberius would build his palace to the north of these structures, directly overlooking the Forum. The most extensive of these palaces is the Domus Flavia, built under Domitian toward the end of the first century AD and covering the whole of the central and eastern Palatine.[15] It was fabulous not only for the scope of its living and meeting spaces, but also for the extensiveness of its gardens and outdoor amenities, including an enclosed garden in the form of a small stadium or hippodrome that could accommodate private races. The spread of the imperial palaces incidentally obliterated or overbuilt the entirety of what was an elite residential neighborhood during the late Republic.

Domitian's Private Racetrack

Palatine Hill beyond Roman Forum

The Domus Flavia overlooked the Circus Maximus, the most famous racetrack in Rome, that sat immediately south of the Palatine. Domitian took advantage of this by creating a lavish, private garden terrace—a kind of perpetual and private box seating for the imperial family. The racecourse would have at one time been surrounded with stone stadium seating raised a safe distance above the action of the chariots.[16] The distinctive feature of circuses or hippodromes was the central *spīna*, which made an open space into an

14. Claridge, *Rome*, 126, 135–44.
15. See further, Connolly and Dodge, *Ancient City*, 218–25; Claridge, *Rome*, 127, 145–57.
16. On the Circus Maximus, see Connolly and Dodge, *Ancient City*, 176–81.

oval track. The most dangerous part of the chariot races were the sharp turns at either end, the occasion for many spectacular wrecks that were no doubt part of the draw of these events. The *spīna* was a prime location for displaying pieces of political propaganda—it was surely not out of a desire merely to decorate that Augustus placed one of the obelisks he brought back from Egypt after his victory over Mark Antony and Cleopatra VII in its center.

Model of Campus Martius

THE *CAMPUS MARTIUS*

A second significantly developed district within the city of Rome was the *Campus Martius*, the "Field of Mars," so named because it was once the site for Rome's military training exercises. That would have been before the southern half of the field was developed into another religious, political, and entertainment district. Four small temples from the earlier Republican period stood near the center of this area.[17] Pompey the Great, once a partner and then a defeated rival of Julius Caesar, had built a theater, expansive portico, and public latrines west of these temples. Pompey's complex also featured a second meeting venue for the Roman Senate (it was here that Julius Caesar was assassinated in 44 BC).[18] North of the four temples, Marcus Agrippa, Augustus' right-hand man, had built a public bath complex and, further to the north, a monumental temple that was later incorporated by the Emperor Hadrian into the famous Pantheon.[19] East of these stood a large park-like area used for the regular voting of the plebs, or citizens of Rome. South of this stood a columned portico built by Augustus in honor of his sister, Octavia, surrounding the sacred precinct of two temples to Jupiter and Juno.[20] Just south of that, Augustus built a second theater in this district in honor of his then heir-apparent, Marcellus.[21] Augustus also allowed his friend L. Cornelius Balbus, a victorious general, to build a smaller theater and portico north of the Portico of Octavia in honor of his pacification of Libya.[22] These theaters would have featured performances of Roman comedy such as those written by Plautus and Terence, tragedy such as Seneca wrote,

17. Claridge, *Rome*, 241–46.
18. Claridge, *Rome*, 239–41.
19. Pescarin, 64–65; Claridge, *Rome*, 226.
20. Claridge, *Rome*, 255–56.
21. Claridge, *Rome*, 275–77.
22. Claridge, *Rome*, 247.

bawdy farces, and pantomimes.[23] Nero would build a public bathhouse in the area northwest of Agrippa's great temple, and Domitian an odeon and stadium, the contours of which remain clearly visible in the Piazza Navona, further west.[24]

Pantheon

THE AVENTINE HILL

Southwest of the Roman Forum on the banks of the Tiber is the Aventine Hill, which had grown to become an important quarter for merchants and manual laborers. This was the major offloading area for shipments coming up the Tiber from the port of Ostia (and later, under Claudius, from the new harbor at Portus just a few miles north of Ostia), with wharves and warehouses lining the Tiber at this point.[25] The Aventine was also one of a number of sites where great amounts of grain were stored to keep the citizens of Rome supplied with their daily rations of wheat for baking bread.[26] An ironic monument to the massive amounts of supplies that passed through the port here is the so-called Monte Testaccio, a 120-foot-high (36.5 m) mountain made from the discarded amphorae and other clay vessels used (chiefly) to bring olive oil to Rome from Spain and North Africa.[27] Other large market areas were to be found in the areas alongside the Tiber north of the Aventine, including a vast livestock market and a produce market.

THE EVOLVING CITYSCAPE OF ROME

Many emperors continued to reshape the Roman cityscape during their reigns, using the public architecture of the city to create monuments to their grandeur and greatness. One story that particularly merits attention—and one that can be plainly read from the architectural landscape of early imperial Rome—is the story of Octavian, who became known as Augustus, Rome's first emperor. Later in the first century AD, Nero reshaped the center of the city to build a colossal palace complex, and Vespasian built the Colosseum, one of the most well-known of Rome's architectural monuments. Other emperors continued building palaces, monuments, and temples.

AUGUSTUS

The story of Augustus is to Rome as the Infancy Narratives of Matthew and Luke are to the Gospels. Augustus' birth was, in

23. See further, Connolly and Dodge, *Ancient City*, 182–89.

24. Claridge, *Rome*, 234–37.

25. Claridge, *Rome*, 403–5.

26. For more on the scope and logistics of sustaining the population of Rome, see Paul Erdkamp, "The Food Supply of the Capital," in *The Cambridge Companion to Ancient Rome*, ed. Paul Erdkamp (Cambridge: Cambridge University Press, 2013), 262–77.

27. Connolly and Dodge, *Ancient City*, 127; Claridge, *Rome*, 402.

the words of an inscription by the provincial council of Asia Minor, also "the beginning of the good news," the inscription employing a form of the Greek word εὐαγγέλιον (*euangelion*), or "gospel, good news," to talk about the significance of Augustus, lauded as a god and bringer of peace, for the world (notably, decades before Luke would write his Gospel).[28] As Luke begins to tell the story of Jesus' birth, he reminds his readers that these events happened under the shadow of Augustus, emperor of Rome from 31 BC to AD 14. This is more than just a date to help readers know how long ago the story took place. It is a subtle but unmistakable invitation to read the story that would follow—the story of a Son of God who would be a savior to the people and usher in a reign of peace and well-being for all nations—over against the story of Augustus, who was painted in very similar hues. Luke's own view of which story is true, of course, is clear from the beginning. God's own angels announce the birth of *this* savior and affirm the promise of peace that *this* Son of God would bring to the world.

Octavian had been adopted by Julius Caesar, who had no son of his own, though Octavian's biological parents were still living.[29] Such adoption of adult children was essentially Julius' way of naming Octavian his successor and heir. After Julius was assassinated, Octavian vowed to avenge his death and punish the conspirators, including the famous Brutus and Cassius. He vowed to build a monumental temple to *Mars Ultor*, or "Mars the Avenger," beside the Roman Forum if he returned victorious—a vow he would begin to fulfill just five years later in the context of creating a massive expansion of the public forum to the north of the Roman Forum and perpendicular to the Forum of Julius, with his temple of Mars Ultor as its showpiece, a project not completed until 2 BC.[30] The majority of the Forum of Augustus stretches under a main, modern road and, therefore, cannot be excavated, but it provided significant new venues for judicial proceedings and government business.[31]

Temple of Mars Ultor

Octavian's partnership with Marc Antony, another loyal client of Julius Caesar, outlived Brutus and Cassius

28. The full text and an excellent explanation of the Priene Inscription can be found in Frederick W. Danker, *Benefactor: Epigraphic Study of a Graeco-Roman and New Testament Semantic Field* (St. Louis: Clayton House, 1982), 215–22.

29. Not counting his illegitimate son Caesarion by Cleopatra VII whom, however, he did not acknowledge as his own.

30. Connolly and Dodge, *Ancient City*, 111.

31. Elisha A. Dumser, "The Urban Topography of Rome," in Erdkamp, *Ancient Rome*, 141; Claridge, *Rome*, 177–80.

only by a decade. Antony's alliance with Cleopatra VII, Egypt's last queen, proved a fatal mistake. Octavian emerged as the protector of Rome's interests and enjoyed the strong support of the Senate and people of Rome, while Antony and Cleopatra were represented as threats to the empire's unity, with Antony being labeled a traitor to his own people. A triumphal arch, of which only the bases and one or two column capitals remain, was built in 29 BC to celebrate Octavian's victory over Marc Antony in the naval battle near Actium two years before.[32] This arch was erected near the center of the Roman Forum adjoining the temple of Castor and Pollux and the temple of the Deified Julius, built in the same year.

The rise of Augustus to sole power was celebrated as the beginning of a new, golden age of peace and stability. "Peace" became the watchword of the new regime, the source of the legitimacy of Augustus' power. Perhaps the most significant monument to the *Pax Augusti*—the Augustan Peace—is the *Ara Pacis* or "Altar of Peace," once erected in the northern portion of the Campus Martius. This particular monument was decreed by the Senate in 13 BC in honor of Augustus' pacification of Spain and Gaul.[33] The altar itself is housed at the top of a flight of steps inside a nearly square monument of about forty by thirty-six feet (12 x 11 m).[34] A carved relief on the two shorter sides of the Altar of Peace displays a religious procession in which Augustus and his extended family take conspicuous part (along with senators, lictors, and priests).[35]

Ara Pacis Augustae, Altar of the Augustan Peace

Augustus had several Egyptian monuments transported to Rome as trophies after his victory at Actium in 31 BC and placed in prominent locations as perpetual reminders of his successful end to civil war. One obelisk from the time of Ramses II was erected in the Campus Martius (or Field of Mars) and used as the needle of a solar meridian, a kind of sundial that marked out the progression of a solar year, allowing the civil calendar to keep in step with the solar calendar. A long strip of metal was laid out beside the obelisk and engraved such that, at noon every day, the shadow of the tip of the obelisk at noon pointed to the date and indicated important seasonal transitions like the solstices and equinoxes. The inscription on the obelisk declared that "The Emperor Caesar Augustus, Son of the Deified, Chief Priest, with Egypt restored

32. Guidobaldi, *Roman Forum*, 37; Claridge, *Rome*, 101–2.
33. Claridge, *Rome*, 207.
34. Claridge, *Rome*, 209.
35. Pescarin, *Rome*, 70–71; Claridge, *Rome*, 210–213.

to the power of the Roman people, gave this as a gift to the Sun."[36]

Augustus also selected a site in the northernmost part of the Campus Martius for his mausoleum. This was a great round, marble-faced brick tomb with a diameter of almost a hundred yards (91.5 m) and rising to a height of perhaps fifty yards (45.75 m) when it was still complete.[37] It would become the site of a massive, block-long inscription celebrating the achievements of Augustus' career, written by Augustus himself shortly before his death—the *Res Gestae Divi Augusti*.[38] While earlier claims that the obelisk of the *hōrologium* would point to the *Ara Pacis* on September 23, Augustus' birthday, appear now to have been mistaken, it remains clear that the two were placed in a clear relation to one another—and to Augustus' mausoleum—creating a triad of monuments to his legacy of peace.[39]

Horologium Augusti Obelisk

An essential claim to legitimate power for Augustus was his adoption by Julius Caesar, and thus his inheritance not only of Julius' estates and wealth, but also of the loyalty of Julius' client base. The fact that the Senate declared his adoptive father to be a god after his assassination improved the legitimacy of Augustus' rule tremendously. In 29 BC, Augustus erected a temple to the deified Julius in the heart of the Roman Forum. Only parts of the podium remain, including the temple's most distinctive feature—a concave area in the front of the podium surrounding the site where the body of Julius was cremated.[40] This temple became a constant reminder of the power that stood behind Augustus' leadership of the empire. The triumphal arch of Augustus, in what was surely no accident, adjoins this temple on its southern side. As the adopted son of Julius, Augustus became

36. Claridge, *Rome*, 216. The inscription is dated to 10 BC. The same inscription was carved into a sister obelisk, once gracing the *spīna* of the Circus Maximus, now standing in the Piazza del Populo.

37. Claridge, *Rome*, 204–5.

38. See page 707 for an image of part of the inscription from a replica. A translation and helpful notes can be found in Danker, *Benefactor*, 256–80. See now also the fresh edition, translation, and rich commentary by Alison E. Cooley, *Res Gestae Divi Augusti: Text, Translation, and Commentary* (Cambridge: Cambridge University Press, 2009).

39. See Peter Henslin, "Augustus, Domitian and the So-Called Horologium Augusti," *Journal of Roman Studies* 97 (2007): 1–20.

40. Guidobaldi, *Roman Forum*, 36; Claridge, *Rome*,100–101.

Remains of Arch of Augustus

Divi Filius, "son of the deified" (in Greek, simply υἱὸς θεοῦ, *huios theou*, "son of a god"), a title included in almost every public inscription.

TIBERIUS, CALIGULA, AND CLAUDIUS

Tiberius, Caligula, and Claudius appear to have altered the cityscape of Rome very little by comparison with Julius and Augustus, though Claudius significantly improved its water supply with a new aqueduct, part of which can be seen in the Porta Maggiore, a great gate on the eastern side of the city of Rome supporting several water channels (only incorporated into the city's walls in the third century AD). The structure bears inscriptions acknowledging the Emperor Claudius for the completion of this branch of the aqueduct system and the emperors Vespasian and Titus for its renovation and expansion.[41] The Senate would vote divine honors to Claudius, after which a massive temple complex was built for his cult southeast of the Roman Forum. All that remains visible today are a few areas of the foundation, incorporated into a later monastic compound.[42]

NERO

Nero, on the other hand, altered the landscape substantially for the sake of his vision of a palace worthy of an emperor. He wanted to join the Palatine Hill to the Oppian Hill, creating a vast complex of

West Side of the Porta Maggiore

41. Claridge, *Rome*, 383, 385.
42. Claridge, *Rome*, 349–50.

palaces, gardens, lakes, and other recreational areas. The fire of AD 64 significantly facilitated his architectural dream, raising widespread suspicion about Nero's own involvement that had to be diverted (Suetonius, *Nero* 38; Tacitus, *Annales* 15.38–42, 44). Having appropriated more than 150 acres (60.75 ha) in the heart of the city, Nero set about creating his *Domus Aurea* ("Golden House") complete with a colossal 120-foot (36.5 m) tall statue of himself as the sun god Helios. Somehow the excessive opulence of the project outpaced even its size. Suetonius describes the walls of the Domus as "overlaid with gold and studded with precious stones and mother of pearl" (*Nero* 31). One cannot help but wonder if John had caught wind of this project and constructed his New Jerusalem in such a way as would mock and put to shame the beast's wildest ambitions.

Arch of Titus

Spoils of Jerusalem, Arch of Titus

VESPASIAN, TITUS, AND DOMITIAN

After the death of Nero, the Roman Empire was plunged again into civil war, this time lasting only a single but devastating year (AD 68–69) at the end of which a new dynasty had emerged—the Flavian emperors Vespasian and, successively, his two sons Titus and Domitian. It was under Vespasian that Jesus' dire predictions of the siege and destruction of Jerusalem as related in Luke 21:20–24, would come to pass. Vespasian, general of the legions in Alexandria, had already begun putting down the Jewish Revolt of AD 66 when his attention was diverted westward in a bid for the emperor's seat. He left his eldest son Titus in charge of the siege of Jerusalem, which he completed by AD 70.

The famous Arch of Titus at the east entrance to the Roman Forum, erected shortly after Titus' untimely death in AD 81, commemorates Titus' successful suppression of the Judean Revolt.[43] Two carved reliefs on the inner walls of the arch show scenes from the triumphal procession awarded to Titus by the Senate immediately following the Jewish Revolt. The first relief shows Titus riding

43. Claridge, *Rome*, 121–23.

in a chariot drawn by four horses, the first horse being led in procession by the goddess Roma herself. Behind Titus stands the winged figure of Victory, holding a wreath over the conquering general's head. The second relief depicts the spoils from the temple of Jerusalem carried aloft (notably the seven-branched candelabra, the gold trumpets, and the table of the showbread), along with several Jewish slaves being led in the triumphal procession awarded to Titus. A dedicatory inscription above the arch reads "The Senate and People of Rome to the Divine Titus Vespasian Augustus, son of the Deified Vespasian."

After successfully bringing an end to the civil wars of AD 68–69 and the Jewish Revolt of AD 66–70, Vespasian constructed the Temple of Peace and its expansive courtyards and colonnades. This became another major northward extension of the Roman Forum, extending the public spaces available for business, imperial administration, and gathering. Vespasian displayed a great variety of artistic treasures within the new temple, including the furniture from the Jerusalem temple that had been brought to Rome (Josephus, *J.W.* 7.158–62).[44] The emphasis on peace in Vespasian's propaganda was directed at presenting him as a new Augustus, whose rise to power was similarly celebrated as bringing an end to civil war and provincial rebellion.

Flavian Amphitheater, Exterior

Under Vespasian, the temple of the Capitoline trio of gods—Jupiter, Juno, and Minerva—becomes important once again. After the destruction of the Jerusalem temple, Vespasian ordered that Jews continue to pay their temple tax as before. The funds, however, would no longer be used in connection with the activity and support of the Jerusalem temple, but rather would be handed over for the restoration and maintenance of the temple of Jupiter, which had been severely damaged in a fire. Thus the tribute that was regarded by Jews universally as due the God of Israel was now to be rendered to Caesar and the principal Roman deities. It is possible that one of the reasons John, the author of Revelation, spoke such strong words

44. Claridge, *Rome*, 171–72. The remains of an artifact of particular importance for reconstructing ancient Rome was discovered in a room inside the Temple of Peace complex—the *Forma Urbis*, a marble map of Rome created in the early decades of the third century. When it was complete, it measured sixty by forty-three feet (18.25 x 13 m) and was affixed to a wall. It is outstanding in its level of detail, showing every shop, every room in a *domus* or public building, every column in every portico. Only a small percentage (10–15 percent) of the original map survives in 1,186 fragments (https://formaurbis.stanford.edu).

against his fellow Jews, calling them a "synagogue of Satan" (Rev 2:9; 3:9), is that he detested the fact that they would buy toleration from Rome at the cost of giving over the money due God for God's worship to the emperors for the support of their demonic, idolatrous religion.

Flavian Amphitheater, Interior

Vespasian also began construction on the massive Flavian Amphitheater, more popularly known as the Colosseum (derived from the fact that it stood right across from the Colossus of Nero, which was reworked after more traditional images of the sun god Helios after Nero's suicide). Vespasian made a powerful statement here, returning to popular use a large piece of the land that Nero had coopted for his *Domus Aurea*. The work was completed under Titus. The whole measures 615 by 510 feet (187.5 x 155.5 m) on its two axes, with the arena floor measuring 246 by 144 feet (75 x 44 m).[45] The seating capacity of its four tiers of bleachers, rising to a height of 150 feet (45.75 m), exceeded fifty thousand.[46] Seats were reserved by social class, with the senators in the lowest (and therefore best) seats, the equestrians (*equites*, "knights") above them, and the *plēbs* in the tiers above them. At the very top, the poorest and slaves enjoyed a distant view of the action. The emperor and special dignitaries like the Vestal Virgins enjoyed a special box in the center of one of the long sides—and the images of the gods a similar box on the opposite side.[47] The arena was equipped with an extensive series of tunnels, lifts, and trap doors that allowed different points of entry for different combatants, beasts, or machinery (it may have once had the capacity to be flooded for the re-creation of naval battles). It had, in other words, the best capacity for special effects available in the first century. It is likely that the project was funded largely from the spoils of the Jewish War, including the proceeds from the sale of tens of thousands of Jewish prisoners of war as slaves.[48] A large gladiatorial training school, the *Ludus Magnus*, stood east of the Colosseum. An underground tunnel gave combatants access to the arena.[49] Titus also constructed a new bath complex just northeast of the Colosseum, a substantial complex covering about two-thirds the area of the Colosseum itself, as a public benefaction—notably extending his father's policy of returning to popular use land that the last Julio-Claudian

45. Connolly and Dodge, *Ancient City*, 192, 202; Claridge, *Rome*, 312.
46. Connolly and Dodge, *Ancient City*, 197; Claridge, *Rome*, 314.
47. Claridge, *Rome*, 314.
48. Connolly and Dodge, *Ancient City*, 192; Claridge, *Rome*, 314.
49. Claridge, *Rome*, 319.

Temple of Vespasian and Titus (right) and Temple of Saturn (left)

emperor had appropriated—and doing so, once again, by providing a highly functional public building (see the testimony of Martial, *Spectacles* 2.5–8).[50]

During his short reign, Titus began construction on a new temple to be dedicated to his deified father, Vespasian, to be located essentially between the ancient Temple of Saturn and the Temple of Concordia. After Titus' early death, his younger brother and successor Domitian, the last emperor of the Flavian dynasty, oversaw the completion of the temple and its dedication to both Vespasian and Titus together.[51] Even though it was "squeezed in" to the space between existing temples, the Temple of the Deified Vespasian and Titus had a commanding location above the eastern part of the Roman Forum. The architrave of the Temple of the Deified Vespasian and Titus was decorated (at least in part) with the tools and sacred vestments of Roman priests, recalling the emperors' own role as Pontifex Maximus, or chief priest, of the Roman world.

LIFE IN ROME

We have focused thus far on essentially the grand, public areas of Rome, the political, religious, and judicial spaces of Rome. But Rome was a city of approximately one million people, and the majority of the cityscape was occupied by their residences, workshops, and supporting structures like the ancient fast-food joints (called *thermopolii*) and taverns (*tabernae*) that largely fed them and the

50. Dumser, "Urban Topography," 147.

51. Claridge, *Rome*, 82. A small carving at the highest point of the underside of the vaulted archway of the Arch of Titus, shows Titus being carried into the heavens on the back of an eagle, a standard image for *apotheosis*, or deification.

hundreds of smaller bath facilities that kept them feeling civilized.[52] (These would come increasingly to be surpassed and replaced by the monumental bath facilities built under Trajan, Caracalla, and Diocletian in the centuries to follow.)

While vast stretches of the city were given over to the public monuments, temples, civic buildings, and entertainment facilities, we must imagine the greater part of the city housing a million people. The most elite lived in private homes that might span half or all of a city block, with some of the frontage rented out to shops of one kind or another, perhaps with living quarters above them for the renters and their families. The *domus* itself was largely a single-story residence with a high ceiling, its rooms arranged around an open atrium in the front half and an open, columned courtyard in the rear half. These openings would provide the greater part of the light and ventilation.

Ara Coeli Insula, 2nd Century Roman Apartment Block near Capitoline Hill

The majority of the population would have lived far more modestly in *insulae*, essentially apartment blocks with the lowest story devoted to workshops, taverns, or other businesses. One particularly unsavory residential area was the Subura, immediately northeast of the Forum of Augustus, which Augustus cordoned off with a thirty-foot-high wall. Apartments on the second floor would have still been relatively comfortable; apartments decreased in size (including the height of the ceilings!) and in number of rooms as one went above that. While many *insulae* would have not climbed above a third story, the remains of a six-story apartment block can be seen on the west side of the Capitoline hill and there is some evidence that a few topped out at eight stories.[53] Most of the residents on the upper floors would not have had the means for cooking or easy access to water, with the result that they would have purchased all their meals at local *thermopolii* and *tavernae* and used the public latrines and other facilities exclusively. The *insulae* would likely be more the world of the house churches that gathered in Rome to hear, for example, Paul's letter and bid for support for his ongoing mission to the West (Rom 15:23–29), though the possibility always exists that a *few* elite families were won to the new faith and opened up their *domus* to the assembly.

The wealth, luxury, and ostentation embodied in the public spaces of Rome and the semiprivate homes of its rulers were the prizes of conquest and political intimidation. They were spoils rather than wages or rewards. The temples dedicated to its deified, deceased rulers

52. On the population of Rome in the late Republican and early imperial periods, see Neville Morley, "Population Size and Social Structure," in Erdkamp, *Ancient Rome*, 29–44.

53. See further, Glenn R. Storey, "Housing and Domestic Architecture," in Erdkamp, *Ancient Rome*, 151–68.

were the ultimate attempts to legitimate Rome's imperialism not just as the will of the gods, but as the achievement of gods. The more prophetic-minded among the early Christians were highly critical of Rome's imperial practices. As John the Seer, for example, contemplated these and other facets of Rome's hegemony over the circle of lands around the Mediterranean—most notably the violence to which the empire resorted as its final argument—he could not believe that the God of Israel, the God of the prophets, would allow such a regime to continue long. The ruins of Rome are a constant reminder not only of Rome's greatness, but of the fact that no empire forged by human beings endures. History proves the common epithet "Eternal Rome" to be a lie, now no more than tourist propaganda, calling us to look to the kingdom of our Lord and of his Christ if we are ever to find a truly stable homeland.

BIBLIOGRAPHY

Carandini, Andrea, ed. *The Atlas of Ancient Rome: Biography and Portraits of the City*. 2 vols. Rev. ed. Princeton: Princeton University Press, 2017.

Claridge, Amanda. *Rome: An Oxford Archaeological Guide*. 2nd ed. Oxford: Oxford University Press, 2010.

Connolly, Peter, and Hazel Dodge. Pages 105–251 in *The Ancient City: Life in Classical Athens and Rome*. Oxford: Oxford University Press, 1998.

Cooley, Alison E. *Res Gestae Divi Augusti: Text, Translation, and Commentary*. Cambridge: Cambridge University Press, 2009.

Danker, Frederick W. *Benefactor: Epigraphic Study of a Graeco-Roman and New Testament Semantic Field*. St. Louis: Clayton House, 1982.

Dumser, Elisha A. "The Urban Topography of Rome." Pages 131–50 in *The Cambridge Companion to Ancient Rome*. Edited by Paul Erdkamp. Cambridge: Cambridge University Press, 2013.

Erdkamp, Paul, ed. *The Cambridge Companion to Ancient Rome*. Cambridge: Cambridge University Press, 2013.

———. "The Food Supply of the Capital." Pages 262–77 in *The Cambridge Companion to Ancient Rome*. Edited by Paul Erdkamp. Cambridge: Cambridge University Press, 2013.

Guidobaldi, Paola. *The Roman Forum*. Milan: Electa, 1997.

Henslin, Peter. "Augustus, Domitian and the So-Called Horologium Augusti." *Journal of Roman Studies* 97 (2007): 1–20.

Leon, Harry J. *The Jews of Ancient Rome*. Rev. ed. Peabody, MA: Hendrickson, 1995.

Morley, Neville. "Population Size and Social Structure." Pages 29–44 in *The Cambridge Companion to Ancient Rome*. Edited by Paul Erdkamp. Cambridge: Cambridge University Press, 2013.

Pescarin, S. *Rome: A Guide to the Eternal City*. New York: Barnes and Noble, 2000.

Smallwood, E. Mary. *The Jews Under Roman Rule: From Pompey to Diocletian*. 2nd ed. Leiden: Brill, 1981.

"Stanford Digital Forma Urbis Romae Project." https://formaurbis.stanford.edu.

Storey, Glenn R. "Housing and Domestic Architecture." Pages 151–68 in *The Cambridge Companion to Ancient Rome*. Edited by Paul Erdkamp. Cambridge: Cambridge University Press, 2013.

CHAPTER 35

PAUL IN SPAIN AND CRETE

Rom 15:23–29; Acts 21–28

Eckhard J. Schnabel

KEY POINTS

- There is sufficient evidence to conclude that Paul was released from his imprisonment in Rome, which allowed him to realize his plan to begin missionary work in Spain.
- There is some evidence that suggests that Paul preached the gospel on the island of Crete.

INTRODUCTION

Paul planned to begin missionary work in Spain after his mission in the province of Asia based in Ephesus, as he explains to the Christians in the city of Rome (Rom 15:23–29). His arrest in Jerusalem and the inconclusive legal proceedings that the Jewish leaders pursued against Paul in Jerusalem and Caesarea, eventually leading to his transfer to Rome (Acts 21–28), made the realization of the plan to go to Spain impossible, at least initially. Paul was a prisoner for two years in Caesarea, then for two years in Rome (AD 57–59/60–62). Luke does not report what happened with the legal case against Paul. The view that a prisoner had to be released if his accusers failed to appear within two years cannot be defended since such a rule was relevant only later.[1] Paul's Jewish opponents in the Jerusalem hierarchy may have decided that winning a verdict against Paul in the imperial court was unlikely; since they did not want to be exposed as *calumniatores* (or slanderers), they may have accepted the less serious option of defaulting, of simply not appearing in

1. Adrian Nicolas Sherwin-White, *Roman Society and Roman Law in the New Testament* (Oxford: Clarendon, 1963; repr., Eugene, OR: Wipf & Stock, 2004), 115–19; Brian M. Rapske, *The Book of Acts and Paul in Roman Custody*, vol. 3 of *The Book of Acts in Its First-Century Setting*, ed. Bruce W. Winter (Exeter: Paternoster, 1994), 322–23.

Rome. Since Nero was not very much interested in the law courts, Paul's case might have been heard by the Prefect of the Praetorian Guard, Sextus Afranius Burrus. It is possible that Paul's case was resolved in Paul's favor, either by acquittal or by default, just before Burrus' death in the spring of AD 62.

PAUL IN SPAIN

Early Christian sources agree that Paul was executed in Rome during the principate of Nero. Two early Christian sources indicate, however, that Paul preached the gospel in Spain, which implies that he was released from prison. Clement of Rome states in a letter written at the end of the first century that Paul "served as a herald in both the East and in the West; and he received the noble reputation for his faith. He taught righteousness to the whole world, and came to the limits of the West, bearing his witness before the rulers. And so he was set free from this world and transported up to the holy place, having become the greatest example of endurance" (1 Clement 5:6–7; author's translation). The phrase "the limits of the West" most probably refers to Spain, thought to be the "end of the world" in the West. Slightly later, but more explicitly, the Muratorian Canon states:

> For the "most excellent Theophilus" Luke summarises the several things that in his own presence have come to pass, as also by the omission of the passion of Peter he makes quite clear, and equally by (the omission) of the journey of Paul, who from the city (of Rome) proceeded to Spain.[2]

Many scholars accept these two passages as historical evidence that Paul was released from his (first) imprisonment in Rome, which allowed him to go to Spain.[3] Paul's journey to Spain was the fifteenth phase of his missionary work, dating around AD 62–64 (see page 702 for a chart of the phases of Paul's missionary work).

Spain (Greek Σπανία [*Spania*], Latin *Hispānia, Spania*) had early contacts with the eastern regions of the Mediterranean world by 1000 BC when Phoenician traders from Tyre and Sidon founded Gades and other cities on the south coast of Spain, including Mainake (Malaga) and Abdera. The reason for this colonization was the rich mineral deposits on the Iberian Peninsula. After the Romans defeated Carthage in 204 BC, they established in 197 BC two provinces in Spain: Hispania Citerior on the east coast, and Hispania Ulterior, which comprised the southeast coast and the Guadalquivir Valley. In the course of administrative reorganizations in 29 and 19 BC, Hispania Ulterior was divided between the senatorial province of Baetica with Corduba as capital, and the imperial province of Lusitania with Emerita Augusta as capital; the northern region of Spain continued to be administered as the province of Hispania Citerior with Tarraco as capital. Famous Spaniards from Spain included Seneca, Quintilian, and Martial. No evi-

---

2. Muratorian Canon, lines 35–39 (*NTApoc* 1:35); see also Acts of Peter 1.

3. Colin J. Hemer, *The Book of Acts in the Setting of Hellenistic History* (Tübingen: Mohr Siebeck, 1989), 390–404; Harry W. Tajra, *The Trial of St. Paul: A Juridical Exegesis of the Second Half of the Acts of the Apostles* (Tübingen: Mohr Siebeck, 1989), 196; Jerome Murphy-O'Connor, *Paul: A Critical Life* (Oxford: Oxford University Press, 1996), 354–63.

dence has yet been found that documents the presence of Jewish communities in Spain in the first century. Some classical scholars take Paul's plans to go to Spain as evidence that Jews must have lived in Spain, which is not necessarily the case since Paul's missionary work did not *depend* on the presence of a Jewish community.[4]

Some have suggested that Paul planned to reach Tarraco and preached the gospel there after he was released. Tarraco was the most important city in Spain during the imperial period. Julius Caesar granted Tarraco the status of a colony (Colonia Iulia Urbs Triumphalis) in 45 BC; Augustus, who had recuperated from an illness in Tarraco, made the city the capital of the province of Hispania Citerior (Hispania Tarraconensis) in 27 BC. The survey of the territory of Tarraco that was concluded in 1990 revealed that the city controlled about 3,300 villages and hamlets in the early Roman period.[5] It is estimated that Tarraco had between ten thousand and fifteen thousand inhabitants, with about sixty-six thousand people living in the villages in the territory of the city. According to local tradition, Paul preached at the site of the chapel that stands in the courtyard of the cathedral, which is built on Roman foundations; Paul is said to have appointed Prosperus, the first bishop of the city. The voyage from Ostia/Rome to Tarraco was about five hundred nautical miles (575 miles [925 km]).

It is a plausible assumption that Paul preached in Tarraco, but there were other cities that would have been plausible sites for missionary work: on the

4. For Paul's missionary work on Spain, see Eckhard J. Schnabel, *Early Christian Mission*, 2 vols. (Downers Grove, IL: InterVarsity Press, 2004), 2:1271–83; Schnabel, *Paul the Missionary: Realities, Strategies, and Methods* (Downers Grove, IL: InterVarsity Press, 2008), 115–21.

5. Josep-Maria Carreté, Simon Keay, and Martin Millett, *A Roman Provincial Capital and Its Hinterland: The Survey of the Territory of Tarragona, Spain, 1985–1990* (Ann Arbor: Journal of Roman Archaeology, 1995).

The Amphitheater of Tarraco

east coast north of Tarraco, he could have reached Barcino, Emporiae (and Caesaraugusta in the interior); south of Tarraco: Saguntum, Valentia, Lucentum, Carthago Nova; on the south coast: Abdera, Malaca, Carteia (and Corduba in the interior); on the Atlantic in southeast Baetica: Gades (and Hasta Regia in the interior). Paul's mission in Spain is the fifteenth phase of his missionary work.

PAUL ON CRETE

A passage in Paul's letter to his coworker Titus suggests that Paul returned to the Aegean after his (first) imprisonment in Rome.[6] He writes, "The reason I left you in Crete was that you might put in order what was left unfinished and appoint elders in every town, as I directed you" (Titus 1:5). There were evidently Christian communities in several cities, perhaps established by Jewish pilgrims to Jerusalem who heard Peter preach on Pentecost (Acts 2:11) in AD 30, were converted to faith in Jesus the Messiah, and returned to Crete to preach the gospel in their home towns.[7] If Paul traveled to Crete after his return from Spain, perhaps to assist Titus, his visit to Crete—the sixteenth phase of his missionary work—would date to AD 64/65.[8]

Philo states in his report of the letter of Herod Agrippa I to Caligula that the Greek islands are "full" of Jewish communities, mentioning Crete in this context (Philo, *On the Embassy to Gaius* 282). One of the wives of Josephus came from one of the first Jewish families of Crete (Josephus, *Life* 427). Tacitus mentions Jewish communities on Crete as well (*Histories* 5.11). Cities on the north coast of Crete include (from west to east): Phalasarna, Kisamos, Kydonia, Rhithymna, Heracleion, Chersonasos, Olous. Around twenty-five miles (40 km) south of Heracleion was Gortyn (modern Agioi Deka), the capital of the province of *Creta et Cyrene*. Gortyn is mentioned in 1 Macc 15:23 as a city with a Jewish community. According to local

6. For Titus see 2 Cor 2:13; 7:6, 13–14; 8:6, 16, 23; 12:18; Gal 2:1, 3; 2 Tim 4:10; Tit 1:4.

7. William D. Mounce, *Pastoral Epistles* (Nashville: Nelson, 2000), 386, mentions this as a possibility.

8. For Paul's missionary work on Crete, see Schnabel, *Early Christian Mission*, 2:1283–87; Schnabel, *Paul*, 121.

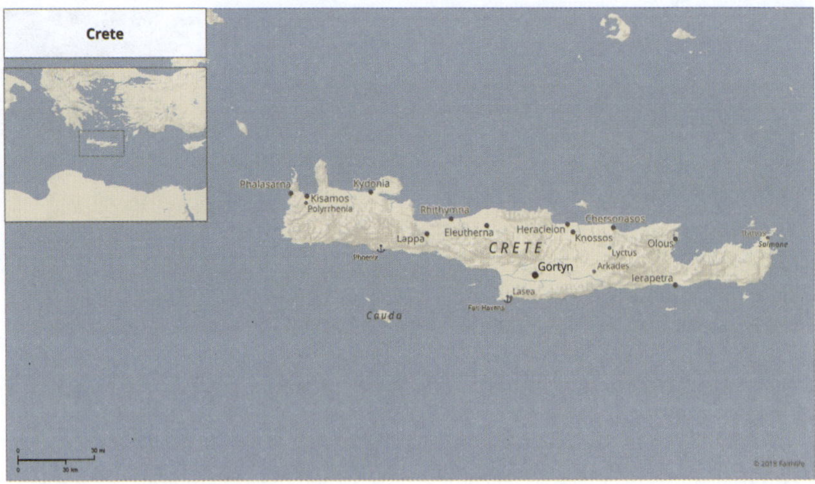

tradition, Titus was the first bishop of the city; the church Haghios Titus was built in the sixth century. The first documented bishop is Philippos in the second century; ten Christians of Gortyn were killed around AD 250 in the persecution under Decius.

Haghios Titus in Heracleion

BIBLIOGRAPHY

Carreté, Josep-Maria, Simon Keay, and Martin Millett. *A Roman Provincial Capital and Its Hinterland: The Survey of the Territory of Tarragona, Spain, 1985–1990*. Ann Arbor: Journal of Roman Archaeology, 1995.

Hemer, Colin J. *The Book of Acts in the Setting of Hellenistic History*. Tübingen: Mohr Siebeck, 1989.

Mounce, William D. *Pastoral Epistles*. Nashville: Nelson, 2000.

Murphy-O'Connor, Jerome. *Paul: A Critical Life*. Oxford: Oxford University Press, 1996.

Rapske, Brian M. *The Book of Acts and Paul in Roman Custody*. Volume 3 of *The Book of Acts in Its First-Century Setting*. Edited by Bruce W. Winter. Exeter: Paternoster, 1994.

Schnabel, Eckhard J. *Early Christian Mission*. 2 vols. Downers Grove, IL: InterVarsity Press, 2004.

———. *Paul the Missionary: Realities, Strategies, and Methods*. Downers Grove, IL: InterVarsity Press, 2008.

Sherwin-White, Adrian Nicolas. *Roman Society and Roman Law in the New Testament*. Oxford: Clarendon, 1963. Repr. Eugene, OR: Wipf & Stock, 2004.

Tajra, Harry W. *The Trial of St. Paul: A Juridical Exegesis of the Second Half of the Acts of the Apostles*. Tübingen: Mohr Siebeck, 1989.

CHAPTER 36

PAUL'S TRAVELS AFTER ACTS

Rom 15:24; Phil 1:25; 2:24; Phlm 22; 1 Tim 1:3; 3:14; 2 Tim 1:16–17; 4:6–8,13,20; Titus 1:5; 3:12

J. Carl Laney

KEY POINTS

- There are four main theories about what happened to Paul after Acts 28.
- Paul's prison epistles and pastoral letters provide information that can be used to reconstruct a likely itinerary of Paul's life and travels after Acts 28.
- Paul's ministry after Acts 28 concluded with a second Roman imprisonment and his martyrdom in the spring of AD 68.

KEY QUESTIONS

The book of Acts concludes with these words about Paul, "And he stayed two full years in his own rented quarters and was welcoming all who came to him, preaching the kingdom of God and teaching concerning the Lord Jesus Christ with all openness, unhindered" (Acts 28:30–31). But was this really the end of the story? Did Paul ever appear before Caesar? If he did, what was the verdict? Was Paul released after his two years of house arrest? Did Paul ever realize his desire to visit Spain (Rom 15:22–23)? Did Paul later return to prison? Was he later executed?

Why would Luke, who is obviously a careful historian, end his account leaving so many questions unanswered? Perhaps Luke didn't know the end of the story. But that would be strange since Paul mentions in his final letter before his death that Luke is with him there in Rome (2 Tim 1:17; 4:11). Perhaps, as William Ramsay suggests, Luke contemplated a third book in which he would complete the account.[1] Darrell Bock suggests that Luke chose to end the book of

1. William Ramsay, *St. Paul the Traveller and Roman Citizen* (Grand Rapids: Christian Classics Library, 2000), 351.

Acts with chapter 28 because the gospel had reached "the highest levels of Rome" and the Great Commission anticipated in Luke 24 had been realized.[2] Although we don't really know what Luke had in mind as he concluded the book of Acts, he wants us to understand that the good news of the "kingdom of God" was being proclaimed (Acts 28:31). There are basically four theories concerning Paul's life after Acts 28.

MAIN THEORIES

1. Paul was tried and executed. According to this view, cited by I. Howard Marshall, Paul was brought to trial, convicted, and executed.[3] It is suggested that Paul's words to the Ephesian elders (Acts 20:25, 37–38) predicted his martyrdom and this was included in Acts to indicate what happened at the end of the two years. For reasons of vocabulary, style, uncertainty regarding their historical context and advanced church organization, it has been argued that the Pastoral Letters (1 and 2 Timothy and Titus) were not written by Paul and don't fit anywhere into the known biographical material provided in Acts, although they may contain fragments of notes that Paul had written.[4] Bart Ehrman suggests that the Pastoral Epistles were forged by second-century Christians who sought to combat the use of Paul's other writings by gnostic Christians.[5] If Paul died at the end of his Roman imprisonment then there is no life of Paul after Acts and the geographical references in the Pastoral Letters have to be squeezed into the historical narrative of Acts or ignored as merely an attempt to make these writings more credible.[6]

2. Paul was placed in a more strict confinement. With a slight variation from the first view, Harrison suggests that at the end of the two years, Paul lost his house arrest status and was placed in a more strict confinement.[7] This view is supported by the fact that Paul was still in Rome when Onesiphorus searched for and found him (2 Tim 1:17). Harrison's arguments against the Pauline authorship of the Pastoral Letters are very adequately answered by Donald Guthrie.[8] According to this understanding, Luke's goal was to report how the gospel had been proclaimed to the ends of the earth

---

2. Darrell L. Bock, *Acts* (Grand Rapids: Baker Academic, 2007), 758–59.

3. I. Howard Marshall, *The Acts of the Apostles* (Grand Rapids: Eerdmans, 1980), 426.

4. D. A. Carson, Douglas Moo, and Leon Morris, *An Introduction to the New Testament* (Grand Rapids: Zondervan, 1992), 360–66.

5. Bart D. Ehrman, *Lost Christianities: The Battles for Scripture and the Faiths We Never Knew* (New York: Oxford University Press, 2003), 240.

6. For a defense of Pauline authorship of the Pastoral Epistles, see Donald Guthrie, *The Pastoral Epistles: An Introduction and Commentary* (Grand Rapids: Eerdmans, 1957), 212–28.

7. P. N. Harrison, *The Problem of the Pastoral Epistles* (London: Oxford University Press, 1921), 127.

8. Guthrie, *Pastoral Epistles*, 212–28.

(Acts 1:8), and having accomplished that goal, he concludes the book.

3. Paul was tried and exiled. According to this view, Paul was tried, found guilty and was punished by exile, probably to Spain.[9] It is pointed out that Paul didn't die after the two years in Rome, for Luke stresses the fact that the Roman officials who had investigated Paul's case had judged that he had done nothing worthy of death (Acts 23:29; 24:26–27; 25:10–11,25; 26:31–32; 28:28); and house arrest (Acts 28:30) would not be appropriate for someone who might be deserving of the death penalty. Clement of Rome mentions Paul's many trials in a letter he wrote to the Corinthian church around AD 96 and reports that Paul "had been driven into exile ... having reached the limit of the west" (i.e., Spain; 1 Clement 5:7 [trans. Lightfoot and Harmer]; see "Jesus' Missionary Commission and the Ends of the Earth"). If it was the Roman and Jewish intent to get Paul out of the way and make him as harmless as possible, Spain would have been a reasonable place for his exile. Going to Spain was Paul's desire (Rom 15:24) and Roman officials may have viewed this as a way to rid themselves of a nuisance.

4. Paul was released and later experienced a second imprisonment. The most plausible view is that Paul was released after the two years of house arrest, engaged in a ministry throughout the Mediterranean world, and then experienced a second imprisonment that ended in his death.[10] It may be that Paul was tried and acquitted, or that the statute of limitations ran out and he was simply released for lack of any formal complaint against him by the Jews of Jerusalem. Evidence for this view is supported by Paul's anticipation of release mentioned in his prison epistles (Phil 1:25; 2:24; Phlm 22) and by early tradition indicating that he traveled to Spain (1 Clement 5:7). According to this view, Paul authored 1 and 2 Timothy and Titus during this period of ministry between his first and second imprisonments before he was martyred in Rome in the spring of AD 68. While Marshall acknowledges that the picture at the end of Acts is "ambiguous," this view has the strong support of the early church historian, Eusebius (*Ecclesiastical History* 2.22 [trans. Lightfoot and Harmer]), and is the basis of the reconstruction of Paul's travels after Acts that is presented here.[11]

POSSIBLE RECONSTRUCTION

Paul's life after his first Roman imprisonment may be reconstructed in various ways based on the available data, but a possible itinerary can be arranged in a

9. John Gunther, *Paul: Messenger and Exile: A Study of the Chronology of his Life and Letters* (Valley Forge, PA: Judson, 1972).

10. F. F. Bruce, *Apostle of the Heart Set Free* (Grand Rapids: Eerdmans, 1977), 444.

11. Marshall, *Acts of the Apostles*, 426.

logical and reasonable manner based on biblical references.[12]

Paul's Release (Acts 28:30). After two years of confinement in Rome, Paul was released. Perhaps the case came to trial and was dismissed or the statute of limitations expired.[13] Paul seems to have anticipated the possibility of his release (Phil 1:19; 2:24) and was making preparations for future travels (Phlm 22).

To Colossae (Phlm 22). Since Paul had written Philemon requesting lodging in Colossae (Phlm 22), he probably headed east after his release from house arrest in Rome. The most logical route to Colossae would have been to sail to Ephesus and then follow the Meander River to the Lycus Valley where Colossae is located. Paul would have then had the opportunity to visit Philemon and assist in reconciling him to his runaway slave, now brother in Christ, Onesimus.

To Ephesus (1 Tim 1:3). Paul may have visited Ephesus on his way to Colossae, but presumably did so on his return. At Ephesus, Paul installed Timothy as his apostolic representative to appoint elders and provide pastoral leadership for the Ephesian congregation. Timothy was instructed to "remain on" at Ephesus after Paul departed for Macedonia (1 Tim 1:3).

To Macedonia (1 Tim 1:3). After making arrangements for Timothy's leadership at Ephesus, Paul departed for Macedonia. He had plans to visit the believers at Philippi and wrote Timothy from Macedonia providing detailed instructions for his pastoral leadership in case

12. Ramsay, *St. Paul the Traveller*, 285; Robert L. Cate, *One Untimely Born: The Life and Ministry of the Apostle Paul* (Macon, GA: Mercer University Press, 2006), 129–34; Homer A. Kent, *The Pastoral Epistles: Studies in I and II Timothy and Titus* (Chicago: Moody, 1958),14–15.

13. Adrian Nicolas Sherwin-White, *Roman Society and Roman Law in the New Testament* (Oxford: Oxford University Press, 1963), 118.

Paul's return to Ephesus was delayed (1 Tim 3:14–15).

To Philippi (Phil 1:25; 2:24). When Paul wrote his letter to the Philippians from Rome, he anticipated his forthcoming release and future ministry among the Philippians (Phil 1:25). He hoped to send Timothy to the church at Philippi (Phil 1:19) and to join the believers there soon (Phil 2:24). The Philippians had a special place in Paul's heart and he would have no doubt visited them while he was in Macedonia.

To Ephesus (1 Tim 3:14). When Paul wrote Timothy from Macedonia, he wrote with the hope of returning to Ephesus soon. But he gave Timothy instructions concerning church polity and practice in case his journey was delayed (1 Tim 3:14). Paul probably returned to Ephesus after his visit with the Philippians and remained there for some time ministering to the Ephesian believers. At this point Paul's travel itinerary after Acts 28 becomes more uncertain, not because of a lack of biblical references, but because there are no direct statements by Paul about where he went next.

To Spain (Rom 15:24; 1 Clement 5:7). Paul clearly anticipated traveling to Spain (Rom 15:24). It is likely that after fulfilling his obligations to visit Colossae and Philippi as planned, he then felt free to realize his desire to minister in Spain. Clement of Rome (ca. AD 35–99) writes in his First Epistle to the Corinthians, "After he had been seven times in chains, had been driven into exile, had been stoned, and had preached in the East and in the West, he won the genuine glory for his faith, having taught righteousness to the whole world and having reached the farthest limits of the West." (1 Clement 5:7 [trans. Lightfoot and Harmer). Although debated, the "extreme limit of the west" is usually understood as a reference to the Spanish peninsula. Michael Holmes regards this as "the Straits of Gibraltar."[14] Kelly suggests that the description given by Clement as a Roman writer "could only mean Spain."[15] Another notice appears in the Muratorian Canon (AD 170), a Latin document consisting of eighty-five lines that was discovered by L. A. Muratori and published in 1740.[16] This ancient fragment contains the oldest known list of the New Testament books. Referring to the Acts of the Apostles, the fragment records, "Luke addressed them to the most excellent Theophilus, because the several events took place when he was present; and he makes this plain by the omission of the passion of Peter and of the journey of Paul when he left Rome for Spain."[17] Paul's journey to Spain was apparently accepted by the early church as a historical fact, as indicated by its mention in several homilies by John Chrysostom, an early bishop of Constantinople (*Homilies on Matthew* 75.2; *Homilies on 1 Corinthians* 13.6; *Homilies on 2 Timothy* [2 Tim. 4:20], and *Homilies on Hebrews*, Argument 2),

14. Michael W. Holmes, ed. *The Apostolic Fathers*, 2nd ed. (Grand Rapids: Baker, 1989), 31, n. 15. For further study see Otto F. A. Meinardus, "Paul's Journey to Spain: Tradition and Folklore," *Biblical Archaeologist* 41.2 (June 1978): 61–63.

15. J. N. D. Kelly, *A Commentary on the Pastoral Epistles* (New York: Harper & Row, 1963), 10.

16. Eckhard, J. Schnabel, "The Muratorian Fragment: The State of Research," *JETS* 57 (2014): 231–64.

17. Henry Bettenson, ed., *Documents of the Christian Church* (London: Oxford University Press, 1967), 28.

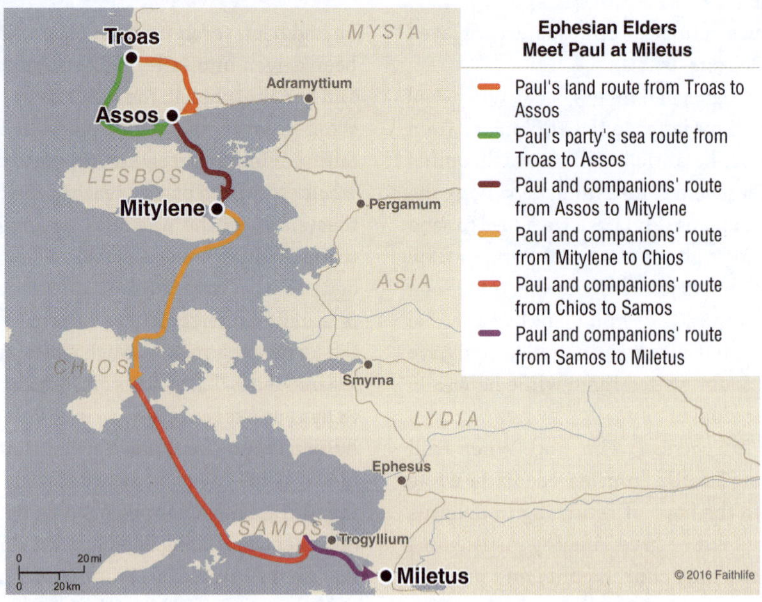

even though no reliable traces of Paul's missionary activity have been found there.[18] The location of Paul's ministry in Spain is not known, but the southern coastal region was the most thoroughly Roman region of the country in the first century.[19] Emil Kraeling suggests that "the extreme limit of the west" referred to by Clement would be the Pillars of Hercules which flank the entrance of the Strait of Gibraltar.[20] If this is so, Paul would have ministered in the region of southern Spain where there were Roman colonies and numerous Greek-speaking people.[21]

To Crete (Titus 1:5). Paul had wanted to winter on Crete during his first journey to Rome (Acts 27:9–11) and may have anticipating having a ministry there. It would have been logical for Paul to have visited Crete on his return voyage from Spain. As Cate observes, "either going to or coming from Spain" Paul made a visit to Crete.[22] After a successful ministry on the island, he departed leaving Titus to complete the follow-up work and appoint elders (Tit. 1:5) as Timothy had been instructed to do in Ephesus.

To Asia Minor (2 Tim 4:13, 20). The details of Paul's itinerary become even less certain at this point, but we do have biblical references that indicate he was in Asia Minor. He wrote Timothy that he left Trophimus sick in Miletus (2 Tim

18. George Ogg, *The Chronology of the Life of Paul* (London: Epworth, 1968; repr. Eugene, OR: Wipf & Stock, 1968), 193.

19. Gunther, *Paul*, 148.

20. Emil G. Kraeling, *Rand McNally Bible Atlas* (New York: Rand McNally, 1956), 462.

21. For other possible interpretations of "the farthest limits of the West," see "Jesus' Missionary Commission and the Ends of the Earth."

22. Cate, *One Untimely Born*, 132.

The Mamertine prison cell where, according to tradition, Paul wrote 2 Timothy shortly before his death.

4:20). Paul had stopped at the harbor city of Miletus to have a conference with the Ephesian elders toward the end of his third missionary journey (Acts 20:15–38). While revisiting the city, his traveling companion Trophimus became ill and had to be left behind as Paul journeyed on. Paul also tells Timothy of his stop at Troas, a city Paul had visited on his second (Acts 16:8, 11) and third journeys (Acts 20:5–6). There at Troas Paul left his cloak, books, and parchments. This may have been due to a quick get-away in his attempt to avoid arrest by Roman authorities.

To Greece (Titus 3:12; 2 Tim 4:20). When Paul wrote his letter to Titus to deal with matters of church order and leadership, he instructed Titus to "come to me at Nicopolis" since Paul had decided to winter there. It appears that he was on his way to Nicopolis in western Greece. Another reference to Paul's ministry in Greece appears in 2 Tim 4:20 where he tells Timothy that "Erastus remained at Corinth." This may indicate that Paul was in Corinth having visited Macedonia and Greece before his arrest and final imprisonment.

To Rome (2 Tim 1:16, 17). It appears from the biblical record that Paul was arrested a second time (2 Tim 1:8, 16, 2:9) and brought to Rome (1:17). Paul's last epistle, 2 Timothy, indicates that his situation was much different than that in Acts 28. During his second imprisonment, Paul was treated more harshly. He writes Timothy, "I suffer hardship, even to imprisonment as a criminal" (2 Tim 2:9). Brian Rapske elaborates on Paul's brief remark with his extensive research on the conditions of life in a Roman prison.[23]

23. Brian Rapske, *The Book of Acts and Paul in Roman Custody*, vol. 3 in *The Book of Acts in Its First Century Setting* (Grand Rapids: Eerdmans, 1994), 195–225,

Basilica of St. Paul Outside the Walls is the traditional location of Paul's tomb. Archaeologists have confirmed the presence of a sarcophagus beneath the altar which may contain the bones of the apostle.

Unlike his first imprisonment where he anticipated his release, now Paul anticipates his death. He writes, "the time of my departure has come. I have fought the good fight, I have finished the course" (2 Tim 4:6–7).

Between Paul's two-year house arrest (Acts 28:30) and his second imprisonment in Rome (2 Tim 1:17; 2:9) he traveled at least 2,350 miles (3782 km) according to the shortest possible itinerary and perhaps much as 2,750 miles (4425 km).[24]

According to Eusebius, Paul's martyrdom took place in the thirteenth year of Nero (AD 67), although Jerome places it a year later. Paul's death probably occurred in the spring of AD 68, for he apparently hoped that Timothy would join him before winter (2 Tim 4:21). Sulpicius Severus preserves an early Christian tradition that Paul was beheaded with a sword during the period when Nero was persecuting believers and having them killed (*Chronicle* 2.29). Eusebius confirms that Paul was beheaded with a sword and buried on the Ostian Way, just outside the gates of the city of Rome (*Ecclesiastical History,* 2.25). Paul's tomb is honored under the altar of the Basilica of St. Paul Outside the Walls in Rome. Because of Paul's life and ministry, the Christian faith would expand and flourish throughout the Roman Empire. The end of Paul's life was but a beginning.

24. Barry J. Beitzel, *The New Moody Atlas of the Bible* (Chicago: Moody, 2009), 253.

BIBLIOGRAPHY

Beitzel, Barry J. *The New Moody Atlas of the Bible*. Chicago: Moody, 2009.

Bettenson, Henry. *Documents of the Christian Church*. 2nd ed. London: Oxford University Press, 1967.

Bock, Darrell L. *Acts*. Grand Rapids: Baker Academic, 2007.

Bruce, F. F. *Paul: Apostle of the Heart Set Free*. Grand Rapids: Eerdmans, 1977.

Carson, D. A., Douglas Moo, and Leon Morris. *An Introduction to the New Testament*. Grand Rapids: Zondervan, 1992.

Cate, Robert L. *One Untimely Born: The Life and Ministry of the Apostle Paul*. Macon, GA: Mercer University Press, 2006.

Conybeare, W. J. and Howson, J. S. *The Life and Epistles of St. Paul*. Grand Rapids: Eerdmans, 1978.

Cruse, Christian Frederick. *The Ecclesiastical History of Eusebius Pamphilus*. Grand Rapids. Baker, 1955.

Ehrman, Bart D. *Lost Christianities: The Battles for Scripture and the Faiths We Never Knew*. New York: Oxford University Press, 2003.

Gunther, John. *Paul: Messenger and Exile; A Study of the Chronology of His Life and Letters*. Valley Forge, PA: Judson, 1972.

Guthrie, Donald. *The Pastoral Epistles: An Introduction and Commentary*. Grand Rapids: Eerdmans, 1957.

Harrison, P. N. *The Problem of the Pastoral Epistles*. London: Oxford University Press, 1921.

Holmes, Michael W., ed. *The Apostolic Fathers*. 2nd ed. Grand Rapids: Baker, 1989.

Kelly, J. N. D. *A Commentary on the Pastoral Epistles*. New York: Harper & Row, 1963.

Kent, Homer A. *The Pastoral Epistles: Studies in I and II Timothy and Titus*. Chicago: Moody, 1958.

Kraeling, Emil G. *Rand McNally Bible Atlas*. New York: Rand McNally, 1956.

Lightfoot, J. B. and Harmer, J. R. *The Apostolic Fathers*. Grand Rapids: Baker, 1989.

Longenecker, Bruce W., and Todd D. Still. *Thinking Through Paul: A Survey of His Life, Letters, and Theology*. Grand Rapids: Zondervan, 2014.

Marshall, I. Howard. *The Acts of the Apostles*. Grand Rapids: Eerdmans, 1980.

Meinardus, Otto F. A. "Paul's Journey to Spain: Tradition and Folklore." *Biblical Archaeologist* 41.2 (June 1978): 61–63.

Ogg, George. *The Chronology of the Life of Paul*. London: Epworh, 1968. Repr. Eugene, OR: Wipf & Stock, 2016.

Ramsay, William. *St. Paul the Traveller and Roman Citizen*. Grand Rapids: Christian Classics Library, 2000.

Rapske, Brian. *The Book of Acts and Paul in Roman Custody*. Vol. 3 in *The Book of Acts in Its First Century Setting*. Grand Rapids: Eerdmans, 1994.

Schnabel, Eckhard J. "The Muratorian Fragment: The State of Research." *JETS* 51 (2014): 231–64.

Sherwin-White, Adrian Nicolas. *Roman Society and Roman Law in the New Testament*. Oxford: Oxford University Press, 1963.

CHAPTER 37

THE SOCIAL AND GEOGRAPHICAL WORLD OF ROMAN CORINTH

Acts 18:1–18; 1 Cor 1:2; 2 Cor 1:1

David A. deSilva

KEY POINTS

- The Isthmus of Corinth, through which both east-west sea trade and north-west land travel would naturally pass, made the location ideal for a major city.
- Greek Corinth was devastated in 146 BC and lay in ruins for a century before being refounded as a Roman colony in 46 BC: Paul's Corinth is not the Corinth of Classical Greece.
- The Isthmus of Corinth was the site of the biennial Isthmian Games, one possible background for Paul's use of athletic imagery (e.g., 1 Cor 9:24–27).
- Corinth's many temples and sacred sites provide the context for Paul's call for Christians to dissociate themselves from the "many so-called gods" (1 Cor 8; 10).
- The dining facilities in the sacred precincts of the Asclepion and the *macellum* or meat market, where meat from sacrificial animals might be sold off, provide context for Paul's discussions of "meat sacrificed to idols" and eating at "the table of demons" (1 Cor 8; 10).
- Inscriptions and monuments bear witness to the culture of "boasting" in Corinth.
- Corinth's eastern port of Cenchreae was home to a Christian congregation under the patronage and direction of Phoebe, a deacon who carried Paul's letter to Rome (Rom 16:1).

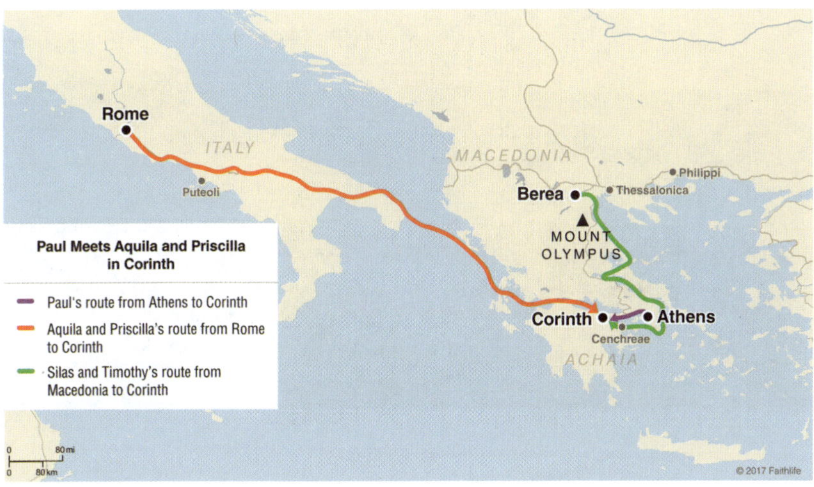

CORINTH IN THE BIBLICAL STORY

After Paul's brief time in Athens, he came to the city of Corinth, which was to become a major focus of his work as a church planter and pastor. Acts provides a rich description of Paul's initial visit to the city (Acts 18:1–18), a visit that spanned at least one and a half years (Acts 18:11), and perhaps even longer depending on how one understands the hearing before Gallio to play into Paul's timetable in Corinth (Acts 18:18). Paul would visit Corinth on at least two more occasions (2 Cor 1:15–17; 12:14; 13:1), writing no fewer than four letters to his converts there—an early letter that has not survived (1 Cor 5:9–11); 1 Corinthians; a painful letter (referred to in 2 Cor 2:1–4); and 2 Corinthians—and writing his letter to the Romans from there (Rom 15:25–28; 16:1, 23).[1] Corinth's participation in the collection for the poor in Jerusalem, an important symbol for Paul of the unity between his churches and the mother church in Jerusalem (Rom 15:25–26), suggests that Paul and his Corinthian congregations were able at last to work through the many difficulties that beset them. The extensive excavations at Corinth coupled with the extensive biblical texts about or addressed to Corinth make for particularly rich connections between the two.

1. On the history of Paul's visits to, and interventions in the congregation at, Corinth, see David A. deSilva, *An Introduction to the New Testament: Contexts, Methods and Ministry Formation* (rev. ed.; Downers Grove, IL: InterVarsity Press, 2018), 491–96, 513–14. It is highly likely that Paul wrote 1 Thessalonians from Corinth as well (1 Thess 1:7–8; Abraham J. Malherbe, *Letters to the Thessalonians: A New Translation with Introduction and Commentary* [Garden City, NY: Doubleday, 2000], 67–74).

Corinthian Canal

THE ROMAN COLONY OF CORINTH

Corinth is a city whose history displays a dramatic "before" and "after." It was a thriving Greek city with an ancient history before it came to an abrupt and violent end in 146 BC as a consequence of its role in the Achaean League's revolt against Rome's intrusion into Greece. Lucius Mummius, a Roman consul and part of the leadership of the Roman forces, allowed his soldiers to destroy old Corinth's walls and defenses, plunder its treasures, massacre its soldiery, and sell many of its women and children as slaves (Pausanias, *Description of Greece* 2.1.2; 7.16.7–10; Strabo, *Geography*, 8.6.23b). While it was not left completely uninhabited (Cicero, *Tusculanae disputationes* 3.53), it was no longer anything like a functioning city.

After laying essentially in ruins for a hundred years, it was founded afresh as a Roman colony—the Colonia Laus Julia Corinthiensis—by Julius Caesar in 46 BC (Dio Cassius, *History* 43.50.3–5). It would only have celebrated its centennial after Paul's first visit was complete. The Roman character of the new city is dramatically displayed in the fact that 101 out of 104 inscriptions found on site from the time of Julius Caesar through the time of Hadrian are written in Latin, with only the remaining three written in Greek.[2] The new colony was first settled primarily with freedpersons—former slaves who, though free, still occupied a social stratum below that of freeborn persons (Strabo, *Geography*, 8.6.23c; Crinagoras, *Greek Anthology* 9.284). As such, it was a city of opportunity for the merchant, craftsperson, and—something rare indeed in the ancient world—the social climber.

THE GEOGRAPHY OF CORINTH

The city of Corinth stands on a narrow isthmus between the Aegean and Adriatic Seas, whence Horace's epithet "twin-sea'd Corinth" (*Odes* 1.7.2). It was well placed to profit from trade between the eastern and western Mediterranean. The city was related closely to two satellite port

2. John H. Kent, *Corinth, Volume 8, Part 3: The Inscriptions 1926–1950* (Princeton: American School of Classical Studies at Athens, 1966), 19.

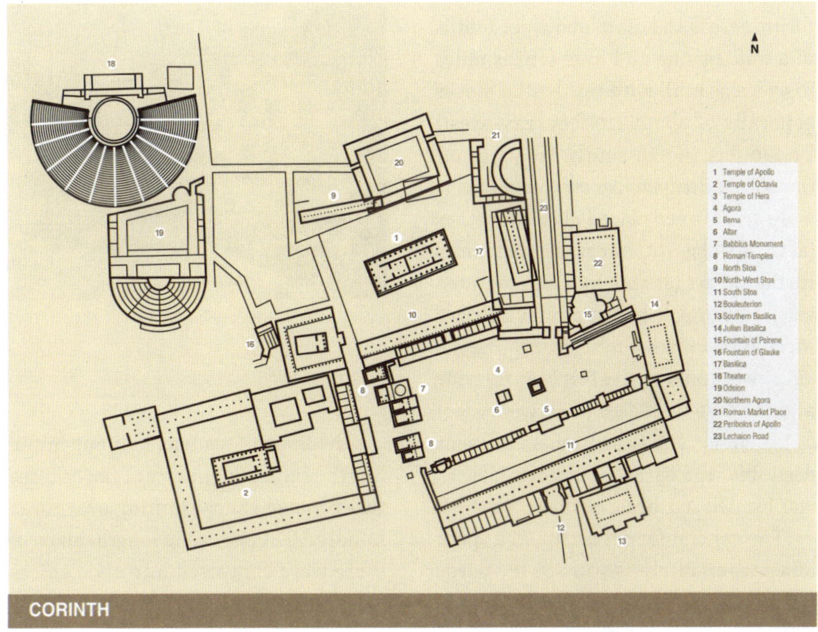

CORINTH

cities: Cenchreae to the east and Lechaion to the north. In Paul's day, ships bearing cargoes from the east unloaded in Cenchreae, sitting on the Aegean. Their goods would be transported over land to the harbor of Lechaion on the west side of the isthmus, the Adriatic, where the cargoes would be loaded onto ships heading for Italy. This facilitated trade between East and West by eliminating the long and often dangerous sea voyage around southern Greece.[3] The costs of transporting the cargoes from port to port through the city, the incidental expenses of sailors and merchants that sought Corinth's entertainments and hospitality, and especially the import and export taxes on the goods passing through all contributed to Corinth's increasing wealth (Strabo, *Geography* 8.6.20a, 22a). It was also ideally located for north-south land travel, as this same isthmus was the only land bridge between northern Greece and the entire Peloponnese. The geography all but predetermined that this would be the site of a thriving city.

The Forum and the City's Layout

The new Roman colony was laid out in a typical grid pattern around a central

3. From the sixth century BC on, smaller vessels, cargo and all, could be loaded onto special carts that would transport them to the other side of the isthmus along a special road (the δίολκος, *diolchos*) built at the narrowest point. The Emperor Nero attempted to cut a canal across the isthmus along this road in AD 67 to make trade even easier (Suetonius, *Nero* 19; Philostratus, *Life of Apollonius* 4.24; 5.19). Josephus (*J.W.* 3.540) reports that the Roman general Vespasian, who was charged with suppressing the Jewish revolt that erupted in AD 66, sent 6,000 Jewish prisoners from Galilee as slaves to labor on the project. The work proved too difficult, however, and was abandoned until modern engineering made it possible in the nineteenth century.

forum across an area of about six-tenths of a mile by one and four-tenths miles (0.97 x 2.25 km), with residential blocks generally of about 120 feet (east-west) by 240 feet (north-south) (36.5 x 73 m), though the *decumani*, or east-west streets, were sometimes placed closer together (at 120-foot [36.5 m] intervals), sometimes further apart (at 480-foot [146 m] intervals), resulting in blocks of varying sizes. Most of the north-south streets (the *cardines*) were only twelve feet (3.65 m) wide, and the east-west *decumani* twenty feet (6 m) wide.[4] The Craneum, an affluent, desirable, and park-like residential area, was located southeast of the Forum.[5]

The central forum occupied a space of approximately 15,500 square yards (13,000 m²), an uncommonly large area.[6] While many Greek cities and Roman colonies had both an administrative forum and a commercial forum, Corinth's forum appears to have served both functions. The forum itself was marked off by columned, covered porticoes on all four sides, behind many of which sat rows of shops rented by artisans and merchants of every kind or shops converted to serve administrative functions in the new colony. Today, the best-preserved strips of shops are to be found along the north side of the western half of the forum, in the far west (though these likely postdate Paul's visit), and along the south.

West Shops

The South Stoa was laid out in the fourth century BC as a row of thirty-three two-roomed shops running over three hundred feet (91.5 m) in length. Many of these were converted into civic offices when the colony was refounded, including an oval council chamber, a public fountain, an archives, and offices for the officials in charge of the Isthmian Games.[7] These Olympic-style games were held every second year and brought tourists into the isthmus in droves. They were celebrated in Corinth itself between 40 BC and AD 50 before returning to Isthmia in AD 50 or 51 (Paul's first year in Corinth!).[8] Their presence in the city's life is a reminder of the prominence of athletic competitions in Paul's world and a possible source of Paul's own use of athletic imagery (e.g., his references to running and boxing in 1 Cor 9:24, 26). It is

4. Jerome Murphy-O'Connor, *St. Paul's Corinth: Texts and Archaeology*, 3rd ed. (Collegeville, MN: Liturgical Press, 2003), 20–22. For extensive discussion, see David Gilman Romano, "City Planning, Centuriation, and Land Division in Roman Corinth," in *Corinth: The Centenary 1896–1996*, ed. Charles K. Williams II and Nancy Bookidis (Princeton: American School of Classical Studies at Athens, 2003), 279–301.

5. Plutarch, *Moralia* 601b; Murphy-O'Connor, *Corinth*, 22.

6. Murphy-O'Connor, *Corinth*, 27.

7. Christopher Mee and Antony Spawforth, *Greece: An Oxford Archaeological Guide* (Oxford: Oxford University Press, 2001), 153; Murphy-O'Connor, *Corinth*, 28.

8. Murphy-O'Connor, *Corinth*, 13.

notable that the wreath given to victors in the Isthmian games was braided from withered celery (Plutarch, *Quaestiones convivales IX.* 5.3.1–3 [*Moralia* 675d–677b]), giving poignancy to Paul's contrast between the "rotting" wreath for which athletes compete and the "imperishable" wreath with which he and his fellow converts seek to be crowned for their victory over the impulses of the flesh (1 Cor 9:25). Paul's mention of the rules governing athletic competitions and the potential for disqualifying oneself from the prize for winning would certainly resonate with spectators of the Isthmian Games (1 Cor 9:27; 2 Tim 2:5).

South Shops

The forum was split into unequal northern and southern halves by a row of shops extending into the center from the eastern side. Halfway down this row, the series of shops was interrupted by a shrine to Ephesian Artemis, whose influence had spread to mainland Greece.[9] Near the center of the forum, in line with this row, stood the rostrum (in Greek, the βῆμα, *bēma*), the public speakers' platform, which is also a likely place at which the Roman governor made public appearances. At the easternmost side of the forum stood a basilica, a large, columned hall that typically served judicial functions in Roman cities. It was adorned with statues of Augustus and his family, including his two grandsons, Caius and Lucius, who were originally slated to succeed him before their untimely deaths made Tiberius' way clear to the succession.[10]

North Market

As the city's economy grew, yet another, larger market area arose to the north of the main forum. This secondary forum consisted of forty-some permanent shops arranged around a central open space for the sale of wares and foods from portable kiosks. One row of these shops has been thoroughly excavated, revealing alcoves of a fairly standard thirteen feet (4 m) high by thirteen feet (4 m) deep, but varying between nine and thirteen feet (2.75–4 m) wide, each with a large doorway of about seven feet (2 m). They appear to have been fitted with lofts

9. Pausanias, *Description of Greece*, 2.2.6; Murphy-O'Connor, *Corinth*, 29.

10. Mee and Spawforth, *Greece*, 153; Murphy-O'Connor, *Corinth*, 28.

accessible by stone steps and wooden ladders. These lofts served as the makeshift residences for the artisans and others working in the shops below.[11]

Paul was the pioneer of "tentmaker ministries." To support himself while in Corinth, he plied his trade as a leatherworker, a main product of his being leather tents. His words to his converts in Thessalonica could equally well have been addressed to the Corinthian congregations that he would plant: "You remember our labor and toil, brothers and sisters; we worked night and day, so that we might not burden any of you while we proclaimed to you the gospel of God" (1 Thess 2:9; see 1 Cor 9:4–6, 12b, 15–18; 2 Cor 11:7–11; 12:12–13). Paul wanted to distinguish himself very clearly from the many marketplace and roadside preachers that his future converts encountered regularly at Corinth, as in any other major city, peddling one philosophy or one religion or another as a means of profiting from those who would listen to and learn from them.

Paul likely spent the majority of his waking hours in Corinth working at his trade in one of the shops recessed behind the stoas surrounding the main forum or north forum (or perhaps in another such row of shops yet to be discovered). He no doubt counted himself fortunate to have found Priscilla (or Prisca) and Aquila, fellow Jews, in Corinth, already well-established in their rented workshop, plying the same trade as his. When the emperor Claudius expelled the Jews from Rome in AD 49, Priscilla and Aquila relocated to the promising city of Corinth and set up shop shortly before Paul's arrival there (Acts 18:1–3; see map on page 465). In Priscilla and Aquila's welcome of the newcomer into their own shop, we see something of the support and partnership that pious Jews were reputed to extend to one another throughout the diaspora, treating fellow Jews as members of an extended family to which such duties were due (Philo, *De specialibus legibus* 1.52).

RELIGION IN ROMAN CORINTH

Corinth, as a typical major city of the Roman world, was home to many temples and religious sites devoted to worship of the traditional Greco-Roman gods. The majority of Corinth's inhabitants worshiped these gods. The main exception was likely the Jewish community in Corinth.

Synagōgē Ebraiōn Inscription

PAUL AND THE JEWISH COMMUNITY

According to Acts, Paul began his preaching among the Jewish community in Corinth, along with their gentile adherents (Acts 18:4–5). While Philo (*Embassy* 281) mentions Corinth as the location of a significant Jewish diaspora population, confirming the impression we get from Acts 18, there is no direct archaeological witness to the first-century synagogue that Paul frequented. The Corinth Museum, however, houses two relics of the city's late-Roman or early-Byzantine

11. Murphy-O'Connor, *Corinth*, 195.

synagogue. One of these is a section of a lintel bearing a partial inscription *[Syna]gōgē hebr[aiōn]*, "Gathering Place of the Hebrews." The inscription was carved on a stone that had a previous life as the cornice of another building and was discovered along the Lechaion Road, though it seems doubtful that the synagogue would have been located in one of the most prominent locations in the center of town.[12] The second is a capital, decorated with menorahs and palm branches, that once adorned the top of a pillar, almost certainly from the synagogue.

Capital Decorated with Menorahs and Palm Branches

Paul's preaching and arguing in the synagogue had two principal effects. First, Paul drew some serious opposition, to the point where he was no longer welcome in the synagogue. Second, Paul enjoyed some significant success. When he left the synagogue, he took with him "a man named Titius Justus, a worshiper of God" (Acts 18:7), probably a gentile God-fearer. The author of Acts tells us that Titius' "house was next door to the synagogue," which may imply that he opened his house up for Paul to continue his ministry. Paul also took with him "Crispus, the official of the synagogue," who "became a believer in the Lord, together with all his household" (Acts 18:8). Those who remained behind in the synagogue no doubt saw Paul as a competitor for the support of gentiles sympathetic to the Jewish religion as well as a source of erosion within the Jewish community itself.

At some point during Paul's first stay in Corinth, members of the Jewish community sought to get this nuisance out of the way. The author of Acts tells us that this took place when Lucius Junius Gallio held the office of proconsular governor of Achaia. A fragmentary inscription from Delphi places Gallio in Corinth during the Roman year spanning from AD 51 into 52, which incidentally becomes an extremely important linchpin for reconstructing the chronology of Paul's ministry.[13]

Gallio Inscription

As the governor's headquarters, the North Basilica located north of the east side of the forum would have been the place where Gallio would have conducted most of his business. According to Acts

12. Victor P. Furnish, *II Corinthians* (Garden City, NY: Doubleday, 1984), 21–22.

13. For text and discussion, see C. K. Barrett, *The New Testament Background: Selected Documents*, rev. ed. (New York: Harper & Row, 1987), 51–52; see also Jerome Murphy O'Connor, "Paul and Gallio," *JBL* 112 (1993): 315–17.

18:12, however, members of the Jewish community brought their accusations against Paul to Gallio at the tribunal, or "Bema," located just east of center in the forum, in line with the central shops. This structure was probably most comparable to a rostrum, a platform from which orators would address the gathered citizenry on public occasions, rather than an official site for judicial activity, which would generally have been more appropriate for the basilica. Only the foundation and part of the first level of the Bema remains, but it was originally a far more impressive two-story building from which the Roman proconsul could address the people and, it appears, occasionally dispense justice.

Bema in Corinth

Members of Corinth's Jewish community charged Paul with introducing unlawful religious customs, something that would typically fall under the jurisdiction of the secular authority. Upon further examination, Gallio ruled that this was all just an internal Jewish affair in which he would not intervene (Acts 18:12–16). The aftermath of Gallio's ruling incidentally reveals something of the marginal status that the Jewish communities of the diaspora could have. First, Gallio is remembered to have "driven them from the tribunal," not only throwing the case out of court but throwing the plaintiffs out of court as well. Second, the author of Acts relates that "then all of them seized Sosthenes, the official of the synagogue, and beat him in front of the tribunal. But Gallio paid no attention to any of these things" (Acts 18:17). Sosthenes, who appears to have succeeded the Christian convert Crispus as "official of the synagogue," becomes the victim of some mob action—we should imagine the non-Jewish residents of the city inflicting this abuse on him for clogging up the justice system with what was, in their opinion, some trifling inner-Jewish matter. Gallio's refusal to act to protect Sosthenes or initiate action against his attackers shows consummate disdain. As the suit against Paul was unsuccessful, he was able to spend "a considerable time" further in that city (Acts 18:18), nurturing the congregation that would prove to be his most difficult over time.

THE TEMPLES OF CORINTH

Paul had proclaimed the existence of only "one God" and "one Lord, Jesus Christ" (1 Cor 8:6), calling people everywhere to give them the exclusive worship that was their due (e.g., 1 Thess 1:9). But Paul was correct that his converts would have to continue to live in the midst of the many "so-called gods in heaven or on earth—as in fact there are many gods and many lords" (1 Cor 8:5). This was a major challenge for Paul's converts in Corinth, which, like every major city in the Roman world, was home to many temples and cults of the traditional gods accepted and worshiped by the vast majority of Corinth's residents.

Overshadowing all of Corinth is the rocky hill known as the Acrocorinth, which once hosted several other temples and sacred sites, similar to the Acropolis of Athens. The goddess Aphrodite had a famous temple resting on the top of the Acrocorinth (Pausanias, *Description of Greece*, 2.5.1; Strabo, *Geography*, 8.6.20c, 8.6.21b). Strabo's report of an army of temple prostitutes deployed by the goddess may represent a misunderstanding of older sources speaking of many bronze statues of women erected in the temple itself. The city and its ports, no doubt, still had a lively sex trade, but probably not more or less than other major seaport cities.[14] Nevertheless, it is noteworthy both that Old Corinth had such a reputation for sexual looseness that Aristophanes could create the verb Κορινθιάζω (*korinthiazō*) to mean "play the whore" (Frag. 354), Plato could refer to a prostitute as a "Corinthian girl" (*Republic* 404D), and comic playwrights could use the title Κορινθιαστής (*Korinthiastēs*) to name their farces about pimps (Athenaeus, *Deipnosophists* 313C, 559A), and that sexual issues are unusually prominent in the Corinthian congregation among Paul's several churches (1 Cor 5:1–2, 9–11; 6:9–11, 15–18; 7:1–2, 9).[15]

Today, there are no significant remains of Aphrodite's temple. In the Christian era, it became a quarry of raw materials for the walls and other fortifications built on the mountain. Throughout its many centuries of occupation, the Acrocorinth was supplied with water by a spring over which was built the Upper Peirene fountain, essentially a barrel-vaulted reservoir accessible by descending steps (Strabo, *Geography* 8.6.21b). Toward the bottom of the Acrocorinth, still south of the city proper, stand the remains of a sanctuary of Demeter and Persephone, goddesses related to the agricultural cycle of the land (Pausanias, *Description of Greece*, 2.4.7, who also describes sanctuaries of Isis, Serapis, Helios, Necessity, and the Mother Goddess in the vicinity).[16]

Perhaps the oldest surviving structure in Corinth is the temple of Apollo. The present temple, a sanctuary whose roof was supported by forty massive Doric columns (six at the front and back, fifteen along each long side), was built around 550 BC on an elevated plateau, the site of an earlier Apollo temple.[17] It overlooked the surrounding Roman-period shops (both the new North Market and the northern shops of the central forum), civic buildings, and porticoes, just as it had the Hellenistic- and Classical-era city of Corinth in past centuries—a physical/spatial symbol of the traditional Greco-Roman gods looking out over, and looking out *for*, the life of the city. For most of Corinth's inhabitants, this would have been a welcome reminder of the gods' sheltering presence. Southwest of the temple of Apollo (and west of the forum) stood a temple to Hera, the wife of Zeus and queen of the gods, once rising above the shops in the northwest corner of the forum. In the square north of the Hera temple and west of the Apollo temple was a public fountain, named the Fountain of Glauke after the

14. Murphy-O'Connor, *Corinth*, 56–57.

15. Greek references are cited in Murphy-O'Connor, *Corinth*, 56–57, who rightly notes, however, that these references all long predate the founding of Corinth, the Roman colony.

16. On the sanctuary of Demeter and Kore, in particular, see further, Nancy Bookidis, "The Sanctuaries of Corinth," in Williams, *Corinth*, 247–59.

17. Mee and Spawforth, *Greece*, 151.

Temple of Apollo

ill-fated princess of Corinth courted by Jason and poisoned by Medea (Pausanias, *Description of Greece*, 2.3.6).

Corinth was also home to a renowned Asclepion, a sacred precinct dedicated to Asclepius, the god of healing, that included a sleeping area where patients would seek a dream vision of the god giving instructions for a cure or miraculously effecting the cure. Votive statues of the afflicted body parts were offered by those who believed to have received healing by the god's intervention. The number and variety of these housed in the Corinth Museum bears witness to the many satisfied customers of the treatments offered in the Asclepion here. The Asclepion was also something of a health spa or country club with recreational areas and multiple dining rooms that could be used by the local elites for entertaining, with invitations sent to guests to dine "at the table of the god."[18] Indeed, social events throughout the city almost always had some such connection with the honoring of one local deity or another. Paul's converts in Corinth would have a difficult time getting along socially *and* avoiding the table of idols (or "demons," 1 Cor 10:21) in every respect at the same time. This would help explain Paul's significant investment in dealing with these challenges in 1 Corinthians 8 and 10.

Several smaller temples and cult sites stood within the forum itself. A temple of Tyche or Fortuna stood in the northwest area of the forum, south of the northwest stoa and its shops (Pausanias, *Description of Greece*, 2.2.8). A head of Tyche, the goddess of good luck, was found on site and is now housed in the Corinth Museum.

Temples of Venus (the mythic progenetrix of Julius Caesar and his line) and Apollo Clarios graced the southwest area

18. Murphy-O'Connor, *Corinth*, 189.

of the forum (Pausanias, *Description of Greece*, 2.2.8), the former at least dating from the time of Augustus.[19] As already noted, a small shrine to Ephesian Artemis interrupted the central row of shops. According to Pausanias (*Description of Greece*, 2.4.5), sanctuaries of Zeus Capitolinus and of Athena once stood in the vicinity of the theater, located some two hundred yards (183 m) northwest of the forum.

Divo Iulio Dedicatory Inscription

There were also some newer gods in Corinth. Julius Caesar, who had refounded Corinth as a Roman colony, was pronounced a god after his death by the Roman Senate. Historically the first Roman to be granted that status, many of his successors would come to be divinized as well. The cult of Julius Caesar, Augustus, and later emperors spread across the Mediterranean as an expression of loyalty and gratitude to the imperial family—and as a bid for imperial favors.[20] A temple to Divus Iulius (the Deified Julius) was located somewhere in the city, probably in the area of the forum itself. A fragment of a dedicatory inscription "To the divine Julius Caesar" as well as several pieces of what might have served as cult statues of Julius were found on site and are housed in the Corinth Museum. Given Julius' personal interest in revitalizing and resettling Corinth (a policy advanced also by his immediate successor Augustus), it is not difficult to imagine the inhabitants of "New Corinth" being quite enthusiastic promoters of imperial cult in their city. A temple was also erected to the west of the forum for the worship of Octavia, the sister of the emperor Augustus and widow of Marc Antony, who abandoned her in favor of Cleopatra VII (Pausanias, *Description of Greece*, 2.3.1). Though little remains of the temple today, its sacred precincts originally covered an area as large as those connected to the temple of Apollo. Imperial games in honor of the reigning emperor were held every fourth

Head of Tyche from Corinth Museum

19. Murphy-O'Connor, *Corinth*, 27.

20. On this phenomenon, see esp. S. R. F. Price, *Rituals and Power: The Roman Imperial Cult in Asia Minor* (Cambridge: Cambridge University Press, 1984); Lily Ross Taylor, *The Divinity of the Roman Emperor* (Middleton, CT: American Philological Association, 1931).

year in conjunction with the Isthmian Games.[21]

CHRISTIANS AND EATING FOOD SACRIFICED TO IDOLS

Jews were historically known for their avoidance of participation in the worship of any gods beside the God of Israel. Many Greeks and Romans actually considered Jews atheists on account of their denial of the reality of any god but their own. Nevertheless, they were a long-tolerated oddity in the ancient world. Paul's gentile converts, however, would have been seen quite differently: their neighbors would regard them as *betraying* the gods of their forebears and fellow-citizens for the sake of their new and quite intentionally chosen devotion to a foreign cult. It is no wonder that some of them, at least, would seek to make a case for "eating food sacrificed to idols" (1 Cor 8:1–4) so as to secure smoother relationships with their neighbors and former associates. If they could just allow themselves to be seen frequenting the temples and joining their neighbors when invited to dinner in the temples' fellowship halls, things would go much more easily for them. Paul, however, draws a sharp line: "what pagans sacrifice, they sacrifice to demons and not to God. I do not want you to be partners with demons. You cannot drink the cup of the Lord and the cup of demons. You cannot partake of the table of the Lord and the table of demons" (1 Cor 10:20–21). Christians cannot compromise their witness to their neighbors that there is indeed only *one* God and *one* Lord.

However, Paul would give them some latitude when it came to buying meat from the marketplace. Corinth had its central meat market, called a *macellum*, in the northeast quarter of the downtown area. This area was approached from the northeast quadrant of the forum through a monumental gateway that opened onto the main road leading to the port of Lechaion, one and a half miles (2.4 km) to the north. Perhaps still a gravel path at the time of Paul's visit, it would soon become a marvelous paved road surrounded by colonnades and covered sidewalks on either side.[22] Walking north through the gate, one first passed by the fountain of Peirene, an important public water source in Paul's time, on the right. The spring-fed reservoir could be accessed through the six archways at the southern side. Its large courtyard was a likely place for pleasant loitering.

Further north sat the *macellum*. By the time Pausanias visited Corinth in the second century, this area had been converted into an enclosed building that might have functioned as a shrine to Apollo (Pausanias, *Description of Greece*, 2.3.3). Some portion of the meat sold here came from animal sacrifices that had been performed in the city's temples. This was an important regular source of revenue for those temples and, in peak holy seasons, one of the few times that meat would be more generally affordable. In 1 Corinthians 10:25 when Paul told his converts to "eat whatever is sold in the meat market without raising any question on the ground of conscience," he was likely referring to this well-known space. Paul claimed that the meat itself was not in any way contaminated by virtue of having come from a

21. Murphy-O'Connor, *Corinth*, 14.

22. Mee and Spawforth, *Greece*, 154; Murphy-O'Connor, *Corinth*, 29.

Fountain of Peirene

pagan sacrifice—though if eating such meat would contaminate the conscience of one's more scrupulous fellow-Christian, Paul did command the more liberal Christians to abstain.

North of the *macellum* stood a bathhouse consisting at least of a *frigidarium* and *tepidarium* at the time of Augustus (the *caldarium*, or sauna, was either renovated or first added in renovations in the mid-first century). Of the bathhouses discovered to date (at least eleven!), this is the only one that dates back to the time of Paul's visit, though it is likely that a Roman city of this size had several at that time.[23]

THE CULTURE OF BOASTING

Because Corinth was a truly new city with no indigenous, landed elite, the military veterans and former slaves ("freedmen" or "freedpersons") that had been settled here by Julius and Augustus had the possibility of significant upward mobility in the midst of a world where such social climbing was strikingly rare. They could become, within a few generations, the local elites, holding civic offices, gaining wealth through trade and business, and establishing a reputation that would have been impossible in many older, established cities. Making a name for oneself—what Paul tends to refer to as "boasting"—was not *just* a "Corinthian thing," but self-promotion was uncommonly at home in Corinth.

Thus, for example, as Corinth grew, its citizens took on more public works and gained public recognition. When one citizen, named Erastus was elected to the office of aedile, the office entrusted with overseeing public buildings and festivals, he showed his appreciation by paving an

23. See discussion in Jane Biers, "*Lavari est Vivere*: Baths in Roman Corinth," in Williams, *Corinth: The Centennary*, 303–19, esp. 305–6.

Erastus Inscription

area northwest of the theater complex. An inscription on the site still provides perpetual testimony to his gift, his name, and his achievement of a high, local public office: *ERASTVS PRO AEDILITATE S.P. STRAVIT*, "Erastus paved this with his own money for the aedileship."[24] This may have been the same Erastus mentioned in Romans 16:23 who served as Corinth's city treasurer (its οἰκονόμος [*oikonomos*], or "city steward"), and who had become part of the Christian congregation in Corinth.

The Babbius monument also exemplifies the self-promoting and self-congratulatory spirit of first-century AD Roman Corinth.[25] Gnaeus Babbius Philenus was a freedman—a former slave—who rose to the offices of aedile, local priest, and *duovir*, one of the city's two chief magistrates. He authorized the construction of this monument to himself as a testimony to his name, success, and benefactions to the city. The monument originally consisted of eight columns arranged in a circle, each bearing an ornate Corinthian capital, all together supporting a cone-shaped roof.

The same spirit of boasting, claiming honor, and calling for recognition would invade the Christian congregations in Corinth. But while boasting was at home in Corinth, Paul was adamant that *competitive* boasting was *not* to be at home in the church (1 Cor 1:31; 4:7; with thick irony, 2 Cor 11:12–12:10). What counted for him was Christ alive in a believer; all that the believer did ought to point to Christ, his character, and his power (which, Paul says, is often most apparent where we have least to boast about; 2 Cor 12:7–10).

THE PORTS OF CORINTH: LECHAION AND CENCHREAE

Each of Corinth's two seaports developed into a small city of its own right (see map on page 182). These ports were named after the two sons born to Poseidon (the god of the sea) and the nymph Peirene. As two of the principal natural water sources of the city of Corinth (the one located atop the Acrocorinth, the other north of the forum) were named after Peirene, it was perhaps natural to name the ports after her children, Leches and

24. S.P. = *suā pecuniā*, "with his own funds."

25. Mee and Spawforth, *Greece*, 151; Kent, *Corinth*, 73.

Road to Lechaion

Cenchrias (Pausanias, *Description of Greece*, 2.2.3).

Lechaion sits one and a half miles (2.4 km) north of Corinth. This was a major harbor installation, outclassed only by Ostia, the principal port of Rome, and Caesarea Maritima, the principal port of Herod's Judea.[26] Two outer harbors were formed by the creation of three large breakwaters, or moles, extending out into the sea. An inner harbor of approximately one hundred thousand square yards (83,613 m²), approached through the eastern outer harbor, was created by massive dredging operations. Temples to Poseidon and Aphrodite once stood in the region of the harbor (Pausanias, *Description of Greece*, 2.2.3).

A road on the south side of Corinth's forum branched off to the east and led to Cenchreae, six miles (9.7 km) distant. The harbor of Cenchreae was created by building two large breakwaters around a natural inlet—a mole on the south side reaching over 100 yards (91.5 m) into the sea to the west, and a mole on the north side reaching down almost 100 yards (91.5 m) to the south. These formed a large, horseshoe-shaped harbor of approximately thirty thousand square yards (25,084 m²) with a wide mouth facing the southeast.[27] Though considerably smaller than Lechaion's harbors, Cenchreae was still sufficient for the high volume of traf-

Cenchreae Harbor, View to North Mole

26. Murphy-O'Connor, *Corinth*, 16.
27. Murphy-O'Connor, *Corinth*, 19.

Interior of Roman Tomb

fic coming to and from Corinth on the Aegean. The entirety of both moles is now submerged.

A bronze statue of Poseidon and a temple to Aphrodite once graced the north mole (Pausanias, *Description of Greece* 2.2.3). Excavations to the north and northwest of the north mole have uncovered residential buildings, small industrial complexes, and a large number of Roman-period underground tombs reminiscent of Macedonian tombs. These were carved into the subterranean rock like apertures into the underworld and opened into large, somewhat rectangular chambers with two levels of niches. Bodies would be laid out to decompose in the larger niches on the lower level; smaller niches on the upper level held ossuaries containing the collected bones of the deceased.

Excavations around the edge of the harbor itself yielded signs of commercial buildings and piers. The remains of the south mole are dominated by a fourth-century Christian church, a testimony to the eventual triumph of the work of Paul and Phoebe in this port city. The outline of the main apse is clearly visible, flanked on the north by what appears to have been a rectangular hall and on the south by a columned portico. This church was built over the remains of a warehouse complex from the Roman period, the first of several such complexes extending out onto the now-submerged south mole. Further out, underwater archaeologists discovered the remains of a complex of fish pools for storing live catches for sale or processing.

A shrine to Asclepius and a temple of Isis stood on the south mole (Pausanias, *Description of Greece* 2.2.3). While the former has not yet been discovered, the mostly submerged foundations of a rounded hall have been identified as part of Isis' temple, partially overbuilt by the fourth-century Christian church complex.[28] Isis was an Egyptian goddess who became a popular object of veneration throughout the eastern Mediterranean during the Hellenistic and Roman periods. She was celebrated as a divine protector whose power could extend life beyond that which the Fates had allotted and offer a blessed afterlife as well. Hers was also a cult in which women could distinguish themselves as priestesses. An annual festival that opened the sailing season in Cenchreae each spring appears to have involved the launching of a new ship laden with offerings to Isis as a kind of first fruits for the profitable season to come (Apuleius, *Metamorphoses* 11.16).

Statue of Isis

Paul, along with Priscilla and Aquila, would leave Corinth for new mission fields by way of Cenchreae (Acts 18:18). The harbor city also became home to a Christian congregation that met in the house of a woman named Phoebe, whom Paul commends in Rom 16:1 as a benefactor and deacon of the congregation there. It was to Phoebe that Paul entrusted the delivery of the letter that contained his most mature theological expression of his gospel, the Letter to the Romans. It was in this context of commerce and cult, profit and paganism, that Phoebe dedicated herself to the support and nurture of a new faith that would come to supplant these older rites.

BIBLIOGRAPHY

Barrett, C. K. *The New Testament Background: Selected Documents*. Rev. ed. New York: Harper & Row, 1987.

Biers, Jane. "*Lavari est Vivere*: Baths in Roman Corinth." Pages 303–19 in *Corinth: The Centenary 1896–1996*. Edited by Charles K. Williams II and Nancy Bookidis. Princeton: American School of Classical Studies at Athens, 2003.

Bookidis, Nancy. "The Sanctuaries of Corinth." Pages 247–59 in *Corinth: The Centenary 1896–1996*. Edited by Charles K. Williams II and Nancy Bookidis. Princeton: American School of Classical Studies at Athens, 2003.

Cadbury, H. J. "The Macellum of Corinth." *JBL* 53 (1934): 134–41.

deSilva, David A. *An Introduction to the New Testament: Contexts, Methods and*

28. For a literary recreation of the activity of the cult of Isis in Cenchreae, see Apuleius, *Metamorphoses*, Book 11.

Ministry Formation. Rev. ed. Downers Grove, IL: InterVarsity Press, 2018.

Furnish, Victor P. *II Corinthians*. Garden City, NY: Doubleday, 1984.

Gill, David W. "Erastus the Aedile." *TynBul* 40 (1989): 293–301.

Harrison, James R., and L. L. Welborn, eds. *The First Urban Churches 2: Roman Corinth*. Atlanta: SBL Press, 2016.

Kent, John H. *Corinth, Volume 8, Part 3: The Inscriptions 1926–1950*. Princeton: American School of Classical Studies at Athens, 1966.

Malherbe, Abraham J. *The Letters to the Thessalonians: A New Translation with Introduction and Commentary*. Garden City, NY: Doubleday, 2000.

Mee, Christopher, and Antony Spawforth. Pages 149–59, 163–67 in *Greece: An Oxford Archaeological Guide*. Oxford: Oxford University Press, 2001.

Murphy-O'Connor, Jerome. "Paul and Gallio." JBL 112 (1993): 315–17.

———. *St. Paul's Corinth: Texts and Archaeology*. 3rd ed. Collegeville, MN: Liturgical Press, 2003.

Papahatzis, Nikos. *Ancient Corinth: An Illustrated Guide*. Athens: Ekdotike Athenon, 1971.

Pettegrew, David. *The Isthmus of Corinth: Crossroads of the Mediterranean World*. Ann Arbor: University of Michigan Press, 2016.

Price, S. R. F. *Rituals and Power: The Roman Imperial Cult in Asia Minor*. Cambridge: Cambridge University Press, 1984.

Romano, David Gilman. "City Planning, Centuriation, and Land Division in Roman Corinth." Pages 279–301 in *Corinth: The Centenary 1896–1996*. Edited by Charles K. Williams II and Nancy Bookidis. Princeton: American School of Classical Studies at Athens, 2003.

Sanders, Guy D. R., Jennifer Palinkas, Ioulia Tzonou-Herbst, and James Herbst. *Ancient Corinth: A Guide to the Site and Museum*. Athens: American School of Classical Studies at Athens, 2018.

Taylor, Lily Ross. *The Divinity of the Roman Emperor*. Middleton, CT: American Philological Association, 1931.

Williams, Charles K. II, and Nancy Bookidis, eds. *Corinth: The Centenary 1896–1996*. Princeton: American School of Classical Studies at Athens, 2003.

CHAPTER 38

THE GEOGRAPHY OF GALATIA

Gal 1:2; Act 18:23; 1 Cor 16:1

Mark Wilson

KEY POINTS

- Galatia is both a region and a province in central Asia Minor.
- The main cities of north Galatia were settled by the Gauls in the third century BC.
- The main cities of south Galatia were founded by the Greeks starting in the third century BC.
- Galatia became a Roman province in 25 BC, and the Romans established colonies in many of its cities.
- Pamphylia was part of Galatia in Paul's day, so Perga and Attalia were cities in south Galatia.

GALATIA AS A REGION

Galatia is located in a basin in north-central Asia Minor that is largely flat and treeless. Within it are the headwaters of the Sangarius River (modern Sakarya) and the middle course of the Halys River (modern Kızılırmak). The capital of the Hittite Empire—Hattusha (modern Boğazköy)—was in eastern Galatia near the later site of Tavium. The name Galatia derives from the twenty thousand Gauls and their families who migrated from Thrace in 278 BC. They had been invited by Nicomedes I of Bithynia to serve as mercenaries in his army. The Galatians were notorious for their destructive forays, and in 241 BC the Pergamenes led by Attalus I defeated them at the battle of the Caicus. The statue of the dying Gaul, one of antiquity's most noted works of art, commemorates that victory.[1] The three Galatian tribes settled in

1. For the motif of dying Gauls, see Brigitte Kahl, *Galatians Re-imagined: Reading with the Eyes of the Vanquished* (Minneapolis: Fortress, 2010), 77–127. For a Roman copy of the original

these cities in Galatia: the Tolistobogii at Pessinus, the Tectosages at Ancyra, and the Trocmi at Tavium (Livy, *History* 38.16.10–12). The Romans became active in Galatia in the second century BC, and in 65 BC Pompey defeated the Pontic king Mithradates VI Eupator, thereby removing his hegemony over the region. A council and tetrarchs ruled until 63 BC when Deiotarus killed his fellow tribal kings and assumed the sole monarchy. Other leaders followed until Rome took direct control of the region in 25 BC after the death of the Galatian king Amyntas (reigned 36–25 BC).[2]

MAIN CITIES IN NORTH GALATIA[3]

Pessinus (modern Ballıhisar) was situated in western Galatia on the west side of sacred Mount Dindymus. In the third century BC the Tolistobogii, the westernmost Galatian tribe, made Pessinus their capital. The city was famous for its shrine of the Phrygian mother goddess Cybele. According to Diodorus Siculus the Phrygian king Midas founded the temple in the eighth century BC (3.59.8). Its priests called Galli were notorious for being eunuchs; however, castration for Romans was forbidden by the Roman Senate and later outlawed by Domitian (Suetonius, *Life of Domitian* 7.1).[4] Cybele's

statue from Pergamum, see the website of the Musei Capitolini in Rome, "Statue of 'Capitoline Gaul,'" http://www.museicapitolini.org/en/collezioni/percorsi_per_sale/palazzo_nuovo/sala_del_gladiatore/statua_del_galata_capitolino.

2. A detailed discussion of Galatia's geography and history can be found in Stephen Mitchell, *Anatolia: Lands, Men, and Gods in Asia Minor* (Oxford: Oxford University Press, 1992), 1:13–58.

3. For a more detailed discussion of these cities, see chapter 46, "Peter's Communities in Asia Minor."

4. This practice has been cited as a background for Paul's comment that those agitating the Galatians should castrate themselves (Gal 5:12); see Susan M. Elliott, *Cutting Too Close for*

cult stone was believed to have fallen from heaven (compare the Ephesian Artemis, Acts 19:35). In 204 BC the Romans brought the black meteorite stone to Rome as a talisman in their fight against Hannibal (Livy, *History* 29.10.4–29.11.9). In 191 BC it was installed in a temple erected on the Palatine Hill to honor the Great Mother (Magna Mater).

Ancyra (modern Ankara) was founded, according to one myth, by the Phrygian king Midas. Situated on a rocky acropolis, it was at the junction of seven key routes. Ancyra became the second metropolis of Phrygia after Gordium. Around 265 BC the Galatian tribe, Tectosages, made Ancyra its capital after receiving the site from the Pontic kingdom.

Tavium (modern Büyüknefes) and its two mounds show continuous occupation since prehistoric times. Around 232 BC the Trocmi, the easternmost Galatian tribe, made it their primary settlement. Tavium sat at an important junction of four highways with an orientation toward Cappadocia and the Euphrates River Basin.

GALATIA AS A ROMAN PROVINCE

In 25 BC a hostile Pisidian tribe killed Rome's client king Amyntas, and Augustus then annexed the province of Galatia (Dio Cassius 53.26.3). He made Ancyra its capital. The new province included not only geographic Galatia but also Pisidia, eastern Phrygia, Lycaonia, Isauria, and Pamphylia. In 6 BC Paphlagonia and in 3/2 BC Pontus Galaticus were also added. Around 22–21 BC Galatia's three northern cities became Roman colonies: Ancyra—Sebasteni Tectosages Ancyrani; Pessinus—Sebasteni Tolistobogii Pessinuntii; and Tavium—Sebasteni Trocmi Taviani. An imperial cult temple for Augustus was started between 10 BC–AD 10 and completed around AD 19/20 by Tiberius. Perhaps the most famous Roman inscription from antiquity—called the "Queen of Inscriptions"—is found on its walls: the bilingual (Greek and Latin) *Monumentum Ancyranum*, or *Res Gestae Divi Augusti* ("Deeds of the Deified Augustus"). Before his death on August 19, AD 14, Augustus composed an account of his personal achievements during his reign. While the original bronze tablets upon which it was engraved in Rome are lost, it is preserved almost in its entirety on the Ancyra tem-

Portion of the *Res Gestae Divi Augusti* from Ancyra

Comfort: Paul's Letter to the Galatians in its Anatolian Cultic Context (London: T&T Clark, 2003), 158–257.

ple.[5] At the Roman colony of Pisidian Antioch (modern Yalvaç) fragments of the Latin text were found at the entrance of the Augustus temple built in the early first century AD, while fragments of the Greek version were discovered in Apollonia (modern Uluborlu).[6] On the temple's southern wall another Greek inscription lists twenty high priests of the Galatian assembly (*κοινόν*, *koinon*) who served during the reign of Tiberius. Further imperial cult activity is evident in Pessinus where a Corinthian imperial cult temple (Sebasteion) was built during the reign of Tiberius (approximately AD 25–35). Tavium hosted games related to the imperial cult that were sponsored by the provincial assembly (*koinon*).

BIBLICAL CITIES IN THE PROVINCE

To contain the hostile Homanadenses in their strongholds in the Taurus Mountains, Augustus founded thirteen colonies with military veterans after 25 BC including Pisidian Antioch and Lystra. In 6 BC he built the *Via Sebaste* from Perga to connect these colonies. Pisidian Antioch was its *caput viae* (roadhead) because it was the apex of the Pisidian triangle.[7] Pacification of southern Galatia was completed by AD 6 by Quirinius (Tacitus, *Annales* 3.48),[8] and the strategic value of a remote site like Lystra began to decrease.

Pisidian Antioch[9] (modern Yalvaç) was one of sixteen cities founded by the Seleucid ruler Antiochus I. It is situated on a plateau in the foothills of the Sultan Mountain range (Sultandağı). The Anthius River (Yalvaç Çay) flows below the acropolis' eastern face. Called Colonia Caesarea Antiochia, it was settled by approximately three thousand veterans of Legions V Gallica and VII and their families, suggesting a total population of around ten thousand. The city was strategically located on the common, or southern, highway that ran from the Cilician Gates to Ephesus. The *Via Sebaste* provided a link to the Mediterranean coast at Pamphylia.

Iconium (modern Konya) was founded as a Phrygian settlement on the western edge of a vast fertile plain. The city became a Roman colony under Augustus; however, the Greek polis was allowed to exist alongside the colony until the time of Hadrian (approximately AD 135) when the Roman colony absorbed the polis. Around AD 41/42 during Claudius' reign the city received the honorific title Claudiconium. Iconium was a major transportation node in south-central Galatia with six roads branching in every direction to major cities.

---

5. See page 707 for an image of a replica with part of the inscription. Alison E. Cooley, *Res Gestae Divi Augusti: Text, Translation, and Commentary* (Oxford: Oxford University Press, 2009), 1–13.

6. Cooley, *Res Gestae Divi Augusti*, 13–18.

7. Barbara Levick, *Roman Colonies in Southern Asia Minor* (Oxford: Clarendon, 1967), 29–55.

8. This is the same Quirinius mentioned in Luke 2:2; see D. S. Potter, "Quirinius," *ABD* 5:589.

9. The site was situated in Phrygia and not Pisidia, therefore it is incorrect to say "Antioch in Pisidia" or "Antioch of Pisidia"; Phrygian Antioch is geographically correct. Strabo identifies it as the Antioch "toward [*πρός*, *pros*] Pisidia" (*Geography* 12.8.14). Luke uses the adjectival form in Acts 13:14 to distinguish it from the other Antioch (Syrian) in his narrative.

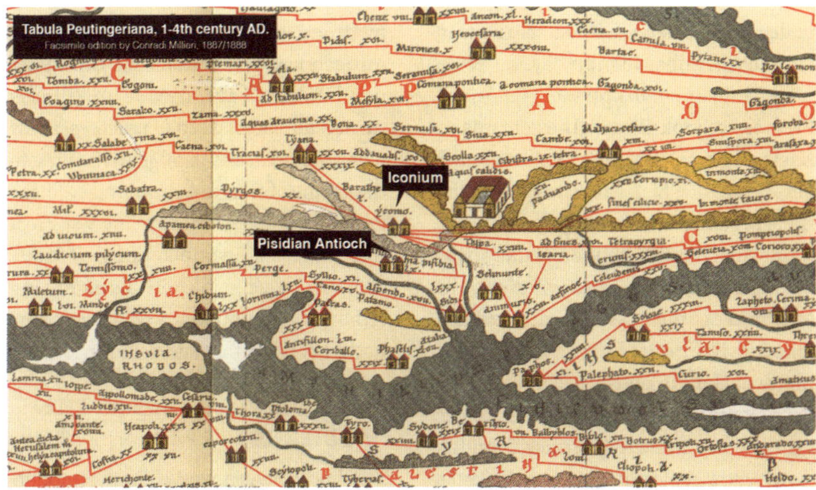

Peutinger Map: Location of Iconium. Note the six roads branching out from the city.

Lystra was twenty-one miles (34 km) southwest of Iconium in the hill country of Lycaonia. It was located on a small rise in a fertile river valley. The initial settlement consisted of approximately one thousand retirees from two Roman legions; the colony's estimated size including women and children was approximately three thousand. Its full name was Colonia Iulia Gemina Felix Lystra. The colonists intermarried with locals as the mixed parentage of Timothy, whose home was Lystra, testifies (Acts 16:1).

Derbe (modern Ekinözü) was a border town in eastern Lycaonia southeast of Mount Boratinon (modern Karadağ). In 36 BC Amyntas defeated Antipater and added Derbe to his realm. Upon the death of this client king in 25 BC, Derbe became part of the province of Galatia. Around AD 41/42 during Claudius' reign the city received the honorific title Claudioderbe. It was located on a branch road that ran southeastward to the Cilician Gates. Laranda was the major town in the region fourteen miles (22 km) to the southwest. In AD 70 the province's boundaries were radically changed by Vespasian, and for military reasons Galatia was then joined to Cappadocia to form a new double province.[10]

North Galatians as the Audience for Paul's Letter

Patristic interpreters understood the audience for Galatians as located in north Galatia. Regarding the provincial reorganization in AD 297, F. F. Bruce writes:

> The province of Galatia was thus reduced to North Galatia, and when the church fathers, in their study of our epistle, read of "the church of Galatia", they

10. Mustafa Adak and Mark Wilson, "Das Vespasiansmonument von Döşeme und die Gründung der Doppelprovenz Lycia et Pamphylia," *Gephrya* 9 (2012): 17–21.

understood "Galatia" without more ado in the sense familiar in their day.[11]

Jerome (*Commentary on Galatians*, Preface to Book II) saw the schisms in Ancyra of his day as counterparts to the heresies with which Paul struggled in the same region.

In his commentary on Galatians, J. B. Lightfoot localized the audience at Ancyra, Pessinus, Tavium, and perhaps Juliopolis. He posited a brief visit by Paul in north Galatia on the second journey to recuperate from illness, then a longer visit while traveling to Ephesus on his third journey. Lightfoot viewed Paul's letter as written on the third journey probably from Ephesus.[12]

For the second journey Robert Jewett projected a route from Iconium running north of the Sultan Mountains to Philomelium rather than south through Pisidian Antioch, for they were "prevented from traveling on the main highway west into Asia." At Philomelium they turned into north Galatia visiting Pessinus, Germa, and Ancyra where they "apparently missionized for a considerable period of time while being detained by illness (Gal. 4:13–14)."[13]

Jerome Murphy-O'Connor holds a modified view, accepting that Pisidian Antioch was revisited on the third journey but that Paul, because of illness, turned northeastward to reach Pessinus where he preached to pilgrims coming to the shrine of Cybele.[14] In summary, those holding the north Galatian view suggest that Paul made an unplanned visit to one or more cities in north Galatia during either his second or third journey (or both) probably for reason of illness.

SOUTH GALATIANS AS THE AUDIENCE FOR PAUL'S LETTER

The book of Acts shows Paul establishing and visiting churches only in south Galatia (Acts 13:14–14:23; 16:1–4). During these journeys he passed through several regions in the province: Pisidia (Acts 14:24), Lycaonia (Acts 14:6, 11), and Phrygia (16:6; 18:23). Ramsay initially favored a north Galatian perspective because of the influence of German scholarship. However, as he began to travel and conduct fieldwork in Asia Minor, especially in the cities visited by Paul on his first journey, he became an ardent advocate of the south Galatian view.[15] Many other scholars have come to agree with Ramsay that Paul vis-

11. F. F. Bruce, *The Epistle to the Galatians: A Commentary on the Greek Text* (Grand Rapids: Eerdmans, 1982), 6.

12. J. B. Lightfoot, *Epistle to the Galatians*, rev. ed. (Andover: Draper, 1870), 27–32. He concedes interestingly: "It is strange that while we have more or less acquaintance with all the other important Churches of St. Paul's founding,—with Corinth and Ephesus, with Philippi and Thessalonica,—not a single name of a person or place, scarcely a single incident of any kind, connected with the apostle's preaching in Galatia should be preserved either in the history or the Epistle" (p. 28).

13. Robert Jewett, "Mapping the Route of Paul's 'Second Missionary Journey' from Dorylaeum to Troas," *TynBul* 48 (1997): 5; Jewett, *Dating Paul's Life* (London: SCM, 1979), 59–60.

14. Jerome Murphy-O'Connor, *Paul: A Critical Life* (Oxford: Oxford University Press, 1997), 161–62; 191–93; for a map see 187 fig. 4.

15. William M. Ramsay, *A Historical Commentary on St. Paul's Epistle to the Galatians* (New York: Putnam, 1900), 1–11; then passim.

ited only the cities of south Galatia.[16] The cities of ethnic north Galatia were reached with the gospel, not by Paul but by Peter and his coworkers. Galatians is often dated as Paul's first letter written from Antioch after his first journey but before the Jerusalem council.[17] However, not all who hold a south Galatian perspective ascribe to its early dating. Keener is one who holds that Galatians was written after the council in Jerusalem.[18]

Several references in Galatians suggest a possible scenario for its composition. After returning to Antioch, Paul and Barnabas announced the results of their preaching mission among the south Galatian cities (Acts 14:27). Later Paul received "news of people who had visited his Galatian mission-field and were persuading his converts there to accept a different form of teaching from that which he had given them."[19] These troublemakers (Gal 1:7; compare 5:10) and agitators (Gal 5:12) knew which cities to visit because of Paul's report in Antioch. That the Galatians had so quickly deserted (ταχέως μετατίθεσθε, *tacheōs metatithesthe*; Gal 1:6; compare 2 Thess 2:2) suggests that only a brief time had passed since his visit.[20] Hans Dieter Betz aptly notes that Paul's use of *tacheōs* "would make little sense, to be sure, if a considerable length of time had passed since the founding of the church" and that the "time reference seems to be the founding of the churches." Paul probably learned about the visit of his opponents from a representative of the Galatian churches who had traveled to Antioch (see 1 Cor 1:11; 16:17). These agitators thus replayed Paul's first missionary journey to preach a "different gospel" to the same churches.

Recent inscription finds have added a new wrinkle to the discussion. A commonly held view has been that Claudius made Lycia and Pamphylia a joint province in AD 43, so Paul's entry to Perga (Acts 13:13) and exit from Attalia (Acts 14:25–26) were from the province of Pamphylia. Boundary lines reflecting this provincial configuration are found in all classical and Bible atlases. Two inscriptions found in Perga suggest otherwise. Burrus and Praesens are named as governors of the joint province *Galaticae et Pamphyliae*. They governed in the late 40s to early 50s, the same time that Paul was evangelizing the area.[21] Pamphylia was therefore part of Galatia during this period. Paul returned to Perga to evangelize at the end of the first journey, and his efforts probably resulted in a church being planted there (Acts 14:25). These believers in south Galatia were probably also part of the audience for his letter. This revised provincial alignment sug-

16. See, for example, Bruce, *Galatians*, 8–18; Ben Witherington III, *Grace in Galatia: A Commentary on St. Paul's Letter to the Galatians* (Grand Rapids: Eerdmans, 1998), 2–6.

17. For example, Richard N. Longenecker, *Galatians* (Dallas: Word, 1990), lxxxviii.

18. Craig Keener, *Acts: An Exegetical Commentary* (Grand Rapids: Baker Academic, 2013), 2:2116.

19. Bruce, *Galatians*, 19.

20. Hans Dieter Betz, *Galatians: A Commentary on Paul's Letter to the Churches in Galatia* (Philadelphia: Fortress, 1988), 47–48.

21. For a discussion of these and other inscriptions that reflect Lycia as a separate province, see Mark Wilson "The Denouement of Claudian Pamphylia-Lycia and its Implications for the Audience of Galatians," *NovT* 60 (2018): 5–7.

Galaticae et Pamphyliae
Inscription from Perga

gests that a new geographical nomenclature is required for ongoing discussion. Pisidian Antioch, Iconium, Lystra, and Derbe were actually middle Galatian churches with Perga and possibly Attalia the true south Galatian churches.[22]

NORTH VERSUS SOUTH GALATIA

Although visits to north Galatia are not recorded in Acts, textual support is sometimes garnered from the translations of Acts 16:6 and 18:23 pointing to a geographic rather than a provincial sense. Luke's language is enigmatic: *tēn Phrygian kai Galatikēn chōran* (τὴν Φρυγίαν καὶ Γαλατικὴν χώραν, Acts 16:6) and *tēn Galatikēn chōran kai Phrygian* (τὴν Γαλατικὴν χώραν καὶ Φρυγίαν, Acts 18:23). Translators understand an adjectival form such as "Galatian region" or "Galatian area," so English versions commonly translate the two phrases as "the region of Phrygia and Galatia" and "the region of Galatia and Phrygia."[23] However, Asterius, bishop of Amasia (died AD 410), was an early commentator who understood these texts to mean that Phrygia was a region and that Galatia was not used by Paul in a geographic sense (*Homily* 8). Recently discovered Greek and Latin inscriptions sustain Luke's use of the Greek *Galatikē* (Γάλατική) and the Latin *Galatica* for the province of Galatia. These are linked with the synonymous terms *eparcheia* (ἐπαρχεία) and *prōvincia* in each of these inscriptions. According to Adak and Wilson, Luke has in mind "obviously the entire greater province of Galatia with all its landscapes united in this administrative unit."[24] So a preferred translation for 16:6 is "the Phrygian region of the province Galatia" and for 18:23 "the territory of the province Galatia and its Phrygian region."[25] As Mitchell observes, "It is hardly con-

22. Wilson, "Denouement of Claudian Pamphylia-Lycia," 17–23.

23. The lexicon BDAG (s.v., Γαλατικός) also suggests such a meaning: "Here probl. the district, not the Rom. Province, is meant."

24. Adak and Wilson, "Das Vespasiansmonument von Döşeme," 9. Original German: "offensichtlich die gesamte Großprovinz Galatien mit allen in dieser Verwaltungseinheit vereinigten Landschaften."

25. William M. Ramsay, *The Cities of St. Paul* (London: Hodder & Stoughton, 1907), 194; compare Glen L. Thompson and Mark Wilson, "The Route of Paul's Second Journey in Asia Minor: In the Steps of Robert Jewett and Beyond," *TynBul* 67 (2016): 223–24.

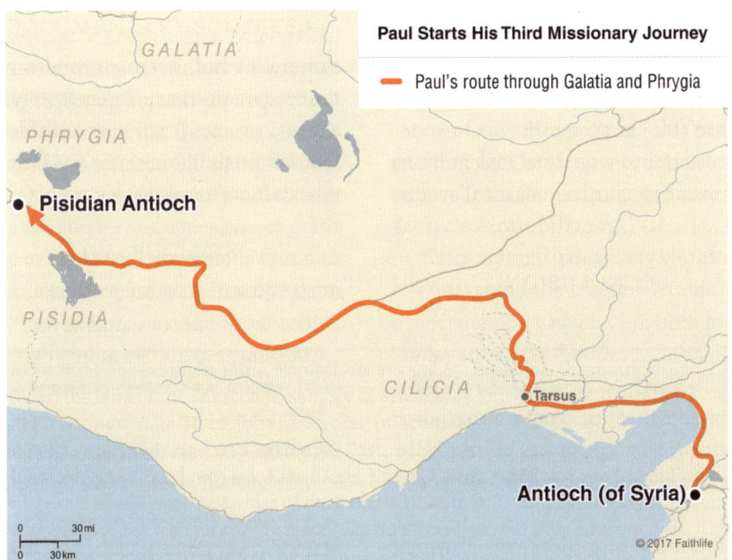

ceivable that the Γαλατικὴ χώρα [*Galatikē chōra*] mentioned here is the region of north Galatia."[26] To propound a north Galatian view and cite these verses from Acts is not consonant with Luke's Greek nomenclature.

On their second journey Paul and Silas added Timothy in Lystra, and the decision of the Jerusalem Council was also announced in Iconium (Acts 16:1–5). But did they visit Pisidian Antioch before the prohibition was received? Paul's purpose for the journey was articulated in Acts 15:36: to revisit the believers in the cities where they had preached during the first journey. From the perspective of Luke's narrative, a visit to Pisidian Antioch was presumed, so a visit directly from Iconium into north Galatia runs contrary to Luke's intention. In Acts 18:23 no specific city names are mentioned. Paul's natural route to Ephesus would have followed the southern highway through the Cilician Gates. He would then revisit the Lycaonian cities of Derbe and Lystra in the province of Galatia, then the province's two Phrygian cities, Iconium and Pisidian Antioch. That the upper, or interior, regions (τὰ ἀνωτερικὰ μέρη, *ta anōterika merē*) of Acts 19:1 must refer to north Galatia, as W. J. Conybeare and J. S. Howson did, is a geographical stretch.[27]

A final argument against north Galatia is the paucity of Jewish communities there. Paul's *modus operandi* in Acts was to visit the synagogue, if one existed, in the cities where he evangelized. In north Galatia no archaeological evidence for Judaism exists from the first century AD. Although literary texts mention Jews and Christians in Galatia in later centuries, "Jewish monuments are rare in

26. Mitchell, *Anatolia*, 2.3.

27. Mark Wilson, "The 'Upper Regions' and the Route of Paul's Third Journey from Apamea to Ephesus," *Scriptura* 117 (2018): 3–5.

Galatia."[28] Granted, an unplanned visit because of sickness or illness would obviate the intentionality seen in Paul's visits to cities with Jewish communities. However, this is only postulated, and Acts mentions only one such medical evacuation: to Derbe (Acts 14:19–20).

CONCLUSION

Whom did Paul address in his letter to the Galatian churches? Was it the ethnic Gauls in north Galatia or the residents of provincial south Galatia? The north Galatian theory continues to have advocates; however, it is saddled with several inherent weaknesses. First, the Jewish population there was minimal. As Mitchell observes, "Jews are hardly attested in any of the cities before the 4th century."[29] With no known synagogues, there was no religious attraction for Paul to travel there. Second, travelers coming from Syrian Antioch through the Cilician Gates to Ephesus would typically pass south of the three main north Galatian cities. While a diversion northward is possible, this hypothesis is conjectural. Third, the book of Acts never describes Paul traveling in north Galatia. Instead it shows the apostle journeying twice through southern Galatia and four times through central Galatia. Fourth, there is evidence that the north Galatian cities were evangelized, but more probably by Peter or his representatives (1 Pet 1:1). Finally, new inscriptional evidence shows that Pamphylia was part of Galatia at the time of Paul's visit. This suggests that the audience of Galatians extended southward rather than northward, thereby including the church in Perga founded on the first journey. This conclusion accords with Mitchell's assessment, "There is virtually nothing to be said for the north Galatian theory."[30]

BIBLIOGRAPHY

Adak, Mustafa, and Mark Wilson. "Das Vespasiansmonument von Döşeme und die Gründung der Doppelprovenz Lycia et Pamphylia." *Gephrya* 9 (2012): 1–40.

Betz, Hans Dieter. *Galatians: A Commentary on Paul's Letter to the Churches in Galatia*. Philadelphia: Fortress, 1988.

Bruce, F. F. *The Epistle to the Galatians: A Commentary on the Greek Text*. Grand Rapids: Eerdmans, 1982.

Cooley, Alison E. *Res Gestae Divi Augusti: Text, Translation, and Commentary*. Oxford: Oxford University Press, 2009.

Elliott, Susan M. *Cutting Too Close for Comfort: Paul's Letter to the Galatians in its Anatolian Cultic Context*. London: T&T Clark, 2003.

Jewett, Robert. *Dating Paul's Life*. London: SCM, 1979.

———. "Mapping the Route of Paul's 'Second Missionary Journey' from Dorylaeum to Troas." *TynBul* 48 (1997): 1–22.

Kahl, Brigitte, *Galatians Re-imagined: Reading with the Eyes of the Vanquished*. Minneapolis: Fortress, 2010.

Keener, Craig S. *Acts: An Exegetical Commentary*. 4 vols. Grand Rapids: Baker Academic, 2012–2015.

28. Philip Niewöhner, "Germia and Vicinity: Western Galatia during the Roman and Byzantine Period," *Araştırma Sonuçları Toplantısı* 28 (2010): 55. He shows an inscribed stele with menorah, dating from Late Antiquity, that was recently found near Pessinus (p. 65 fig. 13).

29. Stephen Mitchell, "Galatia," *ABD* 2:871.

30. Mitchell, *Anatolia*, 2:3.

Levick, Barbara. *Roman Colonies in Southern Asia Minor*. Oxford: Clarendon, 1967.

Lightfoot, J. B. *Epistle to the Galatians*. Revised ed. Andover: Draper, 1870.

Longenecker, Richard N. *Galatians*. Dallas: Word, 1990.

Mitchell, Stephen. *Anatolia: Lands, Men, and Gods in Asia Minor*. 2 vols. Oxford: Oxford University Press, 1992.

———. "Galatia." *ABD* 2:870–72.

Murphy-O'Connor, Jerome. *Paul: A Critical Life*. Oxford: Oxford University Press, 1997.

Musei Capitolini. "Statue of 'Capitoline Gaul.'" Accessed November 30, 2018. http://www.museicapitolini.org/en/collezioni/percorsi_per_sale/palazzo_nuovo/sala_del_gladiatore/statua_del_galata_capitolino.

Niewöhner, Philipp. "Germia and Vicinity: Western Galatia during the Roman and Byzantine Period." *Araştırma Sonuçları Toplantısı* 28 (2010): 47–66.

Potter, D. S. "Quirinius." *ABD* 5:588–89.

Ramsay, William M. *The Cities of St. Paul*. London: Hodder & Stoughton, 1907.

———. *A Historical Commentary on St. Paul's Epistle to the Galatians*. New York: Putnam, 1900.

Thompson, Glen L., and Mark Wilson. "The Route of Paul's Second Journey in Asia Minor: In the Steps of Robert Jewett and Beyond." *TynBul* 67 (2016):217–46.

Wilson, Mark. "The Denouement of Claudian Pamphylia-Lycia and Its Implications for the Audience of Galatians." *NovT* 60 (2018): 1–24.

———. "The 'Upper Regions' and the Route of Paul's Third Journey from Apamea to Ephesus." *Scriptura* 117 (2018): 1–21.

Witherington, Ben, III. *Grace in Galatia: A Commentary on St. Paul's Letter to the Galatians*. Grand Rapids: Eerdmans, 1998.

CHAPTER 39

PAUL'S EARLY MINISTRY IN SYRIA AND CILICIA: THE SILENT YEARS

Gal 1:21; Acts 9:30

Mark R. Fairchild

KEY POINTS

- Two or three years after his conversion, the apostle Paul returned to Tarsus in Cilicia and began a ministry in Syria and Cilicia.
- The ministry in Syria and Cilicia is never mentioned in Acts and only briefly mentioned in Paul's letter to the Galatians (1:21).
- The specifics of Paul's Syrian and Cilician ministry cannot be known, but a plausible scenario can be determined based upon Paul's mission strategies together with an understanding of the history and geography of these regions.
- Paul's experiences in Syria and Cilicia likely affirmed the apostle's call and solidified many of his theological convictions regarding gentile believers.

INTRODUCTION

In his letter to the Galatians, Paul briefly chronicled his ministry in the years following his conversion. In the account, the apostle alluded to his work in Syria and Cilicia (Gal 1:21). The Acts of the Apostles mentioned nothing of this ministry. Acts 9:30 cited Paul's retreat to Tarsus (the chief city of Cilicia), but nothing more was mentioned about Paul until Acts 11:25 when Barnabas traveled to Tarsus to look for Paul and to enlist his help in Antioch. It appears that Paul spent seven to nine years in this ministry in Syria and Cilicia. At a time when Paul was grappling with his new faith, how did this ministry shape his beliefs? Over these several years, where did Paul go and how did these experiences pave the way for Paul's later journeys?

The dating of Paul's travels is an issue that cannot be precisely resolved. We can identify a few solid anchors, such as Paul's visit to Corinth (Acts 18) at the time of Proconsul Gallio (AD 51–52) and the expulsion of Jews from Rome under Claudius' reign (AD 49). Likewise the intervention of Aretas IV the Nabataean king in the affairs of Damascus during Paul's visit (Acts 9; 2 Cor 11:32–33) is also helpful (AD 34–37). But between these dates, it is not easy to pin down the chronology.

Following Paul's conversion around AD 33, the apostle spent some time in Damascus. Later he moved to Arabia (the Nabataean kingdom) and in time returned again to Damascus. In his letter to the Galatians (1:18), Paul claimed that three years later he returned to Jerusalem and visited Peter for fifteen days. According to the Jewish manner of reckoning time (which counted portions of years), this journey to Jerusalem was probably anywhere between one and a half and two and a half years after his conversion. Taking the middle of these dates and times, this puts Paul's visit to Jerusalem at roughly AD 35.

After his short visit in Jerusalem, Paul stated that he traveled to Syria and Cilicia (Gal 1:21). Unfortunately, Paul did not designate how much time elapsed during this journey. In all probability this journey is the same as that mentioned in Acts 9:30, where Paul was sent to Tarsus due to threats he received in Jerusalem. At some point, Barnabas traveled to Tarsus to find Paul and took him to Antioch where they ministered to the church for a full year (Acts 11:25–26). Another time marker in Gal 2:1 states that Paul returned to Jerusalem fourteen years later with Barnabas. This may refer to the famine visit mentioned in Acts 11:30 or it could refer to the Jerusalem Council visit in Acts 15. If this visit refers to the Jerusalem Council visit, the fourteen years would include the time spent on the first mission to Cyprus and Galatia (around AD 45–47). This latter option seems most likely.

The result of this chronological survey suggests that Paul's ministry in Syria and Cilicia involved seven to nine years from AD 35 to roughly AD 42–44. This mission was longer than the time spent on any of Paul's journeys recorded by Luke in Acts. Thus, it is puzzling why so little of this mission was mentioned in Acts or Paul's letters.

Without offering any details, Paul briefly mentioned his mission in Syria and Cilicia in his letter to the Galatians (1:21). The narrative in Acts likewise skipped this period. However, in Acts 15:23 it was stated that the Jerusalem decrees were sent to new gentile believers in Antioch, Syria, and Cilicia. A few verses later in 15:41, it was noted that Paul and Silas began their so-called second mission traveling through Syria and Cilicia "strengthening the churches." These statements were issued with no details, leaving the reader to fill in the blanks. Since Paul's first mission (according to Acts 13:1–14:28) came nowhere close to Cilicia, we have to assume that these churches were established by Paul during the seven to nine silent years after Paul's departure from Jerusalem.

When we consider the places that Paul may have evangelized during this period, we are led by two principles that Paul himself mentioned in his writings. First, Paul claimed that his priority was to visit cities, towns, and villages that had a Jewish presence. This conviction was expressed at the beginning of his letter to the Romans: "For I am not

The Synagogue at Çatıören

ashamed of the gospel, for it is the power of God for salvation to everyone who believes, to the Jew first and also to the Greek" (Rom 1:16; see also Acts 13:46–47).[1] If Acts is to function as a paradigm for Paul's missionary practices, the apostle almost always evangelized places with a Jewish population and began his work by preaching in the synagogue, rather than in the agora or elsewhere. This Jewish priority is consistently mentioned throughout the narratives in Acts: 9:20 (Damascus); 13:5 (Salamis); 13:14 (Pisidian Antioch); 14:1 (Iconium); 16:13 (Philippi); 17:1–2 (Thessalonica); 17:10 (Berea); 18:4 (Corinth); 18:19 (Ephesus); 19:8 (Ephesus); and 28:17 (Rome). In Acts 17:2 Luke declared that this routine was Paul's customary practice. After experiencing opposition from Jews in Pisidian Antioch, Luke conveyed Paul's response: "It was necessary that the word of God be spoken to you first; since you repudiate it and judge yourselves unworthy of eternal life, behold, we are turning to the gentiles." (Acts 13:46).

Second, Paul expressed his desire to preach the gospel in places where others had not shared the message. In his correspondence with the Corinthians, the apostle noted his plan "to preach the gospel even to the regions beyond you, and not to boast in what has been accomplished in the sphere of another" (2 Cor 10:16). Likewise, at the end of his letter to the Romans, Paul expressed his reasons for coming to Rome and Spain. "I aspired to preach the gospel, not where Christ was already named, so that I would not build on another man's foundation; but as it is

1. All Scripture quotations are from the NASB unless otherwise noted.

written, 'They who had no news of him shall see, and they who have not heard shall understand'" (Rom 15:20–21). Here Paul cites Isaiah as support for his policy.

When we apply these principles to an investigation of the places that Paul may have visited during these silent years, we should look first for evidence of a Jewish presence in the locations of Syria and Cilicia. This is not to say that Paul preached exclusively to Jews. There is ample evidence to indicate that Paul preached to non-Jews throughout his ministry. However, Paul's intention was to target Jewish locations as a first priority. There were probably several reasons for this. First, the Jews believed that they were specially commissioned as a priestly nation (Isa 61:6). They were entrusted with the oracles of God (Rom 3:2). And they were uniquely called to minister to the nations: "you will call a nation you do not know, and a nation which knows you not will run to you, because of the Lord your God, even the Holy One of Israel; for he has glorified you" (Isa 55:5).

Second, as a traveling Jew, Paul would be offered hospitality in his travels and would be given an opportunity to address the congregation in the synagogue. And third, at the synagogues Paul would find God-fearers—monotheistic gentiles who were attached to the synagogue. Many of these God-fearers responded positively to the gospel and increasingly the gentiles became the bulk of the population in Paul's churches.

En route to various locations, Paul had to travel through places that had no Jewish population or only a nominal Jewish presence. He would have had to purchase food and provisions at these sites and frequently found lodging in these cities and towns. His conversations inevitably would lead him to share the gospel message with the residents of these places. So, while Paul would avail himself of opportunities to share the gospel with the non-Jewish residents of cities, towns, and villages, these places were of secondary concern when Paul laid plans for his travels. If we are looking for the places where Paul most probably traveled, we need to find Jewish communities.

Geography and Paul's Ministry in Syria

Strabo notes that Cilicia and Syria were divided by Mt. Amanus, a short distance to the north of Syrian Antioch (*Geography* 16.2.1). South of the mountain, the Mediterranean Sea formed the western border of Syria. The Roman province of Syria extended to the east of Mt. Amanus up to the Euphrates River and at times included the territory of Commagene to the north. In AD 17 the Roman emperor Tiberius annexed the Commagene kingdom and added it to the province of Syria. In AD 38 Caligula appointed Antiochus IV as a client king over Commagene and also gave him dominion over a portion of Cilicia. Caligula later revoked this appointment, but in AD 41 the new emperor Claudius restored Antiochus IV as king of Commagene and he ruled until AD 72.[2] At that point Vespasian reincorporated Commagene into Syria.

To the south, the territory of Syria spread as far as Arabia (Nabataea) and included Phoenicia and Judea. When Pompey expanded the Roman Empire to the east in 63 BC, Phoenicia and Judea were

2. F. Miller, *The Roman Near East: 31 BC–AD 337* (Cambridge: Harvard University Press, 1993), 52–53, 59, 81–82.

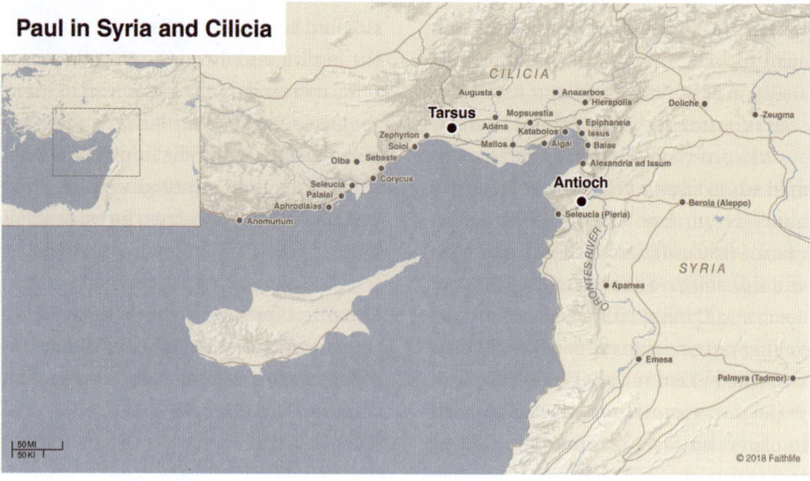

added to the province of Syria. Strabo, writing in the early years of the first century, identified five regions within the province of Syria: Commagene, Seleucid Syria, Coele Syria, Phoenicia, and Judea. Strabo also mentioned that some ancient writers referred to this region by the individual parts (*Geography* 16.2.2). Frequently, Judea and Phoenicia were identified separately from Syria, even though the Romans administratively considered them to be a part of the Syrian province. For those living in or near the province, it was more common to be specific and to refer to the individual regions.

WHERE WAS PAUL LIKELY TO TRAVEL?

Where among these regions of Syria did Paul go? Paul made it clear that Judea was not included in this Syrian ministry. In Galatians 1:21–22 Paul distinguished between Syria and Judea and claimed that he was unknown to the churches of Judea. It is also important to note that Commagene was a client kingdom and was not considered a part of Syria at the time when Paul wrote his letter to the Galatians. Thus, it is not likely that Paul's Syrian ministry involved Commagene. Likewise we can probably eliminate the Phoenician cities of Tyre, Sidon, Berytus, Byblos, and Tripolis. Acts 11:19 indicates that other unknown evangelists reached Phoenicia shortly after Stephen's martyrdom. Paul preferred to minister in places where the gospel had never been preached. The upshot of this is that it seems probable that Paul's reference to his ministry in Syria and Cilicia (Gal 1:21) involved Cilicia and the regions of Seleucid Syria and Coele Syria.

After his conversion Paul preached in the synagogues of Damascus (Acts 9:20) and Arabia (the Nabataean kingdom, Gal 1:17). Then, he was sent away to Tarsus. Several years later, Barnabas was assigned to minister in Antioch (Acts 11:22). Shortly thereafter (11:25–26) Barnabas sought Paul and brought him to Antioch to work with him. But the question remains, where in Syria was Paul doing ministry prior to coming to Antioch?

Tarsus

When Paul was sent back to Tarsus, he probably spent the bulk of his time in

Cilicia. Since Tarsus was his hometown, Tarsus probably served as his home base and his ministry radiated out from there. It cannot be determined how much time he spent in Syria and how far into Syria he traveled. Paul traveled great distances in his later journeys, but the mission in Syria and Cilicia involved smaller distances. Acts 11:25–26 implies that he generally stayed close to his home base. When Barnabas sought Paul to join him in Antioch, he traveled to Tarsus to look for him. The verb *anazēteō* (ἀναζητέω) implies that Paul was not at Tarsus and that Barnabas had to look for him elsewhere in the region. After finding (εὑρίσκω, *heuriskō*) him, they returned to Antioch.

Roman Street in Tarsus

The distance from Tarsus to the northwestern periphery of Syria was ninety miles (145 km). The road passed through Adana and Mopsuestia before traversing the Amanus Mountains. The distance to any of the major cities of Syria was even further. What were the most likely sites for Paul's Syrian mission during this time? Josephus claimed that there were many Jews spread throughout Syria (*J.W.* 7.43)[3] and Paul himself tells us that he specifically targeted Jewish communities.

Antioch

It is likely that Paul was doing ministry in Antioch before (or shortly after) other Christians arrived in Acts 11:19. Paul's seven to nine year ministry in Syria and Cilicia (Gal 1:21) preceded his arrival with Barnabas in 11:26 and it is hard to imagine that he would not have been there prior to the time when he joined Barnabas in Antioch. Departing from Cilicia and turning south on the Roman road, a mountain pass through the Syrian Gates led travelers to Antioch on the eastern side of the Amanus Mountains. Antioch was the largest city in Syria and one of the five largest cities in all the region surrounding the Mediterranean Sea. Moreover, Antioch was the closest large Syrian city to Paul's home in Cilicia and it included a large Jewish population.[4] With such a massive population Paul may not even have been aware that a few other Christians had come to the city and were sharing the gospel. Later, when more Christian refugees arrived in Antioch from Judea and began a ministry among the gentiles, the church numerically exploded (Acts 11:19–21). When Barnabas arrived, Paul was elsewhere in Cilicia. Barnabas soon realized that the work was beyond what

3. Josephus claimed that the Jews were dispersed throughout the world and noted that they were particularly numerous in Syria, especially in Antioch. Elsewhere (*J.W.* 2:561) Josephus asserted that over ten thousand Jews were slaughtered in Damascus during the Jewish-Roman war.

4. E. Schnabel, *Paul the Missionary: Realities, Strategies and Methods* (Downers Grove, IL: InterVarsity Press, 2008), 71, claims that there were between twenty thousand and thirty-five thousand Jews in Antioch at that time, about 10 percent of the population.

he could manage. Paul's familiarity with Antioch and its people may have been a contributing factor in Barnabas seeking Paul in Tarsus, rather than looking for help from Jerusalem.

Orontes River at Antioch

Antioch was located about fifteen miles (24 km) upriver from the Mediterranean coast straddling the Orontes River. The city's Mediterranean port at Seleucia Pieria was likewise evangelized by Paul. It too possessed a sizable Jewish community.[5] This was the port from which Paul, Barnabas, and Mark departed on their Cyprian and Galatian ministry (Acts 13:4).

Beroia

Another likely site of Paul's Syrian mission was the city of Beroia. Beroia (today's Aleppo) was fifty-five miles (88.5 km) due east of Antioch and could be easily reached via a Roman road. A first century Jewish and Christian presence in the city can be inferred from Epiphanius' discussion of a sect of Jewish Christian Nazoraeans at Beroia.[6] Additionally, a silver amulet with Hebrew and Aramaic text dated to the fourth or fifth century AD was found in a tomb at Beroia. The text referred to Yahweh, King David, and the God of Israel.[7] Although the amulet and testimony of Epiphanius date to the fourth century, it is highly likely that the Jewish community in Beroia found its origins prior to the Roman period.

Apamea

Following the Orontes River south of Antioch for another fifty-five miles (88.5 km) Paul likely came to Apamea. That there were a large number of Jews in Apamea is confirmed by Josephus, who

Inscription from the Fourth Century Synagogue at Apamea

5. Few physical remains related to Jews in Antioch and Seleucia are known. An undated plaque with a menorah was found in Antioch and a first century BC or AD ossuary belonging to Eiras from Seleucia was found in Jerusalem. However, little archaeological work has been done in these cities. See David Noy and Hanswulf Bloedhorn, eds., *Inscriptiones Judaicae Orientis, Volume 3: Syria and Cyprus*. (Tübingen: Mohr Siebeck, 2004), 115–17.

6. Epiphanius, *Panarion*, 29. This is supported by Jerome as well, *De viris illustribus* 3.1. See A. F. J. Klijn, *Jewish-Christian Gospel Tradition* (Leiden: Brill, 1992), 14.

7. Noy and Bloedhorn, *Volume* 3, 12.

Palmyra Necropolis

mentioned that the many Jews residing in Apamea were protected during the upheaval surrounding the Jewish war with Rome (*J.W.* 2.479). Evidence of a Jewish presence in Apamea is also confirmed by an ossuary found in Jerusalem bearing the name of Ariston of Apamea.[8] An ancient synagogue built during the fourth century has been discovered in Apamea, but earlier ones from the first century were probably the places where Paul first shared the gospel in Apamea.

Emesa

Further south another 50 miles (80 km) below Apamea lay the city of Emesa and in a southeastern direction the city of Palmyra was located at a distance of 120 miles (193 km) from Apamea. Not much archaeological evidence has been found at Emesa (modern Homs) to indicate an early Jewish presence,[9] but the royal family in Emesa had cordial relations with the Jews to such an extent that the king of Emesa Gaius Julius Azizus agreed to be circumcised in order to marry Herod Agrippa II's sister Drusilla (Josephus, *Ant.* 20.139).

Palmyra

There is much more evidence of an early Jewish presence at Palmyra (Tadmor). David Noy and Hanswulf Bloedhorn list several inscriptions and ossuaries from Beth She'arim and Jerusalem mentioning Jews from Palmyra dating to the second and third centuries.[10] Additionally, several lamps were found at Palmyra containing menorahs along with a doorway inscribed on the lintel and doorposts with the words of Deuteronomy 6, 7, and 29. The houses in this area are dated in the second century, but the inscriptions may have been added later. More certain is the date of an epitaph on the lintel of a tomb in the necropolis at Palmyra. The tomb can be dated to AD 212 and was built by Zenobius and Samuel, sons of

8. Noy and Bloedhorn, *Volume 3*, 114. The ossuary has been dated to the first century BC or AD.

9. According to Noy and Bloedhorn, *Volume 3*, 68, a fourth or fifth century Latin sarcophagus was found in Concordia, Italy inscribed with the name Flavia Optata, wife of a soldier from the royal Jewish Emesene troops.

10. Noy and Bloedhorn, *Volume 3*, Appendix 1, 227–32.

Levi.[11] Even earlier evidence of Jews in Palmyra can be found in a rabbinic reference to a woman Miriam from Palmyra whose daughter had died (Mishnah, `Nazir 6.11).

It is hard to say how deeply Paul penetrated Syria during this early period. If his ministry in this area was shallow, Palmyra may have been beyond Paul's scope. However, the seven to nine year period certainly offered the apostle enough time to evangelize Palmyra. The large Jewish presence at Palmyra indicated by the textual and archaeological evidence could have enticed Paul to make the journey to the city.

Doliche and Zeugma

Instead of going south to Antioch, Beroia, Apamea, Emesa, and Palmyra, an alternate Roman road coming from Cilicia traveled directly east to Doliche and Zeugma. Doliche was located about 95 miles (153 km) northeast of Antioch and another 25 miles (40 km) east of Doliche was Zeugma. The Roman road from Tarsus traversed a direct route to Doliche for 130 miles (209 km). There was a Jewish presence in Doliche, though the size of the Jewish community is unclear.[12] Doliche possessed the sanctuary for Jupiter Dolichenus, the chief deity of the city. The presence of Roman troops at Doliche helped spread the notoriety of Jupiter Doliche so that the deity became one of the most important gods in the empire in the second century AD. Along with the Roman troops, the city also possessed two Mithraea (sanctuaries for the cult of Mithras), a popular mystery religion with the legions.

A mere twenty-five miles (40 km) east of Doliche lay Zeugma. At the time of the construction of the Birecik Dam in 1996, excavators conducted salvage excavations at Zeugma before the city was submerged under the waters of the reservoir. Dozens of beautiful mosaics were extracted from Zeugma and are currently displayed in the Zeugma Mosaic Museum in Gaziantep. Unfortunately, the waters limit the amount of research that can be conducted at Zeugma. Presently, there is no known Jewish presence at Zeugma, but Josephus' comments on the large number of Jews throughout Syria suggests that we cannot discount their presence there. If Paul ministered in Doliche, it is likely that he would have taken the short journey to Zeugma as well.

Roman Mosaic from Zeugma

11. Noy and Boedhorn, *Volume 3*, 76–79.

12. Benedikt Eckhardt, *Jewish Identity and Politics between the Maccabees and Bar Kokhba* (Leiden: Brill, 2012), 207 n. 64. Michael Blömer and Engelbert Winter, *Commagene: The Land of Gods Between the Taurus and the Euphrates* (Istanbul: Homer Kitabevi, 2011), 248–66.

STRENGTHENING THE CHURCHES

Following the Jerusalem Council (Acts 15), Paul chose Silas and passed through Syria and Cilicia "strengthening the churches" (15:41). The verb used here (ἐπιστηρίζω, *epistērizō*) indicates that Paul and Silas revisited churches that had already been established. Paul typically revisited churches that he personally had founded, so the implication is that these were churches that Paul evangelized during the seven to nine year period prior to his journey with Barnabas to Cyprus and Galatia. On this mission Paul's prime objectives were to revisit the churches of southern Galatia that he and Barnabas had established and to travel to Ephesus (Acts 16:6).

The point of departure for Paul and Silas was Syrian Antioch on the northwestern edge of Syria and only fifteen miles (24 km) from Cilicia. No large or midsized Syrian city lay on the direct route between Antioch and Cilicia, Galatia, and beyond. So, for Paul and Silas to revisit churches in Syria, the evangelists had to backtrack to the east and/or the south. It is possible that Luke never intended to include Syrian churches among those that were "strengthened," but if that were the case it would have been better for Luke to omit Syria from the text.

Perhaps the churches in the southern parts of Syria were already visited by Paul, Barnabas, and Silas when they returned from Jerusalem (15:30). Thus, I would tentatively suggest that Paul and Silas made a loop to the east visiting Beroia, followed by a trek northeast to Zeugma. At this point they traveled west to Doliche and on into Cilicia. The apostles may have been following the path of the Judaizers who had unsettled the Antiochene church and then moved on to other Pauline churches.

GEOGRAPHY AND PAUL'S MINISTRY IN CILICIA

When Paul fled Jerusalem, Luke remarked that the disciples brought Paul to Caesarea and sent him away to Tarsus (Acts 9:30). Since Caesarea was the major Mediterranean port for both Jews and Romans, the text implies that Paul sailed to Tarsus, rather than traveling by land.

Cilicia spread to the west of Syria and south of the Taurus Mountains. Cilicia was bounded by the Taurus Mountains on the north and as the mountain range turned to the southwest, the coast followed. At Adana these mountains curved southwest and ran for 170 miles (273.5 km) before turning to the west and then bent northwest running another 70 miles (112.7 km) to the borders of Pamphylia and Lycia. Following the course of the mountains to the south was the sea. Thus, Cilicia encompassed a strip of land with sparsely inhabited mountains to the north, bordered by a band of foothills and a thin strip of flat coastal land terminating at the sea. North of the mountain range on the east was Cappadocia, further west was Isauria and even further west Homonadeis.[13]

Strabo explained that Cilicia was divided into two sections (*Geography* 14.5.1). The eastern portion known as *Cilicia Pedias* (Smooth Cilicia) had a much broader strip of fertile flatland bordering the sea. Over the years the Pyramos, Psaros, Cydnus, and Liparis Rivers deposited alluvial soil in this area resulting in a relatively broader plain before the sea.

13. See *BAGRW*, maps 66, 67, and 68.

Sarcophagus with Menorah at Corycus

Southwest of Soloi (Pompeiopolis) the coastal plain almost disappears. Strabo referred to this region as *Cilicia Tracheia* (Rough Cilicia) for good reason. The Taurus Mountains and foothills rise abruptly out of the sea, leaving little or no flatland. This area is some of the most tortured land in all of Anatolia. Rivers and streams have carved out deep canyons and ravines throughout the land. Massive cliffs and sinkholes pockmark the terrain. Luke referred to Cilicia seven times and Paul once in their writings and they never distinguish between Cilicia Pedias and Cilicia Tracheia.

THE JEWISH PRESENCE IN CILICIA

There are few ancient literary sources that describe life in Cilicia. However, the information that we are able to obtain indicates that there was a sizeable Jewish presence in Cilicia during the first century. Paul himself hailed from Tarsus in Cilicia (Acts 9:11; 11:25; 21:39; 22:3; Gal 1:21) and Acts 6:9 referred to a synagogue of freedmen from Cilicia as well as Cyrene, Alexandria, and Asia.[14] Josephus described a journey of Herod to Elaioussa Sebaste with his sons. Upon returning to Jerusalem he boasted of the benefactions that he bestowed upon the Jews of Cilicia (*Ant.* 16.131–133). Later in the first century Josephus mentioned Alexander, the son of Tigranes, a Jewish king of Armenia who was appointed king of Ketis in Cilicia by Vespasian (*Ant.* 18.140–141). Vespasian's appointment of a Jew to this position suggests that there was a large Jewish population in the area. Much the same can be assumed when Bernice married Polemo, the king of Cilicia, and convinced him to undergo circumcision (Josephus, *Ant.* 20.145–147). Philo as well wrote that Jews had settled throughout Cilicia (Philo, *Legatio ad Gaium* 281–282). Ben-Zion Rosenfeld and Joseph Menirav

14. The Theodotus inscription found near the City of David in Jerusalem probably refers to this synagogue. See page 157 for an image of the inscription.

cite several rabbinic sources that mention synagogues in Tarsus[15] and the fourth century Epiphanius of Salamis passed on the story of Joseph of Cilicia, a Jewish official, who was flogged in the synagogue (*Panarion* 30.11).

There are a number of Jewish archaeological remains in Cilicia with most of those in Rough Cilicia. Some of Turkey's largest cities sit upon the remains of the largest ancient Cilician cities—Adana, Tarsus, and Mersin (Pompeiopolis) and the smaller city of Silifke is the site of Seleucia Ad Calycadnum. It is difficult to excavate these ancient cities. Many other ancient sites were located in the remote foothills and mountains of the Taurus range. Thus, relatively little archaeological work has been conducted in these places of Cilicia. However, the surface remains in the region confirm what the literary sources suggest—that there was a large Jewish presence in Cilicia.

Evidence from Inscriptions and Tombs

Two funerary inscriptions found at Joppa (Israel) refer to Jews in Tarsus: "Judas, son of Joses of Tarsus" and "Herein lies Isaac, elder of the Cappadocian [synagogue], linen merchant from Tarsus."[16] Also, an inscription probably originating from the necropolis at Joppa mentions Theodotus, son of Alexander from the city of Seleucia Isauria.[17] A lead sarcophagus found at Aigai and currently in the museum at Adana contains four menorahs. The sarcophagus belonged to a Jew named Prokla and can be dated to the second to the fourth century.[18]

Both the literary sources and ancient remains suggest a much larger concentration of Jews in Rough Cilicia, specifically between the Lamas and Calycadnus Rivers.[19] The necropolis at Seleucia Ad Calycadnum (Silifke) contains two Jewish tombs: one inscribed with the words "Tomb of a Hebrew" and the other marked with two menorahs and an inscription "Tomb of Theodorus, grandson of Theodorus."[20] Further north up the coast at Corycus, a necropolis contains twelve sarcophagi bearing the names of Jews along with menorahs.[21] Inland at Diocaesarea, there is a tomb that held the remains of "M. Aurelius Zoilos and Diogenes, Jews."[22]

North and inland from Elaioussa Sebaste is an ancient village now known

15. Ben-Zion Rosenfeld and Joseph Menirav, "The Ancient Synagogue as an Economic Center," *Journal of Near Eastern Studies* 58 (1999): 264.

16. Walter Ameling, ed., *Inscriptiones Judaicae Orientis: Kleinasien*, vol. 2 of *Inscriptiones Judaicae Orientis* (Tübingen: Mohr Siebeck, 2004), 531–33, nos. 249–50.

17. Ameling, *Kleinasien*, 523–24, no. 246. Isauria neighbors Cilicia and this reference is likely to Seleucia Cilicia.

18. Ameling, *Kleinasien* , 497–98.

19. Mark R. Fairchild, "The Jewish Communities in Eastern Rough Cilicia," *Journal of Ancient Judaism* 5 (2014): 204–16.

20. Ameling, *Kleinasien*, 521–23, nos. 244–45. Ameling dates these to the fourth century AD.

21. Ameling, *Kleinasien*, 500–520, nos. 232–243. Also listed in J. Keil and A. Wilhelm, eds., *Monumenta Asiae Minoris Antiqua. Denkmäler aus dem rauhen Kilikien*, vol. 3 of *Monumenta Asiae Minoris Antiqua* (Manchester: Manchester University Press, 1931). See also Margaret H. Williams, "The Jewish Community of Corycus: Two More Inscriptions," *Zietschrift für Papyrologie und Epigraphik* 92 (1992): 248–52.

22. Ameling, *Kleinasien*, 499–500, no. 231.

as *Kabaçam*.[23] The ancient name of the village is unknown, but the ruins date to the Hellenistic, Roman, and Byzantine period. On the plastered walls of an underground granary, there was inscribed a large and unusual menorah. The menorah is elongated and shaped like a ship. There are six branches of the menorah flanking a centerpiece consisting of three branches that represent the ship's mast and sail. Elsewhere on the walls of the granary are inscriptions of two ships and a sheep. The granary appears to date to the Roman period and the inscriptions lead us to believe that Jews from *Kabaçam* were involved in the production, transport, and trade of grain. The ancient road from *Kabaçam* leads to the much larger seaside granaries located at *Tirtar Akkale* (ancient name unknown), where one would assume that the grain would be loaded onto cargo ships.

Evidence of Synagogues

There is evidence of ancient synagogues in this area as well.[24] Beneath the Armenian castle walls on the shore of Corycus there lies buried the lintel of what was probably a synagogue. A stylized Byzantine menorah is deeply cut into the lintel. The castle was erected upon the ruins of a Roman agora and the lintel itself may have been the doorway of a shop that was later converted into a synagogue during the Byzantine period.

Inland from Elaioussa Sebaste and west of *Kabaçam* is another unidentified ancient village known locally as *Çatıören*. During the Hellenistic period the site functioned as a fortification guarding the road leading from the interior to the coastal city of Elaioussa Sebaste. Deeply cut ravines on both sides of a central ridge made the site a strategic place to guard settlements further into the mountainous interior. Most of the buildings on the central ridge were polygonally constructed structures dating to the Hellenistic period, including a well-preserved temple to Hermes, a watchtower, and a synagogue. The synagogue has a large crudely inscribed menorah on the exterior surface of the lintel standing next to an inscribed thunderbolt of Zeus. Another smaller menorah can be found on the inside of the lintel. Inside, there is a niche facing south in the direction of Jerusalem. A small mikveh, fed by waters from a cistern higher on the ridge, was attached to the outside walls of the synagogue and a rock-cut staircase led up to a second story of the building. A decree inscribed on the bedrock at the site men-

Menorah Carved into Synagogue Lintel at Corycus

23. The ancient names of many sites in Rough Cilicia are unknown. In what follows, an *italicized font* designates the current Turkish names given to these locations, while the unitalicized normal font designates the known ancient name.

24. Mark R. Fairchild, "Turkey's Unexcavated Synagogues: Could the World's Earliest Known Synagogue Be Buried Amid Rubble?" *BAR* 38.4 (2012), 34–41, 65.

tioned Sabbath keepers, the synagogue official, and others who worshiped at the site.[25]

JEWS AND WORSHIPERS OF THE HIGHEST GOD

A small altar found at Diocaesarea is currently on display in the museum at Silifke.[26] The altar has a five-branched lampstand depicted in relief on the front of the altar. The middle branch holds a star. The sides of the altar contain a pair of ears. Beneath the lampstand is the word ΕΥΧΗΝ (*euchēn*, "vow"), but the words above the altar are damaged and unreadable. This was probably an altar created in fulfillment of a vow to the God who hears. A similar expression can be found on an inscription found at Tanais a colony of the Bosphorean kingdom north of the Black Sea: "In fulfillment of a vow [ΕΥΧΗ, *euchē*] to the Highest God who hears [ΘΕΩ ΥΨΙΣΤΩ ΕΠΗΚΟΩ, *theō hypsistō epēkoō*]."[27] The cult of the Highest God was common in Cilicia and ancient Anatolia.[28] The worshipers of the Highest God were monotheistic gentiles who frequently had associations with Jews in their communities. They often attended the synagogues and they may be identified with the God-fearers mentioned in Acts. Throughout Paul's travels, many of his converts came from the God-fearers (Acts 13:16, 26, 43; 16:14; 18:7).

This unusual altar was found at Diocaesarea and is currently on display in the Silifke Museum

The question is: Does the lampstand on this altar depict a menorah? Rachel Hachlili notes that menorahs can be found containing three, five, seven, nine, and eleven branches, although seven branches are the most common.[29] I follow

25. E. L. Hicks, "Inscriptions from Western Cilicia," *Jounal of Hellenic Studies* 12 (1891): 233–37. Also see *Orientis Graecae Inscriptiones Selectae* 573.

26. Ameling, *Kleinasien*, 498–99, no. 230.

27. Struve, V.V. *Corpus Inscriptionum Regni Bosporani (CIRB)* 1260 (Moscow: Nauka, 1965). Also at Tanais another inscription (*CIRB* 1280) is similar: "To the Highest God who hears" and yet, another dedicatory inscription from Panticapaeum (*CIRB* 64) is similar: "In fulfillment of a vow to the Highest God who hears."

28. Stephen Mitchell, "The Cult of Theos Hypsistos between Pagans, Jews, and Christians," in *Pagan Monotheism in Late Antiquity*, ed. by Polymnia Athanassiadi and Michael Frede (New York: Oxford University Press, 1999), 81–148; Mitchell, "Further Thoughts on the Cult of Theos Hypsistos," in *One God: Pagan Monotheism in the Roman Empire*, ed. by Steven Mitchell and Peter van Nuffelen (Cambridge: Cambridge University Press, 2010), 167–208.

29. Rachel Hachlili, *The Menorah, The Ancient Seven-armed Candelabrum: Origin, Form, and Significance*, (Leiden: Brill, 2001), 200–202.

Serra Durugönül and Ahmet Mörel along with others who believe it is a menorah.[30]

Similar five-branched menorahs can be found at several other locations in this area. Lintels found at unnamed ancient villages located at *Köşkerli, Örendibi*, and *Karaböcülü* all bear similarly shaped five-branched menorahs. Most ancient lintels have no distinctive markings, but those with symbols were important buildings in the community. These menorahs are all set in relief upon lintels of buildings that may have been synagogues.

A menorah is carved into a pilaster of the Athena relief at Sömek. To the left is Zeus' thunderbolt and above that a star and crescent.

Another five-branched menorah was located a short distance from *Örendibi* alongside an ancient road near the village of *Sömek*. This menorah was part of a shrine dedicated to Athena. The centerpiece of the shrine is a five-foot-high rock-cut relief of Athena set in a niche flanked by two pilasters. On both sides of the pilasters there were small busts of unknown figures that were recently removed by treasure hunters. On the right pilaster there remains a star with a crescent below it and Zeus' thunderbolt lower on the pilaster. The menorah is located further to the right. Shrines were commonly located along ancient roads so that travelers could implore the gods for protection in travel.

The presence of the menorah next to pagan symbols is unusual, but not uncommon in this area of Rough Cilicia.[31] As mentioned above, the menorah on the synagogue at *Çatıören* stands next to Zeus' thunderbolt. Likewise, the menorahs at *Köskerli, Örendibi*, and possibly *Karaböcülü* are likewise positioned next to thunderbolts. What was the relationship between these symbols of the Jewish faith and Zeus?

30. Serra Durugönül and Ahmet Mörel, "Evidence of Judaism in Rough Cilicia and Its Associations with Paganism" *Deutsches Archäologisches Institut Abteilung Istanbul* 62 (2012): 303–22. Also Gilbert Dagron and Denis Feissel, *Inscriptions de Cilicie* (Paris: de Boccard, 1987), no. 14; Ameling, *Kleinasien*, 49899, no. 230; and evidently Martin Hengel and Anna Maria Schwemer, *Paul between Damascus and Antioch: The Unknown Years* (Louisville: Westminster John Knox, 1997), 416 n. 824.

31. For that matter, the integration of Hellenistic religious elements with synagogues was not unique to Rough Cilicia or even the diaspora. In some of the synagogues of Palestine one can find depictions of Sol, Helios, and the Zodiac. Beautiful mosaic floors in ancient synagogues at Beth Alpha, Na'aran, Susiya, Hussaifah, Yaphia, Sepphoris and Hamat Tiberias have zodiac circles prominently displayed. These synagogues date to the third century and later, but it is clear that these tendencies existed earlier in many Jewish quarters.

Stephen Mitchell has identified 375 Greek inscriptions that refer to the worship of "the Highest God" (*theos hypsistos*). The bulk of these inscriptions come from Anatolia. Approximately one-third of these identify the Highest God as Zeus. Most of these inscriptions cannot be attached to local Jewish communities, but some of them indicate that the non-Jewish devotees of the Highest God associated with the Jews in their towns and villages. Several early Christian writers mentioned these people: Gregory of Nazianzus, Gregory of Nyssa, Epiphanius of Salamis, and Cyril of Alexandria. Gregory of Nazianzus provides the best description noting that the adherents observed the Sabbath, refrained from the consumption of certain meats, refused to worship idols, and otherwise observed Jewish law. However, they refrained from circumcision and had certain Hellenistic tendencies (*Orationes* 18.5). The similarities to the God-fearers mentioned in the Acts of the Apostles are unmistakable. The *Letter of Aristeas*, a second century BC Jewish writing, probably refers to a similar group of gentile monotheists: "These people worship God, the overseer and creator of all, whom all men worship, including ourselves, O King, except that we all have different names for him, such as Zeus and Yahweh." The connection between Zeus and Yahweh is important in this text because it clearly indicates that some Jews endorsed the faith of non-Jewish monotheists.[32]

The presence of several lintels in Rough Cilicia containing both the Jewish menorah and the thunderbolt of Zeus supports the conclusion that Jews and gentiles worshiped together in this area. The degree of integration between the two groups cannot be known precisely. Two late Hellenistic inscriptions found at *Çatıören* mention two groups of people: the religious members (*hetairois*) and the Sabbath keepers (*sabbatistais*). The larger inscription is a decree that rescinds curses that have been issued against others and levies heavy one hundred drachma fines against anyone who violates the decree of the Sabbath God.[33]

> It was resolved by the religious members and God's | Sabbath keepers, who have gathered together for the worship of the Sabbath *God* to create an | inscribed record which no one can invalidate. And after this is made | let it be strictly observed. If anyone wishes to deposit a curse against someone, | let a curse be deposited against the one who wishes. Protos says to crown | Dis Ibelion as the synagogue official. Of those who are being | condemned in the sanctuaries and who have been inscribed on | the steles and on the curse tablets, let no one be *condemned* nor excised |

32. Arthur Bernard Cook, *Zeus: A Study in Ancient Religion* (Cambridge: Cambridge University Press 1914), 232–237, shows a Phoenician quarter-shekel (probably from Gaza) dated around 350 BC depicting Yahweh as Zeus. Surrounding the head in Phoenician letters is the name Yahweh. Similarly, Cook shows an onyx amulet with Zeus holding his thunderbolt (p. 235) with the words ΙΑΩ ΣΑΒΑΩ (*Iao Sabaoth*) on the back.

33. Hicks, "Inscriptions from Western Cilicia," 233–36. Hicks' transcription was based upon a squeeze made by J. Theodore Bent (Bent, "A Journey in Cilicia Tracheia," *Journal of Hellenic Studies* 12 (1891): 210–11.

> from the record nor dismissed nor removed. And if anyone should deviate or | sin against the Sabbath God he will make payment to | the Sabbath God: one hundred drachmas and to the Sabbath keepers one hundred drachmas and to the city | one hundred drachmas and to the ruler (dynast) one hundred drachmas. This stele is an impartial record of the oath. No one | is to receive *others* into their home on this day. Let the priest distribute the offerings for God | for the maintenance of this place. (author's translation)

What is implied by this inscription is that previous tensions between the "religious members" and the "Sabbath keepers" have been resolved. The non-Jewish religious members were probably worshipers of Zeus Hypsistos and conflicts with the Jews at *Çatıören* resulted in curses that were deposited in the nearby temple of Hermes.[34] This inscription removed those curses and restored relations between the two groups. Additionally, the inscription installed Dis Ibelion as a synagogue official. Dis is a common appellation for Zeus and Dis Ibelion may have been a priest of Zeus Hypsistos. The appointment of this person to the office of synagogue official was a way of enhancing the relationship between the two groups.

Paul's Ministry in Rough Cilicia

Paul's early ministry in this area of Rough Cilicia may have been the stimulus for Paul's understanding that the breadth of God's grace was extended beyond the Jewish community and included non-Jewish people. Paul appears to have been one of the first Christians to fully grasp and articulate this understanding of God's salvation. The inclusion of non-Jews in God's plan of salvation was a massive step forward in Jewish and Christian thought. Acts documents the struggles of Jewish Christian believers in coming to grips with this concept. Peter's ministry to Cornelius and the gentiles gathered together in his house (Acts 10) was not enough for Peter to acknowledge a gentile ministry as a new benchmark moving forward in the future. Later when Peter came to Antioch, Peter's duplicity became evident. Paul confronted Peter with his hypocrisy and harshly rebuked him (Gal 2:11–14). Following his ministry in Rough Cilicia, however, Paul never wavered on the issue. Paul saw little difference between the circumcised and uncircumcised believers in Cilicia, and he realized that God's love and mercy extended to all who would respond to him in faith.

Paul still clung to the hope that the Jewish people would fulfill their mission as a "priestly nation" and minister to the gentile nations. But he also realized that God's mission would not be thwarted by disobedient people: "It was necessary that the word of God be spoken to you first; since you repudiate it ... behold, we are turning to the gentiles" (Acts 13:46). Thus, Paul continued to prioritize his ministry to the synagogues with hopes that responsive Jewish people would fulfill their mission (Rom 1:16).

---

34. The Hermes temple at *Çatıören* was located at the top of the same ridge as the synagogue, less than 110 yards (100 m) away. Hermes was a chthonic deity that transported the deceased and carried messages to the underworld. It was common for people to write curses on tablets and to throw them into the temples of Hermes who supposedly carried them to Hades.

Fortification at Çatıören

So, how far did Paul penetrate into Cilicia? Eckhard Schnabel suggests that Paul visited the cities with a known Jewish presence and lists Anazarbos, Mallos, Soloi, Sebaste, Corycus, Seleucia, and Olba. He also notes that Paul could have visited cities with an unknown Jewish presence such as Baiae, Issus, Katabolos, Aigai, Epiphaneia, Hierapolis, Mopsuestia, Adana, Augusta, and Zephyrion in Smooth Cilicia and the Rough Cilician cities of Palaiai, Aphrodisias, and Anemurium.[35] Of these twenty cities, most of them are coastal cities (thirteen) or cities connected with known major thoroughfares (six). However, the body of work that we piece together from Paul's later travels and from his own words leads us to conclude that Paul did not always take the easy path. If Paul's Syrian and Cilician ministry consisted of a seven to nine year mission, I suspect Paul went deeper into the interior of Rough Cilicia.

The most direct route connecting Tarsus with Syrian Antioch passed through Alexandria Ad Issus, Baiae, Issus, Katabolos, Epiphaneia, Mopsuestia, and Adana. A more southern route would have bypassed Mopsuestia and Adana and added Aigai and Mallos. It can be assumed that Paul would have evangelized all of these cities. North of Adana and Mopsuestia were the cities of Anazarbos and Hierapolis. I would likewise include these cities as likely places for Paul to have visited during this time. Rough Cilicia however, is a bit more complicated. The inland towns and villages were much more remote, and although there was a sizeable Jewish presence there, travel was not easy and there were many dangers.

The inland villages and towns of Rough Cilicia have been scarcely investigated by scholars and archaeologists. Consequently, it is hard to determine how many Jews occupied these mountains and foothills. From the little that is known, the area between the Lamos River and the Calycadnus River had a large number of

35. Schnabel, *Paul the Missionary*, 69.

resident Jews and it is logical to assume that the data cited above is just scratching the surface of what will someday be discovered. I operate under the assumption that the Calycadnus River was the furthest western extent of Paul's reach into Rough Cilicia and that the cities further west—Palaiai, Aphrodisias, Anemurium, Antiochia Ad Cragum, and Coracesium were beyond the scope of Paul's mission. The density of Jews, large number of villages and the difficulties of reaching these places between the Lamos and Calycadnus Rivers was enough to occupy Paul for a long period of time.

This area of Rough Cilicia contains some of the most tortured land in all of Anatolia. The mountains and foothills run close to the shoreline and streams emanating far into the interior have carved deep gorges and canyons that empty into the Mediterranean. Cliffs drop off to the canyon floors as far as 1700 feet (518 m) below. The ancient road on the coast ran in a southwestern direction along the narrow stretch of flatland. In the interior, travel in the same direction was impossible. Instead, all roads into the interior ran in a northwestern direction, climbing, turning, and twisting as the canyons allowed. Most of the modern roads follow the same route. Many sections of the ancient roads can still be found in the region along with several Roman milestones.

Many of the villages and dwellings in this area were constructed for defensive purposes. They occupy strategic positions along the cliffs and places where the occupants could observe movement from the coastal areas into the interior. There are more than thirty watchtowers between the Lamos and Calycadnus Rivers and no doubt many more existed in the past. Even more remarkably, many of the cliff faces have dwellings cut into the rock. Clearly, the residents feared trouble coming in from the coast.

With the exception of Diocaesarea and Olba, none of these settlements contained the usual structures associated with Hellenistic and Roman towns. Absent were the stadiums, theaters, odeons, public baths, water fountains, gymnasiums, and colonnaded streets. Instead, these were austere communities that were designed for protection and survival. Why did these people migrate to these inhospitable regions, why did they erect these rustic communities and what did they fear?

Starting at the end of the second century BC the entire southern coast of Anatolia from Lycia through Pamphylia to Cilicia was controlled by pirates who seized the coastal cities and forced the indigenous residents to pay tribute and to cooperate with them. Many of the native residents fled into the interior and established these crude settlements. Over the years, the Romans sent several of their best military leaders to the area to subdue the pirates and on each occasion the Roman propaganda claimed to eliminate the problem. But these were temporary fixes. The pirates retreated to the security of the mountainous interior and then returned to the coastal cities when the Roman troops departed. The last Roman general, Pompey, claimed to finish the job. However, there is no evidence to indicate that Pompey did anything to the pirates east of Anemurium.[36] By the end of the first century BC and

36. Philip de Souza, *Piracy in the Greco-Roman World* (New York: Cambridge University Press, 1999).

extending into the first century AD, Cilicia was rife with pirates who were deeply entrenched in the coastal cities and had made progress in infiltrating the interior.[37] Cicero was appointed proconsul of Cilicia in 51 BC and was given two legions to subdue the land. In his letters Cicero frequently alluded to the difficulties of fighting with the bandits of the countryside, the rebellious Cilician mountain men and the perpetual hostilities of the inhabitants (*Letters to Friends* 2.10; 15.1; 15.4). Extending even into the first century AD the men of Cilicia and Isauria were described by Cassius Dio as pirates who were creating havoc with their marauding expeditions (*History* 55.28). Paul probably had these places in mind when he described his journeys with dangers from rivers, dangers from pirates, dangers from his countrymen, and dangers in the wilderness, along with sleepless nights in hunger and thirst without food in cold and exposure (2 Cor 11:26–27).

Due to the large presence of Jews in Rough Cilicia, I would presume that Paul began his Cilician ministry in this area, sometime after first evangelizing Tarsus. The coastal road ran for forty-five miles (72.4 km) southwest from Tarsus before reaching Rough Cilicia. Along the way Paul would have passed through Zephyrion and Soli (Pompeiopolis). Rough Cilicia began at the point where the Lamos River emptied into the sea.

Once in the area of Rough Cilicia, Paul could have visited sites relatively near the coast including *Koşkerli*, Kanyteleis, and *Kabaçam* (see map on page 714). These places were agricultural communities and occupied positions that were not easily defended. Traveling up the Lamos River and crossing over three Roman bridges one comes to the fortress of *Sömek* and the settlement of *Örendibi* on the south side of the canyon and the fortresses at *Hüsametli, Yeniyurt,* and *Tapureli* on the north. *Yeniyurt* and *Tapureli* were built at strategic cliff-side locations between 650 and 1600 feet (198–488 m) above the river. Large rock-cut reliefs of soldiers marked the sites. Cliff face rock-cut dwellings litter the canyon walls between these fortresses and ancient roads are still visible leading to *Sömek* and *Tapureli*.

Further to the southwest streams from the mountains formed ravines that deepened into canyons as they approached the coast. At the coast the harbor city of Elaioussa Sebaste was established. A Roman road north led to the fortification at *Çatıören* with its synagogue and *İmirzeli*. On the other side of the ravine to the west another fortress at *Yapılı İn* was dug into the cliff side two hundred feet (61 m) above the valley floor. A large rock-cut relief of a soldier guarded the site and many dwellings were cut into the cliff surrounding the fortress. Yet another fortress was located southeast of *Çatıören* on the cliffs at *Hisarkale*.

A deeper canyon further to the southwest, known by the locals as Satan's Valley, was home to several ancient communities. Above the canyon on the north an ancient road led all the way from the coast to the Olbian kingdom's chief cities, Olba and Diocaesarea. Portions of the road can be seen today and the modern

---

37. Strabo, *Geography* 14.5.10, stated that residents of the interior (the Olbian kingdom) struggled with the pirates. Aba, the daughter of the pirate leader Xenophanes, was married to the priest of the temple of Zeus at Olba. No doubt, this was an attempt to resolve the problem of the pirate raids into the interior.

road follows the same path. The road was a main route to the interior and was guarded by several watchtowers. Starting from the coastal port at Corycus, the traveler would journey north to a fortification at *Adamkayalar* (550 feet [167.6 m] above the valley) preserved with several soldier reliefs. Çambazli, Diocaesarea, and fortresses and watchtowers at *Kurşunlu* and Olba were further to the northwest. Large sections of Roman roads, milestones, and watchtowers are present along the route.

Other routes to Diocaesarea ran along the sides of another deeply cut canyon located further to the southwest. On the northeastern side of the canyon a road ran from Korasion on the coast north to fortresses located at *Paslı* and *Tekkadın* (both of them located 400 feet [122 m] above the canyon floor). On the southwestern side of the same canyon heading northwest from the coast one would encounter ancient towns at *Karakabaklı, Işıkkale, Akhayat, Sinekkale* and the cliffside fortress at *Imamlı* (*Meydankale*—300 feet [91.4 m] above the canyon) before reaching Diocaesarea.

From Seleucia Ad Calycadnum two routes ran north into the mountains. The eastern route ran north to *Imbriogion* and then connected to *Meydankale* and continued north to Diocaesarea. Further to the west, a road led to the fortress at *Karaböcülü* standing 650 feet (198 m] above a valley leading to the Calycadnus River.

Did Paul's ministry involve all of these remote cities, towns, and villages? It is hard to say with any certainty. But, these places fit the criteria that Paul mentioned for ministry: places where nobody else had shared the gospel and places with a Jewish presence. Moreover, these were places close to his home in Tarsus, and the seven to nine years of Paul's ministry in this region afforded him enough time to scrupulously cover the territory.

The watchtower at Kurşunlu (ancient name unknown) guarded a small settlement located about 10 kilometers (6 miles) from Olba along a Roman road leading to the southeast. Over thirty watchtowers can be seen today in the region.

It is common in contemporary scholarship to suggest that Paul's so-called second and third missions followed a route over the Taurus Mountains north of Tarsus through the Cilician Gates and into Isauria, Lycaonia, and Galatia. However, if Acts 15:41's reference to strengthening the churches in Cilicia is understood to involve more than the region of Cilicia Pedias and to have included the region of Cilicia Tracheia, then the course of Paul's travels would have been different. The coastal road from Tarsus extended southwest all the way to Seleucia Ad Calycadnum and beyond. If Paul established churches in Rough Cilicia as far to the southwest

Overlooking a canyon that emptied into the Calycadnus River valley, Karaböcülü (ancient name unknown) was strategically positioned to observe travelers heading into the interior. A half buried lintel with a menorah suggests that a Jewish community resided here.

as Seleucia, the apostle's journey to the Galatian interior probably would have followed the Calycadnus River north through the Taurus Mountains and into Isauria, Lycaonia, and Galatia. It would make sense that Paul would follow up his ministry in these cities, towns, and villages of Rough Cilicia en route to the interior on his later journeys.

The Thecla traditions contribute to this conclusion. Even though the Acts of Thecla (part of the apocryphal Acts of Paul) is overlaid with doubtful legends, in my mind the early date, quantity of traditions, and the strength of these traditions is convincing enough to conclude that Thecla was a historical person converted under Paul's ministry in Iconium. The Acts of Thecla concludes with Thecla traveling to Seleucia and spending her remaining years there.[38] The ruins of three Byzantine churches commemorating Thecla remain there today and the place was a popular pilgrimage site throughout the Byzantine period. The transit of Thecla from Iconium to Seleucia suggests that this route via the Calycadnus River was commonly used in the Roman period. Additionally, the choice of Seleucia as the place of Thecla's

38. Most scholars date the Acts of Thecla in the early or middle of the second century, for example, Stephen J. Davis, *The Cult of Saint Thecla: A Tradition of Women's Piety in Late Antiquity* (New York: Oxford University Press, 2001); Jeremy W. Barrier, *The Acts of Paul and Thecla: A Critical Introduction and Commentary* (Tübingen: Mohr Siebeck, 2009); Barrier, J. N. Bremmer, T. Nicklas. and A. Puig i Tarrech, eds., *Thecla: Paul's Disciple and Saint in the East and West* (Leuven: Peeters, 2017).

final years indicates that a church was established in that place prior to Thecla's journey. This all points back to Paul's ministry in Rough Cilicia during the seven to nine silent years.

CONCLUSIONS

We cannot be certain regarding the specific details of the silent years of Paul's ministry in Syria and Cilicia. Nevertheless, we can posit a plausible scenario of these years based upon the history of those regions, the geography and topography of the land, and Paul's missionary strategies. In his early years, and perhaps until the end, the apostle believed that the Jews were an elect nation that was charged with the task of achieving God's purposes in this world.[39] For that reason, Paul targeted the cities and towns that had a Jewish presence. The Jewish historian Josephus tells us that there was a large Jewish presence in Syria. Literary and archaeological evidence also indicates that Rough Cilicia also had a substantial Jewish population. It is reasonable to assume that Paul visited these cities, towns, and villages.

Paul also tells us that his desire was to preach the gospel in places where churches were not already established. During these silent years, Acts indicates that persecutions drove many Christians north from Judea into the regions of Syria. As they came to Syria, these Christians shared their faith and churches were established. One can assume from this that Paul did ministry in Syria in the early years of this seven to nine year period. But, when more Christians infiltrated Syria and more churches were established, Paul increasingly turned his attention to Cilicia, particularly the region of Rough Cilicia and its numerous Jewish residents.

In Syria and Cilicia Paul became aware of the dangers of ministry. The mistreatment that Paul described in 2 Corinthians 11:23–28 cannot be completely harmonized with Paul's three missions as described in Acts. While writing to the Corinthians, Paul described the harsh travel and abuse that he experienced in all of his missions.

It seems that Paul's perspectives on the gentiles were broadened as a result of his work in Rough Cilicia. Through the close association of gentile worshipers of the Highest God with the Jews in the synagogues, Paul came to realize that God had opened the doors of salvation to uncircumcised people. The Jewish Christians in Judea struggled with this concept, but Paul was decades ahead of the Judaizers.

Perhaps it is going too far to suggest that Paul learned something about reconciliation during this time. In the first century Jewish and gentile relations were terrible and most rabbis forbade close relations with gentiles. We can imagine Paul standing at the inscription in the bedrock at *Çatıören*. Here was a deeply fractured village where Jews and gentiles had hurled curses at one another. But through their common devotion to one God, the community found common ground, reconciled with one another, rescinded all curses, banned future curses, and levied heavy penalties against anyone violating the decree. Was

39. See N. T. Wright, *Paul and the Faithfulness of God* (Minneapolis: Fortress, 2013); Lionel J. Windsor, *Paul and the Vocation of Israel: How Paul's Jewish Identity Informs His Apostolic Ministry, with Special Reference to Romans* (Berlin: de Gruyter, 2014).

this experience in the back of Paul's mind later when he wrote to the Ephesians?

> Therefore remember that formerly you, the gentiles in the flesh, who are called "Uncircumcision" by the so-called "Circumcision" … remember that you were at that time separate from Christ, excluded from the commonwealth of Israel, and strangers to the covenants of promise, having no hope and without God in the world. But now in Christ Jesus you who formerly were far off have been brought near by the blood of Christ. For he himself is our peace, who made both groups into one … so that in himself he might make the two into one new person, thus establishing peace, and might reconcile them both in one body to God through the cross, by it having put to death the enmity. And he came and preached peace to you who were far away, and peace to those who were near; for through him we both have our access in one Spirit to the Father. So then you are no longer strangers and aliens, but you are fellow citizens with the saints, and are of God's household. (Eph 2:11–19)

The ministry in Syria and Cilicia affirmed Paul's call and set the apostle on a course that would not conclude until his death. Paul lived life on the edge, realizing that death could come at any moment. His was a life without material comforts, without the pleasures of a wife and family, and a life of frequent opposition. Yet his was a life of joy, knowing that there were greater rewards in the hereafter. "For to me, to live is Christ and to die is gain."

BIBLIOGRAPHY

Ameling, Walter, ed. *Inscriptiones Judaicae Orientis: Kleinasien*. Vol. 2 of *Inscriptiones Judaicae Orientis*. Tübingen: Mohr Siebeck, 2004.

Barrier, Jeremy W. *The Acts of Paul and Thecla: A Critical Introduction and Commentary*. Tübingen: Mohr Siebeck, 2009.

Barrier, Jeremy W., J. N. Bremmer, T. Nicklas, and A. Puig i Tarrech, eds. *Thecla: Paul's Disciple and Saint in the East and West*. Leuven: Peeters, 2017.

Bent, J. Theodore. "A Journey in Cilicia Tracheia." *Journal of Hellenic Studies* 12 (1891): 206–24.

Blömer, Michael, and Engelbert Winter. *Commagene: The Land of Gods Between the Taurus and the Euphrates*. Istanbul: Homer Kitabevi, 2011.

Çalışkan, Mehmet, Ayşe Aydın, Ümit Aydınoğlu, and Filiz Kerem. *Mersin: Ruins, Castles Museums*. 2nd ed. Mersin: Il Özel Idaresi, 2009. [Turkish]

Cicero. *Letters to Friends, Volume 1: Letters 1–113*. LCL 205. Translated by D. R. Shackleton Bailey. Cambridge: Harvard University Press, 2001.

Cook, Arthur Bernard. *Zeus: A Study in Ancient Religion*. Cambridge: Cambridge University Press, 1914.

Dagron, Gilbert, and Denis Feissel. *Inscriptions de Cilicie*. Paris: de Boccard, 1987.

Davis, Stephen J. *The Cult of Saint Thecla: A Tradition of Women's Piety in Late Antiquity*. New York: Oxford University Press, 2001.

Dio Cassius, *Roman History, Volume VI: Books 51–55*. LCL 83. Translated by Earnest Cary. Cambridge: Harvard University Press, 1917.

Durugönül, Serra and Ahmet Mörel. "Evidence of Judaism in Rough Cilicia and Its Associations with Paganism." *Deutsches Archäologisches Institut Abteilung Istanbul* 62 (2012): 303–22.

Eckhardt, Benedikt. *Jewish Identity and Politics between the Maccabees and Bar Kokhba*. Leiden: Brill, 2012.

Epiphanius. *The Panarion of Epiphanius of Salamis: Book 1 (Sects 1–46)*. Translated by F. Williams. Leiden: Brill, 1997.

Fairchild, Mark R. "The Jewish Communities in Eastern Rough Cilicia." *Journal of Ancient Judaism* 5 (2014): 204–216, 285–288.

———. "Turkey's Unexcavated Synagogues: Could the World's Earliest Known Synagogue Be Buried Amid Rubble?" *BAR* 38.4 (2012): 34–41, 65.

Freely, John. *The Eastern Mediterranean Coast of Turkey*. Istanbul: SEV Matbaacılık, 1998.

Hachlili, Rachel. *The Menorah, The Ancient Seven-armed Candelabrum: Origin, Form, and Significance*. Leiden: Brill, 2001.

Hengel, Martin, and Anna Maria Schwemer. *Paul between Damascus and Antioch: The Unknown Years*. Louisville: Westminster John Knox, 1997.

Hicks, E. L. "Inscriptions from Western Cilicia." *Journal of Hellenic Studies* 12 (1891): 225–73.

Jones, A. H. M. *Cities of the Eastern Roman Provinces*. 2nd ed. Oxford: Clarendon, 1971.

Josephus. *Jewish Antiquities: Books 16–17*. LCL 410. Translated by Ralph Marcus and Allen Wikgren. Cambridge: Harvard University Press, 1963.

———. *Jewish Antiquities: Books 18–19, 20*. LCL 433, 456. Translated by Louis H. Feldman. Cambridge: Harvard University Press 1965.

———. *The Jewish War: Books 1–2, 3–4, 5–7*. LCL 203, 487, 210. Translated by H. St. J. Thackeray. Cambridge: Harvard University Press, 1926–1928.

Keil, J., and A. Wilhelm, eds. *Monumenta Asiae Minoris Antiqua, Volume 3: Denkmäler aus dem rauhen Kilikien*. Manchester: Manchester University Press, 1931.

Klijn, A. F. J. *Jewish-Christian Gospel Tradition*. Leiden: Brill, 1992.

Levinskaya, Irina. *The Book of Acts in Its Diaspora Setting*. Vol. 5 of *The Book of Acts in Its First Century Setting*. Edited by Bruce W. Winter. Grand Rapids: Eerdmans, 1996.

Miller, Fergus. *The Roman Near East: 31 BC–AD 337*. Cambridge, MA: Harvard University Press, 1993.

Mitchell, Stephen. "The Cult of Theos Hypsistos between Pagans, Jews, and Christians." Pages 81–148 in *Pagan Monotheism in Late Antiquity*. Edited by Polymnia Athanassiadi and Michael Frede. New York: Oxford University Press, 1999.

———. "Further Thoughts on the Cult of Theos Hypsistos." Pages 167–208 in *One God: Pagan Monotheism in the Roman Empire*. Edited by Steven Mitchell and Peter van Nuffelen. Cambridge: Cambridge University Press, 2010.

Neusner, Jacob. *The Mishnah: A New Translation*. New Haven: Yale University Press, 1988.

Noy, David, and Hanswulf Bloedhorn, eds. *Inscriptiones Judaicae Orientis, Volume 3: Syria and Cyprus*. Tübingen: Mohr Siebeck, 2004.

Philo. *On the Embassy to Gaius*. LCL 379. Translated by F. H. Colson. Cambridge: Harvard University Press, 1962.

Riesner, Rainer. *Paul's Early Period: Chronology, Mission Strategy, Theology*. Grand Rapids: Eerdmans, 1990.

Rosenfeld, Ben-Zion, and Joseph Menirav. "The Ancient Synagogue as an Economic Center." *Journal of Near Eastern Studies* 58 (1999): 259–76.

Schnabel, Eckhard J. *Paul the Missionary: Realities, Strategies and Methods*. Downers Grove, IL: InterVarsity Press, 2008.

Schürer, Emil. *The History of the Jewish People in the Age of Jesus Christ: Volume 3, Part 1*. Revised by Geza Vermes, Fergus Millar, and Martin Goodman. Edinburgh: T&T Clark, 1986.

Sinclair, T. A. *Eastern Turkey: An Architectural and Archaeological Survey*. Vol. 4. London: Pindar, 1990.

Souza, Philip de. *Piracy in the Graeco-Roman World*. New York: Cambridge University Press, 1999.

Strabo. *Geography: Books 13–14, 15–16*. LCL 223, 241. Translated by H. L. Jones. Cambridge: Harvard University Press, 1929–1930.

Struve, V. V. *Corpus Inscriptionum Regni Bosporani (CIRB)*. Moscow: Nauka, 1965.

Talbert, Richard J. A., ed. *Barrington Atlas of the Greek and Roman World*. Princeton: Princeton University Press, 2000.

Taşkıran, Celal. *Silifke (Seleucia on Calycadnus) and Environs*. Revised edition. Silifke: SİM Matbaacılık, 2010.

Trebilco, Paul. *Jewish Communities in Asia Minor*. Cambridge: Cambridge University Press, 1991.

Williams, Margaret H. "The Jewish Community of Corycus: Two More Inscriptions." *Zeitschrift für Papyrologie und Epigraphik* 92 (1992): 248–52.

Wilson, Mark. "Cilicia: The First Christian Churches in Anatolia." *TynBul* 54 (2003): 15–30.

Windsor, Lionel J. *Paul and the Vocation of Israel: How Paul's Jewish Identity Informs His Apostolic Ministry, with Special Reference to Romans*. Berlin: de Gruyter, 2014.

Wright, N. T. *Paul and the Faithfulness of God*. Minneapolis: Fortress, 2013.

CHAPTER 40

THE MEANING OF "ARABIA" IN CLASSICAL LITERATURE AND THE NEW TESTAMENT

Gal 1:17; 4:25

Barry J. Beitzel

KEY POINTS

- Though cited only twice in the New Testament (Gal 1:17; 4:25), the term "Arabia" is attested nearly two thousand times in classical literature, in widely diverse contexts and by many different writers.
- The word Arabia is found in Old Testament literature, and it is part of a modern dictionary, but one must not uncritically assume that the word denotes the same geographic entity in all these literatures.
- As with his fellow authors of New Testament books, Paul most often employs classical geographic terminology that is contemporary with him.

INTRODUCTION

Near the beginning of his epistle to the Galatian churches, the apostle Paul declares the following:

> But when God, who set me apart from my mother's womb and called me by his grace, was pleased to reveal his Son in me so that I might preach him among the Gentiles, my immediate response was not to consult any human being. I did not go up to Jerusalem to see those who were apostles before I was, but *I went to Arabia*. Later I returned to Damascus. (Gal 1:15–17, emphasis added)[1]

Further in the same epistle, Paul enters into a discussion of the relationship between "the free woman" (Sarah) and

1. See also 2 Cor 11:32–33; Acts 9:23–25. Unless otherwise indicated, Scripture quotations in this essay are taken from the New International Version (NIV).

"the slave woman" (Hagar). The apostle employs figurative/allegorical language (ἀλληγορέω, *allēgoreō*), he claims, in order to compare the two covenants represented by these two wives of Abraham and their descendants. His text reads:

> These things are being taken figuratively. The women represent two covenants. One covenant is from Mount Sinai and bears children who are to be slaves: This is Hagar. Now Hagar stands for *Mount Sinai in Arabia* and corresponds to the present city of Jerusalem, because she is in slavery with her children. But the Jerusalem that is above is free, and she is our mother. (Gal 4:24–26, emphasis added)

The question of the location of "Arabia" in Galatians has historically been thoroughly examined by a wide range of scholarship, whether in commentary form or in periodical literature, with no unequivocally definitive resolution. However, beginning in the last quarter of the twentieth century, a new wrinkle has been introduced into this discussion. So far as I can discern, this recent turn is a separate and entirely modern inquiry that focuses not on biblical exegesis, Pauline theology, or classical history, but instead on the location of Mt. Sinai specifically. This growing discussion is found not in scholarly books or articles but rather in more popular venues—on websites, videos, YouTube videos, or blog posts. In particular, this discussion understands Paul to be making a straightforward and purely geographic assertion—one essentially without nuance of any sort—and, accordingly, it marshals his statement in Galatians to settle the longstanding question of the locations of Arabia and Mt. Sinai: both must be situated somewhere in Saudi Arabia.

This assertion, which has been expressed in two different forms—(2a) premise = a logical form or (2b) premise = a biblical form—can be reduced to the following syllogism:

1. Paul declares that Mt. Sinai is in Arabia; either

- (2a) One learns from any encyclopedia that Arabia geographically identifies the Arabian Peninsula and/or politically designates the country of Saudi Arabia; or
- (2b) The Old Testament without exception always places Arabia in the land of Midian (that is, modern Saudi Arabia); and therefore

(3) Mt. Sinai must be located in Saudi Arabia.

Either form of such syllogistic thinking may account for the title of a recent post on a popular website: "Paul said Mt. Sinai was in Saudi Arabia: Gal 4:25."[2]

Before offering an evidentiary response, I wish to introduce two diagnostic illustrations that will help us better understand the rationale of this modern view, as well as provisionally consider its theoretical viability. First, an illustration from history. A widely recognized authority of logic, David Hackett Fischer, identifies what he calls "the fallacy of the perfect analogy," which "consists in reasoning from a partial resemblance between two entities to an

2. http://www.bible.ca/archeology/bible-archeology-exodus-mt-sinai-arabia-gal-4-25.htm.

entire and exact analogy."[3] Both forms of this modern syllogistic point of view appear to presuppose that the analogy in this case is perfect, exact, and absolute. Second, according to an element of Euclidian geometry, "Things which equal the same thing also equal each other." Simply stated, Euclid's element means that if A = B and B = C, then A = C.

As applied to my essay, a logical entailment of this modern view requires more than simply to demonstrate A = C or C = A. More fundamentally, for the syllogism to obtain fully in this instance without presupposition, B must with certainty equal B. That is to say, the "Arabia" (1) as identified in Galatians must equal the "Arabia" (2a) as identified in an encyclopedia, or it must equal the "Arabia" (2b) found in Old Testament citations. A wide chronological gap involved in both cases—between Paul's first century AD statements and either a sixth to eighth century BC source or a twenty-first century AD source—renders this an exceedingly high hurdle to overcome, even theoretically or even before examining relevant documentary evidence. For this assumed equation to be logically demonstrable or for the analogy to be perfect and absolute, one would be obliged to show with certainty either that Paul was writing or using identical terminology in vogue either during the sixth to eighth century BC or in the twenty-first century AD (a logical nonstarter) or that Old Testament citations or today's encyclopedia definition of Arabia must always apply to precisely the same entity and with precisely the same denotation as at the time Paul penned his Galatians epistle. To be valid and worthy of our embrace, a B = B equation is required to be both perfect and absolute.

In this regard, the clear question to be addressed is not what "Arabia" may denote in the Iron Age or in modernity, but rather what the term "Arabia" would have suggested to a first-century Jew, whether one living in Judea or in the Roman province of Galatia.[4] It is to address this latter necessary consideration that I present my study here.

3. David Hackett Fischer, *Historical Fallacies: Toward a Logic of Historical Thought* (New York: HarperPerennial, 1970), 247–51.

4. It is scarcely relevant what the term "Arabia" may have denoted in the Old Testament. Beyond the obvious issue of anachronism, one must first recognize the hard fact that the Old Testament texts themselves do not consistently specify one and the same region. Thus, for example, as a root designating Arabia/Arab(s), the Hebrew word [*'rb*, ערב] occurs some sixteen times in the Old Testament. When construed as a geographical/regional entity (= "Arabia"), the word occurs in five texts: Isa 21:13 (twice); Jer 25:24; Ezek 27:21; 30:5. The context of the first four of these citations can theoretically point in the direction of the Arabian Peninsula (*Arabia Eudaimon/Felix*, see below) or to the desert area of eastern Nabatea (*Arabia Petraea*, see below), but the context of Ezek 30, which is part of an oracle of doom pronounced on Egypt (30:1–19; for the wider context, see Ezek 29:1–32:32), points unmistakably to a location for Arabia on or near the continent of Africa (perhaps *Arabia ad Aegyptum* or *Arabia Nomos*, see below). It is important to note here that an explicit connection between "Arabia" and biblical Midian, central to the syllogistic model, is nowhere to be found in these texts.

Second, there are four Old Testament texts in which this word is used as a singular gentilic (= "Arab"): (1) Neh 2:19 [Heb: 4:1; LXX: 2 Esdras 14:1]: three individuals hear about the effort to rebuild Jerusalem's walls, and they travel there to accuse Nehemiah of treasonous activity: They are Sanballat (who comes from either Beth-horon or Samaria), Tobiah (who hails from Ammon), and Geshem the Arab (his homeland is unstated but is possibly Kedar, a territory understood by classical writers and modern writers alike to be a locale around Petra or west

DOCUMENTARY SOURCES

The evidentiary data that follow are largely dependent on a computer search available through the *Thesaurus Linguae Graecae* (*TLG*), an electronic data bank that seeks exhaustively to identify and classify all lexical entries and a measure of grammatic or syntactic expressions found in Greek literature, ranging in scope from the time of Homer (late eighth century BC) through the end of the Byzantine period (AD 1453). According to the preface of the canon of the third edition,[5] this ever-expanding data bank now contains lexical entries from the writings of more than 3,100 classical authors.

Since my aim in this essay is to attempt to understand the lexeme "Arabia" as it

across the Sinai [for example, Pliny, *Natural History* 5.12.65; Eusebius, *Onomasticon* 620/118:21]). (For Kedar, the land of the Saracenes, as early as Ptolemy [5.17.3; Nobbe enumeration], see also Michael O'Connor, "The Etymology of *Saracen* in Aramaic and Pre-Islamic Arabic Contexts," in *The Defence of the Roman and Byzantine East*, ed. Philip Freeman and David Kennedy, 2 vols. [Oxford: BAR, 1986], 603–32; Ernst Axel Knauf, "Kedar,"*ABD* 4:9–10; Israel Eph'al, *The Ancient Arabs: Nomads on the Border of the Fertile Crescent, 9th–5th Centuries B.C.* [Jerusalem: Magnes], 223–27; see also John Wilkinson, *Egeria's Travels to the Holy Land*, 3rd ed. [Oxford: Aris & Phillips, 2006], 5.8); (2) Neh 6:1 [LXX: 2 Esdras 16:1]: in a related text, the same three individuals propose to Nehemiah that they should meet him on the Plain of Ono (northwest of Jerusalem, near Philistia), intending to do him harm; (3) Isa 13:20: Babylon will become so uninhabited that not even an "Arab" will pitch his tent there; and (4) Jer 3:2: Judah lies in wait for lovers like an "Arab" in the desert. Again, these texts are problematic for any absolute interpretation. As indicated just above, the Nehemiah texts are most likely referencing somewhere between Petra and western Sinai. The two prophetic narratives appear to be making a rather generic and geographically nondescript reference to the desert per se (see NIV and NLT, "nomad[s]" in both cases). None of these texts reveals an explicit connection to Midian or points us definitively in the direction of Saudi Arabia.

Finally, there are seven Old Testament texts where the Hebrew root *'rb* is used as a plural gentilic (= "Arabs"): 1 Kgs 10:15 = 2 Chr 9:14; 2 Chr 17:11; 21:16; 22:1; 26:7; Neh 4:7 [LXX: 2 Esdras 12:19]. The first of these, a synoptic text, is inexact in context and offers no useful information. The remaining texts in 2 Chronicles are a bit more helpful in our quest. The narrative of 17:11 indicates that Jehoshaphat's neighbors—the Philistines and the Arabs are expressly mentioned by name—come with their gifts to placate the Judahite king. Similarly, the text of 21:16 (also rehearsed in 22:1) juxtaposes the Philistines and the Arabs, and in this case Arabs who are said to be living near the Cushites (perhaps refer in this instance to 2 Chr 14:9, where a skirmish between a Cushite and king Asa is said to have taken place at Mareshah, a town in the Shephelah near Lachish); in this latter event, scholarship tends to locate the Cushite people in the southern Negev and/or in portions of the Sinai peninsula.

Once again linking the Philistines and the Arabs, 2 Chron 26:7 indicates that king Uzziah of Judah was given divine assistance against his foes the Philistines and the Arabs, in this case Arabs who live in Gur-baal, a town or a region said to have been situated either near Petra or west of Edom and in the southern Negev or northeast Sinai (see Randall Younker, "Gurbaal," *ABD* 2:1100; Anson F. Rainey and R. Steven Notley, *The Sacred Bridge* [Carta: Jerusalem, 2006], 218 [map]). Even when most expansive, the realms of Judahite kings Jehoshaphat, Asa, or Uzziah never included Midian or any part of Saudi Arabia. In my estimation, therefore, these sixteen Old Testament texts referencing Arabia/Arab(s) have the cumulative effect of evoking the greatest doubt regarding the oft-repeated claim that "Arabia" in the Bible always and without exception refers to the land of Midian (modern Saudi Arabia).

5. Luci Berkowitz and Karl A. Squitier, eds., *Thesaurus Linguae Graecae: Canon of Greek Authors and Works* (New York: Oxford University Press, 1990), xii; this project is anchored at the University of California at Irvine. See http://www.tlc.uci.edu/index.prev.php/.

would have been understood in a world contemporary with Paul, I have restricted my use of this vast data, chronologically speaking, to the period between Alexander the Great (approximately 333–331 BC) and the time of the Emperor Constantine (approximately AD 325). However, since Alexander's major historians themselves date from the first century BC to the first century AD (Diodorus of Sicily, *Bibliotheca Historica*; Arrian, *Anabasis*; Quintus Curtius, *Historiae Alexandri Magni;* see also Plutarch, *Life of Alexander*), I am able to narrow my time frame to a certain extent. Moreover, in an attempt to circumscribe my purview even more, I rely sparingly on documentation dating after the second Christian century, though I shall include some evidence, so as to take in (1) a brief but relevant discussion of Provincia Arabia, created in AD 106 by Trajan after his apparently peaceful annexation of Nabatea and (2) the testimony of some early Christian writers. Notwithstanding, even this narrowing of scope has left me with more than 1200 classical citations of Arabia. Space will constrain my usage here to only a few of the citations that can speak most unambiguously to the question under consideration.

Another determinative documentary source for my research is *The Onomasticon of Iudaea-Palaestina and Arabia in the Greek and Latin Sources* (*IASH*).[6] Unlike the *TLG* in three significant ways, the *IASH* volumes intend to isolate and classify only geographical names (not all lexemes), they include Latin texts, and they assume a much more geographically restrictive horizon, limited largely to classical sources originating in Syria, Palestine, Sinai, Egypt, and Arabia, and not from across the entire Greco-Roman world. Even with this more limited conceptual and geographical framework, one is still left with almost six hundred attestations of "Arabia," dating between the time of Alexander and the time of Constantine. This leaves me again with the urgent need to be ruthlessly selective in my use of data.

For citations of Arabia found in the New Testament and other early Christian literature I have utilized *A Greek-English Lexicon of the New Testament and Other Early Christian Literature* (BDAG). For attestations of Arabia in Josephus' considerable writings, I have employed the comprehensive concordance of Rengstorf,[7] and for the scattering of references found in the Apocrypha or Pseudepigrapha, I have made use of Metzger.[8] For the numerous citations from the famed Greek geographer, Ptolemy, I have relied on the editions of Nobbe or Stückelberger and Grasshoff (not the fatally flawed English edition of Stevenson).[9] My use of authoritative Greco-Roman cartographic data and sources rests primarily on the *Barrington Atlas of the Greek and*

6. Leah Di Segni and Yoram Tsafrir, *The Onomasticon of Iudaea-Palaestina and Arabia in the Greek and Latin Sources*, 2 vols. (Jerusalem: Israel Academy of Sciences and Humanities, 2017). The editors of the *IASH* series use "Arabia" to reference the relevant historical data, not the modern country.

7. Karl Heinrich Rengstorf, *A Complete Concordance to Flavius Josephus* (Leiden: Brill, 2002).

8. Bruce M. Metzger, ed., *A Concordance to the Apocrypha/Deuterocanonical Books of the Revised Standard Version* (Grand Rapids: Eerdmans, 1982), 31.

9. Carolus Fridericus Augustus Nobbe, *Claudii Ptolemaei Geographia*, 3 vols. (Leipzig: Tauchnitus, 1843–1845); Alfred Stückelberger and Gerd Grasshoff, *Klaudios Ptolemaios,*

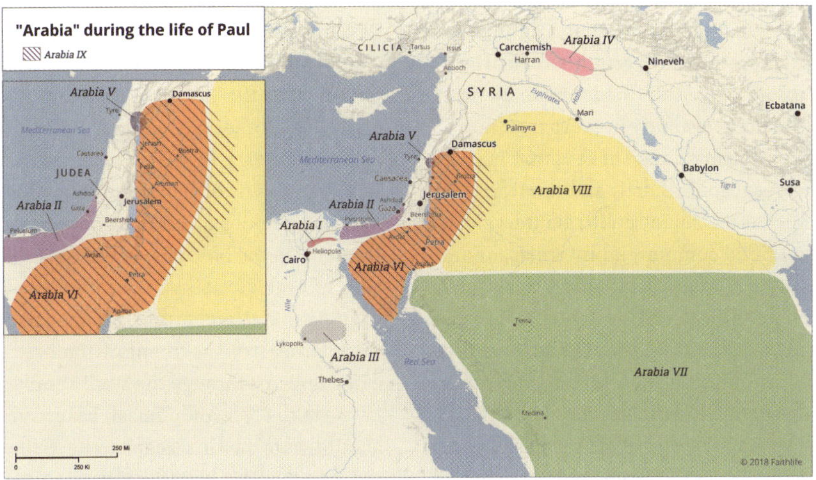

Roman World (*BAGRW*), as well as *Brill's New Pauly: Historical Atlas of the Ancient World* (*BNP*), and *Tübinger Bibelatlas* (*TBA*), together with a host of area-specific maps or specialized digital resources (for example, Digital Atlas of the Roman World).[10]

DOCUMENTARY EVIDENCE

As nearly as I can determine, at least provisionally, classical literature within the general time frame of this essay appears to attest to some nine discrete areas, each denominated as "Arabia" (with or without a qualifier).[11] These areas are located in what today are the countries of Saudi Arabia, Jordan, Syria, Lebanon, Turkey, Israel (Negev), or Egypt (Middle and Lower Egypt; Sinai). At the outset, I need to offer a few caveats and acknowledge several aspects of lingering uncertainty. First in this regard, I am assuming the writers from whom I draw are supplying factual information and that their texts have not been corrupted through transmission. I am assuming a given region may change its territorial extent over time or that differing nomenclature may be employed by a wide array of Hellenistic and Roman sources. I do

Handbuch der Geographie, Griechisch-Deutsch, 2 vols. (Basel: Schwabe Verlag, 2006). The work of Edward Luther Stevenson, *Geography of Claudius Ptolemy* (New York: New York Public Library, 1932) has been known to be severely marred and functionally unusable since the stinging review of Aubrey Diller, in *Isis* 22.2 (1935): 533–39.

10. Anne-Marie Wittke, Eckart Olshausen, and Richard Szydlak, eds., *Brill's New Pauly: Historical Atlas of the Ancient World* (Leiden: Brill, 2010); Siegfried Mittmann and Götz Schmitt, eds., *Tübinger Bibelatlas* (Stuttgart: Deutsche Bibelgesellschaft, 2001); http://dare.ht.lu.se/.

11. With my use of an equal sign [=], I intend to designate that a given area was known in classical literature *both* by the simple term (for example, Arabia) *and* with an accompanying qualifier (for example, Arabia Petraea or "Arabia of the Nabateans"). My use of parenthesized Roman numerals—for example, Arabia (I)—is entirely artificial on my part and is added here for diagnostic purposes only. The sequence of presentation implies no necessary logical or chronological order.

not wish to indicate that a delineation of these nine geographical entities is absolute, well-defined, or can be maintained consistently in every instance. To the contrary, I take as fact that matters of geographical drift and territorial fluidity as a result of political intervention, modified commercial interests, and/or military action, particularly as this may relate to the periphery of a region, occur and may occur more than once over time.

Attempting therefore to portray all these entities cartographically on a single map is a hazardous and speculative enterprise. Even aside from political upheaval or chronological variability, some areas will inevitably bleed together and even overlap, perhaps extensively so. Outer limits of some boundaries (even when well-defined by classical sources) must remain elusive and suggestive. On the other hand, regional overlap or territorial bleeding will take place in what are remote desert regions, bleak and sparsely populated desert regions, where for the most part residents would have possessed a socio-spatial outlook that was tribal and nomadic, but not urban. Here follows a brief summary and analysis of the classical evidentiary documentation related to Arabia.

ARABIA (I) = ARABIA NOMOS—IN LOWER EGYPT

A first century AD letter describes an Egyptian official holding court in several nomes (administrative districts) in the eastern Nile Delta, including Arabia.[12] Ptolemy (4.5.53; Nobbe enumeration) identifies Arabia Nomos as a nome in Lower Egypt, near the Bubastis distributary of the Nile (otherwise known as Sopdu Nome). Ptolemy (4.5.54) also notes the Egyptian towns of Babylon, Heliopolis, and Heroonpolis are said to have been located "on the border [μεθόριον, *methorion*] of Arabia."[13] It is generally assumed that Arabia Nomos was adjacent to the southeastern segment of the Delta, extending east through the Wadi Tumilat between the Nile and Timsah Lake. One should note in this regard the references in the Septuagint of Genesis 45:10 and 46:34 that Joseph's family was to be settled in "the land of Goshen of Arabia" (see also LXX Gen 46:28–29 which twice reads Heroonpolis = Tell el-Maskhuta). The early Christian pilgrim Egeria [7.1] describes her travels "to the land of Arabia, the land of Goshen," a region that is part of Egypt.[14]

ARABIA (II) = ARABIA AD AEGYPTUM ("ARABIA THAT BORDERS EGYPT")—IN THE NORTHERN SINAI

This terminology appears to denote Sinai, especially in its northern and western sectors. A number of sources speaking of northwestern Sinai as Arabia are dealing with military campaigns between Canaan and Egypt, following the Great Trunk Road between Gaza and Pelusium (for example Cambyses; Alexander; Antiochus IV Epiphanes;).[15] The first century AD historian Pomponius Mela apparently envisions Arabia ad Aegyptum when he

12. *IASH* 2.1:153; see also Roger S. Bagnall, *The Oxford Handbook of Papyrology* (Oxford: Oxford University Press, 2009), 522–24 for additional information on Arabia Nomos.

13. See Aristide Calderini and Sergio Daris, *Dizionario dei nomi geografici e topografici dell'Egitto Greco-Romano* (Bonn: Habelt, 1935–1996), 1.2:179–80; *BAGRW* 74.

14. Wilkinson, *Egeria's Travels*, 115. And see *IASH* 2.2:762.

15. See *IASH* 2.1:570–71; 2.1:580. Note also Alexander's frustrating failure ever to incorporate any part of the Arabian Peninsula into his kingdom (*IASH* 2.1:576).

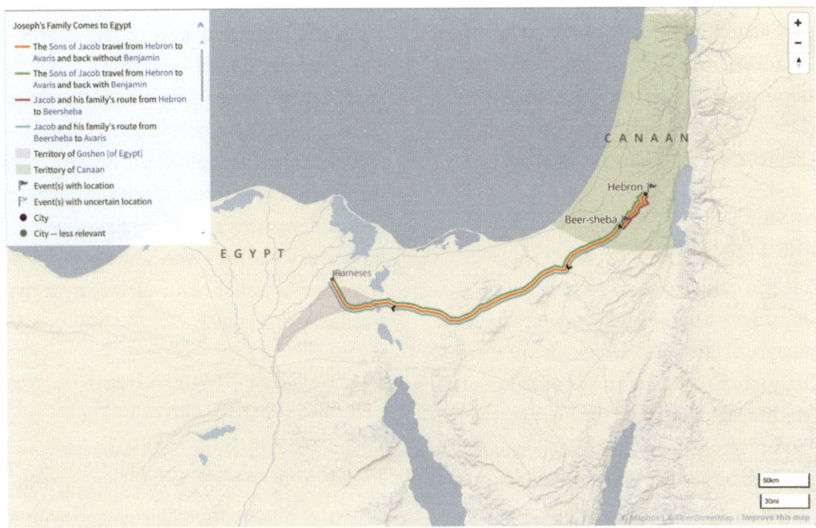

states that beside Egypt, Arabia touches the (Mediterranean) shores for a short piece, to (a point) where the coastline turns northward (and comes) to the land of Syria (*Description of the World* 1.14; compare 1:60; see also Egeria Y3).[16] This same historian also places the coastal city of Azotus/Ashdod and Mt. Casius (el-Kas, on the Mediterranean shore near Lake Serbonis) in this Arabia (1.61; 3.74).[17] This is almost certainly in Strabo's view when he describes desert mountains of Arabia that border and protect Egypt on the east (*Geography* 17.1.53).

ARABIA (III)—IN MIDDLE EGYPT

Several texts and papyri especially from the Ptolemaic era make mention of an "Arabia" located in Middle Egypt near Lykopolis (just north of modern Asyut).[18] Arabia (III), though not well attested and quite ill-defined in its boundaries, apparently extended from the east bank of the Nile eastward across the desert to the vicinity of Thebais, which bordered on the Red Sea.[19]

ARABIA (IV)—IN UPPER MESOPOTAMIA

According to Louis Dillemann and T. A. Sinclair, Persian and Roman sources reference a territory identified as the "land of the Arabs," a region inside upper Mesopotamia, east of the Euphrates River in the district of Viranşehir, between the biblical site of Harran and the Habur triangle, in modern Turkey (compare Strabo, *Geography* 1.26–28).[20] It is conceivable that the third century AD author Philostratus

16. Wilkinson, *Egeria's Travels*, 95.

17. *BAGRW* 70.

18. *TBA* B/V/8; B/V/22.

19. Calderini and Daris, *Dizionario*, 1.2:181–82; Sergio Daris, "Toponimi del Licopolite," *Zeitschrift für Papyrologie und Epigraphik* 47 (1982): 206–10, esp. 207; *BAGRW* 77.

20. Louis Dillemann, *Haute Mésopotamie orientale et pays adjacents* (Paris: Geuthner, 1962), 75–77 (and see fig. X); T. A. Sinclair, *Eastern Turkey: An Architectural and Archaeological Survey*

is envisioning this region when he refers to nomadic Arabs, living in the north between the Tigris and Euphrates rivers (*Life of Apollonius of Tyana* 1.20; compare Cicero, *De divinatione* 1.92, 94).

ARABIA (V)—IN THE ANTILEBANON MOUNTAINS

Several classical sources speak of an auxiliary action taken by Alexander the Great as part of his southward advance, from his victory at Issus in 333 BC, along the Mediterranean coast in the direction of Egypt. According to Arrian—normally taken to be a sober and judicious source—while Alexander was preparing to lay siege to the city of Tyre with both land and sea forces, the monarch took some of his cavalry squadrons and some archers, and he marched against "Arabia towards the mountain range called 'Antilibanus' [ἐπ' Ἀραβίας ... Ἀντιλίβανον, *ep' Arabias ... Antilibanon*]" (*Anabasis* 2.20.4). The comments of Quintus Curtius (*Historiae Alexandri Magni* 4.2.24–4.3.1) enable us to contextualize Alexander's motives in this regard: the Macedonian went to Arabia because he needed to obtain wood for building siege machines capable of attacking the offshore island on which Tyre sat at that time. In any event, Alexander apparently accomplished his mission and then returned to his main force ten days later.[21]

Given the fact that Alexander was able to travel from Tyre to Arabia, accomplish his objective, and in the span of ten days return to his main force on the Mediterranean coast means this Arabia must have been nestled into the Antilebanon range, at a distance not far from Tyre. Israel Eph'al suggests Alexander at this point may have encountered Iturean Arabs who had moved westward and established an enclave near the Antilebanon range.[22]

ARABIA (VI) = ARABIA PETRAEA = ARABIA OF THE NABATEANS—THE SINAI PENINSULA AND SOUTH AND EAST OF JUDEA

Until the Roman annexation of Nabatea in AD 106 by the emperor Trajan, and the concurrent establishment of an official province named Provincia Arabia, Arabia = Arabia Petraea = Arabia of the Nabateans was without doubt the most frequently and the most widely attested territory known across the empire as "Arabia" (Strabo, *Geography* 17.1.21). In very general terms, Ptolemy declared that Arabia Petraea borders Judea on the east and south, and it extends (north) to the border of Syria and (southwest) to the border of Egypt (5.17.1 [Nobbe enumeration]; compare Dio Cassius 68.14.5; Diodorus 2.48.1).[23] Note at this point in his discussion, Ptolemy explicitly differentiates Arabia Petraea from both Arabia Ereme/Deserta and Arabia Eudaimon/Felix.

For us to gain greater specificity of Arabia (VI), it is helpful to recall that

(London: Pindar, 1987), 1.83–85, 94–104; see also *BAGRW* 89.

21. Plutarch (*Life of Alexander* 24.6–10) mentions an expedition by Alexander against the Arabs who live near the Antilebanon mountains. See also Polyaenus, *Stratagems* 4.3.4.

22. Eph'al, *Ancient Arabs*, 100–101 n. 337; Shimon Dar, *Settlements and Cult Sites on Mount Hermon, Israel: Ituraean Culture in the Hellenistic and Roman Periods* (Oxford: Tempus Reparatum, 1993), 14–19, and bibliography; Jan Retsö, *The Arabs in Antiquity: Their History from the Assyrians to the Umayyads* (Hoboken: Taylor & Francis, 2013), 407–8.

23. See also *BAGRW* 70, 76, 83; *BNP* 178–181; *TBA* B/V/8; B/V/17; B/V/18/a-b.

(1) between the first arrival of Roman interests in the Levant (that is, the campaign of Pompey in 64–63 BC, that firmly established and even militarized the expansive province of Syria, and ended with the capture of Jerusalem) and (2) Trajan's creation of the Roman province, there was a span of slightly more than 150 years. Growing hostility and even conflict in this area between the competing political interests of the Nabateans and the Romans (and the latter's clients, such as Herod the Great), in addition to the political ambitions of the Hasmoneans and the Parthians, all become the backdrop for many classical citations of Arabia Petraea during this era.

In this regard, perhaps some considerable preference should be given to the writings of the Jewish historian Josephus (who wrote the most extensive known history of the area, dated to AD 75–95) and the Roman geographer Strabo (who wrote for explicitly geographical purposes and composed an exhaustive geographic compendium of the area, dated to approximately 7 BC). After all, both of these men lived and traveled in this immediate vicinity, both frequently referenced this Arabia, and both wrote precisely from inside the 150-year window, thus rendering both authors as near contemporaries of the apostle Paul. Josephus and Strabo are obviously not the only classical sources available, and their testimony basically accords with other more distant writers (both geographically and/or chronologically distant), but it is fair to say their citations enable one to configure Arabia Petraea with greater detail and specificity, especially in its outermost portions.

From such sources, one can determine that Arabia Petraea centered on its capital, Petra, and extended across northern Transjordan, at times as far north as Damascus, and certainly including such cities as Bostra, Dionysias/Soada, Kanatha, Amathus, and Phaine. Across central Transjordan, Arabia Petraea is said to have included such cities as Adraa/Edrei, Abila, Amman/Philadelphia, Areopolis/Kerak, Eusbus/Heshbon, Jerash, Medeba, Bezer, Zoar beside the Dead Sea, and as far south in Transjordan as Aila/Aqaba, on the northern tip of the Red Sea. Extending across the Negev and into Sinai, Arabia Petraea is said to have included such sites as Eboda/Avdat and Pharanitai/Pharan/Paran, among others (see Strabo, *Geography* 2.48.1, 6; 16.4.2 [where Arabia stands between Arabia Felix and Syria], 21–24; Josephus, *J.W.* 1.125; 1.267; 3.47; 4.173, 454; *Ant.* 4.161; 5.82 [tribe of Simeon was in Idumea, which adjoins Egypt and Arabia]; 12.228–235; 13.392–397; 14.80, 362; 16.347).[24] In biblical terms, therefore, Arabia Petraea would have included the areas of Golan, Bashan, Trachonitis, and Hauran in the north, Decapolis, Gilead, and Perea in central Transjordan, and Ammon, Moab, and Edom toward the south, as well as the Negev and Sinai south of Judea. That Arabia Petraea was thought to have been situated immediately adjacent to Judea is reflected in several Josephus' texts: *J.W.* 5.159–160, where the historian asserts Arabia could be seen from atop the Psephinus' Tower in Jerusalem; *Ant.* 1.419,

24. See *IASH* 2.1:451, 489, 528, 597, 656–57, 659; 2.2:689, 761, 869; Pliny, *Natural History* 5.72; Diodorus 19.94.1; compare Egeria 13.2; 1 Macc 11:16; Jdt 2:25. See also BDAG, 127–128; Uzi Dahari, *Monastic Settlements in South Sinai in the Byzantine Period: The Archaeologial Remains* (Jerusalem: Israel Antiquities Authority, 2000), 5–9.

where Josephus indicates Herod built his fortress at Herodium on the "hills of the Arabian frontier." Even if these two latter texts are considered to be a bit exaggerated geographically, they nevertheless certainly testify to the notion of Arabia Petraea being perceived to have been situated in close proximity to Judea, and not at some far distant point.

A curious Josephus text that could potentially be relevant to this essay states as follows: Apion declared that Moses had ascended a mountain "between Egypt and Arabia, called Sinai," that he remained there for forty days, and that he descended from there to give the Jews their laws (*Ag. Ap.* 2.25; see Exod 24:15–18). Queries linger concerning the validity and purpose of this text, which it seems Josephus himself questions: Is this Apion's own description? Can the text be taken at face value? Why does Apion engage here in what appears very much to be a lengthy aside? Notwithstanding these questions, at the end of the day, whether Apion's "Arabia" should be Arabia Petraea, Arabia Ereme/Deserta, or Arabia Eudaimon/Felix, his text is clear that Mt. Sinai stands *between* (μεταξύ, *metaxu*) Arabia and Egypt.

ARABIA (VII) = ARABIA EUDAIMON/FELIX—THE ARABIAN PENINSULA

Such complimentary descriptive terminology as Arabia Eudaimon/Felix[25] was doubtless given as a consequence of the rare and exotic natural resources found there (for example, frankincense, myrrh, cassia, cinnamon, nard, precious metals, rare forms of wood). As early as Herodotus, Persians are said to have imported one thousand talents (twenty-five tons [22.7 MT) of frankincense from Arabia annually (3.97–115, but see especially 3.97); Pliny speaks of the high prices frankincense and myrrh could command in the west (*Natural History* 12.32.65–71), and on one occasion this first century AD author laments that women from Rome spent as much as 100 million sesterces annually on luxury imports from Arabia (*Natural History* 12.41.84).[26]

The perimeter boundaries of Arabia Eudaimon/Felix are quite clear. According to several classical geographical sources, Arabia (VII) encompassed the entire Arabian Peninsula, bordered on the east by the Persian Gulf (to the mouth of the Tigris and Euphrates Rivers) and on the west by the modern Red Sea (as far north as Aila/Aqaba, where it met Arabia Petraea) (Strabo, *Geography* 16.3.1; 16.4.2; Ptolemy 6.7.18, 27; 8.22.1–2 [Nobbe enumeration]; Marcian of Heraclea, *Periplus of the Outer Sea* 1.17a.11–18). The same three authors also indicate, albeit rather vaguely, that the north side of Arabia Eudaimon/Felix touched on Arabia Ereme/Deserta (see below), but they don't say exactly where. On one occasion, Strabo divided Arabia's various inhabitants by differentiating according to the latitudes (*Geography* 16.4.27). If I may follow such a lead, therefore, and draw a somewhat imaginary east-west line from the northern tip of the Persian Gulf over to the northern tip of the Gulf of Elat/Aqaba, thus approximating 30 degrees

25. Greek *eudaimon* (εὐδαιμων) and Latin *felix* both mean "blessed" Arabia (Strabo, *Geography* 16.4.27; Diodorus 3.46.1; Pliny, *Natural History* 5.12.65; 12.30.51; 12.41.82).

26. The issue of inflation makes comparison with a modern monetary system rather inexact, but if Pliny's figure is not exaggerated and is intended to be taken literally, this may amount to as much as $5–25 million annually in today's dollars.

north latitude, this appears to me to be a fair estimate of where Arabia Eudaimon/Felix met Arabia Ereme/Deserta.

Arabia (VIII) = Arabia Ereme/Deserta—The Arabian Desert

As with Arabia Eudaimon/Felix, the territory of Arabia Ereme/Deserta is well defined in classical literature.[27] Ptolemy's accounts are the most clarifying in this regard (5.19.1–7 [Nobbe enumeration]). Arabia Ereme/Deserta is said to have been bounded on the north by Mesopotamia along the Euphrates river, on the south by Arabia Eudaimon/Felix, on the west by parts of Syria and Arabia Petraea, and on the east by Babylonia and the head of the Persian Gulf.[28]

Known today either as the Syro-Arabian Desert or the Great Eastern Desert, the area defined by Arabia Ereme/Deserta may be said to have stretched from its southern border with Arabia Eudaimon/Felix near the aforementioned 30 degree parallel, northward in a way that tended to follow the 7.9–9.8 inch (200–250 mm) precipitation lines.[29] These rainfall lines run somewhat parallel to the course of the lower Euphrates flood plain, to a point about seventy-five miles (120.7 km) northwest of the site of Mari, where the isohyet lines begin to bend westward and then gradually southwestward and come to abut the eastern extremities of Arabia Petraea in the vicinity of Jebel Druze.[30]

Arabia (IX) = Provincia Arabia—Mostly Arabia Petraea and Part of Arabia Ereme/Deserta

This nomenclature was introduced in the immediate aftermath of Trajan's annexation of Arabia Petraea in the year AD 106. Roughly approximating what had been the Nabatean kingdom (= Arabia of the Nabateans; Strabo, *Geography* 17.1.21), Provincia Arabia in the north was bounded by Syria and the southern Hauran; it extended east into Arabia Ereme/Deserta; on the west it was bounded by Judea (Syria-Palaestina after AD 135), and the new province also took in the southern end of the Dead Sea, southern Transjordan as far as Aila/Aqaba, the Negev, and most of Sinai.[31] This overall provincial outline was modified somewhat in the third century AD, and by middle of the fourth century, part of Provincia Arabia had become known as Arabia Nea.[32]

Perhaps the extent of Provincia Arabia is best known by cities said to have been located in the province: Petra, Bostra, Canatha, Adraa/Edrei, Ashtaroth-

27. Greek *erēmē* (ἐρήμη) and Latin *deserta* both mean "deserted," "abandoned," or "empty."

28. See *BAGRW* 69, 93; *BNP* 87; *TBA* B/V/22; Strabo, *Geography* 16.4.1.

29. A detailed map showing the 9.8 inch (250 mm) isohyet line arching across the Syro-Arabian Desert can be found in P. Sanlaville, "Pays et paysages du Tigre et de l'Euphrate; Réflexions sur la Mésopotamie antique," *Akkadica* 66 (1990): 10 (fig. 2). A slightly more simplified version, showing the 7.9 inch (200 mm) rainfall line, appears in Barry J. Beitzel, *The New Moody Atlas of the Bible* (Chicago: Moody Press, 2009), 22 (map 2).

30. A similar outline is given in D. H. Müller, "Arabia," in Pauly-Wissowa, *Real-Encyclopädie der klassischen Altetumswissenschaft*, ed. Georg Wissowa (Stuttgart: Metzler, 1897), col 345.

31. *BAGRW* 69–71; *BNP* 179, 278; *IASH* 2.2:712–16, 719.

32. See, for example, *IASH* 2.2:873–74. See also Leah Di Segni, "Changing Borders in the Provinces of Palaestina and Arabia in the Fourth and Fifth Centuries," *Liber Annuus* 68 (2018): 247–67.

karnaim, Abila, Areopolis, Philippolis, Jerash, Philadelphia/Amman, Medeba, Baal-meon, Heshbon, Sodom (?), and Dionysias. Almost all of these cities are also mentioned by the early Christian bishop Eusebius in his *Onomasticon* in his attempt to identify sites mentioned in the Bible, especially relating to places listed with territory inherited by the Transjordanian tribes of Reuben, Gad, and east Manasseh, all said by the bishop to have been situated "in Arabia."[33]

Option	Name(s)	Location
I	Arabia Nomos	Lower Egypt
II	Arabia ad Egyptum	northern Sinai Peninsula
III	Arabia	Middle Egypt
IV	Arabia	upper Mesopotamia
V	Arabia	Antilebanon mountains, east of Tyre
VI	Arabia Petraea	Sinai Peninsula and south and east of Judea north to Damascus
VII	Arabia Eudaimon/Felix	Arabian Peninsula
VIII	Arabia Ereme/Deserta	Arabian desert, north of VII
IX	Provincia Arabia	Area of VI and parts of V and VIII

CONCLUSION

It is almost impossible to overemphasize the dramatic, seminal consequences of Alexander's 333–331 BC campaign into the Levant and beyond in terms of the changing linguistic landscape and the widespread adoption of novel geographic nomenclature. In line with this new and pervasive linguistic paradigm, New Testament writers—including Paul, Luke, John, and even Peter, the apostle with perhaps the strongest lingering Jewish inclinations—commonly employ Greek geographic terminology that was contemporary with them, rather than archaic (and perhaps Semitic) nomenclature. Thus, for example, they speak of Cyprus (not Kittim), Crete (not Caphtor), Philippi (not Krenides), Philadelphia (not Callatebus), and so forth; they often use city names of places not founded before the classical period (for example, Thessalonica, Antioch of Syria, Antioch of Pisidia, Alexandrian Troas). New Testament writers make frequent use of Roman provincial names (for example, Macedonia, Achaia, Asia, Pontus, Bithynia, Pamphylia, Cappadocia, Lycia, Galatia, Egypt, Mesopotamia, Dalmatia) or Roman regional/territorial names (for example, Lydia, Pisidia, Mysia, Phrygia), none of which are known to have had currency much before Alexander the Great, and none of which are attested in the Hebrew Bible.

There is no compelling reason to suppose that Paul broke with his normal practice when he indicated he had

33. R. Steven Notley, and Ze'ev Safrai, *Eusebius, Onomasticon: The Place Names of Divine Scripture* (Leiden: Brill, 2005).

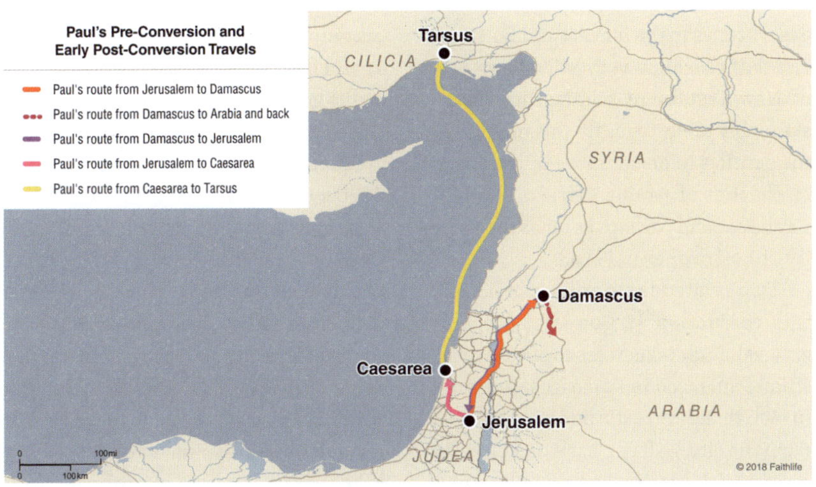

gone "to Arabia" or when he stated that Mt. Sinai was "in Arabia." To the contrary, one notes in the immediate context of his first use of Arabia, the apostle also speaks specifically of traveling on his mission "to (the Roman provinces of) Syria and Cilicia" (Gal 1:21). Paul uses the Greek word "Syria"[34] (a term apparently first applied to the Levant by the Seleucids), not "Aram/Aramea" (the Hebrew lexeme consistently used throughout the Old Testament to designate that broad sweep of land north of northeastern Galilee and the Golan as far as the Taurus mountains and the upper Euphrates river). Paul mentions "Cilicia," not Kizzuwatna or Hatti—terms employed in the preclassical era to denote the territory adjacent to the extreme northeastern corner of the Mediterranean Sea, hemmed in by the Amanus and the Taurus mountains.

To which "Arabia" did Paul go immediately after his conversion? We can reasonably rule out Arabia (I), (II), (III), (IV), and probably (V), and Arabia (IX) was not created until the early second Christian century. But this still leaves (VI), (VII), and (VIII), a wide territorial expanse. However, while these three regions may remain in one's theoretical field of view, logically and contextually they do not stand on equal footing. If, as much contemporary New Testament scholarship maintains, Paul was motivated to go to Arabia primarily to carry out his calling to "preach [Christ] among the gentiles" (Gal 1:16), and in accordance with what we know to have been the urban focus of his itineraries that are recorded in the New Testament, it makes sense to assume Paul went into municipal areas, perhaps reasonably near Damascus, and that he did not press deeply into the remote and largely unpopulated

34. Despite modern English translations, "Syria" is not found in the Hebrew Bible; it is worth noting this name also bears little territorial correspondence to the modern political name.

desert zones to the far east and far south. For that reason, a very wide spectrum of New Testament scholarship understandably seeks to locate this mission to the gentiles in one or more of the dozen or so cities of Arabia Petraea, south of Damascus and perhaps as far as the vicinity of Bostra or even Pella.[35]

Two related texts appear to bolster this conviction (2 Cor 11:32–33; Acts 9:23–25). Both texts refer to strong opposition Paul faced in Damascus, so strong, in fact, that the apostle had to be lowered from the city wall in a basket in order to escape with his life. The diabolical plot apparently occurred between the time Paul returned to Damascus from Arabia and when he went up to Jerusalem (see Acts 9:26–30; Gal 1:18–21). In Paul's own account of the incident, in 2 Corinthians 11:32, he ascribes ultimate responsibility to the governor of Damascus, an appointee of King Aretas. Mentioned with fair frequency in classical literature, this is Aretas IV Philodemos, who is known to have ruled Arabia Petraea from Petra between the dates of 9/8 BC–AD 40/41. On various grounds, New Testament scholars tend to date this attempt on Paul's life around AD 32–35, during the reign of Aretas. Whatever the case, this life-threatening event may be precisely a result of Paul's initial and presumably successful mission to urbanite gentiles of Arabia Petraea, including Nabatean Arabs, regarded by Jews at the time as the descendants of Hagar and Ishmael.[36] The mission rankled local Jews also living in

35. Leading commentary literature adopting this view includes Herman N. Ridderbos, *The Epistle of Paul to the Churches of Galatia* (Grand Rapids, Eerdmans, 1953), 65 and n. 14; Hans Dieter Betz, *Galatians: A Commentary on Paul's Letter to the Churches in Galatia* (Philadelphia: Fortress, 1979), 73–74; Donald Guthrie, *Galatians* (London: Marshall, Morgan & Scott, 1981), 70; F. F. Bruce, *The Epistle to the Galatians: A Commentary on the Greek Text* (Grand Rapids: Eerdmans, 1982), 95–96; Richard N. Longenecker, *Galatians* (Waco, TX: Word, 1990), 34; Paul Nadim Tarazi, *Galatians: A Commentary* (Crestwood, NY: St. Vladimir's Seminary Press, 1994), 50–51; Timothy George, *Galatians* (Nashville: Broadman & Holman, 1994), 124; Thomas R. Schreiner, *Galatians* (Grand Rapids: Zondervan, 2010), 102; Martinus C. de Boer, *Galatians: A Commentary* (Louisville: Westminster John Knox, 2011), 96; Douglas J. Moo, *Galatians* (Grand Rapids: Baker Academic, 2013), 106; Craig S. Keener, *The IVP Bible Background Commentary, New Testament*, 2nd ed. (Downers Grove, IL: InterVarsity Press, 2014), 526, 536; and David deSilva, *The Letter to the Galatians* (Grand Rapids: Eerdmans, 2018), 157–58. Other scholarly treatises proposing this view include Jerome Murphy-O'Connor, "Paul in Arabia," *Catholic Biblical Quarterly* 55 (1993): 732–33; Martin Hengel and Anna Maria Schwemer, *Paul Between Damascus and Antioch: The Unknown Years* (Louisville: Westminster John Knox, 1997), 109–11; Ruth Schäfer, *Paulus bis zum Apostelkonzil: Ein Beitrag zur Einleitung in den Galaterbrief, zur Geschichte der Jesusbewegung und zur Pauluschronologie* (Tübingen: Mohr Siebeck, 2004), 99–102; Eckhard J. Schnabel, *Early Christian Mission* (Downers Grove, IL: InterVarsity Press, 2004), 2:1032–38; Schnabel, "Paul's Missionary Work in Syria, Nabatea, Judea, and Cilicia," chapter 18 in this volume. It strains credulity to imagine that Paul's two uses of "Arabia" should reference differing entities. Even if Paul were making a purely geographical pronouncement in Gal 4:25, which a great many scholars contextually conclude is not the case—given the apostle's allegorical language, laced with a thick dosage of irony having to do with who really are the "free" offspring and the "enslaved" offspring of Abraham—a location sought for Mt. Sinai either in the Negev or across the Sinai peninsula remains in view, since both are situated inside the territory of Arabia Petraea.

36. Hengel and Schwemer, *Paul Between Damascus and Antioch*, 110–13; Schnabel. *Early Christian Mission*, 1032–35. For a detailed treatment of the wording and history of Gal 4:25, its form in various manuscript witnesses, its literary character, and its history in Jewish

the area, adding to the already growing Jewish-Arab antipathy and political discord that existed in the central and northern parts of Arabia Petraea. According to this view, therefore, Aretas' dutiful agent attempted preemptive action against Paul in the name of law and order.

BIBLIOGRAPHY

Bagnall, Roger S. *The Oxford Handbook of Papyrology*. Oxford: Oxford University Press, 2009.

Beitzel, Barry J. *The New Moody Atlas of the Bible*. Chicago: Moody Press, 2009.

Berkowitz, Luci, and Karl A. Squitier, eds. *Thesaurus Linguae Graecae: Canon of Greek Authors and Works*. 3rd ed. Oxford: Oxford University Press, 1990.

Betz, Hans Dieter. *Galatians: A Commentary on Paul's Letter to the Churches in Galatia*. Philadelphia: Fortress, 1979.

Boer, Martinus C. de. *Galatians: A Commentary*. Louisville: Westminster John Knox, 2011.

Bruce, F. F. *The Epistle to the Galatians: A Commentary on the Greek Text*. Grand Rapids: Eerdmans, 1982.

Calderini, Aristide, and Sergio Daris. *Dizionario dei nomi geografici e topografici dell'Egitto Greco-Romano*. 5 vols. + 5 supplement vols. Bonn: Habelt, 1935–1996.

Carlson, Stephen C. *The Text of Galatians and Its History*. Tübingen: Mohr Siebeck, 2015.

Dahari, Uzi. *Monastic Settlements in South Sinai in the Byzantine Period: The Archaeologial Remains*. Jerusalem: Israel Antiquities Authority, 2000.

Dar, Shimon. *Settlements and Cult Sites on Mount Hermon, Israel: Ituraean Culture in the Hellenistic and Roman Periods*. Oxford: Tempus Reparatum, 1993.

Daris, Sergio. "Toponimi del Licopolite." *Zeitschrift für Papyrologie und Epigraphik* 47 (1982): 206–10.

DeSilva, David. *The Letter to the Galatians*. Grand Rapids: Eerdmans, 2018.

Dillemann, Louis. *Haute Mésopotamie orientale et pays adjacents*. Paris: Geuthner, 1962.

Diller, Audrey. Review of *Geography of Claudius Ptolemy*, by Edward Luther Stevenson. *Isis* 22 (1935): 533–39.

Di Segni, Leah. "Changing Borders in the Provinces of Palaestina and Arabia in the Fourth and Fifth Centuries." *Liber Annuus* 68 (2018): 247–67.

Di Segni, Leah, and Yoram Tsafrir. *The Onomasticon of Iudaea-Palaestina and Arabia in the Greek and Latin Sources*. 2 vols. Jerusalem: Israel Academy of Sciences and Humanities, 2015–2017.

Eph'al, Israel. *The Ancient Arabs: Nomads on the Border of the Fertile Crescent, 9th–5th Centuries B.C.* Jerusalem: Magnes, 1982.

Fischer, David Hackett. *Historical Fallacies: Toward a Logic of Historical Thought*. New York: HarperPerennial, 1970.

George, Timothy. *Galatians*. Nashville: Broadman & Holman, 1994.

Guthrie, Donald. *Galatians*. London: Marshall, Morgan & Scott, 1981.

Hengel, Martin, and Anna Maria Schwemer. *Paul Between Damascus and Antioch: The Unknown Years*. Louisville: Westminster John Knox, 1997.

and Christian interpretation, consult Allen Kerkeslager, "Jewish Pilgrimage and Jewish Identity in Hellenistic and Early Roman Egypt," in *Pilgrimage and Holy Space in Late Antique Egypt*, ed. David Frankfurter (Leiden: Brill, 1998), 180–213; Stephen C. Carlson, *The Text of Galatians and Its History* (Tübingen: Mohr Siebeck, 2015), 162–72.

Keener, Craig S. *The IVP Bible Background Commentary, New Testament*. 2nd ed. Downers Grove, IL: InterVarsity Press, 2014.

Kerkeslager, Allen. "Jewish Pilgrimage and Jewish Identity in Hellenistic and Early Roman Egypt." Pages 99–225 in *Pilgrimage and Holy Space in Late Antique Egypt*. Edited by David Frankfurter. Leiden: Brill, 1998.

Longenecker, Richard N. *Galatians*. Waco, TX: Word, 1990.

Metzger, Bruce M., ed. *A Concordance to the Apocrypha/Deuterocanonical Books of the Revised Standard Version*. Grand Rapids: Eerdmans, 1982.

Mittmann, Siegfried, and Götz Schmitt, eds. *Tübinger Bibelatlas*. Stuttgart: Deutsche Bibelgesellschaft, 2001.

Moo, Douglas J. *Galatians*. Grand Rapids: Baker Academic, 2013.

Müller, D. H. "Arabia." Cols 344–359 in vol. 2, part 1 of Pauly-Wissowa, *Real-Encyclopädie der klassischen Altetumswissenschaft*. Edited by Georg Wissowa. Stuttgart: Metzler, 1897.

Murphy-O'Connor, Jerome. "Paul in Arabia." *Catholic Biblical Quarterly* 55 (1993): 732–37.

Nobbe, Carolus Fridericus Augustus. *Claudii Ptolemaei Geographia*. 3 vols. Leipzig: Tauchnitus, 1843–1845.

Notley, R. Steven, and Ze'ev Safrai. *Eusebius, Onomasticon: The Place Names of Divine Scripture*. Leiden: Brill, 2005.

O'Connor, Michael. "The Etymology of *Saracen* in Aramaic and Pre-Islamic Arabic Contexts." Pages 603–32 in *The Defence of the Roman and Byzantine East*. Edited by Philip Freeman and David Kennedy. 2 vols. Oxford: BAR, 1986.

Rainey, Anson F., and R. Steven Notley. *The Sacred Bridge: Carta's Atlas of the Biblical World*. Carta: Jerusalem, 2006.

Rengstorf, Karl Heinrich. *A Complete Concordance to Flavius Josephus*. Leiden: Brill, 2002.

Retsö, Jan. *The Arabs in Antiquity: Their History from the Assyrians to the Umayyads*. Hoboken: Taylor & Francis, 2013.

Ridderbos, Herman N. *The Epistle of Paul to the Churches of Galatia*. Grand Rapids: Eerdmans, 1953.

Sanlaville, P. "Pays et paysages du Tigre et de l'Euphrate, Réflexions sur la Mésopotamie antique." *Akkadica* 66 (1990): 1–12 and fig. 2.

Schäfer, Ruth. *Paulus bis zum Apostelkonzil: Ein Beitrag zur Einleitung in den Galaterbrief, zur Geschichte der Jesusbewegung und zur Pauluschronologie*. Tübingen: Mohr Siebeck, 2004.

Schnabel, Eckhard J. *Early Christian Mission*. 2 vols. Downers Grove, IL: InterVarsity Press, 2004.

Schreiner, Thomas R. *Galatians*. Grand Rapids: Zondervan, 2010.

Sinclair, T. A. *Eastern Turkey: An Architectural and Archaeological Survey*. 4 vols. London: Pindar, 1987–1990.

Stevenson, Edward Luther. *Geography of Claudius Ptolemy*. New York: New York Public Library, 1932.

Stückelberger, Alfred, and Gerd Grasshoff. *Klaudios Ptolemaios: Handbuch der Geographie, Griechisch-Deutsch*. 2 vols. Basel: Schwabe Verlag, 2006.

Tarazi, Paul Nadim. *Galatians: A Commentary*. Crestwood, NY: St. Vladimir's Seminary Press, 1994.

Wilkinson, John. *Egeria's Travels to the Holy Land*. 3rd ed. Oxford: Aris & Phillips, 2006.

Wittke, Anne-Maria, Eckart Olshausen, and Richard Szydlak, eds. *Brill's New Pauly: Historical Atlas of the Ancient World*. Leiden: Brill, 2010.

CHAPTER 41

THE SOCIAL AND GEOGRAPHICAL WORLD OF EPHESUS

Acts 18:19–21, 24; 19:1–41; 20:16–17; Eph 1:1; 1 Tim 1:3; Rev 1:11; 2:1–7

David A. deSilva

KEY POINTS

- Ephesus was a major commercial port city and an important node on the north-south and east-west road system, and thus a strategic hub for the immediate and ongoing work of a missionary/church planter like Paul and his team.
- The worship of Artemis and the city's identity and pride were intertwined from the founding of Ephesus, making devotion to Artemis a natural rallying point against an invasive monotheistic cult.
- Ephesus enthusiastically supported the Roman imperial cult, with a marked upsurge toward the end of the first century as it was awarded its first provincial imperial temple. This is the situation to which John's Revelation would appear to respond most directly for Ephesian Christians.
- The commercial activity of Ephesus, particularly as a collection point for shipments heading west to Greece and Rome, is another important point of connection with Revelation's critique of the Roman imperial economy.

EPHESUS IN THE BIBLICAL STORY

Few cities in the Mediterranean were more important in the story of the emerging church than Ephesus. Shortly after Paul had completed his work of church planting in Corinth (probably in AD 52), he traveled with Aquila and Prisca to Ephesus, stopping only long enough to get them settled there as a kind of advance guard for his future mission in the area (Acts 18:19–21). Apollos would encounter Priscilla and Aquila in Ephesus and be instructed by them in the gospel (18:24–26) before moving on to become a missionary and itinerant teacher in the circle of Pauline churches (see, e.g., Acts 18:27–19:1; 1 Cor 1:12; 3:4–6; 16:12; Tit 3:13).

Paul would return to make Ephesus his home and base of operations for two or three years (AD 53–55), during which time he no doubt became familiar with every yard of the public spaces of this city (Acts 19:1–20:1). He invested a great deal of himself in the evangelization of this city, which was one of the principal cities of the Roman province of Asia, in what is now the westernmost part of Turkey. From this city, members of his team took the gospel to other cities in the province. Ephapras, for example, set out from here to evangelize Colossae, Hierapolis, and Laodicea, and also brought back word to Paul about these mission churches when his guidance was needed (Col 1:7–8; 4:12–13). The Corinthian correspondence and the visits of Paul and his emissaries to Corinth during that period were undertaken from Ephesus.[1] Timothy is remembered to have exercised some important follow-up work in Ephesus, perhaps at some point in Paul's later ministry (1 Tim 1:2).[2]

Ephesus may also have served as a hub for the Christians most directly nurtured by the Johannine literature of the New Testament. Tradition associates the apostle John with Ephesus, as well as John the Elder (the author of 1–3 John).[3] Christians in Ephesus were explicitly included among the congregations addressed by the visionary author of Revelation (Rev 1:11), not only in the oracle of the glorified Christ spoken to them specifically (Rev 2:1–7) but by Revelation as a whole, which spoke a poignant word to Christians in a city so supportive of the Roman imperial cult and Roman economy.[4]

ROMAN EPHESUS: GEOGRAPHY AND DEMOGRAPHICS

The Ephesus known to Paul was located near the mouth of the Cayster River (the Küçük Menderes River) on the shore of a harbor on the Aegean Sea, stretching into the valley between Mt. Pion (Panayır Dağ) and Mt. Coressus (Bülbül Dağ) and up the lower slopes of both hills. The natural harbor, which had to be periodically dredged because of the silting caused by the Cayster River, made Ephesus a major node for shipping in trade between east and west (Strabo, *Geography* 14.1.24). The effects of the constant silting can be dramatically seen from the fact that the ruins of Roman Ephesus now sit three full miles (4.8 km) inland from the Aegean shore.

The location of Roman Ephesus is the result of a decision made three centuries before Paul by Lysimachus, one of the successors to a part of the kingdom of Alexander the Great. A settlement existed in the Homeric period (ca. eighth

---

1. Jerome Murphy O'Connor, *St. Paul's Ephesus: Texts and Archaeology* (Collegeville, MN: Liturgical Press, 2008), 201–2, 235–43.

2. Paul Trebilco (*The Early Christian in Ephesus From Paul to Ignatius* [Grand Rapids: Eerdmans, 2007], 206–9) favors the view that both 1 and 2 Timothy were addressed to Christian communities in Ephesus (though as pseudonymous letters written between AD 80–100).

3. See discussion in Trebilco, *Early Christians*, 241–92.

4. See David A. deSilva, *Seeing Things John's Way: The Rhetoric of the Book of Revelation* (Louisville: Westminster John Knox, 2009), 37–63, 104–9, 198–209, 235–38.

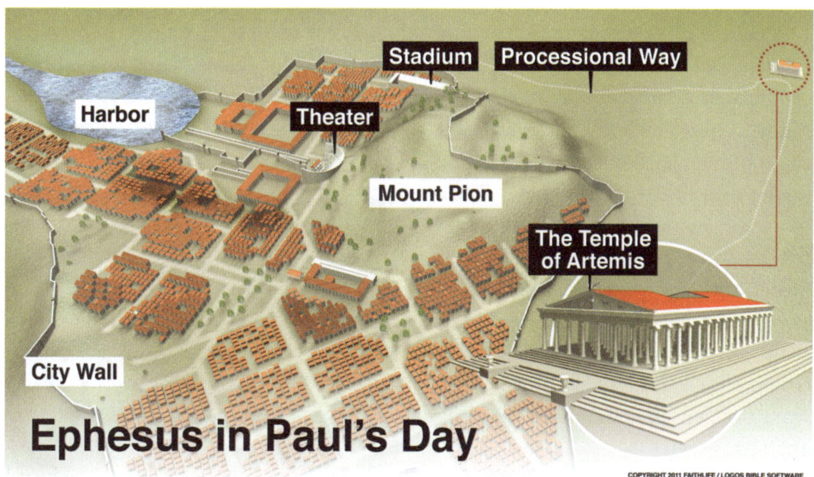

century BC) on the north side of the base of Mount Pion.[5] During the Classical period, the settlement had relocated to an area about a mile (1.6 km) to the northeast, between the base of a third hill (the Ayasoluk) and the famous Temple of Artemis (see below). Lysimachus chose the city's final location to make of Ephesus a major port city and fortified it with a perimeter wall of about six miles (9.7 km) in circumference.[6] Ephesus also came to be a node on a highway running north-south through Roman Asia, and also the westernmost point on a series of highways that led east as far as India (Strabo, *Geography* 14.2.29; Herodotus, *Histories* 5.53–54).[7]

Estimates of the population in the early Roman period generally fall around two hundred thousand people, making Ephesus the fourth or fifth largest city in the empire.[8] Immigration was a huge factor in the growth of the city. Infant mortality was about 33 percent during the first year, 50 percent by the fifth year; the maintenance of the population suggests a steady flow of immigrants.[9]

5. Colin J. Hemer, *The Letters to the Seven Churches of Asia in Their Local Setting* (Grand Rapids: Eerdmans, 2001), 35.

6. See page 711 for a map of ancient Ephesus. Mark W. Wilson, *Biblical Turkey: A Guide to the Jewish and Christian Sites of Asia Minor* (Istanbul: Ege Yayınları, 2010), 199–200; Mark Fairchild, *Christian Origins in Ephesus and Asia Minor* (Peabody, MA: Hendrickson, 2017), 23. I find it highly unlikely that two relocations over the yawning space of eight centuries would have been a meaningful background for the glorified Christ's threat to "move [the Ephesian church's] lampstand from its place" if they failed to repent (Rev 2:5), *pace* Hemer, *Letters to the Churches*, 52–54.

7. Murphy-O'Connor, *St. Paul's Ephesus*, 36–37.

8. Murphy-O'Connor, *St. Paul's Ephesus*, 131–32; Wilson, *Biblical Turkey*, 200.

9. L. Michael White, "Urban Development and Social Change in Imperial Ephesus," in *Ephesos: Metropolis of Asia; An Interdisciplinary Approach to Its Archaeology, Religion and Culture*, ed. Helmut Koester (Valley Forge, PA: Trinity Press International, 1995), 45.

There is no significant archaeological evidence for the presence of Jewish community in Ephesus beyond a handful of inscriptions and other artifacts bearing common, Jewish iconic decorations (menorahs, shofar, lulav, etrog).[10] There is, however, ample literary evidence for the same, particularly in Josephus' *Antiquities*. Josephus documents the exemption from military service, first of the Jews in Ephesus who were Roman citizens (Josephus, *Ant*. 14.228) and then, from 43 BC on, all Jews in Asia (Josephus, *Ant*. 14.225–227).[11]

EPHESUS IN THE TIME OF PAUL

After leaving Priscilla and Aquila in Ephesus to get established, Paul retraced his steps to Jerusalem, Antioch, and finally Galatia and Phrygia (Acts 18:22–23). When he finally returned to Ephesus, he would have entered through the Magnesian Gate, the major opening in the fortification walls on the southeast side of the city. The road through here connected Ephesus with Magnesia on the Meander about fifteen miles (24 km) to the east and thence to an ancient road that led all the way into Babylonia.[12] A short walk would have brought him into the civic forum, the center of the city's government. Here he would have seen a largely open courtyard of about 525 by 190 feet (160 x 58 m) surrounded by columned porches, the most magnificent of which would have been the Basilica Stoa, constructed around 11 BC by Sextus Pollio.[13] This two-story, three-aisled portico was 50 feet (15.25 m) wide,

Basilica Stoa

stretching the entire length of the civic forum on its north side. Its covered area, supported by sixty-seven Ionic columns, would have been a popular place for businessmen and city politicians to meet and conduct business out of the sun or rain. The Stoa was dedicated "to Artemis of the Ephesians, Emperor Caesar Augustus, son of a god, Tiberius Caesar, son of Augustus, and to the Ephesian people" with larger-than-life statues of Augustus and his wife, Livia in an antechamber on its easternmost side.[14]

The city was well supplied with water, with significant amounts being carried in by aqueducts (one of which was also

10. Wilson, *Biblical Turkey*, 216.

11. Murphy-O'Connor, *St. Paul's Ephesus*, 80. See the more extensive references in Josephus, *Ant*. 14.223–227, 228–229, 230, 234, 238–240, 262–264, 301–313, 314–317; 16.27–65; *Ag. Ap*. 2.39.

12. Murphy-O'Connor, *St. Paul's Ephesus*, 35; Wilson, *Biblical Turkey*, 207.

13. Wilson, *Biblical Turkey*, 209; Murphy O'Connor, *St. Paul's Ephesus*, 190.

14. S. R. F. Price, *Rituals and Power: The Roman Imperial Cult in Asia Minor* (Cambridge: Cambridge University Press), 1984), 140, 255; Steven Friesen, *Imperial Cults and the Apocalypse of John: Reading Revelation in the Ruins*. (Oxford: Oxford University Press, 2001), 95–96; Wilson, *Biblical Turkey*, 209.

constructed as a gift to the city by Sextus Pollio). Water was collected in cisterns, one major such node being located on the south side of the civic forum, and

Pollio Aqueduct

distributed throughout the city through clay pipes both to public fountains and private residences.

Several public buildings dominated the civic forum of Paul's day, three of which stood on the north side of the Basilica Stoa. First, the Prytaneion (in the northwest corner of the forum) was the site of the city's sacred hearth—the symbolic fire kept perpetually burning. As a symbol of the city's hospitality, it would have been the place where state dinners were held and foreign dignitaries entertained, but it also remained a place for the worship of several traditional Greek gods and goddesses. Inscriptions on the reerected pillars record the names of the priests—the *Curetai*—who served both in this building and in the Ortygian mysteries of Artemis (Strabo, *Geography* 14.1.20). A small temple of Artemis, the patron goddess of the city, stood next to the Prytaneion. By the turn of the era, part of this temple had been rededicated also to the worship of Julius Caesar. It consisted of a courtyard of about 108 by 95 feet (33 x 29 m) surrounded by colonnades on three of its sides; on the fourth side, a series of seven steps led up to the twin shrines.[15] East of these stands an odeon, a small theater suited for musical performances and poetical recitations. The current structure dates from the second century and also served as the meeting place for the civic council. As excavations have not been undertaken beneath this structure, it is not known whether it was built over an older structure that served as a council hall in Paul's time.

The vast courtyard of the civic forum also became a kind of sacred precinct for a freestanding temple in its midst—a temple dedicated to Augustus and the goddess Roma. The worship of the Roman emperors had become an important expression of loyalty and gratitude to the chief patron of the world on the part of the citizens of Ephesus—as indeed for the whole province of Asia, whose cities vied for what they considered the privilege of constructing such temples to Roma (the divinized personification of the city of Rome itself) and to members of the imperial family. This temple, sport-

Temple of Julius and Artemis

15. Price, *Rituals and Power*, 139, 254; Murphy O'Connor, *St. Paul's Ephesus*, 190–91.

ing single rows of six columns front and back and ten columns on its sides, had a footprint of about fifty by seventy-two feet (15.25 x 22 m).[16]

Paul would have left the civic forum by a single, columned street beginning in its northwest corner and leading eventually to the commercial center of Ephesus. Archaeologists have named this street "Curetes Street" because it begins at the Prytaneion where the *curetai* carried out their duties. In antiquity it appears to have been known as the *Embolos*, the "Wedge," perhaps because it cut diagonally across the city's grid pattern.[17] The street was lined with shops built into recesses behind the colonnades. It is *possible* that Aquila and Prisca had secured one of these spaces in which to ply their trade, though other sites were more likely. The street was also lined with statues bearing inscriptions honoring public benefactors of the city (and thus, incidentally, bearing witness to the cultural importance of honoring them as such). Grander honorary monuments, such as a memorial built to Caius Memmius, a grandson of the dictator Sulla, and a monumental tomb for Sextus Pollio were also to be found on the upper half of this street (the latter being built beyond and below the west end of Pollio's Basilica Stoa).

At the base of Curetes Street stand two blocks of town houses, the second of which sits today under a protective Kevlar roof and has undergone significant restoration, giving visitors a glimpse into the colorfully decorated interior spaces of ancient homes approaching the quality of preservation of homes in Pompeii. The size of these dwellings, the elaborate decorations that adorn them in the way of frescoes and mosaics (e.g., frescoes of the nine muses, a mosaic of Neptune and his bride Amphitrite riding a dolphin), and the provisions for indoor plumbing and even something approaching central heating show these to be the

Curetes Street

16. Wilson, *Biblical Turkey*, 209. There is some debate as to which of the two cult sites was dedicated to the Deified Julius and which to Augustus. Peter Scherrer ("The City of Ephesos From the Roman Period to Late Antiquity," in Koester, *Ephesos*, 4–5) believes the double temple between the Prytaneion and Bouleuterion to have been dedicated to Augustus and Artemis, with the freestanding temple representing the temple Augustus ordered built for Divus Julius and Dea Roma in 29 BC, when Ephesus was made the capital of the province (see, perhaps, Dio Cassius, *Roman History* 51.20.6). Friesen (*Twice Neokoros: Ephesus, Asia and the Cult of the Flavian Imperial Family* [Leiden: Brill, 1993], 11 n. 21; *Imperial Cults*, 101) and Price (*Rituals and Power*, 140, 254), on the other hand, support the reverse.

17. Murphy O'Connor, *St. Paul's Ephesus*, 191.

Terrace House

houses of the rich and powerful citizens of Ephesus. This second block appears to contain six or perhaps seven individual units, most originally enjoying a second story (given the presence of bases of staircases). Two of these individual units measure about four thousand and seven thousand square feet (371.6–650.3 m^2)—lavishly spacious even by modern standards, and all the more so by ancient standards.[18] Paul seems to have made a point of bearing witness to members of this class in the various cities in which he sought to plant churches, since securing such patrons whose homes would be large enough to serve as meeting places for the congregation was essential to the movement's long-term success.

More tomb monuments were to be found at the base of Curetes Street. Just in front of the second block of apartments once sat the Tomb of Arsinoë, a half-sister of Cleopatra VII who was murdered by Marc Antony's soldiers in 42 BC to advance Cleopatra's interests in Egypt. Arsinoë had sought asylum in the Artemision after Caesar was assassinated and was dragged thence and killed.[19] A monument also stood there to honor Androclus, the legendary founder

18. Murphy-O'Connor, *St. Paul's Ephesus*, 193–95. See also Peter Scherrer, *Ephesus: The New Guide* (Istanbul: Ege Yayınları, 2000), 100–113, which includes a richly detailed floor plan of the two apartment complexes on pp. 104–5.

19. Murphy-O'Connor, *St. Paul's Ephesus*, 45–46; Scherrer, *New Guide*, 124. There were conflicting reports concerning this event in antiquity: Appian, *Civil Wars*, 5.1.9 (who locates the murder in Miletus, probably wrongly); Dio Cassius, *History*. 48.24.1–2 (who mistakenly makes the victims Cleopatra's brothers); Josephus, *Ant.* 15.88–90 (generally regarded as the most reliable).

Tetragonos Agora

of Ephesus (see Pausanias, *Guide to Greece* 7.2.6–9; Strabo, *Geography* 14.1.3).

Adjacent to a bath complex that likely postdates Paul's visit, and thus probably also postdating Paul's time in Ephesus, there is an excellent example of an ancient latrine across Curetes Street from the Terrace Houses. Modern visitors are always surprised at the lack of privacy and personal space that the ancients required for such functions.

Less expensive blocks of multistoried apartments, or *insulae*, climbed Mount Pion on the other side of Curetes Street.[20] One of the narrow side streets leading up Mount Pion led to a large complex overlooking the great theater (see below). This might have been the home and (unofficial) administrative center for the governor of the province of Asia (the civic forum serving as the official locus for public administrative business).[21]

Curetes Street opens at its base into a public square that also affords one point of access to the commercial center of Ephesus—the *Tetragonos agora*, or the "Square Market". The agora could be entered here from its southeast corner through a magnificent gate built by Mazaeus and Mithridates, two freedmen (that is, former slaves) of the house of Augustus, in honor of their former master and perpetual patron Augustus, his wife Livia, and Marcus Agrippa (at the time, Augustus' heir apparent). The magnitude of the structure bears witness to the wealth that could be amassed by imperial freedmen during this period.[22]

The agora itself doubled in size during the reign of Augustus to the dimensions of 370 square feet (34.4 m^2).[23] There were sixty or so permanent workshops and stalls, built from stone, surrounding the inside perimeter on three sides. Columned porches on all four sides would have provided an ideal venue for buying, selling, or open-air preaching. These porticoes were impressive two-story structures with stairs at the corners giving access to the upper floor. A side street running north from Curetes Street alongside the agora and past the great theater also gave access to the upper story of these porticoes through a basilica built during the early years of Nero's reign.[24] The vast open courtyard would, of course, have also been filled with vendors' carts and tents. This would have been the likeliest place among those so far excavated for Aquila, Priscilla, and Paul to have set up shop for their long stay in Ephesus. Statues of public benefactors, including members of the imperial household, graced the complex.

20. Murphy-O'Connor, *St. Paul's Ephesus*, 198.
21. Murphy-O'Connor, *St. Paul's Ephesus*, 198.
22. The inscription is datable to 3 BC (Wilson, *Biblical Turkey*, 217).
23. Murphy-O'Connor, *St. Paul's Ephesus*, 197.
24. Murphy-O'Connor, *St. Paul's Ephesus*, 198.

From the commercial agora one could find one's way to the harbor by two paths: one through a gate in the west side of the agora that opened onto a street leading west to the harbor, another through a gate on the north side that led eventually to a broad thoroughfare running between the great theater and the harbor. This street was thirty-six feet (11 m) wide and a third of a mile (483 m) long.[25] It led past storehouses and more venues for vendors and merchants to conduct their business or inspect cargoes and eventually to the harbor itself, which, in Paul's day, was one of the busiest seaports of the Roman Empire. As such, it was also carefully regulated. A massive inscription was found on a slab standing taller than a human being that details the customs regulations of the harbor as well as penalties for smuggling and other infractions. This was a major node in the flow of goods from the East to Rome.

South Gate, Entrance to Agora

Many of the cargoes listed in Rev 18:12–13 could be found arriving in Ephesus from the East for further transportation west, including slaves for the city's slave markets, attested from inscriptions in the Square Market and from regulations concerning slave trafficking on the customs inscription.[26] There were obvious advantages and incentives for merchants and shipowners to favor putting themselves in Rome's service. An inscription in Ephesus reads: "no one is liable to pay tax for goods carried in service to the people of Rome, nor for goods conveyed for religious purposes."[27] The emperor Claudius provided insurance for ships dedicated to delivering grain to Rome, should they be lost at sea, a major incentive in a risky industry. An inscription above the entrance to the somewhat pretentious tomb of one Flavius Zeuxis, a merchantman sea captain from Hierapolis, boasts of his making seventy-two successful trips around the southern coast of Greece to Italy (most likely using Ephesus as his port) in trade with Rome. The Ephesian harbor indeed afforded a distinctive view into the Roman imperial economy that directed a disproportionate percentage of the world's goods—both luxury items and staples—toward "the great city" (Rev 17:18; see esp. also 18:11–20).

At the east end of "Harbor Street" stands the great theater of Ephesus. Originally constructed during the Hellenistic period, it was expanded to its present dimensions over the course of a century beginning in about AD 40.[28] It

25. Murphy-O'Connor, *St. Paul's Ephesus*, 27.

26. Shaner, "Ephesus," 372, 374.

27. See J. Nelson Kraybill, *Imperial Cult and Commerce in John's Apocalypse* (Sheffield: Sheffield Academic, 1996), 66; the translation is my altered version.

28. Wilson, *Biblical Turkey*, 218.

is possible that the city council used this as a meeting place prior to the construction of the odeon. The theater could have accommodated a vast crowd of between twenty-one thousand and twenty-five thousand spectators.[29] Readers of Acts

Theater

will immediately connect this site with the riot that probably convinced Paul that it might be time to move on from Ephesus (Acts 19:21–41). The episode is instructive from a number of angles: the economic interests that were inseparable from questions of religion and conversion; the ease with which civic pride could be connected with the worship of a particular (endangered) deity and harnessed against a foreign cult; and Paul's team's apparent degree of effectiveness in this city.

The street that ran north from Curetes Street past the great theater continued further north to a gymnasium complex that began just diagonally across from the theater and, eventually, to a vast stadium. During the Hellenistic period, this had been a simple earthen stadium like that at Olympia in Greece; it was reconfigured in stone with typical stadium seating over arched passageways during Nero's reign.[30] The stadium was home to the *Ephesia*, an annual series of games drawing competitors from throughout the province and involving both athletic and artistic competitions, including music and dance.[31] Another principal egress from the city's fortifications could be found behind the stadium—the Coressian Gate, from which the Great Artemision would have been clearly visible in the distance.

EPHESUS AND ARTEMIS

As in every major city in the Roman world, the residents of Ephesus were also devoted to many deities. For example, the worship of Cybele is attested in a shrine that stands on the far north side of the Panayir Dağ and evidence of private devotion to Aphrodite, Dionysus, and Isis was discovered in houses throughout the city.[32] Ephesus was known throughout the region, however, as a city especially devoted to Artemis. While Artemis was worshiped in many of the cities of Asia Minor, Ephesus was home to her greatest temple. Today, very little remains of the Artemision, since throughout the Medieval and Ottoman periods the perfectly cut stones of the derelict temple were quarried for new buildings. In

29. For the lower estimate, see Wilson, *Biblical Turkey*, 218; for the higher, Fairchild, *Christian Origins*, 36.

30. Fairchild, *Christian Origins*, 37.

31. Murphy-O'Connor, *St. Paul's Ephesus*, 199.

32. A monumental temple would be erected to Isis's companion Sarapis in the second century AD. On the archaeological evidence for worship of the Egyptian gods, see James C. Walters, "Egyptian Religions in Ephesos," in Koester, *Ephesos*, 281–309.

Paul's time, however, the Great Temple of Artemis was one of the seven wonders of the ancient world (indeed, the crowning marvel among them according to Antipater of Sidon in *Greek Anthology* 9.58) and a major destination for pilgrims and tourists from across the Mediterranean. Its footprint was 220 by 425 feet (67 x 129.5 m), more than four times that of the Parthenon in Athens.[33] Double rows of columns 6.5 feet (2 m) in diameter and 65 feet (19.8 m) high stood around the temple's perimeter, supporting its roof. These were arranged in rows of 8 on the shorter and 20 on the longer sides, to a total of 127 columns (Pliny the Elder, *Natural History* 36.21.95–97). A grand altar stood about 125 feet (38 m) in front of the temple itself.[34] A shrine to Augustus may also have been incorporated into this famous Artemision in the early imperial period.[35]

In addition to being the most prominent religious site in the area, the temple also served major commercial functions: It was an important lending agency, using the proceeds from the lands owned by "the goddess" as capital to be lent out at interest, as well as a sacred depository for major sums of money (Caesar, *Civil Wars* 3.33, 105; Dio Chrysostom, *Orationes* 31.54–55; Aelius Aristides, *Orationes* 23.24). Its activities were supported by an immense staff of priests, functionaries, and temple slaves.

The Artemision sat less than a mile's (1.6 km) walk from the Coressian Gate (the northern gate of Roman Ephesus) and about a mile and a quarter (2 km) from the Magnesian Gate (the city's eastern gate). A calendar of regular sacred processions featuring Artemis connected the city with her temple. One itinerary brought the sacred images of Artemis and other cult images and paraphernalia from the temple to the Magnesian Gate, through the civic agora, down Curetes Street, past the Square Market and theater, and out the Coressian Gate, to return thence to the Artemision. Over 250 participants might be involved in the typical sacred procession, carrying the images on platforms, singing, and carrying out

Statue of Artemis Flanked by Two Deer

33. Murphy-O'Connor, *St. Paul's Ephesus*, 118.

34. Murphy-O'Connor, *St. Paul's Ephesus*, 22.

35. Price, *Rituals and Power*, 254.

various offerings at sacred locations throughout the city.[36]

Although Greek-styled images of Artemis were found in private homes in Ephesus, this was not her public face in Asia Minor.[37] Cult statues and representations of cult images, for example on coins of Ephesus, show her as a mother goddess, flanked by two deer, her chest covered with symbols of fertility. It is debated whether these symbols should be understood as breasts (so Minucius Felix, *Octavius* 23.5), eggs, or even the testicles of bulls.[38] It is clear, however, that the more ancient worship of the Mother Goddess of the region was joined at an early stage with the worship of Artemis. She wears a peculiar headdress on which several buildings are represented—perhaps representing the city of Ephesus itself, with Artemis as its personal patron and protector.[39]

Many inscriptions found throughout Ephesus bear witness to the importance of Artemis (as well as the emperor) for the life of the city. One typical inscription begins with a dedication to both "Ephesian Artemis" and Augustus. Artemis was so closely linked with the prestige and well-being of the city that the city laid particular claim to her as, in some sense, their own. The inscription goes on to honor an Ephesian noble named Vibius Gaius as *φιλάρτεμις καί φιλοσέβαστος* (*philartemis kai philosebastos*), a "friend of Artemis and friend of Augustus." What gives Vibius honor in this city is his piety toward—and perhaps his financial support of—the civic cults of Artemis and the emperor. A great many

Ephesian Coin with Image of Artemis

coins minted in Ephesus bear witness to the city's pride in and identification with their patron goddess.

In such a city, Paul was destined to run into trouble. His proclamation of one and only one God threatened the city's very identity and its claim to fame, not to mention the livelihood of the concessioners like Demetrius whose trade depended on the reputation and worship of Artemis of the Ephesians. Demetrius, a maker of souvenir silver replicas of the goddess Artemis, rallied thousands of the city's citizens to gather in the theater to protest Paul's activity. As one sits in its stands, one can almost still hear the echoes of the chant they took up for

36. Murphy-O'Connor, *St. Paul's Ephesus*, 174–75; see also the brief description of a procession in Xenophon of Ephesus, *Ephesian Tale* 1.2–3 and discussion in Murphy-O'Connor, *St. Paul's Ephesus*, 177–79.

37. Maria Aurenhammer, "Sculptures of Gods and Heroes from Ephesus," in Koester, *Ephesos*, 254, 276.

38. Murphy-O'Connor, *St. Paul's Ephesus*, 7.

39. Murphy-O'Connor, *St. Paul's Ephesus*, 21.

two whole hours: "Great is Artemis of the Ephesians!" (Acts 19:34).

CIVIC DEVELOPMENTS UNDER DOMITIAN

The church Paul and his team planted would continue to grow in this city in the decades following Paul's departure. The church in Ephesus emerges again prominently in Revelation as one of the seven congregations addressed by that text. By then, the point of conflict between the Christian movement and city had moved away from Artemis and more fully toward the worship of the emperors, with the latter becoming a new focus for civic pride and identity.

For most of the first century, Pergamum and not Ephesus was the epicenter of imperial cult in the province of Asia. Augustus and the Roman Senate granted the Pergamenes the honor of building the first temple to the emperor Augustus and the goddess Roma (the deified personification of the city of Rome) in 29 BC, making it the center for the worship of Augustus in the province. Smyrna would be selected from among twelve cities in Asia (including Ephesus and Pergamum) to host the provincial cult of Augustus' successor Tiberius, along with Tiberius' mother Livia and the Roman Senate, in AD 26. Such grants conferred significant honor upon a city above its peers and also became a visible symbol of the emperor's favor toward the city, even as the city proposing (and building and maintaining and operating!) the imperial temple expressed its exuberant gratitude and loyalty toward the imperial family.

Though the provincial capital of Asia Minor, Ephesus would not win the honor of housing the leading temple in the provincial cult of a particular emperor until the late first century AD in connection with the city's bid to undertake a massive temple in honor of the emperor Domitian (ruled AD 81–96). The new temple would be inaugurated in AD 89/90.[40] It is, in fact, unclear whether the temple was to be dedicated to all three emperors of the Flavian family (Domitian together with his deceased and divinized father, Vespasian, and older brother, Titus, both of whom had reigned prior to Domitian) or to Domitian alone.[41] It is clear, however, that the temple was at least rededicated to Vespasian after Domitian's death, for the latter had fallen so significantly out of favor with the Senate as to have suffered the condemnation of his memory—the opposite of the apotheosis that his father

Foundations of Domitian Temple Platform

40. Friesen, *Twice Neokoros*, 41–49. See D. A. deSilva, *A Week in the Life of Ephesus* (Downers Grove, IL: InterVarsity Press, 2020), for a historical novella of the days leading up to this event.

41. This is, in part, dependent on the identification of the cult statue whose remains were discovered on the site (see below).

and brother had enjoyed upon their passing.[42] The temple would be referred to as "Asia's Shared Temple of the Augusti in Ephesus" in inscriptions (particularly inscriptions made by representatives of other cities who thus claimed a share in the temple even while conceding its placement "in Ephesus").[43]

The city fathers selected a prominent plateau on the west side of the civic forum. Engineers artificially extended this plateau to an area of 280 by 210 feet (85.3 x 64 m) by means of a vaulted and arched brickwork substructure to accommodate the grandiose plans for this temple and its surrounding courts and porticoes.[44] A three-story facade faced worshipers arriving from the main approach off Curetes Street. Doric columns stood on the bottom level, Ionic on the middle, and Corinthian on the third—a tribute to the Flavian Amphitheater in Rome, a major construction project begun under Vespasian and completed by Titus. Across the second and third levels, every column bore the life-sized, carved relief of a god, some known from Greek and Roman religion, some local like Attis and Cybele, some imported from the far reaches of the empire like Isis of Egypt, as if the pantheons of every nation had assembled here to bless those who approached to worship at the temple of the living god Domitian.[45] Worshipers would ascend by means of a grand staircase to the temple courtyard.

Domitian Temple Platform

Excavations on the top of the plateau have uncovered parts of the original temple itself, including the raised 80 by 110 foot (24.4 x 33.5 m) platform on which the temple sat, approached on all sides by four steps, and the temple's foundations. The temple had single rows of eight columns front and back and thirteen columns on the longer sides.[46] It was surrounded by a broad courtyard with columned porticoes on three sides. The Ephesus Museum now houses part of the altar that originally stood before the temple, ornately engraved with sacrificial scenes (such as a garlanded bull, bound to the altar and ready to be sacrificed) and scenes commemorating Domitian's military victories. A colossal statue of the emperor, estimated to have stood more than twenty feet (6 m) in height, was housed within the temple, presenting him as the larger-than-life and greater-than-human figure that an emperor was believed and experienced to be. The head and left forearm are all that remain. The identity of the emperor represented

42. Price, *Rituals and Power*, 178, 255.

43. Friesen, *Imperial Cults*, 45–46.

44. Katherine A. Shaner, "Ephesus," in *The Oxford Encyclopedia of the Bible and Archaeology*, ed. Daniel Master (Oxford: Oxford University Press, 2013), 379.

45. Friesen, *Imperial Cults*, 50–51.

46. Shaner, "Ephesus," 380.

by this statue is admittedly a matter of dispute, some favoring Domitian, others favoring his elder brother Titus.[47]

Sacrificial Scene on Altar of Domitian

Another massive construction (possibly an expansion) project beside the harbor to the north of Harbor Street involved an expansive bath and gymnasium complex in preparation for the inauguration of Olympic-style games in honor of Domitian. These facilities—covering an area of over seventy thousand square yards (58,529 m^2) in all, making it one of the largest such complexes of its time—were completed in AD 92/93.[48]

For its extraordinary devotion to the emperor Domitian, Ephesus finally gained the honor of being named νεωκόρος (*neōkoros*) or "temple warden" of a provincial imperial cult in the Roman Province of Asia.[49] The city took evident pride in having achieved this honor, for a great number of public inscriptions would henceforth speak of "the council and people of the temple-warden (*Neōkoros*) city of the Ephesians." Imperial cult was now at the very heart of civic identity and pride. This was no less true for Pergamum whose leaders, after Ephesus had also won this title that Pergamum had enjoyed for over a century, began to refer to their city in inscriptions no longer simply as "the temple-warden city of the Pergamenes," but rather as "the *first-to-be-named*-temple-warden city of the Pergamenes." They responded further by building the monumental temple to Trajan (ruled AD 98–117) on the very brow of their acropolis, for which they were awarded a second neocorate and began to speak of their city as "Twice-named-temple-warden." The cities of Roman Asia Minor boasted of their

Inscription Naming Ephesus *Neōkoros* (Temple Warden)

47. Price (*Rituals and Power*, 187, 197) excludes the possibility that the statue represents Titus on the basis of the existing inscriptions that only name (first) Domitian and (then) Vespasian as the particular *Augustus* worshiped at this site. He claims that the statue "could pass for any of the Flavians" (*Rituals and Power*, 255). Friesen (*Imperial Cults*, 46, 50) regards it as certain that the statue represents Titus, and thus that Titus was a recipient of cult at this site.

48. Friesen, *Imperial Cults*, 74.

49. The city had previously been identified as *Neōkoros* of the goddess Artemis (see Acts 19:35), though this term would come to be applied almost exclusively to the honor of sponsoring a provincial cult of an emperor.

Temple of Hadrian

imperial temples and honors like modern cities might boast about their professional sports teams. Ephesus would press this rivalry even further, however, building a monumental temple to the emperor Hadrian (ruled AD 117–138), identified with "Olympian Zeus," near the harbor. For this, Ephesus was also awarded a second neocorate, adding to the reputation and luster of the city. After this point, however, the Pergamenes began to refer to themselves as "the *first*-to-be-named-*twice*-temple-warden," thus maintaining their edge over their rival city.

Modern readers of Revelation may have difficulty understanding the unpopularity—indeed the resentment and danger—that Christians faced if they took an open stance *against* the worship of the emperor in cities like Ephesus and Pergamum. It may be even more difficult to understand the local enthusiasm for the cults of men-turned-gods. But when we begin to understand how civic identity, civic pride, civic standing in the region, and civic well-being were all tied to the imperial cult, we may begin to appreciate more fully what a threat the Christian gospel was with its call to "fear God and give Him glory" (Rev 14:7)—him, and no other. Nevertheless, John would call the Christians in Ephesus, who would hear John's references to a beast and its organized cult as a trenchant critique of the Roman emperor and the worship offered to him throughout the province and legitimating Roman imperialism, to consistent and uncompromising witness to their neighbors that there was indeed only one God, and that the pretensions of Rome and its emperors were utterly demonic.[50]

BIBLIOGRAPHY

Aurenhammer, Maria. "Sculptures of Gods and Heroes from Ephesus." Pages 251–80 in *Ephesos: Metropolis of Asia; An Interdisciplinary Approach to Its Archaeology, Religion and Culture*. Edited by Helmut Koester. Valley Forge, PA: Trinity Press International, 1995.

deSilva, David A. *Seeing Things John's Way: The Rhetoric of the Book of Revelation*. Louisville: Westminster John Knox 2009.

———. *Unholy Allegiances: Heeding Revelation's Warning*. Peabody, MA: Hendrickson, 2013.

———. *A Week in the Life of Ephesus*. Downers Grove, IL: InterVarsity Press, 2020.

50. On Revelation 13 and the Roman imperial cult, see Friesen, *Imperial Cults*, 135–217; deSilva, *Seeing Things*, 93–116, 193–228, 257–84; *Unholy Allegiances: Heeding Revelation's Warning* (Peabody, MA: Hendrickson, 2013), 21–76.

Erdemgil, Selahattin, et al., *The Terrace Houses in Ephesus*. Istanbul: Hitit Color, 1988.

Fairchild, Mark. *Christian Origins in Ephesus and Asia Minor*. Peabody, MA: Hendrickson, 2017.

Friesen, Steven. *Imperial Cults and the Apocalypse of John: Reading Revelation in the Ruins*. Oxford: Oxford University Press, 2001.

———. *Twice Neokoros: Ephesus, Asia and the Cult of the Flavian Imperial Family*. Leiden: Brill, 1993.

Hemer, Colin J. *The Letters to the Seven Churches of Asia in Their Local Setting*. Sheffield: JSOT Press, 1986. Repr., Grand Rapids: Eerdmans, 2001.

Koester, Helmut, ed. *Ephesos: Metropolis of Asia; An Interdisciplinary Approach to Its Archaeology, Religion and Culture*. Valley Forge, PA: Trinity Press International, 1995.

Kraybill, J. Nelson. *Imperial Cult and Commerce in John's Apocalypse*. Sheffield: Sheffield Academic, 1996.

Murphy O'Connor, Jerome. *St. Paul's Ephesus: Texts and Archaeology*. Collegeville, MN: Liturgical Press, 2008.

Price, S. R. F. *Rituals and Power: The Roman Imperial Cult in Asia Minor*. Cambridge: Cambridge University Press, 1984.

Scherrer, Peter. "The City of Ephesos From the Roman Period to Late Antiquity." Pages 1–25 in *Ephesos: Metropolis of Asia; An Interdisciplinary Approach to Its Archaeology, Religion and Culture*. Edited by Helmut Koester. Valley Forge, PA: Trinity Press International, 1995.

———. *Ephesus: The New Guide*. Istanbul: Ege Yayınları, 2000.

Shaner, Katherine A. "Ephesus." Pages 370–381 in *The Oxford Encyclopedia of the Bible and Archaeology*. Edited by Daniel Master. Oxford: Oxford University Press, 2013.

Trebilco, Paul. *The Early Christian in Ephesus From Paul to Ignatius*. Grand Rapids: Eerdmans, 2007.

Walters, James C. "Egyptian Religions in Ephesos." Pages 281–309 in *Ephesos: Metropolis of Asia; An Interdisciplinary Approach to Its Archaeology, Religion and Culture*. Edited by Helmut Koester. Valley Forge, PA: Trinity Press International, 1995.

White, L. Michael. "Urban Development and Social Change in Imperial Ephesus." Pages 27–79 in *Ephesos: Metropolis of Asia; An Interdisciplinary Approach to Its Archaeology, Religion and Culture*. Edited by Helmut Koester. Valley Forge, PA: Trinity Press International, 1995.

Wilson, Mark W. *Biblical Turkey: A Guide to the Jewish and Christian Sites of Asia Minor*. Istanbul: Ege Yayınları, 2010.

CHAPTER 42

PAULUS GEOGRAPHICUS?

THE SPATIAL (SOMATIC) WORLD OF PAUL'S LETTER TO THE PHILIPPIANS

Phil 1:1–4:23

Michael J. Thate

They are the silences where we see in each departing
human shade some disturbed Divinity.

—Eugenio Montale[1]

KEY POINTS

- The relationship between the body and experiences of space and time provides a way to explore the social and geographical context of Paul's letter to the Philippians
- The dynamics of imitation in Philippi offer insight in relation to Paul, Christ, and the assemblies in Philippi.
- The function of Paul's incarcerated body and its social-spatial effects upon the assemblies in Philippi is an important consideration for interpreting Philippians.
- Philippi's history as a serially colonized space is also relevant for understanding the letter itself.

1. Eugenio Montale, *Cuttlefish Bones*, trans. William Arrowsmith (New York: Norton, 1994), 9.

LANDSCAPES AND INSCAPES

In his *Livro do desassossego*, the Portuguese poet Fernando Pessoa reflects on the relationship between landscapes and states of mind.[2] Which is prior to the other: a landscape or one's spirit or state of mind? Pessoa begins to formulate an answer to this question by posing Henri Frédéric Amiel's aphorism: "a landscape is a state of mind."[3] In Amiel's rendering, landscapes are conditions of spirit. Pessoa, however, objects. Such a position, he avers, is "feebly felicitous" and does little more than produce a "feeble dreamer." Landscapes are landscapes—not states of mind. Undergirding Pessoa's formulation is the conviction of the fundamentality of an external reality. "Quite independently," he states, "the grass grows, the rain waters the grass as it grows and the sun turns to gold the whole field of grass that has grown or will grow; the mountains have been there since ancient times and the wind that blows sounds just as it did to Homer (even if he never existed)."

It is more appropriate, Pessoa suggests, to maintain that *a state of mind is a landscape*; a kind of *inscape*.[4] Such a formulation would contain within itself all the advantages of refusing the "lie of a theory" while embracing "the truth of a metaphor."[5]

THE TRUTH OF A METAPHOR

Pessoa introduces for us a series of complex dynamics to consider in Paul's letter to the Philippians. In particular, how do environmental forces act upon our ways of knowing? How does the shape of space form our *conceptions* of an outside world? And, if a state of mind is a landscape, how does the embodiment of that state of mind relate to landscapes themselves? Moreover, how do the geographies we occupy *occupy us*? Or is this all the wrong way around?

Another series of dynamics is introduced from the world of physics. In 2016, experiments from the Laser Interferometer Gravitational-Wave Observatory reported a detection of the merging of two black holes. Such events, concludes physicist Richard A. Muller, "create new space." They create "new time," too.[6] The power of these insights from the physical world (and, indeed, their relevance for what follows), allows a critical interval from which to position not "a lie of theory" but the truth of a metaphor: that is, time and space *proceed from events*.

These themes of landscape as an external reality, the embodied, internal conceptions by which we imagine and mediate such geographies, and the metaphorical truth that space and time are effects of an event, will guide what

2. Fernando Pessoa, *The Book of Disquiet*, trans. Margaret Jull Costa (New York: New Directions, 2017), 415, §386.

3. The original French is found in Amiel's journal entry from 31 October 1852, and reads: "Un paysage quelconque est un état de l'âme, et qui lit dans tous deux est émerveillé de retrouver la similtude dans chaque détail" (Henri-Frédéric Amiel, *Fragments d'un journal intime*, vol. 1 [Geneva : George, 1897], 62).

4. The concept of inscape dominates the work of Gerard Manley Hopkins. On this topic, see the study of Bernadette Waterman Ward, *World as Word: Philosophical Theology in Gerard Manley Hopkins* (Washington, DC: Catholic University of America Press, 2002).

5. Pessoa, *Book of Disquiet*, 415, §386.

6. Richard A. Muller, *Now: The Physics of Time* (New York: Norton, 2016), 11.

follows. Moreover, in this brief essay on Paul's letter to those conventionally referred to as "Philippians" (Φιλιππήσιος, *Philippēsios*), considerations of the body as both the object of spatial theorizing as well as the subject from which such theorizing proceeds are as necessary as those dealing with the square mileage of ancient Philippi when considering questions of geography and space.[7] Though at first blush the letter appears to offer little by way of standard geographic interests, the dynamics and movements of the letter are themselves driven by a series of spatial, temporal, and somatic concerns.

THEORIZING BODIES IN PHILIPPI

The idea of an originating relationship between bodies and space is a classical one.[8] In Vitruvius' third book in *De architectura*, for example, dedicated and addressed to Augustus, Vitruvius discusses symmetry as it relates to the human body—or, at least, the ideal man—and the body's experience within the city in general and the temple in particular.[9] For Vitruvius, the "ideal man" is the analogy for architectural measure. Reflecting on the "origins" of temple symmetry, he states:

> Nature has composed the human body so that in its proportions the separate individual elements answer to the total form. ... Therefore, when [the gods] were handing down proportional sequences for every type of work, they did so especially for the sacred dwellings of the gods. ... They gathered the principles of measure, which seem to be necessary in any sort of project, from the components of the human body. (Vitruvius, *De architectura* 3.I.4–5)

The "Vitruvian man," therefore, provides a bodily site from which classical understandings of space emerged.[10] Moreover, it is this Vitruvian man that provides the ideal-type experience in cultic contexts. This ideal-type experience consists of a play of manipulations that are dependent upon architectural space's enhancement of cultic experience for ideal bodies. Temple steps (5.4.4), or the placement of cultic statues (4.9.1), for example, are intended to impress upon the ideal body a manipulated sense of divine relationality and proportion. And yet cities were filled with other bodies who could

7. See, for example, George Dodds and Robert Tavernor, eds., *Body and Building: Essays on the Changing Relation of Body and Architecture* (Cambridge: MIT, 2002); and Gaston Bachelard, *The Poetics of Space: The Classic Look at How We Experience Intimate Places*, trans. Maria Jolas (Boston: Beacon, 1994).

8. On this relationship within contemporary theory, see Michael J. Thate, "Paul, Φρόνησις, and Participation: The Shape of Space and the Reconfiguration of Place in Paul's Letter to the Philippians," in *"In Christ" in Paul: Explorations in Paul's Theology of Union and Participation*, ed. Michael J. Thate, Kevin J. Vanhoozer, and Constantine R. Campbell (Tübingen: Mohr Siebeck, 2014), 281–327.

9. See Vitruvius, *Ten Books on Architecture*, trans. Ingrid D. Rowland, commentary and illustrations by Thomas Noble Howe (Cambridge: Cambridge University Press, 1999).

10. See, generally, Indra Kagis McEwen, *Vitruvius: Writing the Body of Architecture* (Cambridge: MIT, 2002). See also, Laura Salah Nasrallah, *Christian Responses to Roman Art and Architecture: The Second-Century Church amid the Spaces of Empire* (Cambridge: Cambridge University Press, 2010), 10–12.

not share in such spatial experiences. Notions of ideal bodies in the Vitruvian sense may thus introduce a barring, or an interval. Municipal planning of the city based upon ideal bodies can become

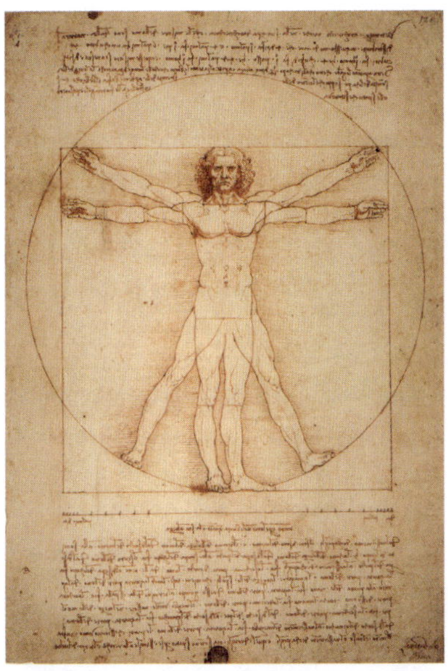

da Vinci's "Vitruvian Man"

a hostile and marginalizing environment for those whose embodied existence do not accord with the proportions of the Vitruvian man.

The imagery of bodies and temples are familiar and foundational in Pauline writings (for example, 1 Cor 3:16; 6:19).[11] Such imagery within Philippians, though latent, is also present (see Phil 1:1). Paul addresses his addressees by fusing cultic (τοῖς ἁγίοις ἐν Χριστῷ Ἰησοῦ, *tois hagiois en Christō Iēsou*) and civic labels (τοῖς οὖσιν ἐν Φιλίπποις, *tois ousin en Philippois*). It is in the latter designation where an "identity" or a "being" is labeled (οὖσιν, *ousin*). This identity, however, is qualified not by a civic polity—and, perhaps, not even by Paul himself—but by the sacerdotal decrees of the assembly (ἐπισκόποις καὶ διακόνοις, *episkpois kai diakonois*). What, if anything, can we make of this slight difference in attribution?

> To all (πᾶσιν, *pasin*) the holy ones in Christ Jesus (τοῖς ἁγίοις ἐν Χριστῷ Ἰησοῦ, *tois hagiois en Christō Iēsou*) the ones who are in Philippi (τοῖς οὖσιν ἐν Φιλίπποις, *tois ousin en Philippois*) with the overseers and deacons (σὺν ἐπισκόποις καὶ διακόνοις, *syn episkopois kai diakonois*)

As opposed to offering definitive answers, perhaps it is most helpful simply to call out the complexity and ambiguity of reference to those living in Philippi. It is this ambiguity, this "being" or "identity" or body that Paul theorizes and affords possibilities for theological reflection. This, then, is the object of Paul's spatial-somatic theorizing: *bodies in Philippi*. That is to say, Paul offers bodies living "in Philippi" a theorized body to which to conform as well as an imagined body from which such theorizing is produced.[12] That body, however, is not "Philippian" as such. As Christ

11. On the body in Paul, see Michael Tilly, "Aspekte der Leiblichkeit im paulinischen Denken," in *Dimensionen der Leiblichkeit: Theologische Zugänge*, ed. Bernd Janowski and Christoph Schwöbel (Göttingen: Neukirchener, 2015), 69–85.

12. "Theory" is that discursive practice that attempts to make visible social relations manifest with respect to their place within fields of power. The production of theory is somatic—that is, it originates from bodies and for bodies. Here see Sara Ahmed, *Queer Phenomenology: Orientations, Objects, Others* (Durham: Duke University Press, 2006); J. K. Puar, *The Right to*

introduced a transvaluation in Paul (see 3:7–11), his address strategically positions "the ones who are in Philippi" (τοῖς οὖσιν ἐν Φιλίπποις, *tois ousin en Philippois*) within a theological frame: the "I" that was no longer is. Within life's remainder there is simply Christ: "to live is Christ" (τὸ ζῆν Χριστός, *to zēn Christos*; Phil 1:21).

Though it appears that the ideal body from which space is theorized is that of Christ Jesus, as the letter progresses a merger with Paul's own somatic experience occurs. Whatever Christic realities may be wrought cosmologically or social-structurally, they are dramatically enacted within the psycho-somatic experience of the apostle (see 1:20–30; 2:12–13). The subject from which this spatio-somatic theory is produced is therefore Paul (and his band of brethren) *as* "servants/slaves of Christ Jesus" (δοῦλοι Χριστοῦ Ἰησοῦ, *douloi Christou Iēsou*). Paul—and the brothers and sisters (οἱ ἀδελφοί, *hoi adelphoi*) with him (see 4:21)—are positioned as the mediators of a grace (χάρις, *charis*) and peace (εἰρήνη, *eirēnē*) from God and the Lord Jesus Christ (1:2). And it is this grace and peace that are extended and explicated for the assembly as a reimagined network of social exchange. There is thus a subtle tension at work in the letter: the body imaging of Paul and that of the provincial leadership of those living in Philippi.

ENVIRONS AND EXISTENCE

Within the genre of commentary writing, commentaries tend to distinguish themselves by taking a particular stance on the specificities of provenance. Questions of date, authorship, and place of writing are of course noteworthy items to include in any commentary. In the case of Philippians, such rehearsed approaches are laced with additional complexity, and, I suggest, potential distraction. The authorship of Paul is relatively straightforward and uncontested.[13] Authorship, of course, is significant. For all we might rage against notions of intent, we persist in reading Paul differently than John or Plotinus. The date is more or less straightforward, too: sometime in the early to mid-50s AD. The chronology of the letter's appearance depends on our estimation of the relevance of Acts 16:11–40 and 20:1–6. The questioning of the historical value of Acts for arriving at a chronology of Paul's travels is rightfully called for in troubling simple pictures of the emergence of the early assemblies.[14] Questioning the historical accuracy of Acts however is different from ruling out its relevance for understanding something about Paul in Philippi. Let's assume a stylized form and late date for Acts in the second century. Does that necessarily rule out its utility for Philippians? What if we read them together for the sake of yielding critical interpretive possibilities for theorizing bodies in Philippi as opposed to making critical-historical claims?

The particulars of the story and the miraculous occurrence within Acts 16 may be literary embellishments. Several themes and the general movement of the scene, however, are worthwhile to

Maim: Debility, Capacity, Disability (Durham: Duke University Press, 2017); D. Schaefer, *Religious Affects: Animality, Evolution, and Power* (Durham: Duke University Press, 2015).

13. Though, see James Moffatt, *An Introduction to the Literature of the New Testament*, 2nd ed. (Edinburgh: T&T Clark, 1912), 165–72.

14. Here see, for example, Daniel Marguerat, *Paul in Acts and Paul in His Letters* (Tübingen: Mohr Siebeck, 2013).

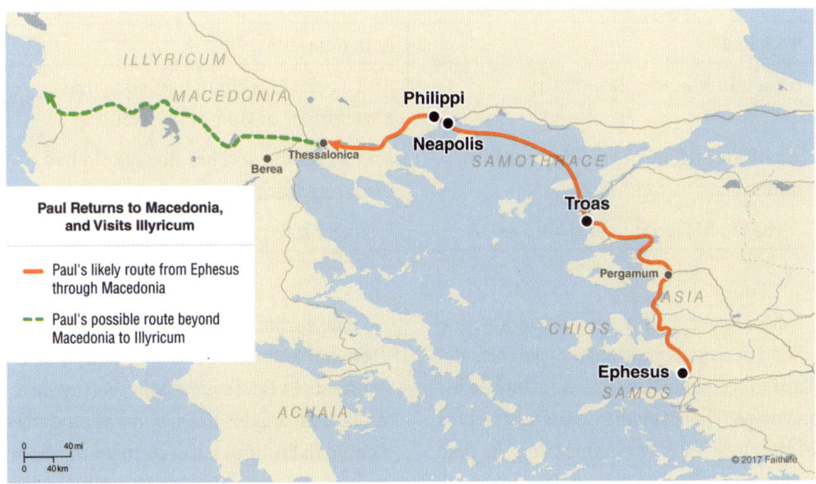

consider. The first is the "vision" (ὅραμα, *horama*) of a "man of Macedonia" (ἀνὴρ Μακεδών, *anēr Makedōn*), pleading with Paul:"Help us" (βοήθησον ἡμῖν, *boēthēson hēmin*; v. 9). After setting sail from Troas, and voyaging through Samothrace and Neapolis, Paul's band arrives at Philippi—"which is a leading city of that part of Macedonia, a [Roman] colony" (ἥτις ἐστὶν πρώτη[ς] μερίδος τῆς Μακεδονίας πόλις, κολωνία, *hētis estin prōtē[s] meridos tēs Makedonias polis, kolōnia*; v. 12). The exact meaning of this text is difficult to parse but its sense is clear: Philippi is an important "place" (*meris*) in Macedonia and also a Roman colony. The duration of the stay is uncertain—perhaps under a week owing to the arthrous reference of the Sabbath. Though surely Paul's band would have encountered "men of Macedonia" along the way and while in Philippi itself, the first people to be mentioned are a gathering of women outside the city gates (v. 13). Perhaps these women were simply washing clothes along the riverside or drawing water. Perhaps this was some form of assembly—maybe even of the cultic sort. The use of *synerchomai* (συνέρχομαι) throughout Acts would suggest such a meeting.[15] Within Paul's writings the expression could be used when referring to "the whole church" (ἡ ἐκκλησία ὅλη, *hē ekklēsia hole*) coming together into a single shared space (1 Cor 14:23). In any case, the first to be named is Lydia of Thyatira, a merchant of some sort (πορφυρόπωλις, *porphuropōlis*), who worshiped God (σεβομένη τὸν θεόν, *sebomenē ton theon*), and whose heart was opened by God to receive Paul's message (v. 14). The sense in which Lydia "worshiped" is, of course, an interpretive challenge.[16] What is clear, however, is the sense in which she reprises the role of the "Macedonian man."

15. See Acts 1:6, 21; 11:12; 15:38; 22:30; 25: 17; 28:17.

16. Compare the ranging uses of the participial form of *sebō* (σέβω) in Acts 13:43, 50; 17:4, 17; 18:7.

Acts 16:9[17]	Acts 16:14–15[18]
A certain Macedonian [man]	And a certain woman named Lydia ... a worshiper of God, was listening.
was standing and appealing for him and saying:	And when she and her household had been baptized, she urged, saying:
"Cross to Macedonia and help us!"	"... Enter into my house and remain."

Moreover, Lydia is said to have prevailed or urged (παρεβιάσατο, *parebiasato*) Paul to return to her house and share his message. This prevailing echoes the plea of the risen Jesus' companions on the road to Emmaus (Luke 24:29).[19] The relevance of Lydia's representation in Acts 16 for the letter to the Philippians is of course contested.[20] Why is she not named by Paul? Or is she simply lumped into the collective of *these* [women] (Phil 4:3)? The significance of her reprisal of the Macedonian man for the purposes of this essay, however, is in its illustration of our earlier comments on the Vitruvian man. A gendered body rests at the center of space's emanations. What began with the gesture of the Macedonian *man* ended with an assembly *chez Lydia* (16:40). Her absence in Paul's letter may therefore say very little about the significance of Lydia *in Philippi* as it does to other concerns and conceptions of Paul's views of an ideal body. Here again, creative tension and interpretative possibilities emerge and clash.

The second theme of note is the tradition that associates Philippi with imprisonment. As Paul's band followed Lydia to a place of prayer, the second person presented in Philippi is a certain young slave girl (παιδίσκην, *paidiskēn*) who hounded them for many days by declaring their mission aloud (vv. 16–18). This "certain young slave girl" appears to have been of significant financial benefit to her lords. Her economic utility for her masters, however, was broken by her exorcism (v. 19). Her owners (οἱ κύριοι αὐτῆς, *hoi kurioi autēs*), enraged by their destroyed property, seized (ἐπιλαβόμενοι, *epilabomenoi*) Paul and Silas and forcefully led them into the agora to face the city rulers (εἵλκυσαν εἰς τὴν ἀγορὰν ἐπὶ τοὺς ἄρχοντας, *heilkysan eis tēn agoran epi tous archontas*; v. 19). Intriguingly, in this second-century text they are presented to the city rulers (τοῖς στρατηγοῖς, *tois stratēgois*) as Jews (Ἰουδαῖοι, *Ioudaioi*; v. 20). The charges leveled against them—again, *as Jews*—is of unsettling the *polis* and introduc-

17. Acts 16:9—*anēr Makedōn tis* (ἀνὴρ Μακεδών τις)
ēn hestōs kai parakalōn auton kai legōn (ἦν ἑστὼς καὶ παρακαλῶν αὐτὸν καὶ λέγων)
diabas eis Makedonian boēthēson hemin (διαβὰς εἰς Μακεδονίαν βοήθησον ἡμῖν)

18. Acts 16:14—*kai tis gunē onomati Lydia ... sebomenē ton theon, ēkouen* (καί τις γυνὴ ὀνόματι Λυδία ... σεβομένη τὸν θεόν, ἤκουεν)

Acts 16:15—*hōs de ebaptisthē kai ho oikos autēs, parekalesen legousa* (ὡς δὲ ἐβαπτίσθη καὶ ὁ οἶκος αὐτῆς, παρεκάλεσεν λέγουσα) ... *eiselthontes eis ton oikon mou menete* (... εἰσελθόντες εἰς τὸν οἶκόν μου μένετε)

19. See examples in BDAG, 759.

20. On balance we should stress that the relevance of Lydia in Acts 16 rests in the literary composition and strategies of Acts and not Philippians.

ing unlawful customs (vv. 20–21). What those exact practices were is unclear. While the Roman penal code prohibited the privatization of unrecognized foreign gods,[21] the larger point of the text appears to be a skillful literary ambiguity raised by the scene on the nature of Paul's message. The relevance of the scene for our concerns in this essay, however, are the reasons and location for imprisonment. The reasons given are civic and economic disruptions within the *polis*; and the location of the temporary imprisonment is Philippi. Again, in terms of historical judgments we need not commit to much here. As far as the pairing of imprisonment and Philippi within a Pauline tradition, however, ranging from the mid-first century to the early second century, perhaps this is grounds for considering a carceral hermeneutic for the letter itself.

The second mention of Philippi is in Acts 20:6. After the uproar (τόν θόρυβον, *ton thorybon*) in Ephesus had calmed (20:1; cf. 19:21–41), a plot (ἐπιβουλή, *epiboulē*) against Paul arose in Greece "from Jews" (ὑπὸ τῶν Ἰουδαίων, *hypo tōn Ioudaiōn*). This is an odd turn. The disorderly charges brought against Paul *as a Jew* in 16:20 now shift to a plot against Paul *by Jews* (20:3). Where this occurred in Greece is difficult to say. It is also unclear what to make of v. 6. Paul wishes to return to Syria through Macedonia (v. 3). Those who travel with him represent a sampling of an emerging universal diaspora community: Pyrrhus' son Sopater from Berea, Aristarchus and Secundus from Thessalonica, Gaius of Derbe, Timothy, Tychicus, and Trophimus of Asia (v. 4).[22] The group separates (v. 5) from those designated as the *we who sailed from Philippi*.[23] The geographic point of divergence thus appears to be Philippi. Again, forming historical judgments of this episode are likely a red herring. The association of a conflict *within Judaism* in Philippi, however, introduces further nuance into the traditions surrounding Paul and Philippi.

IMPRISONED BODIES

In considering the body's relationship with space—both in the sense of bodies *in* space and the bodies *out of which* space emerges—what should we make of the relationship between Paul's letter and Paul's body as an *imprisoned body* at the writing of the letter(s)? Throughout his letter(s),[24] Paul frequently refers to his imprisonment.[25] As opposed to ancient epistolary practices of indicating the date of sending and in some cases their

---

21. See Cicero, *De legibus* 2.8.19; Dio Cassius, *Roman History* 67.14.2; 57.18.5.

22. See Wolf-Henning Ollrog, *Paulus und seine Mitarbeiter: Untersuchungen zu Theorie und Praxis der paulinischen Mission* (Neukirchen-Vluyn: Neukirchener Verlag, 1979), 45–58.

23. On the so-called "we" passages in Acts, see the brief excursus in Richard I. Pervo, *Acts: A Commentary* (Minneapolis: Fortress, 2009), 392–96.

24. There is, of course, significant debate on whether there was a letter or letters. I myself favor a composite letter approach. In this reading, there are basically four separate writings pieced together to form the single letter we have preserved in our NA28 as Philippians.

A (4:10–20) Paul thanking Philippians for their gift sent via Epaphroditus
B (1:1–3:1) Paul's letter of reassurance sent via Epaphroditus upon his return
C (3:2–4:3) polemical letter sent later when Paul is more appraised of situation
Remainder: 4:4–9; and, 4:21–23.

For the sake of simplicity, however, I will treat the letter in its canonical form.

25. Phil 1:7, 13, 14, 19, 30; 2:23, 27; 3:10; 4:10, 14.

Traditional Site of Paul's Philippian Prison

originating place,[26] Paul simply refers to "what has happened to me" (τὰ κατ᾽ἐμέ, *ta kat' eme*). The precise nature and location of this imprisonment is unclear. John Chrysostom, for example, referred to the emperor's "waging war against" Paul (*Homily* 4.58.7–17), perhaps in Rome,[27] Caesarea Maritima, or somewhere else like Ephesus. On the one hand, it makes sense if Paul wrote from a place like Ephesus owing to how its geographic proximity to Philippi would allow for the frequent exchange of letters. Moreover, prisoners within Roman detention (*custodia*) typically were required to provide for themselves.[28] Perhaps the fellowship and partnership between Paul and those in Philippi consisted in part in the latter's material support of Paul while imprisoned. On the other hand, the geographic place from which Paul wrote his letter(s) to Philippi is slightly immaterial. We write out of an uncertain mixing of experience. As I write this sentence in the library of l'École normale supérieure, Paris (and revise it in a café on Rue

26. See the examples listed in Holloway, *Philippians*, 19 n. 147.

27. The Latin Marcionite prologues refer to this provenance.

28. Note the studies of Jens-Uwe Krause, *Gefängnisse im römischen Reich* (Stuttgart: Steiner, 1996); S. Arband, W. Macheiner, and C. Colpe, "Gefangenschaft," in *Reallexikon für Antike und Christentum*, ed. Theodor Klauster et al. (Stuttgart: Hiersemann, 1976) 9:318–45. See also, Brian Rapske, *The Book of Acts and Paul in Roman Custody*, vol. 3 of *The Book of Acts in Its First Century Setting*, ed. Bruce W. Winter (Grand Rapids: Eerdmans, 1994), esp. 209–16; Richard Cassidy, *Paul in Chains: Roman Imprisonment and the Letters of St Paul* (New York: Crossroad, 2001) 124–42. I owe these references to Holloway, *Philippians*.

Hamra in Beirut), the specificity of these places does not necessarily determine the content of this essay's ideas. Surely any thought formed is influenced by place in so far as any idea is met by a bricolage of experience. Geographies may attune and bring discrete points of awareness to writing (and revision), but they also mix with an existing *mélange* of memories. Paul wrote out of the diverse mixture of his Jewish experience as a cosmopolitan and traveler who had encountered the risen Christ in some form.

Paul could speak generally of the shared affliction (θλῖψις, *thlipsis*) he and his band suffered while in Asia (2 Cor 1:8). Their suffering was an excessive burden beyond their natural abilities of coping—causing them to in fact despair of life. A sentence of death was passed within Paul and his crew (αὐτοὶ ἐν ἑαυτοῖς τὸ ἀπόκριμα τοῦ θανάτου ἐσχήκαμεν, *autoi en heautois to apokrima tou thanatou eschēkamen*) that worked an affectual deferral of hope for God's deliverance *after* civic sovereignty's judgments (2 Cor 1:9). This affectual trust worked a cancellation of the sovereignty of worldly judgments, which, in turn, mirrored a deliverance to come (2 Cor 1:10). Paul, as he does with those in Philippi, entreats those in Corinth to see their prayers as an emblem of participation within a wider "many" (2 Cor. 1:11). Paul's imprisonment—and whatever sufferings there may have been beside—is thus a matrix of meeting not only for some future divine deliverance but also frames an aesthetic of longing for release from worldly sovereignty (2 Cor 1:12). This logic or aesthetic of release referenced in 2 Corinthians as occurring in Asia can be seen as traveling throughout the architecture of the Pauline assemblies. The spatial dynamics of Paul's carceral release and its effective hope for divine deliverance *as an episodic sentiment* thus emerged as a kind of existential environment for Paul's ecclesial network.

PHILIPPI AS SERIAL SPACE

How this episodic sentiment would have been heard and contested in Philippi is also complex. This sentiment was *Paul's sentiment*. Considering the occasional nature of the epistle, however, and, indeed, how Paul's missive(s) may have been heard within the complex social milieu of Philippi and the assembly's administrators and leaders, forcefully awakens readers to a cacophony of sound—and, perhaps, other sentiments. The making of place in Philippi was a pastoral procurement. Paul's was but one presence among others. Philippi was itself a place of spatial conflict long before Paul had arrived.[29] Though little is known about Julio-Claudian Philippi, a rich tradition of Thracian cultic practices as well as local economy and commerce met dynamic exchange along the famous trade route of the Via Egnatia. Moreover, as Laura Sallah Nasrallah comments, varying epigraphic and sculptural remains "attest to the honoring of Augustus and his adopted sons Gaius and Lucius Caesar at Philippi both at the time of Paul and later."[30] Such traces remind us of the cosmopolitan intersecting of civic,

29. The classical study is Paul Collart, *Philippes: Ville de Macédoine, depuis ses origines jusqu'à la fin de l'époque romaine*, 2 vols. (Paris: de Boccard, 1937).

30. Laura Salah Nasrallah, "Spatial Perspectives: Space and Archaeology in Roman Philippi," in *Studying Paul's Letters: Contemporary Perspectives and Methods*, ed. Joseph A. Marchal (Minneapolis: Fortress, 2012), 60.

Remains of the Acropolis at Philippi

commercial, and cultic space in such cities. Philippi was thus a contact zone of ethnic deities—ranging from the many lives of Artemis, Sylvanus and Isis—and ethnicities: "Thracians and Thasians, Greeks and Macedonians, Romans and those who had inhabited the area before Philippi's colonial status, and even Romans against Romans."[31] Perhaps most infamous was this latter conflict which stemmed from the civil war between the rival visions of Octavian and Antony on the one hand and Cassius and Brutus on the other. It was in 42 BC, in the lowlands of southwest Philippi, where the latter were defeated. The alliance of the former, however, proved tenuous and treacherous. A series of bronze coins minted by Augustus would associate the victory of 42 BC with his person alone. Earlier numismatic evidence seems to point to Antony as the founder of Philippi and the settler of its denizens. Such memories of an Antonian founding, however, drowned in Actium in 31 BC and were refashioned around the buoyancy of Augustus.[32]

Nasrallah has pointed to the settling of military veterans as a key development within the land of Philippi. Appian (*Bella civilia* 5.12–13) and Dio (*Roman History* 48.4–14) are cited as evidence for a dispossessed and manipulated veteran populace settled within the city. Such veterans, she suggests, "were presumably even more disgruntled, disenfranchised, and ruthless than those sent back to their Italian homeland."[33] Whether they were the descendants of these dispossessed veterans or prior families whose lands might

31. Nasrallah, "Spatial Perspectives," 60.

32. See Collart, *Philippes*, 1.226–27.

33. Nasrallah, "Spatial Perspectives," 61.

have been reappropriated to such veterans, the impact of social maneuvering would likely have been felt among the assemblies of Philippi.[34] Though conquered in 167 BC, the display of a particular form of *romanitas* on display in the *Colonia Julia August Philippensis* marks a visual cue toward the erasure of previous settlements (for example, Pierie and Edoni, Macedonian). Romanization led to "a widespread obliteration of historical memory."[35] The land thus experienced cultural, ethnic, and political change within its own city.[36] Such flux in city demographics, and, specifically, the "new divisions of land and the veterans' other impact on the land and city are important historical contexts within which to read the letters."[37] Amidst varying veteran legacies, moreover, residual rifts may have endured regarding military families loyal to Antony and those to the now-crowned Augustus.[38] Though particulars may well be forgotten, social bodies mark such buried wounds within their psychic and somatic identifications. Memories "tend to be longer than we think."[39]

Paul wrote occasional letters. Provenance and destinations therefore matter. *Place matters*. Paul and his crew address particular persons in particular places within dynamic situations and relations.[40] The mind and frame of reference however are mobile matrices of dynamic and redacted experiences. The complex social situation in Philippi—with its uneven history of dispossession and displacement from the land on the one hand, along with the provincial leadership of the Philippian assembly—help us consider the multiple ways the letter(s) might have been received.[41] Paul's awareness of such issues is not exactly the point—nor in any way discernable. Such sensitivities however alert us to reconsider later traditions about Paul in Philippi and the nature of their partnership and fellowship.

THE LOGIC OF RELEASE

Paul's imprisonment lends a dynamism to the concerns and movements of the letter(s) if we loosen fixed points of author location. The nearer Paul's imprisonment

34. Nasrallah, "Spatial Perspectives," 61. See also, for example, Edgar M. Krentz, "Military Language and Metaphors in Philippians," in *Origins and Method: Towards a New Understanding of Judaism and Christianity; Essays in Honour of John C. Hurd*, ed. Bradley H. McLean (Sheffield: JSOT Press, 1993): 105–27; Joseph H. Hellerman, *Reconstructing Honor in Roman Philippi: Carmen Christi as Cursus Pudorum* (Cambridge: Cambridge University Press, 2005), 64–87. I was first alerted to these studies by Nasrallah, "Spatial Perspectives."

35. Simon Price and Peter Thonemann, *The Birth of Classical Europe: A History from Troy to Augustine* (New York: Penguin, 2010), 8–9.

36. Nasrallah, "Spatial Perspectives," 62.

37. Nasrallah, "Spatial Perspectives," 64.

38. See, generally, Charalambos Bakirtzis and Helmut Koester, eds., *Philippi at the Time of Paul and after His Death* (Harrisburg, PA: Trinity Press International, 1998).

39. Gunnar Olsson, *Abysmal: A Critique of Cartographic Reason* (Chicago: University of Chicago Press, 2007), 4.

40. See Nasrallah, "Spatial Perspectives," 54.

41. Here again, see Collart, *Philippes*; Krentz, "Military Language and Metaphors in Philippians," 105–27; Hellerman, *Reconstructing Honor in Roman Philippi*, 64–87; and Bakirtzis and Koester, *Philippi at the Time of Paul*.

might have been to Philippi the more the frequency of communication, the collection, and other exchanges assumed in the writing make sense. And yet there is something of the affliction experienced in Asia that led to a general mood of despair that is important to bear in mind as a permeating force within Paul's psyche and mediated through particular exchanges (see 2 Cor 1:8). What arises from the specificity of Paul's imprisonment referred to throughout his letters to those in Philippi,[42] for example, is a logic of release. We see this logic at work in allusions to the day of Christ. In 1:6 we read:

> The one who began in you a good work (ὁ ἐναρξάμενος ἐν ὑμῖν ἔργον ἀγαθὸν, *ho enarxamenos en humin ergon agathon*) He will complete (ἐπιτελέσει, *epitelesei*) until the day of Christ Jesus (ἄχρι ἡμέρας Χριστοῦ Ἰησοῦ, *achri hēmaras Christou Iēsou*)

Or, as in 1:10, Paul can speak of the day of Christ as revealing, testing, and judging the current age. It is this age, this spatio-temporal indexing, to which the day of Christ stands opposed (2:15–16; compare Deut 32:5; Wis 2:18). This interval is the space from which the children of God appear as lights to the world (v. 15; compare Dan 12:3; 1 En. 104:2). It is also the point from which they are summoned, and geography is transcended (3:14). Paul's pressing onward toward the "*upward* call of God in Christ Jesus" is not intended as a solitary affair. The language of imitation is implied (see 3:17; 4:9). Being in space and time within Philippi is to be set aside for a being that is in Christ. And, again, the model of this imitation is Paul himself (3:1–11). His arrival and preaching of the gospel marks the event that he fashions as *a beginning of time* (see 4:15). And it is his promised return that marks and disciplines the time that remains for those in Philippi (see 1:27–30; compare 2:25, 27). At least, this is the image and sentiment Paul gives and attempts to instill in his letters.

SOME THEO-GRAPHICAL CONCLUSIONS

We began by inquiring after the relationship between external landscapes and states of mind. Pessoa alerted us to whether or not we should consider the independence of landscapes from our perceptions or states of mind. Perhaps we could push back slightly here against hard and fast distinctions. On the one hand, Philippi as place is independent of Paul's geographic vision or state of mind. And yet Philippi as place consisted of, and was dependent upon, multiple visions. Philippi was serially colonized and resettled. Moreover, the local leadership of the Philippian assemblies had its own traditions and visions for local piety. Paul's geographic vision was but one of many within *and that made up* Philippi and the assemblies of Philippi.

This led us to consider the function of the body in the ordering of space and time. The embodiment of a particular geographical vision is key to understanding the letter(s). The nature of that embodiment appears to be a complex fusion of Christ's cosmic reign and Paul's recapitulation of that reign in his own body and experience. The logic of imitation is thus a subtle blurring of Paul as the image of Christ. Other bodies, however, exist in this spatial imaging of

42. Phil 1:7; 12–14, 16–17, 19, 29–30; 4:14.

Philippi. Traditions like Acts 16 alert us to such bodies that may have been present in Philippi as do Paul's own slurs against those outside his mapping of a spatial piety (see 3:2).

Finally, the implications of such movements are a reworked civic identity and a new sense of belonging. Identity, heritage, communion, ethnicity, and networks of exchange are all transvalued by an "upward calling" and citizenship. That is, the provincial identities of "those in Philippi" are to be replaced "in Christ." The suggestion of this brief essay has been that this is as much a geographic claim as it is a theological one. "In Christ" marks a body politic placed by Paul's own imitation of a being that is in Christ.

BIBLIOGRAPHY

Ahmed, Sara. *Queer Phenomenology: Orientations, Objects, Others*. Durham: Duke University Press, 2006.

Amiel, Henri-Frédéric. *Fragments d'un journal intime*. Volume 1. Geneva: George, 1897.

Arbandt, S., W. Macheiner, and C. Colpe. "Gefangenschaft." Pages 318–45 in volume 9 of *Reallexikon für Antike und Christentum*. Edited by Theodor Klauster et al. Stuttgart: Hiersemann, 1950–.

Bachelard, Gaston. *The Poetics of Space: The Classic Look at How We Experience Intimate Places*. Translated by Maria Jolas. Boston: Beacon, 1994.

Bakirtzis, Charalambos, and Helmut Koester, eds. *Philippi at the Time of Paul and after His Death*. Harrisburg, PA: Trinity Press International, 1998.

Cassidy, Richard. *Paul in Chains: Roman Imprisonment and the Letters of St Paul*. New York: Crossroad, 2001.

Collart, Paul. *Philippes: Ville de Macédoine, depuis ses origines jusqu'à la fin de l'époque romaine*. 2 vols; Paris: de Boccard, 1937.

Dodds, George, and Robert Tavernor, eds. *Body and Building: Essays on the Changing Relation of Body and Architecture*. Cambridge: MIT, 2002.

Hellerman, Joseph H. *Reconstructing Honor in Roman Philippi: Carmen Christi as Cursus Pudorum*. Cambridge: Cambridge University Press, 2005.

Holloway, Paul A. *Philippians: A Commentary*. Minneapolis: Fortress, 2017.

Kagis McEwen, Indra. *Vitruvius: Writing the Body of Architecture*. Cambridge: MIT, 2002.

Krause, Jens-Uwe. *Gefängnisse im römischen Reich*. Stuttgart: Steiner, 1996.

Krentz, Edgar M. "Military Language and Metaphors in Philippians." Pages 105–27 in *Origins and Method: Towards a New Understanding of Judaism and Christianity; Essays in Honour of John C. Hurd*. Edited by Bradley H. McLean. Sheffield: JSOT Press, 1993.

Marguerat, Daniel. *Paul in Acts and Paul in His Letters*. Tübingen: Mohr Siebeck, 2013.

Moffatt, James. *An Introduction to the Literature of the New Testament*. 2nd ed. Edinburgh: T&T Clark, 1912.

Montale, Eugenio. *Cuttlefish Bones*. Translated by William Arrowsmith. New York: Norton, 1994.

Muller, Richard A. *Now: The Physics of Time*. New York: Norton, 2016.

Nasrallah, Laura Salah. *Christian Responses to Roman Art and Architecture: The Second-Century Church amid the Spaces of Empire*. Cambridge: Cambridge University Press, 2010.

———. "Spatial Perspectives: Space and Archaeology in Roman Philippi." Pages 53–74 in *Studying Paul's Letters:*

Contemporary Perspectives and Methods. Edited by Joseph A. Marchal. Minneapolis: Fortress, 2012.

Ollrog, Wolf-Henning. *Paulus und seine Mitarbeiter: Untersuchungen zu Theorie und Praxis der paulinischen Mission*. Neukirchen-Vluyn: Neukirchener Verlag, 1979.

Olsson, Gunnar. *Abysmal: A Critique of Cartographic Reason*. Chicago: University of Chicago Press, 2007.

Pervo, Richard I. *Acts: A Commentary*. Minneapolis: Fortress, 2009.

Pessoa, Fernando. *The Book of Disquiet*. Translated by Margaret Jull Costa. New York: New Directions, 2017.

Price, Simon, and Peter Thonemann. *The Birth of Classical Europe: A History from Troy to Augustine*. New York: Penguin, 2010.

Puar, Jasbir K. *The Right to Maim: Debility, Capacity, Disability*. Durham: Duke University Press, 2017.

Rapske, Brian. *The Book of Acts and Paul in Roman Custody*. Volume 3 of *The Book of Acts in Its First Century Setting*. Edited by Bruce W. Winter. Grand Rapids: Eerdmans, 1994.

Schaefer, Donovan. *Religious Affects: Animality, Evolution, and Power*. Durham: Duke University Press, 2015.

Thate, Michael J. "Paul, Φρόνησις, and Participation: The Shape of Space and the Reconfiguration of Place in Paul's Letter to the Philippians." Pages 281–327 in *"In Christ" in Paul: Explorations in Paul's Theology of Union and Participation*. Edited by Michael J. Thate, Kevin J. Vanhoozer, and Constantine R. Campbell. Tübingen: Mohr Siebeck, 2014.

Tilly, Michael. "Aspekte der Leiblichkeit im paulinischen Denken." Pages 69–85 in *Dimensionen der Leiblichkeit: Theologische Zugänge*. Edited by Bernd Janowski and Christoph Schwöbel. Göttingen: Neukirchener, 2015.

Vitruvius, *Ten Books on Architecture*. Translated by Ingrid D. Rowland. Commentary and illustrations by Thomas Noble Howe. Cambridge: Cambridge University Press, 1999.

Waterman Ward, Bernadette. *World as Word: Philosophical Theology in Gerard Manley Hopkins*. Washington, DC: Catholic University of America Press, 2002.

CHAPTER 43

THE SOCIAL AND GEOGRAPHICAL WORLD OF COLOSSAE

Col 1:2; 1:15–20; 2:6–3:17; 3:18–4:1

Alan H. Cadwallader

KEY POINTS

- The natural setting and fertility of ancient Colossae induced a cosmological geography for the city.
- The Letter to the Colossians reconfigures these elements, even bringing Christian reassurance to the unfathomable threat of earthquakes.
- A city's ancient foundation story regularly combines a death and establishment in/over nature ritualized through a procession to a central temple. These elements are appropriated to provide a contextualized understanding of the Christ-story.
- Colossae's fecund environs and location at the eastern entrance to the Lycus Valley made the prosperous city a ready stopover for the military and for gladiators, both key signifiers of Roman imperial power. The letter appropriates a series of images from both these sources.
- Colossae's prosperity is guaranteed by its rich pasturelands and plentiful water supply. Agricultural metaphors are replete in Colossians and are extended to the designation of the Christ-followers as "fruit-bearers" in deliberate contrast to Roman imperial claims.

ANCIENT COLOSSAE

The ancient city of Colossae in southwest Turkey has only been identified in the last two hundred years (see page 392 for a map of the region). The toponym probably originates from Hittite occupation

The biconical mound that was the center of the city of Colossae, now surrounded by the fertile orchards and crops of the Honaz region of Turkey.

in the second millennium BC, and later was accepted as Greek.[1] The site is now almost completely bare and has not been excavated. The elevation and expanse of the biconical mound belies a simple GPS location (37°47′12.3″ N, 29°15′36.2″ E). It covers 23 acres (9.3 ha) and its apex (1215 feet [379.3 m] above sea level) rises nearly 200 feet (61 m) above the plain, witnessing to a longevity that stamped it as one of the premier cities of southwest Phrygia.

One of Colossae's coins, from the early third century AD, claims that it enjoyed perfect harmony with the gods.[2] As late as the twelfth century, one of its eminent sons, Nicetas Choniates, described it as "a large and prosperous city," repeating the Greek historian Xenophon from 1500 years earlier (Nicetas Choniates, *Chronicles* 178.19, citing Xenophon, *Anabasis* 1.2.6). They reveal Colossians' pride in their enduring place within the cosmos.

COSMOLOGICAL CONSTRUCTIONS

In the first half of the second century, a certain Diodotos of Colossae, eager to further his studies, traveled to Smyrna, a walking journey of just over a week (145 miles [233.3 km])[3]—one day or so more than the 120 mile (193 km) jour-

1. J. Freu, "Les débuts du nouvel Empire Hittite et les origins de l'expansion Mycénienne: À propos d'une nouvelle datation des textes des rois Tuthaliya et Arnuwanda," *Annales de la Faculté des Lettres et Sciences humaines de Nice* 35 (1979): 27.

2. H. von Aulock, *Münzen und Stadte Phrygien*, 2 vols. (Tübingen: Wasmuth, 1980–1987), 2:93, nos. 592, 593.

3. Justinian's sixth-century *Digest of Laws* 2.11.1 reckons a day's journey at twenty Roman miles (that is, about 18.3 of our miles [29.45 km]).

ney that Epaphras took to Ephesus on the "Common Road" [Strabo, *Geography* 14.2.29] to meet with Paul (implied by Col 1:7). Diodotos is described on his epitaph (*ISmyrna* 440) as a *philologos* (φιλόλογος), a student (literally, lover or friend) of learning, a synonym of *philosophos* (φιλόσοφος), philosopher, which, in the form "philosophy" gains its only New Testament mention in Col 2:8. Diodotos, otherwise unknown, died in the course of his studies. At that time, Smyrna boasted a noted teacher of mathematical cosmology, named Theon.[4] For him, numbers were the primary elements of the universe, which combine to create "harmony in the cosmos, good order in the polis, and moderation in the household" (Theon, *Mathematica* 12.19–21).[5] These categories resonate with sections of the Letter to the Colossians: Col 1:15–20—the cosmological foundation; 2:6–3:17—the application to Christian living; 3:18–4:1—the household. The New Testament letter (especially Col 1:15–20) and fragments of evidence related to the site, demonstrate that for the Colossians (as for many in the ancient world), geographical position had to be factored cosmically as well as terrestrially. Everything depended on the cosmic center—tilling, sowing, harvesting, and all manner of agricultural activities.

The letter offered the Christ-groups in Colossae a critical alternative to the cosmological constructions that informed the thought and behavior of Colossae's population.[6] Colossian Christ-followers themselves are "hid with Christ in God" and there lay the pattern for their lives (Col 3:1–3).

EARTHQUAKES

Concern about harmony with the cosmos became acute in the face of earthquakes. The immense forces of the Eurasian, African, and Arabian Plates pressing on Anatolia have an epicenter in the Lycus Valley. The east-west valley, the lowest part of Phrygia, is framed by fault zones along its northern embankment and southern boundary, where the Taurus mountain range steeply rises. Hierapolis lies on the northern faultline, Colossae at the southern line, with Laodicea caught between.[7] In at least two of the cities, ancient seismic activity bequeathed adjustments to the landscape of such significance that they were endowed with mythologically reinforced sacred sites—the Ploutonium of Cybele (and other underworld deities) near the

4. L. L. Thompson, "ISmyrna 753: Gods and the One God," in *Reading Religions in the Ancient World: Essays Presented to Robert McQueen Grant on His 90th Birthday*, ed. D. E. Aune and R. D. Young (Leiden: Brill, 2007), 113–19.

5. The threefold summation is so striking that I give the text from Hillers's edition: καὶ γὰρ αὕτη [i.e., ἡ ὁμόνοια τῶν πραγμάτων ... ἀριστοκρατία τοῦ παντός] ἐν κόσμῳ μὲν ἁρμονία, ἐν πόλει δ'εὐνομία, ἐν οἴκοις δὲ σωφροσύνη (*kai gar hautē* [i.e., *hē homonoia tōn pragmatōn ... aristokratia tou pantos*] *en kosmō men harmonia, en polei d'eunomia, en oikois de sōphrosunē*).

6. See generally, C. E. Arnold, *The Colossian Syncretism: The Interface between Christianity and Folk Belief at Colossae* (Tübingen: Mohr Siebeck, 1995).

7. H. Kumsar, Ö. Aydan, C. Şimşek, and F. D'Andria, "Historical Earthquakes That Damaged Hierapolis and Laodikea: Antique Cities and Their İmplications for Earthquake Potential of Denizli Basin in Western Turkey," *Bulletin of Engineering, Geology and the Environment* 75 (2016): 519–36.

temple of Apollo at Hierapolis;[8] the sacred spring, monolith, and chasm of St. Michael of Chonai (the later name of Colossae) whose story was probably adapted from an earlier Zeus account.[9]

Rock Tomb Shifted by Earthquakes at Colossae

The earthquake of AD 60 was not the only serious seismic event of the first century; a devastating earthquake in AD 17 knocked out Hierapolis' civic mint among other damage to urban infrastructure.[10] Laodicea never really recovered from an earthquake in AD 494. But the earthquake of AD 60 has often been named as the terminal destruction of Colossae. The Roman historian, Tacitus, did report on Laodicea's self-funded rebuilding program after the catastrophe (*Annales* 14.27) but this is likely to be the notice that a center for judicial proceedings (a *conventus metropolis*) would attract, just as Laodicea, but not Hierapolis or Colossae, is included on the third-century Peutinger map of Roman roads. A recently discovered inscription clearly shows that Colossae, while seriously damaged, managed its own recovery through a leading citizen named Korymbos. The pictured white-marble pedestal (originally

Korymbos Inscription

8. F. D'Andria, "Nature and Cult in the Ploutonion of Hierapolis: Before and After the Colony," in *Landscape and History in the Lykos Valley: Laodikea and Hierapolis in Phrygia*, ed. C. Şimşek and F. D'Andria (Newcastle upon Tyne: Cambridge Scholars Publishing, 2016), 189–217.

9. A. H. Cadwallader, "'As If in a Vision of the Night …' Authorising the Healing Spring of Chonai," in *Dreams, Memory and Imagination in Byzantium*, ed. B. Neil and E. Anagnostou-Laoutides (Leiden: Brill, 2018), 265–92.

10. A. Travaglini and V. G. Camilleri. *Hierapolis di Frigia, Le Monete: Campagne di Scavo 1957–2004* (Istanbul: Ege Yayınları, 2010), 9–12, 23.

holding a statue) was set up to honor Korymbos for his munificence in repairing the baths and extending the water infrastructure of Colossae. Part of the inscription reads, "For good Tyche; for Korymbos the patriot (literally, lover of the fatherland)."[11] The letter itself likely alludes to this earthquake in a number of places (for example, Col 2:8, 20 "the elemental forces of the cosmos"), certainly to the experience of earthquakes that threatened confidence and life in the Lycus Valley. The letter provides reassurance that Christian destiny is founded on an unshakeable trust.[12]

SOCIOSPATIAL ASPECTS OF LIFE IN COLOSSAE AND THE LYCUS VALLEY

LYCUS RIVER

The Letter to the Colossians connects the ancient city with Laodicea and Hierapolis (Col 2:1; 4:13, 15). These were a triangle of main cities in a valley that gained its name from its main watercourse, the Lycus River (Çürüksu). The river was crucial to the valley's life, with Colossae receiving the first rush (hence the name Lycus, "wolf") given its height above Laodicea, a welcome addition to its annual 19.7 to 23.6 inches (50–60 cm) of rainfall. Probable remains of part of Colossae's city wall to the north of the city, separating the urban heart from its sweeping necropolis, suggests that Colossae contained the watercourse within its city precincts. Remains of large stone blocks hem a section of the southern riverbank and mark the remains of locally remembered Roman baths. Whether the river and its feeder streams, the nearby spring or the sculpted bathhouse, Colossae held a ready store of water that local Christ-followers might, with care, use for baptism (Col 2:12).

The Lycus fed a substantial body of water between Hierapolis and Laodicea, a shallow, inland fishing expanse (approximately 5.8 square miles [15 km^2], 591–623 feet [180.1–189.9 m] above sea level),[13] roughly matching Lake Huleh in the Galilee. The two adjacent cities, whose control extended to the plain, asserted their rights over such enterprises; friction developed.[14] For all that the mineralized waters were prized for dyeing and the production of the characteristic glistening, black wool (Vitruvius, *De Architectura* 8.3.14), the lake could also sustain aquatic life.

The Lycus lake also functioned as a transit harbor; vessels punted goods to the Meander River, ten miles (16 km) from Laodicea to the west and on to the Mediterranean.[15] This juncture, just

---

11. A. H. Cadwallader, "Honouring the Repairer of the Baths: A New Inscription from Kolossai," *Antichthon* 46 (2012): 150–83.

12. M. Oehler, "Earthquakes and the Elements of the World in the Letter to the Colossians," in *New Documents Illustrating the History of Early Christianity Vol 12: The Lycus Valley*, ed. J. Harrison, et al. (Grand Rapids: Eerdmans, forthcoming).

13. G. Scardozzi, "Ricerche topografiche e telerilevamento," in *Hierapolis di Frigia I: Le Attività delle Campagne di Scavo e Restauro 2000–2003*, ed. F. D'Andria and M. P. Caggia (Istanbul: Ege Yayınları, 2007), 83–84.

14. T. Ritti, E. Miranda, and F. Guizzi, "La ricerca epigrafica: Risultati dell'ultimo quadriennio e prospettive future," in D'Andria, *Hierapolis di Frigia I*, 589.

15. Scardozzi, "Ricerche topografiche," 83–84.

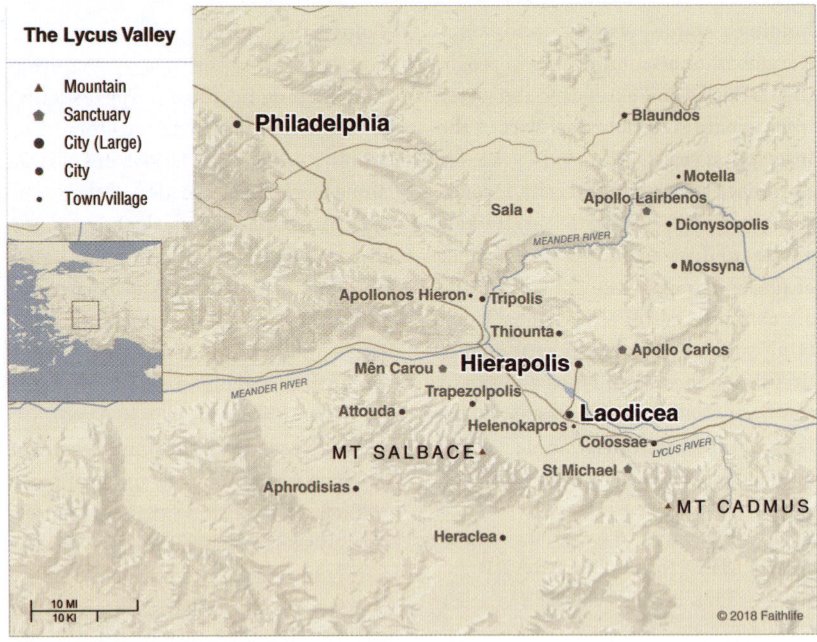

south of the city of Tripolis, marks the western boundary of the Lycus Valley and the administrative divide between Lydia and Phrygia. The river complemented roads for transporting merchandise such as the famous Colossian wool (Strabo, *Geography* 12.8.16; Pliny, *Naturalis Historia* 21.27.51) and the textile designs, styled regionally as "Laodicean."[16] Contact with Ephesus, Smyrna, or Miletus unlocked the world (Laodicean goods are noted in Gaul), just as the customs law of Ephesus (AD 62 but replicating earlier regulations) penetrated 100 miles (160 km) inland. Clothing metaphors in Col 3:9–10 would have been substantially visualized through the famed textile products of the area.[17]

Epaphras appears in the letter as the leader promoting the Pauline gospel of the crucified Christ among the house churches/meeting groups in these cities (Col 1:7, 4:12–13).[18] A day's brisk walk separated them, with Laodicea about 10–11 miles (16–17.6 km) to the west of Colossae and Hierapolis 6 miles (9.7 km) to the northwest of Laodicea on a road skirting the lake. Both Hierapolis and Colossae were accessed by avenues that branched off from the main roadway. The thor-

16. H. Erdemir, "Woollen Textiles: An International Trade Good in the Lycus Valley in Antiquity," in *Colossae in Space and Time* ed. A. H. Cadwallader and M. Trainor (Göttingen: Vandenhoeck & Ruprecht, 2011), 117–18; P. Thonemann, *The Maeander Valley: A Historical Geography from Antiquity to Byzantium* (Cambridge: Cambridge University Press, 2011), 188.

17. R. Canavan, *Clothing the Body of Christ at Colossae* (Tübingen: Mohr Siebeck, 2012).

18. See M. Trainor, *Epaphras: Paul's Educator at Colossae* (Collegeville, MN: Liturgical Press, 2008).

oughfares converged at Laodicea, making it the heart of the valley.

Cosmopolitan Connections

Whether Colossae was always a short detour off the main spine (the ancient "Royal Road"; see Herodotus, *Histories* 7.26–31) connecting the Mediterranean to Persepolis and Susa, is not known. But this was no barrier to Colossae's cosmopolitan connections: Smyrna, Sardis, Keretapa, Aphrodisias, Boubon, Ephesus, Apameia, Attouda, Eumeneia, and Tripolis in addition to its Lycus neighbors are all attested. Another recently published inscription (first or second century AD) honors a certain Markos, named as "chief interpreter and translator of the Colossians."[19] The meaning is disputed but it may indicate that the cosmopolitan life of Colossae, the first city encountered in the Lycus Valley from the eastern Anatolian highlands, demanded linguistic assistance.[20]

View toward Colossae down Syria Street at Laodicea

The letter itself witnesses to a range of ethnic connections: Col 3:11 has the familiar Jew and Greek (see also Gal 3:28; 1 Cor 12:13 though in Colossians, the order is reversed, only here in the New Testament). But it adds Scythian and barbarian into the mix. One Latin name, used as a homonym, is given in 4:11—Justus—adopted because it sounds loosely like Jesus. But it is supplemented with a curious reference to "the only ones ... of the circumcision." It suggests that the Jewish presence in Colossae was minimal.[21] A Latin origin belongs to the names Mark and Luke as well: Col 4:10, 14. The names found on inscriptions and coins show an even broader compass. And, of course, there is the Phrygian petname, Apphia (Phlm 2). Though Colossae had become a Greek-styled polis in the Hellenistic period, ethnic, cultural and onomastic variety is indicated. Part of the intention of the letter is to promote a unity across all this diversity.

Agriculture in the Lycus Valley

Part of Colossae's historic prosperity, shared increasingly by Laodicea and Hierapolis, derived from the fecundity of the Lycus Valley. Critical to this is the connection between a city (*polis*, πόλις) and country (*chōra*, χώρα)/village (*kōmē*, κώμη). When Colossae came

19. Cadwallader, "Two New Inscriptions, a Correction and a Confirmed Sighting from Colossae," *Epigraphica Anatolica* 40 (2007): 109–18.

20. R. Strelan, "The Languages of the Lycus Valley," in Cadwallader, *Colossae in Space and Time*, 77–103.

21. P. Foster, *Colossians* (London: T&T Clark, 2016), 10–16.

under Roman rule after 129 BC, the basic city-hinterland administrative and economic arrangements of Hellenistic times remained, albeit with Roman imperial supervision. In the late Persian Empire, Colossae had been the headquarters for a western satrap's hunting park, baths, and gardens. We can expect the familiar western Phrygian husbandry of livestock—sheep as we have noted already, but also pigs as one stele from Colossae clearly shows (*MAMA* 6.50). Other animals were reared for sacrifices (especially bulls for Zeus, probably the patron deity of Colossae), meat and leather-manufacture (*MAMA* 6.44).

A broken funeral stele, which would have been set up at the grave, has no surviving inscription but suggests that the deceased farmed pigs

Grapes, wine, olives, figs, and probably cherries were all part of the horticultural production at Colossae. One Colossae inscription mentions grain and oil (*IGR* 4.870). Colossae was especially favored by streams of fresh water that flowed through the rich soils into the Lycus River from the south of the city, one from a natural spring that became a Christian pilgrimage site devoted to the archangel Michael (compare Col 2:18). Literary references accent prosperity (Herodotus, *Histories* 7.30; Xenophon, *Anabasis* 1.2.6; Polyaenus, *Strategemata.* 7.16; Diodorus Siculus 14.80.5). Dionysos, always connected with the nature's fecundity, figures prominently on coins and inscriptions. Significant is the emphasis in Colossae's coinage on Artemis the hunter,[22] almost unknown at Laodicea where the sedentary Artemis of Ephesus dominates.

The inscription mentioning grain distribution (*IGR* 4.870) shows how much the surrounding countryside sustained the city's life. The landscape was funneled by architecture, roadways, inducements, and regulation toward ensuring a city's well-being. Agricultural metaphors

A dramatic presentation of Artemis the hunter in full flight in her biga drawn by two deer; reverse of a coin of Colossae dated to the time of the Emperor Commodus (AD 180–192)

22. Von Aulock, *Münzen*, 2:90–93, nos. 553–54, 555–61, 566–74, 586–87, 594–95.

have long been noted in the letter,[23] but the sequence of metaphors in Col 2:6–7 moves from the country into the city. The translations of Col 2:6 (KJV, RSV, NIV, NRSV, etc.), frequently read "As therefore you have received Christ Jesus the Lord, so live in him" taking the word *peripateō* (περιπατέω), meaning "walk," from an Old Testament notion of walking as living one's life. This has merit but loses any sense of the approach to an ancient city, a walk that passes through agricultural cultivation (*rizoō*, ῥιζόω, "rooted"), through the formal city precincts focused on the walls (*epoikodomeō*, ἐποικοδομέω, "established/ founded"), to the heart of the city's life, namely the agora where commercial and sacred pledges were sealed (*bebaioō*, βεβαιόω, "validated/ confirmed").[24]

FOUNDATION STORIES

Something further can be drawn from the reception of a sacred tradition implied by the verb *paralambanō* (παραλαμβάνω, "receive") in Col 2:6 and the outline of that tradition in verses 8–15. Most cities gave thanks for their existence by (usually annual) festive celebrations of their foundation narratives. These foundation stories shaped the identity of the populace (compare Col 2:18–19), often because they were adjusted to engage contemporary needs.[25] Most foundation traditions narrated some element of the colonization of nature to harness its fecundity. Ephesus' foundation story of Androcles had the city established around the spot where he slew a wild boar (Pherecydes, *Fragmente der greichischen Historiker* 3 F155; Pausanias 7.2.8–9). A central temple safeguarded this sacred tradition. At Colossae, one nineteenth-century sketch of the mound places a temple base on the highest part. Colossae's foundation story is not known but the Letter to the Colossians clearly delineates the "oikist" (founder) of the Colossian Christians' identity as Jesus. Celebration and thanksgiving erupt from that foundation (so Col 2:8 "abounding in thanksgiving").

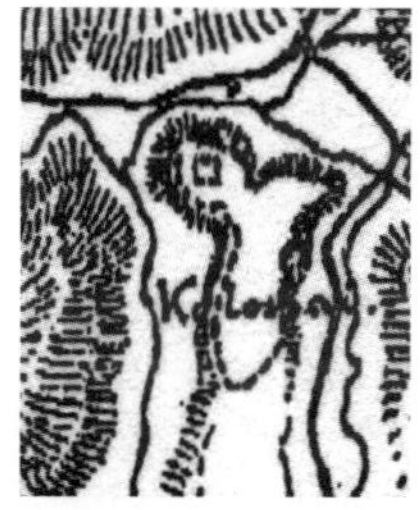

Sketch by Georg Weber (1891) depicting the base of a temple on the mound of Colossae

This sacrality adds a dimension to a rare word used here. The recipients are exhorted not to let anyone "despoil" or "rob" them of their foundational tradition (Col 2:8). The word used, *sylagōgeō* (συλαγωγέω), reduplicates a syllable (-γο- -*go*-) to add intensity. It emphasizes the sacrilegious larceny of a sacred trust,

23. M. Y. MacDonald, *Colossians and Ephesians* (Collegeville, MN: Liturgical Press, 2000), 88.

24. On this last metaphor, see esp. J. D. G. Dunn, *The Epistles to the Colossians and to Philemon: A Commentary on the Greek Text* (Grand Rapids: Eerdmans, 1996), 142.

25. L. Donnellan, "Oikist and Archegetes in Context: Representing the Foundation of Sicilian Naxos," in *Foundation Myths in Ancient Societies: Dialogues and Discourses*, ed. N. M. Sweeney (Pennsylvania: University of Pennsylvania Press, 2015), 41–70.

much like temple-robbery (compare Rom 2:22b, *hierosyleō*, ἱεροσυλέω).[26] The letter has converted the journey to the sacred center of the city's life that reiterates the foundation traditions, into a pattern of life for the Christ-follower: walking with/in Christ, rooted, founded, confirmed, celebrating, and holding the sacred tradition against efforts to breach the inviolability now attached to the body of Christ (Col 2:8, 19). For Colossian Christians, the combination of metaphors collating hinterland and city in a foundation story provided a clear way of comprehending the Christ story. Social geography—the crafting of space to direct people—has been drawn through a careful sequence of metaphors into the service of the gospel (Col 1:5-6).

There is one further aspect of these foundation stories. The cosmopolitan circumstances of many cities in Asia Minor, where diverse ethnic backgrounds were part of the color of urban life, struggled with foundation stories that were built on the easy dichotomies of old Greek sensibilities—of Greek and barbarian in particular. Unlike mainland Greece, the foundation stories in Asia Minor tended to be more ambiguous; they endeavored to accommodate the multiple backgrounds from which the populace hailed.[27] The Letter to the Colossians accents unity through the removal of dualisms as well, not just in the assertion of the unity of all in Christ (Greek and Jew, circumcised and uncircumcised) but in removing any antithetical conjunctions in the syntax: "barbarian, Scythian, slave, free." (Col 3:11). For an author sensitive to his Asian context, Christ is the one who realizes the positive aspirations expressed in flawed foundation stories.

IMPERIAL METAPHORS

MILITARY IMAGERY

Horticulture was frequently bordered, especially on rising and marginal land, by the famed Phrygian products: the pine (*pinus brutia*) and oak (*quercus*). A massive supply chain was built around the appropriation of wood. But wood, with food and water, are the fundamental requisites for the stationing of an army, and imperial estates often claimed woodlands to meet this need.[28] Colossae's few mentions in ancient literature are particularly interested in army stopovers.[29] Two Colossian inscriptions confirm military visits (*IGR* 4.869, 870). With Laodicea as an occasional seat for the Roman provincial governor when the judicial assizes were held, and with all the provinces of the Asia Minor peninsula providing recruits and supplies for the eastern front,[30] the visibility of soldiers would have been pronounced. Military-flavored images are therefore no surprise in the letter: the inversion of "the triumph"

---

26. L. Bormann, *Der Brief des Paulus an die Kolosser* (Leipzig: Evangelische Verlagsanstalt, 2012), 125–26.

27. N. M. Sweeney, *Foundation Myths and Politics in Ancient Ionia* (Cambridge: Cambridge University Press, 2013), 198–203.

28. Thonemann, *Maeander Valley*, 280.

29. A. H. Cadwallader, *Fragments of Colossae: Sifting through the Traces* (Adelaide: ATF Press, 2015), 29–43.

30. S. Mitchell, *Anatolia: Land, Men and Gods in Asia Minor, Volume I: The Celts in Anatolia and the Impact of Roman Rule* (Oxford: Clarendon Press, 1993), 118–42.

where commanders responsible for the death of Jesus are now reduced to captives on display (Col 2:15), and Christ-followers themselves are portrayed in a military line-up, steadfastly holding their ground (Col 2:5).

GLADIATORIAL CONTESTS

The roads also brought a lower status but still distinctly Roman stamp into community life—gladiators. Gladiatorial and venatorial contests remained a sublimated mark of the violence that undergirded Roman control of its empire.[31] A recently discovered section of a two-tiered narrative of gladiator contests suggests that Colossae had a share in this almost-ubiquitous popular entertainment. Death and slave imagery, so familiar to these spectacles, dominated much of early Christianity. In Colossians, a number of references (Col 2:18 *katabrabeuō*, καταβραβεύω, "disqualify," see also 3:15 *brabeuō*, βραβεύω, "rule"; 4:13: *ponos*, πόνος, "physical effort, toil") hint at the appropriation of gladiator imagery for Christian identity.[32] Gladiator contests underscore Roman control of space, a geographical construction of social management that also claimed cosmic authority, frequently personified by a leading Roman official in the prime seat at a theater or stadium. Colossae already attests a theater (a Hellenistic foundation dug into the side of the *höyük*), which may have been modified to accommodate spectacles. The letter to the Christ-followers in the city encouraged them to wrest these imperial metaphors to characterize life under Christ, rather than under Caesar.

Fragment of a gladiator panel found at the site of Colossae

REJECTING IMPERIAL CLAIMS OF COSMIC DOMINION

The emperor Augustus engineered a revolution in governance that included a massive ideological program proclaiming cosmic approval for the emperor. The emperor was credited not merely with dominion over land (and sea) and its produce (a cosmically ordered geography). But precisely because that dominion was (asserted to be) cosmically ordered, the fecundity of the realm was promoted as issuing from the imperial person, "the

31. Compare H. O. Maier, "Reading Colossians in the Ruins: Roman Imperial Iconography, Moral Transformation, and the Construction of Christian Identity in the Lycus Valley," in Cadwallader, *Colossae in Space and Time*, 212–31.

32. A. H. Cadwallader, "Assessing the Potential of Archaeological Discoveries for the Interpretation of New Testament Texts: The Case of a Gladiator Relief from Colossae and the Letter to the Colossians," in *The First Urban Churches* ed. J. R. Harrison and L. L. Welborn (Atlanta: SBL Press, 2015), 41–66.

benefactor of the world." As part of the promotion of stable family relationships held to be at the heart of a stable state, Augustus spread some of this munificent role among family members, most notably his wife Livia (also called Julia). The particular divine association granted Julia was Ceres/Demeter. Demeter was the eastern deity; her particular attribute was fecundity. She was often displayed holding three ears of wheat, and sometimes a cornucopia—symbols of that prosperity. When Colossae's mint was revived in AD 117 at the beginning of Hadrian's reign, the association of Demeter with fecundity and with the women of the imperial family was entrenched.

The key epithet of Demeter was *karpophoros*, καρποφόρος, "fruit-bearer" (*SEG* 54.1479; *IEphesus* 1210). Any coin that held a portrait of the emperor or one of the imperial women on the obverse and the image of Demeter Karpophoros on the reverse was emphasizing the imperial source of fecundity. One coin minted by Philip Antipas, applied the title expressly to Julia herself.[33] The Letter to the Colossians will have none of it. The metaphor of fruitfulness and growth, derived from a horticultural context (see, for example, *PSI* 3.171; *SEG* 31.631), is both democratized by being transferred to the members of the church and also sourced in the good news of Christ Jesus rather than that of the Caesars; moreover the extent of his realm is none other than that claimed by the emperor—the cosmos (Col 1:6, 10). So powerful was this metaphor of *karpophoros*, that long after the letter was written and long after the imperial women had been severed from a connection with Demeter, it became one of the key synonyms for "Christian." Followers of Christ were known as the *karpophoroi*, the fruit-bearers (*SEG* 40.1477).

BIBLIOGRAPHY

Arnold, C. E. *The Colossian Syncretism: The Interface between Christianity and Folk Belief at Colossae*. Tübingen: Mohr Siebeck, 1995.

Aulock, H. von. *Münzen und Stadte Phrygien*. 2 vols; Tübingen: Wasmuth, 1980–1987.

Bormann, L. *Der Brief des Paulus an die Kolosser*. Leipzig: Evangelische Verlagsanstalt, 2012.

Cadwallader, A. H. "'As If in a Vision of the Night ...' Authorising the Healing Spring of Chonai." Pages 265–92 in *Dreams, Memory and Imagination in Byzantium*. Edited by B. Neil and E. Anagnostou-Laoutides. Leiden: Brill, 2018.

———. "Assessing the Potential of Archaeological Discoveries for the Interpretation of New Testament Texts: The Case of a Gladiator Relief from Colossae and the Letter to the Colossians." Pages 41–66 in *The First Urban Churches*. Edited by J. Harrison and L. L. Welborn. Atlanta: SBL Press, 2015.

———. *Fragments of Colossae: Sifting through the Traces*. Adelaide: ATF Press, 2015.

———. "Honouring the Repairer of the Baths: A New Inscription from Kolossai." *Antichthon* 46 (2012): 150–83.

33. F. Strickert, "The Dying Grain Which Bears Much Fruit: John 12:24, the Livia Cult, and Bethsaida," in *Bethsaida: A City by the North Shore of the Sea of Galilee, Volume 3*, ed. R. Arav and R. A. Freund (Kirksville, MO: Truman State University Press, 2004), 149–82.

———. "Two New Inscriptions, a Correction and a Confirmed Sighting from Colossae." *Epigraphica Anatolica* 40 (2007): 109–18.

Canavan, R. *Clothing the Body of Christ at Colossae*. Tübingen: Mohr Siebeck, 2012.

———. "Weaving Threads: Clothing in Colossae." Pages 111–33 in *Fragments of Colossae: Sifting through the Traces*. Edited by A. H. Cadwallader. Adelaide: ATF Press, 2015.

D'Andria, F. "Nature and Cult in the Ploutonion of Hierapolis: Before and After the Colony." Pages 207–40 in *Landscape and History in the Lykos Valley: Laodikea and Hierapolis in Phrygia*. Edited by C. Şimşek and F. D'Andria. Newcastle upon Tyne: Cambridge Scholars Publishing, 2016.

Donnellan, L. "Oikist and Archegetes in Context: Representing the Foundation of Sicilian Naxos." Pages 41–70 in *Foundation Myths in Ancient Societies: Dialogues and Discourses*. Edited by N. M. Sweeney. Pennsylvania: University of Pennsylvania Press, 2015.

Dunn, J. D. G. *The Epistles to the Colossians and to Philemon: A Commentary on the Greek Text*. Grand Rapids: Eerdmans, 1996.

Erdemir, H. "Woollen Textiles: An International Trade Good in the Lycus Valley in Antiquity." Pages 104–29 in *Colossae in Space and Time*. Edited by A. H. Cadwallader and M. Trainor. Göttingen: Vandenhoeck & Ruprecht, 2011.

Foster, P. *Colossians*. London: T&T Clark, 2016.

Freu, J. "Les débuts du nouvel Empire Hittite et les origins de l'expansion Mycénienne: A propos d'une nouvelle datation des textes des rois Tuthaliya et Arnuwanda." *Annales de la Faculté des Lettres et Sciences humaines de Nice* 35 (1979): 7–37.

Hillers, E., ed. *Theonis Smyrnaei, Philosophi Platonici: Expositio rerum mathematicarum ad legendum Platonem utilium*. Leipzig: Teubner, 1878.

Huttner, U. *Early Christianity in the Lycus Valley*. Leiden: Brill, 2013.

Kumsar, H., Ö. Aydan, C. Şimşek, and F. D'Andria. "Historical Earthquakes That Damaged Hierapolis and Laodikeia: Antique Cities and Their Implications for Earthquake Potential of Denizli Basin in Western Turkey." *Bulletin of Engineering, Geology and the Environment* 75 (2016): 519–36.

MacDonald, M. Y. *Colossians and Ephesians*. Collegeville, MN: Liturgical Press, 2000.

Maier, H. O. "Reading Colossians in the Ruins: Roman Imperial Iconography, Moral Transformation and the Construction of Christian Identity in the Lycus Valley." Pages 212–31 in *Colossae in Space and Time*. Edited by A. H. Cadwallader and M. Trainor. Göttingen: Vandenhoeck & Ruprecht, 2011.

Mitchell, S. *Anatolia: Land, Men and Gods in Asia Minor, Volume I: The Celts in Anatolia and the Impact of Roman Rule*. Oxford: Clarendon Press, 1993.

Oehler, M. "Earthquakes and the Elements of the World in the Letter to the Colossians." In *New Documents Illustrating the History of Early Christianity Volume 12: The Lycus Valley*. Edited by J. Harrison, A. H. Cadwallader, R. Canavan, and M. Trainor. Grand Rapids: Eerdmans, forthcoming.

Ritti, T., E. Miranda, and F. Guizzi. "La ricerca epigrafica: Risultati dell'ultimo quadriennio e prospettive future." Pages 583–618 in *Hierapolis di Frigia I: Le Attività delle Campagne di Scavo e Restauro 2000–2003*. Edited by F. D'Andria and M. P. Caggia. Istanbul: Ege Yayınları, 2007.

Scardozzi, G. "Ricerche topografiche e telerilevamento." Pages 67–86 in *Hierapolis di Frigia I: Le Attività delle Campagne di Scavo e Restauro 2000–2003*. Edited by F. D'Andria and M. P. Caggia. Istanbul: Ege Yayınları, 2007.

Şimşek, C. "Urban Planning of Laodikea on the Lykos in the Light of New Evidence." Pages 1–52 in *Landscape and History in the Lykos Valley: Laodikea and Hierapolis in Phrygia*. Edited by C. Şimşek, and F. D'Andria. Newcastle upon Tyne: Cambridge Scholars Publishing, 2016.

Strelan, R. "The Languages of the Lycus Valley." Pages 77–103 in *Colossae in Space and Time*. Edited by A. H. Cadwallader and M. Trainor. Göttingen: Vandenhoeck & Ruprecht, 2011.

Strickert, F. "The Dying Grain Which Bears Much Fruit: John 12:24, the Livia Cult, and Bethsaida." Pages 149–82 in *Bethsaida: A City by the North Shore of the Sea of Galilee, Volume 3*. Edited by R. Arav and R. A. Freund. Kirksville, MO: Truman State University Press, 2004.

Sweeney, N. M. *Foundation Myths and Politics in Ancient Ionia*. Cambridge: Cambridge University Press, 2013.

Thompson, L. L. "ISmyrna 753: Gods and the One God." Pages 101–22 in *Reading Religions in the Ancient World: essays presented to Robert McQueen Grant on His 90th Birthday*. Edited by D. E. Aune and R. D. Young. Leiden: Brill, 2007.

Thonemann, P. *The Maeander Valley: A Historical Geography from Antiquity to Byzantium*. Cambridge: Cambridge University Press, 2011.

Trainor, M. *Epaphras: Paul's Educator at Colossae*. Collegeville, MN: Liturgical Press, 2008.

Travaglini, A., and V. G. Camilleri. *Hierapolis di Frigia, Le Monete: Campagne di Scavo 1957–2004*. Istanbul: Ege Yayınları, 2010.

CHAPTER 44

THE SOCIAL AND GEOGRAPHICAL WORLD OF THESSALONICA

1 Thess 1:1, 9; 2 Thess 1:1; Acts 17:1–9

Philip W. Comfort

KEY POINTS

- The city of Thessalonica was ideally located as a hub for travel within the Roman Empire.
- Thessalonica, as the church whose faith was "heard of around the world" (1 Thess 1:9), was possibly the primary collector of Paul's major letters.
- The church at Thessalonica was also likely the promoter of the term "*parousia*" (παρουσία) used by Jesus to denote his second coming.

INTRODUCTION

Thessalonica was founded around 315 BC by the Macedonian general Cassander who had destroyed around twenty-six towns in the region and then "settled all the inhabitants together in one city."[1] Thessalonica was capital of the second district of Macedonia. It was given many political freedoms by Rome due to its loyalty to Antony and Octavian in the battle at Philippi (in Macedonia), where Cassius and Brutus were defeated. Octavian, the first emperor of Rome (31 BC–AD 14), known as Caesar Augustus, looked favorably on Thessalonica, which was a "free city" (*civitas libera*).[2]

As described by Pliny, the city was situated in the middle of the bend of the Thermaic gulf.[3] In addition to having a good natural harbor, it was geographically central to all of Macedonia. For the purpose of inter-communication with

1. Strabo, *Geography* 7, fragment 21 (LCL); see also Andrew R. Talbert, "Thessalonica," *LBD*.

2. Philip W. Comfort and Walter A. Elwell, eds., "Thessalonica," *Tyndale Bible Dictionary* (Wheaton, IL: Tyndale House Publishers, 2001), 1255.

3. Pliny, *Natural History* 4.10.17.

distant cities, its situation was perfect. The location of Thessalonica was ideal for travel within the Roman empire. A major route went through it to the east and the famous Egnatian Way passed through it.

The Egnatian Way was the Romans' primary route to the east, linking Rome to Byzantium. Thessalonica's geographical position made it a gateway between the churches to the west (as in Italy) and to the east (as in Asia Minor). Also, there is a road that breaks off the Egnatian Way to the south towards Greece and a road to the north that breaks off the Egnatian Way only ten miles west of Thessalonica, providing major access inland, between the Aegean Sea and the Danube River. It is no wonder that the Thessalonians' faith in Christ "was heard around the world" (1 Thess 1:9). Furthermore, the city's prime location makes it an ideal place for bringing Paul's letters together in one codex and dispersing that collection to the churches all around the Greco-Roman world.

Thessalonica had a larger population than any other city in Macedonia and was populated by Greeks, Romans, and Jews who had a synagogue (Acts 17:1). But most of the converts to Christ, through the preaching of Paul, Silas, and Timothy, were Greek-speaking idol-worshiping Macedonians (1 Thess 1:9).[4] The Thessalonians were involved with the worship of Cabiri, the mystic deities of Samothrace. The city was ruled by "politarchs" (according to Luke, in Acts 17:6, using a word not known elsewhere in classical literature—but an inscription still seen in a Thessalonian arch at the western end of the town has the word).[5]

4. Philip W. Comfort, "1 & 2 Thessalonians," in *Cornerstone Biblical Commentary: Ephesians, Philippians, Colossians, 1 & 2 Thessalonians, Philemon*, ed. Philip W. Comfort (Carol Stream, IL: Tyndale House Publishers, 2008), 324.

5. For the inscription, see "Politarch Inscription" in Helmut Koester, ed., *Cities of Paul: Images and Interpretations from the Harvard New Testament Archaeology Project* (Minneapolis, MN: Fortress Press, 2005).

THESSALONICA AND PAUL'S LETTERS

The first point I want to posit is that Thessalonica, because of its socio-spatial-ecclesiastical position, was likely a primary local church that participated in the collection and dispersion of Paul's major letters in one codex. It is generally accepted that the early church collected two different groups of New Testament writings—Paul's major letters (Romans, 1–2 Corinthians, Galatians, Ephesians, Philippians, Colossians, 1–2 Thessalonians—as well as Hebrews)[6] and the four Gospels (Matthew, Mark, Luke, John). The Gospels were collected into one codex by the mid-second century.[7] Paul's letters were collected earlier.

Paul's letters were being collected between AD 60 and 100. There was a well-known collection of Paul's letters at the time Peter wrote 2 Peter, where he categorized Paul's writings as "scripture" (2 Pet 3:15–16). Zuntz believed there was a Pauline corpus by AD 100.[8] Gamble also argued that Paul's letters had been assembled by the end of the first century, and that this collection was circulated in codex form among several churches before the circulation of the fourfold Gospel in codex form.[9]

One of the major reasons I think Thessalonica was one of the primary church-cities to collect the Pauline letters into one codex is the city's geographical situation along a major east-west Roman road and in close proximity to north-south roads that facilitated the further dissemination of the letters. Additional suggestive evidence comes from the extant early New Testament papyri. There are five second-century and third-century papyri that originally were Pauline collections; four of the five contain 1 and 2 Thessalonians: P30 (dated early third century), whose pagination indicates that P30 was part of a Pauline codex; P46 (dated early second century), which has all the major Pauline letters from Romans to 2 Thessalonians; P49 + P65, preserving portions of Ephesians and 1 Thessalonians; P92, preserving portions of Ephesians and 2 Thessalonians. Only P15 + P16 does not include the Thessalonian letters, and that is because only portions of 1 Corinthians and Philippians are extant, with no pagination.[10]

Another reason I think the church in Thessalonica was a major collector of Paul's letters is that the second letter to the church there had Paul's personal signature at the end (2 Thess 3:17) to guard against forgeries (2 Thess 2:2). With this signature they could be the guardian of his genuine letters, comparing the personal handwriting of Paul with other letters brought into the collection.

6. For additional discussion of this process, see Philip W. Comfort, *Encountering the Manuscripts: An Introduction to New Testament Paleography & Textual Criticism* (Nashville: Broadman and Holman, 2005), 34–37.

7. This is explained in full by Comfort, *Encountering the Manuscripts*, 33-34.

8. G. Zuntz, *The Text of the Epistles: A Disquisition Upon the Corpus Paulinum* (London: Oxford University Press, 1953), 271–72.

9. Harry Gamble, *Books and Readers in the Early Church*, (New Haven: Yale University Press, 1995), 53–57.

10. For the text of each of these papyri, see Philip W. Comfort, and D. Barrett, *The Text of the Earliest New Testament Greek Manuscripts* (Wheaton: Tyndale, 2001).

View of Modern Thessaloniki Looking South toward the Thermaic Gulf

At this juncture I need to speak of Silas as the most likely collector of Paul's letters into one codex and his connection with Thessalonica. First, it must be noted that Silas was one of two writers (along with Judas Barsabbas) who composed a letter for the gentile churches from the leaders in Jerusalem and was its emissary traveling with Paul (Acts 15:22–23). Silas (also known as Silvanus) was a leading Christian in the church at Jerusalem; he was a prophet and a Roman citizen.[11] Second, it is very important to note that Silas was co-author with Paul of 1–2 Thessalonians. (I have argued extensively for this in my commentary on 1–2 Thessalonians.[12]) Third, it may have been Silas who, when he was with Peter, assisting with the writing of Peter's first letter (1 Peter 5:12), referred to Paul's epistles as "Scripture" (2 Pet 3:15–16). In short, Silas was Peter's writer for both 1 Peter and 2 Peter. These points indicate that Silas was a writer and therefore very interested in the writings of Paul (especially since he was co-author of 1–2 Thessalonians). This would strongly suggest that, of all Paul's co-workers, Silas would have been the one who collected the Pauline letters. It is also likely that Silas, because of his connection with the Thessalonian church (which maintained a strong testimony in the early centuries of the church), coordinated with this church in collecting Paul's letters. The other possible candidate is Timothy because Paul (while he was in prison) asked Timothy to bring him "his books, especially the parchments" (2 Tim 4:13). This could have included a collection of Paul's writings. But this doesn't have to be interpreted this way (i.e., it could refer to Old Testament texts, and blank writing material), and even if it did, it doesn't preclude the idea that Silas also collected Paul's letters.

As I said before, Thessalonica was centrally located between Rome and Corinth to the south and west, and Philippi (note the communication between Thessalonica and Philippi in Phil 4:16), Ephesus, Colossae, and Galatia to the east—as well

11. Comfort, "1 & 2 Thessalonians," 316–17. See also J. D. Douglas, *Illustrated Bible Dictionary*, 1451.

12. Comfort, "1 & 2 Thessalonians," 315–18.

as being on the Egnatian Way. It was a perfect place to collect all Paul's letters and disperse this collection. Furthermore, since the two letters of Paul and Silas to the Thessalonians were written early in Paul's ministry, around AD 51–52, these two letters were among the earliest writings of the New Testament, if not the very earliest. As the recipients of Paul's (and Silas') first writings, as well as being centrally located between the churches raised up by Paul, the Thessalonians would have been eager to obtain Paul's writings from other churches and thereafter form a collection. The only reason that 1–2 Thessalonians appear last in the Pauline collection is that they were the shortest epistles—the codex was arranged with the longest first (i.e., Romans) and so forth. Otherwise, 1–2 Thessalonians would have been, chronologically speaking, the first in the Pauline corpus.

THESSALONICA AND THE PAROUSIA

The second point I want to address pertains to the Thessalonians' knowledge of the παρουσία (*parousia*, second coming) and how this knowledge must have helped them understand Paul and Silas' use of the word in the Thessalonian epistles (1 Thess 2:19; 3:13; 4:15; 5:23; 2 Thess 2:1, 8, 9). In these passages, Paul and Silas are explaining the meaning of the Lord's second coming (*parousia*) and the rapture of the Christians to a meeting (ἀπάντησις, *apantēsis*) with the Lord in the air. It is very possible that Silas, as one of the seventy or seventy-two disciples of Jesus[13] and as one who would have heard the term *parousia* used by Jesus in his end-time Olivet discourse (Matt 24:3, 27, 37, 39), spoke of the *parousia* when he was with the Thessalonians (2 Thess 2:4) and then used the term again in the Thessalonian letters. In short, Jesus could have been the originator of the term *parousia* as signaling his divine visitation to earth at the end of this age. So Silas (in the Thessalonian letters) used a term known to him from hearing Jesus use it.

The term *parousia* is rich in Hellenistic usage. Primarily, "the word served as a sacred expression for the coming of a hidden divinity, who makes his presence felt by a revelation of his power, or whose presence is celebrated in the cult."[14] Significantly, there was a cult of Dionysus in Thessalonica and elsewhere in the Roman world, who was known as "the god that comes," a god of epiphany. His coming was known as a *parousia* in the centuries before the church and after it (Diodorus Sicilus 3.65.1, first century BC; Josephus, *Ant.* 3.80,203; 9.55, first century AD; Aelius Aristides 48.30, 31, second century AD). The *parousia* was used, for example, of Dionysus's *parousia* on earth—*he tou theou parousia* (ἡ τοῦ θεοῦ παρουσία; Diodorus Siculus 3.65.1). When the Thessalonians heard about the *parousia* of Jesus, the Thessalonians would have immediately connected it to their understanding of Dionysus' coming.

The term *parousia*, as making its first appearance in the early letters to the Thessalonians, caught on in the early churches. In short, the spatial position of Thessalonica (as a gateway to the east and west) promoted the spreading of the term as code for Jesus' second coming. Its presence in writings that are later

13. Comfort, "1 & 2 Thessalonians," 317. See also Pseudo-Hippolytus, *On the Seventy Apostles* 50 (*ANF* 5.256).

14. BDAG, s.v. "παρουσία."

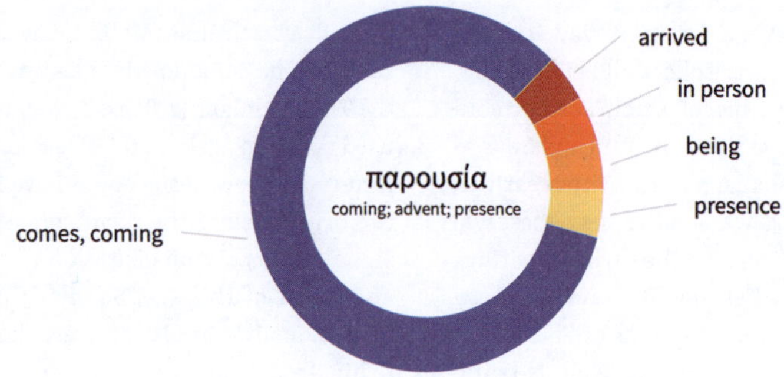

than the letters to the Thessalonians affirms this. The term was used by James (5:7–8), Peter (2 Peter 1:16; 3:4, 12), Matthew (24:3, 27, 37, 39—Jesus' discourse on the end-times would have been earlier than the writing of Matthew's Gospel), and John (1 John 2:28). In all of these writings, which are usually dated by scholars *after* 1–2 Thessalonians, the *parousia* signifies Jesus coming to earth at the end of this age.

The term *parousia* also "became the official term for a visit of a person of high rank, especially of kings and emperors visiting a province."[15] The word was used "from Ptolemaic times onwards to denote the visit of a king, emperor, or other person in authority."[16] For example, P. Paris 26.1, 18 speaks of the visitation (*parousia*) of King Ptolemy Philometor and Cleopatra to Memphis (163/162 BC). Other literature of that period indicates that *parousia* was used of this kind of visitation.[17] The Thessalonians would have understood the second definition of *parousia*, either by the context of Paul and Silas' letters to them or by way of Jesus' use of the term in apocalyptic context (as recorded in Matt 24), which then became a part of oral tradition, spoken to them by Silas, one of Jesus' early disciples. Jesus' usage of the word would have spread among the early churches, especially to and from Thessalonica, which was a gateway (on the Egnatian Way) between the eastern churches and western churches.

Connected to the term *parousia* is the Greek expression *apantesis* mentioned above, which refers to the custom of sending an official delegation out of the city to meet a visiting dignitary.[18] Earlier in their history, some Thessalonians had gone out to meet Octavian after his military victory at Philippi (as noted earlier). They would go out to accompany the dignitary and return with him to the city. For

15. BDAG, s.v. "παρουσία."

16. James H. Moulton and George Milligan, *Vocabulary of the Greek Testament* (London: Hodder & Stoughton, 1930), 497.

17. See P. Tebtunis 48, 14; 116, 57; Ulrich Wilcken, *Griechische Ostraka aus Aegypten und Nubien: ein Beitrag zur antiken Wirtschaftsgeschichte* (2 vols.; 1899; repr., Amsterdam: A. M. Hakkert, 1970), 2:1372, 1481; Adolf Deissmann, *Light from the Ancient Near East: The New Testament Illustrated by Recently Discovered Texts of the Graeco-Roman World*, trans. Lionel R. M. Strachan (London: Hodder & Stoughton, 1910), 372–78.

18. See P. Tebtunis 43.1, 1; Josephus, *Ant.* 13.101.

example, the word in the New Testament was used of the Christian brothers who came out to meet Paul on his way to Rome (they met him at the Forum of Appius) and then accompany him back to Rome (Acts 28:15–16). The implication is that the risen and raptured Christians will leave earth and go to meet the Lord Jesus in the air and then return with him to earth.

CONCLUSION

In summary, Thessalonica's socio-spatial-ecclesiastical position made the Thessalonian church a prime place for collecting Paul's letters and distributing them in one corpus. In the early centuries of the church, Thessalonica was one of the chief strongholds of Christianity and won for itself the title "the Orthodox City."[19] What better way to bolster their reputation than promote the Pauline letters that were the pillars of early Christian doctrine. Furthermore, the church in Thessalonica became the promoter of the circulation of the special term *parousia*, which became a codeword for Jesus' second visitation to earth at the end of this age.

BIBLIOGRAPHY

Comfort, Philip W. "1 & 2 Thessalonians." Pages 312–414 in *Cornerstone Biblical Commentary: Ephesians, Philippians, Colossians, 1 & 2 Thessalonians, Philemon*. Edited by Philip W. Comfort. Carol Stream, IL: Tyndale House Publishers, 2008.

———. *Encountering the Manuscripts: An Introduction to New Testament Paleography & Textual Criticism*. Nashville: Broadman and Holman, 2005.

Comfort, Philip W., and D. Barrett. *The Text of the Earliest New Testament Greek Manuscripts*. Wheaton: Tyndale, 2001.

Comfort, Philip W., and William Elwell, eds. *Tyndale Bible Dictionary*. Wheaton, IL: Tyndale House Publishers, 2001.

Deissmann, Adolf. *Light from the Ancient Near East: The New Testament Illustrated by Recently Discovered Texts of the Graeco-Roman World*. Translated by Lionel R. M. Strachan. London: Hodder and Stoughton, 1910.

Douglas, J. D. *Illustrated Bible Dictionary*. Wheaton: Tyndale, 1999.

Gamble, Harry. *Books and Readers in the Early Church*. New Haven: Yale University Press, 1995.

Koester, Helmut, ed. *Cities of Paul Images and Interpretations from the Harvard New Testament Archaeology Project*. Minneapolis: Fortress, 2005.

Moulton, James H., and George Milligan. *Vocabulary of the Greek Testament*. London: Hodder & Stoughton, 1930.

Tod, M. N. "Thessalonica." Pages 2970–71 in *The International Standard Bible Encyclopaedia*. Edited by James Orr, John L. Nuelsen, Edgar Y. Mullins, and Morris O. Evans. Chicago: The Howard-Severance Company, 1915.

Wilcken, Ulrich. *Griechische Ostraka aus Aegypten und Nubien: ein Beitrag zur antiken Wirtschaftsgeschichte*. 2 vols. 1899. Repr., Amsterdam: A. M. Hakkert, 1970.

Zuntz, G. *The Text of the Epistles: A Disquisition Upon the Corpus Paulinum*. London: Oxford University Press, 1953.

---

19. M. N. Tod, "Thessalonica" in *The International Standard Bible Encyclopaedia*, ed. James Orr, John L. Nuelsen, Edgar Y. Mullins, and Morris O. Evans (Chicago: The Howard-Severance Company, 1915), 2971.

CHAPTER 45

ONESIMUS AND THE SOCIAL AND GEOGRAPHICAL WORLD OF PHILEMON

Phlm 1–25

Alan H. Cadwallader

KEY POINTS

- Colossae as the context for the recipients of the Letter to Philemon requires taking account of the organization of the city, its housing and its environs.
- Paul's imprisonment, probably in Ephesus, and anticipation of a visit, assume considerable mobility among the key players mentioned in the letter.
- Colossae's famous textile industry is reflected in the commercial language that is blended with Christian connotations in the letter; but so also is the slave trade. Both elements are strong indicators of careful organization of space.
- The common business interests of Paul and Philemon suggest contact (leading to conversion) outside of Colossae, and a joint appreciation of what it means to "value-add" to a slave, in this case, a training "in the faith."
- The legal jurisdiction covering most Colossians most of the time was the city's Greek laws—once outside the city's environs, Onesimus became a fugitive, following circuitous (shepherds'?) routes to the incarcerated Paul.

COLOSSAE AS THE GEOGRAPHICAL SETTING FOR PHILEMON

The short Letter to Philemon carries no place-name, but it has traditionally been assigned to Colossae (see map on page 574). There are a number of reasons to support this location. A fifth-century bishop of Cyrrhus, named Theodoret, is famous for his commentaries on the Pauline letters. He mentions that the house of Philemon was still known in his day as a goal of pilgrimage at Colossae (*Patrologia Graeca* 82.613B, 871–72A). Most

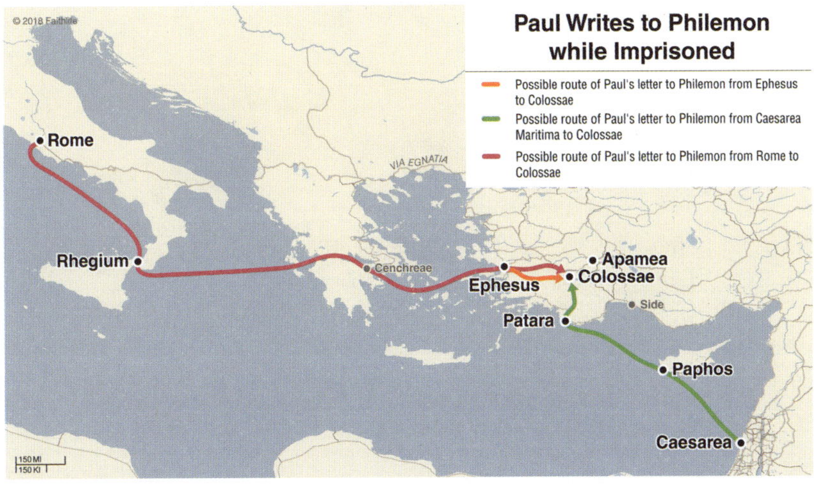

recent commentary focuses on the commonality of the names mentioned in both Philemon 1–2, 10, 23–24 and Colossians 4:7–18.[1] The absence in the Letter to the Colossians of the names of two of the main players in Philemon, namely, Philemon and Apphia, reinforces the assignment of the Letter to Philemon to a Colossian setting. Egyptian papyri letters directed to the same household over time show that when someone dies between letters, the name of the deceased is no longer included in greetings.[2] The implication is that the Letter to the Colossians was written some time after the Letter to Philemon, and that Philemon and Apphia (whether husband and wife is unknown) have both died.

THE LOCATION OF PAUL'S IMPRISONMENT

This only satisfies one of the preliminary questions that have troubled scholarship on the letter. Paul wrote the letter from prison (Phlm 1, 9, 10, 13, 23); but where he is incarcerated is left unsaid. Three possibilities are usually floated: Ephesus, Rome, and Caesarea Maritima. These major cities are increasingly distant from Colossae. Ephesus is 120 miles (193 km) and a six-day direct walking distant; Rome is 1780 miles (2864.6 km) and ninety-seven days' walking distant or 2160 miles (3476 km) and forty-nine days of sea travel from Patara on the south coast of Asia Minor (longer if from Ephesus); and Caesarea Maritima is 962 road miles (1548 km) and fifty-three

1. J. D. G. Dunn, *The Epistles to the Colossians and to Philemon: A Commentary on the Greek Text* (Grand Rapids: Eerdmans, 1996), 37–38; U. Huttner, *Early Christianity in the Lycus Valley* (Leiden: Brill 2013), 80–92.

2. P. Arzt-Grabner, "Everyday Life in a Roman Town like Colossae: The Papyrological Evidence," in *The Lycus Valley*, ed. J. R. Harrison and L. L. Welborn (Atlanta: SBL Press, forthcoming).

In the nineteenth century the building at the top of a hill overlooking the cityof Ephesus was dubbed "Paul's Prison", captured here in 1865 by the Hungarian photographer Alexander Svobodov.

days of travel or 900 miles (1448.4 km) and twenty-six days of travel by road and sea route from Side.

Each option finds support in the New Testament (Ephesus: 1 Cor 15:32; 2 Cor 1:8–10; Rome: Acts 28:16–20; Caesarea Maritima: Acts 23:35; 24:23). Distance (and cost) influences a preference. Given that Epaphras shares Paul's confinement (Phlm 23) and yet is a nurturer of the Christ-followers in the Lycus Valley (Col 4:13); given that Paul's eyes are turned to the western empire when Rome is in his sights (Rom 15: 24); and given that Paul expressed a hope to visit Philemon and other church members (Phlm 22—note the plural "you"), Ephesus appears the most likely. Whether that jail was in the *praetōrium* (the governor's headquarters) or a holding cell in the civic offices (found in every major city along the Meander-Lycus Valley) is unknown. These cells provided the hard edge to the order imposed on the behavior and movement of urban dwellers by the city's topographical and architectural layout. Law-enforcement officers, the *nomophylakes* (νομοφύλακες), reinforced the spatial constraints, incarcerating those who disrupted them.

RELATIONSHIPS OF ONESIMUS, PHILEMON, AND PAUL

Two issues concern Onesimus' relationship to Philemon: was he a fugitive slave,[3] a vagrant slave,[4] a slave seeking a reconciling intermediary,[5] a freedman,[6] or not a

3. J. G. Nordling, "Some Matters Favouring The Runaway Slave Hypothesis in Philemon," *Neotestamentica* 44 (2010): 85–121; A. H. Cadwallader, "Complicating Class in the Letter to Philemon: a Prolegomenon," in *Religion and Class: Ancient Jewish and Christian Writings in their Socio-Economic Contexts*, ed. G. A. Keddie, M. Flexsenhar, and S. Friesen (Atlanta SBL Press, forthcoming).

4. P. Arzt-Grabner, "How to Deal with Onesimus? Paul's Solution within the Frame of Ancient Legal and Documentary Sources," in *Philemon in Perspective: Interpreting a Pauline Letter*, ed. D. F. Tolmie (Berlin: de Gruyter, 2010), 120–35.

5. P. Lampe, "Keine 'Sklavenflucht' des Onesimus," *Zeitschrift fur neutestamentliche Wissenschaft* 76 (1985): 135–37.

6. Huttner, *Lycus Valley*, 103–7.

slave at all?[7] And how was Philemon (and the household) to deal with Onesimus on his return—would he continue as a slave or was manumission likely? In addition, how are we to understand Paul, a prisoner, in his relationship to both Philemon and Onesimus and the Christ-followers listening to the letter (v. 2c)? Whatever decisions are made, commerce in slavery and the control of slaves constitute the critical context for the letter. Hence, the organization and control of space and movement must be addressed.

PHILEMON'S CONNECTION TO PAUL

Frequently overlooked in this broad sketch are the implications of Philemon's movement, both in relation to Paul and to Onesimus. Philemon must have encountered Paul somewhere, and yet the general interpretation of Col 2:1 is that Colossae had not met Paul. The "in the flesh" reference (sometimes omitted in translations) ties strongly to Phlm 16 "in the flesh (and in the Lord)" that speaks of the restoration of Onesimus to Philemon—a personal encounter. The letter indicates that Paul had close Christian and probably commercial ties with Philemon (vv. 17–19). Philemon's adherence to Christ was due to Paul's mediation.[8] One manuscript (Codex Claromantus) adds "in the Lord" to make clear what is meant by "you owe me your very self" (v. 19b). Philemon's conversion must have occurred somewhere else. The letter's striking commercial language indicates a shared linguistic field between Paul and Philemon that, without embarrassment, could be utilized for their Christian relationship as well. Hence, a related question arises about where Philemon purchased Onesimus and why. Slave markets were ubiquitous across the Mediterranean—"the ordinary, daily traffic in slaves" (*Digest* 41.2.44. pr). They were sometimes permanently located in large cities.

PHILEMON'S PURCHASE OF ONESIMUS

Little epigraphical evidence for slaves exists in the approximately thirty inscriptions from Colossae, though the staging of gladiatorial spectacles combined with the household code's emphasis on slaves (Col 3:17–4:1) suggests that future excavation will change this deficiency. Slaves would have been traded at Colossae between individuals of means (sometimes by contractual subletting for specific services) and during the main festivals of the civic religious calendar.

A fragment of a funerary relief displaying the work of a slave trader from Amphipolis in northern Greece

7. A. D. Callahan, "Paul's Epistle to Philemon: Toward an Alternative *Argumentum*," *Harvard Theological Review* 86 (1993): 357–76.

8. Dunn, *Colossians and Philemon*, 340.

But centers for trafficking in human lives existed at Apamea, 55 miles (88.5 km) east on the Royal Road (a three-day walk) and at Laodicea, 10 miles (16 km) to the west. Possibly, though less likely, Philemon might have journeyed south to the port city of Side, 185 miles (298 km) away (over a ten-day walk, half that for a horse-drawn carriage). Ephesus was a closer port city, 120 miles (193 km) to the west, about a six-day walk—longer if taking a punt down the Lycus and Meander Rivers from Laodicea.

Ephesus offered other commercial advantages for trade goods from the Lycus Valley. It is unlikely that Philemon ventured beyond Colossae with the sole goal of purchasing Onesimus, but included it in his general business travel. At the major trade centers, Onesimus—if that was the name provided for the slave—would have been paraded, probably in the commercial agora, compelled to stand naked or loin-clothed on a small platform (a *catasta*), open to physical inspection by Philemon. This pattern of somatic incursion and surveillance was the norm throughout a slave's life.[9] Onesimus was probably labeled by his ethnic origin, identifying body marks and assurances that he was unencumbered by another's proprietorial claims or by a history of flight or vagrancy (this last, a warranty adopted from Roman practice). Any skills Onesimus may have had would have inflated the purchase price. Phrygians, for example, were renowned as workers in textiles, besides being demeaned as sexually promiscuous (Cicero, *Epistulae ad Quintum fratrem* 1.1.16; Martial, *Epigrams* 11.104). We have none of these details, but the ubiquitous trade in slaves makes Onesimus' situation assumed by the Letter to Philemon unexceptional.

SIGNIFICANCE OF THE NAME ONESIMUS

Little can be deduced from the name Onesimus. It is Greek, very common in Asia Minor, and hence could readily refer to multiple individuals among Christ-followers (Col 4:9; see also Ignatius, *To the Ephesians* 1). An elite, free Greek might carry the name,[10] or a slave prostitute at Pompeii (*Corpus Inscriptionum Latinarum* 4.8380). It is extremely rare among Roman freeborn, since it was, to Roman ears, a name that denoted servility.[11] Frequently, masters gave names to slaves that made a joke about a slave's (impossible) virtue. In the letter, the joke operated obliquely. The name Onesimus means "useful," but Paul opposes that with the common stereotype of a slave as "useless" (Phlm 11; compare Matt 25:30; Luke 17:10).[12] It was similar to dub-

9. J. A. Marchal, "The Usefulness of an Onesimus: The Sexual Use of Slaves and Paul's Letter to Philemon." *JBL* 130 (2011): 749–70; S. R. Joshel, "Geographies of Slave Containment and Movement," in *Roman Slavery and Roman Material Culture*, ed. M. George (Toronto: University of Toronto Press, 2013), 99–128.

10. Huttner, *Lycus Valley*, 86–87.

11. H. Solin, *Die stadtrömischen Sklavennamen: Ein Namenbuch*, 3 vols. (Stuttgart: Steiner, 1996), 3:680.

12. M. J. Smith, "Utility, Fraternity and Reconciliation: Ancient Slavery as a Context for the Return of Onesimus," in *Onesimus Our Brother: Reading Religion, Race and Culture in Philemon*, ed. M. V. Johnson, J. A. Noel, and D. K. Williams (Minneapolis: Fortress, 2012), 47–58. A. H. Cadwallader, "Name-punning and Social Stereotyping: Reinscribing Slavery in the Letter to Philemon," *Australian Biblical Review* 60 (2013): 18–31.

A funerary panel of a slave named Onesimus

bing a slave "Malchus" (see John 18:10), a humiliating play on the word for "king"—unimaginable for a slave. Paul claims that the slave Onesimus now displays a real not impossible virtue.[13]

ONESIMUS' SERVICE TO PHILEMON

Crucial is what Philemon was looking for in his purchase. Household and workplace employment are the obvious choices.

PHILEMON'S HOUSEHOLD

Philemon's house (note the singular "your" in v. 2; compare Col 4:15, single owner; Rom 16:5a, joint owners) must have been of considerable size. It could accommodate an assembly of Christ-followers (v. 2c); it had at least one guest room (v. 22) that could be prepared; and it seems to have had a number of free-born residents (permanent or temporary), whether family or friends. Names can be a helpful guide to regions, if not ethnicity, in the ancient world. Philemon and Apphia are both very common names in Phrygia and the neighboring regions of Lydia and Caria.[14] They are also attested in the Lycus Valley, with two inscriptions connected to Colossae displaying the name Apphia. They are almost certainly locals. The name Archippus occurs once at Laodicea and not elsewhere in Phrygia,[15] nor in the West. By contrast, it is common from Greece to the west coast of Asia Minor.[16] Travel and comradeship are indicated in the epithet "our fellow soldier" (Phlm 2b),[17] and this ties him more to Paul and Timothy. Perhaps he occupied another guest-room. Only later was he given a specific charge, indicated in Col 4:17, probably following the death of Philemon and Apphia.

The housing complexes now uncovered off Syria and Stadium Streets at Laodicea indicate the structural arrangements of housing in the region in the first century. Buildings were

13. The Onesimus pictured in the funerary panel above rose to become a manager (an οἰκονόμος, *oikonomos*) of the estate of Aelius Monogenes near Thessalonica in the second century AD. The grave, set up while he was still alive and in a style imitating the graves of freeborn citizens, is also for his wife Nikē, his daughter Onesimē (upper panel), and his mother Euphrosunē (lower panel, far left, seated).

14. See J. S. Balzat et al., *A Lexicon of Greek Personal Names Volume V.B: Coastal Asia Minor; Caria to Cilicia* (Oxford: Clarendon, 2013); and Balzat et al., *A Lexicon of Greek Personal Names Volume V.C: Inland Asia Minor* (Oxford: Clarendon, 2018), under the names.

15. Balzat, *Volume V.C*, "Archippus."

16. Lexicon of Greek Personal Names online (http://www.lgpn.ox.ac.uk/) has 234 examples!

17. V. Balabanski, "Where is Philemon? The Case for a Logical Fallacy in the Correlation of the Data in Philemon and Colossians 1.1–2; 4.7–18," *Journal for the Study of the New Testament* 38 (2015): 8.

An aerial view of the biconical mound of Colossae

adjusted to local topography; comparable housing at Hierapolis follows a square rather than rectangular perimeter.[18] Philemon's house would similarly have been adjusted to local Colossian circumstances—not least factoring the river Lycus flowing through the city, which was fed by nearby streams flowing from south and north into the river. These streams (especially the Ak Su) were channeled to feed water to industries (such as mills, masons' workshops, wool preparation and dyeing) on the north side of the Lycus River. Waterways, especially when much of a city's wealth depended on them, were carefully regulated and policed, as a recent imperial edict found at Laodicea shows.[19]

Large houses also contained (lockable) slave quarters, shop fronts and, sometimes workrooms, inevitably directing goods to the local marketplace. At Colossae, an agora is probably to be understood on the lower section of the biconical hill or to the east of Theater Street that ran north-south past the theater—the *cavea* and a few seats are still visible at the eastern side of the mound.[20]

18. C. Şimşek, "Urban Planning of Laodikeia on the Lykos in the Light of New Evidence," in *Landscape and History in the Lykos Valley: Laodikeia and Hierapolis in Phrygia*, ed. C. Şimşek and F. D'Andria (Newcastle upon Tyne: Cambridge Scholars Publishing, 2016), 11.

19. Şimşek, "Urban Planning," 9.

20. The theater *cavea* is at upper-right of the photograph and one candidate for the agora is on the green section of the mound. The main temple (to Zeus?) was located on the acropolis at top left.

House design maximized the surveillance of slaves.[21] It also reinforced the hierarchies within the household, not only from freeborn down to slaves, but in gradations applied to the slaves themselves—a hierarchy that was usually based on the functions/tasks assigned to slaves,[22] privileging the slave who monitored slave movements and performance.[23] These spatial and status arrangements had practical and honorific consequences—a slave simply could not travel without some sort of supervision. Rarely would such supervision be made metaphorical by an authorizing letter (which, in a sense, the Letter to Philemon is, given that Paul asserts his superiority as an "elder"—v.9). Frequently slaves were tattooed or otherwise branded, or given a "dog-tag" that stigmatized the bearer as owned by another.[24]

A collar that would be fixed to a slave's neck

PHILEMON'S BUSINESS

The issue is where to place Onesimus in this complex of relationships and spatial constraint. One ancient subscript (addition) to the letter calls Onesimus an *oiketēs* (οἰκέτης). Literally, it signals one bound to the household and has been taken to mean a household slave. Indeed, a couple of subscripts turn Onesimus into Apphia's slave, perhaps to exonerate Philemon of direct culpability for his lack of effective oversight (Phlm 14; compare Col 4:1). However, in Asia Minor, *oiketēs* had become a general word for slave, like *doulos* (δοῦλος)—the word used of Onesimus in v. 16. Whether classified as *oiketēs* or *doulos*, such indentured service might as readily be exerted on a rural estate—relevant if Philemon is in the textile business.

This is where an intersection between Colossae's famous industry and a turn of phrase in the letter is evocative. We have seen already the tendency in the letter to blend commercial and Christian language. In v. 13, Paul writes of Onesimus' potential service to the captive author. The word used, *diakoneō* (διακονέω),

21. S. R. Joshel and L. H. Petersen, *The Material Life of Roman Slaves* (Cambridge: Cambridge University Press, 2014).

22. Cadwallader, "Complicating Class," forthcoming.

23. Joshel, "Geographies of Slave Containment," 102–10.

24. The tag with Latin inscription (from Rome) reveals the common assumption about the propensity of slaves to escape: "I have run away; hold me. You will receive a gold coin if you return me to my master, Zoninus" (*Corpus Inscriptionum Latinarum* 15.7194). Translation from M. Wiedemann, *Greek and Roman Slavery* (London: Routledge, 1981), 186.

can mean domestic help (Mk 1:31) but, against the background of Colossae's textile industry, seems to employ a key term from apprenticeship contracts for training in weaving.[25] Paul's own profession is given as tent-making (Acts 18:3). The trade complements the textile industry, whether by weaving (especially for awnings) or the associated trades of felt-making or stitching of hides.

Weaving and related industries were more esteemed in Asia Minor than in the West.[26] Assuming that Philemon caught Paul's drift in his use of commercial language, it suggests that Philemon and Paul shared similar business interests. If so, we can postulate that Philemon's house, with a discrete shop front and workroom, made considerable use of the surrounding environment and productivity of Colossae—its agricultural husbandry, its lavish water supply. Slaves would have been integral to the various components of this enterprise from primary husbandry to cleaning and dyeing, to manufacture, to sale, and preparation for export. Whether Philemon purchased Onesimus because he was already skilled or intended to provide the training himself is unknown. But this notion of increasing the value of a slave is part of Paul's rhetorical strategy (v. 11).

LEGAL JURISDICTION AND RUNAWAY SLAVES

Philemon did not conduct his affairs under the direct jurisdiction of Rome, except when taxes and dues attracted Roman regulation (as in the *portorium*, the transit charge mentioned in the customs law of Ephesus). Rome had a keen interest in tax revenues from the slave trade, but this did not mean that Roman laws touched every aspect of slavery. Rome happily tolerated a plurality of laws, provided there was no fundamental clash with Roman interests.[27] At the temple of Delphi, for example, where slave manumissions are voluminously inscribed, there is the occasional reference to manumission being granted "according to foreign law" (*xenikos*, ξενικός). With Colossae in the Roman imperial period still maintaining its own citizens' assembly (the *dēmos*, δῆμος) and its own council (the *boulē*, βουλή), its Greek-style law code would have covered slave infractions.[28]

A coin of Colossae from the time of the emperor Commodus (AD 177–192) featuring the legend and pictorial representation of the Demos of the Colossians on the obverse, and the sun-god Helios galloping across the sky in his *quadrīga*.

Jurisdiction becomes crucial here, given that local law codes were similarly

25. Arzt-Grabner, "Everyday Life," forthcoming.

26. R. Canavan, "Weaving Threads: Clothing in Colossae," in A. H. Cadwallader, *Fragments of Colossae: Sifting through the Traces* (Adelaide: ATF, 2015), 124–25.

27. Cadwallader, "Complicating Class," forthcoming.

28. S. R. Llewellyn, "The Government's Pursuit of Runaway Slaves," *New Documents Illustrating Early Christianity* (Grand Rapids: Eerdmans, 1998), 8:41–43.

in operation in Laodicea and Hierapolis, a day's journey to the west. Somewhere between these cities, boundary lines of legal enforceability were drawn, even if occasionally these were disputed. Once outside the territorial jurisdiction of Colossian law, Onesimus would not qualify as a vagrant; he would be a fugitive. Indeed, there is some doubt whether the category of vagrant (*errō*, ἔρρω) is recognized in Greek law.[29] Philemon's hope of retaking Onesimus would be dependent on his advertising in the agora or central temple at Colossae offering a reward for a runaway (a potential loss of face, though such advertisements were common [*Digest* 11.4.18a]), and/or hiring an agent to operate on his behalf, which would require, for proper legal process, the agent making application to another local authority wherever a fugitive might be found (*Oxyrhynchus Papyri* 1643). Whether Onesimus actually stole anything (sometimes considered to be the meaning of v. 18) or left empty-handed, he was, nevertheless, a thief, for a slave was the property of another, not of himself (compare Rev 18:13). Allowing for the closest imprisonment of Paul at Ephesus, 120 miles (193 km) away on the most direct route, Onesimus would have had to negotiate the great bulk of that journey as a fugitive, even if he tried to pass as, say, a freedman (compare Cicero, *Epistulae ad familiares* 13.77.3).

TRAVEL AS A RUNAWAY SLAVE

This complicates the journey. Runaway slaves cannot be assumed simply to rush to the nearest large city in the hope of anonymity. Laodicea, now estimated to have had a population of eighty thousand to two hundred thousand, that is, from city precincts to controlled hinterland,[30] was the nearest prospect for an urban disappearance. But runaways are equally likely to conceal themselves as hired labor on some of the vast estates (*Digest* 11.3), especially those privately owned, that filled Asia Minor's landscapes. Some might have sought asylum at a religious sanctuary. There were certainly many such sanctuaries dotted around or just outside the Lycus Valley. But their rights of asylum were often restricted when it came to harboring slaves—priests might simply sell them on to a new master (*SEG* 46.2263).

How Onesimus came into contact with Paul is not known. Suffice to conclude that the journey from Colossae to Ephesus was unlikely to be either direct or immediate. (The "for a while" of v. 15 probably means "temporarily.") The potential for recapture would have been too great with *stationarii* (law enforcers) at various places along the way, especially if Onesimus was tattooed or an agent was hired for the pursuit. Maps of the Roman province of Asia readily record the standard routes for which literary, epigraphical, and material evidence provide considerable information. However, the foundational laborers for the textile industry, namely shepherds, were neither bound by nor interested in the main highways.

Sometimes, friction occurred with crop farmers because shepherds grazed their flocks on cultivated land. One inscription from Dionysopolis, about sixty miles (96.5 km) north of Colossae

29. Cadwallader, "Complicating Class," forthcoming.

30. Şimşek, "Urban Planning," 5.

via Hierapolis, records a proconsular decision in favor of viticulturalists against shepherds whose sheep were damaging their vines (*MAMA* 4.297). Part of the ruling warns local villagers who may have aided and abetted the shepherds. This suggests that some in the local indigenous population, operating at a bare subsistence level and at some remove from main thoroughfares, may have offered some support or at least indifference to runaways.

A damaged epitaph from the region of Lydia for Onesimus who died aged eighteen years.[31]

PAUL'S ADVOCACY FOR ONESIMUS

Onesimus likely knew of Paul's relationship with Philemon. It appears also that Onesimus had not immediately followed his master's conversion (Phlm 10), even though the household became "Christian" (Phlm 2; see also Acts 16:15, 33). This brings us to a remarkable aspect of the letter. Paul returns to the language of commercial exchange when he writes of Philemon having Onesimus back (v. 15). The documentary evidence for the word used, *apechō* (ἀπέχω), offers no clear instance of a welcome of a human being.[32] It belongs to the world of business transactions and has the sense of a payment in full, a return of full value.[33] In the context of slavery, it may refer to a sales contract or to some special training such as we noted in the context of apprenticeships to master weavers. Using the metaphor, Paul has provided a value-adding to the worth of Onesimus the slave by bringing him into the same faith shared by Philemon (hence the language of "beloved brother" v. 16), a faith that Philemon had been unable to confer upon Onesimus. Paul has acted as a master-trainer, enhancing Onesimus' usefulness to both free men (v. 11). The "receipt" of Onesimus "for good, for life" (the meaning of *aiōnion*, αἰώνιον, in v. 15, rather than "forever") is therefore a payment in full of the special enhancement, understood to be gained "in the flesh" as well as "in the Lord" (v. 16c). When Cicero, the great Roman lawyer of the late Republic, estimated the worth of value-adding to a slave (in the case of actor training), he valued the unformed slave at four thou-

31. This Onesimus is recorded as "the sweetest child" of Adaneus and Olympia. The language resonates with that used in Phlm 10, 12 but also confirms how widespread in the region and across status the name Onesimus was.

32. P. Arzt-Grabner, *Philemon* (Göttingen: Vandenhoeck & Ruprecht, 2003), 223.

33. A. Deissmann, *Light from the Ancient East: The New Testament Illustrated by Recently Discovered Texts of the Graeco-Roman World*, trans. L. R. M. Strachan (London: Hodder & Stoughton, 1910), 111–12.

The sanctuary of Apollo Lairbenos

sand sesterces (about one thousand denarii), but the slave who had benefited from the training and renown of his trainer (but not owner) was worth one hundred thousand sesterces. Even if Cicero exaggerated, the parallel is striking, especially with Paul reminding Philemon of the debt of his very self (v.19b).

THE POSSIBILITY OF ONESIMUS' RELEASE

This raises our last, thorny question. Was Paul subtly prompting Philemon to give Onesimus his freedom (given the language of v. 16)?[34] Recall that Philemon was subject to local, Greek law not Roman law. One key method of releasing slaves was by dedicating the slave to a god—in effect a transfer of ownership that freed a slave from the human master. However, he or she remained a slave. This procedure is well-known from a number of sanctuaries in the Greek world, such as one of the most-patronized rural sanctuaries serving the Lycus Valley—the sanctuary of Apollo Lairbenos, thirty-seven miles (59.5 km) by road from Hierapolis up a steep, winding incline to a promontory overlooking the Meander River.[35]

Laodicea, Hierapolis, and Dionysopolis are three of many places from which patrons came to release their slaves to the god Apollo (through inscribed records, called *katagraphai*, καταγραφαί). One such release of a house-born slave named Synphoros, of the town of Motellos, was

34. See generally, Cadwallader, "Name-punning."

35. The sanctuary is perched approximately five hundred feet (152.4 m) above the Meander River (now dammed). Forty-three miles (69 km) to the south, the Meander is joined by the Lycus River.

executed by a citizen named Onesimus, son of Onesimus.[36] Colossae is not yet mentioned there, but just over two miles (3.2 km) to the south of Colossae there seems to have been a rural sanctuary (probably dedicated to Zeus Brontes) where such manumission types might have been similarly recorded.

Such an option, privileging Apollo, was hardly available to the Christ-follower, Philemon,[37] and Onesimus may have had to wait until Philemon's death for a testamentary manumission (and this was not obligatory—slaves could be sold on). We have noted that Philemon's death is a distinct probability. So perhaps the Onesimus of Col 4:9 had honored the training given to a slave (Phlm 15–16) and was now a freedman.

BIBLIOGRAPHY

Arzt-Grabner, P. "Everyday Life in a Roman Town like Colossae: The Papyrological Evidence." In *The Lycus Valley*. Edited by J. R. Harrison and L. L. Welborn. Atlanta: SBL Press, forthcoming.

———. "How to Deal with Onesimus? Paul's Solution within the Frame of Ancient Legal and Documentary Sources." Pages 113–42 in *Philemon in Perspective: Interpreting a Pauline Letter*. Edited by D. F. Tolmie. Berlin: de Gruyter, 2010.

———. *Philemon*. Göttingen: Vandenhoeck & Ruprecht, 2003.

Balabanski, V. "Where Is Philemon? The Case for a Logical Fallacy in the Correlation of the Data in Philemon and Colossians 1.1–2; 4.7–18." *Journal for the Study of the New Testament* 38 (2015): 1–20.

Balzat, J.-S., et al. *A Lexicon of Greek Personal Names Volume V.B: Coastal Asia Minor; Caria to Cilicia*. Oxford: Clarendon, 2013.

———. *A Lexicon of Greek Personal Names Volume V.C: Inland Asia Minor*. Oxford: Clarendon, 2018.

Cadwallader, A. H. "Complicating Class in the Letter to Philemon: A Prolegomenon." In *Religion and Class: Ancient Jewish and Christian Writings in their Socio-Economic Contexts*. Edited by G. A. Keddie, M. Flexsenhar, and S. Friesen. Atlanta: SBL Press, forthcoming.

———. "Name-punning and Social Stereotyping: Reinscribing Slavery in the Letter to Philemon." *Australian Biblical Review* 60 (2013): 18–31.

Callahan, A. D. "Paul's Epistle to Philemon: Toward an Alternative Argumentum." *Harvard Theological Review* 86 (1993): 357–76.

Canavan, R. "Weaving Threads: Clothing in Colossae." Pages 111–33 in *Fragments of Colossae: Sifting through the Traces*. Edited by A. H. Cadwallader. Adelaide: ATF, 2015.

Corsten, T., ed. *A Lexicon of Greek Personal Names Volume V. A: Coastal Asia Minor; Pontos to Ionia*. Oxford: Clarendon, 2010.

Deissmann, A. *Light from the Ancient East: The New Testament Illustrated by Recently Discovered Texts of the Graeco-Roman World*. Translated by L. R. M. Strachan. London: Hodder & Stoughton, 1910.

36. T. Ritti, C. Şimşek and H. Yıldız, "Dediche e *καταγραφαί* dal santuario frigio di Apollo Lairbenos," *Epigraphica Anatolica* 32 (2000): 37.

37. Huttner, *Lycus Valley*, 105–6. *archisynagōgos*

Dunn, J. D. G. *The Epistles to the Colossians and to Philemon: A Commentary on the Greek Text*. Grand Rapids: Eerdmans, 1996.

Huttner, U. *Early Christianity in the Lycus Valley*. Leiden: Brill, 2013.

Joshel, S. R. "Geographies of Slave Containment and Movement." Pages 99–128 in *Roman Slavery and Roman Material Culture*. Edited by M. George. Toronto: University of Toronto Press, 2013.

Joshel, S. R., and L. H. Petersen. *The Material Life of Roman Slaves*. Cambridge: Cambridge University Press, 2014.

Lampe, P. "Keine 'Sklavenflucht' des Onesimus." *Zeitschrift fur neutestamentliche Wissenschaft* 76 (1985): 135–37.

Llewellyn, S. R., "The Government's Pursuit of Runaway Slaves." Pages 9–46 in *New Documents Illustrating Early Christianity*. Edited by S. R. Llewellyn. Vol. 8. Grand Rapids: Eerdmans 1998.

Marchal, J. A. "The Usefulness of an Onesimus: The Sexual Use of Slaves and Paul's Letter to Philemon." *JBL* 130 (2011): 749–70.

Nordling, J. G. "Some Matters Favouring The Runaway Slave Hypothesis in Philemon." *Neotestamentica* 44 (2010): 85–121.

Ritti, T., C. Şimşek, and H. Yıldız. "Dediche e *καταγραφαί* dal santuario frigio di Apollo Lairbenos." *Epigraphica Anatolica* 32 (2000): 1–88.

Şimşek, C. "Urban Planning of Laodikeia on the Lykos in the Light of New Evidence." Pages 1–46 in *Landscape and History in the Lykos Valley: Laodikeia and Hierapolis in Phrygia*. Edited by C. Şimşek and F. D'Andria. Newcastle upon Tyne: Cambridge Scholars Publishing, 2016.

Smith, M. J. "Utility, Fraternity and Reconciliation: Ancient Slavery as a Context for the Return of Onesimus." Pages 47–58 in *Onesimus Our Brother: Reading Religion, Race and Culture in Philemon*. Edited by M. V. Johnson, J. A. Neal, and D. K. Williams. Minneapolis: Fortress, 2012.

Solin, H. *Die stadtrömischen Sklavennamen: Ein Namenbuch*. 3 vols. Stuttgart: Steiner, 1996.

Wiedemann, T. *Greek and Roman Slavery*. London: Routledge, 1981.

CHAPTER 46

PETER'S CHRISTIAN COMMUNITIES IN ASIA MINOR

1 Pet 1:1

Mark Wilson

> KEY POINTS
>
> - Peter himself perhaps did evangelistic work in the provinces addressed in his first letter.
> - These provinces were connected by major sea and land routes still in use today.
> - Cities with royal, religious, and tribal connections were founded along these routes.
> - Jewish communities are documented in Cappadocia, Pontus, and Bithynia.
> - Letters between Pliny the Younger and Trajan indicate that Christianity had spread throughout Bithynia and Pontus by the early second century AD.

THE GEOGRAPHICAL BACKGROUND OF PETER'S FIRST LETTER

The book of Acts presents Peter as its major figure in chapters 1–12 while Paul predominates in chapters 13–28.[1] Peter's travels in Acts are confined to Samaria (8:14), Lydda (9:32), Joppa (9:43), and Caesarea (10:24). Paul mentions a confrontation between them in Antioch (Gal 2:11). Paul's naming of Peter in 1 Corinthians (1:12; 9:5) suggests that he had visited Corinth.[2] Another geographical marker is "Babylon" where Peter wrote his first letter (1 Pet 5:13). Babylon is plausibly interpreted as a cipher for Rome (see Rev 17:5 among others), so 1 Peter was written from the impe-

1. In Acts 15 both men play an important role at the Jerusalem Council.

2. C. K. Barrett, "Cephas and Corinth," in *Essays on Paul* (London: SPCK, 1982), 28–39, is a strong proponent of a Petrine visit there.

rial capital.[3] The letter is addressed to Christian communities in north-central Asia Minor—Pontus, Galatia, Cappadocia, Asia, and Bithynia (1 Pet 1:1). Although these locations seem ill-defined, a closer examination of their socio-political dimensions permits the development of a geographical profile. The likelihood is that Peter himself planted some of the churches in these provinces as he traveled westward.[4] This tradition is preserved in Eusebius' *Church History* (3.1.2). Pilgrims from three of the provinces—Cappadocia, Pontus, and Asia—and one region—Phrygia—were among the diaspora Jews in Jerusalem for the day of Pentecost (Acts 2:9–10). Some were perhaps among the respondents to Peter's message and became early Jesus followers in the region (Acts 2:41; 4:4). From Syrian Antioch the distance to Amisus on the Black Sea was shorter (631 mi. [1015 km]) than to Ephesus on the Aegean Sea (667 mi. [1073 km]).[5] A network of roads had developed in north-central Asia Minor to facilitate intra- and inter-provincial trade and travel. Vespasian reorganized these provinces dramatically beginning in AD 70 so the provincial boundaries before his reorganization are assumed.[6]

3. Paul J. Achtemeier, *1 Peter: A Commentary on 1 Peter* (Minneapolis: Fortress, 1996), 63–64, 354.

4. Carsten P. Thiede posits such a mission but in the early 40s under Claudius (Thiede, *Simon Peter: From Galilee to Rome* [Grand Rapids: Zondervan, 1988], 155). However, such an early date is generally rejected. Stephen Mitchell identifies the evangelist bringing the gospel to these provinces as "the author of 1 Peter" (Mitchell, *Anatolia: Land, Men, and Gods* [Oxford: Oxford University Press, 1992], 2:871).

5. These distances were calculated using http://orbis.stanford.edu/.

6. Christian Marek, *In the Land of a Thousand Gods: A History of Asia Minor in the Ancient World*, trans. Steven Rendall (Princeton: Princeton University Press, 2016), 338–42. For the provincial organization in the 60s, see page 327 map 16; for the Vespasianic reorganization, see page 340, map 18.

The messenger carrying the letter, probably Silvanus (Silas; 1 Pet 5:12),[7] arrived in Asia Minor either by ship or road. Depending on the season, the latter was more dependable. His route followed the Via Appia from Rome to Brundisium.[8] From its port, ferries made a short crossing of the Adriatic Sea to Dyrrachium. There travelers embarked on the Via Egnatia to transit Illyricum, Macedonia, and Thrace (see map on page 584). The distance to Byzantium (later Constantinople) was 1057 miles (1700 km) and took nearly two months.[9] At the harbor Chrysokeras (Golden Horn; modern Haliç) on the Bosphorus (Ox-ford), Silvanus secured passage on a coasting vessel to transport him along the south coast of the Black Sea to Pontus.

The order of the provinces in 1 Peter 1:1 has been judged unhelpful for reconstructing Silvanus' route. Because Cappadocia has no border with Asia, it has been argued that the description is inherently flawed.[10] However, Peter's audience knew the region's geography and that Galatia must be recrossed from Cappadocia to reach Asia. Peter, perhaps to avoid repetition, chose not to repeat Galatia in his list. This order suggested to F. J. A. Hort a delivery route; Colin Hemer later made minor modifications to Hort's suggestion.[11] For example, Hort proposed an entry point at Sinope while Hemer proposed Amisus.[12] The weakness of their reconstructions is the inclusion of the Pauline cities of Iconium and Pisidian Antioch and the Johannine city of Sardis. Peter's provinces are instead oriented toward the Black Sea and center "on northern and eastern churches not reached by the journeys of Paul."[13] While building on these previous proposals, this article presents a more refined view of the route, particularly after Cappadocia.[14]

PONTUS AND ITS CITIES

Pontus is the Greek word for "sea" (Πόντος, *pontos*). The southern coast of the Black Sea (*Pontus Euxinus*, "Hospitable Sea")

7. E. Randolph Richards, "Silvanus Was Not Peter's Secretary: Theological Bias in Interpreting διὰ Σιλουανοῦ ... ἔγραψα," *JETS* 43 (2000): 427–32.

8. In AD 9 when Augustus exiled the poet Ovid from Rome to Tomis, he traveled by sea from Brundisium to the Black Sea (*Tristia* 1).

9. In the fourth century AD Constantine constructed the Milion to mark the starting point of the *Via Egnatia*. It copied the Golden Milestone (*Milliarium Aureum*) that Augustus had erected in the Roman forum. Today a stone from the monument stands opposite the Hagia Sophia in Istanbul.

10. For example, Torrey Seland, *Strangers in the Light: Philonic Perspectives on Christian Identity in 1 Peter* (Leiden: Brill, 2005), 36.

11. F. J. A. Hort, *First Epistle of St. Peter I,1–II,17* (London: Macmillan, 1898), 167–84; Colin J. Hemer, "The Address of 1 Peter," *Expository Times* 89.8 (1978): 239–43.

12. Hort, *First Epistle of St. Peter*, 176; Hemer, "Address of 1 Peter," 241.

13. J. Ramsey Michaels, *1 Peter* (Waco, TX: Word, 1988), 10.

14. Observations here are drawn from my article, Mark Wilson, "Cities of God in Northern Asia Minor: Using Stark's Social Theories to Reconstruct Peter's Communities," *Verbum et Ecclesia* 32 (2011): passim, as well as from my book, Wilson, *Biblical Turkey: A Guide to the Jewish and Christian Sites of Asia Minor* (Istanbul: Ege Yayınları, 2010), passim. For other suggested itineraries see Karen H. Jobes, "'Foreigners and Exiles': Was 1 Peter Written to Roman Colonists?" in *Bedrängnis und Identität: Studien zu Situation, Kommunikation und Theologie des 1. Petrusbriefes*, ed. David S. du Toit (Berlin: de Gruyter, 2013), 36–37.

was divided into three regions—Bithynia, Paphlagonia, and Pontus. The Parthenius River (modern Bartın) separated Bithynia from Paphlagonia, while the Halys River (modern Kızılırmak) separated inland Paphlagonia from Pontus. The Iris (modern Yeşilırmak) similarly emptied into the Black Sea east of Amisus. The forested Paryadres Mountains (modern Küre Dağları), with peaks over 6500 feet (1900 m), separated the narrow coastal plain from the inland plateau, so travel in Pontus was largely done by sea. While a track connected the coastal cities, it was slow and rugged. The roads that ran inland from the coastal cities connected with an east-west Pontic road that, in part, followed the valley of the Amnias River (modern Gökırmak).[15]

A Hellenized Persian named Mithridates I founded the kingdom of Pontus in 302 BC. After three wars the Romans finally defeated Mithridates VI Eupator in 66 BC. In 63 BC Pompey united Pontus with Bithynia to form the new double province *Bithynia et Pontus*. The province had thirteen cities including Amastris, Sinope, Amisus, Amasia, and Zela. Mark Antony reorganized Pontus in 39 bc and established the kingdom of Pontus Polemoniacus in eastern Pontus. Augustus made Bithynia along with most of Pontus a senatorial province in 29 BC. Philo attests to an extensive settlement of Jews throughout Pontus (*Embassy to Gaius* 36).

Portait of Mithridates I on Tetradrachm

Although the Bithynian city of Heraclea Pontica (modern Karadeniz Ereğli) had the first major harbor east of the Bosphorus, Amastris (modern Amasra) was better situated with its double harbor. It was originally named Sesamos (Homer, *Iliad* 2.853). However, around 300 BC Queen Amastris founded a new city for her capital by merging four cities at Sesamos. In 70 BC during the Mithridatic wars, Amastris was captured by the Romans. It became a metropolis of the Pontic assembly and served briefly as capital of the twin province. Pliny the Younger described Amastris as "an elegant and beautiful city" (*Letters* 10.99 [LCL]). A well-preserved road monument stands two and a half miles (4 km) south of Amasra today. Its Greek-Latin inscription identifies Gaius Julius Aquilla as the governor who built the road under the emperor Claudius.[16] Ramsay suggested Amastris as the messenger's entry point because it was Pontus' "chief center at first."[17] Because the road's terminus was Bithynian Hadrianopolis (modern

15. Pompey founded or completed cities after 63 BC along this road; see Mitchell, *Anatolia*, 1:32; 268–69, map 3. Karen H. Jobes believes it is these inland cities also colonized by Claudius that were among the Christian communities addressed by Peter (Jobes, *1 Peter* [Grand Rapids: Baker Academic, 2005], 29–32).

16. The monument in Turkish is called Kuşkayası ("Bird rock"); see Takeko Harada and Fatih Cimok, *Roads of Ancient Anatolia* (Istanbul: Turizm, 2008), 2:196–97, figs. 282–84.

17. William M. Ramsay, "Pontus," in *A Dictionary of the Bible*, ed. James Hastings (Edinburgh: T&T Clark, 1898), 4:17.

Eskipazar) where it joined an east-west road, this hypothesis is unlikely. An inscription recording a benefaction from Aurelios Protektetos for a synagogue (προσευχή, *proseuchē*) in Amastris dates from the third century AD.[18]

Sinope (modern Sinop) was situated on a peninsula whose promontory Lepte/Syrias is Asia Minor's northernmost point and the narrowest distance to the Cimmerian Bosphorus (modern Crimea). Located astride a narrow isthmus, its two deep-water harbors were the best on the Black Sea. Strabo calls Sinope the greatest city of Pontus with its fine walls and public buildings (*Geography* 12.3.11). In 630 BC it became Miletus' first colony (Xenophon, *Anabasis* 6.1.15). Sinope retained its status as an independent free city until 183 BC when Pharnaces I moved his capital here from Amasia. In 67 BC the Roman general Lucullus made Sinope a free city again; in 46 BC Julius Caesar established a Roman colony here. In 14 BC Herod the Great sailed to Sinope to join Marcus Agrippa, Augustus' deputy (Josephus, *Ant.* 16.21–23). They returned by land, passing through Paphlagonia, Cappadocia, and Great Phrygia before arrival in Ephesus.[19] A milestone dating to Vespasian's reign identifies Sinope as the *caput viae* (roadhead) of this road running inland to Paphlagonia.[20] Such overland travel, albeit by the Roman elite, suggests that Silvanus' journey was practicable. The city remained the Roman base for its Black Sea fleet until the third century AD. The Jewish believer Aquila, companion of Paul and husband of Priscilla, was a native of Pontus (Acts 18:2), probably from Sinope or Amisus.

Kuşkayası Monument South of Amasra

Amisus (modern Samsun) was also founded by Milesian colonists in the mid-sixth century BC. It was the terminus of

18. Margaret H. Williams, *The Jews among the Greeks and Romans: A Diasporan Sourcebook* (Baltimore: Johns Hopkins University Press, 1998), 122 V.45; Walter Ameling, *Inscriptiones Judaicae Orientis: Band II, Kleinasien* (Tübingen, Mohr Siebeck, 2004), 314–17 no. 149.

19. Peter Richardson and Amy Marie Fischer using Josephus' provincial and geographical markers, reconstruct a plausible itinerary similar to this reconstruction (Richardson and Fischer, *Herod: King of the Jews and Friend of the Romans* [London: Routledge, 2017], 174).

20. David H. French, *Milestones: Pontus et Bithynia (with Northern* Galatia) in fascicle 3.4 of *Roads and Milestones of Asia Minor* (Ankara: British Institute of Archaeology at Ankara, 2013), 58 no. 19. The earliest milestones date from Vespasian's reign; for maps of the provincial road system see pages 19–20.

Tombs of the Pontic Kings at Amasya

the primary passable road to the Black Sea coast from Cappadocia.[21] Although J. Arthur Munro called it the "alimentary canal" of the Pontic kingdom, his metaphor applies equally to the road's significance for central Asia Minor since it continues southward to the Cilician Gates and Tarsus.[22] Its democratic constitution, suppressed under the Persians, was restored by Alexander the Great in 334 BC. Under the Mithridatic kingdom, the city was enlarged and adorned. After the suicide of Mithridates VI in 63 BC, his son Pharnaces sent his body to Amisus where Pompey finally realized victory over his enemy. He later sent the corpse to Sinope to appease the divine jealousy (Plutarch, *Life of Pompey* 42.2–3). In 47 BC Julius Caesar confirmed the city's free status. Around 36 BC Mark Antony placed Amisus under the control of a local tyrant, but in 31 BC Augustus again made Amisus a free city. In the early first century AD Amisus was the limit of Roman rule with Armenia Minor to the east. Sampsames, usually identified with Amisus, was one of the cities addressed by the Roman consul Lucius on behalf of the Jews (1 Macc 15:23).

GALATIA AND ITS CITIES

Galatia was the region and province south of Pontus. Situated around the headwaters of the Sangarius River (modern Sakarya) and the middle tributary of the Halys River, it comprised a largely level basin in central Asia Minor. The name derives from the many Gauls who migrated from Europe in 278–277 BC to serve as mercenaries for Nicomedes I, king of Bithynia. In

21. D. R. Wilson, "The Historical Geography of Bithynia, Paphlagonia and Pontus in the Greek and Roman Periods: A New Survey with Particular Reference to Surface Remains Still Visible" (B.Litt. thesis, Oxford, 1960), 369–78.

22. J. Arthur Munro, "Roads in Pontus, Royal and Roman," *Journal of Hellenic Studies* 21 (1901): 53–55.

232 BC the three Galatian tribes received fixed boundaries. The Tolistobogii were centered at Pessinus, the Tectosages at Ancyra, and the Trocmi at Tavium. In 63 BC the Tolistobogiian king Deiotarus killed his fellow rulers and became sole monarch. Individual leaders followed until Amyntas bequeathed his kingdom to Rome in 25 BC. Galatia then became a Roman province with Ancyra as its capital. The new province included not only the Galatian settlements but also Pisidia, eastern Phrygia, Lycaonia, Isaurian, and Pamphylia. In 6 BC Paphlagonia and in 3/2 BC inland Pontus were also added to Galatia.

Amasia (Amasya) is situated in the deep valley of the Iris River (Yeşilırmak) and "had a strategic position in the road system leading to the NE frontier."[23] The main north-south route also passed through the city. A milestone from Nerva's reign seemingly indicates Amasia as the *caput viae*.[24] Mithridates I established Amasia as his first capital in 301 BC. In 183 BC Pharnaces I transferred the capital to Sinope, but Amasia remained important since it hosted the shrine of the chief Pontic deity Zeus Stratios. After the Romans captured the city in 70 BC, Pompey granted Amasia city status in the newly created province of Bithynia-Pontus. In 3/2 BC Augustus attached it to Galatia, and Amasia became the capital of the region Pontus Galaticus. The geographer Strabo was born a Roman citizen of Pontic aristocracy in Amasia (approximately 64 BC–AD 23).

Zela (modern Zile) had an important temple of the Persian goddess Anaitis on its acropolis and so was part of a large temple territory ruled by priests. Outside Zela in 67 BC Mithridates VI decisively defeated Gaius Valerius Triarius and killed seven thousand of his men. In 64 BC Pompey defeated the king and established Zela as one of the eleven urban centers of Pontus. A civic organization now replaced Comanian priestly rule, and the lands of the goddess became the new civic territory. Pharnaces II usurped his father's former Pontic kingdom during the Roman civil wars but was defeated by Julius Caesar at Zela in 47 BC. This inspired Caesar's famous words to the Roman Senate: *Veni, vidi, vici* ("I came, I saw, I conquered"). Under Antony in 36 BC the city reverted to its prior temple status and was ruled by Pontic client kings. In 3/2 BC the Romans annexed Zela, which then regained its city status. The city lay on the north-south trunk road.

CAPPADOCIA AND ITS CITIES

Cappadocia was both a region and province in central Anatolia bounded on the east by the Euphrates River (modern Fırat) and on the south by the Taurus Mountains (modern Toros Dağları). Its name is believed Persian: "land of the beautiful horses." This vast treeless plateau was sparsely populated, and the Halys River flows through its northern part. Mount Argaeus (Erciyes Dağı) looms over the region, and tufa formed by volcanic activity is responsible for its "fairy chimney" moonscape. In 301 BC Cappadocia became an autonomous state with its capital established at Mazaca. Its residents were mainly agrarian shep-

23. Stephen Mitchell, "Amaseia," in *Oxford Classical Dictionary*, ed. Simon Hornblower and Anthony Spawforth, 4th ed. (Oxford; Oxford University Press, 1993), 69.

24. David H. French, *Milestones: Cappadocia*, fascicle 3.3 of *Roads and Milestones of Asia Minor* (Ankara: British Institute of Archaeology at Ankara, 2012), 46–47 no. 19.

Mount Argaeus Towers over the City of Kayseri

herds and horse breeders. Hellenization was of little influence except among its rulers, so Cappadocian remained the main language. Strabo records that only two cities existed—Caesarea Mazaca and Tyana (*Geography* 12.2.7). In AD 17 Tiberius established Cappadocia as a Roman province with Caesarea (modern Kayseri) as its capital. Vespasian formed a new superprovince in AD 70 that combined Cappadocia with Galatia and Armenia Minor. Cappadocia was the home of Jewish pilgrims who were in Jerusalem for the Day of Pentecost (Acts 2:9).

Caesarea Mazaca was situated on a low spur rising on the northern side of sacred Argaeus (12,851 ft. [3917 m]). The mountain is frequently depicted on Caesarea's coins. Mazaca served as a capital for Tubal and the Persians in the sixth to fourth centuries BC. Alexander passed through Cappadocia, but his general Perdiccas later secured it for the Greeks. After the death of Seleucus, an independent Cappadocian kingdom was established in 301 BC. The city was renamed Eusebeia in honor of Ariarathes V Eusebes Philopator (reigned 163–120 BC), who sought to promote Greek culture in this backwater. After sacking the city in 77 BC, Tigranes I the Great deported the residents to populate his capital Tigranocerta. The Roman general Lucullus freed them eight years later, and Pompey the Great helped with the city's reconstruction. Archelaus (36 BC–AD 17), a client king of Augustus, again made Mazaca his capital, and in 12–9 BC he changed its name to Caesarea in honor of his patron. In AD 17 Tiberius made Caesarea the capital of the new Roman province. Because of its strategic location, Caesarea served as an important transportation hub with five roads, including the main north-south trunk, converging on the city. A twice-inscribed milestone from the reigns of Titus and Nerva indicates Caesarea as the *caput viae* of the road eastward to Melitene on the Euphrates.[25]

25. French, *Milestones: Cappadocia*, 102–3 no. 66; see also 20 map 5.1. A milestone (p. 31 A7) dating around AD 100 comes from the Caesarea to Tyana route.

GALATIA AND ITS CITIES

The recrossing of Galatia is assumed in Peter's itinerary so coming from Caesarea Mazaca, Tavium (modern Büyüknefes) was the major city in northeast Galatia. Four major roads converged here. Tavium is the probable *caput viae* for a group of milestones dating from Nerva's reign.[26] Around 232 BC the Trocmi, the easternmost Galatian tribe, made Tavium their primary settlement. Augustus founded a colony around 22–21 BC called Sebasteni Trocmi Taviani. A Late Antique cemetery near Tavium contains both Christian and Jewish gravestones including one with a menorah in memory of Sara.[27]

Ancyra (modern Ankara) was the second metropolis of Phrygia after Gordium, and both the Persians and the Seleucids sought to control it. It was situated at the junction of seven key trade routes in northern Asia Minor. Anycra is the *caput viae* for a group of milestones found around the city that date from the reigns of Titus, Domitian, and Trajan.[28] Around 265 BC the Galatian tribe, Tectosages, made Ancyra its capital after receiving the site from the Pontic kingdom. In the early first century BC Mithradates VI Eupator took control of the city until Pompey defeated him in 65 BC. After the Romans annexed Galatia in 25 BC, Augustus made Ancyra the capital of the new province also named Galatia. He founded a colony there around 22–21 BC called Sebasteni Tectosages Ancyrani.

Pessinus (modern Ballıhisar) was an important city in west central Galatia situated beneath holy Mount Dindymus. It held the shrine of the Phrygian mother goddess Cybele until the Romans moved the sacred black stone to Rome in 204 BC (Livy, *History* 29.10.4–29.11.9). In the third century BC the Tolistobogii, the westernmost Galatian tribe, made Pessinus their capital. After the Romans annexed Galatia in 25 BC, Augustus founded a colony at Pessinus around 22–21 BC naming it Sebasteni Tolistobogii Pessinuntii. Pessinus' influence and territory were reduced after Augustus founded the colony of Germa in 17 BC to the northwest. An undated inscription found on the east slope of Dindymus clearly uses the Jewish names Esther and Jacob.[29]

ASIA AND ITS CITIES

The Attalid dynasty ruled western Asia Minor from Pergamum from 283 to 133 BC when Attalus III bequeathed his kingdom to Rome. In 129 BC the Romans established the province of Asia whose boundaries changed considerably over time. By the first century AD it had thirteen juridical districts encompassing ancient regions from the Aegean Sea on the west to the Mediterranean on the southwest and the Propontis (modern Sea of Marmara) on

---

26. David H. French, *Milestones: Galatia*, fascicle 3.2 of *Roads and Milestones of Asia Minor* (Ankara: British Institute of Archaeology at Ankara, 2012), 68–69 no. 45(A); 70–71 no. 47; 71–72 no. 49(A); 78–79 no. 51(C); 84–85 no. 54(B); 86 no. 56; 89–91 nos. 59(B)–60. For maps of the road system in Galatia, see pages 15–16.

27. See Stephen Mitchell, *The Inscriptions of North Galatia: The Ankara District*, vol. 2 of *Regional and Epigraphic Catalogues of Asia Minor* (Oxford: BAR, 1982), 512.

28. French, *Milestones: Galatia*, 27–29 nos. 07–08; 57 no. 35; 59–60 nos. 38(A–B). The first two stones lay between Ancyra and Pessinus. French interestingly notes, "The Flavian date for the paving of the road—*viam stravit*—is some one hundred years later than the creation of the province itself" (11).

29. Mitchell, *Inscriptions of North Galatia*, 133.

Roman Theater at Nicea

the northwest. Synnada was the assize center for the Phrygian region of northeastern Asia. Around 35 BC Octavian guaranteed its large Jewish population the right to send the temple tax to Jerusalem. In AD 30 Jews from Asia were in Jerusalem at Pentecost (Acts 2:9), and some belonged to the Synagogue of the Freedmen (Acts 6:9).

Dorylaeum was situated at Şarhöyük (Şar mound) north of modern Eskişehir in the fertile plain of the Tembris River (modern Porsuk). Located in Phrygia Epictetus (Cicero, *For Flaccus* 17.39–41) and linked administratively to Synnada, Dorylaeum's civic territory bordered that of Bithynian Nicea.[30] Its strategic location commanded the junction of five roads, particularly from Galatia to the east and northwest into Bithynia. Controlling Dorylaeum "ensured easy passage for armies or more peaceful traffic."[31] Paul probably reached Dorylaeum on his second journey, arriving from Cotiaeum to the southwest. Here he was forbidden by the Spirit of Jesus to proceed into Bithynia (Acts 16:7).[32] If the Pauline cities in Asia west of Cappadocia are skipped and Galatia's three northern cities are visited, Silvanus would have naturally

30. A. H. M. Jones, *Cities of the Eastern Roman Empire*, 2nd ed. (Oxford: Oxford University Press, 1971), 65, 160.

31. Clive Foss, "Dorylaion: Bulwark of the Byzantine Frontier," *Greek Orthodox Theological Review* 41 (1996): 39.

32. Glen L. Thompson and Mark Wilson, "The Route of Paul's Second Journey in Asia Minor: In the Steps of Robert Jewett and Beyond," *TynBul* 67 (2016): 230–32; for a map see 231 fig. 4. They had previously been forbidden to preach in Asia (Acts 16:6).

Roman Walls and Byzantium/Constantinople Gate at Nicea

visited Dorylaeum in his circular itinerary. A funerary inscription, undated and found in Judea, mentions a rabbi named Samuel who was a synagogue leader (ἀρχισυνάγωγος, *archisynagogos*) from Phrygian Dorylaeum (*CIJ* 1414).[33]

BITHYNIA AND ITS CITIES

Bithynia was a region and later province in northwest Asia Minor that bordered the Propontis, the Bosphorus, and the Euxine (Black) Sea. The Sangarius River provided a fertile delta, while much of its remaining landscape was mountainous and forested. The Bithynian tribe had migrated from Thrace, and in 298 BC King Zipoetes founded a local dynasty. During the reigns of Nicomedes I and II and Prusias I many cities were founded and Greek culture promoted. The last Bithynian king Nicomedes III bequeathed his kingdom to the Romans in 74 BC. However, Roman rule was not instituted until Mithridates was defeated in 72 BC. Pompey the Great in 63 BC united coastal Pontus with Bithynia to form a single senatorial province. However, each region always retained its distinct identity, hence the official double name—*Bithynia et Pontus*. Bithynia was a rich and highly civilized province. Nicomedia was its political center; Nicea its commercial one. Two important roads crossed Bithynia: one ran eastward from Nicomedia to the inner Pontic region; the second ran southeast from Nicea to Asian Dorylaeum and Galatian Pessinus and Ancyra. The latter became the main land route for European pilgrims to Jerusalem, hence was later called the Pilgrim's Road. Philo mentions the presence of Jews in Bithynia (*Embassy to Gaius* 36).

---

33. Shaye J. D. Cohen, "Epigraphical Rabbis," *Jewish Quarterly Review*, 72 (1981): 14–15. Ameling, *Inscriptiones Judaicae Orientis*, 389–92 no. 184, prefers the restoration of Docimeum, a Phrygian city noted for its marble quarries but more isolated geographically.

Nicea (modern İznik) was situated on the eastern shore of Lake Ascania (İznik Gölü), which helped to connect to its port Cius (modern Gemlik) on the Propontis. Five roads from all directions converged here. Nicea is probably the *caput viae* of a milestone found near Gemlik that dates to Vespasian's reign.[34] The road from Nicea to Dorylaeum was of particular importance "leading as it does to the whole of southern, southeastern and indeed eastern Asia Minor."[35] Antigonus founded the Hellenistic city of Antigonia in 316 BC. After the battle of Ipsus in 301 BC, Lysimachus captured the city; he refounded and named it after his first wife Nicea. Bithynian kings controlled Nicea after Lysimachus' death in 281 BC until the arrival of the Romans in the first century BC. Nicea and Nicomedia vied for the honor of being Bithynia's principal city. In 29 BC Augustus authorized a sanctuary of Dea Roma and Divus Julius to be built in Nicea for Roman citizens (Cassius Dio 51.20.6). A Jewish inscription with menorah dates from Late Antiquity. Its Greek text of Psalm 135:25 LXX (Ps 136:25) is the longest citation of a scripture from the diaspora.[36]

Nicomedia (modern İzmit) lay at the northeastern corner of the narrow Gulf of Astacus (modern İzmit Körfezi), the eastern arm of the Propontis. Lysimachus razed the city of Astacus ("lobster") on the southern shore around 281 BC, and its residents became the first citizens of the new city founded by Nicomedes around 264 BC. With its excellent natural harbor, Nicomedia was Bithynia's major maritime port. Traffic from the Bosphorus into Asia Minor passed through the city. In 74 BC the Bithynian king bequeathed his kingdom to the Romans, who made Nicomedia their provincial capital. As the seat of the provincial assembly (κοινόν, *koinon*), it was Bithynia's most populous city. An imperial cult temple to Rome and Augustus for Greeks was built here in 29 BC (Cassius Dio 51.20.7). Dio Chrysostum's thirty-eighth oration addressed the strife between Nicomedia and Nicea generated by their fierce competition. Several Jewish inscriptions come from Nicomedia including the funerary one of Ulpia Capitylla that mentions a synagogue.[37]

Chalcedon (modern Kadıköy) was situated on the east side of the Bosphorus as Bithynia's westernmost city. This Greek colony was founded around 676 BC. The site was situated between two harbors, the modern bays of Kalamış and Kadıköy. However, Chalcedon had two disadvantages: the Bosphorus currents carried the fish toward the western shore and these same currents made it difficult to land at Chalcedon. Byzantium thus came to overshadow her sister city. Nevertheless, all traffic from the east passed through Chalcedon's port where ferries conveyed them to Byzantium. During the Roman period Chalcedon was a free city. A funerary stele of Jacob son of Leontios with a

34. French, Milestones: Pontus et Bithynia, 70–71 no. 26.

35. Wilson, "Historical Geography of Bithynia, Paphlagonia and Pontus," 338.

36. Steven Fine and Leonard V. Rutgers, "New Light on Judaism in Asia Minor," *Jewish Studies Quarterly* 3 (1996): 7.

37. Williams, *Jews among the Greeks and Romans*, 30 I.108; compare 34 II.4; 130 V.73; see also Ameling, *Inscriptiones Judaicae Orientis*, 324–32 nos. 154–58.

Looking Westward across the Bosphorus to Modern Istanbul (Byzantium)

menorah was found at the nearby port of Chrysopolis (modern Üsküdar).[38]

Byzantium (modern Istanbul) was located on the west side of the Bosphorus. Between 668–657 BC Greeks from Megara and Argos founded the city on seven hills across from Chalcedon. In 340/339 BC its defenders resisted the siege of Philip II of Macedonia, reputedly through the intervention of the goddess Hecate. During the reigns of Augustus, Tiberius, and Nero, Byzantium functioned as a free city. Although situated in Thrace, Byzantium was attached to the province of Bithynia and Pontus (Pliny the Younger *Epistles* 43, 44). Here Silvanus would have completed his rota, perhaps visiting a Christian community there before returning to Rome to bring Peter news of the congregations in northern Asia Minor.

CONCLUSION

Silvanus' suggested itinerary shows parallels with Paul's journeys in Acts. It follows major roads in north central Asia Minor that connected royal, religious, and tribal centers, which later became provincial and regional capitals during the Roman period. Though less populated with Jewish communities than southern and western Asia Minor, Jews were found in the major cities. Peter's first connection with these diasporan communities might date to the day of Pentecost.

Evidence for an early establishment of churches, particularly in Bithynia and Pontus, is found in two second-century sources. Pliny the Younger served as imperial commissioner to Pontus-Bithynia from AD 111–113 and wrote a letter to the Emperor Trajan (*Letters* 10.96). He described the spread of Christianity in this double province. Pliny's testimony is significant because it is the first secular source to describe the practices of early Christian congregations. The demographics of this new movement consisted of many individuals of every age, class, and gender who lived not only in towns but also in villages and rural districts. Some were even Roman citizens. He likens the spread of this "wretched cult" to an infection that must be checked. The socio-religious impact of the movement had caused temples to be deserted, sacred rituals to be neglected, and the meat of

38. Ameling, *Inscriptiones Judaicae Orientis*, 317 no. 150.

sacrificial animals to go unbought. To stem this spiritual plague, he tortured two deaconesses who were slaves and allowed others to escape persecution by having them offer wine and incense to the emperor's statue. Pliny believed that many people could be reformed if given an opportunity to repent. Yet many did not repent, for Lucian, writing a few decades later, said that Pontus was "filled with Epicureans and atheists and Christians" (*Alexander* 25). Pliny's comments show how the Christian movement had expanded both geographically and demographically less than half a century after 1 Peter was written.

BIBLIOGRAPHY

Achtemeier, Paul J. *1 Peter: A Commentary on 1 Peter*. Minneapolis: Fortress, 1996.

Ameling, Walter. *Inscriptiones Judaicae Orientis: Band II, Kleinasien*. Tübingen: Mohr Siebeck, 2004.

Barrett, C. K. "Cephas and Corinth." Pages 28–39 in *Essays on Paul*. London: SPCK, 1982.

Cohen, Shaye J. D. "Epigraphical Rabbis." *Jewish Quarterly Review* 72 (1981): 1–17.

Fine, Steven, and Leonard V. Rutgers. "New Light on Judaism in Asia Minor during Late Antiquity: Two Recently Identified Inscribed Menorahs." *Jewish Studies Quarterly* 3 (1996): 1–23.

Foss, Clive. "Dorylaion: Bulwark of the Byzantine Frontier." *Greek Orthodox Theological Review* 41 (1996): 39–55.

French, David H. *Milestones: Cappadocia*. Fascicle 3.3 of *Roads and Milestones of Asia Minor*. Ankara: British Institute of Archaeology at Ankara, 2012.

———. *Milestones: Galatia*. Fascicle 3.2 of *Roads and Milestones of Asia Minor*. Ankara: British Institute of Archaeology at Ankara, 2012.

———. *Milestones: Pontus et Bithynia (with Northern Galatia)*. Fascicle 3.4 of *Roads and Milestones of Asia Minor*. Ankara: British Institute of Archaeology at Ankara, 2013.

Harada, Takeko, and Fatih Cimok. *Roads of Ancient Anatolia*. 2 vols. Istanbul: Turizm, 2008.

Hemer, Colin J. "The Address of 1 Peter." *Expository Times* 89 (1978): 239–43.

Hort, F. J. A. *First Epistle of St. Peter I, 1–II, 17*. London: Macmillan, 1898.

Jobes, Karen H. *1 Peter*. Grand Rapids: Baker Academic, 2005.

———. "'Foreigners and Exiles': Was 1 Peter Written to Roman Colonists?" Pages 21–41 in *Bedrängnis und Identität: Studien zu Situation, Kommunikation und Theologie des 1. Petrusbriefes*. Edited by David S. du Toit. Berlin: de Gruyter, 2013.

Jones, A. H. M. *Cities of the Eastern Roman Empire*. 2nd ed. Oxford: Oxford University Press, 1971.

Marek, Christian. *In the Land of a Thousand Gods: A History of Asia Minor in the Ancient World*. Translated by Steven Rendall. Princeton: Princeton University Press, 2016.

Michaels, J. Ramsey. *1 Peter*. Waco, TX: Word, 1988.

Mitchell, Stephen. "Amaseia." Page 69 in *Oxford Classical Dictionary*. Edited by Simon Hornblower and Anthony Spawforth. 4th ed. Oxford; Oxford University Press, 1993.

———. *Anatolia; Land, Men, and Gods*. 2 vols. Oxford: Oxford University Press, 1992.

———. *The Inscriptions of North Galatia: The Ankara District*. Vol. 2 of *Regional and Epigraphic Catalogues of Asia Minor* Oxford: BAR, 1982.

Munro, J. Arthur. "Roads in Pontus, Royal and Roman." *Journal of Hellenic Studies* 21 (1901): 52–66.

Pliny. *Letters*. Translated by W. Melmoth. Revised by W. M. L. Hutchinson. 2 vols. LCL. London: Heinemann, 1915.

Ramsay, William M. "Pontus." Page 17 in vol. 4 of *A Dictionary of the Bible*. Edited by James Hastings. 5 vols. Edinburgh: T&T Clark, 1898–1923.

Richards, E. Randolph. "Silvanus Was Not Peter's Secretary: Theological Bias in Interpreting διὰ Σιλουανοῦ … ἔγραψα." *JETS* 43 (2000): 417–32.

Richardson, Peter, and Amy Marie Fischer. *Herod: King of the Jews and Friend of the Romans*. London: Routledge, 2017.

Seland, Torrey. *Strangers in the Light: Philonic Perspectives on Christian Identity in 1 Peter*. Leiden: Brill, 2005.

Thiede, Carsten P. *Simon Peter: From Galilee to Rome*. Grand Rapids: Zondervan, 1988.

Thompson, Glen L., and Mark Wilson. "The Route of Paul's Second Journey in Asia Minor: In the Steps of Robert Jewett and Beyond." *TynBul* 67 (2016): 217–46.

Williams, Margaret H. *The Jews among the Greeks and Romans: A Diasporan Sourcebook*. Baltimore: Johns Hopkins University Press, 1998.

Wilson, D. R. "The Historical Geography of Bithynia, Paphlagonia and Pontus in the Greek and Roman Periods: A New Survey with Particular Reference to Surface Remains Still Visible." B.Litt. thesis, Oxford, 1960.

Wilson, Mark. *Biblical Turkey: A Guide to the Jewish and Christian Sites of Asia Minor*. Istanbul: Ege Yayınları, 2010.

———. "Cities of God in Northern Asia Minor: Using Stark's Social Theories to Reconstruct Peter's Communities." *Verbum et Ecclesia* 32 (2011): 1–9.

CHAPTER 47

GEOGRAPHY OF THE ISLAND OF PATMOS

Rev 1:9

Mark Wilson

KEY POINTS

- Patmos is a volcanic island located off the western coast of Asia Minor.
- The island was a colony of Miletus with a defensive fortress at Castelli.
- The Romans exiled political prisoners to islands in the Aegean Sea.
- Artemis Patmia was its patron goddess whose temple once stood at the site of the monastery at Chora.
- The cave in which John traditionally received his visions continues to function as an Orthodox church.
- Patmos' insularity surrounded by the sea influenced John's apocalyptic visions.

GEOGRAPHICAL SITUATION

Patmos is a volcanic island in the Icarian Sea, a subdivision of the Aegean, and one of the most northern of a chain of twelve Greek islands called the Dodecanese. Strabo (*Geography* 10.5.13) situates it among the islands of Leros, Icaria, and the Corassia. The island is shaped like a seahorse facing right. It has an area of 13.15 square miles (34.05 km^2) and an irregular shoreline of bays and promontories measuring about 37 miles (60 km). Pliny the Elder estimated less: "Patmos is thirty miles [48.3 km] in circumference" (*Natural History* 4.23 [LCL]). At its farthest point north to south the island extends about 8 miles (13 km). Patmos is divided into three sections connected by two low, narrow isthmuses. The northern section is the largest and broadest, spanning 3.5 miles (5.6 km) from Cape Zouloufi to Cape Geranos. The northern isthmus, just above Skala, measures 1230 feet (375 m) across. The southern isthmus at Diakofti is 1007 feet (307 m) across. The island's highest point is the peak, Profitis Ilias, at 883 feet (269 m).[1]

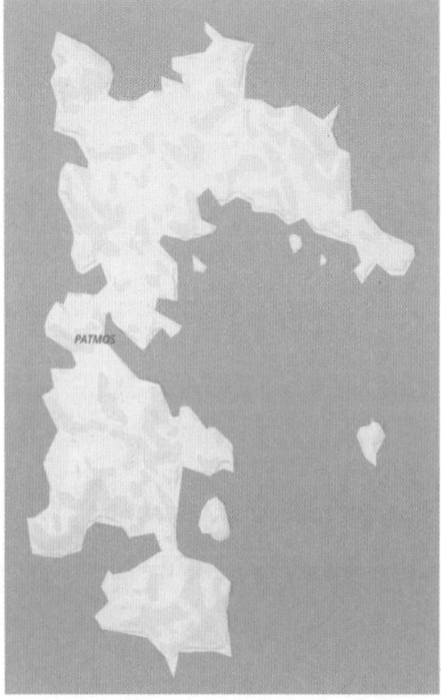

The island of Patmos resembles a seahorse facing right.

Five small islets surround Patmos: Hiliomodi, Saint Thecla, Saint George, Tragonisi, and Prasonisi. Some twenty-five islands and islets are within visual distance of Patmos. Samos looms twenty-two miles (35 km) to the north-northeast. Asia Minor (modern Turkey)—particularly Mount Mycale (Dilek Dağı; 4058 feet [1237 m])—is visible thirty miles (49 km) to the northeast.[2] This fact is existentially significant because John could have seen the land of the Seven Churches from Patmos (see map on page 630). When Paul sailed southward along the western coast of Asia Minor on his second and third journeys (Acts 18:21; 20:15; 21:1), Patmos would be barely discernible on the western horizon.

SETTLEMENT AND POLITICAL SITUATION IN ANTIQUITY

Pottery sherds found around Patmos indicate settlements in the Middle Bronze Age and Mycenean period, while sherds found at the base of Castelli Fortress date to the Late Geometric, Classical, and Hellenistic periods. Phora (modern Skala) in the bay of Panormos developed as the island's port.[3] Few historical sources mention the island. Thucydides (*History* 3.33) mentions that in 427 BC the Athenian general Paches pursued the Spartan fleet under Alcidas as far as Patmos, a natural development since the Spartans were using Miletus and its colonies as a base (*History* 8.79–80).

Anaximenes of Lampsacus, according to Strabo (*Geography* 14.1.6), stated that Leros and Ikaros were colonized by the city of Miletus. Since these islands frame Patmos on the southeast and northwest respectively, Patmos likely also came within the orbit of Miletus. Vanessa Gorman writes, "Most scholars presume that the Milesian influence on the islands—at least on Leros, Lepsia, Patmos,

1. A detailed and scalable map of the island is published online at: http://ontheworldmap.com/greece/islands/patmos/patmos-tourist-map.jpg. It gives the altitude of Profitis Ilias as 896 feet (273 m), apparently adding the monastery's height to the measurement.

2. At the western tip of the Mycale peninsula was the anchorage Trogyllium where Paul's ship was becalmed on his third journey, according to Codex Bezae (Acts 20:15 KJV, NKJV).

3. Phora is shown on map 61 in *BAGRW*.

View eastward from Patmos, Asia Minor is visible in the distance.

and probably on Ikaros as well—must have begun in the late seventh century."[4] Patmos formed part of a second line of islands comprising Miletus' commercial sphere. These Milesian islands shared several common characteristics: "a minimal amount of arable land; in general, they are small, rocky, and undesirable except so far as they facilitated maritime trade."[5] Patmos also played a critical defensive role in protecting Miletus' commercial routes. With Leros and Lepsi, Patmos was a *phrourion* (φρούριον, "military fortress"). Milesian veterans formed an important population within the colony. The island was governed by a phrourarch (φρούραρχος, *phrourarchos*) who served as the commanding officer of the garrison. The island's social, political, and economic life was thus oriented to Miletus for centuries.[6] Pirates were an ongoing menace to these islands. Julius Caesar was kidnapped by Cilician pirates in 75 BC and held on nearby Pharmakonisi for thirty-eight days. After a ransom of fifty talents of silver was paid, Caesar gathered a force at Miletus, captured the pirates, and had them crucified in Pergamum (Plutarch, *Julius Caesar* 2.1–7).

Preserved on the Castelli acropolis are sections of a fortification wall, gate with steps, and three towers built in isodomic style and dating probably to the third century BC. Above the modern church of Saints Constantine and Helena is the northwest tower still standing to eleven and a half feet (3.5 m). Castelli holds a commanding position that overlooks three bays: Skala to the east, Chochlaka to the south, and Merika to the northeast. In 129 BC the Romans gained the former Attalid kingdom and formed the province of Asia. Magie writes, "The new 'Asia,' therefore, extended from the Propontis

4. Vanessa B. Gorman, *Miletus: The Ornament of Ionia* (Ann Arbor: University of Michigan Press, 2001), 50.

5. Gorman, *Miletus*, 49.

6. Grüll Tibor, *Patmiaka: Two Studies on Patmos* (Budapest: Eötvös, 1989), 3.

on the north to the gulf of Cos on the south and included the islands along the coast, which must inevitably have been in close economic connection with the mainland."[7] During the struggle between Marc Antony and Octavian a century later, Patmos undoubtedly served as a base for Antony, as did all of Asia. With the inauguration of the Principate under Augustus in 27 BC and the resulting Pax Romana, the defensive importance of Castelli was reduced. From the Late Republic, Miletus served as the conventus of one of Asia's thirteen administrative districts. An inscription dating to the Flavian period found in Ephesus identifies only five cities attached to Miletus, however, none are on its offshore islands.[8] Since these never gained the status of a *polis* (πόλις, "city"), this omission is expected. The governor conducted a court session (assize) annually in Miletus so it remained a prosperous city.[9] Since Patmos' mainland connection continued through Miletus, its political and economic fortunes also affected the island's residents.

Skala Harbor and the Castelli Acropolis

RELIGIOUS SITUATION

Several religious sanctuaries were significant on Patmos. At Grikos Bay is a rocky promontory called Petra of Kallikatsou. Featuring rock-cut steps, artificial caves for offerings, and cisterns to provide water for sacred ceremonies, the rock functioned as an outdoor sanctuary beginning in the seventeenth century BC. The temple was probably dedicated to Aphrodite. In the Christian period its cavities were used as hermitages from the seventh to the fourteenth centuries.

The anonymous author of the Stadiasmus Maris Magni (#283) mentions an Amazon sanctuary on the island and notes it was 200 stadia (twenty-three miles [37 km]) from the Parthenion of Leros. Where this Amazonian was located is debatable. It has been localized either on Patmos' northwestern tip or near its southern promontory at

Skala

7. David Magie, *Roman Rule in Asia Minor* (Princeton: Princeton University Press, 1950), 1:155.

8. Christian Habicht, "New Evidence on the Province of Asia," *Journal of Roman Studies* 65 (1975): 77.

9. For a full discussion of Asia's conventus lists, see Habicht, "New Evidence," 69–71. Four of the seven churches—Ephesus, Smyrna, Pergamum, and Sardis—were conventus cities.

Cape Vitsilia.[10] The temple of Artemis Parthenos is located at Partheni Bay on northern Leros. From here, a direct sail to Patmos' southern tip is too short to fit the distance in the Stadiasmus, thus suggesting that the Amazonian is better localized on the northwestern coast.

Artemis Patmia was the patron goddess of the island. An inscription found at her temple site (the monastery's location) describes the cult's origin and practice on "the loveliest island of the daughter of Leto."[11] It mentions a foundation myth that Artemis was brought from Scythia by Orestes, the son of Agamemnon, to remove his terrible madness that resulted from the murder of his mother. The Patmian version of the Orestes myth differs from that of Euripides: Orestes overcame his crime by recovering a sacred statue of Artemis in Tauria believed to have fallen from heaven. Boxall concludes, "The Patmos inscription apparently claims that this sacred statue was brought, not to Athens, but to Artemis' own island of Patmos."[12]

The inscription also names Vera, a maiden priestess appointed by the Virgin Huntress herself. She was born on Patmos but raised on Artis (Argos?) and crossed the stormy Aegean to return home to sacrifice goats on the altar of Artemis Patmia. After this she organized a festive celebration and banquet. She also held the honorific title of *hydrophoros* (ὑδροφόρος, "water-bearer"), one fre-

Artemis Temple Inscription

quently found on inscriptions of Miletus and Didyma. An inscription found at the latter's Apollo temple mentions another *hydrophoros* of Artemis Patmia, Aurelia Dionysiodora Matrona (*IDidyma* 492). This office fell to the daughters of the richest families since it entailed many expenses related to the numerous liturgical duties of her annual appointment. One particular duty of the *hydrophoros*

10. Northwestern tip: Johanna Schmidt, "Patmos," in *Paulys Realencyclopädie der klassischen Altertumswissenschaft*, ed. A. Pauly et al. (Waldsee: Druckenmüller, 1949); also *BAGRW*, map 61; southern promontory: Adrienne Mayor, *The Amazons: Lives and Legends of Amazon Warriors across the Ancient World* (Princeton: Princeton University Press, 2014), 308.

11. The inscription (Syll.^{3} 11.52) dates to the third/fourth century AD and is now displayed in the monastery's museum. For a recent reconstruction and interpretation of this lacunose text, see Tibor, *Patmiaka*, 3–6, and H. W. Pleket and R. S. Stroud, "Patmos: Epigram for Versa, Hydrophoros of Artemis Patmia, 3rd/4th cent. A.D.," *SEG* 39:261–62, no. 855.

12. Ian Boxall, *Patmos in the Reception History of the Apocalypse* (Oxford: Oxford University Press, 2013), 233. Boxall is reflecting the discussion of Victor Guérin, Description de l'ile de Patmos et de l'ile de Samos (Paris: Durand, 1856), 17–18, 59.

was to draw water from a sacred spring and pour it on the altar of Artemis.[13]

PATMOS AS A PLACE OF EXILE

In Revelation 1:9 John identifies his place of writing as the "island [*nēsos*, νῆσος] called Patmos." The reason for his presence there is given next: "because of the word of God and the testimony of Jesus Christ." This catchphrase is used in Revelation 6:9 and 20:4 as the reason for the martyrdom of the saints. In the first century AD the Romans often used Aegean islands to exile political prisoners. Among them were Cos, Rhodes, Samos, and Lesbos (Cassius Dio 56.27.1), Gyaros and Andros (Philo, *Flaccus* 1.51, 157, 159), Cynthos/Delos (Tacitus, *Annales* 3:69), and Amorgos and Donousa (Tacitus, *Annales* 4.13, 30; cf. 15:71).[14] There were two types of exiles. First, *deportatio in insulam* was ordered only by the emperor and pronounced against important citizens who fell into disfavor. This banishment was permanent with the guilty losing their civil rights and property. Second, *relegatio ad insulam* could be imposed by a provincial governor, either temporarily or permanently. No loss of Roman citizenship or property need result. John's exile to Patmos was probably the latter, since church tradition suggests that he was later released to return to Ephesus (Eusebius, *Church History* 3.23). John was not sent to Samos, the island nearest to Ephesus, neither was he banished to a more barren island like Gyaros. Instead he was sent to a semi-remote but inhabited island. Even though Patmos was connected to Miletus, John was apparently sent directly from the provincial capital Ephesus since Miletus is not among the seven churches. Church tradition places his exile during the reign of the emperor Domitian and release after his death (e.g., Eusebius, *Church History* 3.20.11; 3.23.1, 6). Because no persecution of Christians under Domitian is recorded by Roman historians, an alternate scenario situates John's exile after Nero's suicide in AD 68 and his release after the fall of Jerusalem in AD 70.[15] The myth of Nero *redivivus* reflected in Revelation 13:3 and 17:8 gen-

Cape Zouloufi

13. For a full discussion of the *hydrophoros* and her duties, see Tibor, *Patmiaka*, 7–9.

14. For more on these banishments see Brian Rapske, "Exiles, Islands, and the Identity and Perspective of John in Revelation," in *Christian Origins and Greco-Roman Culture and Literary Context for the New Testament*, ed. Stanley E. Porter and Andrew W. Pitts (Leiden: Brill, 2012), 326–27.

15. Mark Wilson, "The Early Christians in Ephesus and the Date of Revelation, Again," *Neotestamentica* 39 (2005): 186–89.

Mosaic of John and Prochorus on Patmos

erated its first pretender who appeared on the island of Cynthos/Delos in AD 69.[16] The governor of Galatia, Calpurnius Asprenas, executed him and had his corpse brought to Ephesus where it was displayed publicly (Tacitus, *Histories* 2.8).

John's insularity for an indeterminate period appears to influence the imagery found in his vision.[17] Surrounded by water during his exile, the sea (*thalassa*, θάλασσα) is a dominant image in Revelation with twenty-six references. For John, sea is a symbol of heavenly splendor (4:6; 15:2), God's creation (5:13; 10:6), place of judgment (7:1–3; 8:8–9), abode of the first beast (13:1), domain of commerce (18:17, 19), holding place for souls (20:13), and absent in the new heaven and earth (21:1). Islands are mentioned at the opening of the sixth seal (6:14), and at the outpouring of the seventh bowl every island will disappear (16:20). Franz suggested that John was standing on the sand (*ammos*, ἄμμος) at Psili Ammos when he saw the vision of chapter 13.[18] However, this beach's remote location on the rugged southwest coast

16. For a map showing the "Myth of Nero Redividus or Nero Redux," see Mark Wilson, *Charts on the Book of Revelation: Literary, Historical, and Theological Perspectives* (Grand Rapids: Kregel, 2007), 116, no. 77.

17. The issues concerning the connectivity and insularity of Mediterranean islands through various periods has been a topic of recent scholarly discussion; see, e.g., the ten articles in Anna Kouremenos, ed. *Insularity and Identity in the Roman Mediterranean* (Oxford: Oxbow, 2018).

18. Gordon Franz, "The King and I: Exiled to Patmos, Part 2," http://www.biblearchaeology.org/post/2010/01/28/The-King-and-I-Exiled-To-Patmos-Part-2.aspx.

A variant reading reflected in the KJV and NKJV has John standing on the sandy beach, not the beast.

Cave of the Apocalypse Interior

makes it unlikely that John would have walked there.

PATMOS IN LATER HISTORY

An apocryphal document called the Acts of John attributed to Prochorus probably originated in Patmos and dates to the fifth or sixth century AD. It recounts the writing of Prochorus, a deacon at Jerusalem (Acts 6:5). This text preserves extracts from the original Acts of John, a document deemed heretical by the church fathers (e.g., Eusebius, *Church History* 3.25.6). The story opens with John being directed in a vision to go to Ephesus from Miletus (18). The previous chapters 14–17, now missing, have been reconstructed to depict the departure of John and Prochorus from Patmos after the death of a Roman emperor unnamed but presumed to be Domitian. The two make their way to Miletus by hanging onto a piece of cork oak.[19] Other miracles performed by John on Patmos are recounted in the apocryphal Acts, scenes of which "adorn the exonarthex of monastery's catholicon."[20] The tradition regarding Prochorus remains entrenched on the island, and Orthodox icons depict John dictating his visions to his amanuensis. There are a number of caves on the island in which John could have sought shelter. However, the Cave of the Apocalypse is conveniently situated just below the road, still in use, that ran uphill from the harbor to the Artemis temple. In Late Antiquity this cave became a place of Christian pilgrimage. The Chapel of St. Anne, built around the cave's entrance in the eleventh century, honored the mother of emperor Alexius I Comnenos. This cave sanctuary continues to function as a Greek Orthodox church. In 1088 the monastery at Chora was founded by a monk named Christodoulos who received permission from the emperor. When Comnenos sent Nikolas Tzanzes to the island in August of that year, he saw a chapel honoring John the Theologos standing on the hill where the monastery was soon built.[21]

The earliest basilicas on the island date to the fifth to sixth centuries AD. North of the Skala port and opposite the chapel of Hagios Theologos are scant remains of a Roman structure that, according to local tradition, comprise the baptismal font used by John. Since Patmos was inhabited in John's day, no reason exists to pre-

19. J. K. Elliott, "The Acts of John," in *The Apocryphal New Testament* (Oxford: Clarendon, 1993), 311–47; István Czachesz, *Commission Narratives: A Comparative Study of the Canonical and Apocryphal Acts of the Apostles* (Leuven: Peeters, 2007), 93, 96.

20. Otto F. A. Meinardus, "The Christian Remains of the Seven Churches of the Apocalypse," *BA* 37 (1974): 70.

21. Tibor, *Patmiaka*, 7.

Monastery of St. John the Theologos

clude converts being made during his exile. Joseph Georgirenes, the archbishop of Samos, visited the island in 1677 and reported that the town near Skala was deserted. He was shown among the old ruins "a church yet standing which they say was built in St. John's day and they show something like a pulpit, where they say St. John used to preach."[22] In 1896 the American explorer William Geil visited Patmos. His two maps of Patmos with its two main ports provide important cartographic information for the time. Similarly, his twenty-seven photographs provide visual documentation of its landscape and life in the late nineteenth century. Geil writes, "Standing on some one of the seven mountains of Patmos and looking off over the island with its three hundred and sixty-four churches, one is impressed with the absence of steeples, there being not a single turret or spire on the crescent island."[23] In 1999 UNESCO declared the Monastery of Saint John the Theologian and the Cave of the Apocalypse as World Heritage Sites. In the monastery's museum is displayed Comnenos' foundation chrysobull, a phrourarch inscription from the first century BC, and several ancient manuscripts including a sixth-century vellum copy of Mark's Gospel. Patmos remains the "Holy Island" not only for Greeks but also for Christians around the world.

BIBLIOGRAPHY

Boxall, Ian. *Patmos in the Reception History of the Apocalypse*. Oxford: Oxford University Press, 2011.

22. Joseph Georgirenes, *A Description of the Present of Samos, Nicaria, Patmos and Mount Athos*, (London: Pitt, 1678), 77.

23. William Edgar Geil, *The Island that is Called Patmos* (Philadelphia: Rowland, 1896), 113.

Czachesz, István. *Commission Narratives: A Comparative Study of the Canonical and Apocryphal Acts of the Apostles*. Leuven: Peeters, 2007.

Elliott, J. Keith. "The Acts of John." In *The Apocryphal New Testament: A Collection of Apocryphal Christian Literature in an English Translation*. Oxford: Clarendon, 1993.

Franz, Gordon, "The King and I: Exiled to Patmos, Part 2," http://www.biblearchaeology.org/post/2010/01/28/The-King-and-I-Exiled-To-Patmos-Part-2.aspx.

Geil, William Edgar. *The Island That is Called Patmos*. Philadelphia: Rowland, 1896.

Georgirenes, Joseph. *A Description of the Present of Samos, Nicaria, Patmos and Mount Athos*. London: Pitt, 1678.

Guérin, Victor. Description de l'ile de Patmos et de l'ile de Samos. Paris: Durand, 1856.

Gorman, Vanessa B. *Miletus: The Ornament of Ionia*. Ann Arbor: University of Michigan Press, 2001.

Habicht, Christian. "New Evidence on the Province of Asia." *Journal of Roman Studies* 65 (1975): 64–91.

Kouremenos, Anna, ed. *Insularity and Identity in the Roman Mediterranean*. Oxford: Oxbow, 2018.

Magie, David. *Roman Rule in Asia Minor*. 2 vols. Princeton: Princeton University Press, 1950.

Mayor, Adrienne. *The Amazons: Lives and Legends of Amazon Warriors across the Ancient World*. Princeton: Princeton University Press, 2014.

Meinardus, Otto F. A. "The Christian Remains of the Seven Churches of the Apocalypse." *BA* 37.3 (1974): 69–82.

Pleket, H. W. and R. S. Stroud, "Patmos: Epigram for Versa, Hydrophoros of Artemis Patmia, 3rd/4th Cent. A.D." *SEG* 39:261–62, no. 855.

Rapske, Brian. "Exiles, Islands, and the Identity and Perspective of John in Revelation." Pages 311–46 in *Christian Origins and Greco-Roman Culture and Literary Context for the New Testament*. Edited by Stanley E. Porter and Andrew W. Pitts. Leiden: Brill, 2012.

Schmidt, Johanna. "Patmos." Pages 2174–91 in volume 18 of *Paulys Realencyclopädie der klassischen Altertumswissenschaft*. Edited by A. Pauly et al. Waldsee: Druckenmüller, 1949.

Tibor, Grüll. *Patmiaka: Two Studies on Patmos*. Budapest: Eötvös, 1989.

Wilson, Mark. *Charts on the Book of Revelation: Literary, Historical, and Theological Perspectives*. Grand Rapids: Kregel, 2007.

———. "The Early Christians in Ephesus and the Date of Revelation, Again." *Neotestamentica* 39 (2005): 163–93.

CHAPTER 48

THE SOCIAL AND GEOGRAPHICAL WORLD OF SMYRNA

Rev 1:11; 2:8–11

David A. deSilva

KEY POINTS

- Smyrna, as it was known in the Roman period, was founded under Alexander the Great and his successors, who established the new city as a thriving commercial port.
- Smyrna had a long history of pro-Roman sentiments, building a temple to Roma even while the Seleucid Empire was at its peak and expanding fast in their direction.
- The city showed its devotion through significant involvement in promoting the imperial cult, which was likely a source of stress for Christians in the city.
- Archaeology has not shed light on the role that the Jewish community played in the harassment that the early Christians addressed by John were experiencing or would soon experience.

SMYRNA AND THE BIBLICAL STORY

Smyrna appears only once in the biblical story, as the location of one of the seven congregations addressed by the glorified Christ in the book of Revelation (see Rev 1:11; 2:8–11). The origins of the Christian community or communities there are unknown. We know that one of Paul's associates—Epaphras—took the gospel to Colossae, Laodicea, and Hierapolis, perhaps while Paul was working in the ministry hub of Ephesus (Col 1:7–8; 4:13). It is quite possible that the Christian movement got its start in Smyrna during the same period, all the more as Smyrna was a more important city, and far closer to Ephesus, than any of those cities where Epaphras was known to have taken the gospel.

THE POLITICS OF SMYRNA IN TIME AND SPACE

Although Smyrna has a long history even before the classical age of Greece, the history of the Smyrna that was home to the Christians addressed by Revelation began after Alexander the Great's rise to power. The old city had been built around a defensible peak two miles (3.2 km) distant from the shoreline, thriving until it was destroyed by the Lydian kingdom around 600 BC.[1] The area became little more than a cluster of villages until Alexander and his successors reestablished the city, this time at a small distance removed from the original site (Pausanias, *Description of Greece* 7.5.1–3; Strabo, *Geography* 14.1.37). The new city would not sit on the fortified hill but by the shore, so that it could enjoy the benefits of a natural harbor at the coast. While it would be significantly eclipsed in maritime trade by Ephesus, the harbor remained a great asset and kept Smyrna firmly on the commercial map. The original harbor has since been overbuilt and buried beneath the modern city, with the result that the modern shoreline is now further west and bears no resemblance to its ancient counterpart.

Perhaps because it was a port city and enjoyed trading connections with the west, Smyrna looked more to Rome than to the Greek empires in the east. The city had already built a temple to honor *Rōma*, the deified personification of the city of Rome, in 195 BC—long before it was popular to do so in the region.[2] In 195 BC, the Seleucid kingdom under Antiochus III was at its greatest strength, and Antiochus was keen on establishing his hold over all of Asia Minor. The city of Carthage in North Africa was still a great power in the west and a significant threat

1. Colin J. Hemer, *The Letters to the Seven Churches of Asia in Their Local Setting* (Sheffield: JSOT Press, 1986; repr., Grand Rapids: Eerdmans, 2001), 60–61.

2. Tacitus, *Annales* 4.56; Hemer, *Letters to the Seven Churches*, 70–71.

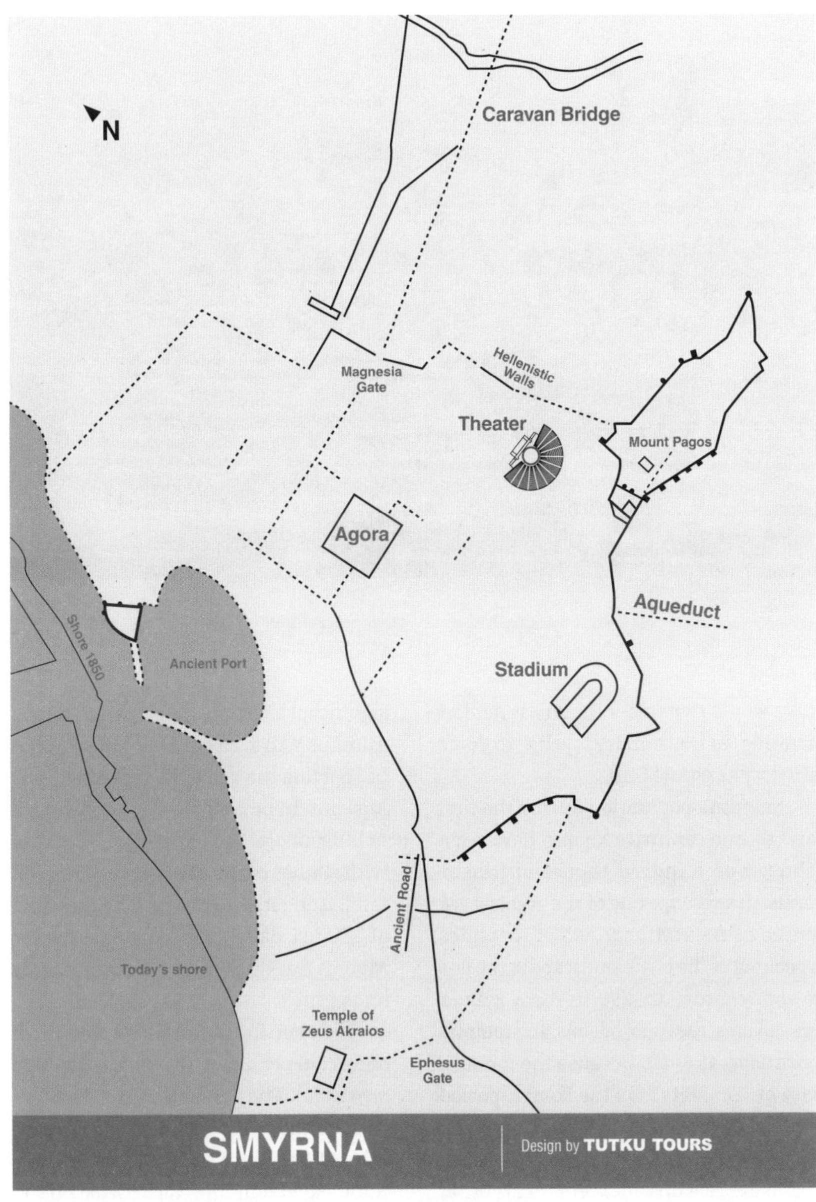

to Rome's power in the Mediterranean. The outcome of their struggle was still uncertain. Smyrna's declaration of its loyalty to the rising power in the west as opposed to the established Greco-Syrian kingdom to the east was a sign of extraordinary faith in Rome and her destiny. This loyalty would be long-remembered. In the first century BC, the Roman senator Cicero spoke of Smyrna as "among our most faithful and most ancient allies" (*Philippics* 11.2.5[LCL]);

Agora Western Stoa Basement

Livy would remember the city as demonstrating "extraordinary loyalty" to Rome (*History* 38.39.11[LCL]).

Smyrna's population during the first and second centuries AD may have risen above one hundred thousand inhabitants.[3] It was once one of the great Greek cities of Asia Minor. Aelius Aristides, speaking of the city's landscape in the late second century AD, lists its many gymnasia, forums, theaters, odeons, and temples (*Orationes* 17.8–11). Because the modern city of İzmir sits atop the Roman-period city of Smyrna, very little of the ancient city has been excavated. Today, the most extensive remains uncovered are those of the state agora, or civic forum. The city had been devastated by an earthquake in 178 AD, with the result that the older forum had to be rebuilt under, and with significant aid from, the emperor Marcus Aurelius.[4] An arch still bears the portrait of Faustina the Younger, wife of Marcus Aurelius, in honor of the imperial household's support. The agora was once graced with statues of members of the imperial family; one statue base bearing the name of "Fadilla, daughter of Augustus Caesar Marcus Aurelius Antoninus" still stands on the site.

The civic forum was built around an open court of about 400 by 260 feet (122 x 79.25 m). The east and west sides were lined with two-story, colonnaded porticoes. On the north side stood a two-story colonnaded building constructed on the pattern of a basilica (essentially three long, covered aisles, with the central aisle—the nave—being wider and taller than the two outside aisles), running the length of the

3. Mark Wilson, *Biblical Turkey: A Guide to the Jewish and Christian Sites of Asia Minor* (Istanbul: Ege Yayınları, 2010), 310.

4. Willson, *Biblical Turkey*, 313.

Agora Basilica Basement

forum and sporting a depth of about 90 feet (27.5 m). The basilica was erected over a foundation of an arched, vaulted basement. This basement served as a shopping arcade, which could be entered from the main road behind the forum so as to preserve the decorum of the basilica and civic areas above. An altar to Zeus once stood in the center of the forum, a reminder of the watchful care of the gods and the obligations of the city to its protectors. Part of the facade of this monument now stands in the History and Art Museum in İzmir. It shows, in deep relief and in figures significantly larger than life-size, Poseidon, seated, with Demeter and Artemis standing beside him.

Literary references suggest that there were also two prominent temples in the city marking the uppermost and lowermost ends of a road known as "The Golden Way"—a temple to Zeus and a temple to Cybele, the Phrygian mother goddess and a kind of patron goddess of Smyrna, to judge from coins minted in the city. Smyrna also had a cult of Dionysus, judging from a local inscription recording that a certain Dionysicles, son of Metrodoros, began to serve as priest of Dionysus during the presidency of a certain Alexander.[5]

New Smyrna was well supplied with water, brought by aqueducts to vast cisterns located on the hill above the city and distributed thence to public and private sites throughout the city. A large theater was carved into the side of the hill overlooking the city and its harbor.

5. Craig R. Koester, *Revelation: A New Translation with Introduction and Commentary* (New Haven: Yale University Press, 2014), 272; see also Aelius Aristides, *Orationes* 20.20, 23.

While this is now the site of a sprawling residential area that prevents excavation, a few rows of seats are still visible between the houses. Some of the more ornate seats reserved for dignitaries have also been recovered. The platform of the stage building has also been recently excavated. It is thought that the theater was once able to accommodate sixteen thousand spectators. The ancient stadium has also been located on an artificially leveled area of the hill descending from Mount Pagus.

Like Ephesus and Pergamum, its sister cities with whom it engaged in an ongoing sibling rivalry, Smyrna showed significant devotion to the Roman emperors in the form of worship known as the imperial cult. This is not at all surprising for a city that prided itself on its particular loyalty to Rome and, therefore, to Rome's rulers. It would also make the question of loyalty—of "faithfulness unto death"—a principal issue for the Christians living within its jurisdiction, as they would come more and more to be forced to choose between loyalty to Caesar and loyalty to Christ.

By the early decades of the third century AD, Smyrna had been awarded the honor of being named νεωκόρος (*neōkoros*) or "temple warden" of a provincial imperial cult site, three times. The city was eager to publicize the fact, as a popular coin minting featuring the three imperial temples on its reverse demonstrates (see image on page 707). Smyrna had won her first neokorate in AD 26, when she successfully petitioned the Senate for the honor of erecting a temple and establishing a cult for Tiberius, his mother Livia, and the Senate of Rome, beating out ten rival cities for the award (Tacitus, *Annales* 4.55–56).[6] The city received a second neokorate in connection with a new temple to Hadrian, emperor from 118 to 137 AD.[7] Smyrna's exuberance for this emperor is evident from the titles used to describe him in an inscription, found in the civic forum: "The emperor Trajan Hadrian Caesar Augustus, Olympius, Savior, and Founder." The title "Olympius" equated Hadrian with the god Zeus; the title "founder" attributed to Hadrian a new beginning, a new era, for Smyrna; the title "savior," of course, refers to Hadrian as the city's deliverer using language that was already becoming prominent also in Christian circles to speak of Jesus' accomplishments and significance. Smyrna would win a third

Agora Inscription Naming Hadrian as Olympius and Savior

6. S. R. F. Price, *Rituals and Power: The Roman Imperial Cult in Asia Minor* (Cambridge: Cambridge University Press, 1984), 64–65, 258.

7. Price, *Rituals and Power*, 67, 258.

neokorate with its successful bid to build a temple to Caracalla, the son of and successor to Septimius Severus, in the early third century.[8]

Several inscriptions found in the civic forum attest to the prominence of the imperial cult and its priests in this city. One inscription, in which Smyrna boasts of its greatness in the midst of other cities of Asia on account of its having received the honor of a neokorate three times, honors a certain Julius Menecles Diophantus, the chief priest of the imperial cult, for gladiatorial games that he provided for five days at his own expense. Another inscription graced the base of a statue of Claudius Aristophanes Aurelianus, a chief priest of the imperial cult prior to the city's third neokorate.

The piecemeal efforts at archaeology in İzmir have yet to uncover evidence of the Jewish community that figures so prominently in the glorified Christ's oracle to the Christians in Smyrna (Rev 2:8–11). Inscriptional evidence is also largely lacking until the second century AD. Nevertheless, it seems quite plausible that Smyrna enjoyed the same organized Jewish presence that many of her sister cities did throughout the early Roman period.

THE CHURCH IN SMYRNA

In the middle of the second century, Smyrna would become the scene of a great drama of faith as Polycarp, the elderly bishop of the Christian congregation there, was brought to trial in the arena before the provincial governor. The governor might not have known the details of Christian faith and practice, but he knew that it drew people away from giving the gods—including the emperors—their due, and that this Christ and his kingdom was a rival to Rome and her emperors. This could not be tolerated in the city of Rome's "oldest and most faithful allies." The governor therefore gave Polycarp an ultimatum:

Inscription Honoring a "Temple Warden of the Emperors"

"Swear by Caesar's fortune; change your mind; say, 'Away with the atheists'," or face death in the stadium (Martyrdom of Polycarp 9.2).[9] The local police chief urged the old man, "What harm is it to say 'Caesar is Lord' and to offer a sacrifice?" (Martyrdom of Polycarp 8.2). But Polycarp could not bring himself to show disloyalty to so great a benefactor as

8. Price, *Rituals and Power*, 258.

9. Translations from the Martyrdom of Polycarp are the author's own.

Wreaths on Grave Stele

Jesus: "For eighty-six years I have served him, and he has wronged me in no way. How, then, can I revile my king, who rescued me?" (Martyrdom of Polycarp 9.3). As a result, the elderly bishop was burnt at the stake and, when the fires failed to do the job, stabbed to death.

Issues of loyalty to the emperor and the traditional gods were a major factor in the growing tension between Christians and the civic authorities throughout Asia Minor and its surrounding provinces—witness the famous correspondence between Pliny the Younger, governor of Bithynia and Pontus, and the emperor Trajan from about 110 AD (Pliny, *Epistulae* 10.96–97). It is likely that these would have been at the fore of the trials that the glorified Christ predicted for the near future of the Christians in late first-century Smyrna.

John called the Christians in Smyrna, as in the other six cities he addressed, to take up a position of no compromise with the domination system of Rome, with its self-glorifying and self-deifying claims. Under the coercive pressure of being thrown into prison, the glorified Christ urges his followers not to yield to the demands to prove themselves loyal subjects of Rome and her emperor, but rather loyal subjects of God and his Messiah: "Be faithful to the point of death, and I will give you the crown of life." The "crown," better visualized here as a "wreath," was a familiar image in Smyrna and throughout the Greco-Roman world. It was given to the winning athlete; it adorned the military conqueror. It also showed up in funerary settings, as the bodies of the deceased were frequently adorned with gold-leaf wreaths even as their grave steles often sported wreaths in carved relief. Such wreaths were testimonies to a life well-lived, the value and virtue of which were sealed by death, not ended by it. Whichever of these backgrounds John had in mind, his message is clear: dying for loyalty to Jesus did not mark one as a deviant or as a loser, but rather as a winner, a conqueror, a person who lived and died virtuously, and who would continue to live and enjoy honor in the greater empire of God.

BIBLIOGRAPHY

Ascough, Richard S., ed. *Religious Rivalries and the Struggle for Success in Sardis and Smyrna*. Waterloo, ON: Wilfrid Laurier University Press, 2005.

Bagnall, Roger S., Burak Yolaçan, Roberta Casagrande-Kim, Akin Ersoy, and Cumhur Tanriver, eds. *Graffiti from the Basilica in the Agora of Smyrna*. New York: New York University Press, 2016.

Fairchild, Mark R. *Christian Origins in Ephesus and Asia Minor*. Istanbul: Arkeoloji ve Sanat Yayınları, 2015.

Hemer, Colin J. *The Letters to the Seven Churches of Asia in Their Local Setting*. Sheffield: JSOT Press, 1986. Repr., Grand Rapids: Eerdmans, 2001.

Koester, Craig R. *Revelation: A New Translation with Introduction and Commentary*. New Haven: Yale University Press, 2014.

Price, S. R. F. *Rituals and Power: The Roman Imperial Cult in Asia Minor*. Cambridge: Cambridge University Press, 1984.

Wilson, Mark. *Biblical Turkey: A Guide to the Jewish and Christian Sites of Asia Minor*. Istanbul: Ege Yayınları, 2010.

CHAPTER 49

THE SOCIAL AND GEOGRAPHICAL WORLD OF PERGAMUM

Rev 1:11; 2:12–17

David A. deSilva

KEY POINTS

- Pergamum was a hub of imperial cult in the province of Asia Minor, the site of the provincial temple of Roma and Augustus, authorized in 29 BC and inaugurated in 19 BC.
- Though some scholars associate the temple of Rome and Augustus with the "throne of Satan" (Rev 2:13), the distinctive altar of Zeus on the brow of the acropolis may have been more in John's view, given his equation of demons with the Greco-Roman gods and, therefore, Satan with their chief (see Rev 9:20–21).
- The popular support for the idolatrous rituals that pervaded Pergamene society, particularly for the imperial cult that had become such a source of civic identity and pride for the city, helps explain the motivation of the Christian teachers whom John calls "Nicolaitans" and followers of the teaching of "Balaam" to develop a theological rationalization for accommodation.
- Exploration of the temple of Sarapis revealed the ancient technology by means of which priests could make their idols seem to speak to the worshipers.
- Pergamum was incidentally the location where parchment appears to have been first developed and from which it continued to be exported throughout the Roman period.

Pergamum Acropolis

PERGAMUM IN THE BIBLICAL STORY

Pergamum appears only once in the New Testament Scriptures, the Christian congregation (or congregations) there being addressed by John in Revelation (Rev 1:11; 2:12–17; see map on page 630). In the oracle to this congregation, the glorified Christ speaks of Pergamum ominously as the location of "the throne of Satan" and the place "where Satan dwells" (Rev 2:13). Antagonism toward the Christian movement appears to have been particularly high there, resulting in the murder (whether as a result of official proceedings or back-alley action) of a Christian named Antipas.[1] An inner-Christian movement seeking to make room for some degree of participation in their neighbors' idolatrous rites appears to have gained a foothold in that environment (2:14–15). Nothing at all is known of the origins of the Christian community there. It is possible that members of Paul's team or of the congregations he planted in Ephesus, 110 miles (176 km) to the south, carried the gospel to other major cities in their province, as Epaphras had evangelized Colossae, Laodicea, and Hierapolis (Col 1:7–8; 4:12–13), but this is merely conjecture.

A Jewish community, at least one of small to moderate size, appears to have existed in Pergamum and might have provided the seedbed for the fledgling church there, as so frequently in the Mediterranean diaspora. The evidence for this Jewish community's existence is almost entirely literary. Josephus (*Ant.* 14.247–255) preserves a decree of the

1. On Antipas and persecution in the background of Revelation, see David deSilva, *Seeing Things John's Way: The Rhetoric of the Book of Revelation* Louisville: Westminster John Knox, 2009), 50–55; Roland H. Worth, *The Seven Cities of the Apocalypse and Roman Culture* (New York: Paulist, 1999), 112–30; Worth, *The Seven Cities of the Apocalypse and Greco-Asian Culture* (New York: Paulist, 1999), 124–25.

city council of Pergamum in favor of the Jewish people, essentially acknowledging and pledging support for the stipulations laid down by Rome concerning the Jewish state in Judea under John Hyrcanus I (high priest and head of state from 134–104 BC). The decree is quite vague and mentions nothing about a Jewish presence in Pergamum itself, but it seems highly likely that the Judean embassy would only have stopped in Pergamum on its way home to Judea from its audience with the Roman Senate because there was a Jewish community in the city that they wished to visit.[2]

In 59 BC, the governor of Asia, L. Valerius Flaccus, was accused of misappropriation of funds, including a large sum of money that had been collected by Jewish communities throughout the province for the purpose of supporting the Jerusalem temple (that is, the "temple tax" paid by adult male Jews throughout Israel and the diaspora). In the details of the charges, we learn that a small amount of the money in question had been appropriated from Jews in Pergamum, suggesting at least a small Jewish community resident in the city and its environs (Cicero, *Pro Flacco* 28:66–69). Flaccus appears not to have been guilty of misappropriation; rather, he was enforcing an earlier edict prohibiting the transport of gold out of the province. This, in turn, tells us something of the Jews of Asia Minor's devotion to the temple and to their fulfillment of their obligation that expressed their connection to the temple, since they were willing to defy a recent edict in order to continue their practice.[3]

Finally, we might mention one important second-century AD artifact that attests to a Jewish presence in Pergamum—a small altar or table bearing an inscription that seems most naturally to speak of the God of the Jews: "God, (the) Lord, the 'one who is' forever. Zopyros (dedicated) the altar/table and the lampstand with the lamp to the Lord."[4] The designation of God not with any known name of the Greek pantheon, but by the titles familiar from the Jewish Scriptures ("Lord," frequently; "the one who is," Exod 3:14), renders it highly likely that Zopyros was a devotee of the God of Israel (though his own ethnicity cannot be determined).

THE CITY OF PERGAMUM

Many of the monuments and inscriptions on hand to be seen even in first-century Roman Pergamum would have kept the residents mindful of the dynasty of the Attalid kings, close allies of Rome from their beginnings, that had ruled Pergamum prior to 133 BC. In the struggles between Alexander's offspring and generals following Alexander's death, Lysimachus, a former commander and close confidant of Alexander, gained control of western Asia, including Pergamum. He entrusted a great amount of his war chest to his friend and steward, Philetaerus, in the stronghold of Pergamum. Philetaerus served Lysimachus faithfully for two more decades but, in the ongoing strife between the successors, revolted against Lysimachus and allied himself with the Seleucid kings as their client. After his

2. Paul R. Trebilco, *Jewish Communities in Asia Minor* (Cambridge: Cambridge University Press, 2006), 7–8.

3. Trebilco, *Jewish Communities*, 14–16.

4. Trebilco, *Jewish Communities*, 163.

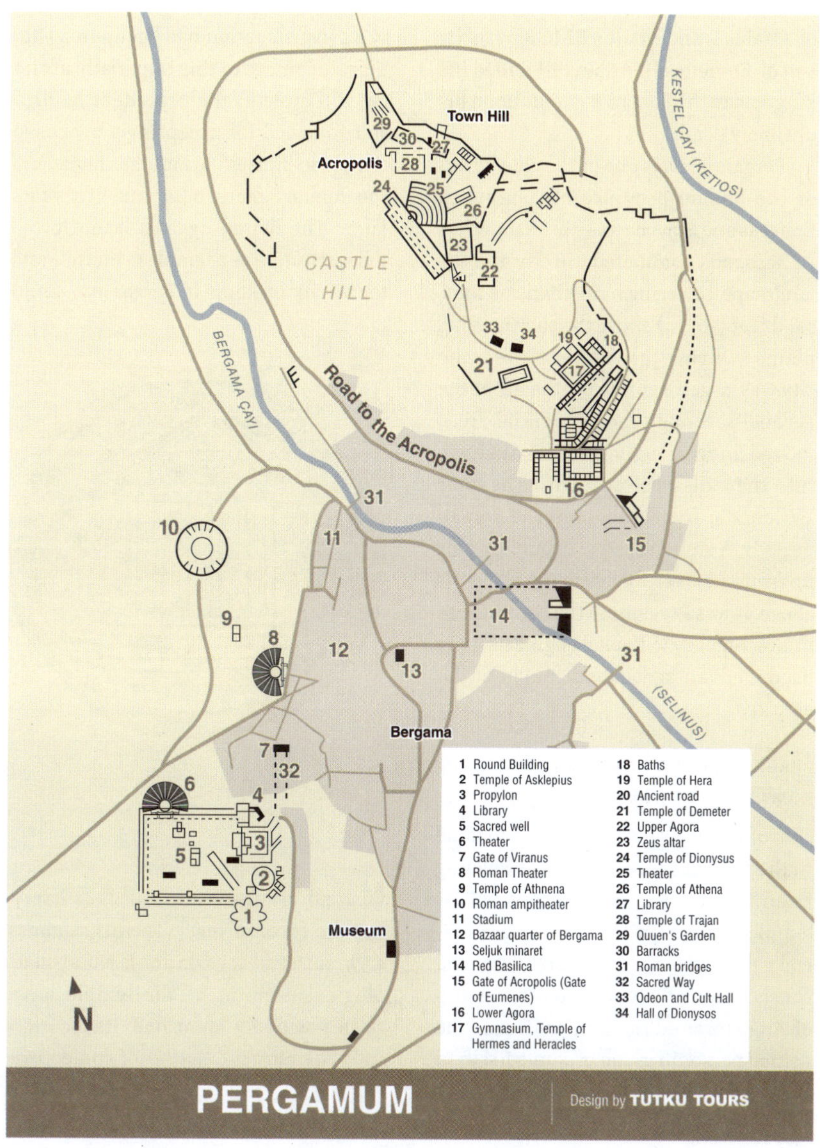

death, his nephew and heir, Eumenes I (263–241 BC), successfully broke away from the Seleucid overlords and established a kingdom of Pergamum, taking the title "king." He was followed, in turn, by Attalus I (241–197 BC), a nephew of Philetaerus by another brother, who protected Pergamene independence from both the ambitious Seleucids and the Galatians in central Anatolia; Eumenes II (197–159 BC), son of Attalus I, who was instrumental in leveraging Roman power against the Seleucid Antiochus III, destroying Seleucid ambitions of ever retaking Asia; Attalus II (159–138), the brother of Eumenes II and younger son of Attalus I; and Attalus III (138–133), the son of Eumenes II. Attalus III willed his kingdom to the Roman Republic upon his untimely death.[5]

Pergamum was one of the chief cities of the Roman province of Asia, with Ephesus and Smyrna as its primary rivals. Its acropolis dominated the city and the landscape, towering more than one thousand feet (305 m) above the surrounding plains.[6] During the Attalid period, the city was largely confined to the hill of the acropolis, though the residential areas moved increasingly and expansively into the valley below during the later Hellenistic and throughout the Roman periods. A siphon system brought water up from the rivers below to the acropolis above. It was Pergamum that introduced this technology to Roman engineers, who used it advantageously throughout the empire.[7]

PERGAMUM AND THE ROMAN IMPERIAL CULT

One of the city's greatest claims to fame in the province was the honor of having been named νεωκόρος (*neōkoros*) or "temple warden" of the provincial imperial cult in Asia for its construction and consecration of a temple to the worship of Augustus and the goddess Roma, the deified personification of Rome itself, in 19 BC (construction had begun in 29 BC). Tiberius refers to this imperially authorized temple as the precedent he himself followed for accepting a proposed temple to himself, his mother Livia, and the Roman Senate in Smyrna fifty years later: "The divine Augustus did not forbid the institution of a temple to himself and to the city of Rome in Pergamum, and I view all his deeds and words as carrying the force of law" (Tacitus, *Annales* 4.37, author's translation). No archaeological remains of the temple have been positively identified; its location in Pergamum is a matter of conjecture,

Coin of Pergamum with Temple to Augustus

5. Strabo, *Geography* 13.4.1–2; Colin J. Hemer, *The Letters to the Seven Churches of Asia in Their Local Setting* (Sheffield: JSOT Press, 1986; repr., Grand Rapids: Eerdmans, 2001), 79–81. A fuller account of the Attalid kingdom of Pergamum can be found in *Cambridge Ancient History*, ed. F. W. Walbank et al., 2nd ed. (Cambridge: Cambridge University Press, 1970–2005), 7.1:426–32; 8:324–334, 373–380.

6. Hemer, *Letters to the Seven Churches*, 78.

7. Mark Wilson, *Biblical Turkey: A Guide to the Jewish and Christian Sites of Asia Minor* (Istanbul: Ege Yayınları, 2010), 281. On the water supply system of Pergamum, see, further, Dora Crouch, *Water Management in the Ancient Greek Cities* (Oxford: Oxford University Press, 1993), 43–46, 104–8, 329–33.

though the agora at the foot of the acropolis is suggested as a potential location.[8] A resident of Pergamum named Telephus had written an extensive treatise on this famous temple in the second century AD, but this document is also unfortunately lost to posterity.[9] Coins issued by the provincial council of Asia under Augustus, Claudius, and Domitian feature the facade of this temple and reveal something of its contents. It was apparently a temple with four columns supporting its front architrave, housing two cult images. Augustus appeared standing in military armor; Rome stood next to him, draped in a feminine toga, holding a cornucopia as a symbol of prosperity, and extending a victor's wreath over Augustus' head. As the seat of the provincial cult of Augustus, an association popularized on the currency of the province, this temple and its activity has been one candidate for identification as the "throne of Satan" in Rev 2:13.[10]

Smyrna would also win the title *neōkoros* for the temple to Tiberius, Livia, and the Senate in 26 AD, and Ephesus would finally win the title for the temple it consecrated to the Flavian emperors (Vespasian, Titus, and Domitian) in 89 AD.[11] Ephesus appears to have been the first of these major cities to flaunt its recent acquisition of the title in civic inscriptions both within its municipality and abroad. The Pergamenes, however, were very sensitive to their place in the pecking order among the cities of Asia and so began to assert their more ancient honor in their own civic inscriptions. One such inscription in the ancient gymnasium in Pergamum honoring the director of the facility (the "gymnasiarch") identifies the city and its leaders as "the council and the people of the Pergamenes, the first to be awarded the title of 'temple warden'" (*neōkoros*). Pergamum thus claimed preeminence over its rival for having been thus distinguished first in the province.

Gymnasiarch Inscription

The Pergamenes were not content merely to have been "first" to win this honor. Shortly after Ephesus had won this title for its temple to Domitian, Pergamum invested in an equally massive temple to Trajan, who ruled as emperor

8. S. R. F. Price, *Rituals and Power: The Roman Imperial Cult in Asia Minor* (Cambridge: Cambridge University Press, 1984), 137.

9. Price, *Rituals and Power*, 133.

10. Hemer, *Letters to the Seven Churches*, 87; Wilson, *Biblical Turkey*, 285.

11. See David A. deSilva, "The Social and Geographical World of Smyrna."

Aerial View of the Temple of Trajan

from 98 to 117 AD. This temple and its precincts were placed conspicuously at the center of the side of the acropolis overlooking the city below. An artificial extension of the temple's platform using the barrel-vaulted arch technique found also in the substructure of the temple of Domitian in Ephesus allowed the new temple to jut out upon the artificial brow of the acropolis. Set on a podium ten feet (3 m) high, with a footprint of sixty by eighty feet (18.25 x 24.4 m) and rising to a height of sixty feet (18.25 m), the temple to Trajan towered above the worshipers and passers-by, a testimony to the city's enthusiasm for the emperor and estimation of his greatness. Its architrave was supported by six columns on each of its shorter sides and ten on its longer sides. The temple sat in the midst of a courtyard of 220 by 170 feet (67 x 51.8 m) and was surrounded by tall colonnaded porticoes on three sides, with no colonnade obscuring the view of the temple from below. For its pledge and display of loyalty, the city was awarded the title of *neōkoros* a second time and thus enjoyed renewed preeminence. Civic inscriptions bear witness to the city's pride: its civic body began to refer to itself in inscriptions as "the council and people of the Pergamenes, twice awarded the neokorate."

Ephesus continued the competition after Trajan's death, building a temple consecrated to Trajan's successor, Hadrian, who ruled from 117 to 138 AD. For its support of and loyalty to the emperor, Ephesus won *its* second neokorate and began to name itself "twice *neōkoros*" in its civic inscriptions. The city fathers of Pergamum, however, did not relinquish their claim to preeminence in the province on the basis of having been awarded its second neokorate *first*. Inscriptions found in the city Asklepion speak of "the people and council of the first-to-be-twice-named-*neōkoros* city of the Pergamenes."

This story of civic competition is recounted here in order to demonstrate how strong were the connections between civic identity and pride and

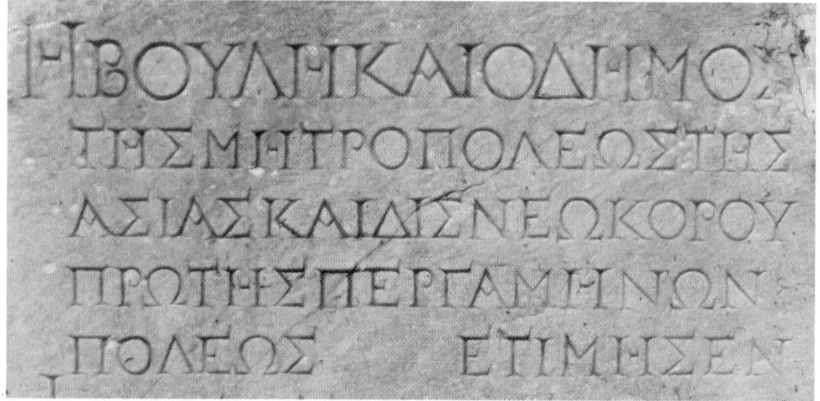

An inscription at the Asklepion in Pergamum boasts the city's place of honor as the "first-to-be-twice-named-*neōkoros*."

support for the imperial cult. While this competition appears only to have begun in earnest during the reign of Domitian, specifically following the erection of Ephesus' temple in 89 AD, it attests to the growing investment of the local elites in the imperial cult and the relationship of imperial cult to a city's regional prominence at the very time that Christian witness *against* the legitimacy of imperial cult and resistance to participation was becoming sharper. Even if John would not have identified an imperial cult site as the "throne of Satan," the conflict between the Pergamenes and the Christians can certainly be attributed, in part at least, to their differing views of this particular cult.

THE ALTAR OF ZEUS AND THE TEMPLE OF ATHENA

The cult of the emperor and Roma was but one facet of religion in the city of Pergamum. Several traditional Greco-Roman gods were worshiped in splendid temples studding the acropolis and spread throughout the city below. Many of the religious sites atop the acropolis would have been prominently visible even from far away. In the first century, before the temple of Trajan was constructed, the altar of Zeus and temple of Athena crowned the brow of the hill. The altar of Zeus, located on the southern crest of the acropolis, was without a doubt the most distinctive and most prominently visible structure overlooking Pergamum. Construction was begun in the early- to mid-second century BC under Eumenes II, possibly in connection with his victory over the invading Galatians. The massive throne-like altar complex resembled an open-air temple, with columned porticoes flanking its staircase and surrounding its inner courtyards. The whole had a footprint of about 120 by 110 feet (36.5 x 33.5 m), and it rose to a height of 40 feet (12 m).[12] The sacrificial altar sat within the inner courtyard, which was approached

12. Wilson, *Biblical Turkey*, 285.

Foundation of the Altar of Zeus

by a wide, grand staircase. The reconstructed monument now sits in the Pergamum Museum in Berlin. The altar was adorned with nearly four hundred linear feet (122 m) of frieze, its scenes carved about seven feet (2 m) high. The frieze around the structure's perimeter depicted the mythological battle between the Olympian gods and the giants, with Zeus and Athena prominently featured on the front side. An interior frieze told the story of Telephus, the mythic founder of Pergamum.[13] An L-shaped agora or forum was set just below the precincts of the altar of Zeus. The identification of some of the buildings as warehouses makes it likely that this particular forum served as a commercial center in the old city.[14]

On a plateau just above the altar of Zeus sat the temple of Athena, originally constructed in the fourth century BC.[15] The forty-by-seventy-foot (12 x 21.3 m) temple itself appears to have had a double sanctuary, with the deities facing in opposite directions. As Zeus and Athena were both the protectors of Pergamum, it would make sense for Zeus to have been the second deity worshiped at this site. The temple itself was built close to the edge of the acropolis, with a large courtyard extending away from the precipice. The sacred precincts were expanded with colonnaded porticoes and an elegant gate (called a propylon) bearing the inscription "King Eumenes [II] to Athena Victory-Bearer." The false balcony of this gateway was decorated

13. For a detailed account of the monument, see Volker Kästner, "The Architecture of the Great Altar of Pergamum," in *Pergamon,Citadel of the Gods: Archaeological Record, Literary Description, and Religious Development*, ed. Helmut Koester (Harrisburg, PA: Trinity Press International, 1998), 137–61.

14. Tevhit Kekeç, *Pergamon* (Istanbul: Hitit Color, 1990), 36.

15. Kekeç, *Pergamon*, 37.

with reliefs of shields and weaponry, probably representing the weapons of the defeated Gauls in Galatia, as this was the major threat during Eumenes II's time. The facades both of the temple and the propylon have been reerected in the Berlin Museum, along with a cult statue of Athena.

Eumenes II also established a library adjacent to the sacred precincts of Athena. If the library did indeed contain two hundred thousand scrolls at one point, a good portion of these would have had to have been stored someplace other than the five rooms of the library complex.[16] That certain ancient kings took special pride in possessing great—indeed, the *greatest*—libraries is exemplified in the rivalry of Ptolemy II, king of Egypt and patron of the great library of Alexandria, and Eumenes II. Upon learning of Eumenes' ambition, Ptolemy significantly curtailed the exporting of papyrus. This is reputed to have led, in turn, to the invention of parchment (called *pergamena* in Pliny, *Natural History* 13.21.70), a writing medium made from the scraped skins of goats, and the development of the codex.[17] Pergamum itself became a major exporter of parchment thereafter. The palaces of the Attalid kings lay to the north and east of the library and Athena temple. These generally followed the peristyle pattern—rooms for various purposes arranged around a central, open-air courtyard, the courtyard itself being surrounded by columned porticoes. These palaces came to serve as barracks for soldiers, with some areas converted into storerooms and arsenals. A heroon (a shrine to a hero), likely dedicated to the ruler cult of the Attalid kings, stood at the south edge of the line of palaces and Athena temple.[18] This consisted essentially of a courtyard leading to the shrine, with a number of smaller rooms and a fellowship hall. It appears to have been built in the midst of (and to some extent *over*) a residential area.

ADDITIONAL PUBLIC BUILDINGS AND RELIGIOUS SITES

A great theater was built into the steep hill southwest of the Athena temple—indeed, this is the steepest theater in the province of Asia. It was begun in the third century BC and eventually renovated and expanded during the Roman period to accommodate ten thousand spectators in eighty rows of benches.[19] A pathway leading north-northwest from the stage area of the great theater led to a temple of Dionysus, appropriately linked to the activities of the theater. The performance of Greek tragedies and the worship of Dionysus were often connected, as in the Greater Dionysiac Festival in Athens, in honor of which Sophocles, Aeschylus, and Euripides wrote their famous plays, including *Oedipus the King*, *Agamemnon*,

---

16. Kekeç, *Pergamon*, 40; Mark R. Fairchild, *Christian Origins in Ephesus and Asia Minor* (Istanbul: Arkeoloji ve Sanat Yayınları, 2015), 165.

17. See page 712 for more information on parchment. Plutarch (*Antony* 58.5) recounts that Mark Antony presented Cleopatra with the two hundred thousand scrolls of Pergamum's library, Asia Minor being within Mark Antony's jurisdiction, but it is far from clear if this involved the physical transfer of the library to Egypt. On the library at Pergamum, see Lionel Casson, *Libraries in the Ancient World* (New Haven: Yale University Press, 2001), 48–53.

18. Fatih Cimok, *Pergamum* (Istanbul: Turizm Yayınları, 1993), 9; Kekeç, *Pergamon*, 28–29.

19. Fairchild, *Christian Origins*, 162, 165; Wilson, *Biblical Turkey*, 285.

Theater and Temple of Dionysus

and *The Bacchae* (respectively). The temple, itself about forty by sixty-five feet (12 x 20 m), sat atop a podium fitted with a tall staircase of twenty-five steps.

Following the main road down from the upper toward the lower acropolis, one passes a Hellenistic-period bathhouse and exercise area and, further down, a complex consisting of a small Roman bath, an odeon (a small music and lecture hall), and an opulent cult room honoring a Pergamene named Diodoros Pasparos from the first century BC, as well as some oil, grain, and wine shops.[20] One does not have to travel far, however, before coming to another complex of major cultic sites. On a large shelf halfway down the southern slope of the acropolis sit the expansive precincts of the temple of Demeter, the goddess of abundance, especially of an abundant harvest. The complex as a whole occupies a space of about 125 by 250 feet (38 x 76 m). The altar proper (about 25 x 8 feet [7.6 x 2.5 m]) sits in the middle of the precinct with the remains of the sanctuary of the goddess behind it. The altar was adorned with sacrificial scenes, such as a relief of a priestess of Demeter, standing between torches beside the altar, preparing to sacrifice a bull to the goddess. One major difference between ancient temples and modern religious practice is that the worshipers tended to gather respectfully *outside* the house of the god, with the rituals and sacrifices conducted on an altar in front of the god's house. The temple of Demeter was originally built by the predecessors of the Attalid kings—Philetaerus and his brother Eumenes (father of Eumenes I) in honor of their mother. It was expanded and renovated

20. Kekeç, *Pergamon*, 54.

Temple of Demeter

by their successors. One significant improvement was the creation of stadium seating along the northern side of the courtyard sufficient to accommodate about eight hundred worshipers.[21]

East of the temple of Demeter sat a temple of Hera, the wife of Zeus. An inscription found *in situ* shows this temple to have been built by Attalus II (159–138 BC). Building it atop a platform approached by twelve steps helped to make the smallish temple more impressive. A modest cult hall dedicated to Dionysos, the main building measuring about seventy-five by thirty feet (23 x 9 m), was located nearby in the midst of what was a (rather exclusive) residential area.[22]

The temple of Hera overlooked the grand gymnasium and bath complex of Pergamum, the first iteration of which was constructed under Eumenes II, but which continued to be expanded and modified throughout the Roman period.[23] Because of the nature of the landscape, the complex featured a three-tiered plan. The uppermost tier housed the principal facilities—the sprawling *palaestra* (a courtyard where all the principal exercises and combat sports were practiced) and two bath complexes. The *palaestra* was surrounded by colonnaded porticoes on at least three of its sides, which was in turn surrounded by halls that could be put to various uses (including educational purposes). The complex was furnished with a one-thousand-seat odeon in its northwest corner, and a small temple to Asclepius. The bath

21. Cimok, *Pergamum*, 54.

22. See discussion in Ulrike Wulf-Rheidt, "The Hellenistic and Roman Houses of Pergamon," 299–330 in Koester, *Pergamon*, 229–330.

23. Wilson, *Biblical Turkey*, 286.

Upper Gymnasium and Palaestra

complexes followed the typical course of the Roman bath, including cold pools, warm pools, saunas, and rooms for massages and cleansing one's skin with olive oil and a good scraping with strigils. A second, lower tier offered a running track for the younger teenage boys; the third and lowest tier was allocated for children, including an exercise area and classroom spaces. A temple to Hermes and Heracles, the patron gods of the gymnasium and athletics in general (no doubt because of their representation of speed and strength, respectively) was part of the middle gymnasium complex. Another agora or forum of about 120 by 200 feet (26.5 x 61 m), surrounded by the customary four columned porticoes, was constructed below and south of the gymnasium as part of Eumenes II's expansion of the city. Eumenes also created a new perimeter of defensive fortifications around his expanded city, the principal access point—the Gate of Eumenes—was located just west of the forum. The entryway was guarded from above by soldiers stationed on three towers.

One other monument merits mention, namely the Serapeion, or "Red Hall," located about five hundred yards (457 m) south of the acropolis. Built in the second century AD under Hadrian, this massive temple was likely dedicated to the Egyptian deities Sarapis (Osiris), Isis, and Harpocrates (Horus). The shrine had a footprint of approximately two hundred by eighty feet (61 x 24.4 m) and rose to a height of at least sixty feet (18.25 m), approached through a broad forecourt surrounded by columned porticoes.[24]

24. Kekeç, *Pergamon*, 75.

The Serapeion, or "Red Hall"

Only the brick substructure remains—any marble has long since been repurposed. Although built after Revelation was written, the construction of such a magnificent edifice to the Egyptian gods suggests a devotee base that had been growing in Pergamum for several decades. The chief point of interest for readers of Revelation is that one of the statues within this temple was found to have an apparatus of piping that allowed a hidden priest to make it appear that the cult image could speak to its worshipers. John's vision of a local beast causing a cult image of the first beast to speak (Rev 13:15) was not beyond the special effects technology of his time.

Beginning in the Hellenistic period, but increasingly in the Roman period, the major residential areas of the city spread from the lower slopes of the hill into and across the valley beneath the acropolis, all under the watchful eyes of the gods above, even as the modern city of Bergama does today (sporting a population of one hundred thousand, perhaps not far off from the population in the first century). To the southeast of the acropolis lie three principal public buildings from the Roman period—an amphitheater (one of the few in Anatolia), a stadium, and a theater, all making the public entertainments of the Roman period more accessible to the resident population.

THE ASKLEPION

Further to the southeast of the acropolis lies an Asklepion, a kind of religious healing resort dedicated to Asclepius, the son of Apollo and the god of medicine and healing, whose interventions would be sought in these sanctuaries. There were many such facilities in the ancient world, another celebrated one being located in Corinth. An eight-hundred yard (731.5 m) road lined with columned porticoes led from the bottom of the acropolis to the Asklepion, terminating in a small forecourt of sixty feet (18.25 m) squared, equipped with a central round altar, then opening into the sanctuary's main courtyard of about four hundred by three hundred feet (122 x 91.5 m), surrounded by wide, columned porticoes on the north, west, and south sides. Off the northwest

Forecourt, Colonnade, and Theater at the Asklepion

corner of the courtyard stood a theater capable of seating over three thousand spectators. The southwest corner was furnished with spacious latrines. A library and reading room stood in the northeast corner. The pavement of the main courtyard was interrupted by several small pools, no doubt for a variety of healing treatments. In the mid-second century, a temple to Asclepius was built along the east side. In the center of the courtyard was the entrance to a long tunnel running diagonally southeast into the circular *abaton*, the "hospital" proper where patients would sleep in the hope that the god Asclepius would reveal, or even effect, a cure in a dream.

"Satan's Throne" in Pergamum

The association of Asclepius with the serpent, found coiled about his staff and, as a result, a common decorative feature running throughout the Asklepion, has led a few scholars to associate this complex with the "throne of Satan."[25] In favor of such an identification might be the fact that Asclepius came to serve as the visual representation of the city itself on coins and in carved reliefs on inscriptions—for example, in coin mintings or adorning inscriptions celebrating the ὁμόνοια (*homonoia*), the "agreements" worked out, between Ephesus (represented by the distinctive Artemis Ephesia) and Pergamum (represented by Asclepius).[26] Against the identification is the much closer parallel between the official imperial ideology of

25. For example, Fairchild, *Christian Origins*, 155–56.

26. On the importance of *homonoia*, or "concord, agreement," between the three great rival cities of Asia—Ephesus, Smyrna, and Pergamum—as they negotiated their pecking order with their shifting fortunes, see Dio Chrysostom, *Orationes*. 34.48; Ursula Kampmann, "*Homonoia* Politics in Asia Minor: The Example of Pergamum," in Koester, *Pergamon*, 376–77.

the rule of Jupiter enacted through his agents, the emperors, and John's subversion of the same as the rebellion of Satan enacted through his agents, the beasts.

Many scholars believe that John was speaking about the distinctive landmark the altar of Zeus when he said that Pergamum was home to "Satan's throne" (Rev 2:13).[27] Jews were known to identify the pagan gods with demons, claiming that those who worshiped idols were really worshiping demons (Bar 4:6–7; 1 Cor 10:19–21; Rev 9:20–21). Identifying the Greeks' chief god, Zeus, with Satan, the chief of the demons, would have been a natural extension of this tendency. If John is thinking of a particular monument in Pergamum as "Satan's throne"—indeed, a distinctive monument that would set "Satan's throne" in Pergamum as opposed to one of the other seven cities John addresses—the great altar of Zeus seems to me the likeliest candidate.[28] In John's deconstruction of the official view that Rome and its emperors rule by the will of Jupiter/Zeus and were destined by the chief of the gods to bring order, peace, and rule of law to the known world (see, e.g., Virgil, *Aeneid*, 1.236–37; 4.232), John asserts that "the dragon," who is Satan (Rev 12:9), stands behind the many-headed beast that exercises authority over the peoples, nations, and languages of the world, and that receives worship from its awestruck subjects (Rev 13:1–4, 7–8). The temple of Roma and Augustus in Pergamum is a manifestation of the cult of the beast and its image, not of the dragon that gives the beast its power.

Whether John had in mind the great altar of Zeus, the centers of the imperial cult, which he would describe as worship of the beast and its image, or the acropolis as a whole as a cluster of sacred sites that would be abhorrent to John, Pergamum would indeed have seemed to him a stronghold of Satan, perhaps the location of his very seat of power as he deceived humanity to take what was due God and give it instead to sticks and stones and pretentious human rulers. The investment of the city in these cults, however, also explains why their inhabitants would not be disposed to tolerate a movement of people in their midst who claimed that all their temples, their sacrifices, and their piety was a sham—or worse. It is surely no coincidence that the theological program of the rival Christian teachers whom John labels "Nicolaitans" and identifies with Balaam, the historic prophet of compromise (see Num 25:1–3; 31:15–16), found a following among the Christians of this city.[29] The pressure was indeed great to find a way to pay lip service to the gods of their neighbors while holding on to their (private?) belief in one God and his Messiah. John rightly saw in Antipas, who was killed in some fashion because of his profession of one God to the exclusion of all others (Rev 2:13), the shape of things to come for Christians who refused to bow, as John saw it, before Satan's throne.

BIBLIOGRAPHY

Aune, David E. *Revelation 1–5*. Dallas: Word, 1997.

27. For a summary of views on the subject, see David E. Aune, *Revelation 1–5* (Dallas: Word, 1997), 182–84.

28. deSilva, *Seeing Things John's Way*, 43; Kästner, "Architecture of the Great Altar," 143.

29. Further on the Nicolaitans, see deSilva, *Seeing Things John's Way*, 59–63, 138–40; for a contrary view, see Worth, *Greco-Asian Culture*, 125–30.

Casson, Lionel. *Libraries in the Ancient World*. New Haven: Yale University Press, 2001.

Cimok, Fatih. *Pergamum*. Istanbul: Turizm Yayınları, 1993.

Crouch, Dora. *Water Management in the Ancient Greek Cities*. Oxford: Oxford University Press, 1993.

deSilva, David A. *Seeing Things John's Way: The Rhetoric of the Book of Revelation*. Louisville: Westminster John Knox, 2009.

Fairchild, Mark R. *Christian Origins in Ephesus and Asia Minor*. Istanbul: Arkeoloji ve Sanat Yayınları, 2015.

Hemer, Colin J. *The Letters to the Seven Churches of Asia in Their Local Setting*. Sheffield: JSOT Press, 1986. Repr., Grand Rapids: Eerdmans, 2001.

Kampmann, Ursula. "*Homonoia* Politics in Asia Minor: The Example of Pergamum." Pages 373–94 in *Pergamon,Citadel of the Gods: Archaeological Record, Literary Description, and Religious Development*. Edited by Helmut Koester. Harrisburg, PA: Trinity Press International, 1998.

Kästner, Volker. "The Architecture of the Great Altar of Pergamum." Pages 137–61 in *Pergamon,Citadel of the Gods: Archaeological Record, Literary Description, and Religious Development*. Edited by Helmut Koester. Harrisburg, PA: Trinity Press International, 1998.

Kekeç, Tevhit. *Pergamon*. Istanbul: Hitit Color, 1990.

Koester, Helmut. *Pergamon, Citadel of the Gods: Archaeological Record, Literary Description, and Religious Development*. Harrisburg, PA: Trinity Press International, 1998.

Price, S. R. F. *Rituals and Power: The Roman Imperial Cult in Asia Minor*. Cambridge: Cambridge University Press, 1984.

Trebilco, Paul R. *Jewish Communities in Asia Minor*. Cambridge: Cambridge University Press, 2006.

Walbank, F. W., et al. *Cambridge Ancient History*. 2nd ed. Cambridge: Cambridge University Press, 1970–2005.

Wilson, Mark. *Biblical Turkey: A Guide to the Jewish and Christian Sites of Asia Minor*. Istanbul: Ege Yayınları, 2010. Esp. pp. 279–93.

Worth, Roland H. *The Seven Cities of the Apocalypse and Greco-Asian Culture*. New York: Paulist, 1999.

———. *The Seven Cities of the Apocalypse and Roman Culture*. New York: Paulist, 1999.

Wulf-Rheidt, Ulrike. "The Hellenistic and Roman Houses of Pergamon." Pages 299–330 in *Pergamon,Citadel of the Gods: Archaeological Record, Literary Description, and Religious Development*. Edited by Helmut Koester. Harrisburg, PA: Trinity Press International, 1998.

CHAPTER 50

THE SOCIAL AND GEOGRAPHICAL WORLD OF THYATIRA

Rev 2:18–29

Mark Wilson

KEY POINTS

- Thyatira is the third city of the seven churches of Revelation.
- The city was a Lydian fortress later refounded by the Macedonians as a military colony in the third century BC.
- Thyatira was situated at a major intersection with intraprovincial and interregional connections.
- Trade guilds played a major role in civic life with Lydia being a purple dealer in Philippi.
- Eating food sacrificed to idols at pagan temples was a major issue in its Christian community.

GEOGRAPHICAL SITUATION

Thyatira (modern Akhisar) was situated in the northwestern part of Lydia[1] amidst a broad, fertile plain along the Lycus River (modern Gördük), a northern tributary of the Hermus River (modern Gediz) (Pliny, *Natural History* 5.115).[2] Its elevation is 338 feet (103 m) above sea level. Strabo noted a claim by some, surely mistaken, that it was the farthest most city of Mysia (*Geography* 13.4.4). Various ancient traditions declared that its name

1. For an excellent map of the geography of ancient Lydia, see Christopher H. Roosevelt, *The Archaeology of Lydia, from Gyges to Alexander* (Cambridge: Cambridge University Press, 2009), 39, fig 3.4.

2. See the map of the province of Asia on page 392. The personification of a reclining river god Lycus appears frequently on the reverse of imperial-period coins.

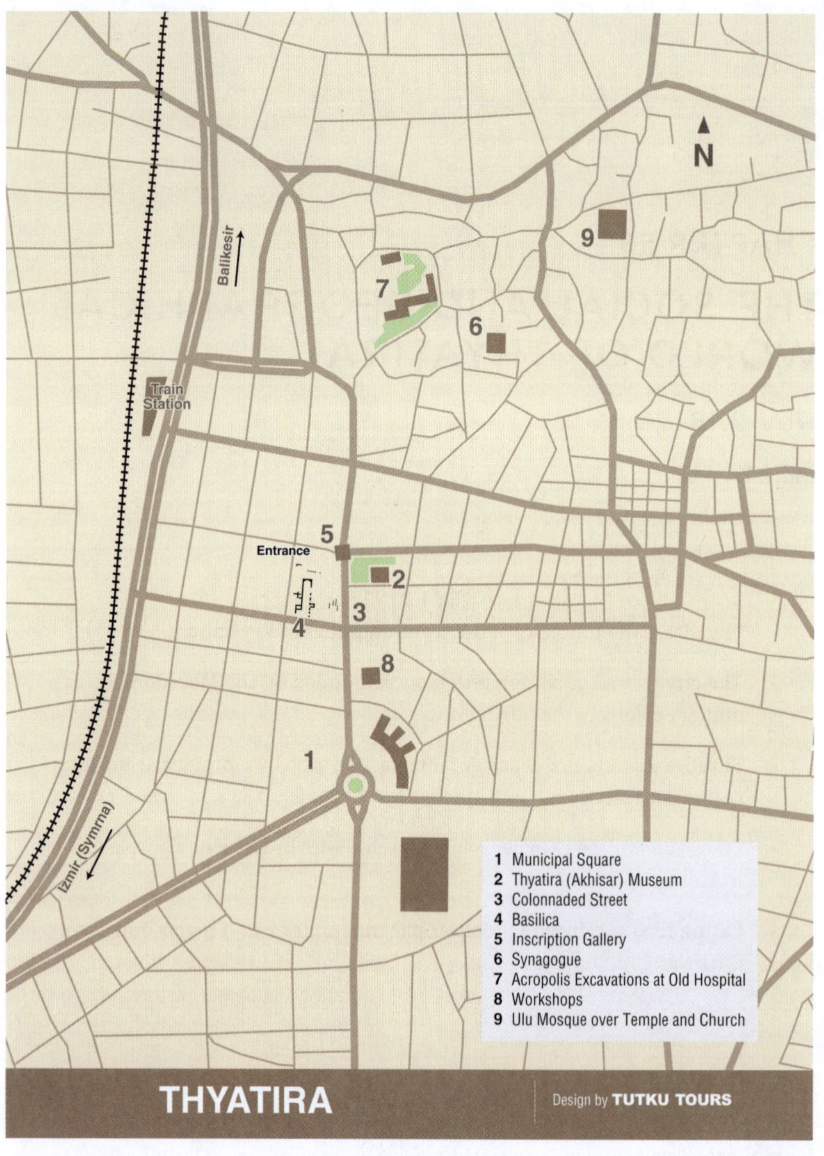

was formerly Semiramis, Pelopeia, and Euhippia. However, as Getzel Cohen notes, "it is doubtful if these names were ever actually used."[3] Its name is probably Asiatic and derived from "teira," the Lydian word for "fortress" or "stronghold," hence the Greek form *Thyateira* (Θυάτειρα). Stephanos (under the entry for "*Thyateira*") suggests unconvincingly that its probable founder Seleucus

3. Getzel Cohen, *Hellenistic Settlements in Europe, the Islands, and Asia Minor* (Berkeley: University of California Press, 1995), 238, 239–40.

I named the city after his daughter.[4] The acropolis, today called Hastane Hüyüğü (Hospital Mound), was first settled in the Early Bronze Age, as pottery remains show.[5]

Located at an important road junction, Thyatira was situated between Sardis to the southeast (35 miles [56 km]) and Pergamum to the northwest (52 miles [83 km]). It lay along the imperial road improved in 129 BC by the Roman governor Manius Aquillius, which started in Pergamum, then at Laodicea merged with a branch coming from Ephesus. The order of the final five of the seven churches tracks this route, so the messenger delivering the Apocalypse would have used it (see map on page 630). Another major road linked Smyrna to the southwest (56 miles [90 km]) and Bithynian Prusa to the northeast (150 miles [240 km]). In 281 BC the battle of Corupedium was fought to the south between the two Diadochi kings, Seleucus I and Lysimachus. After his victory Seleucus I resettled Lydian Teira with Macedonian officers and soldiers to form a military colony (Strabo, *Geography* 13.4.4; see also *OGIS* 211). This became one of the oldest Hellenistic settlements in Asia Minor.[6] Surrounding villages undoubtedly belonged to its territory (*χώρα*, *chōra*). Several later milestones discovered in this *chōra* give measurements to Thyatira as the roadhead (*caput viae*). One reads "seven miles [11.25 km] from the most splendid and greatest (city of) Thyatira."[7]

HISTORICAL SITUATION

Because of its strategic location, Thyatira witnessed many other battles. During the third century BC the Galatians, Seleucids, and Attalids struggled over Thyatira. The Seleucids held the city in 190 BC since the army of Antiochus III, before the battle of Magnesia, was camped *circa Thyatiram* (Livy 37.8.7; 37.37.6; 37.38.1). With the defeat of the Seleucids, Thyatiran delegates surrendered to the Romans (Livy 37.44.4). However, the treaty of Apamea awarded its control to the Attalids in 189 BC, who ruled for over a century (Polybius 21.45.10).

Because of its vulnerability, the city was invaded by Prusias of Bithynia in 150 BC and later besieged by the pretender Aristonicus in 131 BC who resisted the bequest of the Attalid kingdom to Rome (Strabo, *Geography* 14.1.38). In 129 BC Thyatira was incorporated into the Roman province of Asia. It was located within the *conventus* of Pergamum, one of the thirteen administrative and judicial centers of the province (Pliny, *Natural History* 5.116).[8]

4. Cohen, *Hellenistic Settlements*, 240.

5. Information regarding the ongoing archaeological work in Thyatira can be found on the excavation's mostly Turkish web site http://thyateirakazisi.com/.

6. Christian Marek, *In the Land of a Thousand Gods: A History of Asia Minor in the Ancient World*, trans. Steven Rendall (Princeton: Princeton University Press, 2016), 195.

7. David H. French, *Milestones: Asia*, fascicle 3.5 of *Roads and Milestones of Asia Minor* (Ankara: British Institute of Archaeology at Ankara, 2014), 239 no. 130, 254 no. 137E, 256–59 no. 140; for the translation see Hasan Malay, *Researches in Lydia, Mysia and Aiolis* (Vienna: Österreichischen Akademie der Wissenschaften, 1999), 60–61 no. 53.

8. Christian Habicht, "New Evidence on the Province of Asia," *Journal of Roman Studies* 65 (1975): 70, 78, 80.

Arches from Colonnaded Street at Thyatira

During the First Mithridatic War in 84 BC the Roman general Sulla confronted his rival Fimbria who held Thyatira. Fimbria surrendered the city, and his troops were added to Sulla's army (Plutarch, *Sulla* 25.1). Fimbria received safe passage to Pergamum where he fell on his sword in the temple of Asclepius (Appian, *Mithridatic Wars* 9.60).

Around 27 BC Thyatira was among some Asian cities struck by an earthquake (Agathias, *Histories* 2.17.1, 9). Their appeal to Augustus for relief was referred to the Roman Senate, and in 24 BC the future emperor Tiberius argued its case, resulting in aid to rebuild the city (Suetonius, *Life of Tiberius* 8). During the Imperial period the citizenry (δῆμος, *dēmos*) and private donors expanded the civic space with colonnades (like the one visible in Akhisar today), an ornamental gateway, and gymnasia.

After Caracalla visited the city in AD 214, he made it an assize town to conduct judicial hearings (*OGIS* 517). Because of this privilege, the city honored Caracalla as Founder and Benefactor. In AD 218 his successor Elagabalus gave permission to C. Perlius Aurelius Alexander to hold a "sacred game" (*iselasticus*) in the city involving athletic and musical competition. It was sponsored by the trade guild of fullers. On the inscription the name of the emperor

Bust of Emperor Caracalla

Antoneinon, aka Elagabulus, was erased. After Elagabulus' assassination in AD 222, the Roman Senate decreed the damning of his memory (*damnatio memoriae*), and his name was erased from all public monuments.[9]

Thyatira was typical of cities in Asia Minor where women such as Iulia Iuliana and Iulia Menogenis held public offices. Others had sacral duties in priesthoods and high priesthoods. The responsibilities of these offices were somewhat fluid and varied among cities.[10] Thyatira has been called a "minor" town among the seven churches, but as seen, this was clearly not the case.[11]

COMMERCIAL SITUATION

As in other Asian centers of textile production, trade guilds were prominent in Thyatira. These included wool dealers, potters, linen weavers, tanners, leather workers, and coppersmiths. Inscriptional evidence reveals their influence in civic affairs.[12] Prominent among these guilds were dyers mentioned in several inscriptions (*TAM* V.2.991.5-8). Its purple dyers were noted throughout the empire: in Thessalonica an inscription mentions Menippus of Thyatira who was honored by the purple-dyers there (*IG* X.2.1.291).[13] Lydia was a purple dealer (πορφυρόπωλις, *porphyropōlis*) from this city whom Paul met in the Roman colony of Philippi (Acts 16:14-15, 40).[14] Since Thyatira was

Bust of Emperor Elagabalus

9. This inscription now stands in Akhisar's archaeological park; it (pp. 37-38 no. 29) and nineteen other new inscriptions of Thyatira (nos. 16-35) have been published by Malay, *Researches in Lydia, Mysia and Aiolis*, 33-46.

10. Sviatoslav Dmitriev, *City Government in Hellenistic and Roman Asia Minor* (Oxford: Oxford University Press, 2005), 180, also nn. 214-15.

11. G. W. Clarke, "The Origins and Spread of Christianity," in *The Augustan Era*, vol. 10 of *Cambridge Ancient History*, ed. Alan K. Bowman, Edward Champlin, and Andrew Lintott, 2nd. ed. (Cambridge: Cambridge University Press, 1996), 858.

12. David Magie, *Roman Rule in Asia Minor to the End of the Third Century after Christ* (Princeton: Princeton University Press, 1950), 1:48-49.

13. Another inscription found in Philippi mentions a purple dyer from Thyatira named Antiochus son of Lycus. Regarding its authenticity, see Gennadi A. Sergienko, *"Our Politeuma Is in Heaven!": Paul's Polemical Engagement with the "Enemies of the Cross of Christ" in Philippians 3:18-20* (Carlisle: Langham, 2013), 86-87 no. 4.7, esp. n. 74.

14. Teresa J. Calpino, *Women, Work and Leadership in Acts* (Tübingen: Mohr Siebeck, 2014), 198 argues that Λυδία (*Lydia*) is better understood as "the Lydian lady," understanding it as a

Murex Shells and Purple Dyed Textiles

inland, purple dye from mollusks had to be imported. A deep scarlet dye was also obtained from the local madder root, an organic dye still used for carpet production in Turkey today. Dyers used much water, so they were usually located at the edge of the city.[15] Their work also produced both a strong odor and polluted wastewater. Such activity was probably localized near the Lycus River northwest of Akhisar. Here at the village of Medar/Ovaköy an inscription (*TAM* V.2.991) was discovered that praises Marcus son of Menander for paying for an aqueduct that undoubtedly benefited the dyers by providing an adequate supply of water.

RELIGIOUS SITUATION

The city's primary deities were Apollo Tyrimnus and Artemis Boreitene. In the second century BC they along with Athena were featured on Thyatira's coinage. In the Roman Imperial period other gods and goddesses appeared including Heracles, Cybele, Tyche, Nike, and even Serapis.[16] Apollo Tyrimnus had a sanctuary "outside the city" (*TAM* V.2.1001). His full name, Helius Pythius Tyrimnaeus Apollo (*TAM* V.2.976), represented a syncretistic conception of Lydian, Macedonian, and Greek deities. What Artemis' local epithet Boreitene means can only be conjectured; perhaps

toponym. However, the three other examples of women cited with the personal name "Lydia" undercut her assertion.

15. For a discussion of porphyrology, see David Graves, "What Is the Madder with Lydia's Purple? A Reexamination of the Purpurarii in Thyatira and Philippi," *Near East Archaeological Society Bulletin* 62 (2017): 4 tab. 1 for dyers in Thyatira; 10 for the issue of odors. For a list of other inscriptions mentioning purple dyers and dealers, search for "purple" on the webpage *Associations in the Greco-Roman World*, http://philipharland.com/greco-roman-associations/?s=purple.

16. For examples, see the Wildwinds.com page on "Ancient Coinage of Lydia, Thyateira," http://www.wildwinds.com/coins/greece/lydia/thyateira/i.html.

it is derived from a village in the city's territory.[17]

On its civic coinage the busts of emperors began to appear *seriatim* starting with Claudius in the first century AD. The reverse of a coin featuring Vespasian on the obverse has an unidentified tetrastyle temple on the reverse.[18] Neighboring Pergamum had Asia's first imperial cult temple in 29 BC. A locally organized civic cult of Rome and Augustus was dedicated sometime before 2 BC (*TAM* V.2.902–3). A coin issued circa AD 100 features the draped bust of the goddess Roma.[19] In AD 110 a second imperial temple was constructed in Pergamum to honor Trajan.

The demos of Thyatira erected a stele to honor its neighbor for being Asia's first city to be twice honored as an imperial temple guardian (νεωκόρος, *neōkoros*; compare Acts 19:35).[20] The oracle at Didyma instructed Thyatirans how to avoid further pains and casualties inflicted by the offended Moon Goddess by prescribing offerings to certain gods and heroes. Didyma was approximately 140 miles (225 km) away, which shows how far supplicants would travel to receive prophecies for themselves or their communities.[21]

A Jewish community probably lived in Thyatira. Two thousand Jewish families from Mesopotamia were settled in Lydia and Phrygia by Antiochus III around 210 BC (Josephus, *Ant.* 12.148–153). So the Jewish populace would have come from these colonists.[22] An inscription (*CIJ* II.752) dating from the second century AD names Fabios Zosimus and his wife Aurelia Pontiane, who erected a sarcophagus for themselves and "placed it on a holy site, which is before the city by the *sambatheion* in the Chaldean precinct alongside the public highway."[23] The sepulcher's ambiguous language has generated much controversy regarding its meaning. Williams writes,

> Some see it as the direct equivalent of the *sabbateion* mentioned in Josephus, *Jewish Antiquities* 16.164 and conclude that a synagogue is indicated here and Fabios Zosimos was a Jew. Others connect the word with the Chaldaean Sibyl, Sambethe, and think that a pagan

17. Cohen, *Hellenistic Settlements*, 242.

18. *RPC* II.939. See an image of the coin at the webpage *Asia Minor Coins* (Coin ID #13053), http://www.asiaminorcoins.com/gallery/displayimage.php?pid=13053.

19. See the image of coin BMC 18 at Wildwinds.com (http://www.wildwinds.com/coins/greece/lydia/thyateira/i.html).

20. This inscription still stands on Pergamum's acropolis next to the Trajan temple.

21. Addressed to the "Macedonians," the inscription is probably Hellenistic with perhaps a later reinscribing during the Roman period; see Hasan Malay and Georg Petzl, *New Religious Texts from Lydia* (Vienna: Österreichischen Akademie der Wissenschaften, 2017), 31–37 no. 3.

22. Colin J. Hemer, *The Letters to the Seven Churches of Asia in Their Local Setting* (Sheffield: JSOT Press, 1986), 247 n. 21, believes that Thyatira was never under Seleucid control at this time so could not have received Jews. However, by this time Attalus I had been confined to Pergamene territory and Antiochus III had reestablished control of Sardis; see John Ma, *Antiochos III and the Cities of Western Asia Minor* (Oxford: Oxford University Press, 2000), 246.

23. Margaret H. Williams, *The Jews among the Greeks and Romans: A Diasporan Sourcebook* (Baltimore: Johns Hopkins University Press, 1998), 175 no. VII.47; see also Walter Ameling, *Inscriptiones Judaicae Orientis: Band II, Kleinasien* (Tübingen, Mohr Siebeck, 2004), 297–302 no. 146.

> shrine (possibly belonging to Sabbath-worshippers) is indicated here. Whatever the truth, Jewish influence is unmistakeable.[24]

Lydia, whom Paul met in Philippi (Acts 16:14), had probably become a God-fearer through this Jewish community; however, no remains of a synagogue have been found.

Christianity perhaps arrived in Thyatira in the 50s, for Luke writes that residents of Asia heard the gospel during Paul's time in Ephesus (Acts 19:10). One of the earliest Christian inscriptions yet found (early third century) came from nearby Chorianos (modern Akselendi). Aurelius Gaios openly identifies himself as a Christian along with his wife Aurelia Stratoneikiane.[25] It is remarkable that a century before Christianity is legalized, Christians around Thyatira are publicly declaring their faith. The prophetic "Phrygian heresy" called Montanism took over the community in the late second century and dominated for 112 years (Epiphanius, *Refutation of all Heresies* 51.32–33). According to Epiphanius the Thyatiran church was restored to orthodoxy around 335 (*Panarion* 33.1-5, 8–10).[26] Papylus, a deacon from Thyatira, was martyred in Pergamum along with Carpus, bishop of Gordos, most likely during Decius' persecution in AD 250.[27]

THYATIRA IN LATER HISTORY

The site's location was lost until the seventeenth century. The British consul in Smyrna, Paul Rycaut, began to visit the seven churches in October 1669. His party visited Tire, then widely believed to be Thyatira. However, he discovered no such a tradition among the local Greeks nor any archaeological confirmation, so he concluded that the site should be northeast of Smyrna as the literary evidence suggested. On October 8, 1670, after a visit to Pergamum, Rycaut rode into Akhisar where he saw "Pillars and broken Stones with rare Sculptures, and on certain Inscriptions, which at a distance were so fair, that they seemed almost legible." Upon seeing the city's name on inscriptions, he realized that Thyatira had been found.[28] Numerous objects of Thyatira are found in the archaeology museum at Akhisar and in the provincial archaeological museum at Manisa.[29]

---

24. Williams, *Jews among the Greeks and Romans*, 201–2 n. 60.

25. William Tabbernee, *Montanist Inscriptions and Testimonia: Epigraphic Sources Illustrating the History of Montanism* (Macon, GA: Mercer University Press, 1997), 100–104. Whether the inscription is Montanist is debatable; it also lacks the characteristic "Christians for Christians" formula.

26. For the issues related to Epiphanius' dating, see Tabbernee, *Montanist Inscriptions*, 136–38.

27. This later date is contra Eusebius (*Church History* 4.15.48) who puts it in the 160s; see Tabbernee, *Montanist Inscriptions*, 140-41.

28. Paul Rycaut, *The Present State of the Greek and Armenian Churches, Anno Christi, 1678* (London: Starkey, 1679), 72, 73–74. In this volume Rycaut presents a fifty-page review (pp. 30–80) of the present state of the seven churches, the first scientific publication about them. Rycaut had been commissioned by Britain's Royal Society to "inquire after these excellent Works of Antiquity, of which that Country is full"; see Mark Wilson, "Smyrna: The Open Door to Rediscovering the Seven Churches," *Ekklesiastikos Pharos* 89 (2007): 78.

29. For statues of Athena and Nike see Münteha Dinç, "Manisa Müzesi'ndeki Hellenistik - Roma Dönemi Heykelleri," in *Manisa Müzesi Heykeltıraşlık Eserleri*, ed. Serra Durugönül (Mersin: Mersin University, 2015), 33–34, 37.

Column Bases for Roman Colonnaded Street

SOCIAL AND GEOGRAPHICAL REALITIES OF THE THYATIRA LETTER

The Thyatiran message is the central letter of the seven and the longest. It is also the only letter to refer to the other six churches (Rev 2:23). Three allusions—Jezebel (Rev 2:20; compare 1 Kgs 16:31–21:25 passim), rod of iron (Rev 2:27; compare Ps 2:8–9), and morning star (Rev 2:28; compare Num 24:17)—presumed a background in the Jewish Scriptures to interpret. The command not to eat food sacrificed to idols (Rev 2:20) required compromised Christians to forgo banquets at pagan temples where such food was served. Trade guilds also gathered for festive banquets, so to withdraw from such dining occasions invited economic ostracization. The large ashlar blocks in the southeast corner of Ulu Mosque suggest that the structure was formerly a pagan temple where such banquets occurred. The building was later converted into a church and then to a mosque.

BIBLIOGRAPHY

Ameling, Walter. *Inscriptiones Judaicae Orientis: Band II, Kleinasien*. Tübingen: Mohr Siebeck, 2004.

Ascough, Richard A., Philip A. Harland, and John S. Kloppenborg. *Associations in the Greco-Roman World: An Expanding Collection of Inscriptions, Papyri, and Other Sources in Translation*. Accessed November 26, 2018. http://philipharland.com/greco-roman-associations/

AsiaMinorCoins.com. *Asia Minor Coins: An Online Index of Ancient Greek and Roman Coins from Asia Minor*. Accessed November 26, 2018. https://www.asiaminorcoins.com/

Calpino, Teresa J. *Women, Work and Leadership in Acts*. Tübingen: Mohr Siebeck, 2014.

Clarke, G. W. "The Origins and Spread of Christianity." Pages 848–72 in *The Augustan Era*. Vol. 10 of *Cambridge Ancient History*. Edited by Alan K. Bowman, Edward Champlin, and Andrew Lintott. 2nd ed. Cambridge: Cambridge University Press, 1996.

Cohen, Getzel. *Hellenistic Settlements in Europe, the Islands, and Asia Minor*. Berkeley, University of California Press, 1995.

Dinç, Münteha. "Manisa Müzesi'ndeki Hellenistik - Roma Dönemi Heykelleri." Pages 30–96 in *Manisa Müzesi Heykeltıraşlık Eserleri*. Edited by Serra Durugönül. Mersin: Mersin University, 2015.

Dmitriev, Sviatoslav. *City Government in Hellenistic and Roman Asia Minor*. Oxford: Oxford University Press, 2005.

French, David H. *Milestones: Asia*. Fascicle 3.5 of *Roads and Milestones of Asia Minor*. Ankara: British Institute of Archaeology at Ankara, 2014.

Graves, David. "What Is the Madder with Lydia's Purple? A Reexamination of the Purpurarii in Thyatira and Philippi." *Near East Archaeological Society Bulletin* 62 (2017), 3–29.

Habicht, Christian. "New Evidence on the Province of Asia." *Journal of Roman Studies* 65 (1975): 64–91.

Hemer, Colin J. *The Letters to the Seven Churches of Asia in Their Local Setting*. Sheffield: JSOT Press, 1986.

Ma, John. *Antiochos III and the Cities of Western Asia Minor*. Oxford: Oxford University Press, 2000.

Magie, David. *Roman Rule in Asia Minor to the End of the Third Century after Christ*. 2 vols. Princeton: Princeton University Press, 1950.

Malay, Hasan. *Researches in Lydia, Mysia and Aiolis*. Vienna: Österreichischen Akademie der Wissenschaften, 1999.

Malay, Hasan, and George Petzl. *New Religious Texts from Lydia*. Vienna: Österreichischen Akademie der Wissenschaften, 2017.

Marek, Christian. *In the Land of a Thousand Gods: A History of Asia Minor in the Ancient World*. Translated by Steven Rendall. Princeton: Princeton University Press, 2016.

Roosevelt, Christopher H. *The Archaeology of Lydia, from Gyges to Alexander*. Cambridge: Cambridge University Press, 2009.

Rycaut, Paul. *The Present State of the Greek and Armenian Churches, Anno Christi, 1678*. London: Starkey, 1679.

Sergienko, Gennadi A. *"Our Politeuma Is in Heaven!": Paul's Polemical Engagement with the "Enemies of the Cross of Christ" in Philippians 3:18-20*. Carlisle: Langham, 2013.

Tabbernee, William. *Montanist Inscriptions and Testimonia: Epigraphic Sources Illustrating the History of Montanism*. Macon, GA: Mercer University Press, 1997.

Wildwinds. *Ancient Coins: Roman, Greek, Byzantine and Celtic Numismatic Reference for Attribution and Values*. Accessed November 26, 2018. http://www.wildwinds.com/

Williams, Margaret H. *The Jews among the Greeks and Romans: A Diasporan Sourcebook*. Baltimore: Johns Hopkins University Press, 1998.

Wilson, Mark. "Smyrna: The Open Door to Rediscovering the Seven Churches." *Ekklesiastikos Pharos* 89 (2007): 75–87.

CHAPTER 51

THE SOCIAL AND GEOGRAPHICAL WORLD OF SARDIS

Rev 1:11; 3:1–6

David A. deSilva

KEY POINTS

- Sardis was a flourishing city located on a major east-west highway during the Persian, Hellenistic, and Roman periods.
- Like many of its sister cities, Sardis exhibited strong pro-Roman sentiments, seen in its bid to house provincial imperial cults and in the prominence of the imperial cult in its second- and third-century architecture.
- The Jewish community in Sardis had ancient and strong roots and was likely well-established from the Hellenistic period. If one can extrapolate from its fourth-century synagogue, it had been better integrated into the life of its city than was true for many Jewish diaspora communities.
- Very little has been discovered in Sardis to shed light on the origins of, or challenges to, the Christian community there in the late first century beyond these generalities.

SARDIS IN THE BIBLICAL STORY

The city of Sardis intersects with the biblical story at only two points. The first is a passing reference in Obad 20, which names Sepharad (סְפָרַד, *sefared*) among the cities into which Israelites had already been dispersed in exile. Sepharad appears to be related to the Persian name for the district and its leading city, Shparda, a name that also appears in Aramaic in a bilingual inscription (Aramaic and Lydian) in Sardis itself.[1]

1. Mark Wilson, *Biblical Turkey: A Guide to the Jewish and Christian Sites of Asia Minor* (Istanbul: Ege Yayınları, 2010), 307; Paul R. Trebilco, *Jewish Communities in Asia Minor* (Cambridge: Cambridge University Press, 2006), 38. The text and translation of the inscription

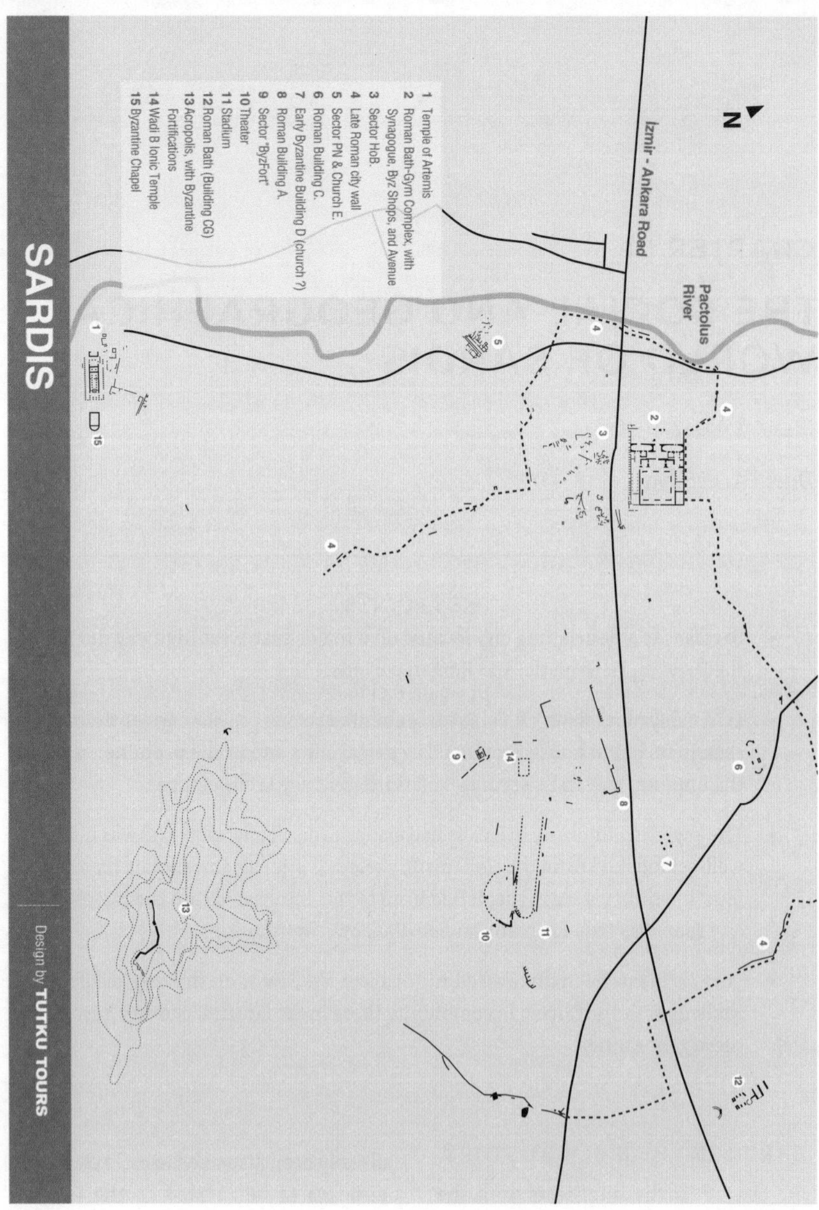

The second is the more significant, as John names the Christian community or communities in Sardis among the recipients of his revelation (see Rev 1:11), addressing them specifically—and none too flatteringly—in one of the seven oracles (Rev 3:1–6). Sardis sits sixty miles (97 km) east of Smyrna and thirty-five miles

can be found in Mariona Vernet Pons, "The Origin of the Name Sepharad: A New Interpretation," *JSS* 59 (2014): 297–313, esp. 304.

(56 km) southeast of Thyatira, within the horseshoe-shaped circuit of these seven congregations that John the prophet may have traveled before his removal to the island of Patmos (see map on page XXX).

ROMAN SARDIS

Sardis had a legendary past as the seat of the kingdom of Lydia. It was situated beside the Pactolus River, whose sands, rich in gold dust, gave the city a constant source of wealth. Coins made of electrum, a gold and silver alloy, were minted here as early as the seventh century BC (Herodotus, *Histories* 1.94).[2] One of its kings, Croesus, became proverbially associated with wealth—and with folly, for provoking the Persians and losing his kingdom (Herodotus, *Histories* 1.47–91). The Persians extended their "Royal Road" into their newly conquered territory, linking Sardis, capital of the empire's westernmost satrapy, with the capital city of Susa some fifteen hundred miles (2414 km) away to the east (a short stretch of this well-paved road has been uncovered along the south of the synagogue complex).[3] This located Sardis on a major trade and communications route that persisted into the Roman period, positioning the city for ongoing prosperity.

Sardis was a major urban center with upwards of sixty thousand residents during the Roman period. Unfortunately, very little of first-century Sardis, such as might illumine the context and situation of the Christian church addressed by John, has been uncovered. The most impressive archaeological remains postdate the New Testament period by a century or more. The acropolis, with the most ancient remains predating the Persian invasion, has yielded little archaeological fruit, having been subject to centuries of erosion and collapse.

TEMPLE TO ARTEMIS

The oldest structure of significance is the temple to Artemis, built about two-thirds of a mile (1 km) west of the acropolis. The worship of Artemis was popular throughout the cities of Roman Asia, nowhere more so than in Ephesus. The temple of Artemis in Sardis, however, was a marvel—the eighth largest temple in the Greek world, with eight grand Ionic columns supporting its roof on the east and west sides, and twenty columns on each of the longer sides. The temple's footprint is about 300 x 160 feet (91.5 x 48.75 m), covering twice the amount of ground as the Parthenon in Athens, its roof once rising to a height of over 80 feet (24.5 m). A large stone altar sits in front of the temple (to the west), as was typical throughout the ancient world—the temple was the house of the deity; worshipers gathered respectfully outside for the rites and sacrifices.

Construction on this temple (which replaced an earlier Artemis temple on the site) began in 334 BC, shortly after Alexander wrested control of Asia Minor from the Persians, but it suffered major interruptions. It remained operational but unfinished until the second century AD, when the temple was rebuilt and rededicated to include the cult of the living emperor, Antoninus Pius, and his deceased wife, Faustina. The temple's structure was altered to create two sanctuaries. It is unclear how the sacred

2. Colin J. Hemer, *The Letters to the Seven Churches of Asia in Their Local Setting* (Sheffield: JSOT Press, 1986; repr., Grand Rapids: Eerdmans, 2001), 131.

3. Wilson, *Biblical Turkey*, 297.

Temple of Artemis

spaces were divided. One theory is that the front-facing sanctuary remained sacred to Artemis with the rear-facing sanctuary dedicated to Antoninus and Faustina; another posits that the rear-facing sanctuary was dedicated to Zeus and Antoninus, with Artemis and Faustina sharing the front-facing sanctuary.[4] Sardis had previously sought the honor of hosting a provincial temple of the imperial cult. After Tiberius granted significant aid to the city (ten million sesterces plus tax relief for several years) in the wake of the great earthquake of 17 AD that rocked the region, Sardis competed a decade later with her sister cities for the honor of building the provincial temple to honor Tiberius, losing out to Smyrna. The temple to Antoninus and Faustina won the city the title of νεωκόρος (*neōkoros*, "temple warden") of the provincial imperial cult for the first time. The cult images of the imperial couple were massive: the heads alone measured a yard (1 m) from chin to crown.[5]

The temple structure was situated close by the Pactolus stream, which ran a fairly straight course to the north and west of the city. A structure tentatively identified as a shrine to Cybele sat about five hundred yards (457 m) north-northeast of the Artemis temple, also in close proximity to the Pactolus. Worship of Cybele, identified as the "Great Mother" goddess, is well attested in Lydia and Asia in general, famous for her eunuch priests.[6]

CIVIC ARCHITECTURE

About five hundred yards (152.5 m) northeast of the acropolis sat two structures

4. S. R. F. Price, *Rituals and Power: The Roman Imperial Cult in Asia Minor* (Cambridge: Cambridge University Press, 1984), 151–52. Wilson (*Biblical Turkey*, 298) prefers the second configuration.

5. Price, *Rituals and Power*, 187.

6. Hemer, *Letters to the Seven Churches*, 138–39.

Cult Stele of Cybele

essential to entertainment during the Roman period: the theater and stadium. Only the general contours of the theater, plus the massive retaining walls that supported its seating at the open ends, remain to be seen today, the vast majority of the seating itself having been removed and repurposed. The theater opened out over one end of the stadium complex, which remains itself largely unexcavated save for a few lengths of the broad arched passageway that once led under, and gave access to, the seating.

The most prominent building left standing in ancient Sardis is the reconstructed gymnasium, standing a little over a thousand yards (915 m) north of the acropolis and northeast of the Artemis temple. The present structure was built in the mid- to late-second century AD, but there was, no doubt, a gymnasium in the city for centuries prior to that, for the gymnasium, which combined emphases on education and athletics, was the primary institution for forming the next generation into good Greeks in every Greek or Hellenized city. This gymnasium had an expansive square forecourt—called a *palaestra*—consisting of a field of over two hundred feet (61 m) long on each of its four sides, the whole once surrounded by porticoes sporting one hundred columns facing the interior.[7] This was the location of the facility's athletic fields where wrestling, boxing, running, discus-throwing, and other events were practiced.

Little of the original architecture of the forecourt remains (see page 713 for a reconstructed view). The massive entrance hall separating the *palaestra* from the bath house, however, has been painstakingly reconstructed. The breathtaking ornamentation of the hall, together with its pious dedicatory inscription to the members of the imperial household, has led archaeologists to suspect that it functioned not only as a grand vestibule, but also as a site for the celebration of imperial cult rituals. The dedicatory inscription appears to come from the Severan period, or the early third century, as it makes mention of Septimius Severus, Caracalla, and Caracalla's mother, Julia Domna.[8] The inscription also bears proud witness to the fact that, by this time, Sardis had been awarded the title *neōkoros* (νεωκόρος, the designation of "temple warden" of the cult of a deified emperor) not once, but twice. The cities in Roman Asia regarded this title as a principal claim

7. Wilson, *Biblical Turkey*, 302.

8. Wilson, *Biblical Turkey*, 302.

Gymnasium

Dedicatory Inscription on Sardis Gymnasium

to fame. Inscriptions in Ephesus and Pergamum show that the inhabitants of these cities regarded their enjoyment of the title *neōkoros* as the second most important feature of the city after the city's name itself (and they exhibit an uncommon rivalry with one another in regard to which city was awarded the title, and how many times, first).

Immediately inside the structure behind the marble hall was a shallow swimming pool, or *natatorium*. This may also have functioned as the *frigidarium*, or "cold plunge," of the bath complex. The rooms behind, which still lie in ruins, would have offered the remainder of the typical features of a Roman bath—a *tepidarium*, a *caldarium* (essentially a sauna), and dressing rooms and spaces for massages. Lecture halls and classroom spaces were likely also part of the complex, perhaps in the wings to either side of the marble hall.

THE JEWISH SYNAGOGUE

The third most prominent site in Sardis is a Jewish synagogue, dating in its present form from the fourth century AD.[9] The Jewish community in Sardis significantly predates this structure. Aside from the passing reference in Obadiah 20, Antiochus III is known to have relocated two thousand Jewish families from Syria and Babylon to the western frontier regions of his empire, including the region of Lydia and, no doubt, its capital city Sardis (Josephus, *Ant.* 12.149–51). Josephus also records decrees by Roman officials confirming the traditional rights of the Jewish community in Sardis, including the right of assembly, adjudicating internal affairs, and collecting funds for the Jerusalem temple (Josephus, *Ant.* 14.235, 259–61; 16.171). The present synagogue building no doubt had many predecessors, though quite probably not in this prominent a location.

The synagogue consists of two principal rooms—an interior hall of about two hundred feet by sixty feet (61 x 18.25 m) and a forecourt of about eighty by sixty feet (24.4 x 18.25 m), the forecourt being furnished with a central fountain. The main hall was able to accommodate around a thousand worshipers. While the synagogue is rich in inscriptions (over eighty were recovered) and, therefore,

9. Lloyd Gaston, "Jewish Communities in Sardis and Smyrna," in *Religious Rivalries and the Struggle for Success in Sardis and Smyrna*, ed. Richard S. Ascough (Waterloo, ON: Wilfrid Laurier University Press, 2005), 19–20.

Interior Hall of Sardis SynagogueShowing the *Nomophylakion*

in insights into the place of the Jewish community in Sardis, the existing evidence is centuries later than Revelation (which notably makes no mention of the Jewish community in Sardis as a significant factor in the situation of the Christians there, unlike the oracles to Smyrna and Philadelphia). An astounding feature of the synagogue is its placement adjacent to the gymnasium complex itself, as well as its ornate decoration and construction. This suggests that, by the late third or early fourth century AD, the Jews of Sardis were very much at home, quite prosperous, and accepted by their gentile neighbors to a very high degree. This is somewhat unusual in the ancient world, given typical anti-Jewish prejudice among gentiles and the not infrequent eruptions of violence against local Jewish communities. The Jewish community here was well-integrated into the life of the city.

Central Table with Eagle on Base

The most distinctive feature of a synagogue was the *nomophylakion* (νομοφυλάκιον), now referred to as an "ark," in which the Torah scrolls were housed.[10] Two niches, located in the rear (the east end) of the main hall, originally served this purpose. The synagogue had a central table for the reading of the Torah scrolls and accompanying scriptures (the *haftorah*). The two bases of the table sport a pair of Roman eagles. This is quite strange, first of all given the fact that Jews tended to avoid depictions of animals or people in fulfillment of the second commandment; it is also surpris-

10. The term itself appears in a nearby inscription. See Trebilco, *Jewish Communities*, 51.

Byzantine Chapel near Temple of Artemis

ing given the fact that the Romans had by this time twice devastated the Jews' homeland (in 70 and 135 AD), and the eagle was the most prominent symbol of Rome. Statues of lions decorated the central space of the main hall as well, likely repurposed from the defunct shrine of Cybele, a goddess often portrayed flanked by a pair of lions. Even if they were reimagined as representations of the Lion of Judah, identified with the tribe of Jews in Sardis who designated themselves the *Leontioi* (λεόντιοι), the carved depiction of animals in a synagogue shows a remarkable accommodation of the second commandment to Greco-Roman religious artistic practices.[11] The mosaic designs in the floor, however, were all of the more typical geometric designs with no images. The elders of the synagogue enjoyed a place of honor in semicircular seats at the far front of the main hall (the far west end). This area might also have served as a kind of community council chamber, being crafted in imitation of the typical civic council chamber, or *bouleuterion* (βουλευτήριον).

The forecourt of the synagogue also sported an ornate mosaic floor, again rich in geometric patterns but not in images. Several inscriptions have been laid within the mosaic. One, for example, reads "Aurelius Polyhippos, a God-fearer, having prayed, fulfilled [his vow]." Gentile adherents of the synagogue like Polyhippos may have paid for some portion of its decoration as thank offerings for answered prayers. A row of Byzantine-period shops, some of which enjoyed running water, has been excavated along the street that runs adjacent to the south wall of the synagogue and gymnasium complex.

11. For *Leontioi*, see Trebilco, *Jewish Communities*, 44–45.

Inscription at Sardis Synagogue

THE CHURCH IN SARDIS

The Christians whom the glorified Christ chastened in the fifth of the seven oracles that opened Revelation appear to have taken heed to Christ's warning. The church continued its living witness into the second century and beyond, until the Sassanid invasion destroyed Sardis and scattered all its inhabitants in 616 AD. The most dramatic archaeological witness to this is the fine Byzantine chapel in the southeast corner of the precincts of the temple of Artemis. Worship of Christ significantly outlasted the worship of Artemis in this city. A smaller church structure has been uncovered in the near vicinity of the shrine to Cybele, another sign of the growth and, indeed, the victory of the Christ-cult over the others that had enjoyed such widespread devotion in the city and surrounding region for so long.

BIBLIOGRAPHY

Gaston, Lloyd. "Jewish Communities in Sardis and Smyrna." Pages 17–24 in *Religious Rivalries and the Struggle for Success in Sardis and Smyrna*. Edited by Richard S. Ascough. Waterloo, ON: Wilfrid Laurier University Press, 2005.

Fairchild, Mark R. *Christian Origins in Ephesus and Asia Minor*. Istanbul: Arkeoloji ve Sanat Yayınları, 2015.

Hemer, Colin J. *The Letters to the Seven Churches of Asia in Their Local Setting*. Sheffield: JSOT Press, 1986. Repr., Grand Rapids: Eerdmans, 2001.

Pedley, John G. *Ancient Literary Sources on Sardis*. Cambridge: Harvard University Press, 1972.

Pons, Mariona Vernet. "The Origin of the Name Sepharad: A New Interpretation." *JSS* 59 (2014): 297–313.

Price, S. R. F. *Rituals and Power: The Roman Imperial Cult in Asia Minor*. Cambridge: Cambridge University Press, 1984.

Trebilco, Paul R. *Jewish Communities in Asia Minor*. Cambridge: Cambridge University Press, 2006. Esp. pp. 37–57.

Wilson, Mark. *Biblical Turkey: A Guide to the Jewish and Christian Sites of Asia Minor*. Istanbul: Ege Yayınları, 2010.

CHAPTER 52

THE SOCIAL AND GEOGRAPHICAL WORLD OF PHILADELPHIA

Rev 1:11; 3:7–13

Mark Wilson

KEY POINTS

- Philadelphia was sixth of the seven churches of Revelation and the newest of the cities.
- The city was founded by the Attalid kingdom of Pergamum in the second century BC.
- It was situated on a major road with intercity and interregional connections.
- Earthquakes often damaged the city, which was then rebuilt with the help of Rome.
- The city was home to a Jewish community with a synagogue.

GEOGRAPHICAL SITUATION

Philadelphia was located along the northeastern slope of the Tmolus Mountains (Boz Dağları) in the southeastern part of Lydia.[1] The mound Gavurtepe, three tenths of a mile (.5 km) east of modern Alaşehir, was the initial settlement site on the southwestern side of a broad valley some six miles (10 km) wide.[2] The Cogamus River, named by Pliny the Elder

1. See page 392 for a map of the Roman province of Asia that includes Philadelphia. For a map of the geography of ancient Lydia, see Christopher H. Roosevelt, *The Archaeology of Lydia, from Gyges to Alexander* (Cambridge: Cambridge University Press, 2009), 39 fig. 3.4. However, the city of Blaundos and territory eastward is usually situated in Phrygia.

2. Recep Meriç, *Hermus (Gediz) Valley in Western Turkey: Results of an Archaeological and Historical Survey* (Istanbul: Ege Yayınları, 2018), 147. Gavurtepe was later used as a necropolis from the late Hellenistic period onward.

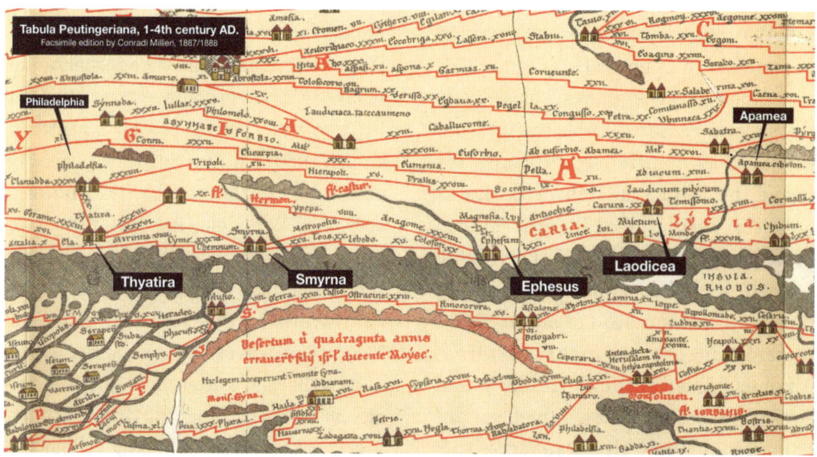

Peutinger Map: Philadelphia to Apamea

(*Natural History* 5.30), joined the Hermus River (modern Gediz) twenty-five miles (40 km) northwest of Philadelphia. Strabo confusingly places Philadelphia first in Phrygia and later in Mysia (*Geography* 12.8.18; 3.4.10). The site may perhaps correspond with that of the earlier Lydian city of Callatebus (Herodotus, *Histories* 7.31).[3]

Philadelphia commanded the road that led up the Cogamus, then crossed a watershed over two thousand feet (610 m) high before descending into the Meander Valley. There it joined the Southern Highway near Laodicea. In 480 BC Xerxes marched to Sardis along this route after stopping at Celanae/Apamea and Colossae (Herodotus, *Histories* 7.26, 30–32). In 399 BC Cyrus the Younger with his ten thousand marched this route in reverse departing from Sardis; he then crossed into the Meander Valley and past Colossae before reaching Apamea (Xenophon, *Anabasis* 1.2.5–6). Sardis (modern Sart) lay only thirty miles (48 km) northwest of Philadelphia, while Tripolis on the Meander (modern Yenicekent) was the final city in Lydia some forty miles (64 km) to its southeast. The northwest gate of Tripolis was called the Philadelphia Gate, indicating its orientation to that city. Philadelphia lay along the imperial road constructed in 129 BC by the Roman governor Manius Aquillius that started in Pergamum, then at Laodicea merged with a branch coming from Ephesus. The final five of the seven churches listed in Revelation 1:11 are given in an order that tracks this route, which suggests the messenger delivering the Apocalypse would have used it (see map on page 630). Aquillius' road eventually terminated at the Pamphylian port of Side.

A track left the Southern Highway at Apamea and ran northwest past the Phrygian city of Blaundos. Eckhard Schnabel has suggested that Paul descended from these "upper regions" before passing Philadelphia on his way

3. Alan H. M. Jones, *Cities of the Eastern Roman Empire*, 2nd ed. (Oxford: Clarendon, 1971), 54, 92.

into the upper Cayster River valley before descending to Ephesus (Acts 19:1).[4] This circuitous detour to Ephesus is unlikely for several reasons. First, traffic from Apamea, as mentioned, typically followed the Southern Highway as far as Laodicea. Ignatius, the bishop of Antioch, most likely followed the southern route when he passed through Philadelphia on his way to Smyrna around AD 110.[5] Since the most direct route to the coast from Apamea passed through Laodicea and continued westward down the Meander Valley, it is likely that Paul took this route to Ephesus rather than through Philadelphia.[6] The fourth-century Peutinger map depicts Philadelphia as a major way station situated at an important road junction.[7]

SETTLEMENT AND POLITICAL SITUATION IN ANTIQUITY

The city was the newest among the seven churches and was established by Attalus II king of Pergamum (reigned 159–138 BC) probably as a garrison town in reaction to the invasion of the Gauls in 168 BC. As the "most important of the Pergamene foundations,"[8] its most common Greek ethnic designation (or demonym) was *philadelpheus* (φιλαδελφεύς), occasionally *philadelphēnos* (φιλαδελφηνός); its Latin form was *Philadelphini*. The Macedonian shield on its civic coinage confirms that Philadelphia originated as a military colony with its first settlers probably coming from the nearby Macedonian colony of Kobedyle (Bebekli).[9] Its civic territory (χώρα, *chōra*) was extensive, including many villages that extended southward to the Meander River at Tripolis and covered the Cogamis Valley as well. Barclay's attempt to position the city as an "open door" for Greek culture and language to neighboring barbarous peoples ignores the hellenization of the region that had begun centuries earlier.[10] The city's name comes from a curious incident regarding Rome's dealings with the Attalids. When Attalus II traveled to Rome in 167 BC, the Roman Senate attempted to turn him against his older brother Eumenes II (reigned 197–159 BC). Livy describes the outcome: "after disappointing the hopes of those who had supposed that he [Attalus II] would accuse his brother and seek a division of the kingdom, he left the senate-house" (45.20.3 LCL; see also Polybius 30:1–3). For remaining loyal, he earned the nickname "Philadelphus," so Philadelphia reflects the love between the two brothers. In the

4. Eckhard Schnabel, *Early Christian Mission* (Downers Grove, IL: InterVarsity Press, 2004), 2:1200.

5. William R. Schoedel, *Ignatius of Antioch: A Commentary on the Letters of Ignatius of Antioch* (Philadelphia: Fortress, 1985), 11.

6. This view is fully articulated in Mark Wilson, "The 'Upper Regions' and the Route of Paul's Third Journey from Apamea to Ephesus," *Scriptura* 117 (2018): 1–21.

7. An online version of the Peutinger map is available at http://peutinger.atlantides.org/map-a/.

8. David Magie, *Roman Rule in Asia Minor to the End of the Third Century after Christ* (Princeton: Princeton University Press, 1950), 1:124.

9. Getzel Cohen, *Hellenistic Settlements in Europe, the Islands, and Asia Minor* (Berkeley: University of California Press, 1995), 227.

10. William Barclay, *The Revelation of John* (Philadelphia: Westminster, 1976), 1:140.

Roman imperial period Philadelphia used the Actian calendar; like other Lydian cities, it reckoned civic dating from the battle of Actium in 31 BC.

In 129 BC, when the Senate voted to accept Attalus III's bequest of his kingdom to the Romans, Philadelphia became part of the province of Asia. Roman Asia was divided into thirteen administrative districts called assizes or *conventus*, and Philadelphia was located within that of its rival Sardis (Pliny, *Natural History* 5.111 [30]). An inscription found in Ephesus dating to the Flavian period similarly placed Philadelphia in the assize of Sardis.[11] In the second century AD Philadelphia finally became the principal city of a new assize (Aelius Aristides, *Orations* 50.96–98). Greek cities were typically divided into tribes, a division of the male citizenry called the *dēmos* (δῆμος).[12] That Philadelphia had seven tribes (unnamed) is known from a third-century AD inscription (*CIG* 3422).[13] The seating arrangements of a city's tribes in a theater was sometimes inscribed on its rows such as at Hierapolis. The tribes gathered in the theater for meetings of the assembly (ἐκκλησία, *ekklēsia*; compare Acts 19:39). Perhaps the fourfold division of humanity often mentioned in Revelation—nation, language, tribe (φυλή, *phylē*), and people—reflects a Greek perspective of humanity's composition (Rev 5:9; 7:9; 11:9; 13:7; 14:6).

Philadelphia's city wall had a rectangular plan with intermittent defensive towers. Though not well preserved, its masonry style dates it probably to the late third century AD (with later reconstructions).[14] The summit of Philadelphia's acropolis (Toptepe) stands at 3135 feet (955 m) and loomed 200 feet (61 m) above the city. On its east side the *cavea* of the theater is visible; however, only the foundations of the stage building remain. A stadium that opened east toward the city was built into the northern end of the acropolis. In it games were held honoring Zeus Helios and Anaitis, a Persian goddess who was assimilated to Cybele and Artemis in Lydia.[15] An alliance (ὁμόνοια, *homonoia*) coin of Domitian (reigned AD 81–96) shows the city goddesses of Ephesus and Philadelphia crowned and shaking hands. That of Ephesus holds a

11. Christian Habicht, "New Evidence on the Province of Asia," *Journal of Roman Studies* 65 (1975): 70, 75.

12. John K. Davies, "Phylai," in *Oxford Classical Dictionary*, ed. Simon Hornblower and Anthony Spawforth, 4th ed. (Oxford: Oxford University Press, 1993), 1178–79.

13. For an image and translation of the inscription, see "Honors by a Tribe of Wool-workers for Aurelius Hermippos (after 212 CE)" on the webpage *Associations in the Greco-Roman World*, http://philipharland.com/greco-roman-associations/honors-by-a-tribe-of-wool-workers-for-aurelius-hermippos-after-212-ce/.

14. For the probability that these walls replaced the Hellenistic walls as well as a further description, see Özcan Erdoğan, "The Remains from Late Antiquity and the East Roman Periods and Their Location within the Lydian City of Philadelphia: New Comments," *Mediterranean Journal of Humanities* 5 (2015): 254–59.

15. Christian Marek, *In the Land of a Thousand Gods: A History of Asia Minor in the Ancient World*, trans. Steven Rendall (Princeton: Princeton University Press, 2016), 162, 516.

Philadelphia Acropolis

scepter while the Philadelphian goddess holds a small statue of Artemis Anaitis.[16] Architectural elements now resting atop the southern end of the acropolis once belonged to a temple of Zeus or Dionysus, but its foundation is now covered by a park.[17]

Philadelphia was situated in an earthquake region called the Catacecaumene ("burnt land"). Strabo states that because of the frequent seismic activity few people lived in Philadelphia but rather in the country as farmers (*Geography* 13.4.10). Grapes grew abundantly in the volcanic soil, and vineyards dotted the countryside, even as today. Bunches of grapes appearing on civic coinage from the Claudian period testify to the soil's fertility.[18] In addition to agriculture, the city's prosperity derived from wool workers, linen workers, cobblers, and dyers. It also was probably a center of textile production like its neighbors Hierapolis and Laodicea.[19] Inscriptional evidence identifies guilds in the city associated with these trades.[20]

In AD 17 a damaging earthquake struck twelve Lydian cities including

16. Barbara Burrell, "Iphigeneia in Philadelphia," *Classical Antiquity* 24 (2005): 241–42; fig. 11b. This interpretation differs from that identifying the goddesses as Tyche and the small statue as Artemis Ephesia.

17. Inci Turkoğlu, "Philadelphia in Lydia," in *Proceedings of the International Congress on Cultural Heritage and Tourism, May 19–21, 2017*, ed. Necmi Uyanık et al. (Konya: Nobel Bilim, 2017), 550.

18. For an illustration, see the coin RPC S2-I-3039A on the Wildwinds.com page for "Roman Imperial Coins of Claudius," http://www.wildwinds.com/coins/ric/claudius/RPC_S2-I-3039A.jpg.

19. Peter Thonemann, *The Maeander Valley: A Historical Geography from Antiquity to Byzantium* (Cambridge: Cambridge University Press, 2011), 186–87. However, in note 40 he concedes that direct evidence of textile production "is not abundant."

20. For further on these guilds, see Thonemann, *Maeander Valley*, 186 n. 40.

Philadelphia. The emperor Tiberius granted tax relief for five years and also gave ten million sesterces to rebuild the cities (Tacitus, *Annals* 2.47). Strabo's description of the city as abandoned because of earthquakes seems overstated. Otherwise, why would the emperor appropriate money to rebuild Philadelphia if it were largely deserted? Rome's mint in AD 22–23 issued a coin depicting Tiberius as a god wearing a laurel wreath to celebrate the restoration of these cities. In thanks, Philadelphia along with the other eleven cities erected a monument in AD 30 in Rome's Forum of Julius Caesar. A personification of Philadelphia was among those representing each city depicted on a base upon which a statue of Tiberius stood. Sardis and Magnesia ad Sipylum flanked the dedicatory inscription on its front with Philadelphia on the right side in the third position. This monument was apparently destroyed in the fire of AD 80. Fortunately, a copy with dedication was made by the Augustales of Puteoli, and this base is now displayed in the Naples National Archaeological Museum.[21] Philadelphia received a new name twice: after AD 17 it was called "Philadelphia Neocaesarea" in gratitude to Tiberius, and later named "Flavia Philadelphia" after the wife of Vespasian (reigned 69–79) when the emperor gave financial assistance following another earthquake. Under Elagabalus it was given the right to call itself a metropolis.[22]

The personification of Philadelphia (at left) from the Tiberius statue base on display at the Naples Museum. The name Philadelphia can be easily read at the bottom left.

RELIGIOUS SITUATION

The city's religious traditions are reflected on its coins. In the first century BC these featured Artemis, Zeus, Dionysus, and the Dioscuri. In the first century AD additional deities such as Hecate, Apollo Kitharoidos, Asclepius, Cybele, and Nike began to appear.[23] An inscription (*SIG* 3.985) dating around 100 BC mentions a shrine erected by Dionysius at the direction of the goddess Agdistis in a dream from Zeus. In it were cultic altars for at least ten gods and goddesses. Men and women, slave

21. Cornelius Vermeule, "The Basis from Puteoli: Cities of Asia Minor in Julio-Claudian Italy," in *Coins, Culture and History in the Ancient World: Numismatic and Other Studies in Honor of Bluma L. Trell*, ed. Lionel Casson and Martin Price (Detroit: Wayne State University Press, 1981), 90–91.

22. Barbara Burrell, *Neokoroi: Greek Cities and Roman Emperors* (Leiden: Brill, 2004), 128.

23. Images of coins of Philadelphia can be viewed online at the Wildwinds.com page "Ancient Coinage of Lydia, Philadelphia (Philadelphia Neokaisareia)," http://www.wildwinds.com/coins/greece/lydia/philadelphia/i.html.

and free were required to take an oath to live within strict ethical guidelines in the context of their sacrificial offerings.[24] Inscriptions indicate that the city had a priest of Rome and Augustus as early as 27/26 BC, but no imperial cult temple was built until AD 214 when Caracalla visited the city and granted permission for Philadelphia to call itself *neōkoros* (νεωκόρος, "temple warden"; *IGR* 4.1619).[25]

A Jewish community lived in Philadelphia. Two thousand families were settled in Lydia and Phrygia around 210 BC as military colonists (Josephus, *Ant.* 12.148–153). So the city's Jewish population probably came from these settlers. No remains of a synagogue have been found, although a Greek inscription dating to the third century AD and found east of Philadelphia mentions a "synagogue of the Hebrews." The legs of a funerary table found in Philadelphia for Judas and Hesychios display menorahs, lulav, and etrog on them.[26]

PHILADELPHIA IN LATER HISTORY

An early tradition suggests that Paul appointed his Jewish kinsman, Lucius (Rom 16:21), as bishop of Philadelphia. However, according to the Apostolic Constitutions, the city's first bishop, Demetrius, was appointed by John.[27] Ignatius visited the city around AD 110 and later wrote a letter from Troas to the church, whose leaders are unnamed (*Philadelphians* 1).[28] He warned them not to listen to anyone expounding Judaism (*Philadelphians* 6), suggesting the ongoing influence of the Jewish community. He also instructed them to appoint a deacon to join the embassies of other Asian churches to travel to Syrian Antioch and congratulate the church there for achieving peace and reconciliation (*Philadelphians* 10).

The travel network among churches established by Paul and the other apostles is shown to continue in the postapostolic period. Ammia and Quadratus were Christian prophets who ministered in Philadelphia during the reign of Hadrian (Eusebius, *Church History* 5.17). Eleven Christians from Philadelphia were martyred with Polycarp in Smyrna around AD 156 (Martyrdom of Polycarp 19.1). John Lydus (born AD 490) was a well-known Byzantine administrator from the city. Though nominally a Christian, he celebrated the city's ties to pagan antiquity; by the fifth century "Philadelphia had earned special distinc-

24. Stanley Stowers, "A Cult from Philadelphia: Oikos Religion or Cultic Association?" in *The Early Church in Its Context*, ed. Abraham J. Malherbe, Frederick W. Norris, and James W. Thompson (Leiden: Brill, 1998), 287–301.

25. Burrell, *Neokoroi*, 126–29. For more on the pagan religious background, see Özcan Erdoğan, "On the History of Religions in Philadelphia in Lydia until the End of Late Antiquity," *Mediterranean Journal of Humanities* 4 (2014): 172–73.

26. Walter Ameling, *Inscriptiones Judaicae Orientis: Band II, Kleinasien* (Tübingen: Mohr Siebeck, 2004), 202–8 nos. 49–50; for photographs of the table legs, see p. 569, figs. 11–14.

27. O. F. A. Meinardus, "The Christian Remains of Seven Churches of the Apocalypse," *BA* 37 (1974): 80.

28. The Philadelphians were so divided, according to Allen Brent, "that Ignatius could not name the bishop, presbyters, and deacons in this church." (Brent, *Ignatius of Antioch: A Martyr Bishop and the Origin of Episcopacy* [London: T&T Clark, 2009], 40).

Church of Saint John

tion for its temples and festivals."[29] Thus John proudly writes about his hometown: "The school of Proclus called Philadelphia 'little Athens' because of their enthusiasm for it" (*de Mensibus* 58). The Byzantine Church of Saint John dating to the sixth century provides the most visible remains in Alaşehir today with three piers of this large basilica still standing.[30] In 1390 Philadelphia was the last Byzantine outpost in Anatolia to fall by surrendering to Bayezid I. Numerous objects of Philadelphia including inscriptions and statues of various gods are found in the provincial archaeological museum at Manisa.[31]

SOCIAL AND GEOGRAPHICAL REALITIES OF THE PHILADELPHIA LETTER

Christianity likely came to Philadelphia in the latter half of the first century. Luke writes that Jews and Greeks throughout Asia heard the gospel during Paul's time in Ephesus (Acts 19:10). John's letter to the church in Philadelphia is rich in local imagery. The "synagogue of Satan" (Rev 3:9), as in Smyrna, seemingly refers to opposition from the local Jewish leadership. The victors in Philadelphia are promised that in God's heavenly temple they would be columns (Rev 3:12).[32] Columns of limestone, granite, or

29. Michael Maas, *John Lydus and the Roman Past: Antiquarianism and Politics in the Age of Justinian* (London: Routledge, 1992), 30.

30. Erdoğan, "Remains from Late Antiquity," 266–71.

31. For inscriptions see Hasan Malay, *Greek and Latin Inscriptions in the Manisa Museum* (Vienna: Österreichische Akademie der Wissenschaften, 1994), passim; for statues see Münteha Dinç, "Manisa Müzesi'ndeki Hellnistik - Roma Dönemi Heykelleri," in *Manisa Müzesi Heykeltıraşlık Eserleri*, ed. Serra Durugönül (Mersin: Mersin University, 2015), 60–64, 66–67.

32. The Greek word *stylos* (στῦλος) is better translated "column" since in discussions of Greco-Roman architecture "pillar" is never used to describe the vertical supports of a temple.

marble were ubiquitous in ancient temples. Their style could be either monolithic or drum (round blocks), unfluted or fluted (grooved). By design, temples were often the most secure structure in a city, especially in earthquake-prone ones like Philadelphia. The promise of being a column suggests strength and stability. The promise of new Jerusalem (Rev 3:12) was interpreted literally by the Montanists, whose prophetic movement is believed by some to have started around Philadelphia in the late second century AD. However, this "Phrygian heresy" is better localized fifty-three miles (86 km) east of Philadelphia around their center at Pepouza. Nevertheless, Montanism had many followers in and around Philadelphia for centuries.[33]

BIBLIOGRAPHY

Ascough, Richard A., Philip A. Harland, and John S. Kloppenborg. *Associations in the Greco-Roman World: An Expanding Collection of Inscriptions, Papyri, and Other Sources in Translation.* Accessed November 26, 2018. http://philipharland.com/greco-roman-associations/

Ameling, Walter. *Inscriptiones Judaicae Orientis: Band II, Kleinasien.* Tübingen, Mohr Siebeck, 2004.

Barclay, William. *The Revelation of John.* 2 vols. Philadelphia: Westminster, 1976.

Brent, Allen. *Ignatius of Antioch: A Martyr Bishop and the Origin of Episcopacy.* London: T&T Clark, 2009.

Burrell, Barbara. "Iphigeneia in Philadelphia." *Classical Antiquity* 24 (2005): 223–56.

———. *Neokoroi: Greek Cities and Roman Emperors.* Leiden: Brill, 2004.

Cohen, Getzel. *Hellenistic Settlements in Europe, the Islands, and Asia Minor.* Berkeley, University of California Press, 1995.

Davies, John K. "Phylai." Pages 1178–79 in *Oxford Classical Dictionary.* Edited by Simon Hornblower and Anthony Spawforth. 4th ed. Oxford; Oxford University Press, 1993.

Dinç, Münteha. "Manisa Müzesi'ndeki Hellnistik – Roma Dönemi Heykelleri." Pages 30–96 in *Manisa Müzesi Heykeltıraşlık Eserleri.* Edited by Serra Durugönül. Mersin: Mersin University, 2015.

Erdoğan, Özcan. "On the History of Religions in Philadelphia in Lydia until the End of Late Antiquity." *Mediterranean Journal of Humanities* 4 (2014): 171–79.

———. "The Remains from Late Antiquity and the East Roman Periods and Their Location within the Lydian City of Philadelphia: New Comments." *Mediterranean Journal of Humanities* 5 (2015); 251–74.

Habicht, Christian. "New Evidence on the Province of Asia." *Journal of Roman Studies* 65 (1975): 64–91.

Jones, Alan H. M. *Cities of the Eastern Roman Empire.* 2nd ed. Oxford: Clarendon, 1971.

Maas, Michael. *John Lydus and the Roman Past: Antiquarianism and Politics in the Age of Justinian.* London: Routledge, 1992.

Magie, David. *Roman Rule in Asia Minor to the End of the Third Century after Christ.* 2 vols. Princeton: Princeton University Press, 1950.

33. William Tabbernee, *Montanist Inscriptions and Testimonia: Epigraphic Sources Illustrating the History of Montanism* (Macon, GA: Mercer University Press, 1997), 53.

Malay, Hasan. *Greek and Latin Inscriptions in the Manisa Museum*. Vienna: Österreichische Akademie der Wissenschaften, 1994.

Marek, Christian. *In the Land of a Thousand Gods: A History of Asia Minor in the Ancient World*. Translated by Steven Rendall. Princeton: Princeton University Press, 2016.

Meinardus, O. F. A. "The Christian Remains of Seven Churches of the Apocalypse." *BA* 37 (1974): 69–82.

Meriç, Recep. *Hermus (Gediz) Valley in Western Turkey: Results of an Archaeological and Historical Survey*. Istanbul: Ege Yayınları, 2018.

Roosevelt, Christopher H. *The Archaeology of Lydia, from Gyges to Alexander*. Cambridge: Cambridge University Press, 2009.

Schnabel, Eckhard. *Early Christian Mission*. 2 vols. Downers Grove, IL: InterVarsity Press, 2004.

Schoedel, William. *Ignatius of Antioch: A Commentary on the Letters of Ignatius of Antioch*. Philadelphia: Fortress, 1985.

Stowers, Stanley, "A Cult from Philadelphia: Oikos Religion or Cultic Association?" Pages 287–301 in *The Early Church in Its Context*. Edited by Abraham J. Malherbe, Frederick W. Norris, and James W. Thompson. Leiden: Brill, 1998.

Tabbernee, William. *Montanist Inscriptions and Testimonia: Epigraphic Sources Illustrating the History of Montanism*. Macon, GA: Mercer University Press, 1997.

Thonemann, Peter. *The Maeander Valley: A Historical Geography from Antiquity to Byzantium*. Cambridge: Cambridge University Press, 2011.

Turkoğlu, Inci. "Philadelphia in Lydia." Pages 549–61 in *Proceedings of the International Congress on Cultural Heritage and Tourism, May 19–21, 2017*. Edited by Necmi Uyanık, Şafak Ünüvar, Tugay Arat, and Ceyhun Ç. Kilinç. Konya: Nobel Bilim, 2017.

Vermeule, Cornelius. "The Basis from Puteoli: Cities of Asia Minor in Julio-Claudian Italy." Pages 85–101 in *Coins, Culture and History in the Ancient World: Numismatic and Other Studies in Honor of Bluma L. Trell*. Edited by Lionel Casson and Martin Price. Detroit: Wayne State University Press, 1981.

Wildwinds. *Ancient Coins: Roman, Greek, Byzantine and Celtic Numismatic Reference for Attribution and Values*. Accessed November 26, 2018. http://www.wildwinds.com/

Wilson, Mark. "The 'Upper Regions' and the Route of Paul's Third Journey from Apamea to Ephesus." *Scriptura* 117 (2018): 1–21.

CHAPTER 53

THE SOCIAL AND GEOGRAPHICAL WORLD OF LAODICEA

Rev 3:14–22

Cyndi Parker

KEY POINTS

- The letter to Laodicea uses rich images to communicate not only to the church in Laodicea but also to other residents in the Lycus Valley.
- Laodicea was the prominent city in the Lycus Valley due to its location on the trade routes, its fertile agriculture, and its rich textile industry.
- The Laodicean church is called "lukewarm," which is a rebuke on the ineffectiveness of the church.
- The church of Laodicea viewed themselves as rich, prosperous, and in need nothing, but God saw the opposite in them and invites them to experience fulfillment in him.

INTRODUCTION

Laodicea is the last of the seven churches addressed in Revelation (3:14–22). Similar to the other letters, the greeting begins with a descriptive character of Christ (v. 14) and concludes with "He who has an ear, let him hear what the Spirit says to the churches" (v. 22, see also 2:7a, 11a, 17a, 29; 3:6, 13).[1] The conduct of the Laodicean church is judged, and the people are described as neither hot nor cold. Their lukewarmness will result in being spit out of God's mouth (vv. 15–16). The church says they are rich, prosperous, and in need of nothing, but God says they are poor, blind, and naked (v. 17). Only God can provide the gold, garments, and eye salve necessary to flourish (v. 18). The motivation for the Lord's reproof stems from his love for the church (v. 19). The letter concludes with

1. Unless otherwise, noted biblical quotations are from the NASB.

two images of restored relationship—a shared meal (v. 20) and a shared throne (v. 21). This letter is rich with images pertinent to the residents of Laodicea, and the interpretation of these images deserves special attention.

GEOGRAPHY

The western part of Asia Minor consists of four east-west valleys that drain the Phrygian highlands into the Aegean Sea. The southern most of the east-west valleys is the Meander River Valley, which is anchored on the west by the port cities of Miletus and Ephesus further north (see Acts 20:15–38). At the eastern end of the Meander River Valley the Lycus Valley breaks off to the southeast. Near the junction of the two valleys sits the city of Laodicea.[2] In this area, the Lycus Valley is six miles (9.7 km) wide but gradually narrows to two miles (3.2 km) wide in the east.[3]

Through the junction of the Meander and Lycus Valleys run important roads.[4] One is the trunk route that runs from Ephesus or Miletus on the Aegean Sea, through the Meander Valley, into the

2. For detailed information of the geography of the Lycus Valley and the growth of the cities within it, see Celal Şimşek and Francesco D'Andria, eds., *Landscape and History in the Lykos Valley: Laodikeia and Hierapolis in Phrygia* (Newcastle upon Tyne: Cambridge Scholars Publishing, 2017).

3. Sherman Johnson, "Laodicea and Its Neighbors," *BA* 13 (1950): 2–3.

4. For details of New Testament road networks see *BAGRW* with particular attention to plates 61, 65–66, and 67.

Lycus Valley, and ultimately to Syria.[5] At the Lycus Valley junction a traveler also has the choice to turn northwest to reach Philadelphia or south over the mountains to the coast. Laodicea sat at this junction and grew in significance and wealth due to its location. These roads were a part of a larger communication network that made circulating letters among the seven churches of Revelation easy. A messenger could travel from Ephesus north along the coast to Smyrna and Pergamum, and then overland to Thyatira, Sardis, Philadelphia, and Laodicea, making geographic sense of the listed order of the churches in Revelation (see map on page 630). A turn west through the Meander Valley takes the messenger back to the coast.[6]

The Lycus River Valley contained three primary cities, Colossae, Hierapolis, and Laodicea. Given the interconnected nature of these cities, a brief discussion of each is warranted. In the narrow, eastern portion of the valley was Colossae, the oldest of the three cities and one that flourished in the fifth and fourth centuries BC. The city was built on a mound above the floor of the valley near the cold-water springs that supplied water for the residents. Colossae was a trade center for wool and dyeing, and although the city flourished due to its location on the southern trade route, it was later eclipsed by Laodicea.[7]

Hierapolis was built three hundred feet (483 m) above the valley floor on the northern hills of the Lycus Valley. The city was renowned for its warm medicinal springs located on the edge of the city facing the valley floor. The high mineral content of the thermal waters calcified on the edges of the pools creating dramatic terraces and turning the hillside into what looked like a frozen waterfall.[8] These cascading white cliffs over which thermal waters dripped into the valley were visible from Laodicea. Along with these mineral hot springs, Hierapolis was known for wool, metal working, and stone cutting.[9]

Thermal Waters of Hierapolis

The third significant city in the Lycus Valley was Laodicea. The city was located at the opposite end of the Lycus Valley from Colossae (11 miles [17.7 km]), and a short distance south from Hierapolis

5. *BAGRW*, 4; Anson F. Rainey and R. Steven Notley, *The Sacred Bridge* (Jerusalem: Carta, 2006), 382; Carl Rasmussen, *Zondervan Atlas of the Bible*, rev. ed. (Grand Rapids: Zondervan, 2010), 239.

6. Ulrich Huttner, *Early Christianity in the Lycus Valley* (Brill, 2013), 152.

7. Johnson, "Laodicea and Its Neighbors," 5.

8. Colin J. Hemer, *The Letters to the Seven Churches of Asia in Their Local Setting* (Sheffield: JSOT Press, 1986), 182.

9. Hemer, *Letters to the Seven Churches*, 12.

(6 miles [9.7 km]).[10] By the second century BC, Laodicea eclipsed Colossae as the dominant city in the valley. Laodicea was built on a plateau one hundred feet (30.5 m) above the valley floor on the south side of the Lycus River.[11] To the north and the west of the city, the Lycus Valley widened and ultimately joined the broad fields of the Meander Valley. To the south and the east the views were aborted by the high mountains. No fresh water springs were near Laodicea, although two small tributaries of the Lycus River were nearby. Since those streams dried up in the summer months, the residents of the flourishing city relied primarily on a clay-pipeline siphon system that carried water from springs to the south, which continue to supply the nearby.[12]

Siphon System Leading to Laodicea

HISTORY

Laodicea grew out of the small town of Diospolis. It gained prominence and size between 261 and 253 BC when Antiochus II rebuilt the city and named it after his wife Laodice. The city came under Roman control in 133 BC and continued to develop in wealth and importance due to its fertile territory, famed textiles, and prominent location on the southern trunk road.[13]

The Lycus Valley was in an earthquake-prone area. One quake demolished Laodicea in AD 17, and Tiberius sent money to rebuild the city. Another devastating quake occurred in AD 60, but, according to Tacitus, while Hierapolis and other cities rebuilt with the help of Rome, Laodicea refused imperial funds choosing to rely on its own wealth to restore itself (Tacitus, *Annales* 14.27).[14] Although the attitude of self-sufficiency was respected by Rome, the church of Laodicea would be rebuked for such self-reliance.

ARCHAEOLOGY

The manner in which the residents rebuilt the city after the earthquake in AD 60 is evidence of their affluence. Recent excavations and restorations have been ongoing in the ancient city for thirteen years under the leadership of Professor Celal Şimşek of the Pamukkale University Archaeology Department. It is a huge site and many of the remains

10. Rainey and Notley, *Sacred Bridge*, 382.

11. Edwin Yamauchi, *The Archaeology of New Testament Cities in Western Asia Minor* (Grand Rapids: Baker, 1980), 135.

12. Mark Wilson, email message, July 9, 2019; see also M. J. S. Rudwick and E. M. B. Green, "The Laodicean Lukewarmness," *Expository Times* 69.6 (March 1958): 177.

13. Hemer, *Letters to the Seven Churches*, 180.

14. See also Celal Şimşek, "Urban Planning of Laodikeia on the Lykos in the Light of New Evidence" in Şimşek, *Landscape and History in the Lykos Valley*, 5.

speak to the wealth and sophistication of the Roman city.[15]

Laodicea had three city gates corresponding to its external connections via the road system—the western gate to Ephesus, the northern gate to Hierapolis, and the eastern gate to Syria. The city contained a Greek-style theater (not yet

15. For an English summary of Şimşek's archaeological findings see Şimşek, "Urban Planning of Laodikeia," 9–51. Also, see Huttner, *Early Christianity in the Lycus Valley*, 159–60.

Ephesian Gate

excavated) and a smaller Roman theater with an odeon (see image on page 694). A stadium for gladiatorial games was dedicated to Vespasian and Titus by a wealthy family. The city also contained a large forum and temple—likely belonging to the imperial cult—that were depicted on coins minted in the city (see an image of a temple on page 691). In AD 123/124 the emperor Hadrian dedicated a gymnasium and bath complex.

Also visible on adjacent hills are remains of a siphon-style aqueduct that brought water to the city from Denizli in the south. Similar to the hot waters of Hierapolis, the water carried through the aqueducts to Laodicea had a high mineral content, as evident by the calcareous deposits that have blocked sections of the pipe. Water was collected in water towers from which it was distributed to the city's residents.[16]

Archaeology demonstrates that Laodicea was a city where stadiums were built for games and major regional events, small theaters were replaced by larger ones, and huge temples were dedicated to the emperor.[17] Not all of these structures were built by the time of the writing of the letter in Revelation, but this amount of ambitious expansion speaks to the robust development of Laodicea that was well underway. The letter written to Laodicea as well as the other six churches were addressed to Christians living in large and cultured cities in the Roman Empire.

LOCAL INDUSTRY

By the time of the writing of the letter in Revelation to Laodicea, the city's prominent position on the trade route had turned it into a wealthy city of commerce. The city was a banking center that minted its own bronze city coins. Some gold artifacts such as rings and Byzantine gold glass were also found in the excavations.[18] A large Jewish community flourished in Laodicea as is evident by the sizable amounts of gold sent back to the temple in Jerusalem. Cicero reports that in 62 BC Laodicea's governor seized

16. Strabo described the water as hard though potable (Strabo, *Geography*, 13.4.14). See also Şimşek, "Urban Planning of Laodikeia," 8–9.

17. Huttner, *Early Christianity in the Lycus Valley*, 159–60.

18. Huttner, *Early Christianity in the Lycus Valley*, 164. For a more detailed discussion of the banking center of Laodicea see Hemer, *Letters to the Seven Churches*, 191–94.

twenty pounds of gold sent by Jews in the region to Jerusalem—a substantial sum potentially the equivalent of the offering of 7,500 Jewish freemen.[19]

Bronze Coin Minted in Laodicea

Similar to Colossae and Hierapolis, Laodicea was known for textiles. The expensive garments made from the black wool of local long-haired black sheep was one of Laodicea's most important exports (Strabo, *Geography*, 12.8.16).

Circumstantial evidence suggests a medical school was possibly located in Laodicea which specialized in dispensing collyrium—a type of dark, powdered eye shadow used in eye salves and cosmetics.[20] Northwest of the city was a famed temple and school of medicine of Men Karou where Phrygian stone was ground and used as an eye salve (Strabo, *Geography*, 12.8.20). Also nearby was the medical school in Carura where the famous ophthalmologist Demosthenes Philalethes practiced. The proximity of the two medical schools and the abundance of powdered Phrygian stone near the city suggest that Laodicea was a medicinal center as well.[21]

THE CHURCH IN LAODICEA

The church in Laodicea was likely established during Paul's ministry in Ephesus when during the course of two years "all who lived in Asia heard the word of the Lord, both Jews and Greeks" (Acts 19:10). It was likely Epaphras and not Paul who evangelized the cities in the Lycus Valley (Col 1:6–7; 4:12–13).[22] Christian communities throughout the Lycus Valley were closely connected and shared letters from Paul. Notice in Colossians that all three of the cities in the Lycus Valley are mentioned together (Col 2:1; 4:13, 15–16). The recognized connection between the communities in the Lycus Valley further suggests that the letter to Laodicea in Revelation 3:14–22 may have been intended for the wider Christian community outside the city limits.

WHAT DOES IT MEAN TO BE LUKEWARM?

The opening comments of the letter to Laodicea include an unfavorable evaluation of the Laodicean church calling the people *lukewarm* (χλιαρός, *chliaros*). Their deeds are observed, but since they are neither cold nor hot but rather lukewarm, they will be spit out (Rev 3:15–16). The scholarly interpretation of these verses, specifically the *lukewarm* connotation, has varied in past years. The ambiguity comes from the hot and cold

19. David Aune, *Revelation 1–5*, (Dallas: Word, 1997), 249; Hemer, *Letters to the Seven Churches*, 182; Yamauchi, *Archaeology of New Testament Cities*, 137. See also Cicero, *Pro Flacco*, 28–68.

20. Yamauchi, *Archaeology of New Testament Cities*, 145 n. 28; Huttner, *Early Christianity in the Lycus Valley*, 170–71.

21. Huttner, *Early Christianity in the Lycus Valley*, 172–73.

22. Aune, *Revelation*, 250; Hemer, *Letters to the Seven Churches*, 181.

Temple A at Laodicea

adjectives that connote a preferred state of being in contrast to the lukewarmness that is negative. However, these temperature adjectives do not come with a noun, so the object must be inferred based on context. A brief summary of scholarly suggestions for *who* or *what* is lukewarm will be discussed below,[23] but first, a word of caution is deserved here. The descriptive terms in this letter must not give way to the temptation to isolate the concrete references to Laodicea. If the assumption is that the letters are intended to be circulated, then the context must be familiar to those who not only know Laodicea's environs and reputation but who themselves are able to relate to the images.

In the late third century AD, Victorinus of Pettau wrote a Commentary on the Apocalypse of the Blessed John in which he attributed the temperature metaphor to the intensity of a person's faith.[24] "Cold" was the antagonism of nonbelievers, and "hot" was the fervor of believers. Thus, "lukewarm" referred to those who compromised their beliefs, or rather, "became all things to all people."[25] Pettau concluded that God prefers people to be on one extreme or the other but not in the compromising middle.

23. Aune says "hot" is negative and "cold" is positive for a person's self-control, and Ford suggests that "lukewarm" is a metaphor of spiritual apathy in which a person's religious fervor cools after conversion. Both scholars state that the metaphor is taken from Laodicea's water supply that was tepid and less desirous than the hot or cold springs in nearby cities. See Aune *Revelation*, 257; and J. Massyngberde Ford, *Revelation* (Garden City, NY: Doubleday, 1975), 418–419. Huttner, *Early Christianity in the Lycus Valley*, 156 n. 64 traces the history of the scholarly view of the lukewarm reference relying on assumed information about the aqueducts.

24. William Weinrich, ed. and trans., *Latin Commentaries on Revelation: Victorinus of Petovium, Apringius of Beja, Caesarius of Arles, and Bede the Venerable* (Downers Grove, IL: InterVarsity Press, 2011).

25. Weinrich, *Latin Commentaries*, 6.

The interpretation that "lukewarm" meant the Laodicean church lacked religious zeal is problematic. Cold and hot are taken as equally commendable alternatives, so it is not logical to conclude that antagonism toward God is on par with fervor for God. There is no biblical support for such a conclusion nor that the indifference of a nonbeliever is preferable in God's sight to a half-hearted believer. Likewise, it is difficult to defend that temperatures refer to a person's temperament or to the spiritual state of a person.[26] Certainly as one reads within the apocalyptic context of the text, such a conclusion does not make sense.

The difficulty of translating the temperature analogies is compounded by textual problems. *Zestos* (ζεστός), meaning "hot," is found in the New Testament only in Revelation 3:15–16, although a similar Greek word is used in Acts 18:25 and Romans 12:11. *Zestos* is sometimes used figuratively to describe the passions of people, but it does not describe an individual's character. *Psychros* (ψυχρός), meaning "cold," is used in Revelation 3:15–16 and also in Matthew 10:42. Although *psychros* can be used in a metaphorical sense, it is rarely used of a person. The Greek word for "lukewarm" (χλιαρός, *chliaros*) is rare. In the New Testament *chliaros* is used singularly in Revelation 3:16, which is the only time in all sources when the term is applied to a person.[27] Therefore, the rare use of these words will not help modern readers uncover the original, assumed reference, but they do point to the unlikely nature of these adjectives as descriptions of a person's religious fervor.

In the late 1800s, Sir William Ramsay suggested that the local context of Laodicea should be used to understand the letter. The temperature analogy, therefore, must refer to the water system.[28] The phrase "because you are lukewarm ... I will vomit you out of my mouth" (v. 16) prompts many to agree that water is the intended referent due to the elaborate aqueduct systems and water towers supplying the city with water. Thus, the lukewarmness alluded to the quality of the city's water supply. The hot springs of Hierapolis were praised for healing qualities, and the cool spring water of Colossae was refreshing. To make the temperature analogy work, scholars presumed the water coming through the aqueduct to Laodicea was lukewarm and useless.

This argument is also problematic. Laodicea received water through the aqueduct from Denizli, but there is no evidence for the temperature or quality of that water. It is assumed that the travel time through the aqueduct made the water undesirable, but this conclusion would not make Laodicea unique among

26. As stated by Aune, *Revelation*, 257; and Ford, *Revelation*, 418–419. See also Rudwick and Green, "Laodicean Lukewarmness," 176; Huttner, *Early Christianity in the Lycus Valley*, 157.

27. Detailed discussions of extrabiblical uses of these three temperature words can be found in Stanley Porter, "Why the Laodiceans Received Lukewarm Water (Revelation 3:15–18)," *TynBul* 38 (1987): 144–46.

28. William Ramsay, *Cities and Bishoprics of Phrygia* (Oxford: Clarendon, 1895) and *The Letters to the Seven Churches and Their Place in the Plan of the Apocalypse* (London: Hodder and Stroughten, 1904). The assumption that the temperatures refer to the city's water supply is now assumed in many publications. Cf. Hemer, *Letters to the Seven Churches*, 188; Porter, "Why the Laodiceans Received Lukewarm Water," 143–44, 147; Rainey and Notley, *Sacred Bridge*, 382; Rasmussen, *Zondervan Atlas of the Bible*, 239.

other cities that also get water from aqueducts. There is no evidence of aqueducts carrying hot water from Hierapolis nor cold water from Colossae, so assumptions about the cooling or heating of water in the aqueducts is guess work. Importantly, the hot water of Hierapolis was known for medicinal reasons but *not for drinking*. Therefore, the waters of Laodicea would be better for drinking than the water from Hierapolis.[29] Yet the verse states that the lukewarm are "spit out." The conclusion that "lukewarm" is in reference to the quality of drinking water available in Laodicea still relies on too much guess work and deserves to be questioned.

A recent interpretation posited by Craig Koester refines the above argument by explaining the ancient view that hot and cold waters had positive medicinal benefits while lukewarm water was considered to be emetic (that is, something that induces vomiting).[30] Koester thinks there are feasting parallels between the hot, cold, and lukewarm references in verses 15–16 and the image of Jesus coming to dine in verse 20. Depicting Jesus knocking at the door suggests that an accepted invitation leads to a shared meal that demonstrates acceptance and fellowship.[31] The earlier analogy of hot and cold should be interpreted according to favorable temperatures of liquids served at a meal (thus hot and cold being preferable), making lukewarm a reference to tepid water used to purge the stomach. Koester concludes that the message to Laodicea is at first threatening (the current emetic effects of the deeds of the church) but then concludes on a hopeful note using feasting imagery to encourage repentance in the church.[32]

Clare Rothschild agrees that ancient medicine is the appropriate lens through which to understand the rebuke of Laodicea but does not agree that feasting images are intended. Both cold and hot were connected to health and were among the four potent medicinal elements that formed the basis of creation (along with dry and wet). Rothschild suggests *potency* not *extremes* are being discussed in Revelation 3. While cold and hot are potent and effective elements, the lukewarm middle ground was judged to be inert and powerless.[33] Therefore, the Laodicean church lacked *potency*.[34] The church of Laodicea, represented by its works, was not effective like the four medicinal elements of creation, but instead caused illness and required purgation by lukewarm water.[35] Rothschild

29. Rudwick and Green, "Laodicean Lukewarmness," 176–78; Craig Koester, "The Message to Laodicea and the Problem of Its Local Context: A Study of Imagery in Rev 3:14–22," *NTS* 49 (2003): 409–10.

30. Huttner, *Early Christianity in the Lycus Valley*, 157–58; Koester, "Message to Laodicea," 415; Clare K. Rothschild, "Principle, Power, and Purgation in the Letter to the Church in Laodicea (Rev 3:14–22)" in *Die Johannesapokalypse: Kontexte—Konzepte—Rezeption*, ed. Jörg Frey, James A Kelhoffer, and Franz Tóth (Tübingen: Mohr Siebeck, 2012), 261.

31. Koester, "Message to Laodicea," 413.

32. Koester, "Message to Laodicea," 416.

33. Huttner, *Early Christianity in the Lycus Valley*, 158; compare Rothschild, "Principle, Power, and Purgation," 261.

34. Rothschild, "Principle, Power, and Purgation," 261.

35. Rothschild, "Principle, Power, and Purgation," 283.

Hellenistic (West) Theater

suggests the letter to Laodicea rebukes the church for its impotency, not for its lack of religious conviction. Despite the respect and wealth and regard of the city, Christ is nauseated by the church of Laodicea.[36]

Koester and Rothschild build their arguments in different ways, but their conclusions are similar. The letter to Laodicea claims that the works of the church are ineffective.[37] The hot, cold, and lukewarm comparison is one of healthy versus unhealthy or potent versus impotent. Therefore, it is not the spiritual temperature but the ineffectiveness of the church that is condemned.

The following verses (Rev 3:17–18) expand on what it means for the church to be lukewarm. The imagined condition of the people was of affluence and without need of anything. And, historically the city did enjoy financial independence. In the aftermath of a destructive earthquake, Laodicea's prosperity allowed residents to refuse Roman imperial money to rebuild their city. The Laodicean church's context was that of a city of great wealth and honor. Yet the end of verse 17 describes the reality of the true condition of the church. "You are the one who is wretched, pitiable, poor, blind and naked!" A shocking contrast to how the church viewed itself! The church of Laodicea thought that they were rich, prosperous, and in need of nothing, but God saw the opposite in them. In their self-reliance they were coming up empty.

What resolution is available to a church that so wrongfully evaluated their state of being? The solution is to buy refined gold to be rich, white garments to be dressed, and eye salve to see (Rev 3:18). The true needs of the church can only be supplied by Jesus himself.[38]

36. Rothschild, "Principle, Power, and Purgation," 291.

37. Rudwick and Green arrive at the same conclusion even though stating "cold" and "hot" refer to the water brought by aqueducts to Laodicea, see "Laodicean Lukewarmness," 178.

38. Hemer, *Letters to the Seven Churches*, 195–96.

If the Christian church of Laodicea was familiar with Jewish traditions, then these allusions refer to Old Testament metaphors that symbolized purification and right standing with God.[39] However, they also clearly hit upon the reality of those in this mercantile city. Laodicea was the financial center in the area, and they exported black wool and (perhaps) eye salve. Products such as these made the citizens wealthy. The contradiction between the wealth created from Laodicea's products and the true wealth attained by going to God is poignant. However, these products are not specific only to Laodicea[40] making the comparison relatable to all people in the region. Self-reliance led to ineffective deeds, but reliance on God led to true health and vitality of the church.

POSSIBILITY OF A RESTORED RELATIONSHIP

The letter concludes with two images of a restored relationship. The first is of Jesus standing at the door and knocking. Although Jesus is outside, he is waiting for the invitation to enter and to eat around the table. "If anyone hears my voice and opens the door, I will come in to him and will dine with him, and he with me" (Rev 3:20). The emphasis on eating "with" each other highlights the intimate fellowship created around food. The second image of a restored relationship is the imperial image of sharing a victorious throne—an image not uncommon in Revelation. The kingdom posture threatened the position of the Roman emperor whose temple was in the city. Jesus' promise to share the throne subverts the emperor's role and emphasizes God's dominion over Rome.[41]

The letter to the church of Laodicea is a clear rebuke for the ineffectual and impotent behavior of the church due to its own self-reliance. The church's self-perception is the opposite of their reality as described by God, and yet an offer is made for reconciliation. The letter concludes with a call for the church to accept complete reliance on Jesus who offers an invitation for a restored relationship producing a powerful outcome.

BIBLIOGRAPHY

Aune, David. *Revelation 1–5*. Dallas: Word, 1997.

Decker, Timothy L. "'Live Long in the Land': The Covenantal Character of the Old Testament Allusions in the Message to Laodicea (Revelation

39. Refined gold in Ezek 22:18–20; Zech 13:9 Mal 3:3. Purity of white garments in Ps 51:7; Eccl 9:8; Dan 7:9; 11:35; Isa 1:18; Rev 7:19. Having eyes to see or restoring sight to the blind is a common analogy in the Old Testament although no references use eye salve in direct connection with the restored sight. See Huttner, *Early Christianity in the Lycus Valley*, 164–66. A lengthy discussion of possible Old Testament references is found in Timothy L. Decker, "'Live Long in the Land': The Covenantal Character of the Old Testament Allusions in the Message to Laodicea (Revelation 3:14–22)," *Neotestamentica* 48 (2014): 423–37; and Hemer, *Letters to the Seven Churches*, 184–86.

40. Ephesus was also a banking center along with Pergamum. Medicine was produced at Pergamum, Smyrna, and Ephesus. Ephesus, Smyrna, Sardis, Thyatira, Philadelphia, Hierapolis, and Colossae all were connected to textile trade. See Koester, "Message to Laodicea," 417–18; Hemer, *Letters to the Seven Churches*, 200.

41. Hemer, *Letters to the Seven Churches*, 207; Huttner, *Early Christianity in the Lycus Valley*, 181.

3:14–22)." *Neotestamentica* 48 (2014): 417–46.

Ford, J. Massyngberde. *Revelation*. Garden City, NY: Doubleday, 1975.

Hemer, Colin J. *The Letters to the Seven Churches of Asia in Their Local Setting*. Sheffield: JSOT Press, 1986.

Huttner, Ulrich. *Early Christianity in the Lycus Valley*. Leiden: Brill, 2013.

Johnson, Sherman. "Laodicea and its Neighbors." *BA* 13 (1950): 1–18.

Keener, Craig S. *Revelation: From Biblical Text to Contemporary Life*. Grand Rapids: Zondervan, 2000.

Koester, Craig R. "The Message to Laodicea and the Problem of Its Local Context: A Study of the Imagery in Rev 3:14–22." *NTS* 49 (2003): 407–24.

Porter, Stanley E. "Why the Laodiceans Received Lukewarm Water (Revelation 3:15–18)." *TynBul* 38 (1987): 143–49.

Rainey, Anson F., and R. Steven Notley. *The Sacred Bridge*. Jerusalem: Carta, 2006.

Ramsay, William. *Cities and Bishoprics of Phrygia*. Oxford: Clarendon, 1895.

———. *Letters to the Seven Churches and Their Place in the Plan of the Apocalypse*. London: Hodder and Stroughten, 1904.

Rasmussen, Carl. *Zondervan Atlas of the Bible*. Revised ed. Grand Rapids: Zondervan, 2010.

Rudwick, M. J. S., and E. M. Green. "The Laodicean Lukewarmness." *Expository Times* 69.6 (March 1958): 176–78.

Rothschild, Clare K. "Principle, Power, and Purgation in the Letter to the Church in Laodicea (Rev 3:14–22)." Pages 259–91 in *Die Johannesapokalypse: Kontexte—Konzepte—Rezeption*. Edited by Jörg Frey, James A. Kelhoffer, and Franz Tóth. Tübingen: Mohr Siebeck, 2012.

Şimşek, Celal. "Urban Planning of Laodikeia on the Lykos in the Light of New Evidence." Pages 1–52 in *Landscape and History in the Lykos Valley: Laodikeia and Hierapolis in Phrygia*. Edited by Celal Şimşek and Francesco D'Andria. Newcastle upon Tyne: Cambridge Scholars Publishing, 2017.

Şimşek, Celal, and Francesco D'Andria, eds. *Landscape and History in the Lykos Valley: Laodikeia and Hierapolis in Phrygia*. Newcastle upon Tyne: Cambridge Scholars Publishing, 2017.

Strabo. *The Geography of Strabo*. Translated by Horace Leonard Jones. LCL. Cambridge: Harvard University Press, 1924.

Tacitus, Cornelius. *The Complete Works of Tacitus*. Translated by Alfred John Church. Edited by Moses Hadas. New York: Modern Library, 1942.

Weinrich, William, ed. and trans. *Latin Commentaries on Revelation: Victorinus of Petovium, Apringius of Beja, Caesarius of Arles, and Bede the Venerable*. Downers Grove, IL: InterVarsity Press, 2011.

Yamauchi, Edwin. *The Archaeology of New Testament Cities in Western Asia Minor*. Grand Rapids: Baker, 1980.

MAPS, IMAGES, AND CHARTS

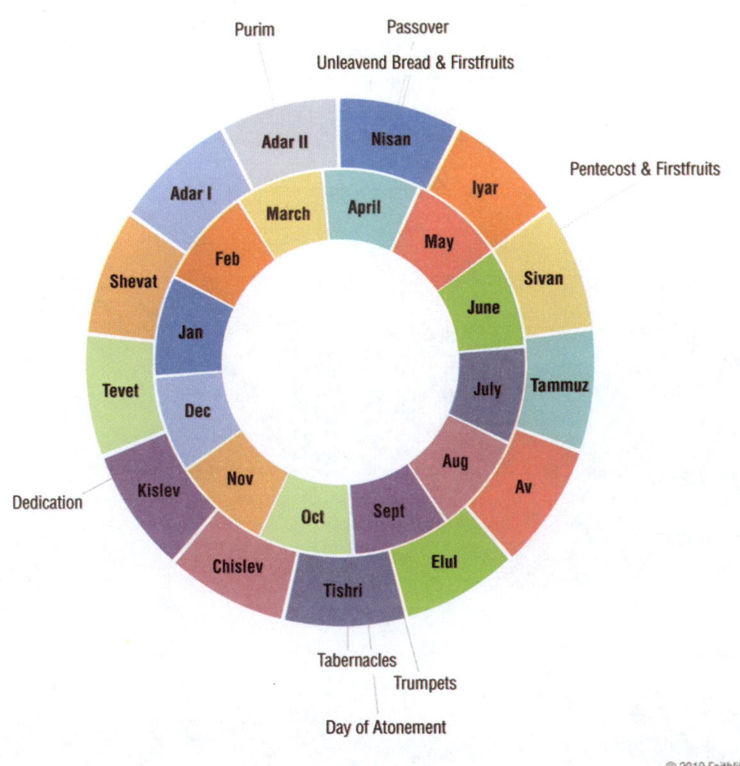

Gamla Synagogue

Masada Synagogue

Herodion Synagogue

Magdala Synagogue

Trajan's Column (Cichorius Plate) Scene 23 (center): Making a Road through the Forest

Trajan's Column (Cichorius Plate) Scene 56 (left): Road-building in the Mountains

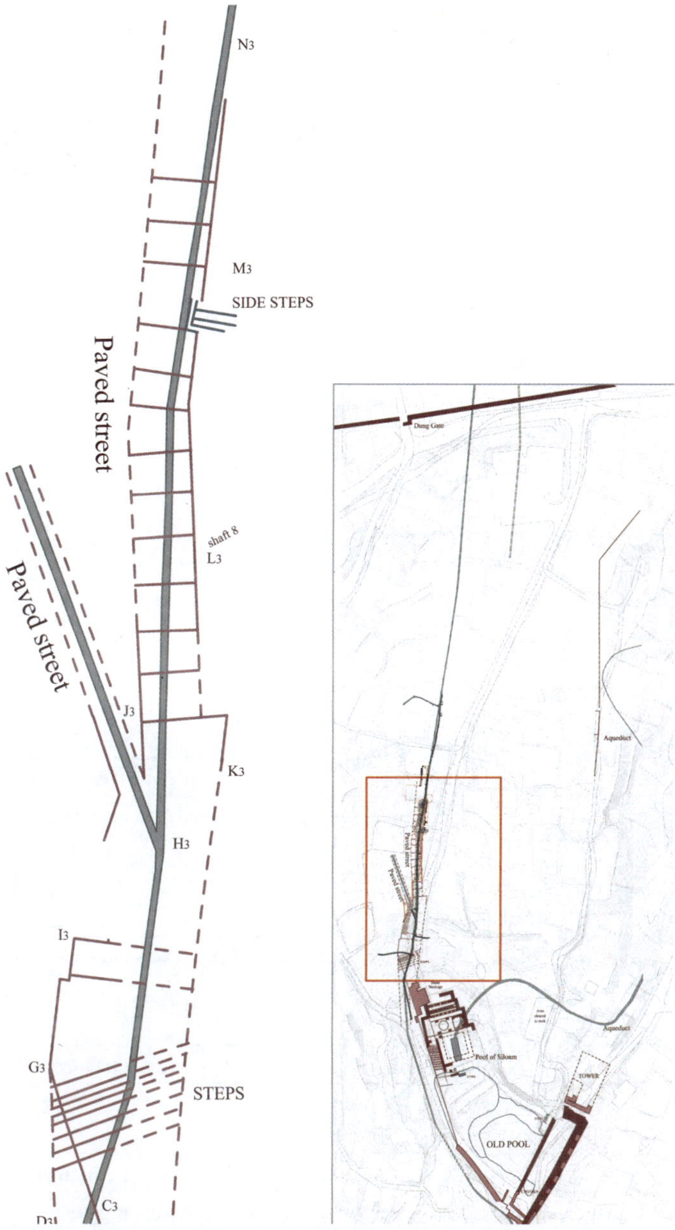

Fig. 1: Site plan of the stepped street by which the Pool of Siloam was accessed.

Hippodrome at Caesarea Maritima

The Periods of Paul's Missionary Work

PERIOD	LOCALE	PASSAGES	YEARS
Period 1	Damascus (Syria)	Acts 9:19–21; Gal 1:17; Acts 9:23–25	32/33
Period 2	Sakkaia? Bostra? Petra? (Arabia/Nabatea)	Gal 1:17; 2 Cor 11:32	32–33
Period 3	Jerusalem (Judea)	Acts 9:26–29; Rom 1:16	33/34
Period 4	Tarsus? Anazarbos? (Cilicia)	Acts 9:30; 11:25–26; Gal 1:21	34–42
Period 5	Alexandria? Seleucia? Antioch (Syria)	Acts 11:26–30; 13:1	42–44
Period 6	Salamis, Paphos (Cyprus)	Acts 13:4–12	45
Period 7	Antioch, Iconium, Lystra, Derbe (Galatia)	Acts 13:14–14:23	45–47
Period 8	Perga (Pamphylia)	Acts 14:24–26	47
Period 9	Philippi, Thessalonica, Berea (Macedonia)	Acts 16:6–17:15	49–50
Period 10	Athens, Corinth (Achaia)	Acts 17:16–18:28	50–51
Period 11	Ephesus, Sardis? Pergamum? (Asia)	Acts 19:1–41	52–55
Period 12	Dyrrhachium? Apollonia? (Illyricum)	Rom 15:19	56
Period 13	Caesarea (Judea)	Acts 21:27–26:32	57–59
Period 14	Rome	Acts 28:17–28	60–62
Period 15	Tarraco? Gades? (Spain)	1 Clement 5:5–7	63–64?
Period 16	Kydonia? Polyrrenia? (Crete)	Titus 1:5	64–65?

Augustus seated colossus from the Herculaneum Augusteum. A similar colossus would have sat within the temple at Pisidian Antioch.

Agricultural Cycle of the Levant/Palestine

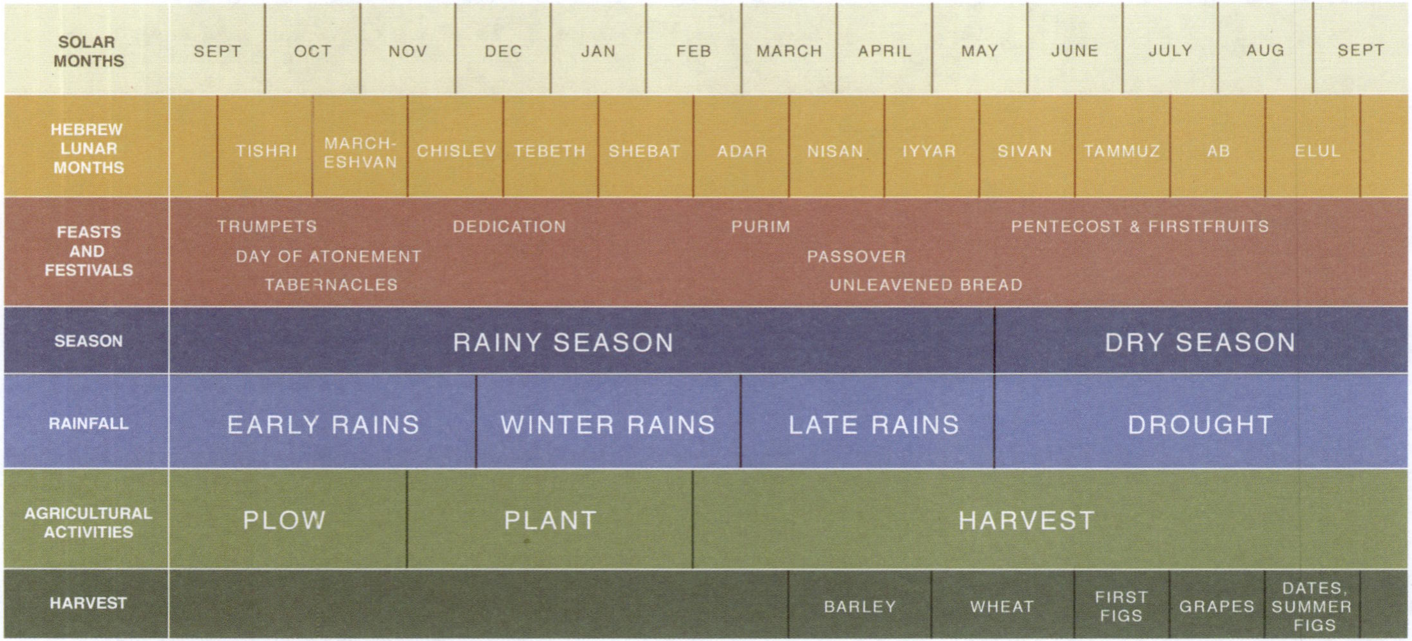

SOLAR MONTHS	SEPT	OCT	NOV	DEC	JAN	FEB	MARCH	APRIL	MAY	JUNE	JULY	AUG	SEPT
HEBREW LUNAR MONTHS	TISHRI	MARCH-ESHVAN	CHISLEV	TEBETH	SHEBAT	ADAR	NISAN	IYYAR	SIVAN	TAMMUZ	AB	ELUL	
FEASTS AND FESTIVALS	TRUMPETS DAY OF ATONEMENT TABERNACLES			DEDICATION		PURIM		PASSOVER UNLEAVENED BREAD	PENTECOST & FIRSTFRUITS				
SEASON	RAINY SEASON								DRY SEASON				
RAINFALL	EARLY RAINS		WINTER RAINS				LATE RAINS		DROUGHT				
AGRICULTURAL ACTIVITIES	PLOW		PLANT			HARVEST							
HARVEST							BARLEY		WHEAT	FIRST FIGS	GRAPES	DATES, SUMMER FIGS	

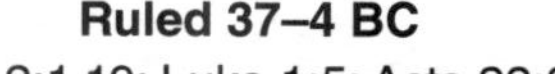

King Herod (Herod the Great; Herod I)
Ruled 37–4 BC
Matt 2:1-19; Luke 1:5; Acts 23:35

Archelaus
Son of Herod the Great by Malthace
Ruled 4 BC–AD 6
Matt 2:22

Antipas
(Herod Antipas)
Son of Herod the Great by Malthace
Ruled 4 BC–AD 39
Matt 14:1–12; Mark 6:14–29; 8:15;
Luke 3:1, 19–20; 8:3; 9:7–9; 13:31; 23:7–15;
Acts 4:27; 13:1

Philip
(Philip the Tetrarch)
Son of Herod the Great by
Cleopatra of Jerusalem
Ruled 4 BC–AD 34
Luke 3:1

Agrippa I
(Herod Agrippa I)
Grandson of Herod the Great,
son of Aristobulus IV and Berenice
Ruled AD 37–44 [or 41–44]
Acts 12:1–23

Agrippa II
(Herod Agrippa II)
Great-grandson of Herod the Great,
by Aristobulus IV, by Agrippa I
Ruled AD 48–100
Acts 25:13–26:32

Herodian Dynasty Family Tree

Mosaic inscription from the House of Eustolios describing his work as a benefactor of Kourion.

Another mosaic inscription from the House of Eustolious attributing the strong structure of the house to the "signs of Christ."

Inscription Dedicated to "Jupiter, Best and Greatest"

RES · GESTAE · DIVI · AVGVSTI ·

Res Gestae Divi Augusti Replica

Coin Celebrating Smyrna's Thrice Awarded Neokorate

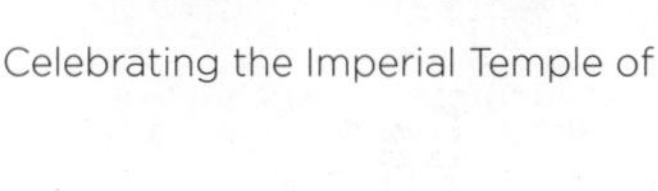

Coin Celebrating the Imperial Temple of 26 AD

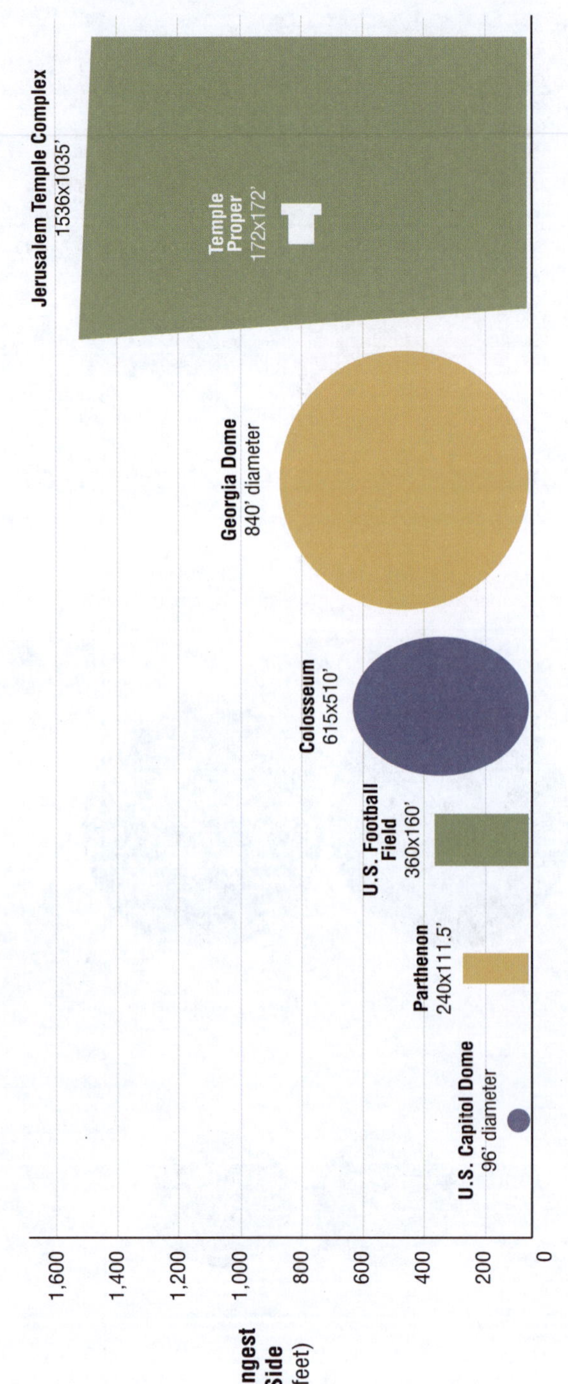
Temple Mount Size Comparison
Longest Side (feet)
0
200
400
600
800
1,000
1,200
1,400
1,600
U.S. Capitol Dome
96' diameter
Parthenon
240x111.5'
U.S. Football Field
360x160'
Colosseum
615x510'
Georgia Dome
840' diameter
Jerusalem Temple Complex
1536x1035'
Temple Proper
172x172'
Copyright 2018 Faithlife

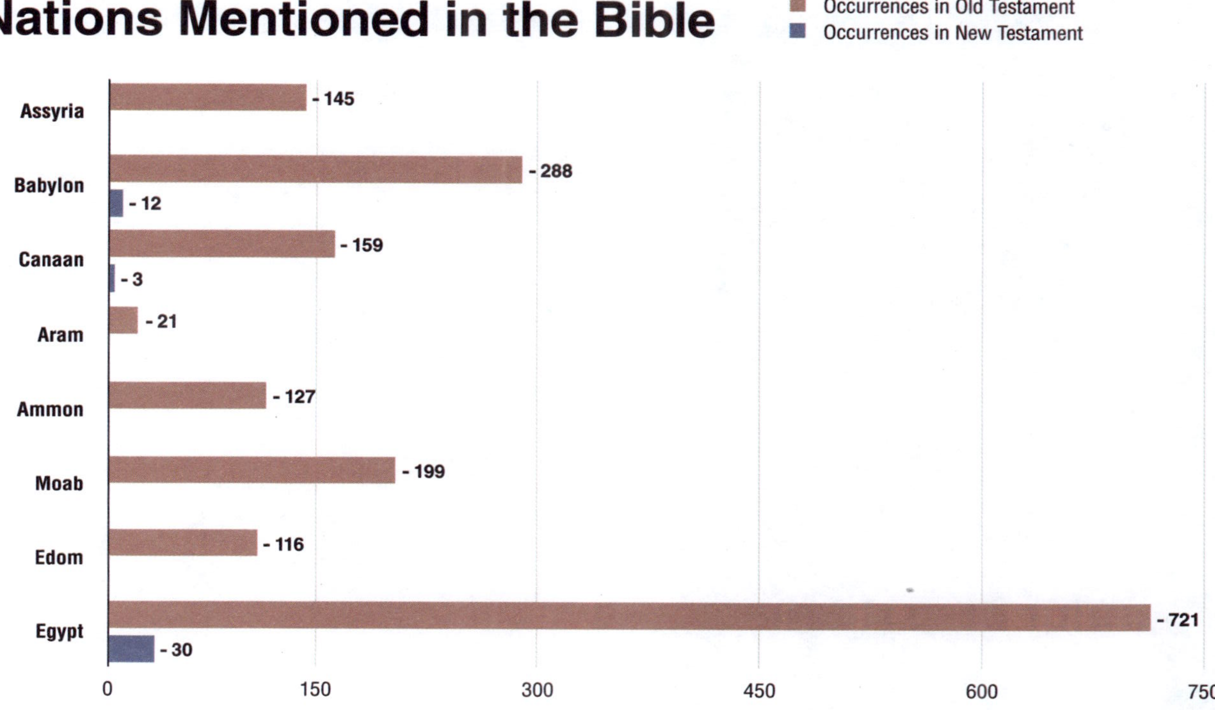

Nations Mentioned in the Bible
Occurrences in Old Testament
Occurrences in New Testament
Assyria
- 145
Babylon
- 288
- 12
Canaan
- 159
- 3
Aram
- 21
Ammon
- 127
Moab
- 199
Edom
- 116
Egypt
- 721
- 30
0
150
300
450
600
750
Copyright 2018 Faithlife

1–Domus Septimi Severi
2–Temple of Jupiter Victor
3–Domus Livia
4–Temple of Magna Mater
5–Temple of Divis Julius
6–Colossus of Nero
7–Temple of Castor and Pollux
8–Temple of Vesta
9–Curia Julia
10–Temple of Saturn
11–Temple of Juno Moneta
12–Temple of Jupiter, Juno, and Minerva
13–Temple of Venus Genetrix
14–Temple of Mars Ultor

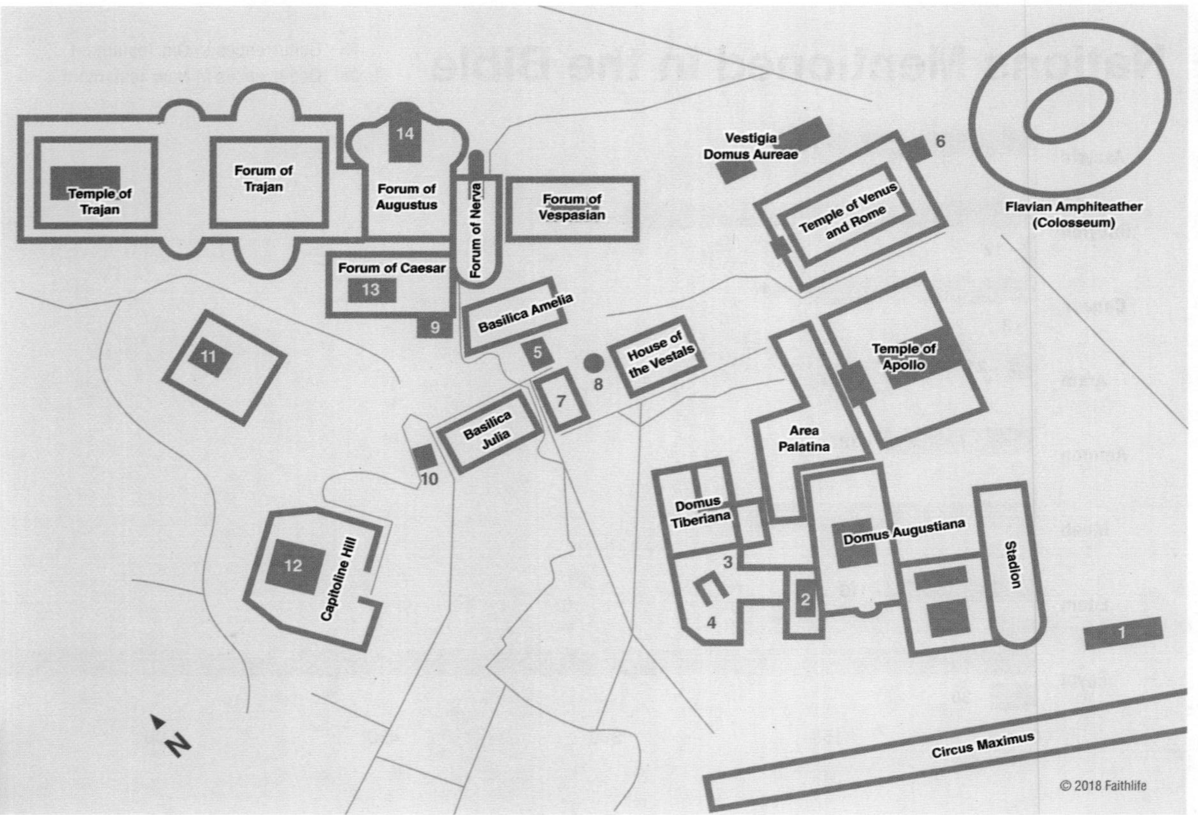

ROMAN FORUM

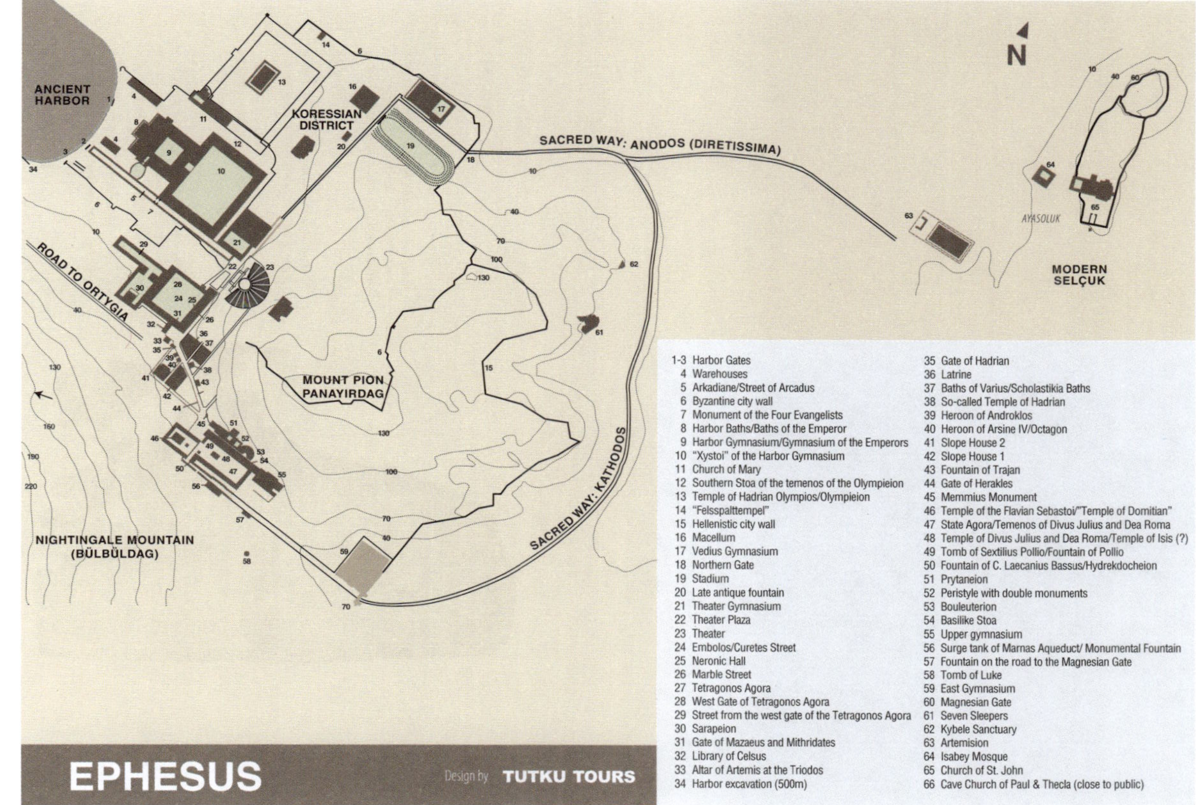
ANCIENT HARBOR
KORESSIAN DISTRICT
SACRED WAY: ANODOS (DIRETISSIMA)
N
ROAD TO ORTYGIA
MOUNT PION PANAYIRDAG
SACRED WAY: KATHODOS
MODERN SELÇUK
AYASOLUK
NIGHTINGALE MOUNTAIN (BÜLBÜLDAG)
EPHESUS
Design by TUTKU TOURS
1-3 Harbor Gates
4 Warehouses
5 Arkadiane/Street of Arcadus
6 Byzantine city wall
7 Monument of the Four Evangelists
8 Harbor Baths/Baths of the Emperor
9 Harbor Gymnasium/Gymnasium of the Emperors
10 "Xystoi" of the Harbor Gymnasium
11 Church of Mary
12 Southern Stoa of the temenos of the Olympieion
13 Temple of Hadrian Olympios/Olympieion
14 "Felsspalttempel"
15 Hellenistic city wall
16 Macellum
17 Vedius Gymnasium
18 Northern Gate
19 Stadium
20 Late antique fountain
21 Theater Gymnasium
22 Theater Plaza
23 Theater
24 Embolos/Curetes Street
25 Neronic Hall
26 Marble Street
27 Tetragonos Agora
28 West Gate of Tetragonos Agora
29 Street from the west gate of the Tetragonos Agora
30 Sarapeion
31 Gate of Mazaeus and Mithridates
32 Library of Celsus
33 Altar of Artemis at the Triodos
34 Harbor excavation (500m)
35 Gate of Hadrian
36 Latrine
37 Baths of Varius/Scholastikia Baths
38 So-called Temple of Hadrian
39 Heroon of Androklos
40 Heroon of Arsine IV/Octagon
41 Slope House 2
42 Slope House 1
43 Fountain of Trajan
44 Gate of Herakles
45 Memmius Monument
46 Temple of the Flavian Sebastoi/"Temple of Domitian"
47 State Agora/Temenos of Divus Julius and Dea Roma
48 Temple of Divus Julius and Dea Roma/Temple of Isis (?)
49 Tomb of Sextilius Pollio/Fountain of Pollio
50 Fountain of C. Laecanius Bassus/Hydrekdocheion
51 Prytaneion
52 Peristyle with double monuments
53 Bouleuterion
54 Basilike Stoa
55 Upper gymnasium
56 Surge tank of Marnas Aqueduct/ Monumental Fountain
57 Fountain on the road to the Magnesian Gate
58 Tomb of Luke
59 East Gymnasium
60 Magnesian Gate
61 Seven Sleepers
62 Kybele Sanctuary
63 Artemision
64 Isabey Mosque
65 Church of St. John
66 Cave Church of Paul & Thecla (close to public)

Parchment

Parchment was made from the skins of goats, sheep, and cattle.

The word **parchment**, from the Greek *pergamenos*, is linked to the ancient city of Pergamum, well-known for its production (and the possible origin) of the writing material.

Though parchment was likely more expensive than papyrus, it was more durable which eventually made it the preferable material for manuscripts.

Around AD 400, parchment became the primary material on which manuscripts were written.

Vellum

A special type of parchment made from very fine animal skins is called **vellum**. It was often dyed purple and used for special copies of manuscripts.

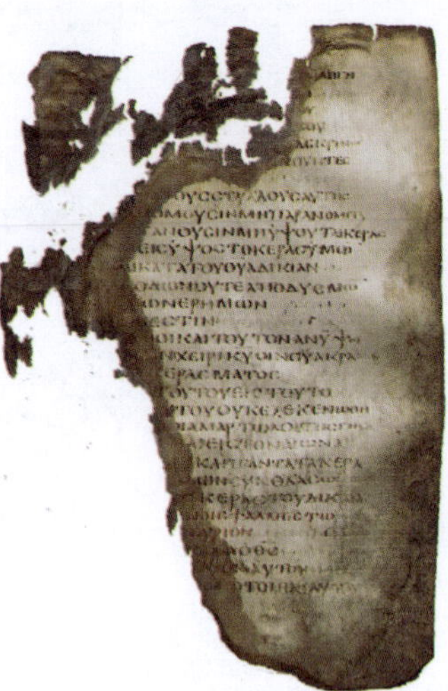

Section of Psalms in Washington Manuscript II

Learn more

Factbook: Parchment

Aerial View of the Gymnasium and *Palaestra* at Sardis

Reconstructed View of the Gymnasium and *Palaestra* at Sardis

KIZILGEÇİT
TAPURELİ
Hisarkale
Soldier relief
Hüsametli
Üç Ayaklı rustic villa
KAYACI
Soldier relief
Tapureli Fortress
Watchtower
Road
Veyselli
Soldier relief
Yeniyurt Fortress
Watchtower
YENİYURT
Eşekderesi Roman Bridge
Araplı Veyseli
Sömek Roman Bridge
Roman Bridge
Warrior Reliefs
Roman Road
Watchtower
Fortress
Sömek Warrior Relief
Sömek Athena Relief with Menorah
Koşkerli Ören Yeri
TABİYE
ERDEMLİ
YEĞENLİ
Seydili
Seydili Ruins
ESENPINAR
Sömek
Roman Road/ Milestone
Relief
Tomb
Tower
2 Watchtowers
Tomb
Watchtower
UZUNCABURÇ (Diocaesarea)
Watchtower
Olba
CAMBAZLI
Örendibi Menorah Lintel
Lamos Cay Relief
Yanıkhan
KOCAHASANLI
Church
Kurşunlu Kale
Watch-tower
Milestone
Öküzlü
Roman Road
BATISANDAL
LİMONLU
Roman Road Along Modern Road
Karaahmetli
Kırağıbucağı
Kanyteleis Watchtower
Watchtower
Imirzeli Ören Yeri
Tırtar Akkale Graneries
Roman Road & Reliefs
KUMKUYU
HÜSEYİNLER
Keşlitürkmenli
Roman Road
Watchtower
Çatıören
Kabaçam
Mancınıkkale
Reliefs
Watchtower
Roman Road
Ovacık
Watch-tower 2
Watch-tower 1
Watchtower
Hisarkale
Yapılı In Reliefs
Meydankale
RomanRoad
Gömeç Watchtower
Ören Yeri
Hıdırlı
Theater
İMAMLI
Tekkadın Watchtower
Watchtower
Adamkayalar Reliefs
Watch-tower
Watchtower
AYAŞ
Elaiousia Sebaste
YENİBAHÇE
Hasanlılar Church
KIZKALESİ (Korykos)
Karaböcülü
Watchtower
Watchtower
Mezgitkale
Paslı
Karadere
Cennet Cehennem
Watchtower
Sinekkale
Aşağı Dünya
Işıkkale
BÜKDEĞİRMENİ
Roman Road
NARLIKUYU
Mosaic Museum
Karakabaklı
Imbriogion Demicili
Susanoğlu (Korasion)
Göksu
ATAKENT
ATAYURT
Mediterranean Sea
SİLİFKE
Seleucia Ad Calycadnum
Göksu
ARKUM
BURUNCU
KURTULUŞ
TAŞUCU
Göksu
EASTERN ROUGH CILICIA
Prepared by
TUTKU TOURS
TURKEY & THE MEDITERRANEAN
N
S
E
W

CONTRIBUTORS

Dr. Barry J. Beitzel is Professor Emeritus of Old Testament and Semitic Languages at Trinity Evangelical Divinity School in Deerfield, Illinois, USA. He holds a PhD in Ancient Near Eastern Studies from Dropsie University in Philadelphia. He obtained a postdoctorate in Ancient Near Eastern Geography from the Université de Liège, Belgium, and has engaged in postdoctoral archaeological work through UCLA in eastern Syria. Dr. Beitzel is the author of *The New Moody Atlas of the Bible* (Moody Press, 2009). His publications on Near Eastern geography have appeared in a variety of monographs and journals, from *Biblical Archaeology Review* and *The Bulletin of the American Schools of Oriental Research* to *Iraq: The British Institute for the Study of Iraq*. Dr. Beitzel's maps appear in *National Geographic, The Biblical Word: An Illustrated Atlas, The Holman Bible Atlas, The NIV Study Bible, The ESV Study Bible,* and in several monographs.

Dr. John A. Beck (PhD, Trinity International University) has taught courses in Hebrew and Old Testament at various colleges and universities for more than twenty-five years. For more than twenty of those years, he has been teaching field studies in Israel, Jordan, and Egypt that explore the relationship between geography, culture, and the way the biblical authors express themselves. Beck spends most of his year writing books and documentaries. He is a permanent adjunct faculty member at Jerusalem University College in Israel. His books include: *The Land of Milk and Honey, God as Storyteller, Zondervan Dictionary of Biblical Imagery, The Baker Illustrated Guide to Everyday Life in Bible Times, The Discovery House Bible Atlas, The Baker Bible Book of Maps, Charts, and Timelines,* and *The Holy Land for Christian Travelers*. Forthcoming book-documentary releases include *Along the Road: How Jesus Used Geography to Tell God's Story* and *Land without Borders: How God Guides You Through the Wilderness*. Beck lives in Wisconsin.

Dr. Todd Bolen is Professor of Biblical Studies at The Master's University in Santa Clarita, CA. For more than a decade, he lived and taught at the university's Israel Bible Extension (IBEX) campus near Jerusalem, and he continues to instruct undergraduate and seminary groups in Israel. Bolen is the creator of the *Pictorial Library of Bible Lands* (18 volumes) and the *Historic Views of the Holy Land* (17 volumes). He is currently leading a team of researchers in creating the *Photo Companion to the Bible* with the goal of illustrating nearly every verse in Scripture. He was a contributing author to *Jesus: A Visual History*, by Donald L. Brake, and he wrote the notes for 2 Kings in the *Zondervan NIV Study Bible*.

Dr. Alan H. Cadwallader is a Research Fellow at the Center for Public and Contextual Theology at Charles Sturt University, Canberra, Australia. His doctoral monograph, published as *Beyond the Word of a Woman* (a study of the Syrophoenician woman's encounter with Jesus in Mark 7) won the Australasian Theological Book of the Year award in 2008. His field and archival research into the site of Colossae in the Lycus Valley began in 2000 and he has regularly published new inscriptions, discoveries, and analyses related to the site. He coedited a collection of new interpretations of the site in 2011 (*Colossae in Space and Time*) and released *Fragments of Colossae* in 2015, which won the Biblical Archaeological Society Book of the Year award for best popular archaeology publication in 2017. He is currently coediting a major collection on the Lycus Valley for the series *New Documents Illustrating Early Christianity* and writing a monograph on the major Byzantine story associated with Colossae, the Story of St Michael of Chonai.

Dr. Philip W. Comfort (DLitt et Phil) has taught English, Greek, New Testament, and Religion at many colleges, including Wheaton College and Coastal Carolina University. He has authored many books about the New Testament manuscripts, the New Testament literature, and translations of the New Testament. He was translator and coordinating editor of the New Testament of the New Living Translation. He is currently retired and lives in Pawleys Island, South Carolina.

Dr. David A. deSilva (PhD, Emory) serves as Trustees' Distinguished Professor of New Testament and Greek at Ashland Theological Seminary. He is the author of over twenty-five books, including *An Introduction to the New Testament* (InterVarsity Press, 2004), *Introducing the Apocrypha* (Baker Academic, 2002), *Honor, Patronage, Kinship & Purity* (InterVarsity Press, 2000), and *Paul's Letter to the Galatians* in the New International Commentary to the New Testament series (Eerdmans, 2018). Over the course of the past decade, he has spent several months in the Eastern Mediterranean investigating the material culture of the New Testament.

Dr. Mark R. Fairchild (PhD, Drew University) is Professor and Chair of the Department of Bible and Religion at Huntingdon University. His recent publications include *Christian Origins in Ephesus and Asia Minor* (Hendrickson, 2017), "Laodicea's Lukewarm Legacy: Conflicts of Prosperity in an Ancient Christian City" (*Biblical Archaeology Review*, March/April 2017), "The Jewish Communities in Eastern Rough Cilicia" (*The Menorot of Limyra and Judaism in Asia Minor: Archaeology, Visual Culture and Literature. Journal of Ancient Judaism*, Volume 5, 2014), "Why Perga? Paul's Perilous Passage through Pisidia" (*Biblical Archaeology Review*, November/December 2013), and "Turkey's Unexcavated Synagogues: Could the World's Earliest Known Synagogue Be Buried Amid Rubble?" (*Biblical Archaeology Review*, July/August 2012). Professor Fairchild has traveled to Turkey numerous times over the past twenty years undertaking research on the ancient cities of Anatolia.

Dr. Benjamin A. Foreman received his MA from the Hebrew University of Jerusalem and his PhD from the University of Aberdeen (2009). He has lived in Israel since 2001 and is a faculty member at the Israel extension of The

Master's University (IBEX), where he teaches historical geography and biblical history. He also travels to Hungary on a yearly basis and is a guest lecturer of Manners and Customs and Psalms at the Word of Life Bible Institute. He has participated in several archaeological digs in Israel and is the author of *Animal Metaphors and the People of Israel in the Book of Jeremiah* (Vandenhoeck & Ruprecht, 2011).

Dr. Joshua W. Jipp (PhD, Emory) is Associate Professor of New Testament at Trinity Evangelical Divinity School. He is the author of *Saved by Faith and Hospitality* (Eerdmans), *Christ is King: Paul's Royal Ideology* (Fortress), and *Divine Visitations and Hospitality to Strangers in Luke-Acts* (Brill).

Dr. J. Carl Laney served from 1977–2018 as Professor of Biblical Literature at Western Seminary in Portland, Oregon. Laney was introduced to the land of the Bible in 1973 during his studies at the Jerusalem University College (formerly the Institute of Holy Land Studies). Since that experience he has given special attention to the geographical, cultural, and historical background of the Bible, writing his ThM thesis at Western Seminary on "The Geopolitics of the Judean Hill Country" and his ThD dissertation at Dallas Theological Seminary on "Selective Geographical Problems in the Life of Christ." Laney's studies in Israel have included excavations at Tel Qasile, Tel Jezreel, and Bethsaida. Since 1992 he has been taking students to Israel to participate in the short-term program at the Jerusalem University College. Laney's book, *Concise Bible Atlas: A Geographical Survey of Bible History*, is published by Hendrickson.

Dr. Chris McKinny received his PhD from Bar-Ilan University (Israel). His dissertation focused on the historical geography and archaeology of the town lists of Judah and Benjamin in the book of Joshua. Chris is also a core staff member of the Tel Burna Archaeological Project and currently involved in several other writing and research projects. His past projects include *My People as Your People: A Textual and Archaeological Analysis of the Reign of Jehoshaphat* (Lang, 2016) and *The Regnal Chronology of the Kings of Israel and Judah* (BiblePlaces, 2015). In addition to this academic research, Dr. McKinny has served as an adjunct faculty member at the Israel Bible Extension Campus (IBEX) of The Master's University, and has led numerous field tours throughout Israel for undergraduates, graduates, and laypeople.

Dr. Cyndi Parker is the Clark Assistant Professor of Biblical Studies at Biblical Theological Seminary. She holds a PhD in Theological and Religious Studies from the University of Gloucestershire, and teaches in churches and universities around the world. Her research interests include biblical views of place, biblical history and geography, and the correlation between theology and ecology (with particular interest in food justice). Dr. Parker lived in Jerusalem for five years teaching Historical Geography of the Bible at Jerusalem University College, and has led dozens of trips to Israel. She continues to develop innovative educational trips to Israel, seeking to inspire students of all ages through experiential education.

Dr. Elaine A. Phillips is Distinguished Professor of Biblical Studies at Gordon College in Wenham, MA, where she has taught since 1993. She holds a PhD in

Rabbinics from the Dropsie College for Hebrew and Cognate Learning. She and her husband, Perry (also a contributor to the *Lexham Geographic Commentary*), studied and taught at the Institute for Holy Land Studies (now Jerusalem University College - JUC) from 1976–1979 and are adjunct faculty with JUC, serving as field instructors for the three-week course in Historical and Geographical Settings of the Bible. In addition to field study in Israel, her areas of interest and scholarly writing include the books of Exodus and Esther, biblical wisdom literature, and hermeneutics. Her book-length commentary on Esther is included in *The Expositor's Bible Commentary*, edited by Tremper Longman III and David Garland. She authored *With God Nothing Is Impossible* (Deep River, 2014), tracing narratives of key women in the Bible as their stories unfolded in the Promised Land. Her latest publication is *An Introduction to Reading Biblical Wisdom Texts* (Hendrickson, 2017), designed for inquisitive laypersons.

Dr. Perry G. Phillips, after receiving his PhD in astrophysics from Cornell University where he became a Christian as a graduate student, attended Biblical Theological Seminary, where he earned his MDiv before heading to the Institute of Holy Land Studies, now Jerusalem University College (JUC), to complete his M.A. in Hebrew language. After his MA, Dr. Phillips remained at JUC where he taught historical geography to groups of students from around the world. Dr. Phillips has taught over sixty groups in Israel, off and on, and continues to teach historical geography together with his wife, Dr. Elaine Phillips (also a contributor to the *Lexham Geographic Commentary on the Gospels*).

Dr. Eckhard J. Schnabel (PhD, Aberdeen) is Mary F. Rockefeller Distinguished Professor of New Testament at Gordon-Conwell Theological Seminary. His recent publications include *Early Christian Mission* (InterVarsity Press, 2004); *Paul the Missionary: Realities, Strategies, Methods* (InterVarsity Press, 2008); *The Book of Acts* (Zondervan Exegetical Commentary on the New Testament, Zondervan, 2012); *The Trial and Crucifixion of Jesus* (with D. Chapman; Mohr Siebeck, 2015); *Der Brief an die Römer* (Brockhaus, 2015/2016); *The Gospel of Mark* (InterVarsity Press, 2017); and *Jesus in Jerusalem* (Eerdmans, 2018).

Dr. Mark L. Strauss (PhD, Aberdeen) is University Professor of New Testament at Bethel Seminary San Diego, where he has served since 1993. He is the author/coauthor of fifteen books and many articles, and editor/coeditor of forty volumes. His works include commentaries on Mark's Gospel in the *Zondervan Exegetical Commentary Series* (2014) and *Expositor's Bible Commentary*, vol. 9 (2010) and on Luke in the *Illustrated Bible Background Commentary* (2002); *Jesus Behaving Badly* (InterVarsity Press, 2015); *How to Read the Bible in Changing Times* (Baker, 2011); *Four Portraits, One Jesus* (Zondervan, 2007) and *The Davidic Messiah in Luke-Acts* (Sheffield Academic, 1996). He serves as Vice Chair of the Committee on Bible Translation for the *New International Version* and as an associate editor for the *NIV Study Bible*.

Dr. Michael J. Thate has embarked on something of a nomadic, cross-disciplinary existence since obtaining his PhD in Religious Studies from Durham University in 2012. His first position was as a lecturer in New Testament Interpretation at Yale Divinity School, where he also was a postdoctoral visiting fellow. From there he moved to Princeton University where he again was a postdoctoral researcher / lecturer, this time in ethics at the Center for the Study of Religion and the Religion Department. A recent recipient of the Alexander von Humboldt award, Dr. Thate spent time between the Institut für antikes Judentum und hellenistische Religionsgeschichte at Tübingen University and in the Centre international d'étude de la philosophie française contemporaine at the École normale supérieure, Paris. He is currently at Princeton University as an Associate Research Scholar working on labor disputes from antiquity to modern times. Additionally, he is a visiting fellow at the Center for the Study of World Religions at Harvard Divinity School where he is undertaking new research on time, technology, and messianism in twentieth-century philosophy. Dr. Thate's first book, *Remembrance of Things Past?* (Mohr Siebeck, 2013) was a social history of the rise of history-as-science in nineteenth- and twentieth-century German universities and the emergence of the "historical Jesus" discourse it produced. His second book, *The Godman and the Sea* (University of Pennsylvania Press, 2019), reads varying representations of the sea in antiquity and early Christianity through the rubrics of desolation and trauma. Dr. Thate is currently finishing a book on the sense of smell in antiquity.

Dr. Mark Wilson received an MA in Biblical Studies at Regent University and a DLitt et Phil from the University of South Africa (Pretoria) where he serves as a Research Fellow in Biblical Archaeology. He is an Associate Professor Extraordinary of New Testament at Stellenbosch University. He is also an Adjunct Professor in New Testament at Ridley College and Regent University. He has authored a commentary on *Revelation* (Zondervan), *Charts of the Book of Revelation* (Kregel), and *Biblical Turkey: A Guide to the Jewish and Christian Sites of Asia Minor* (Ege Yayınları). He contributed the "Acts" and "Revelation" sections for the *ESV Archaeology Bible*. He has published numerous articles on the geography and Roman roads related to Paul's journeys. Dr. Wilson regularly leads study trips for groups to biblical sites in Turkey, Greece, Italy, Malta, and Cyprus. He is the founder of the Asia Minor Research Center in Antalya, Turkey, where he lives with his wife Dindy.

Rev. Dr. Paul H. Wright is President of Jerusalem University College/Institute of Holy Land Studies. Dr. Wright has lived full-time in Jerusalem since 1997, where he has taught classes in biblical historical geography and on the cultural backgrounds of the Bible to thousands of students in Israel. He received his PhD in Bible and Ancient Near East from Hebrew Union College, Cincinnati, OH. Dr. Wright has published numerous books on topics related to the landed context of the Bible with the Israeli publisher Carta and is the author of the *Rose Then and Now Bible Map Atlas* with Rose Publishing.

SUBJECT INDEX

Polybius xix(n5), 415, 657, 676

SCRIPTURE INDEX

Old Testament

Micah

Haggai

Zechariah

Malachi

New Testament

Matthew

Mark

Luke

John

Acts

Romans

1 Corinthians

2 Corinthians

Galatians

Ephesians

Philippians

Colossians

1 Thessalonians

2 Thessalonians

1 Timothy

2 Timothy

Septuagint (LXX)

Apostolic Fathers

Acts of the Apostles

Old Testament Pseudepigrapha

Josephus

Rabbinic Literature

IMAGE ATTRIBUTION

Page 7. Model of Herod's Temple. Image by Juan R. Cuadra. Public Domain. Via Wikimedia Commons.

Page 13. Mount Gerizim. Image by Daniel Warner. Copyright 2004 The Virtual Bible. Used by permission.

Page 16. Reconstructed Map of Eratosthenes Depicting the Ancient World (ca. 2nd century BC). Image by J. F. Horrabin. Public Domain. Via Wikimedia Commons.

Page 21. Valleys of Hinnom (Left), Tyropoeon (Center), and Kidron (Right) in Jerusalem. Image by Daniel Warner. Copyright 2004 The Virtual Bible. Used by permission.

Page 23. Jerusalem in the First Century. Illustration by Leen Ritmeyer. Copyright Ritmeyer Archaeological Design (www.ritmeyer.com). Used by permission.

Page 24. Southern Wall of the Temple Mount. Image by Oren Rozen. Licensed under CC BY-SA 3.0. Via Wikimedia Commons.

Page 25. Southern Wall of the Temple Mount (Model). Image by Daniel Ventura. Licensed under CC BY-SA 4.0. Via Wikimedia Commons.

Page 26. Pool of Siloam (Lower Basin). Image by Abraham. Public Domain. Via Wikimedia Commons.

Page 27. Temple Mount from Southwest. Image by Dan Lundberg. Licensed under CC BY-SA 2.0. Via Wikimedia Commons.

Page 30. Double and Triple Gates Buildings. Illustration by Leen Ritmeyer. Copyright Ritmeyer Archaeological Design (www.ritmeyer.com). Used by permission.

Page 31. Herodian Hall from Model of Jerusalem. Image by Dan Lundberg. Licensed under CC BY-SA 2.0. Via Wikimedia Commons.

Page 33. Herodian Street in Front of Western Wall of Temple Mount. Image by Daniel Warner. Copyright 2004 The Virtual Bible. Used by permission.

Page 34. The Antonia Fortress (illustration). Illustration by Leen Ritmeyer. Copyright Ritmeyer Archaeological Design (www.ritmeyer.com). Used by permission.

Page 36. Herod's Palace from Model of Jerusalem. Image by Berthold Werner. Public Domain. Via Wikimedia Commons.

Page 38. Antonia Fortress from Model of Jerusalem. Image by Ariely. Licensed under CC BY 3.0. Via Wikimedia Commons.

Page 46. Judean Hill Country. Image by Maglanist. Public Domain. Via Wikimedia Commons.

Page 48. Mount Ebal (Right) and Mount Gerizim (Left). Image by Barry J. Beitzel. Copyright 2014 Faithlife / Logos Bible Software.

Page 54. Reconstructed Map of Eratosthenes Depicting the Ancient World (ca. 2nd century BC). Image by J. F. Horrabin. Public Domain. Via Wikimedia Commons.

Page 56. Roman Theater at Gades. Image by Emilio J. Rodríguez Posada. Licensed under CC BY-SA 3.0. Via Wikimedia Commons.

Page 58. Mosaic Floor Visible in the Ruins of the Archaeological Site at Chersonesos. Image by A. Savin. Licensed under CC BY-SA 3.0. Via Wikimedia Commons.

Page 59. Nubian Pyramids at Meroë. Image by Ron Van Oers. Licensed under CC BY-SA 3.0. Via Wikimedia Commons.

Page 59. Temple Ruins at Musawwarat. Image by Vaido Otsar. Licensed under CC BY-SA 4.0. Via Wikimedia Commons.

Page 61. Dharmarajika Stupa (Buddhist Monument) at Taxila. Image by Sasha Isachenko. Licensed under CC BY-SA 3.0. Via Wikimedia Commons.

Page 63. Coin Depicting Gondophares, the Indo-Parthian King. Image by Classical Numismatic Group (www.cngcoins.com). Licensed under CC BY-SA 2.5. Via Wikimedia Commons.

Page 74. Mount of Olives. Image by Daniel Warner. Copyright 2004 The Virtual Bible. Used by permission.

Page 80. Mikveh near Southern Steps of Temple Mount. Image by David A. deSilva. Copyright 2017 David A. deSilva. Used by permission.

Page 82. Cenacle, Traditional Site of the Last Supper. Image by Marco Plassio. Licensed under CC BY-SA 3.0. Via Wikimedia Commons.

Page 84. Courtyard in Front of the Cenacle with Dormition Abbey on Mt. Zion. Image by Britchi Mierla. Licensed under CC BY-SA 4.0. Via Wikimedia Commons.

Page 87. Pieter Bruegel the Elder's "Construction of the Tower of Babel." Image by Pieter Bruegel. Public Domain. Via Web Gallery of Art.

Page 88. Summit of Mount Sinai. Image by Mohammed Moussa. Licensed under CC BY-SA 3.0. Via Wikimedia Commons.

Page 99. "Jews and God-fearers" Inscription on Theater Seat at Miletus. Image by Barry J. Beitzel. Copyright 2014 Faithlife / Logos Bible Software.

Page 100. Pool on the Gangites River, Possible Location of Lydia's Baptism. Image by Sarti Design. Copyright 2011 Logos Bible Software.

Page 107. Remains of Synagogue at Dura-Europos. Image by Marsyas. Licensed under CC BY-SA 3.0. Via Wikimedia Commons.

Page 109. Outer Courtyard of Synagogue at Sardis. Image by David A. deSilva. Copyright 2016 David A. deSilva. Used by permission.

Page 110. Elephantine Island. Image by Barry J. Beitzel. Copyright 2014 Faithlife / Logos Bible Software.

Page 111. Island of Crete. Image by Barry J. Beitzel. Copyright 2014 Faithlife / Logos Bible Software.

Page 117. Western Wall. Image by David A. deSilva. Copyright 2017 David A. deSilva. Used by permission.

Page 118. Jesus and Disciples in Solomon's Colonnade by James Tissot (c. 1886). Image by James Tissot. Public Domain.

Page 119. Model of Herod's Temple. Image by David A. deSilva. Copyright 2017 David A. deSilva. Used by permission.

Page 120. Remain's of Robinson's Arch. Image by Barry J. Beitzel. Copyright 2014 Faithlife / Logos Bible Software.

Page 122. Temple Balustrade Inscription. Image by Barry J. Beitzel. Copyright 2014 Faithlife / Logos Bible Software.

Page 123. Fragment of Temple Warning Inscription. Image by David A. deSilva. Copyright 2017 David A. deSilva. Used by permission.

Page 129. Delos Synagogue. Image by Carl G. Rasmussen. Copyright 2018 Carl G. Rasmussen (www.HolyLandPhotos.org). Used by permission.

Page 138. Megiddo Mosaic. Image by Nicky Davidov. Copyright Israel Antiquities Authority. Used by permission.

Page 139. Earliest Papyrus of Jude (P72). Image by Mediatus/Kopie eines Originalbriefes. Public Domain. Via Wikimedia Commons.

Page 145. Bust of Claudius. Image by Eckhard J. Schnabel. Copyright 2018 Eckhard J. Schnabel. Used by permission.

Page 145. Coin Depicting Herod Agrippa I. Image by Classical Numismatic Group (www.cngcoins.com). Licensed under CC BY-SA 3.0. Via Wikimedia Commons.

Page 147. Possible Site of the Philippian Jail. Image by Sarti Design. Copyright 2011 Logos Bible Software.

Page 149. Bema at Corinth. Image by David A. deSilva. Copyright 2014 David A. deSilva. Used by permission.

Page 152. Bust of Nero. Image by cjh1452000. Licensed under CC BY-SA 3.0. Via Wikimedia Commons.

Page 157. Theodotus Synagogue Inscription. Image by Oren Rozen. Licensed under CC BY-SA 4.0. Via Wikimedia Commons.

Page 159. The Upper City (#1), Lower City (#2), and City of David (#3) of 1st Century Jerusalem. Image by Daniel Warner. Copyright 2004 The Virtual Bible. Used by permission.

Page 161. Location of Theodotus Inscription. Image by Chris McKinney. Copyright 2019 Chris McKinny. Used by permission.

Page 162. Aerial of Southern End of the City of David. Image by Bill Schlegel/BiblePlaces.com. Copyright Bill Schlegel / BiblePlaces.com. Used by permission.

Page 165. Corner Steps of Pool of Siloam. Image by Barry J. Beitzel. Copyright 2014 Faithlife / Logos Bible Software.

Page 176. Golden Milestone (*Milliarium Aureum*). Image by MM. Licensed under CC BY-SA 3.0. Via Wikimedia Commons.

Page 177. Trajan's Colomn (Cichorius Plate) Scene 19 (center): Building a Bridge. Image by Conrad Cichorius. Public Domain. Via Wikimedia Commons.

Page 178. Ancient Roman Bridge in Aleppo, Syria. Image by Bertramz. Licensed under CC BY-SA 3.0. Via Wikimedia Commons.

Page 179. Votive Altar with Inscription *salvos ire*. Image by Mark Wilson. Copyright 2018 Mark Wilson. Used by permission.

Page 184. Republican Milestone from Side Erected by Governor Manius Aquillius. Image by Mark Wilson. Copyright 2018 Mark Wilson. Used by permission.

Page 197. Sea of Galilee and Surrounding Terrain. Image by אילה סעדיה Pikiwiki Israel. Licensed under CC BY-SA 2.5. Via Wikimedia Commons.

Page 198. Roman Road from Jerusalem to Beth-guvrin. Image by Davidbena. Licensed under CC BY-SA 4.0. Via Wikimedia Commons.

Page 205. Peutinger Map: Five Routes Leading to Caesarea. This is a derivative of a public domain image: https://commons.wikimedia.org/wiki/File:Tabula_Peutingeriana_-_Miller.jpg. Via Wikimedia Commons. The image was cropped and labeled.

Page 209. View from the Ruins of Herod's Palace Looking Toward the Harbor at Caesarea Maritima. Image by Sarti Design. Copyright 2011 Logos Bible Software.

Page 212. Aerial View of the Ruins of Caesarea Maritima. Image by Meronim. Licensed under CC BY-SA 3.0. Via Wikimedia Commons. Labels added.

Page 213. Aerial View of Caesarea Harbor. Image by Barry J. Beitzel. Copyright 2014 Faithlife / Logos Bible Software.

Page 215. Barrel-Vaulted Warehouse. Image by David A. deSilva. Copyright 2018 David A. deSilva. Used by permission.

Page 216. Pillars from the Upper Level of Praetorium. Image by Sarti Design. Copyright 2011 Logos Bible Software.

Page 217. Restored Theater at Caesarea. Image by Barry J. Beitzel. Copyright 2014 Faithlife / Logos Bible Software.

Page 218. Aqueduct Along the Beach at Caesarea. Image by David A. deSilva. Copyright 2018 David A. deSilva. Used by permission.

Page 219. Pontius Pilate Inscription. Image by BRBurton. Public Domain. Via Wikimedia Commons.

Page 223. Peutinger Map: Damascus to Tiberias. This is a derivative of a public domain image: https://commons.wikimedia.org/wiki/File:Tabula_Peutingeriana_-_Miller.jpg. Via Wikimedia Commons. The image was cropped and labeled.

Page 227. Straight Street in Damascus. Image by New York Public Library. Public Domain. Via Flickr.

Page 230. Roman Triumphal Arch on "Straight Street." Image by Bernard Gagnon. Licensed under CC BY-SA 3.0. Via Wikimedia Commons.

Page 230. Temple of Zeus in Damascus. Image by DIMSFIKAS. Licensed under CC BY-SA 3.0. Via Wikimedia Commons.

Page 233. Basalt Street in Tarsus. Image by Barry J. Beitzel. Copyright 2014 Faithlife / Logos Bible Software.

Page 238. Aerial View of Joppa. Image by Barry J. Beitzel. Copyright 2014 Faithlife / Logos Bible Software.

Page 239. Aerial View of Caesarea Maritima. Image by Abraham Graicer. Licensed under CC BY-SA 4.0. Via Wikimedia Commons.

Page 247. Praetorian Guard. Public Domain. Via Logos Bible Images.

Page 248. Roman Soldiers. Public Domain. Via Logos Bible Images.

Page 249. "The Centurion." Image by James Tissot. Public Domain.

Page 250. Roman Standard Bearer. Public Domain. Via Logos Bible Images.

Page 251. Roman *Testudo* (Tortoise) Formation. Image by Christian Chirita. Licensed under CC BY-SA 3.0. Via Wikimedia Commons.

Page 252. Trajan's Column. Image by Barry J. Beitzel. Copyright 2014 Faithlife / Logos Bible Software.

Page 253. Ballista. Public Domain. Via Logos Bible Images.

Page 253. Catapult. Public Domain. Via Charles Barnes, *The People's Bible Encyclopedia* (1912).

Page 255. Front Interior of Synagogue at Capernaum. Image by David A. deSilva. Copyright 2014 David A. deSilva. Used by permission.

Page 256. Hasmonean Palace, Model of Jerusalem. Image by Berthold Werner. Public Domain. Via Wikimedia Commons.

Page 258. Model of Jerusalem. Image by Daniel Case. Licensed under CC BY-SA 3.0. Via Wikimedia Commons.

Page 260. Caesarea Maritima. Image by Barry J. Beitzel. Copyright 2014 Faithlife / Logos Bible Software.

Page 262. Archaeological Remains at Paphos. Image by Barry J. Beitzel. Copyright 2014 Faithlife / Logos Bible Software.

Page 272. Tetradrachm Bearing Image of Antiochus I Soter. Image by David A. deSilva. Copyright 2014 David A. deSilva. Used by permission.

Page 273. Bust of Antiochus III. Image by Auguste Giraudon. Public Domain. Via Wikimedia Commons.

Page 273. Bust of Caesar Augustus (Octavian). Image by David A. deSilva. Copyright 2015 David A. deSilva. Used by permission.

Page 274. Bust of Gaius Caligula. Image by Louis le Grand. Licensed under CC BY-SA 3.0. Via Wikimedia Commons.

Page 276. Cave church of St. Peter. Image by Barry J. Beitzel. Copyright 2014 Faithlife / Logos Bible Software.

Page 280. Wheat Field in Upper Galilee. Image by H2o. Public Domain. Via Wikimedia Commons.

Page 283. Locust. Image by Dror Feitelson Pikiwiki Israel. Licensed under CC BY 2.5. Via Wikimedia Commons.

Page 285. Terrain near the Dead Sea. Image by Barry J. Beitzel. Copyright 2014 Faithlife / Logos Bible Software.

Page 287. The Negev. Image by Andrew Shiva. Licensed under CC BY-SA 4.0. Via Wikimedia Commons.

Page 291. Head of Agrippa Based on Depiction from Coin. Image by Todd Bolen/ BiblePlaces.com. Copyright Todd Bolen/BiblePlaces.com. Used by permission.

Page 293. Promontory Palace of King Herod. Image by Barry J. Beitzel. Copyright 2014 Faithlife / Logos Bible Software.

Page 294. Aerial View of the Ruins of Caesarea Maritima. Image by Meronim. Licensed under CC BY-SA 3.0. Via Wikimedia Commons. Labels added.

Page 295. Hippodrome of Caesarea. Image by Sarti Design. Copyright 2011 Logos Bible Software.

Page 296. Location of the Temple of Roma. Image by Lior Golgher • ליאור גולגר. Licensed under CC BY-SA 3.0. Via Wikimedia Commons.

Page 300. Salamis on the Island of Cyprus. Image by Barry J. Beitzel. Copyright 2014 Faithlife / Logos Bible Software.

Page 305. Stadium at Perga. Image by Barry J. Beitzel. Copyright 2014 Faithlife / Logos Bible Software.

Page 306. *Galaticae et Pamphyliae* Inscription from Perga. Image by Mark Wilson. Copyright 2018 Mark Wilson. Used by permission.

Page 313. Salamis Gymnasium. Image by Barry J. Beitzel. Copyright 2014 Faithlife / Logos Bible Software.

Page 315. Fifth Century Statue of Aphrodite from Cyprus. Image by Ophelia2. Public Domain. Via Wikimedia Commons.

Page 315. Kourion. Image by Michal Osmenda. Licensed under CC BY 2.0. Via Flickr.

Page 316. Sanctuary of Aphrodite. Image by Nikodem Nijaki. Licensed under CC BY-SA 3.0. Via Wikimedia Commons.

Page 317. L. Sergius Paulus Inscription from Pisidian Antioch. Image by Mark Fairchild. Copyright 2018 Mark Fairchild. Used by permission.

Page 325. Anatolian Moon God, Men. Image by David A. deSilva. Copyright 2015 David A. deSilva. Used by permission.

Page 325. Apse of Fourth Century Church of St. Paul. Image by David A. deSilva. Copyright 2015 David A. deSilva. Used by permission.

Page 326. Part of the aqueduct leading water into Antioch. The shifting terrain has buried almost all trace of the lower course of arches. Image by David A. deSilva. Copyright 2015 David A. deSilva. Used by permission.

Page 327. Shops or Offices on the *Decumanus Maximus*. Image by David A. deSilva. Copyright 2015 David A. deSilva. Used by permission.

Page 328. Foundations of the Augusteum. Image by David A. deSilva. Copyright 2015 David A. deSilva. Used by permission.

Page 329. *Res Gestae Divi Augusti* Inscription. Image by David A. deSilva. Copyright 2019 David A. deSilva. Used by permission.

Page 330. Fragments of an inscription ascribing divine honors to the emperor. Image by David A. deSilva. Copyright 2015 David A. deSilva. Used by permission.

Page 337. Agora at Philippi. Image by Sarti Design. Copyright 2011 Logos Bible Software.

Page 338. Shop Ruins at the Thessalonica Agora. Image by Sarti Design. Copyright 2011 Logos Bible Software.

Page 342. Ruins of Corinth. Image by Sarti Design. Copyright 2011 Logos Bible Software.

Page 345. Mars Hill in Athens. Image by Carolyn Sugg. Licensed under CC BY 2.0. Via Flickr.

Page 347. Bust of Socrates. Image by Derek Key. Licensed under CC BY 2.0. Via Wikimedia Commons.

Page 351. Athenian Acropolis and Its Many Temples. Image by Evangelos Methenitis. Licensed under CC BY-SA 4.0. Via Wikimedia Commons.

Page 356. Tomb of Absalom, Kidron Valley. Image by Praisethelorne. Licensed under CC BY-SA 3.0. Via Wikimedia Commons.

Page 358. Parthenon. Image by David A. deSilva. Copyright 2014 David A. deSilva. Used by permission.

Page 360. The Areopagus (Mars Hill). Image by Sarti Design. Copyright 2011 Logos Bible Software.

Page 361. Roman Forum. Image by Florestan. Licensed under CC BY 3.0. Via Wikimedia Commons.

Page 365. Propylaia Leading to Acropolis. Image by Barry J. Beitzel. Copyright 2014 Faithlife / Logos Bible Software.

Page 366. Temple of Hephaestus. Image by David A. deSilva. Copyright 2014 David A. deSilva. Used by permission.

Page 371. Brick remains of a Roman town. Image by Barry J. Beitzel. Copyright 2014 Faithlife / Logos Bible Software.

Page 373. Bust of Alexander the Great. Image by David A. deSilva. Copyright 2014 David A. deSilva. Used by permission.

Page 374. Pharos of Alexandria. Image by Hermann Thiersch. Public Domain. Via Wikimedia Commons.

Page 375. Plan of Alexandria c. 30 BCE. Image by Faithlife. Copyright 2018 Faithlife. This work is a derivative of https://commons.wikimedia.org/wiki/File:Plan_of_Alexandria_c_30_BC_Otto_Puchstein_1890s_EN.svg. Original by Philg88. Licensed under CC BY-SA 3.0. Via Wikimedia Commons.

Page 376. Roman Triumphal Column "Pompey's Pillar." Image by Alberto-g-rovi. Licensed under CC BY-SA 3.0. Via Wikimedia Commons.

Page 379. Roman Odeion at Alexandria. Image by Nivycubbins. Licensed under CC BY-SA 3.0. Via Wikimedia Commons.

Page 390. Theater at Ephesus. Image by David A. deSilva. Copyright 2014 David A. deSilva. Used by permission.

Page 393. Remains of Roman Harbor at Troas. Image by Barry J. Beitzel. Copyright 2014 Faithlife / Logos Bible Software.

Page 395. Assos. Image by KureCewlik81. Public Domain. Via Wikimedia Commons.

Page 399. The Antonia Fortress. Illustration by Leen Ritmeyer. Copyright Ritmeyer Archaeological Design (www.ritmeyer.com). Used by permission.

Page 401. Illustration of Herod's Palace at Caesarea. Illustration by Leen Ritmeyer. Copyright Ritmeyer Archaeological Design (www.ritmeyer.com). Used by permission.

Page 403. Downward View at Myra. Image by Barry J. Beitzel. Copyright 2014 Faithlife / Logos Bible Software.

Page 404. Kaloi Limenes. Image by Barry J. Beitzel. Copyright 2014 Faithlife / Logos Bible Software.

Page 406. St. Paul's Island. Image by Barry J. Beitzel. Copyright 2014 Faithlife / Logos Bible Software.

Page 406. The ancient harbor at Caesarea Maritima from which Paul sailed for Rome. Image by Barry J. Beitzel. Copyright 2014 Faithlife / Logos Bible Software.

Page 408. Bay of Naples with Mount Vesuvius in the Background. Image by Rum Bucolic Ape. Licensed under CC BY-ND 2.0. Via Flickr.

Page 413. 13th Century Mosaic Depicting the Pharos Lighthouse of Alexandria. Public Domain. Via Wikimedia Commons.

Page 418. Granary at Myra. Image by Barry J. Beitzel. Copyright 2014 Faithlife / Logos Bible Software.

Page 421. Harbor at Cauda. Image by Barry J. Beitzel. Copyright 2014 Faithlife / Logos Bible Software.

Page 423. St. Paul's Island and Bay. Image by Barry J. Beitzel. Copyright 2014 Faithlife / Logos Bible Software.

Page 425. Statue of St. Paul on St. Paul's Island. Image by Barry J. Beitzel. Copyright 2014 Faithlife / Logos Bible Software.

Page 428. Appian Way. Image by Livioandronico2013. Licensed under CC BY-SA 4.0. Via Wikimedia Commons.

Page 433. Depiction of Roman Eagle on Globe. Image by David A. deSilva. Copyright 2018 David A. deSilva. Used by permission.

Page 434. Basilica Julia. Image by David A. deSilva. Copyright 2014 David A. deSilva. Used by permission.

Page 435. Curia of Julius. Image by David A. deSilva. Copyright 2014 David A. deSilva. Used by permission.

Page 435. Temple of Castor and Pollux. Image by David A. deSilva. Copyright 2014 David A. deSilva. Used by permission.

Page 436. Coin Depicting Temple of Jupiter Capitolinus. Image by David A. deSilva. Copyright 2014 David A. deSilva. Used by permission.

Page 437. Domitian's Private Racetrack. Image by David A. deSilva. Copyright 2014 David A. deSilva. Used by permission.

Page 437. Palatine Hill beyond Roman Forum. Image by David A. deSilva. Copyright 2014 David A. deSilva. Used by permission.

Page 438. Model of Campus Martius. Image by Theatrum Pompei Project. Public Domain. Via Wikimedia Commons.

Page 439. Pantheon. Image by Barry J. Beitzel. Copyright 2014 Faithlife / Logos Bible Software.

Page 440. Temple of Mars Ultor. Image by David A. deSilva. Copyright 2014 David A. deSilva. Used by permission.

Page 441. *Ara Pacis Augustae*, Altar of the Augustan Peace. Image by David A. deSilva. Copyright 2014 David A. deSilva. Used by permission.

Page 442. Horologium Augusti Obelisk. Image by David A. deSilva. Copyright 2014 David A. deSilva. Used by permission.

Page 443. Remains of Arch of Augustus. Image by David A. deSilva. Copyright 2014 David A. deSilva. Used by permission.

Page 443. West Side of the Porta Maggiore. Image by David A. deSilva. Copyright 2014 David A. deSilva. Used by permission.

Page 444. Arch of Titus. Image by David A. deSilva. Copyright 2014 David A. deSilva. Used by permission.

Page 444. Spoils of Jerusalem, Arch of Titus. Image by David A. deSilva. Copyright 2014 David A. deSilva. Used by permission.

Page 445. Flavian Amphitheater, Exterior. Image by David A. deSilva. Copyright 2014 David A. deSilva. Used by permission.

Page 446. Flavian Amphitheater, Interior. Image by David A. deSilva. Copyright 2014 David A. deSilva. Used by permission.

Page 447. Temple of Vespasian and Titus (right) and Temple of Saturn (left). Image by David A. deSilva. Copyright 2014 David A. deSilva. Used by permission.

Page 448. *Ara Coeli Insula*, 2nd Century Roman Apartment Block near Capitoline Hill. Image by Ursus. Public Domain. Via Wikimedia Commons.

Page 453. The Amphitheater of Tarraco. Image by Mark.thurman92. Licensed under CC BY-SA 3.0. Via Wikimedia Commons.

Page 454. Haghios Titus in Heracleion. Image by Jebulon. Public Domain. Via Wikimedia Commons.

Page 461. Mamertime Prison Cell. Image by J. Carl Laney. Copyright 2018 J. Carl Laney. Used by permission.

Page 462. Basilica of St. Paul Outside the Walls. Image by Berthold Werner. Public Domain. Via Wikimedia Commons.

Page 466. Corinthian Canal. Image by Barry J. Beitzel. Copyright 2014 Faithlife / Logos Bible Software.

Page 468. West Shops. Image by David A. deSilva. Copyright 2014 David A. deSilva. Used by permission.

Page 469. North Market. Image by David A. deSilva. Copyright 2014 David A. deSilva. Used by permission.

Page 469. South Shops. Image by David A. deSilva. Copyright 2014 David A. deSilva. Used by permission.

Page 470. *Synagōgē Ebraiōn* Inscription. Image by David A. deSilva. Copyright 2014 David A. deSilva. Used by permission.

Page 471. Capital Decorated with Menorahs and Palm Branches. Image by David A. deSilva. Copyright 2014 David A. deSilva. Used by permission.

Page 471. Gallio Inscription. Image by Barry J. Beitzel. Copyright 2014 Faithlife / Logos Bible Software.

Page 472. Bema at Corinth. Image by David A. deSilva. Copyright 2014 David A. deSilva. Used by permission.

Page 474. Temple of Apollo. Image by David A. deSilva. Copyright 2019 David A. deSilva. Used by permission.

Page 475. *Divo Iulio* Dedicatory Inscription. Image by David A. deSilva. Copyright 2018 David A. deSilva. Used by permission.

Page 475. Head of Tyche from Corinth Museum. Image by David A. deSilva. Copyright 2018 David A. deSilva. Used by permission.

Page 477. Fountain of Peirene. Image by Barry J. Beitzel. Copyright 2014 Faithlife / Logos Bible Software.

Page 478. Erastus Inscription. Image by David A. deSilva. Copyright 2014 David A. deSilva. Used by permission.

Page 479. Cenchreae Habor, View to North Mole. Image by David A. deSilva. Copyright 2018 David A. deSilva. Used by permission.

Page 479. Road to Lechaion. Image by David A. deSilva. Copyright 2018 David A. deSilva. Used by permission.

Page 480. Interior of Roman Tomb. Image by David A. deSilva. Copyright 2018 David A. deSilva. Used by permission.

Page 481. Statue of Isis. Image by David A. deSilva. Copyright 2018 David A. deSilva. Used by permission.

Page 485. Portion of the *Res Gestae Divi Augusti* from Ancyra. Image by Carole Raddato. Licensed under CC BY-SA 2.0. Via Flickr. The image was cropped.

Page 487. Peutinger Map: Location of Iconium. This is a derivative of a public domain image: https://commons.wikimedia.org/wiki/File:Tabula_Peutingeriana_-_Miller.jpg. Via Wikimedia Commons. The image was cropped and labeled.

Page 490. *Galaticae et Pamphyliae* Inscription from Perga. Image by Mark Wilson. Copyright 2018 Mark Wilson. Used by permission.

Page 496. The Synagogue at Çatıören. Image by Mark Fairchild. Copyright 2018 Mark Fairchild. Used by permission.

Page 499. Roman Street in Tarsus. Image by Barry J. Beitzel. Copyright 2014 Faithlife / Logos Bible Software.

Page 500. Inscription from the Fourth Century Synagogue at Apamea. Image by Daderot. Public Domain. Via Wikimedia Commons.

Page 500. Orontes River at Antioch. Image by Barry J. Beitzel. Copyright 2014 Faithlife / Logos Bible Software.

Page 501. Palmyra Necropolis. Image by Gianfranco Gazzetti. Licensed under CC BY-SA 4.0. Via Wikimedia Commons.

Page 502. Roman Mosaic from Zeugma. Image by Barry J. Beitzel. Copyright 2014 Faithlife / Logos Bible Software.

Page 504. Sarcophagus with Menorah at Corycus. Image by Ingeborg Simon. Licensed under CC BY-SA 3.0. Via Wikimedia Commons.

Page 506. Menorah Carved into Synagogue Lintel at Corycus. Image by Ingeborg Simon. Licensed under CC BY-SA 3.0. Via Wikimedia Commons.

Page 507. Unusual Altar Found at Diocaesarea. Image by Mark Fairchild. Copyright 2018 Mark Fairchild. Used by permission.

Page 508. Menorah Carved into a Pilaster of the Athena Relief at Sömek. Image by Klaus-Peter Simon. Licensed under CC BY-SA 3.0. Via Wikimedia Commons.

Page 511. Fortification at Çatıören. Image by Zeynel Cebeci. Licensed under CC BY-SA 4.0. Via Wikimedia Commons.

Page 514. Watchtower at Kurşunlu. Image by Mark Fairchild. Copyright 2018 Mark Fairchild. Used by permission.

Page 515. Karaböcülü Overlooking a Canyon. Image by Mark Fairchild. Copyright 2018 Mark Fairchild. Used by permission.

Page 540. Basilica Stoa. Image by David A. deSilva. Copyright 2014 David A. deSilva. Used by permission.

Page 541. Pollio Aqueduct. Image by David A. deSilva. Copyright 2014 David A. deSilva. Used by permission.

Page 541. Temple of Julius and Artemis. Image by David A. deSilva. Copyright 2014 David A. deSilva. Used by permission.

Page 542. Curetes Street. Image by Sarti Design. Copyright 2011 Logos Bible Software.

Page 543. Terrace House. Image by David A. deSilva. Copyright 2014 David A. deSilva. Used by permission.

Page 544. Tetragonos Agora. Image by David A. deSilva. Copyright 2014 David A. deSilva. Used by permission.

Page 545. South Gate, Entrance to Agora. Image by David A. deSilva. Copyright 2014 David A. deSilva. Used by permission.

Page 546. Theater. Image by Barry J. Beitzel. Copyright 2014 Faithlife / Logos Bible Software.

Page 547. Statue of Artemis Flanked by Two Deer. Image by David A. deSilva. Copyright 2014 David A. deSilva. Used by permission.

Page 548. Ephesian Coin with Image of Artemis. Public Domain. Via *Helps to the Study of the Bible* (1896).

Page 549. Foundations of Domitian Temple Platform. Image by David A. deSilva. Copyright 2014 David A. deSilva. Used by permission.

Page 550. Domitian Temple Platform. Image by David A. deSilva. Copyright 2014 David A. deSilva. Used by permission.

Page 551. Inscription Naming Ephesus *Neōkoros* (Temple Warden). Image by David A. deSilva. Copyright 2014 David A. deSilva. Used by permission.

Page 551. Sacrificial Scene on Altar of Domitian. Image by David A. deSilva. Copyright 2014 David A. deSilva. Used by permission.

Page 552. Temple of Hadrian. Image by Mars Hill Church. Copyright 2011 Mars Hill Church. Used by permission.

Page 557. da Vinci's "Vitruvian Man." Image by Leonardo daVinci. Public Domain. Via Wikimedia Commons. Modified version of source: https://commons.wikimedia.org/wiki/File:Uomo_Vitruviano.jpg. Blurring of center.

Page 562. Traditional Site of Paul's Philippian Prison. Image by Mark Hoffman. Copyright 2015 Mark Hoffman. Used by permission.

Page 564. Remains of the Acropolis at Philippi. Image by Sarti Design. Copyright 2011 Logos Bible Software.

Page 570. Biconical Mound of Colossae. Image by Alan H. Cadwallader. Copyright 2018 Alan H. Cadwallader. Used by permission.

Page 572. Korymbos Inscription. Image by Alan H. Cadwallader. Copyright 2018 Alan H. Cadwallader. Used by permission.

Page 572. Rock Tomb Shifted by Earthquakes at Colossae. Image by Alan H. Cadwallader. Copyright 2018 Alan H. Cadwallader. Used by permission.

Page 575. View toward Colossae down Syria Street at Laodicea. Image by David A. deSilva. Copyright 2015 David A. deSilva. Used by permission.

Page 576. Broken Funeral Stele. Image by Alan H. Cadwallader. Copyright 2018 Alan H. Cadwallader. Used by permission.

Page 576. Artemis on a Coin of Colossae. Image by Reinhard Saczewski / Münzkabinett of the Staatliche Museen. Copyright Staatliche Museen, Berlin. Used by permission.

Page 577. Sketch by Georg Weber (1891) depicting the base of a temple on the mound of Colossae. Image by Georg Weber. Public Domain.

Page 579. Fragment of a Gladiator Panel from Colossae. Image by Alan H. Cadwallader. Copyright 2018 Alan H. Cadwallader. Used by permission.

Page 586. View of Modern Thessaloniki Looking South toward the Thermaic Gulf. Image by Sarti Design. Copyright 2011 Logos Bible Software.

Page 592. 1865 Photograph by Alexander Svobodov. Image by The J. Paul Getty Museum. Public Domain. Via www.getty.edu.

Page 593. Fragment of a Funerary Relief. Image by Alan H. Cadwallader. Copyright 2018 Alan H. Cadwallader. Used by permission.

Page 595. Funerary Panel of a Slave named Onesimus. Image by Alan H. Cadwallader. Copyright 2018 Alan H. Cadwallader. Used by permission.

Page 596. Aerial View of the Biconical Mound of Colossae. Image by Alan H. Cadwallader. Copyright 2018 Alan H. Cadwallader. Used by permission.

Page 597. A collar that would be fixed to a slave's neck. Image by Carole Raddato. Licensed under CC BY-SA 2.0. Via Flickr.

Page 598. Coin of Colossae from the Time of Commodus. Image courtesy of Classical Numismatic Group (www.CNGcoins.com).

Page 600. Damaged Epitaph from the Region of Lydia. Image by Alan H. Cadwallader. Copyright 2018 Alan H. Cadwallader. Used by permission.

Page 601. The Sanctuary of Apollo Lairbenos. Image by Alan H. Cadwallader. Copyright 2018 Alan H. Cadwallader. Used by permission.

Page 607. Portait of Mithridates I on Tetradrachm. Image by Classical Numismatic Group (www.cngcoins.com). Licensed under CC BY-SA 3.0. Via Wikimedia Commons.

Page 608. Kuşkayası Monument South of Amasra. Image by Vikiçizer. Licensed under CC BY-SA 4.0. Via Wikimedia Commons.

Page 609. Tombs of the Pontic Kings at Amasya. Image by Zeynel Cebeci. Licensed under CC BY-SA 4.0. Via Wikimedia Commons.

Page 611. Mount Argaeus Towers over the City of Kayseri. Image by Carole Raddato. Licensed under CC BY-SA 2.0. Via Flickr.

Page 613. Roman Theater at Nicea. Image by QuartierLatin1968. Licensed under CC BY-SA 3.0. Via Wikimedia Commons.

Page 614. Roman Walls and Byzantine/Constantinople Gate at Nicea. Image by Barry J. Beitzel. Copyright 2014 Faithlife / Logos Bible Software.

Page 616. Looking Westward across the Bosphorus to Modern Istanbul (Byzantium). Image by Barry J. Beitzel. Copyright 2014 Faithlife / Logos Bible Software.

Page 621. View Eastward from Patmos. Image by Mark Wilson. Copyright 2018 Mark Wilson. Used by permission.

Page 622. Skala. Image by David A. deSilva. Copyright 2014 David A. deSilva. Used by permission.

Page 622. Skala Harbor and the Castelli Acropolis. Image by Barry J. Beitzel. Copyright 2014 Faithlife / Logos Bible Software.

Page 623. Artemis Temple Inscription. Image by David A. deSilva. Copyright 2014 David A. deSilva. Used by permission.

Page 624. Cape Zouloufi. Image by Mark Wilson. Copyright 2018 Mark Wilson. Used by permission.

Page 625. Mosaic of John and Prochorus on Patmos. Image by David A. deSilva. Copyright 2014 David A. deSilva. Used by permission.

Page 626. Cave of the Apocalypse Interior. Image by Mars Hill Church. Copyright 2011 Mars Hill Church. Used by permission.

Page 627. Monastery of St. John the Theologos. Image by Mars Hill Church. Copyright 2011 Mars Hill Church. Used by permission.

Page 631. Smyrna. Map by TUTKU TOURS. Copyright 2018 TUTKU TOURS. Used by permission.

Page 632. Agora Western Stoa Basement. Image by David A. deSilva. Copyright 2015 David A. deSilva. Used by permission.

Page 633. Agora Basilica Basement. Image by David A. deSilva. Copyright 2015 David A. deSilva. Used by permission.

Page 634. Agora Inscription Naming Hadrian as Olympius and Savior. Image by David A. deSilva. Copyright 2015 David A. deSilva. Used by permission.

Page 635. Inscription Honoring a "Temple Warden of the Emperors." Image by David A. deSilva. Copyright 2015 David A. deSilva. Used by permission.

Page 636. Wreaths on Grave Stele. Image by David A. deSilva. Copyright 2015 David A. deSilva. Used by permission.

Page 639. Pergamum Acropolis. Image by David A. deSilva. Copyright 2014 David A. deSilva. Used by permission.

Page 641. Pergamum. Map by TUTKU TOURS. Copyright 2018 TUTKU TOURS. Used by permission.

Page 642. Coin of Pergamum with Temple to Augustus. Public Domain. Via Logos Bible Images.

Page 643. Gymnasiarch Inscription. Image by David A. deSilva. Copyright 2018 David A. deSilva. Used by permission.

Page 644. Aerial View of the Temple of Trajan. Image by Barry J. Beitzel. Copyright 2014 Faithlife / Logos Bible Software.

Page 645. An inscription at the Asklepion in Pergamum boasts the city's place of honor as the "first-to-be-twice-named-*neōkoros*." Image by David A. deSilva. Copyright 2014 David A. deSilva. Used by permission.

Page 646. Foundation of the Altar of Zeus. Image by David A. deSilva. Copyright 2014 David A. deSilva. Used by permission.

Page 648. Theater and Temple of Dionysus. Image by Barry J. Beitzel. Copyright 2014 Faithlife / Logos Bible Software.

Page 649. Temple of Demeter. Image by David A. deSilva. Copyright 2014 David A. deSilva. Used by permission.

Page 650. Upper Gymnasium and Palaestra. Image by David A. deSilva. Copyright 2014 David A. deSilva. Used by permission.

Page 651. The Serapeion, or "Red Hall." Image by Mars Hill Church. Copyright 2011 Mars Hill Church. Used by permission.

Page 652. Forecourt, Colonnade, and Theater at the Asklepion. Image by Dennis Jarvis. Licensed under CC BY-SA 2.0. Via Wikimedia Commons.

Page 656. Thyatira. Map by TUTKU TOURS. Copyright 2018 TUTKU TOURS. Used by permission.

Page 658. Arches from Colonnaded Street at Thyatira. Image by Klaus-Peter Simon. Licensed under CC BY-SA 3.0. Via Wikimedia Commons.

Page 658. Bust of Emperor Caracalla. Image by Marie-Lan Nguyen. Licensed under CC BY-SA 2.5. Via Wikimedia Commons.

Page 659. Bust of Emperor Elagabalus. Image by Carole Raddato. Licensed under CC BY-SA 2.0. Via Wikimedia Commons.

Page 660. Murex Shells and Purple Dyed Textiles. Image by David A. deSilva. Copyright 2015 David A. deSilva. Used by permission.

Page 663. Column Bases for Roman Colonnaded Street. Image by Ian W. Scott. Licensed under CC BY-SA 2.0. Via Flickr.

Page 666. Sardis. Map by TUTKU TOURS. Copyright 2018 TUTKU TOURS. Used by permission.

Page 668. Temple of Artemis. Image by David A. deSilva. Copyright 2016 David A. deSilva. Used by permission.

Page 669. Cult Stele of Cybele. Image by David A. deSilva. Copyright 2015 David A. deSilva. Used by permission.

Page 670. Dedicatory Inscription on Sardis Gymnasium. Image by David A. deSilva. Copyright 2016 David A. deSilva. Used by permission.

Page 670. Gymnasium. Image by David A. deSilva. Copyright 2016 David A. deSilva. Used by permission.

Page 671. Central Table with Eagle on Base. Image by David A. deSilva. Copyright 2016 David A. deSilva. Used by permission.

Page 671. Interior Hall of Sardis Synagogue Showing the *Nomophylakion*. Image by Sarti Design . Copyright 2011 Logos Bible Software.

Page 672. Byzantine Chapel near Temple of Artemis. Image by Mars Hill Church. Copyright 2011 Mars Hill Church. Used by permission.

Page 673. Inscription at Sardis Synagogue. Image by David A. deSilva. Copyright 2016 David A. deSilva. Used by permission.

Page 675. Peutinger Map: Location of Philadelphia. This is a derivative of a public domain image: https://commons.wikimedia.org/wiki/File:Tabula_Peutingeriana_-_Miller.jpg. Via Wikimedia Commons. The image was cropped and labeled.

Page 678. Philadelphia Acropolis. Image by Mark Wilson. Copyright 2018 Mark Wilson. Used by permission.

Page 679. Personification of Philadelphia. Image by Mark Wilson. Copyright 2018 Mark Wilson. Used by permission.

Page 681. Church of Saint John. Image by simonjenkins. Licensed under CC BY-SA 2.0. Via Flickr.

Page 686. Thermal Waters of Hierapolis. Image by David A. deSilva. Copyright 2015 David A. deSilva. Used by permission.

Page 687. Siphon System Leading to Laodicea. Image by Mark Wilson. Copyright 2019 Mark Wilson. Used by permission.

Page 688. Laodicea. Map by TUTKU TOURS. Copyright 2018 TUTKU TOURS. Used by permission.

Page 689. Ephesian Gate. Image by David A. deSilva. Copyright 2016 David A. deSilva. Used by permission.

Page 690. Bronze Coin Minted in Laodicea. Public Domain. Via Logos Bible Images.

Page 691. Temple A at Laodicea. Image by Sarti Design. Copyright 2011 Logos Bible Software.

Page 694. Hellenistic (West) Theater. Image by David A. deSilva. Copyright 2015 David A. deSilva. Used by permission.

Page 698. Gamla Synagogue. Image by David A. deSilva. Copyright 2014 David A. deSilva. Used by permission.

Page 698. Masada Synagogue. Image by Oren Rozen. Licensed under CC BY-SA 3.0. Via Wikimedia Commons.

Page 699. Herodion Synagogue. Image by Deror avi. Licensed under CC BY-SA 3.0. Via Wikimedia Commons.

Page 699. Magdala Synagogue. Image by David A. deSilva. Copyright 2016 David A. deSilva. Used by permission.

Page 700. Trajan's Colomn (Cichorius Plate) Scene 23 (center): Making a Road through the Forest. Image by Conrad Cichorius. Public Domain. Via Wikimedia Commons.

Page 700. Trajan's Colomn (Cichorius Plate) Scene 56 (left): Road-building in the Mountains. Image by Conrad Cichorius. Public Domain. Via Wikimedia Commons.

Page 701. Fig. 1: Site plan of the stepped street by which the Pool of Siloam was accessed. Image by Israel Antiquity Authorities. Copyright 2013 Israel Antiquities Authority. Used by permission.

Page 702. Hippodrome at Caesarea Maritima. Image by Carole Raddato. Licensed under CC BY-SA 2.0. Via Wikimedia Commons.

Page 703. Augustus Seated Colossus from the Herculaneum Augusteum. Image by David A. deSilva. Copyright 2015 David A. deSilva. Used by permission.

Page 705. Herodian Dynasty Family Tree. Diagram by Todd Bolen. Copyright 2018 Faithlife / Logos Bible Software.

Page 706. Another Mosaic Inscription from the House of Eustolious. Image by Carole Raddato. Licensed under CC BY-SA 2.0. Via Wikimedia Commons.

Page 706. Inscription Dedicated to "Jupiter, Best and Greatest." Image by David A. deSilva. Copyright 2015 David A. deSilva. Used by permission.

Page 706. Mosaic Inscription from the House of Eustolios. Image by Wknight94. Licensed under CC BY-SA 3.0. Via Wikimedia Commons.

Page 707. Coin Celebrating Smyrna's Thrice Awarded Neokorate. Image courtesy of Classical Numismatic Group (www.cngcoins.com).

Page 707. Coin Celebrating the Imperial Temple of 26 AD. Image courtesy of Classical Numismatic Group (www.cngcoins.com).

Page 707. *Res Gestae Divi Augusti* Replica. Image by David A. deSilva. Copyright 2015 David A. deSilva. Used by permission.

Page 711. Ephesus. Map by TUTKU TOURS. Copyright 2018 TUTKU TOURS. Used by permission.

Page 713. Aerial View of the Gymnasium and *Palaestra* at Sardis. Image by Barry J. Beitzel. Copyright 2014 Faithlife / Logos Bible Software.

Page 714. Eastern Rough Cilicia. Map by TUTKU TOURS. Copyright 2018 TUTKU TOURS. Used by permission.

PROJECT STAFF

EDITORIAL STAFF

Douglas Mangum
Jessica Parks
James Spinti

PRODUCTION STAFF

Andrew Curtis
Justin Marr
Abigail Salinger

INFORMATION ARCHITECTURE

Sean Boisen

COVER DESIGN

Peter Park

MAP DESIGN

Ben Vander Woude